Developmental Psychology

Developmental Psychology

Little, Brown and Company

AN INTRODUCTION SECOND EDITION

Howard Gardner

BOSTON   TORONTO

For Kerith, Jay, and Andrew
with love

Library of Congress Catalog Card No. 81-82653

ISBN 0-316-30380-1

9 8 7 6 5 4
HAL

Published simultaneously in Canada
by Little, Brown & Company (Canada) Limited

Printed in the United States of America

CREDITS

The author gratefully acknowledges permission to use material from
the following sources.

Page 1: Judith D. Sedwick/The Picture Cube. *Page 3:* Illustration courtesy of The Bettmann Archive. *Page 10:* From Lynn S. Liben, "Long-term Memory for Pictures Related to Seriation, Horizontality, and Verticality Concepts," *Developmental Psychology,* 1981, *11,* 797. Copyright 1981 by the American Psychological Association. Reprinted by permission of the publisher and author. *Page 13:* Top right and bottom, courtesy of Judith Sedwick; left, courtesy of Irvin de Vore Anthro Photo.

Page 24: Top, Sam Sweezy/Stock, Boston; bottom, © Ellen Shub, 1976. *Page 25:* Top left, Michal Heron; bottom left, Dr. Landrum B. Shettles; top right, Henry E. F. Gordillo; bottom right, Mary D. Ainsworth.
Page 27: Suzanne Szasz. *Figure 1.1:* Harry F. Harlow, University of Wisconsin Primate Laboratory. *Figure 1.2:* Harry F. Harlow, University of Wisconsin Primate Laboratory. *Figure 1.3:* From "Love in Infant Monkeys" by Harry F. Harlow. Copyright © June 1959 by Scientific American, Inc. All rights reserved. *Figure 1.4:* Left, Suzanne Szasz; right, Leonard Lee Rue III/Monkmeyer. *Figure 1.5:* Jan Lukas/Photo Researchers. *Figure 1.6:* Henry E. F. Gordillo. *Figure 1.7:* Mary D. Ainsworth. *Figure 1.8:* From H. R. Schaffer and P. E. Emerson, "The Development of Social Attachments in Infancy," *Monographs of the Society for Research in Child Development,* 1964, *29,* serial no. 94. By permission of The Society for Research in Child Development, Inc. *Figure 1.10:* Adapted from M. D. S. Ainsworth

and S. M. Bell, "Attachment, Exploration and Separation: Illustrated by the Behavior of One-Year-Olds in a Strange Situation," *Child Development, 41,* 49–67, 1970. By permission of The Society for Research in Child Development, Inc. *Figure 1.11:* Harry F. Harlow, University of Wisconsin Primate Laboratory. *Figure 1.12:* Marvin E. Newman. *Figure 1.13:* Joanne Leonard/Woodfin Camp. *Figure 1.14:* Derived from Erik H. Erikson, *Childhood and Society,* 2nd Ed., copyright 1950, © 1963 by W. W. Norton & Company, Inc.; *Insight and Responsibility,* copyright © 1964 by Erik H. Erikson; *Identity, Youth and Crisis,* copyright © 1968 by W. W. Norton and Company, Inc., with permission of the publishers, W. W. Norton & Company, Inc., The Hogarth Press, and Faber and Faber Ltd. *Figure 1.15:* Mary D. Ainsworth.

Page 57: Erika Stone/Peter Arnold, Inc. *Figure 2.1:* Top left, Arthur Tress/Photo Researchers; bottom left, Suzanne Szasz; right, George Zimbel/Monkmeyer. *Figure 2.2:* Judith Sedwick. *Figure 2.5:* George Zimbel/Monkmeyer. *Figure 2.8:* Miriam F. Mednick.

Page 93: Anna Kaufman Moon. *Figure 3.2:* Dr. Landrum B. Shettles. *Figure 3.3:* From H. Prechtl and D. Beintema, "The Neurological Examination of the Full-Term Newborn Infant," *Little Club Clinics in Developmental Medicine,* 1964, no. 12 (London: Spastics Society Medical Information Unit and William Heinemann Medical Books, Ltd; Philadelphia: J. B. Lippincott Co.). By permission. *Fig-*

(continued on page 654)

Foreword

There are three of everything, of course, and that includes varieties of developmental psychologist. There is a variety that is only incidentally concerned with children, the psychologist whose interests center on a single topic, such as first-language acquisition or the perceptual constancies, and who becomes involved with children because his topic reaches its peak of importance sometime in childhood. For this sort of psychologist, children or, more exactly, certain childhood years are little more than a locus.

There is also the child psychologist proper. This sort of psychologist can tell you a lot of interesting things about children of a given age and also some quite specific things about a limited number of individual children. What you are told may derive from research, but child-centered psychologists are not limited to research; they will have a large fund of close acquaintance with children of every age. Integrating simultaneous developments, they put back together the child segmented by topical analysis.

The third variety is the rarest. This is the general theorist of human development: Jean Piaget, Erik Erikson, Heinz Werner. The general developmentalist attempts to formulate laws that are not limited to one sort of content, to synthesize as much as possible of human development. In one way, the general developmentalist resembles the content-centered analyst; both seem a little detached, the generalist downright Olympian. The person who is in there mixing it up with Dick and Jane on a daily basis is the child psychologist.

All three kinds of developmental psychologist have made discoveries worth knowing. But because they are three distinct kinds—in their interests, methods, and goals—it is a daunting challenge to put their work together. When the author of this book was a graduate student, he showed a startling inclination to be all three kinds of psychologist at once. He had a particular content focus, a very original one: the child's comprehension and use of symbols. Howard Gardner was, in the same years, very much a child psychologist. Readers of his experimental and theoretical papers were always surprised to learn that the same man spent a good deal of time just becoming acquainted with children: giving piano lessons, teaching classes in elementary school, learning from his own children. The general developmental theorist also made an early appearance. There were in those days, and are still, quite a few developmental psychologists on the faculty of Harvard University. And they offered good courses on moral development, language development, personality development, and so on. Howard Gardner asked several of his professors why, with so many developmental psychologists, there was no integrative seminar, no course on the general theory of development. Probably, each of us pronounced it a splendid idea and then withdrew into his foxhole. So Howard Gardner organized the seminar himself, together with like-minded peers.

In Howard Gardner's previous distinguished books, one or another of the three kinds of developmental psychologist could be said to be dominant. In the book you hold in your hands, the three have operated in perfect balance, and a structure has been found that accommodates all of developmental psychology. That structure is explicitly set forth in the Introduction: a stagewise progression that incorporates content specialties by becoming an epigenetic progression; it copes with cross-cutting issues by introducing interludes. The author is the one to describe all this. The only thing I am better positioned to do than he, is to report on how well the design works. That is for readers to say, and I am one.

It can never be taken for granted, of course, that a design will succeed. We have all seen elaborate outlines at the start of a book or a lecture course that even when scrupulously adhered to do not exactly "work." That is, they do not do much for the content. But a structure that works confers upon a stretch of exposition the blessed property of readability. Sentences do not plod along like weary foot soldiers, but strain forward, one upon another, each prepared for and half anticipated, and demanding to be read now. And integrating over time into an enduring memory. This effect cannot be achieved by using common words or short sentences or sensational content or even the first person singular. Only structure can do it, and the structure must be organic. It is so in this book.

What makes structure succeed, what makes it organic, is, of course, almost totally mysterious. In a book intended to be used as a text, however, I think we can identify at least one precondition. The author must have mastered his content—the important experiments and phenomena and theories—until all these exist in his mind in a state of high cognitive mobility. This renders him able to place each bit where it will be most tellingly felt; to select, subordinate, and dramatize, and not simply to reel everything off. I honestly did not think that one author could bring the whole of developmental psychology into such a state of readiness. But the author of this book has done it and done it on a more comprehensive scale and with greater penetration than has anyone else.

In fact, it seems to me that every intention succeeds. The reader is refreshed by the alternation of cognitive and affective topics and, as the book builds, develops a sense of wholeness, a sense that no aspect of human development has been slighted. Beginning each major discussion with the description of interesting concrete phenomena, the author engages us at once in thinking with him and trying to guess what is ahead. The interludes are experienced as a relaxation, not because they are less involving, but because they cross-cut the main design and show us other patterns.

All this emphasis on structure may suggest a feeling of relentlessness which is, in fact, totally absent. One experiences the book as continually fresh and surprising. The things that most delighted me are not likely to be exactly the same as the things that will most appeal to you, but you may want to watch for them. The start of the Introduction, growing out of a childhood memory of Jean Piaget's, is a brief, deft example of how structure brings life to prose. The diary entries concerning the Gardners' daughter Kay and her Big Bear must charm everyone. The sustained tension between cognitive-structural theory and environmental-learning theory does much to unify the book. The analysis of studies that seem to confound Piagetian theory is not only up-to-the-minute, but brilliantly perceptive. The inclusion of Douglass Carmichael's work on the appreciation of irony, along with a discussion of formal operations and moral reasoning, in the chapter on adolescent thought is fresh and revealing. The discussion of early infantile autism is superb. There is an invented colloquy among seven kinds of developmental psychologist, puzzling over how children learn to recognize melodies across transpositions of key. It is intended to reveal the interplay of fact and theory in developmental psychology, and it is stunningly successful. But if you let this tempt you to read things out of order, you will cheat yourself of the monumental effect, when it is read where it has been placed, of the Epilogue: "The Self Across the Life Span."

One effect was not planned: the impression we form of Howard Gardner's feeling for children. I notice it whenever he uses the word "youngsters," a word seldom heard or read today, but used very often in his book. As used, it seems to be a compound of protective affection, wondering admiration, and helpless enchantment. You will find that the author takes special pleasure in turning up something that is better developed in children than in adults; for instance, eidetic imagery. You will notice that though no research can be said to have proved that violence on television harms children, the author, nevertheless, has an uneasy feeling that it does and is careful to point out that the research that has been done is still not very directly relevant to the issue. My guess is that it is the author's concern for children, his admiration of them, and respect for their individuality that prevents *Developmental Psychology* from ever sounding remotely like a "baby book."

Yes, there are three of everything and that includes varieties of developmental psychology. In this book, however, the three become one, a single seamless narrative.

Roger Brown
Harvard University
August 1981

A Note to Instructors

In writing *Developmental Psychology,* I have sought to compose a comprehensive yet readable introductory text, one that gives a feeling for children of different ages and clarifies the processes of human development. The specific kind of book I have written reflects my own vision of developmental psychology—a vision I have shared with all readers in the Introduction. This note explains why I believe such a book is needed, how the book has been designed to meet those needs, and how it might be adapted for different forms of instruction. I have also noted new features of the second edition.

RELATION TO OTHER TEXTBOOKS

In reviewing other developmental psychology textbooks, I have discerned several characteristics that diminish their usefulness. To begin with, many tend to be encyclopedic: in a commendable but misguided effort to be comprehensive, they overwhelm the nonprofessional reader with hundreds of studies. Complementing this feature is a kind of theoretical blindness or agnosticism: either theories are avoided altogether, or each makes a scheduled appearance, only to disappear thereafter. Additionally, most texts fail to convey the texture of developmental psychology—its most interesting problems, its most salient phenomena, its dominant points of view. And rarely does one receive the feeling that author and reader are genuinely collaborating in an exploration of difficult issues.

A final and especially troublesome characteristic of many developmental texts is the failure to provide a coherent organization of the field. Authors have either embraced the age-stage approach, thereby obscuring the way events unfold within a single domain of development, or they have favored a topical approach, which fails to convey a sense of the child as a whole during each stage. What is needed is a framework that integrates the field's facts, theories, concepts, and themes into a single coherent story of human development, thus giving at once a sense of the whole and a feeling for process.

These are serious indictments. They explain the widespread dissatisfaction I detected some years ago among instructors of developmental psychology, their disappointment about the gap between the exciting field in which we are all engaged and the lackluster nature of most texts. In this book I have sought to respond to the problems outlined above, with the goal of providing a more effective account of the field—*our* field.

CHARACTERISTICS OF THIS TEXT

In my view the major innovation in this text is its organization. In an effort to capture the strengths of both the age-stage *and* the topical approaches, I have devised an epigenetic structure: the book has five parts corresponding to the major developmental stages, but the focus within each part falls on those issues (such as the role of attachment or the effects of schooling) and on those domains (such as language or moral development) that appear most crucial during that period of life. This approach, which seems to capture more of the natural course of development than either the age-stage or the topical organizations, highlights issues and domains when they are most important, while deemphasizing topics of lesser importance during that stage. For instance, language development is accentuated in the preschool years, moral development in adolescence; and milestones in these areas are reviewed more briefly during other stages.

The epigenetic approach has yielded several consequences for the book's organization. The first two chapters of each part deal with two major domains of development during that stage: cognition and affect, individual factors and social factors, the world of physical objects and the world of persons. The final chapter generally contains a more comprehensive discussion of that stage of development, including, when practical, an attempt to synthesize the two domains traced in the opening chapters. In addition, each part begins with a discussion of vivid phenomena that seem to exemplify that period of life, and then moves to the important but sometimes drier factual material relevant to the stage. Thus Chapter 1 focuses on the concept of attachment as a means of exploring the infant's initial ties to the world of social objects, and Chapter 2 traces the course of sensorimotor intelligence in a parallel consideration of the infant's initial contacts with the world of physical objects. These cognitive and affective themes, which will characterize the entire course of development, should help awaken students' interest in and appreciation of the details of genetics and early physical, perceptual, and motor development presented in Chapter 3.

In the chapters themselves, intensive discussions of major issues are interwoven with less-detailed surveys of other topics. Rather than mentioning briefly all the research that supports or disconfirms a position, I have preferred to examine representative studies in some depth and then allude to other research. This combination of narrow and broad focus—an alternative to the more typical ency-

clopedic survey in which all topics and studies are weighted equally—should provide students with a textured understanding of the most central issues in developmental psychology. Moreover, because of the constant interplay among the several developmental domains mentioned above, students can gain a genuine feeling for the recurring and cumulative aspects of development.

Because they transcend or cut across the stages and the domains of development, some crucial topics do not fit readily into the epigenetic structure of the text. Although they are often treated in a text's first chapter or two, I have placed these topics in interludes between the parts, for I feel that students will gain more from such discussions if they have already begun to explore the substance of development. Accordingly, the history of child study forms an initial interlude: having met some theorists and pondered some issues in the field, students can now discover where these lines of study began. The next interlude, a review of the concept of development, comes after students have become familiar with developmental processes. A consideration of atypical development—the subject of the third interlude—is based on knowledge of the normal course of development. And, finally, the synoptic view of theories and methods in the concluding interlude follows the application of each one during discussion of appropriate topics.

Like any other author, I would like to have my vision apprehended as a totality; and I hope that the way themes have been organized will appeal to all who might assign this book. But some instructors, because of scheduling constraints, personal preferences, or their own vision of the field, will doubtless wish to omit some chapters or rearrange others. Accordingly, I have written this book to allow flexibility in its use. The self-contained interludes can be read at almost any point in the course, so that instructors who are accustomed to starting, say, with history and the concept of development can simply assign those interludes first. By the same token, the chapters within each part can also be rearranged. For instance, instructors who wish to begin their treatment of infancy with prenatal development or genetics can assign all or the opening sections of Chapter 3 before Chapter 1; those who prefer to treat cognitive matters before the concept of attachment can simply reverse the order of the first two chapters. And instructors who want to teach a short course in developmental psychology can assign just the Introduction and the opening two chapters of each part (11 chapters in all), while still preserving the vision I have sought to articulate here.

I believe that any work of this scope benefits from a point of view, a theoretical orientation. Even as an author owes it to colleagues to put his theoretical cards on the table, a concern with theoretical issues creates a framework for students, making explicit what is often implicit and providing analytic tools for dealing with future issues. My own perspective in this book is that of the cognitive and structural schools. This vantage point leads to an emphasis on cognitive investigations, with an inevitable reduction of attention to other orientations. But I have introduced other theories, particularly the environmental-learning point of view, and have sought to be even-handed in assessing the contributions of each. Indeed, whenever necessary, the inadequacies of the cognitive-structural view are noted, and phenomena are accounted for either in terms of another theory or by means of a possible rapprochement with other theories.

Most of us in developmental psychology have been struck by the dynamic growth of our area of study, the important discoveries made within the field as well as the increasing connections being forged with other disciplines. Unquestionably, the major stimulant to

this growth has been the application of scientific methods of study—both imported from other disciplines and devised specifically for the study of children. A major goal of this text is to enable students to understand these contributions and, to the extent that it proves possible, to participate themselves in the practice and the further development of this science.

At the same time, however, it would be lamentable were developmental psychology simply to ape *science,* in the narrow sense of that word. The study of children, and of developmental psychology, benefits from a variety of approaches that reflect the manifold ways individuals can make sense of experience. History, art, and literature help us understand both how children think and how adults think (and have thought) about childhood. Children's own thoughts, behaviors, and testimony can be illuminating. And numerous practical, and even political, issues concerning children, such as the effects on children of their mothers' working or the possible negative consequences of schooling, assume the important role of connecting the subject matter of a text with the press of daily decisions. All these sources of insight, suggestive supplements to the growing wealth of scientific information, combine to yield a fascinating and exciting discipline, one with tremendous potential for informing most aspects of our lives. If students can share in the excitement of the field and connect it with their daily lives, my aspirations in writing this text will have been fully realized.

FEATURES OF THE SECOND EDITION

Instructors familiar with the first edition will readily assimilate the present volume. The organization of the book has remained substantially the same. Most of the major themes and motifs have also been retained.

Yet in another sense, the second edition of

Developmental Psychology is a wholly new book. In preparing this edition I have read exhaustively through the contemporary literature in developmental psychology and have sought to bring the text totally up to date. Every chapter has been reworked, a few have been completely rewritten, and nearly every sentence of the book has been altered in order to make this edition as authoritative as possible. Indeed, half of the references that are cited appeared after the first edition and many are from the 1980s.

Over and above minor reworkings, shifts of emphases, and correction of errors, this edition differs from the first in three principal ways, each reflecting shifts which have taken place since the middle 1970s. First, while Piaget's work remains central, I have taken a more critical approach to his theoretical constructs and have surveyed evidence which calls into question some of his claims. Piaget remains a dominant figure, but he is no longer the dominating presence in developmental psychology. As a counterpart, I have paid more attention to alternative accounts: I survey the increasingly popular information-processing approach to cognition and also treat those theorists, both nativist and empiricist, who question the existence of stages and other qualitative changes in development.

Finally, and perhaps most importantly, this edition places far more emphasis on recent work in the areas of social development, social cognition, and social behavior. Included are an account of the leading theories as well as a broad survey of what has been discovered about social activities and relations throughout childhood. Chapters 5 and 8, both of which focus on social aspects of development, have been extensively redrafted and Chapter 12, a more theoretically oriented account of social development, is an entirely new essay.

ACKNOWLEDGMENTS

Even more in this edition than in the first, I have come to appreciate the indispensable role played by colleagues in the writing of a book. I have been thrilled by the reaction of readers, seasoned professors as well as undergraduates, who wrote or told me their reactions to the book and their suggestions for improvements. Even when I have not been able to follow their leads, I remain in their debt. A number of colleagues read and commented on whole sections of the manuscript and I owe them a special debt of gratitude: Helen Benedict, Michigan State University; Lloyd Borstelmann, Duke University; Nancy Cook, University of Washington; William Damon, Clark University; Shirley Feldman, Stanford University; John Gibbs, Ohio State University; Stanley Kuczaj, University of Minnesota; Leighton Stamps, University of New Orleans; Hoben Thomas, Pennsylvania State University; Michael Tomasello, Emory University; and Phyllis Weaver, Harvard University. For additional help, I'd like to thank Michael Cole, Tom Davies, and Elissa Koff.

By far the most technical and voluminous area of developmental psychology these days is the area of language acquisition. Despite good intentions, I no longer have a comprehensive grasp of this field. Therefore, I was most delighted when Ellen Winner agreed to assume primary responsibility for the redrafting of Chapter 4. My own assessment of her achievement has been confirmed by a number of reviewers who consider it the best short summary of this area currently available.

My colleagues across the river at Little, Brown and Company have continued to thwart any inclinations on my part to treat the publisher as the foe. They have handled their end of this complex project with skill, facility, and friendliness. I am especially indebted to my editor, Mylan Jaixen, and also to Sally Stickney, Victoria Keirnan, and particularly Elizabeth Schaaf for their impressive editorial skills and assistance in the various phases of this project. My deepest gratitude to each of them. The adjuncts to this book, the *Study Guide, Instructor's Manual,* and *Test Bank,* have been ably prepared by P. S. Associates and Kathleen M. White at Boston University.

Typing was done in a most accommodating and careful manner by Judy Fram, Celia Shneider, Debra Kaufman, and Elynn Finkelstein.

For their pivotal roles in the preparation of the first edition, I would like once again to thank Jane Aaron, Albert J. Becker, Roger K. Bufford, Joan Burns, Pauline R. Christy, Marvin W. Daehler, Carol S. Dweck, Helen Jones Emmerich, David Feldman, Marian Ferguson, Kathleen Field, Hiram E. Fitzgerald, Judith Fram, James Garbarino, Judy Gardner, Jean Berko Gleason, Murray Grossman, Elaine E. Holder, Blake Keasey, Hope Kelly, Charles Liberty, Kenneth Livingston, Harry MacKay, Frederick J. Morrison, Deborah Otaguro, Freda Rebelsky, Anne Rosenstiel, Tina Schwinder, Karen Sheingold, Sheldon White, Ellen Winner, and Mary Virginia Wyly.

Again my loving gratitude goes to my children, Kerith, Jay, and Andrew, who have taught me much about child development, who allowed me to describe their antics, and even to play with their names, and have waited—now twice—with bemused patience for "their book" to be finished.

Roger Brown has represented an ideal to me in scholarship, writing, and personal integrity since I had the good fortune to become his student some fifteen years ago. I am honored and humbled by his generous foreword to this edition.

The most important contributor to this book has been Eve Mendelsohn, my assistant, colleague, and friend. Working on a daily basis with me and with Little, Brown, she has handled all aspects of the preparation of this book that I could possibly foist upon her. And she has carried out her diverse assignments with unbelievable skill, loyalty, and flair. Perhaps this book could have been reworked without Eve's help, but it could never have been done so well or so quickly. Her contributions appear on every page and they inform the substance as well as the trimmings of this text.

Howard Gardner

Cambridge, Massachusetts
September 1981

Brief Contents

Contents

CHAPTER TWO
Gaining Knowledge About the World *57*

CHAPTER THREE
From the Fetus to the Discovery of Self *93*

INTERLUDE

The Origins of Child Study *136*

PART II

The Preschool Years *154*

CHAPTER FOUR (with Ellen Winner)

Language Development *157*

CHAPTER FIVE

Entering the Social Realm   *199*

CHAPTER SIX

The Playing Child *231*

INTERLUDE

The Model of Development in Psychology *256*

The Years from Five to Seven *274*

CHAPTER SEVEN

Communication with Others and with Oneself *277*

CHAPTER EIGHT
Influences of the Family, the Community, and the Society *305*

CHAPTER NINE
The Symbols of the Young Artist *338*

INTERLUDE
Another Perspective on Human Development *368*

PART IV
Middle Childhood *384*

CHAPTER TEN
The Intellectual Revolution of Middle Childhood *387*

CHAPTER ELEVEN

Skills and Schooling *424*

CHAPTER TWELVE

Relations with Other Selves *459*

INTERLUDE
Theories and Facts in Developmental Psychology *491*

PART V

Adolescence *508*

CHAPTER THIRTEEN
Thought During Adolescence *511*

CHAPTER FOURTEEN
The Experience of Adolescence *541*

EPILOGUE
The Self Across the Life Span *579*

Themes of Developmental Psychology

Lord, I do not remember living this age of my infancy. I must take the word of others about it and can only conjecture how I spent it even if with a fair amount of certainty—from watching others now in the same stage.

  –St. Augustine

I was not even a year old perhaps. . . . I can see my mother taking me in her arms, then she puts me down again. . . .

  –A mnemonist quoted by Alexander Luria

Suppose you wish to learn the fundamentals of physical chemistry, acquire a classical language, or investigate the intricacies of economic theory. You are likely to enroll in a course, or perhaps devise a program of reading for yourself. With each of these subjects a body of knowledge is assumed to exist; you tackle it, in the hope of advancing from relative ignorance to the point where you can think intelligently about molecular bonds, intransitive verbs, or the balance of payments. If you insisted that you could acquire these subjects without study, or that you already knew about them from experience, you would be thought a bit mad. There is no reason to believe that these subjects can be mastered without effort and study.

When it comes to the field of psychology, claims of "know-

1

ing all there is to know" may at first seem more plausible. After all, psychology is the study of thought processes, feelings, behaviors; should not anyone who has thought, felt, and behaved for many years, and especially anyone who has reflected on these psychological processes, be an expert? And what of developmental psychology—the investigation of children's thoughts, feelings, and behaviors, and of the ways these evolve throughout life? Because we have all been children, can we not consider ourselves experts in the discipline? Having already experienced childhood—having thought, felt, and behaved as children, and having subsequently reflected on our experiences—we may already possess the central insights of the field of developmental psychology.

Yet we are no longer children, and so our knowledge about childhood must be housed somewhere in our memories. Access to our childhood depends, first, on playing back memory's internal filmstrip and, second, on interpreting what was happening at the time the frames were shot. It becomes crucial, therefore, to determine how accurate our memories of childhood may be. Only if they are reasonably faithful can we place any confidence in them, and thus in our "natural" expertise about developmental psychology.

The Reliability of Memory

One can find testimony from surprising sources regarding the extent and reliability of our memories of childhood. The English novelist Charles Dickens has his David Copperfield remember events from early infancy:

The first objects that assume a distinct presence before me; as I look far back, into the blank of my infancy, are my mother with her pretty hair and youthful shape, and Peggotty, with no shape at all, and eyes so dark that they seemed to darken their whole neighborhood in her face. . . . I think the memory of most of us can go farther back into such times than many of us suppose, just as I believe the power of observation in numbers of very young children to be quite wonderful for its closeness and accuracy [*David Copperfield*, 1930, pp. 12–13].

Such claims are not confined to fiction. A Russian mnemonist (a person with nearly total recall) reports faithful memories of the first months of life:

I was not even a year old perhaps. . . . I can see my mother taking

A scene from *David Copperfield*. While personal recollections in a work of fiction present the author with an opportunity for sheer invention, such fictional memories may also prove revealing about the kinds of events and experiences that individuals are likely to recall from childhood.

I BEGIN LIFE ON MY OWN ACCOUNT, AND DON'T LIKE IT.

me in her arms, then she puts me down again. . . . I sense movement . . . a feeling of warmth, then an unpleasant sensation of cold. . . . This is the sense I had of my mother: up to the time I began to recognize her, it was simply a feeling "this is good." No form, no face, just something bending over me, from which good would come [Luria, 1968, pp. 76–77].

Such evidence from the pen of a great writer or from an expert "memorizer" has an undeniable persuasiveness. Yet the case for a reliable memory of one's childhood would gain in power if more scientific evidence could be collected in its favor. A highly relevant source of data comes from the neurosurgeon Wilder Penfield who, by electrically stimulating brains during surgery, enabled patients to recall previously unremembered incidents in their lives. Penfield has concluded that the brain contains a permanent store of all that has happened in the individual's life. As he explained: "There is, hidden away in the brain, a record of the stream of consciousness. It seems to hold the detail of that stream as laid down during each man's waking conscious hours. . . . In this record are all those things of which the individual was once aware" [1958, p. 58].

So far, the evidence we have reviewed favors the proposition that we have reliable and fairly complete memories from early life. And so, up to this point, the field of study called developmental psychology itself remains in jeopardy. But since, as you have no doubt observed many times, memories can also be deceiving, they cannot be expected to provide a reliable guide to one's earlier experience. As an example of such deceptiveness, we can consider an early memory related by Jean Piaget, one of the most important contributors to developmental psychology:

I was sitting in my pram, which my nurse was pushing in the Champs Elysées, when a man tried to kidnap me. I was held in by the strap fastened around me while my nurse bravely tried to stand between me and the thief. She received various scratches, and I can still see vaguely those on her face [1962*a*, p. 188].

Piaget clung to this memory until he was about fifteen. Then his parents received a letter from his former nurse, confessing her past sins and returning the watch she had been given as a reward for protecting the infant Piaget. In fact, she had made up the whole story, even faking the scratches. Piaget speculates: "I therefore must have heard, as a child, the account of this story, which my parents believed, and projected it into the past in the form of a visual memory, which was a memory of a memory, but false" (1962*a*, p. 188).

To confirm his speculation, Piaget devised a set of laboratory experiments that would test the reliability (or unreliability) of children's memories (Piaget, 1968; Piaget and Inhelder, 1973). In a typical study, he showed children an array of ten sticks arranged from the shortest to the tallest as shown in the drawing at left. He asked the children to examine the array closely because they would be asked to draw, describe, or recreate it at a later date.

A week later the children were asked to reconstruct the array from a set of sticks. Only the seven-year-olds succeeded in reproducing the original design. As these drawings illustrate, the children offered a variety of incorrect responses.

After six months, children were asked to reconstruct the array once again. Although younger children usually did not produce the array correctly, their designs were closer to the original than those they had made after a week. In fact, there was a clear sequence: those who had made the middle pattern after a week made the bottom pattern after six months; and those who originally constructed the bottom pattern were making the top one. Three-fourths of the children in one study had a better recollection of the original array after six months than after one week. And despite the time lapse, not a single child displayed a poorer memory.

These results strongly challenge commonsense notions of memory, including the accounts of faithful memory presented

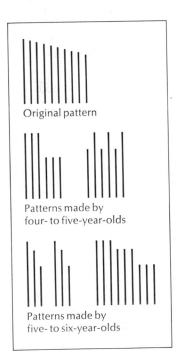

Original pattern

Patterns made by
four- to five-year-olds

Patterns made by
five- to six-year-olds

by Dickens, Penfield, and the Russian mnemonist. In Piaget's view, children do not simply form a correct or incorrect mental photograph of the original array that can be retained and retrieved at any later time. Rather, they make the best sense they can of the array when they first see it. Then, whenever they are asked to reproduce the array, they do so in a way that reflects their understanding of arrays of sticks at that particular moment in their lives.

But what is there to understand in a series of sticks ordered from longest to shortest? What seems self-evident to adults goes unappreciated by young children, who are unaware that the second stick is shorter than the first but taller than the third, and so on. The most three- or four-year-olds understand is that there is a group of sticks, and so that is all they can possibly store in memory. And the five-year-old, although noting some differences in size, does not yet appreciate their ordering.

Over time, as children's understandings of principles of order develop, their reconstructions of the original array become increasingly ordered. They make increasing sense of their fragmentary recollection, so that the recollection itself apparently passes through stages of improvement. The result, paradoxically, is that children's reproductions become more like the original the longer it has been since they saw the original. Memory does not, by itself, improve over time; rather, the child's *understanding* of order improves. And this enhanced understanding is revealed in later tests of recall.

Piaget's dramatic demonstration raises many questions about what memory is and is not. This study has stimulated a whole line of research (see, for instance, Liben, 1974, 1975*a, b,* 1976, 1977, Maurer et al., 1979) and has yielded a number of findings that challenge certain facets of Piaget's argument. For instance, the paradox of "improving memory" occurs only when there is an intrinsic order in the original array—memory does not improve for a random assortment of sticks or an arbitrary design. Yet, whatever the subtleties and problems of Piaget's original study, his experiments seem to demonstrate decisively that one's memories of childhood are not completely reliable: it is no less difficult for us to recall a time when we were unable to do arithmetic (and therefore could not pay a bill), or when we relied on our parents to fulfill every need (and therefore never had to work to achieve a goal), than it is for children to recall with accuracy an array whose construction they do not understand. It has even encouraged a critical examination of the strong claims put forward by the surgeon

Penfield (Neisser, 1967). Ironically, and yet appropriately, this ingenious investigation in developmental psychology provides a strong rationale for the existence of, and the need to study, the field of developmental psychology.

Piaget's studies also show that efforts to understand a psychological phenomenon can legitimately begin almost anywhere—with a surgical procedure like Penfield's, with memory of a childhood incident like Piaget's, with a piece of fiction or a report by a person with unique powers. But establishing the validity of one's notions requires that they be tested by experiment. Such a procedure is currently being applied to Piaget's views on memory and to hundreds of other ideas about human development. And this process from idea to experimental demonstration to subsequent refinements to the proposing of new ideas forms the mainstream of contemporary developmental psychology.

Building a Science of Developmental Psychology

So long as scholars simply collected anecdotes about children or recalled their own childhoods, knowledge about the processes of human development accumulated slowly and unreliably. The study of children as a science began less than a hundred years ago when the methods used by scientific researchers in other disciplines were applied to children. Before long, the field had acquired serious researchers, important findings, and a charter to guide further investigation.

A SCIENTIFIC APPROACH

Developmental psychology attempts (1) to devise methods for studying organisms as they evolve over time; (2) to collect facts and figures about individuals of different ages, backgrounds, and personalities; and (3) to construct a theoretical framework that can account for the observed behaviors as well as for the changes occurring throughout the life cycle. Developmental psychologists typically investigate children, though adults and other developing organisms (ranging from mice to monkeys) are also considered. Researchers usually focus on people's behaviors and thought processes, though other aspects like physiology or neurology may also be taken into account.

Although the particular steps of a research program naturally depend on the researcher, and on the nature of the problem being investigated, an overview of certain fundamental

steps and procedures will enable you to evaluate the observations and experiments to be presented in the following chapters. We will attempt such an overview by sketching how a
typical study in developmental psychology might be conducted.
And, to flesh out this example, we will refer back to Piaget's
study of memory, even speculating about what might have
been on Piaget's mind when he conducted his research.

OBSERVATIONS, HYPOTHESES, AND OPERATIONAL DEFINITIONS

Psychological investigation usually begins with **systematic observations** of behavior—the collection of facts. Individuals
trained to observe behavior record what they have seen and
heard as carefully and completely as they can. They try to disregard any personal feelings about the phenomena in question
and to refrain from imposing an interpretation. As we saw
above, Piaget stepped back, observed, and then reflected on his
own experiences. And as we shall see later, he also carefully
observed his three children and drew on his impressions in
designing more elaborate experiments.

But observations, however intriguing they may be, represent
only a foundation upon which controlled experiments are built.
Based on an observation, a deduction from a general theory, or
a response to another investigator's claim, the psychologist's
first step is to formulate a **hypothesis.** A hypothesis is a precise
statement or proposition that attempts to explain the phenomenon in question, or to trace the relations between two or
more phenomena. The subsequent experiment must either help
prove or disprove the hypothesis. If there is no way the hypothesis could be proved wrong, it is of scarce interest to the
scientific community; after all, one could cling to the hypothesis regardless of how any (or all) experiments happen to turn out.

We can see the experimental method in action by returning to
Piaget's study. Provoked by his own experience, Piaget speculated that children's memories are sometimes unreliable. To
establish this observation's validity (or truth) and to determine
its generality (the extent to which it applied to a cross section
of children observed under different conditions), Piaget had
first to state a hypothesis and then to undertake an experiment
that would either support or discredit the hypothesis. Given
the general nature of his first hunch, Piaget might have hypothesized that "Children's levels of understanding determine
the contents of their memories" or "Memories improve over
time." Each hypothesis could have suggested a somewhat different line of experimentation.

Let us suppose that Piaget hypothesized "Children's memories of a display seen at time A but measured at time B reflect their understanding at time B of displays of that general type." The next step is to form an operational definition of (or to **operationalize**) the crucial terms within the hypothesis—that is, to define experimental procedures that can stand for the major terms in the hypothesis. Unless this is done, other investigators will be able neither to confirm that the hypothesis has actually been tested nor to test the hypothesis in their own laboratories. In Piaget's hypothesis, the crucial terms would be "memory," "display," and "understanding." (In contrast, such terms as "children," "time A," and "time B" could be defined in various ways without altering the basic design of the study.) In Piaget's study, the operational definition for "memory" was the child's physical manipulation of a set of sticks at some time after the original presentation of the sticks. The operational definition for "display" was an ordered set of sticks. The operational definition for "understanding" was the particular pattern of sticks arranged by the child—whether a seemingly random production, a pattern featuring some short and some long sticks, a partially ordered array, or, the highest level, a correctly ordered sequence of sticks. Piaget might also have administered a separate test of understanding (for example, asking the child to describe the array to another child) but, as it happens, he did not do so.

Though these operational definitions seem sensible, and did yield provocative results, the same hypothesis could have stimulated alternative operational definitions. For instance "memory" might have been singing, "display" a series of musical tones, and "understanding" the particular pattern of tones sung back by the child. Such a set of definitions might well have yielded different results—for instance, the memory for the tones might have deteriorated or remained constant over time. Because of these limits in operational definition, any experiment—no matter how inspired—can constitute only a single strand of evidence in support of a hypothesis. If a hypothesis is to be strongly confirmed, and if the theory on which it is based is to be validated, a series of experiments and a variety of operational definitions are essential.

CONDUCTING A STUDY

Once a hypothesis and operational definitions have been arrived at, researchers must lay out an exact set of procedures and then treat all subjects identically. They must define the

population (or group) in which they are interested (say, American school-age youngsters drawn from the middle class), from which they select a sample of subjects in an unbiased way. This ensures that any conclusions are not restricted to the particular subjects seen (for example, ones known personally by the experimenter, or ones who go to a special school) but can be confidentially applied to the entire population (for example, all middle-class schoolchildren in America).

The specifics of the experimental design determine how the subjects are grouped and how measures of behavior will be taken. Let us suppose that Piaget had become interested in how children's memories for a series of sticks seen at time A change over one-month intervals. The children could be retested every month for six months (time B to time G) and their responses (understanding) at each time of testing could be categorized.

Suppose further that the children showed steady improvement over the six-month period. Could Piaget conclude that his hypothesis had been confirmed? Not really, beause the children may actually have been trained (or have become bored or otherwise affected) by the monthly testing. Thus, in addition to this **experimental group,** it would be necessary to set up one or more **control groups.** Children in the control group, selected at random from the same population, would be shown the original stimulus but they would not be retested again until time G at the end of six months. If children in both groups produced similar arrays after six months, Piaget could infer that the monthly testing was not affecting the experimental group; instead, it provided an accurate and more detailed assessment of children's memories and understanding at each time. If, however, the performances of children in the experimental and control groups differed at time G, then the repeated opportunities to arrange sticks probably did affect ultimate performance: conclusions derived from the experimental group about the "natural course" of memory would be suspect.

Of course, even if the results bore out Piaget's hypotheses, they could be challenged. One reasonable objection would be that the study tests only memory for an array of sticks and might have little generality to other kinds of displays. As it happens, other displays have been looked at and the picture put forth by Piaget retains some validity.

One of the most intriguing variations tested subjects' memories of drawings of liquid-filled containers that had been tilted at various angles (Liben, 1975a). It turns out that this is a difficult task, and that many subjects will initially draw the liquid

Kindergartners and fourth graders were shown these stimuli. One week later and then five months later, they were shown the same, but incomplete, drawings and were asked to complete them. Correct completion required that the children understand horizontality by adding a horizontal liquid line. (Liben, 1981)

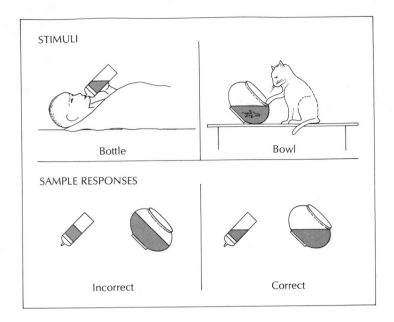

STIMULI

Bottle

Bowl

SAMPLE RESPONSES

Incorrect

Correct

so that it is parallel to the base of the container, rather than parallel to the horizon (see the figures). Consistent with Piaget's analysis, memory for the appearance of the water level improves over time; and so subjects' drawings at later intervals may prove closer to the original display than subjects' drawings directly following exposure to the original display. Interestingly, improvement occurs here chiefly with subjects of an older age (about the age of nine); for younger subjects, the whole concept of "horizontality" is apparently sufficiently complex or confusing that they are not yet in a position to benefit from the passage of time. They continue to draw the liquid parallel to the base of the container.

CONCEPTUALIZING THE DESIGN AND ANALYZING THE DATA

In order to think clearly about their experimental design and to analyze their data properly, scientists (including psychologists) have adopted a way of conceptualizing their studies. They speak of manipulating **factors,** or **variables,** in order to determine how such manipulations affect a subject's behavior. The factor varied by the experimenter is called the **independent variable:** in our specimen study, the time elapsing between the presentation of the stimulus and the request for recall is completely controlled by the experimenter. Reflecting the effect of this experimental manipulation is the **dependent variable:** in our study, the children's behavior (the particular ways in which they arrange the sticks) is presumed to depend on the amount of time elapsed after original presentation.

If the children produce the same arrangement of sticks regardless of the amount of elapsed time, then the independent variable of elapsed time has not affected the dependent variable of memory. If, however, memory does reflect the effects of time, then (as hypothesized) the dependent variable has been affected by the independent variable. To ensure the validity of the findings, one must be certain that no other factors contributed to the results. As we have seen, a control group can indicate which effects are attributable to the independent variable and which (if any) to such extraneous factors as unintended training across sessions.

Once all the children's behaviors have been collected and scored (in this case, characterized as exemplifying one or another memory pattern sketched above), the experimenter can determine whether the hypothesis has in fact been confirmed. Occasionally, the results speak for themselves. But in general it is advisable to subject the collected data to **statistical analysis**—mathematical procedures that indicate whether the results may be attributable simply to chance, or whether they differ enough from chance to confer some causal power on the independent variable. If, at time B, 85 percent of the children make patterns identical to those they make at time G five months later, then time is unlikely to have made a statistical difference and any effects should probably be attributed to chance. If, on the other hand, 85 percent of the children make displays at time G that are closer to the original than those they made at time B, then elapsed time will have been shown to exert a significant effect on memory.

Having properly operationalized the hypothesis, used control groups, and secured and analyzed the data, the experimenter returns to the original hypothesis to judge its validity. No single study can establish a hypothesis (though it might invalidate one). But by judiciously evaluating the data, by relating them to findings in other studies (for example, those testing the depiction of liquids), and—perhaps most important—by performing two or three follow-up studies suggested by the original observations, the experimenter can certainly make progress in assessing the hypothesis and in evaluating the theoretical framework within which it was formulated or analyzed.

For the most part, developmental psychologists have focused on performances by subjects of a given age. Like Piaget, they have assumed that children of the same age can be readily grouped together. But an important area of study concerns the existence of and explanation for **individual differences:** responses that may differ consistently among subjects of the same age. One factor that often gives rise to differences among individuals is social class background; for instance, subjects from a middle-class background may score at a different level or use different strategies from those drawn from an upper-class or lower-class background (we will look at such social class differences in Chapter 8). Another important, and often controversial, area involves differences between males and females. As it happens, males perform consistently better on tasks involving the depiction of horizontal liquids than do females (Harris, Hanley, and Best, 1975; Liben and Signorella, 1980; Thomas, Jamison and Hummel, 1973). The issue of sex differences will be discussed in Chapters 5 and 8, and we will revisit the problem involving horizontal liquids in Chapter 14.

In carrying out programs of research, whether they focus on group differences across ages or individual differences within age groups, experimenters generally choose between two research designs. They may elect to take periodic measures of the same group of subjects over a long period of time; in doing so, they will be using the **longitudinal method.** Alternatively, researchers may elect to examine several age groups during a single brief interval of time: in this case they will be adopting a **cross-sectional method.** As it happens, Piaget has drawn on facets of both designs. He used different groups of subjects during a relatively short time span, but secured data on the same subjects at various intervals over a six-month period. Although this hybrid design may at first be disconcerting, its existence conveys a very important point. In fact, no psychological experiment ever proceeds completely "according to the book": there are always exceptions, deviations from past practices, and novel problems in the design of materials and the analysis of data. And this unexpectedness, far from being frustrating, constitutes part of the challenge and excitement of all scientific research.

OTHER SOURCES OF INSIGHT

Controlled experiments provide the most important data for a science of developmental psychology. But other approaches also contribute to our understanding of children and of the developmental process. In all probability, the chief nonexperi-

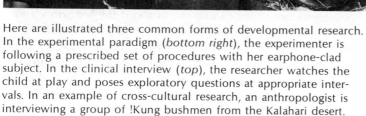

Here are illustrated three common forms of developmental research. In the experimental paradigm (*bottom right*), the experimenter is following a prescribed set of procedures with her earphone-clad subject. In the clinical interview (*top*), the researcher watches the child at play and poses exploratory questions at appropriate intervals. In an example of cross-cultural research, an anthropologist is interviewing a group of !Kung bushmen from the Kalahari desert.

mental approach used by psychologists derives from work in clinical settings such as hospitals, schools, or asylums. Here the sustained and intimate relation between individual patients and a physician, therapist, or other clinical worker engenders a detailed and deep understanding of a single individual that nicely complements more superficial but more reliable information secured experimentally.

Sometimes such a relationship culminates in a single case study. Sometimes a researcher will group results from several similar (or instructively contrasting) case studies. At still other times, observations made initially in a clinical or therapeutic setting will give rise to a standard experiment.

The clinical research tradition has many offshoots, but we will be concerned in this book with only two of them. The **clinical approach** includes researchers from the psychoanalytic or psychiatric tradition, particularly Sigmund Freud and his followers. These investigators work chiefly with disturbed children or adults whom they seek to help with psychotherapy.

In his initial research conducted in the 1920s, Piaget pioneered the second offshoot, called the **clinical interview.** In this procedure, lengthy interviews are conducted with normal individuals in order to arrive at a detailed understanding of a person's mental processes. These interviews usually begin with a prescribed set of questions (or issues), but they are deliberately structured loosely so that the researcher can follow up promising leads or unexpected responses.

Although there are dangers in relying on one's introspections, recollections and thoughts about childhood can certainly be valuable. Fictional accounts of childhood, books written for, by, or about children, autobiographies, and even carefully conceived paintings of children can provide insights into their lives, particularly facets that do not lend themselves to the strict, quantitative measurements of scientifically oriented researchers.

Disciplines other than psychology may also contribute. Historians can enlighten us about children in diverse cultures. Sociologists can provide information about the behaviors and attitudes of groups of children as well as about the social forces that influence whole societies or eras. Biologists can instruct us about children's bodies, and physicians, psychiatrists, and social workers can help us see the effects of physical and mental health or illness. Finally, philosophers concerned with the nature of knowledge can encourage and help us to examine important but often ambiguous concepts like "development," "stage," "memory," or "understanding."

The theoretical, cultural, and scientific issues of childhood are crucial but somewhat removed from our daily experience. What of the more practical issues of child care and education? Should children be subjected to strict discipline? Should they be sent to day-care centers? Should they be allowed to watch violence on television? Science can provide a range of responses to questions like these, but decisions must ultimately be made by individual parents or citizens, drawing on their common sense, their life experiences, and, to the extent that it seems appropriate, their interpretations of research findings. Some familiarity with the "hows" and "whats" of research can aid us in deciding which findings are important and which are misleading, trivial, or incorrectly interpreted.

The Approach of This Book

STAGES OF LIFE, DOMAINS OF DEVELOPMENT

Let us suppose that two people are preparing to spend a year in Japan. One of them studies Japan's history, from its first recorded accounts in the fifth century to the present. The other focuses by turns on different aspects of Japanese life, starting with government and moving on to religion, mythology, geography, and so on.

In roughly the same way, one can adopt different approaches to developmental psychology. On the one hand, development can be seen as a series of principal life stages (phases or steps) beginning with infancy and extending to the adult years. In a book based on this approach one identifies the principal features of each life stage and then relates each stage to the ones preceding and following it. Consideration of each stage includes important aspects of the child, ranging from physical capacities to awareness of others to intellectual capacity.

The contrasting (and equally prevalent) approach to development is a topical one. A book based on this approach focuses on the important domains of development, one at a time. One chapter may be devoted to intellectual development, one to social development, one to physical development, and so forth. Within each chapter (or more than one chapter, if the topic warrants such attention), the book begins with infancy and surveys the whole course of development.

Each of these approaches has definite assets, but neither is ideal. Following the child through stages makes it difficult to keep track of growth in a single domain like intellectual development. On the other hand, focusing on individual domains makes it difficult to discern the relations among simultaneous events, so that one loses sight of the infant or adolescent as a whole.

In this book, I have sought to combine the strengths of the stage and domain approaches. The general progression is by stages, with each of the five principal parts of the book devoted to a major period of childhood: infancy, the preschool years, the beginning of school, middle childhood, and adolescence. Each part presents a general picture of what the child is like at that age, although any ages given are approximate, because there are no precise timetables regulating all children. By the same token, I have often introduced examples of particular children, including my own youngsters. To provide a proper balance among "typical" children, and to be consistent with the rhythm of the book, the pronoun used to refer to single children will be alternated from feminine to masculine across parts of the book.

Although this approach should yield a comprehensive picture of each stage, I have not attempted to cover *all* facets of development during each stage. Instead, I have singled out the domains that assume special importance during each stage. Language, for instance, figures in a person's life from the first babblings to a dying sigh. But the major changes and spurts in language development occur during the toddler years, roughly between the ages of two and five. Thus language development is examined in detail in the second part of the book. Although touched on at several other stages, the child's emerging linguistic capacities are treated most comprehensively at the stage during which they are most salient.

A similar strategy determines how the other major developmental domains are treated. For instance, we will focus on the infant's knowledge of the physical world; the toddler's evolving family and peer relations; the communication ability of the child entering school; the rapid acquisition of skills valued by the culture during middle childhood; and the adolescent's developing moral and scientific reasoning. When a topic has overriding importance, as does social development, it receives detailed treatment in several of the stages. Thus, the reader of this book should become familiar with children at each stage of development, while also securing detailed knowledge of the central events occurring in each major domain of development.

FACTS AND ISSUES

In tackling any field of study, one needs pegs on which to organize information. In history, names and dates prove useful; in chemistry, the formulas for compounds and the rules of equations serve as building blocks. And in developmental psychology, it is crucial to have some facts about children, especially facts about the variations among children of different ages, abilities, backgrounds, and personalities.

But facts alone have little use. Data on the heights of children, the number of words they speak, or the kinds of games they play are readily forgotten; they acquire significance and become worth committing to memory only when they are put together to tell a story and lead to informative conclusions. Can changes in height be tied to changes in brain structure or to the amount of stimulation in early childhood? Will the number of words spoken reflect the child's underlying understanding of events? Does the type of game favored relate to the child's temperament and motivation? Only in answering such questions do barren facts come to life and achieve a meaningful place in one's own thinking about a subject.

The actual facts of child development are seldom disputed. However, the field of child development is pervaded by deep disagreements over *which* facts are important, *how* they ought to be related, and *what* conclusions they lead to. An honest look at the discipline must examine the contrasting points of view, or theories; show how they might differ in their interpretations of specific findings; and indicate which practical and theoretical implications follow from these interpretations. A primary aim of this book is to do just this. Whenever possible, the various differences will be introduced through a central issue drawn from life—such as why a boy might grow up thinking of himself as a girl, or whether adolescence must be an emotionally turbulent time—thereby making the controversies concrete and meaningful.

My goal in presenting the competing claims, theories, and conclusions is not to impose a mindless eclecticism in which every view is equally valid. Nor is it to destroy all points of view. Rather, it is to expose you to the range of thinking in this growing discipline and, when possible, to bring about a tentative synthesis among several views, showing how seemingly disparate elements may be integrated into a single, encompassing orientation.

THEMES, TENSIONS, AND ORGANIZING PRINCIPLES

Let us return for a moment to our Japan-bound travelers. Suppose that their trip has been completed and that now, some years later, they are looking back on their experiences. No doubt they will remember isolated facts—perhaps the population of Kyoto—and dramatic experiences—for example, the time they got squeezed in Tokyo's mobbed subways. But their year will probably come to be organized in memory according to overriding themes or patterns characteristic of Japanese society—the charming politeness of most Japanese, the care taken in dress and gardening, the gains and costs of industrialization.

In my view, one's understanding and appreciation of any experience—or any field of knowledge—depend as much on the themes and organizing principles that pervade the domain as on the specific facts or details that have been committed to memory. And so, in this book, even as we encounter myriad experiments and details, we will maintain a *thematic* approach to the discipline—searching for principles, patterns, tensions, and issues around which thoughts about developmental psychology can reasonably be organized.

In my own efforts as a developmental psychologist, I have been strongly influenced by the **cognitive-structuralist** point of view, expressed in the writings of Jean Piaget and various of his colleagues and followers. These researchers view the child as an active organism who, over time, constructs his or her knowledge of the world. They also believe that development can be usefully described as a series of stages, or steps, that succeed one another in an orderly fashion. The cognitive-structural approach will be contrasted to **environmental-learning theory,** which sees the child as passive and malleable, heavily influenced (or formed) by the environment. The environmental learning theorist prefers to regard development as a continuous process and to stress the continuities between animal and human, between child and adult (see Brainerd, 1978*c*; J. Langer, 1969; Reese and Overton, 1970).

Bearing in mind my own theoretical leanings, I have attempted to sketch both points of view in some detail and to delineate the advantages and limitations of each. Quite often, we will find that the two views are not irreconcilable. Instead, a cognitive-structural approach may prove more illuminating for some facets of an issue, whereas the environmental-learning approach may prove more appropriate for other aspects. Occasionally, other theoretical orientations have been introduced. When possible, I have sought to blend the views into a sensible synthesis.

Several other tensions that have pervaded discussions in developmental psychology will crop up in the following pages. The first is between cognitive and affective approaches. Psychologists partial to a **cognitive** interpretation focus on children's mental processes—on their ability to reason and solve problems. Those partial to an **affective** approach focus on children's feeling life—on their "lived" experiences, emotions, and ties to other persons. Researchers interested in *social development* have allegiances to both cognition and affect, though much of the work on social development reviewed here has a definite cognitive flavor.

A second tension exists between *biological* and *cultural* (or social) approaches. A biological approach focuses on children's genetic heritage, on their neurological and physiological constitution, and on the natural stages of development that characterize all human beings. A cultural (or social) approach minimizes the individual's biological predisposition, and highlights the contributions of the environment in general, of other individuals in the society, especially one's own family and friends, and of the customs, values, and standards of the particular culture in which an individual is raised.

A final tension is encountered between *universal* and *individual* approaches. Many scholars whose work is reviewed here search for universal properties—traits and behaviors that characterize normal children throughout the world. Others, focusing on the differences among individual children, search out the origins of these differences, their evolution, and their ultimate significance for the life of the individual.

These tensions are reflected in the organization of this book. In each of the five parts, the first chapter highlights one approach (for example, a cognitive view of the child), and the second chapter highlights an alternative view (for instance, an affective or social view of the child). In most of the parts, the final chapter will tie the two approaches together or introduce another, more comprehensive view of the child.

At places in this book, some other devices are also offered as a means of organizing the enormous body of information about childhood. To begin with, each stage of development covered here is characterized with a central image of the child: the infant as a well-equipped stranger to a new world (Part I); the toddler as a player (Part II); the child entering school as an artist (Part III); the schoolchild as a skill builder (Part IV); and the adolescent as a young scientist or philosopher (Part V). In no sense should children be reduced to the image of their age, but the image may suggest what is distinctive about the stage.

A second device involves the notion of three systems that develop during childhood: the perceiving system, which includes the perceptual discriminations the child can make; the making system, the actions of which the child is capable; and the feeling system, the child's sensations and emotions. We will see how these evolve and how they interact on two levels: first, in infancy, on the level of physical and social objects (Chapter 3), and then, a few years later, on the level of symbols—words, pictures, numbers (Chapter 9). These three systems, which together constitute all the child's capacities, provide a convenient way of organizing disparate facts about the child's competence and, more generally, of viewing the child's development.

Three systems do not make a person; they must somehow combine into an organized whole that can function smoothly and can eventually reflect upon or conceive itself. This crucial process of integration can be seen in the development of a sense of self. Though the mature sense of self forms only in adolescence, its roots can be observed much earlier, in the memorable moments when children recognize their reflection in the mirror, or say their own name. In tracing the evolution of the child's sense of self, we will follow an important thread—one that can serve as a suggestive metaphor for the entire process of human development.

INTERLUDES

Human development is a story, and the natural growth of the child provides a consistent, coherent, and often compelling narrative. Yet some aspects of developmental psychology that cut across the ages and domains of the discipline fall outside a chronological approach. Some of these themes have been treated in separate, brief chapters, called interludes, that are featured between the major parts of the book.

The first interlude treats the history of childhood and child study, indicating how conceptions of children have changed over time and how folk wisdom gradually yielded to a more systematic, scientific discipline. In the second interlude we will examine the concept of development, beginning with its original application in biology and focusing on its uses, implications, and limitations in psychology. The third interlude shows how children who differ quite markedly from their peers can provide an alternative perspective on human development, at times supplementing and revising formulations based exclusively on the study of the "normal" child. In the fourth interlude we will compare and contrast the theories and methods of seven psychologists as they ponder a single research finding about children. Besides summarizing the theoretical tensions encountered elsewhere in this book, this interlude raises questions about the nature of scientific inquiry in developmental psychology. Finally, in the Epilogue, our interlude between this book and the world beyond, we will consider briefly some principal events of the adult years and recapitulate, in conclusion, the development of the sense of self throughout the human life cycle.

A First Signpost

Each chapter in this book ends with "signposts," a brief section providing the kind of information valued by travelers in the course of a journey. Signposts will include a look back to prior chapters, a summing up of the main themes and questions discussed in the chapter, and a preview of the coming chapters. Here, however, the urge is to look only forward, to begin our search for the essence of developmental psychology. So rather than reviewing the state of the field and the plan of this book, let us examine some of the difficulties and rewards to come.

The puzzles of development are subtle and complex; and there may never be a complete formula for its ultimate mysteries. The very nature of the developmental process may elude living creatures who are themselves (ourselves) always in the process of developing, of becoming. Indeed, our very act of understanding alters our future development, even as that development in turn alters our own understanding. And, to complicate the undertaking further, the objects of our study—children—are themselves developing very rapidly in a world we cannot hope to understand fully.

The lure of studying developmental psychology is twofold. First, there is the intriguing question of how the infant grows into a capable—and sometimes exceptional—adult. Of course, all possibilities are built into the newborn's genetic heritage, but no one could use that heritage to predict just where the child would go and what heights (or depths) would eventually be attained. In a way, human development represents the ultimate instance of pulling oneself up by one's own bootstraps: children's own constructive efforts, undertaken in a supporting environment, culminate in an increasingly complex person and in the emergence of a developed sense of self. To be sure, the achievements of each successive stage of development are logical; yet they are not simply inevitable outcomes of the individual's potential at the beginning of the stage. Unexpected events interact with predispositions to yield an unexpected (and thus more intriguing) product. And this unique product provides the input for the "bootstrapping" that continues during each succeeding developmental stage.

Complementing the fascination of the developmental process is a second lure: the excitement of observing a field of science that is rapidly acquiring new insights and that is marked and sustained by eager argument and substantive debate. Cognitive-structuralists and environmental-learning theorists care deeply about the issues of growth, and their discussions often carry considerable intellectual power. Productive syntheses have sometimes resulted from these (and other) tensions in the field. And because developmental psychology is still a young and growing field, it is possible for a newcomer to appreciate the debates, to learn from them, to participate in them, and even to make significant contributions to their resolution.

Even as developmental psychology is evolving, your understanding of this book and your command of developmental psychology should undergo similar growth. Conversations with friends and teachers, observations of children, and your other reading should make important contributions. I hope this book will neither confirm the obvious nor confound all your expectations, but rather serve to stimulate your thinking, encourage discussion and argument, and eventually allow you to go beyond the tentative summations and syntheses provided here.

With this overview of developmental psychology and this preview of your text, we are ready to consider the first stage of life—the two years of infancy. We turn first to the crucial relationship between infant and parents, a relationship that promises to color, if not control, the child's entire life. And because this relationship seems rooted in our biological evolutionary heritage, we begin with an examination of the attachment between the infant monkey and its mother.

PART I

Infancy

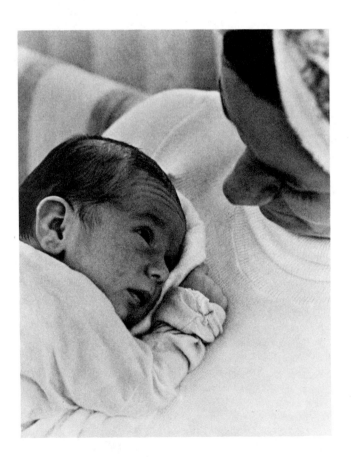

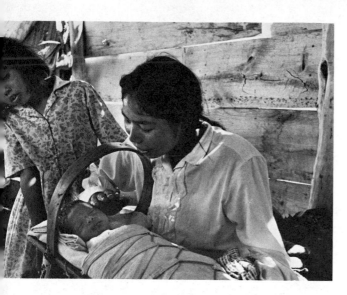

The newborn child faces two major challenges: to become acquainted with the social world of other people and to gain understanding of the physical world of objects. The first of these begins when the child recognizes the existence of other people and, most particularly, the principal caretaker, usually the mother. The resulting bond of attachment and sense of trust will have important consequences for the child's later well-being.

To understand the physical world, the child must build upon basic ways of processing information, which eventually yield complex ideas about the attributes and behavior of objects and their existence in space and over time. This "sensorimotor" intelligence is a product of the interaction of the child and her environment. Upon this foundation the increasingly advanced cognitive levels of childhood and adulthood are constructed.

Infants are strangers to the world, but they are, fortunately, well equipped to master its challenges. Their genetic heritage, the nine months spent in the mother's womb, and their capacities to perceive, to act, and to feel all combine to bring about the affective and cognitive advances that mark the first two years. By the end of their second year children have begun to know the world and to gain a sense of their own place in it.

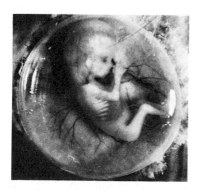

CHAPTER ONE

Bonds of Attachment

A child forsaken, waking suddenly,
Whose gaze afeard on all things round doth rove,
And seeth only that it cannot see
The meeting eyes of love.

  –GEORGE ELIOT

I'm interested in the social and psychological conditions that enable a woman to be a good mother and a man to be a good father.

  –JOHN BOWLBY

If anthropologists discovered a culture in which newborn children did not form intimate attachments to adults, the news would make headlines in the scientific community. After all, newborn infants are helpless—they need support and sustenance from mature humans. For most infants, the caretaker will be the mother, who has already housed her offspring. Equipped with food and warmth to sustain the child, she is strongly inclined to aid the child in the first days of life. Whatever happens later, the first weeks belong to mother and child.

Because the attachment between mother and child is so predictable, there is a tendency to take it for granted. But though an uncriti-cal acceptance of attachment may be wise for mother and child, it is risky for researchers. And so scientists have come to pose several complex and profound questions about the nature and the purpose of attachment. The mother must provide food, of course; but if attachment is to occur, must she also provide smiles, messages, and that most elusive but prized possession—love? Is the mother-child bond present from birth, or does it build slowly, and, if so, how does it evolve? How long does it normally last? Who can partici-pate in the bond? What costs accrue if a bond does not form? Must the child's natural mother be involved in bonding, or could the baby be cared for exclusively by the father, by a group of other adults, or even by other children?

In this chapter we will examine some prominent thinking and research on these and related questions. When possible, we will report on laboratory studies of human attachment. Often, however, the relations between caretaker and child are not fit subjects for experimental manipulation. One cannot (and would not want to) alter a caretaker's relationship to a young child to satisfy scientific curiosity. For this reason it is important to dwell on two other sources of information. The first is the pathbreaking research into the effects of maternal deprivation on infant monkeys, conducted by Harry Harlow and his associates. The second, which complements Harlow's work and extends it to humans, is John Bowlby's studies of children raised in institutions.

Although the bond between infant and mother is intriguing in its own right, its ultimate importance for the study of human development rests on its consequences for the person later in life. We will consider which conditions of early childhood are likely to bring about a healthy relationship among individuals and a sense of trust that can endure throughout life.

Before we become immersed in the details of mother-child relations, one matter needs airing. Whether the child's mother is the only, or even the best, possible caretaker is itself a subject for study, and later in the chapter we will examine the child's relationship with other adults, including the father. When we speak of the "mother" throughout this chapter, it is not to prejudge this sensitive issue (about which researchers know little) but to describe the current situation. The fact is that young infants are almost always and everywhere cared for by their mothers. Adopting a more neutral term, such as caretaker, nurturer, or mothering organism, seems both awkward and possibly misleading.

Harry Harlow's Studies of Attachment in Monkeys

For many years Harry Harlow had been one of the most prominent and insightful investigators of animal behavior in this country. While he focused primarily on primate learning—how monkeys solved problems (Harlow, 1949)—he occasionally encountered intriguing behaviors that seemed unrelated to his stated research goals. For instance, after separating young monkeys from their mothers so they would not be exposed to disease, Harlow noticed that the offspring became physically healthy but seriously impaired socially. Another time Harlow noted that monkeys often became quite attached to soft cheesecloth diapers in their cages. Finally Harlow visited an institution where he saw human infants huddling pathetically in corners (Harlow, 1973).

At first Harlow did not pursue or relate these scattered observations because they seemed symptoms of the affective (or feeling) life, and he was studying cognitive (intellectual or problem-solving) capacities. Yet, what began as incidental impressions of affective life eventually became central in Harlow's research. Piecing together the bits of behavior he had witnessed, he launched a series of epoch-making studies that probed the role of the mother monkey during the early months of her offspring's life, the needs she fulfills, the services she supplies, the degree to which she is indispensable. These studies helped to explain why monkeys cling to diapers, why seemingly healthy monkeys may become maladjusted, why institutionalized human babies may fail to develop normally. Most tellingly, they suggested explanations for the powerful mother-child bond in human family life.

MONKEYS WITH SURROGATE MOTHERS

In the view of the mother-child relationship traditionally held by behavioral researchers—

particularly by proponents of environmental-learning theory (see page 18)—the mother is satisfying the child's basic physiological needs (see Dollard and Miller, 1950). The baby is an organism that needs its stomach filled, and nothing more. The mother, a source of food, becomes associated with all forms of gratification. Whatever intimate relations and profound attachments might eventually evolve between them rest on this initial gratification of need.

Because (for better or worse) experimental manipulations are tolerated with nonhumans, Harlow could put this widely accepted theory to a test. He created two kinds of **surrogate** (or substitute) mothers (Harlow, 1958). The first, called the "cloth mother," consisted of a cylinder of wood covered with a sheath of terry cloth. The second, the "wire mother," was simply a wire cylinder. (See Figure 1.1.) Within twelve hours after birth, four newborn rhesus monkeys were placed alone with the cloth mother, another four with the wire mother. The cages were constructed so that each monkey had the option of "visiting" the other surrogate mother.

Each mother was provided with a bottle holder so that the baby could nurse on it. For experimental purposes, therefore, the two mothers were essentially the same, except one had a softer, more comfortable surface that might soothe or attract the young monkey. And of course it did. What was more unexpected, and scientifically revolutionary, was that even when nourishment was provided only by the wire mother, the infant still spent most of its time clinging to the cloth mother (see Figure 1.3). Thus, not only does warmth exert an attraction independent of mere gratification of a physical need, but baby primates become more attached to a source of warmth (or "contact comfort") than to a source of food. Anticipating the implications of this finding, Harlow quipped, "Man cannot live by milk alone" (Harlow, 1958, p. 678).

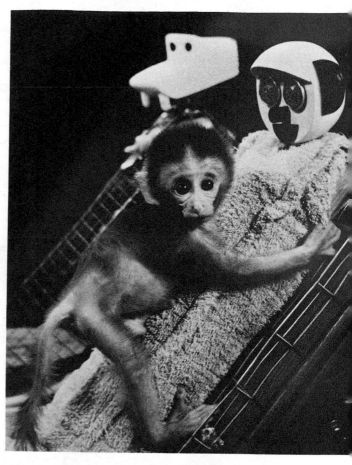

Figure 1.1. A baby monkey demonstrates a clear preference for the soft contact comfort of a surrogate cloth mother; the unappreciated wire mother can be seen in the background.

Normal human and monkey infants will withdraw from a fearful object into the bosom of their caretaker. Would infant monkeys reared by the surrogate mothers do the same? To find out, Harlow deliberately frightened the infants. In one study, a moving windup bear toy with large, contrasting features was presented to the infants in their cage (Harlow and Zimmerman, 1959) (see Figure 1.2). When frightened by this "bear-monster," infants raised exclusively by the cloth mother initially clung tightly to their "mother" and then gradually ventured forth. On the other hand, infants raised exclusively on the wire mother shoved the fearful object

Figure 1.2. Remaining close to its surrogate cloth mother, a baby monkey looks warily at the "bear-monster" provided by the Harlow research team. Eventually, the monkey may venture forth to explore this strange creature.

Figure 1.3. Whether fed on a wire or a cloth mother, infant monkeys spend an overwhelming amount of their time clinging to the cloth mother. The comfort furnished by soft contact proves far more seductive than the site where nourishment has been obtained. (Harlow, 1959)

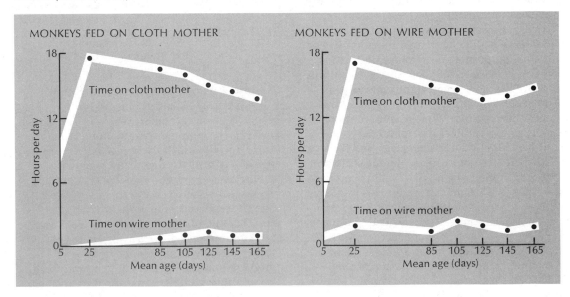

away, but they neither clung to nor otherwise embraced the wire mother. Instead, in a manner akin to the institutionalized human infants that Harlow had observed, they clutched themselves and rocked back and forth, threw themselves on the floor, or rubbed against the sides of the cage. These findings confirmed the importance of the contact comfort provided by the cloth mother, as well as the lack of appeal of the wire mother.

Harlow also wanted to determine the strength of the bond between surrogate mother and child. He found that after a period of separation monkeys "raised" by cloth mothers maintained an attachment (Harlow and Zimmerman, 1959). They were comforted by the reappearance of the mother and returned to it when it was reintroduced. In frightening situations, infants ran to where the cloth mother had been and awaited its return. In sharp contrast, infants raised with a wire mother showed little preference for it and were not calmed by its appearance.

By the end of his initial series of studies, Harlow had apparently isolated a crucial variable: the opportunity for the infant to have comforting physical contact with a soft object. Yet it hardly seemed possible that mothers (whether human or monkey) merely provide a soft place of repose. Indeed, when Harlow took into account other behaviors, a less blissful picture emerged. For instance, in one study of seven females raised by surrogate mothers, five were either abusive or indifferent toward other monkeys; only two interacted adequately; and none could copulate normally. Experimental manipulations had rendered the monkeys incompetent as adults.

ISOLATED MONKEYS

A next logical, if somewhat heartless, step was to assess the total contributions made by the mother, whether biological or surrogate. Harlow and Harlow (1969) imposed conditions of utmost deprivation: monkeys were raised in a metal chamber, in complete isolation from humans or other monkeys. Attainments of such monkeys would clearly not depend on having a single caretaker, and any behavior deficits would probably result from the absence of a mother figure.

Motherless rearing produced an even bleaker picture than rearing by a wire surrogate. Monkeys clutched their own bodies compulsively. They rocked or paced repetitively and spent an inordinate amount of time putting objects into their mouths. When later exposed to other monkeys, they were usually apathetic, staring vacantly in their cages and ignoring the activities of others. At times they acted aggressively toward both observers and themselves—biting their own hands, arms, feet, or legs. This self-directed aggression differed completely from the behavior of normal peers and even of the surrogate-raised monkeys. The isolated monkeys reminded Harlow of the most deprived institutionalized human infants he had seen.

The extent and duration of these bizarre behaviors reflected the length of the isolation. Monkeys in solitary confinement for the first three months of life were retarded socially when initially returned to monkey society, but with the help of new mothers or peers they generally recovered to normal or near-normal levels. But monkeys who had been isolated for a whole year could not be helped. These monkeys never played with others or displayed proper sexual behavior. They were socially so backward that normal animals perpetually mistreated them, rendering them confused and helpless. Even their aggression was inappropriate. For instance, they sometimes engaged in near-suicidal threats against much larger adult males or attacked and bit younger monkeys. They appeared to dread all normal social contacts.

Despite their sexual inadequacy, a few of the motherless females did become pregnant (Harlow and Harlow, 1962). Their behavior as mothers turned out wholly abnormal. They paid no attention when their infants were removed from the cage, though such a separation usually engenders the most violent reaction from a normal mother. Those who nursed their children often abused them violently. Quite possibly, they did not know how to mother because they had never themselves been mothered.

At the conclusion of his first decade of study, Harlow (1971) was convinced of the centrality of the infant-mother bond in primates. The moral he drew—that mothering is central to normal development in *all* primates—was widely publicized and widely viewed as authoritative. Much more recently, the work of a number of researchers, including that of Harlow's own group, has questioned the strongest of the early claims. We will consider some of these modifications later. But the most powerful claims concern-

Figure 1.4. For both human and baboon, many moments of contact over a period of months form the basis of attachment between mother and child. Yet despite the similarities between species, there are so many differences that generalizations from one to the other can only cautiously be made.

ing *human* attachment—those proposed during the past two decades by John Bowlby—fit in well with and drew on the initial findings from the Harlow laboratory. While monkeys clearly differ from humans, carefully studied cases in the animal world can illuminate what we know about our own species. Bearing this in mind, let us therefore examine the main points of Bowlby's position.

John Bowlby's Studies of Human Attachment

ORIGIN OF THE STUDIES

In the 1940s the United Nations World Health Organization asked John Bowlby, a British psychiatrist, to study the effects of mother-child separation in early childhood. After reviewing available evidence (for example, Ribble, 1944; Spitz and Wolf, 1946), Bowlby and his colleagues spent considerable time observing children who had been apart from their parents for a long period, including youngsters in nurseries and hospitals where there was no stable mother-substitute. In addition, they conducted intensive interviews with psychologically ill adolescents and adults in order to locate possible sources of their illnesses in the experiences of early childhood.

In 1951 Bowlby and his colleagues reported that normal infants who have been separated prematurely from their mothers are unable to relate satisfactorily to any person and are afraid to play, venture forth, explore, discover the world beyond their own skins, or even discover themselves. Bowlby reached this conclusion: "What is believed to be essential for mental health is that the infant and young child should experience a warm, intimate and continuous relationship with his mother (or permanent mother-substitute) in which both

find satisfaction and enjoyment" (Bowlby, 1966, p. 11).

Individuals who worked with children in clinical settings and others concerned with child care acclaimed Bowlby's work. But the reaction of researchers studying child development was more restrained. Although few directly challenged Bowlby's observations, many commented that he had not analyzed the *reasons* for the ill effects of separation. Moreover, critics noted that Bowlby's conclusions about the mother's importance involved a sizable extrapolation from his data.

Convinced that he had described a most powerful factor in human development, Bowlby decided to address competing views. These include claims by some environmental-learning theorists (for example, Gewirtz, 1961) that the mother serves only the baby's physical needs or that the tie to the mother is completely learned (and hence readily unlearned). Also at issue was the psychoanalytic assertion (A. Freud, 1949; Klein et. al. 1952) that the child's attachment to the mother is simply a "fixation" on the mother's breast, a means for reducing instinctual drive, a desire to return to the womb, or a need to cling to any available object. Bowlby also confronted claims that, although separation might indeed contribute to abnormality, its consequences need not be dire and in fact might be counteracted.

INSIGHTS FROM ETHOLOGY

In his search for a theoretical orientation that would account for all his findings, Bowlby became impressed by the analytic framework of **ethology,** at that time a new line of behavioral investigation (Lorenz, 1957; Tinbergen, 1951). Unlike workers in the environmental-learning tradition, who favor controlled studies in the laboratory, ethologists study the organism in its natural habitat. Such naturalistic observations of an organism are deemed crucial to a proper understanding of its most important behaviors—aggression, sexual relations, and other interaction between species members.

Ethologists do not, however, simply report everything a duck, fish, or monkey does. They are guided by specific hypotheses about just what factors in the environment determine a pairing, an aggressive or threatening gesture, or the location of a nest. Once their hypotheses have been tentatively confirmed in the animal's natural habitat, ethologists may then devise miniature experiments on the scene (see Eibl-Eibesfeldt, 1970).

Suppose, for example, that an ethologist interested in waterfowl has determined that ducks follow their mothers from an early age, that they will not follow other organisms after the first days of life, and that this early "attachment" is of prime importance in ducks' learning and socialization. Here, then, careful observation has uncovered an important set of behaviors. Suppose further that informal observations suggest that the infant duck is initially attracted by either a clucking sound, a moving target, or the tactile warmth provided by contact with another organism. These rival explanations could then be tested by experimental intervention. To determine which factor stimulates the following behavior, the ethologist would intervene in a young duck's world. If *motion* seemed to be the key variable, the investigator might prevent the mother duck from moving and see whether the duckling nonetheless remained close to its mother. Another moving target (say, a painted balloon) might then be placed in front of the duckling to see whether the duckling would follow this target instead. By such manipulations the ethologist would eventually determine which single element, or which combination, brings about the offspring's enduring following of its parent.

In this example the ethologist tries to determine which factors or **releasers** in the environment cause the infant to become **imprinted** on or permanently bonded to a mother figure (see Lorenz, 1957). Perhaps the duckling can be imprinted on a tape recording, in which case sound is serving as a releaser. Or perhaps the duckling will become attached to a source of warmth like an electric blanket. Or perhaps the releaser is a ducklike decoy or a human being who moves in a ducklike manner. In fact, by mimicking the strutting of a bird, ethologist Lorenz (1957) managed to make himself the object of a jackdaw's attachment: this jackdaw eventually regarded humans as parents and even as sexual companions!

In addition to studying the process and effect of imprinting, ethologists also examine the time during which such early behaviors emerge. In particular, they are looking for **critical periods,** fixed intervals during which pivotal events must occur, or releasers be encountered, if a certain lasting consequence is to ensue. For instance, Lorenz believes that a duck must imprint on its mother (or some other object) within the critical period of the first three days of life if a permanent attachment is to result. By the same token, Harlow has contended that monkeys must form enduring attachments during the first year of life.

Many researchers (for example, Corter, 1973; Oyama, 1979; Rajecki, Lamb, and Obmascher, 1978; Scott, Stewart, and DeGhett, 1974) urge caution in applying concepts of critical periods and imprinting directly to human beings. They prefer to speak of **sensitive periods,** fairly circumscribed times during which important milestones are most apt to occur, or are likely to occur in their most characteristic form. Yet the spirit of the ethologists' analysis has appealed to many students of the mother-infant relationship, and especially to John Bowlby.

THE COURSE OF ATTACHMENT AND SEPARATION

In his book *Attachment and Loss* (1969), Bowlby reexamined through the ethologist's lenses many of his earlier observations of the mother-infant bond. At first the infant's and parent's behaviors are quite simple and predictable: they resemble the stereotyped sounds and movements nonhumans display during bond formation or imprinting. The human infant's grasping, crying and sucking, the mother's cooing and hugging—these dominate the earliest social interactions. Soon, however, these behaviors are replaced by finer patterns of response. A single yelp becomes a variety of modulated cries; sucking is modified to fit specific objects; clinging is replaced by faithful following with the eyes.

In Bowlby's view, each of the infant's behaviors is designed to result in physical (and, eventually, psychological) closeness to the mother. The baby clings to the mother; the crying child signals fright and a need for comfort; the child following the mother with limbs or eyes seeks to maintain contact with her. The ultimate origins of this attachment, buried in the evolution of the species, may forever elude scientists. Bowlby, however, believes it reflects the fact that, over millions of years, the infant's best hope for survival has lain in proximity to a caring mother.

During the early weeks of life, the behaviors that maintain closeness are not directed

Figure 1.5. In the first phase of attachment, at around four months, the infant maintains intimate contact with the mother, and both feel pleasure. The foundation is laid for the stronger and more discriminating bond that will be formed during the second half-year of the infant's life.

Figure 1.6. A more active phase of attachment begins when the infant reaches out to members of her family. Soon, even more active forays will be made into the world beyond.

Figure 1.7. At the age of thirty-five weeks, when the attachment bond is strong, this Ugandan child shows distress at the prospect of being separated from his mother.

at a particular caretaker. But by the second half of the first year, the child clearly recognizes a primary caretaker (usually the mother), and unique styles of interaction with that person have evolved. Now one may speak of an **attachment** or an **attachment bond:** an affectional tie enduring in nature, specific in its focus—comparable in suggestive ways to the duckling's imprinting on its mother.

When a bond specific to one person has been formed, disruptions can be disturbing. Children a year old react with special vehemence when this bond is challenged. For instance, a child who encounters a stranger, even when the mother is present, may fret, cry, move away, or otherwise display anxiety.

So long as the mother remains nearby, this **stranger anxiety** will pass, but if the mother withdraws or the stranger comes too close, anxiety may be heightened. More profound distress—**separation anxiety**—is apt to occur whenever the child is suddenly separated from the mother. If such separation persists, as when the mother is hospitalized or dies, there are likely to be severe psychological costs.

Bowlby has outlined a sequence of events that typically follows long-term separation during the second year of life. At first the child protests, perhaps shouting, screaming, or running about wildly—marshaling all resources in an attempt to recapture the mother. Here is what happened when ten children were separated from their parents:

Eight of the children were crying loudly soon after their parents' departure. Bedtime was also an occasion for tears. The two who had not cried earlier screamed when put in a cot and could not be consoled. . . . One little girl, who arrived in the evening and was put straight to bed, insisted on keeping her coat on, clung desperately to her doll, and cried "at a frightening pitch." Again and again, having nodded off from sheer fatigue, she awoke screaming for her mother [Bowlby, 1973, p. 8].

During a second phase (the period of despair), such children are continually preoccupied with their mothers. Now, however, their behavior reveals increasing hopelessness. The children sit unoccupied, with mournful faces. As a defense against feelings of abandonment, the children build up extreme resentment against their mothers. For this reason, such a child will fly into a despairing rage if any traces of the mother appear. These children have fallen into so brittle a state that they cannot cope with reminders of earlier, more secure days.

Only after some months can the children relate to others and seemingly forget their own mothers. This detachment is often welcomed as a sign that the children can finally cope realistically with the lack of a parent. But such behavior masks damaging, long-range consequences: in managing to get along without their mothers, the children may sacrifice the ability to sustain enduring relationships with *anyone*. Should a child's mother return after the period of detachment, the child may turn away or show disinterest, seeming hardly to know her. If the separation has not been too long—perhaps only a few months—and if the mother can gradually reestablish the relationship, permanent damage can be averted. If, however, too much time has elapsed, or the separation has occurred during a particularly crucial (critical) period, the most ardent efforts of the caretaking parent may prove futile. (Bowlby, 1980).

If anxiety in the presence of a stranger or extreme reactions to separation were isolated phenomena, Bowlby's theory would be of scant interest. But in fact these behaviors have been observed among humans the world over (see Ainsworth, 1967; Lester et al., 1974) and even, in somewhat limited form, among nonhuman primates (Harlow, 1971). Moreover, as Bowlby (1980) has recently argued, the mourning in later life that follows loss of any beloved individual closely resembles that undergone by young children following the loss of a parent. Apparently we are dealing with compelling phenomena—ones that demand explanation.

THE MEANING AND FATE OF ATTACHMENT: BOWLBY'S CONCLUSIONS

Early attachment to a mother-figure is crucial; the absence or disruption of such an attachment signals subsequent difficulty. But the close tie between infant and mother is not permanent, and during the second, third, and fourth years of life it will gradually slacken. Bowlby views this gradual separation in ethological terms, as a natural step occurring when the needs that once dictated a close relationship have been satisfied. As the child becomes able to walk, talk, and actively explore the environment, direct access to the mother is no longer appropriate and contact can be maintained by various means at greater distances. So long as situations arousing anxiety are infrequent, the child can endure increasingly lengthy absences from the mother, secure in the knowledge that maternal support is available if needed. And the child gradually learns that contact need not be so frequent. Going it alone, or with the help of peers, the child can now find fulfillment elsewhere for many of the needs originally satisfied exclusively by the mother. In fact, the strong relationship formed with the mother may come to serve as a model for future relationships.

According to Bowlby, the latter part of the third year of life marks a crucial change. Until then, most children seem to be upset by the departure (or impending departure) of their mothers. Even if they do not cry for long, they search for substitutes, demand the attention of other adults, or sob longingly for their mothers. In contrast, by the end of the third year, most children will accept a mother's temporary absence without protest, playing in the meantime with objects or other children. They will also accept substitute attachment figures, such as teachers or relatives. Nonetheless, during times of stress throughout childhood, children will continue to search for their mothers or for other valued individuals.

Bowlby underlines the mother's role as a central and indispensable figure in the life of the child. This is probably the most controversial part of his theory, in part because he has picked out the female parent, in part because he has stressed the importance of a single figure. Could not the father substitute quite satisfactorily for the mother? Might not the same roles and needs be supplied by more than one figure, as apparently happens in other cultures?

Bowlby offers several reasons for singling out the mother. For one thing the mother's unique role in childbearing makes her the obvious candidate to care for the child. In his view the mother is also predisposed toward caretaking activities—such as the cuddling and singing that accompany feeding—which will promote the attachment bond. Her activities are likely to compel attention at a time when, like the imprinting animal, the child is prone to pick out and focus on a single individual. Neither the father nor a group can fill all these roles as adequately as the mother.

In Bowlby's view, if the attachment drama is appropriately enacted, it should culminate in confidence, self-reliance, maturity, and the ability to form enduring and successful attachments to one's own mate and offspring. In contrast, individuals who fail to forge secure relationships with their mothers may become unstable adults who will lack the strength that derives from a secure attachment and will fail to develop into competent parents.

Further Research on Attachment

Bowlby's work has become the point of departure for research and theorizing about the relationship between infant and mother. Some researchers have tried to verify Bowlby's claims in naturalistic settings. Others have worked in the experimental laboratory to help flesh out the details of attachment. But not all the evidence supports Bowlby's position. Critics have pointed out problems, introduced alternative theoretical considerations, and pon-

dered the implications of new research findings with primates. We will turn now to these different perspectives.

STUDIES SUPPORTING BOWLBY

The essential points of Bowlby's portrait of the attachment process have been widely supported. For example, two Scottish researchers, H. R. Schaffer and P. E. Emerson (1964), followed sixty infants for over a year. Besides verifying that most infants develop strong attachment to the mother in the second half-year of life (see Figure 1.8), these researchers also found that a child's attachment to other individuals, such as the father, in no way lessened attachment to the mother. Indeed, the more people a child was attached to, the more intense the attachment to the mother was likely to be. In a slight rebuff to Bowlby, however, Schaffer and Emerson described a small group of infants with stronger attachment to their fathers.

On this side of the Atlantic, Sally Provence and R. C. Lipton (1963) studied seventy-five children in an American institution. They found that children mistreated or ignored during their first year of life were severely retarded both intellectually and socially. Such youngsters made gains the following year if they received effective maternal care and were reintegrated into a family life. For instance, they began to respond to other people and to perform more adequately on measures of mental skill. Nonetheless, these children still exhibited difficulties, apparently because of their earlier deprivations. They were less able than children reared in normal homes to form enduring emotional relations with others, to control strong aggressive impulses, and to engage in play and other imaginative behaviors. Perhaps most tellingly, they displayed very little self-esteem. Lacking flexibility and confidence about themselves, they seemed completely unable to react deliberately and appropriately when faced with a difficult situation, such as a move to a new neighborhood. The striking contrast between these children and youngsters from normal homes led Provence and Lipton to reaffirm Bowlby's conclusion: Regular ties and attachment to the mother are a necessary ingredient in the normal development of the individual and the maturation of an adequate sense of self.

MARY AINSWORTH'S WORK WITH INFANTS IN UGANDA

The studies of Bowlby, Schaffer and Emerson, and Provence and Lipton were conducted mostly with infants raised in Western society. To determine whether patterns of attachment are similar in radically different social settings, Mary Ainsworth (1967; 1977*a, b;* 1979) spent several months observing two dozen infants in the Ganda tribe of Uganda, in Africa. Her study provided striking support for the main lines of Bowlby's thesis. Using sixteen measures of attachment, including the child's crying when the mother left the room and delight upon her return, Ainsworth discovered that most children were clearly attached to their mothers by the age of six months. Most began to fear strangers during the last quarter of their first year, though a few children did so as early as eight months (cf. Kagan, 1979).

Ainsworth also identified a few youngsters who were insecurely attached or, perhaps because they were slow developers, had not yet become attached by their first birthday. These children cried a great deal, fussing and demanding much attention, even if they were near their mother. Apparently, they did not regard her as a secure base from which to explore the world. These unattached youngsters seemed just like those in the West described by Bowlby and other researchers.

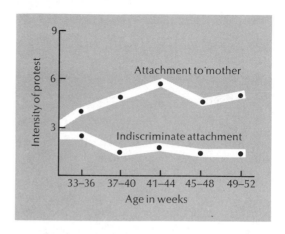

Figure 1.8. During the first half-year of life, children rarely protest when a person leaves their visual field. A general form of protest—fussing and crying—begins to accompany such a departure at six or seven months. This nondiscriminating reaction gives way toward the end of the first year of life to strong protest at the departure of specific individuals, most often the mother; the attachment bond has now been forged. (Schaffer and Emerson, 1964)

Although Ainsworth amplified and modified Bowlby's claims in several ways, for example documenting significant differences among infants in the type and intensity of attachment, her findings basically reinforce the thrust of Bowlby's position. Both regard the early months as a period of undiscriminating attachment. Then after six months or so, the infant recognizes her caretaker with whom she establishes a specific style of interaction. By age one the child both initiates and breaks off contact with her mother, who has become a central anchor point from which the child ventures out into alien domains. Ainsworth adds that while greeting her mother with enthusiasm, the child of this age responds to strangers by staring into space or warily examining them. In a final phase which extends to the second year, the child shows severe tension in the presence of a stranger, clinging tightly to her mother for long periods and actively resisting any lessening of contact with the caretaker.

In trying to isolate the variables that correlate with an early and successful attachment, Ainsworth came to distinguish among three types of babies. Those in group B were securely attached: they used mothers as trusted bases from which to explore, they were distressed by separation, and they sought close contact with their mothers when reunited with them. Babies in group C were insecurely attached: they were uncomfortable even during normal play, excessively distressed by separations, and ambivalent when reunited—seeking intimate contact and yet also resisting it. Finally, in sharp contrast, babies in group A failed to become attached: they rarely cried during separation episodes and actually avoided their mothers when they were reunited.

In general, the most successful attachments featured mothers who were confident about their supply of milk or who felt positively about breast feeding, and mothers who described their childrearing practices effectively. These "successful" mothers showed sensitivity to their children's signals of need and distress. Having few competing interests or concerns, they interacted enthusiastically with their offspring. They tended to adjust their behavior to the child's rhythms and tempos rather than imposing their own preferred pace upon the child.

As a result, group B infants formed a "working model" of the mother as generally reliable and accessible. In contrast, group A and C babies, cared for by mothers who disregarded their signals or responded to them inappropriately, had little basis for believing their mothers were dependable. Hence, they either became overly anxious about their mother's whereabouts or elected to avoid her altogether.

THE EARLIEST MOMENTS OF ATTACHMENT: INTIMATE DIALOGUES

The roots of attachment may extend back much further in the infant-mother relationship. Based upon extensive experience with newborn babies in the delivery and nursery rooms of hospitals, Marshall Klaus and John Kennell (1970) have put forth a radical proposition. In their view contact between mother and child during the first hours, and perhaps even the first minutes, of a baby's life may have crucial and positive long-term consequences. They have observed that mother and newborn are in an unusual state of alertness during the first moments of life. If given the opportunity for bodily and eye contact during this period, mother and child can forge a bond of intimacy. Mothers who have had this postbirth interaction are more likely than other mothers to display affection to their infants when they are observed some months later. There are also suggestions that such early contact may have cognitive as well as affective implications; for example, influencing the way in which mothers talk to two-year-olds (Flaste, 1977b). Clearly, in addition to helping the child become attached to her mother, the mother's actions are helping forge a strong attraction and attachment to the child who, until a few moments before, was very much a mystery to her.

Some researchers have challenged these strong claims (Leiderman and Seashore, 1975; Rutter 1979a; Whiten, 1977), and certainly more research is needed before a "critical period" version of the first hours of life is accepted. Yet there is growing consensus that mothers and infants in our culture readily enter into intimate dialogues with one another from an early age (Beebe and Gerstman, 1980; Brazelton, 1976; Kaye et al., 1979; Oates, 1978; Stern et al., 1977; Trevarthen, 1977;

Tronick et al., 1980) and perhaps even during the newborn period (Peery, 1980). Analysis of slow-motion films of these interactions reveals that they are exquisitely tuned and timed (Brazelton, 1976). Initially, as part of "pseudo-dialogues," the mother responds to the infant's spontaneous behavior, chiming in with oral responses, smiling and gesturing back in an exaggerated fashion to the child. The mother then waits for a response, and when a response is forthcoming, she will initiate some variation of the initial sequence. Usually the infant will attend carefully, as if trying to "take in" the whole display, and will behave quite differently toward a human than toward an inanimate object.

Figure 1.9. Bowlby outlines the normal development of the attachment bond. The ultimate outcome is competent caretaking behavior by the adult who was once a securely attached child.

BASIS OF ATTACHMENT	Evolutionary basis	Infant's best hope for survival lies in proximity to caretaker.
	Early weeks	Infant is predisposed to achieve closeness to people.
	Second or third month	Infant reacts to other people and environmental events; indiscriminate attachment to every individual and smiling face.
ATTACHMENT BOND FORMED	Six months	Infant seeks mother and reacts especially to her.
	Nine to twelve months	Infant maintains attachment link over some distance; increasingly takes initiative in contacts; begins to fear strangers.
GRADUAL SEPARATION FROM MOTHER AND ATTACHMENT TO OTHERS	Twelve to twenty-four months	Mother is the central figure for the infant; infant experiences tension in the presence of a stranger.
		Long-term separation from the mother will lead to protest, then despair, then relative detachment.
	Later part of third year	Child accepts temporary absence of mother without protest and will accept substitute attachment figures.
	Adulthood	Attachment bond is basic in the development of a self-reliant, mature adult able to form stable relationships. If no bond was formed in early life, the adult is likely to be unstable and anxious.

By acting as if the infant were already an active communicator, by trying to find and remain on the child's "wavelength," and by filling in pauses, the mother in fact helps genuine communicative interaction come into being. Within a few months the rhythmic synchrony between vocalization and hand and arm movement of mother and child has become most impressive; it seems like a precursor of genuine conversation. By the end of the first year of life, the child has become a full-fledged partner in such dialogues, often initiating them, turning them into games, using them to direct attention and achieve goals (Ninio and Bruner, 1978).

EXPERIMENTAL STUDIES OF ATTACHMENT AND SEPARATION

Clinical and naturalistic studies have furnished a broad and convincing outline of the course of attachment from its earliest moments, but only carefully framed experimental studies can unravel the specific variables involved in its manifestations. And only through studies involving experimental manipulations can the specific claims made by Bowlby, Ainsworth, and others be reliably assessed.

Not all facets of Bowlby's position lend themselves readily to experimental verification. Some, such as his speculations on the evolutionary roots of attachment, cannot be tested at all. Experimental manipulations of other claims, such as his account of the effects of lengthy separation, would be totally unethical. For these reasons investigations that bear specifically on his theory of attachment are at a premium. As we have seen, Bowlby places importance on the forms of anxiety said to accompany separation from the mother or confrontation of a stranger. Devising the appropriate experimental conditions and performing the appropriate manipu-

lations should make it possible to determine whether separation and stranger anxiety are as pervasive as claimed, whether they occur similarly across different children, and which factors influence the child's reactions.

In a series of studies Harriet Rheingold (1969), a leading experimental researcher of attachment, sought to re-create the stressful experience of separation from the mother. She introduced nine-and-one-half-month-old infants into a strange but harmless environment: a small, empty room that presented little to attract the children's attention and equally little to provoke their fear. The infants were observed over several periods, sometimes alone and sometimes with their mothers.

Children who were placed in the room without their mothers refused to explore the room and showed considerable distress, often whimpering or crying. In contrast, the children whose mothers remained in the room explored willingly and vocalized pleasantly. After their mothers left, these infants explored less vigorously and eventually began to cry, but they were still much more at ease than those children whose mothers had never stayed behind. Apparently, the one-time presence of a mother can render an anxiety-provoking situation somewhat less threatening.

Further manipulations revealed that neither toys nor a friendly but strange adult could alleviate the children's distress. In fact, the appearance of a stranger proved even more upsetting to the children, who may have perceived the unfamiliar adult as posing an additional threat. Apparently, only the presence of a beloved figure can convert a strange, somewhat threatening environment into one that invites exploration. Across situations, the mother serves as an anchor point from which active exploration can proceed (see Figure 1.10). Even a film of the mother proves more comforting than a stranger,

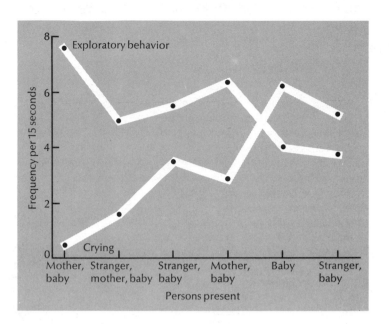

Figure 1.10. The reactions of the year-old child are a sensitive barometer of who is present in the room over a period of a half hour. Crying increases and exploration of the environment decreases as a joint effect of the absence of the caretaker and the presence of strangers. (Ainsworth and Bell, 1970)

whether presented live or on film (Passman and Erck, 1978).

A number of researchers have focused specifically on the behavior of children confronted with a stranger. Shirley Feldman and Margaret Ingham (1975) compared the effects of companions like the mother, the father, or a recent acquaintance. As expected, one-year-old children placed in a strange situation were more likely to play, less likely to cry, and generally more secure with their parents than with an acquaintance. Indeed, attachment behaviors of remaining close to the caretaker were heightened when a stranger entered the room. But two-year-old children in the same situations surprised the researchers. Although generally more playful, they were more anxious and less willing to interact with the stranger when accompanied by their parents than when accompanied by the recent acquaintance. Situations comforting at age one may thus produce some anxiety at age two. In studying attachment, one must expect interactions between the children's age and their reactions in the presence of different adults.

While the primary attachment is directed toward individuals, some forms of attachment extend to physical objects as well. Objects to which children have developed an attachment can sometimes substitute for a mother: those infants who are attached to a pacifier can, when given the pacifier, engage in more play and endure longer separations from their mothers (Passman, 1977). In situations involving strangers, children prove more likely to play with a toy that a mother has manipulated than one she has shunned. Sometimes the same object can carry radically different valences: when a mother at home puts on a mask, her child will smile and laugh; but when the same event occurs in the unfamiliar laboratory setting, the child becomes distressed (cf. Rinkoff and Corter, 1980; Sroufe, Waters, and Matas, 1974).

The child's underlying attachment to her mother will affect performance in problem-solving situations. Children with different attachment histories were presented with a challenging task in which they had to weight down a lever with a block in order to reach candy in a Plexiglas box. Securely attached

"B babies" seek and receive help as needed. Insecure "C babies" fall apart at the task: their mothers increase the amount of their directiveness but the quality of their assistance decreases markedly. Not surprisingly, the involvement of both mother and unattached "A baby" remains low throughout the task (Sroufe, 1979).

Eventually the anxieties undergone by most children in the experimental setting become alleviated. Hildy Ross (1975) shows that the fearful or cautious reactions initially directed by one-year-old infants toward adult strangers disappear rapidly as the adults become familiar over a series of four-minute trials. Weinraub and Lewis (1977) describe the alleviating effects of a mother's explanation that she is leaving and her advice on what to do while she is gone. Alison Clarke-Stewart (1975a) indicates that infants are more likely to play with a stranger if the mother has interacted playfully and pleasantly with that stranger. Moreover, she reports that two-year-old children frequently regard adult strangers as highly interesting, worthy of more attention than their own mothers. And so, even as they remain close to their mothers, youngsters of this age are more likely to look at strangers, imitate them, play with them, and show positive emotions toward them (for instance, by smiling three times as frequently). Finally, Carol Eckerman and Judith L. Whatley (1975) report that, when confronted by two adults, one wholly novel, the other somewhat familiar, ten-month-old infants are more likely to smile at the wholly novel adult.

PRIMATES, MULTIPLE CARETAKERS, FATHERS, AND PEERS: REVISIONS OF BOWLBY'S POSITION

The various experimental findings expand and modify the specific claims made by Bowlby and his associates. For instance, the nature and degree of stranger anxiety across a group of infants turn out to be more complicated than Bowlby had suggested (see Rheingold and Eckerman, 1973). None of the results we have reported thus far, however, poses a fundamental challenge to the view of attachment developed in the last quarter century. Recently, some research has raised more fundamental questions and criticisms.

Primates Revisited. Bowlby's original formulations drew on the picture of mother-child relations as reported in Harlow's classic studies. More recent research had demonstrated considerable differences across primate species (Sackett et al., 1981) and modulated this picture in other ways.

As to the question of the unique status of the mother, adult male rhesus monkeys, while sometimes quite rough, can apparently serve as adequate caretakers (Mitchell, Redican, and Gomber, 1974). Moreover, adult males behave differently toward their own offspring than toward those of other monkeys, engaging in play (though relatively little grooming) with them. Adult males are more concerned with their male offspring than with their daughters: and they act so as to encourage their male infants to leave home-base and explore further (Suomi, 1977).

Even peers can serve as reasonably adequate substitutes for a primate mother. In one investigation monkeys were raised in complete isolation until three months. Within a few days after exposure to other juveniles, the previously isolated monkeys began to behave quite appropriately (Griffin and Harlow, 1966). In a more dramatic investigation, Novak and Harlow (1975) subjected four infant monkeys to a full year of isolation—treatment generally believed to devastate a monkey for all time (Rowland, 1964). Thereafter, the experimenters allowed the isolated monkeys to look at one another and then at nonisolated monkeys. Next the isolated monkeys played with one another. Finally, the isolated monkeys were introduced to "therapist" monkeys, normal animals younger than the isolated ones who were supposed to play with and draw them out.

Amazingly enough, these therapist monkeys lived up to their labels. The play of the previously isolated monkeys became more social. Their self-stimulation and rocking decreased dramatically and their behavior came to resemble that of normal nonisolated monkeys (see also Chamove, 1978). When seen at the age of three, following further opportunities to interact with age-mates, these monkeys were able to participate appropriately and effectively in nearly all social situations (Novak, 1979). It appears, then, that ample contact with other immature members of the species can totally reverse the effects of a year's isolation. In fact, deprived monkeys may even

Figure 1.11. A monkey whose early months were spent in isolation is being comforted by a normal "therapist" monkey. Harlow's recent demonstration that peers can aid in the rehabilitation of abnormally reared primates not only has stimulated a reconsideration of his earlier studies of social isolation but has also suggested possible applications in human psychopathology. (Suomi and Harlow, 1971)

become adequate mothers (Ruppenthal et al., 1976). Intriguingly, such motherless mothers are likely to perform their maternal functions in a superior fashion with a second child or after they have had practice with another infant.

ALTERNATIVE CARETAKING ARRANGEMENTS

While rearing by a single mother is the arrangement of choice in contemporary Western society, other arrangements have often been used in other cultures, ranging from the communes of China to the kibbutzim of Israel. Working in an East African agricultural village, Herbert and Gloria Leiderman (1974) compared several dozen infants raised in two kinds of homes. Some children were reared in **monomatric** (single-mother) households in which chores and interactions were handled at least 75 percent of the time by one individual—the mother. Others were raised by two or more people in **polymatric** (many-mother) households where the natural mother was involved in principal childrearing activities less than 50 percent of the time. The households were roughly equivalent in other ways, so the effects of single versus multiple mothering could be assessed directly.

Basically, the Leidermans found that the caretaking arrangements had no profound effects upon the offspring. Moreover, any differences tended to cancel one another out. For example, infants reared in polymatric households responded more anxiously to strangers, perhaps because they felt slightly less secure than those reared consistently by a single caretaker. But these same children received higher scores on a number of cognitive tests, such as finding a hidden object or securing an object by pulling a string. Especially important is the fact that the children most helped by polymatric rearing were those from less affluent homes. Apparently, the additional caretakers provided helpful "surplus"

Figure 1.12. At Kibbutz Mishmar Ha'emak in Israel, youngsters eat lunch in the company of nurses who are specially trained in the care of children. Whether these caretakers are as effective and as loving as the child's natural parents is still a controversial matter.

social stimulation, which was not required by children from more affluent homes. In fact, an attachment to more than one individual may have survival value in an environment where physical and social dangers are pronounced.

Such cross-cultural considerations assume additional importance nowadays, since almost half of all American mothers work outside the home and the day care for their 7.5 million preschool children is a constant concern. Just what might be the effects of a caretaking situation in which the American child spends the majority of her waking hours in an alternative caretaking arrangement?

Jerome Kagan and his colleagues (Kagan, Kearsley, and Zelazo, 1978) conducted a major longitudinal study comparing children in day-care settings with a matched group of children remaining at home with their mothers. All the children came from intact homes, and the day-care facility was staffed by very competent, nurturing caretakers. The researchers began making comparisons when the infants were only three and one-half months old, and they continued to measure various aspects of language, cognitive func-

tioning, and attachment until the children were twenty-nine months old. Although the infants' ethnic backgrounds and social classes often combined to produce very complex effects, no significant differences between groups of children could be attributed simply to home versus day-care rearing. In particular, in spite of the daily separation for the day-care infants, there were no differences in measures of attachment to the mother.

It should be stressed that the majority of day-care centers in the United States have neither the quantity nor the quality of the caretakers in the Kagan study. Whether the same effects would be produced in a day-care setting of inferior quality is simply not known. And other studies have noted that caretakers in a day-care situation in no way substitute for mothers (Farran and Ramey, 1977), that children reared in day-care settings are less likely than mother-care children to interact with a stranger (Ragozin, 1980), and that infants receiving day care are more likely to display anxious and avoiding behavior when confronted with a stranger (Vaughn, Gove, and Egeland, 1980). Nonetheless, on the basis of the scanty research carried out until now, there is little reason to challenge quality day care (see Belsky and Steinberg, 1978; but also Fraiberg, 1977).

The Role of the Father. Findings obtained in cross-cultural and day-care settings call into question the necessity for a single mothering figure. Yet in each of these places the caretaking figures are still women. Can fathers handle caretaking?

The accumulating evidence suggests that they do just fine (Belsky, 1979). In an important early study conducted in a maternity ward, Parke (1972) showed that fathers and mothers differed very little in how they reacted to their babies. Shortly thereafter, Kotelchuk (1973, 1976) demonstrated that infants were also democratic: they exhibited equivalent upset when mother or father left the room and they were faced with a stranger. Michael Lamb documented few differences in signs of attachment when children played alone with one parent and then the other (1976). Nonetheless, when direct competition obtains between parents, most children are more likely to display stronger attachment behaviors toward the mother (Cohen and Campos, 1974; Lamb, 1976). And when, as in Guatemala, the father spends very little time with the child, he is treated more like a stranger (Collins, 1979; Konner, 1977).

As potent bonds between child and father have been convincingly documented, attention has turned to differences in the *ways* in which mothers and fathers interact with children. This has proved to be a fertile ground for investigators. As early as two months, fathers play differently with their children than mothers do: they do not sit as close, they speak in more adult terms, and they are more likely to engage in touching games (Flaste, 1976; Lamb, 1977*a*). In early dialogues with their infants, mothers are typically smooth and low-key,

Figure 1.13. As fathers in our society become increasingly involved in infant care, the attachment bonds between them and their children are bound to grow stronger. Yet the ways in which children are attached to males may differ from the traditional forms of attachment to female caretakers.

while fathers are more playful and given to sudden shifts in level of excitation, from peaks of involvement to valleys of minimal attention. Fathers seem to expect, and often to get, a more heightened playful response, including brighter eyes and more vivid facial expressions (Brazelton, 1976).

The father, then, may come to play a different role in the life of the child. Mothers highlight the caretaking response and the control of inner feelings, while fathers initiate vigorous play and model the oscillation from greater to less self-control (Brazelton, 1976; Clarke-Stewart, 1978). In addition, fathers treat boys and girls differently: after the first year of life, human fathers (like other male primates) begin to pay special attention to their sons and, to some extent, withdraw from their daughters. Sons begin to develop preferences for the male parent at this time (Lamb, 1977*b*); and infants of this age are more upset by the departure of the same-sex than of the different-sex parent (Weinraub and Frankel, 1977). These findings indicate that while parents of both sexes can perform adequate caretaking functions, mothers and fathers are by no means interchangeable; both play important, complementary, and perhaps indispensable roles in the lives of children (Belsky, 1979). As Michael Lamb (1979) has put it, a social system that incorporates redundancy has a greater probability of success than one that relies on a single socializing agent.

More General Criticisms. The lines of investigation we have reviewed suggest the need for a more general critique of Bowlby's theory. Findings from the laboratory as well as observations of childrearing in other cultures and in other species challenge Bowlby's strict account of the course of attachment. It now appears that early development may proceed by various routes. Neither a single mothering figure nor stranger and separation anxiety appear as crucial or as inflexible as had been thought.

One may also criticize Bowlby's adoption of the language and assumptions of ethology (see Corter, 1974). In particular, Bowlby's comparison of the human infant-mother relationship to imprinting in birds seems strained. Not only is there little "hard" evidence to suggest a critical period in the development of mother-child interaction; but without the kind of experimental manipulations permitted with ducks or geese, it seems ill-advised to view the child as imprinted on her mother. Whatever validity the imprinting position has for lower animals—and even that position is controversial (Moltz, 1960; Rajecki et al., 1978)— its application to human attachment is premature at best. And if one of Bowlby's major theoretical frameworks is called into question, this poses difficulties for acceptance of his overall position.

It may also be that the mother's role is unnecessarily magnified in Bowlby's account. Often, what is automatically attributed to the mother could be plausibly linked to other factors. For example, the difficulties faced by institutionalized children hardly need be attributed solely to the lack of a mother. The dismal conditions in many of these places are in themselves sufficient to yield the wretched children described by Bowlby and his colleagues. Moreover, the mother can be viewed simply as a very interesting social or physical object, one who reinforces by being colorful, active, stimulating, and beneficent. Perhaps an equally pleasant father, sibling, or even a well-equipped machine could provide what the mother ordinarily furnishes (see Bijou and Baer, 1965; Gewirtz, 1961). The child's active role in forging the attachment link could unfold in a variety of settings.

Other issues of importance are neglected by Bowlby. For example, it has now been shown in a variety of species that infants will become attached to a caretaker even if the caretaker mistreats it (Egeland and Sroufe, 1981; Rajecki et al., 1978). Bowlby's ethological position offers no adequate account of this phenomenon. Furthermore, a problem of increasing concern within our society is that of child abuse—the practice by some parents of administering harsh physical abuse to the child (see the box). This issue is also skirted

in Bowlby's writings (Segal and Yahraes, 1979; Starr, 1979, for example).

Finally, the course of attachment seems to be far more varied than Bowlby suggests. Given Bowlby's account, one might infer that stranger and separation anxiety are universal phenomena; that the mother must serve as the original and principal caretaker; and that a decisive shift in the strength of the bond

The Cycle of Abuse

Gruesome tales of child abuse are reported every day. We hear of infants and children who have been severely beaten and bruised, left alone or even handcuffed and chained in a closet, willfully burned by cigarettes, denied food, and sexually abused by their parents. Preliminary findings of the Incidence Study conducted by the Children's Bureau of the U.S. Department of Health and Human Services indicate that at least half a million children are abused each year in the United States. Experts do not believe that those figures reflect an increase in child abuse in the past years, but awareness and concern have increased dramatically and inspired both new programs and new research.

This battered child syndrome, as it is called, usually occurs as part of a cycle. Almost all abusive parents were themselves battered or neglected as children. Researchers cite several psychological factors that may be responsible for the cycle of child abuse (Kempe and Kempe, 1978). There is evidence that people repeat the experiences from their first two years of life, although those experiences may be absent from conscious memory. The parent who was abused as an infant remains tormented by subconscious feelings that are somehow tied to and reenacted in the present parent-child relationship. Those who are abused as youngsters and receive inadequate love and nurturing grow up having a powerful desire to fulfill their unsatisfied needs. As adolescents, their strong need for love leads them to premature and poor relationships that often result in early and unhappy marriages. With each failure the need for love grows more intense. Finally, they turn to their children to fill the void—to satisfy their lack of love and self-approval. The children cannot meet these inflated expectations; they become the target of conflict, frustration, and disappointment; and the cycle of child abuse continues.

(For readings on child abuse, see Inglis, 1978; Kempe and Kempe, 1978; Starr, 1979.)

occurs at the age of two and one-half. Actually, attachment is far more flexible: the severity of separation and stranger anxiety varies markedly among children; these forms of anxiety prove quite sensitive to manipulations; multiple caretakers, and possibly male parents as well, can adequately assume the mother's role; and the various age markers proposed by Bowlby and Ainsworth are, at best, rough approximations (Rheingold and Eckerman, 1973).

If Bowlby's work presents such problems, why focus attention on it? A first answer is that Bowlby placed the mother-child relationship and the attachment bond squarely at the center of research and discussion about young children. Moreover, he fashioned a full-fledged framework for the study of the issue, thereby coordinating a vast number of studies and providing persuasive refutations of earlier accounts. In turn, Bowlby's work has stimulated hundreds of further studies—which, by and large, have reinforced his central claims. And even if research has raised difficulties about part of his original formulation, discussions continue to be couched in terms of the issues he first formulated. By offering a coherent and convincing account of the most important human social relationship, Bowlby has earned a place as one of the major figures in the psychology of infancy.

Early Attachment, Later Growth

Although Bowlby and his followers have illuminated the dynamics of attachment, they have provided little empirical evidence regarding its consequences in later life. This lack is understandable in view of the difficulty of carrying out long-term studies. But scattered evidence documenting some consequences has recently begun to accumulate. Secure attachment has been shown to be positively related to social competence, persistence in tasks, and problem-solving ability in preschool children (Matas, Arend, and Sroufe, 1978) and school-age children (Rutter, 1979a). Conversely, diffuse attachment in early life predicts inept and impaired relationships with adults and other children during the early school years (Tizard and Hodges, 1978). Probably the strongest evidence for the importance of early attachment would be evidence tracing events of later life directly and explicitly to those of early childhood. Here the work of Erik Erikson (1963) is particularly illuminating.

As a practicing psychoanalyst, Erik Erikson, like Bowlby, has been deeply influenced by the theories and techniques of Sigmund Freud (1938a; 1965a). But whereas Bowlby has focused on the first years of life, a period when psychotherapy is not possible, Erikson has spent most of his professional life in intensive therapeutic sessions with patients of different ages. Working with young children, he has pioneered in the development of play therapy; working with adolescents, he has focused especially on the problems of identity that emerge during the teenage years (Erikson, 1963). Erikson has also pondered the circumstances that yield leaders—those who made positive contributions, like Gandhi or Martin Luther, as well as those who have wreaked destruction, such as Adolf Hitler (Erikson, 1959, 1968, 1969).

In the course of his work with patients and his biographical studies of historical figures, Erikson has developed a model of stages of life through which all normal individuals will pass (see Figure 1.14). We will examine this

Figure 1.14. *Opposite:* Erik Erikson has described eight central life crises, each of which may yield a more or less favorable outcome, thereby laying the groundwork for the next developmental stage. (Erikson, 1963, 1964a)

Life crisis	Favorable outcome	Unfavorable outcome
FIRST YEAR		
Trust—mistrust	Hope. Trust in the environment and the future.	Fear of the future; suspicion.
SECOND YEAR		
Autonomy—shame, doubt	Will. Ability to exercise choice as well as self-restraint; a sense of self-control and self-esteem leading to good will and pride.	Sense of loss of self-control or sense of external overcontrol; the result is a propensity for shame and doubt about whether one willed what one did or did what one willed.
THIRD THROUGH FIFTH YEARS		
Initiative—guilt	Purpose. Ability to initiate activities, to give them direction, and to enjoy accomplishment.	Fear of punishment; self-restriction or overcompensatory showing off.
SIXTH YEAR THROUGH PUBERTY		
Industry—inferiority	Competence. Ability to relate to the world of skills and tools, to exercise dexterity and intelligence in order to make things and make them well.	A sense of inadequacy and inferiority.
ADOLESCENCE		
Identity—confusion about one's role	Fidelity. Ability to see oneself as a unique and integrated person and to sustain loyalties.	Confusion over who one is.
EARLY ADULTHOOD		
Intimacy—isolation	Love. Ability to commit oneself, one's identity, to others.	Avoidance of commitments and of love; distancing of oneself from others.
MIDDLE AGE		
Generativity—stagnation	Care. Widening concern for what has been generated by love, necessity, or accident; for one's children, work, or ideas.	Self-indulgence, boredom, and interpersonal impoverishment.
OLD AGE		
Integrity—despair	Wisdom. Detached concern for life itself; assurance of the meaning of life and of the dignity of one's own life; acceptance that one will die.	Disgust with life; despair over death.

model in some detail in Chapter 14. At this point it is important to indicate that Erikson sees each stage of life—infancy, the toddler years, adolescence, and so on—as marked by a pivotal struggle, issue, or crisis that every individual must confront and somehow resolve. The individual who successfully negotiates the crisis acquires strength for dealing with subsequent crises. However, the individual who is unable to deal successfully with the crisis of a particular stage will continue to be haunted, in a sense, by this irresolution, and her progress will be slowed or even thwarted at each subsequent stage. To be sure, no life crisis is ever completely resolved or fully failed; what varies across individuals (and stages) is the *degree* to which the crisis has been successfully managed. And failures need not be completely crippling; one mission of therapy is to help an individual compensate for crises that have been poorly managed.

THE CRISIS OF BASIC TRUST

Erikson believes that all infants experience a profound tension between feelings of trust and of mistrust, a tension that must in some way be resolved during the opening two years of life. He rests his claim on two independent yet complementary sources. First, there are observations of infants who are in the early years of life. Some two-year-olds are remarkable for their capacity to handle problems and losses that arise; they seem to have developed in infancy a sense of trust, a feeling that all is right with their world. Other toddlers are notable for their constant difficulty in relating to others, in devising and achieving goals for themselves, in attaining moments of calm, in avoiding anxiety. These infants seem to lack a sense of basic trust.

Erikson's other source of information is retrospective. As a consequence of his treatment of dozens of adolescents, he has discerned recurrent constellations of traits. He finds a clear division between those who have long had and those who have long lacked a sense of basic trust. Unfortunately, Erikson has not had the opportunity to follow patients from birth to maturity in order to monitor on a regular basis their degree of trust. Yet the kinds of clinical observations made by him and by other psychoanalysts (Bettelheim, 1967; Mahler, Pine, and Bergman, 1975; Sullivan, 1953) support the hypothesis that the degree of trust acquired early in life has reverberations many years later. Indeed, this assumption has become a constant, though not unchallenged, notion of clinical psychology (see Crews, 1975; Kagan and Klein, 1973; for critical comments).

For Erikson, as for Bowlby, the first years of life center about the child's relationship to a caretaker, almost always the natural mother. At first, the child must establish a comfortable and close relationship. Then she can gradually withdraw from the mother and approach strangers, secure in a feeling of trust. Coming to rely on the sameness and continuity of others as well as on her own body, skills, and urges, the child can now face the world. But if, for whatever reason, such relationships are not satisfactorily established, the child will be plagued by a lack of trust, by active feelings of mistrust. In the most extreme cases, the result is a mental breakdown that prevents individuals from entering into meaningful relationships with others (Erikson, 1963).

THE QUALITY OF MOTHER-CHILD INTERACTION: A CONTROVERSY

One of Erikson's most important ideas is that basic trust cannot be attained by applying a simple formula—so much time spent with the baby, so many loving words, so many well-intentioned providers in the home. Instead, the child's trust depends on the *quality* of her

Figure 1.15. The course of attachment is remarkably similar across cultures. Having forged a successful attachment bond and developed a sense of trust, this two-year-old Ugandan child can now explore securely on his own.

relationship with the mother. Here Erikson echoes an idea hinted at by Bowlby and Ainsworth. Bowlby (1958) indicates that children are likely to become attached to individuals who spend relatively little time with them but who respond to them readily and sympathetically when they cry. Ainsworth (1967) stresses that those interactions which are characterized by mutual delight (rather than by routine care) lead to an effective attachment bond.

If we accept that the quality of interaction between mother and child determines whether the child will be equipped to face later life with confidence, we may have found the emotional key to the child's development. Skeptics however, are likely to protest that "quality of interaction" says nothing because it cannot be measured and manipulated experimentally. Only the *quantity* of interaction can be a subject for scientific investigation—say, by comparing the length of time mothers spend with their children or the amount of vocal interchange between them. The vague concept of "quality" brings us back to prescientific days; we are dealing with unknowable forces, and we remain unable to obtain explanations.

Those who stress the quality of interaction may offer several responses to this criticism. They can say, in effect, that unable as we are to define quality precisely, we can at least know it when we see it. Trained judges should be able to observe a mother and her child and to agree on whether their interaction exhibits the appropriate qualities of attachment or trust. Other defenders of quality might say that we are dealing with human properties that are by their very nature beyond the power of scientists to measure.

One should be able to specify *which* of the mother's acts are likely to lead to attachment and trust, and which are likely to thwart attachment, culminating eventually in pervasive mistrust. A few signs heralding "genuine" attachment are the persistence of eye-to-eye contact between mother and child; the mother's sensitivity to the child's signals and her ability to respond immediately and appropriately; and consistency in the mother's treatment of the child. Once such behaviors are isolated, they need to be related to independent measures of attachment (such as proximity to the mother), basic trust (such as ability to accept separations), and later adjustment (such as successful relations with other individuals). Ideally, studies will be longitudinal: the same children will be followed over several years.

Cross-cultural research again is relevant. James Chisholm (1980) spent three hundred hours observing Navajo mothers and children together. Attachment theory might have dictated dire consequences for these children, who spent most of the day on a cradleboard, tightly swaddled, virtually immobile, and with little opportunity to interact with others. Yet mother-infant attachment proved quite normal. Various compensating factors—the proximity of mother and child, the mother's quick response to the infant's cry, and the intimate play when the child was released from the cradleboard—underscored the plasticity and the robustness of the mother-child bond.

Going beyond the anecdotal and cross-cultural evidence, several researchers have demonstrated clusters of behavior associated with effective and ineffective mothering. Alison Clarke-Stewart (1975b) was able to trace infants' cognitive and social competence to several interrelated factors of good mothering. Looking at and talking to the child, responding to the child's distress and social expressions, playing with objects, expressing positive feelings and suppressing negative feelings—all these summed up to a single factor that Clarke-Stewart labeled "optimal maternal care" and that, in turn, yielded "competent infants." In a similar fashion, Burton White (1975) has isolated numerous characteristics of competent and "super" mothers. It should be consoling to those of the Bowlby-Erikson persuasion that aspects of good mothering in fact form a coherent set of behaviors; and it should be a relief to more skeptical scientists that at least some of the suspected contributors can be measured.

Our review of attachment may yield a moral. Most of the great issues probed by developmentalists are not new ones. As often as not, they can be found in a culture's art, literature, philosophy, and folk wisdom. Yet until imaginative researchers look at these impressions critically, following leads and verifying or even disconfirming intuition, we will not be able to separate the common sense from the common nonsense. A judicious combination of clinical insights and rigorous experimental procedures should culminate in a science that can illuminate long-standing puzzles.

Signposts

In our first look at the newborn child we have focused on one of the most striking and pervasive of all human behaviors: the attachment bond between the child and the initial caretaker—usually the mother. We have sought to determine whether the bond occurs universally, the extent to which it is based on the nourishment supplied by the mother, whether it follows the same course in all infants, and how the bond affects the child's subsequent development.

Our first clue came from Harry Harlow's studies with infant monkeys. These investigations established that attachment does not occur simply because the mother supplies the infant's nourishment: the warm and comfortable surface she provides is also crucial. Harlow and his associates have also documented the severe consequences of long-term maternal deprivation: compulsive behaviors; apathy toward other monkeys; aggression toward observers; self-inflicted injuries; and (in monkeys isolated for as long as a year) a failure ever to play, engage in normal sexual behavior, or care for their own infants properly when pregnancy and birth do occur.

The Harlow findings can be interpreted in terms of the discipline of ethology, the study of animals in their natural environment. An ethological account of attachment stresses that the organism must be exposed at an early age to releasers in the environment—stimuli like warmth, sound, or movement—that promote a permanent bond to the releaser's source, usually the mother. The ethological approach also stresses the rather fixed time, usually called a critical period, during which such imprinting must occur.

Building on the work of Harlow, and also inspired by ethology, John Bowlby has provided the fullest portrait of human attachment. Bowlby believes that the infant's behaviors are designed to enhance closeness to the mother; given a normal run of events, a strong bond will form between infant and mother by the second half of the first year of life. In Bowlby's view the caretaker should be the mother because she bears the child, is predisposed to caretaking activities, and is most likely to spend time with the child during the critical period.

Much of Bowlby's contribution lies in a description of the normal course of attachment. At the end of the infant's first year, when attachment is at its height, the infant will be made quite anxious by possible threats to the bond—for instance, the presence of a stranger or a separation from the mother. The bond remains strong during the second year but begins to weaken during the third year when the child, now secure in the world, is able increasingly to venture forth and form new relations with other individuals.

Finally, Bowlby sketches the dire consequences of failure to form an attachment bond or of a lengthy disruption of the link between mother and child. Either is likely to produce a child who lacks a secure mooring in the world, is perpetually anxious, and will experience difficulties forming enduring relations with other individuals. In contrast, the child who forms the normal bond with the mother should eventually achieve self-reliance and maturity and become a competent and loving parent.

Many researchers have sought clinical and experimental evidence of the validity of Bowlby's claims. Studies of infants in institutions confirm the costs suffered by a child deprived of a strong attachment bond. Cross-cultural work with Ugandan children and their mothers documents a similar course for attachment in a very different setting. Observations of very young infants flesh out the "dialogic" nature of early mother-child communication. Experimental studies confirm the existence of separation and stranger anxiety. To be sure, at certain ages children are much more accepting of strangers and much less fearful of separation than Bowlby has suggested. Moreover, the context in which children play and interact with unfamiliar persons and objects can significantly affect and modulate their attachment behaviors.

Other, more serious objections have also been raised to Bowlby's formulation. The importance of the mother in attachment has been challenged by the findings that motherless infant monkeys can be rehabilitated by "therapist" peers, that multiple mothering works effectively in some cultures, that day care can function smoothly in our culture. In addition, increasing evidence suggests that strong attachment links exist between children and their fathers. The course of human attachment seems less rigid, and more subject to individual and cultural differences, than a strict ethological model would allow.

Although some of Bowlby's specific claims have thus been questioned, his belief in the importance of a strong and caring relation between child and caretaker is widely accepted. Researchers concur that the quality of the relationship between infant and caretakers is probably more important for the child's ultimate welfare than the sheer quantity of time spent together or nourishment dispensed. Indeed, in Erik Erikson's view, every infant confronts a crisis of trust during the first two years of life. Those who develop a feeling of trust have a good chance of negotiating subsequent crises and of realizing effective interpersonal relations throughout life. Those who fail to develop a trusting relationship with their caretakers and their environment will be perennially plagued by doubt and will have difficulty in finding a niche within their community.

However complex and compelling it may be, the relation between child and caretaker is only a page in the chapter of infancy. Equally impressive and important is the speed and thoroughness with which the infant comes to know the physical world—its objects, their properties, the frameworks of time and space in which bodies move. We will examine this complex undertaking in the next chapter. Our main guide will be Jean Piaget, the developmental psychologist whose view of cognitive development will assume an important role in the rest of this book. But we will also make an initial acquaintance with the environmental-learning theorists, whose approach to the acquisition of knowledge forms an instructive contrast to Piaget's.

CHAPTER TWO

Gaining Knowledge About the World

Early mental development is no less than conquest by perception and movement of the entire practical universe that surrounds the small child.

–JEAN PIAGET

All we have to start with in building a human being is a lively squirming bit of flesh. . . . Parents take the raw materials and begin to fashion it in ways to suit themselves. This means that parents, whether they know it or not, start intensive training of the child at birth.

–JOHN B. WATSON

The major challenge facing newborn children is to come to know the world in which they live. This assignment may not seem difficult; after all, the world is so familiar that we take for granted its many facts and aspects. We know there are objects of various types: rocks, trees, and animals; books, records, and films; women, men, and children. We expect these to behave in customary ways: a rock falls to the ground when dropped; a tree changes in form over the years; men and women often marry and have children. Above all, we believe that objects are permanent:

they will continue to exist in some form, even if hidden from us for a considerable time.

We also understand some of the forces governing these objects. Actions have specifiable consequences: for example, a stone will skip on water if it strikes the surface with a given force and at a specific angle; a missile launched at sufficient speed will result in an apparent, though only temporary, defiance of the laws of gravity. We know that objects exist in a spatial framework: no two objects can occupy the same place; the same object will look different when seen from another angle; we can approach a goal by one route and return by a different path to the point of origin. And we acknowledge the principles governing temporal organization: a specific event can occur before or after another but not at both times; there are objective measures of time, which often differ from our subjective impressions of speed.

Finally, we have detailed knowledge about the contents of our world. We know the color of hair and the sound of voice associated with many persons in our lives. We come to expect pleasure from the taste of ice cream or the sight of a loved one. We anticipate painful experiences like the heat of a burning match or the sting of an inoculation. And we associate a rich set of meanings with the symbols of our environment: a certain pattern of musical notes marks a birthday celebration; a specific configuration of lines depicts the country's flag.

Coming to know these and countless allied things is the task facing the child. Coming to understand how the child acquires such knowledge is one mission of developmental psychology.

Competing Views of Cognition

Psychologists are deeply divided about *which* aspects of knowledge are most important to study and *what* the ultimate sources of this knowledge might be. To help portray these disputes, we will draw on two behaviors familiar to us from our description of the affective life of the infant. In the first, a four-month-old child is handling a ball as her mother leaves the room. The child does not react but simply continues to play. In the second, a one-year-old is also playing with a ball. When her mother leaves the room, she at once stops playing, begins crying, and suffering from separation anxiety, keeps crying until her mother returns. These simple behaviors have radically different meanings for opposing psychological schools.

WHAT SHOULD BE STUDIED?

To begin with, psychologists disagree on which aspects of the child's knowledge are most important to study. Psychologists associated with the environmental-learning tradition (for example, Bijou and Baer, 1965; Gewirtz, 1969; Rosenthal and Zimmerman, 1978) are interested in the specific contents of the child's world. In their view we should concentrate on which objects the child fears or loves, remembers well or forgets, and on how such pleasures and pains, memories and omissions come about. In considering our two examples, the environmental-learning theorist is likely to focus on children's associations between their mothers and their own feelings. According to this view, the four-month-old in our example has not yet formed strong associations between her mother and pleasure, and she therefore does not react negatively to her mother's absence. The year-old child, however, has long since come to associate her mother with pleasurable feelings and her mother's absence with negative feelings. Her pain and her reactions are immediate and sharp.

Psychologists of the cognitive-structural school (for example, Bruner, Olver, and Greenfield, 1966; Flavell, 1977; Kohlberg, 1969; Piaget, 1970) focus on a wholly different set of questions. In their view, children's associations with specific objects and events should take a backseat to the rules and patterns governing the physical world. These psychologists try to illuminate how a child comes to understand that there are objects at all, that specifiable laws govern cause and effect, that experiences unfold over time and occupy space. Thus, the cognitive-structuralist sees the four-month-old in our example as incapable of understanding that any animate or inanimate object continues to exist after it has gone out of sight. She does not react to her mother's disappearance because she cannot conceptualize an absent figure: for her, out of sight means out of mind. The one-year-old, however, has begun to develop a model of the world in which objects continue to exist despite their physical absence. This child therefore reacts strongly when a valued object disappears and continues to make her feelings known until the object returns.

The two schools are strikingly different. The cognitive-structuralist focuses on the very elements that the environmental-learning theorist takes for granted: the existence of objects and an understanding of the laws of nature that govern their behavior. The environmental-learning theorist attends to elements ignored by the cognitive-structural school: the specific features of an object (for example, its size and color) that control the child's attention and have significant consequences for her well-being and her feelings. Furthermore, those of the environmental-learning tradition maintain that though the amount of accumulated experience differs, the four-month-old and the one-year-old have similar relations to the world. Cognitive-structuralists believe such children only eight months apart hold fundamentally—or qualitatively—different views of the world.

TRADITIONAL VIEWS ON THE ULTIMATE SOURCES OF KNOWLEDGE

Even as psychologists differ about which aspects of knowledge are worth studying (see Furth, 1981), they disagree profoundly about how this knowledge is obtained. It would be most convenient if this dispute paralleled the one just sketched, but as it happens the lines of contention are somewhat differently drawn. On the one side stand again the environmental-learning theorists. In their view the newborn is equipped with little, if any, specific knowledge about the world. The world contains what needs to be known, and all knowledge derives from experiences undergone in the world. Hence the environmental-learning

position is also called **empiricism** (from the Greek *empeiria:* experience). The infant's task is to make for herself a copy of the real world and then form associations to this replica (Rorty, 1980). In this view the child slowly builds up an image of the mother as a result of lengthy exposure to her in the real world. Then feelings of pleasure gradually become associated with this inner model.

The opposing set of views is usually called **nativism.** Nativists like T. G. R. Bower (1974a), Jerry Fodor (1975), and Noam Chomsky (1980) see the problem of attaining knowledge as an essentially trivial one. In their view knowledge is part of one's birthright: at birth children possess all the knowledge they will ever need. Some nativists assert that the information is already built into each human brain and children must simply gain access to it. In a somewhat weaker version of the theory—one held by many ethologists (see Chapter 1)—children possess at birth all the structures or rules they need to attain knowledge; although they still must secure specific data or encounter specific "triggering events" from the environment. But in neither of these nativist accounts does the child copy the external world; rather, the relevant version of the world already exists in the brain at birth. Nativists would explain separation anxiety as an inborn and universal tendency that does *not* depend on lengthy exposure to a mother or caretaker. At four months this tendency simply has not yet developed or "matured" and so the child will not exhibit overt separation anxiety. By age one, however, all normal infants should protest regardless of the particular events they happen to have experienced.

THE INTERACTION VIEW OF KNOWLEDGE

Although the cognitive-structural school is squarely opposed to empiricism on the issue of *what* should be studied, most of its proponents stand midway between empiricism and nativism on the sources of knowledge (see Flavell, 1977; Furth 1981; H. Gardner, 1981; Piaget 1970). Briefly stated, they believe that knowledge of the world, whether general or specific, entails neither a simple reading of the outside world (as empiricists would say) nor the emergence of a built-in property of the brain (as nativists would have it). It is, rather, the product of an *interaction* between two sets of features. On the one hand are the child's ways of knowing—her mental capacities or, more technically, **mental structures.** These are the means, such as simple motor actions and sensory processes, that have evolved over many millennia for analyzing experience. On the other hand, there are those aspects or properties of the world that the child is capable of perceiving and understanding at a given time in her development.

Both sets of features are constantly changing. The child's ways of knowing alter continually as a result of experience and maturation of the nervous system. For instance, the one-month-old can "know" the mother primarily through the senses of taste and touch; the one- or two-year-old has a well-developed model of the mother, including numerous traits and labels that she can apply to her parent. By the same token, the properties of the world accessible to the young child are constantly expanding. The one-month-old sees a world of mostly unrecognizable shapes. The one-year-old readily identifies many objects, persons, and events. As the cognitive-structuralist puts it, all knowledge may be thought of as the product of an interaction between the child's current ways of knowing the world and the various facets of the world to which she is at that time sensitive.

We can think of these rival views in terms of the following images. The empiricists see all knowledge housed in the world; the initially "blank" child simply reads off what she needs to know. The nativist sees all knowl-

edge housed in the child's brain; the child merely waits for it to unfold over time. But the cognitive-structuralist views the acquisition of knowledge as a highly active, or constructive, interaction between the human subject (with her ways of knowing) and the objects she is confronting. The child is continuously devising models about what the world is like, and she is constantly testing these models in the world and changing them accordingly. If the nativist's child is like a sage who knows all, and the empiricist's child is like a mimic who copies all, then the cognitive-structural child is like an enterprising scientist, an unwitting Newton or Einstein, who theorizes, tests hypotheses, and revises them in the light of recent results.

Although the child's models are constantly being modified, it would be a mistake to assume that the world is just there, that it is waiting to reveal itself once the child has abandoned various faulty constructions. For—and this is the most important as well as the knottiest part of the cognitive-structural claim—what the child can know about the world at any time is specified (and limited) by the ways of knowing that have evolved in the child's mind (see Figure 2.1). Like a computer that can process only one or two programming languages, the four-month-old has limited ways of knowing—a few actions like sucking, a few perceptual processes like focusing on round, facelike targets. That child can know the world's objects—whether mothers or balls—only through exploiting these scant cognitive resources. The ways of knowing expand slowly, but the one-year-old has a sufficiently comprehensive knowledge of objects and their behaviors to appreciate the significance of the mother's disappearance.

Among the mental structures the child has acquired during the intervening eight months are rules about what happens when objects disappear, procedures for searching for lost

Figure 2.1. Infants' ways of knowing—or schemes—change as they grow older: a newborn approaches a nipple, ready to begin sucking; a five-month-old reaches for and grasps an object; and an eight-month-old, her face suffused with intention, crawls toward a spoon.

objects, means for remembering locations, and the ability to scan an area visually in a systematic and exhaustive fashion. With these new ways of knowing, the child passes from a fragmentary model of the world to models that are increasingly rich, comprehensive, and accurate. Indeed, like a scientist in diapers, the one-year-old may "hypothesize" that the mother will soon return and then become upset when that expectation is violated. Yet despite these mental advances, the individual can never reach the promised land of full knowledge. Like a computer that can process many but not all possible languages, we all remain limited by the ways we can know anything, and there may be many mental capacities that have simply been denied to our species.

Jean Piaget:
A Guide to Cognition

The first and beyond doubt the most acclaimed representative of the cognitive-structuralist school is the Swiss scientist Jean Piaget, who died in 1980 at the age of 84. Piaget's views are not easy to understand. His concepts and terminology are initially forbidding; moreover, many of his claims either go beyond or apparently contradict common sense. Indeed, they have had a revolutionary impact in psychology. In addition to undermining "popular psychology," Piaget's concepts challenge much of the environmental-learning and the behaviorist points of view that once dominated American psychology (see pages 150-152). Piaget's contribution cannot be fully appreciated in a single reading; but by studying his examples carefully it is possible to get a feeling for his view of the child.

What, briefly, was the nature of the revolution Piaget helped to bring about? To begin with, in opposition to the view of the child as a passive reflection (or copy) of the world, Piaget stressed the child's active role in gaining knowledge. Then, against the claims of both nativists and empiricists, he emphasized the interactional aspects of knowledge acquisition—how the child's manner of knowing changes and what consequences these changes have for the child's resulting view of the world. And in opposition to both historical beliefs and much current speculation, Piaget argued that the child's world diverges from the adult's and that children of various ages differ radically from one another. Discussion of the stages of cognitive development proposed by Piaget will be an important part of this book. (Readers who want to investigate further can consult Flavell, 1963; Furth, 1981;

H. Gardner, 1981; Piaget and Inhelder, 1968. Critical treatments can be found in Brainerd, 1978*b*; Bryant, 1974; Fodor, 1975; Gelman and Gallistel, 1978.)

PIAGET'S METHOD OF INVESTIGATION

Before we turn directly to Piaget's view of infancy, we should recognize certain limitations in the approach he consciously adopted. First, Piaget was interested primarily in cognitive (problem-solving reasoning) capacities. Focusing mostly on children's perceptions and performances, he paid virtually no attention to children's emotions—how they feel, how attached, anxious, or apathetic they are. (Thus the themes of Chapter 1 held little interest for Piaget.) Nor did he concern himself with what motivates children to prefer one activity at one time, another at a later moment. Furthermore, Piaget had a highly specific idea of what developed cognition is like. He was interested in the knowledge and skills of the competent scientist, especially the physicist and the mathematician. Accordingly, he focused on cognitive capacities that sound like chapter headings in a scientific textbook: the principles of causality, the behavior of objects, knowledge of probability, and so on. Even when looking at infants, Piaget telegraphed his own concerns by examining children's notions of time, space, causality, and the behavior of objects rather than, say, their aesthetic or ethical capacities.

Like any other investigator, Piaget built his conclusions upon his method of investigation. For instance, Piaget's studies of infancy amounted to hundreds of little tests conducted with his three children, Jacqueline, Lucienne, and Laurent. These tests were not formal experiments; for the most part Piaget simply played with his children, using household objects. Those wedded to fancy equipment, large samples of subjects, relevant control groups, disinterested observers, and statistical tests find much to criticize in Piaget's procedures.

Yet it would be wrong to conclude that Piaget did not know what he was doing or that he was a sloppy researcher. The playful actions and interactions detailed in his three volumes on infancy (1954, 1962a, 1963) had a definite purpose—to test specific hypotheses about the development of ways of knowing and of knowledge. Moreover, Piaget's criteria for attributing knowledge to the child were very strict. Some observers might have credited understanding if the child showed any (or occasional) success with a task. But Piaget attributed a capacity to a child only when that capacity had been demonstrated regularly and in spite of strong incentives to do something else. In other words Piaget stacked the deck against the child: according to his strict scientific conscience, the only convincing sign of knowledge was correct performance under trying circumstances. Though this approach has been criticized by those in search of early evidence for childhood competences, it is certainly scientifically prudent. Piaget was unlikely to overestimate the child's capacities, and his research strategy is likely to illuminate whatever qualitative differences may exist among children of different ages.

Taken one by one, Piaget's observations may not seem dramatic. But crucial insights accrue as one observes the Piaget children's changing responses to the "same" objective stimuli or situations over several months. Indeed, if the ultimate test for scientific merit lies in the appropriateness of the methods used and the reliability of the conclusions drawn, then Piaget's apparently casual investigations emerge as some of the best-substantiated research in all of developmental psychology.

THREE ASPECTS OF CHILDREN'S BEHAVIOR

Three features of children's behaviors are continually stressed in Piaget's writings. First, he describes children as **egocentric**—not because they think about themselves a lot but rather because children are incapable of separating their own perspective from that of other people. In fact, nearly all of Piaget's several dozen books can be read as a lengthy account of how the child slowly sheds egocentrism—a gradual **decentration** as she becomes aware of how the world looks to other people and how their views differ from her own. And in a similar spirit, the egocentric infant can be seen as attributing all consequences to her own behavior, only gradually coming to recognize a world apart from her own actions and conceptions.

A second principal feature—one touched on above—is Piaget's view of the child (and the adult) as possessing a set of ways of knowing the world. Whereas general ways of knowing are often called mental structures, the child's specific ways of knowing are usually called **schemes.** (In the case of older individuals, the term **operations** is usually favored, as we will see in Chapter 10.) As a first approximation, one can think of the infant's schemes as her primary recurring behaviors toward objects. An infant's major schemes would include motor acts such as sucking and simple perceptual processes such as looking at areas of adjacent light and darkness. But the scheme is not bound up in any specific motor action. Rather, the scheme amounts to the general—or formal—aspects of such an action, that set of features which remains constant across different instances (or realizations) of a specific physical action (or, later, of a specific mental operation). Thus the child's scheme for sucking is not the set of physical parameters underlying any particular suck but those characteristics that exist across—and therefore define the nature and limitations of—all the child's potential sucks during a given time. By the same token the adult's scheme for writing her name is not restricted to any particular set of movements or any particular autograph. Not only do signatures vary across time but also, deprived of her right hand, an individual can sign with a pen in her left hand or even in her foot or mouth.

Reverting to our simpler usage of the term *scheme,* we can say that the child's principal schemes in the first weeks after birth are sucking and looking. It follows that the child can know objects only as she can suck and look at them. But schemes develop and change; they grow more complex and organized; they become increasingly differentiated from and integrated with one another; they eventually involve internal or mental representations. Indeed, by the age of two the child combines various schemes toward objects into a highly general scheme—or cognitive structure—called by Piaget a **sense of object permanence.** This general scheme allows the child to think of a ball even when it disappears from sight. Later, even more intricate schemes evolve, basically composed of thought rather than of actions. For example, schemes of reading and of representing concepts in your mind allow you to absorb information from a text. By this much later point in development, it is more accurate to think of schemes as patterns of thinking within the brain rather than as sets of motions carried out in the physical world.

In considering how schemes change with time, we encounter a third Piagetian theme: the twin processes of **assimilation** and **accommodation** (see Figure 2.2). These two processes are the only means by which children can revise their models of the world. Given an initial set of schemes, the child comes to know objects and situations either by *assimilating* the object to an already existing scheme, or by *accommodating* that scheme to the object or situation at hand.

To understand this favorite pair of Piagetian terms, imagine an infant confronting two types of nipples—those found on bottles and those on her mother's breasts. Suppose, in addition, that the infant is equipped with a scheme for sucking that is well-fitted to her mother's nipples. If she is to receive milk in an efficient and satisfying manner from the bottle as well, she has only two options. She can either reshape her mouth to fit the bottle or she can reposition the bottle to fit the shape of her mouth. In altering her mouth and the associated sucking, she reshapes or *accommodates* the initial scheme to fit the new object. Alternatively, as the child finds (or remakes) sources of nourishment—for instance by grasping the bottle's nipple at an unusual angle—her initial scheme remains serviceable and does not require alteration. In doing so she is said to *assimilate* the object to prior schemes.

According to Piaget, assimilation and accommodation apply to all acts of knowing, but the stress on each may differ across acts. Every attack on the nipple involves both processes, but assimilation is highlighted with the mother's nipple, accommodation with the bottle. The processes also occur at different levels of sophistication, ranging from infantile sucking to adult learning: as noted before, the latter instances of assimilation or accommodation of schemes occur with thought processes rather than with physical actions in the world.

Consider, for instance, the writing and reading of this text. In conveying Piaget's principal ideas, I must attempt to accommodate to his views (else I will distort them). At the same time I must assimilate his views to my current ways of knowing (else I will alto-

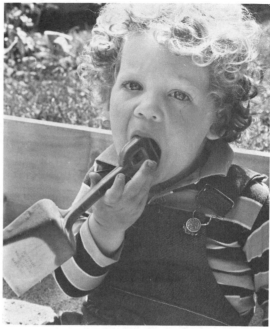

Figure 2.2. Eric, a two-year-old at play with a toy shovel, offers examples of Piaget's two major ways of knowing. In the first scene, Eric assimilates the shovel to his customary schemes for eating from a spoon. In the accompanying scene, Eric accommodates the shape of his mouth to the unexpectedly large dimensions of the handle.

gether miss their significance). By the same token, you must use the schemes you already possess (for instance, your thoughts about what a child is like) to enter Piagetian territory. In this sense you must assimilate Piaget to your previous schemes. But then, to interpret Piaget's ideas and gain his message, you must also accommodate—that is, alter—your schemes so they accord as closely as possible to his views. All acts of knowing—homely or profound—are products of complementary assimilation and accommodation. And, according to Piaget, the optimal breakthroughs of understanding occur when neither process dominates but rather when both are in balance or **equilibrium.**

A final point, crucial to an appreciation of Piaget and central to the presentation in this

book: A biologist by training, Piaget considered the acquisition of knowledge to be deeply rooted in the physiological functioning of the organism. As such, it must be a continuous process, with assimilation and accommodation occurring perpetually and schemes constantly changing. At the same time, we cannot say simply that the developing child accrues increasing knowledge or more finely differentiated schemes. Rather, at specifiable points in development, schemes become organized (or reorganized) in fundamentally new ways. And these fundamental reorganizations profoundly alter the way in which the child knows—and understands—the entire world of objects and persons.

Once a whole family of schemes has altered, new cognitive structures have formed and the child has achieved a new stage of development. Though some structures and stages are not very significant, others involve a fundamental reorganization of the whole world. In later chapters, following our treatment here of the sensorimotor stage, we will examine the major stages of cognitive development described by Piaget: the symbolic, preoperational, or intuitive stage (ages two to seven); the concrete operational stage (ages seven to eleven); and the formal operational stage (adolescence). These stages are briefly introduced in Figure 2.3.

There are two corollaries to the stage approach. First, the stages must occur in the same fixed sequence or order: stage B must follow stage A in every individual. Second, the attainment of a new stage in one domain will affect all other domains of knowledge. And so, acquisition of knowledge about the permanence of objects decisively alters the child's understanding of other concepts like space, time, and causality. Although these "stage-sequence" corollaries are accepted by many cognitive-structuralists, it is better to regard them as hypotheses to be confirmed—or refuted. In other words, one should entertain the possibility that the order of stages is not constant across all individuals. And one should consider the possibility that attainment of a new stage in one domain has few if any consequences in other spheres of knowledge. (We will consider these points further in Chapters 9 and 10).

THE SENSORIMOTOR SUBSTAGES

How did Piaget actually view the newborn child? At the moment of birth the child is a bundle of reflexive behaviors, patterns of action that are automatically triggered by certain conditions of stimulation (Piaget, 1963). Prick an infant's foot and her knee flexes;

touch an infant's eye and it closes. Sensory systems such as vision are working but are sensitive chiefly to gross variations such as contrasts of light and dark. When in pain or in need of nourishment, the infant cries. There are also a few more highly organized and flexible responses, such as sucking. Even the newborn will search for a nipple and will adjust (or accommodate) the sucking scheme to the nipple's size and the degree of flow.

In one sense, reminiscent of the empiricist position, the newborn knows nothing, or next to nothing, about the world. But in another sense, reminiscent of the nativist account, every newborn has the potential to know all. For, equipped with these reflexive schemes and with the all-important biological capacities to assimilate and to accommodate, the child will eventually construct—or build models of—the world.

And, in fact, development begins immediately. Every act of sucking, looking, or crying builds on schemes used in previous episodes and, in turn, lays the groundwork for later schemes. Before long, the newborn's behavioral schemes—in our loose sense, the actions of which she is capable—will reflect the particular conditions under which the schemes have typically been employed. For instance, if there is little light, the child will look at an object for a considerable period of time. If there is much light, glances will be briefer. If milk is plentiful and easily evoked, sucking will quickly become regular and efficient. If, however, sucking is not followed by nourishment, the child will move her head, perhaps suck more vigorously, or cease to suck and instead explore the object with the lips or tongue. Soon the child will suck numerous objects, such as a blanket, a pillow, a hand, or a pacifier. And the child will accommodate the sucking scheme to the properties of each object.

Stage	Description	Some specific achievements
SENSORIMOTOR *Birth to eighteen months:* Motor activities and sensory impressions from which mental operations are later derived.	The infant learns to differentiate herself from the external world; she learns that objects exist even when they are not visible; time and space come to exist independently of her own actions; she gains some appreciation of cause and effect, past and future.	If an object is hidden, the infant will search for it. The infant can make detours and retrace her steps to reach a goal.
PREOPERATIONAL OR SYMBOLIC *Eighteen months to seven years:* Representation, mental imagery, use of speech.	The child becomes able to represent something with something else—in speech, play, gestures, and mental pictures. Egocentrism declines as the child becomes more able to take other people's perspectives into account.	The child can represent, draw, or describe her path to a goal.
CONCRETE OPERATIONAL *Seven years to eleven years:* Internalized actions can be reversed; logic based on objects and states that can be manipulated.	The child becomes capable of a certain logic—of mentally undoing a mental or physical action so long as manipulable objects are involved. She can relate dimensions, appreciate that some aspects of objects remain the same despite changes in appearance, and classify elements into hierarchies.	The child can make or interpret a simple map; the perspective of another viewer can be appreciated.
FORMAL OPERATIONAL *Beyond eleven years*—Reasoning, freed from the concrete, can be based on purely verbal or logical statements.	The adolescent can reason on purely verbal or logical statements. She can relate any element or statement to any other, manipulate variables in a scientific experiment, and deal with proportions and analogies. She can construct whole systems of belief, become actively engaged in the world of ideas, and reflect on her own activity of thinking.	The adolescent can solve a geometric proof; she can explain the trajectory of a rebounding ball in terms of physics.

Figure 2.3. This chart presents, in brief form, the four major stages of cognitive development, as described by Jean Piaget. We shall discuss the details of each stage, as well as its implications and limitations, at appropriate points in the text.

As part of normal biological functioning, organisms will at times repeat actions even in the absence of an obvious reward or consequence. Piaget's children Lucienne and Laurent occasionally continued to suck even after the nipple had been removed (1954). Like earlier researchers (Baldwin, 1897), Piaget called such repetition of an act a **circular reaction:** the completion of one cycle (or circle) of the act leads automatically to a repetition (with slight but inevitable modifications) of the same act. Some circular reactions highlight assimilation: for instance, sucking is reproduced in virtually identical form, irrespective of the materials being sucked. Accommodation can also be highlighted. At such times each act of sucking differs so as to fit the physical configuration of the object being sucked.

The first extended period of life was called by Piaget the **sensorimotor stage.** This term reflects Piaget's belief that knowledge is initially built up from direct motor actions on the world and from immediate sensory perceptions of the world. In other words Piaget saw knowledge as deriving from the child's perceptions (which rely on sensory organs, particularly sight) and motor activities (which rely on various limbs and organs, particularly the hand). (In subsequent stages of cognitive development, overt actions become less important, and the operations of thought come to the fore. See Figure 2.3.)

According to Piaget's general account (1963) of the development of intelligence, the sensorimotor stage consists of six steps, or substages. During these substages the child gradually becomes able to define practical goals and to proceed in an increasingly systematic fashion to achieve them. We will first consider the general properties of these substages. Then we will note how they are manifest in one specific conceptual acquisition, the central capacity to recognize that objects continue to exist in time and space even after they have disappeared from sight (Piaget, 1954). Finally, we will discuss some attempts to explain the compelling phenomena described by Piaget.

Substage 1: Activating Reflexes. As we have noted, in the first substage of sensorimotor intelligence the child activates reflexes like sucking, swallowing, crying, and moving the arms or legs. At the beginning of the substage, the reflexes appear in inflexible fashion. By the end of the substage, however, the infant can adapt them somewhat to different circumstances. No longer will all realizations of a scheme be virtually carbon copies of one another: each one will reflect the conditions under which it was elicited.

Substage 2: Primary Circular Reactions. Once the child no longer acts reflexively with objects but begins instead to coordinate separate facets of a behavioral pattern, she has entered the second substage. For instance, when one-month-old Laurent begins to cry with hunger, his arms initially flail about. But later he begins to bring the arms closer to the mouth. His hands brush against his face, his mouth is wide open, and he tries to gain satisfaction by placing his hand in his mouth. Though Laurent's hands never reach his mouth, Piaget sees in this sequence the first signs of a connection between movements of the arms and attempts at sucking. We see here the barest beginnings of goal-directed behavior; the child appears to be acting in order to gain nourishment. Contrasting with the reflexes of substage one, the repetition of this attempt to secure a goal constitutes a **primary circular reaction.** There is also increasing indication that assimilation (converting objects into pre-existing schemes for sucking) is beginning to become separate from accommodation (adapting one's schemes for sucking to diverse objects). For instance, the specific shape of the object now affects the operation of the scheme.

Substage 3: Preserving Interesting Sights. During the third sensorimotor period, typically at the middle of the first year of life, circular reactions are finally put to specific use. Instead of mere repetition, repetition limited to smoothing out, or repetitions centering about the body, the circular reactions become increasingly devoted to goals of the moment, especially to preserving interesting sights and experiences. While primary circular reactions are generally restricted to motions of the body, **secondary circular reactions** signal some intention or recognition on the part of the child and are generally directed toward the manipulation of external objects. The child repeats an action not only for its own sake, but also because of its apparent consequences in the external world. What the child sees begins to influence what she does. Moreover, the particular scheme invoked by the child reflects some aspect of the situation at hand.

A good example occurs when five-month-old Lucienne sees a doll. She begins to move her feet. As Piaget moves the doll closer, Lucienne shakes her feet more vigorously. What is intriguing is the child's apparent belief that her shaking brings about the doll's approach. What appears to be intention on the child's part can also be seen as superstitious or magical behavior, for the child's shaking of course has no actual connection to the doll's location. Indeed, sometimes a child will emit all the schemes at her disposal in a frantic effort to continue or revive an interesting sight. Seven-month-old Laurent, captivated by a tin box his father is playing with, alternately looks at it, laughs, turns toward the box, shakes his arm, draws himself up, strokes his coverlets, and shakes his head.

Two limitations of the secondary circular reactions are worth noting. First, the infant has no goal initially: the goal has been discovered only by accident, and the means for achieving it are by no means fully appropriate. Second, the child's reactions are limited to schemes that have apparently worked in the past. The child can neither invent new schemes nor successfully coordinate ones that have already evolved.

Substage 4: Combining Schemes to Achieve a Goal. A fourth substage called **coordination of secondary schemes** is launched toward the end of the first year. Now the child begins to *combine* secondary circular reactions and to apply them more and more appropriately in new situations. Such activity presupposes an established intention as well as the related ability to execute a plan in order to achieve a goal. The plan need not be formulated with logical precision, but the child must have sufficient access to and control of her schemes to order them sensibly.

Consider some examples. Piaget presents ten-month-old Laurent with a cigar case and then covers it with a cushion. Revealing his goal, Laurent deliberately picks up the cushion to look for the cigar case. With one hand he removes the cushion, with the other he tries to grasp the cigar case. The child can now coordinate two separate schemes—one for lifting and one for reaching—in order to gain a desired objective. Similarly, nine-month-old Jacqueline watches her mother sew a piece of material. Earlier, Jacqueline might have kicked or laughed to keep this interesting sight going. Now, however, she searches for her mother's hand, places it in front of the material, then shakes the hand so that her mother will continue sewing.

By the fourth substage, changes have also occurred in the ways children explore new objects. Earlier the child would simply run through her repertoire of schemes randomly, regardless of whether they were appropriate. By the end of the first year, however, the child favors those schemes which, based on past evidence, are likely to have the desired result. Thus, handed an unfamiliar cigarette case, Jacqueline explores its numerous facets:

At first [she] examines it very attentively, turns it over, then holds it in both hands while making the sound *apff*. After that she rubs it against the wicker of her bassinet, then draws herself up while looking at it, then swings it above her, and finally puts in into her mouth [1963, p. 253].

Substage 5: Evolving New Schemes. In the fifth sensorimotor period, occurring around the start of the second year, children no longer rely on established schemes for confronting a problem or obstacle. Rather, now much more interested in objects' actual properties, they evolve new schemes specifically tailored to the novel aspects of the object or situation. In deploying these **tertiary circular reactions,** children are now more than mere technicians. They have become imaginative sensorimotor "engineers." No longer condemned to repeat schemes that happened to have worked on an earlier occasion, children can now alter or refine prior schemes in order to come to grips with the unfamiliar facets of a situation and then to attain a goal.

In one instance at fourteen months, Jacqueline finds that a certain movement of her fingers causes a box to tilt. Then, like a budding experimenter, she varies the conditions of this movement until she hits on an effective way of tilting the box back up. Another time, she spies a toy cat perched on the woodwork of her bassinet but located beyond her reach. Whereas earlier she had failed to reach the object, she now finds that she can use a stick to move the cat slightly and push it within

reach. Armed with such tertiary circular reactions, children can improvise and combine sensory and motor schemes for nearly any contingency (Piaget, 1963).

Indeed, by the fifth substage it may seem that children have attained all the schemes needed for sensorimotor knowledge of the world. After all, they are already capable of just about any action that a nonlinguistic animal can execute. But a crucial item is still missing: these children have neither mental images nor symbols. Thus they can neither think of elements removed in time and space nor perform mental actions or transformations upon elements in their presence. Accordingly, children at the fifth substage are restricted to physical actions using objects within their field of attention.

Substage 6: Devising New Means through Mental Combinations. These missing elements are supplied at about eighteen months, when children enter the sixth period. No longer restricted to experimenting "out in the open" with sensorimotor acts presently at their disposal, they can now carry out these actions implicitly, arriving at solutions by devising "mental combinations." Now they can consider various possible actions, locations, or uses of an object "in the head," and then frequently arrive directly at the (sometimes unique) solution to a problem. What occurs is a kind of internal experimentation, a mental exploration of ways and means, of alternative schemes. This newly evolving ability to imagine objects and actions leads to the appearance of "insight" behavior: like the bulb that suddenly lights, the solution to a problem abruptly makes its appearance in the "real world."

Two examples can ease us into this pivotal substage. Our first features a capricious Papa Piaget who hides a chain inside a matchbox, leaving a small opening. At first, daughter

Lucienne, now sixteen months, tries to turn the whole box over. Then she attempts to grasp the chain through the opening, and eventually she secures a small amount of chain with her finger. But when her father reduces the opening even further, Lucienne finds that neither of these procedures works. First a pause and then Lucienne

looks at the slit with great attention; then several times in succession she opens and shuts her mouth, at first slightly, then wider and wider. Soon after this phase of thinking, Lucienne unhesitatingly puts her finger on the slit and, instead of trying as before to reach the chain, she pulls so as to enlarge the opening. She succeeds and grasps the chain [1963, p. 338].

This illustration captures the child in transition between the fifth and sixth substages. So long as running through one's present arsenal of schemes solves a problem, the child has no need to invent new means through mental coordination. Such a mental inventory becomes necessary when present schemes prove inadequate and is possible when the child has evolved a way of representing the world to herself. The problem confronting Lucienne is how to widen the box so that the chain will come out. In gradually widening her mouth, she displays the beginnings of the capacity to take a mental inventory. She is on the brink of conceptualizing or imagining the scheme of "widening" without having to enact it fully in the world. And within a short time, she should be able to represent this scheme entirely internally, without any public display.

Our second illustration portrays just such a fully developed ability to devise schemes "in one's head" and arrive at insightful behavior. In this example, eighteen-month-old Jacqueline faces an impasse. She arrives at a closed door that she cannot open because she is holding a blade of grass in each hand:

Jacqueline stretches out her right hand toward the knob but sees that she cannot turn it without letting go of the grass. She puts the grass on the floor, opens the door, picks up the grass again and enters. But when she wants to leave the room things become complicated. She puts the grass on the floor and grasps the doorknob. But then she perceives that in pulling the door toward her she will simultaneously chase away the grass which she placed between the door and the threshold. She therefore picks it up in order to put it outside the door's zone of movement [1963, p. 339].

The ability to represent things of the world via mental imagery—as Jacqueline has done by eighteen months—is perhaps the central achievement of human intellectual development (see Kosslyn, 1980; Langer, 1942). This capacity ultimately allows us to use symbols such as words or pictures to stand for elements not immediately available to our senses. Only with this kind of representation can we conceive of persons, objects, and events beyond our present reach.

THE CHILD'S PROGRESS

In about eighteen months, the child once equipped only with reflexes has mastered the objects and events of her daily environment. From this angle the gap between the newborn and the eighteen-month-old is certainly qualitative and staggering. Yet Piaget evolved a vocabulary, a set of problems, and some ways of looking at the child that make the steps between substages seem credible and not even dramatic. Indeed, sometimes the transition seems so natural that it is difficult to state succinctly why a new period has begun.

Here we encounter a central and recurring dilemma in developmental psychology. Changes from one day to the next are never overwhelming; if noticeable at all, the differences are only in degree, or quantitative. As we noted in the last chapter, the child can hardly be described as unattached one day and then attached the next. Nor does the child one day grope publicly to solve a problem and the next day do it privately, in the mind. But viewed from sufficient distance, such changes are striking indeed. Contrast the child of four months who will smile at anyone with the infant of a year who cries for mother alone; compare the reflexive newborn and the purposeful two-year-old "mental experimenter." Viewed in this light, any theory that denies qualitative changes in the course of development seems inadequate (as does any theory that minimizes gradual daily increments and alterations). One of Piaget's accomplishments was to provide a framework for conceptualizing how the quantitative change from one enactment of a scheme to the next gradually gives rise to a qualitative difference and the attainment of a wholly new stage.

Piaget's sequence of sensorimotor substages can be applied equally to the child's interactions with physical objects, with persons, with events witnessed, and with experiences undergone. As already noted, Piaget also applied this framework to the initial understanding of space, time, and causality—three specific avenues of development that are closely interconnected (Piaget, 1954). We will take a closer look now at one of the most intriguing progressions he outlined, the formation of the object concept. Figure 2.4 (page 74) outlines the way this object notion develops in relation to other domains of intellectual development and its ramifications for the child's sense of space, time, and causality.

Constructing a World of Objects in Space

We take objects—and the laws that govern their behaviors—for granted. Of course, the world is made of many objects that cannot occupy the same place at the same time. And undeniably, they can be shifted or removed entirely from sight while continuing to exist. In fact, the beliefs that objects have a persistent identity and that they continue to exist in time and space form cornerstones of our thought. Just consider the consequences if objects suddenly ceased to be or suddenly appeared out of nothing. Such a state is even difficult to imagine, except perhaps in science fiction.

THE EARLY SUBSTAGES

These notions about objects may seem evident to us, but as Piaget demonstrated, infants do not share such a sense of object permanence (Piaget, 1954). As far as we can determine, for newborns in *substage one* objects do not exist at all apart from their immediate physical interactions with them. Nor does the stable identity and the permanent existence of objects dawn on newborns after a few days or even a few months in the world. Rather, the child's understanding of objects is a long and multileveled process—an active construction of a theory about the world—that unfolds over the eighteen months of the sensorimotor stage.

At the core of the **object concept** is the understanding that objects continue to exist when one can no longer see them. Piaget therefore scrutinized how infants behave when objects are removed from sight. During the *second substage* of sensorimotor intelligence, children show no special interest or awareness when objects vanish. Though they may sometimes notice when a nipple or a parent comes into view, they give no sign of understanding that objects exist outside their own activities. Indeed, when an object is removed from sight (or feel or smell), a child displays no schemes of searching. Instead, the schemes center about whatever remains nearby. The infant behaves as if the object no longer exists.

Only at the *third substage,* when secondary circular actions signal specific intentions, do children appear to form some expectations about how the world is organized. Then, for the first time, they are able to anticipate where an object may fall or to reach for an object that has been partially hidden. And only then, armed with a desire to maintain interesting sights, do they become motivated to act when an attractive object disappears from sight. For instance, Piaget drops a paper ball into six-month-old Laurent's crib. The child searches for it, but only in front of him—just where he had grasped it before. When Piaget drops the object outside the crib, Laurent simply repeats the circular action, continuing to search only in Piaget's hands. Here we see again the magical procedures characteristic of the third stage. The child acts as if he expects that any action on his part—whether relevant or not—will secure the desired consequence.

THE LATER SUBSTAGES

A dramatic change marks the subsequent substages. Now, for the first time, children will search actively and with some appropriateness for a hidden object. No longer are they wholly restricted to previous actions or to the object's most evident locations. Secondary schemes are coordinated as the children exhibit persistent energy in pursuing a goal—the missing object.

Even here, however, the transition is gradual. During the *fourth substage,* children tend to search for the object in the place where they looked last. This stage gives rise to a fascinating behavior that Piaget was the first to describe:

At 0.10 (18) [that is, when she is ten months and eighteen days old] Jacqueline is seated on a mattress with nothing to disturb or distract her (no blankets, etc.). I take her parrot from her hands and hide it twice in succession under the mattress on her left in [point] A. Both times Jacqueline looks for the object immediately and grabs it. Then I take it from her hands and move it very slowly before her eyes to the corresponding place on her right, in [point] B. Jacqueline watches this movement, very attentively, but at the moment when the parrot disappears in B, she turns to her left and looks where it was before, in A [1954, p. 51].

It is difficult to believe that the child continues to look for the object at *A,* even after she has seen it moved to *B*. For this reason, many researchers have skeptically tried to replicate the phenomenon (often called the "*A,* not *B*" behavior). Since everyone finds the phenomenon in some form, researchers have devoted considerable energy to uncovering its causes.

Piaget entertained several hypotheses. One theory is that the child has simply forgotten that the object was moved and is therefore going back to its original place. Adults themselves engage in such absentminded behavior when, for example, they search for a wallet in the closet after having moved it to the bureau. A second explanation is that the child's sense of space is immature; she cannot locate "invisible" objects within her unrefined organization of space. A third theory holds that the child has not yet developed the same sense of an object that an adult has. The object is just a particularly striking sight for the child, and her behavior in its absence is best viewed as superstitious rather than logical.

Piaget did not seek to prove or disprove any of these explanations. Rather, he arrived at the formulation—typical for him but infuriating to those in quest of an unequivocal explanation—that these three explanations are just three ways of talking about the same state of affairs. Children are mired in a world of practical actions. What they know is linked to what they can do, and so knowledge of objects is confined to those actions customarily directed toward those objects. Such children have not yet advanced to organizing

Figure 2.4. Each of the six substages of sensorimotor intelligence has its own characteristics. These general features are recapitulated in the first column. How the substages are realized in the area of the object concept is reviewed in the second column. Then, in columns 3 to 5, a brief summary of the principal manifestations of these substages in the domains of space, causality, and time is provided. It should be noted that each of these domains undergoes its own characteristic development but that many structural relations obtain across domains. Details on each of the specific developmental trajectories can be found in Piaget's *The Construction of Reality in the Child* (1954).

	General characteristics	Object
SUBSTAGE 1	*Activating reflexes.*	Objects have no independent existence.
SUBSTAGE 2	*Primary circular reactions:* assimilation becomes separate from accommodation.	No interest in vanishing object; objects exist only as parts of actions.
SUBSTAGE 3	*Secondary circular reactions:* preserves interesting sights; actions are repeated because of consequences; "magical behavior."	Anticipates where object may fall; reaches for partially hidden object; searches for object just seen; associates object with others' actions.
SUBSTAGE 4	*Coordination of secondary circular reactions:* schemes are directed toward goals.	Pursues hidden objects presumed to be at previous site; *A*, not *B* phenomenon.
SUBSTAGE 5	*Tertiary circular reactions:* new schemes evolved to achieve goals.	Monitors all visible displacements, occasionally reverts to original site of object.
SUBSTAGE 6	New schemes devised through mental combination.	Takes invisible displacement into account; represents object mentally.

Space	Causality	Time
No single organized space; just a collection of separate spaces related to specific sensorimotor schemes (e.g., visual space, tactile space).	No sense of cause and effect; at most, relates events to needs and tensions (as in conditioning).	Any sense of time is completely "practical," linked to feelings of effort and need; simply *does* things in a certain order.
Initial awareness of spatial relation between objects; still defines all spaces in terms of actions.	Perceives own acts (sometimes wrongly) as having effect; magical sense of causality; feeling of efficacy relating to acts.	Elementary sense of before and after as part of action; recollects immediate past; own acts remain central to sense of time.
Appreciates relation between object in front of and behind a barrier; interested in displacements of objects seen from different perspectives.	Appreciates means-ends relations; uses others to achieve effects.	Emergence of ability to remember events in which own acts are not central; continues to confuse time and space (as in A, not B phenomenon).
Apprehends body as occupying space; now moves objects all around and studies relations among them.	Appreciates that cause is external to self; takes into account spatial factors in cause-effect.	Retains more events and an event series for longer intervals; more differentiation of time from own actions.
Own movements and those of an object represent internally differentiated routes to the same goal.	Infers cause from effect and effect from cause by mental representation.	Can recall remote events; represents past and future; time exists apart from individual experiences.

events in time, understanding the structure of space, or attributing a permanent existence to objects. The object theory of the one-year-old, in other words, is part of the child's general way of conceptualizing the world (her way of knowing) at this substage: time, space, and causality are just different facets of the emerging but not yet mature object concept.

Whatever its causes, the "*A, not B*" behavior yields in the *fifth substage* to an ability to attend to all displacements occurring within the child's visual field. If an object is shifted from *A* to *B* to *C,* and the child witnesses all these movements, she will dart right for the object. No longer does the object adhere to its prior origin; no longer is the child's search for the object tied to her previous behaviors. The child can now take into account what has most recently happened to the object, and she can sometimes invent new schemes (or tertiary circular reactions) to aid in a search.

Yet this mastery is not absolute. If the number and types of displacements are too complicated to be readily assimilated, children may revert to the more primitive behaviors of the fourth substage. For instance, when the object is not immediately found in its new location (because it has been well hidden there), children are likely to search at the original location. They reject the recent evidence of their senses in favor of the more primitive theory that the object remains where it was. And moving the object to a hiding place beyond ready access also thwarts the search. Children not yet capable of mental imagery again return to the object's original position and eventually stop searching altogether. Indeed, as Paul Harris has shown (1975*b*), even when the object remains visible behind a locked Plexiglas door, children may resume their search at the old location. These phenomena underscore that the fifth substage is not so far divorced from the fourth. The child still lacks conviction that the object continues to exist when it is not in its expected location.

The full-blown object concept emerges during the *sixth substage,* when children are capable of mentally representing information. At this time they can account for nonvisible as well as visible displacements of the object. That is, they can conceptualize the object even if it remains hidden across several displacements. No longer does behavior depend on what has been seen most recently or on what is known about the customary address of the object. Notice Jacqueline's behaviors at eighteen months:

> Jacqueline watches me when I put a coin in my hand, then put my hand under a blanket. I withdraw my hand closed; Jacqueline opens it, then searches under the coverlet until she finds the object. I take the coin back, put it in my hand and then slip my closed hand under a cushion situated at the other side. . . . Jacqueline immediately searches for the object under the cushion. . . . I complicate the test as follows: I place the coin in my hand, then my hand under the cushion. I bring it forth closed and immediately hide it under the coverlet. Finally I withdraw it and hold it out, closed, to Jacqueline. Jacqueline pushes my hand aside without opening it (she guesses that there is nothing in it, which is new); she looks under the cushion, then directly under the coverlet, where she finds the object [Piaget, 1954, p. 79].

Evidently Piaget's daughter is aided decisively by her new capacity to represent actions mentally. She is now aware of the full range of places where the object might be; she can make an educated guess whether Piaget may have hidden it in his hand; and she persists in her search, because she knows that the object *must* continue to exist somewhere. Clearly, having traversed a series of six steps, the child has arrived at a qualitatively different level of understanding. She now appreciates that the world of objects continues to exist, despite transformations, displacements, and the sleight of hand of a father at play (or at work!). The zenith of sensorimotor intelligence has been achieved.

Piaget dismissed certain attempts to explain the source of this knowledge. It has not come about through deduction or through simple "reading-out" of inborn knowledge as a nativist might claim. Were that the case, the child would not need to pass through the many trial-and-error gropings, looking unsystematically in numerous places for the object or simply waiting until it reappeared. Nor would she fall prey to the "*A,* not *B*" trap. Instead, like a student solving a geometric proof, the child could simply reason about where the object *must* be.

Equally inadequate is the empiricist claim that the child arrives at the object concept simply by relying on a series of earlier instances. For if only the behaviors associated with prior experiences had been in effect, children should never be able to locate objects whose displacements they had not seen and never effect the transition from *A* to *B*. Instead, they would be restricted to searching only where objects had been encountered before. Even more emphatically, this simple accrual of past experiences could account neither for the *certainty* with which Jacqueline persists in the search nor for the *disbelief* with which she confronts her playing father. A child conforming to strict empiricist principles would always have to entertain the possibility that the object had disappeared forever.

Piaget adopted a complex interactionist view. According to this perspective, the child has actively constructed her knowledge of the object—first drawing on the primitive reactions and schemes at her disposal and then combining actions and reactions in increasingly systematic ways. Eventually, and inevitably, the child makes certain assumptions about how objects behave, formulates specific

hypotheses, and tries them out. For instance, children first search for an object in its most likely place. When this hypothesis repeatedly proves inadequate, they eventually try out other schemes, such as searching in a new location. Through a combination of close watching, heightened ability to appreciate how events unfold over time, more reliable knowledge of what can happen to objects, and the emerging ability to have mental representations, children's efforts are crowned with increasing success.

The children's experimentation, again, is neither purely deductive nor purely trial and error. Rather, at each stage children assimilate by drawing on current schemes and by building on the knowledge acquired during past stages. At the same time they accommodate, revising schemes and devising new solutions at difficult impasses. Only when they are able to represent to themselves the possible locations of the object and its continued existence despite its disappearance do they succeed in completing a theory "on the existence of objects in a spatial and temporal framework."

EXTENDING AND REVISING PIAGET

Not even Piaget would have claimed that his descriptions adequately explain the emergence of object permanence. We still do not fully understand why substage-five children become able to disregard the object's original location, or how substage-six children can represent events in their heads. Through ingenious experimentation several researchers have helped untangle the mysteries of the later stages of the object concept, especially the enigmatic "*A,* not *B*" (Bower and Paterson, 1972; Gratch, 1976; Moore, 1973; Schuberth, Werner, and Lipsitt, 1978). And they have made some progress. It has been shown, for example, that the infant is

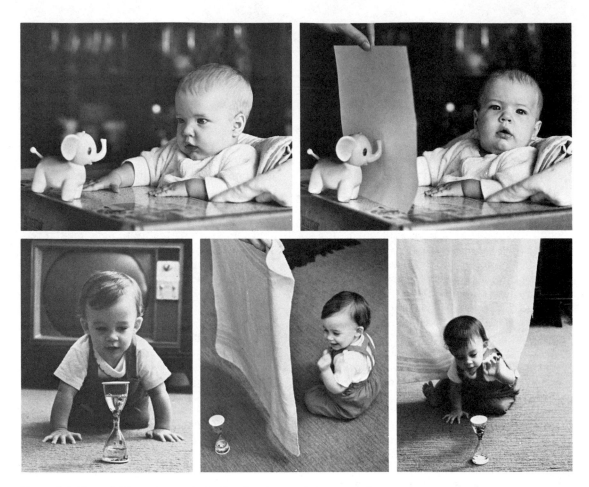

Figure 2.5. Two children demonstrate the developmental course of object permanence. The first child, failing to search for a toy once it has disappeared from view, apparently does not know that objects continue to exist when they are out of sight. But the second child, retaining interest in the hourglass even when it is hidden and then fetching it from behind the barrier, clearly understands the permanence of objects.

hampered by her tendencies to repeat the same motions of her body (always reaching to her left) and to rely excessively on a single landmark (always pulling the cloth near the vase) (Acredolo, 1979; Butterworth, 1976). Infants are helped in overcoming these persistent tendencies if they themselves are moved to a new location (Bremner, 1978); if they are provided with diverse cues that signal the location of an object (Cornell, 1979); or if they are allowed to move around the area before they begin the search (Benson and Uzgiris, 1981).

The role of memory has also been clarified. Infants prove more likely to head for the correct location if they are allowed to search immediately than if a delay has been imposed (Cornell, 1978). Yet memory cannot be the whole answer to the pull toward *A,* for infants will search at the wrong location even when the sought-for object remains visible at its new site (P. Harris, 1975*a*).

Finally, the somewhat artificial "*A,* not *B*" display has been re-created in situations more reminiscent of real life (Corter et al., 1980). In one study children's mothers first left a playroom via exit *A.* Then on a later occasion, the mothers departed via exit *B.* Echoing findings obtained with toys and berets, the majority of the infants searched at the initial doorway—exit *A.* These findings cast doubt on certain critiques of the standard Piagetian task: one cannot attribute children's failures to search at *B* to their lack of familiarity with the hidden object or to their feeling that the experimenter is simply engaged in a game. Indeed, the major difference between this "real-life" version and the standard task is the great distress shown by the nine-month-old children at the mothers' failure to reappear at *A*—solid proof that "*A,* not *B*" is not a trivial phenomenon devoid of "real-world" significance.

Even as parts of a puzzle of object permanence are clarified, fresh enigmas arise. For example, Paul Harris (1975*a, b*) has modified the "*A,* not *B*" task by making the object at *B* visible but impossible to grasp. He finds one-year-old children *more* persistent than younger children in approaching the original location (point *A*) after the object has been placed behind a transparent but locked door (point *B*). To explain this finding, Harris proposes that infants, like many adults, develop theories that blind them to useful data. Thus the year-old infant, after extensive groping, may persist in overlooking the visible object at *B* and in continuing a fruitless search at *A.* The younger child, on the other hand, will be more sensitive to the fresh information—the

sight of the desired object behind the locked transparent door. Accounting for such paradoxical findings may make the task of theorists even more difficult.

Although most students of infancy have marveled at the ingenuity of Piaget's studies, at least some commentators feel that he unduly minimized the child's knowledge during the first years (Bower, 1974*a*; Chomsky, 1980; Gelman, 1978; Mehler and Bever, 1968). Recall that Piaget set very strict criteria for attributing knowledge to a child; for instance, he did not grant knowledge of the object concept unless the child followed an object through several nonvisible displacements. One can counter Piaget by saying that you can fool anyone with a difficult enough test. Piaget's methods make the child perform poorly because they make unrealistic demands on the child's ability to attend, her memory for events, and her motor and sensory capacities. Accordingly, critics have devised simpler tasks to show that children actually possess the necessary competences earlier than Piaget would have allowed. For instance, Bower (1974*a*) has shown that infants can search successfully for objects hidden behind vertical screens but fail to search when the objects are covered by clothes (as in the usual Piagetian procedure). And through training he and Paterson (1972) have accelerated by three to four months the achievement of the final stages of the object concept. Bower's finding suggests that infants have the object concept but may not exhibit it under certain conditions.

Indeed, changing the conditions of an experiment may make younger children appear to have knowledge that Piaget would have denied them. But in some respects this enterprise misses the point of Piaget's studies. The fact is that Piaget was indifferent to ages. It was not crucial to his theory whether a child arrived at an object concept at one year or at eighteen months. What was important was that in every case a certain history of experience and sufficient maturation of the nervous system must precede the object concept. Moreover, there are no shortcuts; anyone who achieves this concept will have had to pass through the prior five substages. It is worth noting that efforts to disprove Piaget have generally been directed toward lowering the age of object permanence. So far, no one has introduced evidence that reorders the sequence of substages or allows one or more to be skipped.

A final crucial point must be borne in mind. Piaget was interested in several domains of physical knowledge, of which the object concept is but one. As shown in Figure 2.4, he traced the development of these concepts throughout the sensorimotor period. And he firmly believed that the events in these domains are intimately (or "structurally") connected. When children become able, in the fifth substage, to invent new means of problem-solving, this capacity has immediate reverberations in their sense of time, space, and the like. So too, the emergence of mental representation qualitatively affects all developing forms of knowledge. Whereas environmental-learning theorists might view progress in each domain as a direct reflection of the child's particular experiences in that realm, with no necessary implications for other realms, Piaget found it artificial to separate these domains. In his view they represent mere surface varieties of the same underlying entity: the child's world view, or cognitive structures, during a particular period of development.

The claim that all these domains are intimately connected confers tremendous strength on Piaget's other claims. Indeed, far more than a series of specific claims, Piaget's framework amounts to a world view that places great weight on the general way a child of a certain age constructs the world

(see also Langer, 1979). And here is where a true challenge to Piaget's views might be mounted. For now, perhaps the best way to test the power of this world view is to confront it with another. And so, in this book as in developmental psychology as a whole, we may pit Piaget's structural view of infant cognition against the environmental-learning approach.

The Environmental-Learning View of Cognition

The strength of Piaget's position is its demonstration that all normal children, irrespective of family background or specific experiences, will inevitably attain certain levels of understanding about their world, our world. But huge areas of knowledge are bypassed in this account. What particular schemes will be developed by children in different cultures, social classes, or families? How do children acquire the words of their language? Why does one child prefer the object hidden under the blue cloth, while another always grabs the checkered one? Why does Johnny fear snakes, Tommy rabbits, and Susie nothing at all? Why, in the same family, does one offspring become a teacher, the second an auto mechanic, the third a writer? Piaget's theory provides little insight into these questions, perhaps because he considered them irrelevant to the processes of scientific thought that he wished to illuminate.

But just these questions are often of pressing interest to parents, educators, and scientists. Our theories about thinking and learning are more frequently oriented toward these questions than toward the curious phenomena like object permanence that intrigue cognitive-structuralists. In comparing individuals, we want to know why they behave so differently even in similar situations.

For many decades, one way of explaining individuals' differences has been favored in our corner of civilization. According to the environmental-learning point of view, which had its origins in British philosophical writings of the seventeenth and eighteenth centuries, most individuals are quite similar at birth and have the potential to end up as similar adults. However, they are treated differently, undergo varying experiences, receive rewards for disparate behaviors. And as these varied "treatments" accumulate over years, they give rise to diverse results. One person lives in a supportive environment and she grows up cheerful; another resides in a punitive environment where she is mistreated, and she grows up bitter. What begins as merely one of a hundred behaviors is repeated and rewarded until it becomes an entrenched habit, typifying that individual. Nothing is inevitable about this at the start; the same individual could have been totally different if her experiences and reactions had followed another course.

But given an initially "blank slate," how does the child eventually form complex behaviors, habits, and concepts? The basic notion of this empiricist philosophy is the **association of ideas.** Elements, objects, or concepts that co-occur, or that occur in a regular sequence, become associated with one another. And soon one member of a pair naturally prompts the other element or behavior.

Clearly, this point of view differs radically from Piaget's. A theory predicated on the association of ideas has no need for, and will be unfriendly to, distinct substages, qualitative changes, and interaction of the individual's schemes with an environment understood (or known) at a certain cognitive level. Rather, the environment is viewed as an objective *given.* And, in turn, the individual is a passive recipient of sensory impressions transmitted from external objects, a simple vessel designed by nature to experience sensations, ef-

fect associations, and then build up ideas and habits through their combination.

Founded on these philosophical moorings, two principal research traditions arose early in this century. Even today, the environmental-learning tradition is dominated by these two schools, one favoring classical conditioning methods and the other operant (or instrumental) conditioning. (Another offshoot, observational learning, is of limited relevance to infancy. It is discussed in Chapter 5.) Experimenters in both schools initially worked with animals but soon adapted their experimental model to adults, to children, and eventually to infants. Moreover, the two schools have held the same broad goals: to uncover basic laws that govern learning and then to illustrate how the laws can account for all principal forms of behavior. And both schools have strongly resisted the notion that internal structures (like schemes, object concepts, or mental images) exist within the child's mind. Let us look, then, at these two approaches.

CLASSICAL CONDITIONING

Ivan Pavlov, a physiologist by training, knew that the taste of food caused a dog to salivate. He asked what would happen if a bell were sounded at, or slightly before, the presentation of food. According to the empirical philosophical tradition, such repeated pairing should eventually forge a link, an association, between the bell and the food. And, in fact, such a bond is the outcome of **classical conditioning,** which is outlined in Figure 2.6.

A special vocabulary has grown up to describe Pavlov's study (1927) and its many successors. At first, one requires only an element (or **stimulus**) that naturally elicits a certain behavior from an organism (a **response**). When this pairing of stimulus with response occurs without any training or special conditions—as in a reflex—the bond is said to be

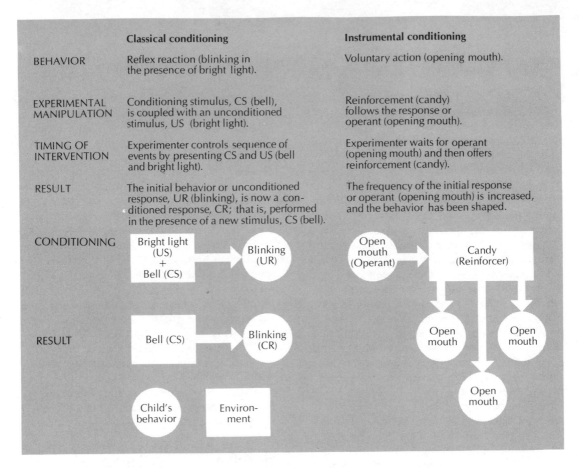

Figure 2.6. Through appropriate manipulation of task variables, an experimenter can bring about the two major forms of environmental learning: classical conditioning and instrumental conditioning.

unconditioned. Thus, in Pavlov's study, the **unconditioned stimulus** (US) of food produced the **unconditioned response** (UR) of salivation.

Next the unconditioned stimulus of food is repeatedly paired (or associated) with another stimulus, one—like a bell—that is originally neutral and does not of itself ordinarily induce salivation. Eventually, a link is formed between the two stimuli of bell and food and, more important, between the bell and salivation. Hence one now has a **conditioned stimulus** (CS)—the bell—and a **conditioned response** (CR)—salivation in the wake of the bell's

sound. In Pavlov's study, a dog came to salivate when it heard the bell, even in the absence of food.

Many variations of this procedure have been tried. After the conditioned link has been formed, the dog may salivate not only to a loud bell but also to related sounds such as a soft bell or a loud buzzer. If so, **generalization** of the stimulus has occurred. On the other hand, if the conditioned stimulus continues to be presented but without any food, the dog may eventually cease to salivate. If so, the conditioned response has been **extin-**

guished. And if the same stimulus is presented over and over again, the subject may eventually cease to pay attention to it. If so, the subject has **habituated** to the stimulus. Only a heightening of the stimulus (say, a louder bell) is likely to elicit or reactivate a response.

The method and terminology devised by Pavlov and his followers were soon applied to experimentation with young children. In one of the first studies with infants, Dorothy Marquis (1931) attempted to establish conditioned responses in newborn infants. From the very first time they were fed, ten infants received their bottle (US) either at the same time or shortly after they heard a buzzer (CS). Sucking (UR) naturally follows presentation of a bottle. Marquis wanted to know whether sucking (CR) would eventually follow the buzzer alone.

At regular intervals from the second to the tenth day of their lives, the infants' reactions were noted whenever a buzzer was sounded. Although both the experimental conditions and the manner of testing were complicated (and eventually controversial), Marquis found evidence that the sound of the buzzer alone eventually elicited conditioned responses— sucking movements and a general increase in activity. Because other sudden stimuli, such as a hammer striking the end of a tin can, did not elicit comparable responses, the results could not be explained away as a usual or unconditioned response to any loud sound. Here, then, was tentative evidence that conditioned responses could be formed even in newborn infants. Embracing the philosophical presupposition of environmental-learning theory, Marquis concluded that "systematic training of human infants . . . can be started at birth" (1931, p. 492).

Recently, these claims have received some modest support: several investigators have demonstrated that the heart rate of at least some two and three day old infants can be altered through variations of classical-conditioning procedures (Clifton, 1974; Crowell et al., 1976; Stamps, 1977; Stamps and Porges, 1975).

OPERANT OR INSTRUMENTAL CONDITIONING

The other branch of the environmental-learning tradition, sometimes called **behaviorism,** was also launched early in the century (Thorndike, 1913; J. B. Watson, 1919). It currently takes its lead from B. F. Skinner's dramatic demonstrations with pigeons and rats (Skinner, 1974). This American psychologist constructed a small soundproof box containing a lever or a key, a place for receiving food, and (sometimes) a light (Skinner, 1938, 1953). Sooner or later, an animal placed in the box would push the lever. As soon as it did, food would be forthcoming. **Instrumental conditioning** (see Figure 2.6) always depends on an **operant,** a behavior, such as lever pressing, which is already in the animal's repertoire. When this operant appears for the first and subsequent times, it can be **reinforced** by such desirable elements as food or praise. These rewards increase the likelihood of the reinforced behavior (or operant) occurring once again.

If a desired operant is not readily obtained, the animal's behavior can be **shaped.** That is, through careful reinforcement (and nonreinforcement), the experimenter can obtain a behavior of great specificity. Suppose a somewhat diabolical experimenter wants the animal to emit only complete bar presses with its left paw. Initially, any pressing of the bar will be reinforced; but subsequently, the animal will be reinforced only when it carries out a complete bar press; and still later, reinforcement only follows complete bar presses with the left paw. In this manner, exotic patterns can be quite readily shaped.

An experimenter might also shape behavior unintentionally. If, just before emitting the behavior that the experimenter has chosen to reinforce, an animal emits a behavior that is actually irrelevant to whether it receives reinforcement, the irrelevant behavior will eventually accompany the relevant behavior in a highly reliable fashion. This type of shaping has been compared to superstitious behavior in humans. People who go through a little ritual before taking an exam or placing a bet may recognize the mechanisms involved here.

Operant conditioning employs **schedules of reinforcement**—prescribed plans governing the conditions under which reinforcement will, or will not, be provided. Shaping proceeds in general according to continuous reinforcement; in such cases, every desired operant is reinforced. However, other schedules of reinforcement, utilized for other purposes, are less regular. Reinforcement can occur a proportion of the time (fixed ratio schedule), at predetermined intervals (fixed interval schedules), or at varying ratios or intervals (variable ratio or variable interval schedules) (see Figure 2.7). Paradoxical patterns sometimes result from patterns of reinforcement. For instance, if a rat is regularly reinforced for pressing the bar with its right paw and reinforcement is then discontinued, the behavior will rapidly be extinguished. If pressing with the right paw has been reinforced at only irregular or variable points and reinforcement is then discontinued, the rat will continue to emit the operant (press the bar) for a much longer time. This is because irregular reinforcements introduce uncertainty about whether and when reward will be received. People who have returned time and again to a pay phone that occasionally returns change can attest to the potency of irregular reinforcements.

Like a clever animal trainer, an ingenious experimenter can produce astonishing behavioral patterns. Suppose that one wants a rat to scratch the wall twice before pressing the lever. To extract this behavior, one simply ceases to reinforce the bar pressing alone, saving all reinforcement for the rare but happy occasion when the animal happens to scratch the wall twice before pressing the bar. Then, as copious reinforcement is forthcoming, the likelihood of paired scratching and the bar pressing will steadily increase. Instrumental conditioning is sometimes a long and tedious process, but remarkable effects can eventually be attained. Through careful shaping of each of the behaviors involved, Skinner has trained pigeons to play Ping-Pong and even to decode a set of colored shapes in a way that he, at least half-seriously, terms "reading" (Epstein, Lanza, and Skinner, 1980).

The operant model has proved extremely popular. Efforts to change human behavior—to improve the deportment of delinquents, to teach basic skills to retarded children, or even to help students learn high school chemistry—have used operant conditioning, sometimes with dramatic effectiveness. The reinforcements are as various as candy, nickels, a kiss, a gold star, or simply the chance to continue engaging in a desired activity. The model has also been used to good effect in basic research. For instance, Harriet Rheingold and her colleagues investigated the origins of communication in infants (Rheingold, Gewirtz, and Ross, 1959; but see also K. Bloom, 1979). Experimenters waited until three-month-old children began to make sounds, and then immediately and enthusiastically reinforced well-formed sounds (or operants) by smiling, making "tsk, tsk" sounds, and lightly tickling the infants' stomachs. Next the experimenters quieted and maintained an expressionless face until the children's next sounds, when the procedure was repeated. Over two days a large increase occurred in the number of

SCHEDULES OF REINFORCEMENT

Name	Example	Result/effect
CONTINUOUS Every response is reinforced.	The child is paid every time she washes a dish.	The child will continue to wash the dishes as long as she is paid. When payment stops, she will soon stop washing the dishes.
FIXED RATIO Every nth response is reinforced.	The child is paid every time she washes five dishes.	The child works hard, washing as many dishes as possible within a short time, thus receiving more pay. The higher the ratio (the more dishes she must wash for payment), the harder she will work.
VARIABLE RATIO Reinforcement comes after a certain number of responses, but that number changes.	The child is paid after washing four dishes, then eight, then six.	The child will continue to wash dishes, but behavior may be erratic since she does not know when payment will come or how her work will affect when she will be paid.
FIXED INTERVAL The child is reinforced the first time she performs the response after a given period of time.	The child is paid for washing the dishes every hour.	The child works harder (washes more dishes) toward the end of every hour when she knows she will be paid. After she is paid, she will work less hard. Thus, the longer the time interval, the less she will work.
VARIABLE INTERVAL The reinforcement comes after a certain interval of time, but the length of the interval varies.	The child is paid for washing dishes after one hour, then after fifteen minutes, then after two hours.	The child will continue to wash the dishes again. Behavior may be erratic and superstitious as she tries to anticipate payment.

Figure 2.7. Different plans or schedules of reinforcement can be applied in instrumental conditioning. Each one serves to train the desired behavior in a particular way.

sounds made by the infants. And when, after the two days, the experimenters stopped reinforcing vocalization, the children's sounds returned to approximately their original level. Like Marquis some years before, the Rheingold group showed that an infant's behavior could be significantly modified by altering the conditions of her environment.

CLASSICAL AND INSTRUMENTAL CONDITIONING APPLIED TO INFANTS

In addition to their common philosophical origins, the two forms of conditioning share numerous other properties. In each case, an experimenter seizes upon a link that is (or becomes) available—whether food and saliva, or a bar press and a food pellet—and then manipulates the link (for instance, by adding a conditioned stimulus or by invoking a schedule of reinforcement). Again, in each case, desired behaviors can be increased by rewards, and undesired ones can be extinguished by withdrawing rewards. Patterns of generalization and extinction also characterize both forms.

Yet certain crucial differences must also be borne in mind. Classical conditioning begins with *reflex* reactions—like salivation to food—and builds on these givens. Instrumental conditioning, on the other hand, typically uses as a point of departure a learned or *voluntary* action—and one that may not readily emerge. Indeed, considerable shaping is often necessary before the operant assumes a desired form. There is also a difference in the degree of activity associated with the animal. Classical conditioning deals mostly with the organism's reactions to events in the environment with the experimeter controlling the sequence of events. Instrumental conditioning, in contrast, waits until actions are performed by the organism on its environment. It is also worth recalling differences in the kinds of experi-

mental manipulations typically (though not invariably) favored. Classical conditioning studies typically imitate the kinds of procedure used by Pavlov (such as food paired with bell or buzzer), whereas instrumental studies often use Skinner's technology (for instance, pressing of a lever followed by reinforcement.)

Beyond doubt, the behavior of young children can be conditioned by both methods. Hundreds of studies document this assertion (see Fitzgerald and Brackbill, 1976; Hulsebus, 1973; Kessen, Haith, and Salapatek, 1970; Millar, 1974). Yet proponents of environmental-learning approaches have also tried to determine how soon conditioning can take place and whether one form of conditioning is more effective than, or succeeds earlier than, the other.

Much controversy has surrounded these issues. While proponents of the environmental-learning theory underscore the importance of early demonstrations of learning, critics question whether these laboratory-secured demonstrations reveal anything about how these processes unfold during normal (nonexperimental) development and whether a response that must be continuously reinforced bears any resemblance to those that emerge naturally and continue to be emitted in the absence of regular reinforcement. To this criticism, defenders of conditioning studies point out that many important processes are best investigated under controlled (if somewhat artificial) laboratory conditions: even if conditioning cannot explain all forms of learning, it describes well the acquisition of some of the most important and basic forms of human behavior (Kaye, 1981).

In general, critics have directed their sharpest attacks at the significance and the robustness of classical conditioning obtained shortly after birth (Sameroff, 1971). Studies employing instrumental conditioning have been somewhat more favorably re-

Figure 2.8. In this study using instrumental conditioning, the operant was turning the head to the left, as in the top picture. An experimenter saying "Peekaboo" reinforced the operant, bringing about a feeling of pleasure (bottom picture). But the power of such a reinforcer can decline as the baby grows accustomed to and then bored with it. (Bower, 1966)

ceived. For instance, Sameroff (1968) has shown that the operant of sucking can be modified by presenting (or withholding) milk. Siqueland (1968) has demonstrated that babies' head turning can be similarly modified. Moreover, by combining instrumental and classical conditioning methods, Siqueland and Lipsitt (1966) successfully conditioned head turning to certain sounds. However, these early forms of conditioning—and related behaviors like habituation (see Jeffrey and

Cohen, 1971)—are often difficult to obtain and prove unreliable and transient.

By the third or fourth month of life, much more robust, and often quite complex, forms of conditioning can be obtained. Some of the most impressive conditioning feats were accomplished by Hanus Papousek (1967), a Czechoslovakian pediatrician. In one experiment, when a bell sounded, milk appeared to the left of the infant's head; when a buzzer sounded, milk was furnished to the right. In this way Papousek combined operant and classical techniques: he paired various conditioned stimuli (a bell and a buzzer) with an unconditioned stimulus (milk), which in turn served as a reward for an operant behavior (head turn).

Using such setups and varying the conditions of reinforcement, Papousek produced behavioral patterns of surprising intricacy. For instance, in one study he conditioned four-month-old infants to make two turns to one side consecutively. In other studies infants were trained to alternate turns to the left with turns to the right, and even to alternate double turns to the left with double turns to the right.

Given such dramatic demonstrations using traditional conditioning techniques, one might think Papousek reluctant to assign "cognitive stances" of a Piagetian sort to the infant. After all, if infants can be conditioned to run through such tricky maneuvers in the first six months of life, why adopt the cognitive-structural view of the child as a painstaking constructor of knowledge? In fact, however, Papousek has come to view his experimental procedures as providing incentives for the child to devise strategies and solve problems. As he describes it,

In observing our subjects closely in conditioning experiments, and by recording their facial and affective responses, we gained the impression

that in their conditioned behavior, more complicated cognitive processes were involved than
just the summing of experiences from trial to
trial. The infants seemed to look as though they
were solving problems, experimenting, seeking a
correct solution [Papousek and Bernstein, 1969,
p. 242].

Infant strategies that impressed Papousek included looking for the milk on the same side
as on the previous trial; expecting the milk to
emanate first from the left and then from the
right; and always turning to one side and
then spontaneously correcting the response if
the milk were not soon presented on that
side.

Papousek's effort to synthesize environmental-learning and cognitive-structural approaches reflects a healthy trend in developmental psychology. Another ambitious
attempt at convergence is found in the
writings of Arnold Sameroff (1971, 1972).
Sameroff suggests that instrumental conditioning can occur in the opening days of life
because infants' existing behaviors, or
operants, are there, available for manipulation by the reinforcing investigator. In contrast, classical conditioning is elusive, in
view of infants' difficulties in forming an
association between the new stimulus (CS)
and their repertoire of unconditioned behaviors (US→UR).

Sameroff's explanation is instructive. Instrumental conditioning uses only existing, well-
organized patterns of behavior, such as sucking. In Piagetian terms, the behavioral scheme
is already present; all the infant must do is
accommodate to fresh contingencies (more
milk if she sucks harder). But in classical conditioning, the infant must initially perceive a
novel stimulus (say, a bell) to which she has
no ready-made response. Then, after this
process of accommodating and assimilating,
the child must accommodate another scheme

(say, sucking or turning) to that new stimulus
before securing a desired reward (milk).

According to Sameroff's analysis this latter
sequence of events requires an ability to accommodate, and to coordinate schemes, at a
level beyond the first sensorimotor substage.
For instance, if a bell (CS) is rung before food
(US) in order to condition sucking in response
to the bell, the infant first has to recognize
the bell as a unit, differentiate it from the
food, and discriminate it from other sounds.
Then she has to perceive the relationship between the presence of food and the bell she
just heard. And finally the infant has to relate
the bell to feelings of hunger and satiation,
previously associated with food. These tasks
are viewed as far more demanding than
merely altering the rate of sucking in order to
achieve more regular reinforcement. Instrumental conditioning is effective whenever existing schemes can be used in their present
form—when no new behaviors are at issue
and the ability to adopt reflexes characteristic
of Piaget's first substage suffices. Classical
conditioning, however, requires the child to
create new schemes and then to combine and
rearrange them. Such recognition and coordination draw on skills (such as secondary circular reactions) that appear only in subsequent periods of sensorimotor intelligence.

Complementary Perspectives

Although the backgrounds of cognitive-structural and environmental-learning theory differ, legitimate bridges can be built between
them. Indeed, rather than viewing the two
approaches as irreconcilable, it seems sensible
to consider them as somewhat complementary. For instance, the two approaches tend to
focus on different behaviors. The cognitive-
structuralist school focuses primarily on central strategies (like circular reactions) and on

conceptions (like the nature of objects) that are found across diverse domains of knowledge and are acquired in diverse settings around the world. Changes are examined over many months. The environmental-learning school, in turn, is more interested in how specific behaviors or associations can be acquired and then altered. Behaviors particular to a given environment or even a specific experimental situation are often probed. Trials are spread over minutes or, perhaps, a few days.

The attitude toward behaviors also differs. The cognitive-structuralist sees the *"A,* not *B"* phenomenon of the fourth substage as a necessary step in the development of the object concept, one that must occur in the sequence just where it does. The environmental-learning theorist resists notions of necessary steps and fixed sequences. Instead, the learning theorist might strive to show that *"A,* not *B"* behavior could be delayed, skipped, or even shifted to a different place in the sequence, depending only on how the contingencies of reinforcement are arranged. Or such a theorist might devote attention to the day-by-day occurrences and "learnings" that ultimately shift the child's behaviors from *A* to *B* (Cornell, 1978). Indeed, a full understanding of *"A,* not *B"* behavior may ultimately require insights from both schools: one may need to take into account not only the child's overall cognitive level but also her history of reinforcements.

In contrasting these points of view (summarized in Figure 2.9), we must consider the possibility that they have been designed to deal with two different classes of events. Perhaps environmental-learning theory should restrict itself to the particular forms taken by individual behaviors: why one child salivates in the presence of the mother, the other in the presence of the father, still a third in the presence of red colors, green bottles, dark rooms, or scary strangers. Perhaps cognitive-

structural theory should restrict itself to the general course of intellectual development: how the child acquires a sense of time or space; what steps precede the invention of a new scheme; or how the child devises a mental image. Were this division of labor adopted, we would not attempt to synthesize the points of view. Rather, we would allow them, like two conquering nations, simply to divide the spoils of development.

The impulse behind each school also differs. Cognitive-structuralists seek to account for "natural developments" and regard interventions and training with a suspicious eye. Hence, they favor naturalistic observation and "ecologically valid" studies. Environmental-learning researchers are interested in the effects of manipulations and tutoring—they are skeptical about claims regarding "natural patterns of growth." Hence, they favor controlled laboratory manipulations.

Yet neither school can afford to ignore the other. Notably lacking in the conditioning literature are well-worked-out notions of when and why certain forms of conditioning are possible, what elements are suitable for conditioning at different points in the developmental course, (Seligman, 1970), and why certain strategies appear and disappear in the manner that they do. By the same token, the cognitive-structural account has lacked sufficient indication of why children reach the same stage at widely differing ages; why competences arise first in relation to certain objects (screens rather than boxes; mothers rather than toy ducks) and only later in relation to others; which features of objects are seized on in forming schemes and which are ignored. These questions, although perhaps not central for Piaget, must be resolved before the sensorimotor account of cognition can be comprehensive.

For such reasons, the integrative lines of study and argument undertaken by Papousek,

THEORIES OF HUMAN KNOWLEDGE

Nativism	Empiricism	Interactionism
Knowledge is part of one's birthright; at birth a child already possesses all the knowledge she will ever need.	The world contains what needs to be known, and all knowledge derives from experiences undergone in the world.	All knowledge is acquired by constructive interaction between the human subject and the physical or social object.

THEORIES OF HUMAN DEVELOPMENT

	Environmental-learning	Cognitive-structural
SOURCES OF KNOWLEDGE	Empiricism: Knowledge is attained through experience in the world.	Interactionism: Knowledge is attained through the interaction of the individual and his environment.
ASPECTS OF THE CHILD THAT ARE STUDIED	The specific contents of the child's world; the learning of associations between objects and events; the acquisition and alteration of specific behaviors.	The child's overall view of the world; learning of rules and patterns governing the physical world.
SAMPLE QUESTIONS	How does a given child come to fear certain objects? What causes a child to cry when her dog leaves her? Why do certain children become dishonest? Why does one child but not another spend a lot of time drawing?	When and how does the child know that objects continue to exist when she does not see them? How does the child understand justice? How does the three-year-old understand and represent space? The seven-year-old? What developmental stages or changes characterize all children's drawings?

Figure 2.9. The theories devised by environmental-learning and cognitive-structural theorists reflect the different issues in which they are interested and their diverse concepts of human knowledge. Together, their two perspectives provide a comprehensive picture of the child's mental growth.

Sameroff, and other researchers (for example, Cornell, 1978; J. S. Watson, 1972) hold promise. Cognitive-structural theory provides just that portrait of children's overall competences within which their particular capacities for learning can be better documented. By the same token, learning theory can supply a richly textured picture of the child's entire behavioral repertoire—preferences, fears, personal traits, changes over time—which fleshes out the rather spare description of a stage of cognitive development.

Finally, methods developed by one school can be exploited by researchers in the other camp; for example, conditioning techniques have been employed by researchers addressing the cognitive-structural agenda (Bower, 1974*a*; Wagner et al., 1981). Indeed, as one review of this field concluded, the exciting task of the next generation of researchers will be to enlarge and complicate various models of learning to make room for the complexity of each infant (Kessen, Haith, and Salapatek, 1970).

Signposts

To complement our opening examination of human attachment, we focused in this chapter on pivotal issues in cognitive development—how the child comes to know the objects and persons in the world about her, their attributes and properties, their regularities and exceptions. We have traced the child from a time when she may possess nothing but some rules for processing information until she has acquired a basic idea of how objects work in time and space.

As background for our discussion of cognition, we considered two sources of controversy among developmental psychologists. First, scholars disagree about which aspects of the child's knowledge to study. The environmental-learning school stresses the importance of specific features in the child's envi-

ronment and specific experiences undergone by the child. The cognitive-structural school focuses on the child's understanding of the physical properties of objects, temporal and spatial relationships, and laws of cause and effect.

The second disagreement concerns the actual source of knowledge. Environmental-learning theorists (or empiricists) believe that all knowledge derives from experience in the world. Nativists hold that all necessary information and response patterns exist in the brain from birth. Cognitive-structuralists, midway between these extremes, view knowledge as resulting from an interaction between the child's current ways of knowing (or mental structures) and those facets of the external world that the child can perceive and understand.

Jean Piaget, the foremost representative of the cognitive-structural school, saw the infant as an active problem solver, seeking to make sense of the world. Starting with schemes, particular ways of knowing her environment, and equipped with the twin capacities to assimilate objects to an existing scheme and to accommodate an existing scheme to new circumstances, the child actively constructs her sensorimotor intelligence during her first two years. From a point of total egocentrism—where she cannot perceive herself as a separate entity—the child gradually gains distance from the objects and persons about her.

The course of sensorimotor intelligence during infancy constitutes the first of Piaget's four major stages of cognitive development. It consists of six ordered substages that characterize the course of intellect in every domain of knowledge: (1) activation of the reflex behaviors present at birth; (2) primary circular reactions, when assimilation and accommodation separate; (3) secondary circular reactions, when actions are repeated in an effort to sustain desired consequences; (4) coordination of schemes in order to attain a goal; (5) tertiary circular reactions, when new schemes are devised to achieve a goal; and (6) the capacity to achieve mental representations. This fixed sequence of substages can be observed in several domains of intellect, including the development of sensorimotor understanding of time, space, and causality.

Central to Piaget's description of infant cognition is a sense of object permanence: the understanding that objects continue to exist even when they are not in view. Although the achievement of object permanence entails the same substages, it includes a paradoxical feature during the fourth substage: the phenomenon of *"A, not B"* behavior, when the child searches only where she last searched for an object, and not at the location to which she subsequently saw it moved.

Researchers have critically examined various phases of Piaget's account. Some have introduced distinctions, examined factors, or tried experimental manipulations that did not figure in his initial descriptions of *"A, not B."* Others have discovered new phenomena that complicate Piaget's account; for example, one-year-old children prove more likely than younger children to search for an object where they last searched, even when the object is visible elsewhere. Still others, like T. G. R. Bower, believe that children may achieve sensorimotor intelligence earlier than Piaget maintained. But so far no one has introduced evidence that Piaget's substages can be reordered or that any can be skipped.

Piaget's focus on the child's active construction of knowledge contrasts with the environmental-learning theorists' perspective. These theorists emphasize the child's passive acquisition of specific associations, fears, preferences, and the like, through some form of conditioning. In classical conditioning (favored by followers of Ivan Pavlov), one begins with a reflex reaction (unconditioned response) and pairs whatever elicits it naturally (unconditioned stimulus) with some other (conditioned) stimulus, eventually producing a conditioned response. In instrumental conditioning (favored by followers of B. F. Skinner), one reinforces an operant (a behavior the individual can already produce) in order to increase the likelihood that the behavior will be repeated. Although both forms of conditioning use rewards to increase or extinguish behaviors, they differ in procedure. Young infants can be conditioned by both methods, but newborns seem more susceptible to instrumental than to classical conditioning.

Despite theoretical disagreements between the schools, some researchers have successfully combined Piagetian and environmental-learning insights. Such efforts have indicated how the effectiveness of conditioning may be influenced by the child's sensorimotor capacities and how the child's mental life may in turn be influenced by her specific conditioning history. Thus, the two approaches are complementary: cognitive-structuralism illuminates the general properties of knowledge, whereas environmental-learning theory shows how specific items of information are acquired and then used to further expand the knowledge base.

The preceding chapter on attachment and this one on cognitive development may suggest a split infant: one concerned primarily with feelings and the world of people, the other with the intellect and the world of objects. What we need now is a fuller portrait of the infant—a description of the equipment with which she begins her life, a consideration of the effects of early experience, an account of what she can perceive, make, and feel over the opening years of life, and a characterization of pivotal behaviors that involve cognitive and affective facets. It is fitting that our consideration of the complete infant should start with the very beginning of life.

CHAPTER THREE

From the Fetus to the Discovery of Self

The very first sensation which an infant gets *is* for him the outer universe. . . . The Object is one big blooming buzzing Confusion. That Confusion is the baby's universe. . . .

   –WILLIAM JAMES

If we only learn to let live, the plan for growth is all there.

   –ERIK ERIKSON

All of us have encountered a new place, whether in the course of visiting a city, arriving at college, or living in another country. The welter of striking initial impressions makes the first days a time of maximum learning and discovery. Later, our learning continues and perhaps also deepens, as we sort out our experiences and refine our impressions.

In such encounters with new environments, we are aided by two principal factors: our preparation and the tools or techniques available at the new site. The more knowledge we have about the place, the more we are likely to gain from our experiences there.

And, once in the new environment, we will make deeper and more rapid discoveries if we remain alert, learn the local lingo, and draw on acquaintances or informants.

In instructive ways this entry of an adult into an alien environment parallels a newborn baby's course. At birth, each infant is a stranger to the external world, but each has been superbly prepared for this entry as a result of genetic heritage and nine months inside the mother's womb. Once birth has occurred, learning proceeds at a staggering rate. Although aided by inherited equipment and by capacities unfolding in the womb, the child's early development will be significantly influenced by specific experiences in the external world and by the help she is given. In fact, during her first months, the child goes through as many changes and developments as in all subsequent years. Unless there are severely damaging circumstances, the course of development will continue smoothly so that a remarkable transition will have occurred by the end of two years: from a microscopic cell the organism will have been transformed into a human who can perceive many features of the world, conduct numerous complicated actions, and undergo a wealth of significant feelings. And the two-year-old will have taken the first and most important steps in forming a sense of self.

In the opening chapters of this section on infancy, we have considered in some detail two aspects of early development. First we examined the formation of attachment between parent and child, thereby gaining insight into the affective (or feeling) life of the child. Then we turned our attention to cognitive matters—how the child perceives and acts on the world of physical objects, and what knowledge derives from such actions.

Although the affective and cognitive approaches may have appeared as rival dimensions of development, no such clear-cut distinction can actually be maintained. In fact children's feelings play an important role in what (and how) they perceive and how they act on the physical world; children's knowledge in turn colors their affective experience. Accordingly, the time has come for us to consider the infant more comprehensively. On the one hand, we need to follow the details of development from conception until the conclusion of infancy, in order to determine what children can and cannot do at various times and in various spheres. On the other hand, we need to tie together the various aspects of the child—to see the ways in which perceptions,

actions, and feelings interact in important behaviors and experiences.

Ultimately, of course, development is continuous; nature brooks no absolute breaks. Yet an examination of certain discrete aspects will aid us in understanding the events of development. To begin with, we will describe the human being before birth—the course of the zygote, embryo, and fetus cushioned within the womb—and we will examine the genetic factors that control the processes of development. Then, having considered these biological factors, we will turn our attention to events occurring after birth, giving special attention to the emergence of the human being as a psychological creature. We will review the perennial but vigorous debate on the nature and extent of the newborn infant's knowledge. This will entail a discussion of the important effects of early experiences and, equally, a description of how the child's capacities to feel, perceive, and act evolve during infancy and become intermeshed. Finally, we will consider some of the more complex capacities achieved by the infant, concluding with a brief examination of the young child's most important creation: a beginning sense of self.

As we ponder the vast changes that occur in the early months of life, it may be helpful to think of the newborn child as a "well-equipped stranger." Even as adults are often strangers in a new environment, young children are completely unfamiliar with the persons, objects, and events that constitute their initial experiences on earth. At the same time, however, infants are superbly equipped for their mission: prepared by biological and genetic heritage, aided by the comfortable and enriched environment of the womb, supported by family and culture, and guided by the abilities to perceive, act, and feel that are part of the birthright of every human being.

Our Biological Heritage

FROM CONCEPTION TO BIRTH

Life begins at conception, when a sperm cell contributed by the father fertilizes the ovum or egg furnished by the mother (see Figure 3.1). A **zygote,** or fertilized egg, is formed. Only 1/200 inch in diameter, the zygote has coded within it all of the information needed for the eventual growth and functioning of the mature organism. The central portion, or **nucleus,** of the zygote divides in a process during which the cell's information-bearing material duplicates itself. These cells then also divide, giving rise to four cells. Then, through repeated division, more and more cells are formed. Within several weeks, sufficient division and differentiation among kinds of tissue have occurred so that the features and overall form of the human organism are readily recognized.

Figure 3.1. After fertilization, it takes ten to fourteen days until the zygote is firmly implanted in the wall of the uterus.

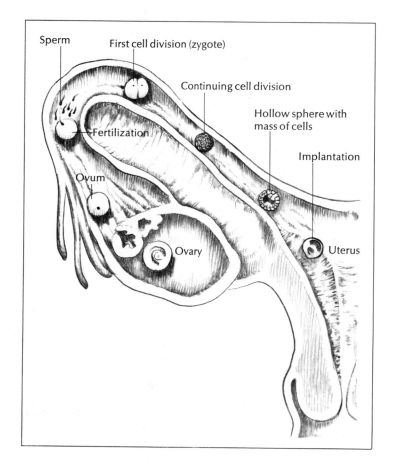

Sperm

First cell division (zygote)

Continuing cell division

Hollow sphere with mass of cells

Fertilization

Implantation

Ovum

Ovary

Uterus

Scientists have obtained amazingly detailed knowledge about the phases through which the fetus passes in the months before birth. Most of this information has been obtained from studying organisms that have been removed from the mother for medical reasons or that have become detached from the wall of the mother's uterus and, in a process of spontaneous abortion, have been expelled from the body (Hooker, 1963; Landreth, 1967). Age determination can only be approximate for any fetus, but if enough immature organisms are examined, the regularity of growth and the precise time at which various organs emerge can be confirmed. In addition, when a fetus is surgically removed from the mother, one can conduct tests in order to discover the organism's sensitivity to types of stimulation. For instance, sensitivity to touch is determined by placing hairs of different weight on the skin of the fetus.

Embryo and Fetus. During the **germinal period,** which is between a week and two weeks long, the fertilized egg travels down to the uterus and is firmly implanted there. Then the **embryonic stage** begins. During this period, which lasts about eight weeks, the organism (or **embryo**) increases in size by about two million percent. At first, the cells organize into a hollow sphere; the body itself develops out of a mass of cells on one side of this sphere. By the end of the second week, three discrete layers have already formed. From the **ectoderm,** or outer layer, develop the sensory organs, the nervous system, and the outer layer of skin, hair, nails, and part of the teeth. From the **mesoderm,** or middle layer, evolve the muscles, the skeleton, and the excretory and circulatory systems. And from the **endoderm,** or inner layer, grow the gastrointestinal tract, the vital organs (such as the liver and the lungs), and various glands. A system of blood vessels connecting the outlying organs

with the heart is established by the end of the first month.

During the *second month,* the embryo grows to about an inch long, and its features become recognizably human. The face is more defined. Fingers, toes, and external genitals are recognizable, and in the male embryo the testes begin to produce androgens, hormones that govern the development of male characteristics. A tail, which was prominent earlier, begins to recede. Nerve cells have developed in the spine. And, as a consequence, early signs of behavior can be detected: some motion occurs in the primitive limbs; the embryo responds to tactile stimulation. By the end of the second month, major portions of the musculature of the trunk and the limbs have developed.

During the *third month,* the beginning of the **fetal period,** electrical activity can be detected in the brain (Rosen, 1978) and signs of behavior are increasingly clear. Various reflexes have developed. For instance, if the fetus is dropped a few centimeters, its muscles automatically contract. Stimulating the palm of the hand causes the fingers to close quickly though incompletely; electrical stimulation makes the limbs move. The thumb and forefinger are apposed so that the fetus could, in theory, grasp an object. And the heart rate is so regular that patterns characteristic of adults can be discerned. Instead of moving in unison, legs now move separately. And, during motion, the arm on one side moves more extensively backward than the arm on the opposite side. These independent movements testify to the differentiation of bodily functions.

In the *fourth month,* the fetus comes increasingly to resemble the newborn infant (see Figure 3.2). By thirteen weeks, the fetus is three inches long. By sixteen weeks, it has attained a size of four and one-half inches. And during the fourth and fifth months, the

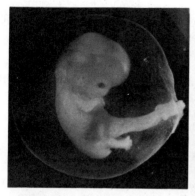 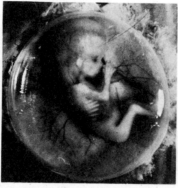 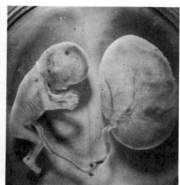

Figure 3.2. The embryo at eight weeks (*at left*) is about one inch long. Although it still has some fishlike characteristics, it is beginning to develop limbs. The fetus at fourteen weeks (*center*) is about three and a half inches long; fingers have already developed. The fetus at sixteen weeks (*right*) is about four and a half inches long; notice the umbilical cord connecting the body to the placenta.

basic bodily structures of the organism are completed. The face is more sculptured; external genitals are now distinctive and sexual gender can be readily determined. Bones are well outlined; blood is forming in the bone marrow; nerve cells are multiplying rapidly. The head now moves independently of the rest of the body—nodding, tilting, retracting, and rotating. Skin is everywhere sensitive to stimulation; limbs are movable at every joint; movements are now graceful and delicate. The four-month-old fetus can make most of the responses that are eventually elicited from the newborn baby.

By the end of the *fifth month,* the basic bodily structures of the human organism as well as many behavioral patterns have been well established. Stimulation of different parts of the brain will evoke appropriate bodily responses. Facial responses (including eye movements) tend to accompany head and mouth movements, and these responses al-

ready anticipate the newborn baby's emotional expressions. Reflexes at this age include sucking, swallowing, and hiccoughing. Fingers are active, though there are no objects to grasp; eyes blink even in the absence of irritation. The fetus now weighs about ten ounces and is about ten inches long. And it already possesses about twelve billion nerve cells, all that will be needed to attain the heights—and the depths—of human cognitive and emotional experience.

Despite this striking physical and behavioral resemblance to the newborn infant, fetuses born before the end of the fifth month rarely live. To survive premature delivery, a fetus should be about twenty-four to twenty-eight weeks, or *six to seven months*. By this crucial time, there has occurred a further increase in size: the fetus at twenty-eight weeks is about fifteen inches long and weighs about two and one-quarter pounds. (Owing to improved medical procedures, some infants weighing but a pound and a half prove viable; however, the risks of being permanently handicapped are high in this population. See Henig, 1981.) By the sixth month, the respiratory apparatus—particularly the nostrils and the lungs—becomes strengthened and coordinated. Various endocrine glands, whose secretions control important bodily processes, become active. Most important, the brain continues to develop; indeed, it has been claimed that the fetal brain begins to "live" at about twenty-eight to thirty weeks, or *seven to eight months* (Purpura, 1975). Important connections between nerve cells emerge, making possible more complex and better-integrated activities.

Once the brain has developed to a certain point, the organism may be considered a "psychological" as well as a "biological" creature: in addition to acting, the fetus may also perceive and feel. It is extremely difficult, however, to determine what information (if any) is being perceived by the sense organs of the fetus and what feelings (if any) the fetus experiences. Beyond question, the sensory organs undergo elaborate development during the fetal stage. Indeed, the antecedents of the human eye begin to develop in the second and third weeks of life; eye movements as well as opening and closing of the lids occur by the sixth month. Yet, because the retina of the fetal eye has not been exposed to normal light, it seems unlikely that the infant is capable of sight as we know it. By the same token, hearing mechanisms seem well developed during the latter months of fetal life; for instance, the heart rate changes when the fetus is exposed to loud noises or to classical music (Newton and Modahl, 1978). But because the outer ear is closed, and the middle ear is filled with liquid, the fetus may not hear sounds of normal intensity. Finally, although the embryo exhibits various facial expressions, we have no way of determining whether these correlate with "felt" bodily states. It is worth noting, however, that when pregnant women enter rooms with bright lights and harsh noises, their six-month-old fetuses are startled. In contrast, soft lights and sounds apparently attract the fetuses, and these reactions occur independently of the mother's own reactions (Brazelton, 1981). Moreover, the development of the nervous system at thirty-eight weeks seems sufficient to allow the detection of pain (Scarf, 1976).

The Maternal Environment. Though fetuses of seven months may experience feelings, the superb environment of the mother's uterus makes it unlikely that fetuses undergo discomfort under normal conditions. Temperature, chemical balance, orientation with respect to gravity, and atmospheric pressure are carefully controlled. The **placenta,** a fleshy disc that attaches the embryo to the uterine wall, serves as a way station for transmitting nutrients—like oxygen, water, and sugars—to the fetus and for returning waste-laden blood to the mother. Although the mother's blood supplies all the raw materials for growth, the embryo itself begins to manufacture complex amino acids, carbohydrates, and other materials required for nourishment and growth during the weeks following conception.

Under normal conditions, the maternal environment ensures a comfortable and uneventful fetal development. However, unhealthy influences may cause problems, especially during the first two months after conception. These deleterious influences range from excessive intake of certain drugs, to various unexpected diseases, to severe states of anxiety—each of which can induce abnormalities in the developing fetus. Table 3.1 summarizes a number of damaging influences the fetus might encounter. Similarly, if the mother undergoes severe stress, the fetus will kick violently, exhibiting up to ten times more

Table 3.1. SOME MATERNAL CONDITIONS ENDANGERING THE CHILD

Mother's condition or behavior	Estimated degree of risk (high = 3; low = 1)	Possible effect on embryo, fetus, or newborn
Malnutrition	3	Fetal growth retardation; malformation; less developed brain; greater vulnerability to disease
Smoking one pack or more per day	1	Fetal growth retardation; increased fetal heart rate; prematurity
Moderate daily use of alcohol	1	Growth deficiency; developmental lag
Rubella (German measles) in early pregnancy	3	Cataracts; deafness; heart defects; mental retardation
Other viral infection: measles, mumps, hepatitis, influenza, chicken pox, herpes	1	Malformation; fetal death; prematurity; fetal growth retardation; disorders and infection in the newborn
Exposure to X ray	3	Retardation; bone defects in skull; spinal and eye defects; cleft palate; limb deformities; increased risk of cancer?
Incompatibility of maternal and fetal blood	2	Jaundice; anemia; death
Use of antibiotics	2	Discolored teeth; inhibition of growth; hearing loss
Use of thalidomide and other tranquilizers	3	Hearing defects; limb malformations; defects of the heart, eyes, intestines, ears, and kidneys; cleft lip or palate
Excessive use of vitamins	1	Congenital anomalies; cleft palate
Use of analgesics	2	Respiratory depression
Use of aspirin in large doses	1	Respiratory depression, bleeding
Use of anesthetics or barbiturates	2	Respiratory depression
Use of cortisone	1	Birth defects; cleft palate
Use of drugs for diabetes control	1	Birth defects
Use of anticonvulsant drugs	1	Heart defects; brain, nervous system, and intestinal malformations; mental retardation; cleft lip and palate; bone defects
Use of anticoagulants	1	Abnormalities of cartilage, mental retardation
Narcotic addiction	2	Growth deficiency; withdrawal syndrome; respiratory depression; death

activity than normal (Newton and Modahl, 1978).

Experiences beyond the uterus may also affect the fetus. Ando and Hattori (1970) studied two groups of babies: those who had spent their fetal period near the noisy Osaka airport in Japan, and those who had moved near the airport just before birth. They found that 58 percent of newborns in the first group slept soundly, and only 6 percent awakened and cried when planes flew overhead. In sharp contrast, only about 10 percent of the babies in the second group slept soundly, and about half of them awoke and cried when an airplane passed overhead. Though it is difficult to fix the precise cause of this difference (perhaps the parents themselves behaved differently), babies in the first group may well have become acclimated to noise during their nine months in the uterus.

In infants who have survived nine full months within the uterus, breathing, heart rate, temperature, blood pressure, and other systems are now well regulated and integrated. The infant is well equipped to withstand changes in the less predictable environment beyond the uterus. There is no longer any need for the organism to remain within: like the chick who pecks at the egg, the fetus is poised for transition to the outside world.

THE GENETIC HERITAGE

Just what accounts for the stunning regularity in human development? Without doubt, the information contained in the egg and sperm is the initial determining factor. Contained in the nucleus of the egg, are twenty-three **chromosomes** that carry the child's genetic heredity. Only in these two **germ** (or reproductive) **cells** are there just twenty-three chromosomes: the zygote formed by the union of egg and sperm and all other bodily cells (the **somatic cells** that make up the bones,

nerves, and muscles of the organism) contain forty-six chromosomes or twenty-three pairs. In these somatic cells one chromosome in each pair is donated by the mother, the other by the father. Each time the cell divides, every new cell receives the identical set of forty-six chromosomes, or twenty-three pairs.

Each chromosome is itself a string of twenty thousand **genes,** large and complex molecules that carry within their structure the traits of parents and transmit them to offspring. The genes themselves are composed of **deoxyribonucleic acid** (DNA). Sometimes called the "substance of life," DNA contains the elaborate information—or set of instructions—needed to perform all activities of living matter. In addition to replicating itself, DNA directs the formation of chains of proteins, which in turn form new tissues and organs, regulate other genes, and control the operation of enzymes crucial in body processes.

Despite these regularities in genetic heritage, many factors combine to ensure that humans will differ from one another. To begin with, in the course of life, every female produces several hundred eggs and every male produces many billion sperm cells. Then, the zygote and all succeeding cells each contain about one million genes, which are the basic unit for hereditary transmission. Since the genes contributed by each parent can be combined in any number of ways, each child represents an accidental combination of countless possible parental features. The odds are astronomical against parents producing two offspring who resemble each other completely—unless they are both produced by a division of the same zygote, as happens in the case of **monozygotic** (identical) **twins.** (See Chapter 8.)

In one sense, of course, all behaviors and capacities can be attributed to the child's genetic endowment—the particular combination of genes received from the parents. Some behaviors and conditions, however, are specifically associated with genetic factors. Perhaps foremost, one's sex is determined by the chromosomal arrangement of one of the twenty-three chromosome pairs. The female's pair contains two chromosomes (both called X), whereas the male's contains an X and a Y chromosome. Because the mother has XX, her egg always contains an X chromosome. The father's sperm, however, may carry either an X or a Y chromosome. If an X-bearing sperm fertilizes the egg, the offspring will be a girl (XX); if a Y-bearing sperm fertilizes the egg, the offspring will be a boy (XY). This fact may clarify why each egg and each sperm contains only twenty-three chromosomes: it is the *combination* of germ cells that determines the offspring's gender.

Various pathological conditions result from abnormalities in the sex-regulating chromosomes. Genes present in the female (X) chromosome may, when they combine with the male (Y) chromosome, cause specific "sex-linked" disorders passed from mother to sons. Color blindness, some kinds of night blindness, and hemophilia (a disease in which the blood does not clot) are examples. Irregularities can occur in other chromosomes as well. Down's syndrome or mongolism, a severe form of retardation, results from an extra chromosome. In theory, either parent could carry the deviant chromosome. It turns out, however, that mothers over age forty are more likely to have children with Down's syndrome. Geneticists believe that the syndrome may result from a chromosomal deformity in the egg. Some other genetic diseases are listed in Table 3.2.

The processes and rules of genetics as well as the kinds of genetic experiments that are now being conducted with many species constitute a complex and rapidly changing science that we cannot review here. (For reliable summaries, see Cavalli-Sforza, 1977; McClearn

and DeFries, 1973; Scarr-Salapatek, 1975; Stern, 1973.) But a few major points from genetics deserve mention. First, genes contribute to the emergence and nature of every human trait from the color of the eyes and the thickness of hair, to the individual's ultimate intelligence and creativity. Every cell in the body contains exactly the same genetic information as every other cell; but cells use the information in different ways at different times of development (otherwise, the organism would simply be a conglomeration of identical units, and differentiation of organs could never take place).

A second crucial point involves the distinction between the **genotype,** the total genetic makeup contributed by the parents, and the **phenotype,** the individual's observable characteristics that eventually emerge. A given genotype—one's birthright—can give rise to an infinite number of phenotypes that vary in size, form, personality, abilities, and so on. This variety in phenotypes results from the fact that genes never influence behavior directly; instead, they direct the production of the chemicals and the unraveling of processes that actually form bodily structures. Indeed, development may be thought of as the process by which a genotype comes to be expressed as one or another phenotype. Only one of many possible phenotypes emerges, and the particular phenotype is determined by the environment (in the uterus as well as out of it) within which development takes place. In other words genes always operate in environments (internal and external), and their ultimate expression is modulated by these environmental factors. Thus the limits of intelligence are fixed by the genotype, but the actual intelligence achieved reflects the diverse environments, ranging from the cells in the fetus to the postnatal individual and cultural influences on growth, through which the information carried in the genes is expressed.

Table 3.2. SOME GENETIC DISEASES

Disease	Description
Breast cancer (female)	Cancer in breast at maturity; surgical removal of tumor may save life.
Cri du chat syndrome	Missing part of chromosome number 5. Results in abnormal head and face, mewing cry of newborn, retarded mental and physical development.
Cystic fibrosis	Appears in infancy or later; mucous glands produce sticky mucus clogging lungs and stomach.
Diabetes	Pancreas fails to produce sufficient insulin; excessive sugar accumulates.
Down's syndrome (mongolism)	Extra chromosome number 21. Severe physical and mental retardation result. May survive to adulthood or old age.
Hemophilia	Blood lacks a vital clotting agent.
Huntington's chorea	Symptoms begin between ages thirty and fifty; personality changes, nervous twitches, progressive deterioration, and death within fifteen years.
Klinefelter's syndrome (male)	Additional X chromosome. Inability to produce sperm results; mental retardation may also result.
Muscular dystrophy	Appears in first five years of life; muscle tissue is replaced by globules of fat; death by age twenty-five.
Neurofibromatosis (Von Recklinghausen's disease; Elephant Man's disease)	Disorder of the central nervous system. Skin discolorations and multiple benign tumors on or under the skin may progress to noncancerous tumors of the nervous system and brain, impairing hearing, sight, and movement. Treatment by surgery.
Phenylketonuria (PKU)	Inability to metabolize the amino acid phenylalanine, leading to mental retardation if not treated.
Sickle cell anemia	Blood lacks ability to carry oxygen, resulting in impaired development and many secondary symptoms leading to death before age forty; black persons are particularly susceptible.
Spina bifida (Open spine)	Defect of the central nervous system. May result in paralysis of the legs and lack of bowel and bladder functions.
Tay-Sachs disease	Enzyme deficiency, causing progressive brain deterioration and death by age five, Eastern European Jews are particularly susceptible.
Thalassemia	Fatal hereditary blood disorder similar to sickle cell anemia. People originating from the Mediterranean region are especially susceptible.
Turner's syndrome (female)	Missing second X chromosome, resulting in failure to develop mammary glands, wide hips, and bodily hair, as well as some cognitive difficulties.

Thus the child's ultimate phenotypical intelligence is the result of a long, complex process under the influence of diverse factors. (We will return in Chapter 8 to the controversial issue of whether—and to what extent—intelligence can be said to be inherited.)

One other genetic principle should be noted. Some traits are **dominant;** they will emerge in the phenotype whenever a certain gene is contributed by either parent. Dominant traits include brown or hazel eyes; the blood types A, B, and AB; and high blood pressure. Other traits are **recessive,** emerging only when similar genes are provided by both parents. Blue eyes, blond hair, and straight hair are recessive traits. It is because of the existence of dominant and recessive traits that two people with identically colored brown eyes may have different genotypes. One person may have two genes for brown eyes; the other may have one brown-eye and one blue-eye gene. Whereas brown eyes will emerge so long as either parent contributes the dominant brown-eye gene, blue eyes can emerge only if each parent has the recessive blue-eye gene and only if the child received this recessive gene from each parent. It should be noted that more complex traits, the sort that psychologists study, are rarely under the control of single genes; very little is known about the factors of heredity and dominance that influence more complex traits like intelligence, temperament, or personality.

THE NEWBORN

Armed with excellently developed bodily structures, an impressive array of reflexes, and all the information required for further development already encoded in its genes, the fetus of nine months is indeed well equipped to enter the world beyond its mother's womb. This newborn, on the average weighing about seven pounds and about twenty inches in length, is proportioned somewhat differently from the adult: the head constitutes about one-quarter of the baby's overall length, compared to about one-seventh in the normal adult. The feet are disproportionately long and bent inward at the ankles. The infant may look a bit scrawny, with thin, dry skin. She may have a flat nose, a high forehead, and a receding jaw. But all the body structures, including all nerve cells, are present and ready to begin functioning.

Just what are the capacities on which the newborn can draw in initial encounters with the external world? Certainly the most prominent are the numerous **reflexes**—all of which have, or once had, distinct survival value. Among the clearly adaptive reflexes are those involving breathing, blinking, vomiting, coughing, and sneezing. Three prominent reflexes are related to feeding: infants **root** (turn head and mouth in the direction of a stimulus, like a nipple, that has been applied to the cheek); they **suck** when an object is placed in their mouths; and they **swallow** milk and other substances.

Several other reflexes, although less clearly keyed to adaptation, are useful in diagnosing a baby's chances to survive and thrive (see Figure 3.3). In the **Moro reflex,** infants react to a sudden change in head position or other disruptive stimulation by flinging their arms out to the side, extending their fingers, and then returning their arms to the middle of the body, as if in an embrace. The Moro reflex may be a legacy from a time millions of years ago when our predecessors lived in trees and had much to fear from falling great distances, much to gain by latching onto their mothers. Although the Moro is expected in newborns, it should disappear after the first few months of life. Indeed, when the Moro persists until the age of one, the infant's nervous system may not, and perhaps may never, appropriately inhibit such a "primitive response"; the

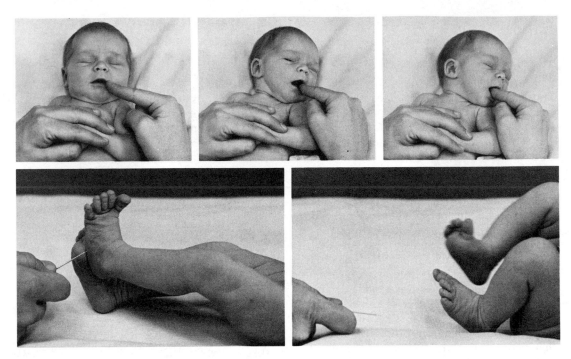

Figure 3.3. Reflexes are a major feature of the newborn's behavioral repertoire, indices of great importance in ascertaining the health of the infant. In the rooting response at the top, touching the side of the infant's mouth causes the head to turn toward the stimulus and the mouth to begin sucking. In the Babinski response (*bottom*), stimulation of the sole of the infant's foot causes the toes to spread out. These reflexes slowly disappear over the course of infancy, yielding to various learned patterns and skills.

inability to suppress nonfunctional behaviors signals developmental difficulties. Among other regularly monitored reflexes are the **grasp reflex,** when infants latch on firmly to a finger or stick placed in their hands; the **Babinski reflex,** when the toes spread out following stimulation of the sole of the foot; and the **swimming reflex,** paddlelike movements of the arms and legs made by infants when placed in water. The baby's overall reflex profile, taken together with assessment of heart rate, color, breathing, and muscle tone, is an important part of the routine testing done on nearly every newborn infant (Apgar, 1953; Apgar and James, 1962; Brazelton, 1978).

Although the bodily reflexes are a main part of the infant's equipment during her first days in the world, other behaviors are also noteworthy. From shortly after birth, the baby's eyes can follow an object or a light placed in the center of her visual field. Facelike configurations elicit special interest. The baby exhibits various limb and trunk movements, including kicking, lifting and turning the head, waving the arms, and flailing about. These behaviors are initially uncoordinated, but they form the basis for more skilled and better-coordinated movements.

Newborn infants seem able to distinguish among various tastes and odors, including the odor of the mother (Macfarlane, 1975). They react positively to sweet tastes, negatively to salty, sour, and bitter tastes (Lipsitt, 1976; Nowlis and Kessen, 1976). They turn away from strong odors, such as that exuded by ammonium hydroxide (Rieser, Yonas, and Wikner, 1976) and react with special vigor to any stimulus that interferes with breathing (Lipsitt, 1979). The skin of the lips is especially sensitive to touch, the skin on the trunk, thighs, and forearms somewhat less so. Though hearing seems somewhat less developed than the other sensory systems, babies from the first day of life do turn toward loud sounds, including speech (Bridger, 1961; Butterworth and Castillo, 1976; Crassini and Broerse, 1980; Wertheimer, 1961). And they have the equally valuable capacity to shut out disturbing or repetitive sights or sounds.

When we consider what the newborn's feelings might be, we are obviously speculating. Round-the-clock observations by Peter Wolff (1966) indicate that infants pass through a graded series of **states of arousal.** These states are characterized by definite facial expressions and sets of behaviors. **Regular sleep** is marked by slow, even breathing and a minimum of facial and bodily movements. **Irregular sleep** is marked by quick, uneven breathing and frequent movements. **Periodic sleep,** which is intermediate between regular and irregular sleep, features rapid, shallow breathing alternating with deep, slow breathing. In the state of **alert inactivity,** the infant's face is relaxed; eyes are open and have a bright, shining appearance; breathing is regular; there is much visual following and exploring. In this state, one likely to occur after feeding or elimination, the infant will often stare at a face or a spot of light. In the state of **waking activity,** featuring frequent spurts of diffuse motor activity, breathing is irregular and the infant may be either silent, moaning, grunting, or whimpering. Finally, in the state of

crying vocalization, movements are diffuse, eyes may be tightly closed, and the baby may cry. Though the nature of these states differs somewhat across infants, each generally lasts for a predictable amount of time. (The average time is perhaps about twenty minutes, though individual states can range from seconds to a few hours.) Moreover, during the first days of life the states succeed each other in a rather fixed order.

The infant's experiences vary, we can speculate, depending on the current state of arousal. Pleasurable feelings might be associated with alert inactivity. At this time, needs have been met and the infant is busily processing information about the world. In contrast, painful experiences could be expected during phases of crying, which may be related to hunger, pain, or excessive heat or cold. Indeed, an infant's hunger contractions may be more vigorous than an adult's, and hence more painful (Hurlock, 1975). Variations in the pitch, intensity, and continuity of an infant's cries may indicate the degree and perhaps even the source of distress (Ostwald, 1972). Particular patterns of crying are also associated with certain specific diseases and with mental retardation.

The Contributions of Early Knowledge and Early Experience

Despite differences in their genetic heritage and in the environment of the uterus, most newborns have the same equipment. Even infants who are premature, or who suffer from one or another developmental abnormality, conform in most particulars to our general description. To be sure, there are important individual differences in **temperament** among infants (see the box). But the full significance of these differences emerges only later.

Table 3.3. TEMPERAMENTAL DIFFERENCES AMONG TWO-MONTH-OLD INFANTS

Temperamental quality	Rating	Example: Two-month-old child
Activity level Proportion of inactive periods to active ones.	High	Moves often in sleep. Wriggles when diaper is changed.
	Low	Does not move when being dressed or during sleep.
Rhythmicity Regularity of hunger, excretion, sleep, and wakefulness.	Regular	Has been on four-hour feeding schedule since birth. Regular bowel movement.
	Irregular	Awakes at a different time each morning. Size of feedings varies.
Distractibility The degree to which extraneous stimuli alter behavior.	Distractible	Will stop crying for food if rocked. Stops fussing if given pacifier when diaper is being changed.
	Not distractible	Will not stop crying when diaper is changed. Fusses after feeding, even if rocked.
Approach/withdrawal The response to a new object or person.	Positive	Smiles and licks washcloth. Has always liked bottle.
	Negative	Rejected cereal the first time. Cries when strangers appear.
Adaptability The ease with which a child adapts to her environment.	Adaptive	Was passive during first bath; now enjoys bathing. Smiles at mother.
	Not adaptive	Still startled by sudden, sharp noise. Resists diapering.
Attention span and persistence The amount of time devoted to an activity, and the effect of distraction on the activity.	Long	If soiled, continues to cry until changed. Repeatedly rejects water if wants milk.
	Short	Cries when awakened but stops almost immediately. Objects only mildly if cereal precedes bottle.
Intensity of reaction The energy of response, regardless of its quality or direction.	Intense	Cries when diapers are wet. Rejects food vigorously when satisfied.
	Mild	Does not cry when diapers are wet. Whimpers instead of crying when hungry.
Threshold of responsiveness The intensity of stimulation required to evoke a discernible response.	Low	Stops sucking on bottle when approached.
	High	Is not startled by loud noises. Takes bottle and breast equally well.
Quality of mood The amount of friendly, pleasant, joyful behavior as contrasted with unpleasant, unfriendly behavior.	Positive	Smacks lips when first tasting new food. Smiles at parents.
	Negative	Fusses after nursing. Cries when carriage is rocked.

Source: Adapted from A. Thomas, S. Chess, and H. G. Birch, "The Origin of Personality," *Scientific American* 223 (1970).

Temperament

Observe the newborns at a hospital nursery. In one cradle rests a passive, still infant, while the child beside her kicks and squirms; one baby is easily distracted by surrounding noise, another seems oblivious to it; one child readily adapts to change, while her neighbor resists change of any kind. Though seemingly minor, these differences reflect general styles of behavior or temperament. Since temperament is a central aspect of an individual's personality and a principal influence on her ability to function in diverse surroundings, it has proved of great interest to students of development.

Even at birth, infants display surprisingly consistent temperaments. But will these change over time and, if so, which factors prove most crucial in bringing about such change? Before one could begin to approach these questions, it was necessary to develop a systematic and reliable way of measuring temperament. Alexander Thomas and Stella Chess (Thomas, Chess, and Birch, 1970; Thomas and Chess, 1977) did just that in an often-cited longitudinal study of 136 children from infancy to adolescence. Drawing on structured parent interviews and on-site observations, these investigators obtained detailed accounts of children's behavior. They then isolated nine distinct components of temperament, such as activity level and attention span, on which a child (or adult) could be scored as high, medium, or low (see Table 3.3).

Thomas and Chess found that the 136 behavioral profiles clustered into three general types of temperament. "Easy children" displayed a positive mood and regularity in bodily function; they were adaptable, approachable, and their reactions were moderate or low in intensity. At the other extreme, "difficult children" were slow to adapt and tended to have intense reactions and negative moods; they withdrew in new situations and had irregular bodily functions. The "slow to warm up" children, situated in the middle, initially withdrew but slowly adapted to new situations; they had low activity levels and tended to respond with low intensity. The majority of the children, 40 percent, fell into the "easy" group; 15 percent were "slow" and ten percent were "difficult"—the remaining 35 percent did not fit into any of the three categories.

Why is one infant "easy" and another "difficult" or "slow"? The origin of temperament remains a puzzle and a debate. The fact that these behavioral differences are present at birth suggests, though it does not prove, that temperament is genetically determined. Studies of twins further support this theory. Torgersen (1974) found that at two months of age identical twins were more similar to each other than dizygotic twins. Furthermore, they tended to remain similar while the fraternal twins became increasingly different.

Cross-cultural data indicate that ethnic differences in temperament may be at least partly inborn rather than the result of socialization. When Daniel Freedman (1979) compared Caucasian and Chinese infants, he found striking differences in temperament. Chinese babies were far more adaptable and amenable than the Caucasians, who showed more annoyance and
(*continued*)

complaining. The children were all born in the same hospital; their mothers were the same age, had been given the same drugs, and came from the same middle-income bracket. Everything seemed the same and yet, forty-eight hours after birth, before any socialization could have occurred, the children were clearly different. Similar studies of Navaho and Japanese children (Caudill and Frost, 1972; Chisholm, 1980) have yielded comparable findings in support of the "biosocial" explanation of temperament differences.

Some studies suggest that certain prenatal and perinatal factors, such as the mother's general emotional health and her attitude toward her pregnancy, may affect an infant's temperament (Sameroff and Kelly, n.d.) For example, adopted boys whose biological mothers were psychiatrically disturbed exhibited more "difficult child" symptoms than adoptees with normal mothers. However, more definitive evidence of these influences is still needed.

Although temperamental individuality seems to be established at birth, environmental factors play a crucial role in determining the changes a person's behavioral style may undergo. In a relatively stable environment, behavior is apt to remain consistent. The infant who cries intensely when bathed may have equally intense reactions when playing peek-a-boo a year later (perhaps screaming, perhaps laughing), and at seven years she may stomp her feet indefatigably at mild frustrations. But with changing circumstances, there may be a corresponding behavioral alteration. One boy, for example, who was cheerful and highly active as an infant spent his childhood in a discordant and unhappy home environment. In later years, his school performance worsened and his motivation waned. By age seventeen he was apathetic and inactive.

But a particular environment will not have the same effect on every child. The same discordant home atmosphere may have caused another child to lash out in an intense and highly active manner. It is this interplay of child and environment (or perhaps of nature and nurture) that Thomas and Chess see as crucial: "If the two influences are harmonized, one can expect healthy development of the child; if they are dissonant, behavioral problems are almost sure to ensue" (Thomas et al., 1970, p. 108).

Turning to the practical implications of their work, Thomas and Chess recommend that parents moderate childrearing styles to suit their offspring's temperament. "Difficult children" need consistent, patient, and objective parents who can handle their instability and slowness. "Slow to warm up children" do best with a moderate amount of encouragement coupled with patience; parents and teachers should let these children adjust to change at their own pace. Finally, though no child should become so accustomed to one particular pattern that she cannot adjust to alternative ones, children with an "easy" temperament tend to adapt and to do well under various styles of rearing.

Until the time of birth, then, the genetic heritage exerts its influence in a direct and fairly unmodified form. Yet, once the child leaves the comfort of the uterus, the genetic inheritance becomes increasingly modulated by the effects of the external world—the sights and smells, the persons and objects, the tempo and sequence of events in the world constitute the kinds of experience with which the "stranger" becomes increasingly familiar.

Heated controversy revolves around the issue of how best to characterize the knowledge that the infant brings to the world. Few will defend the classic descriptions of the baby's world as a "blank slate" (see the Interlude on the origins of child study) or a "blooming, buzzing confusion": we have observed that the newborn already knows how to do many things and exhibits behaviors that are decidedly rule-bound. But how much further should one be permitted to go in characterizing the newborn's knowledge?

The more sophisticated we get in measuring performances, the more capable the newborn baby appears. But exhibition of a behavior under special experimental or eliciting conditions does not mean that it will appear regularly in the child's repertoire, nor that it has the same meaning for the infant as for the adult. We shall encounter claims that infants one or two months old are able to imitate adult models, to classify colors in the same way as adults, and to walk when but a few weeks old. But since these behaviors sometimes are fragile, or drop out, or cannot reliably be obtained by all investigators, developmentalists are generally reluctant to conclude that the newborn's behavior is "the same" as the adult's (though it seems more similar than it did ten or twenty years ago!).

Regardless of the ultimate decision on what the newborn "really" knows, clearly her knowledge is strongly affected by the environment in which she is reared. Because it is not

possible to vary experimentally the environments of newborn infants, our evidence on the effects of initial environments and early experiences comes chiefly from experiments with animals. Rosenzweig (1966) provided the first clues. Young rats raised in "enriched environments"—where they had the opportunity to play with ladders, wheels, and mazes—performed better on tasks and were otherwise healthier than those reared in an environment that provided ample food but lacked any other "enriching" features. When, after eighty days, the animals were killed and their brains examined, the researchers found that the cerebral cortex (outer mantle of the brain) of the enriched rats weighed on the average 4 percent more than that of the impoverished rats.

Additional research has confirmed that animals reared in an enriched environment are better off than those that are not (see Bennett, 1976; Denenberg, 1969; Greenough, 1981; Levine, 1969). Two precautions must be noted, however. First, one can sometimes reverse the ill effects of early deprivation simply by placing a deprived animal into an enriched environment, particularly if this is done before the animal reaches maturity (Bernstein, 1979). Second, neither the enriched nor the deprived rats perform as well, or have brains as highly developed, as rats in a normal, nonlaboratory environment. Apparently, all laboratory animals are deprived in comparison with those in the jungle or in the streets.

In a less experimentally controlled fashion researchers have documented the important contribution of early experiences to the overall development of the human infant (cf. Landauer and Whiting, 1963). In one such study, thirty premature infants weighing less than five pounds were divided into two groups (Rice, 1975). As soon as they were brought home from the hospital, the children in the first group were stroked and massaged

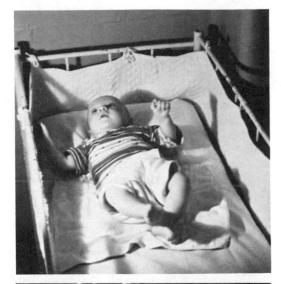

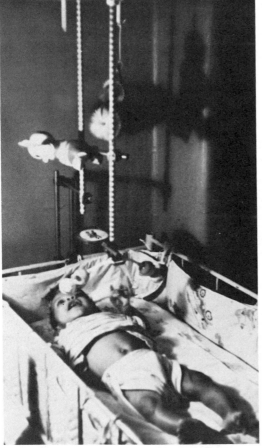

Figure 3.4. Institutionalized infants, whose environment is usually drab, pass more rapidly through perceptual and motor milestones, and can exhibit more sustained attention, when their cribs contain items they can touch with their hands and explore with their eyes. (B. White, 1971)

for considerable periods each day for a month. Infants in the control group received no special stroking. The stroked infants developed more rapidly, gained more weight, and even scored higher on the widely used Bayley Scales of Infant Development. Other experimenters working with premature and other "high risk" infants have reported similar gains following programs of early stimulation (Lodge, 1976; Siqueland, 1973). Working in an institution for children whose families were unable to care for them, White (1967) produced striking results. One group of infants was administered twenty minutes of extra handling each day, given additional exercise, permitted to explore the ward visually, exposed to highly contrasting colors and to numerous geometric forms against a white background. The other group simply rested in the normal dull environment of the institution. The "enriched" children learned to grasp an object with a single smooth, accurate movement forty-five days earlier than the unstimulated children—an impressive spurt at so early a point in life.

It is depressingly easy to document the ill effects of a deprived environment. In addition to the evidence on institutionalized children already reviewed in Chapter 1, massive evidence indicates the pernicious and pervasive effects of malnourishment, poor diet, child neglect, child abuse, and parental drug addiction (Cravioto and DeLicardie, 1975; Lester, 1976). While some researchers feel that certain ill effects can be reversed, or at least ameliorated (Clarke and Clarke, 1977; Kagan and Klein, 1973), no one would seriously recommend anything but a normal or enriched environment for a child.

Where environments are inadequate, governmental and private agencies have often intervened. Programs like Project Head Start, designed in the 1960s to provided disadvantaged preschoolers with educational experiences, have generally yielded meager results (Bereiter, 1972; Miller and Dyer, 1975; but see also Zigler and Muenchow, 1979). But while the results of such compensatory effort programs have been modest in the short run, it is possible that they may exert positive effects in the long run. Thus, the High-Scope Study in

Ypsilanti, Michigan, documented significant improvements in social adaptation and high school academic scores or job status for those children who had attended preschools a decade before as compared to those who had not (Kleiman, 1980). In addition, similarly motivated efforts—for instance, the television show for preschool children called *Sesame Street*—have succeeded in their more circumscribed goals of teaching numbers, letters, and object classification (Ball and Bogatz, 1972). And, on occasion, massive interventions have produced massive effects. For example, the Milwaukee Project (Garber and Heber, 1977) spurred spectacular IQ gains in disadvantaged children; and the Talent Education (Suzuki) method of teaching children in Japan to play

Figure 3.5. Each culture has its own views about environments suitable for infants. For example, among the Navajos, infants are tightly swaddled during most of the day. If there is consensus within a culture about the appropriate way to rear children, there will be no ill effects from such diverse practices—be they swaddling of infants among the Navajo or the encouragement of mobile exploration in our own society.

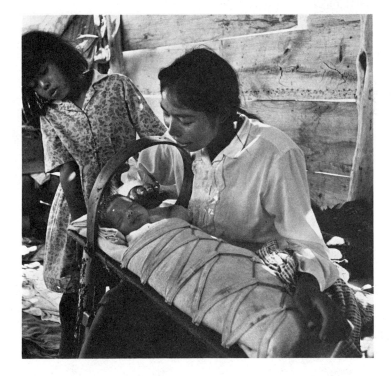

the violin has spawned a generation of highly gifted young violinists (Suzuki, 1969; Taniuchi, 1980).

Though results of studies with animals can only be extended with caution to human children, the collected evidence from research on animals and children suggests some general principles. The potential to behave in certain ways can be substantially modified by early experiences. Such early experiences, moreover, can have effects not only in later childhood but even extending to the adult years and to one's offspring (Denenberg, 1969). The timing of stimulation or deprivation may be crucial; in general, deprivations (or stimulations) during the first months of life are more fateful than equivalent ones later on (Curtiss, 1977; Goldman, 1979; Hirsch, 1981; Levine, 1969; Scott, Stewart, and De Ghett, 1974). The early days and weeks of life are also the time of greatest plasticity: injuries or deficits during this period are generally more susceptible to recovery or compensation than comparable injuries at a later point in development (Goldman, 1979; Goldman-Rakic, 1981). Finally, although early experiences may be pivotal, no single experience need be decisive—one way or the other—and the effects of early trauma can often be reversed.

We have now viewed the fetus in the months before birth and considered in a general way the effects of earliest experiences on the child's course of development. As we have seen, each newborn infant first uses the sensory and motor capacities that have evolved in the prenatal period, and goes through the sequence of arousal states that has been programmed in her nervous system. But with every passing day, each of these biologically based predispositions is increasingly affected by the child's experiences in the external world, and the various biological systems become increasingly meshed and integrated.

Developing Systems: Distinctions, Connections, Interactions

The accomplishments of infants are so enormous—indeed staggering—that it would take many pages simply to catalog them. As they progress from a bundle of reflexes, almost totally ignorant of the specific contents of the world, to a point where they can understand words, walk, grasp, find objects, and solve puzzles, nearly every aspect of their behavioral repertoire undergoes profound changes. The most that we can hope to accomplish in this survey is to describe certain behaviors, capacities, and trends that seem pivotal; analyze certain responses that are especially important in the child's experience; and consider some ways in which the child's sense of self evolves during the opening years of life.

As a convenient way of grouping these diverse capacities, we will speak of three ways, or systems, of interaction with the world: perceiving, making, and feeling. First we will describe how each system evolves during the opening months of life; then we will examine some of the ways these systems interact.

The first system—that of perceiving—detects differences in the external world. Our hands, mouths, and above all our superbly keen eyes and ears help us sense information about the world and, over time, make increasingly fine distinctions among these sensory data. The second system—that of making—entails our actions upon the physical and social world. Using our vocal chords, feet, limbs, and especially our hands, we can act on and combine objects, devise patterns or messages, and transmit them to others—all in order to alter our environment. (In the view of some researchers, notably Piaget, it is the combination of perceptions and actions that constitutes the core of the cognitive domain.)

The third system—that of feeling—involves the sensations, emotions, or affects that we experience within our skin. These include bodily sensations as well as emotions: pain or pleasure, hunger or fullness, happiness or anger, tension or relaxation, jealousy or pride. Sometimes these feelings can overwhelm us. At other times we may go for long periods without noticing any feelings or changes of feeling. Whereas both perceiving and making depend on some commerce with the external world, feeling is invisible to others and experienced by us alone. To be sure, certain external signs (cries, sighs, and smiles) may suggest feelings. But whereas discriminations can be reliably observed, feelings can only be inferred, and require confirmation (or disconfirmation) by the experiencer herself.

Our three systems provide a convenient summary, a way of organizing an army of facts about infants, but, *it must be stressed,* no more than that. In fact, a plausible case could be made that the infant begins life as a single organized biological totality—one that reacts to stimulation "as a whole." According to this rival account, the infant only slowly, over time, becomes capable of distinguishing among percepts, acts, and feelings.

Nor is it likely that scientists will eventually decide that one point of view (say, the view that there exist three discrete systems that ultimately connect with one another) is right and that the rival point of view (that the infant is an undifferentiated whole who eventually exhibits discrete percepts, acts, and feelings) is wrong. Rather, these are simply complementary ways of conceiving of the young child, each properly emphasizing some facets while necessarily neglecting or minimizing others.

But *which* image one adopts is not simply a matter of taste. At this writing scientists

differ profoundly on the extent to which the newborns's specific behaviors actually interact with one another. For instance, those who believe that newborns can imitate adult models necessarily assume that perceptual and making mechanisms are closely interconnected or even "one"; those skeptical about infant imitation believe that the interaction of perception and action builds up slowly.

Similarly, within the realm of perception, some researchers believe that the infant's sensory modalities are intimately interrelated and that the infant can readily connect an object seen with an object felt—such researchers are sympathetic to the notion of "amodal" or "cross-modal" ways of perceiving. An equally vociferous set of researchers doubts that the infant can readily relate information from one sensory mode to another; according to this view, the building of intersensory connections takes time and experience.

While these debates are still raging, we cannot issue a verdict. But we can take a look at the scorecard.

PERCEIVING

The organs of perception—eyes, ears, nose, taste buds, and the instruments of touch—have been designed to enable the infant to discriminate information in the external world. At first the distinctions infants make are relatively gross and approximate, but with time infants can make quite subtle differentiations. Because the visual system has been the most thoroughly studied, and because its principles are often echoed in other sensory systems, we will focus on children's growing ability to make sense of the world presented to their eyes.

With every month, the visual skills of the human infant become more impressive, but even at the beginning the infant is remarkably well equipped. Newborn babies can move their eyes toward (or away from) a source of light. They seem able to use both eyes together, to focus on a target, to follow objects, and to switch their attention to a new target (Hershenson, 1964; Lipsitt, 1979). A newborn who is shown a blank visual field will scan it, in an apparent effort to detect an element of contrast. When a black equilateral triangle is introduced into the field, the infant will select one angle in the figure and stare at it; edges and corners prove particularly attractive. Infants will also scan a vertical black-and-white edge, although they are likely to ignore the same configuration when it is horizontal (Kessen, Haith, and Salapatek, 1970). The infant seems "wired" at birth to focus on areas of contrasting colors, particularly black and white; in addition, specific cells in the brain respond to lines and edges, thus making areas of high contrast especially compelling for the newborn (Haith, 1976; Hubel, 1979).

To be sure, there are limits. Because the muscles that control the shape of the lens are weak, infants have difficulty adjusting their focus to varying distances and controlling the amount of light that enters their eyes (Haynes, White, and Held, 1965; Peiper, 1963). And their tracking is highly inefficient: eye movements are still jerky, darting across distances that often prove too great or too abbreviated to permit continued and accurate monitoring of objects (Appleton, Clifton, and Goldberg, 1975; Pipp and Van Giffen, 1981).

While the newborn baby spends about 5 percent of her waking time scanning the visual environment, the child of two and one-half months spends about 35 percent of her time at this pursuit. Her ability to control head and eye movements, to bring objects into focus, to track a stimulus smoothly, and to maintain attention has increased dramatically (B. White, 1971). By this time she is also able to process a wide variety of patterns and forms and to exhibit clear-cut preferences among them.

The practice of "watching babies watch" received tremendous impetus when Robert Fantz (1958) hit on a simple but workable technique that explores (and exploits) preferential perception. He presented infants with two stimuli that differed on specifiable dimensions and then observed which stimulus the infants looked at longer. If the infants did not attend or if they attended equally to both stimuli, then no conclusions about preferences could confidently be drawn. But if the infants attended to one stimulus more than another, one could infer that they "preferred" that stimulus. Fantz also noted that, shown the same or similar stimuli repeatedly, infants would eventually "habituate" to these targets and cease looking at them. Exposure to a novel pattern would reactivate visual interest. This phenomenon made it possible to study which stimuli were considered equivalent, which dissimilar, by observing the infant.

Using such techniques, investigators found that infants as young as two weeks can detect the difference between a gray patch and a square composed of one-eighth-inch-wide stripes. By eight weeks, infants prefer a bull's-eye to a set of stripes (Fantz, 1958), and they look at three-dimensional forms more than at two-dimensional ones (Fantz, 1965; Polak, Emde, and Spitz, 1964). By three months, infants will look longer at very thin stripes than at a gray patch (Fantz, 1965). And by four months, infants will prefer a facelike configuration (a circle containing a few strategically placed shapes) to a bull's-eye or a simple round form (Fantz, 1961).

There are also other ways to study infants' perceptual practices. One elegant method used by Thomas Bower (1974a) involves conditioning infants to respond to certain stimuli. Subjects a few months old are rewarded with a "peek-a-boo" when they respond to one object (for instance, by turning their heads), but they receive no reward for responding to another object. (Such a technique assumes that the infants have the capacity to prefer either of the stimuli.) Using this method, Bower has explored another perennial question: whether infants perceive the so-called **perceptual constancies** as adults do. These include, for example, **size constancy** (an object remains the same object even when its distance from the observer is varied and it looks smaller) and **shape constancy** (the object remains the same even when its orientation or spatial form changes and it looks as if it is shaped differently).

Consider the case of size constancy. Suppose an infant has been conditioned to respond to a cube (A) at a distance of two feet. If an infant responds only to the physical size the cube occupies on the retina (the light-sensitive surface at the back of each eye), then she will perceive the cube moved three feet away as different (because it then occupies a smaller size on the retina). Infants would also perceive a smaller cube (B) moved closer as equal in size to A (because at one foot cube B occupies the same retinal space as does cube A at two feet). But if the infants follow the laws of size constancy, they will continue to respond to cube A regardless of how near or far away it is: their conditioned response will have generalized to all instances of cube A.

In several studies Bower has found that infants appreciate constancies of size and shape, perhaps even from birth. Indeed, Bower (1974a) even contends that the ability to detect depth—long believed to be built slowly from perception of flat objects—may be present at birth. His results run counter to the traditional environmental-learning theory account of perceptual development, which claims that the constancies are acquired through the gradual and painstaking accrual of experi-

ences. When first reported, these findings created considerable stir. Following the initial excitement, however, certain investigators (for example, Salapatek, 1973) have had difficulty replicating Bower's results and voice some skepticism about his claims.

Color. Talk of black-and-white form might imply that infants are insensitive to color. In fact, the color-perception skills of young infants turn out to be remarkably well developed and surprisingly similar to those of adults. In a series of ingenious studies, Bornstein (1978) has demonstrated that infants divide up the color spectrum much like adults do and that they rely on cues of hue rather than cues of brightness. Bornstein used pairs of stimuli that were equivalent wavelength distances from one another. In some cases the pairs crossed color boundaries (from, say, blue to green), but in other cases they remained within the same color category (navy versus light blue) as defined by adults. Four-month-old infants reacted similarly to two shades of hue drawn from the same adult category (for example, all blues), but they treated those taken from different but adjacent categories as different from one another. Moreover, Bornstein's results suggest that the structure of the infant's color categories resembles that of the adult: that is, both infants and adults will choose the same "focal" blue (or green) as the "defining" or "prototypical" member of the category.

Bornstein's studies help to answer a classical philosophical question: Is the way in which we see and classify colors determined by the categories built into our language or is it a basic property of our perceptual system? Bornstein's studies clearly suggest that our language is molded to fit our color perception, and not vice versa. A recent study by Jones-Molfese (1977) raises the possibility that such categorical responding may even be present in babies less than one day old—certainly before much language has been heard! And a study by Burnham and Day (1979) documents that young infants use color cues to help them recognize objects. But some researchers consider the evidence from color studies consistent with less dramatic claims (for example, that infants can distinguish red from green but no more) and stress the need for further research (Werner and Wooten, 1979).

Figure Perception and Faces. During the opening weeks of life, the infant focuses primarily on specific features of stimuli, features that in general cannot be expected to have much significance for the child. Moreover, those features on which children focus seem to reflect the unfettered operation of their visual systems. But a child who has gone beyond simple features to recognizing forms, and who prefers those forms resembling a face, has attained a new level of development. Indeed, the crucial time is at hand when the child will be able to respond specifically to the faces of those about her.

Determining when faces are recognized *as faces* is very difficult. One must be ingenious; one must offer definitions of such scientifically elusive terms as *seeing, recognizing,* and even *faces;* and one must be able to distinguish between the perception of elements that are related to one another in a specifiable manner and the perception of a mere circle, or a mere pair of eyes, or features that are not properly related to one another. How does one prove that a child who smiles at her mother recognizes her as being different from all other individuals? Or that the child is focusing on the arrangement of all the mother's features, rather than merely on hair color or shape of nose? Because of such difficulties, debates on the emergence of facial perception continue to abound.

Despite the dispute, most students of visual perception agree that a crucial development, occurring at some point between six weeks and three months, alters the infant's perceptual system. Rather than merely preferring certain patterns, the child becomes able to focus on and assimilate complete geometric figures or forms and to detect disruptions of these organized patterns (Bergman, Haith, and Mann, 1971; Cook, Field, and Griffiths, 1978; Schwartz and Day, 1979). No longer is the child's perception a partial sampling of the array. At three months she is more exhaustive, perceiving a whole circle, square, or checkerboard as instances of these geometric categories. Most important, the child perceives a facelike configuration (for instance, a circle with several features in it) as a whole. Whereas the child fixated before on any array possessing certain facelike properties, she can now differentiate reliably between a human face and other dummy forms that merely feature an oval shape or two black eyelike dots (Maurer and Barrera, 1981). As Bower summarizes, "The pattern is no longer just a collection of elements but is, in fact, a whole in a mysterious sense" (1969, p. 219).

Almost no one doubts infants' special sensitivity to faces, but just what brings about the heightened capacity to perceive and respond to human faces is not known. It may be that the infants can deal with larger units than before, or that they have better memories for patterns they have seen before (Salapatek, 1973). Whatever the reason, they no longer need to focus on isolated features or parts; they can now take in an entire organized form or **figure.**

We can piece together scattered clues about how the recognition of faces comes about. The interest of newborns in areas of strong contrast probably pulls them to the area of eyes (Goren, 1975), and the brightening that characterizes eye-to-eye contact

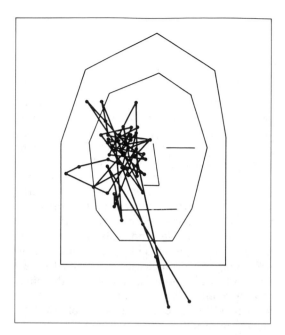

Figure 3.6. The scanning pattern demonstrates that the seven-week-old is especially attracted to the eyes of a face, suggesting an appreciation for the meaning of the facial pattern. Later in infancy, the gaze becomes less concentrated, though it still focuses on internal features. (Hainline, 1978)

probably keeps them there. By the age of one month, infants are already more likely to look at features when they have been arranged in a facelike configuration than when the same features are scrambled—but this effect evaporates when the features are enclosed by a border or bounding shape. By two months the child will look more at the facelike configuration, even when it is so bounded—thereby showing an ability to treat the various pieces as part of the same object (Maurer and Barrera, 1978). Other investigators also report a dramatic increase in face looking at around the age of two months: the eyes are still attractive but now the child's gaze can commute between the features and the boundary (Hainline, 1978). By ten weeks the child is no longer captured by the facial features, scanning all areas for approximately the same

amount of time. And by three months the ability to see a face *as a face* seems securely established: indeed there are claims that a three-month-old can already discriminate a smiling from a frowning face (Barrera and Maurer, 1981; Keane and Swartz, 1981).

Schematic Images and Discrepancies. The ability to see a group of elements in relationship to one another is most apparent in heightened abilities to see faces, but it soon extends to other familiar figures ranging from the rattle with which the parents play to mobiles hanging above their cribs. In an effort to clarify the nature of such figure perception, researchers have studied the ways in which children come to recognize mobiles, faces, and other familiar forms. Jerome Kagan (1970) contends that infants capable of perceiving figures inevitably construct a mental representation of events or experiences. After sufficient experience with any object, a **schematic image** (also called a **schema**)*—a mental representation somewhat like a caricature—is built up, highlighting the most distinctive elements of the experience. From then on, other perceptual experiences are processed or assimilated with reference to that schematic image. If a stimulus differs materially from an existing schematic image, yet is not totally remote from it, it is said to be **discrepant** from that image. For instance, a face without eyes or one with scrambled features is discrepant from the typical schematic image for a face; a mobile that has been changed in size, shape, or color is discrepant from the "standard" mobile. By exposing babies to stimuli such as mobiles or depictions of faces, and by then systematically varying the arrangement of features on subsequent presentations, Kagan and his colleagues

*Schema, or schematic images, should not be confused with the behavioral schemes described by Piaget (see page 63).

have gathered considerable evidence to support his belief that moderate discrepancies—such as changes in shape, orientation, or other specific distinctive features—command the most attention.

Clearly, the establishment of a schema requires adequate memory from one day to the next. Not surprisingly, around the age of three or four months, infants exhibit an increase in their ability to remember novel presentations. Such a mnemonic capacity is most likely to be demonstrated when the conditions of the initial presentation are faithfully re-created (Enright, 1981; Fagan, 1973; Fagan, 1981; Fagen et al., 1981; Fagen, Rovee, and Kaplan, 1976; Olson, 1979). Experimentation can reveal just what is (and is not) remembered. In one study, five-month-old infants were familiarized with a three-dimensional Styrofoam figure. The infants were tested at various temporal intervals with versions of the figure that differed from the original along one or more dimensions. On immediate testing infants proved able to remember shape, color, size, and orientation. They retained only color and form after ten minutes and only form after twenty-four hours (Strauss and Cohen, 1978). By this age a hierarchy has emerged of what is important, or defining, in a form.

Because schematic images are so crucial for children, discrepancies can be expected to exert powerful effects. Here lurks a possible explanation for why four-month-olds smile at scrambled faces, why eight-month-olds love peek-a-boo games, or why the face of a stranger is so fascinating to the child of six months or fifteen months. Once a figure (or schematic image) has been established, other stimuli are perceived in relation to it—and modest departures prove especially alluring. Kagan's theory explains why infants overexposed to one stimulus are likely to prefer a novel one eventually. As a corollary to the discrepancy theory, it has sometimes been

contended that as they grow older infants will prefer increasingly complex stimuli (Appleton, Clifton, and Goldberg, 1975). But despite the appeal of this notion, efforts to measure complexity convincingly have not always produced results consistent with this claim.

The ability to recognize novel figures and to detect alterations in them underscores the remarkable differentiation of which the infant has become capable. And, indeed, comparable progress has been made in yet other areas of perceiving, for example, in the ability to see depth through stereopsis. Moreover, the child of four months can read meaning not only from real-life objects; she is also able to decode information from pictures. She can recognize the resemblances between objects seen in real life and those presented in photographic or line-drawing form; and she displays the equally important capacity to differentiate between a presentation via pictures and a presentation from real life (Dirks and Gibson, 1977; Fantz, Fagan, and Miranda, 1975; Rose, 1977; Strauss, DeLoache, and Maynard, 1977). (According to DeLoache, Strauss, and Maynard [1979] infants prefer a real doll to a two-dimensional depiction.) In any case, it is in judging the depth and distance solely from pictorial cues that infants may need special training (deLoache et al., 1979); otherwise pictures "speak" directly to them.

Finally, by the age of seven or eight months, children are able to form concepts of some complexity simply through visual presentation. For instance, presented with a series of faces and challenged to master various concepts, infants of this age can learn to respond to the broader concept of "female faces in general," to a specific female face, irrespective of its orientation, or to facial moods like happiness or surprise (Caron and Caron, 1981). And even more impressively, infants aged ten months are able, when presented with several members of an arbitrarily constructed set of schematic faces, to abstract out an average or "prototypical" member of that category. Evidence for existence of the prototype comes from the fact that infants will habituate to prototypical instances and will prefer novel instances—ones that do not possess the features of the prototype (Sherman, 1981; Strauss, 1979, 1981). In a manner comparable to adults, infants of less than a year are apparently able to ferret out the various features of the category (like nose width, nose length, eye separation, and head length) and to evaluate individual instances in terms of the extent to which they embody these various features. Clearly, they've come a long way from edges and contours.

Audition. Testing auditory perception is more difficult. As the stimulus is evanescent and not readily localized, simple preference and habituation paradigms are generally inapplicable. Nonetheless, progress in evaluating infant audition is beginning to occur and findings seem comparable in many respects to the picture obtained in the visual realm. For example, at birth infants will orient to a continuous sound source and show a significant bias toward turning in the direction of the sound (Crassini and Broerse, 1980; Mendelson and Haith, 1976; Muir and Field, 1979).

In the two major areas of sound—music and language—infants are very well prepared. As in the case of color perception, young infants seem "wired" to divide the language spectrum as adults do—for example, hearing all p's as different from all b's (see Eimas et al., 1971; Eimas, 1976; Trehub, Bull, and Schneider, 1979; and Chapter 4 for further details). Infants as young as a month can be reliably trained to recognize a word that has been repeated (Ungerer, Brody, and Zelazo, 1978). In the case of music, infants can by the age of three months organize a series of taps into rhythmic configurations, distinguishing

(..) from (. ..) (Demany, McKenzie, and Vurpillot, 1977). By five months they can recognize a pattern of pitches, sorting out instances where the melody is the same and only the key has been changed from instances in which the actual pitches in the melody have been scrambled (Chang and Trehub, 1977; Trehub, Bull, and Schneider, 1979). And, suggesting that their musical precocity is not just perceptual, six-month-old infants have sung back tones at the correct pitch, a finding that causes difficulty for those skeptical of infant imitative capacities—and anguish for those of us who still can't carry a tune (Kessen, Levine, and Wendrich, 1978)!

CONNECTIONS AND ASSOCIATIONS ACROSS PERCEPTUAL MODALITIES

Sophisticated discriminations within the perceptual systems—for example, within the auditory and visual modalities—have clearly been demonstrated in young infants. But what about the ability to relate discriminations from different perceptual systems to one another—to recognize the identity between a ball that is seen and a ball that has been felt; to detect that a voice just heard comes from a visible individual; to appreciate that a property like intensity or continuity can be represented in a number of sensory domains?

At the end of the seventeenth century William Molyneux asked the great English philosopher John Locke whether a man born blind but experienced in touch, and suddenly allowed to see as an adult, could distinguish a cube from a globe by vision alone. In proper empiricist fashion, Molyneux and Locke concurred that he could not: as Locke put it, "the blind man, at first sight, would not be able with certainty to say which was the globe, which the cube, whilst he only saw them, though he could unerringly name them by touch" (Locke, 1961).

For centuries, Locke's was the prevailing wisdom among scientists. Students of infancy provided ample documentation that infants could first make discriminations within one sensory modality (say, vision) but could only gradually learn to associate or connect the visual impression with that gained via another sensory modality, such as touch (Gottfried et al., 1977; McGurk, Furnure and Creighton, 1977; Rose, Gottfried, and Bridger, 1981).

Recently, however, a growing number of findings have called the classic empiricist view into question. These results suggest that the links between sensory modalities are less remote than was once thought and even hint that infants may be wired to effect certain translations with little or no difficulty (Mendelson, 1979). An early study documented that infants as young as one month became upset when their mother's voice came from a speaker located a distance from where she herself was talking (Aronson and Rosenbloom, 1971; see also Bechtold, Bushnell, and Salapatek, 1979). Four-month-old infants have succeeded in forming **bimodal schemes** (schemes involving two sensory modes—see Lawson, 1980; Lyons-Ruth, 1977): trained to respond to an object that produced a characteristic sound (the auditory mode), they became disoriented when the sound now accompanied a seen novel object (the visual mode). To demonstrate an even more complex intermodal ability, Spelke (Spelke, 1979; Spelke and Owsley, 1979) simultaneously showed four-month-old infants two films, one of a bouncing toy kangaroo, the other of a bouncing monkey. The filmed objects moved at different rates, but the infant heard a single sound from a central speaker. Results indicated that the infants looked significantly longer at the film associated with its proper sound: sensitive to both visual and auditory rhythm, they could assess synchrony. (see Menten and Cohen, 1979).

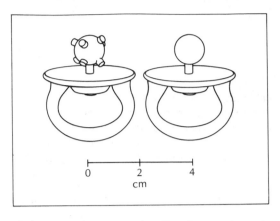

Figure 3.7. Infants in Meltzoff and Borton's study looked at a jagged styrofoam form longer than at a smooth one after sucking the pacifier on the left. The infants looked at the smooth form after sucking the one on the right.

The possibility that Molyneux and Locke were totally in error is raised most sharply by a recent study by Meltzoff and Borton (1979). These investigators allowed twenty-nine-day-old infants to suck on one of two pacifiers, either a smooth round one or one with jagged rubber nubs on it. After a period of exploration, the infants saw one of two dense styrofoam forms (round or jagged) that matched the pacifiers in physical appearance. The infants clearly demonstrated the effects of their previous sucking, looking reliably for longer periods at the form resembling the one they had mouthed. It seems reasonable to conclude they were able to distinguish the abstract properties of "roundness" or "jaggedness" within each sensory modality and then to effect appropriate links across vision and touch.

If infants are "wired" to make associations across sensory modalities, the question arises as to which properties can be so linked—or, as some have phrased it, What is the "amodal" or "polymodal" nature of perception? Various investigators have claimed that young infants can connect across sensory modalities experiences that share "high intensity," "rigidity," or "continuity" with one another (Bower, 1964, 1966a; Gibson, Owsley, and Johnston,

1978; Lewkowicz and Turkewitz, 1980; Wagner et al., 1981). Decoding the "language" used by the nervous system in making such links will be a tricky business, whether these predicates are inborn or acquired early. But the cracking of such a code should enlighten us about "the language of thought" (Fodor, 1975). And it may also suggest the basic building blocks that later allow the higher forms of human creative thought, ranging from the creation of metaphor in language ("Shall I compare thee to a summer's day?") to the devising of analogies in science (the process of evolution viewed as a branching tree).

MAKING

Just as the eyes can illustrate the way in which the child perceives the world, the hands provide telltale cues about the way the child makes (or performs) actions. In discussing the "making system," the system that acts upon the environment, we will examine the ways in which infants use their limbs and other organs to act on, and to organize, the objects in their world. To some extent, we have already encountered the making system: in his treatment of the development of intelligence and in his description of various circular reactions, Piaget showed how crucial concepts grow out of the manual operations of the child. However, here we will downplay inferences about cognition, considering instead the actual principles whereby actions become more highly organized and increasingly flexible in the opening years of life.

In the first days after birth, the child (through her making system) issues forth with assorted actions, which only gradually come under the control of external stimulation. Some seem from our view quite primitive and uncontrolled—witness the way an irritated infant flails and thrashes about (Figure 3.8). Others, including some of the reflexes

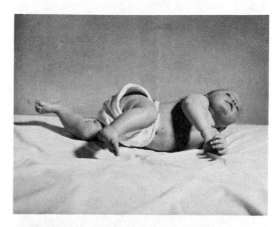

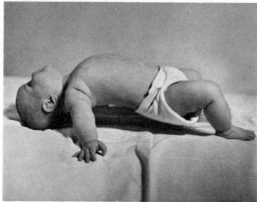

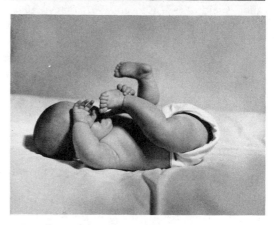

Figure 3.8. A six-month-old's pure making activity includes body and limb movements that will later contribute to complex making patterns (such as jumping or doing a somersault) and the solution of problems (such as escaping from a narrow space).

described above, appear organized, entailing smoothly unfolding components that can eventually be differentiated from one another. Indeed, when held under their arms so that the balls of their feet can touch the ground, newborn infants will begin to walk and can even ascend a flight of stairs. And if the newborn child is given a few weeks' practice in stepping, she will not only continue this behavior but actually increase by a factor of four the number of steps that she can take (Zelazo, 1976). Quite possibly, such exercise transforms a reflex into a useful, instrumental behavior. Consistent with this speculation are findings that those cultures that stress early exercise prompt precocious motor maturity (Konner, 1973; Zelazo, 1976).

Sucking. The sucking response has come under special study, perhaps because of its utility and its elaborate organization in newborns. In fact, much of our knowledge of infants' "making" comes from examinations of their sucking (see Kessen, 1967; Piaget, 1963). Initially the infant's sucking is a reflexive response to the placement of an object in or near the mouth. The infant will automatically and efficiently root toward the object. The eyes will shut, and motor activity will diminish. Assuming that the object lends itself to sucking, the action begins with uniform pressure and at a rate of about two sucks per second. At first, this rate is not affected very much by environmental feedback.

By the age of four weeks or so, the infant's sucking is becoming differentiated and increasingly sensitive to environmental events (Bruner, 1968; Wolff, 1968). If, for instance, the child is nourished only when making lapping movements with the mouth, then the suctioning part of the sucking behavior will eventually be extinguished (Kessen, 1967). The child can also alter the length of the pauses between sucks if an interesting visual display is presented. But if the disruption becomes too great, the infant will "shut off" external stimulation and sucking will resume its compulsive, inflexible form.

By the time the baby is several months old, sucking has become exquisitely sensitive to a range of events. It has become integrated with various perceptual schemes and feeling states. It can serve intelligent activities that could not have been built into the organism. Again, a reflex has achieved instrumental status. For instance, Ilze Kalnins and Jerome Bruner (1973) have shown that two-to-three-month-old infants can learn over a few sessions to suck faster (or slower) in order to make a blurry colored film clear. Indeed, infants' control of their sucking behavior is in its own way as versatile as a pitcher's mastery of a curve ball or a slider.

Other Forms of Making. Sucking is perhaps the most highly organized pattern in the newborn's repertoire, and in its decreasing rigidity and increasing sensitivity to environmental contingencies it exemplifies operation of the making system. But other, more gradual forms of development can also characterize the making system.

Take for instance the newborn's hand movements. At first, all such movements are extremely clumsy, imprecise, and unrelated to the perceptual world. When at about two months children first try to reach for objects in their visual field, their swiping motions are gross (White, Castle, and Held, 1964). They lack the ability to oppose fingers and thumb so that the object can be neatly grasped. By the age of two and one-half months, they become increasingly agitated by the sight of an object, rapidly lifting and lowering their upper torso, and swiping, often with fists clenched, more nearly in the direction of the object. Swiping slows down and becomes more precisely controlled, so that four-month-olds edge slowly toward the object with hand stretched open, and often with mouth agape as well. When they touch the object, their fingers curl around it and they usually put it in their mouth. By five and one-half months, children have a smooth and efficient reach. Visually guided reaching suffers a temporary decline at the age of nine months, as children begin to look away from the target while reaching (Bushnell, 1981). However, this decline signals an imminent advance: by the age of one year, children are capable of a more precise ballistic movement with which they can coordinate thumb and fingers in a precise pincer movement, reaching out to pluck a single chocolate chip lying on a table (Halverson, 1931). And by eighteen months the child can anticipate events sufficiently to be able to catch moving objects (von Hofsten and Lindhagen, 1979).

At first, the child's acts are isolated—a sweep of the hand, a turn of the head. Once mastered, these acts become part of more complicated sequences. In learning to drink from a cup, for instance, the child combines the once discrete acts of grasping, turning the head, lapping liquids, and so on. After drinking has been perfected, this sequence, in turn, is embedded in a larger sequence like eating or brushing teeth, thereby becoming enmeshed in an increasingly organized set of behavioral patterns. Thus these integrated patterns, whose smoothness may be reminiscent of reflexes, actually result from a gradual synthesis of diverse components.

While acts such as sucking and grasping dominate the infant's "making" behavior, her thought process, which becomes central in later life, may emerge by means of the same principles. A single, discrete mental operation (say, adding two numbers) eventually becomes part of a more complicated mental exercise (for instance, computing a square root).

Indeed, the making system is an integral part of the individual's general capacity to

Figure 3.9. In an example of the sophisticated making activity common in the second year of life, a child appropriately grasps and carefully places rings on a peg.

recognize and solve problems. Problem solving of every sort involves choice and coordination among behaviors with reference either to material objects and physical actions or, later, to symbolic representations (Newell and Simon, 1972). The crucial differences between the infant and the adult are found in the degree to which "making" is integrated with other developing systems and in the materials the individual typically encounters. Whether there may exist some areas where principles of making differ in later life—for instance, adults are said to have undue difficulties acquiring new languages or learning to ski—is an intriguing but largely unexplored issue (Hebb, 1949; Lenneberg, 1967; Luria, 1966).

FEELING

Although perception and action have been much studied, the feeling system remains uncharted territory. The most common and time-honored way to treat feelings is to posit a small set of feelings, or emotions, in the infant and then to trace the later emergence of more finely differentiated emotions.

For example, the behaviorist J. B. Watson (1919) described three primitive emotions present at birth: fear (in response to threatening stimuli and accompanied by crying and clutching); anger (in response to frustrating experiences and marked by stiffness and a blue face); and love (in response to soothing stimulation and graced by smiling). Katherine Bridges (1930) found the newborn characterized by an "undifferentiated excitement." In the following weeks this excitement divided into feelings of distress, delight, and, once again, excitement. Within months, distress broke down into fear, anger, and distress; delight into delight, joy, and affection; and excitement once again survived. Further distinctions led by the third year of life to such subtle emotional reactions as anger, envy, jealousy, and disappointment. Even more sophisticated versions of this approach have been proposed recently (see Izard, 1971; Young and Décarie, 1977).

It is certainly reasonable to speculate, with these authorities, that infants' emotional lives are initially undifferentiated and become more fine-grained as they encounter diverse situations and gain knowledge. With the advent of more sophisticated recording and scoring techniques, researchers have devised reliable methods of judging infants' reactions. Evidence grows that infants have a range of facial and bodily expressions from very early in life and that these can be judged with some reliability. Thus Hiatt and Campos (1977) found that adults could reliably judge happiness and, to a lesser extent, surprise and fear in infants as young as three months of age. Carroll Izard and his colleagues (1980) distinguished eight reliably different emotions in the facial expressions of children ranging in age from one to nine months: interest, joy, surprise, sadness, anger, disgust, contempt, and fear. Of course, one must bear in mind that these labels represent adults' best

guesses: we cannot affirm what the child is actually experiencing.

Other approaches may also elucidate the child's feeling life. One can simply describe the child's facial and bodily expressions objectively (for example, a full smile) without giving them names (for example, joy) and attempt to correlate these external indices with information about the child's current experiences. One can focus instead on the infant's general state of arousal (as Peter Wolff has done; see p. 105). Again, in describing the feelings undergone by a child evolving from deep sleep to alert inactivity, one refrains from characterizing the child's feelings in terms of the emotions used to characterize adults. One can focus on apparent temperamental variations in children, calling attention to the regularity (or irregularity) of changes in their expressions and states of arousal. In such an account, some children emerge as well regulated and calm, others as chaotic and uncomfortable (Escalona, 1968). These differences in temperament can be recognized in early infancy, are quite stable throughout infancy (Thomas et al., 1963; Yarrow, 1979), and may well have a genetic basis. For instance, Oriental infants consistently emerge as calmer, less changeable, and steadier than Western infants. Unlike Western infants, they exhibit few overt motions and are able to cease crying immediately (Freedman, 1976). Each of these approaches focuses on indices that can presumably be related to feelings while refraining from using definitions in adult terms.

Children's reactions can indicate salient and significant experiences. Just as a child's visual attention to an object signals the extent of her interest, so too smiles, frowns, crying, and placid contentment reflect how a child feels in a particular situation. Indeed, the infant of four months who smiles readily at adult faces indicates a feeling of pleasure

Figure 3.10. The infant's variety of facial expressions in a brief period suggests a range of feelings that rivals that of adults.

expressed affects to environmental stimulation. Thus, Cohn (1981) has amassed evidence showing that when infants as young as three months observe their mother acting in a depressed manner, they will protest, act wary, and exhibit other negative and disorganized expressions.

All the preceding approaches begin with the child's overt expressions. It is also plausible to begin with a model of the child's needs and desires and then to draw inferences about the child's feelings from the manner in which these needs are (or are not) fulfilled. These inferences can be checked against overt behavior. For example, if a hungry child finally receives food, she is likely to experience pleasurable feelings or almost no feelings at all. If, however, she receives no nourishment, then uncomfortable or even painful feelings may result.

Our treatment of the feeling system is admittedly speculative. Perhaps the child's experiences coincide with different states of arousal. Perhaps the child feels varying degrees of pleasure (or satiation) and pain (or frustration). Perhaps the child's feelings accompany certain cognitive states; for instance, the heightened tension and ultimate release entailed in solving a problem (Gunnar-Vongnechten, 1977). Or perhaps certain basic emotions dominate. Drawing on this last assumption, we will shortly explore the developmental course of a few feelings and behaviors that have emotional significance in the lives of children.

INTERACTIONS AMONG THE SYSTEMS

By classifying behaviors in terms of three separate systems we have taken scientific license. After all, certain reflexes in the newborn suggest an interaction of systems right from birth: the child who roots when touched on the cheek is acting in response to a perceived

that distinguishes her sharply from the infant who wails or the infant who fails to exhibit any reaction at all. The last-mentioned children—unable to form a relationship with their caretakers—are often severely disturbed. Sometimes it proves possible to relate these stimulus; the child who cries when pricked is presumably experiencing pain.

But, you might contend, these behaviors are simply reflexive and, as such, lie outside the psychologist's proper focus. And, you might point out, the evidence that the child can establish novel (non-wired-in) connections at birth is still scanty. Perhaps, then, the fiction of three systems is useful.

Maybe so, but one line of evidence suggests that certain nonreflexive links between systems may be established almost without effort. Once again, the strongest claims comes from Meltzoff and his colleagues (Meltzoff and Moore, 1977). These investigators believe that infants between two and three weeks of age can imitate both the facial and the manual gestures of a model, a skill involving both the perceiving and the making systems. Moreover, some of these imitations involve behaviors that the infant cannot possibly see herself perform—for example, sticking out the tongue (cf. also Gardner and Gardner, 1970; Zazzo, 1957). In the view of Meltzoff and his colleagues, infants have an innate ability to represent the behavior of a model and their own behavior in terms of a supramodal code, a code common to both the modalities of vision and proprioception (sensitivity to the internal reactions of one's body). An active process of matching one's own behavior to that of a model is mediated by an abstract representational system.

If this were the case, it would make short shrift of most traditional accounts of developmental psychology and certainly cast doubt on the utility of a three-systems approach. Not surprisingly then, when Meltzoff presented these findings at the Society for Research in Child Development, there followed as heated a discussion as I have ever heard at a scientific meeting. Other scholars attributed the findings to everything from faulty experimental design and inappropriate statistics to primitive reflexes or innate release mechanisms. Most popular was the belief in an inborn proclivity to stick out a tongue in response to certain arousing stimuli coupled with skepticism about claims that infants can match particular body regions of a model to nonvisible regions in their own body (cf. Gardner and Gardner, 1970; Jacobson and Kagan, 1979).

There is another possibility, however, one that may help us organize several findings reviewed here. Certain abilities that eventually flower in human beings may exist in newborns in a primitive form that can be evoked under special eliciting conditions. Included here could be early walking, imitation, and supramodal and cross-modal matching. These behaviors are by no means identical to the later variants, which evolve as a result of considerable practice in the world, learning from experience, and differentiation within and across each of the three individual systems. On the other hand, these precursors may well exploit some of the same mechanisms in the nervous system and be elicited under at least some of the same conditions as the later variants. They serve as a kind of sneak preview of what is likely to come (see the interlude on the model of development in psychology). And if properly stimulated and maintained, they may turn out to have direct links to more full-blown behaviors that develop later (Bower, 1978; Mehler and Bever, 1968; S. Strauss, 1980).

Three Complex Behaviors

The three systems can aid us in unraveling and making sense of some prominent behaviors in the infant's repertoire. Such behaviors are rarely, if ever, simple and unchanging in meaning. On the contrary, a baby's smiling or frowning, fear or joy, hand shaking or head

Figure 3.11. Thanks to the swimming reflex, even very young children will kick their legs and paddle their arms when placed in water.

shaking alter significantly in meaning during development, becoming connected to a variety of perceptions, feelings, and activity and frequently bearing several meanings even within a single developmental period. For these reasons careful study of a single behavioral pattern does more than highlight a specific stimulus or situation; it may furnish important clues to the child's view of the world. As we conclude our introduction to the well-equipped stranger, we will examine three key infant behaviors: the smile, the fear response, and the attainment of object permanence with respect to other persons.

THE SMILE

Of the various responses at the child's disposal none is more intriguing than the smile. Indeed, whenever another individual looks at an infant more than two months old, the child is likely to smile. But what does this behavior signify? Does it reflect feelings of well-being, a public announcement of a pleasant emotion? Or is it a cognitive signal—the baby's declaration that she perceives the other person or an attempt to communicate knowledge (and its accompanying feelings) to the world? In this winning facial gesture may be locked clues to the world of the infant.

Various elements of smiling have been studied, sometimes together, sometimes apart. Even at thirty weeks after conception, premature infants will smile when sleeping, when touched, or when a glass is tapped (Bower, 1969, p. 165). Blind as well as sighted babies will smile shortly after birth, particularly when their eyes are moving rapidly. But are these *real* smiles? Most psychologists agree that they are not—that facial muscles are merely being maintained in a certain position. So researchers contrast the reflexive or meaningless smiling of premature and newborn infants with the more social smiling of later infancy (Robinson, 1969; Wolff, 1963).

The first "true smiling," which begins in the second month, can be induced by almost any stimulation, though smiling is especially likely when the stimulus is moving and can excite several senses (Ambrose, 1961). During these early months, the primary requirement for soliciting a smile seems to be a visual facelike pattern: two eyes against an oval background are generally effective, though the addition of other facial features will increase the likelihood of a smile (Ährens, 1954). Four-month-old babies will smile at any facial configuration, and, in Jerome Kagan's opinion (1971), this early smiling is linked to recognition of anything familiar rather than to recognition of specific individuals (but see Fogel, 1981, for a suggestion that the mother is more successful than a stranger at eliciting smiles). At four months infants are likely to react with smiles to familiar displays like mobiles; yet as the weeks pass by, smiling becomes more specifically linked to (and reserved for) the presence of a human being, particularly a human face. And it may be that young children already smile in discriminable ways to their mother's face, a checkerboard pattern, and a playpen game (Bower, 1978). Only through experimental variations can it be determined which visual—and nonvisual—features of the stimuli are governing the smile.

By the age of five months, familiar faces reliably evoke smiles while strange ones draw little reaction. In succeeding months, an infant's awareness that a strange face is not her mother's may be nonreinforcing and cause fear or discomfort (Ambrose, 1961). Once the infant establishes the mother (or father) as the primary caretaker, the child may avoid or fear all noncaretaking figures—in this way smiling serves to reinforce the attachment to the mother (Eibl-Eibesfeldt, 1970).

These responses to faces have also been explained in terms of the schematic image-discrepancy theory introduced earlier in this chapter. Stimuli moderately discrepant from a schematic image are interesting to babies; babies therefore experience pleasure (or satisfaction) in "assimilating" the discrepant stimuli to fit an existing schematic image. In terms of our three systems, the *perception* of a discrepant stimulus results in an initial *feeling* of tension. But once the infant aligns the stimulus to her prior schema, she smiles (an *act*) and experiences pleasure (another *feeling*).

Distress at the sight of a stranger can also be considered from this perspective. Whereas the initial tension gives rise to satisfaction when the mother is recognized, anxiety may result when the child discovers that the face is not that of the valued caretaker. Or stimuli that exceed a certain level of discrepancy may evoke feelings of discomfort.

Studies of smiling chart the diverse meanings the response can carry at different ages. Initially a reflex or a response to diverse stimulation, the smile becomes associated, as time goes on, with pleasant experiences, valued individuals, recognition of objects, the exploration of persons, and, eventually, satisfaction or delight at the solution of a problem (Eckerman and Rheingold, 1974; Sroufe and Waters, 1976). Some of these experiences are cognitive, others affective, so an interpretation from only one of those stances would probably not account for all meanings.

L. Alan Sroufe and Everett Waters (1976) have combined both the cognitive and affective aspects of the smile by describing it as a reliable indicator of the release of tension. At all ages the smile seems to develop after a similar sequence: (1) the child desires to be engaged with novel forms of stimulation; (2) the child makes initial efforts to know or to assimilate built-up tension; (3) if the surrounding context is fairly comfortable, a smile is likely to ensue on a correct cognition or solution.

Following this account, we can readily observe intricate interactions among the developing systems. At first the smile can be seen as a fairly pure instance of making—a mere facial gesture devoid of ties either to the perceived world or to internal feelings. By the child's second or third month, the act of a smile has tentative links to the other systems: facelike visual perceptions are more likely to prompt the smile, pleasurable internal feelings to accompany it. Smiling becomes increasingly specific during the middle months of the first year, being reserved first for facelike configurations, particularly those a little different from an established schematic image, and later for strongly valued individuals. At these times, when the child smiles in pleasure from the recognition of an object, the three systems are operating in harmony.

THE FEAR RESPONSE

A revealing and analogous account can be given of the infant's fear responses (Lewis and Rosenblum, 1975). Infants may react with fear and anxiety to a sudden change in their environment, to separation from their mother, or to the presence of a specific, harmful person. Initially, fears occur following a sudden alteration in the level of stimulation. Later, toward the end of the child's first year, fear occurs in response to specific losses or to particular individuals who have in the past upset the child.

Despite the apparently opposite feelings associated with them, fear and smiling may be elicited by the same type of event: encountering a strange stimulus that calls for recognition. In the case of the smile, cognition yields pleasure; in the case of fear, cognition results in avoidance, alarm, or extreme anxiety. A single feature (such as a mask) may elicit a smile in one situation (when viewed at home) and fear in another (when viewed in an unfamiliar environment). Apparently, children are aroused when their expectations are violated or when novel stimulation appears. Whether the resulting emotion (and release of tension) is positive or negative depends on the context

in which the stimulus is encountered as well as on the child's interpretation of the stimulus (Lewis, 1975; Sroufe and Waters, 1976). Perhaps a smile occurs when the stimulus is easy to assimilate, whereas fear results when the stimulus proves difficult or even impossible to assimilate (Kagan, 1975). Finally, one stimulus—say, a stranger—may simultaneously arouse both an affiliative response (desire to be near another person) and a withdrawal response (desire to avoid the unknown). The salience of each response depends on the situation, including the presence of the mother and the particular actions of the stranger (Rebelsky, 1976).

Whatever the ultimate explanations of fear, this set of behaviors once again exemplifies the interaction of systems. A rich behavior with clear affective overtones becomes increasingly intertwined with perceptions of the world. Initially fear results directly from a discrepant stimulus but later it involves considerable interpretation of the surrounding situation.

RESPONSES TO VALUED PERSONS

In the previous chapter we examined in some detail the sense of object permanence—the awareness that an object continues to exist in time and space even when it cannot be perceived directly. Following Piaget, our approach was indifferent to the identity of objects; that is, we assumed that the object concept develops in approximately the same way and with the same speed regardless of the object in question.

To test this assumption, Thérèse Gouin-Décarie (1965) followed ninety infants in the process of attaining object permanence. And she discovered that the infants showed the behaviors associated with knowledge of object permanence first with reference to their mothers, then with reference to persons in general, and finally to inanimate objects. Acknowledging the mother's unique familiarity and importance, Piaget accepted Gouin-Décarie's revisions of his object theory.

"Objects" toward whom the child has developed strong emotional ties have thus been shown to pave the road for cognitive advances. The child's attachment to the mother seems to invest permanence in her, even while other objects are yet regarded as impermanent. Indeed, the feeling system may take the lead in facilitating the child's initial sense of object permanence. In a territory that might be considered exclusively the domain of perceptions and actions, affective considerations turn out to matter (see also Bertenthal and Fischer, 1978).

The Beginnings of the Sense of Self

Guided by the image of a traveler visiting a new territory, we have sought to sketch the well-equipped stranger—first as a physical entity and bearer of genetic inheritance, then as an actor influenced by early experience, one whose developing systems increasingly interact and who engages in highly complex activities involving all three systems. Yet we have not touched on one of the most critical processes of the child's first years, as subtle as it is important: the development in the child of a sense of herself. Here, and at several subsequent stages of childhood, we will pause to consider the extent to which children have combined various facets of their existence into a coherent sense of self.

The possible ingredients of a developed sense of self have long intrigued psychologists (Baldwin, 1897; Cooley, 1909; Erikson, 1963; James, 1950; G. H. Mead, 1934; Sullivan, 1953).

To begin with, these researchers suggest, one must be aware of one's own body: its dimensions, its appearance, its condition. Second, one should use language appropriately with reference to oneself: know one's own name, employ words of personal reference, indicate which descriptions apply to the self and which do not. Third, one should know one's personal history: one's needs and desires, the skills acquired, the events that have happened. This knowledge entails the ability to assume the role of others: to see oneself as others do; to construct a sense of self modeled on the attitudes and perspectives of others; to organize mentally one's own experiences and beliefs.

These ingredients sum up, objectively, to a sense of self. But for many observers, a fully developed sense of self includes an intensely subjective component: a feeling of comfort and satisfaction with who and what one is. A mature sense of self involves being at peace with what one is like, with what one has been, with what one expects to become. Not that this means freedom from anxiety or problems; indeed, a mature sense of self also involves a capacity for confronting and accepting difficulties and limitations. With this acceptance, however, should come a measure of serenity. One must come to terms with what one is in light of one's own values as well as in light of the behaviors and roles esteemed by society. To please only one's self is to be egocentric; to conform slavishly to what others demand is to deny one's own impulses. Achieving a sensitive balance between one's own aspirations and those of the surrounding community is one of the central challenges of human development (Erikson, 1963).

Laden with this description, we may seem light-years away from the average infant. After all, lacking any means for "thinking about" herself, the newborn has little if any distance from self or from other individuals.

The three-month-old will react differently to a peer than to a reflection of herself—but this distinction in all likelihood reflects the greater unpredictability and responsiveness of the "other" (Field, 1979). Yet the two-year-old already has developed some of the basic competences that figure in a sense of self, including correct use of words of self-reference and awareness of her own body (see Bretherton, 1980).

To secure empirical information on the beginnings of this central phenomenon of life, researchers Michael Lewis and Jeanne Brooks (1975) focused on two important facets of the infant's sense of self. In one series of studies, they examined the one-year-old child's ability to refer appropriately to pictures of familiar individuals. Somewhat surprisingly, they found that children learn labels for their fathers first, and then a few months later learn labels for their mothers. Confronted with pic-

tures of themselves, many youngsters initially call themselves simply "baby." They start to use their own names shortly before they reach two years of age. Children begin using personal pronouns at two and a half years, and by the age of three nearly all children can refer to pictures of themselves using both their names and the appropriate personal pronouns.

It appears, then, that children most easily name those individuals at some distance from themselves. The father, usually less involved in the child's life (and perhaps also more often referred to by name), stands out as a more distinct figure and is most readily labeled. Closer involvement with the mother makes her somewhat less easy to conceptualize as a distinct entity. (To confirm this hypothesis, one should secure information on children who were closer to their fathers than to their mothers. Lewis and Brooks believe that in

Figure 3.12. The child's fascination with her reflection in a mirror provides an important contribution to the emerging sense of self. Only when the child realizes that she controls her own reflection, but not those of others, can she successfully distinguish herself from those about her.

such cases mothers would indeed prove easier to name.) Finally, it is worth noting that children develop last the ability to refer to themselves. This feat seems most difficult because it requires both the ability to detach oneself from the entity with which one is most familiar and to take (for a time) the perspective of another individual.

Correct reference to oneself is only a single facet of the sense of self. A second and more revealing index, one not dependent on linguistic ability, is the ability to recognize oneself as different from other persons. Building on ingenious work with chimpanzees (Gallup, 1977), Lewis and his colleagues examined the reactions of infants to their own reflections (Lewis and Rosenblum, 1975). Their basic approach involved coloring a child's nose secretly with rouge and then positioning her in front of a mirror. If the child believes the reflection to be that of another child, she may be aroused by the rouge but there is no reason why she should touch her own face. If, however, the child recognizes the reflection in the mirror, then she may well touch her own nose.

Children rarely touched their noses before rouge had been applied, but many did so afterward. Trends with age were dramatic: nine- or twelve-month-olds did not touch their noses, whereas eleven of sixteen twenty-one-month-olds and twelve of sixteen two-year-olds did so. The latter children also acted silly and coy or touched the mirror image when they saw the rouge; the combination of reactions suggests that this early aspect of reflecting on one's own person emerges during the second year of life. Parallel evidence for an eruption of consciousness of self comes from the work of Amsterdam and Greenberg (1977) whose twenty-month-old subjects acted in embarrassed, admiring, and coy ways when viewing a videotape of themselves.

Such research provides information about more objective indices of self. Supplementing these studies are important insights gained from two major traditions in the study of infancy, the affective and cognitive approaches to which the previous two chapters were devoted.

The development of object permanence seems an intimate companion, if not a prerequisite, of developing a sense of self (Bertenthal and Fischer, 1978). First, it seems quite implausible to think of oneself as a coherent and lasting entity unless one is aware that entities of any sort can in fact continue to exist and undergo change while remaining in something of the same form (Piaget, 1954). By the same token, one's ability to develop the needed distance from self rests on the capacity to adopt the perspectives of other people and to see that they consider one to be a lasting entity.

Knowing facts about oneself represents one facet of the sense of self; evolving a feeling of appropriateness concerning one's own activities and experiences is its essential complement (Erikson, 1963). We have seen that an important contributor to well-being is an adequate attachment to the mother and the resulting evolution of basic trust. And, in most cases, the child's own display of affects serves as the most reliable index of the feelings she experiences about herself (Demos, 1975). If the child has formed a meaningful attachment to the mother—feeling comfortable in her arms yet confident enough to venture forth and to weather the anxieties evoked by the presence of strangers and the absence of familiar persons—then the child should be permeated by a sense of basic trust. An initial phase of selfhood will have been effectively completed—the child feels, if not yet articulately, that she is human, just like others.

If, on the other hand, such attachments and feelings have not formed or if they have been disrupted, then the child will become mistrustful. The self may assume a pathetic and unhealthy taint. If the attachments have been formed to alien entities, the sense of self will be correspondingly anomalous: thus, a chimpanzee trained by humans to use sign language apparently disdained other chimps as "black bugs" and considered himself human. And a chimpanzee raised in isolation showed no awareness of self whatsoever (Gallup, 1977). Correspondingly, in the most severe cases the child may prove unable to develop any sense of self. Such a child will remain pathetically linked to or totally isolated from others, living in a world of delusion and alienation.

In journeying from the union of egg and sperm to the emergence of a sense of self, we have traversed the vast territories that infants themselves cross. Given an adequate genetic heritage, normal reflexes and predispositions, a reasonable environment, and a few caring individuals, the child will make staggering progress. Nor do special talents seem to be required to bring about a healthy child and a strong sense of self. As Erik Erikson reminds us: "We must learn not to break [the child's] spirit by making him the victim of our anxieties. . . . To develop a child with a healthy personality, a parent must be a genuine person in a genuine milieu. . . . If we only learn to let live, the plan for growth is all there" (1959, p. 100).

Signposts

Our examination of the first period of life began with consideration of children's affective states, specifically their deep and significant tie to their mothers. Next, and by contrast, we shifted our attention in the second chapter to another facet—children's "construc-

tion" of the physical world, their acquisition of knowledge about its salient features, their ability to learn connections, associations, and varied patterns of behavior. But even summed, these aspects do not yield a unified picture of the infant. Thus, in this chapter we have tried to gain a fuller picture of the child. We have seen how nine months of fetal development and her genetic heritage equip the baby for life in the world; examined the states and capacities of the newborn child; and traced the unfolding and integration of abilities during the first two years of life.

We found that during the nine months from conception to birth the fetus undergoes astonishing changes. The zygote, or fertilized egg cell, harbors information-bearing material in its nucleus. As the cell divides again and again, the embryo increases in size and its tissues become differentiated. As development proceeds, diverse behaviors become possible and the fetus begins to look like a human infant. Not enough is known about the feelings and perceptions of a fetus to say definitely that it is a psychological as well as a biological creature. But by the time of birth, the baby's capacities to perceive and respond are as fully developed as her tissues and organs.

Although maternal environments affect fetuses differently, most fetuses experience a similar course of prenatal development. Explaining this similarity as well as the uniqueness of each individual required that we examine genetic inheritance. Genes, which carry all inherited characteristics from both parents, can combine in infinite ways. What we inherit (our genotype) is but one possible, accidental combination. What we become (our phenotype) is but one possible group of traits to arise from a given genotype; influences of the environment both before and after birth determine our observable characteristics. Thus, although certain limits are set at the moment of conception, we develop in diverse ways over a lifetime within the range those limits allow.

Inherited characteristics and the course of prenatal development combine to produce an individual equipped with distinctive physical traits, possessing numerous reflexes, and subject to various states of arousal. The potent influence of the early environment on development—for good or ill—has been suggested by experiments with animals and by observations of and experiments with human infants. Yet, if not too extreme, the negative effects of early experiences can be reversed.

Initial experiences are registered through three developing systems of interaction with the world. Within the perceiving system the infant's sense organs convey information about the external world. In seeing, for instance, the infant first responds compulsively to contrasts but then becomes able to choose what to look at. By the third month, the infant can focus on an entire form or face and eventually perceive discrepancies from expected forms. Particular faces and facial expressions, as well as more complex and abstract kinds of patterns, can be reliably recognized later in the first year of life. The making system features the infant's use of her limbs to act on and modify surrounding objects. Isolated hand and arm movements, at first clumsy and unrelated to perceived stimuli, later become smooth sequences responsive to the infant's surroundings. The same principles apply to the making, whether physical or mental, involved in solving problems. Finally, the feeling system, which involves emotions and sensations, seems also to differentiate from generalized excitement and programmed states of arousal into more specific and flexible feelings as the individual encounters and responds to diverse situations.

While the three systems provide a useful way of organizing the growing encyclopedia of knowledge about early development, they may obscure other instructive ways of conceiving of this period. For example, from another vantage point the child is better viewed as a single organized totality, which gradually differentiates into a group of separate, though interacting, systems. Certainly, accumulating evidence suggests considerable flexibility and interconnections across systems from the first. Initially the infant may be "wired" to effect certain connections within her perceptual systems—for example, linking shapes she can see to those she can touch or taste. There may be a prepotent tendency to link major systems—as would occur, for example, in cases of early imitation of adult models. We suggested a reconciliation of these positions: grant the young infant some primitive forms of systemic interaction, but distinguish this reflexive form from later emerging, more flexible means of connecting sensory modalities or systems with one another.

The three systems assume psychological importance when they are interacting smoothly—when acute perception of patterns, flexible motor acts, and feelings responsive to the external world come together in complex behaviors. Smiling, for example, is first reflexive and meaningless, then evoked by almost any stimulation, and later appears chiefly in response to familiar faces, preeminently the mother's. Fear responses also develop, first following sudden changes in level of stimulation, later associated with specific losses or with threatening individuals. Both fear and smiling result from attempts to deal with unfamiliar stimuli and, indeed, the same stimulus may evoke opposing emotions in contrasting contexts. A third response, to valued people, may actually stimulate cognitive development: emotional ties to the mother stimulate the infant to acquire a sense of object permanence—the first the child achieves. Thus, contrary to Piaget's initial view, object permanence may not develop uniformly with respect to all objects.

While the perceiving, making, and feeling systems are becoming integrated in complex behaviors, the infant is also developing a sense of self. Most aspects of the mature sense of self will have to await later cognitive and affective milestones, but two-year-olds are already aware of (and sometimes amused or embarrassed by) the separateness of their own bodies, can recognize their reflections, and can refer to themselves using words. These advances may depend on a developed sense of object permanence and on the basic trust that results from a secure attachment bond.

The birth of the self marks the end of the first period of development: these children have begun to know the world and their place in it. But so far their knowledge is sensorimotor, entirely related to the world of physical objects. They know only what they can perceive, what they can do, and what they can feel. In the following years, youngsters will transcend this practical knowledge through symbols like words, pictures, and gestures, achieving the capacities to represent knowledge mentally, to pattern themselves after parental models, and to create a world of play. The task begins when they learn language, the central symbol system for all humans. The mysterious yet fascinating processes of language acquisition thus command our attention when we consider the toddler in Chapter 4.

Now that we have viewed the beginnings of childhood and gained an initial feel for developmental psychology, it is appropriate to step back and consider the origins of the discipline. And so, in our first interlude, we will examine the history of child study.

The Origins
of Child Study

Society has always had divided opinions about children. Some peoples
have thought of them simply as playthings. Some cultures have considered them to be small versions of men and women; with wayward
extrusions, perhaps, that needed to be cut off or hammered in to
achieve the adult model; unfinished, perhaps, and in need of rich lessons of adult understanding and decorum. . . . Other cultures and individuals have and do look upon children as a race apart, as a group that
exists as an independent unit, one that may sometimes be regarded with
envy and sometimes with amused indifference, a group to be controlled,
to be cared for as needed, and to be kept as much apart from the world
of adults as possible.

—JEAN KARL

It was 1762, and the Archbishop of Paris was extremely per-
turbed. He had just read a book that he judged dangerous to
society. In a lengthy letter, he warned good Christians against
the work, condemning it as "calculated to overthrow natural
law, and . . . false, scandalous, full of hatred toward the
Church and its ministers, derogating from the respect due to
Holy Scriptures and the traditions of the Church, erroneous,
impious, blasphemous, and heretical" (quoted in Steeg, 1886,
p. 2). Once the archbishop's attack had been published, the
Parliament of Paris ordered that the author of the book be ar-
rested and that the book itself be burned. The author fled, first

to Geneva and then to Berne, but he was forced to keep moving when his book was outlawed in these cities also.

The essay that shocked the Church, agitated political leaders, and raised havoc among those able to read it was *Emile: Concerning Education,* the story of a boy's growth by the Swiss-French philosopher Jean-Jacques Rousseau (1712-78). History has confirmed the archbishop's impression of its potency, for Rousseau's description of Emile's growth did indeed launch a revolution in the way children are viewed.

Two Basic Views of Childhood

JEAN-JACQUES ROUSSEAU'S CONTRIBUTION

At the time of *Emile*'s publication, young children in Western society were considered to be unformed adults, insignificant and simple creatures with little mental life of their own. Society's job was to teach children how to be proper adult members of the community. Starting shortly after infancy, children were subjected to strict punishments for their misdeeds; and, before long, the more privileged children received formal instruction in religion, ethics, history, reading, and writing. Following such education the children would proceed directly and smoothly into an adult niche, for instance, serving as merchants, clergy, or teachers, and becoming proper God-fearing citizens.

But in *Emile,* Rousseau declared that "nothing is known about childhood. The wisest people are so much concerned with what grown-ups should know that they never consider what children are capable of learning. They keep looking for the man in the child, not thinking of what he is before he becomes a man" (Rousseau, 1962, p. 5). Focusing on the childhood of Emile, Rousseau described the capacities of the young child and traced their development during five complete stages of life. He analyzed how the child's potential can be most fully realized, so that he becomes "not a magistrate, a soldier, or a priest, . . . but a man" (p. 4). Emile—an imaginary child whose parents have turned over his education to a tutor (Rousseau)—comes to stand for Every Child.

During the first stage of life described by Rousseau, Emile has no will, no ideas, no habits. The adult's immediate impulse to mold the unformed child is wholly wrong. The only habit Emile needs is that of avoiding all habit. Nature (especially his own natural inclinations) will be his guide in learning to eat, to walk, and even to talk.

From Rousseau's *Emile.*

During the second stage, between the ages of two and twelve, nature continues to hold the strings governing Emile's development. All his thought proceeds through his sense organs, which perceive each experience accurately and compare diverse impressions spontaneously. The *world* is Emile's book, the truest source of knowledge, and he learns best from direct, practical experiences in this world. The tutor's task is primarily preventive: to isolate the boy from the potentially harmful influence of other persons, especially from the meddling practices and preachings of adults and from the pressures of the institutions of society. Emile takes his time, avoids stuffing his mind, and allows experiences to unfold at their own pace. As a result, his manner remains open and free.

When Emile arrives at the threshold of adolescence, between twelve and fifteen, he acquires new physical strength and vigorous mental powers. His thinking remains practical, he does not dwell on ideas for their own sake. Yet he can now ponder several elements at the same time, and his extensive experience has stimulated him to derive more abstract notions of space, number, and quantity. Although he considers book knowledge useless, the tutor does introduce Emile to *Robinson Crusoe*—the story of a ship-wrecked Englishman who managed to procure food, safety, and a semblance of well-being. The tutor believes that Daniel DeFoe's book will serve as Emile's model during the rest of his life.

It is only during the fourth stage, from the age of fifteen until adulthood, that Emile mixes with other people, including peers. At last, he supplements his direct knowledge of the world with reading and formal instruction. As he confronts ethical and political issues, he reasons and develops his own opinions about such important but controversial matters.

Emile's education concludes in a fifth stage, the years of courtship and marriage in his early twenties. Rousseau's hero falls in love and wants to marry, but his love must be tested. He is sent abroad, where he can learn of other life-styles and gain needed perspective on his own feelings and desires. When he returns, still sure of his love, Emile learns from his tutor that the time for carefree interaction with nature is past, that he must make vital decisions about his future life and about what kind of an adult he wants to be. Emile does marry and soon has a son whom he will try to educate just as he was educated. With these words, and with the circle of development once again launched, Emile's education comes to an end.

Clearly, Emile's childhood and education departed from the established views of the eighteenth century. Rousseau asserted that children are separate individuals with their own capacities, feelings, and thoughts. So long as these are understood, respected, and left unmolested by parents and society, children will follow a definite natural plan on their road to adulthood. They will seek out important experiences and instructive objects, and they will draw the proper lesson from them. But to do so they should be removed from civilization and raised instead in direct contact with unpredictable but benevolent nature. Rather than leaving instruction to rigid and punitive teachers, parents should assume the burdens of educating their own offspring; they should allow them to master their own lessons at their own rate in a manner appropriate to their own stage of development. Even religious instruction should be postponed until adolescence; and then the youth should be allowed to decide which religion, if any, is most reasonable. In these and other iconoclastic views, the philosopher counseled the opposite of what all past history had dictated. He threatened the very fabric of civilization.

JOHN LOCKE'S DIFFERENT VIEW

Although Rousseau's recommendations were revolutionary, the philosophical exercise in which he engaged was not unprecedented. Earlier, other respected scholars had recorded their views about the nature of childhood and the optimal means of education. Foremost was the English philosopher John Locke (1632-1704), whose influential perspective had become the "establishment" view. Rousseau was motivated in part by a desire to present an alternative view of human development and education. And indeed, between them Rousseau and Locke anticipated the two major schools of thought in developmental psychology.

Both Locke and Rousseau felt that infants have unformed minds, that their early experiences have a crucial effect on their later life, and that children's education should be taken seriously. But there the resemblances end. In Locke's view, the child was an incomplete adult who was likely to be governed by strong passions. These passions and urges needed to be controlled by the community's wise adults who, aided by the powers of reason, created a carefully controlled environment.

In a famous phrase, Locke announced that the mind of the child was a *tabula rasa* or blank slate. What was etched on that slate would be determined by the specific behaviors produced and the rewards furnished by parents and teachers. A staunch believer in habit, Locke stressed the benefits of practice and drill, whether in learning the alphabet, mastering

Scriptures, or acquiring a regular schedule of bowel movements. More generally, Locke accepted most goals of society: he sought effective and palatable means for realizing them—for supplanting natural passions with the sweet light of reason.

PHILOSOPHICAL BEQUESTS TO CURRENT DEVELOPMENTAL PSYCHOLOGY

On fundamental issues, then, Rousseau's beliefs differed markedly from Locke's. Whereas Locke saw society as a necessary (indeed, principal) aid in the education of the child, Rousseau spurned the desires and models provided by most adults. Whereas Locke favored habit and drill, Rousseau rejected them (except for the habit of avoiding all habits). Whereas Locke relied on the reason of man, Rousseau turned to the forces of nature. And whereas Locke found the child's natural impulses dangerous, Rousseau saw children as valued innocents who must be protected from the destructive inclinations of their society. Thus, although both men realized that children required special treatment, it was Rousseau who for the first time attempted to adopt their world view and their personal interests.

In many ways, these eminent philosophers set the stage for a fundamental division in developmental psychology. Foreshadowing the environmental-learning approach, which his writings in part inspired, John Locke questioned whether children have any character or potential of their own. He believed that children, basically passive, could be molded in almost any way. It was the duty of the society's wisest members to educate the young through reward and punishment of behaviors and the instillation of habits.

Indirectly but equally decisively, Rousseau made a bequest to the cognitive-structural school. Rousseau saw children as active rather than passive agents, developing according to a natural plan through qualitatively different stages. At each stage they possessed a characteristic mental view and a parallel way of knowing. Children themselves were best equipped to determine which experiences were valuable; they possessed the necessary mental capacities to interact with the objects and events of their environment and to derive from them crucial principles or lessons. They had little need for active supervision or training: the task of the larger society was simply to allow their natural plan of growth to unfold.

Equating Locke's view with environmental-learning theory, or Rousseau's with cognitive-structuralism, is to some extent an oversimplification. After all, each school has had its own lengthy history; each draws its conclusions chiefly from experiments; each now realizes, as neither Locke nor Rousseau did, the intricate ways in which natural inclinations interact with environmental pressures. Nonetheless, one must marvel at the extent to which Locke and Rousseau anticipated current scientific and educational debates—an especially striking achievement, because concepts of childhood and education had scarcely existed in preceding centuries.

Childhood in History

There have always been children, and no doubt they have always provided joys and caused sorrows, represented hopes and aroused anxieties. Scattered mentions of children can be found in ancient Greek and Roman philosophy and myths and in the Bible. Yet the meaning of children, and of childhood, may have been entirely different until just the last few centuries.

THE MIDDLE AGES

The French cultural historian Philippe Ariès (1962) observes that during the Middle Ages (that is, approximately from the fifth to thirteenth centuries), childhood was not considered to be a separate era of life. To be sure, adults liked (or disliked), helped (or abandoned) children; but they did not think of children as having their own needs, fears, or ways of looking at the world. As a vivid illustration of this phenomenon, Ariès notes that children were not ordinarily depicted in drawings and paintings. And when they were, they appeared as little adults, without the characteristic features, musculature, and proportions of childhood and without costumes, games, or activities of their own. Children were barred from any social life until they reached six or seven, at which time they entered society immediately at the adult level. They began to participate in the rituals, games, and crafts of the larger society; they were equipped to serve in battle; they were spoken to (and understood) in the adult manner; they were thought to experience the same feelings and harbor the same thoughts as adults.

To some extent, such denial of childhood reflected more general features of this remote era. In general, most individuals were not introspective, not concerned with educational, philosophical, or psychological issues. Survival itself was their major preoccupation, along with the religious life and especially the hope for happier times in the afterlife. An individual's niche within the society was preordained. Literacy was

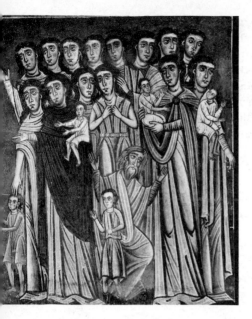

From a twelfth-century painting; the artist is unknown.

extremely rare because education was restricted to the tiniest minority and even then was focused almost exclusively on religious matters (Taylor, 1949).

Not that all aspects of life were fixed and tragic. There were festivals and ceremonies; periods of triumph as well as times of hardship. And, though society as a whole was highly stratified, individuals from different classes—clergy, knights, peasants, serfs—lived in the same areas and mingled frequently, in a rich and varied street life that almost disappeared later on. But both the concern with sheer survival and the informality of daily contacts led to the same consequence: children were taken for granted, used as they could be used, with little regard to what their own mental or emotional life might be like.

THE BEGINNING OF THE MODERN ERA

Changes in the aftermath of the Middle Ages decisively altered social life, including the ways children were perceived and treated (see Stone, 1974; Kessen, 1979; Greven, 1979). In the following six centuries, important economic, political, social, and religious movements (growth of the towns, the discovery of new lands, the intellectual Renaissance, the religious Reformation, the Industrial Revolution, and the American and French revolutions) all combined to reduce the influence of the Church, to loosen the social fabric, and to provide fresh opportunities for those in lower social and economic positions. Now one's skills and knowledge, actions and achievements would determine one's ultimate place in society; and merchants, bankers, lawyers, physicians saw that one's place in society was not necessarily preordained.

These diverse factors brought about a decisive alteration of social life. With greater mobility, extended families were less likely to remain together, and family units became smaller and more private. Street life declined; personal interactions were by and large restricted to those in similar occupations or social positions. And the child became increasingly central in the family's view. Children had a better chance than before of surviving to adulthood, and they could now aid their family and improve its prospects. By acquiring skills and knowledge as children, including the mastery of reading and writing, individuals could rise rapidly in the society. Such success was especially crucial in Protestant societies, where obtaining earthly wealth and prominence was viewed as evidence that one was among the elect and would achieve ultimate salvation. It is perhaps not coincidental that the earliest "child psycholo-

That children were beginning to have their own toys and to engage regularly in play with one another can be seen in these details from the painting *Children's Games* by the sixteenth-century Flemish master Pieter Brueghel.

gies"—those of Rousseau and Locke—emerged in Swiss and British societies that treasured worldly success.

The art of the seventeenth century reflected these changes in family life. Children became the focus of family portraits, and portraits of individual children proliferated. Parents displayed keen interest in their children's habits and language, as evidenced in this rhapsody by one Mme. de Sevigné:

> Our daughter is a dark-haired, little beauty. She is very pretty indeed. Here she comes. She kisses me, she recognizes me, she laughs at me, she calls me just plain *Mama*. . . . She does a hundred and one different things; she caresses, she slaps, she makes the sign of the cross, she begs pardon, she drops a curtsy, she blows a kiss, she shrugs her shoulders, she dances, she strokes, she holds her chin. . . . I watch her for hours on end [quoted in Ariès, 1962, p. 49].

Children were no longer miniature adults—they now had their own costumes and their own activities. And whereas once they had simply been apprentices or field hands, increasing numbers now attended school.

TRENDS IN EDUCATION

The few children who attended school during the Middle Ages received mostly formal religious instruction, along with certain "liberal arts" like grammar, music, and astronomy. For most children, however, basic skills like counting were usually acquired at home or in an apprenticeship or not at all.

A woodcut of a seventeenth-century schoolmaster with some of his charges.

During the sixteenth, seventeenth, and eighteenth centuries, an increasing proportion of children (including some girls) enrolled in school. They were offered more subjects, including sciences, foreign languages, and applied disciplines such as law. Rules of conduct were strictly and harshly enforced. Children were seen as weak, impulsive creatures, and their masters were charged with molding their character to conform to societal values. In the process children did acquire a set of disciplines (as well as discipline), but their achievement was purchased at the cost of pursuing their individual interests, raising their own questions, evolving at their own pace, and experimenting with different approaches. Eventually the strictness of education (and its associated view of childhood) engendered its own reaction.

Both Locke and Rousseau reacted to this rigidity. While writing from within the establishment and endorsing the mission of the schools, Locke sought more humane methods of training and more skilled methods of inculcation. In contrast, Rousseau, who was writing from outside the establishment, raised more fundamental questions regarding both the subject matter taught by schools and the conception of childhood they reflected. But neither Locke nor Rousseau was primarily an educator and so, although their general conceptions were influential, it was left to others to influence more directly the practices of the school.

While Locke was beginning to pen philosophical treaties, a Moravian bishop, John Comenius (1592-1670), was already combating tedious and ill-motivated procedures for training in languages. For example, he taught Latin and Greek by placing useful sentences in the modern and the classical languages side by side. He also insisted that a new language be taught naturally (like the mother tongue), with topical conversation, the inclusion of songs and verses, and the generous use of pictures. His *Orbis Pictus* (1657; English version, 1968), a book illustrated with familiar objects and common actions, was the most popular textbook in Europe for more than a century.

Nearly two centuries later, the Swiss educational reformer Johann Pestalozzi (1742-1827) exerted an equally decisive influence on classroom practice. Expanding on Rousseau's ideas about the development of mental powers, Pestalozzi published a series of books that emphasized training children to observe correctly, to express their ideas clearly, and to appreciate the multiple relationships among elements. Instead of using rote methods, he insisted on conveying to the child—often through vivid, sensory experience—the basic ideas of a subject matter. Like Rousseau, Pestalozzi believed that the child's mental processes changed in the course of development. He felt that education should reflect these mental stages and should help foster self-education.

Joining efforts with their philosophically oriented contemporaries, educators like Comenius and Pestalozzi fashioned a school system more truly responsive to young children's special needs and abilities. Their efforts contributed importantly to a separate discipline of pedagogy, which, in turn, helped to fuel the emerging discipline of child study.

TRENDS IN CHILDREN'S LITERATURE

Only after the printing press was invented in the fifteenth century did literacy increase and writings become widely disseminated among adults. And it was only decades later that books were written expressly for children. The first ones were either schoolbooks like Comenius's *Orbis Pictus;* folktales like Tom Thumb or Reynard the Fox, which were thought to appeal particularly to youngsters; or somber tracts (especially prevalent in the American colonies) designed to teach children moral virtue and warn them of their fate "if they did not walk in the ways of the godly and wage war with the devil" (Kiefer, 1948, p. 3).

Only in the nineteenth century did books come to be written and designed primarily for children's pleasure and amusement (Harvey-Darton, 1960). Simultaneously, children appeared more frequently as the subject of literature written either for adults or for children. Often, however, children were used symbolically, as in these lines by William Wordsworth:

A child, more than all other gifts
That earth can offer to declining man,
Brings hope with it, and forward looking thoughts.

In the latter half of the nineteenth century, some authors became known chiefly for their children's books: Robert Louis Stevenson described Treasure Island, and Beatrix Potter related the tales of Peter Rabbit and his friends. Other authors made children the dominant figures of their works, often presenting them with complexity and subtlety: Charles Dickens wrote of David Copperfield's and Oliver Twist's worlds; Mark Twain described the antics of Tom Sawyer and Huck Finn; and Lewis Carroll conveyed Alice's bizarre experiences.

Writing about and for children has, of course, continued and expanded in this century. Authors addressing an adult audience continue to use children symbolically (like Günter Grass

From Comenius's Orbis Pictus.

(1)

Orbis Sensualium Pictus,

A World of Things Obvious to the
Senses drawn in Pictures.

Invitation.   I.   Invitatio.

The Master and the Boy. | *Magister & Puer.*

M. Come, Boy, learn to . be wise. | M. Veni, Puer, disce sapere.

P. What doth this mean, *to be wise?* | P. Quid hoc est, *Sapere?*

M. To understand rightly. | M. Intelligere recte,

in *The Tin Drum*), for satirical purposes (Vladimir Nabokov in *Lolita*), and to arouse empathy (James Agee's *A Death in the Family*). And literature for children is a major industry, producing countless storybooks, picture books, textbooks, and magazines (Lane, 1971), some of which are now based on television programs.

IMPROVING TREATMENT OF CHILDREN

Despite their increasing importance in family and in literary life, children were rarely recognized as separate legal, political, or medical entities. This was due in part to the extreme fragility of their existence. Poor health care, squalid living conditions, and epidemic outbreaks could be counted on to level much of the youthful population (and adult population) of a community.

The fragility of human life had legal repercussions. Until recently, parents maintained virtually total control over their offspring. They could without penalty educate them, beat them, consign them to slavery, and even, in extreme circumstances, kill them (deMause, 1975). After the Industrial Revolution of the early nineteenth century, youngsters came to be regarded as the readiest and least costly source of labor and were often made to work in factories for twelve hours or more a day. Only in the mid-nineteenth century were children under ten excluded from the coal mines in England.

Until the eighteenth century, limited medical knowledge and the dearth of physicians resulted in scarce medical care for children. Nor did parents' attitudes encourage medical practitioners. As one physician of the time remarked: "Children, while in their infancy, especially if the young family is numerous, and the parents in straightened circumstances, are not thought of sufficient consequence to be attended to, unless some sudden or violent illness happen to give an alarm" (Armstrong, 1783, p. 6).

Anticipating legal trends, concern for children's health began to increase in the early nineteenth century. The standard of living was gradually rising. Parents displayed greater interest in their children and held hopes for preserving their health. Progressively oriented public figures urged better treatment for the disadvantaged, be they poor, blind, or young. Epidemics were better controlled. Medical knowledge was accruing, and for the first time whole books dealt with children's diseases. A few medical practitioners began to specialize in common childhood diseases (like scarlet fever); others, becoming aware of the special nature of children's capacities and thoughts, began to specialize in their mental ailments. By the end of the nineteenth century, the disciplines focusing on the child's body and those concerned with the child's mind were becoming joined.

THE RISE OF SCIENCE

One of the most important trends to occur since the Middle Ages has been the establishment of scientific inquiry as a principal and respected activity in Western civilization. Of course, curious individuals had always probed the mysteries of nature, and the ancient Greeks especially had made advances in astronomy and medicine. But excessive awe of the ancients, an unthinking adherence to dogma, and rampant superstition all thwarted substantial accumulation of knowledge for the fifteen centuries after classical times.

In the sixteenth century, however, the social, religious, and educational trends described above increased and allowed the active resumption of scientific inquiry. New facts were constantly uncovered and systematically recorded—even when, as with Columbus's discovery that the world was round, they violated established wisdom. More important, certain principles of scientific inquiry became widely accepted. There was growing interest in experimenting, devising hypotheses, determining their accuracy, and building theories that integrated past observations and led to new lines of inquiry. By the early eighteenth century, astronomers and physicists like Nicolaus Copernicus, Galileo Galilei, and Isaac Newton had laid the foundations of modern science, and there developed an increasing respect for scientific inquiry and an eagerness to apply scientific discovery to technological advances. There was widespread feeling that knowledge could continue to increase and that humanity's lot would continue to improve.

Although physics and chemistry were well launched by the eighteenth century, the most significant contribution to modern biological science did not occur until 1859, when *On the Origin of Species* by Charles Darwin (1809–82) was published. The different plant and animal species were no longer seen as God's inviolable creation. Instead, Darwin posited an evolutionary process that had over millions of years given rise to plants and animals in their present form.

Based on decades of rigorous reasoning and painstaking study of living organisms in diverse settings, Darwin's bold thesis contested the prevailing notions that humans are creatures apart from all other animals and that an external force (like God) directs evolution. Instead, he emphasized the continuity among species (such as apes and humans), the transmission of traits through heredity, and the random flavor of evolutionary processes. Included also in Darwin's formulation was a concern with the functions of various behaviors and expressions, the competition for existence among members of a species and across species, the pivotal role of the environment in modulating the struggle, and the appearance of occasional, unanticipated mutations that would have the edge in the struggle for existence. As a result of these revolutionary notions, investigators became interested in the links between humans and other species, between one's own genetic pool and that of one's offspring, and between the infant and the adult organism.

The Founding of Developmental Psychology

The events sketched above furnished the background necessary for a science of child development. On a general level, there was the increasing interest in children and the rise of scientific inquiry. Accumulation of information about population trends, diseases, education, and public welfare called attention to the particular situation of children (White, 1979). On a more specific level there were concrete questions about how best to train and educate children. Finally, and of most direct relevance, was the maturing of the discipline of biology, which became explicitly concerned with the evolution of organisms. When these trends were joined toward the end of the nineteenth century, a psychology of human development was an inevitable dividend.

BABY BIOGRAPHIES

The first phase in the history (or prehistory) of child development might aptly be called the age of baby biographies (see Kessen, 1965). In the late eighteenth century, physicians, psychologists, and loving relatives (like Mme. de Sevigné, quoted above) began to prepare comprehensive diaries in which they reported on a daily or even hourly basis happenings in a child's physical, mental, and emotional life.

One of the better, and briefer, baby biographies was in fact Charles Darwin's diary (1877) of his son's development. Darwin first described the infant's reflexes, contrasting them with behaviors that are subsequently learned. He then examined the child's sensory systems and how they are used—noting, for example, that his son gazed at a candle on his 9th day, attended to a bright-colored tassel on his 49th day, and on his

132nd day tried to seize objects that he saw. Darwin next surveyed the emergence of the principal emotions, including anger, pleasure, well-being, and affection, and the development of children's "higher senses," including reasoning powers, memory, curiosity, shyness, imitation of sounds and actions, morality, and language.

With this single diary or case study, Darwin had in fact submitted an agenda for future research. His and other baby biographies proved an excellent trigger for launching a movement that was badly in need of solid facts detailing what children of different ages could (and could not) do. Yet there was an equal need for someone who could provide organization and direction for the field.

G. STANLEY HALL'S CONTRIBUTION

G. Stanley Hall's deep interest in children and his delight in sponsoring courses, societies, and educational reforms proved a valuable combination for the emerging discipline of child study, or developmental psychology (see Grinder, 1967; G. S. Hall, 1923; D. G. Ross, 1972). Hall (1846-1924) provided forums and journals through which researchers in child study could make their findings public. As the first head of the American Psychological Association and the first president of innovative Clark University in Worcester, Massachusetts, he was in a unique position to put child study on the map.

With great energy and conviction, Hall embraced Darwin's evolutionary approach, making it the foundation of his own developmental view of psychology. Whether looking at the animal, the child, the adult, or even a social unit, Hall would search for a basic form of behavior. He would observe how both pressures in the environment and events within the organism jointly contributed to change and development. For instance, focusing on memory he would examine the development in children of the capacity to remember; trace its evolution across species from the simplest animal to the mature adult human; or consider how a group or a culture stored information in its collective memory. "We really only know things," insisted Hall, "when we trace their development from the farthest beginning through all their stages to maximal maturity and decay. Thus we shall never truly know ourselves until we know the mind of animals and most especially those in our line of descent" (quoted in Grinder, 1967, p. 215).

Hall was one of the first psychologists to conduct empirical research with children. Primarily through questionnaires, he would solicit children's views on many topics, ranging from

G. Stanley Hall

play and dolls to religion and sex, and then collate the responses, sum up percentages, make comparisons across ages, and interpret the overall significance of the findings (Hall, 1907). He ultimately conducted nearly two hundred studies of children's behaviors, attitudes, and conceptions. Although no single study was definitive, taken together they provided an initial feeling for how children viewed particular topics. Hall's influence survives today in the continuing research on many of these specific topics as well as in the general empirical activity that characterizes the field. Moreover, by describing children of different ages he pioneered in those tasks of fact finding and systematic observation that are important building blocks of any science.

Hall's interest in theoretical issues, natural for a Darwinian, also contributed to his influence. It was necessary to explore the concept of development as it pertained to children and to consider the relationships among various forms of development. Hall always tried to place his and others' data into a systematic framework and to relate them to other fields such as sociology, biology, philosophy, and education. Indeed, development became a "cause" for Hall; whether studying problem solving, memory, or doll play, he could not resist tracing its evolution and relating it to topics of widespread concern within American society.

Profoundly interested as well in pedagogical questions, Hall focused his teaching on the child's concerns and level of understanding. He pondered the medical and clinical aspects of child study in order to discover their implications for the child's physical, mental, and emotional well-being; in the process he became an advocate of the child's rights and helped create a climate in which the psychological needs of the child were taken seriously. He expanded the boundaries of child study to later periods of life, including adolescence and senescence. And, in 1909, Hall induced Sigmund Freud and his colleague Carl Jung to come to America and introduce the newly developing and highly controversial field of psychoanalysis. Hall's support of the then-radical psychoanalysts had an important influence on psychology and on intellectual history. Once again, Hall was in a key position at an important moment in the development of child study.

THE EMERGENCE OF ENVIRONMENTAL-LEARNING THEORY

G. Stanley Hall's influence on developmental psychology can be discerned today in the organismic view of development (see page 259), in the idea of stages of development, in comparisons of animals and humans, and in the focus on children's conceptions of diverse subjects. Yet, paradoxically, Hall's contributions were for years largely unrecognized, partly because many of his views—and his rather grandiose way of expressing them—ran directly counter to the psychological movement that shortly afterward became dominant in America: environmental-learning theory.

We have already encountered characteristics of the intellectual descendants of John Locke: their emphasis on environmental influences, their skepticism about a natural course of development, their belief in drill and training. In Chapter 2, we encountered other features of environmental-learning theory: a belief that development is basically continuous, without stages; a reluctance to locate an individual's behaviors within an all-inclusive framework; an avoidance of sweeping theoretical statements. Environmental-learning theorists steer clear of introspective or verbal accounts, favoring instead highly controlled experimental situations. In conducting investigations, they state a hypothesis explicitly, vary one factor at a time, analyze the data conservatively, and employ proper controls so that the effects of each variable can be judiciously evaluated. They are deeply suspicious of factors that defy careful definition and measurement, whether they are the unconscious motivations of psychoanalysis or G. Stanley Hall's levels of developmental organization.

Given these attitudes and goals, we can hardly be surprised that most environmental-learning theorists were uncomfortable with Hall's methods and ideas. To be sure, Hall also sought to apply scientific methods to child psychology, but his conceptions of science were much broader than those adhered to by the strict environmental-learning theorist. Unfortunately for Hall (and his reputation), American psychologists during the early part of the century were decidedly more sympathetic to environmental-learning theory. Because of the influence of the Russian Ivan Pavlov and the Americans J. B. Watson and (later) B. F. Skinner, the approach and assumptions of environmental-learning theory became entrenched as *the* American psychology for almost half a century.

A PRODUCTIVE ECLECTICISM

Hall did return to influence indirectly the cognitive-structuralism of Jean Piaget and his followers, a movement that can trace its roots to Rousseau's writings and that is now as pervasive as environmental-learning theory. As we noted in Chapter 2 and have seen here, cognitive-structuralists focus on the constructive mental abilities of the child, on stages and a natural course of development, and on the relations among developmental studies in various disciplines. The tension that has prevailed between the environmental-learning and cognitive-structural schools thus reflects fundamental differences in the way their proponents conceive of human nature and human experience, tensions that persist today. For educational, historical, and scientific purposes, it is useful to keep these fundamental positions in mind.

Yet the two views are not wholly incompatible; in fact, they converge in several areas. Both environmental-learning theorists and cognitive-structuralists concur on the need for unbiased observations collected under controlled conditions, the value of systematic comparisons among organisms, and the desirability of analyzing the purpose, function, and goal of behaviors. Both are proud adherents of the rational scientific tradition and, more specifically, descendants of Charles Darwin's biological and evolutionary ideas. Both groups use the scientific method in their research. Moreover, as we saw in Chapter 2, the cognitive-structural and environmental-learning perspectives are to some extent complementary. For instance, while the environmental-learning approach is particularly useful for understanding how a child remembers specific items of information, the more clinical cognitive-structural approach seems more useful in characterizing a child's moral judgments. Finally, both approaches have moved away from either making grand statements with no experimental support or drawing no inferences at all from massive experimentation.

In this interlude we have encountered complementary perspectives on child study, namely, the historical, literary, and artistic view on the one hand and the scientific view on the other. In part this dual focus is essential because children existed long before the scientific method arose. Yet the complementary approach remains valuable even *with* science. The intuition, imagination, and feeling of the nonscientist may often illuminate aspects of childhood just as convincingly (and faithfully) as the scientist's measurements can. We have seen one such instance in *Emile,* that influential and insightful study written by a philosopher who had never heard of scientific psychology. Many others can be found in paintings, books, and films that are addressed to children or that use children as their subjects.

In fact, child development should and does draw on all realms—combing literature, history, philosophy, or intuition to find ideas for scientific study, or evaluating an experimental finding by resorting to history or literature to ascertain

Family Group by Henry Moore (1948–49). In the modern era, male and female parents are seen as sharing equally in child rearing, whereas earlier times (and earlier art) featured mother and child alone. (Collection, The Museum of Modern Art, New York. A. Conger Goodyear Fund.)

whether things were always so. Many researchers are investigating broad areas such as children's feelings, imaginative powers, political attitudes, and conceptions of themselves. And in doing so, scientists have been consulting earlier writings from different disciplines, even reevaluating their own arguments in the light of these perspectives (see, for instance, Olson, 1976). Some researchers have attempted to organize children's literature, relating themes and characters to historical forces operating during the book's composition, linking the stories heard by children to their subsequent political and social behavior (for example, Bettelheim, 1976; McClelland, 1961). There is renewed interest in the history of childhood, fresh research on education, law, and medicine pertinent to children in our culture and in other cultures (see, for example, deMause, 1975). Scientific insights gleaned in past decades will certainly contribute to a fuller understanding of the children (and adults) of earlier times. And insights gained from familiarity with the full range of children (fictional as well as real, ancient as well as modern) will just as surely inform scientific investigations of childhood.

PART II

The Preschool Years

The most notable feature of children aged two, three, or four—and possibly the most important—is their ability to use language. Within a matter of months, they become able to express wishes, ask questions, follow commands, and even understand simple stories. Before long, they are speaking in complex sentences and creating tales of their own.

Preschool children are also exploring the interpersonal world, particularly the behaviors and values of their parents. They attend to the actions they see, the words they hear, the values and standards that others espouse; more generally, they come to identify in many ways with their parents. Children also adopt a sex-role identification during this period. And they internalize in conscience and in moral standards those behaviors approved by society.

Although both linguistic and social advances are crucial, children of this age stand out for their playfulness. In play, the preschooler tries out various roles and selves, infuses physical objects with imaginary existence, and experiments at the boundary of fantasy and reality. This activity may well serve as the key avenue of transition from pure sensorimotor behavior to the use of symbols for communication and self-expression.

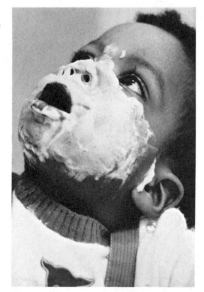

CHAPTER FOUR

Language Development

... For I was no longer a speechless infant but a speaking boy. This I remember and have since observed how I learned to speak. ... It was not that my elders taught me words ... in any set method; but I, longing by cries and broken accents and various motions of my limbs, to express my thoughts ... did ... practice the sounds in my memory. ... And thus by constantly hearing words, as they occurred in various sentences, I collected gradually for what they stood. ... Thus I exchanged with those about me these current signs of our wills, and so launched deeper into the stormy intercourse of human life.

–St. Augustine, *Confessions*

By the age of five, all normal children come to master many aspects of the language spoken in their environment. Moreover, they accomplish this without any formal language instruction. One might conclude, therefore, that language is a fairly simple system. But on examination, the rules underlying language prove so complex that no scholar has yet fully described them. In fact, it has been estimated that ten linguists, working full-time for ten years to analyze the structure of the English language, could not program a computer to learn language (Moskowitz, 1978); yet normal children (and some retarded children) acquire

language with apparent ease in the first few years following infancy. Many attempts have been made to account for how the child learns such a complex set of rules in so short a time. Nearly all the experts believe that traditional theories of learning—for example, those put forth by environmental-learning theorists—have failed to account adequately for language acquisition (Chomsky, 1959). Alternative approaches, such as those put forth by cognitive-structural theorists, have been helpful in accounting for the initial emergence of language but have not proved particularly helpful in explaining the later course of lan-

Ellen Winner was the co-author of this chapter.

guage development. Until now, the explanation of language acquisition has defied standard accounts of human development.

To gain some idea of the child's heroic accomplishment in learning language, simply read the conversation in the language of Tee-Bee in Table 4.1 while covering up the translation on the right. Of course, the process by which we adults figure out this written code is in many ways different from the process the child uses in mastering language. In some ways the child's task is easier because he learns language in a rich social context. But in other ways the child's task is far more difficult. For instance, the adult already has a first language and can master Tee-Bee by attempting to map this new language onto the first one. Moreover, this newly invented language is written out so that we can refer to it, study it, and compare one utterance to another. Finally, when the child hears spoken language, he is exposed to other sounds occurring at the same time (the dog barks, music on the radio); yet the child must distinguish between speech sounds and other environmental sounds, and he must figure out which of the many ongoing events is the topic of the conversation in which he is involved.

The Elements of Language

SOUND, MEANING, ORDER, USE

Just what is it that the language-learning child must master? Students of language describe four crucial aspects (L. Bloom, 1980; Dale, 1972, deVilliers and deVilliers, 1978; Gleason, 1965, McNeill, 1970*b*). As a start, the child must master the sound system of language (called **phonology**). As part of this task, the child must learn to produce the sounds of his language. He must also perceive the speech sounds, or **phonemes,** correctly. He must ignore those variations in speech sounds that do not signal a difference in meaning (for

example, *fenz* spoken by the mother versus *fenz* uttered by the father); and he must attend to other sound variations that do mark a difference in meaning ("bada" versus "dada," which differ only in their initial phonemes).

A second crucial capacity is mastering a word's meaning by relating it to objects or events in the world (**semantics**). In the case of words that refer to objects, children must learn that some refer only to one object (proper nouns). The child in the Tee-Bee dialogue, for instance, must learn that *Tiko* refers only to the family dog (no. 4). He must also learn that most other words that refer to objects refer to an entire class of objects (common nouns); *colot* refers to any apple and even to a picture of an apple.

An even more difficult task is to learn terms such as *more* and *less* or *this* and *that,* whose correct use depends on context. For instance, the same glass can have either *napile* (more) juice than a cup or *taner* (less) than a pitcher. Similarly, correct use of *pin* (this) and *pan* (that) depends on the distance of the object from the speaker (no. 10). A glass next to me is *this* glass for me, but it is *that* glass for someone at the other end of the table.

Grasping the sound system of language and understanding the meaning of words is not all that the child must accomplish. In most languages, including Tee-Bee, the child must also notice the order in which words are arranged. Otherwise, he is likely to equate phrases like "Dada fenz Mama" (Father likes Mother) and "Mama fenz Dada" (Mother likes Father), despite their differences in meaning. The rules governing which words may be combined, the order in which they may occur, and the way words may be inflected (using, for example, the suffixes *-ing, -ed, -s*) constitute the **syntax** (or grammar) of language.

The study of syntax may seem a rather dry topic, but the child's acquisition of the intricate rules governing different kinds of utter-

Table 4.1. A DIALOGUE IN TEE-BEE

Utterances in Tee-Bee	Action during utterance	English translation
1. *Mother:* "Mama fenz colots."	Mother sitting next to child, looking at him.	"Mother likes apples."
2. *Father:* "Dada fenz Mama."	Father enters the room smiling.	"Father likes Mother."
3. *Mother:* "Mama fenz Dada."	Mother smiles back and and kisses Father.	"Mother likes Father."
4. *Mother:* "Tiko, shhh."	Tiko, the dog, barks.	"Tiko, be silent."
5. *Father:* "Ju bada colot."	Father points to a bowl of fruit.	"I want an apple."
6. *Mother:* "Cono pepes?"	Mother speaks without looking up.	"What are you saying?"
7. *Father:* "Ju pepata, ju dena colot."	Father speaks emphatically with slight irritation.	"I said, I desire an apple."
8. *Mother:* "Bado tonor?"	Mother pours juice into two glasses.	"Do you want some juice?"
9. *Father:* "Ka."	Father nods.	"Yes."
10. *Mother:* "Bado pin el pan?"	Mother points to each glass.	"Do you want this one or that one?"
11. *Father:* "Ju bada ta sel taner. Ji teser ta sel napile."	Father points to glass that is only half-filled.	"I want the one with less. You take the one with more."
12. *Child:* "Colo."	Child points toward bowl.	"Appo."
13. *Mother:* "Ku ne peres ja taker colota?"	Mother speaks to Father.	"Why don't you give him a piece of apple?"
14. *Father:* "Rin-rin."	Father hands over apple to child.	"O.K."
15. *Child:* "Colo, colot, whee!"	Child says pleasurably.	"Appo, apple, whee!"
16. *Mother:* "Conem pan?"	Points to paper Father is carrying.	"What is that?"
17. *Father:* "Pan mem teeber bel!"	Father opens up the paper.	"That's my new magazine!"
18. *Child:* "Teeber, belber, bee, bee."	Child apparently lost in his own world.	No evident meaning in Tee-Bee or English— apparently just sound play.

ances strikes many observers as fascinating. Were language somehow deprived of syntax, we would be forced to communicate in single, unrelated words. Given syntax, we can generate an infinite array of messages from finite words: "The horse kicked the boy," "The boy kicked the horse," "Did the horse kick the boy?" "The horse didn't kick the boy." "The boy was kicked by the horse," "The boy wasn't kicked by the horse," and many more. Furthermore, by repeating a single syntactical element (such as the relative clause), one can produce a grammatical utterance of indefinite length, although it may be incomprehensible: "The horse that kicked the boy that fed the cow that ate the grain . . ."

Besides the crucial building blocks of phonology, semantics, and syntax, we must also consider the uses of language (called **pragmatics**). The pragmatic aspects of language consist of the rules that tell us how to use language effectively. For instance, the child must learn to include information in his utterance that his listener needs to know in order to understand him. If when our Tee-Bee child wants an apple he utters "colo" (no. 12) with a falling rather than a rising intonation, his parents may think he is simply showing that he knows the name for apple rather than asking for an apple. The child must also learn how others are using language. Thus when the mother says "Why don't you give him a piece of apple?" the child must recognize that the mother is asking the father to give the child a piece of apple; she is *not* asking the father to explain why he does not give the child a piece of apple!

Psycholinguistics: A Hybrid Field

The study of language acquisition combines the fields of linguistics and psychology. While linguists have traditionally focused on the rules of language (much as one might describe the rules of a game), psychologists have examined how we use language in order to gain certain ends (much as one might describe why people play games). However, in recent years the field of linguistics has exerted a profound influence on psychology.

In the mid-1950s, the linguist Noam Chomsky revolutionized the field of linguistics. Chomsky (1957) argued that the goal of linguistics should be to determine the underlying rules of language that generate *all* of the grammatical sentences of the language and *none* of the ungrammatical ones. In a series of influential works, Chomsky (1957, 1965, 1980) has analyzed the syntax of English at a highly abstract level and has proposed a complex set of rules designed to yield all possible grammatical utterances while at the same time ruling out all incorrect ones.

Linguists and philosophers have also described the phonological rules of language (Chomsky and Halle, 1968; Jakobson and Halle, 1956), the semantic rules (Katz, 1972), and the pragmatic rules (Searle, 1970). These analyses have had an important effect on the field of psychology. For in describing the rules of language, linguists make an implicit psychological claim: these rules must somehow be a part of our knowledge, for otherwise we could not use and understand language. Thus, psychologists have become interested in trying to determine how these rules are represented in the mind and whether, in fact, these rules are psychologically plausible. The results: a hybrid field called **psycholinguistics,** which focuses on adult linguistic knowledge, and a subfield called **developmental psycholinguistics,** which focuses on how children acquire the rules of language.

It is the questions posed by developmental psycholinguistics that will occupy us throughout this chapter. What capacities must the child have in order to master the rules of phonology, semantics, syntax, and pragmatics? How is it possible for the child to master the complex rules of language? Does language acquisition depend primarily on specifically linguistic skills, or does it call upon more general cognitive, problem-solving capacities? Is the child innately equipped with fundamental linguistic knowledge, or is language acquisition a matter of starting from scratch? As we will see, these questions have been addressed by a number of different methods, ranging from intensive longitudinal case studies of a few children (paralleling Piaget's studies of his own children) to cross-sectional experimental studies with many subjects.

We begin by examining the earliest stages of language acquisition—the mastery of the sound system. The infant's ability to perceive and produce the sounds of his language will be shown to be largely under the influence of maturational factors. Turning next to the child's first words, often spoken one at a time, we will see how difficult it is to pin down just how much linguistic knowledge underlies such utterances. The child is remarkably adept at making his needs known, even when he can only say one word at a time.

Our major focus then falls on the two aspects of language that have been most thoroughly studied by psycholinguists. We turn first to the puzzles surrounding the acquisition of syntax; we will see that the child's early grammatical rules, while different from those of the adult, develop in a highly ordered sequence of stages. However, the means by which children come to grasp adult syntax remain in dispute. We turn next to the other major building block of language competence, that of semantics. Here our focus falls on the development of word meanings. We will see that children are able to learn new words at an astonishing rate, but the meanings of their words often differ from adults' meanings.

In the latter part of the chapter, we turn our attention to two areas of language acquisition that were largely ignored in the initial Chomsky revolution: the child's sensitivity to

the pragmatics (or uses) of language, and **metalinguistic skill,** the ability to reflect upon the rules of language.

At the conclusion of the chapter, our attention turns to the relation of the child's language competence to his overall cognitive capacity. Here we focus on the relationship between language and thought. We will see that while in many ways language depends on other nonlinguistic cognitive skills, the acquisition of language may also stimulate advances in cognition.

The Earliest Stages of Language

HEARING AND PRODUCING THE SOUNDS OF LANGUAGE

The study of language acquisition usually starts with children's first single words at about a year of age and charts their dazzling progress over the next two years to complex syntactic forms carrying many different meanings. But the first twelve months of life are also relevant to language development.

From a very early age, infants can distinguish between speech sounds and other environmental sounds such as coughs, the bark of a dog, instrumental music, and the clanging of pots and pans (Hutt et al., 1968). Moreover, infants appear to perceive speech sounds categorically, as do adults. To understand what is meant by categorical perception, we must consider for a moment an aspect of the sound system of language. Phonologists have determined that the sounds /b/ and /p/ are closely related: they are produced in much the same way by the vocal apparatus. However, to utter /b/, the vocal chords begin to vibrate at the same time as the lips separate; to utter /p/, the vocal chords vibrate only after the lips open. This lag between the parting of the lips and the vibration of the vocal chords is called **voice onset time** (VOT).

Figure 4.1. It is unlikely that babbling has any meaning, or even serves any communicative function. Still, the practice the babbling infant receives in producing the sounds of language forms a necessary first step in language production.

Researchers have found that both adults and infants perceive sounds in categories that are defined by a specific range of VOT. Any sound within a given VOT range (−40 milliseconds to +25 milliseconds) is perceived as a /b/, while one with a VOT of +30 milliseconds is heard as /p/ (Liberman, 1970). Two sounds whose VOTs differ by 20 milliseconds are heard as the same sound if they are within the /p/ range but can be readily distinguished as two different sounds if they span the boundary between the /p/ and the /b/ range. Without the ability to perceive speech sounds categorically, language would appear chaotic—the word *baby* (or the Tee-Bee word *bada*) pronounced with slightly different VOTs by different people would be perceived each time as a different word with a different meaning!

One might expect the ability to categorize speech sounds to take a long time to develop. Yet by monitoring rates of sucking while various sounds were played, Peter Eimas and his colleagues have discovered that even one-month-old infants perceive speech categorically (Eimas et al., 1971). Changes in their rates of sucking indicate that infants draw the line between /b/ and /p/ precisely as adults do, at the +25 millisecond boundary. This finding indicates either that infants are born with the ability to perceive speech categorically or that they require only the most minimal exposure to speech before this capacity emerges. However, in light of the recent finding that infants can perceive phonological boundaries not used in their culture (Eimas, 1976), it is far more likely that this ability is present at birth. Whether such perception is made possible by specific linguistic feature detectors in the brain (as Eimas claims), or whether it is due to a physical property of the human ear that language happens to exploit, is a question that has not yet been resolved (cf. Kuhl and Miller, 1975; Trehub, 1979).

Like their perception of the sounds of language, infants' production of speech sounds also seems to be powerfully biologically determined. At about three to four months, children universally begin to babble sounds that approximate speech. Interestingly, the onset of babbling occurs at the same time even in children who are deaf or who have deaf parents who cannot respond to their babbles (Lenneberg, Rebelsky, and Nichols, 1965).

While babbling in hearing children gradually increases until it peaks between nine and twelve months, the babbling of the deaf child soon ceases, most probably because of lack of auditory feedback.

According to early theories of babbling (for example, Mowrer, 1960), the infant babbles all of the sounds in all the world's languages. The range of babbled sounds is then gradually narrowed as a result of selective reinforcement by the parents, who respond only to those sounds that occur in their own language.

There are a number of problems with this claim. To begin with, some sounds that are frequent in adult language also crop up regularly in early babbling (for example [g], [k], [h]) but are infrequent in later babbling and in the child's first words (Leopold, 1953; Winitz and Irwin, 1958). Mowrer's theory cannot predict why sounds that are frequent in the adult language should decrease in frequency for the babbling child. A second problem is that the order in which sounds emerge in babbling seems to have little to do with any kind of reinforcement on the part of the parent. Although researchers have been able to increase the amount of babbling by rewarding such production of sound, no studies have shown that the range of sounds produced can be altered by external reinforcement (Dodd, 1972). Thus the course of babbling appears to be determined less by the environment than by biological maturation. Here is one instance of the inadequacy of environmental-learning theory in accounting for the course of language acquisition.

Does babbling serve any function for the child? Babbling infants sometimes appear to be trying to communicate a specific message: their babbles often mimic the intonational patterns of adult sentences (deVilliers and deVilliers, 1978). Most likely, though, babbling reflects the child's general state of excitement (Menyuk, 1971). When children want a particular object, such as food or a toy, they usually vocalize, reach for the desired object, and (later) point to it. Babbling may also reflect sheer pleasure in playing with the sounds of language or in exercising the vocal tract.

Thus, nature appears to have superbly prepared the child to master the sound system of language. Infants discriminate accurately among speech sounds and ignore differences that are not relevant in their language. And they are able to produce a wide variety of sounds from many languages.

The Meanings of the Child's First Words

Somewhere between the ages of twelve and eighteen months, the child begins to demonstrate the capacity to represent objects and events (Piaget, 1962a). (See also Chapters 2, 7, and 9.) For instance, the child can now represent events in memory, remembering something that occurred at an earlier point in time; he can search for and retrieve an object even though it has been hidden from view; and in his symbolic play, he can use one object to stand for an imagined object (pretending, for example, that a wooden block is a car). Piaget has argued that the ability to represent information internally is a general cognitive capacity that makes symbolization possible across a range of symbol systems. On this account, the child's first words should emerge at about the same time as he begins to engage in other nonlinguistic symbolic activities. In fact, children appear to utter their first words sometime between the ages of twelve and eighteen months—at approximately the same time that they begin to demonstrate the ability to symbolize in nonlinguistic domains (Bates, 1976, 1979).

By the age of eighteen months or so, most children are producing dozens of words, usually spoken one at a time. At various moments young speakers of English will be heard uttering such recognizable sounds as "doggie," "apple," "come," "no," "milk," and "allgone." When the child says "apple," there are many ways to interpret this utterance. He may simply be labeling an apple, he may mean that he wants an apple, he may be asking whether the object on his plate is an apple, or he may be asserting that the apple has fallen on the floor. The intended meaning is usually conveyed by the child's intonation as well as by the nonverbal context.

Because the child's single words often appear to be more than simple labels, some investigators have argued that these single words signal some knowledge of the parts that make up a sentence. That is, a single word utterance is said to correspond in the child's mind to an entire proposition. The child conceives of an entire sentence, including, for example, an actor executing an action. But because of relatively superficial problems such as limited vocabulary or memory or motor limitations, he can only utter one word at a time.

This argument has been put forth most boldly by Greenfield and Smith (1976). Single words are said to correspond to one of the semantic constituents of a sentence (for example, the agent of a sentence, the "doer" of the action), while the other constituents (such as the recipient of the action or the action itself) are supplied by the nonlinguistic context. Consider the child who sees a dog run into the room and bite a cat, and who then says "doggie." Greenfield and Smith would argue that this entire event has been structured by the child in terms of semantic categories such as "agent" (the dog), "action" (bite), and "patient" (the object acted upon, in this case the cat). Because he is as yet unable to utter all three constituents ("Dog bite cat"), the child simply inserts one of these words into the structured framework *dog bites cat*. By uttering "doggie," the child is choosing to label the agent. He could also have chosen to label the patient, "cat," or the action, "bite." However, Greenfield and Smith have found that the child usually labels the aspect that is new and changing; in this case the dog, but not the cat, is the new object.

Does the child's word *doggie* really have the semantic structure of "agent"? Does the child in fact conceive of semantic categories such as agent and patient? More conservative interpretations have been offered by Lois Bloom (1973) and John Dore (1975, 1979). Bloom argues that children at the one-word stage have the motor skills necessary to say

Figure 4.2. "Top" says the child. Does that mean "I want to play with the top," or is it just a label for the object? Both kinds of interpretation of holophrases, which children utter in their second year, have been defended.

two words at a time (for instance, Bloom's daughter attached the nonsense word *widə* to many of her one-word utterances); moreover, children have enough vocabulary to say more than one word about an event (since they often utter successive single words about one event, such as *Daddy, eat, peach*).

Why, then, are words uttered in isolation at this stage? According to Bloom there is only one reasonable explanation: The child does not yet have any knowledge of how to relate words to each other within a sentence. The child has a rich conceptual representation of events, objects, and the relationship among objects. However, he does not yet know the *linguistic* code for mapping his mental representation of the relationship among objects onto the grammatical relations among words. Simply because we as adults can assign the utterance to a semantic category (agent, patient) does not mean that it has such status for the child. It is not until the child begins to combine words that we ought to grant him a knowledge of sentence structure, reasons Bloom.

Dore (1979) argues that single-word utterances are global references to situations. When the child says "doggie," he is referring to the entire event rather than simply to the agent of the action. In brief, there is no strong evidence that the child splits up events into categories corresponding to semantic categories. Dore also points out that investigators have ignored what the child is trying to do when uttering a word. He suggests that one-word utterances be interpreted as "speech acts." Single words do not correspond to sentences. Rather, through the use of different intonations, the child expresses a variety of different pragmatic intentions such as requesting, answering, demanding, or greeting. The child who says "doggie" when he is petting a dog may be labeling. When he says "doggie" with a rising intonation as the dog walks away he may be asking where the dog

is going. And when he says "doggie" in a stern falling intonation, he may be ordering the dog to come to him. By attending to intonation and nonverbal context, adults can expand the child's single word into an entire sentence corresponding to what the child intends. But this does not mean that the child has knowledge of such a sentence. We will return to the question of how children use language when we discuss the development of pragmatic skill.

Striking individual differences have been found in the uses to which children put their first words. Katherine Nelson (1973, 1981*a*) has found that some children employ words primarily for reference. When they say a word, they are likely to name an object ("ball"), to designate one of its properties ("round"), or to make some kind of comment about it ("allgone"). Other youngsters, however, use words to express a feeling or wish (a happy "hi") or to attempt to gain sustenance from the environment (an insistent "more"). These talkers are also more likely to mention other people ("Daddy") or to use stereotyped expressions ("goody-goody"), which may indicate a primary concern with relations among people and with emotional life. The two types of children use their single word utterances differently and employ different strategies in learning to express meaning. And the kinds of sentences they speak later may continue to reflect these different strategies and stresses (Starr, 1975). Other individual differences in speech styles have also been noted (K. Nelson, 1981*a*). Individual differences in language acquisition may well be a product of differences in the linguistic environments of the children learning language. Some variations have been traced to the educational status of the parents (K. Nelson, 1973), sibling birth order (K. Nelson, 1973), and social class (Allen, 1977).

As we have seen, the interpretation of one-word utterances is a psycholinguistic battleground. Some investigators feel that these words indicate a knowledge of sentence categories, while others feel that they simply indicate a knowledge of how to use words globally to convey one's needs. Once the child begins to combine words, it becomes clearer that he is using linguistic categories. But as we shall see in the next section, whether the child's early linguistic categories are as abstract as those of the adult is also controversial.

The Acquisition of Syntax

LINGUISTIC RULES AND LINGUISTIC CATEGORIES

Knowing a language cannot just mean possessing a very long list of memorized sentences, for this would not allow us to compose and understand new sentences. Knowing a language means possessing a set of rules that allow us to generate novel grammatical sentences readily ("As he ran away from the screaming crowd, the man was struck by the truck") and that prohibit us from generating ungrammatical sentences ("As he ran the screaming crowd away from, the man was struck the truck by"). And they allow us to distinguish between sentences that are essentially grammatical though nonsensical ("Colorless green ideas sleep furiously") and those that honor neither syntax nor sense ("Sleep ideas furiously green colorless").

The rules of syntax tell us how units can be combined. These units are not single words but rather abstract categories such as "subject" or "object of verb." Take the sentence "The *truck* hit the *man*" and its passive form, "The *man* was hit by the *truck*." We might assume a simple rule: switch the second and the last words to make a sentence passive. But consider a sentence such as "The *truck* with a drunken driver hit the *man*." If we follow the above rule, we would get "The *man*

with a drunken driver was hit by the *truck*." Thus the rule for passive construction cannot operate on categories as narrow as words in certain positions.

To make a long story very short, sentences are more than strings of words. They have internal structure, and their words form natural clusters, called constituents. One such cluster is the "subject." In our first example, the subject was "truck," but in our second example, the full subject, which includes all associated modifiers of "truck," was "the truck with the drunken driver." It is on categories such as these, rather than on individual words, that grammatical rules operate. They tell us, for instance, that to make a sentence passive we must reverse the subject of the sentence and the object of the main verb.

The adult's ability to perform complex **transformations** of sentences, such as changing from active to passive voice, tells us that he possesses grammatical rules that operate on abstract grammatical categories such as "subject." The child's earliest word combinations tell us that he too possesses grammatical rules. But the child's rules, and the categories on which they operate, appear to be very different from those of the adult.

In the following section we take up two questions. First, what rules do children of different ages use to generate sentences? Second, how does the child eventually arrive at adult rules and adult grammatical categories? The determination of how children, in just a few years, are able to extract the highly complex and abstract rules of syntax is not easy, and not devoid of controversy.

Figure 4.3. *Opposite:* In this overview, we can see the rapid flowering of a typical child's linguistic abilities. These language milestones follow their own logic, but they also reflect the child's more general cognitive advances during the first half-decade of life.

	Description	Examples
FIRST YEAR		
Categorical perception	Infants as young as one month categorize speech sounds in the same way as do adults.	
Babbling	At three-to-four months, children begin to babble. The order in which speech sounds emerge in babbling follows a regular sequence that seems to be independent of reinforcement and of the frequency of sounds that occur in parental speech. By the first year's end, the infant has mastered the sounds of his own language and usually produces his first words.	Baba Didi Geh-geh Mama
SECOND YEAR		
Holophrases	By the time he is eighteen months old, the infant says dozens of words, one by one.	
Duos	Toward the end of the second year, the child begins to speak in paired words, or duos, reflecting knowledge that the child has acquired on the sensorimotor level.	Allgone ball. More ball. Adam hit. My ball.
THIRD YEAR		
Modulation of meaning	The child begins to add grammatical morphemes to his sentences. Sometimes the child overgeneralizes the rules for morphemes, yielding "errors of growth."	I walking. Adam walked. Adam runned. Two mouses.
	At two and a half, the average size of a child's vocabulary is around 400 words; his vocabulary then increases very rapidly. Words may be learned in one or two exposures.	
FOURTH YEAR		
Correct but noncomplex language	Although the grammatical morphemes are now known, the child does not use many grammatical devices in one sentence, nor does he favor passive sentences, conditionals, or verb phrases with *have*. He begins to use the future tense.	
	By the time the child is three or so, he uses negatives with auxiliary verbs; by the time he is four, he asks questions in adult form.	Will Adam go? Adam can't go. Why is she crying?
	By the time the child is three and a half, the average vocabulary is over 1000 words.	
FIFTH YEAR		
Language increasingly resembles adult models	Longer and more complex relative clauses appear and two or more ideas are regularly expressed in one sentence. The child shows some distance from, or "metalinguistic awareness" of, his language.	I see what you made. You think I can do it, but I can't. You shouldn't say it that way.

THE CHILD'S GRAMMATICAL RULES

The Rules Underlying the First Word Combinations. As we have seen, many investigators feel that we are justified in assuming that the child has knowledge of syntax only when he begins to combine words. And this is precisely what children begin to do toward the end of their second year, although some individual differences may exist with respect to the precise time when children begin to tackle syntax seriously (L. Bloom, 1980).

In Part I of this book, we noted that during early infancy children become able to discriminate among persons and among objects; to execute discrete acts and combinations of actions; and to experience various feelings. Later, they increasingly draw this knowledge together as they relate perceptions and accomplishments, feelings and events into a stable physical and social world in which people and objects continue to exist over time and when removed from sight. Thus by eighteen months of age, children have begun to understand the nature of actions, objects, and causes in the world. They understand that individuals carry out actions using objects and that these actions have consequences for the objects.

Is it mere coincidence that children achieve this knowledge at about the same time as they first use words in combination? Perhaps not. Psycholinguists have garnered evidence to suggest that the child's first two-word combinations (**duos**) convey this knowledge acquired during the first eighteen months of life (see L. Bloom, 1970; Bowerman, 1973; R. Brown, 1973; Golinkoff, 1975; Schlesinger, 1971). The child, it seems, is now capturing in the symbol system of language those concepts and relations known before only on a practical, sensorimotor level.

Just what meanings are captured in children's duos? According to Roger Brown (1973), at least eleven forms of sensorimotor knowledge are regularly evident in children's two-word utterances. Among them are forms of reference, including *naming* ("That doggie" or "It cookie"); *recurrence,* reflecting the knowledge that a subject or activity can be prolonged or otherwise enriched ("More book," "More milk"); and *nonexistence,* reflecting the knowledge that an existing element can disappear from a situation ("Allgone Mommy" or "No bird"). Besides the forms of reference, there are also sets of relations, including agent-action, a person acting ("Johnny fall" or "Mommy run"); and agent-object, a person performing actions upon objects ("Daddy ball," as "Daddy throws a ball"). Table 4.2 lists all eleven forms of the duo.

A word of caution is in order, however. While adults may analyze two-word utterances into such semantic categories, it is possible that these utterances mean something different to the child. After all, children conceptualize the world differently from adults and may choose to talk about it differently (Howe, 1976). However, studies demonstrating that prelinguistic infants possess categories such as "agent" and "recipient" (Golinkoff and Kerr, 1978; Grace and Suci, 1981) provide support for the psychological reality of Brown's analysis. (See also Zachry, 1978, who demonstrated a relationship between the nonlinguistic categories of late infancy and the first sentences of the child.)

It appears, then, that children's first word combinations refer to just those meanings they have constructed during the first eighteen months of life. But these early sentences suggest another question: What rules is the child using and what are the categories on which these rules operate?

Consider the following duos; "Doggie bite," "Mommy eat," and "Hit ball." If we treat these utterances purely on a theoretical plane, as a linguist might, we could analyze these sentences in a number of ways. At one extreme, the child could have a set of rules that operate on specific individual words (when *doggie* is combined with *bite* put *doggie* first). Or rules could operate on broader semantic categories such as "agent," "action," and "patient." These are called semantic categories because they are defined by their meaning (agents refer to those things that initiate actions; patients refer to those things that are affected by an action). A rule operating on such categories might state: agent comes before action ("Doggie bite") and action comes before patient ("Hit ball").

Another possibility is that the child's rules may operate on even broader syntactic categories—"subject," "verb," "object." A category such as "subject" is broader than that of "agent" because "agent" includes only those things that carry out actions (dog biting, people running). Subjects, however, include things that do not participate in actions ("*New York* is a city"). Unlike an agent, a subject is defined entirely by position in a sentence and is not tied to meaning in any way. Similarly, the category "verb" is broader

Table 4.2. DUOS

Type	Understanding implied by duo	Example
Naming	There exists a world of objects, whose members bear names.	It ball. There doggie.
Recurrence	A substance or activity can be prolonged, made to reappear, added to, or otherwise enriched or lengthened.	More ball.
Nonexistence	An object can disappear from a situation.	Allgone ball. No doggie.
Agent-action	People do things.	Johnny fall.
Action-object	Objects are acted upon.	Put truck. Change diaper.
Agent-object	A person can perform actions on an object.	Johnny stone. Me milk.
Action-location	An action can occur in a specific place.	Sit chair. Fall floor.
Object-location	An object occupies a specific place.	Book table.
Possessor and possession	People possess objects.	My ball. Adam ball.
Attribution	Objects have characteristics.	Big ball. Little story.
Demonstrative entity	One of a set of objects can be specified.	That ball.

Source: Derived by permission of the author and publishers from Roger Brown, *A First Language: The Early Stages* (Cambridge, Mass.: Harvard University Press, 1973). Copyright © 1973 by the President and Fellows of Harvard College.

than that of "action," because verbs need not refer to actions ("John *thinks,*" "New York *is* a city"); and the category "object" is broader than that of "patient," since things that are not affected by an action may still be objects ("John sees *New York*"). If the child's rules operate on abstract, meaning-free categories such as "subject," "verb," and "object," then he may have a rule that specifies that subjects come before verbs and verbs come before objects.

We have seen that at least three types of rules and categories will yield the same sentences. Not surprisingly, there has been considerable controversy about which rules are actually invoked by children. In the 1960s because of the strong influence of Chomskian linguistics, linguists and psycholinguists attributed highly abstract categories to the child (Chomsky, 1965; McNeill, 1966). It was assumed that the child who says "Doggie bite" and "Hit ball" has rules that specify the order in which to place abstract categories such as "subject," "verb," and "object."

In the 1970s psycholinguists began to wonder whether they might be adopting an excessively adult-centered approach. Simply because we as adults can analyze the child's sentences into categories of "subject," "verb," and "object" does not mean that the child is using these categories. A number of investigators now believe that in fact the child's initial categories are much narrower and more concrete than those of the adult (Bowerman, 1976; Braine, 1976; deVilliers, 1980; Maratsos and Chalkley, 1980; Maratsos, Kuczaj, and Fox, 1978). Braine found that children often begin by using what he called "limited-scope formulae." A child might say "Hit ball," "Hit boy," and "Hit daddy," but never say "See ball," "Kiss boy," or "Kick daddy," despite the fact that he knows each of these words. From this evidence, Braine argues that there is good reason not to assume that the child is using a broad, all-purpose rule like "verb + object."

According to the most parsimonious interpretation, the child is using the rule "hit + *x*": the first word is always *hit,* but any entity can be fitted into the *x* slot.

While many of the child's initial grammatical rules may be tied to specific words (such as *hit*) there is evidence to suggest that he also uses somewhat broader *semantic* categories such as "agent" and "action." (Bowerman, 1976; deVilliers, 1980; Maratsos and Chalkley, 1980). For instance, the child may say "Mommy run," "Daddy run," "Mommy kiss," "Baby eat," and "Doggie bite." If the child produces many such sentences, each with different words, in which the first word is always an agent and the second is an action, there is justification for concluding that he has the broader rule "agent + action." However, there are two reasons why we are not justified in saying that the child is using the broadest category "subject." First of all, there are many kinds of subjects that the child never uses (nonagents, as in "*New York* is a city"). Second, given a choice between a broader and a narrower interpretation, it is preferable in science to use the simpler interpretation.

Two recent pieces of experimental evidence strengthen the claim that, even beyond the two-word stage, children's grammatical categories are narrower than those of adults. Maratsos et al. (1978) tested four- and five-year-olds' abilities to understand active and passive sentences in which the subject was an agent (for example, "Grover washed Ernie" and "Grover was washed by Ernie") and others in which the subject was an experiencer (for example, "Grover liked Ernie" and "Grover was liked by Ernie"). After hearing each sentence, children were asked, "Who did it?" When sentences were presented in the active voice, children answered correctly for each type of sentence. But in the case of the passive form, the children's performance was significantly worse for sentences in which the subject was an experiencer. This suggests that children are employing rules that operate on narrow, meaning-based categories such as "agent," but are not yet using broad categories such as "subject" that can encompass experiencers as well as agents.

A similar finding with a new twist was reported by deVilliers (1980). In this study, children were shown pictures of animal scenes, such as a pig licking a sheep. Descriptions of these pictures were presented in the passive voice ("The sheep was licked by the pig"). The children were then asked to describe similar pictures. In some of the pictures the animals were performing actions on objects (a monkey biting an alligator) while in others the animals were engaged in some nonactive situation (a lion reading a book). DeVilliers found that children generalized the passive rule to active situations more often than to nonactive ones. Thus while the children would readily say, "The alligator was *bitten* by the monkey," they were less likely to utter a passive sentence with a nonaction verb such as "The book was read by the lion" or "The hat was worn by the monkey." This finding suggests that children's rules first operate on the category "action" rather than the broader one "verb."

Thus the child's first sentences seem to be based on rules that apply either to individual words (like *hit*) or to semantically based categories (like "agent" or "action"). Even when the child expands his semantic categories into more abstract ones, the semantic category may remain represented as the most prototypical form of the abstract category. We will return to the notion of prototypes later when we examine the child's early word meanings.

The Modulation of Meaning. While children's initial sentences are limited to two words, there does not appear to be a distinct three-word stage. Once children can combine more than two words, their sentences may be three, four, or even five words long. However, the average length of a child's sentences increases steadily with age.

Children's early multiword sentences have often been called "telegraphic" (R. Brown, 1973). Just as in a telegram we omit small function words such as *the,* the young child might say "Baby eat cookie" rather than "The baby eats the cookie." However, very soon after children start to combine words, their speech becomes less and less telegraphic. They begin to include a group of small particles that subtly modulate the meaning of what they say. Roger Brown (1973) describes this phase as the period of "grammatical morphemes." **Morphemes** are the smallest units of meaning. They include all words (*mother, ball, who*) as well as any parts of words that carry meaning (*un-, -ed, -ing*). At this stage, the child begins to use little grammatical function words, prefixes, and suffixes that indicate which objects, actions, and agents are meant and how they relate to one another. These morphemes, "like an intricate sort of ivy, begin to grow up between and upon the major construction blocks, the nouns and verbs, to which [the first stage of language development] is largely limited" (R. Brown, 1973 p. 249).

Brown and his colleagues have described fourteen important morphemes and have examined the meanings they carry and the precise order in which children acquire them. (They are shown in Table 4.3.) Reviewing longitudinal speech samples of three children named Adam, Eve, and Sarah, Brown found that the rate at which these morphemes were acquired varied. However, remarkably, the three children acquired these morphemes in virtually the same order—in fact, in the very order listed in Table 4.3—even though the children did not know one another, were drawn from different social classes, racial backgrounds, and sexes, and mastered language at varying rates. The impressive parallels in the order of morpheme acquisition have been confirmed in a cross-sectional study with twenty-one subjects (deVilliers and deVilliers, 1973). Here, in these little endings and words, we encounter the best evidence yet of the orderliness of language learning.

Having documented this striking regularity in the order of morpheme acquisition, Brown sought reasons for its occurrence. He found that the morphemes acquired early are not necessarily those that the child hears most frequently. Rather, the order of acquisition seems to depend on the complexity of the meaning of each morpheme. To use appropriately such forms of the verb *to be* as *am* and *are,* for example, the child must first master

Table 4.3. GRAMMATICAL MORPHEMES IN CUSTOMARY ORDER OF ACQUISITION

Morpheme	Meanings expressed or presupposed	Examples
Present progressive	Temporary duration	I walk*ing.*
in	Containment	*In* basket.
on	Support	*On* floor.
Plural	Number	Two ball*s.*
Past irregular[a]	Earlierness[b]	It *broke.*
Possessive inflection	Possession	Adam*'s* ball.
Uncontractible copula[c]	Number; earlierness	There it *is.*
Articles	Specific-nonspecific	That *a* book. That *the* dog.
Past regular	Earlierness	Adam walk*ed.*
Third person regular	Number; earlierness	He walk*s.*
Third person irregular	Number; earlierness	He *does.* She *has.*
Uncontractible progressive auxiliary	Temporary duration; number; earlierness	This *is going.*
Contractible copula[d]	Number; earlierness	That*'s* book.
Contractible progressive auxiliary	Temporary duration; number; earlierness	I*'m* walk*ing.*

Source: By permission of the author and publishers from Roger Brown, *A First Language: The Early Stages* (Cambridge, Mass.: Harvard University Press). Copyright © 1973 by the President and Fellows of Harvard College.

[a] Formation of past tense by means other than *-ed.*

[b] Denotes understanding that an action or state may occur before the time of utterance.

[c] Use of the verb *to be* as a main verb without contraction.

[d] Use of the verb *to be* as a main verb with contraction.

the meanings of verb tenses and singulars and plurals. The syntax of the later morphemes also entails mastery of certain relations acquired earlier. Ideally, one would want to know whether semantic complexity or syntactic complexity contributes more to the order of morpheme acquisition. Unfortunately, these two forms of complexity are highly correlated: both yield roughly the same predictions. Future studies of morpheme acquisition in other cultures may help to clarify which of these competing explanations is more tenable (see Slobin, 1973).

Errors of Growth. So far we have considered how children's grammar comes to approximate that of the adult. Underlying such an approach is the assumption that, with development, the child makes fewer grammatical errors. However, this is not always the case, and this paradox yields rich dividends for the student of children's language. In fact, the occurrence of errors may offer evidence that the child's knowledge of grammar is becoming increasingly systematized. For instance, an often cited **error of growth** is that of the child who initially says "I ran," later begins to say "I runned," and still later returns to "I ran." (R. Brown, 1973). The occurrence of the incorrect "runned" is evidence that the child has extracted the -ed rule for the past tense, but has simply applied this rule too broadly.

Bowerman (in press) has documented many such errors of growth. To cite just one example, while playing a rough-and-tumble game, one three-and-a half-year-old called out "uncapture me" (meaning, "let me go"). This utterance is evidence that she understood the usage of the prefix -un, although she applied it to a verb to which it is not prefixed in English.

Errors such as these are rarely found in the earliest stages of language acquisition. Rather, they occur as the child goes beyond a superficial analysis of language (where he simply repeats forms that he has heard) and begins to extract its underlying rules. When these rules are applied too broadly (or overgeneralized) characteristic errors of growth are made. The child knows the rule but not the precise domains to which the rule can be applied. As exceptions to these rules are mastered, such errors drop out of children's speech.

The Mastery of More Complex Constructions. Even armed with fourteen morphemes, the child has by no means acquired language completely. Among the constructions still to be mastered are **wh- questions** such as *what, who, why, when,* and so on. ("Who is the boy teasing?" "What are you looking at?"); negation ("The boy is not teasing anyone," "Why isn't he teasing anyone?"); passives ("The girl was teased by the boy."); tag questions ("The boy is teasing her, *isn't he?*" "The boy is not teasing her, *is he?*"); and relative clauses ("The boy that teased the girl is my brother.").

Ursula Bellugi (1967) examined the acquisition of negation by the three children—Adam, Eve, and Sarah—studied by Brown (1973). One day Adam announced that he had a watch. When Bellugi said that she did not think he owned a watch, Adam insisted that he did. "What do you think I am, a no boy with no watch?" he asked. Clearly, Adam knew something about negation. But his idea of how to construct a negative sentence differed from that of an adult.

As can be seen in this example, children do not always utter negative sentences in correct form. And their incorrect forms are often surprisingly resistant to correction. Moskowitz (1978) reports a child who said, "Nobody don't like me." His mother corrected him by saying, "Nobody likes me." The child, however, repeated his original version. After his mother had repeated the correct form eight times, the child said, "Oh, nobody don't *likes* me."

Bellugi discovered that children pass through several distinct stages as they acquire the negative form: In the two-word stage, children combine an initial negative word (*no* or *not*) with another word, yielding utterances such as "No doggie" or "Not drink." Even when children are able to combine more than two words, they continue to place the negative word in the initial position, yielding sentences such as "No doggie bite" or "Not doggie drink." Next, children produce sentences in which the negative word is placed at some point inside the sentence, yielding, for example, "Doggie no bite." Still later, with the mastery of auxiliary verbs and contractions at about the age of three, children are able to say "Doggie doesn't bite."

What does this sequence tell us about the rules the child is using? Bellugi, along with McNeill (1970*a*), proposed the following interpretation. The child first uses a rule that says: Place the negative word first, then utter a positive statement. Later the negative marker comes to be placed inside the statement. This account has been disputed by Bloom (1970), who claimed that when the negative word occurred in the first position, the child was not negating the proposition that followed; rather, he was negating a proposition that had been uttered before. Thus, "No doggie bite" does not mean "The dog doesn't bite." Rather, it means something like "No, *I'm not going to pet that dog,* he bites." Because the negative term refers back to a previously stated or implied proposition, such uses are called *anaphoric.*

DeVilliers and deVilliers (1979) disagreed with both of these accounts and proposed a more complex view. They found that sentences beginning with a negative word sometimes negate the proposition that follows (as Bellugi claimed) and sometimes negate a pre-

viously uttered proposition (as Bloom argued). Moreover, children appear to use different forms of negative sentences to express different meanings. Some children construct sentences with the negative word in the first position in order to express the meaning of *rejection* ("No Eric come in my house"); but when they want to *deny* the truth of a statement, they place the negative inside the sentence ("It's not sharp.").

The deVilliers compared their son Nicholas' use of negatives to that of two of Brown's subjects, Adam and Eve. Contrary to what emerges in many other aspects of language acquisition, they found striking individual differences in the relationship between the form of the negatives constructed and the semantic function that these sentences served. Moreover, these individual differences were direct reflections of parental speech styles. For example, Adam's mother used negative sentences more often to deny something ("No, it's not cold out") than to reject something ("Don't do that"). Moreover, her denial sentences tended to begin with a "no," while her rejection sentences most often began with a "don't." These same patterns recurred in Adam's speech. In contrast, when Eve's mother and Nicholas's parents began a sentence with "no," this most often expressed rejection rather than denial ("No, let Daddy do it first"). Consequently, the rejection negatives of Eve and Nicholas were also produced with an initial "no." We can conclude that children at first reserve specific forms for specific functions. Only with development do children come to recognize that one syntactic form (for example, a sentence with a negative placed inside) can be used to express different meanings (in this case, denial *and* rejection).

Probing the Child's Understanding. So far we have treated the child primarily as a nonstop monologuist. But language is clearly a two-way undertaking. Children must be sensitive to the language they hear even as they must produce words on their own.

To what extent does the child of eighteen months or two years understand the linguistic flow directed to him? This is a very difficult issue to unravel. In studying language production, we have the child's own words to go on. But in examining comprehension, research must proceed almost exclusively on inference. We may assume that a two-year old child attends to and understands at least generally what we say. Otherwise he would rarely carry out our commands or answer questions. But how much more specific can we be? If we say "Get the ball" and the child brings us the ball, has he done so because he understands the whole utterance, or just the word "ball," or only because he has been called on to do something and the ball is handy? (See Chapter 7.) Does the child understand the importance of word order, or the difference in meaning between "Daddy hit Johnny" and "Johnny hit Daddy"?

To assess the child's understanding, one may simply read transcripts of conversations and attempt to deduce what has (and has not) been understood. But this method is not sufficiently reliable. Even when one has been with the child, ascertaining the extent of comprehension proves difficult. Enterprising experimenters have therefore devised indirect methods for assessing comprehension. One of the most common methods is to ask children to carry out commands. Manipulating the order of words and the kinds of cues (or miscues) provided in the context makes it possible to assess what the child does and does not understand.

As a general rule, studies have shown that the child can understand certain structures before he is able to produce them (Huttenlocher, 1974; Petretic and Tweney, 1977; Sachs and Truswell, 1978). Huttenlocher studied one

fourteen-month-old who produced no words but who was able to respond in an appropriate nonverbal fashion to questions such as "Where is your shoe?" To make sure that the child was not simply responding to one word (such as shoe), the experimenter also asked "Where is Mommy's shoe?" Similarly, Sachs and Truswell have shown that children who themselves could only produce one word at a time were able to obey multiword instructions such as "Tickle the bunny," "Tickle Raggedy," and even instructions requesting odd activities such as "Tickle the book." Because the instructions involved contrasting elements (tickle the bunny/Raggedy; kiss the bunny/Raggedy), they could not be understood by attending to only one word. And, of course, all nonlinguistic cues as to the meaning of the instructions were eliminated. These studies indicate that children who do not yet combine words may sometimes be able to attend to a number of words in order to understand an utterance.

While two-year-olds can respond to sentences that require understanding of more than one word, they do not display sensitivity to word order. Wetstone and Friedlander (1973), for instance, showed that children of this age respond in the same way to "Show the clown to Mommy" and "Mommy clown the show." The Wetstone-Friedlander research raises an intriguing question. We know that children's own speech honors correct word order to an extraordinary degree. Why, then, should these same children appear so insensitive to the word order of other speakers? Perhaps speech is controlled by mechanisms quite separate from those governing linguistic comprehension (see Goodglass and Geschwind, 1976). Whereas the children's own speech emphasizes syntax (following a regular order as a matter of course), their monitoring of others' language focuses heavily on semantics (picking out key words). If the child can

Figure 4.4. A common means of testing language comprehension is to supply some familiar objects and ask the child to act out a command. Here, the child has been asked to act out active and passive sentences: "The truck is following the car" and "The car is followed by the truck." A four-year-old is likely to interpret the passive sentence incorrectly: the order of words, rather than the inflections of the passive voice, governs the child's response.

glean meaning from what is said, word order is of minimal interest and may safely be ignored.

Although young children focus initially on familiar and highlighted words, it is not long before they become sensitive as well to the order in which sentence constituents typically occur. For instance, in a sentence composed of noun-verb-noun, the first noun is usually the agent of the action ("The man hits the ball," "The truck hits the car"). Thomas Bever (1970) demonstrated that children as young as two and three recognize this regularity. Evidence comes from children's overgeneralization errors. Given toy animals and sentences such as "The cow kicks the horse," children correctly make the toy cow into the agent, kicking the horse. But given a passive sentence such as "The horse was kicked by the cow," children of two and three make the horse do the kicking. (See Figure 4.4.) Thus they reveal that they use a strategy in which the first noun is interpreted as the agent. This

strategy works perfectly for sentences in the active voice, but when overgeneralized to passive sentences it leads with equal regularity to error.

HOW DOES SYNTAX DEVELOP?

Between the years of approximately two and five, the child adopts progressively more complex and abstract rules with which to produce and understand sentences. And, by the age of five, he has almost fully mastered adult syntax. There are only a few constructions that continue to pose problems for children, and these are all mastered by the age of nine or ten (C. Chomsky, 1969).

But we still have not confronted a challenging question: How does the child manage to figure out the exceedingly intricate and abstract syntax of his language, and how does he manage to do this in so short a time? No one has yet proposed an entirely satisfactory answer to this question. But a review of the principal attempts will provide an instructive view of major controversies in the area. Not surprisingly, they reflect the major theoretical traditions in developmental psychology (see Chapter 2). We will first review nativist explanations of language acquisition and then consider opposing explanations that focus on the importance of the special kind of environmental input the child receives.

The Nativist Claim. In one popular account, the acquisition of language has been attributed to the human biological makeup. Struck by the undeniable fact that other animals are intelligent but that only humans talk, researchers have pointed to a unique human feature: the brain's left cerebral hemisphere, which has an area specifically devoted to language (Lenneberg, 1967). This has encouraged the claim that humans are uniquely predisposed to have language, and that, despite claims to the contrary, chimpanzees are not (see the box and Figure 4.5).

The biological approach has spawned the claim that language acquisition may depend upon exposure to language during a "critical period" (Lenneberg, 1967). If a child for some reason heard no language until after puberty, then he might never begin to speak. This claim was challenged by the discovery of an abused child by the name of Genie (Fromkin et al., 1974). Although she was isolated at the age of two and was not exposed to language until she was discovered at the age thirteen, Genie was able to learn some aspects of language after puberty. However, given that certain aspects of syntax have remained beyond her reach, we cannot discard the notion of a critical or perhaps a "sensitive" period during which the brain is especially susceptible to mastering language.

Even if the brain is especially prepared to acquire language during the childhood years, the task of learning a first language remains enormously complex. This task might be facilitated, however, if the child were to come equipped with certain predispositions that he might bring to bear upon any language. Drawing on evidence from many different languages, Slobin (1973) has made such a proposal. According to Slobin, the child brings a set of strategies or "operating principles" to the learning task that determine which aspects of language are mastered most readily. For instance, children appear to be predisposed to pay special attention to the ends of words, thus rendering suffixes easier to learn than prefixes. As evidence, Slobin compared children learning the article form (*a, the*) in Bulgarian and English. In Bulgarian, articles are suffixes attached to the ends of words, while in English, articles precede the word to which they apply. Slobin reported that children learning Bulgarian acquire the article form early, while children learning English acquire it quite a bit later. Further support for this operating principle comes from experiments by Kuczaj (1979), which demonstrate that children are predisposed to learn suffixes rather than prefixes.

Other operating principles proposed by Slobin include the strategy of attending to the order of words. As evidence, he noted the tendency of even very young children to remain faithful to the word order of their language. Still another operating principle is the child's belief that grammatical markers should make sense. As evidence for this, Slobin pointed to the difficulty children have with arbitrary grammatical markers (such as the gender of articles in French, *le, la*) as compared with markers that correspond to something in the world (such as the plural form).

Slobin argues that the child brings certain information-processing strategies to the task of learning language. A more radical version of the nativist claim has been put forth by

Figure 4.5. Researchers have tried to teach chimpanzees to communicate through sign language. Here Bruno is taught to make the gestural signal for "baby."

Those Communicating Chimps

While language was once assumed to be the exclusive province of humans, psychologists have recently sought to demonstrate linguistic competence in animals. Using a variety of methods, a number of researchers have made the bold claim that chimpanzees and gorillas can be taught some form of language. Gardner and Gardner (1971) taught American Sign Language (ASL) to Washoe, a chimpanzee that they reared from infancy. Patterson (1978) taught ASL to Koko, a gorilla. Rumbaugh and his associates (Rumbaugh et al., 1974) taught a chimpanzee named Lana to type symbols on a computer, while Premack (1976) used an artificial language of plastic tokens with his chimpanzee subjects.

In each case these researchers claimed that their subjects were able to do much more than simply memorize strings of symbols. Premack used his token system to demonstrate sophisticated logical abilities, problem-solving skills, and social understanding (Premack, 1976). The other researchers made claims of varying strength that their primate subjects had mastered the rudiments of grammar, allowing them to generate novel utterances and even exhibit metalinguistic awareness.

The initial popular reaction to their claim was almost euphoric—humans were no longer unique in the animal kingdom. But within the scientific community, a reaction against these bold claims has begun to set in. Some scholars believe that the animals have not really learned language but are simply responding to subtle, unconscious, nonlinguistic cues on the part of the experimenters (Chomsky, 1976; Sebeok, 1979). Others have carefully examined all of the "utterances" of some of these chimpanzees and have found that most of them were direct imitations of a previous utterance by the experimenter (Terrace et al., 1979). As a result, some of the original researchers have considerably muted their claims, especially the claim that chimpanzees can acquire syntax. However, this research has clearly demonstrated that nonhuman primates possess sophisticated logical abilities, and that they are extremely clever at communication, even succeeding at convincing supposedly skeptical scientists that they are capable of humanlike language.

Noam Chomsky (1975), who argues that at least some knowledge of language must be innate, that certain syntactic rules and abstract linguistic categories must be part of the infant's native endowment. On what grounds does Chomsky make such a claim? The grounds are logical rather than empirical. Chomsky maintains that the rules and the categories (such as "subject of the sentence") that the adult uses are far too abstract for the child to learn from the input he receives. Thus the only plausible alternative is that the child is innately predisposed to extract the rules from the sentences that he hears.

Consider the example "Mary asked the mechanic to fix her car." We can turn this into a question and ask "Which car did Mary ask the mechanic to fix?" We have moved the element "car" up to the front of the sentence. But consider another sentence: "Mary asked the mechanic to fix her car and her TV." To turn this into a question, we must move the entire phrase "her car and her TV" to the front, yielding "Which car and TV did Mary ask the mechanic to fix?" If we just moved part of this phrase, "car," then we would get an ungrammatical sentence, "Which car did Mary ask the mechanic to fix and her TV?" Chomsky noted that, remarkably, children appear to perform this operation correctly and seemingly without effort or special practice. Given a unit such as "her car and her TV," the child somehow knows that either the entire phrase gets moved or it must be left alone.

In light of the observation that children seem to grasp such highly abstract rules at an early age and because they even get many intricate exceptions correct, Chomsky maintains that this knowledge must be innate. A new and controversial branch of study, called "learnability theory" (Wexler and Culicover, 1980; for a review see Pinker, 1979) has been developed in support of this view. Learnability

theorists attempt to prove formally that, given the sentences the child hears, there is simply no way the child could figure out the correct rules in so short a time if he proceeded purely by inference. Therefore, certain rules, those that occur in all human languages, must be quite literally "there from the start." (See the box on Twin Speech.)

The Environmentalist Claims. We can never prove that the child lacks a certain kind of knowledge. It is always possible he knows something that he does not yet reveal or that we do not know how to elicit. Those who have argued against the nativist position have therefore not attempted to prove that the child knows nothing of language at birth. Rather, they have tried to show that it may be unnecessary to posit innate knowledge. In brief, contrary to Chomsky, they take seriously the possibility that syntax can be learned from scratch, and perhaps even by nonhuman primates.

Even before Chomsky put forth his nativist claim, psychologists had attempted to demonstrate that language was entirely learned and that no innate knowledge was necessary. The explanation of language acquisition rested on two traditional standbys, imitation and reinforcement. (See Figure 4.6.) Children imitate the sentences they hear and they are corrected when they make a mistake (Mowrer, 1960; Skinner, 1957).

How does this traditional view stand up in light of the evidence? Let us first consider the notion of reinforcement. Roger Brown and Camille Hanlon (1970) examined whether parents approved or disapproved of their children's correct and incorrect utterances. They noticed that when children made syntactic errors such as "mices" or "they sings," parents understood their children and did not correct them. It was only when children made factual errors (such as calling a horse a dog)

Twin Speech

Four-year-old Virginia asks, "Dugon, thosh yom dinckin, du-ah?"

"Snup aduk, chase-dipanna," her sister replies.

What is this apparent nonsense? It is certainly not English, nor German, nor any other known language. It isn't really baby talk either. It is an example of an intriguing and potentially revealing phenomenon known as "twin speech" or "idioglossia."

Grace and Virginia Kennedy are identical twins from California who, until the age of six, spoke only their own private language. Although they could understand both the English and German spoken by others, they remained unable, or at least unwilling, to speak either language. Idioglossia has been found among other twins, but it usually disappears at an earlier age and accompanies other, more normal speech.

Little is known about how and why such speech develops. The Kennedy girls lived in rather isolated circumstances; they were cared for by their German grandmother, stayed home most of the day, and knew few other children. This unique language first appeared at about seventeen months and slowly developed into a full communication system. No one else, not even their parents, could decipher the conversation, but the two girls apparently understood each other perfectly. Experts who have examined the speech find that it has many of the markings of a "real" language: verbs, nouns, tenses, and even a structured syntax. It is not a composite of English and German, although it has some sounds in common with both.

Grace and Virginia now attend separate schools where they are in special speech handicap classes. With this help they are learning to speak English and to communicate with others. Scientists, however, remain perplexed as to the cause and significance of idioglossia. Some psycholinguists point to the invention of such systematically structured speech as evidence that some syntactic knowledge is inborn (see Gorney, 1979; Howes, 1977).

Virginia and Grace Kennedy. (Robert Burroughs/NYT PICTURES)

Figure 4.6. Parents can reinforce their children's use of language in many small ways, both consciously and unconsciously. Contrary to the traditional view of how language is learned, however, specific reinforcements do not seem to explain the child's learning of language.

that parents corrected their offspring. Parents seem to see (or "listen") right through the child's faulty grammar to his meaning, and it is only when the meaning is wrong that they step in to set things right, particularly for the young child. It seems, then, that children are not reinforced for producing grammatically correct utterances. Accordingly, it is difficult to account for their continuing syntactic progress in terms of the traditional principles of learning.

If the child is not corrected for faulty syntax, perhaps he still learns language by trying to imitate what he hears adults say. How can this claim be tested? One way is to compare the grammar of utterances that the child imitates with those that he produces spontaneously. If new grammatical forms enter the child's repertoire through imitation, then we would expect imitated utterances to be grammatically in advance of the child's spontaneous utterances. This is because we would expect that before children on their own utter a sentence with a given rule (such as negation), this form would first appear in one or more imitated utterances.

In an early study, Ervin-Tripp (1964) compared the syntax of utterances that were spontaneous with those that were imitative and found no difference between the two. She concluded that the child only imitated those forms that he already had figured out how to produce by some other mechanism. However, more recent studies, relying on more fine-grained analyses, have demonstrated that imitation may indeed play a progressive role. Bloom, Hood, and Lightbown (1974) compared the spontaneous and imitative speech of six children in the earliest stages of language acquisition. They found that some children imitated new words in grammatical constructions that they had already mastered. However, other children imitated constructions that contained familiar words, although they had not yet mastered them in their spontaneous speech. These constructions then entered their productive repertoire.

This study suggests that while imitation is highly selective (the child does not imitate everything he hears), it may in fact help at least some children learn syntax (see also Whitehurst, 1977). Just how imitation may help has been discussed by Ruth Clark (1977). She hypothesizes that once the child has imitated a given form, he is more apt to notice it the next time he hears it uttered by an adult. And by paying extra attention to this form, the child will begin to extract its grammatical structure.

In the past few years, a rather different approach has been taken by investigators who seek to demonstrate that the child could indeed learn language without any innate linguistic knowledge. Researchers have begun to examine the special nature of both the nonlinguistic and the linguistic environment of the child. Perhaps here we can find some fresh clues as to how the child conquers language.

The child does not learn language in isolation. He learns it as he interacts with other people. How important is such interaction to the acquisition of language? It may well be necessary. Moskowitz (1978) reports a case of a normal child whose parents were deaf and who thus communicated with him through sign language. They also exposed him to television so that he could learn spoken English. While this child had no difficulty mastering sign language, which he learned as he interacted with his parents, he proved unable to learn spoken English from television. At least in this case, sheer exposure to spoken language, without accompanying social interaction, was not enough for language to be acquired.

Not only is language mastered in the context of social interaction, but this interaction is also highly structured. And it may be that just this structure makes language acquisition possible. One investigator who has carefully studied the nature of the context of language acquisition is Jerome Bruner (1975a, 1978). Bruner points out that language is first encountered in the context of highly ordered interactions with an adult. Moreover, long before the child utters his first word, he has mastered the rules of nonverbal dialogue with his caretaker. The child knows how to make his needs understood, and he also knows how to interpret the intentions of his caretaker. The prelinguistic communicative framework thus provides the setting for the acquisition of language. (See Chapter 1.) Bruner believes that the linguistic functions the child must eventually master are first acquired in nonverbal communication. For instance, the child acquires the ability to *refer* through games that involve pointing to objects. In that way

the child first masters a function nonverbally; then, in the same communicative context (such as a pointing game), he comes to manifest this function in language, by naming the object in question.

While Bruner as well as other researchers (for example, Bates, 1976; Halliday, 1975) have focused on the nonverbal interaction patterns into which language is slotted, others have examined the special nature of the verbal input the child receives (Moerk, 1979; Newport, 1977; J. Phillips, 1973; Schneiderman, 1981; Snow, 1972, 1979). When adults address other adults, they ordinarily speak rapidly, use complex sentences, refer to objects and events that are not immediately present, and often break off in the middle of a sentence to begin a new one. But when adults speak to children, they modify their language quite radically; they speak at a slower rate, use much simpler syntax, refer to objects in the immediate vicinity, and rarely utter an incomplete sentence.

These modifications are probably carried out without conscious planning on the part of the adult. In fact, they are carried out by mothers, fathers, nonparents, and even by four-year-olds talking to two-year-olds (Shatz and Gelman, 1973). The same kinds of modifications have been found to be used by adults in other languages, though there may be exceptions (Schieffelin, 1979). Thus the child is confronted from the start by short, simple, grammatical models of the language that he must learn. Simplified speech seems to be particularly effective in eliciting the child's attention. For instance, Fernald (1981) and Fernald and Kuhl (1981) have shown that four-month-olds would rather hear adult-to-child speech than ordinary adult speech; they propose that this preference is due to the expanded pitch contours used in adult-to-child speech.

Investigators have demonstrated that certain aspects of the linguistic input facilitate language growth (Furrow, Nelson, and Benedict, 1979; Cross, 1978). To examine such a relationship, analyses of child and parental speech must be made at several points in time. One can then determine whether certain aspects of parental speech style heard at an early point in time correlate with advances in the child's language at a later point. If parents differ in their speech styles, and if certain speech styles (but not others) correlate with advances in the child's speech at a later point in time, one can pinpoint which aspects of parental speech do, in fact, facilitate the acquisition of language.

Newport, Gleitman, and Gleitman (1977) carried out such a study and reported only a few facilitating effects of simplified speech. However, in a more recent study, Furrow et al. (1979) reported a number of significant relations between mothers' speech when the children were one and one-half years old and the speech of the children nine months later. Simpler parental language (such as the use of short sentences and concrete nouns) predicted greater linguistic advancement in the child, while more complex language (such as the use of pronouns rather than nouns or the use of contractions) did not correlate with linguistic gains in the child.

While studies have shown that simplified speech does facilitate language acquisition, they have not shown that such input is *necessary* for language to be acquired. This claim is difficult to test. Since most children (at least in our culture) are exposed to modified speech, we cannot know whether they could learn language without such simplification. Here is where cross-cultural work proves invaluable. A recent study by Schieffelin (1979) has shown that among the Kalui of New Guinea, children are not exposed to simplified speech. Instead, they are given more direct instruction in language, such as numerous opportunities to parrot adult expressions. And yet, Kalui children learn language just as chil-

dren from any other culture do. Possibly, then, direct instruction is a form of tutelage that can substitute for simplified speech.

Even if it can be shown that simplified speech is necessary for language acquisition, such speech input may not be sufficient. As learnability theorists would argue, even with simplified speech the child might not master language without some built-in linguistic knowledge or processing strategies. While the research on parental speech styles weakens some of the more extreme nativist claims, it does not, as yet, allow us to rule out the nativist position.

Another way to investigate the role of linguistic input in language acquisition is to manipulate experimentally the language environment of the child and observe the effects of such manipulation. Some intriguing experiments by Keith Nelson (K. E. Nelson, 1980, 1981; Nelson, Denninger, and Messé, 1981) have pinned down just which aspects of the linguistic input may be most relevant to the task of learning syntax. Nelson noticed that mothers sometimes reply to their children's utterances by recasting them: the parent repeats the child's sentence, maintaining the basic meaning but altering its syntactic structure. For instance, if the child says "Dog jump," the parent may reply "Yes, the dog jumped, didn't he?" Could it be that the slight discrepancy between the child's original utterance and the parent's recasting causes the child to compare the two utterances and pay special attention to the parental form?

To test this hypothesis, Nelson intervened experimentally with two groups of children. Adults responded to children in group 1 by recasting their verbs into more complex forms. For instance, when a child asked, "Where it go?" the adult replied, "It will go there," thus putting the child's verb in the future tense. (Verbs were recast into the future, past, or conditional tense.) Children in group 2 had their utterances cast into complex questions. For instance, a child who said "The donkey ran" was told "The donkey did run, didn't he?" Here the adult added a "tag" question onto the child's sentence with the phrase "didn't he?" Other complex question forms used in recasting were "wh-" questions (who? what? etc.) and negative questions. At the end of five one-hour intervention sessions, mastery of both complex verb forms and questions was assessed. The findings demonstrated that children acquired only those forms that they received in recast form. Children who heard recast verbs advanced in their use of verb forms but not of questions, while children who heard recast questions advanced in questions but not verb forms. Exposure to recast sentences appears to help the child master the syntactic construction in question.

In the ordinary course of language acquisition, recastings may occur infrequently. Nelson argues that this does not matter. The necessary conversational events for the child's advances in syntax may be relatively rare, but what is most important is that they be just a bit discrepant from the child's most recent utterance. Such discrepancy will then elicit the child's attention and will be coded.

Thus investigators have shown that at least some, though perhaps not all, components of what adults say to children influence the acquisition of syntax. We see that children are unlikely to acquire language without learning it in the context of social interaction, and we know that children are universally exposed to a very special form of speech. But whether any aspects of the speech children hear are necessary or sufficient in order for language learning to occur, or whether they simply render language acquisition somewhat easier for the child, is not yet known. Nevertheless, by examining the influences on the child, we can begin to document the various aids that children ordinarily use to grasp the language that they hear around them.

The Development of Word Meaning

By the age of six, children know approximately fourteen thousand words. Since the process of word learning begins during the second year of life, it has been estimated that the preschool child masters nine words a day—almost one new word every waking hour (Carey, 1977a). And these words are rarely explicitly taught or defined. Rather, the child must grasp their meaning simply by noticing how and when they are used.

Susan Carey demonstrated that preschoolers are very skilled word learners. She exposed three- and four-year-olds to a novel color word, *chromium*, which was used to refer to the color olive. Before the experiment, these children described olive-colored objects as either green or brown. In the ordinary context of a nursery school day, the teacher said once to each child something like "You see those two trays over there. Bring me the chromium one. Not the red one, the chromium one." This was the child's only exposure to this new word, although he may conceivably have heard the teacher addressing a similar question to another child. At no time was the word ever defined in any other way for the child.

One week later, children were asked to select the "chromium" color from an array of nine colors. Almost half of the children selected the olive color. Thus, with only the most minimal input, children had begun to map this new word onto the domain of colors. Carey has called this "fast mapping."

Within the six-year-old's vocabulary there are, of course, many different types of words, some of which may be easier to master than others. DeVilliers and deVilliers (1978) distinguished several types of increasingly difficult words that the child must learn, including proper and common nouns and relational adjectives. Of this group, proper nouns (*Mommy, Grandma*) prove the easiest to acquire. Since each proper noun refers to only one object, the child simply has to make a one-to-one mapping of word and object. Common nouns refer to an entire class of elements (*dog* refers to all dogs). These words pose a somewhat greater challenge: now the child must map one word onto many objects. Finally, the most difficult words are relational adjectives (*more, less*). These apply to properties defined by a relative rather than an absolute standard. As we have illustrated, the same quantity of juice may be either *more* or *less* depending on the quantity to which it is compared. Here we will consider the various problems encountered by children mastering two kinds of words, common nouns and relational adjectives.

COMMON NOUNS:
WHY IS A HORSE CALLED "DOGGIE"?

The first common nouns used by the child typically refer to things that move and change and to things with which the child can interact (K. Nelson, 1973, 1979). The child is more likely to refer to a dog that he plays with than the much less interesting, static kitchen table.

There is more than one way that the child could refer to a dog. He could call it an "animal," a "dog," or a "collie." Roger Brown (1958) and Jeremy Anglin (1977) have found that children usually begin by using names that are of an intermediate level of generality—"dog"—rather than a more abstract term ("animal") or a more specific term ("collie"). This intermediate level of naming, which has been called the **basic object level** (Rosch, 1974), probably reflects parental naming practices.

When children do learn the more abstract, superordinate terms such as *animal*, they tend to first apply such terms to the most prototypical members of the category (Anglin,

1977; Mulford, 1979). The most prototypical members of a category are those members considered by the community to be the "best examples" of the category in question. For instance, most would agree that a collie is a better example of a dog than a Chihuahua. Thus, a collie is the more prototypical dog. There is high agreement among members of a culture as to what constitutes a more or a less prototypical member of a category (Rosch, 1973, 1974, 1975).

Given the category "animal," most adults would agree that a horse is a more prototypical member of this category than a butterfly. And children are more likely to call a horse "animal" than they are to label a butterfly "animal." Anglin showed that this was true even when the prototypical member of a category was less familiar than a nonprototypical member. Thus children were more likely to apply the name "animal" to a centipede than to a butterfly—yet surely children are far more familiar with butterflies than centipedes! As we suggested in the case of syntax, here is evidence that the child structures what he learns in terms of categories with highly typical members and less typical members.

One of the most often noted characteristics of early words is that they are "overextended." Thus, the child may not restrict the word *dog* to dogs, but may also apply *dog* to horses, cows, and cats. Sometimes these words apply quite widely. For example, Clark (1973) has reported one child who used the word *moon* to refer to (among other things) the moon, round marks on the window, round postmarks, and the letter O. And another child used *bird* to refer to sparrows, cows, dogs, cats, and then all moving animals.

One of the first attempts to account for such usage was proposed by Eve Clark (1973). She argued that overextensions occurred because the child's word meanings contained only the most general features of the adult definitions. The child who calls horses, cows, elephants and dogs all "doggie," Clark argued, believes that *doggie* simply means "four-legged" and "moves." The word *doggie* has only these two features, while for the adult the meaning of this word can be characterized by a much longer list of features (barks, wags its tail, is furry, and so on). According to Clark, the child applies the word *doggie* to all (and only) those things that possess these two features, gradually adding more features to the word. Consequently, since each new feature further restricts the domain of application, the word is applied to an increasingly narrow set of possible objects or referents. Eventually the child's criteria should come to match those of the adult.

Eve Clark's explanation has come under fire. One problem is that children often overextend in production but not in comprehension (Gruendel, 1977; Huttenlocher, 1974; Thomson and Chapman, 1975). For instance, the same child who uses *doggie* to refer to a dog, a horse, and an elephant may perform accurately when shown pictures of these three animals and asked to point to the dog. If he points only to the dog and never to the horse or elephant, there must be more to his meaning of dog than "four-legged" and "moves."

Why, then, does this child overextend when he himself is doing the naming? One possibility is that he does not know the word *elephant* (or does not have it in his active vocabulary). He knows that this animal with a long trunk is not a dog, but it seems somewhat *like* a dog (it has four legs and moves). Since he happens to know the word *doggie,* he uses this to refer to the elephant. Clark (1978) has revised her theory in light of such evidence and has suggested that overextensions may occur in the service of communication: when children lack a word that they need in order to converse, they simply reach into their mental lexicon for the next best

word. The child who calls an elephant "doggie" may thus not have an incomplete meaning of the word *dog* at all.

There is another reason children may overextend their words. The child who calls a crescent-shaped moon a "banana" may know the word *moon* but may choose to say *banana* in order to indicate that the moon is *like* a banana. Evidence that in some cases the child is actually using words in this analogical or metaphorical way has been offered by Nelson (K. Nelson et al., 1978), Rescorla (1980), and Winner (1979). Indeed, one of the striking aspects of early reference is its creativity. Children not only stretch their language to fill lexical gaps (Clark, in press), but they also deliberately choose to name objects in novel ways even when they know their "real" names. Examples of such early metaphorical use of words include calling a streak of skywriting "a scar on the sky," calling freckles "cornflakes," and calling a red and white stop sign "a candy cane" (Winner, McCarthy, and Gardner, 1980).

What are the bases on which words are overextended? Clark (1973) suggests that words are usually overextended on the basis of perceptual attributes. According to this view, when the child learns the word *ball* in the context of a brightly colored beach ball, he should apply this word to objects that look like the beach ball (to other round and/or bright objects). It is also possible that the child might overextend on the basis of function. In this case, he should apply the term *ball* to objects that *act* like balls—that can be rolled, thrown, and kicked (dice, stones, empty boxes).

There is no simple answer to this question. Children sometimes overextend on the basis of perceptual attributes and they also overextend on the basis of function. However, most overextensions appear to be perceptually based (Bowerman, 1977).

One of the difficulties in answering this question is that form and function are often confounded (things that can be rolled are also usually round). In order to tease apart form and function, Gentner (1978) devised an experiment using two novel objects that differed from each other in both form and function. The "jiggy" was a blue and yellow box with an orange face. When a lever was pressed, the eyes and the nose moved up and down. The "zimbo" had a red base and a clear sphere filled with candy. When its lever was pressed, candy came out. Once children had mastered the name and function of both objects, they were shown a third "hybrid" object that looked like a jiggy but functioned like a zimbo (that is, its lever produced candy). After being shown how the hybrid worked, children were asked what it should be called. Preschool children felt that it should be called a jiggy, thus extending on the basis of form. Children between ages five and fifteen felt that is should be called a zimbo, thus extending on the basis of function. And adults said that it was a jiggy, thus responding just like the preschoolers. A similar set of studies by Tomikawa and Dodd (1980) also demonstrated the perceptual bases of early word meanings. These findings suggest that, as Clark originally proposed (1973), children first use perceptual aspects of objects as a basis for extending words. Despite the fact that the preschoolers in Gentner's study were fascinated by the functions of these objects, they named on the basis of the objects' looks. Gentner suggests that perhaps children extend on the basis of what they best understand. In the preschool years, static perceptual aspects of objects, although perhaps less interesting to the child, may be understood better than dynamic, functional aspects. It may be that the older children in Gentner's study were mastering how things work and thus extended on the basis of function. Adults, who under-stand each aspect equally well, then return to form as the basis of their extensions.

RELATIONAL ADJECTIVES: DOES "LESS" EVER MEAN "MORE"?

Several years ago a team of researchers at the University of Edinburgh in Scotland became interested in children's understanding of the relational adjectives *more* and *less* (Donaldson and Wales, 1970). In one of their studies preschool children were shown two cardboard trees with hooks from which apples could be hung. Before the experiment began, apples were hung on the trees. Then, when the children were shown the two trees, they were asked, "Does one tree have more [apples] on it than the other?" or "Does one tree have less [apples] on it than the other?" A child who answered "Yes" was asked to point to the tree with more (or less). If a child answered "No" he was asked, "Is there the same number of apples on each tree?" Sometimes the trees were stocked with equal numbers of apples, sometimes unequal numbers. A child who answered that both trees held the same number would be asked to rearrange the fruits so there would be more on one tree than on the other or so there would be less on one than the other.

Preschool children were able to answer correctly when asked to point to the tree with more apples. But when asked to point to the tree with less apples, they tended to point to the tree that, in fact, had more apples. These findings were interpreted as evidence that children do not initially distinguish between the meanings of *more* and *less*. Rather, when children first hear *less,* they assume it means the same as *more.*

Eve Clark (1973) believed that the confusion of *less* and *more* could be explained in the same way as she initially explained over-extensions of nouns. The child's meanings of *more* and *less* are incomplete, that is, *more* and *less* simply mean "some kind of *amount.*" The child has not yet differentiated the two words into positive and negative poles—he has not yet attached the semantic feature "plus" to more and "minus" to less.

But why, then, should both terms mean *more* rather than *less* to the children? Clark maintains that children use opposites to refer to the most noticeable end of the dimension to which they pertain. Both *more* and *less* pertain to amount, and having *more* of something is more noticeable (and, in most cases, more desirable) than having less of it. Thus, to a child, both terms refer to *more.*

According to Clark's hypothesis, once the child acquires the feature of polarity and attaches a positive meaning to *more* and a negative meaning to *less,* these errors should disappear. This hypothesis has also been used by Clark to account for findings that appear to show that children also confuse other relational adjectives, such as *big* and *little, tall* and *short, fat* and *skinny.* The child is said to first acquire a very general meaning for each pair (he knows, first, only that *big* and *little* both refer to size, *tall* and *short* both refer to height, *fat* and *skinny* both refer to width). This leads him to confuse these opposites. Once he acquires the features of positive and negative polarity, these confusions drop out.

Since Donaldson and Wales carried out their study in 1970, many more studies of *more* and *less* have been conducted in order to test alternative explanations for children's failure to identify *more* and *less* correctly (Bartlett, 1976; Brewer and Stone, 1975; Carey, 1976, 1977b; Ehri, 1976; Kavanaugh, 1976; Palermo, 1973; Richards, 1979; Sinha, 1978; Townsend, 1976; Townsend and Erb, 1975). According to the major competing hypothesis, the child who points to the tree with more apples when asked to point to the one with less has not, in fact, confused the word *less* with *more.*

Rather, the child pays more attention to the arrays that have more objects and points to these because they are more noticeable (Huttenlocher, 1974; Palermo, 1974). Thus the child points to the tree with more not because he thinks *less* means *more,* but because he has a nonlinguistic response bias to choose the more plentiful array.

A number of studies testify that children do indeed have a bias to point to the array with more. For example, Trehub and Abramovitch (1978) showed three- and four-year-olds arrays of objects such as nuts, sticks, and flowers. The arrays were in pairs, and one had more than the other. Asked to point to the one with more or less, many children pointed to the larger array. When the children who always pointed to the one with more were asked simply to point to either one (without using the words *more* or *less*) they also pointed to the one with more.

The existence of these response biases suggests that children may not actually believe that *less* means *more.* While children do appear to understand *more* before they understand *less* (Weiner, 1974), there is no good evidence that they go through an initial period of interpreting *less* as *more.* Rather, when asked to point to the tree with less apples, since they do not know the meaning of less, they simply fall back on their nonlinguistic bias to point to the more noticeable array (the one with more).

As for confusions of the other polar adjectives, again recent studies suggest that children do not treat the negative member as if it meant the positive one. Given tasks with only two choices (a tall block and a short block identical in width) and asked to point to one member (say, the short one), children do indeed point to the tall block. But when shown an array of objects varying in several dimensions, children are more likely to confuse dimension (height versus width) than polarity (tall versus short) (Brewer and Stone,

1975; Carey and Considine, 1976). Carey and Considine presented children with four blocks: tall, short, wide, and narrow. Thus the blocks varied in terms of both dimension and polarity (the tall and the short blocks represented the two polarities of height; the wide and the narrow blocks represented the two polarities of width). Asked to point to one of the blocks (say, the skinny one), the child could make several types of errors: he could point to the wide block (in which case he would have confused polarities [wide versus narrow] but not dimension); or he could point to the short one (in which case he would have confused dimension [width versus height] but not polarity, since thin and short are both negative ends of their respective dimensions). Carey and Considine found that on such a task the child is more likely to make dimensional than polar errors. Asked to point to the skinny block, the child may point to the short one but he is unlikely to point to the tall one. Confusing *short* and *skinny* tells us that the child respects the polarity of these terms, since both are negative polarity terms. The child does not confuse *short* (negative) with *wide* (positive). It also tells us that the child is uncertain about the difference between dimensions (width, height). Thus, contrary to Clark's original position (1973), children appear to differentiate polarity before dimension. And, contrary to the original interpretation of the *more/less* studies, children seldom attribute the opposite meaning to a word.

The Development of Pragmatic Skills

We have reviewed some of the problems that the child confronts in mastering three building blocks of language—its sound system, its grammatical rules, and its meanings. But, as mentioned earlier, knowing a language involves more than mastering these three components; one must also know how to *use* language.

Long before they are able to use language to communicate, children can communicate in other ways (Bates, 1976, 1979; Escalona, 1973; Ninio and Bruner, 1978). The six-month-old who wants to focus his mother's attention on a toy picks up the object and shows it to her. Within a few months the infant will simply point to the toy and then turn to check that his mother is looking in the right direction (Bates, 1976). When infants show or point to objects, or even try to reach for them while looking pleadingly at an adult, they are using a nonlinguistic form of communication to capture the attention of another person.

Prelinguistic children seem to use gesture to communicate in two different ways. When they point to an object, they are *declaring* that the object is present. When they reach toward an object that is out of reach, they are *requesting* that object (Bates, 1976; Bruner, 1975b; Dore, 1973). Thus the prelinguistic infant has mastered two central communicative functions—declaring and requesting. And the child's early words appear to be used in the service of these same communicative functions (Antinucci and Parisi, 1973; Bates, 1976; Greenfield and Smith, 1976; Halliday, 1975).

The child's first words are often accompanied by gestures. These gestures help make the child's linguistic intentions clear. But even at the one-word stage, the child's use of intonation can be used to make sense of what he is trying to say (Dore, 1975). For instance, when the child says "ball," it is generally clear to the adult whether this is a query (Is that a ball?), a command (Give me the ball), or a declaration (That's a ball). The means by which the child renders his intention clear is intonation. "Ball" as a query may be said with a rising intonation; as a command, it is uttered with a falling intonation.

If one- and two-year-olds are able to flag their utterances so that their listeners know how these utterances are intended, does this mean that the child is deliberately taking his listener's perspective into account? Does he flag his utterances because he knows that otherwise his listener may be misled? There is no need to attribute such sophistication to the child. Our ability to understand the child at the one-word stage is most likely due to the simple fact that we as adults are skilled interpreters of children's linguistic intentions. Moreover, we do not rely solely on intonation. Most often, just as the child exploits contexts in decoding adult utterances, the adult seizes upon the nonlinguistic context as a clue to the child's meaning. Thus, "ball" said as the child is reaching for a ball just out of reach is clearly a request; "ball" said as the child points at a picture is a declaration; and "ball" said with a smile while pointing at a little green pea on a plate may well be an early form of both metaphor and humor.

Thus even very young children succeed (sometimes unintentionally) in making their communicative intentions clear. When it comes to understanding the communicative intentions of other people, a different set of skills is required. In order to "get the point" of what someone says to him, the child must be able to figure out how the speaker is using words. Suppose the child's mother, hoping to get her child to put away his toys, says to him, "Why don't you put the teddy bear in the toy box?" Without a sense of how his mother is using these words, the child could easily be misled. That is, he might think that his mother is quite literally asking him to explain why he does not put his teddy bear in the toy chest. Without an awareness of the intention behind an utterance, the listener might interpret such commonly uttered "indirect requests" literally and offer an explanation for his failure to carry out the action.

Does the child in fact ever get so misled? Remarkably, children as young as two rarely appear to miss the point of indirect requests (Shatz, 1978). There are at least two ways to explain this. We might attribute considerable sophistication to the child, granting him the ability to decode the speaker's intention. But a far simpler explanation is offered by Shatz: the child simply interprets utterances as requests for action when the context makes it appropriate to do so. That is, the child simply interprets any verbalizations addressed to him in the appropriate context as requests to carry out some plausible action with an object to which both he and the speaker are attending. Because the child is biased to respond to language with action, it often appears that he understands more than he does. While the child may appear to be sensitive to how the speaker is using language, this sophistication may in fact be illusory.

By the age of three, the child demonstrates the ability to adopt the listener's point of view. A study by deVilliers and deVilliers (1974) examined the comprehension and production of complex constructions called deictic expressions (for example, my/your, this/that). The meanings of deictic expressions change depending on who uses them and the nonlinguistic situation in which they are used. For instance, if two people are on opposite sides of a screen, "this" side of the screen for the speaker is "that" side for the listener. A speaker uses these terms from his own perspective; to understand such terms, the listener must adopt the perspective of the speaker.

The deVilliers devised a game in which experimenter and child sat on opposite sides of a table with a wall dividing the table in half. On each side of the wall there was a cup. While the child closed his eyes, the experimenter hid an M&M under one of the cups. The child was then told that the candy was on "this" side (or "that" side) of the wall. In order to locate the candy, the child had to realize that when the experimenter said "this side" the reference was to the side nearest the experimenter. In brief, the child had to realize that "this side" for the experimenter was "that side" for the child, and vice versa.

Two-year-olds had difficulty with this task. When they were told that the candy was on "this" side, they often wrongly reached for the cup on their own side, thus revealing that they had not adopted the speaker's perspective. However, by the age of three, children proved able to adopt the speaker's perspective and reached for the correct cup.

Studies by Ackerman (1978) and by Eson and Shapiro (1980) support the view of the child suggested by the deVilliers' study. Ackerman showed that first graders can make contextually sensitive interpretations of indirect speech acts. And Eson and Shapiro showed that between the ages of four and four and one-half, children become able to infer the speaker's intention even when the literal meaning of the statement yields few cues. For instance, given a piece of paper with a blank circle and given two markers, one red and one blue, and told "Don't color the circle red," four-and-one-half-year-olds are able to recognize that they are being asked to color the circle blue.

Thus, at least by the age of three or four, the child appears to be quite sensitive to the pragmatics of language. But there are other aspects of language use that are far beyond the ken of preschool-age children. The ability to detect that a statement is intended sarcastically and to distinguish a sarcastic remark from a dishonest one, or the ability to distinguish kidding from taunting, for instance, calls upon a level of pragmatic sensitivity that may well emerge only in the preadolescent years (Demorest, Silberstein, and Gardner, 1981).

METALINGUISTIC SKILL: THE ABILITY TO REFLECT ON THE FORM OF LANGUAGE

We have seen that the preschool child is able to use language in a highly rule-governed way. But is the child of this age aware of the rules that govern his speech and, more generally, of the whole realm of language? Or is he like Molière's Monsieur Jourdain, who spoke prose throughout his life without ever realizing it? The ability to reflect about language, rather than simply to use it, is called **metalinguistic skill.** Metalinguistic awareness involves a number of different kinds of understanding: the recognition that speech sounds (such as /b/) are different from other environmental sounds (such as a cough); that only some speech sounds create permissible words (*dog* is a word but *dom* is not); that words are arbitrarily related to their referent (that a dog could have been called *cat* and a cat could have been called *dog*); that words must occur in a certain order ("Eat the cake" but not "Cake the eat"); and that certain combinations are nonsensical, even though their order is correct ("Drink the milk" but not "Drink the chair").

To assess metalinguistic awareness in the *adult,* one can simply present the listener with a series of sentences, some of which are ungrammatical, and ask him to decide which ones are grammatical. Asking the child to make such grammaticality judgments may prove somewhat more problematical, as exemplified by this exchange reported in Brown and Bellugi (1964):

Experimenter: Adam, which is right, "two shoes" or "two shoe"?

Adam: Pop goes the weasel!

While it is difficult to elicit metalinguistic judgments in young children, such judgments may sometimes emerge spontaneously. For instance, when the two-year-old daughter of the psycholinguist Helen Tager-Flusberg was taught the word *spool* she commented, "Oh, dis a spool. Dat like school!" In order to elicit metalinguistic judgments systematically, investigators have devised games involving a puppet who cannot speak properly. The child is asked to detect the puppet's errors and to correct them. Using such a paradigm, Smith and Tager-Flusberg (1980) found that, on a range of metalinguistic tasks, children as young as three and four possess some awareness of the rules underlying language. The children proved able to identify a sound such as /b/ as a speech sound (as opposed to the sound of a cough) and they identified a phonemic string such as *chair* as a word (but recognized that *plek* was not a word). They had some awareness of the arbitrary nature of the word-referent relationship: asked whether a carrot could be called a *gok,* most children readily assented. And they also proved able to make grammatical judgments: they agreed that it was permissible to say "two cats" but rejected as silly a puppet who said "two chairer." Metalinguistic awareness on all tasks was found to be highly correlated with the child's level of language comprehension.

The ability to judge the correctness of word order was investigated by Gleitman, Gleitman, and Shipley (1972). They presented three two-and-one-half-year-olds with different types of sentences. Some of the sentences were well formed ("Eat the cake") and some were presented in reversed word order ("Box the open"). Children were asked to decide if a sentence was "good" or "silly."

All three children exhibited some ability to distinguish between deviant and well-formed sentences. Two of the three children were also able to offer corrections of the reversed-order sentences. However, almost all of the corrections changed the meaning, along with the grammar, of the sentences. Thus, "Box the open" was changed to "Get in the box" rather

than "Open the box." This suggests that the ability to detect that a sentence sounds wrong may emerge before the ability to recognize just which rules have been violated.

To determine whether children are in fact better able to detect semantic than syntactic violations, deVilliers and deVilliers (1972) asked two- and three-year-olds to judge and correct two types of sentences. One type violated syntactic rules of word order ("Cake the eat"). The other type was syntactically correct but violated semantic rules of meaning ("Drink the chair"). All children were able to detect errors of the latter type, but only those who were beyond the linguistic level of two-year-olds could judge and correct syntactic violations. Moreover, before they could offer direct word-order corrections they made alterations that changed the meaning of the sentences (changing "House a build" to "Live in a house," for example).

The greater difficulty of perceiving syntactic, as opposed to semantic, deviations has also been demonstrated in a study comparing metalinguistic skill in normal children and in children with special difficulties in learning language (Liles, Shulman, and Bartlett, 1977). While children with language disorders do as well as normal children when asked to detect semantic violations, they have much greater difficulty when asked to detect syntactic deviations such as word-order violations.

These studies suggest that awareness of syntactic rules is not typically found in two-year-olds. However, a year or two later, children prove able to make appropriate judgments about word order (deVilliers and deVilliers, 1972; Smith and Tager-Flusberg, 1980). But all of the studies reviewed so far asked children to make judgments about sentences and to make these judgments out of context, a rather demanding task. And so Eve Clark and Elaine Anderson (1979) used a different measure of metalinguistic awareness. They searched for instances of "spontaneous repairs" in the child's speech—instances in which the child made an error, recognized it, and spontaneously corrected it. They found that children between two and three do make such repairs. One child (aged two years, eight months) said, "The *kitty cat* is—de de spider's kissing the *kitty cat*'s back." Here the child began with the wrong word order, placing the object first, and then corrected himself. In a similar example, a child aged two years, eleven months said, "*She*—he didn't give her any food." Such utterances provide evidence that even two-year-olds may have some ability to reflect upon the rules of word order.

Although the rudiments of metalinguistic skill can be found as early as age two, this ability continues to develop during and even beyond the elementary school years (Forrest and Waller, 1979; Ryan and Ledger, 1979). Many forms of verbal humor, such as puns and riddles, depend for their success on the recognition of ambiguity (for example, that *bank* has two meanings), and thus such humor can only be appreciated once a rather sophisticated level of metalinguistic skill has been attained (see Chapters 11 and 13).

Metalinguistic skill appears to be related to reading ability (Bohannon, 1979; Ehri, 1979; Forrest and Waller, 1979; Gleitman and Rozin, 1977; Golinkoff, 1976; Ryan, in press). Perhaps the fact that one must attend to the printed word in learning to read helps the child shift attention from meaning to other aspects of language, or to language itself. Of course, as Ryan and Ledger (1979) suggest, the relationship could be bidirectional: that is, a higher level of metalinguistic awareness may help the child learn to read, as well as the reverse.

Language and Thought

Among the issues debated by philosophers, linguists, and psychologists, the relationship between linguistic and nonlinguistic capacities is a longtime favorite. In the terms of the developmental psycholinguist, the question is: Does language acquisition proceed relatively independently of other cognitive skills, or is there a significant relationship between language and thought? And if the two are related, what is the nature of this relationship? Does language acquisition depend on prior cognitive achievements, or do cognitive attainments depend on the development of linguistic ones?

Chomsky has argued that language is basically independent of thought (Piatelli-Palmarini, 1980; see also McNeill, 1970*b*). As discussed earlier in this chapter, Chomsky maintains that linguistic categories are "wired in" to the brain at birth. Language does not need to be learned: it simply unfolds. All the child needs is minimal exposure to the speech of his culture. This minimal exposure "triggers" language development, which is believed to occur independently of other intellectual activities. The fact that language develops in substantially the same way irrespective of the child's intellectual skill (excluding, of course, severely retarded children) is considered evidence in support of the thesis that language is an independent "organ of the mind."

Psycholinguists have challenged this view from two perspectives. Some have a position diametrically opposed to Chomsky, arguing that language depends on nonlinguistic cognitive achievements; and others have pointed to a bidirectional relationship between language and thought. We will examine these positions in turn.

The view that language depends on thought has been put forth by Piaget (1967) and others working in the Piagetian tradition (Bates, 1976; Cromer, 1974; Furth, 1966; Macnamara, 1972). In the view of Piaget, language is a transparent cover placed over thought, a verbal reflection of the individual's nonlinguistic knowledge: Language advances can never by themselves spawn cognitive advances; rather, cognition determines language acquisition.

To test whether language development is indeed powerless to elicit cognitive growth, one of Piaget's colleagues, Sinclair-de-Zwart (1967), taught four-, five-, and six-year-olds the correct meanings of *more* and *less*. She then tested whether this linguistic advance would bolster children's performance on a cognitive test requiring conceptual understanding of quantity. Results showed that this "language therapy" had little effect. In nearly every summary of his theory, Piaget cited this failure to improve cognitive performance as evidence that advances in language are by themselves never sufficient to stimulate advances in cognition. Further support for this position comes from Furth's studies (1966) of deaf children who lack language. By demonstrating that the cognitive development of deaf children is similar to that of hearing children, Furth's studies suggest that cognitive growth occurs independently of language.

Scholars in the Piagetian tradition (Cromer, 1974; Langer, 1981; Sinclair, 1971) have collected evidence that language does not stimulate cognitive development. Moreover, they have also tried to show that the reverse relationship obtains—that is, that cognition determines language. These researchers have pointed to the fact that linguistic and nonlinguistic categories are often formally similar to each other and that the nonlinguistic categories emerge prior to the linguistic ones. This line of evidence suggests that linguistic categories simply "map onto" previously established cognitive ones. For instance, the child first acquires the nonlinguistic concepts of "action" and "concrete object"; later he acquires the concepts "verb" and "noun." Because the nonlinguistic concepts emerge first, and because the linguistic concepts appear so similar, it is argued that linguistic concepts grow out of, and are made possible by, nonlinguistic ones. Thus, while Chomsky and his associates

argue that such linguistic categories are innate and require nothing but minimal exposure to language in order to emerge, Piagetians argue that linguistic categories such as "verb" and "noun" are only attainable once the child has mastered parallel nonlinguistic knowledge (Piaget, 1980).

Other psycholinguists have argued that the relationship between thought and language is less unidirectional than Piaget held. Without rejecting the view that there are a number of cognitive prerequisites for language, these investigators hold that certain linguistic advances may also stimulate cognitive ones.

One such view (roughly sketched in Figure 4.7) was proposed by Lev Vygotsky, a Russian psychologist. Vygotsky (1962) contends that thought and language are initially separate

Figure 4.7. Many developmentalists ponder the relationship between language and thought. Vygotsky believes that speech and thought are originally separate streams that ultimately become fused into a single meaningful amalgam.

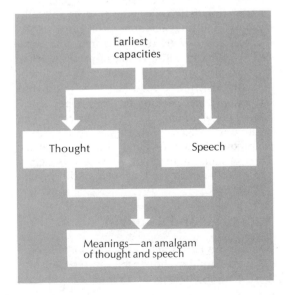

streams that develop for a time in parallel. That is, children form stable sensorimotor concepts before beginning to speak intelligibly or to understand. Similarly, they master the sounds, tone, and many words of the language before placing linguistic resources in the service of their thought.

At about the age of two, however, the independent streams join and the child's behavior changes. The child becomes curious about words and begins naming everything within sight, touch, and hearing. Vocabulary increases geometrically, several words being added each day. The child seems conscious of the symbolic property and power of language. The two lines are now inextricable. Thought becomes verbal, speech becomes rational.

Vygotsky describes certain processes in which language and thought are particularly blended. They include **inner speech,** in which the child uses language as an aid in reasoning; verbal thought, forms of reasoning that are particularly dependent on words (such as those used in political or ethical disputes); and concept development, in which words in the child's possession (such as *animal* or *fruit*) come gradually to direct the way he classifies elements (such as worms or peaches) or expresses ideas. (In Chapter 11 we shall look more closely at the steps of concept development.)

Similar arguments concerning the bidirectional relationship of language and thought have been made recently by Karmiloff-Smith (1979*a,b*), Maratsos (1981), Maratsos and Chalkley (1980), and Schlesinger (1977). An initial point stressed by these investigators is that one cannot explain all linguistic concepts by saying that they map directly onto nonlinguistic ones. For instance, Maratsos and Chalkley point out that while many verbs refer to actions (*run, jump*), not all verbs do so (*know, wish*). Moreover, certain adjectives refer to how people act (for example, *reckless*). Surely, in a nonlinguistic sense reckless is

more like *run* or *jump* than it is like a static adjective such as *red* or *big*. Thus we cannot account for the mastery of a category such as "verb" or "adjective" by simply saying that it grows out of, and maps directly onto, a non-linguistic category. Maratsos and Chalkley argue that children extract linguistic categories by attending not only to meanings of words but also to the "contexts of occurrence" within a sentence. Thus, verbs but not adjectives can be followed by *-ed;* adjectives regularly precede and modify nouns while verbs typically do not. Recognizing this can help the child form the linguistic categories "verb" and "adjective."

Thus many linguistic categories do not have precise parallels outside of language. Moreover, the formation of certain linguistic categories may actually occur prior to the formation of nonlinguistic ones. For instance, according to Schlesinger, the child may initially possess only a vague distinction between people and objects. Then, by noting that his language treats people differently from things (by placing articles such as *a* and *the* in front of common nouns but not proper ones), the child may come to make a sharper conceptual distinction between people and things.

Another investigator, Karmiloff-Smith (1979*a*) has observed that children spontaneously invent certain incorrect linguistic forms and that these forms may help the child master certain conceptual distinctions. For instance, she has found that, given a word with several meanings, children first use it to refer to only one of its senses. As they learn that the word has two meanings, they begin to "overmark" the distinction between the two meanings. While this overmarking is, in one sense, a linguistic error, it may help the child consolidate a conceptual understanding of the two meanings.

Consider one of her examples (which is based on a study with French children but which translates readily into English). The word *same* can be used to refer to similarity in kind ("We are wearing the same dress") or it can indicate identity ("I wore the same dress yesterday"). Children at first use *same* to refer only to the same kind. Given toy props and asked to act out sentences such as "The girl pushes a cow and then the boy pushes the same cow," three-year-olds made the boy push a cow of the same kind, but never the identical cow. By age five, children become aware of the dual meaning of *same*. In order to eliminate possible confusion, children in Karmiloff-Smith's study invented incorrect ways of clarifying the difference in meaning. While three-year-olds correctly said "This one is the same," meaning the same kind, five-year-olds said "This is the *same of* cow." This overmarking later disappears and the child allows one word to mean one thing in one context and another thing in another context.

The existence of such "errors of growth" also sheds light on why the child bothers to advance to adult forms of syntax. It is often said that one motivation stimulating language acquisition is the fact that more fully developed syntax allows the child to be better understood. But if successful communication is the guiding force of language development, it is difficult to understand why the child who first used a term such as *same* correctly would begin to use it incorrectly. It is also often said that the child is motivated to match his language to what he hears. But again, such a theory cannot explain why errors would develop after forms have been used correctly. Karmiloff-Smith takes a wholly different tack. She argues that the language learner is motivated by a powerful urge to discover structure and regularity in his linguistic environment, irrespective of any instrumental gains such as communication. Created in a Piagetian image, the child works on his language as he works on his physical environment—he tries to understand both by classifying their nature and by organizing their salient features into a coherent system. Children introduce these ungrammatical markers not primarily for communication purposes, then, but rather for themselves, as part of their effort to get a grip on the linguistic input.

Karmiloff-Smith (1979*b*) also found evidence of overmarking in nonlinguistic contexts such as a task in which children had to notate the correct route on a map. She argues that overmarking is not specific to language but is a general procedure used to cope with any system that the child must come to understand. Language is a "problem-solving space" for the child in just the same way as is his physical environment. Both challenge the child to perceive the similarities *and* the differences among their constituent elements. While some authorities see language and thought as wholly independent, and others see cognition as providing the motor for language, Karmiloff-Smith's cognitive-structural perspective treats both processes as arenas in which the child's most general modes of acquiring knowledge are given free rein. On this account, the child acquiring the language of Tee-Bee is not simply trying to learn Tee-Bee in order to be able to communicate his needs better; instead, he is motivated to discover the rules underlying Tee-Bee to impose order and regularity on his complex linguistic environment.

Signposts

A dialogue in the invented tongue of Tee-Bee introduced us to what is perhaps the preschool child's major cognitive task—mastering the language spoken in his surroundings. Such mastery entails four principal aspects of language: phonology, or sound in language; syntax, or grammar; semantics, or meaning; and pragmatics, or the use of language to accomplish various purposes. Insights into these aspects have come from linguists (such as Noam Chomsky), who analyze the rules of languages, and psychologists, who study how such rules are represented in the mind of the language user. This background set the stage for our method of study, developmental psycholinguistics, focusing on how children acquire these rules.

Young children pass through several stages of language learning. First, they babble a multiplicity of sounds and these sounds emerge in a fixed sequence. Then they utter their first words. These single words seem to contain a variety of meanings, though how meaningful they are is disputed. Finally, children begin to combine words into primitive sentences. Children's two-word utterances, or duos, apparently capture their sensorimotor knowledge of the world—that understanding of objects and actions we first encountered in Chapter 2. Though the precise linguistic knowledge underlying duos remains a controversial issue, the rules and the categories underlying these early sentences appear to be much narrower and less abstract than those underlying adult sentences.

Many striking features characterize children's language production. Roger Brown and his colleagues have documented the remarkable speed and regularity with which children acquire the major grammatical morphemes, such as plurals, possessives, and articles, and the principal syntactical constructions, such as questions and negatives. But not all aspects of development are equally straightforward. For instance, two-year-olds can understand more than they can produce; not until three do they appear sensitive to the contrasts in meaning signaled purely by word order. Moreover, growth does not always entail improve-

ment. Three-year-olds will make more errors than two-year-olds, but these "errors of growth" signal a greater appreciation of underlying syntactic rules.

Theorists have offered rival explanations for children's impressive ability to learn syntax. Some embrace the extreme nativism of Chomsky, while others offer environmental explanations based on the special nature of the linguistic input that the child receives. An extreme nativism remains a logical possibility, but evidence has accumulated that the nonlinguistic precursors to verbal dialogue and the various simplifications used in talking to children make unmistakable contributions to their acquisition of language.

In order to discover how well children grasp meaning in language, we shifted our attention from syntax to semantics. Examining the phenomenon of overextension, we saw that children may overextend for many reasons, ranging from unavailability of words that they understand to the desire to create a verbal metaphor. We then considered the acquisition of the relational terms *more* and *less* and concluded that, while children learn and use *more* before *less,* they rarely confuse the meaning of *less* with *more.* Rather, errors in word use tend to reflect nonlinguistic response biases as well as confusions between dimensions like height and weight.

Our next assault on aspects of language involved pragmatic skills. We found that prelinguistic infants can communicate successfully without language; and that by three or four, children are skilled language users. Children of this age are often able to adopt their listener's perspective in order to make their message clear, and they are surprisingly sensitive to the indirect requests uttered by others. We saw that the ability to reflect on the form of language, rather than look through it to its meaning, can sometimes be found in children as young as two. However, this metalinguistic awareness continues to develop throughout the elementary school years.

We concluded with a consideration of just how language and thought are related. Our review suggested that language is neither entirely independent of thought (as Chomsky contends) nor entirely dependent on thought (as Piaget maintained). Instead, language and thought may mutually influence each other. Vygotsky has pointed to the merging of the once independent strand of language and thought; various investigators have distinguished those linguistic aspects that simply map onto nonlinguistic concepts from those linguistic aspects that are learned from noting the linguistic contexts in which they occur; and Karmiloff-Smith has shown how certain vague conceptual distinctions can be captured and clarified by linguistic emphases, which in turn feed back into the child's general understanding of the topic at hand.

Once equipped with the symbol system of language, the child may approach the world on an entirely new level of sophistication and expertise. However, there are other realms of development as well, each marked by its own problems and potentials. The child's involvement with other people, his exposure to behavioral patterns of the culture as a whole, and his acquisition of appropriate sex-role traits begin to assume great importance. Essential here are those mechanisms that aid the child in acquiring desirable behavioral patterns, especially imitation and identification. Although these cannot account for linguistic development, they are crucial in determining the child's relationship to the rest of society. In the next chapter, our point of departure will be the sometimes shocking behaviors exhibited by a group of youths growing up in the absence of adult supervision. This example will lead to a consideration of some pivotal events in the affective and social realms that occur at the same time as the child is acquiring language.

CHAPTER FIVE

Entering the Social Realm

A highly developed and organized human society is one in which the individual members are interrelated in a multiplicity of different intricate and complicated ways whereby they all share a number of common interests . . . and yet, on the other hand, are more or less in conflict relative to numerous other interests which they possess only individually, or else share with one another only in small and limited groups.
—GEORGE HERBERT MEAD

In his allegorical novel *Lord of the Flies,* the British novelist William Golding describes the experiences of a group of English schoolboys who find themselves marooned on an island during a war. At first the boys act their parts as civilized young Englishmen, choosing a leader (the sensible and considerate Ralph), laying out a set of rules, attempting to relate to one another in a friendly manner. But before long, baser instincts emerge. Teasing gives way to taunts and then to shouts, the need to hunt becomes the thrill of spilling blood, play turns to violence, and two of the boys, including the gentle and empathetic Piggy, are killed in a grisly fashion. Group spirit of cooperation gives way to a life-and-

death struggle between rival forces of boys: when the adventurous, vengeful, and blood-thirsty Jack gains ascendancy over Ralph, the thin veneer of civilization has completely eroded.

Lord of the Flies raises a number of important, but disturbing, questions. What factors give rise to the cooperativeness and generosity initially displayed by the boys? Why do these break down so rapidly? How can one explain the varying proclivities toward aggressiveness found within the small group of boys? Are there ways of controlling the aggressive and violent streaks soon exhibited by some of the boys? To what extent are the behaviors of these boys a particular function of their sexual identity: would a group of girls, or a mixed group of children, have acted in the same way? Are the youngsters correct that, as one of the boys put it, they've become "just like animals"? Must we concur with Golding's pessimistic conclusion that he has traced "defects of society back to the defects of human nature" (Golding, 1962, p. 246) or should we endorse Rousseau's view that society corrupts the innocent?

In this chapter we will focus our attention on the processes whereby young children interact with other individuals as they come to enter society. We will consider the acquisition of positive or **prosocial behaviors,** like **altruism,** where one individual (or group) engages in actions designed to help another individual or group without the prospect of immediate external rewards (Mussen and Eisenberg-Berg, 1977). We will contrast these with destructive or **antisocial behaviors,** for example, when one individual intentionally inflicts injury upon another. And we will consider one of the most important forms of participation in adult society—the achievement of sex roles, where individuals come to display a certain set of behaviors and to consider themselves part of a given sex group.

In considering the ways in which children acquire these crucial patterns of behavior, we will review, in roughly historical order, four principal theoretical orientations that have been invoked by behavioral scientists: (1) the strict biological, or sociobiological, view, a contender for explaining human behaviors at least since the time of Charles Darwin; (2) the view according to psychoanalytic or Freudian theory, which was influential in behavioral sciences in the early part of the century; (3) the social-learning point of view, which at various points has been the chief competitor of the psychoanalytic view; (4) the cognitive-structural perspective, rival to both psychoanalytic and social-learning theories, which has come to the fore in the last decade or so. In considering these orientations, we will note an increasing emphasis on the child's own interpretation of persons and events in his social milieu. These four points of view have not necessarily treated all of the behaviors that we are examining here: but we will show how each has evolved a characteristic mode of explaining social activities. At the end of the chapter, we will designate certain promising contemporary ways of explaining early social development, approaches that successfully synthesize some of the major strands of the four theoretical positions.

The Contributions of Biology

Nearly all theoreticians begin their consideration of social behaviors by acknowledging the contributions of biological factors. But many do no more than acknowledge these factors before moving on to an environment-centered account of the sources of prosocial, antisocial, and sex-role behaviors. The contributions of biology are of course most evident in the area of sex, for every normal individual is born with a clear membership in either the male or female sex group. As we saw in Chapter 3, if an X chromosome from the mother joins with a Y chromosome from the father, the resulting zygote will undergo a preordained course, during which time the fetus will acquire the external genital organs of a penis and a scrotum. If the father donates an X chromosome rather than a Y chromosome, the fetus will become female and will acquire a vagina, a clitoris, and labia. These developments during intrauterine life are under the control of hormones. After birth, sexual characteristics—for example, the greater proportion of muscle tissue in males, the greater amount of fat and the more rapidly maturing bones of girls—continue under hormonal guidance.

The events of conception, the fetal period, and various hormones secreted through puberty constitute the principal biological contribution to a person's sex. Such biological facts are givens—nature's way of ensuring that the next generation will be able to mate and have offspring. Yet, increasingly, scientists are distinguishing **sex** from **gender** (Unger, 1979); an individual may be biologically a member of one sex, and yet consider himself (and be considered by others) as belonging to the other sex. In such a case the individual's gender will not coincide with his sex.

The most dramatic example of this occurs in cases where the individual has all the features of one sex group and yet, through a combination of factors, comes to think of himself (or herself) as belonging to the opposite sex. A well-known case is that of the British writer James Morris. Known for his journalism and travelogues, he had achieved international celebrity in 1953 when he accompanied explorers part way up Mount Everest. Then in 1973 Morris shocked the public by announcing that he had been receiving sex-change treatments. Beneath his seemingly rugged, tough exterior, Morris had secretly wished to be a woman. In fact, since the age of three he had felt he had been born into the wrong body. His *sex* had been masculine; but his *gender* or **psychosexual identity** was feminine.

Morris's feminine desires eventually became so intense that he resolved to transform his sex. Initially, he received hormone treatments that changed his secondary sexual characteristics, such as beard growth and voice pitch. Ultimately, he underwent a complete sex-change operation that removed his genitals and supplied him with a vagina. The surgery simply aligned sex and gender. James Morris had become Jan Morris—she was now emotionally, psychologically, and physically a woman (Morris, 1974). Explaining the case of J. Morris, and others with anomalous sex-role

identities, should provide a daunting challenge to every theorist of social development.

For well over a century, one group of social scientists believed that biological factors provide the best, and most parsimonious, explanation for social behaviors. Certainly, when it comes to explaining sex-appropriate behavior the biological point of view has seemed plausible. But recently a vocal group of scientists has endorsed the field of **sociobiology,** a new discipline somewhat related to ethology, which seeks to demonstrate the determining role of biology in other prosocial and antisocial behaviors as well. Making the argument that human beings are by nature aggressive has been relatively straightforward (though not, to be sure, uncontroversial). But sociobiologists go on to argue that humanity's prosocial inclinations—the tendency to be altruistic or cooperative—are encoded in one's gene structure to the same extent as the color of one's eyes or the tendency to be color-blind.

Stimulated by impressive studies with insects and other infrahuman species, these researchers underscore the selective advantage in evolution of sacrificing one's own niche, or even one's own life, in order to increase the likelihood that one's genes will survive (E. O. Wilson, 1975). Honeybee workers will lay down their lives in order to repel an intruder and ensure the survival of their colonies; mother birds will act as if their wings are broken to draw a predator's attention away from her helpless young ones; chimpanzees will help their conspecifics by leading others to food. All these efforts are undertaken to increase the probability that close relatives will survive. The great British biologist J. B. S. Haldane was asked whether he, as an evolutionist, would give up his life for his brother. His reply: "For one brother? No. But for three brothers, yes . . . or nine cousins" (quoted in Barash, 1978).

While not necessarily embracing the sociobiological position totally, many psychologists

Figure 5.1. In making a transition from James to Jan, J. Morris underwent not only a sexual operation but also a change in clothing, hair style, and other obvious gender features. More subtle changes in body position, gesture, and facial expressions can also be seen in this series of photos.

stress the contributions of biological factors to social behaviors. They note that certain differences in behavior can be discerned shortly after birth: for example, female infants are more sensitive to sound, more startled by loud noises, while infant boys are from the first more awake, more active motorically, and more irritable (Moss, 1967; Phillips, King, and DuBois, 1978). And they speculate that these differences are best attributed to genetic factors (Freedman, 1976; Restak, 1979a; Schmeck, 1980; Witelson, 1977; Wittig and Peterson, 1979). In time these genetically programmed differences give rise to different styles of play and different styles of interaction with humans and with toys (Smith and Lloyd, 1978). In a way reminiscent of *Lord of the Flies*, boys as young as three or four will naturally establish pecking orders, ranking themselves in terms of toughness and tending to overrate their toughness (even as girls do not undertake such comparability spontaneously, and when asked to do so, favor lower ratings for themselves) (Freedman, 1976). It should be stressed that while these sex differences are reliably found, they do not indicate a dichotomous division, with boys being one way and girls another. Indeed, the overlap between girls and boys is considerable on all of these variables; the variations only reflect differences in the mean amount of activity.

The evidence in favor of the sociobiological interpretation of insect behavior is persuasive but many critics are much less sympathetic as regards its application to the human realm (Gould, 1976; Gregory, Silvers, and Sutch, 1978; Tieger, 1980). In the view of these critics, the invoking of genetic principles is both unnecessary and possibly wrongheaded. Human beings are capable of learning rules and becoming part of cultures that can have widely divergent values and behaviors, and these can readily override whatever tendencies toward pro- or antisocial behaviors might be encoded in the genes. How else, ask such critics, can we account within the same species for cultures that are known for their peacefulness, generosity, cooperativeness, and nonaggressiveness, like the Hopi Indians, and at the same time for a culture like the Ik tribe of Uganda, which displays treachery, scheming, and murderousness as a way of life (Mead, 1935; Mussen and Eisenberg-Berg, 1977; Turnbull, 1974)? The sociobiological answer to this line of criticism has not been recorded. In one possible line of reasoning, the altruistic way would be seen as the norm, encoded in the gene, while the antisocial behaviors would be seen as genetically encoded reactions to severe stress—much like the actions of a normally peaceful animal when its life, or the lives of its children, is at stake.

Sociobiology represents a relatively new attempt to account for socialization—the way in which the young child's behaviors and attitudes come to be formed, by inherent factors and by parents, family members, and other individuals and institutions of the surrounding society. Even atypical sexual behavior, such as homosexuality, is seen by sociobiologists as a genetically determined proclivity (E. O. Wilson, 1978). But there are also three other participants in the debate—the Freudian (**psychoanalytic**), the environmental-learning (or **social-learning**), and the **cognitive-structural** schools. In our review of these positions, it is logical that we begin with the psychoanalytic. Freud's approach stands out: it was the first to gain widespread attention; it has been extremely influential for decades (though less so today); it developed an explanation of identification, the major psychological mechanism that has been proposed for explaining the in-

creasing resemblance between the behavior of young and old; and it put forth a leitmotif that we follow in our discussion—that the behaviors treated here, sex-role as well as prosocial and antisocial, are to some extent interdependent. For these reasons and despite its controversial nature, Freud's approach remains our best point of departure.

The Classical Theory of Identification

Trained originally as a neurologist in the 1870s, Sigmund Freud became increasingly interested in the psychology of human behavior. He noted that many bizarre behaviors displayed by his patients resulted from prior traumatic experiences rather than from physical disorders. For instance, a patient with a paralyzed arm might lose that symptom once he was able to describe and thus relive a prior anxiety-provoking experience. From such insights Freud gradually developed a new form of treatment for emotional trauma and personality disorders. **Psychoanalysis** involves "talking out" old experiences, analysis of dreams, and free association. After making sense of their past, patients can better cope with how they feel today.

Freud also developed a now-famous theory of the human personality and the human mind. The theory stresses the importance for later development of events in early childhood; the centrality of unconscious motivations (the factors, invisible to an individual, that actually prompt his behavior); and the importance of **defense mechanisms,** such as repression (forgetting anxiety-producing experiences), regression (exhibiting earlier, more primitive forms of behavior), and sublimation (engaging in a substitute activity, like painting, rather than satisfying basic drives). Absolutely central to all of Freud's work is the assertion that sexual factors motivate behavior and, if not adequately expressed, can cripple a person's personality (S. Freud, 1938*b*, 1957, 1965*b*, *c*).

SIGMUND FREUD'S PSYCHOSEXUAL VIEW

Though Freud did not himself work with young children, he had an abiding interest in early childhood. Analyzing the recollections of his adult patients, Freud concluded that children pass through a series of stages, summarized in Figure 5.2, each of which could have important ramifications for adult neuroses. Indeed, he was among the first scientists to insist on the importance of the events of a child's first year.

The Oral Stage. Freud proposed that a substance, called **sexual** or **libidinal energy,** governs important behaviors throughout life. During the first year or so, called the **oral stage,** the child's libidinal energy is centered in the area of the mouth. This region is associated with important behaviors such as sucking, with crucial drives such as hunger, and with potent psychological states such as gratification. A child whose needs are unsatisfied (or, for that matter, overindulged) during this period will become an "oral personality"—craving oral satisfaction (in food and in love), perhaps addicted to drugs, searching for trust and relatedness that can never be achieved.

The Anal Stage. If the child's needs are satisfied during the oral stage, libidinal energy will come to focus next on the organs of excretion. This **anal stage** in the child's second or third year coincides with a central event in his life—the start of toilet training. Strong feelings of pleasure or anxiety surround occasions for elimination. If the child can cope with the drives of retention and elimination that dominate this period, development will proceed smoothly. Those youngsters who can-

not negotiate these situations may be preoccupied with cleanliness, orderliness, and possessing goods throughout life. Obsessive and compulsive traits may pervade their "anal personalities."

The Oedipal Stage. Generating much controversy in his day, Freud asserted that between the ages of four and six—the **Oedipal stage**—libidinal energy comes to center about the genitals. Children are subject to sexual longings similar to those that had been attributed only to adults during Freud's time. Children have strong psychological feelings about their sexual organs and these feelings will color later psychological and sexual development.

Concentrating on the male child, Freud defined sexual issues prominent in the four- or five-year-old. A boy is preoccupied with and proud of his penis, yet fears both the possibility of castration and the superior size of his father's penis. He wishes to get rid of his father's penis and he longs for a larger one of his own that he can use, in grown-up fashion, to help gain other possessions.

Sometime between the ages of three and six a child must come to grips with his sex role as well as his relation to his parents and to his society. Focusing again on the male child, Freud dealt with the unconscious strivings and conflicting feelings that haunt the child of this age. He is growing, yet dwarfed by his parents. He craves parental attention, but he cannot always command it. Most significantly, he strives to remain intimate with his parents, especially his mother, yet he is expected (and, in part, desires) to venture forth on his own.

Freud spotted a convenient solution to these conflicts in the Greek myth of King Oedipus. Oedipus unknowingly killed his father, thereby removing his chief rival to his mother's affection. By then marrying his mother, Oedipus ensured a permanent tie to

Stage	Form of gratification	Possible results of conflicts or frustration of gratification
ORAL First year	The infant obtains gratification by stimulation of the oral area—by putting things in the mouth or by biting.	Adult may be overly acquisitive, always attempting to take things in (as seen in drug addiction, excessive eating, smoking) or overly dependent on others. Orality might also be expressed in aggression, as in the case of a very sarcastic or cynical person.
ANAL Second through third year	The child obtains gratification by exercise of anal musculature—by elimination or retention.	Two extremes may result: an adult who is messy and wasteful, or one who is preoccupied with cleanliness, orderliness, and possession of goods. Obsessive and compulsive traits may pervade the individual's personality. Overcautiousness, stinginess, and introversion may result. The adult may suppress emotions excessively.
OEDIPAL Fourth through sixth years	Gratification through manipulation and stimulation of genitals.	For adult males: may be inordinately tied to mother; male homosexuality may result. For females: lack of castration anxiety leads to inadequate superego development. Female homosexuality may also result.
LATENCY Seventh year through puberty	Libido submerged; it does not localize itself in any bodily area.	Adult may be withdrawn, overly individualistic, or deviant.
GENITAL Adolescent and adult years	Gratification in the genital area in adult form, through reproductive functions.	

Figure 5.2. Psychosexual development according to standard Freudian theory.

his beloved nurturer, guaranteed that no one else could compete for her affection, and established himself as the most potent male figure (shades of *Lord of the Flies!*). Noting that variations of this myth recur in other ages and cultures, Freud contended that it captures a central psychological truth: every young boy envies his father's intimate relationship with his mother. He unconsciously wants to eliminate his father so that he can have his mother all to himself.

Identification. But what is possible in myth is not always plausible in life. The child can neither have his mother nor kill his father, and he begins to feel guilty about these "bad thoughts." He can relieve his guilt and anxiety about these unseemly feelings toward his father by striving to become just like him. Thus, through **identification** the boy elects to resemble the dominant male figure in as many respects as possible.

Two important consequences accompany this identification with the parent. First, the child begins to adopt not only the behaviors but also the attitudes, opinions, and standards of the elder generation. Second, the male child chooses the sex role he will assume in later life. By identifying with the father, the boy elects to go through life as a member of the group of males and to fulfill the accepted male role in sexual encounters.

If fully achieved, such an identification is irreversible. The person will always view himself as male. But if it is somehow incomplete—if the child does not satisfactorily navigate the Oedipus phase—he may end up with a full-blown Oedipus complex and even in adulthood continue to fear his father and desire his mother. Or he may even, like James Morris, come to identify so completely with his mother that he thinks of himself as having her gender.

Identification as described by Freud became one of the most powerful ideas in psychology. By incorporating the features of one or both parents, the child, girl as well as boy, comes to resemble them. Indeed, children eventually **internalize** aspects of their parents and society, becoming able to follow their standards independently. They do what their parents *would* do. Or, in cases where insufficient identification produces alienation, children do just what their parents would *not* do rather than following a more neutral, third course. Aggressive and other antisocial behaviors, a part of the human condition according to Freud's pessimistic account (1961), become extremely likely in such cases.

By virtue of identification, children acquire a conscience, or **superego** (Freud, 1965*b*) that induces them to feel unhappy or guilty if they should violate the expectations of others. This portion of their mental personality holds up very high standards of behavior and exacts feelings of severe regret and guilt when those standards are not met. Prosocial behaviors derive directly from the dictates of the superego (just as antisocial behaviors are inevitable in the absence of a developed superego). The superego serves also as a link to the past: by incorporating the values of his parents, the child is incorporating their superegos, which in turn were derived from preceding generations.

Despite many problems and great controversy (which we shall review in the next section), Freud's account of early psychosexual development and identification has endured. It is still a point of departure for most discussions of the acquisition of sex-role identity, perhaps because the theory successfully organizes a mass of events generally considered crucial in the world of the three-to-six-year-old child. Until a more plausible account has been devised, Freud's is likely to retain its prominence in discussions of these matters.

CRITIQUE OF FREUD'S THEORY

Responses to Freud's theory have ranged widely. Some psychologists and psychoanalysts find his position so persuasive that they still embrace it. Others, although generally sympathetic, have softened Freud's heavy emphasis on sexual factors. Erik Erikson, for example, says little about lusting for one's mother and speaks instead of a crisis during the preschool years between a desire to take the initiative and a feeling of guilt about one's own actions and thought (Erikson, 1963) (see Figure 1.14). Others accept the concept of identification but adopt other explanations for it. And still others question the utility of any such concept.

One of the most important criticisms of Freud's ideas is that the Oedipus tale cannot be applied to little girls' behaviors. After all, if the development of the little girl exactly parallels that of the little boy, then she too

Figure 5.3. The opportunity to observe the actions of his father, to imitate them and participate in them, is a crucial ingredient in the little boy's eventual identification with the male sex role.

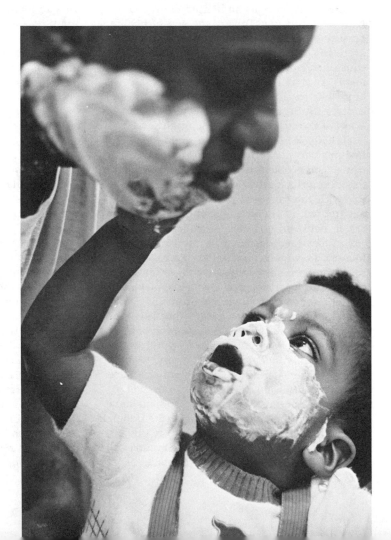

should end up identifying with her father and achieving a male sex-role identity. On the other hand, a simple reversal of the process in which girls would seek the father's affection cannot be invoked either, because girls as well as boys have a strong initial attachment, based on nurturance and dependency, to their mothers. The problem, then, is to devise a theory that recognizes the common libidinal ties in infancy and also outlines a path for little girls in which they end up identifying with their mother.

Aware of this flaw, Freud proposed various explanations with, as he himself conceded, indifferent success. Toward the end of his life, he seemed to favor the idea that the little girl gradually becomes angry at her mother, because her mother does not satisfy all her needs, and, more specifically, because she holds her mother accountable for her lack of a penis (S. Freud, 1965b). **Penis envy** becomes a major motivator for the young girl and eventually leads her to seek a strong love attachment to her father, the possessor of a penis. The problem with this explanation is that the girl's motivation to ultimately identify with the same-sex parent cannot be equated with the boy's fear of castration, which helps bring about masculine identification. Indeed, Freud had difficulty isolating any factor that would ultimately bring about identification with the mother. He therefore embraced the weak solution that girls, lacking anxiety about castration, remain in the Oedipal situation of "mother-hate, father-love" for a long time, and through a repression of the love of father, eventually break away from this bind only incompletely. This conclusion was consistent with Freud's general prejudice that women developed less fully than men.

All but the most convinced Freudians have rejected his attempts to generalize the Oedipal theory to girls. Some, who also reject the male version of the theory, accept Freud's concept of identification and attempt to ex-

plain it in other ways. In one account the greater power of adult authority figures is seen as making the child highly anxious. To eliminate these anxieties, the child tries to become as similar as possible to the potent adult (Bronfenbrenner, 1960). Through such **identification with the aggressor,** children merge their identities with, and strive to become like, the individuals whose powers they most fear (A. Freud, 1946). This position provides a ready-made explanation of antisocial behaviors.

A cousin to this account is the **status envy** view of identification (Parsons, 1955; J. W. M. Whiting, 1960). Again, the young child is struck by a parent's tremendous resources: great power, wealth, skill, intelligence, and so forth. But the child does not so much fear these attributes as genuinely admire and covet them. Hoping eventually to have the same privileges, the child assumes the characteristics of the adult. Here is an avenue for explaining more prosocial behaviors.

A third, somewhat different, view emphasizes the child's observation of the parents and particularly of their responses to diverse experiences (Kagan, 1958). The child gradually comes to share these reactions. When the parent is pleased by a turn of events, the child becomes pleased; when things go badly, the child becomes depressed. After a while, having sufficiently internalized the parents' reactions, the child no longer needs to observe such reactions in order to anticipate and share them.

Despite their differences, these accounts all affirm that identification accounts adequately for the child's increasing resemblance to adults. But what of empirical attempts to support one version or another, or to verify the theory of identification in general? Neither Freud nor his followers were much interested in testing the theory; they were content to rely on the recollections of adults in therapy that made up the original body of evidence.

And it must be said that investigations by other researchers do not strengthen one's confidence in the theory (see Mischel, 1970). For instance, orthodox Oedipal theory received a blow many years ago when the anthropologist Bronislaw Malinowski (1929) showed that a boy need not rival his father. In the Trobriand Islands, what rivalry there is exists between son and maternal uncle; relationships with the father are casual and benign throughout childhood. At least in its traditional form, Oedipal theory is undermined by this cross-cultural investigation. Analogously, experimental attempts to document the efficacy of a potent model in inducing identification have not always been successful (Bryan and Walbeck, 1970). Even a massive study conducted two decades ago by Robert Sears and his colleagues (Sears, Rau, and Alpert, 1965) could neither support nor refute Freud's principal contentions. Given this indefinite state of things, it is no wonder that the whole concept of identification has been increasingly criticized.

Some Approaches to Imitation

Researchers in the environmental-learning tradition examined the literature and arguments about identification and were scandalized by the vaguely defined concepts and unsupported assertions (see Miller and Dollard, 1941). Why not wipe the slate clean, they asked, and use only the concepts that were logically necessary and could be empirically verified?

One of these concepts—**imitation**—had been proposed to explain language learning during early childhood (see Chapter 4) and seemed appropriate to social behavior as well. Adults perform various behaviors and children see them. If suitably reinforced, children will engage in such activities; if not so reinforced, or if reinforced for other acts, they will cease to

do so. To explain the writer James Morris, for example, there is no need to invoke Oedipal strivings or status envy. Here is simply an individual who has not been adequately reinforced for behaving as a male, or who has been reinforced for feminine behaviors and attitudes. Different reinforcements would have produced a quite different individual.

THE TRADITIONAL ENVIRONMENTAL-LEARNING VIEW

Initially, members of the environmental-learning school put forth the simplest possible explanations for the acquisition of prosocial or antisocial behavior. Neal Miller and John Dollard (1941) argued that children learn to behave like adults by imitating them and, further, that the very act of imitation has to be learned—and can be unlearned. In fact, in a series of studies and demonstrations, they tried to show that a young child's first imitation occurs by accident. That is, the child's first imitative act is merely a coincidental repetition of something someone nearby has just done. Should that imitation be reinforced—say, the pleased parent provides a piece of candy—the imitation will continue. On the other hand, if reinforcement is not forthcoming, or if nonimitative behaviors are reinforced, the child will no longer imitate.

By and large, these findings meant that children would resemble their parents to the extent—but only to the extent—that they were so reinforced. This is an instrumental conditioning explanation, such as we first saw in Chapter 2. According to it, James Morris may have accidentally produced an operant—for instance, playing with a doll—that was reinforced by his parents. As the operant was strengthened through repeated reinforcements, young Morris may have eventually fallen into a pattern of feminine thought and behavior. Following the same line of argument, an aggressive child is one who happens to have been rewarded after he hit another child (or who failed to receive a reward following his rescue of a child in pain).

ALBERT BANDURA'S SOCIAL-LEARNING STANCE

One especially controversial element in the Dollard-Miller point of view is the claim that particular imitative behaviors emerge only when they have been shaped step by step by another individual. A psychologist from within the environmental-learning camp who has vigorously attacked this position is Albert Bandura (1969, 1974, 1977, 1978) of Stanford University. Bandura points out that this approach, if taken literally, is entirely implausible. For the environmental-learning account to be correct, an individual learning to speak would have to be reinforced for every sound that he uttered; a child learning the game of baseball would require separate reinforcement for every movement, swing of the bat, or step toward first base. Nor, according to the traditional account, would the purposes of these enterprises ever become clear. How would the child come to understand that utterances (such as the promise of a gift or the threat of punishment) have long-term effects, or that the purpose of a ballgame is to score the most runs over the course of nine innings?

Clearly, Bandura suggests, something is radically wrong with the Dollard-Miller account of social learning. What these investigators completely overlooked is that individuals can learn a great deal simply by observing sequences of behaviors engaged in by others, taking note of the consequences of these behaviors for the individuals involved, and then, at a subsequent time, carrying out the series of behaviors witnessed. To accomplish this feat, children cannot simply form a separate response to each observed stimulus. Rather, they must be able to represent to themselves a whole pattern of responses (say, jumping

across the hopscotch board and then back again) and its consequences; then they must try to produce the modeled pattern as a single coherent set of behaviors. Increasingly with age, the child can represent "types of behaviors" or "abstract regularities" (for example, outwitting one's opponents) rather than simple sequences of action (for example, winning at hopscotch) (Rosenthal and Zimmerman, 1978).

In Bandura's view, this ability to observe and then to produce (or reproduce) behavioral sequences draws on at least four skills:

1. Careful attention to the model, observing appropriate and distinctive features of the performance.
2. Retention to the critical features of the modeled behavior.
3. Adequate duplication of the model.
4. Justification of the imitative act in terms of external, internal, or vicarious rewards.

Bandura finds these processes at work in all kinds of imitation, from the modeling of an isolated act to the reproduction of complex and intricate prosocial or antisocial patterns. If this is so, it is difficult to justify two distinct processes, one called "imitation" and restricted to single acts, the other called "identification" and reserved for more general patterns of responses. In Bandura's view, sex-role identity comes from repeated observation of appropriate models (see Perry and Bussey, 1979). But in contrast to what most traditional identification theorists would hold, there is nothing irrevocable about the sex-role behavior patterns of a girl or boy. Thus Bandura might attribute James Morris's experience to his long-term observation of female behavior as a young child, coupled with a strong motivation to adopt those patterns of behavior. So long as this motivation persisted, Morris favored feminine behaviors. But if either the models or the source of motivation had been radically altered, he should have begun to acquire a masculine sex-role identity.

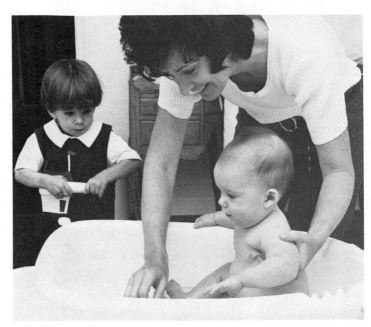

Figure 5.4. Watching his mother bathe the infant, this little boy would seem to have met at least three of Bandura's prerequisites for imitation of behavior: he is watching carefully, he can probably remember the important aspects of the behavior, and he is probably able to perform the motions of bathing the infant. Whether he will learn and imitate this behavior pattern perhaps depends on whether Bandura's fourth criterion is met: Is he motivated to learn this pattern of responses?

Bandura feels no compulsion to invoke a sociobiological or psychoanalytic view of aggression as an inescapable part of the human condition. Nor is there any need to assume that aggression only follows upon frustration (cf. Dollard and Miller, 1950). According to social-learning theory, children witness numerous aggressive acts committed both by individuals whom they know and by models in the mass media. Youngsters clearly know how to be aggressive (Bandura, 1965). And if they are asked, following an aggressive demonstration, what they have seen, children are only too willing to offer a blow-by-blow description.

Whether they will in fact carry out such actions will depend, however, on the consequences that have greeted the antisocial behaviors they witnessed. If aggressors have been previously punished, of if less risky means exist for securing desired goals, aggressive acts are unlikely to surface. But if, as is often the case, aggression has been rewarded—if victors have gained tangible rewards or received approval from others—and if alternative paths are not evident, aggression may be the preferred mode of behavior. Just such a state of affairs may have prompted the increasingly hostile actions that the boys in *Lord of the Flies* direct towards one another.

Bandura has provided various demonstrations to support his intuitively appealing conceptions. In his most famous studies, to which we will return in Chapter 8, a model knocks down a rubber doll and children are given the opportunity to do the same; this demonstration documents children's tendency to imitate a model's behavior in every particular (Bandura and Walters, 1963). Interestingly, even when children do not on their own initiate the behaviors, they show the capacity to do so when explicitly requested (Bandura, 1965). Yet, despite the power of Bandura's demonstrations, there may be serious difficulties with his claims. Cognitive-structuralists in fact believe that Bandura's social-learning analysis misses the whole point of what imitation and identification are really about. The dispute between the two groups can be better illustrated after we have considered some of the basic tenets of the cognitive-structural approach to socialization.

A Cognitive-Structural Approach to Social Behavior

So far we have seen how the psychoanalytic view of identification and certain learning views of imitation seek to explain the child's acquisition of sex-role identity and selected prosocial and antisocial behaviors. Perhaps the strongest and most persuasive statement of the rival cognitive-structural position has been articulated by Lawrence Kohlberg (1966, 1969). And because he directly addresses the psychoanalytic and social-learning views, his approach provides an instructive comparison to the theories introduced above.

Figure 5.5. Each of the major theorists of imitation and identification offers a different flow chart of the process. Notice the stress on affective factors in the views of Freud and of Miller and Dollard compared to the initiating role of perception assumed by the Bandura and Kohlberg positions.

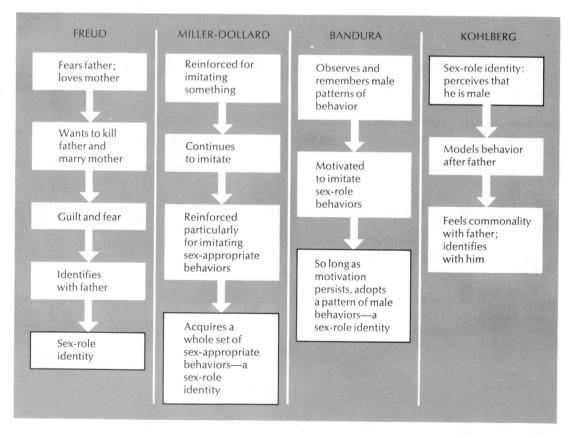

LAWRENCE KOHLBERG'S COGNITIVE VIEW

Kohlberg sees identification as a cognitive-structural process involving imitation of the most general forms of a model's behavior. As such, contrary to the claims of traditional learning theory, identification does not depend on particular motives or reinforcements, nor must it involve fidelity to specific details of a model's behavior. Instead, children have enduring tendencies to imitate their parents, to conform to their parents' expectations, to idealize one or both parents, and to derive self-esteem from their parents' competence or status. Moreover, these tendencies will overrule the contingencies of any reinforcement situation, so that a child is unlikely to imitate a model if that model's behavior runs completely contrary to an internalized parental value.

In opposition to the traditional Freudian view, however, identifications are not seen as totally irreversible. Consistent with the "constructive view" of the child favored by cognitive-structuralists, identifications are more profitably regarded as solutions to developmental tasks, solutions that may themselves be abandoned when the child acquires greater cognitive sophistication. For example, a young boy identifies with his father because he perceives similarities between himself and his father, admires his father's competence, and wants to resemble the father. Yet at a somewhat later age, he may cease to identify strongly if the father fails to fulfill certain expectations or if the child no longer perceives as strong a resemblance between himself and his father. Complete identification with parental authority is to be expected in the early years when children are incapable of distancing themselves from their parents or of instituting subtle changes in behavior or motivation. But such total identification becomes less and less likely during the middle childhood and adolescent years, when children have acquired greater distance from their elders.

According to Kohlberg's cognitive-structural view, children's attitudes toward social and sexual questions must always reflect their general level of understanding. Just as the year-old infant began to appreciate the permanence of objects, so the three- of four-year-old gradually begins to appreciate certain identities that persist across long times and vast spaces. A plant begins as a small seedling and grows eventually into a large bush or flower. A human starts as a small infant and eventually becomes an imposing adult. But the large plant retains features of the small plant, and the large person preserves features of the small person. For example, body parts remain, even though their size and shape may change (see deVries, 1969).

Among a person's most enduring features are those defining his or her sexual nature. The child learns that certain physical properties, behaviors, life-styles, occupations, and expressions correspond with being (and being called) a man or a woman, a boy or a girl. Adult gender identity, in Kohlberg's words, is a "basic cognitive reality judgment and not a derivative of social rewards, parent identifications, or sexual identifications" (1966, p. 93). The key to sex-role identification lies in the child's realization that he is a boy or that she is a girl, because he or she possesses crucial attributes exhibited by others of the same sex. The following actual exchange between two youngsters captures the difference between a child who has begun to appreciate these identity relations and another who has not:

Johnny (age four and one-half): I'm going to be an airplane builder when I grow up.
Jimmy (age four): When I grow up, I'll be a Mommy.
Johnny: No, you can't be a Mommy. You have to be a Daddy.

Jimmy: No, I'm going to be a Mommy.
Johnny: No, you're not a girl, you can't be a Mommy.
Jimmy: Yes, I can [Kohlberg, 1966, p. 95].

KOHLBERG'S COMMENTS ON OTHER THEORIES

Kohlberg's theory differs sharply from the Freudian view. For Freud, the boy's identification with his father results from strong, uncontrollable feelings. Loving his mother but fearing competition or retaliation from his father, he elects to act and feel like his father. By contrast, Kohlberg focuses on the child's understanding of his or her own traits. Sex role is viewed as a mental deduction, based on the child's knowledge of certain regularities that endure.

Kohlberg's theory is equally remote from the environmental-learning tradition. First, he differs from those who deny the concept of sex-role identification. In Kohlberg's view, the child does, at the age of four or so, make an essentially irrevocable decision to be male or female. Second, Kohlberg differs from certain social-learning theorists who allow some forms of identification but who attribute these behaviors to such factors as status envy, in which the boy views the father as a major rewarder and controller of power (J. W. M. Whiting, 1960). In the social-learning view, as in the psychoanalytic, the child's acknowledgment of his sex-role identity is the final step of the process.

For Kohlberg, however, cognition is primary. And so, flipping these rival accounts of identification on their heads, Kohlberg begins with the child's knowledge that he or she is and *will remain* a boy or girl. A boy, for instance, first perceives his physical and behavioral likeness to other males and then begins to model his behavior after his father and other men. The resulting feeling of similarity follows, rather than precedes, the imitative

behavior. According to this theory, James Morris somehow perceived more similarities between himself and women than between himself and men. Despite the ordinarily compelling cues of the culture and of his anatomy, he could therefore insist on his essential femininity.

In support of his cognitive developmental view, Kohlberg (1966) points to the fact that many three-year-olds know which types of objects (such as razor blades or dresses) belong with each sex, and also whether they themselves are boys or girls (see Kuhn, Nash, and Brucken, 1978; Mussen, 1969; but also Bussey, 1981; Lloyd, 1981). This knowledge is present at a time when, in the classical Freudian view, children still identify primarily with their mothers. Children deemed the most advanced on tests of intelligence and cognitive level turn out to perform best on these tasks of sexual awareness and (as predicted by the theory) also display the most consistently appropriate identification patterns. Further, the same relationship between cognitive level and sex-role awareness is found even among children who do not have fathers in their homes and among retarded children, who behave more like their mental-age counterparts (younger children with normal IQ) than like chronological-age counterparts. According to Kohlberg, these results would be difficult to account for by the other major theories. Whereas his view predicts the link between knowledge of the world and one's sex-role identification, the other theories ignore cognitive factors and instead trace identification and sex-role identity to the degree of attachment between parent and child or to the extent of status envy or fear of aggression.

THE KOHLBERG PERSPECTIVE ANALYZED

Certainly, the role played by cognition in the acquisition of sex roles has been amply documented by research conducted since Kohlberg

Figure 5.6. Little boys in our society are far more likely than girls to play avidly with trucks and wagons. These play preferences are determined in large part by the social approval meted out by parents: if such play were modeled by women, and approved of in little girls, this apparent difference in play preference might well disappear.

first propounded his theory. Toddlers, and even infants, are able to distinguish reliably between the two sexes (Lewis and Brooks, 1975). Nursery school youngsters are more likely to imitate those behaviors that have been labeled as appropriate for their sex than just any behavior produced by a model of the same sex (Masters, Ford, Arend, Grotevant, and Clark, 1979). And children's awareness of gender and their ability to label "girls" and "boys" reliably despite changes in hairstyle or dress relate to their cognitive level, rather than to the sex role they happen to favor for themselves. Such a finding is difficult to square with any view except cognitive-structural theory (Liben and Signorella, 1980; Marcus and Overton, 1978).

And yet it may be that, as a cognitive-structural spokesman, Kohlberg has at once complicated and oversimplified the processes involved in sex-role learning. On the one hand, they may be more straightforward than Kohlberg has realized. Strong, possibly biologically influenced proclivities guide an individual toward behaviors that are consistent with culturally approved sex roles (Arnold, 1980; Gutmann, 1975). Boys tend to be more muscular, competitive, concerned with dominance, and physically active than girls. Girls may be less aggressive and more given to quiet structured activity (DiPietro, 1981; Maccoby 1980; Maccoby and Jacklin, 1974). Play patterns also reflect sex membership from early childhood (Fein et al., 1975) and are strongly reminiscent of those encountered in other primates. Because these trends, however caused, are routinely reinforced by the society, individuals receive at least a gentle push toward the sex role expected by the society (Adams, 1980; Langlois and Downs, 1980). If, as is surely the case with lower animals, nature has predisposed organisms to behave in sexually appropriate manners, cognitive explanations may be superfluous.

On the other hand, sex-role identification may also be more complex than Kohlberg suggests. According to his analysis, if three-year-old James Morris had correctly matched object and sex and correctly reported his own sex, he would have been judged as having formed the basic identifications and his future course as a male would have been guaranteed. In fact, however, there may be crucial differences between how a child parries questions about sex role, how he handles sex-typed materials, and how that child actually feels and later acts with reference to his own sexual roles (Eisenberg-Berg, Murray, and Hite, 1981; Wehren and DeLisis, 1981).

Moreover, the steps in mastering gender prove quite complex: children are likely until school age to remain uncertain as to whether an individual will remain the same sex if his or her appearance changes dramatically (for example, if a boy lets his hair grow long and wears a skirt) (Emmerich et al., 1977). And the course may also prove subtler, more mysterious, and of longer duration than is suggested by the Kohlberg formula. Youngsters initially associate sex roles with physical traits (such as hair length) or types of activity (for example, baseball) and only later appreciate the role of social and psychological factors (for example, favored emotional or interpersonal traits like kindness) in traditional sex-role identities (Damon, 1977, 1981). Indeed, as Jan Morris exemplifies, processes of sex-role identification may continue to change throughout life. Masculine and feminine thoughts, behaviors, and attitudes may come to the fore at different times, significantly affecting interaction with the world. Patterns of fantasy and play can (and often do) partake of characteristics of both sexes, suggesting that normal youngsters possess an element of bigenderism and a proclivity to attend to features of both sexes (Bradley et al., 1978; Bryan and Luria, 1978; Freud, 1938b; Money and Ehrhardt, 1972; Slaby and Frey, 1975). And, indeed, there may be in many adults a significant degree of **androgyny,** an identification with both masculine (*andr* = male) and feminine (*gyne* = female) sex roles (see Bem, 1974).

We seem in an unpalatable position. Although promising leads crop up in several theories, none of the points of view about identification seems authoritative. But recent formulations about specific prosocial behaviors may suggest a more adequate approach to these complex issues. Though not directed specifically at the question of how boys become men and girls become women, they contain interesting clues about processes of socialization in early life.

Kohlberg himself has focused on the origins of sex-role identity and has said relatively little about the acquisition of specific prosocial or antisocial behaviors. Nonetheless, from his writings and from accounts from other cognitive-oriented social theorists (Damon, 1977; Hoffman, 1970; Maccoby, 1980), it is possible to piece together the kind of account with which he might be comfortable.

A cognitive-structural view of the acquisition of behaviors like altruism or destructive aggression place relatively little importance on the sheer incidence of such behaviors. Indeed, a cardinal assumption of this position is that one cannot simply observe a behavior and declare that it is prosocial, antisocial, or, for that matter, socially neutral. To assess the nature and significance of an action, it is essential to observe the context in which it occurs and to assess its meaning to the child who has performed it.

Consider, for example, the following hypothetical incident. A child observes a model hitting a doll and receiving an award. Shortly thereafter, the child proceeds to hit a doll (or another child). A psychoanalytically oriented observer might describe such an action as a result of identification and might even designate it as "identification with the aggressor." A social-learning theorist would indicate that the child has seen aggression rewarded and so is incorporating this antisocial behavior into his repertoire.

But the cognitively oriented theorist would raise a whole different set of questions. What is the child's understanding of the action? Does he know that it is antisocial to hit another person or object? Does he know that hitting will hurt the other child? Can he put himself in the role of the model or of the child whom he has struck? What are his goals in carrying out his action and what does he think about the action he has carried out? What would the child say if told that he had done something wrong? Would he try to atone for his action? How would he justify it to someone else?

According to the cognitive-structural view, it only makes sense to deem the action aggressive if the child is aware of the damaging consequences of his action and nevertheless intends to carry it out. (By the same token, an action, no matter how generous it seems, can only be called altruistic if the child is aware of the beneficial consequences of his actions, intends to carry them out, and is not doing so merely to gain rewards.) The child's mental construction of the event becomes all-important: the actual physical parameters of the act, like its frequency, recede in importance.

Another cardinal assumption of this position is that the child will pass through a set of stages with respect to those actions that others term aggressive. Each stage will reflect the child's overall understanding of behavior and of the relation among individuals. Thus at an early stage, where the child has little sense of other individuals, of their rights and feelings, his aggression will be completely instrumental: it will be carried out to gain possessions and with little feeling for (or even awareness of) others involved.

By the time he enters school, the child will have attained some awareness of the consequences of his actions and some sense of how others will feel. This will lead in most cases to a decline in the incidence of aggressive acts and also to a shift in the occasions that prompt aggressiveness. The child is less likely to lash out aggressively in a struggle over objects; but he is more likely to act in an anti-social fashion if his pride has been hurt or if he feels he has been treated unfairly. And, by the same token, the means will change: his aggression is less likely to take the form of physical abuse and more likely to be couched in hostile verbal terms. Capacities to empathize come to balance aggression and children begin to consider alternative means (including flattery) to secure their ends. Finally, children become more sophisticated in the means they fashion to hurt their chosen victims (Hartup, 1974; Maccoby, 1980).

In some respects the cognitive-structural and the social-learning points of view seem to be on totally different wavelengths. Cogni-

tive-structuralists belittle the action itself and focus on its purposes and its meaning; social-learning theorists have little patience with underlying motives and instead attend to the appearances and the consequences of actions. Cognitive-structuralists focus on behavioral propensities that are relatively enduring but that will necessarily be altered by the attainment of higher levels of understanding; social-learning theorists see behavior as more evanescent and strongly reject the notion of stages that must follow, one upon another, in logical order.

A Clash Between the Social-Learning and Cognitive-Structural Approaches

It is of some interest to consider instances where the social-learning and cognitive-structural points of view have come into direct collision with one another. Probably the best known instance of such a collision occurred over some studies of children's moral judgment. Let us therefore take a closer look at what the fuss was all about.

In the late 1920s Jean Piaget became interested in the ways in which children of different ages (and cognitive stages) reacted to and interpreted various moral dilemmas. And so he described to children two sequences of behaviors and asked the children which one featured the "naughtier boy" (Piaget, 1932). In a sample item, Johnny is coming to dinner and on the way he inadvertently knocks over a tray and breaks fifteen cups. In the comparison story, Henry is trying to steal some cookies against his mother's instructions. While engaged in this act, he accidentally knocks over and breaks a single cup.

Piaget discovered an intriguing phenomenon. Children up to the age of eight or nine focused exclusively on the objective amount of damage that resulted. Taking an "objective orientation," they concluded that Johnny was naughtier, because he broke more cups. Past this age, children were able to take into account the child's intention. On this score, Johnny emerged as a relatively innocent offender, while Henry, intent on an antisocial act, deserved more punishment. Piaget's ten-year-old subjects successfully adopted a "subjective orientation."

In classic cognitive-structural fashion, Piaget maintained that he had outlined a stage sequence. Children below a certain age have an objective, "eye-for-eye" view of the world and so they will focus on consequences, not on intentions. Older children, having a grasp of intentions and motivations, will be more sympathetic to an innocent offender. They will be partial to Johnny.

As we will see later (Chapter 12), various criticisms can be leveled against the Piagetian study, whether or not one is sympathetic to the cognitive-structural point of view. But a basic objection was raised by Albert Bandura and Frederick McDonald (1963) who doubted altogether the need for concepts like "level of learning" or "stage of development." Convinced that they could explain the children's judgments via a social-learning analysis, they exposed matched groups of children, all of whom had already taken Piaget-style tests of moral judgments, to a number of experimental conditions in which adult models gave various responses to similar dilemmas. Of special interest were those situations in which the model spewed forth reasons that ran counter to the children's own customary style of reasoning. Thus, children of an objective persuasion heard subjective-style reasons, while those of a subjective leaning were exposed to a litany of objective assessments.

Even in cases where there was no reinforcement for adopting the style of respond-

ing modeled by the adult, children showed a strong tendency to do what their model had done. Training more than doubled the number of responses that resembled those of the model. These findings constituted a strong challenge to a cognitive-structural stance. First of all, ensconced at a given stage of development, children's responses should show more resistance to a model. Second and even more damaging, while a shift to a higher level of reasoning might be tolerated by a cognitive-structural perspective, there is little reason to expect (and much difficulty in accounting for) a pattern of results where children of a higher subjective level revert to the more primitive objective level. Stage progressions should only advance in one direction.

It should be no surprise that Piagetians vigorously challenged the Bandura and McDonald claims. Some have commented on the deficits of the experimental design and report (Cowan et al., 1969; Kuhn, 1973). Bandura and McDonald attended to the children's choice of the naughtier person but not to the reasons they offered for their choice. From the Piagetian perspective, the choice itself is not nearly so informative as the type and level of reasoning.

A second response has been to replicate the experiment and to reanalyze its results. After such a replication, Jonas Langer and his colleagues (Cowan et al., 1969; J. Langer, 1975) reported that it was very difficult to classify children's judgments according to the system used by Bandura and McDonald. They found that the moral judgments of half the children remained the same even after exposure to the model. Some children were extremely distressed by the model's responses and asked the experimenter what to do. Most important, although the children's choices may have changed, the *explanations* they gave did not. For instance, "objective" children might say that Henry, who broke only one cup, was naughtier than Johnny (subjective response) because the single cup he broke was very expensive (objective reason). Langer concluded that the modeling technique confused the children, causing them to mimic the model without understanding the underlying reason for the judgment.

Another perspective on the Bandura-McDonald claims comes from studies that have looked in greater detail at the relation between stage of moral reasoning and exposure to models at other levels (Keasey, 1973; Rest, Turiel, and Kohlberg, 1969; Rothman, 1976; Turiel, 1966, 1969; Walker, 1981). These studies have used the more complex model of moral judgment devised by Kohlberg (see Chapter 13 for details). Though the pattern of results is tricky, in general findings support the cognitive-structuralists' claims: movement to the next higher stage of development is possible when the child is exposed to models of that stage; exposure to stages more than one level above the child's own stage has relatively little effect; and children show little attraction to views below their own level of moral judgment. They may, for the sake of a reward, mouth less-advanced judgments, but they will not "really" change the way in which they apprehend the events of the social world.

These cognitive-structural studies pose difficulties for the Bandura-McDonald view: if children are predisposed to imitate models, and if other conditions of reinforcement are held constant, then they should espouse with equal enthusiasm (and equal competence) all possible levels of reasoning. This does not happen. The problem is that social-learning theory—in its traditional *or* its observational form—ignores the child's level of cognitive development. In fact, observational-learning theorists attribute to children the potential to imitate whatever they perceive, including the behavior and thought patterns of a more mature person. Until adherents of this view provide evidence that children have genuinely assimilated—rather than merely echoed—a moral perspective some levels above their own, cognitive-structuralists will accept the findings of Piaget's original demonstration.

A more formal presentation of the cognitive-structural view has been put forth by Deanna Kuhn (1973). Using Piaget's theory of cognition as a point of departure, she notes that children can copy (or accommodate to) a model only if it can be related to their current level of cognitive functioning. Therefore, the first factor to be determined in any treatment of imitation is the child's level of mental functioning. Once this is known, the analyst can predict with some confidence what sorts of behaviors the child may be able to imitate and what sorts may prove beyond duplication.

Applying Kuhn's framework to moral judgment, we may assume that, say, seven-year-olds are at a stage where they can appreciate only *objective* dimensions of a stimulus and not yet assimilate underlying subjective or intentional factors. Faced with a parent who reasons at a more sophisticated level, the child can imitate certain surface features—the parent's voice, style of dress, customary comments, daily habits, and the like. Yet the child will fail to reproduce the adult's attitudes, prejudices, or beliefs. These features, lying below the surface, stand beyond the child's current level of cognitive functioning. The most he can do is repeat, without understanding, some of the adult's common ways of speaking.

When it comes to moral judgments, the cognitive-structural approach seems to me to have the upper hand. The way in which a child construes issues like motivation, intent, and consequences cannot be radically altered by the simple expedient of exposure to a way of speaking that differs from the child's own orientation. But when it comes to other areas of social behavior, ranging from aggression to empathy, the scorecard is much more mixed. In these realms, the child's thoughts and behaviors seem to be a complex compound of his level of understanding, his biological predispositions, the particular models to which he is exposed, and the pattern of reward he has received. The most convincing and comprehensive account of these events is likely to come from a judicious blending of insights from each theoretical perspective.

Clues Toward a Possible Synthesis

MARTIN HOFFMAN'S DESCRIPTION OF ALTRUISM

Motivated by the increase in violence in our own country, and spurred by accounts of how most individuals are unlikely to aid an individual who has been injured, researchers have joined policy makers in attempting to inculcate prosocial behavior in children (Rushton, 1979). A favorite means is epitomized by Mister Rogers, the hero of a television show for preschoolers, who devotes much time to the modeling of prosocial behaviors like **empathy**—sharing the feelings experienced by another person—and **altruism**—making sacrifices for another without any immediate expectation of reward. But can such displays be appreciated by children? And if imitated, will they be understood and generalized appropriately to other situations?

To approach these questions we need a theory—and relevant data—about the development of altruistic and other prosocial tendencies. From the perspective of this chapter, we would like such a theory to be eclectic, to partake of relevant insights from several traditions. Altruistic and empathetic behaviors are good vantage points for such a theory, inasmuch as they incorporate strong affective as well as cognitive features. One individ-

Figure 5.7. Most children have the inclination to perform altruistic or helping behaviors. Here, Amy helps her younger sister, Suzanne, learn how to roller skate.

ual who has devoted considerable effort to explicating altruism and empathy from an integrated perspective is Martin Hoffman. Hoffman finds clues for the beginning of altruism in the child's earliest behaviors (Levine and Hoffman, 1975; Sagi and Hoffman, 1976).

During the first stage, in early infancy, the child attends to and is stimulated by the strong behaviors of others in the environment. Infants cry when others cry or laugh when others laugh (Simner, 1971). This contagion may result from conditioning, in which cues of pain or displeasure from another person become associated with the child's own past experiences of pain. Hoffman regards the

Figure 5.8. According to sociobiologists, animals are programmed to perform altruistic behaviors in order to protect the future of their species. Here a mother penguin guards her young ones.

result as a rudimentary form of empathy. Repeated demonstrations that even two-day-old infants cry vigorously at the sound of another infant's screaming—more than they will cry at a computer-generated cry—suggest that children can experience empathetic distress long before they are believed to have any cognitive appreciation of the existence of others. In fact, at this age children may even confuse the distress and pain of others with their own.

A major change occurs after the first year, when the child gradually becomes aware of himself as different from others. Confronted by someone in pain, the child now realizes that it is the other and not he who is actually in distress. And for the first time, the child's concern for self-comfort gives way, at least in part, to concern for the other. Having perceived another person as distinct, the child is now in a position to relieve that person's distress. Maternal modeling is probably the most effective way to encourage empathetic responses on the part of the young child (Rheingold, 1979; Zahn-Waxler, Radke-Yarrow, and King, 1979).

Because the ability to sort out his own feelings from those of others is still primitive, the child will not yet act completely appropriately. For instance, a child may offer his doll to his father when he looks sad. But by the age of two and one-half, the child is sometimes sufficiently aware of the other person's separateness to give the other what the other wants. Thus a boy may know enough to bring a teddy bear to his crying sibling and to offer a kiss to his sobbing parent. The child of this age will typically display empathy toward an injured individual but may not do anything to help (L. W. Hoffman, 1979).

A later level of altruistic behavior matures during middle childhood, after the child has entered school. Now he becomes aware not only that others have feelings of their own, but also that these occur within a larger set of experiences. Capable of appreciating the existence of classes of individuals, a child now shows strong concern for the general condition of others, not just for their momentary state. Ultimately, children become able to comprehend the plight of an entire group, which makes possible their meaningful involvement in social or political innovation. As their cognitive level has advanced, children's responses have become more appropriate, more enduring, more differentiated, and more sensitive to the overall facts of a situation. Yet if novelist William Golding's understanding of human nature is accurate, this altruism may prove brittle at times of stress.

Hoffman's eclectic formulation about altruism points up a number of specific issues, which researchers have begun to address. Particularly illuminating in this regard is a study conducted by Marion Yarrow and her associates (Yarrow, Scott, and Waxler, 1973). One group of preschoolers spent a considerable period of time with a caretaker who was consistently nurturant and empathetic; a matched group spent comparable time with the same caretaker who in this instance acted consistently aloof. Following two weeks of interaction, modeling sessions began. Some youngsters from each group viewed the caretaker in a pretend play situation in which she aided toy creatures who were in distress. The remaining youngsters viewed the model both at play and while aiding individuals who were genuinely in distress—for example, an adult visitor who had banged her head against a table.

Following these exposures to helping behavior by their former caretaker, children were given the opportunity to be altruistic. On a first occasion they had the opportunity to display helpfulness to toy creatures and to "real-life" victims. Then, two weeks later, they were taken to a neighborhood home where this time they had the opportunity to help a mother and a baby.

The results suggest a number of principles. First, those children who have been exposed to extensive modeling on the part of a nurturant caretaker were far more likely to help the mother and the baby in the home setting than children in the other group. At least in real life, there is a Mister Rogers effect. Such training has also proved effective in other contexts, particularly when children have had the opportunity to role-play the victim (Iannotti, 1975; Staub, 1971).

In the Yarrow study, modeling of helpfulness only with the toy creatures proved less effective than "live helping." In fact, in tests two days after training, those who had seen only the toy creatures came themselves to the aid of the toy creatures but not to individuals troubled in "real life." Possibly the Mister Rogers effect requires "real-life" instances to be effective in real life (see Stein and Friedrich, 1972). Further supporting this point, young children are more likely to imitate live models than those observed on television (McCall, Parke, and Kavanaugh, 1977; Yates and Mischel, 1979); apparently, symbolic or mediated presentations are relatively ineffective.

The question arises: Are empathetic and altruistic behaviors on the part of young children simply superficial imitations or do they reflect a genuine understanding of, and sympathy for, the other? That an altruistic response may sometimes be based on superficial factors is suggested by Gove and Keating (1979) who documented the difficulties experienced by young children in taking into account the subjective needs of characters in stories. Rybash, Roodin, and Hallion (1979) found that kindergartners were unable to take into account the intention of an actor in deciding upon a suitable punishment. And Eisenberg-Berg and Lennon (1979) have shown that children who describe themselves as empathetic on a verbal measure are actually less likely than other children to exhibit spontaneous prosocial behavior: apparently the self-described empathizers are simply more aware of what is socially desirable. It seems that the difficulties in perceiving intentionality detected by Piaget and his colleagues limit the young child's altruistic behaviors.

On the other hand, the child's own experienced affect may well play a critical role in the development of prosocial behaviors. Kindergartners show increasing understanding about others' emotions following reflections on their own reactions to the feelings of other individuals (Hughes, Tingle, and Sawin, 1981). And children are more likely to experience guilt if they have previously developed empathy toward the victim (Thompson and Hoffman, 1980). In a series of complex but important experiments (for further details, see the box) Aronfreed and his colleagues (1968) examined the way in which children learned an important aspect of socialization—how to punish or criticize oneself when one has done something wrong. They found that the precise moment during the learning procedure when the child experienced strong affect was crucial in determining whether the desired self-critical social behavior was in fact mastered. In other words, learning this behavior depended on its being linked to a strong feeling of anxiety; in fact, Aronfreed's study suggests that the experience of affect under very specific circumstances may be necessary if the individual is to cognize and to master the desired

Aronfreed's Account of Prosocial Behavior

How do children learn what they should and should not do? And how do they learn to characterize their deeds and misdeeds? Such were the questions addressed in a series of ingenious studies conducted by Justin Aronfreed in the mid-1960s (1968). After children performed a simple task (pulling a lever), an experimenter indicated whether they had done the job a good way, called "red," or an evil, "blue," way. While in some cases only the labels "red" and "blue" were used; at other times a punishment (such as a loud buzzer) or praise either accompanied or followed the labeling. Aronfreed wanted to ascertain in which of the experimental manipulations children would learn to apply the labels to their own performance (eventually saying "Uh-oh, I did it the 'blue' way"). He found that only those who had heard the label immediately after a punishment acquired such self-critical behavior. Those who were not punished or who were punished simultaneously with labeling never adopted self-labeling.

Aronfreed concluded that the timing of punishment and verbal criticism is crucial in the acquisition of self-critical behavior. A child is most likely to realize that he has acted wrongly and thus to adopt self-critical behavior when he is first punished and then told why his act was wrong. The verbal criticism serves to explain the punishment and thereby to reduce the anxiety it has produced. In the future the child will recall the event as a unit, label it as a misdeed and, it is hoped, refrain from repeating it. If, on the other hand, verbal criticism comes first, it cannot reduce the anxiety caused by the subsequent punishment. The child will not associate critical labeling with reduced anxiety and is unlikely to be self-critical in the future. The best way to teach a child what he should and should not do is to punish him first and immediately thereafter explain the reason for the punishment. Moral: Spank, then speak!

behavior. And his own experimental manipulations suggest that such learning may well be under the control of the researcher, or, in more natural circumstances, the parent, the teacher, or the television model.

A final question, raised insistently by *Lord of the Flies,* concerns the interrelations among various prosocial behaviors. Do they go hand in hand, such that a child who is cooperative in one situation is likely to prove empathetic or altruistic in others? Or does each virtue stand in relative isolation? There is considerable evidence that mothers who are themselves nurturant and prosocial are more likely to have children who exhibit prosocial behaviors (Barnett et al., 1980; Bryant and Crockenberg, 1980). And across a number of studies, a modest degree of intercorrelation has been found between one variant of prosocial behavior and another (see Mussen and Eisenberg-Berg, 1977; and studies reviewed therein). Setting good examples seems to have at least some carryover from one situation to the next, although the consistency in actual behavior may be less pronounced than the consistency in talking about it (Kohlberg, 1969; Mischel, 1968).

TYING TOGETHER THE PIECES: THE ISLAND REVISITED

Returning to our fictional lads on the Pacific island, let us see if we can account in a more satisfactory fashion for their experiences: how they first behaved as youngsters, how they acquired their prosocial behaviors, why these behaviors tended to break down, even as individual differences among the boys tended to endure. We will speculate as well on what the experiences of a group of girls, on a similar island in the Atlantic Ocean, might have been like.

Beginning with the biological, we can assume that the boys were predisposed (perhaps mediated by sex hormones) to display certain motor actions and sensitivities to external stimuli. These predispositions were noted in some fashion by mothers, who in turn behaved toward their sons in a manner somewhat differently than they would have behaved toward their daughters—thereby heightening any naturally occurring differences.

By the age of two or three, the boys were already playing in somewhat different ways from their female counterparts: engaging in more rough-and-tumble play and considerable constructive activity with blocks, while a comparable set of girls would more likely be involved in nurturant behavior with dolls. Both identification, of the Freudian sort, and imitation, of the social-learning variety, will contribute to these sex-appropriate behaviors (DiPietro, 1981). Clearly these lines of behavior are strongly mediated by the culture; in fact, it is possible to heighten or lessen such stereotypical behaviors by varying the kinds of objects and opportunities in a preschool environment (Fagot, 1978; Katz, 1979).

The child's own perception of self and environment becomes crucial by this age. The world is categorized in many ways, among which the classification of individuals and objects as "boy" and "girl" is especially prominent. Children become sensitive to and enamored with this distinction at an early age, often embracing its most stereotypical forms—for instance, superheroes in the case of males.

But this cognitive activity is not divorced from affective circumstances. Discrimination of sex and sex-related objects and behaviors is often greeted by the label "good" for appropriate sex behavior; the labeling of "bad" often obtains in the opposite situation. (Such labels are also applied to specific prosocial and antisocial patterns of behavior.) Children not only are strongly influenced by these patterns of social reward or disapproval but come to resist counterstereotypical presentations, as when a doctor is presented as a female and a nurse as a male (Cordua, McGraw, and Drabman, 1979; Liben and Signorella, 1980). By school age, this combination of cognitive and affective factors ("I am like my father") ensures a coming together of gender and sex roles. (For exceptions, see the next section.)

During the school years children can benefit increasingly from symbolic as well as real-life presentations of desirable conduct; and so the models presented in books or on television parallel those available in the family, in the school, and among peers. There are also consistent individual differences, reflecting not only the behaviors of prominent models but also the contexts in which the child usually finds himself (Barrett, 1979) and, quite possibly, physiological and genetic factors as well. Thus in *Lord of the Flies,* Piggy, the intelligent but unassertive and empathetic youngster, is seen as more feminine than the aggressive and powerful Jack. By the same token, there are sufficient consistencies within each individual's customary behaviors to justify considering one individual—for instance Ralph, the chief—as relatively prosocial in outlook and another, say his rival, Jack, as essentially aggressive and antisocial. Perhaps Ralph had available to him alternative ways to success while Jack was consistently rewarded for aggressive actions. And perhaps, in the absence of positive adult role models and reinforcement of prosocial behaviors, the destructive behaviors of Jack became the norm.

What of girls on our imaginary island? Less likely, I should think, to gravitate toward a strong hierarchical organization, a leader with a group of followers, or flirting with aggressive and destructive acts. More likely, I should think, to foster nurturant, caring, and cooperative activities. But would this neces-sarily be the case? One line of study suggests that girls are better at giving responses that are considered socially desirable, but no more likely to actually exhibit altruistic behavior (Shigetomi et al., 1979). And consistent with sociobiological theory, the tendency to engage in prosocial activity, or rhetoric, might well dissipate, given an unfavorable turn of events.

Transsexualism Revisited

And what of those relatively rare individuals who do not follow the normal course of sex-role identification? Can the variety of perspectives reviewed in this chapter illuminate the course of an unusual individual—for example, our writer, J. Morris?

Taking into account the host of biological and cultural factors that we have reviewed, we can tentatively suggest that the person's ultimate gender identification should involve at least three contributing factors:

1. *Perceived similarity to other individuals, adult and child.* In most cases, this will be consistent with one's given sex. But when parents have treated the child in an unusual way, or when the child is in fact quite different from others of the same biological sex, he may well align with the opposite sex (cf. Zucker et al., 1979).
2. *Biological characteristics.* These range from the possession of certain external sexual organs and hormones to the degree of inborn aggressiveness or passivity. Biological characteristics will also tend to be consistent in sex and gender. But in rare cases, one's biological characteristics may be abnormal or may be interpreted as being different from others of the same sex. Here the culture assumes an important role, for either a child or an adult may arrive at an interpretation of given physical factors that is at odds with the child's biological nature.

Domain	Difference
PHYSICAL AND MOTOR	After about four years, girls no longer grow faster than boys.
	Girls slow their growth less in response to malnutrition or disease.
	By about three, boys are more proficient at tasks requiring strength.
COGNITIVE AND EMOTIONAL	Boys show a greater tendency for outbursts of negative emotion in response to frustration. The frequency of such outbursts declines more rapidly in girls than in boys.
	Girls more quickly exhibit preferred use of the right (or left) hand.
	Some objects may arouse fear more rapidly in girls than in boys.
SOCIAL AND PLAY BEHAVIOR	Boys engage more in large-muscle or "gross motor" activity.
	Boys engage in more rough-and-tumble play.
	Girls tend to be more obedient to adults but not to peers.
	Boys engage in more positive social interaction with age-mates.
	Boys receive more pressure against engaging in sex-inappropriate behavior.
	Boys receive more punishment but probably also more task-appropriate praise and encouragement.
	Boys and girls tend to prefer toys and activities that adults consider appropriate for their sex; for example, girls sew, draw, or play at housekeeping; boys play with guns, blocks, toy trucks, or do carpentry.
UNFOUNDED BELIEFS ABOUT SEX DIFFERENCES	That girls are more "social" than boys.
	That girls are more suggestible.
	That girls have lower self-esteem.
	That girls are better at rote learning and simple repetitive tasks; boys at tasks that require analytic thinking.
	That girls are more affected by heredity, boys by environment.
	That girls lack achievement motivation.
	That girls are auditory, boys visual.

Figure 5.9. The discovery of general, valid differences between girls and boys is a pursuit surrounded by controversy. This chart lists some of the most well-established differences among preschool children, as well as certain alleged differences for which no reliable evidence exists. (Maccoby and Jacklin, 1974)

Just such a course is likely to happen in instances of **hermaphrodity,** in which the child actually possesses some traits of both sexes (Money, 1971). The interpretation made by the culture can strongly affect the child's ultimate decisions regarding sex role. Indeed, the way the hermaphroditic child is treated in the opening years of life may be crucial in determining both how they act and how they feel about themselves (Hampson, 1965).

3. *Affective linking of positive or negative feelings with specific patterns of behavior and thought.* A child's behaviors elicit reactions from others. If the child behaves in a pattern consistent with his biological sex and this behavior is rewarded, positive feelings will result and appropriate sex-role typing will likely follow. If, however, others provide inconsistent or contradictory reinforcements, the child may well develop positive feelings for the opposite-sex identity or negative feelings for the same-sex identity. Aronfreed's studies suggest how this could happen. If at a crucial time a sex-role behavior is labeled as appropriate or inappropriate, this designation might have a significant and lasting effect on the impressionable young child.

Jan Morris does not herself provide sufficient autobiographical evidence to test this formulation. Nonetheless, applying the model one might arrive at the following analysis. If all factors pointed to same-sex typing, then the child would clearly assume the appropriate sex role. If all three factors pointed to opposite-sex typing (as might happen if a person belonged biologically to one sex but all external features and reinforcement patterns placed that person in the opposite sex), there would be unambiguous identification with the opposite sex (Bentler, Rekers, and Rosen, 1979).

This may happen in certain forms of homosexuality. If, finally, some factors point to one sex role and others to the opposite, confusion and anxiety may reign. This seems to have happened to James Morris: he looked masculine and was rewarded for male behaviors, yet he perceived himself to be like a woman and experienced anxiety at his male **sex-role identity.** The consequences could range from extreme emotional illness to a conscious decision, like that made by James Morris, to align one's sex with one's gender. What little empirical evidence exists on transsexualism suggests that early environmental factors can tip the ultimate sex-role identification in either direction and that, by the age of four or five, the child's primary identification has been rather firmly fixed (R. Green, 1974; Martino, 1977; Money, 1976; Stoller, 1975).

BEHAVIORS AND THOUGHTS

Though we have not tied all loose threads in the complex questions of socialization, we may have made some progress. We have brought out distinctions between the child's imitation of the single act of a model and broader behaviors dependent on the child's perceived generalized similarity between himself and a model. Whether, in the last analysis, one favors two separate terms—*imitation* and *identification*—may be a matter of judgment on which competent researchers will differ. But the developing child's tendency to adopt general behavioral patterns and understandings that cut across specific instances is certainly well documented.

The central conflict in the field, the tension between the cognitive-structural and social-learning approaches, has also been instructive. To begin with, the ways in which modeling occurs and imitation follows may well prove similar across diverse forms of behavior. And, as social-learning suggests, a child can acquire many sorts of novel sequences, prosocial as well as antisocial. But *which* behaviors are focused on, *which* behaviors are modeled and which are not, seems to depend on the child's cognitive level. So long as certain behaviors remain outside the child's conceptual network—because he has not yet attained the appropriate mental level—the child will not correctly and comprehensively model those behaviors. Once a child is capable of diverse behaviors, then the particular one he selects can be determined externally.

The social-learning point of view is concerned primarily with *behavior:* actions are crucial in determining what one represents both to oneself and to others. From this perspective, James Morris was a male as long as he behaved like one, regardless of what he might have been thinking. He began to assume the female identity once he began to adopt female patterns of action. Cognitive theorists pay much less attention to the individual's actions, attempting instead to understand how various thoughts and attitudes are organized. If James Morris thought of himself as a woman, then his sex-role identity was essentially female, no matter how he acted.

In conclusion, it is important to raise the possibility that the gap between social-learning and cognitive-structural theory may not be as wide as we have suggested here. Particularly in the recent work of Albert Bandura, considerable attention is paid to the way in which the child cognizes—or represents—the situations in which he is involved. Indeed, when one takes fully into account the child's representation of the whole situation, his ability to foresee outcomes and to modulate his behavior accordingly, the infusion of cognitive factors into an environmental-learning framework is striking indeed. Somewhat surreptitiously, much of the Piagetian critique has crept into social-learning theory, circa 1980.

Clearly the gap between behavior and thought can—and must—be bridged. Thought processes are obviously also behaviors (though not overt ones); furthermore, all inferences about such internal processes must rely on the study of overt behaviors. And just as evidently, behaviors are not mindless; they do not just happen. They reflect classifications, choices, prejudices, desires, and perceptual discriminations. To imitate, a person must perceive a target and comprehend it at some level, or the most tempting reinforcement will have little effect. By the same token, a person cannot mysteriously acquire a developed cognitive structure. Understanding is rooted in reactions to the full gamut of contacts with the world. And the elements the person comes into contact with, as well as the reinforcing experiences (positive and negative) that accompany these experiences, help to determine how one's own world view will eventually materialize. Our goal here has been to examine the interaction of such thoughts and actions in an amalgam of behavioral patterns important for society.

Signposts

During the toddler stage, children build on their practical knowledge of the world both through further direct actions on objects and, increasingly, through the use of symbols such as language. Children learn a great deal from their culture, and particularly from members of their family, about appropriate prosocial behaviors and attitudes and about antisocial behaviors such as aggression. Over the course of this period they gradually develop a conscience. And they must come to think of themselves as belonging to a specific gender and to act consistently with that self-definition. In this chapter we considered several theoretical orientations that have sought to account for these important events of the preschool years.

The first and, in the view of some, the most vital contribution to socialization comes from the individual's biological makeup. This is most obvious in the case of the individual's sexual membership but, according to sociobiological theory, also figures significantly in the emergence of prosocial behaviors (like altruism) and antisocial behaviors (like aggression). The verdict on sociobiology is not yet in, but it is certain to constitute part of discussions for some time to come.

The child's adoption of prosocial behaviors and his acquisition of appropriate sex-role identity are closely linked, in the classic theory of Sigmund Freud, to the concept of identification. Freud postulated a series of psychosexual stages (oral, anal, and Oedipal) culminating in the Oedipal crisis, through which all children must pass in early childhood. A predictable course of desires, frustrations, and compromises causes the child to identify in terms of sex role with the parent of the same sex and to adopt the values of the elder generation. Failure to follow this course and to develop an appropriate superego often signals aggressive and other antisocial behaviors. We noted that Freud never successfully explained girls' identification with their mothers. Furthermore, cross-cultural study has somewhat undermined the Oedipal pattern Freud proposed for boys. Thus, useful as it is, the Freudian model does not answer all our questions. Nor have other efforts to account for identification—as resulting from a desire to be similar to a powerful, feared adult, to an admired and envied parent, or to the most readily and frequently observed model—satisfied critical observers.

In their own efforts to explain the child's acquisition of sex-role and prosocial attitudes, environmental-learning theorists focus on simple imitation rather than Freudian identification. Children observe interesting events and repeat them, either because they are explicitly rewarded for doing so or because imitation is intrinsically rewarding. Traditional learning theorists such as Neal Miller and John Dollard see each step of a behavior as separately learned; social-learning theorists such as Albert Bandura believe that the child can observe and acquire large segments of behavior at a single exposure and that even sex-role patterns need not be permanent or irreversible. Although these environmental-learning approaches can account for much of behavior, they have tended to overlook crucial restrictions imposed by the child's particular level of understanding. This defect has been stressed by cognitive-structuralists such as Piaget, who hold that children can meaningfully imitate only the behaviors and attitudes they can assimilate.

Rival interpretations of imitation and identification have yielded different models of sex-role identity. Cognitive-structuralists like Lawrence Kohlberg stress that children must first recognize their similarity to others of the same sex and that feelings of general identification will flow from this understanding, even in the absence of particular motives or reinforcements. However, such an unabashedly cognitive viewpoint may slight the role biological predisposition plays in humans, as in other animals. And it overlooks instances in which sex-role identification may be inconsistent with objective knowledge about one's sexual characteristics. Social-learning theorists, if they allow the concept of identification at all, regard feelings of anxiety, weakness, or desire as the motivation for identifying with one or another parent. Psychoanalytical observers following Freud point to a biological heritage and the need to satisfy certain libidinal drives.

At times the social-learning and cognitive-structural approaches have directly clashed. With respect to moral judgment, for example, social-learning theorists feel that children can learn, through the observation of models, to reason at a variety of levels of sophistication. Cognitive-structuralists, on the other hand, feel that children must pass naturally through an ordered sequence of stages; they may learn to mimic other higher stages or to parrot lower stages in order to receive a reward, but these manipulations will not affect their "genuine" level of understanding. A review of the evidence in the various areas of social development under consideration here provides some support for both positions but reveals that neither, in itself, is fully adequate.

Possibly, then, a more complex and multifaceted approach is needed. Such an approach would consider biological as well as cultural factors and focus on the continuing interaction between what children know and what they feel. Important hints concerning such an approach emerge from certain studies of prosocial behaviors. Studies of altrusim and empathy document an early stage where the infant responds to signs of distress; stages during early childhood in which the roles of various nurturant individuals prove influential; and a later time during the school years when the child's cognitive level permits understanding of the intention of an individual and the structure of an entire situation. Affective factors play a role here as well; understanding is most likely to go beyond the superficial when the child can truly share the feelings of an individual in distress. Such an account helps to explain some of the behaviors exhibited by a collection of young boys marooned on a desert island; it also provides hints about certain behaviorial differences that might obtain among the boys themselves and certain ways in which they might differ from girls trapped in an analogous situation.

Issues related to acquisition of sexual and social attitudes and behaviors are thrown into sharp relief by transsexual individuals who, despite the physical evidence of their own bodies, view themselves as members of the opposite sex. Through the case of British writer J. Morris,we have evaluated the different interpretations of sex-role identity. One's ultimate sex-role commitment seems to be a joint product of one's self-perceptions and relations with others; the objective biological facts of one's body and behavior; the models one has observed; and one's conditioning history, whereby emotions become coupled with specific behaviors and thoughts.

Thus, even as toddlers are mastering language and other symbol systems of the culture, they are acquiring sexual and social behaviors that will endure over a lifetime. In each of these pursuits the children are becoming increasingly a part of their cultural setting. But toddlers are, above all, players: play is the activity that dominates their waking hours and at which they seem especially at home. In the concluding chapter of this section, we will see the child engaged in play and surrounded by valued play objects. By considering diverse interpretations of such activity, we will assess the significance of play in the life of the young child.

CHAPTER SIX

The Playing Child

I'm a playing boy, not a working boy.
  –JERRY, AGE 4

Children's playings are not sports and should be deemed as their most serious actions.

  –MONTAIGNE

At the age of fourteen months, my daughter Kay received a twelve-inch-tall toy koala bear. Over the next several years, the stuffed animal assumed an increasingly special place in Kay's life, until it was participating in nearly every family activity. Kay called on the bear constantly as a friend, as a partner, as a sibling, as an actor in little play scenes of her devising, as a target of her feelings, both positive and negative—and her experiences with this inanimate but lifelike object help to illuminate the behaviors we usually call "play." Here we will review some entries from a diary I kept during Kay's first years. As you read these entries, you can perhaps share my own puzzlement as I tried to figure out why Kay

selected the bear, what needs and purposes it fulfilled, and whether these diverse activities should all be thought of as play.

1:4:12 [in the twelfth day of the fourth month of her second year]—Kay starts to take the bear along when she walks about the house. She names him "Bear." She hugs "Bear" frequently.
1:6:15—Bear now goes to bed with Kay every night. Kay drags around both Bear and "Blanket" inside and outside the house. Mommy and Daddy always check that Bear and Blanket are in Kay's bed before she goes to sleep. Bear is no longer a comfortable object: it is now a bosom companion.

1:7:20—Bear is momentarily lost. Kay stands in bed screaming, "I want Bear!"

1:9:2—We get a new "infant seat" in the car. Kay is reluctant to sit in it herself. Finally she runs into the house, gets Bear, and makes Bear sit in the seat first.

1:9:10—Kay asks us to rub noses with Bear—the ultimate token of affection.

2:0:0—On her second birthday Kay gets another bear. Promptly christened "Little Bear," in contrast to Bear, who is renamed "Big Bear."

2:1:20—Kay takes one of her favorite books off the shelf, sits down on the floor, and pretends to read the book aloud to Big Bear.

2:4:2—Big Bear is lost for an afternoon. Kay is very upset and several times during the afternoon runs around the house screaming, "Find my Big Bear. I want Big Bear." Efforts to assuage her with Little Bear or with her blanket are to no avail.

2:5:8—By now Kay has two more bears, which she names "Biggest" and "Tiny." She informs me, "They're a family. Big is the daddy, Little is the mommy, Tiny is the baby." "Who is Biggest?" I ask. "He's another Daddy."

2:5:15—Kay pretends that she is Big Bear and that Big Bear is Kay. "Hi, Kay" she says and is then delighted when I mimic the voice of Kay.

2:6:8—I hear strange squeaking in the room and I ask Kay what's the matter. "Big Bear's talking," she declares. Big Bear, it turns out, has a high, squeaky, almost incomprehensible voice, which resembles a series of flute sounds. But, when pressed, Big Bear also emits understandable words like "I want my Mommy," and "I'm going to go outside now."

2:6:20—Someone put crayon marks all over the wall of Kay's room. When I inquire, Kay tells me "Big Bear did it. I'm going to give you a spanking, Big Bear." Big Bear is not actually whipped. But in the days following, nearly all misdeeds are attributed to Big Bear and he is frequently admonished. "Now don't do that, Big Bear, or I won't tell you a story at night." The words with which Big Bear is admonished are eerily familiar.

2:9:12—Returning from a trip, I'm informed, "Big Bear missed you."

2:10:7—Kay now has a new imaginary character named Funty. Funty has no physical dimensions; she lives only in stories. Her presence in no way dampens Kay's attachment to Big Bear.

2:11:8—On the first two days of school, Kay is tremendously upset and refuses to let her mother leave the classroom. Before going to school on the third day, she asks to bring Big Bear along. This is a perfect solution: she bravely enters the classroom without protest.

2:11:15—Big Bear becomes the subject of a song, chanted to the tune of "Frère Jacques." It goes: "Big Bear's coming, Big Bear's coming, How are you, How are you?"

2:11:18—Big Bear is going to have a birthday party. By a strange coincidence it is scheduled to occur on the same day as Kay's birthday. Big Bear will get lots of presents.

3:0:2—When Kay's birthday arrives, Big Bear's birthday celebration is forgotten in the excitement of the day. But Big Bear does sit right alongside Kay at the birthday table. Later Kay gives her beloved stuffed animal some stones, calling each one a different present.

3:1:15—Big Bear cannot be found. It is surprising and instructive to hear Kay say to Little Bear, "Now *you* be Big Bear."

3:5:29—Kay is asked to help with the garbage but refuses. "Big Bear is very busy doing his work," we are told.

3:11:1—Kay has a bad dream at night. A wolf has eaten up Big Bear and Kay. The next day Big Bear is kept close at hand.

3:11:5—Big Bear has lost all of his hair by now. Not to mention his appendages. Finally a foot and then a leg fall off and all the stuffing falls out. Kay says that she will give Big Bear away tomorrow. But she never does. Instead Mother sews Big Bear's leg back on and he returns to the wars.

4:2:17—Kay asks me to tell her a bedtime story. This time it's not about Kay, or about Funty, or about Peter Pan, or any of the usual nocturnal characters. Kay wants a story about Big Bear.

4:4:11—Told a story about a giant who scared all the people, Kay declares, "Big Bear will get the giant."

4:8:27—Big Bear now goes to school regularly with Kay.

5:4:2—For the first time Kay goes to school without Big Bear. She is not greatly disturbed by his absence.

6:5:3—Kay has not played with Big Bear for days. But when severely punished, she cries for Big Bear.

Drawing conclusions from a single case study is risky, especially when the subject is one's own child. As an exercise in developmental psychology, however, it is useful to try to characterize the changing nature of the relationship between Kay and her Bear.

Although Kay paid little attention to the bear initially, by the middle of her second year she began to form an attachment toward it. Kay's strong reactions whenever Bear was missing—similar to her earlier anxiety when she had been separated from her parents—heralded the important role Bear was assuming. The animal's distinctiveness was confirmed on Kay's second birthday, when he received a special name. And even more potent evidence of Big Bear's separate personlike identity was his increasing involvement in Kay's daily activities. Big Bear was read to, spoken to, and included in dramas. Soon he was invested with his own voice, family responsibilities, and behavioral routines.

By her third year, Big Bear's life was becoming intertwined in a new way with Kay's. When criticized or punished, Kay no longer bore the blame alone, but instead began to attribute misdeeds to Big Bear and to punish him for what he had allegedly done. The animal not only fulfilled needs for comfort and companionship but also served as a convenient target on which to deflect unhappy moments and feelings. Big Bear also assumed a larger role in Kay's fantasy life, becoming a protagonist in little stories, songs, and eventually drawings. Indeed, for a time, he seemed a constant in all of Kay's imaginative play.

During Kay's fourth year, however, some signs emerged that Big Bear was not all-powerful as before, and these continued until her seventh year. Big Bear began to figure less prominently in Kay's fantasy. Other bears could be substituted in his absence. Indeed, Kay even toyed with the idea of getting rid of Big Bear, but could not bring herself to do so. This was presumably because Big Bear continued to serve important functions, particularly when Kay was frightened, sad, or lonely. Dispensable when things were going well, Big Bear remained essential as a source of comfort, particularly when Kay indulged in imaginative fantasy.

Kay's bear participated in her making, perceiving, and feeling life, on the sensorimotor level as well as in the symbolic world that was increasingly capturing her interest. Such attachment to one or more objects is typical for toddlers, although hardly universal. And Kay's waning interest in Bear is also typical, although some people continue their attachment until their adult years.

Many observers would say that Kay's involvement with Big Bear is "play," and, indeed, many of her activities during this period do have an unmistakable flavor of play. Kay shifts rapidly from one situation with props to another. She imbues the stuffed animal with lifelike properties. She repeats familiar activities like parties in abbreviated form. She refuses to accept full responsibility for misdeeds carried out in make-believe. And her moments of enjoyment with Big Bear are colored by lighthearted expressions and moods. Yet characterizing these behaviors as play—even describing the three-year-old as a "player"—raises numerous questions.

Defining Play

As ordinarily used, the term **play** denotes a variety of activities. There is the initial experimentation with a new object—whether it is a teddy bear or a video camera—when one is exploring various facets and possibilities. There is the mastery involved in games such as basketball or chess. There is a warm-up before a more serious activity, such as fiddling with a paintbrush before beginning a portrait. There is the invention involved in acting out fantasies or fashioning imaginary characters and situations. There are the ornamentations imposed on a finished product, such as the curlicues affixed to a signature.

Few people would object to calling these activities "play," but may commentators have not been so restrictive (see Caplan and Caplan, 1973; Huizinga, 1955.) They have instead viewed almost all the toddler's activities as play, and have attributed all development during this period to the child's unique (and perhaps temporary) flair for playing. The problem with such broad usage is that it robs the word of any practical use in describing behavior, particularly during early childhood. It seems preferable, then, to begin defining *play* by saying what it is *not*.

Behaviors that are better excluded from the domain of play include those that satisfy pressing biological needs, such as eating, drinking, or escaping from pain; those that are part of a fixed ritual like a religious ceremony; or those designed to overcome an immediate obstacle, such as pushing away a child who is reaching for a desired toy. Even these boundaries prove slippery, however, for children often treat mealtime or religious ceremonies simply as welcome occasions for exploring, experimenting, or fantasizing.

We can get an initial handle on the nature of play by contrasting it with problem-solving and then examining the roles of play in problem solving (Gardner, 1971). Suppose a teacher presents several kindergartners with some forms drawn on a sheet of paper and tells them: "Here are some squares and some circles. Put together the group of circles with the group of squares having the same number in it. For instance, put together the *two* squares with the *two* circles." The teacher has now set a task that the child can approach in various ways.

A child who produces the correct answer right away has engaged in pure problem-solving behavior. In contrast, the behavior of a child who ignores the problem completely—instead getting up from the table and moving across the room—cannot be characterized as either playing or problem-solving. Usually, however, children have some idea of what is being asked and some desire to use the given materials, even when they do not understand—or do not care about—exactly what the teacher is requiring. Using the given materials as a point of departure, the child may engage in a variety of activities that can be called "play."

Figure 6.1. Children equipped with scissors and paper can engage in different kinds of play. In balancing a cut-out form on her nose, the girl at left is illustrating exploratory play. By producing paper dolls according to a prescribed formula, the girl at right exhibits rule-governed play.

One child may toy with some behavioral patterns or making schemes he has previously evolved. He may note the circles and then, practicing a form he has recently begun to draw, begin to produce varied ellipses. Or he may call on behaviors that can be performed with paper, cutting out designs of his own liking or crumpling the paper. In such instances, the child is engaged in **exploratory play** (see Figure 6.1). The materials are simply a stimulus, a point of departure for rehearsing behaviors he is in the process of mastering and now has a fresh opportunity to enact. The behaviors are not directed toward a goal.

We can, adopting Piaget's approach, view such exploratory play as assimilatory activity. Just as the infant can assimilate an object like a ball to a number of schemes that he has already developed, such as sucking, mouthing, throwing, or rolling, so too the somewhat older child may exploit the circles and squares as an occasion to try out the schemes that are most prominent in his current arsenal.

The child alone takes the initiative and decides what to do. In fact, the child is more likely to continue exploring, and to try out a great range of schemes, if adults remain in the background, refrain from selecting the game, and don't offer a reward (Swann and Pittman, 1977).

While exploratory play can—and perhaps should—proceed in unpredictable ways, it does not at all unfold in a random fashion. Corinne Hutt (1966) studied children's play when they are presented with an unfamiliar but complex object—for example, a red rectangular box with four brass legs, topped by a perpendicular stick that can be moved in different directions and that will under various conditions emit novel sounds or visual sights. At first, Hutt found, children actively investigated the object, trying to discover what it could do. After initial exploration, they shifted to another approach: using the toy in repetition or game playing, while simultaneously searching for other objects to explore. Once the object had assumed a relatively peripheral role in the child's world, he would investigate it only if he hit upon a new property, such as the un-expected sounds or sights that followed upon a certain movement of the stick.

Returning to our circles and squares, consider another child who proceeds from the assigned task to an activity already mastered. He might draw an organized sequence of circles, then an analogous series of squares, then a set of triangles. Or he might fold the paper in a geometrical pattern and cut it in a certain way to produce a chorus line of dolls. This child is following rules derived from his culture. He is engaging in **rule-governed play** (Garvey, 1977).

In such rule-governed play, processes of accommodation have come to the fore. Rather than trying out a variety of novel schemes, the child instead accommodates the object(s) to a scheme that has already been well mastered: for example, a familiar routine, a ritual, or a game. Sometimes the rules are ones that the child imports from a realm of importance to him: this occurs when the child engages in pretend play, by simulating a trip to the store or the presenta-tion of a birthday cake. At other times the rules are drawn from a game within his cul-ture, in which case a set of rules has already been defined by others and the child is simply expected to abide by them (Hay, Ross, and Goldman, 1979). Often such games have a so-cial origin, commencing in interchanges with other individuals, dating back to the mother-child dialogues of early infancy and, eventu-ally, including one's siblings, peers, and stran-gers. But whether there are several individu-als involved and whether the pursuit of victory is important prove less crucial in de-fining rule-governed play than the fact that the objects have been injected into a single set of procedures that must be strictly hon-ored.

Here, then, is one "rough-and-ready" way of dividing the universe of tasks into play and problem solving. If, in a desire to try out his own emerging schemes, the child loses sight of the problem that was posed, or if the child substitutes a set of cultural rules or pro-cedures for the task at hand, the child is playing.

As part of this effort to introduce play, we can present another distinction. Consider, now, the situation where Kay is involved in a little dramatic scenario, for example, feeding Little Bear at a birthday party. As Piaget (1962*a*) pointed out many years ago, this kind of "pretend" or "symbolic play" certainly is rule-governed: Kay follows regular procedures for feeding, including setting the table, pour-ing the milk, washing the dishes, handing out presents, and the like. It may also contain bouts of exploration, for example, if Big Bear and Little Bear are knocked together, rolled across the floor, or allowed to "leapfrog" over one another.

In such dramatic scenes, two further facets of play are realized. The Bear (which is, after all, but a manufactured product) is allowed to represent an individual with a particular role, in this case a "birthday child." Here is an in-stance of Role Play, and in various vignettes Bear can assume the roles of mother, feeder, comforter, victim, and so on. Note that physi-cal objects with no trace of animateness can also assume roles, as when the stones "stand for" birthday presents. Then, in addition, in portraying an imagined meal, Kay is enacting or re-creating a small drama or scene—the procedures that typically unfold in daily life when individuals interact with one another in a given context, such as a birthday party.

We thus encounter two facets of play. One facet contrasts unregulated experimentation (exploratory play) with faithful honoring of a set of procedures (rule-governed play). An-other facet exists within the realm of sym-bolic or pretend play. Here we can contrast the **role** or roles that a given person (or physical object) can play at any moment in time, with the little dramatic **scenes** or scenarios that unfold over time.

We have not fashioned an impeccable definition of play but we have introduced some relevant distinctions: these can help to describe Kay's interaction with Big Bear, as well as the classroom exercise involving squares and circles. With these initial distinctions in hand, we will in this chapter examine the characterizations that prominent students of child development have offered about play activities. We will then review research on the distinctions we have introduced between the roles of individuals, the roles of objects, and the scenes that are typically enacted in play. Finally, after touching on some other important dimensions of play—ranging from individual differences to affective components—we will offer a sketch of how play develops during the first years of life.

Scientists Explain "Big Bear": Some Theories of Play

In invading the territory of play, one may proceed along three separate avenues. One may *define,* as in the attempt we just made to delineate kinds of play and to isolate play from other activities. One may *conduct research* on specific forms of play (we will introduce various relevant empirical studies throughout this chapter). But, given difficulties in defining and conceptualizing play (Berlyne, 1960; Rubin, Fein, and Vandenberg, in press; Sutton-Smith, 1979*a*; Weisler and McCall, 1976), it is a third approach that may be most important at this time. That approach is to *theorize* about a circumscribed set of play activities. In this section, we shall investigate the surprisingly diverse ways in which

theorists of play might interpret Kay's activities with a once furry creature named Big Bear.

TRANSITIONAL OBJECTS

Many theorists (for example, Winnicott, 1971) would call Big Bear a **transitional object,** an inanimate physical entity to which a child becomes attached and with which the young child performs elaborate sequences designed to fulfill certain needs and desires. During the opening months, as we have seen in Part I, children direct their strongest feelings and attachments to human caretakers. Other objects will acquire enduring importance or fulfill significant roles only after a sense of object permanence has fully evolved, during the second year.

By age three, children venture forth into the world, move away from the caretaker, and interact more with others. This move outward, along with heightened recognition of right and wrong and growing competition with peers, creates feelings of ambivalence even as it engenders increasing self-awareness. The child's sense of self slowly emerges as he seeks to find his place (a place for himself). At this time, the child spends more time alone, thinking and fantasizing. And during these moments he may seek the comfort and companionship of a special, loved object.

A common, though by no means universal, practice at this age is the formation of an intimate attachment to one or perhaps two new objects, an animal such as Big Bear, an item of clothing such as Mommy's scarf, a blanket such as that dragged about by Linus in the comic strip "Peanuts." Sometimes these relationships are long-lived. At other times they are brief, soon replaced by some new object or, perhaps, by nothing at all. And sometimes, as in the case of Kay's Funty, they can exist completely in the realm of fantasy.

The transitional object becomes an important part of the child's play activities. It may participate in the child's own miniature world, a more manageable and more benevolent version of the complex real world. In this way, the transitional object can help the child solve emotional or social problems.

DONALD WINNICOTT'S VIEWS OF TRANSITIONAL OBJECTS

Donald Winnicott (1964, 1971, 1977), a British psychiatrist, made transitional objects the focus of his research. He viewed the transitional object as the child's first possession that is not merely a part of the body, like the child's own thumb or the mother's breast. In Winnicott's words, "it is not the object itself . . . that is transitional: it represents the infant's transition from a state of being merged with the mother to a state of being in relation to the mother as something outside and separate" (1964, p. 168).

Winnicott saw the role of transitional objects as varying from child to child. Some children find them acceptable substitutes for their mothers. They may rely on objects particularly when sad or alone. Others require that their mothers be present if they are fully to savor the objects. In most cases, the exact condition and precise location of the object matter a great deal to the child. Smell, texture, and shape are so important that the child strenuously resists any efforts on the part of others to clean the object or otherwise alter its appearance or condition. Probably the child does not yet know which features of objects are accidental and can be changed without affecting the object's identity; the child may also be loath to part with the object during cleaning times. Moreover, the fact that the object *has* shape or smell is important; without some vitality it would cease to function effectively.

Figure 6.2. Blankets, rattles, dolls, bears, all may serve as transitional objects. Even as this little girl is consoling her transitional object—the ubiquitous teddy bear—that bear may well be comforting her own sad feelings, as all good transitional objects should do.

Paradoxically, the child often uses the object as a target of both affectionate caressing *and* destructive attack, because (unlike humans, who fight back) the bear, blanket, or book will endure all treatments and mistreatments. But by the child's rules, the object must have enough substance to survive attacks. The child must not feel omnipotent.

Winnicott saw the transitional object not only as the child's first possession; it is also his first creation. Such creation is possible only when the object is differentiated, at least to some extent, from the child's own person. Then the child can invest in it what is important—ideas, emotions, hopes, and fears. Because the object belongs only to the child, no one else can presume to alter it in any way. Winnicott reported that in their childhoods, creative artists were much more likely than nonartists to have had transitional objects or imaginary companions (a kind of transitional object that exists only in words or images). Perhaps one can use these tangible or imaginary objects to learn how to instill in an alien body a valued portion of oneself.

Although in the normal course of events transitional objects recede into the background by the school years, some trace of them survives longer. In fact, as Kay's behavior reminds us, the adoption and, later, the gradual relinquishing of the transitional object can re-create, with a few years' gap, the child's initial relation to his mother. Sometimes the original transitional object can itself be supplanted, perhaps by a puppet (Sanders and Harper, 1976) or even a musical instrument (Suzuki, 1969). True, the adult who retains a teddy bear or an imaginary companion is rare and might be thought neurotic. Yet in Winnicott's view, some of the most profound experiences of later life—such as involvement with mystical events, religious figures, or artistic masterpieces—are akin to a person's attachment to a transitional object. In each of these instances the individual is sustained by something greater, a creation of his own mind that achieves transcendental importance.

An ingenious empirical effort has been made to study the function of transitional objects. Richard Passman and his colleagues (Passman, 1976; Passman and Weisberg, 1975) have examined how two- and three-year-old children with a prior attachment to a blanket behave when left alone with the blanket, with a favorite toy, or with their mother; and they have compared the behavior of such children to that of children with no attachment to a blanket. Youngsters attached to a blanket play as calmly when alone with their blanket as when alone with their mother, and they play more calmly when alone with their blanket than when alone with a favorite toy. In

contrast, children without a blanket-attachment play comfortably only in the presence of their mother. Performance on novel learning tasks is also better among children who have blanket-attachment than among those who do not (Passman, 1977). Under conditions of separation, however, even children attached to a blanket gain little comfort from it when placed in a stressful situation (in this study a dark and noisy room with a strange woman blocking the exit). Under such anxiety-provoking conditions, there may be no adequate substitute for the mother.

Whatever their import in our own culture, transitional objects are not a necessary part of human development. In one sample the incidence of attachment to transitional objects emerges as greatest among American children, lowest among Korean children, and intermediate in Korean youngsters reared in the United States (Hong and Townes, 1976). These differences are attributed to childrearing practices, particularly at the time of going to sleep. Attachment to inanimate objects may be lower in a cultural or social group where infants receive a large amount of physical contact, including breast feeding, particularly at the hours surrounding bedtime.

A focus on transitional objects offers a suitable approach to play, particularly since play itself can be considered a kind of transitional activity en route to the "serious" realities of school and work. But other authors who have considered transitional objects only incidentally add important ingredients to our analysis of this activity.

PLAY AS COPING

One major approach to play assumes that its guises of dreaming, fantasizing, and imaginative invention represent the child's effort to cope with the problems of daily life (S. Freud, 1958; Gould, 1972). A child who receives inadequate attention or has a desperate need for more love and cannot gain it from others may turn for solace and love to the objects and characters of play. Such play can express the child's major anxieties. By the same token, through play a child can remake the world to fulfill his dreams and fantasies: mud pies sweeten into fudge, dragons shrink into plastic figurines that can be knocked down at will. Such play can assuage the child's hurt feelings and aid him in tolerating a difficult situation or delaying gratification (Singer and Singer, 1980). For those who view play as coping, a transitional object replaces loved ones who have abandoned the child or defends against the threat posed by a new sibling. A child with all needs met and all fears allayed would have little need for a transitional object.

However, the child needs a certain measure of security and ego strength to play at all. If he is excessively aroused, so insecure that he will not venture forth, or terrified by any change in his milieu, the child may be unable either to explore or to play according to rules. In fact, this is the unhappy fate of certain seriously disturbed children (Hutt, 1979; Lewis, 1979). In cases where the very possibility of play is threatening, it may be especially important to allow the child to control the toy or game; by this means a potentially frightening object can be converted into a less threatening one (Gunnar-vongnechten, 1978). Achieving this measure of security is crucial for therapy involving disturbed children: the improvement that sometimes results from peer play, role playing, or pretend play of course presupposes some willingness to play at all.

Others who view play as coping behavior stress its constructive as well as its defensive uses. Some psychoanalysts, notably Erik Erikson, have used this approach. In one case report Erikson (1963) describes his work with four-year-old Ann, who has withdrawn from her family. When she initially spurns Erikson, the therapist does not try to talk her out of

her shyness, as others might do. Instead, he plays. On hands and knees, he constructs a simple house of blocks complete with characters, including the familiar mother urging her child to go to the bathroom.

But will the familiar and less threatening situation allow Ann to reveal the nature of her problems? She watches the scene with increasing fascination and suddenly springs into action:

She relinquishes her thumb to make space for a broad and toothy grin. Her face flushes and she runs over to the toy scene. With a mighty kick she disposes of [the mother]; she bangs the bathroom door shut and she hurries to the toy shelf to get three shiny cars, which she puts into the garage beside the man. She answered [Erikson's] question: she, indeed, does not wish the toy girl to give her mother what is her mother's, and she is eager to give to her father more than he could ask for [Erikson, 1963, p. 50].

The speed and bluntness of Ann's expression of inner feelings is dramatic. Ann's activities convince the therapist that she is experiencing ambivalent feelings about her mother, most especially over demands about toilet training. Numerous similar cases document how a child's difficulties may be communicated compellingly through play (see Wickes, 1968).

In sessions with normal youngsters, Erikson (1963) has documented a most intriguing phenomenon. Given an odd assortment of toys, children are asked to construct an "exciting scene" based on an imaginary movie. Typically, after some thought, the children arrange the toys in a quiet and purposeful manner, as if following the dictates of some potent inner logic. And surprisingly often, the scenes created by children serve as a metaphor for their lives: their chief concerns and interests, their goals and fears, their style of life can be discerned. The scenes can also uncover the child's difficulties as well as his hidden strengths. Visiting his players many years later, Erikson was amazed at the extent to which their adult life-styles had been implicit in the themes of their childhood play (Erikson, 1977). For instance, one man who, as an adult counselor, helped rebellious teenagers control their feelings had as a youngster built a cage in which wild animals were securely kept. Here we see objects of play helping the child to dramatize issues that are central in his life rather than merely compensating for life's deficiencies.

In Erikson's view, play is an attempt to master a complex reality, to capture strengths as well as difficulties, and to communicate them to oneself and to others. Indeed, Erikson proposes that

the child's play is the infantile form of the human ability to deal with experience by creating model situations and to master reality be experiment and planning. . . . He relives the past and thus relives left-over affects. He anticipates the future from the point of view of a corrected and shared past [Erikson, 1963, p. 222].

Thus play can be constructive even for the well-adjusted child, because it helps to clarify options and anticipate outcomes. In this view, an object like Big Bear gives Kay an opportunity to replay themes important and potentially anxiety provoking in her life—separation, harm, and loss—and thereby gain some mastery over them. Whether interpreted as a defense against problems or as a coping behavior, such views treat play primarily as the child's way of dealing with affective predispositions. As we shall now see, others view play as a means of learning about the physical world or as a means of attaining a physical or a cognitive skill.

PLAY AS A PARTNER IN SKILL BUILDING

Scientists associated with the cognitive-structural school have approached play quite differently. In his pioneering writing on the subject, Piaget (1962a) assimilated play to his general preoccupation with knowledge, highlighting the assimilatory aspects of typical exploratory play, but noting as well the accommodation involved in the mastery and deployment of rules. A more broad-based view of play as a means of attaining cognitive skill is held by Jerome Bruner and his colleagues (Bruner, 1972; Bruner, Jolly, and Sylva, 1976).

Proceeding from observational studies of young children and of various nonhuman primates that engage in considerable exploratory play, Bruner attributes to play a crucial role in the development of physical and cognitive skills in young children. Play features experimentation with smaller acts that can eventually be combined into a well-orchestrated higher-order skill. Thus a two-year-old who is given a set of Tinkertoys will first, in approved exploratory fashion, tinker with each toy separately. Then, over the next weeks, he will try out various motor schemes, such as banging the pieces together or lining them up. Within a few months, the child will, with increasing confidence, combine pairs of sticks. And ultimately, after many months of exploration, the child will be able to combine the pieces to create complete constructions.

Such play allows the child to learn about spatial relations, mechanics, and the like—all in an informal and nonthreatening setting. Unrestricted by external rules, the child is free to experiment, to order and reorder objects, to try new combinations, to practice, refine, and ultimately master his actions. Consistent with the operation of the making system (see Chapter 3), the child can master each specific move in Tinkertoy play before having to coordinate various moves into a smooth sequence of combined acts.

These separate facets all come together in the child's ability to use tools, an ability that dramatically increases the child's power and enables him to transform the environment. Indeed, deprived of the opportunity for free

Figure 6.3. Like most forms of play, this game of stacking forms serves a variety of functions. The little boy is mastering fine motor movements, learning to look carefully at plastic forms, improving his ability to balance tiny objects, producing a pleasing physical pattern, and gaining a feeling of accomplishment from a task well done.

play, children may not develop the ability to use tools in a constructive fashion.

A demonstration of how play can contribute to problem solving and tool use comes from some recent studies by Bruner and his associates (Sylva, Bruner, and Genova, 1976). Children aged three to five were instructed to fetch a piece of colored chalk from a latched box that lay out of reach. The problem could be solved only by clamping two sticks together and then extending them into the box.

The Bruner group found that children who were merely allowed to play with the materials solved the task as rapidly as children who had seen the entire solution modeled by an adult; furthermore, the playing children were more successful than children who had seen only part of the solution modeled.

Others have documented further cognitive dividends from play. Preparatory to a task where they would have to join two sticks with a block in order to retrieve a marble, children were given either training directly relevant to the task or the opportunity to play with the materials (Smith and Dutton, 1979). While training and play groups performed equally well on the task at hand, the children with play opportunities proved more successful at solving a new, more complex task, involving three sticks, two blocks, and a marble located at a greater remove. In a series of studies, Vandenberg (1980) has replicated the major findings of the Bruner and Smith teams. But Vandenberg's failure to obtain the same results when he used subjects of different ages and employed different tasks raises the question of whether play necessarily aids in all problem solving.

Extensive opportunity to play with objects has been correlated with a number of other desirable outcomes: greater creativity and imaginativeness (Feitelson and Ross, 1973); emergence of classifactory skills (Rubin and Maioni, 1975); the ability to produce varied uses for objects (Dansky and Silverman, 1973); and more divergent (innovative) thinking (Pepler, 1980). Heightened fantasy has been related to spurts in cognitive development (Singer and Singer, 1980; Saltz, Dixon, and Johnson, 1977). Memory for a list of objects has improved when children have had the opportunity to use these objects in dramatic play (as compared to using the objects in more conventional rule-governed play) (Gobbel and Rider, 1981). Children who at six months of age were judged to have a better quality of play—displaying more attention, more continuity and more rule-governed uses of objects—turned out to perform better on cognitive measures at a year of age (Jennings et al., 1979). It must be noted, however, that not all attempts to document the efficacy of play have been successful. Accordingly, some authorities retain a healthy skepticism about the direct benefits of play for various cognitive ends (Brainerd, 1980*a*; Saltz, 1980; Vandenberg, 1980; Yawkey, 1981).

What of a longer-term effects of play? In a study that probably deserves a footnote in the Guinness book of records, Hutt (Hutt and Bhavnani, 1972) tracked down and revisited the children whose exploratory play she had studied five years earlier. She found that nonexploring in early childhood relates to lack of curiosity and adventure in boys and to difficulties in personality and social adjustment in girls. Conversely, boys (and to a lesser extent girls) who had been active explorers while toddlers were more likely to score high on tests of creativity and more likely to be judged as curious and independent by their teachers. Hutt's study clearly demonstrates a relation between one form of exploration examined with preschool children and subsequent personality and cognitive style. In studies whose results echo these findings, children from disadvantaged backgrounds have shown dramatic upsurges in their overall performances when they have been given supplementary dosages of play (Smilansky, 1968).

These studies contribute to a picture of exploratory play as a potent partner in the acquisition of skills and the solution of problems. But such forms of play are not only helpful in early life. Place a child in the background as you consider the testimony of no less an authority than the physicist Albert Einstein: "This combinatory [exploratory] play seems to be the essential feature in productive scientific thought—before there is any connection with logical construction in words or other kinds of signs that can be communicated to others" (quoted in Piers, 1973, p. 137).

LEV VYGOTSKY ON THE ROLE OF PLAY IN DEVELOPMENT

There is, to be sure, a gap between the child's exploratory play with transitional objects and the theoretical physicist's exploratory grouping of symbols, Yet both of these players also participate fully in more rule-governed play. Extending the cognitive-structural viewpoint to its furthest point, the Russian investigator Lev Vygotsky (1967) sees play as a key propeller of overall development. Vygotsky focuses particularly on the rules of play. Confronted by a difficulty, the child unconsciously creates an imaginary situation that he can handle better. Crucial to this play situation are rules, a set of procedures the child follows with painstaking fidelity so long as the "game" is in effect.

As a means of contrasting play and nonplay situations, Vygotsky recalls an anecdote reported by James Sully, a nineteenth-century English psychologist. Sully tells of two sisters, aged five and seven, who one day agreed to "play sisters." The two girls tried to enact rules that would help them comprehend their own personal situation. They walked about holding hands, engaged in various family activities, and made remarks like "My sister and I act the same; we are treated the same, but others are treated differently." As Vygotsky remarks, "What passes unnoticed by the child in real life becomes a rule of behavior in play" (1967, p. 9).

Vygotsky focuses on the primitive symbolic representations prevalent in the play of young children. A child fetches an object such as a stick. Declaring that it is a horse, he proceeds to ride around on it. Vygotsky points out that children's ordinary activities reflect the conventional uses of familiar objects—the mundane functions of silverware, soap, clothing. But when a child grabs a stick and dubs it a horse, he no longer honors the usual traits of the stick (or of the horse). Instead, he is governed by internal representations—by ideas or rules or symbols. The stick—a physical object—has become a lever for prying the meaning of a horse away from its usual embodiment in a large animal with its characteristic sight, feel, and smell.

What has happened? A complete reversal: At first the object's customary use dominated; now the child's ideas determine the significance of the object. All this can be a very difficult business, for the child must swallow his momentary desires and force himself to conform to his new rules. He must resist the impulse to use the stick to whack his sibling. Rules now dictate that the stick be treated as a horse.

Vygotsky concludes that play is not children's predominant activity. Indeed, it stands apart from their usual behavior. Play should instead be considered a leading contributor to developmental progress. During play, children learn to follow rules and eventually divorce themselves from total domination by the objects' and events' present context. Now the children can refer to events and experiences removed in time and adopt a hypothetical or pretend stance toward the present.

Indeed, play creates a "zone"—often termed the "zone of potential development"—in which higher steps of development can unfold. The child may behave at a cognitive level above that typical for his age—for instance, going through some of the motions of reading or writing for the first time. In fact, a good way to assess the child's potential for development at a given moment is to observe the distance between his customary activities and the heights reached during play.

There are also, according to Vygotsky, some general developmental trends governing the course of play. In the second or third year of life, the imaginary situation is very similar to the real one (a sister stands for a sister; a toy horse for a real horse). Gradually, distances emerge so that eventually almost anything can stand for almost anything else. And play becomes increasingly internal, going from talking to oneself to fantasy and, eventually, to abstract thought. The older child plays by inventing stories and scenarios, by daydreaming, by manipulating symbols and concepts in both exploratory and rule-guided ways. Far from fading away, play lingers as an alternative to everyday reality, continuing to color the child's work in school and many rule-governed activities in later life.

Few acid tests have been conducted with respect to Vygotsky's claims but at least one line of research provides suggestive support for it. The ability to understand conservation of matter—to appreciate, for example, that the amount of liquid remains the same even if it is poured into a container of quite different dimensions—is considered by many psychologists an important milestone in development, one that is not ordinarily reached until the school years, and one resistant to early training. Working with four-year-olds, who clearly did not yet grasp conservation, Claire Golomb (Golomb and Cornelius, 1977) gave them intensive practice in various kinds of pretend games in which, for example, they had to distinguish between how something looks and what it really is. Thereafter, the players exhibited dramatic improvement in the ability to conserve, while no differences were observed in various control groups.

Golomb suggests that play can be the "cutting edge" of development, introducing children to difficult concepts that they cannot readily apprehend in daily life and thus laying the groundwork for the eventual (or even rapid) acquisition of such concepts. Similar results documenting improvement in perspective taking following play have also been reported by other researchers (Burns and Brainerd, 1979). But of late, some researchers have challenged the "play causes cognitive spurts" claim (Brainerd, 1980*a*; Guthrie and Hudson, 1979); and so Golomb's intriguing results must be considered tentative rather than definitive.

In addition to its cognitive facets—play as rule following, play as symbolic transformation, play as an arena for experimentation with more advanced schemes—Vygotsky is keenly sensitive to the affective components of play. We have seen that he locates the original motive for play in the child's reaction to a difficult or perplexing situation. For the most part, however, it is not specific frustrations but generalized affects (difficulties with adults, customary disappointments) that stimulate play. Further, since pleasure accompanies the rules honored in a contrived situation and motivates future play, affective factors can also provide considerable incentive for playful activities.

Avoiding a one-sided interpretation of play as either strictly the alleviation of frustration or solely an aid to reasoning, Vygotsky instead takes into account the cognitive, motivational, and affective facets of play and the amazingly complex purposes to which this activity can be put. Furthermore, Vygotsky contends that not all behaviors of preschool children are play and in fact insists that play differs in many ways from children's normal activity. Finally, Vygotsky's approach seems applicable to the issue of transitional objects. Children "create" these objects at a time when they are confronting unsettling life changes. And for several years the objects not only help gratify desires but also serve to usher in the dominance of rules and symbols in children's lives.

OBJECTS, ROLES, THEMES

Using as a point of departure one child's play with a single "created" object, we have examined the principal theoretical accounts of play—exploratory as well as rule-governed—and certain empirical studies that address the claims of theory. While these accounts differ in their stress, they do not contradict one another. Many activities qualify as play, and it is scarcely surprising that a variety of perspectives can be brought to bear upon it.

By the age of two or three, however, interaction with a transitional object is but a single, and no longer the predominant, play activity of a young child. Much time is spent in play with common household objects and in the enactment of specific roles and scenes, which can be drawn from daily life (Sachs, 1980), from the child's imagination, or from narratives presented in a book or on television. To convey the flavor of this play, which assumes a prominent place with many children, I will describe a play task that has proved informative and then consider some research that has helped illuminate the principal features of this task.

The props are simple: a toy girl, a lion, and a set of blocks that can serve as a house. When children of different ages are provided with these props, and given the opportunity to create a little story, a series of stages can be anticipated. Before the age of two, the child is likely simply to manipulate the objects, even if a dramatic scene has been modeled by an experimenter. The lion and the girl are simply stuffed into the playhouse. The lion is not imbued with ferocious qualities, nor is the girl rendered sweet, peaceful, or frightened. In fact, if wooden blocks were substituted for figures, the same behaviors would occur.

A few of the narrative implications of these props become evident to the child by the age of two and one-half or so. Now the child will hold the lion and make it approach the girl, perhaps roaring menacingly (Rubin and Wolf, 1979, p. 23). The child may direct an experimenter to put the girl inside the house: "Girl in house . . . go bed." Then the child will knock the house over, and the whole event may be repeated several times.

Though a child at this age will sometimes try to resolve a problem that has been posed by an experimenter—for instance, the lion attacking the girl—he does it through direct action. He will step in and rescue or punish the girl himself, rather than accomplish this by using the props. There are other limitations as well. For example, the characters are completely one-dimensional: the lion is capable of physical intimidation, nothing else, and the girl is frightened, that is all. If the experimenter attempts to complicate the story—say, by indicating that the lion is lonely and would like to be comforted—this information will completely bypass the child/player.

In contrast, with just this trio and perhaps a prompt from an adult, children of three or four will act out elaborate scenarios. They may play with the objects individually, incorporating them into their own domestic routines, or they may enact a vignette, most typically the events that occur when the lion attacks the little girl and she must somehow be rescued.

By the age of four or five, the child can approach this scene in an even more sophisticated manner. Seldom resorting to action himself, the child will accomplish changes of scene solely through the characters themselves. He is becoming sensitive to the possibilities of dual roles and of ambiguities: the lion can be ferocious but also lonely; the girl can be frightened but also ingenious in plotting her escape. There is also the possibility of changes in character: the lion can become kind or repentant, and he can be portrayed as

a father as well as an attacker. Achieving these more sophisticated understandings requires initial mastery of at least three skills: the use of physical objects to stand for (or symbolize) different real-life objects; the appreciation of various roles that can be played by persons, or by their "prop" representatives in play; and an acquaintance with the chief features of particular "scene" plots that can be expressed in "pretend" or "symbolic" play (Winner and Gardner, 1979; Wolf, in press).

Objects. Play by young children often involves the use of objects, particularly familiar ones scooped up from around the house. At times the objects are used in their proper fashion, as when the child gives a tea party using real spoons. At times tiny replicas are used, as when the child plays with a miniature tea set. But how adaptable are children? What will count as a spoon or a cup, and when will it cease to count?

Initially, children pay little attention to the particular object used—as we saw, at first they treat the props as if they were simply blocks. Physical "sparkle" rather than potential for representation dictates choices (Rosenblatt, 1975). However, by the age of two or so, the actual physical form of the object becomes important. Children want to use objects that bear a reasonable physical resemblance to the referent that they are symbolizing. A cup can be used as a potty seat, a hat, or a ladle (Fein, 1979b, p. 71). At the age of three, the child has developed a firm notion of what counts as a prototype or model representation of an object: it becomes possible to rank objects in terms of the ease with which they will be accepted as substitutes for a cup, a hat, or a potty seat (Fein, 1979b, p. 70; Jackowitz and Watson, 1980). Both the customary form of the referent and the function to which it is put are relevant factors, with replicas that share both form and function being much more readily accepted.

After the age of three or four, however, the particular form of the object ceases to matter as much (Elder and Pederson, 1978). As meaning comes to dominate over objects, almost anything can stand for anything else. Indeed, it may sometimes be easier to pretend when the association is more obscure: and so, for entirely different reasons, older children prove as adaptable as those one- or one-and-a-half-year-old children who are still at a prerepresentational stage (Fein, 1979*b*).

Roles. Just as physical objects can represent a range of meanings, so, too, humanlike props, ranging from dolls or puppets to animate objects like animals or siblings, can assume various roles in children's play. We have seen that Kay's furry friend initially inhabits the persona of Big Bear and that Big Bear himself comes to fulfill various roles, from friend of Kay and Little Bear to parent of Little Bear to substitute for Kay at times of partying, playing, or punishment. Indeed, children eventually are able to attribute to the same puppet or transitional object a number of roles, such as lion-aggressor *and* lion-father, or Bear-friend *and* Bear-victim.

We can see in the development of role playing the same set of factors that were at work in the realm of object substitution. Initially the child is impervious to any potential for role enactment: props are simply occasions for exploratory play. In social play, the child can fulfill a role as long as it is frozen—for example, saying peek-a-boo—but he has little flexibility in stepping into another role. We might say that the child is performing typical actions rather than assuming roles.

By the age of two most children can make a doll serve as an independent agent (Rubin and Wolf, 1979; Watson and Fischer, 1980).

A toy lion can go for a walk or attack a little girl. The two-year-old can also adopt two roles in a simple game—for example, being the chaser as well as the individual who is chased. And a prop can assume the role of "patient" as well as "agent": when the baby doll is hurt, Kay can put a Band-Aid on it and soothe it. Later stages, which emerge approximately at yearly intervals, include the following milestones: the child can enact a **social role** by making a prop (say a doctor doll) perform fitting behaviors (act appropriately toward a patient doll); and the child can manipulate the **intersection of social roles** in an individual (the doctor doll can also be a father and act appropriately toward his daughter). Thus with age children become able to enact a greater variety of roles, including roles in which they could not actually have participated in real life, such as wife and husband (Garvey and Berndt, 1975). And, with that special flavor that makes play of the young so charming, children of five or six are quite willing to attribute a whole array of humanlike properties to inanimate objects, thus giving rise to "talking brooks," "clouds that wander about," and "angry mountains" (Piaget, 1965*a*; Winner et al., 1980).

Worthy of special mention is the role of the imaginary playmate, the creature (like Kay's Funty) who is invented out of whole cloth but may eventually assume a major role in the child's fantasy life. According to one school of thought, such playmates could be seen as a sign of difficulty, loneliness, or even pathology; indeed, "hearing voices" and hallucinating may be considered pathological symptoms in adults. However, empirical studies of children with imaginary playmates indicate that often these creations prove quite beneficent: they correlate with intelligence, mental health, and, eventually, even a life of creative output (Caldeira, Singer, and Singer 1978; Fraiberg, 1959; Pines, 1978). Most important, children with imaginary playmates show no difficulty in distinguishing "make-believe" from "real".

Scenes and Themes. The objects and the roles of play are the building blocks of a play sequence (Sachs, 1980). Initially, these entities are absorbed into a sequence that bears a strong resemblance to the activity of daily life. In fact, in most cases the initial scripts are the simplest domestic scenes of importance to the baby—putting the child to bed, feeding the child, having dinners, perhaps going shopping. (Fenson and Ramsay, 1979; Rubin and Wolf, 1979; Nicolich, 1977, 1978). Initially these scripts are limited to the repetition of the most general properties of the situation, those events that typically occur; only later are children able to recreate the idiosyncratic features of one particular instant of the scene (K. Nelson, 1981*b*).

Pretend play expands rapidly in the number of subjects that can be treated and in the complexity with which scenes are enacted. Single acts give way to sets of acts, to whole scenes, and to scenes joined together to make a drama. A wider, if not yet exotic, set of themes is possible—teacher-student interactions, trips, birthday parties, weddings, religious rituals. (Nicolich, 1977, 1978). There is also a greater tendency to devise problems for solution, such as the classic victim in distress, the child who can't find his way home, or the threat by the monster. Finally, the child becomes less dependent upon the props of symbolic play and can sustain a narrative solely, or primarily, in oral language.

Nonetheless, the capacity to treat the narrative as entirely apart from the child's own wishes and drives remains elusive. As we've seen, in dealing with narrative materials young children have a strong tendency to want things to come out in a certain way. If someone or something is not arrayed as they would like, children are prone to interfering,

even (or especially) if the requisite materials for achieving their desired result are not present in the narrative itself. Hence the little girl is rescued just because she or the experimenter is kind, rather than by an increase in her own guile or a change of heart on the part of the threatening lion.

A formidable challenge facing the young child is to build up and then respect a boundary around the story, to treat the story as an entity having its own rules that he can exploit for desired ends but that he should not—according to those rules—circumvent. This task can involve considerable skill in the management of the resources of the story—knowing what the objects, the roles, and the themes allow and forbid. Whether a general proclivity for fantasizing—having imaginary playmates in an imaginary world—aids children or serves as an impediment toward forging the boundary between reality and fantasy is not yet known; nor is it clear that "premature" congealing of the boundary is necessarily a desirable developmental goal.

SOME FLAVORS OF PLAY: INDIVIDUAL DIFFERENCES, AFFECTIVE COMPONENTS, LANGUAGE

Now that we have considered the ingredients of the complex behavioral sequences of young players, we can turn our attention to certain factors that may modulate individual play schemes. We touch, in turn, on some of the key differences found among young players and on the relation between play and two vital features of the young child, his language and his affect.

Individual Differences. Nearly all researchers report differences between players of the two sexes. (Cramer and Hogan, 1975; Fein et al., 1975; Harper and Sanders, 1975; Rubin et al., in press). Indeed, the principal bone of contention is not whether girls play differently from boys—almost everywhere they do—but rather where these differences originate.

As we've come to expect, some researchers emphasize the biological substrate underlying differences in playing. Relying on information from primates and other animals, they stress the greater amount of rough-and-tumble play among males the world over and relate it to hormonal level (Blurton-Jones and Konner, 1973; P. K. Smith, 1977; Young, Goy, and Phoenix, 1964). The heightened activity level of young boys is taken as evidence in favor of their proclivity toward physical activity, play with more dynamic objects, and identification with more aggressive heroes (Tauber, 1979).

But the major differences between boys' and girls' play can also be accounted for readily in terms of modeling by parents, peers, and others in the child's environment. Rheingold and Cook (1975) have documented, for example, clear differences in the toys parents give to daughters and to sons. In fact, the choice of toys even reflects family makeup: children with no siblings of the opposite sex are more likely to play with toys normally associated with the opposite sex than children with cross-sex siblings. Possibly, single or same-sex children feel greater liberty (and a stronger need) to indulge their curiosity about what it is like to be a member of the opposite sex than children in a family where opposite sex roles can be observed (Tauber, 1979). Interestingly, while young girls often (and perhaps increasingly) engage in activities that are considered typically masculine (playing superheroes), young boys are less prone to indulge in pursuits that are considered feminine (playing with dolls) (Singer and Singer, 1980).

Some authorities have discerned two contrasting styles of play with toys (Shotwell, Wolf, and Gardner, 1980; Wolf and Gardner, 1979). Emphasizing the dramatic possibilities in play, some children use neutral objects like blocks or sticks to stand for persons and show a proclivity for acting out little scenes even when they have not been called on to do so. In contrast, other children attend to the physical patterns or configurations into which sticks or blocks can be arranged and may actually resist being drawn into a narrative mode. Calling attention to related dimensions, Jennings has contrasted children who like to play chiefly with objects with children who prefer to play with other individuals. Object-oriented children perform better on tasks assessing the classification of physical objects but, interestingly, an orientation toward people does not result in higher performance on tests assessing social knowledge (Jennings, 1975).

Language. Clearly, language plays an important role in much of play. Storytelling, play with props, and various verbal rituals where the child alternates lines with another individual or where he himself repeats linguistic formulas all presuppose competence in language (Sutton-Smith, 1979*b*; Garvey, 1979; Chukovsky, 1968; Kirschenblatt-Gimblett, 1979). Children who are precocious in language or who, like dramatists, rely heavily on language prove expert in this kind of play.

But what of the more general relation of linguistic ability to play? A number of investigations have confirmed that the stages of symbolic play—the ability to enact simple sequences with objects and roles—correlate significantly with the child's linguistic competence. Perhaps the same psychological mechanisms are entailed in carrying out a sequence of actions with props and gestures and being able to encode these sequences in language (Bates, 1979; Nicolich, 1977; Wolf, in press). Explicit announcements that he is playing or that he is engaged in "pretend" also underscore the child's sophistication in play; and although these "winks" that he is playing need not be conveyed by language (Bateson, 1955), typically they are.

Recently, a few investigators have sought to correlate the child's playing style and level of play with the kind of language he uses. Drawing on the distinction between referential and expressive language (see Chapter 4), Rosenblatt (1975) has shown that a child's sophistication in play correlates with the amount of referential language in his speech. Supporting this conclusion, Fein (1979*b*) reports that children whose language is largely expressive are likely to remain for a longer period of time at the simplest level of play. Apparently, even if counter to intuition, expressiveness in language does not translate into sophistication in play.

Affect. Though there has been little experimental research on the affective significance of play, two tentative conclusions can be drawn (Gould, 1972). First, children who have undergone stress or who have experienced conflict are prime candidates for "acting out" these themes shortly thereafter in their play (A. Freud, 1965; Matthews, 1977). Second, whether or not they are disturbed in any way, young children gravitate toward themes known to be affectively toned for them: attachment and loss, victory and defeat, hurting and being hurt. While not their only themes, these are the ones least likely to be missing from play (Bettelheim, 1976).

Piecing Together the Puzzle of Play

A DEVELOPMENTAL PORTRAIT

From the various strands of research reviewed here, we can sketch the principal milestones through which children pass during their "playing years." Until the age of eighteen months to two years, play remains sensorimotor. The child engages in dialogues with his mother but these consist of highly over-learned, ritualistic encounters. There is much solitary play with objects such as toys, but this play largely takes the form of exercise or repetition of simple schemes (Rubin and Maioni, 1975).

A great divide is passed at the age of two, when children can approach the world in a symbolic fashion. The child can now let objects stand for other objects: he can himself assume roles, have props act as independent agents, and enact simple stories or schemas. By this time the child, beyond the point of simple exploratory play, can also follow rules. However, these rules are primarily ones that he imposes himself and that follow his own proclivities for making sense of the world: for the most part they are not rule systems that have been devised by the larger culture. Nonetheless, a number of important trends occur in the wake of the symbolic revolution. The child can engage increasingly in fantasy or pretend activities. No longer tied to physical objects and their habitual uses, he can allow other objects to stand for familiar referents and can eventually dispense altogether with a material base. Flights of fantasy can take place, imaginary characters can be invented. Yet, paradoxically, at the very same time the child is firming up the boundary between reality and fantasy. He is less likely to step inappropriately across these realms, less likely to resolve problems within a bounded story by recourse to direct actions. And, through various conventions that refer to play activity, the child can signal to others that he is pretending (Garvey and Berndt, 1975).

Play becomes increasingly social. After a time of merely looking at others, or playing in parallel, without any exchanges, simple interactions begin to take place. At first these interactions may be quite rigid but soon they involve some give-and-take and, ultimately, genuine turn-taking and cooperation (Whiteside, Busch, and Horner, 1976).

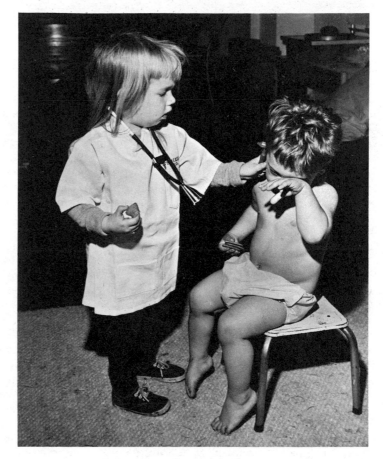

Figure 6.4. This reenactment, through pretend play, of a familiar sequence in the doctor's office gives both children an opportunity to practice behaviors and roles that they have not previously fully understood and mastered. One measure of the sophistication of play is the child's ability to switch roles in the course of play and appropriately enact the other role in the interaction.

It is not easy to determine how much time children spend in their various play pursuits, and the figures differ significantly across children and across populations. Nonetheless, some estimates have been put forth (Rubin et al., in press). Among the youngest children, play with single objects occupies about 90 percent of activities at age eight months, but it is down to less than 20 percent by the age of eighteen months. The slack is picked up by play with pairs of objects, by enactment of short sequences, and by the rapid rise in representational play in the second year of life. In somewhat older children, the amount of pretend play rises steadily, from 9 percent at age three to about 25 percent at ages five and six. Interactive pretend play mimics this trend at about the same rate, from 4 percent of all play at age three to 21 percent at age five. There are also some suggestive U-shaped trajectories in the data of early play. Perhaps the most intriguing is the finding that solitary play declines steadily from a high of 13 percent at age three to a low of 6 percent at age five; among six-year-olds, solitary dramatic play is on the rise, consisting of 19 percent of all pretend activities. This increase in solitary play may reflect children's private rehearsals of the new social games in which they have recently become involved.

Only with the advent of the school years does the child participate fully in the games of his society. Accommodation has now come to the fore and the child can follow rules faithfully, sometimes even too rigidly. The child is also now able to reflect on the nature of play. Indeed, when asked to do so, school-age children show a gradual decline in references to objects and props and an increase in references to the use of imagination, hence recapitulating the sequence they themselves have gone through a few years before (Chaillé, 1978). But now we are anticipating a later part of our story.

THE MANY USES OF PLAY

In addition to undergoing a developmental sequence, play itself contributes to development. For in play children try out a whole range of roles, acts, and behaviors, become familiar with them, and test their own and others' reactions to them. Such experimenting allows children to step into another's shoes: a decline in egocentrism and an increased sensitivity to rights and obligations ordinarily ensues (Piaget, 1932). Children also can embrace, at least tentatively, the behaviors and roles that feel most comfortable; confronting options, they begin to combine traits into the kind of person they would like to be. And, indeed, in pretend play children experiment with diverse facets of self, even as they can reveal to the sensitive observer certain features of the self that have already evolved.

As we've seen, a transitional object such as Big Bear often assumes a crucial role. The child's own creation, it is comfortably present when he is alone and engaged in reverie. Capturing facets of the child and other people, it can be experimented on in various ways. And because the object does not hit back, walk away, or otherwise reject the child, it can be explored with minimum risk and maximum latitude. Through play, and especially through the transitional object, the child receives an invaluable opportunity to make a trauma-free break from the initial caretaker and to form an enduring relation with another object. Acting out behaviors, wishes, emotions, and difficulties allows the child eventually to combine them more harmoniously and to face more directly the complex physical and social world. Most important, the transitional object serves as an experimental ground where sequences of rules and rituals can be attempted and perfected, combined and recombined, for their own sake and in the service of subsequent problem solving.

Figure 6.5. As children enter school, they spend an increasing amount of time in rule-governed games. Adhering to the rules is as important to these children as the diverse physical and social pleasures gained from such activities.

Even as Big Bear is a transitional object, play serves as a transitional activity. Children's play inhabits a land between awareness of the self and the other, between the world of objects and the world of symbols, between physical entities and meanings, between thoughts and feelings. It is dual because it can assume different roles. The child is beginning to discover activities and thoughts that are public, shared by others, tangible, "real." Yet another, equally significant domain is not so public. Remaining invisible to others unless reference is made to it, this territory consists of internal representation, of imaginary characters and figures, of pretense and fantasies and appearances. Eventually, because societal functioning demands a border between these regions of the psyche, the child must work out an equitable division between them.

The distinction between public and private worlds could not possibly be drawn by an infant, for whom all things are equally real (or equally apparent). But the playing toddler has the opportunity, initially, to make what is apparent to him accessible to the world—and, at the same time, to take what is real to others and absorb it into an imaginary world. Indeed, as the anthropologist Gregory Bateson (1955) indicated, play becomes possible only if one participant can signal ("wink") to the other that an act is meant in other than its usual sense. What has traditionally had one meaning takes on another, for the sake of play. This ambiguous, paradoxical, and norm-suspending character of play has been succinctly captured by Susanna Millar (1968). She observes that in play one explores what is familiar, practices what has already been mastered, becomes aggressive in a friendly manner or excited about nothing, and initiates social behavior in situations where it has not been called for.

In the opinion of most observers, the long period of play in human childhood is a princi-pal source of the accomplishments eventually attained by adults (Bruner, 1972; Lorenz, 1971). And, as many theorists have noted, play persists beyond childhood. In adulthood a free and easy activation of previous schemes (as occurs in brainstorming or free association) can prove very helpful in deciding what procedures to use in solving a problem. This is the kind of playful exploration to which Einstein and many other scientists have alluded (see Hadamard, 1945). Similarly, we can draw on rule-governed forms of play, both in recreational games and when—as in writing out a geometric proof—an approximate solution to a problem is converted into a form that others can comprehend and evaluate. And finally, several activities in which we have a deep interest—particularly art forms—continue to exert their hold on us throughout life.

This special blend of meaningful involvement without total commitment, which characterizes early exploratory behavior, continues in later years to produce a piquant pleasure and to enrich the mind. Indeed, if we could borrow from Kay's experiences with Big Bear, applying diverse schemes to new undertakings and old problems as freely and cheerfully as she does, we might be able to experience the preschooler's daily conceptual breakthroughs. Problems would become an occasion not for destructive worry, but for constructive play.

Signposts

Much of the child's energy during the preschool years is devoted to mastering language and acquiring appropriate social and sex-role behaviors. Nonetheless, it is illuminating to characterize children of this age as players. Their activities are exploratory, pleasurable, and not oriented toward goals—just those pursuits we commonly call "play." But considering all children's behaviors as play robs the word of explanatory value. Thus it seems preferable to differentiate play from other forms of behavior, and particularly from pure problem solving. And, in considering play itself, some further distinctions prove helpful. In exploratory play children focus on flexible experimentation, using schemes that they are in the process of mastering, even when those schemes are not strictly relevant to the task at hand. In rule-governed play children apply schemes already mastered, even in contexts where they are not necessarily appropriate.

Within the realm of sequences involving objects of play, a further distinction suggests itself. We can speak of different *roles* that an object or replica can assume at any given moment and the particular theme, story, or *scene* where the roles are being enacted.

Children's transitional objects—inanimate objects invested with personality and feeling—prove especially revealing about the dynamics of play. They also provide an opportunity for the child to experiment, to act out feelings without risk, and to formulate rules and rituals, all necessary skills in the complex physical and social world. Donald Winnicott sees such objects as a principal vehicle for detaching oneself from one's parents and for constructing an independent existence and self. Theorists like Erik Erikson, who are interested primarily in personality and emotion, view transitional objects mostly as a means of coping, of satisfying wishes, or of warding off threats. But they recognize the constructive as well as the defensive uses of transitional objects: the child uses play to dramatize and communicate about positive as well as negative concerns.

In contrast to these researchers who emphasize the affective role of play, cognitively oriented theorists like Jerome Bruner focus on how play reflects or serves the child's reasoning and how it promotes the flowering of problem-solving and other skills. In the re-

laxed, pressure-free context of play, children explore spatial relations, perform sequences of acts, rehearse components of tasks, and eventually gain the vital skill of using tools. Experimental work documents that playful experiences with objects can increase the likelihood that children who use these materials will subsequently solve novel problems.

Finally, Lev Vygotsky has proposed an appealing theory of play that combines its affective and cognitive aspects. In his view, the child uses play to cope with recurrent difficult situations, to try out more highly organized forms of behavior, and to ease the transition from a world dominated by practical objects to one imbued with symbolic meaning. This perspective seems to fit the transitional object especially well. Created by the child in response to disturbing life changes, the transitional object ushers in the dominance of rules and symbols in the child's life. Vygotsky makes strong claims about play's contribution to development. Though difficult to test experimentally, these claims receive some support from research suggesting that pretend play can actually speed the onset of important cognitive milestones such as understanding of conservation of matter.

Filling out the picture presented by leading theorists, researchers have examined the principal components of play sequences as well as various modulating factors. The ability to use objects to stand for other entities passes through stages, in which physical objects can first be used freely to represent anything, then must resemble their referents in various physical particulars, and, ultimately, can once again be used in a more freestanding fashion. The child initially can assume—or have his props assume—only one or two simple domestic roles. But eventually the child can enact a variety of roles through the use of props and negotiate a set of complementary roles within the same prop. At the beginning, the scenes in play are very simple but these too also gain in number, variety, and departure from prototypicality in the years following early childhood.

As Piaget noted, all children pass through the same general sequence of play—from pure exercise to early forms of symbolic or pretend play to later more socialized and rule-governed forms. But individual differences obtain as well. Girls and boys exhibit different toy preferences and different degrees of aggressiveness at play. And at least within our culture children can be distinguished from one another in the degree to which they focus on patterns as opposed to narratives and in their orientation to objects as opposed to persons. Play proves to be integrally related to the child's linguistic style and competence, and the child's pattern of language use—for example, expressive versus referential—may signal the child's playing competence. Finally, though experimental evidence has yet to accumulate, considerable clinical data suggest a close link between the child's affective life and the themes and tempo of his play.

Child's play clearly has its purposes: greater mastery of the world, more adequate coping with problems and fears, superior understanding of oneself and one's relationship to the world, an initial exploration of the relations between reality and fantasy, an arena in which intuitive, semilogical forms of thought can be freely tested. Accordingly, by about the age of five and after several years of "serious" play, the child is on the verge of mastering the physical and symbolic worlds and has begun to find a niche in the social world.

The toddler's world is the scene of many changes, but so many more occur in the ensuing years that psychologists speak of the shift between five and seven. We will examine this dramatic shift in Part III. In an initial chapter we will see how the child's language capacity becomes increasingly enmeshed with, and eventually dominates, his behavior. Then, in the next chapter, we will focus on the dominant social events of the period, including the child's relations with family members, peers, and the world at large. Finally, following up the survey of play we have just completed, we will consider the child as an artist—an image that represents our attempt to capture the essential spirit of the five-to-seven period.

Throughout the previous chapters we have encountered examples of development—children of different ages evolving skills and capacities in diverse domains. But what is the process of development like? How do psychologists conceptualize its mechanisms and its stages? These issues will concern us in the next Interlude.

The Model of Development in Psychology

The more perfect the creature becomes, the less similar to one another are *its* parts.

—JOHANN GOETHE

Nearly everyone is intrigued by how the human egg becomes fertilized and over nine months divides and divides again; we marvel at the stages through which the fetus passes before becoming a newborn baby. Biologists and embryologists have not only charted the daily progress of the embryo and fetus; they have also identified the stages of development, the possible substances that organize the growth process, and the overall orderly plan whereby specific organs and systems appear at the proper point in development. And, not least, they have constructed a theoretical framework within which to consider these processes.

Let us take a closer look at this approach. To begin with, development is seen as continual **differentiation**: if conditions are suitable, a diffuse whole of a given size and shape separates into parts of more specific form and function. (For in-

Larval, pupal, and butterfly stages of *Papilio machaon brittannica* (swallow-tailed butterfly).

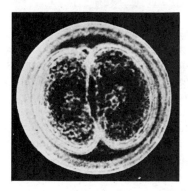

Human organism thirty hours after fertilization, three and one-half days into the germinal period, and at twenty-eight days.

stance, over the first four weeks of human life, initially identical cells give rise to a separate head, tail, heart, liver, and gastrointestinal tract.) Along with differentiation, development also entails **integration:** parts that were once isolated come together to form a new, better-organized system. (For instance, in the newborn there is little coordination between seeing, hearing, and moving; but in the infant of six months or a year, considerable integration of these components proves the rule.) Thus as different parts of the body become interconnected, a far more flexible organism emerges.

Biologists do not apply the term *development* to every natural event. Thus simple organisms (like sponges or algae) that increase in size simply by replicating their structure, without undergoing significant differentiation or reorganization, are not considered examples of development. The developing organism must assume a more complex organization over time; it will reach a mature form that is maintained for a period of self-regulation and there will eventually be a period of aging, which may entail disintegration and loss of differentiated capacities.

The model of development used in biology is so attractive that scholars from many other disciplines have borrowed it. For instance, studies of social, economic, and political organization often discuss the degree of a system's development, contrasting "underdeveloped" or "less developed" social units with "more developed," "highly developed," or even "postdeveloped" units. Not surprisingly, psychologists who study human growth have also been drawn to the model or metaphor of physical development.

The application of developmental terminology to a child's physical growth is entirely appropriate. But when the concept of development is applied to something so seemingly intangible as a child's cognitive or emotional growth, such usage becomes more problematic. Is it really proper to compare the child's greater problem-solving skills or more evolved friendships to the emergence of the head and the heart from undifferentiated cells? As we will see, the importation of the biologist's vocabulary to the individual's behavior and thought is not without controversy. But first it seems appropriate to examine a view within child psychology that embraces the full use of the term (and the theory) of development.

Heinz Werner's Organismic-Developmental Approach

In the early part of the century, psychology became firmly entrenched as a scientific discipline committed to the empirical investigation of mental phenomena (see pages 148–153). As part of this movement, Charles Darwin's ideas about evolutionary processes were particularly influential: psychologists contrasted the simpler mental phenomena characteristic of animals and children with the more advanced mental capacities of the adolescent and adult. Considerable attention was also directed toward the mental capacities of primitive peoples, as well as of individuals suffering from brain disease or from severe emotional disorders.

As compelling observations were obtained about each of these (and other) groups, pressure built to relate these phenomena to one another. Rising to the challenge was the German psychologist Heinz Werner, who had zealously collated findings about the mental and emotional capacities of various groups of different ages and capacities. Then, attempting to synthesize his data, Werner reasoned as follows: Principles of development have been observed in plants and animals; children's physical growth clearly passes through steps; therefore, it should be possible to conceptualize mental stages along similar lines. Thereupon Werner (1948) outlined a comparative psychology of mental development—the **organismic-developmental approach**—within which one could order forms of mental thought along such dimensions as complexity and differentiation. The approach was **organismic,** because it emphasized the coherence of and interactions among processes within the organism; it was **developmental,** because it assessed each organism's status at a certain moment in terms of its degree of development.

THE ORTHOGENETIC PRINCIPLE

The basic tenet of the organismic-developmental approach is a general developmental or **orthogenetic principle.** As formulated by Werner, "the orthogenetic principle states . . . that whenever development occurs, it proceeds from a state of relative globality and lack of differentiation to a state of increasing differentiation, articulation, and hierarchic integration" (Werner, 1957, p. 126). Inherent in this principle is a sense of direction. An organism always starts as a single whole with some minimal organization and moves, for at least a period, toward a better-organized structure consisting of discrete and integrated parts.

The orthogenetic principle has been deliberately formulated to be so general that it can apply to a host of diverse areas: a cell, a person, a city, and even an economy. In earlier chapters we have encountered familiar examples of such physical and psychological development—for instance, the development of the visual system (Chapter 3). To fully assess the power of the orthogenetic principle, therefore, we should consider an example that lies beyond the usual range of application: the formulation of friendships.

At first, two strangers meet; they talk for a while, perhaps participate in the same activity, and then draw some preliminary conclusions about their feelings toward one another. Alice thinks that Bob is a kind person with a nice sense of humor. She hopes to see more of him. Bob finds Alice a bit cold but stimulating and intelligent. He is also inclined to continue the relationship. In terms of the orthogenetic principle, Bob and Alice have global views of one another, punctuated with a few isolated impressions that have yet to coalesce into an organized pattern.

Alice and Bob meet again, and their impressions are expanded somewhat. Alice learns that Bob has recently suffered several disappointments but has tried to cope with them thoughtfully. She now finds him more profound, but somewhat less humorous. Perhaps Bob's initial humor was an attempt to ingratiate himself. This time, Bob realizes that Alice's knowledge is really somewhat superficial; she knows something about everything, but not a great deal about anything. But he finds her to be warm and genuinely helpful to him in confronting one of his problems. The original coldness was perhaps a strategy to avoid becoming too intimate early in the relationship. The friendship has now moved into a new stage: each participant has registered several, sometimes conflicting, impressions about the other, and these impressions have not yet been combined into a consistent and coherent view of the other individual.

In the end, after numerous and varied encounters, Alice and Bob become close friends. Each is now quite aware of the other's strengths and weaknesses. Alice finds that Bob gained profound insights from his difficult experiences. Although he has occasional depressions, he wears this stress gracefully and continues to be a delightful companion. Bob learns that Alice is usually friendly and sympathetic. Only when she feels ill-at-ease does she resort to superficial bragging and defensiveness. Bob feels that he has been strengthened by his friendship with Alice.

The friendship between the two people has now passed through a definite development, one reflecting each person's understanding of the other. Each participant is known to and accepted by the other as a complex and multifaceted person. Not all facets are equally appealing, but they are consistent and, taken together, they make sense, form a composite picture, and can be accepted on their own terms. Thus, the friendship—a developmental phenomenon in the same sense as the growth of a plant or the evolution of the child's mind—has become a differentiated as well as an integrated whole.

END-STATES AND STAGES

In addition to stating and illustrating the orthogenetic principle, Werner introduced several other concepts that are central to a developmental perspective. One such crucial term is **end-state**—a full description of the features toward which development tends, the characteristics that make up the fully developed form. Only armed with a description of the end-state of development can one delineate the steps or stages along the way and ensure that one has really specified the appropriate developmental progression (see Langer, 1969).

An illustration drawn from the biological realm may clarify the necessity for an end-state. Because a tail is an important feature of the developed mouse, the details of its emergence and subsequent growth must occupy a significant place in an account of the development of the embryo of a mouse. In humans, however, where tails are unimportant, such emphasis is not necessary. On the other hand, because linguistic capacities are crucial in the adult human, the end-state features relevant to language would command attention in the study of the human. Researchers would invest considerable energy in describing the stages culminating in the human ability to

understand and produce sounds, while neglecting sound production and discrimination in the mouse.

The description of an end-state proves highly significant in
psychology. For example, if one assumes that the competent
adult is like a scientist, then in considering the child's mental
development one will focus on the capacities—like solving
mathematical problems or formulating experimental hypotheses—that count in physics or chemistry. If, on the other hand,
one considers the artist to be a more appropriate adult end-
state, one is likely to focus on children's abilities to respond
sensitively to a painting, to create a metaphor, or to carve a
wooden necklace. (see Chapter 9)

The delineation of stages or steps is part of any end-state
analysis. Indeed, once one has defined the end-state of the developed organism, one directs both theoretical and empirical
inquiry toward describing the steps leading to this ultimate
realization. Thus the developmentalist describes the stages of a
friendship, an attachment bond, an object concept, or linguistic
mastery. As we will see later, researchers differ on whether to
treat the phases en route to the end-state as full-fledged
stages, as simple steps, or as substages. But nearly all agree
that some set of preliminary structures must precede attainment of an end-state. Customarily, developmental psychologists lay out such a set of stages. And the sequence, particular
features, and names of stages are all drawn up in the light of
the defined end-state.

INTERACTIONISM AND EQUILIBRIUM

Loyalty to an orthogenetic principle and focus upon an end-
state are particular staples of Werner's approach. Other concepts stressed by Werner have also been embraced by developmental psychologists, particularly Jean Piaget and others of his
cognitive-structural school. Two of them, *interactionism* and
equilibrium, have gained a great deal of attention.

We can approach interactionism by recalling the two opposing views of development presented in Chapter 2. The environmental-learning theorist holds that the developmental course is
determined almost entirely by the organism's particular experiences in the world, and neither specific stages nor prescribed
sequences can be anticipated. In contrast, the nativist holds
that the rules for development are inscribed in the genetic
code, and the organism will inevitably pass through a sequence
of stages. At most, the environment "triggers" processes that
are set to go.

In between these extreme positions, scientists like Werner and Piaget have adopted **interactionism,** a point of view that sees all development as a product of *both* individual predispositions (genetic factors, past history, current stage, proclivities of the species) *and* forces in the environment (other individuals, social factors, cultural tradition, training methods). All growth results from a rich and perpetual interplay between these two necessary and equally potent forces; the interplay ultimately comes to include the individual's perception of his own environment and his own actions upon the environment as well as the environment's adjustments to particular individuals. Nowadays, nearly all scholars at least pay lip service to interactionist views. Yet when it comes to controversial issues—for example, the factors determining an individual's intelligence—only a minority of researchers actually holds strictly to an interactionist perspective.

The second key developmental concept, encountered in the discussion of sensorimotor development in Chapter 2, is **equilibrium** (also called **equilibration**) (Kitchener, 1978; Moessinger, 1978). Mental and behavioral development, no less than physical development, is seen as inextricably linked to the individual's existence as a biological organism. Each individual must continually interact with the environment to achieve a balance among the external forces of the world and the internal forces of his own mind and body. But such harmony will not emerge automatically: after periods of crisis, conflict, or difficulty, some process within the individual must strive toward reestablishing a sense of balance and proportion.

Developmentalists see equilibrium (or a tendency toward equilibrium) as a basic property of organic matter, one that keeps the psychological organism on a fairly even keel. When one is physically ill, the body's recuperative powers strive to reintroduce a state of health. Analogously, when one has experienced mental or emotional stress, forces of equilibrium bring one back to a state where stable functioning is again possible. The child who is distraught by his mother's disappearance may suck his thumb, become attached to a blanket, or even repress the memory of his mother.

Although equilibrium is clearly necessary and, overall, advantageous, the individual would never develop if all forces tended toward equilibrium and none toward change. Many developmentalists maintain that advances to a higher developmental stage are most likely to occur when the organism is in a state of **disequilibrium,** when some cognitive structures are competing with others. If the organism is to avoid being mired in the cement of a given stage or substage, there may have to be some intrinsic pulls toward disequilibrium or a heightened sensitivity to potential conflicts. For instance, Piaget's daughter Jacqueline would never have achieved a sense of object permanence if she had not felt a tension between an object seen at point A and its eventual reemergence at point B. Only through the temporary disequilibrium of the intermediate stages did she progress to a new plane of equilibrium when she fully understood and accepted the permanence of objects. Development can be considered a perpetual duet, with the voices of equilibrium and disequilibrium alternately taking their turns.

WHAT DEVELOPMENT IS—AND IS NOT

So far in our discussion, development has been viewed as a process that unfolds in a single direction over a period of time. For the most part, this serves as an adequate shorthand formulation of developmental processes in animals and humans. But several qualifiers should be added (see Kaplan, 1967; Langer, 1969, 1970). First we must understand that development is not equivalent to change over time. Indeed, development can be seen at a single moment: one can consider two organisms or entities, compare them on a number of dimensions, and indicate which of the two is "more" or "less" developed. Two ten-month-olds can be contrasted on a task of object permanence. If one child is at stage 4, and the other is at stage 5, the latter is considered "more" developed. By the same token, one can look at two friendships, two nations, two computer programs, two forms of government, and—again applying a set of criteria—judge which is more developed. Development emerges as a criterion for evaluation, one that can apparently be applied in as objective a manner as size, strength, or shape.

Even as development can be studied at a single moment, change itself does not denote that a developmental process is at work. As we have noted, some organisms grow larger simply by replicating cells, but they do not therefore (or thereby) develop. And a rock's erosion from running water—clearly a change over time—also falls outside our use of the term *developmental.*

Applying this stricture to human development, we can see that certain claims fail to qualify as developmental. For instance, suppose an extreme environmental-learning theorist maintains that the young child is simply an adult who knows fewer facts. Should the child's growth be seen simply as repetition of the same process of accretion—learning of new facts— there would be no differentiation, no integration, and hence, in our terms, no development. By the same token, were the claim made that a child is simply born with a certain level of trust and never thereafter alters this level, the affective course of the child would not be viewed as genuinely developmental.

Though development cannot be equated with changes over time, it is important to underline that developmental psychologists constantly track the factor of time. Some observe change over long periods, extending to the evolution of a species; others focus on the time span of an individual organism; still others chart changes over seconds or even milliseconds, following, say, the course of perception or learning within a single experimental trial. But in each case, the psychologist in the organismic-developmental school can honor the orthogenetic principle, the need for an end-state reached through a series of stages, and the twin concepts of interactionism and equilibrium.

The Controversies over a Developmental Approach

In describing a conception of development, we have adopted the point of view of the committed developmentalist. But many in the field of developmental psychology would not allow Werner (or Piaget or their colleagues) to serve as their mouthpiece. It is time to turn the floor over to those who are critical of Werner's ideas and, more generally, of the developmental position outlined above.

TOO VAGUE OR TOO AMBITIOUS

Perhaps the most frequent criticism of Werner's position centers on its triviality or vagueness. To some, the formulation seems so loose and general that it can explain very little. Others find its terms vaporous. Leland van den Daele has pointed out that development might be said to proceed not from Werner's "relative globality and lack of differentiation" to "increasing differentiation, articulation, and hierarchic integration," but, equally soundly, "from a state of relative elementalism and differentiation to a state of increasing globalization, dedifferentiation, and signification" (1974, p. 12). T. G. R. Bower (1976) sees development as proceeding from "abstract" to "specific" knowledge. The fact that these definitions do not seem obviously in error, even though they are virtually the opposite of Werner's, demonstrates the difficulties of gathering convincing empirical evidence for or against Werner's position.

If the orthogenetic view appears too vague to some, it seems too ambitious to others. Werner and others are proposing an analytic principle that can be applied to children, to cells, to brain-damaged individuals, to animals, to political systems, to friendships found in diverse cultures around the world. Yet how can we assert that a few general principles apply to all these processes, particularly when we scarcely understand any one of them? Each may be distinct. Or some may be related, whereas others may require entirely different explanatory principles. Proponents of this position find it more profitable to search for differences among processes because, once established, differences cannot be erased. Ironically, they are calling for a differentiation among this family of developmental processes—a recognition that the development of a child might instructively be distinguished from the development of a friendship, a society, or the concept of development itself (Langford, 1975).

DEVELOPMENTAL STAGES AND END-STATES

The focus in developmental theory on end-states and accompanying stages of development has also collected its share of criticism, some of which cuts to the core of child development.

The Moral Argument. One serious critique of the developmental view questions the notion of a set of stages that unfailingly lead to a mature end-state. Once stages have been ranked, the conclusion follows with virtual inevitability that one stage is better than another (see B. Kaplan, 1967, 1971). And, because theorists of development cannot escape their own time and concepts, those who have the opportunity to define the end-state and its stages and the techniques used to measure achievement (typically scholars from the industrialized West) are bound to end up in the most favorable position, whereas those who disagree or differ with their analysis are left in the least favorable spot (Cole and Means, 1981). (Indeed, organismic-developmentalists generally think of their theories as more advanced than such "primitive" views as sheer nativism or empiricism.) Furthermore (say the critics), even if one stage could be reliably established as more advanced, such evaluation risks stigmatizing the person or group designated as less developed. Indeed, the very enunciation of an end-state is equal to glorifying a certain mode of behavior. Thus the developmentalist who favors a scientific end-state is honoring the

scientist (while downgrading the artist); the scholar who selects artistry as an end-state is sanctifying the artist (while
minimizing the achievements of the butcher, the baker, and
the candlestick maker). Who is to say that "our" end-state is
preferable to that favored in ancient Greece, contemporary
Russia, or a preliterate aboriginal society?

The alternative approach avoids any talk of stages or end-
states. To the extent that distinctions must be made, the analyst should simply describe different patterns of behavior, without deeming any as more developed or more advanced than
any other. Different phases in the development of the embryo,
a friendship, or a child's mind would be considered as objectively as possible. In fact, to avoid making judgments, and to
prevent notions of stages and end-states from clouding one's
perceptions, one might simply define a beginning state and let
neutral observation reveal what happens next (see Kagan, 1971).

The organismic-developmental school has an answer to
these objections. According to Bernard Kaplan (1970), a student of Werner's, those who would scuttle stages and end-
states represent a pure organismic position untempered by a
developmental perspective. Although both analytic frameworks
emphasize organized and differentiated wholes and their relationship to their parts, the pure organismic view spurns stages
and end-states in favor of simple descriptions of different patterns of behavior. But, Kaplan says, such a position proves difficult to defend. For one thing, such apparent objectivity overlooks the fact that one pattern routinely follows another, and
that behaviors of the later pattern are more flexible and adequate. Moreover, if all patterns (or stages) were in fact equal,
one would never be justified in attempting to influence a
human or social entity, no matter how harmful or self-destructive its behavior might be. One could not maintain, say, that
slavery is less advanced than freedom; that a state of health is
preferable to a siege of cancer; nor that children with a sense
of object permanence can more adequately cope with their
environment than children who lack this capacity. Having declared that all stages are equal, one is not free to add that
"some are more equal than others."

Wernerians also rally to defend the notion of end-state.
They argue that every investigator concerned with human
growth selects an end-state, whether consciously or not. In
deciding to study anything, one assumes first that the process
or element under scrutiny is important and, second, that understanding its course will be instructive. Thus, because an
end-state is defined at least implicitly, there is every reason to

define it consciously and explicitly. Then progress (or lack of progress) toward explaining the process can be more readily evaluated.

Quantity Versus Quality. The notion of developmental stages generally entails an assumption that development features qualitative changes; each stage is seen as distinct from others. But as we noted in Chapter 2, many would argue that development consists primarily of quantitative, piecemeal changes. In particular, those sympathetic to an environmental-learning position find it more useful to view human growth as simply the gradual acquisition of more complex responses, without any fundamental reorganization of capacities.

As some of Werner's followers have pointed out (for example, Langer, 1970), one's conclusion on this issue will reflect one's perspective. Viewed from sufficient distance, the child who can only crawl differs qualitatively from the child who can stand, and the child who can stand differs qualitatively from one who can run, skip, or jump. Yet from a much closer position, it would be impossible to state that a qualitative change had occurred at any given point. Under minute-by-minute examination, qualitative changes tend to evaporate, and the basic continuity of development becomes most impressive. Most controversy about qualitative versus quantitative changes would probably cease if the observer's temporal and spatial points of reference were taken into account. Yet some changes do seem most appropriately described as qualitative. Consider, for instance, when one stage (for example, the ability to use symbols) proves difficult to account for in terms applied to an earlier one (the time when all knowledge is embedded in sensorimotor schemes); or when there are no intermediate stages between earlier and later forms (as when a young woman begins to menstruate).

The issue of continuity resurfaces when one ponders the relations between different points in the development of a single behavior (see Brim and Kagan, 1980; Bower, 1976). Consider, for example, the smiles of a newborn baby, the year-old infant, and the mature adult. From a continuity point of view, these are all smiles and, therefore, identical behaviors prompted by identical stimuli. But perhaps the infant's smile is totally unrelated to the adult's. Perhaps the infant's smile should be related to the adult's sigh, because both are primarily release of energy. Or perhaps the infant's widening eyes should be related to the adult's smile, because both signify enjoyment and understanding. In that case, the actual continuity extends between infants' widening eyes and adults' smiles, and the smiles of the two are discontinuous.

The question of the relation between apparently similar behaviors encountered at different moments in development has been raised most sharply in discussions of so-called U-shaped curves of development (Bower, 1974b; Bowerman, in press; Gardner, 1979b; Gardner and Winner, 1981; Siegler, in press; Strauss and Rimalt, 1974; Strauss and Stavy, 1979). In numerous domains, certain behaviors emerge early in life, only to disappear for a time and then reappear later. We can trace this U-shaped pattern with a few examples. The ability to imitate facial expressions and to "walk" appears in newborn babies, wanes during the first year of life, and then reappears later. While two-year-olds will utter correct plurals such as "mice," at three they may overgeneralize linguistic rules and say "mouses" instead. And preschoolers exhibit impressive artistic skill and expressiveness that disappears during the "literal stage" of middle childhood and may reemerge during adolescence or adulthood.

At issue is the relationship between the two ends of the U. In one camp some observers believe that the mature forms of behavior are closely tied to, or perhaps dependent upon, the

As shown by these works done by primary school children, some children's art work bears an uncanny resemblance to modern art, especially the works of Picasso, Klee, and others interested in "primitive" modes of artistic expression. These resemblances have led investigators to speak of a "U-shaped" curve in the development of artistic skill.

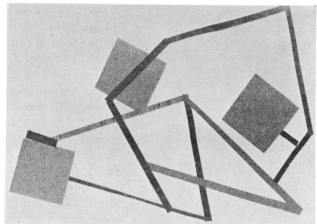

earliest forms (Mehler and Bever, 1967). In an opposing camp are observers who find no relationship between the two ends or who consider any relationship to be superficial rather than deep (Klahr, in press).

How to determine who is correct in any given case proves very difficult. One empirical method has been proposed: if the two behaviors are in fact related, procedures that preserve or extend the early form of the behavior (for example, intensive training) should result either in the avoidance of the "dip" in the U or in the more rapid acquisition of the mature form of the behavior (Bower, 1974*b*). In the absence of such costly demonstrations, which have rarely been attempted, the best procedure is simply careful analysis. Any psychologist bent on tracing genuine continuities in the underlying structure of the two surface behaviors must attend to the properties, the context, and the ends of each. Only when each of the candidate behaviors is well understood and the points of similarity (and difference) can be clearly stated does the assertion of a genuine U gain in persuasiveness.

The Usefulness of Stages. Many psychologists do not find developmental stages a particularly powerful or even useful concept (Brainerd, 1978*c*). Poking fun at stage theorists, Leland van den Daele (1969) points out the unreliability of the distinction:

Milestones, phases, and ages
render general gauges,
while periods, levels, and stages
require pages and pages [p. 303].

Making a similar point, William Kessen (1966) indicates that some people use *stage* in a "literary-evocative way," as when the child is spoken of as being in the "chimpanzee stage." Others regard *stage* as a paraphrase of age ("the child is in stage *X*" equals "the child is *Y* years old"). Some employ it as a paraphrase for observation (the child is in the "negativistic stage"), as a description of the environment (the "school-age stage"), or as a shorthand way of relating the child to a theory of development (the psychoanalytic discussion of oral, anal, and genital stages).

All analysts want to make sense of their data by simplifying and relating disparate phenomena; at the very least, positing stages is a convenient way to do so. In addition, it sometimes proves possible to specify the factors that characterize each stage and thereby to indicate the differences between individuals who have just entered a stage, those who are embedded deeply within a stage, and those most likely to move to a higher stage (D. Feldman, 1980; Strauss and Rimalt, 1974). Such analyses hold genuine promise for explaining, in detail, the "stuff" of human development—how changes actually come about in the living, thinking, child.

However, there are dangers. It is all too easy to improvise stages—for instance, of crawling, standing, walking, running, and jumping. But these do not really simplify. They do not tie together separate but empirically relatable phenomena, nor does any notable clarification result from invoking them. They are simply a way of elevating the commonplace.

The solution seems to be the one arrived at time and again in the formulation of scientific theories: Devise a fit between data and theoretical concepts, a compromise between stages so general that they cannot be tested (the stage of childhood), and stages so specific that the trees prevent sight of the woods (the stage of six-word utterances). Stages are most useful when they cut across seemingly disparate areas of knowledge and experience to uncover important but not obvious commonalities. Whatever their profound differences, these criteria seem to have been most convincingly met by Jean Piaget's stages of cognition (Chapters 2, 10, and 14), Lawrence Kohlberg's stages of moral development (Chapter 13), Sigmund Freud's stages of sexual development (Chapters 5, 11, and 14), and Erik Erikson's stages of life (Chapters 1 and 14).

The Contributions of the Developmental View

Despite the objections to it, the organismic-developmental school has provided helpful ways of thinking about psychological issues. The orthogenetic principle (with its associated concepts) clarifies discussions about childhood. And the orientation can be extended beyond the study of children to illuminate other areas of psychology, for instance, the kinds of behavior seen in drug-induced states. Indeed, in its most general form, it may even illuminate quite different domains such as literary style or economic trends. The primary purpose of such broad application is not to classify systems or individuals as "better" or "worse," "more advanced" or "less advanced," but to enable comparisons to be made at all. To the extent that the developmental perspective does facilitate comparisons, it will have

Pablo Picasso, Mother with dead child on ladder. Dated "May 9, 37 (III)."

Pablo Picasso, Mother with dead child on ladder. Dated "May 10, 37 (V)."

Pablo Picasso, detail from *Guernica*, 1937.

Pablo Picasso, *Guernica*, 1937.

One can see development in an artist's output, both over the course of his life and within a single work. Pablo Picasso made over two hundred sketches in preparing his modern masterpiece *Guernica,* and it serves as an excellent instance of creative development within a symbol system. Shown here are two of these sketches, a detail from the final mural and the complete mural.

served its purpose. For, in a sense, comparisons and contrasts are what any scholarly endeavor is about.

Like any initial approximation, the developmental view has limitations. For one thing, it is only a metaphor with which to think about human growth. And although the growth of the child's mental or emotional powers is in many ways reminiscent of the flowering of a plant, this is by no means the only relevant model. An entirely different family of insights might come about if one were instead to view the child as a machine such as a computer.

Even if the biological metaphor provides the most appropriate way to study human growth, one must determine how far to extend the analogy. One must ascertain whether, and in what respects, the development of behavior or thought might differ from the development of the nervous system. One must decide whether the model applies equally to the social, emotional, cognitive, and moral realms or for that matter, to different domains of cognition (D. Feldman, 1980). And one must assess whether, in championing the model of development, one always wants to accept its associated baggage: an end-state, qualitatively different stages, the process of equilibrium.

But the ultimate test of the classical formulation of development will be its success or lack of success in organizing a significant amount of data. To begin, one must examine the facts about behavior in children and see whether they indeed reflect the orthogenetic principle. Then, looking further, one must see whether the same set of principles also extends to other domains allegedly subsumed by developmental analyses: the perception of stimuli, the behavior of brain-damaged patients, the growth of a friendship, even one's own increasing mastery of a subject.

In the last analysis, those who criticize the developmental model for being too ambitious, and call instead for a specification of differences among individuals and groups, may have identified the most productive avenue of research. But even if the developmental model requires revision, its attempts to conceptualize human growth in scientific terms, to outline the major characteristics of development, and to suggest commonalities among diverse populations have enhanced thinking and research in the field.

PART III

The Years from Five to Seven

Between the ages of five and seven, the child experiences important physical, cognitive, social, and emotional changes. The reasons for these changes—which psychologists call the five-to-seven shift—are still being debated, but most observers single out these children's newfound abilities to use language to control their own behavior and to influence the behaviors of others. More generally, this period is characterized by declining egocentrism and the emergence of the ability to communicate effectively with others.

The child's social circle is also broadening beyond parents and siblings to encompass peers, teachers, the media of communication, and other societal institutions. Heredity may influence their capacities and performances, but relationships at home and with peers, social-class background, and media (like television) also make crucial contributions to development. Clearly, the person the child is becoming reflects these diverse social forces.

These are the years when children start school and when they are becoming increasingly competent in using symbols—words, pictures, numbers, gestures, and the like. Because they can capture meanings in symbols and fashion effective works of art, children between five and seven resemble young artists. They can invest part of themselves in symbols and can fashion expressive symbols that inform and delight other persons.

CHAPTER SEVEN

Communication with Others and with Oneself

Every function in the child's cultural development appears twice: first between people, then inside the child.

—LEV VYGOTSKY

Throughout the time he is learning to speak, the child is constantly the victim of confusion between his own point of view and that of other people.

—JEAN PIAGET

It is the developmental psychologist's lot to administer tests and tasks to children. Infants and young toddlers are often difficult to work with because they do not recognize a task as such; in working with them one must structure the environment so they have no option but to confront the task and perform in a measurable way. The naiveté of young subjects imposes a special obligation on experimenters to treat subjects sensitively and not to take advantage of them. In contrast, adolescents can be so savvy about tests and tasks that they may well figure out the hypothesis of the study. With subjects who are not naive, the results of the investigation may

be of doubtful use. Sometimes the experimenters have to be careful, lest these knowing subjects take advantage of them!

This extreme difference between infants and adolescents is hinted at by significant changes occurring at about the start of the school years—between the ages of five and seven. Children of two, three, or four confront a psychologist's task as they would any other task or game; they often go about their business, interacting minimally with the experimenter, paying little attention to his or her desires, showing only intermittent attention to the stimuli and marginal awareness of the problem posed. Their use of language is not yet integrally tied to the rest of their behavior. It often seems an ornament or punctuation to what they would or would not do anyway.

Six- or seven-year-olds are very different. Almost immediately aware that a task has been posed, they proceed to meet its demands in a reasonable and logical way. And their language has become much more fully integrated with the rest of their behavior. They listen to what others say and they carry out directions promptly. They ask questions when they do not understand. They strive to supply useful information to a listener. They may well cue themselves using language ("First I'll do this, then I'll do that"), and they may "rehearse" words to aid their memories.

Consider, as an example of these differences, how my children reacted when I asked them to play a game with me as an informal experiment. I had two hand puppets—one a personlike figure representing the doctor, the other a little rabbit who was to be the patient. Four-year-old Kay was initially enthusiastic about the game. She put the doctor puppet on her hand and began to greet it. But, not knowing what else to say, she simply repeated what the rabbit (played by my hand) was saying. Soon, she removed the puppet from her hand and began to jump up and down while holding it under her arm. When I asked her to put on the rabbit puppet instead, she repeated the words we had previously spoken. But she was unable to continue the conversation and soon she began to sing a song she had learned the previous morning.

Jerry, at seven, reacted to the game in an entirely different way. First he assumed the role of doctor with considerable appropriateness, saying things like "Roll up your sleeve so I can give you a shot," "Nurse, would you help me," and "It's time to weigh you now." We enacted a plausible exchange between doctor and patient. Then, when I suggested that we exchange puppets, Jerry readily

agreed. He took the rabbit, said, "Now I'll be the bunny," and was able to assume the radically different role without difficulty: "Oh, it hurts," "Could I have a lollipop," and "I just love to have carrots." Not only could Jerry carry on a sustained conversation using appropriate phrases; he could also assume the role of the other protagonist, thereby showing that he could put himself in someone else's place.

These differences are a few of the changes that occur during the so-called **five-to-seven shift.** Sheldon White (1965, 1970a) has collated the diverse alterations that reportedly occur during this period among children all over the world (see also Super and White, 1970; White and Olds, 1964).

A partial sampling of this list indicates its richness and variety. Children blinded before the age of six never report visual memories, whereas children blinded thereafter do. Children younger than seven are more susceptible than older children to Pavlovian conditioning. The ability to tell left from right emerges at about age six or seven. On a word-association task, preschool children usually respond with a word that follows the given word (for instance, "bite" as a response to *dog*) whereas by seven children usually mention another member of the same lexical class (responding "cat" to dog). Children's ability to plan their maneuvers before beginning a drawing emerges at about age six or seven. And children at about six experience accelerated physical growth. Further illustrations of the five-to-seven shift are given in Table 7.1.

These changes lead White to conclude that a fundamental reorganization in the child's mental life is occurring at this time. White does not attribute all the changes to a single cause, but he mentions several candidates: a significant reorganization of the brain, the child's superior linguistic ability, the ability to take the role of other persons, the emergence of certain logical operations described by Piaget, and the influence of social and cultural factors remolding the child's conception of herself.

Research done since the five-to-seven shift was first enunciated has increased our understanding of the events that occur at this time. Changes are less dramatic than White thought: many of the trends he described have their origins in events occurring during the second, third, and fourth years of life, and many continue to alter in the years ahead. We should, then, think of the period five-to-seven in a symbolic sense—as a watershed that represents a set of trends occurring gradually between the preschool and the school years.

What are some of the primary trends occurring at this time? A number of them have typically been cited by researchers: (1) the decline in egocentrism, as exemplified by the child's increasing ability to see the world through the eyes of others; (2) the gradual decline of "private" or "egocentric" speech—the practice of young children of muttering aloud to themselves, apparently with little regard for the impact of their words on others; (3) the emergence of verbally guided behavior—the use of language explicitly for purposes of planning and guiding their own behavior; (4) the flowering of effective communication skills—the increasing ability to

Table 7.1. SOME OTHER CHANGES IN BEHAVIOR ASSOCIATED WITH THE FIVE-TO-SEVEN SHIFT

Before the five-to-seven shift	After the five-to-seven shift
If the preschool child's face is touched at the same time as her elbow, wrist, or hand, she will report only that her face was touched.	At about age six, the child will be able to report that both her face and elbow (or wrist or hand) were touched.
Four-year-old children who have lost a limb never report that they continue to feel the "phantom limb."	Children eight or older who have lost a limb always report sensing a "phantom limb."
If preschool children are shown two patterns and asked which one is most like a third, many will choose the one similar in color.	After six, most children's choice of what patterns are similar will be guided by similarity of form, not of color.
If younger children are shown a medium-sized square drawn on a square sheet of paper and then are asked to draw the smallest and largest squares possible on the paper, they will draw squares only slightly larger and smaller than the square they are shown.	Regardless of the size of the square on the page, children older than seven or eight have no problem drawing a very small and a very large square.
For preschool children, rewards must be fairly immediate and sensual; the children are most sensitive to praise and attention.	Older children are rewarded by the information that they have been correct; they adopt an internal standard of performance.

Source: Derived from Sheldon H. White, "Evidence for a Hierarchical Arrangement of Learning Processes," in L. P. Lipsitt and C. C. Spiker (eds.), *Advances in Child Development and Behavior,* Vol. 2 (New York: Academic Press, 1965), pp. 195–210; and from "Some General Outlines of the Matrix of Developmental Changes between Five and Seven Years," *Bulletin of the Orton Society* 20 (1970), 41–57.

describe things in such a way that they will be comprehensible to other persons, and at the same time the ability to become effective listeners and questioners, communicators to others, and communicators to themselves.

These changes are so apparent that they have been acknowledged by nearly all investigators of early childhood. Many commentators cite the central role played by the child's growing linguistic capacities. However, the factors that give rise to the various shifts, and the best explanation for them, are subjects of controversy. In the following pages we shall examine the principal points of view.

We shall begin by considering one intriguing line of explanation for the shift: that certain physical changes occurring in the child's brain may cause it. Then, as we consider phenomena of the sort just mentioned, we will review explanations put forth by a number of major theoreticians and theoretical schools: the cognitive-structural view on egocentrism as propounded by Piaget; the sociocultural view of cognition as held by Vygotsky, Luria, and other members of the Soviet school; the emphasis by certain American scholars on mediation; and, finally, a converging consensus on the principal components of effectiveness in communication as emerging from the work of a number of empirical researchers, such as John Flavell.

Clues in the Nervous System

CORTICAL DEVELOPMENT

Even before birth, the child's brain approximates its adult size and weight more closely than does any other organ. At birth the brain is 25 percent of its adult weight, and by age five about 90 percent of its adult weight (Tanner, 1970). Thus an increase in size does not account for the changes that occur *after* five.

More relevant than bulk is the development of the outer surface of the brain, called the **cerebral cortex.**

As Figure 7.1 shows, the adult cerebral cortex has several principal zones. Toward the front of the brain, in a region called the **frontal lobes,** is the narrow motor strip that directs all our voluntary bodily movements, such as chewing, running, and grasping. The motor strip is the first cortical area to mature, probably during the opening month or two of life (Rose, 1973). During the succeeding months, several other areas of the cortex—together called the **primary sensory cortex**—begin to function: the primary visual cortex responds to all visual stimulation; the primary auditory cortex responds to all sound stimulation; and the parietal region responds to touch and to variations in body position.

The primary sensory areas record the isolated sense data of objects—colors, lines, sounds. Other, **secondary processing areas,** adjacent to the primary areas, are needed to realize the object's significance or meaning. Roughly speaking, the primary areas record that an object is round and has a sweet taste and a hard surface. The secondary areas, which develop later in the first year of life, enable us to construe the object as an apple (Geschwind, 1964, 1967).

Appreciation of more complex meanings and of the connections between disparate sensory experiences depends on the maturation of cortical areas that lie between the zones serving each sensory system (or mode). These **cross-modal zones,** which are maturing during the second, third, and fourth years (Tanner, 1970), are considered essential for appreciating the connections and relations among objects, as well as sequences of events. In humans the primary and secondary processing areas primarily relay information from the environment to the cross-modal zones, which in turn integrate impressions into an organized expe-

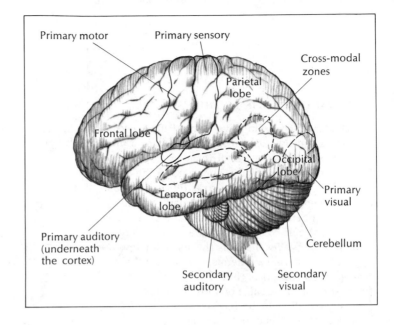

Figure 7.1. Information obtained from the study of brain-damaged patients, who have lost certain behavioral capacities, and from surgical operations, in which parts of the cortex are stimulated, have enabled anatomists to specify the functions served by various parts of the human brain.

rience. A principal cross-modal zone nestled between the parietal, temporal, and occipital lobes can be seen in Figure 7.1. When matured, this zone allows the child to associate the sound "ap'l" with the sight of the fruit and its taste, smell, and smooth texture.

But how do maturational changes in the child's brain relate to the behavioral changes described by Sheldon White? To answer this question, it helps to think about the child's mental processes during these periods. During the first years, the child acts and reacts primarily in relation to immediate physical objects. But by the later preschool years, the child's behavior is increasingly dominated by symbols. Several investigators, among them Norman Geschwind (1964), believe that symbol use depends on the maturation of the cross-modal zones. According to their argument, the infant's reaction to sensory input—sights, sounds, smells—is primarily a response to its pleasurable consequences. If pleasure accompanies these experiences, the child will seek them; if pain results, the child will try to avoid them. Aspects of experience involving pleasure and pain exploit primarily the con-

nection between the sensory areas and the structures underlying the cerebral cortex. But once the cross-modal zones allow connections to be formed among the cortical sensory areas themselves, further possibilities arise: Now children may react to percepts that have meaning only because they are connected to other percepts. Thus a sound can represent a sight, as when the sound "mēt" designates a piece of animal flesh. Or a sight can represent a tactile sensation. The printed word *fur* may give rise to a tactile sensation, because the cross-modal zones connect the visual percept to the feel of animal hair.

Geschwind has pointed out that the greatest brain growth in human primates, as compared to nonhuman primates, is in the cross-modal zones. These zones arose late in evolution and also mature quite late in the child's life, probably not completely until the fifth year of life. The fact that symbolic activity increases rapidly during the very same period suggests that the child's emerging domination by symbols (and especially by linguistic symbols) may reflect specific events in the nervous system.

DOMINANCE OF THE LEFT HEMISPHERE

Another facet of brain development may also underlie cognitive advances. The human brain is composed of two symmetrical hemispheres. The symmetry is not only apparent to the eye (as Figure 7.2 shows) but also extends beyond the surface; some corresponding parts of the two hemispheres (for example, the left and right visual cortexes) govern the same behavioral functions. Yet perhaps the most intriguing feature of the two hemispheres (and their respective cortexes) is that their overall functions are *not* identical. For most individuals (and nearly all right-handed persons), the left hemisphere is considered dominant in two ways. First, it controls the activity of the right part of the body—the more important half for the vast majority of people, who are right-handed. And second, the left hemisphere is crucial for all language and language-related activities as well as for many other cognitive capacities (Gazzaniga, 1970).

The nature of this dominance can be clearly demonstrated. Persons who have sustained sizable injuries to the right hemisphere will be impaired in moving the left side of the body, but their language will remain essentially normal. In contrast, persons with even a small injury in certain portions of the left hemisphere will suffer impaired linguistic performance, and a large injury will render them entirely unable to use or understand words. Although the right hemisphere is also dominant for some tasks—for instance, those involving musical perception, fine discriminations of shape and texture, and visual-spatial abilities such as drawing complex forms—its dominance for these functions is not nearly so decisive as that of the left hemisphere for language (H. Gardner, 1975).

So much for the state of affairs in adults. In children, dominance does not seem to be clearly established during their early years. Although whether a child will be left- or

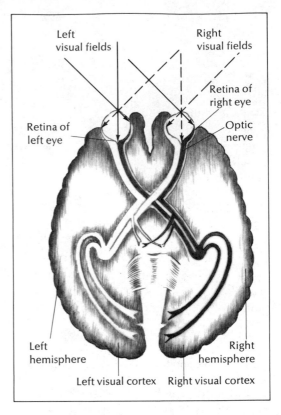

Figure 7.2. This view of the undersurface of the brain reveals its peculiar "crossed" nature. That is, images of objects to the left of the perceiver are projected onto the right surface of both retinas and, from there, are transmitted to the visual cortex in the right hemisphere of the brain. Images of objects on the individual's right side make their way, by an analogous path, to the individual's left visual cortex.

right-handed can usually be determined within the first year or two (and perhaps earlier; see Bresson et al., 1977; Caplan and Kinsbourne, 1976; Entus, 1975; Michel, 1981), most children seem able to use both hands with equal facility until the age of four or five. More revealingly still, children up to the age of twelve or so can sustain large injuries in the left hemisphere, including loss of language capacity, and later reestablish language to nearly normal levels (Lenneberg, 1967).

This finding strongly suggests that abilities are organized differently in the young brain than in the adult brain. Dominance seems not to be strongly established, and capacities like language may exist (or be represented) in both hemispheres. Further, the preadolescent's brain seems to have considerable potential for recovering damaged functions, though it cannot, so far as we know, generate replacement nerve cells.

The considerable plasticity in the nervous system of the young organism does not mean, however, that the location of affective and cognitive capacities has been randomly determined (Davidson and Fox, 1981; Dennis and Whitaker, 1977; Geffen and Wale, 1979). Indeed, increasing evidence suggests that the proclivity of the left hemisphere to be dominant for language (in most persons) and for the right hemisphere to be dominant for music (in most persons) has been laid down at birth (Best and Glanville, 1978; Caplan and Kinsbourne, 1976; Lewkowicz and Turkewitz, 1981; Molfese and Molfese, 1979; Segalowitz and Chapman, 1980; but see also Vargha-Khadem and Corballis, 1979). Moreover, as tools for measuring dominance have improved, some researchers have concluded that dominance for certain language, motor, and sensory functions may be well established by the age of three or four (Etaugh and Levy, 1981; Hiscock and Kinsbourne, 1980; White and Kinsbourne, 1980). Thus, while these functions can, in the case of injury, be taken over by other portions of the brain during early childhood, actual dominance and lateralization may be established at an extremely early point in life.

Nonetheless, it may still be useful to distinguish between the basic lateralized organization of the human nervous system, established early in life, and the actual dominance by the left hemisphere as indexed by handedness in daily activities. Speculatively, one might correlate the solidification of left hemisphere dominance in the child's brain with the emergence of a new cluster of behaviors between the ages of five and seven.* Especially intriguing is the possibility that left hemisphere dominance, which is intimately tied to language capacity, facilitates the linguistic control of behavior that assumes such importance in the years from five to seven. Support for this speculation comes from several studies indicating that children who develop hemisphere dominance early are most successful at a number of the tasks studied by Sheldon White, whereas children with retarded or "mixed" dominance have difficulty with the tasks (Benton, 1959; Cruikshank and Hallahan, 1975; Mount et al., 1981; S. White, 1970*a*).

THE DANGERS AND DIVIDENDS OF "NEUROLOGIZING"

The parallels between brain organization and psychological function are sufficiently neat and attractive that it is tempting to "neurologize"—to account for milestones of development in terms of what is going on in the brain (Wertlieb and Rose, 1979). But this position can be dangerous, because it assumes that a correlation between a behavior and a region of the brain (or brain structure) explains a process. At most, however, the presence of a certain brain structure may prove a necessary antecedent for a behavior, never by itself a sufficient one. Language may not be learned without certain structures in the temporal lobe; but even with those structures, a person needs considerable experience in order

---

*There may be parallel solidification of the right hemisphere at a later point in development; some investigators have proposed that the ability to perceive a face as a single organized whole (or gestalt) may depend upon certain neural centers in the right hemisphere that mature only in the preadolescent years (cf. Carey, Diamond, and Woods, 1980; Moscovitch, Strauss, and Olds, 1980).

to learn language (Curtiss, 1977). And, as we saw in Chapter 3 in examining how early stimulation affects rats, the actual maturation of brain structures may well depend on the organism's interactions in the environment.

There is yet a further danger. If one takes models of neural maturation too literally, one may be blinded to important phenomena. For instance, if one believed that only a child with matured cross-modal areas could learn to read (connecting visual signs with spoken words), one might then overlook the minority of children who are able to read as early as age two (Fowler, 1962; Huttenlocher and Huttenlocher, 1975). It seems preferable instead to let the psychological facts take the lead here. If a child can perform a function, it is up to the neurologist to explain how (and where) that can be accomplished in the child's brain— rather than to establish, by neurological decree, what that child can or cannot do (Nolan and Kagan, 1978).

To be sure, the child's brain is integrally connected with all thoughts and behaviors. Moreover, as we acquire more detailed knowledge of the maturing nervous system, we will undoubtedly achieve fresh insights into how skills can (and cannot) be acquired (Milner, 1967). But any explanation of the shift between five and seven must take into account not only changes in the nervous system, but also in the child's environment, parental models, motivations to achieve certain goals, and basic cognitive and social skills. Let us turn now to some of these other considerations.

EGOCENTRIC SPEECH AND EGOCENTRIC BEHAVIOR

Although aware of the changes occurring in the brain, most psychologists have elected to interpret the five-to-seven shift in terms of psychological variables—children's behaviors

and thoughts, the pressures and models of their immediate environment, and the broader influence of their culture. The cognitive-structural school, in particular, has focused on a broad cluster of behaviors involving the child's ability to view herself as others see her and to assume the perspective of other individuals. As in other examinations of the cognitive-structural perspective, we shall begin with trail-breaking work by Jean Piaget.

JEAN PIAGET'S STUDIES AND SOME RECENT CONTRIBUTIONS

Egocentric Speech. In his very first book on child psychology, *The Language and Thought of the Child* (1955; original version, 1923), Piaget described an intriguing phenomenon. He had observed many youngsters speaking aloud in the presence of others but directing their remarks to no one in particular. Piaget called this curious behavior **egocentric speech,** a reflection of his view of the young child as egocentric (see Chapter 2). Like other aspects of children's behavior at this time, egocentric speech was seen as a sign of their immersion within their own mental world: their inability to separate their own perspective from those of other people.

Piaget described several manifestations of egocentric speech. As an example, he told children stories and then asked them to relate the stories to others. Children aged four or five failed utterly in this task. On the one hand, they tended to repeat, to dwell on, and even to invent details. On the other hand, they left out the central points, referred to characters without naming them, or shifted at will their designations of specific characters. The mistellings made it impossible for listeners to appreciate the story. After all, the story of Goldilocks makes little sense when the storyteller forgets to mention that Goldilocks was found sleeping in the little bear's bed or confuses the bears with each other.

Piaget thought that egocentric speech serves no apparent function in the child's behavior, so there is no reason for it to survive. As children grow older and more aware of the distinctions between themselves and others, egocentric speech declines and then eventually fades away.

Lev Vygotsky's View. Piaget's pioneering demonstrations that young children use speech differently from adults and that children seem unable to adopt others' points of view gained him an international reputation. But the Soviet psychologist Lev Vygotsky disagreed with Piaget's interpretation. In Vygotsky's view (1962), egocentric speech represents an important and perhaps necessary stage in children's development. By talking aloud, children are in fact thinking for themselves—trying out ways of conceptualizing a problem and then reaching a solution. Vygotsky supported this view by documenting an increase in egocentric speech when a child is attempting to overcome an obstacle or solve a puzzle (see also S. H. Goodman, 1977, 1981; Wertsch, 1977, in press). Such speech seems to accompany the child's explorations, to take for granted the topic at hand, and to focus instead on new and potentially useful information that has come to her attention—for example, the shape of a missing piece. Far from just fading away, egocentric speech goes underground to become **inner speech,** a form of language spoken to oneself that Vygotsky identified closely with the pure thought of adults (see Chapter 4).

Egocentric speech has another positive side: it represents the child's admittedly primitive efforts to remain in contact with other people, to share ideas, to participate in their social world. To prove this point, Vygotsky showed that children's egocentric speech declined when they were placed in a room with peers who spoke a foreign language or who were deaf and mute. Here, then, was evidence that supposedly egocentric speech was actually responsive to an audience. Clearly, there was more to egocentric speech than Piaget had realized.

Vygotsky saw that language played a crucial part in the changes occurring at the start of the school years. Indeed, in response to Vygotsky, Piaget admitted that he had failed to take into account some of the cognitive and social value of egocentric speech (see Piaget, 1962*b*). He now recognized that events before the age of six or seven made necessary contributions to the increase in communicative competence seen at that time.

Other Demonstrations of Egocentrism. Piaget soon documented egocentrism in areas other than language (Piaget, 1932; Piaget and Inhelder, 1968). One striking demonstration came in the so-called three-mountains task. Children varying in age from four to twelve viewed an arrangement of three model mountains along with a set of photographs taken from various positions around the display (see Figure 7.3). The children's task was to remain at one spot and select the photograph that reflected how the scene would look from other perspectives (represented by other chairs) in the room. In a slightly more demanding version of the problem, the children were asked to reproduce the view of another person by manipulating a set of movable mountains.

To solve this problem, a child had to appreciate—and recognize in a picture—the relationship among the mountains from her own perspective, then mentally shift that relationship in line with a different point of view. Although children under nine or ten had little problem choosing the photograph that captured their own perspective, they had clear difficulties solving the other tasks. Piaget took

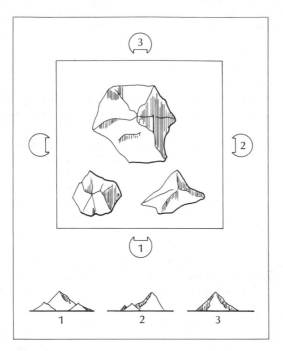

Figure 7.3. In the three-mountains problem, a classic measure of egocentrism, a child is positioned at location 1. She must then select from a group of drawings the view of the mountains that would be seen by persons at locations 1, 2, and 3.

their difficulty as evidence of enduring egocentrism—the child's imprisonment in her own momentary perspective.

Demonstrations of egocentrism came from other laboratories as well. For example, Diana Korzenik (1972) asked children to draw objects so that another child could identify them. She found that children aged five or six made drawings that failed to include features necessary for identification; seven-year-olds were able to modify their drawings in light of their peers' difficulties. In a study to which we will return later, Robert Krauss and Samuel Glucksberg (1969) asked a child to describe one of a series of squiggles so that another child would be able to pick it out from that series. Once again, the typical four- or five-year-old, rather than describing the decisive differentiating features, would mention features common to several squiggles, give idiosyncratic names (like "Daddy's shirt"), and neglect telltale details. Older elementary school children came through with flying colors.

EGOCENTRISM REEXAMINED

Until a few years ago, this picture of marked egocentrism in the preschool years was widely accepted. But recently new tasks and more subtle measurements have suggested a decline in egocentrism at far younger ages than Piaget and others had claimed. For instance, Helene Borke (1975) has demonstrated that three- and four-year-olds can solve the three-mountains task if more familiar elements and methods replace those used by Piaget. Borke introduced the character of Grover from television's "Sesame Street," and youngsters watched him take a ride around in a fire engine. Children were asked how the scene would look to Grover at various stops on his trip and then asked to turn a movable version of the scene until it captured Grover's current perspective. If they responded incorrectly, the examiner took them by the hand and showed them Grover's perspective.

Familiarized with the task, youngsters viewed a series of displays, including sets of familiar objects (horses, cows, wagons) and a papier-mâché replica of Piaget's trio of mountains. The children again were asked to rotate the display until it corresponded to Grover's point of view, but on these test trials they were not allowed physically to assume Grover's position.

Grover's views were anticipated correctly by 79 percent of the three-year-olds and 93 percent of the four-year-olds; in contrast, only 42 percent of the three-year-olds and 67 percent of the four-year-olds were able do respond appropriately on the original three-

FIVE-YEAR-OLD'S DRAWING OF "JUMPING"

The child was talking to himself as he drew: ". . . He's off the ground . . . should I put him on the ground? He just learned to jump higher . . . he is on his way down, see, he's bending his legs. . . ." The experimenter asked if the other child would guess correctly and he answered . . . "She'll guess because he's way up here. If she watched *I Love Jeanie* then she must watch *The Flying Nun*. . . . This man is jumping. . . . That's the ladder and he got up to get a kitty and then see his knee. . . . Marcy probably watches *The Flying Nun* so she'll know he's jumping!"

When asked why the other child didn't guess the picture right away, he answered,

"Because she didn't know the word and it's kinda hard to think. She would have guessed faster if I put the word on the paper."

SEVEN-YEAR-OLD'S DRAWING OF "JUMPING"

When asked if the other child would be able to guess the word from his first picture, this seven-year-old said, "No, because he looks like he's walking. . . ." He decided to draw a new picture, shown at right. When then asked if the other child would guess what this drawing was, he said, "Kind of . . . 'cuz he looks more off the ground and more like jumping."

Figure 7.4. The ability to take the point of view of another person appears across a range of symbolic media, including drawing. In these pictures and texts, we see two attempts by children to draw a picture of "jumping" so that another child can guess what has been depicted. The five-year-old proves much less successful than the seven-year-old in anticipating which sorts of cue will aid a peer in making the correct guess. (Korzenik, 1972)

mountains task à la Piaget. Part of the difficulty with the three-mountains display seems to have been purely perceptual: it was difficult for the children to distinguish among highly similar topographical landmarks. Motivation seems also to have been a factor: "Sesame Street" is more likely than mountain ranges to engage preschoolers. The form of the response is yet another factor: children communicate their awareness of another's view much more easily when they can turn a display than when they have to "translate" a photograph or construct their own models (Huttenlocher and Presson, 1973). Borke concluded that preschool children are not inherently egocentric. Presented with tasks and a mode of response appropriate for their age range, they perform well on Piaget-style tests of egocentrism.

Using a variety of tasks, other investigators have further questioned Piaget's claims. In fact, demonstrating declines in egocentrism has become a major activity for developmental psychologists. Four-year-olds understand that a secret is shared by those who have seen an event but not by those whose eyes were shut (Mossler, Marvin, and Greenberg, 1976). Two-year-olds have been found to adjust *what* they say and *how* they say it depending on whom they are addressing at a given moment (Menig-Peterson, 1975; Shatz and Gelman, 1973; Starr and Eshleman, 1975; Wellman and Lempers, 1977). They prove able to orient pictures so that others can see them (Lempers, Flavell, and Flavell, 1975). And the child who has once worn opaque goggles or rose-colored glasses will appreciate the difficulties experienced by the mother when she has donned such spectacles (Novey, 1975; Liben, 1978).

Clearly, a flat verdict of "preschool egocentrism" is an oversimplification. The degree of apparent egocentrism can be dramatically shifted by varying the task. If cues are easily perceived, if the materials used are familiar, if the differences between perspectives are dramatic, if the context is clear and the mode of response readily available to the child, egocentrism seems to wane early (Gelman, 1978, 1979; Herman, 1979; Schachter and Gollin, 1979). But if these facilitating characteristics are not present, egocentrism may last much longer. In fact, in one complicated variation of Piaget's three-mountains task, only eight of twenty sixteen-year-olds achieved a maximum score (Flavell, Botkin, and Fry, 1968). What emerges, overall, is a reliable association between the difficulty of a task and the amount of egocentric behavior (Flavell, Botkin, and Fry, 1968; Higgins, 1977; Lempers, Flavell, and Flavell, 1975; Urberg and Docherty, 1976).

Given this evidence, can we properly speak of a decline in egocentrism between the ages of five and seven? Should we instead talk of a gradual shift from the age of one until one's dotage (S. White, 1975)? Or might it be that preschoolers are not completely egocentric—that is, they are capable of assuming another's view and may well do so in a naturalistic situation but they are unlikely to do so in a more formal school or experimental situation? Piaget's tasks require this initiative on the part of the child, whereas in studies like Borke's the child is led by the hand to a nonegocentric view. Thus the breakthrough at about the start of school seems to be this: faced with a novel task, the child no longer needs to be guided out of the land of egocentrism. More fully aware that others have discrete points of view, children, on their own, adjust their behavior to the situation or audience. The repeated demonstrations that this initiative occurs around age six or seven gives Piaget's descriptions continued usefulness. And the occasional egocentric behavior displayed by all of us—whether we expect too much of our audience or forget what it was like to be a child—reminds us that we never actually reach the promised land free of egocentrism.

SIGNALS, FISHES, AND BULBS: THE SOVIET VIEW

In the 1920s just about the time that Piaget and his associates were studying egocentric speech among the nursery school children in Geneva, Lev Vygotsky and his colleague Alexander Luria were formulating their own brand of cognitive-structural psychology in Soviet Russia. Like Piaget, they documented a series of important phenomena, which in spite of considerable reinterpretation continue to suggest the nature of the changes occurring throughout early childhood.

The principal point of departure for the Soviet school of psychology was the work of Ivan Pavlov. Basing his conclusions on his renowned studies of salivation in dogs, Pavlov assumed that both human and animal behaviors are triggered by an elementary system of signals (or stimuli) called the **primary signal system** (Pavlov, 1927). Pavlov also detailed a **secondary signal system,** based on the primary system, that eventually comes to the fore in humans. Whereas in animals higher mental processes result from individual experience, the basic forms of mental development in humans come through one's experiences of other people, for example, in speech. As Luria later described it, humans are ultimately a product of both signal systems, the first concerned with direct perception of sensory stimuli, the second involved with systems of verbal elaboration and drawing upon knowledge of the culture. (This way of putting things is consonant with our earlier discussion of brain connections in early childhood; and indeed, the Soviet school has always been sympathetic to a search for the neurological underpinnings of behavioral change.) Both Luria and Vygotsky came to focus on the contributions of language to cognitive development, the ways in which emerging linguistic capacities influence and eventually control the child's behavior, and, more generally, the manner in which the surrounding culture supplies information and examples that ultimately make possible self-guided activity.

Vygotsky died of tuberculosis when he was only thirty-eight, but his student and friend Luria carried his ideas forward (Luria, 1979; see also H. Gardner, 1980b). Many of Luria's own notions grew out of a series of experiments in which he examined how children respond to linguistic stimuli and how the functions of language change over the course of development (Luria, 1961).

Luria's experiments involved issuing simple commands to children of different ages. For example, he confronted children with one or more objects and said, "Give me the fish." Six-month-old children simply looked at the experimenter, whose command apparently attracted their attention. During the second half-year, children might also respond to the command by looking at the fish or at any other attractive object lying about. By the age of one or one and one-half, children nearly always oriented to the fish; if it was nearby and they were not otherwise occupied, they handed over the fish as commanded. Thus in younger children a linguistic command would direct a child's attention to an object, but language as a meaningful system did not seem to be directing particular forms of behavior. Rather, the language was **impelling speech,** which simply stimulated the child to do *something,* not necessarily what was called for. Only at the age of two or so could children reliably carry out this simple command.

Luria then complicated the task in various ways. For instance, he would explore under what conditions children would press a rubber bulb. Sometimes the command was expressed in a conditional form: "When the light comes on, press the bulb" or "When the light comes on, don't press the bulb." Children younger than two and one-half would look at the light when they heard the word "light" and press when they heard "press." They paid no attention to the relationship between the clauses, instead allowing their behavior to be directed by their knowledge of individual words or phrases. And asked to stop, they often would just press harder. The potential of language to inhibit or postpone action in a specific way only came later. Similarly, when asked to "Press twice," children would often perseverate (or continue to press persistently). Language still lacked the potency to both initiate and then terminate a set of actions. Children sometimes uttered a rhythmic phrase, like "Go, go," to help trigger a specific and appropriate action.

Only by the age of five or six were children able to initiate or halt a series of actions solely by following a verbal instruction with precision. Language not only initiated behavior; it could now guide the specific lines of action ("Press twice"), it could terminate action ("Don't press"), and it could stimulate a planned sequence entailing both a start and a conclusion ("Press until the light changes color"). Finally, the speech that once had to be uttered aloud could now begin to move inward: external or egocentric speech, prompts like "Go, go" no longer prove essential for directing activities. Children talk to

Figure 7.5. How language gradually comes to control behavior can be seen in these two records from Luria's bulb-pressing experiment. Children have been asked to press a bulb when the red light goes on, but to stop pressing when a green light goes on. Sasha, the younger subject, is unable to resist pressing the bulb; language has an impelling function for him, irrespective of the meaning of a particular "second signal." But Vasilii, five and a half years old, proves able to press in the presence of the red light and to refrain from pressing when the green light goes on. (Luria, 1961)

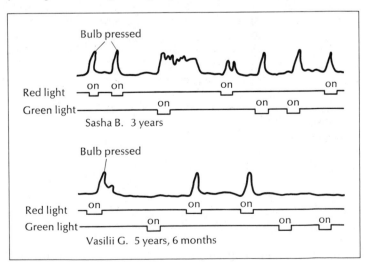

themselves, making plans by means of inner speech; meanings now dominate over the sounds and rhythmic patterns of the words.

Luria's description of the steps involved in the gradual control of behavior by language is persuasive. John Flavell, a sympathetic critic, stated, "Luria's is just the sort of developmental theory that most developmental psychologists (this writer included) both want to believe and find it easy to believe: the theory tells a developmental story that is at once dramatic and easy to grasp (it makes an interesting and readily communicable class lecture or textbook section, for example)" (1977, p. 68).

Unfortunately, however, as Flavell documents, many of the specific claims in Luria's description have not been validated by research in other laboratories. Miller, Shelton, and Flavell (1970) found that the command "Squeeze" did not help the child to respond correctly to the positive light, nor did "Don't squeeze" cause difficulties. In Flavell's view, children do have a general tendency to act—to squeeze and to talk when given the opportunity to do so—and they must learn to control both these impulses; but Luria's sequence simply does not emerge in Flavell's laboratory. Nor did it emerge in Meacham's (1978) or in Rondal's (1976) laboratory, although these investigators did find that overt verbalization helped children to remember their goals and that the rhythmic aspects of speech corresponded to the tempo of the child's actions.

If the specifics of the Luria-Vygotsky account have fared so poorly (but see Wertsch, 1977; Wozniak, 1972, for a more sympathetic discussion), why pay attention to the theory? It is possible, of course, that the theory holds more water than the experiments would suggest or that it describes what happens naturally over the course of development, though not what happens in an experimental context. To accept the theory on this basis, however, would be to lean over too far in its favor.

It seems to me that the theory has continued to attract interest because, even though its specific claims may be problematic, the Soviet school has called attention to a whole set of phenomena that demand to be taken seriously—the child's initial failure to listen to what is said, her tendency to persevere, her increasing capacity to regulate her own behavior—and has offered one relatively unified account of how these phenomena are related to one another. As we shall see, these phenomena have challenged other researchers, who have so far failed to construct an adequate alternative formulation. As Albert Einstein is said to have once remarked, "Old theories are never disproved by facts. They are only replaced by newer and better theories."

But there is, perhaps, a deeper reason for the survival of the theory (Cole, 1979; Wertsch, in press). More so than other developmental psychologists, Luria and Vygotsky have called attention to two important aspects of development. They have documented the increasingly regulative role played by language in all behavior; and they have underscored the contributions to cognitive development of various manifestations of the society, including symbol systems, games, notations, and the models provided by other individuals, particularly parents and teachers.

The theorists describe the culture's role in the development and eventual fate of the secondary signal system. For in their view, it is culture—that body of wisdom, customs, and rituals evolved over many centuries—that decisively separates humans from other animals (and older children from infants). In furnishing language, in facilitating its appropriate use, and in defining the words and topics of greatest value, the culture makes crucial contributions to the child's ability to regulate her own behavior. And the transmissions of the culture are most evident in the interaction of the adult and the child: the adults who talk to the child constitute models for how the child should talk to herself—at first aloud, then silently. In this manner, the outside culture instills in the child the means to continue (or suspend) action, exert her will, become a conscious and full agent.

Indeed, according to the Soviet account, voluntary behavior is viewed as a complex interaction between the biologically developing systems (such as the cortical zones that serve language and the cross-modal association areas that permit various secondary signals) and the cultural illustrations of how to communicate. Language is *the* means of capturing and conveying the concepts, processes, and ideas that are most valued by the culture and that will eventually inhabit (in fact, constitute) the individual's mental world. At work is the elegant interplay between the external influences stressed by the environmental-learning theorists and the child's constructed mental capacities, which preoccupy the cognitive-structuralists.

The Soviet position is enhanced by its constant attention to the neurological processes that facilitate the secondary signal system's regulation of behavior. Luria (1966) and Vygotsky (1967) believe that the infant and young toddler are under the control of the primary sensory functions of the cortex—they are pulled by the sights, sounds, and, later, the objects of the immediate environment. Thus the young child will sooner reach for what is close at hand or what is physically attractive than for what a word such as *fish* symbolizes. By the fifth year of life, however, the cross-modal zones come to dominate the sensory areas and the secondary signal system prevails. Linguistic sounds, gestures, and other signs become imbued with meaning. Now children reach for what they are told to reach for, rather than for the closest object. The brain thus sponsors a pivotal event of

development during the first decade of life: the coming to the fore of symbolic regulation of behavior.

Symbolic regulation, however, does not complete the story of child development. Even though behavior comes to be controlled by symbols, the child may still be unable to plan ahead, to think in terms of long time spans, to relate past and future. Such achievements are the particular province of the frontal lobes, the structures at the front of the brain that receive and synthesize inputs from other portions more directly concerned with routine acts and percepts. Except for the early developing motor strip, these synthesizing frontal structures probably do not develop fully until the later years of childhood and adolescence (Nauta, 1971; S. White, 1970a). At first, children's behavior is controlled by stimuli in their immediate surroundings. Then, in the middle years of childhood, the culture and the symbol system tell children what to do with their lives. But eventually the child can develop, perhaps in the frontal lobes, a metaphor that stands for herself. It is that self—an internalized representative of the individual's previous experiences and of cultural values—that ultimately determines what the person will do in life.

A MOLECULAR VIEW: MEDIATION IN THE SOLUTION OF PROBLEMS

Because of their breadth and vision, the Piagetian and the Soviet schools are the two most influential examples of a cognitive-structural approach to communication. The Piagetian approach is perhaps the broader, relying on such themes as egocentrism; the Soviet school is more focused, in its utilization of the Pavlovian signal systems and in its attempt to relate stages of growth to specific centers in the brain. Yet in their terminology and their examples both seek to encompass the gamut of developmental phenomena. Perhaps challenged in part by the difficulties involved in such a large-scale or **molar** approach to these phenomena, investigators in the environmental-learning tradition have also tried to explain the five-to-seven shift (Kendler and Kendler, 1970; Reese, 1962; Spiker, 1960). They too have tried to account for the increasing power of language, children's growing ability to attend to the diverse dimensions of a situation, their more ready commerce with other individuals and objects. But, unlike cognitive-structuralists, they have eschewed broad or "molar" concepts like egocentrism and tasks like perspective taking. Instead, they have studied the fundamental properties of the five-to-seven shift primarily in highly controlled experimental situations.

We have called this view **molecular** because in contrast to the molar orientation of cognitive-structuralists, the environmental-learning approach holds that explanations are best constructed out of small units or particles. Paralleling their work with infants, environmental-learning researchers have attempted to describe the behavior of older children in terms of specific stimuli and responses and have sought to avoid global explanatory constructs and the imputing to children of internal structures or schemas.

THE TRANSPOSITION PROBLEM

A task called the transposition problem provides a good introduction to the molecular approach (Stevenson, 1970; S. White, 1970b). Transposition is very simple: Children must respond to one of two stimuli, and they are rewarded whenever they select the one the experimenter has designated as "appropriate." In a typical transpositional study, children are shown two circles of different sizes: C-big and C-bigger. They must select C-bigger, the larger circle, in order to obtain a reward.

Once the child has been trained, or conditioned, to choose C-bigger, the pair is changed. Now the child is shown C-bigger and a new, even larger circle, C-biggest. The child has never been told "Pick the bigger circle"; she has simply been trained through rewards to select a particular circle. The crucial question is: Will the child continue to pick the particular circle she has been conditioned to pick (C-bigger) or switch to the new one (C-biggest)? If the former, the child is responding to a specific, previously reinforced choice. If the latter, the child is responding not to a particular circle but to the concept "larger than." In this case, the child is transposing—shifting her response from one circle to another.

The way children approach such tasks alters around the age of four or five. In many studies, the governing assumption has been that three- or four-year-olds respond simply on the basis of physical appearance, whereas the behavior of six- or seven-year-olds is monitored by language. When given the second pair, the older children conceptualize the situation anew and then use an appropriate linguistic description ("larger than") to control their subsequent behavior.

If C-biggest is much larger than C-bigger (say, five inches larger), the change is very blatant, and children of varying ages will continue to pick C-bigger as they were trained to do (Stevenson, 1974). However, the more interesting question centers about children's behaviors when C-biggest is, say, one inch larger than C-bigger, thus creating a new pair of circles relatively similar to the original pair.

Margaret Kuenne (1946) hypothesized two possible routes a child could take to make a choice (see Figure 7.6). She could simply note a specific circle and always select the circle of that precise physical dimension. Or she could note the relationship between the two circles

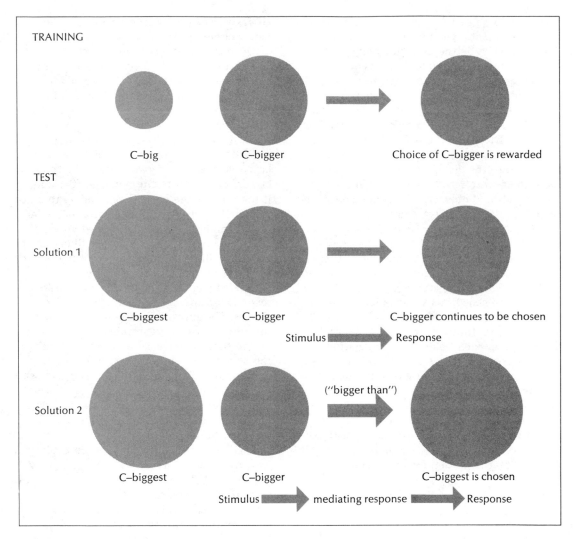

Figure 7.6. In the training phase of a transposition problem, a child is rewarded for selecting the bigger of two circles (*C-bigger*). During the subsequent test phase, she is presented with *C-bigger* and a still bigger circle (here called *C-biggest*). A child incapable of mediating will continue to select *C-bigger;* the mediating child, who has responded on the basis of noting the "bigger" circle, will now select *C-biggest.*

(relative size) and codify that concept in symbolic form (as in the expression "the larger circle"). Kuenne speculated that school-age children who relied on language in regulating their behaviors would tend to adopt this naming strategy and thus select the larger circle.

Kuenne's study confirmed this hypothesis. Focusing on physical identity, preschoolers chose the same circle across trials. In contrast, children aged five or six tended to draw on a relationship like "larger than" as a guide to their behavior and so were less tied to the absolute properties of the circles. In fact, they often transposed (or shifted) to the new and larger circle (C-biggest) even when it differed significantly in size from the original one. Moreover, in follow-up conversations, none of the three-year-olds but nearly all five- and six-year-olds could verbalize the relationship "larger than." Here was further confirmation of the role played by language: children's behavior is apparently revolutionized when they become able to devise concepts like "larger than" and invoke them to direct their actions.

Kuenne's work inspired major revisions of the classical environmental-learning theory. The steadfast notion "a single stimulus gives rise to a single response" yielded to the view that, as a result of the forming of a concept (like "the larger one") or the application of a verbal label ("choosing the bigger"), responses to a single stimulus can differ. This "mediationist" view closely parallels Pavlov's concept of a secondary signal system. According to mediationists, a child can recode—label or mediate—the stimulus during the interval between its initial presentation and her ultimate response. The **mediating response** newly categorizes the stimulus and, in turn, guides the child's response. The mere addition of a mediating response between the stimulus and the response may seem a minor change in the classical theory. But, in fact, the acknowledgment of covert events within the mind represented a major break. For once the concept of a single mediating response was allowed, nothing prevented the addition of other internal mediations—and a developmental psychology potentially as complex as that tolerated by the cognitive-structuralists.

THE REVERSAL SHIFT

Two major proponents of the mediationist school are Howard H. Kendler and Tracy Kendler (1962, 1970). These researchers see the mediating response as the central factor in the child's shift from the sensorimotor level to a level of symbolic representations (T. Kendler, 1972). Yet while adopting some of the cognitive-structuralist emphasis on stages, the Kendlers continue to rely on the simple tasks associated with the environmental-learning school and, in particular, on a task called a reversal shift.

In a typical reversal-shift experiment, the stimuli presented to children differ simultaneously in two dimensions—say, brightness (black versus white) and size (large versus small). At first the children are trained to respond to all stimuli that epitomize one pole of one dimension. For instance, they must always choose the *black* stimulus, regardless of its size.

After this discrimination has been learned, the attribute leading to a reward is changed (say, from black to white), usually without warning, as outlined in Figure 7.7. This is called a **reversal shift,** because the relevant dimension (brightness) remains the same but the value rewarded has been reversed (white rather than black). In other variations, the basis for the reward is shifted from one dimension (brightness) to a pole of the other, previously irrelevant dimension (size). Now the child is rewarded for choosing the large one, irrespective of brightness. This is called a **nonreversal shift.**

Figure 7.7. During the initial discrimination of a reversal shift problem, a child is always rewarded for choosing black. When a reversal shift is subsequently called for, the child will then always be rewarded for choosing the opposite, or white dimension. When a nonreversal shift is called for instead, the child will be rewarded for attending to the formerly irrelevant dimension of size. Children capable of mediation find it easier to execute a reversal shift than a nonreversal shift, because they can simply negate the rule that they had been following. (Kendler and Kendler, 1962)

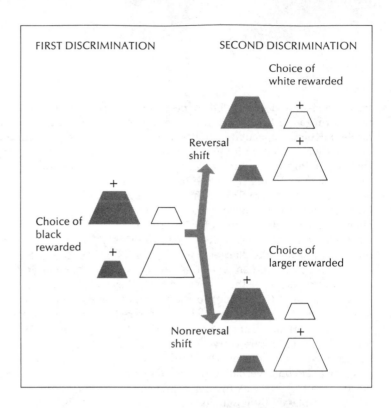

A Mediation Account. Different versions of environmental-learning theory predict different results on this task. In the classical Pavlovian view, there is a direct link between external stimulus and outward response. Thus a reversal shift that required a complete about-face should be more difficult to learn than a nonreversal shift. A response that has been always positively reinforced (say, choosing black) now becomes wrong, and the child must instead make the very response (choosing white) that has consistently been negatively reinforced or extinguished. Such radical shifting of behavioral patterns should prove time-consuming and difficult.

But according to the Kendlers' version of mediation theory, the school-age child should learn a reversal shift fairly easily. Having mediated her earlier responses with a phrase like "Choose the black and not the white,"

the child need only to remediate her responses slightly by saying something like "Do the opposite" or "It was black, now it's white." Conversely, children should find the nonreversal shift more formidable and time-consuming. They must abandon their original strategy (of attending to mediating brightness) while at the same time adopting new mediations (noting size) and changing their overt responses.

The Kendler's numerous studies generally support the mediationist view. They find that children who are more verbal and more cognitively advanced tend to perform better on a reversal shift, whereas children who are deficient verbally and cognitively tend to master the nonreversal shift more efficiently. And there is even some direct evidence that verbalization aids reversal shift tasks. Tracy Kendler (1972) has shown that kindergarten children who are required to explain their responses verbally are more likely to perform reversal shifts successfully than those who are not required to verbalize. However, children have sometimes mastered the shift while offering incorrect verbal characterizations of what they are doing (T. S. Kendler, 1964).

The Kendlers have also been corroborated by other lines of research. For instance, a large number of studies indicate that children on their own may fail to produce the required mediating response but if stimulated to do so will go on to perform tasks at a higher level (Bray and Justice, 1977). Other researchers document the increasing use with age of various mediating strategies, but stress that oral utterances do not necessarily signal mediation

and that vocalization may sometimes actually interfere with correct performances (Conrad, 1972).

Still other researchers see no need for invoking the construct of verbal mediation. For instance, David Zeaman and Betty House (1963) contend that the key to reversal shift lies in children's processes of attention. All depends on whether children are attending to relevant dimensions; explanations in terms of verbal labeling are superfluous (see also Bacharach and Luszcz, 1979). And Thomas Tighe and Lois Tighe (1972) find the key to reversal problems in the ability to discriminate which features of the stimuli are actually relevant to the solution. The Tighes have shown that pretraining in discriminating

Figure 7.8. Had Johnny possessed verbal mediators, indicating that stores are closed on Sundays, he would have spared himself a frustrating trip to the candy store.

among stimuli in terms of varying dimensions allows children to focus on dimensions ("brightness") rather than on the properties of a single object ("being black"); and this embracing of more general concepts in turn yields better performance on the target task. Once again, an explanation in terms of verbal mediators proves superfluous.

OPENING PANDORA'S BOX

Each viewpoint reviewed here—verbal mediation, attention, and discrimination—was devised to account for an experimental demonstration and, more broadly, to explain some compelling changes in children's behavior around the age of six. Each view can cite evidence in its favor. Yet it is difficult to evaluate different views because the factors of labeling, attending, and discriminating prove most difficult to disentangle. Attending may depend on labeling; discriminating may depend on attending; labeling may depend on discriminating; and so on. What are claimed to be competing positions may turn out instead to be points on the same circle. Moreover, it is not possible to control variables adequately, for one cannot guarantee that children will or will not use language implicitly, attend where they should, or have experienced the appropriate history of perceptual discriminations.

The environmental-learning approach set out to locate a simple process that captured the essentials of a phenomenon, to understand that process completely, and then to apply that understanding to more complex problems. But the approach has run into problems. The reversal and transposition problems are important only because of their implications for general development. Yet in trying to capture what is central to children's development, in trying to characterize changes in language and behavior around the ages of five to seven,

the environmental-learning school has slipped beyond the pure molecular view to take on issues of molar complexity. (See also the discussion of Bandura's work on pp. 210–211.) For instance, although inserting a single mediating response within the stimulus-response link may still be molecular, the same cannot be said for mediating chains that contain not just one or two but numerous internal mediating responses. And these have become familiar sights in the writings of mediationists (see Osgood, 1957).

Thus the mediation view has opened a Pandora's box of complexity. As Harold Stevenson, who has thoughtfully reviewed the literature, concludes: "As more and more data have come in, theoretical notions about reversal-non-reversal problems have met the same fate as the early ideas about transposition: the problems have proved to be so complex that none of the theories is capable of handling the essential results" (1970, p. 889). In fact, despite its different origins, the mediation view now includes many of the same concepts and ponders many of the same demonstrations as the cognitive-structural school.

Attempts at Synthesis

Because both the molar and molecular perspectives are so complex, siding with one or the other may be a matter of personal taste. One may either begin at the molecular level and follow its increasing complexity or start with the molar problem and try to parcel out the central component factors. Or perhaps the two views can be more closely aligned (see Berlyne, 1965; Gholson, 1980). Sheldon White (1965, 1970a, b) embraces the notion that the two approaches are suitable for different problems, time constraints, and developmental levels. In his review of the literature White finds the explanatory models of the molecular, environmental-learning school most useful for dealing with animals, abnormal or retarded children, and normal children younger than about five; in each case behaviors are more primitive, under control of immediate stimuli, and proceeding in a rapid, inflexible fashion. By the time children enter school, however, they approach problems differently, using language and complex reasoning capacities productively and systematically. For this age, the molar, cognitive view becomes more appropriate.

Yet, as White sees it, the schoolchild never abandons the simpler approach, because the more mature approach does not completely supplant the earlier one. Instead, the two are "stacked" or arrayed so that either one or the other will be mobilized. When the individual is under pressure, the more elementary system may go off. Thus, even a normal adult may behave like a preschool child when fatigued, in a hurry, unable to concentrate, faced by stimuli that are too difficult to assimilate, or—on occasion—simply bored. On the other hand, when conditions are more favorable, giving the individual leisure to reason, the primitive system will be inhibited in favor of the high-level conceptual system.

CONSENSUS ON COMMUNICATION

A disarmingly simple procedure devised some fifteen years ago by Robert Krauss and Samuel Glucksberg (1969) has illuminated some of the issues involved in the five-to-seven shift. The standard Krauss-Glucksberg experiment is reminiscent of a telephone conversation between two physically remote individuals who are both able to examine the same display. In a typical version two youngsters are seated opposite each other at a table, with a board or shield obscuring their vision of each other. Both of the children have identical sets of arbitrary designs. One of the youngsters—*the speaker*—is instructed to describe a target design in such a way that the other youngster—*the listener*—can guess which design the speaker has in mind. If the listener fails on the first round, he may have the right to ask questions, or the speaker may have the option of providing further or different cues.

As often happens in the first round of such studies, children below the age of five or six do not do well. Speakers give cues that are not sufficiently discriminating, and the listener often fails to appreciate the implications (or lack of implications) of the cues. Children aged eight or nine, on the other hand, are clever at offering cues that effectively discriminate among the designs just as the listeners will swiftly call the speakers to task whenever their cues are inadequate.

Modifications of the Krauss-Glucksberg paradigm have proved as popular among developmental researchers as variations on Piaget's three-mountains theme. Children the world over have been asked to communicate about designs and objects of every conceivable size, shape, description, and degree of similarity to one another. All manner of cuing, feedback procedures, and training techniques have been used. Children, adults, and stooges have been drafted. And with the accumulation of experimental data, some clear indications have arisen about the extent of childhood egocentrism in this simple (yet somewhat naturalistic) "telephone call" situation.

What findings have regularly emerged? With age, children are better able to detect the features of the stimulus that are truly discriminating and they are more sensitive to the characteristics of the individual who is listening. Older speakers are better able to direct the attention of the listener to appropriate cues (Higgins, 1977), more aware when the failure of a listener is really due to the inadequacy of the speaker's own cues (Markman,

1977), and more successful at revising their cues in the wake of feedback from the listener.

The initial studies focused on the abilities of the speakers to choose adequate cues and to revise their cues when necessary. More recently, researchers have examined the development of skills in listeners and the ability of children (acting the role of onlookers or eavesdroppers) to judge *where* the fault of an inadequate communication lies (Robinson, 1978; Patterson and Massad, 1980; Patterson and Kister, in press). These studies have shown that young listeners are as impaired as young speakers: they are unlikely to appreciate that speakers may be offering undiscriminating cues. They do not know which questions to ask, or which alternatives to offer, in an effort to secure more helpful cues. Paradoxically, children learn from the mistakes of peers more than from mistakes of adults. If adults provide incompetent messages, children tend to assume that the message was adequate and to blame themselves; perhaps for adaptive reasons, they are not so respectful or charitable toward their peers (Sonnenschein and Whitehurst, 1980). In general, older children are more likely to request clarification (Patterson and Kister, in press).

In "eavesdropping" on communicative sequences, young children also prove deficient. They tend to judge the effectiveness of a communication solely in terms of whether the listener guessed correctly rather than in terms of the quality of the cues. In general, they tend to blame the listener for failures. Only if the speaker's message was blatantly inconsistent with the target card are they likely to notice it. Older children, on the other hand, are able to attribute fault and credit accurately, even when a faulty message happens to culminate in success.

Armed with better information about where young children are deficient, research-ers have been able to isolate factors that lead to enhanced performance and to devise training programs that enhance the communicative skills of the younger subjects. The providing of systematic listener feedback may train children in effective speaking skills (Patterson and Kister, in press). Listeners bent on providing useful feedback should pinpoint their difficulties with a particular message, their frustration with the cues, and the kinds of information they are seeking (Peterson, Danner, and Flavell, 1972).

As in earlier research, it is possible to demonstrate communicative skills at an early age if the task has been stripped down to its essentials. Bearison and Levey (1977) employed only two potential referents, and their six-year-olds performed quite well on the task. Also echoing earlier research, children communicate more effectively if they are placed in a naturalistic situation involving familiar people, and if their motivation to succeed is high (Cooper, 1980). Indeed, under such real-life conditions, children spontaneously request clarification of ambiguous messages at a much earlier age than one might expect from laboratory studies (Patterson and Kister, in press).

One can even raise the question of whether the difficulties shown by children in these kinds of tasks might evaporate if a different mode of childrearing were adopted. Robinson and Robinson (1977) point out that young children are rarely placed in a position where adults have to depend on what the youngsters say. Usually the child's message is quite clear from the nonverbal context. Nonverbal looks of confusion also help (Mossler et al., 1978). In fact, it is chiefly in school that a premium is placed on the crisp and effective communication of novel information. Understanding about communication might develop much earlier if children were given more relevant information at their level of understanding about how well they were communicating;

they need to be told explicitly about the failures as well as the successes of communication. One needs to ask: is it the child or the adult who is egocentric (Robinson, 1978)?

ONCE AGAIN, THE SHIFT

It should be patent that the five-to-seven shift is a much more complex trend than had been anticipated (and than those of us in search of neat and tidy development would like). In each of the phenomena that we have considered—the private speech evoked in the solving of puzzles, the egocentrism displayed in solving the three-mountains task, the difficulties entailed in the control of actions by verbal commands and the failure of listeners and speakers to be attuned to one another—we have seen a simple recipe of "failure to succeed" replaced by a far more complex set of factors and equations. The origins of the various behaviors under investigation can usually be located in the second or third year of life, the time when children first begin to use language. If powerful cues, straightforward tasks, and naturalistic situations are provided, high levels of success are often found by the age of four or five (Klahr, 1979). On the other hand, when the task is new, the materials somewhat complex, the load on perception or memory challenging, the amount of planning or reflection significant, then children well beyond our fabled shift may continue to encounter difficulties with the tasks. The way in which the phenomenon is *operationalized* by the researcher often turns out to be the biggest variable of all.

It may be possible to offer some general guidelines about the steps through which children pass in their transition to the mature forms of communication and problem solving we have examined here. Our guide is James Wertsch (1977, in press), a psychologist influenced by the Soviet school. His data describe the sequence through which children pass as they attempt to solve puzzles with the aid of verbalizations from cooperating adults.

At an initial stage, the child fails even to appreciate that the language used by the adult is related to the task at hand. During a second stage (see Luria's "impelling speech"), the child is aware that the adult language relates to the task but does not understand its content or purpose well enough to make use of the adult's words. By a third level the child can follow hints given by the adult and is already altering her behavior in light of what the other person has said. This is the time when adult intervention can make the biggest contribution to growth, often spelling the difference between success and failure. Only by a fourth stage, however, is the child able to direct her behavior successfully by herself, having internalized from earlier encounters the kinds of messages and hints that are generally appropriate and helpful in the situation in question. The shift from regulation by another to regulation by the self has been completed.

Wertsch's synopsis is obviously most relevant to the kinds of simple parent-child interchanges examined by the Soviet school. And yet the transition he talks about may help to illuminate our other phenomena as well. In Piagetian perspective-taking tasks, the child must appreciate that other individuals have views different from her own; this knowledge can come about only as a consequence of considerable interactions with such other persons. In the bulb-pressing and fish-pointing games, the child must translate the adult's command into her own internal language and then carry out the sequence in the requested manner. And in the Krauss-Glucksberg telephone exchange situation, the child can only succeed if she has internalized the particular demands that are made on other participants in the exchange and can draw on this knowledge in effecting her own directions, questions, or evaluations. Buried everywhere, in apparently solitary voluntary action, is the history of many previous interactions with representatives of one's culture.

Can we (and should we) salvage our analysis in terms of a five-to-seven shift? I think that, at least provisionally, we should. Part of psychology is concerned with documenting what can be found in the laboratory and teasing apart the variables that bring about specific results. All well and good. But part of psychology—and perhaps the better part—must account for the kinds of behaviors that are seen normally in the course of everyday living. The kinds of phenomena studied by Piaget, Vygotsky, Flavell, the Kendlers, and Krauss and Glucksberg are somewhat artificial, yet all are based upon (and inspired by) behaviors that one sees every day. Moreover, if we can believe parents, teachers, and clinicians, these behaviors do undergo a significant change at about the start of school—and this may perhaps be the reason that school commences, the world over, at about the same time. Rather than attempt to dissolve or dismiss this fact of life, we must keep it in mind, even though the end result of our research may be to uncover an unexpectedly complex picture of developmental processes.

Signposts

In the years after infancy, sometimes with astonishing speed, children gain mastery over the various symbols used in their culture. We witnessed in Chapter 4 children's remarkable progress with language. And now in this chapter we considered a pivotal milestone: children become able to use language not only to refer to objects and events, but also to control their own behavior and to direct the behavior of others.

Using language to direct behavior is one of the most crucial skills perfected between the ages of five and seven. (Indeed, the beginning of schooling in diverse cultures at about this time may reflect the fact that instruction and communication can for the first time proceed on a verbal level.) However, as Sheldon White has shown, numerous other physical, cognitive, emotional, and social events also mark the decisive five-to-seven shift. White suggests several possible causes for these changes: increasing linguistic ability and the dominance of language, the capacity to take the role of others, social and cultural influences, and so on.

Our search for a key to the five-to-seven shift led us initially to consider crucial changes in the nervous system that occur during this period of development. We described the maturation of the brain's regions that interrelate sensory perception (for instance, allowing the sound of a word to evoke sensory impressions of the object it refers to), and we noted the emergence of left hemisphere (linguistic) dominance. But the neurological view may by itself oversimplify or minimize psychological factors. And so we examined other points of view as well—two molar cognitive-structural approaches, the molecular environmental-learning perspective, and a variety of other research traditions.

The cognitive-structural point of view, which focuses on the child's increasing ability to take into account the perspective of others, draws its inspiration from Piaget's studies but has gone beyond them in instructive ways. In his original studies Piaget had examined the young child's egocentric speech: the unstructured talk that apparently reflects an inability to break out of an egocentric mental world and an incapacity to distinguish one's own perspective from that of others. Piaget concluded that egocentric speech serves no useful purpose and fades away as the child grows older. But Lev Vygotsky offered evidence that egocentric speech is an early and revealing form of thinking aloud to oneself, a crucial behavior that eventually becomes transformed into adult thought. And Vygotsky's position has gained acceptance among many cognitive-structuralists.

Piaget's original work also suggested that egocentrism begins to decline during the years around the start of school. But more recent studies have also challenged this point, and it is now realized that the decline of egocentrism begins by the second or third year of life. Nonetheless, the ability to adopt on one's own the perspective of others—as opposed to waiting until these alternate points of view are pointed out—does seem to blossom after the first five years of life.

A second slant on the five-to-seven shift comes from the Soviet school of psychology. In this account symbolic activity is viewed as an interaction between biological development in the brain and cultural pressures to communicate, to plan ahead, and to reflect upon oneself as a person. Its two chief proponents, Lev Vygotsky and Alexander Luria, have stressed the extent to which language comes to control behavior after the opening years of life, and Luria developed a quite detailed acccount of the shift of language from an impelling to a regulative function. Many of the specifics of Luria's account have been called into question. Nonetheless, the Soviet school is worth taking seriously, because of its concern with important issues like voluntary action and self-regulated behavior; its illumination of the ways in which the directions and programs of other people are eventually internalized by the child; and its insightful combination of biological, linguistic, and cultural features of development.

Seemingly in sharp contrast to the broad Piagetian and Soviet approaches is the molecular environmental-learning view, which studiously avoids general concepts like "commu-

nication" or "egocentrism." Adherents of this tradition have relied on a number of demonstrations, such as transposition and reversal-shift problems, to document the appearance around the age of six of a mediating response—an internal representation that intervenes between the external stimulus and the child's outward response. Noting that the child begins to exhibit mediating responses at the same time as other changes in communicating and conceptualizing occur, mediation theorists claim that this novel behavior marks the shift from functioning at the sensorimotor level to behaving in terms of symbolic representation. The molecular approach offers a viable alternative to the structural point of view; but as it has evolved over years of research, it has itself become increasingly complex and, as a consequence, less remote from cognitive-structuralist teachings.

An interesting effort to reconcile these contrasting views comes from Sheldon White, who postulates (in accordance with the molecular view) that young children's behaviors are controlled by immediate stimuli, whereas those of older children reflect (in accordance with the molar view) more complex reasoning capacities. Even in adulthood, the more primitive stimulus-dominated mode may come to the fore under various pressures, although it is inhibited under normal conditions. In this view, the behaviors of the five-year-old remain, but they become dominated by those of the older child.

A view of the five-to-seven shift that is derived from data more than theory grows out of the studies of interpersonal communication inspired by Robert Krauss and Samuel Glucksberg. These investigators initially documented the difficulties experienced by youngsters in communicating information to one another when, in a telephone-style interaction, they were unable to see one another directly. A spate of studies has documented the growing ability of the child-speaker to adjust her cues in the light of the specifics of the array and the listener's responses and the growing ability of the child-listener to interrogate the speaker in an informative way. What emerges is a portrait of the development of communicative skills that points out its multiple facets and seems faithful to the kinds of situations confronted by children and parents in daily life.

The many changes in the child's cognitive and communicative capacities between four or five and seven or eight are impressive indeed. Though the changes are more gradual than a "five-to-seven" formula might imply, their ultimate impact is significant. However, they are not all that goes on in the child's life at

this time. Armed with a genetic heritage, the child is moving increasingly into the world, subject to the influence not only of the parents but also of the siblings and other family members, the people in the immediate neighborhood, and the larger institutions of society such as school, church, and communications media. Some of these factors affect most children in the same way; others exert quite different effects, depending on the child's social class. By the same token, some influences are generally benign, whereas others—like a steady diet of television—may have potential for destructive as well as constructive results. In the following chapter, we will examine the rich and varied social fabric in which children from five to seven are enmeshed.

CHAPTER EIGHT

Influences of the Family, the Community, and the Society

I looked into his eyes and saw a reflection of myself. I wanted to scream or cry, but all I could do was laugh.

—JIM SPRINGER, LOOKING AT HIS IDENTICAL TWIN WHOM HE HAD NEVER SEEN

When they were only four weeks of age, the identical twins who later became James Arthur Springer and James Edward Lewis were separated from one another and adopted by different families. And apart they remained for thirty-nine years, until they were reunited in February 1978. Upon coming together, they were astonished to find the large number of features they shared (Chen, 1979).

Each had been married to and then divorced from a woman named Linda. In each case their second wives were named Betty.

During childhood, each owned a dog named Toy.

Springer's son was named James Allan. Lewis's son was named James Alan.

They had held similar jobs, both working as deputy sheriffs, and shared many common interests, principally involving visual-spatial skills.

Their smoking and drinking patterns were nearly identical. Their medical histories were strikingly similar. In addition to having identical pulse rates, sleep patterns, and blood pressure, they both suffered from the same headache syndrome, which had begun at the age of eighteen in each case (Holden, 1980). Considering the vast number of similarities, of which but a few have been listed here, Thomas Bouchard, head of the University of Minnesota team that investigated the twins declared, "The probability of two people independently being given the same name is not that rare. But when you start to compound the coincidences, they become highly unlikely very quickly. In fact, I'm flabbergasted by some of the similarities" (Chen, 1979, p. 114).

The two Jameses are not the only pair of twins who exhibit such a close resemblance despite a long separation. Robert Shaffran and

Separated at birth, the Mallifert twins meet accidentally.

Eddy Garland, twins separated six months after birth, rediscovered each other at the age of nineteen. They turned out to have identical IQs and the same tastes in music, food, and sports; and both smoked too much (*New York Times,* September 19, 1980).

It might seem that these sets of identical twins, with the same genetic inheritance but different rearing environments, provide incontrovertible evidence of the dominant contribution of heredity to various aspects of intelligence and personality. However, this is not a necessary conclusion. It could be that, by chance, the twins happened to have been adopted by individuals who treated them in similar ways; and certainly both were reared within American culture, which provided more similar situations than if they had been raised in, say, Europe or Central America.

An even more critical case exists: that of Oskar Stohr and Jack Yule, separated at the age of six months. Yule had grown up in Trinidad with his father while Stohr had gone with his mother to Eastern Europe. Thus, in addition to being reared in different cultures, Oskar had been reared by a woman and Jack by a man. The twins were finally reunited at the age of forty-seven. According to Bouchard, "Jack and Oskar clearly have the greatest differences in background I have ever seen among identical twins reared apart . . . no question about it. Their differences are overwhelming: different religions, different languages, different qualities of child rearing" (Chen, 1979, p. 118). Still there were similarities: both excelled at sports and had difficulties with math; both spoke at the same rate of speech and displayed the same temper; they had similar appetites and certain peculiar habits, such as fidgeting with other people's rubber bands and paper clips and flushing the toilet before *and* after using it.

Such pairs sharply raise one of the most dominant and perennial questions in the whole area of human development: what are the contributions of hereditary and environmental factors to the development of the person? By and large the twin evidence tends to favor the hereditary position. Yet one could look at members of the same family who, while not having the same genetic configuration, are also strikingly similar to one another. Students of the American scene, for example, often point to the sons of Joseph and Rose Kennedy and note the unusual intelligence and drive, capacity for hard work, aggressiveness, family loyalty, and political ambition; there are also certain less attractive features such as ruthlessness and chauvinism that have often been commented upon. These features, found among the four sons (and also, with appropriate variation, among the daughters), are evidence for the potent influences of environmental factors. And still other commentators note that adopted children often come to resemble their adoptive parents, even though there is no reason to suspect that the genetic inheritance of such adopted youngsters is any more similar to their parents' genetic makeup than that of any two individuals selected at random from the general population.

In this chapter, while continuing our focus on the young school-age child, we will consider a number of candidate influences on development. First, we shall review the relative contributions made by heredity and environment to behavioral attainments. Then, after discussing the child's genetic heritage, we shall turn our attention to several external influences on development. We shall examine different methods of childrearing, the disruptive influences caused by divorce or other forms of parental absence, and the relations that obtain among siblings. Moving beyond the family we shall consider the effects of the peer group, social class, and the mass media, especially television. In examining these processes of socialization, we shall be adopting the perspective not only of the developmental psychologist but also of the social psychologist, the sociologist, and the anthropologist. Such an expanded perspective is appropriate at this time, for it is just at the age of five to seven that children regularly leave their parents and venture for substantial periods of time into the larger community.

Every behavior has genetic roots, and every behavior is subject to social influence. For any of the identical twins' traits—or of our own—we could debate the relative contributions of heredity (nature) and environment (nurture). But disputes are most intense and most important when they concern behaviors or attributes of great significance to the society. Thus we shall single out for special attention the factors that may give rise to intellectual performance and to potentially problematic behaviors such as aggression. Our goal will not be to prove that heredity or environment is the true or primary cause of either; the issue is far too complex to permit so simple a solution. Indeed, most social scientists now agree that one should direct attention to the *ways* in which hereditary (genetic) and environmental (external) factors interact in the formation of all human traits. Accordingly, we shall view the ways in which many social factors—immediate as well as remote—combine to mold the child's genetic potential.

Heredity Versus Environment

THE CONTROVERSY

People have argued endlessly about the source of various traits. Some attribute honesty to genetic inheritance; other emphasize the examples of family members, the influence of peers, or perhaps even the values held within a sector of society. A similar argument has been echoed in discussions about particular instances, like the Kennedys: some commentators highlight the genetic union of the Kennedy and Fitzgerald clans (both gifted in business and politics) whereas others have stressed the environmental influences of an ambitious family, excellent schooling, and the like.

In no area of human achievement has there been greater controversy about the relative contributions of heredity and environment than in the study of intelligence. Because there has been much controversy and especially because this issue has strong social and political overtones, it is important to keep straight the crucial points in the controversy (see Scarr-Salapatek, 1971, 1972, 1975). Two issues are disputed: the validity of tests of intelligence and the extent to which intelligence can be attributed to genetic inheritance. Tests of intelligence, and particularly the IQ (or intelligence quotient) test, consist of questions probing an individual's capacity to solve problems, understand words and passages, complete puzzles, and the like. Such tests have been used in Europe and America for years but have increasingly been accused of cultural bias. That is, the knowledge required to do well on these tests is valued and available in some portions of our society but not in others. We shall treat the nature and validity of contemporary intelligence tests in Chapter 10, when we consider the cognitive development of the schoolchild.

The second major controversy—the degree to which intelligence, however tested, can be said to be inherited—is even more volatile. Some authorities (for example, Eysenck, 1971; Herrnstein, 1973; Jensen, 1969, 1979) have held that most of a person's intelligence is determined genetically. A larger group of scholars (for example, Block and Dworkin, 1976; Hirsch, 1970; Kamin, 1979, 1980; Lewontin,

1970) have taken the position either that one's preference on tests of intelligence is influenced chiefly by environmental factors or that the relative contribution of the two factors cannot be disentangled. In the view of this latter group, from the moment of conception every facet of an individual's development is affected by external factors, ranging from the environment of the mother's womb to the nature and tempo of the culture in which the child happens to be reared. Any discussion of strictly genetic contributions to as complex a trait as intelligence is considered futile.

TWIN STUDIES

The science of genetics is complicated, and we will not expand on our brief survey in Chapter 3. However, nature does provide a promising method for making at least a rough assessment of the relative effects of heredity and environment and the extent to which environment can mold genetic potential. The key lies in keeping heredity constant. It is not enough to study offspring of the same parents, because each child has a unique genetic endowment. Only children who come from the same union of egg and sperm—**identical** or **monozygotic** (one-egg) **twins**—share identical heredity. One can safely conclude that differences between such twins are caused by environmental factors.

A number of comparisons can help fix the effects of environment. One can contrast identical twins with each other or with their siblings. One can compare the degree of difference between identical twins with the degree of difference found between **fraternal** or **dizygotic** (two-egg) **twins.** Though the product of separate eggs and sperms, fraternal twins should otherwise have been treated similarly (or roughly as similarly as identical twins). Or one can compare adopted children who have been raised in the same household with adopted children subjected to different environments (Willerman, 1979).

Such studies indicate that identical twins are consistently more similar across a variety of measures. Moreover, monozygotic twins tend to become more similar to each other with age, while dizygotic twins become less similar, more like two siblings a year or two apart (R. S. Wilson, 1978). However, it is also likely that parents treat monozygotic twins somewhat more similarly than they treat dizygotic ones, thus contributing to the patterns of each type (Lytton, 1977). For instance, identical twins may well have temperaments that are highly similar and these, in turn, evoke more similar responses from parents and others.

In all, it seems fair to conclude that heredity makes a significant contribution to children's development (Newman, Freeman, and Holzinger, 1937; R. S. Wilson, 1974, 1977, 1978). However, that contribution differs across traits: identical as well as fraternal twins resemble each other most in their physical traits, somewhat less in intelligence, and less still in personality and emotions (Goldsmith and East, 1981). But the order may also reflect the ease of testing the various traits. Although we can see clearly whether two children look alike, we may be less able to pin down subjective factors like personality. Differences between types of twins can also be noted in social interactions: common heredity predicts the quality of infants' responses to strangers more reliably than it predicts infants' responses to family members (Plomin and Rowe, 1979). These patterns can be used as indices of the extent to which traits are influenced by the environment.

Studies of identical twins raised in different environments most accurately probe the extent of environmental contribution. If twins continue to resemble each other despite years

in distinctly different environments, the case for the environment would seem to become weaker. In a review of literature on this topic, Robert Woodworth (1941) found that if identical twins were separated but raised in similar environments, the differences in intelligence proved negligible. But identical twins' performances on an intelligence test could differ markedly if their environments were very different. Among nineteen sets of identical twins, the largest difference in intelligence test scores was 24 points. In this case, the twin with the higher score had been raised in a prosperous farming region, had gone to college, and had become a schoolteacher. Her low-scoring twin grew up in the backwoods and had received only two years of regular schooling. In nearly all other cases, the difference in score was 10 points or less (the average was 7.6 points). Bouchard finds much the same trends in his sample of twins reared apart. Most pairs of twins have scores that are extremely close to each other. But there is one difference of twenty points, again reflecting two vastly different upbringings (P. Watson, 1980). Environmentalists as well as hereditarians can take some comfort in these findings.

Clearly, the difference in intelligence among identical twins reared apart (7.6 points) is less than that found among unrelated individuals. (The chance of sampling two persons at random who were reared separately and finding their IQs to be 15 points apart is about .5.) However, the differences are greater than those encountered between identical twins reared together (about 3 points). Other studies report a mean difference in IQ of 5 points for identical twins reared together, 6.5 points for identical twins reared apart, and 11 points for dizygotic twins reared together (Scarr-Salapatek, 1975).

Such studies serve as a reasonable assessment of the environmental effect on a fixed heredity. Still, as we have noted, twins who look exactly alike may well be treated some-what alike, perhaps even if raised in separate environments. Therefore, their environments may actually be more similar than those of fraternal twins or of siblings born at different times.

STUDIES OF SOCIALIZATION

In the vast majority of cases, where there are no twins, it is not possible to assess directly the contribution of hereditary factors. Further, because of the complications noted above, and because some people have made unwarranted inferences about racial differences in IQ scores, most psychologists are extremely wary about speculating on the heritability of intelligence (Block and Dworkin, 1976). Making a virtue out of necessity, psychologists have generally opted to study environmental factors, trying to determine how family members and the persons, institutions, and norms of the larger society influence children's behavior, and also considering how children may affect their environments.

Most studies of socialization take a broad view of the context in which the human develops. Although laboratory studies of aspects of socialization are possible (see Chapter 5), psychologists studying this process usually rely heavily on systematic observations, case studies, clinical interviews, and other more naturalistic measures.

We have already considered several examples of environmental contributions to development. As we saw in Chapter 3, maternal behaviors such as smoking or community fixtures such as noisy airports can influence the human fetus. Moreover, in Chapter 1 we noted how in the early months of life infants' relationships to their initial caretakers affect the formation of basic trust. And in Chapter 5 we observed how parents' behaviors and attitudes affect children's activities and the emerging sex-role identity of toddlers. During the

opening years of life, when the child is so vulnerable and malleable, monopolization by parents—eventually shared by brothers and sisters—is perhaps as it should be. But by their fourth or fifth year, children are already venturing beyond their homes. Thus, although developmental psychologists must start by looking at the nuclear family, they must eventually move outward to assess the effects of peers, social-class membership, and society's institutions. We shall also follow this path.

The Family Unit

Many investigators interested in socialization have tried to work with an important, yet manageable, unit of influence: and, not surprisingly, they have looked first at the role of the biological family. Scholars concerned with the family have several approaches, including examinations of evolutionary contributions, styles of child rearing, the effects of broken families, and the texture of sibling relations. Certainly, these approaches overlap to some extent, yet they can be usefully teased apart.

AN EVOLUTIONARY PERSPECTIVE

Considering the family as a biological unit, some scientists have searched the childrearing practices of baboons, chimpanzees, and other primates for clues about human family relations (see Bruner, Jolly, and Sylva, 1976; deVore, 1965; Hinde, 1974). Their studies have usually entailed intensive observation of the mother-child pair, the relations among peers, and the emergence of a dominance hierarchy among males in the group.

Some general characteristics of human social growth can be gleaned from observations of primate groups in their natural habitat (Omark and Edelman, 1973). Like human infants, young primates leave their mothers periodically and are increasingly attentive toward peers, but they do so much earlier, usually after the first few months of life. Mothers encourage offspring, particularly males, to venture forth into the troop. In general, juvenile primates form clusters that are organized by sex. Young males assemble at the edge of the troop and play roughly with one another, whereas the young females gather in small groups within the troop, usually near the older females. Although primates of both sexes play vigorously, males' play is more rough-and-tumble, heavily tainted with aggression, and more likely to result in a fixed dominance hierarchy, with some individuals emerging as pivotal, others habitually adopting a submissive role. And males are less likely than females to associate with adult females.

We saw in Chapter 1 the fate of primates raised under various conditions of deprivation. Rhesus monkeys reared without mothers cling to one another rather than venturing forth, and what play they engage in is passive and unsophisticated (Suomi and Harlow, 1976). Analogously, monkeys reared by their mothers but deprived of contact with peers tend to be excessively aggressive and unable to conduct simply playful attacks. Monkeys raised in isolation have difficulties interacting with other monkeys, whereas those reared with peers and mother are able to interact in trios and in larger groups (Anderson and Mason, 1974). Monkeys separated from peers will display signs of deep depression (Suomi and Harlow, 1972). Moreover, groups of normally raised monkeys are likely to have well-worked-out dominance hierarchies. Possibly because the members can take into account a greater amount of social information about each of the other monkeys, relations are also more stable in normally raised groups.

Differences in rearing history also influence how female monkeys will themselves eventually mother. Whereas normally raised mothers tend to overprotect their firstborn, socially deprived mothers tend to ignore or severely mistreat their first offspring (Mitchell and Schroers, 1973). When a socially deprived mother has a second offspring, however, she usually treats the child adequately. Correspondingly, normally reared mothers tend to be less protective of their second born. Monkey fathers, too, show typical behavior patterns: younger males overpunish or overprotect their offspring, whereas older (and also more accomplished) males do not. Perhaps as a result of these patterns, the social and emotional characteristics in a group of firstborns vary more than do those of later-born monkeys.

As we shall see, these and other differences observed in primates are generally consistent with patterns found in observations and studies of human infants (see Hinde, 1974). These consistencies provide one justification for studying primate rearing. Not only do common findings suggest a biological basis for certain childrearing patterns; but also the possibility for experimentation with monkeys holds promise for deeper understanding of human family and peer relationships.

STYLES OF CHILDREARING

Of course, direct focus on the human family unit is also desirable. Many studies have examined parents' behaviors toward their children, and some styles of parenting have been repeatedly observed. Whether the data are based on case studies, naturalistic observations, or experimental investigations, parents can be classified with reasonable constancy as warm or hostile, consistent or inconsistent in their handling of misbehavior, overprotective or neglectful, anxious or relaxed, and generally effective or ineffective (Baumrind, 1971; Becker, 1964; Schaefer, 1959, 1965; Sears, Maccoby, and Levin, 1957).

Probably the dimension of parental behavior to undergo the most intensive examination is the degree of control the parent exerts over the child. As a first approximation one can distinguish between a **restrictive** parent, who sets firm and narrow guidelines for behavior, punishes infractions vigorously, and discourages the expression of impulses, wishes, or desires for autonomy; and a **permissive** parent, who is reluctant to set firm guidelines, sets wide ones if at all, is lax in punishing infractions, and encourages the child to express ideas and fulfill her own wishes, even if some infringement on the rights of others may result. In contrasting these extremes of behavior control, it is important to attend as well to the degree of communication the parent directs toward the child. A relatively restrictive parent who communicates effectively to her child the reasons for her actions is likely to produce a child who is competent and self-assertive; restrictiveness in the absence of effective communication is likely to produce children who are obedient, suggestible, somewhat withdrawn, and lacking in curiosity, originality, and displays of affection (see Baldwin 1955; Baumrind, 1967).

A study of nearly four hundred American families, conducted some years ago, provided considerable information about these dimensions (Sears, Maccoby, and Levin, 1957). The Sears study, based largely on intensive interviews with mothers, established that parents tend to be consistent in their degree of restrictiveness, and it produced a portrait of the effects of restrictive or permissive parenting that has been largely corroborated by subsequent investigators (Becker, 1964; Bronson, 1972; Kagan and Moss, 1962; Schaefer, 1959).

According to these studies, restrictive parents have children who are obedient, polite, and generally conforming. Permissive parents have children who are more disorderly, aggressive, expressive, and uninhibited. Interestingly, both kinds of parents tend to be somewhat more permissive toward boys than toward girls, especially in their toleration of aggressive behaviors. There is also a tendency for each parent to make more severe demands on a child of the same sex and to be somewhat more indulgent toward a child of the opposite sex (Lingle, Gonska, and McGilli-cuddy-DeLisis, 1981; Maccoby and Jacklin, 1974), as well as a tendency on the part of fathers to treat their sons with greater confidence and consistency (Radin, 1981; Ziegler, 1981).

Extreme permissiveness combined with inconsistent discipline tend to result in emotionally disturbed or delinquent children. On the other hand, children of overstrict parents may appear submissive while harboring vast resentment and frustration. As adults, these victims of repressive upbringings may lash out against others or become self-aggressive or even suicidal. Apparently, a strict environment produces outward conformity at the cost of an inner turmoil that may eventually surface.

Parents' restrictiveness may also interact with the amount of warmth (or, alternatively, of hostility) they show toward their children. For instance, permissive but hostile parents tend to have openly aggressive children, whereas restrictive but warm parents have shy, dependent, and less-creative children. But when hostility is coupled with restrictiveness children are most likely to inhibit aggressive tendencies or to turn aggressive interactions against themselves (Becker, 1964; Kagan and Moss, 1962; Sears, Maccoby, and Levin, 1957).

Because excessive aggressiveness is a serious problem within our society, and perhaps across cultures, the roots of this behavior have been of particular interest to psychologists. While scholars claim that a tendency to aggressiveness is innate, and perhaps uncontrollable (Freud, 1927; Lorenz, 1966), many have a more optimistic view, feeling that aggression is neither necessary nor inevitable (Kuo, 1967; Scott, 1958; Skinner, 1953). The fact that aggressiveness is not noticeable in every individual and differs widely from one society to another at least holds open the possibility that it can be better understood and, possibly, better controlled.

In one classic study, Sears, Maccoby, and Levin (1957) sought to discover parental antecedents of aggression. They interviewed several hundred mothers and performed numerous statistical correlations between stated childrearing practices and stated resulting behaviors. Highly permissive parents tended to have highly aggressive children, for when the children got their way by acting in an aggressive fashion, their behavior was reinforced. But parents who physically punished aggression also had aggressive children, apparently because punishments increased the children's frustration and thus incited more aggression (see Dollard et al., 1939).

Further analysis revealed that children were more likely to become aggressive when parents were highly anxious about childrearing, had low self-esteem, were dissatisfied with their current situation, and disagreed with each other about procedures of child training. Those parents who were restrictive but not very punitive had the least aggressive offspring; those who were permissive but also punitive had the most aggressive children. Becker (1964) has described similar findings in somewhat different terminology: parents whose disciplinary techniques are love-oriented, featuring much praise and punishing by withdrawal of love, have unaggressive children. In contrast, parents whose disciplinary methods are power-oriented, featuring generous dosages of the cane, have children who turn out to be noncooperative and aggressive (Segal and Yahraes, 1979).

The dynamics of these combinations of parental behaviors can be quite complex, and the processes by which they affect children still are not well understood. Moreover, be-cause most of these generalizations are based largely on studies of an earlier generation of families, they should be treated cautiously. Nonetheless, it seems reasonable to conclude that extremes of parental behavior are nonproductive; that parental permissiveness and strictness will always produce some aggressiveness in the children, but that the way in which it is expressed will vary; and that warmth and effective communication spiced with a moderate degree of control seems to produce children who are relatively happy and well adapted in this society.

According to psychologist Diana Baumrind (1967, 1971), exclusively restrictive and exclusively permissive styles of parenting are equally destructive. She has studied a wide range of parental styles and has pinpointed their consequences in children (see Figure 8.1). In her view, both types of parents have an unrealistic picture of their children, seeing them as dominated by egotistic and impulsive forces. Whereas strict or authoritarian parents think the child's tendencies must be constrained, the permissive parents tend to glorify these primitive expressive tendencies as refreshing and natural. Neither group takes into account their children's stage of development—for instance, the desire in early childhood to conform to parental models or the inability at that time to reason properly when faced with a parental command. Baumrind endorses "authoritative" and "harmonious" parents who are more inclined to see the rights and duties of parents and children as complementary. Such parents take into account their children's needs (as well as their own) at a given point in their development before deciding whether to act and how to handle the need. They are careful to introduce a calm and comfortable tone into interactions and deliberations. Yet, while being warm, conscientious, and supportive, they exert clear controls over their children's behavior and

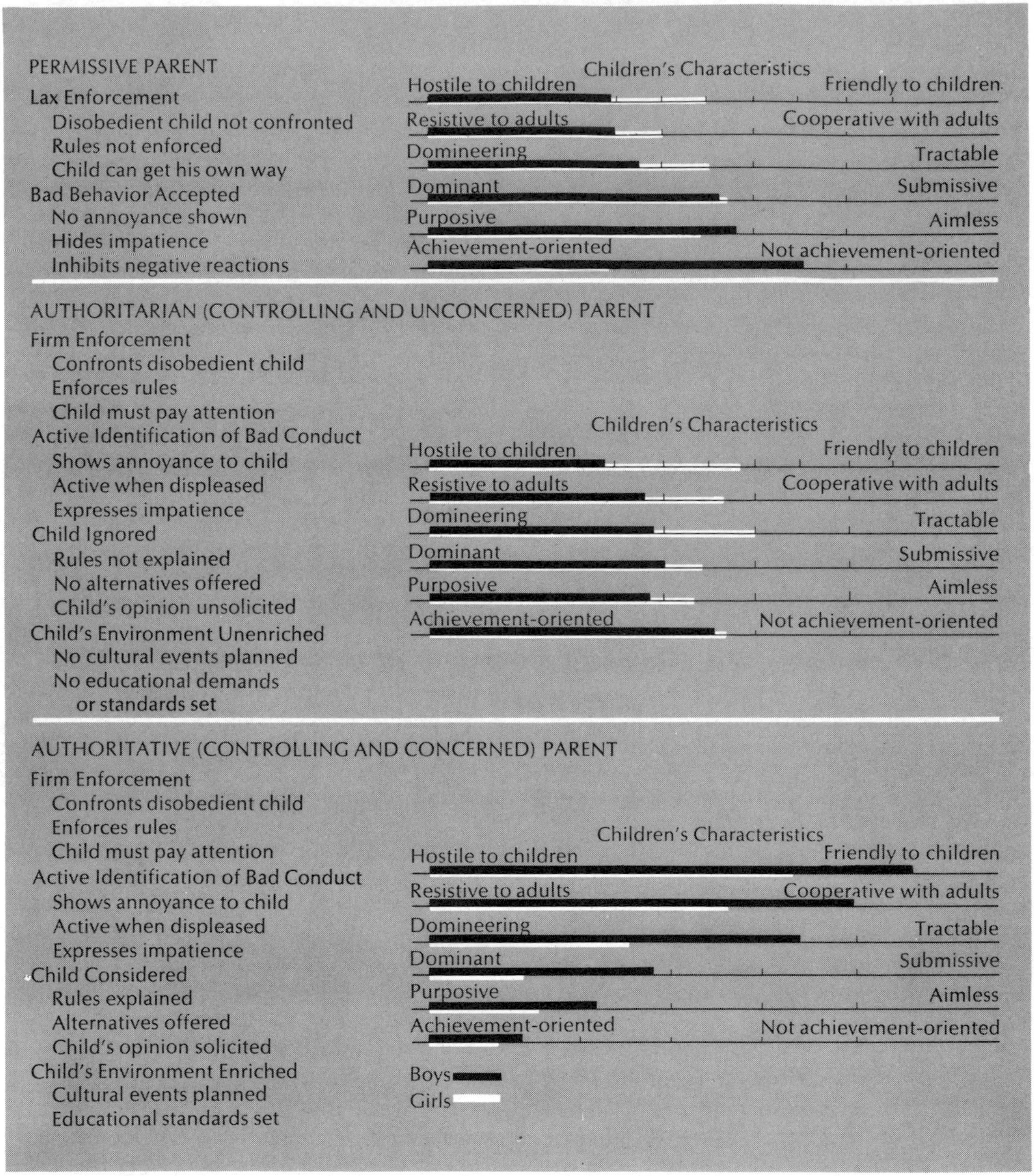

PERMISSIVE PARENT

Lax Enforcement
  Disobedient child not confronted
  Rules not enforced
  Child can get his own way
Bad Behavior Accepted
  No annoyance shown
  Hides impatience
  Inhibits negative reactions

Children's Characteristics

Hostile to children — Friendly to children
Resistive to adults — Cooperative with adults
Domineering — Tractable
Dominant — Submissive
Purposive — Aimless
Achievement-oriented — Not achievement-oriented

AUTHORITARIAN (CONTROLLING AND UNCONCERNED) PARENT

Firm Enforcement
  Confronts disobedient child
  Enforces rules
  Child must pay attention
Active Identification of Bad Conduct
  Shows annoyance to child
  Active when displeased
  Expresses impatience
Child Ignored
  Rules not explained
  No alternatives offered
  Child's opinion unsolicited
Child's Environment Unenriched
  No cultural events planned
  No educational demands
    or standards set

Children's Characteristics

Hostile to children — Friendly to children
Resistive to adults — Cooperative with adults
Domineering — Tractable
Dominant — Submissive
Purposive — Aimless
Achievement-oriented — Not achievement-oriented

AUTHORITATIVE (CONTROLLING AND CONCERNED) PARENT

Firm Enforcement
  Confronts disobedient child
  Enforces rules
  Child must pay attention
Active Identification of Bad Conduct
  Shows annoyance to child
  Active when displeased
  Expresses impatience
Child Considered
  Rules explained
  Alternatives offered
  Child's opinion solicited
Child's Environment Enriched
  Cultural events planned
  Educational standards set

Children's Characteristics

Hostile to children — Friendly to children
Resistive to adults — Cooperative with adults
Domineering — Tractable
Dominant — Submissive
Purposive — Aimless
Achievement-oriented — Not achievement-oriented

Boys
Girls

Figure 8.1. Diana Baumrind has identified distinct styles of parenting, each yielding children with their own characteristic styles of behavior. In general, parental styles exert similar effects on girls and boys; it is intriguing to speculate why, in certain instances, similar parental attitudes have contrasting effects on male and female offspring.

expect the child to behave as maturely as possible. And, if they feel that the child is "in the wrong," they indicate the proper behavior. Baumrind's conclusion confirms those of other authorities on childrearing: parents should honor a golden mean somewhere between always dictating what needs to be done and always leaving decisions to the child.

More focused studies have examined the effects of specific parental behaviors on social as well as cognitive tendencies. Parental agreement about childrearing correlates with the popularity of children in nursery school (Block and Morrison, 1978). Excessive maternal directiveness slows down the attainment of milestones in intellectual development, possibly by reducing the child's scope for exploration and for learning from the results of her actions (Hatano, Miyake, and Tajima, 1980). Authoritarian fathers have sons who cannot themselves tolerate ambiguity, are generally anxious, and are relatively ineffective in cognitive functioning (Harrington, Block, and Block, 1978). In contrast, parents who treat their children in problem-solving situations as being more capable and more resourceful, who offer considerable warmth and positive comments as well as occasional models of how to perform, are likely to have children who are themselves more competent in dealing with the complexities of everyday life (Mondell and Tyler, 1981).

Such correlations demonstrate that consistent parental patterns—whether benign or harmful—have predictable effects. Yet it is crucial not to overinterpret these results. For one thing, parents are often inconsistent in their behaviors across situations (Grusec and Kuczynski, 1980), and may base their behaviors upon different principles or cues (McGillicuddy-DeLisis, 1981). For another, the same behaviors do not always yield the same effects: thus, maternal protectiveness during the first years of life will lead to passive behaviors on the part of male, but not female,

schoolchildren (Kagan and Moss, 1962b). In certain cases the effects of peers can override the parental models (Hartup, 1976b). Unfavorable experiences in early life may be counteracted by more positive events later in childhood (Kagan, 1979; Rutter, 1979a).

Finally, there is a small but fascinating group of youngsters who have grown up in physically, psychologically, and emotionally deprived circumstances but who nonetheless develop in a normal and sometimes even outstanding fashion (Flaste, 1977b; Rutter, 1979a). Such children call attention to an important but as yet little-investigated facet of growth, the contributions made by the child herself to social growth. While the effects of parental behaviors upon children are evident, and certainly worthy of study, it is equally important to examine the effects of the child's own temperament and behaviors and to determine how they act upon and mold the behaviors of parents (Buss, 1981). Parent-child interactions are truly interactions: science has much to learn from those "invulnerable" children who have the strength to guide their own development (see the box).

THE FAMILY AS A SYSTEM

Another approach, which first evolved in the study of the mentally ill, views the family as an interacting **system:** all members have an enduring relationship with one another and, as in any organic entity, actions, changes, and events in the system will exert effects throughout.

Considering patterns of childrearing, a practitioner of the family-system approach focuses not only on parental effects upon children but also on how a parent's behavior is molded by the child's responses and by the reactions of others in a family. For instance, a permissive father may become more restrictive if he feels he lacks control over his child. If mother and father agree in such cases, their

Invulnerable Children

Paul and Frank have grown up in severely deprived circumstances. They live in slums and come from families plagued by physical illness as well as economic and emotional hardships. Paul suffers severe psychological consequences; Frank thrives and blossoms. Why? What makes a lucky few apparently immune or "invulnerable" to the stresses that may devastate others?

Whereas, in the past, research tended to focus on pathologic or disturbed individuals, in recent years several investigators have shifted their attention to these so-called invulnerable children. It is hoped that more knowledge about these "superkids" will lead to better preventive and therapeutic measures for the less resilient. Researchers, led by James Anthony (1974), Norman Garmezy (1976), and Michael Rutter (1979a, b), have sketched an initial profile of the invulnerable child.

Children like Frank and Paul who are beset by a range of hardships are said to be "at risk." They may suffer from physical handicaps or chronic illness. They may have schizophrenic, psychotic, or physically disabled parents; they may live in single-parent homes or have been separated from their parents entirely. Some have been reared in institutions, others come from financially and socially impoverished homes.

Against this bleak background, those who seem immune to the risks share a number of characteristics. Since early childhood, they have had a good relationship with at least one adult. If a parent is not available, able, or willing to fulfill this role, another adult (such as a teacher or a family member) takes the parent's place. The child knows or learns how to use this adult for support and encouragement, without becoming dependent. "Superkids" are generally relaxed, sociable, and have many friends. Furthermore, they tend to succeed in their endeavors and often display unusual creativity. At times, these children may need and create their own haven, perhaps in an attic or a tree house, where they are autonomous and detached from their harsh surroundings. But they do not flee; for, in order to gain competence and confidence and in order to build up invulnerability, children need to face challenges.

No child can withstand unlimited stress. The greater the number and severity of her hardships, the less likely she is to be invulnerable. Conversely, if just one stress can be alleviated, the child has a better chance of being able to conquer those that remain. Experts caution, however, against premature optimism. No one knows if these invulnerable children will still thrive as adults in fifteen or thirty years.

behaviors are likely to reinforce each other. In contrast, parental disagreement may cause bickering that will severely strain family relations. The status and the strength of the parental relation can be potent influences upon the experience of the child (Belsky, 1981); in fact, conflict between parents may prove more detrimental to children than excesses of either permissiveness or restrictiveness.

Part of seeing the family as a system involves a focus on the phases through which families regularly pass (see Zilbach, 1968). At first, two newly united individuals learn to live together in a common household. In the second phase the first child is born, and in the third phase the child goes to school. In subsequent phases other children are born, they grow up, leave home, and set up their own families. Each of these milestones causes perturbations within the family system.

In addition to charting the highlights of these phases, one can monitor the status of both the family's crucial functions (providing shelter and food) and the roles assumed by specific individuals (such as the potentate or the passive individual). And one can also examine disruptions in regular family patterns: a move to a new town, divorce, illness, or death. The challenge confronting the family-system approach is to capture accurately the torrent of events in the family and to trace their effects without producing an analysis so complex that it proves difficult to follow, interpret, and use. Clearly, families' sagas ranging from those captured on television soap operas to the equally dramatic adventures of the Kennedy clan offer rich material for a systems analysis.

DISRUPTIONS OF THE FAMILY

Current estimates indicate that about 40 percent of the marriages of young adults will end in divorce, and about half of all youngsters born in the 1970s will at some time live in the home of a single parent. Disruption of the family unit has always been seen as a malignant event and most researchers see no reason to question the basic point that it is usually preferable for the nuclear family to remain together. Yet given the ravishes of war, disease, and especially divorce, psychologists have necessarily had to examine the ways in which children react to such stresses and the range of outcomes that might result (Hetherington, 1979; Wallerstein and Kelly, 1974, 1975). And in view of the increasing experimentation in alternative life-styles, such as group living, rearing by a father, or child-bearing without marriage, psychologists have begun to direct their attention toward a whole set of nontraditional family units.

By far, the most studied form of family disruption is the divorce. Initially the effects of divorce are painful for nearly all children, but the precise reactions thereafter depend upon several factors (Kurdek, in press). First is the age of the children. Since young children see themselves as the cause of all events in their lives, they tend to blame themselves for divorce. They will often mourn the lost parent, even as they will continue to fantasize that he or she will return. Older youngsters are better able to assess blame and responsibility and will only rarely turn this punitiveness inward. Also, they have more personal resources, interests, and friendships on which to draw during the period following separation.

Events occurring within the family unit before and after the divorce are another crucial factor. If family life before the separation has been marked by severe conflict, the separation is sometimes greeted with relief by all concerned and the child may actually thrive. In general, a hostile parent is more detrimental than an absent parent. The relationship between the parents after the separation is perhaps even more important. If the parents

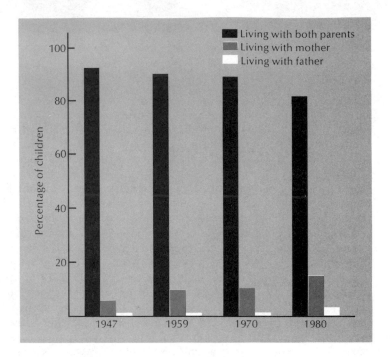

Figure 8.2. Although the overwhelming majority of youngsters live with both of their parents, the number of children in one-parent homes has increased steadily over the last thirty years. Factors at work in the larger society will determine whether this trend continues, levels off, or is reversed. (U.S. Bureau of the Census, 1961, 1968, 1969, 1973, 1976, 1979, 1980)

speak ill of each other, and turn the children against the other parent, the effects will be far worse than if parents refrain from such accusations and both remain in regular contact with the children. The resources of the single parent in terms of financial security and psychological support are also crucial. If the single parent's own burdens increase significantly after the separation, the children are apt to bear the brunt and to suffer. On the other hand, if ample support systems are available, if the single parent can maintain firm but sensible discipline, encourage independent behaviors, and remain on good terms with the departed spouse, signs are much more hopeful for the children's well-being. Still other factors include the attitudes toward divorce of the surrounding community and the individual child's personal competences and psychological understanding (Kurdek, Blish, and Siesky, 1981).

Divorce consists of a number of phases, including the initial disorganization that follows upon separation (which often includes a regression at school and in play), experiments with various kinds of coping mechanisms, and, finally, the attainment of a new state of equilibrium (Hetherington, 1979). Each of these phases has its own characteristics, perils, and opportunities. The long-term effects are of course the most important and yet the least understood. In general, boys seem to suffer more than girls both in school and at home, and they exhibit more behavioral disorders. This may be because, in most cases, the father leaves the home; by this action, he can no longer be a logical or stable model for identification and, indeed, he has become a model for disruptive behavior. It is also possible, however, that boys are in general more sensitive and more likely to show the effects of any disruption by "acting out."

Many but not all of these effects are repeated, particularly among boys, when the father is no longer present for other reasons, which range from death to extended travel to imprisonment (Shinn, 1978). In cases of death, the mourning will be deep but there will be no antagonism or recrimination to contend with. In the case of a lengthy separation, the eventual return is crucial with children old enough to understand that the separation is not permanent; but if the father has left because of criminal behavior there is a significant chance that the child himself will become delinquent (Rutter, 1979*a*; Sack, 1977). Cognitive effects may also occur: growing up in a house with a single female parent tends to heighten boys' success on verbal tests while lowering their performance on spatial and mechanical tests, traditionally the province of males (Chapman, 1977). Authorities differ in their assessment of the cognitive or personality changes in women consequent to the absence of a father (Hainline and Feig, 1978; Hetherington, 1979), and they have yet to investigate motherless families. Nor have they addressed the important question: In a society with changing sex roles, will it remain preferable in cases of family disruption to be a girl?

Figure 8.3. Younger siblings often want to follow in their older siblings' footsteps—and older siblings often want to enlist the participation of their younger siblings—even when the activity in question may not be quite suitable.

BIRTH ORDER AND SIBLINGS

A fourth approach to family study focuses specifically on the children—on the family situation when the child was born and on her place among the other children (or siblings) in the family. There is consensus that siblings affect each other tremendously (Sutton-Smith and Rosenberg, 1970) and that their influence is especially intensive and extensive in a society like ours where tradition and parental authority are waning (Riesman, Glazer, and Denney, 1950; Seeley, 1956). Some of the influence they have on each other results simply from the order of their birth.

A look at diverse cultures throughout centuries will show that children are often treated differently as a result of their birth order (Rosenblatt and Skoogberg, 1974). According to European law, the firstborn male received all or most of his father's property, thus keeping the family trust intact. In modern times, Stanley Schachter (1959), among others, has experimentally investigated the effects of birth-order position. He invited college women to participate in an important scientific study in which they would receive painful but harmless electric shocks. Schachter's real concern was whether, when given the choice, students preferred to pass the time before the experiment alone or with others. Quite unexpectedly, he found that preference was related to birth order. Firstborn women showed a stronger desire to wait with others, while those born later were content to be alone.

Schachter speculated that firstborns tend to be ministered to whenever they are in distress, so that they come to link the sight of other persons with reduction of anxiety. Accordingly, firstborns had a greater "need for affiliation" and sought company as they awaited their fate. In contrast, later borns are raised by mothers who can no longer attend to every bruise—whether real or imaginary—and who are too busy always to come when called. These children learn to allay their anxiety at least in part through their own efforts. And so they were content to remain alone.

A Composite Portrait. Schachter's intriguing results have stimulated considerable research on the multifaceted effects of birth-order position. Drawing on the findings of numerous studies of siblings (Sutton-Smith and Rosenberg, 1970; Zajonc and Markus, 1975), we can now sketch a composite portrait of the child representing each sibling position. Naturally, there are many exceptions, but the patterns are fairly typical, at least within our society.

Firstborn children are characterized by two somewhat inconsistent features. On the one hand, having parents who expect much of them, they tend to be highly motivated, ambitious, and successful, to adhere to rules, and to have highly developed standards and considerable organizational ability. From early infancy, they receive and emit more behaviors than other children (Booth, 1981; Kilbride, Johnson, and Streissguth, 1977; Lewis and Kreitzberg, 1979; Snow, 1981). They are especially likely to succeed in fields where seriousness, intellectual prowess, and high goals are valued. Yet, on the other hand, firstborns do not have the self-confidence that might be expected of successful persons. They are more likely to need others around them and are more fearful and sensitive to pain. They are less able to cope with anxiety, and they are quite dependent on parents and other people. They tend to be cautious and conservative (Finley and Cheyne, 1976). While successful in school, they are not particularly popular

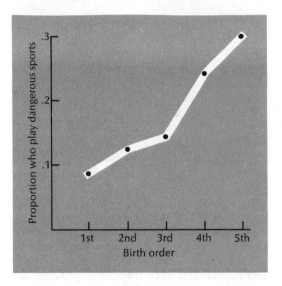

Figure 8.4. One reason for the growing fascination with a child's birth-order rank is the often unanticipated effects that seem associated with the accident of birth. One such example comes from the work of Richard Nisbett: a child's birth order turns out to be directly correlated with the likelihood that he will participate in a dangerous sport, like football, rugby, or soccer. In contrast, participation in sports such as baseball or crew appear unrelated to one's birth-order rank. (Nisbett, 1968)

(Lyons, 1979). (See also Figure 8.4.) This paradox may explain why firstborn children are often uncertain of their roles and are more likely than middle children to turn to psychotherapy (Garner and Wenar, 1959).

Even more dependent and achievement-oriented than the firstborns, only children have often been viewed as "super firstborns." Their parents often make strong demands on them and the children often satisfy these high demands. Because they remain at the center of attention, they may become quite adroit at pitting one parent against another to get their own way. They are likely to become quite self-centered, viewing themselves as unfairly treated and refusing to cooperate if they do not get their own way. They often have difficulties in relating to peers. And they often seek out the company of adults. Interestingly, they are more likely than firstborns to display traits normally associated with the opposite sex (Segal and Yahraes, 1979).

At the polar extreme of the sibling hierarchy are the children born last in a family. In some ways, last borns resemble firstborns, for they too are likely to be the center of attention for a long time and to be somewhat spoiled. However, rather than maturing quickly, as first borns usually do, last borns may remain quite babyish. Moreover, because they are not given responsibility, they are unlikely to develop feelings of independence: as the littlest in the family, they may feel inferior to the other, stronger family members, sometimes even becoming discouraged with their relatively paltry achievements and giving up in despair. They are as prone as firstborns to have personal problems and to seek psychiatric help. However, unlike firstborns, they are often quite popular, possibly because they develop interpersonal competence through the constant need to negotiate, accommodate, and tolerate (Segal and Yahraes, 1979).

And what of middle children? They may feel unloved and imposed upon because they have never been at the center of attention. They are caught in the middle, unable to recap the benefits incurred by being oldest or youngest. They are quite likely to perceive themselves as less skilled than the firstborn. As a result, they often turn to nonacademic endeavors, such as sports or the arts, preferring physical and action-oriented pursuits. They are also more likely to pick up unconventional ideas or philosophies, possibly as a means of getting back at an oppressive older figure. In fact, over 90 percent of the scientists who first supported Charles Darwin's biological notions in the nineteenth century were younger siblings (Sulloway, 1972). Re-

ceiving less attention than their siblings, middle children often become more cooperative with their peers and less dependent on their elders. Even as young children they are more likely to talk to strangers, whereas firstborns restrict their conversation to their mothers. Overall, middle children are usually easygoing, cheerful, and gentle, not anxious, not overconcerned with achievement.

Evaluating Birth-Order Studies. Everyone can think of (and some can peer in the mirror at) exceptions to these sketches. It must be remembered that these are only typical portraits; they yield no specific predictions about a specific individual. Each pattern can be modulated by many factors: the size of the family; its social, economic, and personal characteristics; the number of years between the children; and so on (Trotter, 1976). For instance, second-born children are more likely to be treated as firstborns if born much later or if their sex is different from the firstborn's.

Finally, many of these conclusions rest on tenuous findings. Results based on questionnaires and self-reports are usually less reliable than systematic observations or experimental manipulations by impartial researchers. Studies tended to concentrate on middle-class families. Moreover, statistical correlations were usually between birth order and personality trait: that is, they indicate that children who occupy place x in the birth order are likely, as a group, to score high on trait A and low on trait B. Longitudinal studies focusing on the family dynamics that lead to this profile of scores would be more reliable. And greater confidence could also be achieved if studies were conducted on the way children of different birth-order positions solve problems or interact with one another.

Nonetheless, the fact that patterns can be found for each of the major birth-order positions is powerful evidence that a child's place within the family will have a significant influence on her development. In the future more precise experimental studies may yield firmer insights about the significance of birth order. For instance, one recent study found that older sisters are more likely than older brothers to help a younger sibling solve a problem by offering explanations, providing feedback, and the like (Cicirelli, 1975). Children from larger families sought and received more help from one another than children from small families did, and mothers were more likely to aid children who had older brothers than children who had older sisters. Siblings prove more likely to interact with one another when only one parent is present than when both are present (Lamb, 1979) and older children can serve as attachment figures for their younger siblings (Stewart, 1981). Younger siblings attend to and often imitate their older siblings, while older siblings are more likely to initiate behaviors—both antisocial like aggression and prosocial actions like teaching—toward their younger sibs (Abramovitch, Corter, and Lando, 1979; Pepler, 1981; Vandell, 1981). These findings indicate that we need to (and can) go beyond a simple list of traits to understand the dynamic relations among children in various birth-order positions.

THE KENNEDYS REVISITED

One yardstick against which to assess various approaches to the family is the extent to which they successfully illuminate a particular family. Returning to ponder the remarkable saga of the Kennedys, we can call on each of these perspectives in turn and identify its relevant features.

From the evolutionary perspective, the Kennedy sons may be compared to a strongly male-oriented primate group (R. Kennedy, 1974; Whalen, 1965). The family extolled masculine virtues, encouraged the boys to go out in the world, and emphasized combative phys-

ical activity. As typically occurs in primate tribes, the males were clearly dominant in the family. And, within the tribe of Kennedy males, there seems also to have been a definite order of dominance, based largely on age: when the dominant male died, the next in line assumed his post.

Rose and Joseph Kennedy, the parents, clearly evolved a particular style of childrearing (R. Kennedy, 1974). They were highly demanding of their youngsters and yet compassionate regarding failure so long as the children tried their best. Authoritarian features such as strict schedules and stringent demands were modulated by a more permissive atmosphere during meals and periods of play. Especially important was that the parents apparently agreed on methods of childrearing and consistently supported each other's decisions. Indeed, as we saw earlier, this consensus and consistency may have been as important as any specific feature of their parenting style.

Events in the lives of the Kennedy children underscore the usefulness of a family-as-system approach. The oldest brother, Joseph, Jr., was slated to go into politics but was killed in an accident during World War II. The next brother, John, stepped into his older brother's shoes, eventually becoming President. When John was killed, Robert was next in line, and indeed he entered a presidential campaign before being assassinated. And when Robert was killed, Edward stepped forward as a political leader and a possible presidential candidate. Here we see how changes have reverberations throughout a family system. Each time a brother was killed, the roles of the survivors were altered. At the same time, throughout their many tragedies, the Kennedy family has consistently drawn together, showing a pervasive thread of unity within the family system.

The Kennedy children seem to be fertile ground for an analysis of birth-order position. The oldest offspring, Joseph, was the serious and intellectual one. The second son, John, was at first somewhat nonacademic, but as often happens with second borns, he quickly assumed the role of leader and intellectual when his older brother died. The third son, Robert, exemplifying a child in the middle, was known as an activist and a physical enthusiast; he was gregarious and somewhat more pragmatic than his elder brothers. Edward seems to have suffered from many of the difficulties that confront the baby in the family. He was a spoiled youngster, had difficulty maturing, and sometimes displayed a tendency to be discouraged and to "throw it all away" (Burns, 1976). How well he has handled responsibilities as the last Kennedy son remains a controversial matter.

The Community

In considering the child's place midst parents and siblings, we have examined the narrowest circle within which socialization takes place. But shortly after infancy, and with increasing frequency once they begin to attend school, children enter into daily contact with a wide sphere of humanity: neighbors, relatives, peers, and other individuals, as well as with institutions in the community. Not only are they placed in a situation characterized by many rules and regulations, but they now must form relations with other adults—teachers, custodians, police—and, especially, with others of their own age.

Each of these factors in the community contributes to the child's subsequent development, although individual children will be influenced differently in diverse social settings. Because of our interest in the factors molding young Americans, we shall focus on forces of undeniable importance in our society. First we shall examine the effect of the peer group—a factor that becomes increasingly central as children develop. Then we shall consider a

less visible but equally potent influence: the individual's social-class background. This influence is especially crucial because it cuts two ways: social-class factors influence not only the child's own behavior but also the way others treat (and respond to) the child.

THE PEER GROUP

Traditionally, the family has exerted the largest influence on the child's development. Indeed, earlier in our own history and in many other contemporary cultures, children have had only intermittent contact with other children outside their families until they are seven or so. Today, however, the influence of peers seems to be rising sharply. Researchers have accordingly focused on the effects of peers at different ages, of opposite sexes, and in diverse cultures.

Groups of young contemporaries arise spontaneously in every culture, even when peer interaction is not deliberately encouraged (Hartup, 1970). This interaction may reflect the strong tendency among primates (including humans) for such grouping, which generally occurs by age and sex. As children's egocentrism declines and their ability to adopt the perspective of others grows, they can engage in more organized and sustained kinds of activity—such as games—with their peers. A shift can then be noted from a mere collection of children who happen to be playing in tandem to a genuinely cohesive group (Piaget, 1932).

Specific changes have been observed in peer relations during children's early years. Even in infancy, children will look attentively at peers (Eckerman and Whatley, 1977) and will sometimes behave differently toward them than toward their mother (Young and Lewis, 1979), for example, directing a greater variety of facial expression toward the mother, more abrupt, intense, and active motor movements toward the peer (Fogel,

Figure 8.5. Young schoolchildren enjoy one another's company and form friendships, usually with others of the same sex. Such peer contact plays an important role in introducing a youngster to the games, stories, jokes, and tricks of society.

1979). Contact with peers continues to rise during the second year of life, although children still do not seem to recognize the special needs, wishes, and point of view of a peer. They often pattern their interaction after their relations with adults—expecting from other children what they get from adults and naturally being somewhat disappointed. They smile, vocalize, and offer a peer the same toys they would present an adult. Or children at this early age may treat other children as interesting objects—pinching them, squeezing them, or pushing them down the stairs (Hartup, 1970; Maudry and Nekula, 1939).

Despite these limitations, a significant amount of peer interaction can be observed by the age of two (Hay, 1979; Mueller and Lucas, 1975). In a study in which two children and their mothers were placed in a room with several toys, the children were more likely to interact in some way with each other than to play by themselves. In over 60 percent of the recorded observations, they touched the same objects as their peers, imitated their actions,

exchanged toys, or somehow coordinated their play to perform a common task or to elaborate a social game. Peer relations began as children interacted physically over specific objects. Shortly, however, they were both directing smiles, vocalizations, and offers of toys toward one another. And before long these two-year-olds were approaching each other with the clear intent of beginning a social interaction (Eckerman, Whatley, and Kutz, 1975).

Studies with nursery school children document that the amount of peer interaction correlates highly with age and, to some extent, with intellectual competence (Feiring, 1981). In all situations observed, the older children are more likely to participate in activities requiring cooperation and active interchange. They less often play alone or sit by idly, watching others. They begin to seek attention and praise from peers. They adopt complementary roles, rather than simply playing in parallel (Mueller, et al., 1977). They behave in a much more coordinated fashion with a toddler whom they already know (Mueller and Brenner, 1977). And by the age of three or four, dominance hierarchies, based on perceived toughness, have already emerged (Sluckin and Smith, 1977; P. K. Smith, 1978; Zivin, 1977); highly stable cliques, linking children of the same sex and ages, can also be observed (LaFreniere, 1981). Children exhibit clear likes and dislikes, with common activities and physical proximity contributing to liking, **aggression** and unusual behavior leading to antagonism (Hayes, 1978).

Insight into young children's sensitivity to their peers emerges from a study of four- and five-year-olds at play with a simple marble game (Hartup, 1964). Either a peer who was a best friend or a peer who was disliked told the player how she was doing. Paradoxically, the child performed better when the disliked peer was approving. Researcher Willard Hartup suggests that children tend to talk and be distracted when their friends are present, and that their anxiety in the company of a disliked child may itself be motivating. Moreover, the youngsters have already received positive reinforcement from their friends, whereas the response from the disliked peer proves both unexpected and novel. Whatever the explanation, however, it is noteworthy that preschoolers' performances are in fact influenced by their attitudes toward their peers and their peers' attitudes toward them. Dorothy Blitsen (1971) in fact suggests that the kind of competitiveness aroused by contact with peers may have positive social implications. Children learn what patterns of behavior are important for others and can take these into account in fashioning their own reactions, attitudes, and goals.

Further changes mark the years past early childhood. In the course of playing games, school-age youngsters become much more oriented toward others, they compare themselves with others in terms of skill and stature, and they typically respond competitively (Graziano, 1978; Read and Jenness, 1974; Ruble, Feldman, and Boggiano, 1976). Children in the early school years agree with one another about both the structure and dominance hierarchies and the relative popularity of members of their class, though these rankings seem to be largely independent of one another (Wynn and Lawrence, 1981). Curiously, older peers are less likely to clarify miscommunications or to reciprocate overt expressions of feeling—hence younger children emerge as more successful communicators of friendship (Gottman and Parkhurst, 1977). This may go along with the finding that with age children are less likely to expect friends to be pleasurable and to provide entertainment; instead, they expect that their friends will be of use to them (Reisman and Shorr, 1978).

As we have noted in Chapter 5, forms of aggression also change with age (Hartup, 1974; Maccoby, 1980). Preschool children favor **instrumental aggression:** this form arises out of immediate frustrations with the physical world and usually terminates when a desired object has been obtained. When one preschool child is insulted by another, a physical response often results: in fact, the insulted child is likely to hit back about half the time.

Grade school children favor **hostile aggression:** this form, directed primarily toward persons rather than objects, usually follows a threat to the child's self-esteem, when the child perceives that she has been intentionally wronged. When annoyed or frustrated, rather than hitting back, grade school children are more inclined to reciprocate with an insult of their own or perhaps with some version of the childhood jingle: "Sticks and stones may break my bones, but words can never hurt me." As children gain the capacity to carry out acts in their fantasy life and to express their feelings in words, they become better able to deflect impulses that might physically harm another person: instead, they inflict injury upon their tormentors with psychological weapons.

A few sex differences have been noted. Young girls, and especially newcomers in a class, are more likely to orient toward teachers, while young males orient toward same-sex peers (Feldbaum, Christenson, and O'Neal, 1980). Youngsters are more likely to direct positive *and* negative social behaviors to playmates of the same sex. Girls often experience specific difficulties with boys, who typically ignore their prohibitions and do not allow them to control a situation (Jacklin and Maccoby, 1978).

Parental behavior also influences children's interaction with peers. For instance, if the mother is dominant in the household, a boy's relations with his peers are likely to be aggressive and unfriendly. But if the father is dominant, the boy is likely to be more forceful in initiating friendships and to exert considerable power in the peer group. Families marked by affectionate relationships are more likely to have children who are fond of other children and who are themselves liked by others (L. W. Hoffman, 1961).

Nowadays, there is considerable concern about whether peers may exert too much influence on one another, coupled with uncertainty about whether influence is necessarily for the good. On the positive side, expecially at younger ages, play with peers contributes to the development of social skills (Hartup, 1976b, 1977; Vandell, 1979), while inadequate peer play correlates with social and emotional problems (Hartup, 1977; Scarlett, 1980). At a somewhat older age, membership in a social organization correlates positively with an individual's level of moral judgment (Keasey, 1971). Problems can arise, however, when the behaviors and attitudes of peers prove inconsistent with parental and cultural norms. In cultural settings where these standards are at

odds, concern about peer domination tends to be most pronounced.

Various cross-cultural studies have touched on this tension between the pressures of peers and the norms of society. Bronfenbrenner (1970) found that Russian children are more likely than their American, German, or English counterparts to resist peer pressure that runs contrary to adult standards. The latter group proved least resistant. A child's age, the amount of peer interaction, and the extent of adult supervision that accompanies it influence the behavior of youths who have been subjected to these contrasting types. For example, American eight-to-sixteen-year-olds are more apt to conform to peer pressure if their parents are unlikely to learn about it (Bixenstine, DeCorte, and Bixenstine, 1976). Finally, peers seem to play an increasingly dominant role as children mature; thus, sixth, eighth, and tenth graders are less likely than third graders to resist their peer models or to judge their behavior as wrong.

The actual effects of peer influence can be most clearly examined in societies where the peer group has deliberately been designated as a principal contributor to the socialization process. Both the Israeli kibbutz and the Chinese day-care center deemphasize traditional parental authority, stress the peer's influence (see Figure 8.6), and plan educational policy around the group rather than the individual or the parents. Studies in such peer-centered societies have generally (but not always) documented less competitiveness and a weaker sense of tradition than is found among, say, Israeli children raised in traditional homes (Bettelheim, 1969; Kessen, 1975; Rabin, 1965; Shapira and Madsen, 1969; Spiro, 1965). These studies of nontraditional family arrangements fail to reveal pathology among the children as a result of this upbringing. In fact, they suggest that peers may exert a beneficial effect on one another (see Hartup, 1976a).

Figure 8.6. In the People's Republic of China, peers are explicitly used by the society to aid socialization. Here, row monitors in a primary school are carrying out a morning inspection in which general cleanliness as well as length and neatness of hair are routinely checked.

SOCIAL CLASS INFLUENCES

By the time children first go to school, the influence of peers and siblings has already become pronounced. But what of more global influences—ones less visible, perhaps, but nonetheless pervasive? In particular, what about the effects of children's general background and environment—the ethnic origin, educational level, and social class of their parents and of other adults in their lives? In examining the Kennedys, for example, we would have to consider their rise from poor immigrants to millionaires; their Irish-American, Roman Catholic heritage; their New England upbringing; and their education in parochial schools and Ivy League universities. Also pertinent would be the values of their teachers and peers and, of course, the currents and countercurrents in American society during their lives.

These factors, added together, undoubtedly have significant effects. Studies of biological

siblings and even twins raised in different environments (Scarr-Salapatek and Weinberg, 1976) strongly suggest that the Kennedy children might have become rather different adults had they been born to tenant farmers living in Georgia and gone to work after completing the eighth grade in a one-room schoolhouse. Yet, we cannot evaluate each factor's precise contribution. We cannot assess, for example, whether the Kennedy competitiveness comes from parental example, ethnic heritage, or sibling rivalry. But the important generalization can be made: social influences unquestionably do matter.

Life in Different Classes. A common way of analyzing the community's influence on development involves considering an individual's **social class.** Although the definition of social class is controversial (Hollingshead, 1957; Sims, 1952; Warner, Meeher, and Eells, 1949), it generally designates a group of people whose background, education, occupations, and income are similar. The **upper class** includes those of wealthy background, often with a Yankee heritage, who are highly successful executives or professionals. The **middle class** includes moderately successful professionals who have substantial income but little inherited wealth; for instance, skilled white-collar workers and technicians. The **working class** comprises blue-collar, lower-level white-collar, and semiskilled workers whose income is near the national average. Working-class individuals are more likely than middle-class individuals to have been born abroad or to come from recent immigrant stock. The **lower class** includes those whose incomes are near subsistence level because of frequent unemployment or job changing; its members include a disproportionate number of non-whites.

Any attempt to squeeze people into one of four neatly labeled groups necessarily creates generalities and minimizes individual differences. Nonetheless, we can use this framework to chart some effects of belonging to different social classes.

In a thorough discussion, Robert Hess (1970) describes lower-class life in metropolitan society in contrast to middle-class life in suburbia (see also O. Lewis, 1966; Liebow, 1967; Seeley, 1956; Whyte, 1956). Middle-class people have their basic needs satisfied, whereas lower-class individuals must constantly worry about food and shelter. Unlike the lower class who tend to feel powerless and lack self-confidence, the middle class feel they can attain their material goals. They feel secure in the society whose values they share, in contrast to lower-class people who feel more out of place and more alienated.

Under the impact of these feelings, parents from low socioeconomic backgrounds will convey low self-esteem and passivity and often considerable frustration to their children. These parents are unable to provide adequate financial support and individual attention to their commonly large family. Frequent desertion by one parent takes both psychological and material tolls on the child. And deep and constant problems of sheer survival may affect parents' treatment of their children.

Middle-class families, smaller on the whole, maintain high expectations for each of their youngsters. Parents will often make sacrifices to help their children achieve these goals while also encouraging independence. The children will accordingly have a more positive self-image. The growing number of breakups of middle-class marriages is more likely to have psychological rather than material effects on children, though some reduction in standard of living can be expected.

Lower-class parents also view their children differently and act differently toward them than middle-class parents do (Baumrind, 1971; Hess, 1970; O. Lewis, 1966; Snow et

al., 1976; Wedemeyer, 1976). Parents with fewer advantages are less permissive and less tolerant of drives and impulses. They hold lower expectations for their children and provide less appropriate stimulation in the form of toys, experiences, and daily conversation. They are likely to stress obedience, cleanliness, and neatness, and they may mete out physical punishment arbitrarily. Middle-class parents, in contrast, are more likely to think of children as eager to learn, cooperative, happy, and healthy. They are more likely to be tolerant of their children's ideas and wishes, to reason with them, and less likely to be authoritarian or overmoralistic. Interestingly, differences in social class rearing patterns may be more evident with respect to boys. For instance, parents of a lower socioeconomic status are more likely than parents of a higher socioeconomic status to use direct power assertions with their boys: the two socioeconomic groups do not differ in the degree to which they assert power over their daughters (Zussman, 1977).

Making overall assessments of self-esteem and happiness is extremely difficult—perhaps even impossible—yet it clearly seems more pleasant to grow up in a middle-class household where there is enough to eat, where opportunities are plentiful, and where one receives significant attention and love from two parents. At the same time, we must not neglect signs that middle-class life in contemporary society also entails costs (Coles, 1980b; Lasch, 1979; Whyte, 1956). For one thing, conformity has often numbed American middle-class society; families attempt to attain all the possessions that their neighbors have and feel grossly inadequate when they do not. For another, the emphasis on youthfulness stimulates a terror of growing old, ugly, or infirm.

As psychiatrist Robert Coles (1980b) has shown, middle- and upper-class children are not immune from stress and conflict. The excess of choices and material possessions can prove confusing and even frightening for children. Those who are forced to move from place to place may experience a feeling of rootlessness. And as affluent children become aware of their special status, they often wonder whether others respond to them because of their personal traits, or because of their social position. Children may resolve this plight with a healthy desire to help others and to share their possessions. Or they may simply become guilty about their privilege or may reject it angrily and embrace a wholly different life-style (Erikson, 1959).

Even as upper- and middle-class children have difficulties and dilemmas, lower-class children may have some advantages. In lieu of the ambitious, achieving atmosphere, working-class children (particularly of recent immigrant stock) may experience intimate and affectionate personal ties within the family or even the neighborhood. Moreover, these children often have a more realistic and sophisticated notion of how the overall society operates. They often perceive the significance of interpersonal conflicts more rapidly and more accurately than middle-class youngsters do. They can often act decisively and properly in a difficult situation, and they recognize the importance of having power (Coles, 1967; Hess, 1970). If such youngsters have talent, they are often better equipped than the more pampered middle-class children to forge a lasting place for themselves within a highly competitive and fast-changing society.

Experimental Studies. The above findings are based primarily on observations and interviews, and even journalistic impressions. Because they are difficult to conduct, more controlled studies in which parent-child interactions are examined in a structured situation are at a premium. One such study found that middle-class mothers are more likely than working-class mothers to help their children solve problems, to request verbal feedback rather than physical compliance, to give specific instructions, and to use special techniques to motivate a skilled performance (Hess and Shipman, 1965). Apparently, middle-class mothers regard their children as effective social agents who exert control over their own behavior; lower-class mothers have less belief in their own efficacy and transmit their insecurity to their children (Kagan, 1979). Another research team discerned differences in the kinds of language used by mothers: middle-class mothers were more likely to expand on their children's utterances and to point out features in the environment; but they were less likely to issue commands or to indicate what should be done (Snow et al., 1976). Some investigators have drawn on such evidence in order to claim that language is used in a fundamentally different manner across social classes (Bernstein, 1970). However, careful examination of the use of language in diverse social classes suggests that these differences are only superficial and that the dialect favored by lower-class persons can accomplish all the ends and transmit all the information typically captured in the language of a middle- or upper-class person (Labov, 1969).

Children from different social backgrounds also perform differently in cognitive tasks. Almost without exception, children from middle-class backgrounds surpass their lower-class counterparts; performance differences are greater on measures of linguistic or academic skills than on tasks assessing perceptual or practical skills (Hess, 1970). At least one contributor to these differences is quite revealing. When given feedback by an experimenter, middle-class children typically assume they have responded correctly; lower-class children draw the opposite conclusion—that their answer should be changed (Simmons, 1980). This finding suggests a complex interaction between social class, cognitive ability, and one's self-esteem and self-confidence (Cole and Means, 1981). Children from lower-class families seem less well adjusted, at least as measured by tests of personality and emotional stability. They are more likely to get into trouble and eventually to end up in jail or in some equally unhappy condition.

Research Difficulties. It is extremely difficult to determine whether these consistent differences reported by observers and replicated in formal testing reflect differences in opportunities (for example, better school), models (parents who are more accomplished in the areas being tested), cultural bias of the tests (which are almost always devised by members of the middle class), motivation (middle-class children being more bent on achieving success), feelings of efficacy (Gelfand and Hartmann, 1977; Kagan, 1979), or some combination of these factors. Nor is it easy to evaluate the data on which the above conclusions are based.

To begin with, the information on styles of parenting comes largely from questionnaires, which are difficult to interpret. Observational studies are more desirable but even the most conscientious observer has difficulty avoiding value judgments and subjective assessments. Furthermore, there are few oportunities to observe in the homes of lower-class families, and there are few trained investigators from that background to enter into such homes. Although structured laboratory studies are generally desirable, they are sometimes only marginally related to real-world situations and they tend to be more readily handled by middle-class parents. Important variables may also be confounded: for example, social class and ethnicity correlate with one another, and it is difficult to determine whether specific behavioral patterns reflect the availability of material possessions or the customs of different cultural groups (Chan, 1981).

The cultural bias of cognitive tests must also be carefully considered. In a striking documentation of this fact, a psychologist devised a verbal multiple-choice test requiring knowledge of the lore found in lower-class black communities (Dove, 1968). (For sample items, see the box on the chitling test.) Not surprisingly, middle-class white children performed quite poorly on the test (even as lower-class American blacks understandably have done poorly when asked for the author of *Romeo and Juliet* or for the definition of *lien*). As Allison Davis and Robert Havighurst have pointed out, different social groups have substantially different kinds of cultural experiences, different in the kinds of things with which the children deal, in the vocabulary and language with which the children will be familiar and in the attitudes and values which determine what problems seem important to the children. . . . The differences in IQ or scores on the tests may be a reflection merely of [a] bias in the test materials and not of basic differences in the real abilities of children from the different backgrounds [quoted in Hess, 1970, p. 510].

Despite the individual weaknesses that we've noted, studies of many different kinds, taken together, may produce reliable findings about social influences. Naturally, it is more difficult to study molar variables such as "parental attitude" or "community influence" than specific behaviors such as puzzle solving or spanking. Yet the overwhelming importance of childrearing and the progress that has been made so far dictate continued study of this complex area (Cochran and Brassard, 1979; Rutter 1979a).

A few tentative generalizations have been put forth by Urie Bronfenbrenner (1979), a developmental psychologist actively concerned with the effects of socialization. In Bronfenbrenner's view, certain factors—occupational status, size of family, and amount of schooling—can be counted on to contribute reliably to the ultimate outcomes of childrearing. A second set of factors—the number of parents in the home and the extent to which the child is exposed to adults rather than to peers— sometimes matters. And still other factors— such as the use of day care and the employment status of mothers—turn out to have only marginal effects. Taking a somewhat different tack, the anthropologists Carolyn Edwards and Beatrice Whiting (1980) point out that each culture must decide how children will spend their time; who will rear, teach, and discipline them; with whom they will be allowed to play; how much independence and how much responsibility will be assigned to each at different points during childhood.

The Chitling Test

The verbal world of black children is often different, in predictable ways, from that of their white peers. Yet IQ tests administered to groups of children have traditionally assumed the linguistic and experiential background of the white middle class. Many people believe that this culture bias explains the finding that blacks, on the average, score lower than whites on such tests. To dramatize the point, sociologist Adrian Dove (1968) devised the Counterbalance General Intelligence Test, nicknamed the Chitling Test, which contains multiple-choice items like these:

1. A "handkerchief head" is: (a) a cool cat, (b) a porter, (c) an Uncle Tom, (d) a hoddi, (e) a preacher.
2. Which word is most out of place here? (a) splib, (b) blood, (c) gray, (d) spook, (e) black.
3. A "gas head" is a person who has a: (a) fast-moving car, (b) stable of "lace," (c) "process," (d) habit of stealing cars, (e) long jail record for arson.
4. "Bo Diddley" is a: (a) game for children, (b) down-home cheap wine, (c) down-home singer, (d) new dance, (e) Moejoe call.

Not surprisingly, white children perform worse than blacks on this test of the lore of urban black life. This and other demonstrations of the bias inherent in group IQ tests have led to a ban on their use in California, Washington, D.C., Philadelphia, and New York City; and Massachusetts is considering a similar ban (Fiske, 1977). The issues are complex, however, and a complete abandonment of mental testing seems unlikely (Sowell, 1977). In the meantime it behooves us all to understand better the nature, uses, and misuses of these instruments.

Answers to test questions: 1(c); 2(c); 3(c); 4(c).

Even though it may not always be possible to pinpoint the exact effect of each of these factors, the wide differences among adults (and children) reared in China, Uganda, Mexico, and the United States indicate that these "decisions by the culture" do matter.

Influences of the Communications Media

In no area of socialization have there been greater changes in the recent past than in the media of communication. In traditional times the norms and values of the culture were transmitted to children primarily through the individuals in the immediate social surrounding. But now nearly all children in the industrialized world spend a great deal of time receiving messages from various communications media: books, magazines (read by others and read by the children themselves), movies, radio, and, above all, television. Nearly everyone has an opinion about the effects of television on the socializing process, and particularly heated discussions surround the effects of television on the aggressive behavior of children. By reviewing the high points of this dispute, we can gain some insights about the more general effects of the media—for good and for ill. And we can consider an issue of importance to scientists and other citizens: are the results of developmental research pertinent to debates of societal import?

First, some facts. Nearly every American child watches television, and the average viewing per day ranges from two to six hours (Liebert, Neale, and Davidson, 1973; Lyle and Hoffman, 1972). Most children are subjected daily to televised examples of aggressive and violent behavior performed by cartoon characters, by human actors, or by real people in the news. It has been estimated that by graduation from high school the average American child has seen 18,000 televised murders (Brody, 1975). It seems possible that children's aggressiveness is significantly affected by what they absorb from television and other media.

One point of view is that any form of aggression portrayed in the media can have a disastrous effect on the level of aggression in the world (Wertham, 1954). Proponents of this view trace the apparent increase in crime and violence in our society directly to a loss of respect for people and for property. And the fact that the sharpest rise in crime and violence has apparently occurred while the media have been gaining in importance is taken as proof of the source of the trouble. Were violence and aggression expelled from all media, children and adults alike would emerge as less aggressive.

The contrasting point of view contends that the rise in violence or aggression, if indeed it is on the rise, reflects complex social factors of which the media are only a symptom (Fogelson, 1970; Harrington, 1964). Those holding this view claim that televised aggression may actually purge viewers' aggressive impulses, thus reducing antisocial behavior in the long run. Further, normal persons will not be significantly affected by what they watch, and persons with decidedly aggressive tendencies will become aggressive no matter what (or whether) they watch. A variant of this view—common among civil libertarians—concedes that aggression may occasionally be prompted by television, but considers this a small price to pay for allowing individuals to entertain and educate themselves as they choose. The very fact that people choose to view violent displays suggests that television serves a valid function.

ALBERT BANDURA'S POWERFUL DEMONSTRATION

The empirical question of whether the media affect aggressiveness would seem an ideal subject for social science research. And at first, the answer seemed rather clear. Impressive studies by Albert Bandura and his colleagues (for example, Bandura and Huston, 1961; Bandura, Ross, and Ross, 1961, 1963) revealed that young children were intrigued by displays of violence and that, given the opportunity, they would readily mimic them. As we saw in our earlier discussion of observational learning (in Chapter 5), children are remarkably quick at imitating striking behaviors. In a typical study children of different ages were allowed to watch a live or filmed model or a cartoon in which the hero made aggressive verbal statements or played aggressively with a toy. (For example, the model would repeatedly knock down the inflated rubber toy called a Bobo doll.) Then the children were left in a room full of toys while their behavior and words were observed and recorded. In one study after another, the chil-

dren imitated the model's behavior—whether it had been aggressive or gentle. Imitation was even more pronounced and more widespread if the model's actions brought a reward, and it declined correspondingly in the absence of rewards. And if a live model had acted kindly toward the child, the tendency to imitate was heightened further. Even in those cases where the children desisted from imitating the model, they revealed on subsequent questioning that they knew exactly what the model had done and could demonstrate it if they were asked to do so.

Has the case against violence on television been proved? The Bandura studies suggest that it has been, but a more careful look reminds us how far removed the studies are from the phenomenon under consideration. In such studies, there is never any real injury to person or property. Long-term effects of the

Figure 8.7. Notice how faithfully the little girl copies the model in one of Albert Bandura's many studies of modeling.

modeled behaviors are minimal (Feshbach, 1970). Nor does either the model's or the children's aggression appear to have any adverse consequences for themselves or for others. Thus the studies do not tell us whether the child would imitate an aggressor who actually does damage or one who was severely reprimanded by a respected authority.

DOES TELEVISION ENCOURAGE AGGRESSIVE BEHAVIOR?

What happens if shows varying in aggressive content are shown in a more natural setting? Seymour Feshbach tackled just that question (Feshbach and Singer, 1971). He managed to secure control over the entire viewing diet of preadolescent and adolescent boys in three private schools and in four residential centers. For six weeks the boys saw either all aggression laden-shows (Westerns, crime shows) or all nonaggressive shows (situation comedies, talk shows, benign cartoons, and the like). Feshbach used numerous measures of aggressive attitudes and acts to assess the effects of these different video regimens.

In a set of unexpected and dramatic findings, those youngsters on a "bland" diet showed more aggression, while the boys who viewed the aggressive programs actually demonstrated *reduced* aggression. Parallel trends were observed at all ages. Moreover, declines in aggressive behavior were greater for boys who were initially aggressive, especially for those who had scored above the mean on a measure of hostility. The boys who had seen aggression on television also became less verbally aggressive toward authority and peers.

Feshbach and Singer's study immediately gained wide notoriety. Resonating with classical theories about the "cathartic" effects of viewing aggressive displays, and bolstered by another large-scale study that failed to docu-

ment effects of antisocial models on television (Milgram and Shotland, 1973), these findings gave considerable comfort to those who do not want to meddle with the often violent content on television. And it contributed to the very moderate conclusions reached by a governmental body charged with evaluating the effects of violence on television (Rubinstein, 1978; Surgeon General's report, 1972).

More recently, however, the negative effects of a large diet of televised violence, particularly on the behaviors of young children, has been amply and quite persuasively documented by a substantial body of research (Rubinstein, 1978; Singer and Singer, 1979a). Consider, for example, a naturalistic study in which preschool children's viewing was monitored for an entire year. A significant correlation was found between the amount of viewing of shows featuring a high level of activity and aggression and the amount of aggressive behavior displayed by children in spontaneous play in nursery school and day-care settings (Singer and Singer, 1979a). The pattern of aggressive behavior was likely in families that featured lax control of viewing habits, conventional sex-role orientation, traditional values, and relatively limited cultural interests. In contrast, in the case of heavy-viewing children who exhibited little aggression, parents encouraged the viewing of prosocial programs (like "Sesame Street" and "Mister Rogers' Neighborhood") and also involved their children in a wide range of cultural activities. Interestingly, children in the "prosocial" viewing group also turned out to be the most imaginative; perhaps they translated volatile impulses into fantasy.

A long-term follow-up study further documents the effects of viewing aggressive displays. After a ten-year hiatus, Lefkowitz, Eron, Walden, and Huesmann (cited in Singer and Singer, 1979a) revisited youngsters whose viewing habits had originally been studied in the third grade. The results: the greater the preference of boys for violent television at age nine, the greater their aggressiveness both at that time and at age nineteen.

These recurring patterns suggest that more positive role models on television may exert beneficial effects on children. Lynette Friedrich and Aletha Stein (1973) exposed preschool children to aggressive cartoons ("Batman" and "Superman"), constructive prosocial programs ("Mister Rogers' Neighborhood"), or neutral films (say, of children living on a farm). While children exposed to the aggressive programs proved less likely to obey rules and less able to tolerate delays of gratification, youngsters who had viewed the prosocial programs persisted longer at tasks, were more likely to obey rules, and more willing to delay gratification than those who viewed neutral programs. Such prosocial behavior was especially likely among children of above-average intelligence. Extending beyond the social realm, several additional lines of research have documented considerable intellectual gains by preschool children who regularly view "Sesame Street," a children's show that presents cognitively oriented materials in an entertaining format (Rubinstein, 1978).

As always, it is necessary to play the card of age. In general, younger children are more likely to take at face value and to imitate what they see on television. Preschool children consider commercials as "real" and "true" as news or documentary programs; they fail to comprehend the disclaimers on commercial products or the fact that much of what they see has been performed by actors. In addition, they do not take into account the motives behind an action (Collins, Berndt, and Hess, 1974); thus they will imitate actions equally, whether they are positive or negative, motivated or wanton. In contrast, older children soon learn to display a cynical attitude toward commercial messages on television, to appreciate the difference between a staged and a genuine event, and to note the intentions behind an action. It is probably not accidental that Feshbach's dramatic findings occurred with older children; these subjects knew how to interpret the meanings of the aggressive acts on television and were much less likely to treat them simply as actions to be imitated. Indeed, some critics have reinterpreted Feshbach's findings as evidence that the youths, deprived of their usual television fare, became frustrated and *that* is why their aggressive output increased (Liebert, Neale, and Davidson, 1973; Rubinstein, 1978).

Evaluating the Media Research. We have seen that televised aggression is most likely to affect younger children whose ability to distinguish between reality and fantasy is not yet well established, whose tendency to imitate is most pronounced, and whose understanding of the causes prompting aggression is less well developed. The differences in reaction, which highlight the children's level of understanding of television fare, caution against equating television's effects on children at different developmental stages.

The studies also suggest that televised aggression may affect children who are already predisposed toward aggression—but in different ways. Whereas younger aggressive children may become more aggressive, older children may become less so. What may have a strong effect on a four-year-old may have little effect, or perhaps even the reverse effect, on an adolescent.

In 1961, after the first wave of studies of television and children, Schramm, Lyle, and Parker concluded:

For some children, under some conditions, some television is harmful. For other children under the same conditions, or for the same children, under other conditions, it may be beneficial. For most children, under most conditions, most television is probably neither particularly harmful nor particularly beneficial [1961, p. 1; in Rubinstein, 1978].

Twenty years of studies since that time have clearly deepened our knowledge of the effects of particular kinds of television fare. The negative effects of aggressive displays have been convincingly documented. And we have seen from "Sesame Street" that steady watching of a well-designed children's show may bring about positive effects on children's learning.

Nonetheless, it probably remains true that children's personality and behavioral profiles have not been dramatically changed simply by virtue of watching American television—a medium that, after all, is a microcosm of the society as a whole. It may be, as various commentators have suggested, that television watching has affected children's attitudes toward various phenomena, ranging from the essential humanity of individuals from alien cultures to the merits of waging war, and that the rapid pace and generally unchallenging character of most television fare has affected the ways in which children process information and use their imaginations (Kelly and Gardner, 1981). Convincing evidence has yet to be gathered on these matters, however.

Signposts

In the previous chapter we witnessed the evolution of playful preschoolers into cognitive schoolchildren who approach tasks in an increasingly reflective manner and who can use language to control their own and others' behavior. In this chapter we have shifted our attention to the larger environment and have sought to unravel its various effects on the child.

Using the rare cases of identical twins reared apart as a point of departure, we pondered the extent to which children's intellectual and personality characteristics arise from genetic or environmental factors. Most scientists now adopt a cautious approach to this issue and embrace neither "nature" nor "nurture." They realize from studies of identical twins that intellectual potential is to some degree inherited, yet they also underscore that tests of intelligence may be culturally biased. And they point out that significant differences can be brought about by environmental factors, even in individuals who have the same genetic inheritance.

Next we examined the ever-widening set of influences that modulate the child's genetic inheritance. In considering the role of the immediate family, we found that parents' styles of childrearing—measured by characteristics like restrictiveness, permissiveness, warmth, hostility, and communicative effectiveness—can powerfully influence a child's development. When we viewed the family as a system, we obtained insights into the family's crucial functions, the phases families pass through, and the child's own effect on the parents. We noted the harsh emotional effects that can be wrought by disruptions in the family, as well as certain factors—like support systems—that can modulate the chaos and stress.

Studies of siblings document the results of interactions among members of a family and reveal constellations of traits that reflect one's birth-order position. Firstborns emerge as successful and adultlike, but often insecure; last borns resemble firstborns in some respects, though they tend to be more babyish and also more popular; middle-born children, often "caught in the middle," are less achievement-oriented and more at ease than their siblings at the extreme ends of the birth-order array. Although such generalizations about the effects of order of birth are better viewed as statistical trends than as predictions about individuals, they prove generally reliable and can help to account for patterns observed in families like the Kennedys.

Turning to the role of the wider community, we considered the increasing importance during the school years of children's interactions with members of their peer group. Youngsters begin interacting with peers from the opening years (if not months) of life, but the styles of interaction available and the amount of interaction—positive as well as disruptive—increase at least through the preschool years. Hierarchies of dominance and cliques are well established by this time. The influence of peers has often been viewed as injurious to communal standards, but peers can also serve as a valuable agent of socialization, particularly in the absence of parental models.

An equally potent factor in individual development is social class membership. Again, the popular view stresses the negative effects of a lower-class background, but less biased examination reveals the pitfalls of a middle-class background. Because this form of research relies heavily on questionnaires and on observations by middle-class researchers, findings on social class background must be viewed with caution. Nonetheless, it seems clear that certain social factors, such as amount of schooling, and certain cultural factors, such as the amount of responsibility given a child, will affect adult behavior and personality.

To parallel a focus on the agents of socialization, we can also examine the effects of certain culturewide forces, such as the media of communication. In contemporary American society, the most pervasive medium is undoubtedly television. Insight can be gained by considering the effects of certain kinds of pro-grams—for example, prosocial and aggressive programs—on subsequent behaviors of children. While research in this area is laden with perils and ambiguities, evidence has mounted that the amount of a child's aggressive or prosocial behavior can be influenced by how often she has viewed such behaviors on television. Still, the child's prior behavioral proclivities remain a crucial variable in the equation, and the same modeled behaviors can exert different effects, depending upon the age and understanding of the young television viewer. Clearly, the various agents of socialization, ranging from parents to media of communication, operate upon the child as a complex and interacting system, whose overall effects can only be predicted if each of their respective contributions has been taken into account.

Our focus on socialization has surveyed the broad range of influences on the child's behaviors and attitudes. Yet we must not lose sight of children's personal evolution within the cultural milieu. Whatever their family or social class, children between five and seven are developing their own styles of thinking and being, becoming increasingly independent, planning behaviors, interacting with a wider social world, capturing experiences in words and other symbols. This overall orientation, in its freshness and enhanced power, confers a very special flavor on the child. In attempting to convey this flavor, it seems useful to think of the child at this point in life as a participant in the arts, one who can create imaginative works and appreciate the artistic efforts of others. Let us therefore turn our attention to the various forms of symbol use, artistic and otherwise, found among children of this age.

CHAPTER NINE

The Symbols of the Young Artist

A highly intelligent and gifted boy of six years of age combined the qualities of the artist and the scientist in himself in the most delightful way. One day he experimentally opened the case of the piano and spent hours examining its structure and watching the action of the hammer on the wire, and the relation of the striking of the key to the movement of the hammer. A day or two later he told me that his mother said to him that "When the hammer struck the wire, a little fairy that was in the wire came out and sang."

–Susan Isaacs

. . . the world of an adult made it hard to be an artist.

–William Empson

Before his first birthday, my son Jerry received a set of toy blocks that had pictures of animals as well as various numbers and letters etched on them. As befits an infant, he enjoyed touching these blocks, knocking them together, throwing them across the room, but so far as I could tell he paid relatively little attention to the squiggles on them.

Over the next several years, however, these blocks came to assume a diverse set of roles in his life. By the age of a year and a half, he could clearly recognize the pictures on the sides of the blocks, and when asked to pick the block with a "dog" on it, he handed over the correct one. He also could say the words "block" and "dog" and for the most part used these words correctly. Both the sound "dog" and the picture of the four-legged creature were functioning as symbols for canines in our neighborhood.

As a young player, Jerry used the blocks in numerous ways. Sometimes, as a two-year-old, he would grab onto a large block, glide it back and forth along the floor, grunting "vroom, vroom" as if the block were a plane taking off. Once when he was three, he grabbed a large block and a small block, said "This is the mommy and this is the baby," and led both blocks off to a pretend store to buy an ice cream cone.

The blocks were conscripted to the service of other symbol-using activities. When a catchy tune was played on the record player, Jerry would beat time with a block or bang against it with a pencil or Tinkertoy. Given a set of colored markers for his third birthday, Jerry drew various forms on the blocks. Within a year or so, the blocks were profusely decorated with circles, squares, dotted patterns; by the time Jerry was four, miniature versions of human beings, suns, and "doggies" could also be seen.

Of course, Jerry also built with the blocks, erecting towers of every conceivable size and shape. It was fun to build these up, even more fun to knock them down. Increasingly, the towers came to resemble shapes in the world—a skyscraper in Boston, a castle from a storybook—and increasingly they were enmeshed in stories featuring dragons, dinosaurs, and daredevils.

An avid viewer of "Sesame Street," four-year-old Jerry could name numbers and letters and had also learned to read a few words and recite a few number facts. But his ability to use these conventional symbols did not really take off until he entered kindergarten. At this point, now age five, he used his blocks to write out small words like *dog* and *coke,* to join numerical symbols in appropriate ways ("two 3s make 6"), and to classify the blocks according to consistent principles (putting together all the tall blue blocks, and so on).

By this time he was a full-fledged symbol user. He could use his blocks, as well as many other objects in his environment, to build representations of the "real world," to create scenarios of play as backdrops against which to

draw pictures of objects, and to construct verbal or numerical messages. Nor did all of Jerry's symbol-using activity require blocks. By age five he could also create little stories, purely with words; and he could sing a variety of songs taught to him by others, as well as create little ditties on his own. He had come a long way from the infant whose ways of knowing blocks were restricted to placing them in his mouth or lobbing them out of his crib.

Mastering Symbol Use and Becoming an Artist

In the months following infancy, Jerry was acquiring mastery in the use of symbols. Any element can function as a **symbol** when it is used to refer to, represent, depict, or denote some element in the world, or when it is used to express or exemplify some property or quality of experience. No element is in itself clearly symbolic or nonsymbolic; the way the element is used determines whether it functions as a symbol. My pencil does not function as a symbol when I use it to write, but when I make it stand for a birthday candle (as Jerry once did), then the pencil has become a symbol.

Some elements, such as body parts and food, seldom take on a symbolic role. Others, such as words, pictures, musical scores, and Morse code, serve primarily as symbols and rarely assume any other function. Some symbols, like words or representational pictures, are meaningful because they **denote** elements in the world; other symbols, like symphonies or abstract pictures, are meaningful because they express feelings or abstract properties (a "lively" tune, an "angry" or "rich" design).

We must remember how common and accepted some symbols are: from the numbers

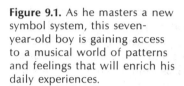

Figure 9.1. As he masters a new symbol system, this seven-year-old boy is gaining access to a musical world of patterns and feelings that will enrich his daily experiences.

on the alarm clock that awakens us, to the street signs that direct our daily passages, on to the Muzak lulling us to daydream, ours is a world pervaded—even dominated—by symbols.

Most symbols do not function alone. Rather, they belong to **symbol systems,** such as spoken or written language, traffic directions, and mathematical systems. Symbols are presented (or embodied) in a **medium**—a material or apparatus used to convey a message. A verbal symbol, or word, can be presented in writing or speaking. A musical phrase expressing gaiety can be conveyed by the voice or by an instrument, perhaps a trumpet or a flute. A story can be presented on television, on the radio, or in storybook form.

The ability to use symbols appropriately and to appreciate symbolic reference most clearly separates humans from other organisms in the animal kingdom. Thus, the ad-

vent of this capacity is the most fundamental and far-reaching revolution in a child's life, a revolution that opens the door to countless worlds of experiences. No longer restricted to the present moment or to customary associations, the child is free to consider multiple meanings and implications and the numerous relations among symbols. Without symbols, children (like most animals) are merely skilled pragmatists, able to act only with reference to given physical objects. With symbols, they can represent and contemplate, create and annihilate many worlds. And they can also become immersed in cognitive activities such as the sciences, religion, politics, or the arts. Symbols come to dominate and direct behavior; their growing prominence is what the five-to-seven shift is mainly about.

Although symbols pervade every area of human knowledge and activity, they are clearly paramount in the arts. In dancing, acting, painting, sculpting, writing literature, and composing music, artists must fashion symbols so as to capture and convey the nuances of ideas and feelings to their public. Sometimes the symbols are fashioned by a single individual; sometimes, as in the example of a ritual or fairy tale, they have been formed by many individuals over the course of history. Once we have recognized humans as symbol-creating and symbol-decoding creatures, it is but a small step for us to assert that the symbol user is capable of artistic practice. Jerry's miraculous voyage illustrates this assertion. As he became able to represent knowledge in symbolic forms, he began reacting to and creating artistic symbols (like drawings) as well as other symbols that could serve aesthetic purposes (like words used in stories and poems).

At what point do children participate in the **artistic process?** When a child writes the number 4 as the sum to a problem, she is using symbols, but her behavior is not in itself aesthetic. If she writes the number so as to call attention to the bold intersection of lines or to contrast two colors, she is using the symbol system artistically. It is at times when a symbol is apprehended on a number of levels, when every detail matters, or when unaccustomed links are found that aesthetic experiences are most pronounced and most valued (Goodman, 1968).

Even as two- or three-year-old children resemble players, children aged five to seven can be seen as youthful artists. Not that they have the skills to be virtuosos or to interpret artwork at a sophisticated level (H. Gardner, 1973; 1980*a*). But they *have* absorbed the fundamentals of symbolic creation in art forms; they can respond to works of art; and they exhibit the spontaneity in expression and openness to new experience that typifies the creative artist (Ghiselin, 1952; Koestler, 1964).

As artist and performer, the child creates pictures and stories, sings songs, dances, and collects and presents these works to others. As an audience member, the child experiences feelings aroused by art objects and eagerly cultivates these experiences. Only when it comes to the critic's role of comparing works and discussing them according to traditional canons of analysis has the child not yet become involved in the artistic process.

There is another reason for focusing on the arts. Any discussion of child development needs to consider an end-state or goal. Most developmental treatments choose as their end-state scientific excellence, as Jean Piaget has done, or the healthy personality, as Sigmund Freud and Erik Erikson have done. But participation in the arts can also serve as an instructive end-state for the developmental process that we have been examining. In the first place, the various art forms cut across the cognitive and affective domains emphasized, respectively, by Piaget and Erikson. In any discussion about the arts, it is as pointless to overlook feelings as it is to ignore the rich cognitive components. Furthermore, although scientific activity has generally been restricted to isolated pockets within a few societies, nearly everyone in every culture is somehow involved in the arts. For these reasons, artistic participation seems a reasonable end-state for development. And because five- to seven-year-olds seem to exemplify several properties of the artistic participant (deep immersion in symbolization, an openness to unusual associations, a keenness in discrimination), viewing these children within an aesthetic framework can be revealing.

In earlier chapters we saw how children come to know the physical world *directly*, through the evolution and interaction of three systems: perceiving, making, and feeling. Following the description of sensorimotor development, we focused on the acquisition of language, that symbol system that plays a crucial role in cognition and expression in all human cultures. In this chapter we will direct our attention more generally to the use of symbols during what Piaget has termed the **symbolic** or **preoperational (intuitive)** stage. We shall reconsider the fundamental developmental processes of making, perceiving, and feeling as they occur in various symbolic activities. Our emphasis will fall on two forms of symbolization that in our culture play an especially important role in the life of the preschool child: drawing pictures and telling stories.

Following this review of principal forms of artistic symbolization, we shall turn our attention to a crucial theoretical question: Do children possess certain central cognitive skills that allow them to advance equivalently across the range of symbolic media (as one committed to a cognitive-structural view of the symbolic stage might suppose)? Or do advances depend more on the specific symbols, media, and sensory systems being used (as might be expected in an empiricist or environmental-learning approach)? In addressing these questions, we will dwell on research in which the same kinds of information are presented in rival symbol systems or media and observe the effects of these presentations on children's comprehension and performance. Finally, we shall return to children's creative and imaginative skills, examining how symbols help them create new worlds and, equally important, a sense of self. Throughout the chapter, we shall keep in the background a view of the child as young artist, but we will not place every act, perception, and feeling in an aesthetic context. After all, the purpose of such a metaphor is not to restrict our view of a complex organism; its purpose is to highlight some recurring patterns that may help organize diverse kinds of information and insights.

The Developing Systems on the Symbolic Level

In Chapter 3 we described three systems—making, perceiving, and feeling—whose development during the first years of life consists in their elaboration and gradual but inevitable intermingling. The challenge facing the child during the next period of life—between the ages of two and seven—is to recapitulate previous development, this time on the level of symbols.

THE DRAWING

Visual Depiction. The human capacity to make lines and shapes that resemble actual objects is one of the most remarkable symbolizing activities, one that does not seem to be found in other organisms. In every culture where children begin to draw in the first years of life, the drawings pass through a similar sequence of stages (Kellogg, 1969; Schaefer-Simmern, 1948). When they are about two years old, children make scribbles, straight or curvy lines that wander back and forth. Sometimes the scribbles are made hastily and with heavy pressure. At other times they glide gracefully across the page, almost resting in midair. In all, children's scribbles seem to fall into at least a dozen basic patterns.

After scribbling for a time, children begin to draw lines on the paper in various arrangements. Although the drawings are not yet attempts to portray specific objects, two-year-olds will occasionally point out (or "invent") a resemblance between some of these lines and objects they know. And if given an incomplete form, such as a circle with two eyes inscribed inside, they will place a nose or a mouth inside properly (Golomb, 1980; Wolf and Gardner, 1979). By the time they are two and one-half, children regularly create on their own certain common shapes, such as crosses and circles, out of the basic scribbles and lines. Gradually they evolve certain drawing formulas, or customary visual patterns with which they are particularly comfortable and to which they periodically return. Also at about this time, children begin to appreciate that a bounded area on a piece of paper can be read as a solid object and that marks within this area "stand for" elements inside or on top of the visual object they have created.

Some time during the third or fourth year, children move on their own from producing such fixed patterns to explicitly representing facets of their world: people, faces, buildings, animals, vegetation, and other common objects. At last there is a recognizable link between the particular shape fashioned by the child and the form or contour of the object being depicted. Symbolization has arrived in the area of drawing. Still, at this stage, children often do not detect and label the parallel between drawing and object until they have completed the drawing: they must *make* a form before they can *match* that form to the world (Gombrich, 1960; Lowenfeld, 1957). By the time they enter school, however, they generally declare their intention beforehand and revise the drawing until they have achieved an adequate resemblance. And they can combine simple forms (circles and rectangles) to produce more complex objects (trains, human figures).

By the age of five, most children know that a drawing can capture experiences, and they are quite capable of representing familiar objects and elements. Having mastered the basic rules of symbolization in the medium of drawing, they follow a reliable set of procedures for rendering familiar schemas. For example, in first producing "tadpole" figures, they make a circle with two protruding lines (legs) underneath. Some months later, they will add a second circle for the body and another pair of protruding lines, to function as arms (Goodnow,

1977; Freeman, 1980). As preschoolers they will place a limb first on the right side, second on the left side of the central circle. And by the time they enter school, they are likely to have adopted canonical ways of depicting objects, drawing humans from the front, dogs and cars from a side perspective (Ives and Houseworth, 1980).

During the following years, their drawings undergo further significant changes. Pictures begin to suggest stories, series of events, more intricate scenes and experiences, and even personal feelings (Wilson and Wilson, 1977). Children aged seven or eight become increasingly preoccupied with realistic representations of the world about them and impatient with symbols that are not realistic (like those seen in abstract painting). They become more skilled at composing a picture, distributing elements across the canvas or page, blending colors, and producing a consistent and appropriate texture. By the age of ten or eleven, they can vary thickness of line, shading, or mix of color in a purposeful way, thereby achieving a variety of intended graphic effects (Carothers and Gardner, 1979). Having mastered the basic rules of picturing the world, children will now elaborate on them. And although the importance of drawing differs from child to child, attaining the capacity to present ideas and feelings, fears and hopes in a drawing is an important and meaningful milestone for most youngsters of school age (Coles, 1967; Erikson, 1963; Fraiberg, 1959).

One useful way of assessing children's symbolic competence is to observe how they perform in the presence or absence of a model. One may, for instance, show a child a toy cat that has many unusual features and ask the child to draw it. Before the age of seven or eight, children are poor at this task (Luquet, 1927; Piaget and Inhelder, 1956). They tend to draw the cat for which they have a graphic formula (the single-colored cat they know in the one canonical orientation they have mastered) and to ignore the strange features of the cat in front of their eyes. Older children can adapt their customary formula in order to capture idiosyncratic features of the model.

A neat demonstration of this tendency comes from the work of Freeman and Janikoun (1972), who asked children to copy a cup. The cup was positioned so that the handle (a defining feature of the cup) was not visible, and a flower painted on the side (a nondefining feature) faced the child. Younger children drew the cup that they knew how to draw—a typical view from the side with the handle visible—rather than the cup they saw. The older the children were, the more they tended to include the flower and to exclude the handle from their drawings. The crucial shift to a more faithful rendering of the perceived stimulus usually occurred between the years of seven and eight. Here is evidence that young children cannot yet dissociate what they know to be true about an object from the demands of a particular drawing assignment. However, if their attention is explicitly directed to the deviant aspects of a stimulus, for example, that the handle areas are not visible or that it must be viewed from an unusual angle, they are more likely to make a faithful copy (Cox, 1978; Light and MacIntosh, 1980; Pariser, 1976).

Though the progression in art, at least until school age, is one of the most regular in all of child development, there are exceptions. For example, if children do not have the opportunity to draw until they reach school age, they may pass through the early stages in very short order and perhaps skip some altogether (H. Gardner, 1980a). And there may be a few children, such as the autistic child, Nadia (see Figure 9.2 and the interlude, Another Perspective on Human Development), who, despite intellectual or emotional abnormalities, are

nonetheless able to draw objects and scenes in a highly realistic and apparently nonschematic way (Selfe, 1977). Whether such **idiot savants** are producing works of art by processes different from those used by most children has generated controversy among art educators (Arnheim, 1980; Pariser, 1976; Park, 1978; Wilson and Wilson, 1977).

Figure 9.2. Some youngsters who suffer severe emotional and intellectual handicaps nevertheless excel in one area of competence. This impressive sketch, which features both realistic perspective and striking expressiveness, was done by Nadia, an autistic child, at the age of five and one-half years.

Learning to Read Pictures. At first it may seem that a child should have no problem understanding pictures. After all, since pictures look like what they depict, a child should be able to recognize a picture of anything she knows. But this view proves too simple. A picture differs in many ways from the real object: it is flat, lacking cues of texture and depth; it usually differs radically in size from the real object; it can be folded or bent; and so on. Though infants are able to recognize simple pictorial depictions (see Chapter 3), they are less likely to attend to pictures than to three-dimensional objects and they are less successful in deriving information from pictorial depictions (Bower, 1974a). And although toddlers read regular pictures, more unusual representations of objects can throw children off (Arnheim, 1954; Elkind, 1969; Goodman, 1968; Hudson, 1967). For instance, when shown a line drawing of a human being composed of several fruits (apple as head, bananas as legs) most adults but few six-year-olds can discern the human (Elkind, 1969).

Accordingly, a debate has emerged on whether children can learn to read pictures naturally, or whether some form of informal teaching is required (E. Gibson, 1969; Gombrich, 1960; J. M. Kennedy, 1974). To find out, Julian Hochberg and Virginia Brooks (1962) kept an infant from exposure to pictures for nearly two years. They removed pictures from the child's home, took off labels from cans and bottles, kept picture books out of sight, and, in the rare instances when a picture appeared, refrained from labeling its subject matter. The crucial question: When exposed to pictures for the first time, just before the age of two, would the child know what they designated?

For the most part, the child knew. Whether presented as line drawings or as photographs, most pictures were correctly identified. Apparently, the child needs little tutelage in order to make sense of pictorial representation, or at least to label it.

Yet children do require education with respect to what *should* be discriminated in pictures. Studies of children's sensitivity to artistic styles document a recurring pattern. When asked to put together drawings by the same artist, children below the age of ten will group paintings in terms of subject matter (for example, putting together all landscapes or all portraits). They seem distracted by the content of the picture, incapable of attending to the ways (or style) in which that subject matter has been portrayed, and they show little inclination on their own to put together all the paintings that feature a bold brush stroke or a pointillistic technique (H. Gardner, 1972). Children in the early school years prove equally insensitive to other pivotal aspects of pictorial depiction: for instance, they seem insensitive to the way in which line can be used for expressive purposes and to the arrangement of objects within a picture (Carothers and Gardner, 1979; Gardner, in press). And while they can "read" an organized pictorial scene, they have considerable difficulties deciphering the spatial relations that obtain among objects in a scene that lacks a clear organizing principle (Mandler and Robinson, 1978).

Of course, these difficulties might be due to the fact that children receive little training in how to view pictures: after all, style sensitivity is not a required subject in most elementary schools! It therefore becomes crucial to determine whether children have the capacity, if not the inclination, to attend to these non-subject-matter aspects of drawings. Calling children's attention to such stylistic features proves of some help (Silverman, Winner, and Gardner, 1976) but usually more active forms of training are necessary (H. Gardner, 1972) if the performance of children six or seven years of age is to improve substantively.

Whether for biological or cultural reasons, children's tendencies to view pictorial works as pictures of *something* (or of *somebody*) prove very tenacious.

Children's Scanning Strategies. Concentration on subject matter is only one feature of children's perception of pictures. They also have characteristic strategies for scanning pictures. For instance, Norman Mackworth and Jerome Bruner (1970) found that, in looking at pictures, six-year-old children use many small eye movements rather than a few broad ones. Consequently, as Figure 9.3 illustrates, they usually fail to sample a display as fully or systematically as adults (see also Lasky, 1974) and their scanning patterns also seem more diffuse and less well organized. Moreover, children do not always notice informative aspects of pictures, so that, failing to see that a creature had wings, they might misidentify a bat as a squirrel. Similarly, in interpreting out-of-focus pictures they will sample only one or two spots and jump to erroneous conclusions. Yet, paradoxically, when they do sight an informative area they may become so seduced by it that they fail to scan other portions of the picture (see also Gaines, 1973).

Further information about how children scan visual arrays comes from some intriguing work by Lila Ghent Braine and her colleagues (Braine, 1978; Braine, Lerner, and Relyea, 1980). (See Figure 9.4.) Braine's point of departure is the observation that normal adults initially focus on one feature of a figure and then, in an effort to identify it, move around to adjacent features. Braine's work suggests, however, that children younger than four or five instead focus on a dominant feature and then scan downward. Thus, when shown an abstract figure, these youngsters tend to regard it as right side up when its most dominant feature is at the top and the dominant lines are vertical, and as upside

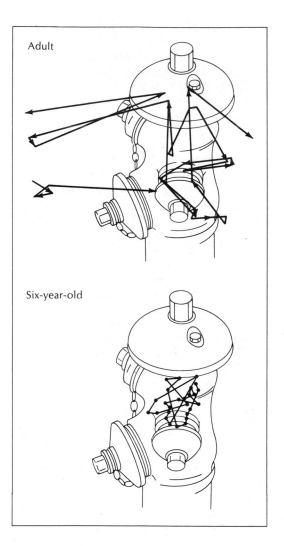

Figure 9.3. Confronting a fire hydrant, the mature adult viewer makes a few broad eye movements, which sample all of the most "informative" aspects of the display. In contrast, the young schoolchild makes numerous small eye movements that often fail to take into account salient portions of the display. (Mackworth and Bruner, 1970)

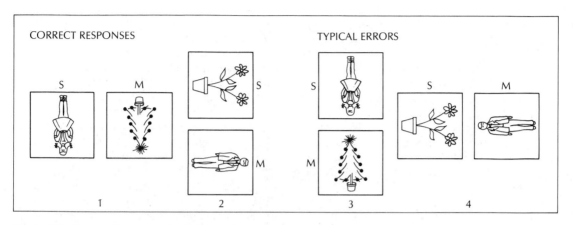

Figure 9.4. To test their sensitivity to the orientation of a figure, young children are shown a standard card (S) in either an up/down (as in 1 or 3) or a sideways (as in 2 or 4) orientation. They are then asked to turn a matching card (M) to the same orientation and place it either underneath or beside the standard. Up/down orientations are generally matched correctly when the two cards are side by side (1) and incorrectly, in mirror image, when placed one above the other (3). Conversely, sideways orientations tend to be matched correctly when the cards are placed one above the other (2) and in mirror image when placed side by side (4). One explanation of these common response patterns is that children place comparable parts near each other: tops near tops and bottoms near bottoms. This strategy sometimes results in "mirror image" errors. (Braine, 1978)

down when the dominant feature is at the bottom. As a result, when the identifying features are at the top, but not dominant, children are likely to overlook (or underlook!) them and, hence, fail to recognize the figure. In addition, because of their practice of proceeding downward from dominant features, children will often (though not always; see Prather, 1981) fail to detect differences among objects that they judge to be upside down in orientation. After age four or five, however, children define the top of any figure as the focal feature and scan downward. By follow-

ing this procedure, they are far more likely to figure out what it is they are seeing.

Braine's studies suggest that children develop certain perceptual strategies that they apply to all stimuli. If the strategies prove serviceable, they will be retained. If they prove unwieldy or result in the loss of significant information, they will be modified or perhaps even abandoned. When scanning figures, children retain downward processing for all vertically oriented figures, but by making the top the original point of departure they ensure that they will sample the whole figure.

It is worth recalling that analogous perceptual strategies can be observed in other symbolic media. For example, we saw in Chapter 4 that children aged two or three initially assume that the first noun in a sentence is the actor and the second noun is the object of the action (Bever, 1970). This strategy is retained until it becomes clear that it is often unreliable, as in comprehending passive sentences ("John was hit by Mary") in which the actor-object relation is reversed. By the age of three and one-half or four, most children have given up this strategy.

A few other perceptual proclivities merit mention. Children exhibit considerable difficulty in discriminating among and remembering various kinds of oblique lines, particularly when these are mirror images of one another (Bryant, 1973, 1974; Corballis and Zalik, 1977; Fisher and Heincke, 1981; Olson, 1970); apparently the eye abhors a mirror. Discrimination among faces presented in photographs also poses problems, particularly if the same person is photographed wearing different hairstyles or different clothing (Carey and Diamond, 1977). Children find it difficult to search complex arrays, particularly in the presence of competing background cues (Day, 1978), and are generally unable to exploit whatever organizing structure exists in such arrays (Chipman and Mendelson, 1979). But if young children are at a disadvantage in most perceptual tasks, they also possess certain gifts. They may be more successful at recognizing depth relations in certain kinds of stereoscopic pictorial displays (Dowd et al., 1980) and they may possess forms of photographic (or **eidetic**) imagery (Leask, Haber, and Haber, 1969). Skeptics are invited to play the game of "Concentration" with a six-year-old.

Feelings in Drawings. The creation of objects in graphic arts is clearly important in the lives of young children, though at least in our society the significance of drawing appears to wane during the school years. Young children may have difficulty confronting their feelings in words: during the preschool period, drawings can serve as a vehicle for children to examine and act upon their feelings. At the age of four, my son Jerry was able to deal with themes of conflict, aggression, and power by becoming deeply involved in the drawing of superheroes. Perhaps in parallel fashion, my daughter Kay at a slightly older age became enamored of horses and horse riding, using these themes to explore her own feelings about action, caring, and the control of powerful drives.

Few clinicians doubt that drawings serve the feeling life of the child (Alschuler and Hattwick, 1969; Bettelheim, 1976; Coles, 1967; Erikson, 1963). Yet the knowledge of feelings embedded in drawings appears to be implicit. Conscious, intentional use of the medium in order to communicate feelings of, say, anger or glory is a development that waits upon the school years and, often, the mastery of certain cultural conventions. We encounter a paradox that at the very time when the child learns to *hide* her feelings from other individuals (Buck, 1976; Flaste, 1977*a*; Saarni, 1979) she becomes able to communicate her feelings with greater effectiveness in her symbolic products (Carothers and Gardner, 1979; Scarlett, 1980). But perhaps this is not so paradoxical: as direct expression of feelings becomes less appropriate (and direct feelings less likely to enter drawings through overflow), the child's ability to manipulate the medium is

Figure 9.5. *Opposite:* As children gain competence in various symbol systems, they often convey powerful emotions in their artistic creations. Here children who lived in Northern Ireland during recent political unrest express the felt turmoil in their drawings.

enhanced. And, of course, the range and subtlety of feelings that offer themselves for symbolization increase for some time to come
(Flaste, 1977a; Saarni, 1979).

STORYTELLING

Rivaling the image of the scribbling toddler is
the view of the attentive youngster seated
next to a parent who is reading aloud a picture book or retelling an ancient fairy tale.
Since time immemorial children have listened
avidly to, enjoyed, and been suitably frightened by the stories related by their elders.
And from early on in their own lives, children
create and enact stories, at first using the
simple objects and props of their environment
as an entry point, soon creating little narratives purely with words. Beyond question,
stories play an important, indeed a central
role in the lives of young children everywhere, even as they involve individuals of all
ages (or the child in all of us). But whether
children actually understand the stories they
hear and whether their involvement with stories has the same flavor that it will have later
on are questions that have challenged researchers.

As compared to, say, words or pictures,
stories resist ready experimental investigation:
they are long and often complex structures
that unfold over time, and they are therefore
difficult to analyze in detail. Nonetheless, researchers have been guided by certain general
features of narratives. First of all, stories have
fairly predictable structures. They include settings, problems to be solved, plans set forth
by characters, feelings experienced by these
characters, tentative solutions, and in the end,
a resolution that returns the characters to a
state of equilibrium. There are also certain
recurrent contents: the tiniest son who gains
victory over the others, the evil stepmother
who is vanquished, the two lovers who are

finally reunited, on earth or beyond. Children's own spontaneous stories and their understanding of others' stories can be analyzed
in terms of these characteristic forms and
contents.

Let's consider first the stories told by children. As we've noted earlier, children's stories
are initially stimulated by familiar objects of
play and typically feature common domestic
scripts (going to bed, having dinner). But they
rapidly undergo structural complexity. Looking at the spontaneous narratives of children
ranging in age from three to twelve years,
Botvin and Sutton-Smith (1977) ferret out
seven different levels of complexity. The earliest narratives (level one) feature the juxtapos-
ing of several proper nouns and a few simple
actions:

The little duck went swimming. Then the crab
came. A lobster came. And a popsicle was playing by itself [page 379].

At subsequent levels, the child becomes able
to posit a central dilemma and to handle a
pair of characters who undergo a series of
interactions with one another. Subplots may
intervene between the opening and closing
episodes. A typical level-four story reads:

There was this friendly lion in Asia but he was
captured and brought to a zoo. Then the lion
escaped. He was walking down the road and a
truck tried to run him over, but he managed to
get out of the way. He began to get hungry so
he ate a rabbit. The end [page 381].

Later high-level stories, obtained from children aged eight to twelve, add an important
further component: a hierarchical organization in which some portions of the plot are
subordinate to others. In a typical story a
character in pursuit of a guiding or central
mission (for example, escape from a powerful
evil individual) becomes involved in a series
of adventures along the way; still her main

mission is never lost sight of, and she eventually vanquishes her nemesis.

The steady increase in structural complexity is paralleled by changes in the experiences undergone by protagonists. Consider, for example, the classic plot where a small and apparently powerless person is besieged by a ferocious force, perhaps a monster. In the earliest stories the strong force is so overwhelming that the narrating child cannot exploit literary structures to defeat or fend off the monster. Thus the small person is either vanquished or saved by a sudden solution—the monster goes away or is changed into a fairy. In a more sophisticated version, the child becomes able to draw upon the resources of the narrative to reduce pressure at least temporarily: for example, the small person hides or the monster is tied down. Still, the possibility for later calamity remains all too real (Sutton-Smith, 1975; Sutton-Smith, Botvin, and Mahoney, 1976).

Only at the age of eight or nine does the child become able to conjure up a satisfactory narrative solution to this state of affairs. Now there can be a genuine change in the behavior of the villain (he may recognize the folly of his evil ways), the capacities of the protagonist (she is clever enough to entrap the powerful but dim-witted villain), or the relation between the two characters (faced with an even greater threat, they become allies). Moreover, a state of equilibrium is achieved and there is no reason to think that the problem will recur the next day. This indeed is the meaning behind the phrase "And they lived happily ever after."

Negotiating this sequence of stages proves to be a lengthy process, requiring considerable linguistic, cognitive, and aesthetic sophistication. The child is aided by familiarity with many stories on which she can draw in her spontaneous narratives; yet in the absence of general mastery of the structure and forms of the story, she may mimic the superficial features (lots of violence or certain odd-sounding names, for example) rather than the underlying structural forces (the tension between two characters with opposing goals). And even when the child has mastered the forms indicated here, further obstacles can prevent genuine narrative mastery. Like the young child who is drawing, the child spinning narratives must master techniques of style, expressivity, and compositional balance. Then, within the narrative modality, she must become aware of the intentions and motivations of her characters and be able to create situations in which these motivations are embodied rather than simply announced (Rubin and Gardner, 1979). The need to handle more than two characters and a number of interrelated problems—the bane of readers of spy stories—is a further complicating factor in the mastery of narrative. And, finally, there is the capacity to utilize different genres—to tell a story that qualifies as an adventure, a mystery, a fairy tale, a shaggy dog story—and to fashion parodies of these underlying forms. Such achievements require a mastery that is beyond most children, and, in fact, beyond many adults.

The Perception and Comprehension of Narratives. In seeking to understand the understandings of children, psychologists have been aided by story grammars (Bower, 1976; Rummelhart, 1975). These are formalizations of the relations among elements (such as character, setting, sequence of events) that are thought to characterize a proper story, much as certain relations among elements (such as subject, predicate, and object) are thought to characterize a proper sentence.

Armed with a story grammar, the psychologist has available to her a number of techniques for probing narrative understanding. She can tell a story and ask the child to repeat it, noting which features of the grammar are eliminated, which retained or expanded.

She can delete or reorder elements of the story and observe effects on the recall. Or she can present incomplete stories and see which grammatical elements are added, transformed, or simply forgotten. Not surprisingly, psychologists have documented a greater sensitivity with age to the principal grammatical features of stories. And some of the details of this increasing tendency prove illuminating.

The following "story" emerges (Fitzhenry-Coor, 1977; Glenn, 1977; Mandler and Johnson, 1977; McConaughy, 1978; Stein, 1979). Young children (aged four to six) will remember the main characters of the story, the event that launched the story, and the ultimate outcome. Actions are well preserved. Children are much less likely to keep track of the various attempts made by the characters en route to the final outcome and they almost never note the internal reactions (the plans and feelings and reactions) of the characters. The physical predominates, the psychological seems invisible.

Other differences exist between novice and accomplished story comprehenders. For the young child the causal relations among events remain obscure, whereas the narratives of older children highlight the chains of causal connections. Similarly, as narratives become more sophisticated, the goals of characters and the motivations that lead to events are difficult for younger subjects to handle (McConaughy, 1978). Younger children are likely to be discombobulated when events of a story are related in a misordered fashion or when important features have been deleted; older subjects prove able to make corrections in ordering and to infer elements that are missing but should be there (Rubin and Gardner, 1979; Stein, 1979).

Despite these differences, children as young as four or five have mastered the essentials of a story. When "stripped-down" versions are presented, in sentences or in pictures, when the relations between events are made explicit (rather than left to inference), when canonical forms are honored, and when children are asked explicitly about aspects that they did not themselves recount, the differences cited above are reduced or disappear altogether (Brown and Murphy, in press; Stein, 1979). They also show some appreciation of the boundary between fiction and reality and of the existence of an author (Hay, 1981; Scarlett and Wolf, 1979; Silberstein, 1981).

A particularly telling demonstration comes from Fitzhenry-Coor (1977), who examined children's ability to make subjective judgments of morality (see Chapter 5). This investigator demonstrated that at least some of the difficulties exhibited by young children in judging the morality of behaviors had nothing to do with their moral standards. Instead, the judgments reflected the subjects' understanding of the stories themselves. Thus when children did not understand the stories, they tended to ignore the intentions of characters and to make "objective" moral judgments (the biggest offense merits the most severe penalty, irrespective of motivation). Once a character's intentions were spelled out, the children were able to take the intentions into account and to make more sophisticated "subjective" attributions. Moral: Children may differ from one another less in their basic comprehension of a story than in their ability to draw the inferences that adults make nearly automatically. Once inferences have been spelled out, comprehension becomes virtually equivalent between youthful and experienced listeners.

Nonetheless, there are still areas of comprehension where youngsters lag behind. Taking a Piagetian tack, Miller (1979) presented children with short vignettes featuring characters with conflicting goals (for example, the cat wanted to eat the mouse, the mouse wanted to escape). He documented an inability on the part of young children to appreciate the core of the story: that only one of the protagonists could attain her goal. Young children either believed that both of the protagonists could gain their goals or that it was in the order of things that a particular protagonist *had* to gain her goal: "The cat has to eat the mouse." Only children aged nine or ten appreciated that, depending upon the events in the story, either of the protagonists might gain the goal but that no solution could satisfy both. When it comes to understanding the nature of stories, appreciation of complex motivation, assimilation of diverse genres, and the mastery of aesthetic aspects, a considerable developmental progression may be necessary.

The Feelings of Stories. It is difficult to overstate the effect (and the affect) of narratives on a child. A four-year-old becomes so enamored of a certain story that she wants to hear it (and no substitutes, please!) over and over again. She is happiest in the presence of this story and crestfallen if the book containing it is in any way damaged. Another youngster of the same age may become so fearful of a character in a book or television show that she breaks down uncontrollably whenever that character is even mentioned. In fact, sometimes the reaction can be uncanny. When my son Jerry watched a videotape of me on television while I was sitting next to him, he became so upset that I had to shut off the television. Somehow, crossing the boundaries between "stories on television" and "interactions in real life" was too overwhelming to handle.

Part of this excessive emotional effect derives from preschool children's initial difficulty in making fine discriminations about people. Characters tend to strike them as all good or all evil and children's reponse is similarly unmodulated (Bettelheim, 1976; Demos, 1974).

Furthermore, the concrete symbols of fairy tales (wicked wolves, disobedient children) embody many of the charged issues that confront the child (Oedipal feelings, sibling rivalries, and boundaries between good and evil). With their multiple levels of affect-laden meaning, such symbolic characters can understandably upset the child.

But probably an equally potent factor in the child's reactions are the difficulties experienced by all preschool children in discriminating between reality and fantasy. Subjected daily to an assortment of relatives, monsters, historic persons, fairy-tale characters, and puppets, the child cannot reliably determine how real (or unreal) each of these figures may be. Indeed, the whole notion of what is real and what is fantastic is too complex for the child to grasp. As a consequence, the preschool child is forever uncertain about whether a witch might really devour her, whether a parent might suddenly disappear, whether Santa Claus has the same status as the milkman, the president, the Easter bunny, or God (Morison and Gardner, 1978). Even eight-year-olds (if not eighty-year-olds) retain some uncertainty about Santa Claus.

Although sometimes a source of difficulty, the child's vulnerability to potent emotions may also be invigorating. In the grip of a strong emotion, a child may fashion a story, picture, song, or play that has great importance for her, as well as considerable effect on those who behold it. The single dominant emotion may organize the child's somewhat scattered behaviors, structuring them so they gain great power. For instance, in the wake of a frightening thunderstorm, a child of six or seven may produce a gloomy and chaotic black abstract painting that captures the mood, as well as the appearance, of the awe-inspiring event. Such symbolic expressions resemble significant artworks, which also evoke potent emotional reactions. The twin features of a strong emotional response to certain works and the capacity to fashion a powerful expressive symbol lend further reasonableness to our characterization of the child as a young artist.

OTHER ARTISTIC SYSTEMS

Drawings and stories are central in the lives of children in our culture, and they may be similarly pivotal in other cultures as well. But clearly symbolic development progresses in other domains, both those of an artistic taint and those of general communicative significance. As revealed in our opening description of Jerry, children during the first several years of life are also advancing in three-dimensional depiction (portraying the world through clay, playdough, or building blocks); in the expression of meaning via gesture, dance, and mime; and in the mastery of other symbol systems, ranging from drama to music.

In each of these domains a history of the child's progress can be written, and in each case we see a surprisingly regular series of stages. The child first goes beyond simple motor and perceptual acts to master the basic building blocks of the particular symbol system. A basic capacity to symbolize emerges by the age of three or four: the child can enact scenes through mime, build houses or forts with blocks, construct snakes or pots with clay. There follows a regular infusion of models from the culture and an increasing ability to handle more complex, multifaceted, or psychological aspects of the symbol system. Sometimes, as in the case of storytelling, emphasis falls on the representational aspects of symbolization. At other times, as in the case of music, emphasis centers on the expression of various emotions and feelings, as children convey their moods by choice of register, pitch, rhythm, rising or falling contours, and the like. And in some art forms, such as

dance or three-dimensional construction, one encounters a balance between representation and expression, between form and content.

Symbol use is not restricted to artistic forms. In fact, in Western culture other symbol systems often come to the fore. Even as the child is learning to draw and tell stories, she is also discovering the properties of the number system and learning relevant cultural codes—the names and the written forms of the numbers—in order to capture and convey her numerical understanding. Numbers are but one notational system. Either on her own or with help from parents, peers, and teachers, the child is also learning about other symbolic codes—maps, diagrams, musical notations, codes, game formats, and the like. And most important, she will shortly learn how to read and write and become able to exploit this form of symbolic communication as a principal—and often *the* principal—means of acquiring and disseminating knowledge.

Effects of the symbolic revolution prove profound and permanent. From a world dominated by actions, percepts, and feelings the child comes to inhabit a world dominated by symbols. These symbols, moreover, come to carry as much weight as the direct unmediated aspects of experience. The child who once reacted with fear only to a genuine physical threat can now experience an equivalent amount of fear as a result of a scary story, a threatening picture, or a jarring musical composition. The child who once gained pleasure primarily from direct physical stimulation now experiences pleasurable emotions in response to songs, stories, and scenes on television. And, perhaps most significant, children at the threshold of school can now present their own deeply felt emotions in words, pictures, and other forms of symbolic play.

In an earlier chapter we introduced the guiding fiction of three developing systems that increasingly interact with one another.

Taking another page from the same guide-book, we may speak of the development within each symbol system of the capacities to perceive, to make, and to feel. Recapitulating the events of the first year or two of life, we can discern an increasing interplay in young children between these various capacities, at first within specific symbol systems and eventually across the diverse systems. Just as the child becomes able to connect the stories she hears and loves to the ones she creates, so too she eventually becomes able to join narrative knowledge gained in the domain of language to narration in the pictorial, gestural, and even the musical domains. Similar forms of interplay occur in the opposite direction, as aspects of musical organization can infuse the child's narrative competence. Many of the most outstanding products of the artist's imagination—for example, Picasso's painting of Guernica or Giuseppe Verdi's musical adaption of the plays of Shakespeare—exploit this permeability of the membranes between various symbolic forms, a process of mixing media that is under way by the time the child takes her first steps to school.

The Effects of Specific Media

Up to this point our examination of symbolic development has been consonant with a cognitive-structural line: we have assumed a child who develops in across-the-board fashion in a range of symbolic systems (Bruner, 1964; Piaget, 1962a; Werner and Kaplan, 1963). Adopting this viewpoint, we would expect that the child's ability to use one object to represent another or to perceive style in one artistic media should have a relatively ready and immediate impact on the child's capacities in working with other symbol systems.

However, a wholly different view of symbol development holds that relations among symbol systems cannot be assumed and need to be established. In this view, embraced by many supporters of environmental-learning theory and also by some cognitive-structuralists, each medium entails (and demands) a separate set of skills. Thus a child's progress (or difficulties) in drawing with pencil or sculpting with clay has few implications about her symbolic skills in writing poetry or composing music.

PAINT, PENCIL, CLAY

Representation in Multiple Media. Claire Golomb (1973, 1974) contrasted the "general-symbolic" with the "specific-medium" view. To verify one or the other, she asked children aged three to seven to represent the human figure in several media: drawing, clay, and puzzle pieces. And she found that the children's organization and articulation differed markedly depending on the nature of the task.

In the drawing task, most three- and four-year-olds produced tadpole figures with a few simple strokes (see Figure 9.6). A strong version of the cognitive-structural theory would predict that the children would then represent humans as tadpoles in all other media. But, in fact, their style of attack and their productions varied widely across media. Using cardboard puzzle pieces, children made more sophisticated figures with more and better integrated parts. On the other hand, they became so engrossed with the "stuff" of clay that they sometimes produced nothing at all. Performance on other tasks, such as copying a model, yielded similar differences (Golomb, 1973). Some examples are shown in Figure 9.6.

Overall, a subtle interaction is at work between the children's knowledge and the actual steps they must take to express this knowledge in different media (Taylor and Bacharach, 1981). For instance, children who draw tadpoles will nonetheless choose more

Figure 9.6. These versions of the human figure, gathered by Claire Golomb, illustrate the strikingly different "concepts" and levels of integration that emerge from children's renditions in diverse media of expression. (Golomb, 1974)

complex human figures when given a choice. And, given pieces to fit together as in the puzzle task, they produce figures that are intermediate in sophistication between the preferred complex figure and the simple tadpole that they draw.

Golomb's findings clearly refute the theory that the child's cognitive level imposes itself on all tasks, regardless of symbolic medium.

There are undeniable differences across media and across tasks within a given medium. The child's conceptual level must interact with the experience and demands of each medium. To be sure, as Jerry approached his third birthday he could represent symbols at a new level of sophistication: but at first his performance with music far outstripped his modeling with clay.

Producing Lines in Diverse Media. Following a line of thinking similar to Golomb's, David Olson (1970) was perplexed that four- and five-year-olds can recognize diagonal lines when they cannot yet produce them in any medium. Olson wondered whether children would be able to produce a diagonal line in diverse media once they had mastered it in one medium. To find out he asked children to produce diagonals in three ways: (1) on one of three kinds of checkerboard: (2) on bulb boards (pressing buttons to light bulbs, which do not then remain lighted); and (3) with a toy designed to teach "diagonality." Contrary to what a strict cognitive-structuralist might predict, Olson found only loose associations among the tasks. For instance, one bright youngster who could easily distinguish among lines of different orientation and could readily produce a horizontal line, a letter *E*, or a letter *H* on the bulb board gave a random and confused response when asked to copy a diagonal on his bulb board.

Apparently, perceptual skills, whether with physical or symbolic objects, routinely outstrip productive skills. In fact, perceiving seems a necessary prerequisite to making: not until children have made the relevant discriminations can they capture relevant features in a making act. But how long will this process take and with what media will success eventually come?

It turns out that a regular order of difficulty emerges across the media Olson studied. For example, constructing the diagonal proves easier with the checkerboard, where the checkers remain in place, than with the bulb board, where the bulbs do not remain lit. Both boards limit the elements of the response. The freehand drawing task, which allows an unlimited set of possibilities, is most difficult. Here we recall some of the distinctions Golomb discerned when she had children copy, select, and assemble human forms.

Olson's study suggests that psychologists and educators should concentrate more on the specific demands of each medium. A medium should be conceptualized as offering the opportunity for a range of making activities, each of which demands certain perceptual information and yields specifiable patterns and options. Accordingly, Olson urges abandonment of the idea of general capacities (or general intellectual abilities) underlying all media. Rather than looking for underlying operations, Olson feels one should enumerate the options confronting an individual in a given task within a given medium and examine how well the individual can select among them.

Learning the Tricks of the Trade. With her eye on the question of "general skills" ranging across media, Jacqueline Goodnow has studied children engaged in a variety of symbolic tasks. In one, children were asked to draw a set of dots that would describe a sequence of sounds (Goodnow, 1971*a*). To accomplish this task, a child had to understand that a dot could stand for a sound, that a left-to-right direction represented a first-to-last time order, and that a larger space between dots was equivalent to a longer interval between sounds. Most kindergarten children appeared to understand the first two principles, but only first and second graders grasped the third. As a result, kindergartners drew a dot, waited until the next tap, and then drew a second dot right next to the first. Lapse of time dictated a pause in drawing but did not translate into a spatial gap.

Like David Olson and Claire Golomb, Goodnow minimizes the importance of a general capacity like knowledge of a figure, understanding the diagonal, or perceiving rhythms. At most, certain cognitive understandings are necessary prerequisites for success on specific experimental tasks; they are not sufficient. Goodnow calls attention instead to the importance of learning the "tricks of the trade": knowing when and whether a skill should be used, how to evaluate whether it is being used properly, and how to secure independent confirmation of performance. For example, a child may be able to discern crucial features of a tapped rhythm and to leave a space between dots; but she must also be aware of the cultural convention (or "trick") of notating pauses with spaces before she can construct a bridge linking these islands of knowledge. Goodnow challenges educators to alert children to the tricks, which are taken for granted by (often egocentric) adults and which children must thus pick up on their own. In this view the acquisition of knowledge consists of a series of many small tasks to be mastered in a variety of media and symbol systems, rather than the natural development of all-purpose concepts and understandings that will transfer spontaneously to new contexts.

STORIES IN DIVERSE MEDIA

In yet another effort to evaluate the effects of media, Laurene Meringoff (Meringoff, 1980; Meringoff, et al., 1981) has examined the abilities of young children to comprehend and reproduce the same narratives presented in different media of communication. The principal comparisons have centered on stories presented in storybook form compared with stories aired on television.

In such studies the identity of the story chosen and the quality of the particular enactment in each medium are crucial elements: it is all too easy to bias a study so that one medium will come out looking superior to another. Indeed, ideally such research should aim not to prove that children perform better in one medium than another, but rather to delineate differences in performances that diverse media may elicit.

Studies by Meringoff and her colleagues (see also Greenfield et al., 1981) suggest that even when the same sound tracks are used, television focuses children's attention on actions of characters while a radio or storybook format directs attention to the quality of the language. Children are more likely to consider television a self-contained experience and to base answers on what they have seen in the video format; in contrast, when they have received a storybook version they are more likely to draw on their own personal and on "real world" experience. The provision of information to more than one sensory channel is also a crucial variable. When information presented to the eye and ear is redundant (a pictured person or event is also described verbally), the child's performance improves. But when the information presented to the eye and the ear covers different topics, younger children become confused, are unable to process it, and exhibit less adequate comprehension than when a single channel has been stimulated (Kelly and Meringoff, 1979).

EVALUATING THE MEDIA POSITION

The point of view put forth by these investigators is attractive: it provides a needed corrective to an account of cognitive development that disregards the actual materials used in tasks. But the contrast between general skills like symbolic representation (or understanding diagonals) and specific skills like sensitivity to the properties of clay (or mastery of bulb boards) may not be as sharp as they have drawn it. A clue comes from Olson's own work (1970). One teacher told Olson that she could train three-year-olds to make a diagonal with checkers. First the teacher demonstrated: Step-by-step she built the diagonal walking around the board, nodding and shaking her head appropriately each time she neared and veered from a correct square.

Olson tried the teacher's method with seven three- and four-year-olds. All four who succeeded in the task nodded and shook their heads in the process. Olson interprets the children's precocity as confirmation of his theory: the head motions helped dramatize the alternative choices available in the medium and thus highlighted the advantages and liabilities inherent in each.

But a cognitive-structural interpretation is also possible. Such commentators would concede that in order to perform correctly the child must have some familiarity with the medium, in this case a checkerboard, and the teacher is providing just that degree of familiarity. The young children who succeeded in producing a diagonal may have been mimicking without understanding, or they may already have had the basic operation for diagonality and needed only a brief nudge with a checkerboard. As Piaget has put it, the operation is there but there may be some *décalage* or lag between different tasks that assess the operation. Conversely, a child who failed even after repeated practice with the checkerboard would probably fail with all other variations of the problem as well. The underlying knowledge required to appreciate diagonality has not yet emerged.

In comparing media, it is essential to take into account the amount of practice an individual has had. Media differences prove of scant scientific (or educational) interest if they can be undone by brief training or sensitization. If, for example, a child who has little experience listening to radio performs poorly on a radio condition, one cannot draw any conclusions about the medium per se; what is needed is familiarization with radio, followed by a repetition of the same test. Once these training and practice effects have been controlled for, it should be possible to determine the genuine effects of each medium upon performance and whether these effects have a

significant or only a marginal impact on the child's performance and knowledge (Case, 1975, 1980; Fischer, 1980; Olson, 1974).

We see, then, that the two positions have very different emphases. The specific-medium school downplays central across-the-board understandings and highlights the mastering of the principles involved in using each particular medium. The general-symbolic camp emphasizes a single central form of understanding and believes a brief familiarity with a new medium should permit requisite transfer of the concept. In all probability, both a general level of understanding *and* some acquaintance with specific media and tasks are necessary for correct performance (Oppenheimer and Strauss, 1975). Learning would be frighteningly inefficient (perhaps even hopeless) if no general skills, independent of specific task and medium, existed. And yet no skill is powerful enough to be realized apart from experience with the particular task or medium. What remains to be determined in each particular case is whether the child's general understanding can evolve simply from practice with one medium or whether the child must achieve a separate mastery of the concept in a number of different media.

Symbols, Media, and Senses

THE EFFECTS OF THE SENSES

We have complicated our discussion of symbols and symbol systems with a consideration of the various media in which symbols can be presented. The two topics are quite different yet interrelated: a symbol like a word may appear in the different media of written and oral literature, whereas a medium like a brush and paint may embody the different symbols of words, pictures, or musical notes. Now, if we are to capture with some fidelity the range of factors affecting the development of the young child, we must add yet a further complicating factor: the specific sense or senses to which the symbolic message is presented. Only by sorting out these factors can we determine whether proficiency in a certain domain—say, painting—reflects its membership in the symbol system of pictures, the medium of oil painting or the sense of vision.

Experimental investigations with animals, children, and adults have documented that an organism's performance is affected by whether the eye, the ear, the hand, or some combination of channels receives a message (J. J. Gibson, 1966; Pick and Pick, 1970; Stevens, 1951). Numerous studies have compared the ease of information processing in two different senses and determined how readily the same information can be transferred from one sense to another. For instance, a person will be trained to make a visual discrimination (such as choosing the larger of two cubes) and then will be asked to master the same discrimination using touch alone. In general, the findings from such studies indicate that it is easier to master a comparison when only a single sense modality is involved, especially when it is vision (Birch and Lefford, 1963; Chase and Calfee, 1969; Galin et al., 1979). A comparison is more readily mastered in two sense modalities when both are used at the same time rather than successively. Performance is best when the stimuli are simple and when no interference follows their presentation. And, finally, as usual, older children perform better than younger ones (see Cronin, 1973; Jarman, 1979).

Although these findings have received considerable support, none of them is definitive. In fact, it is nearly always possible to design a comparison that is easier across senses than within senses, or a stimulus that is more readily handled by one sense in one task but more difficult to handle in another task. As a result of this inconclusiveness, Jacqueline Goodnow (1971b) suggests that researchers abandon their interest in determining which sense is faster or better and investigate instead the precise manner by which information is discriminated within and across given senses.

Goodnow (1971b) mentions a few tentative findings on the way information is processed by different senses. In comparing letterlike forms, a person can discriminate a change in the curve of a line more readily with the eye than with the hand, but the hand can more readily pick up a change in overall orientation of a form. In a related vein, different senses pick different stimuli features as focal: the eye seems more sensitive to vertical lines, the hand to loops; and people find it more difficult to remember a distance they have felt than one they have seen. Yet experience also enters into the equation, for blind people sometimes exhibit a more sophisticated sense of touch than do sighted people. Finally, older children prove able to use their hands together in a complementary way—one hand supporting, the other exploring a target object—whereas kindergartners cannot.

Clearly, studies of information processing need to take into account the sense organs being stimulated, the type of medium being employed, and the symbol system conveying the information. Sorting out these factors will challenge even the cleverest psychologist, and providing a rigorous definition of each dimension may pose an equivalent challenge to a philosopher. Moreover, these factors may shift in relative importance across individuals or during an individual's development, considerations that further muddy the picture of human cognition (H. Gardner, 1977; Jarman, 1979; Luria, 1966). And cultural experiences with any of them may also change. For instance, a contemporary child may be heavily involved with television, whereas intimacy with that medium was not possible only a few decades ago. Who dares assert that six hours in front of the television each day does not affect the kinds of information a person can handle and the way that information is handled?

STRUCTURES UNDERLYING DIVERSE MEDIA

Researchers sympathetic to the cognitive-structural position continue to look for principles of knowing that cut across diverse symbol systems. Rather than denying differences across media and across symbol systems, they have taken these as a point of departure; they have then searched for analogous principles that are necessary in each symbol system and that work in ways appropriate to that symbol system.

One of the most active researchers in this area is Patricia Greenfield (Beagles-Roos and Greenfield, 1979; Greenfield, 1978). In one study Greenfield and Schneider (1977) asked children to construct a mobile from straws that interconnect. The models contained several sections and subdivisions resembling in formal complexity such linguistic entities as sentences or narratives (see Figure 9.9). Examining the children's attempts to reproduce this model, the researchers found at work certain principles that also characterize a child's developing linguistic ability: in particular the ability to organize elements into a complex hierarchical structure (see Beagles-Roos and Greenfield, 1979) and the increasing capacity to interrupt one part of a sequence in order to turn attention to, and to complete, another. Such parallels in the construction of sentences and mobiles count, in Greenfield's view, as evidence for an "amodal organizer," which can be manifest across diverse materials. As she phrases it:

Just as the three-year-olds build isolated parts of the mobile, so do children form isolated two-word propositions when they first begin to combine words. . . . A (later) stage is the hierarchical integration of two two-word propositions into an embedded three-word sentence, similarly the hierarchical integration of parts of the mobile into a double-branched structure is the final stage in the development of our tree structure [Greenfield and Schneider, 1977, page 311].

A broader-gauged effort to discern structures underlying the diverse course of several symbol systems comes from work in which Dennie Wolf and I have been engaged (Wolf and Gardner, 1981). We have suggested that children pass through a series of "waves of symbolization" at approximately one-year intervals between the ages of one and one-half and five. Each wave consists of the emergence of a specific psychological structure, which is most noticeable in one or two symbol systems but which also has reverberations across a range of symbol systems.

According to this "wave" account, at about the age of eighteen months children become able to organize their knowledge of actions and roles into a symbolic sequence. The primary instance is found in language and pretend play (see Chapters 4 and 6), where children can say or enact "Baby sleeping" or "Mommy give cookie," but in their efforts to draw or build they also gravitate to "enactive representations," as when they "draw" a truck by animating a crayon or marker and saying "Vroom, vroom." A second wave of symbolization occurs at about the age of three. The principal novel capacity at this point involves the child's ability to capture spatial relations in a medium like drawing or clay: children can now create representations of human figures and of other simple objects. Also part of this "mapping wave" is the capacity to capture relations of relative size or distance in other media. For instance, the child can alter her voice "up" or "down" properly when singing a song or can vary speed and bodily movements appropriately when executing a dance.

A more precise and "digital" form of mapping constitutes a third wave of symbolization at about the age of four. Now the child is able to count accurately and to appreciate simple numerical relations. This capacity has widespread reverberations across symbol systems. In drawing, children now get the number of features in a face or digits in a hand correct; in singing, they can correctly reproduce rhythm and re-create pitch intervals; in stories, they can keep track of three characters and attribute to each a specific personality and set of actions.

Finally, by about the age of five or six, the child becomes able to use culturally devised symbol systems, like written language or other notations. Similarly, the child can capture an already acquired basic knowledge of symbol systems in such a "second-order" symbol system. Now the child can add to her knowledge of words (a first-order symbol) the ability to write a word down; here the written (or second-order) symbol denotes the spoken (or first-order) symbol, which in turn denotes the object or event in the world. Once this second-order symbolization has been achieved, a productive Pandora's box has been opened; symbol systems can piggyback on one another, giving rise to the most complex forms of scientific or artistic expression.

Efforts like those of Greenfield and of Wolf and Gardner seek to preserve the principal insights of the media position, while at the same time conferring as much power as possible upon psychological processes that can range across diverse materials. Whether the candidate processes they nominate can withstand careful testing across diverse materials remains to be determined.

FAITHFULNESS AND FLUIDITY IN THE YOUNG CHILD

Midst talk of media and senses and of psychological structures and processes, we risk losing track of the young child, her own powers, her own world. In fact, the child at the

threshold of school displays a number of remarkable sensitivities and capacities that we must mention before returning to her artistry.

At one extreme is the ability to be entirely faithful to the forms of experience. The most striking instance is **eidetic imagery,** a capacity that about 10 percent of children possess in strong form and perhaps a majority have in adulterated form (Haber, 1979; Haber and Haber, 1964; Leask, Haber, and Haber, 1969). Loosely speaking, eidetic imagery is photographic memory; eidetikers can continue to scan a visual display even after the display has been removed from the visual field. Though this capacity may sometimes get in a person's way, it is a clear asset in cases where the ability to retain experiences in their pristine form is important. Many children have a remarkable ability to remember their experiences in pure form, often for months or even years.

At the opposite extreme from faithful retention of experiences or symbols is the tendency to transform them. Many young children show a strong capacity for **synesthesia,** the ability or tendency to translate an experience perceived in one sense directly, and perhaps automatically, into another (Marks, 1975; Revész, 1923; Wagner et al, 1981; Werner, 1948). Preschool children often associate numerals with abstract geometric forms or letters, and specific tones or tactile sensations with specific colors and shapes. Sometimes they may make more exotic associations, as in the case of one five-year-old I knew who consistently matched letters of the alphabet to phrases on the piano (H. Gardner, 1973, 1974).

In a way synesthesia represents a transforming approach to symbols: the child apprehends an element clearly intended for one sense and translates it into another sense that is not being directly stimulated. Yet the large number of children who possess synesthesia and the surprising regularity and effortlessness with which they make associations might indicate that the connections are formed almost automatically in the mind (and perhaps also in the brain). Maybe children's perceptions are so ordered that a stimulus to one sense readily evokes sensations of an earlier experience (for example, in terms of size or contrast). Maybe synesthesia is actually closer to eidetic imagery than to transformation, more an instance of faithful retention of a stimulus than of conceptual classification or reclassification. Finally, synesthesia may represent a very special moment in the child's development between the simple fusion (or confusion) of experiences at age two or three and the literalness of adult classifications acquired at seven or eight (H. Gardner et al., 1978). The age of synesthesia—at about four or five—may be a time when the child is no longer confused but is still open to fresh associations between domains. Such domains, although not identical, do share properties of force, tension, power, openness, or harmony—like the sound "ah," a bright day, and a patriotic song.

The Creative World of the Child

In speculating about the roots of synesthesia, we touch on the most fascinating aspect of children between five and seven. Midway between infancy and adolescence, they often possess an imagination, creativity, and artistic sensitivity that younger children lack and that older children will often lose. For the most part they are graceful in body and in expression, they exhibit a sense of balance and proportion in their daily activities, they have achieved a working knowledge of different artistic symbol systems. They can give free rein to their imaginations, yet they no longer move with total abandon from reality to fantasy and back again. They greatly enjoy playing with symbols, yet they are not as uncriti-

cally and exclusively occupied with these activities as the younger playing child. Overall, they respond with an open mind and a free spirit to the rhythms, colors, tones, and phrases of life.

THE ORIGIN OF ARTISTIC INCLINATIONS

But to what extent are children in deliberate control of their artistic pursuits? The artlike activities, for example, the linguistic play of the two- or three-year-old do not seem conscious. Rather, they are an integral (perhaps even a necessary) part of coming to know the symbolic world. In contrast, the stories and drawings of an eight- or nine-year-old are clearly conscious productions. The child approaches them with intention, goals, and preferences. Older children sharply distinguish reality from pretense; they are preoccupied with producing symbols (like drawings) that are true to life; they are suspicious of the free and imaginative connections wrought by adult artists and by younger children.

But it is difficult to be certain about the creative lives of children between five and seven. Though they usually seem in command, there are times when they are so at the mercy of the situation—confused, mesmerized, excessively excited—that it seems premature to consider them full-fledged participants in the arts. And on a conscious level, the extent to which they can appreciate nuance and subtlety remains unclear (Winner and Gardner, in press). It is in their production, more than in their perceptions, that they resemble the mature artistic practitioner.

Even among so-called normal children, the penchant for artistry and imaginativeness varies significantly. Youngsters run the gamut from the straight forward and matter-of-fact child to one who is shy and stifled to those so preoccupied by real life matters that they bypass artistic inventiveness entirely.

We can identify some of the factors that predispose children to be artistic (Eisner, 1976; H. Gardner, 1973; Getzels and Csikszent-mihalyi, 1976; Malone and Beller, 1973; Singer, 1973; Wallach and Kogan, 1965). A strong intrinsic interest in one or another artistic symbol system is certainly a useful point of departure. It helps if the child comes from a supportive and reinforcing environment that offers consistent and rich opportunities. "Only" children who are frequently left to themselves are more likely to create imaginary companions than are children who have several siblings and little time to themselves. Powerful experiences and involvement with specific symbols are likely to ignite artistic expression. The child who listens to records every day and then has the misfortune to lose a treasured pet is likely to compose a song in its memory.

CREATING THE WORLD: CREATING THE SELF

Exploiting various symbol systems, media, and senses, the child between ages five and seven is busily creating. First, she creates (or re-creates) the world known by others, using the symbols, the rules, and the rituals of her culture. Later, the child creates new worlds. Employing words, pictures, and gestures, she fabricates fresh, often attractive, configurations of her own.

But in addition to fashioning products, children are also creating a self. Still showing signs of egocentrism, unable to act independently or to separate herself from others, the preschooler's self-existence is not yet truly confirmed. Between the ages of five and seven, this egocentrism has begun to wane and children are gaining distance from themselves. Their performance improves on communicative tasks; they show themselves capable of assuming the roles of other individuals (Flavell, Botkin, and Fry, 1968). They are apt to talk about themselves, their plans, fears, needs, and hopes, and they can act with greater decisiveness. At this age the child regularly looks back on her past, to "What I did when I was little." And she begins to look forward, to "The next time we go there." Such statements are not mere repetitions of what others have said; increasingly they reflect the child's own assessment of what *she* (as a person) wants of life and how *she* (as a person) thinks of herself.

There is no moment when the formation of self begins, no point when it ceases. The ability to remove oneself from one's own body, to regard oneself similarly to the way one looks at others is a perpetual process, one never stilled until death. Through words and other symbol systems, an individual creates a symbolic entity (the self) that refers to a material entity (the physical being with its attendant feelings). The various symbols devised by the culture present a range of options (roles, traits, activities) from which children must make important life choices. And their activities with different symbolic media allow children to try out a variety of roles from which they will ultimately construct a sense of self that makes sense to themselves and to others as well. Most children of this age are, to some extent, artists with words or pictures. All normal children don an artist's garb in creating their own selves.

Despite the many changes we have observed, a continuous thread extends from the first feelings of attachment and trust in infancy right through to the notions of identity so crucial during adolescence. Midway in childhood it is possible to discern both ends of this thread, for as the youngster enters school she draws on what is known and has been experienced, on a new facility with symbols, and on a special affinity with artistic creativ-

Figure 9.7. As this Nigerian youngster joins in a community dance, she can draw on the symbol systems that are intelligible within her community even as she discovers a means of expressing her own feelings.

ity in order to form the image of self that she will carry with her through the ensuing years.

Signposts

In earlier chapters of Part III, we considered specific aspects of children aged five to seven: their increasing capacity to communicate and their responses to various agents of socialization. In this chapter, we have sought to capture the broader spirit of school-age children by viewing them as young artists. And because participation in the arts requires the capacity to use symbols, we have examined how children come to use various symbols and how this capacity for symbol use in turn reshapes their world. Indeed, we noted that participation in the arts, like scientific excellence and the healthy personality, can be seen as an end-state, a goal toward which development tends.

Following a practice established in Part I, we returned to the three developing systems—making, perceiving, and feeling—but this time we examined the systems as they operate on the level of symbols. We focused in special on two domains of symbolization of particular moment for young children. First we considered the regular set of stages through which children's drawings pass—perhaps the world over—and we considered those properties of drawing skill, like the ability to create a realistic scene, that enter only later into the child's repertoire. We also noted certain strong proclivities in children's perceptions—for instance, a search for a focal point in a visual array—as well as clear deficits in detecting patterns of complexity and subtlety.

Our attention turned next to storytelling. Over time, the stories told by children increase in structural complexity and in the extent to which potent contents—like heroes and villains—are properly handled. Story grammars permit an analysis of the child's level of comprehension. Here, too, certain aspects of story meaning, such as the internal reactions of characters or the causal relations among episodes, prove difficult for young children to master. Nonetheless, when stories are stripped down to essentials, and relations among characters or episodes are made explicit, the core of a story can be understood by a four-year-old.

Similar progressions characterize other symbolic media, both those within and outside of the arts. Processes of making, perceiving and feeling are at work with symbols and symbol systems in each domain. Development at this stage features increased interactions of these systems, both within particular symbolic domains and, increasingly with age, from one symbol system to another.

But there are different kinds of symbols, different media in which the symbols appear, and different senses to which the symbols appeal. As a counterpoint to the view of symbolization as a single capacity that cuts across any setting and material, we considered an approach that emphasizes the crucial effects of *specific* symbols, media, and senses. According to this view, children do not readily apply large, all-purpose concepts encountered initially in one or another medium. Instead, whether they are mastering the diagonal or representing the human figure, children must master a series of many small skills and construct knowledge anew in each medium.

Although this "medium-specific" view provides an important corrective, symbolic competence in the end seems to reflect both general capacities (such as understanding of narrative relations or ability to handle hierarchical relations) and specific experiences (exposure to radio, use of colored markers) with the full range of symbols, media, and senses. There may in fact be waves of symbolic competence that exert effects over several symbol systems. In the end, separating out the effects of factors like symbols, media, and senses and understanding multichannel behaviors like synesthesia remain extremely challenging.

A central picture of the child between five and seven can be discerned. Having mastered the culture's symbols, the child can now combine them into imitations of existing products as well as refreshingly original creations. Certain factors predispose children to be artistic: a supportive setting wherein imaginative play is encouraged; a consistent environment offering diverse enrichment opportunities; frequent time to be alone; powerful emotional experiences; and prolonged involvement with specific symbols. Yet despite differences in inclinations, talent, and predisposing factors, the majority of children at this age can be considered true creators of an imaginative world. Their stories, drawings, and forays into singing, dance, and drama reflect a balance between procedures adopted from the culture and their own dominant ideas and emotions. And their most important creation, one that exploits their capacity to use symbols, is their sense of self, the symbolic entity that reflects the child's understanding of the individual personality inhabiting the physical being.

Equipped with the gifts of the artist, a sensitivity to the surrounding culture, an ability to communicate and conceptualize using language, a developing relation to others in their society, and a burgeoning sense of self, children of six or seven stand out from toddlers. In many ways, they have already taken the decisive step toward adulthood. And yet, in other ways, they remain unformed. Having acquired, with relatively little formal tutelage, a basic competence with a variety of symbols, the child must now become more intimately involved with the traditions and norms of society. It is time to enter school; to convert rough capacities into fluent and disciplined skills; to partake fully of the games, rituals, and serious practices of society; and to integrate individual style with the needs of the community. In Part IV we will observe the preadolescent child becoming assimilated into the larger society, going to school, developing a range of operations and skills, and becoming an increasingly effective member of various social groups.

So far—in an emphasis appropriate for a survey of developmental psychology—we have focused on traits and processes that characterize every normal child. Yet sometimes special insights can be gained by attending to populations that differ from the norm. In our next interlude we will consider one such difference, and its significance for an understanding of all children.

Another Perspective on Human Development

The importance of these cases [of infantile autism] to the development of a science of psychology would seem to be vastly beyond what their relatively rare occurrence in the general population would suggest.

–SEYMOUR SARASON AND
THOMAS GLADWIN

The great variety of human environments, as manifested in several thousand cultures, each with its own language, provides the best evidence that human beings can develop in a number of ways. The profound differences in values, life-style, and tempo between wandering nomads in the plains of Arabia, Eskimo seal trappers in the Arctic zones, urban dwellers in overpopulated Tokyo, and cattle ranchers in the American West are difficult to grasp, let alone to explain in a satisfactory way. A psychology that purports to explain the behaviors, feelings, and thoughts of these diverse citizens of the world confronts a difficult task.

Despite these vast differences, some principles of development seem applicable across diverse populations. Most of what is known about individual physical development confirms the essential identity of all human beings, which overwhelms the tiny racial differences that have been reported (Lewontin, 1970). When it comes to the realms of intellectual and emotional development and social growth, the issues are more vexing and the results far from conclusive. Yet certainly this book, if not the entire field of developmental psychology, exists because of the faith that there exist interesting characterizations applicable to all growing human beings.

Or, perhaps, nearly all. Owing to the ravages of disease, to highly unstable or hostile environments, or to genetic abnormalities, some children are destined to be very different from their peers. In some cases these differences are reversible, in others not. Some of the disorders are primarily emotional, others are social, and still others affect all or some of the child's thinking skills.

It is important to understand these disorders. On a theoretical level we need to determine whether deviations can be explained within the compass of the theories developed primarily to explain the growth of the normal majority, or whether more comprehensive or even wholly new theories are required. On a practical level, procedures to help those children—in many cases coming from families close to our own—may well depend upon a superior understanding of what has gone wrong with them and what may still remain "right."

Books could be (and have been) written on every major disorder known to plague human development. Any effort to summarize findings from all these domains would take many pages. Here we will concentrate on an especially bizarre condition called *infantile autism,* which has fascinated many observers. Besides offering a crucial perspective on some key issues of normal development, our study of infantile autism will also allow us to examine central themes in the study of exceptional children. We will encounter the question of whether autism is primarily biological or psychological in origin, and we will examine different views on how it should be treated. We will offer a contrasting view of another disorder, *anorexia nervosa,* which primarily affects adolescent girls. At the end we will view these issues more broadly through other lenses on development.

The Controversy over Infantile Autism

LEO KANNER'S ORIGINAL DESCRIPTION

Autism was identified as a distinct behavioral disturbance only in the 1940s, when Leo Kanner (1943, 1944) defined the basic characteristics of the disorder. The first case he described was a preschooler, Paul G. The history provided by Paul's mother indicated that he had had a normal birth and, except for a great deal of vomiting during his first months (possibly a sign of some physiological abnormality), had passed smoothly through the milestones of the first year. He was a slender, healthy-looking, and attractive child whose face looked intelligent and alive. But his behavior had become increasingly unusual.

As soon as Paul entered a room, he began to play appropriately with physical materials, and he was extremely dexterous. He would describe what he was doing with the objects, saying, for instance, "Cutting paper" or "The engine is flying." He also spoke phrases whose meaning was unclear. But he would seldom respond when someone spoke to him, proceeding instead as if nothing had happened. None of his remarks bore any apparent communicative value. He was indifferent to others, no matter how they treated him. And even when he allowed them to lead or dress him, he paid no attention at all.

For a noncommunicator Paul had a surprisingly rich vocabulary. His linguistic syntax was satisfactory, except that—most intriguingly—he never uttered the pronouns *I* or *me* and he never referred to himself as Paul. Instead he compulsively repeated just what others said to him, invariably retaining the word *you* used by others in addressing comments to him. He knew and repeated many songs, nursery rhymes, and other passages, but again without communicative intent or value. He was able to count and to name colors, two bits of evidence that proved he was not feebleminded. Often he would run in circles, repeating phrases ecstatically. But when interrupted he would break out into a vicious temper tantrum.

Another case described by Kanner was four-year-old Charles N. As an infant he had been slow and inactive, and, rather than creeping first, he simply stood up and walked one day shortly after his first birthday. Otherwise, he had passed normally through the developmental milestones.

Charles's vocabulary was ample, but like Paul he always avoided the first-person pronouns *I* or *me*. In fact, nearly all that he said involved repetition or echoing. Charles's musical abilities were astonishing. At one and one-half he was able to distinguish among eighteen symphonies and to identify the composer by name as soon as the first movement began. Although uncooperative when tested, he gave clear indications of his intellectual competence. And he was very agile with his hands, able to investigate skillfully a variety of objects. Yet, like Paul, Charles remained completely remote from other individuals. He might mimic a voice or sing, but otherwise he would avoid all involvement with others.

Kanner described sixteen boys and four girls, each of whom displayed highly similar symptoms. Thirteen of the twenty children could speak, but they did not use language to convey meanings. Instead, most of what they said featured parrotlike repetition of what they heard, including personal pronouns. Because of their excellent rote memories for poems, songs, lists of presidents, and so on, the children often appeared initially to be prodigies.

A striking feature was the children's obsessive distaste for the slightest change in their environment or routine. Only they themselves could make alterations. Proof of their extraordinary memories was the accuracy with which they could detect even the minutest change in a familiar pattern, for example, the relocation of a flowerpot. Their uniformly accomplished skills with inanimate objects underscored their perceptual acuity and suggested a desire to exhibit mastery in at least one domain of experience.

In total contrast was the incompetence of the youngsters in interpersonal relations. Playing alone, the children looked placid, almost sublimely happy, and they often accompanied themselves with monotonous humming and singing. But in the company of others, they became serious, anxious, tense, even terrified. Conversations simply did not occur. Adults and other children were always spurned in favor of objects, and the children never looked at an adult's face. Only if something was changed against their will did the children struggle and become angry. Even then, they did not address the offender, and they became placid again as soon as the wanted object or situation was introduced.

Kanner noted another remarkable facet: Very few of the parents could be described as loving or warmhearted. Even the fairly happy marriages were cold, rather formal relationships. Yet the parents were also highly intelligent and skilled. Among parents or close relatives of autistic children were numerous physicians, scientists, writers, journalists, artists, and critics. Indeed, nine of the twenty families were listed in *Who's Who in America* or in a companion volume called *American Men of Science.*

Kanner's reports were immediately recognized by others who had seen the same symptoms, and they were soon adding their cases to the records. Although Kanner resisted suggesting causes of the disease he called **infantile autism,** a general interpretation of the disorder shortly gained widespread acceptance. Clinicians influenced by the psychoanalytic or personality psychology traditions tended to attribute autism to the unusual surroundings in the child's home and to atypical behavior on the part of the parents, particularly the mother. For instance, Margaret Mahler (1965) speculated that autistic children had not developed clear perceptions of their mother and therefore remained unresponsive to her. Being distant from their mother meant that the children did not form a sense of themselves as distinct from other persons or other objects. Still, the mother remained an important figure and controller of resources. And so, in a state of panic over the threat of separation from her, the children remained at (or regressed to) a state of being psychologically "one" with the mother, and never became capable of separate, voluntary action in the world. Mahler linked this pathological condition to repeated interpersonal traumas, such as extreme overstimulation by the mother followed by actual or perceived abandonment.

BERNARD RIMLAND'S BIOLOGICAL ARGUMENT

In the early 1960's, twenty years after its initial discovery, infantile autism was widely believed to be traceable to forces in the children's households. However, the psychologist Bernard Rimland (1964, 1972, 1975) argued very strongly and persuasively that infantile autism should be seen as a congenital or inherited personality disorder rooted within the baby, *not* as the result of parents' behaviors. In his view, autism is the product of a highly abnormal nervous system.

Evidence for Rimland's Position. To support his view, Rimland emphasizes the striking similarity among most reported cases of autism. For instance, during the first year of life autistic children display repetitive and ritualistic behavior such as rocking. Their isolated existence is marked by surprising cognitive strength but complete failure in verbal communication with others. Autistic children are uniformly uninterested in people and correspondingly preoccupied with objects. Their parents are usually highly intellectual and accomplished individuals.

Besides the dramatically regular and predictable pattern of symptoms, Rimland cites other evidence that autism is a biological condition. Autistic children seem to be behaviorally abnormal within weeks after birth, so that any parental influences would have to occur in the womb or immediately in the postnatal period. The symptoms are highly unique and specific, a state of affairs rarely encountered in psychologically based disorders. Such a symptom picture typically reflects injury in a particular center or centers in the brain. Psychological factors would be more likely to result in a scattered pattern of behaviors, including ones frequently encountered in otherwise normal persons. Socially based disorders usually show up in degrees of severity between normal and extreme, but infantile autism features no such gradations.

Evidence about the families of autistic children also favors Rimland's biological interpretation. Siblings of autistic children are almost always normal, a fact difficult to explain if parental behavioral patterns and interpersonal relations have caused the damage. There are three or four times as many autistic boys as girls, a ratio typifying many disorders thought to be of neurological origin, such as stuttering or the reading difficulty called dyslexia. And, finally, while nearly all fraternal twins in the autistic literature include one normal child, almost all autistic twins are identical twins (*New York Times,* April 24, 1977). Because identical twins have precisely the same genetic constitution and would presumably exhibit the same neurological disturbances, this fact strongly supports a genetic determination of infantile autism.

Speculation and Controversy. Having argued on these and other grounds for the biological basis of autism, Rimland speculates about its specific cause. In his view autistic children are unable to relate new stimuli to remembered experience; therefore, they can neither understand relations nor deal in abstractions. Moreover, because they cannot understand relations, they cannot gain pleasure from a repeated relation to their mother. And just as they have no deep affection for the individual(s) to whom they should be closest, they are also not aware of a similarity between themselves and others.

Though recognizing certain forms of intelligence in autistic children, Rimland speculates that a deficiency in their brains makes them unable to use their skills meaningfully and renders them unaware of the feelings of others. In Rimland's phrase autistic children have a "high-fidelity transmission" to their brain storage areas, which results in highly specific responses (including phenomenal memory, perception, reading) but very few nonspecific relations. Forewarnings of their own atypical brain structure can be seen in the youngsters' intelligent parents; these individuals are often introverted, superbly able to inhibit emotions, and capable of highly critical analysis. The very cerebral specialization that gives the parents excellent scientific and analytic abilities may paradoxically leave

Joey, one of the autistic children with whom Bruno Bettelheim worked, thought of himself as a human machine. Over the course of his treatment he produced numerous drawings that exemplified this mechanical feeling. In this self-portrait, the body has no substance but is formed of electrical wires.

their children vulnerable to an inability to perceive any relations among elements.

Rimland's work has been well received and is highly influential. Many observers who once embraced a psychological interpretation of autism now believe that the biological or neurological approach must be taken seriously. Evidence from a number of laboratories suggests that the brains of autistic children, and in particular their cerebral lateralization, may be deviant. Rimland skillfully related a mass of previously isolated findings and assembled a set of arguments to support the biological position. At the same time his analysis also casts light on the relation of autism to other psychoses and on the general way in which the brain processes and interprets experience.

Yet Rimland's biological argument has also engendered controversy. A number of individuals from a psychodynamic background have not been convinced by his arguments and have questioned the reliability and consistency of his data. Even those in agreement concede that Rimland has amassed neither critical biological evidence nor a satisfactory biological explanation of this enigmatic condition.

By far the most vocal opponent of Rimland is the Austrian-born psychoanalyst Bruno Bettelheim. Bettelheim (1967, 1974) has devoted a large part of his clinical practice to treating a condition that he considers to be autism and has for many years headed an institution devoted to such treatment. According to Bettelheim, normal development requires that children initiate schemes of all sorts and that these schemes will elicit responses from other persons. Autism begins, in his view, when children realize, unconsciously, that their actions and interactions with other persons are ineffective, if not disastrous. The circumstances that prompt an autistic reaction may occur during any one of several periods: in the first months of life, when children should be establishing a bond with their mother; during the next period when, already knowing their mother, they should be undergoing stranger anxiety; or during the second year, when children can physically enter into relations with or actively withdraw from, others.

Bettelheim concedes that some children may be predisposed to autism because of innate oversensitivity or fragility. But he maintains that events after birth—the interactions with parents in particular—will determine which of the children with autistic tendencies will become autistic and which will not. Bettelheim holds the parents responsible even when abnormal behavior occurs in the first months of life. The child receives signs from the parents that they do not want and do not love their child. In such cases a highly sensitive and intelligent infant notices and responds precociously to the parents' hostility, thereby embarking on the fatal course to autism.

To bolster his argument, Bettelheim cites a number of factors. First, he indicates that an abnormal nervous system does not in itself prove that autism is biologically caused. The damage may actually have been caused by the noxious environment. Second, certain features of autism prove difficult to explain in terms of a biological argument—for example, the fact that children will readily repeat "You want milk" but not "I want milk," perhaps changing it to "You want milk."

Bettelheim also draws heavily on experiments and theories in developmental psychology. He analogizes autistic youngsters to Harlow's deprived monkeys, whose desperate state has been demonstrably caused by an uncaring mother (see Chapter 1). And he compares the hapless children to other casualties of Erik Erikson's first stage of development—youngsters who lack basic trust and therefore completely reject the world (also see Chapter 1). Finally, and most passionately, Bettelheim indicates that autistic children can recover, especially after being removed from their damaging parental environment and placed instead in a supportive environment. He considers this recovery pattern as evidence against the biological position.

Despite Bettelheim's impassioned defense of the "psychogenic" origins of autism, the majority of experts now believe that autism is primarily caused by a biological factor, perhaps genetic, perhaps neurological (Ornitz, 1978; Rutter, 1974; Rutter and Schopler, 1978). The principal lines of evidence lending credence to the biological account are the uniqueness of the condition, the data on the identical twins, and the accumulating evidence on brain abnormalities in autistic children. Researchers now believe that the "specialness" of the autistic family has been overemphasized in the past and that it may be a reaction to, rather than the cause of, autism. Some experts believe that the children described by Bettelheim are actually schizophrenic rather than autistic. Still others believe that his cases may be biologically based autistic children who nonetheless benefit from a highly structured and highly caring environment. The fact that something is caused by biological factors does not, of course, mean that it is insusceptible to therapy.

An interactionist approach to autism can be instructive (J. C. Schwartz, 1979). It may well be that autism is induced by biological factors, that is not in any sense the parents' fault, but that the ultimate fate of the autistic child still depends on the quality of his environment. John Bowlby suggests that "autism has a very big organic [biological] component . . . but for the autistic child, development turns enormously on whether the child has a good relationship with the mothering figure. In fact, you could argue that the more damaged the child, the more important these things are" (Evans, 1977, p.7).

TREATMENT FOR AUTISM

Even if his ultimate explanation of autism proves to be flawed, Bettelheim has taught us much about the factors that can aid such children. His deep convictions about the condition stem from his own experiences working intensely with autistic children for many years. He and his staff at the Orthogenic School in Chicago have devised a "total milieu" in which autistic children abandoned as hopeless by other clinicians can be treated (Bettelheim, 1974). Every feature of the child's environment is carefully chosen (color and shape of furniture, types of art objects, arrangement of rooms). No child, however ill, is admitted unless she wants to come. The staff makes every effort to establish (or reestablish) feelings of trust and confidence in the child. The staff is available to patients day and night, and members meet regularly to discuss and "work through" their own feelings.

Bettelheim concedes that this "superadequate" environment has helped some children very little, even after years of therapy. Still, as a result of months spent in the extrasecure and extraloving environment, many of Bettelheim's patients have been helped a great deal, often to the extent that they can return to their homes and lead healthy and full lives.

Bettelheim sees autistic children as in need of a sense of self, one that can begin to emerge only after the children begin to interact with other persons. As the therapy begins to take effect, they dare to look at others, thereby affirming for the first time that other individuals exist. They show feelings of hope; they begin to use pronouns correctly. They start to behave as if their relations to others have consequences, as if they can achieve wishes and goals. This awakening generally occurs at first with reference to the individual whose role most resembles the mother's.

Behavior Modification. Ivar Lovaas (1971, 1974, 1977), an expert in behavior modification, has focused on the skills lacking in autistic children. In proper behaviorist fashion, Lovaas has skirted the controversial question of the causes of autism and concentrated instead on modifying abnormal behaviors by regular use of aversive conditioning methods. Rather than merely reinforcing or shaping a child's desired activity, Lovaas in a more directive fashion punishes the child for undesirable behavior.

Lovaas describes a girl whose behavior was self-mutilative; for instance, she would hit her head against steel cabinets. Most parents and therapists would normally react to this behavior by rushing to calm the child, thereby reinforcing this behavior. Lovaas rejects this natural impulse and instead favors striking the child, hard, each time the behavior occurs—indeed, such severe punishment eventually extinguishes the behavior altogether. In Lovaas's words, "We sort of specialized in treating self-mutilative kids. We took in some of the worst cases that the state hospitals could provide. We used electric shock and spanking as punishment. The procedure was simple—we just set up a contingent punishment for self-mutilative behavior" (1974, p. 79).

Lovaas's approach can also bring about desirable cognitive behaviors. For instance, in training mute children to speak, the Lovaas team use discrimination procedures to evoke vocal imitation. At first, children are positively reinforced for all sounds; then only for imitating what the adult says; then for producing sounds that have not been previously presented. The next goal is to bring the children to view their own verbal behavior as self-reinforcing. And a final step is to prompt children to speak appropriately in diverse situations and to say things other than those that have been specifically taught. Although success at getting children to produce some sounds is far greater than success at obtaining meaningful language, breakthroughs have been reported even in this latter, most difficult endeavor (S. L. Harris, 1975; Lovaas et al., 1966; Prizant, 1978). But genuinely spontaneous language and activity have continued to elude the Lovaas team (1977).

Clearly, Lovaas's approach to rehabilitation differs drastically from Bettelheim's. Whereas Bettelheim focuses on changing the overall environment of the child and on developing strong interpersonal bonds, Lovaas is concerned chiefly with altering specific behaviors—eliminating undesirable operants and shaping desirable ones—and will use standard conditioning means to secure these ends. Not surprisingly, the two clinicians do not see eye-to-eye; in fact, they have openly criticized each other (Bettelheim, 1967; Lovaas, 1974). Yet those of us who have less stake in the dispute can note certain parallels in their positions: each clinician believes in a highly structured environment (though the manner of structuring differs); each surrounds himself with a staff that is totally committed to the mode of treatment. Perhaps clinical work with autistic youngsters dictates therapeutic procedures more strongly than it constrains theoretical persuasions.

A Contrasting Syndrome: Anorexia Nervosa

The controversy over the origins of infantile autism and over its proper treatment has not yet been resolved. Yet the importance of autism for an understanding of human development can readily be seen. We are reminded of the central role assumed by qualities like trust and the sense of self when we learn of autistic children who lack them completely. We note how curiously disembodied are capacities like reading, speaking, or counting, when they are practiced by an individual who does not appreciate their significance. And we see the power of environmental factors when we learn that a severely disturbed individual can be brought much closer to the norm through the rigorous application of a therapeutic technique. To the extent that biological factors contribute to autism, we are reminded of the pivotal consequences for behavior of neurological structures. In a parallel fashion, to the extent that interpersonal factors are at work, we are reawakened to the importance of relations between children and their caretakers.

But, as we noted at the start of this chapter, infantile autism is by no means the only perspective from which to evaluate standard accounts of child development. It is instructive to consider, as a contrasting case, another highly unusual disorder, called **anorexia nervosa.** Whereas autism occurs in early life and affects primarily males, anorexia nervosa (anorexia for short) occurs typically in adolescence and affects females much more often than males (estimates indicate that from 90 to 95 percent of the anorexic population is female). It is particularly common in girls from privileged backgrounds: indeed, one British study documents ten times as great an incidence among private school girls as among a comparable public school population (Bruch, 1978*a*).

The primary symptom of anorexia nervosa is a refusal to eat, followed by a decrease in weight that may be so extreme that the youth starves, or threatens to starve, to death. Anorexic youths go to great lengths to deny this behavior, insisting that they are normal in weight or perhaps even slightly on the chubby side. Asked to estimate the size of animate and inanimate objects, they show a selective tendency to overestimate the size of their own bodies (Slade and Russell, 1973). Curiously, they display great interest in cooking and other food-related themes. Yet at the same time, they will hardly nibble at foods, will often induce vomiting in themselves after they eat, and will engage in exercise to the point of exhaustion, all in an apparent (if unconscious) effort to keep their weight as low as possible.

Like infantile autism, anorexia has long been viewed in psychodynamic terms (Bruch, 1978a, b). More recently, increasing attention has been paid to some of the metabolic changes that accompany (or perhaps help to precipitate) anorexia (Halmi, 1978), and there are even suggestions of abnormal brain structure, at least in the males who suffer from the disorder (Nussbaum et al., 1980). Still, the pendulum has not swung so far as to indicate that anorexia is caused by genetic or neurological factors. Instead, most experts feel that the origins of anorexia, at least for the classical female patient, lie in a particular family constellation: accordingly, therapeutic attempts must build upon this basis.

According to Hilda Bruch, one of the leading analysts of anorexia, the anorexic child is characteristically favored by her parents; often she is considered to be perfect. The parental marriage is ostensibly a happy one, but often there is underlying discord: parents use the child as a means of securing that affirmation and affection which they do not get from their spouse.

Being treated as if one is perfect and having to serve as a substitute love object for both one's parents places great stress on the child. She comes to feel that she is not in control of her own life and that she cannot possibly live up to the expectations of others. Then, often precipitated by a relatively minor crisis during adolescence, the youth begins to engage in the food-related behaviors and rituals that culminate in an anorexic condition. Along with other experts, Bruch sees this behavior as a desperate attempt on the girl's part to gain control over some area of her life, to show that she can achieve at least one form of perfection—having the body size and shape of her choice. Clearly, there is also a desire to avoid growing up and achieving mature sexuality, to avoid having to face the world, to risk revealing one's own inefficacy. The anorexic youngster receives certain immediate rewards; in fact, menstruation ceases. Moreover, the tables are turned elsewhere: the child is no longer regarded as perfect, parents are greatly agitated, and the girl has exerted control (at last) in one area of her life.

The regular set of bizarre symptoms that constitute anorexia reminds one of autism—a readily recognized syndrome. And, like autism, it responds best to a therapeutic intervention in which the whole milieu of the child is involved. The child must first be made cognizant of the extremely self-destructive behavior in which she is engaged; she must be made to understand that if she does not eat, she will certainly die. At the same time, however, her own feelings of self-adequacy and efficacy need to be confronted and, whenever and however possible, bolstered. The tensions and conflicts within the family may have been precipitating, or at least contributing, factors and they must also be confronted. If each of these elements in the equation falls into place, chances of a cure rise. Unfortunately, however, many anorexic youths starve to death.

At present, then, anorexia is considered a disorder with primarily psychodynamic origins, though one that may well have definite physiological concomitants. Its cure is still approached primarily through psychiatric means. Whether a more biologically based explanation may at some time be forthcoming cannot yet be anticipated.

Conclusion: Other Lenses on Development

Autism and anorexia nervosa are remarkable and highly unusual conditions. For that very reason they throw out in sharp relief some of the most basic issues of human development, such as the need for trust and the importance of self-control. Researchers have also gained insights into the human condition through the study of different and less astonishing populations. One can study emotionally disturbed children with neuroses (like a fear of death) and psychoses (like schizophrenia) to gain further insight into children's affective life. Or one can look at behavioral disorders such as hyperactivity (see Chapter 11). One may examine extremes in intellectual ability— retarded children who have few mental skills and prodigies who are gifted in several areas—for fresh insights into cognition (Feldman, 1980). These examples help us discover how skills are acquired as well as the extent to which cultural factors (such as the society's attitude toward various gifts) fix the level of a child's ultimate achievement. **Idiot savants,** individuals of overall modest ability who excel in one isolated area like mathematics, and children with specific learning disabilities who are otherwise normal or even gifted may illuminate a single

Some youngsters exhibit striking excellence in one isolated area. One such child created drawings reminiscent of mature artists. This impressive self-portrait was done at age ten.

disturbed or spared ability and its relation to others. And one may use observation as well as experiment in different cultural settings to see whether and how different forms of socialization (such as the commune or the kibbutz) influence children's affective and cognitive lives. Only such comparisons can reveal whether children the world over feel and reason in the same way despite the diverse circumstances and environments in which they grow.

These perspectives touch on some of the same issues that came up in the cases of autism and anorexia. There is, first, constant debate about the relative contributions of biological (including genetic) as against psychological factors. Nonetheless, some conditions (such as mental retardation) are widely regarded as the result of biological factors (see Table 3.2), whereas others (including many neuroses) are generally deemed the result of psychological or interpersonal conditions.

The universal language of drawings has proved of special importance in comparisons among groups of children. In general, scholars
have been impressed by the parallels among children's drawings the
world over. Thus, the scribbles by a Nepalese boy (bottom), who
had never before used paper or crayons, strongly resemble those
found in American nursery schools. By the same token, the top left
drawing, made by a ten-year-old living in an orphanage in Taiwan,
shares features with drawings found in classrooms in Western countries. On the other hand, drawings can also signal special difficulties
or pathologies. The top right drawing of "a baby drinking the
mother's milk from the breast," produced by a young schizophrenic
girl, has been interpreted as reflecting her desire to "incorporate"
her mother and to assume the dual role of mother and infant.

Contrasting cases of clear biological and psychological causa-
tion can help in assessing the relative role of these factors in
normal development, as well as in controversial conditions like
autism.

Second, one repeatedly encounters tension over the optimal
treatment for the disadvantaged or the diseased. There are
those predisposed toward psychodynamic methods directed at

the whole person, whereas others favor behavioral methods directed specifically at encouraging desirable and eliminating undesirable actions. Here, too, treatment seems fairly clear-cut in some cases: the severely retarded respond well to behavioral techniques, whereas complex personality disorders like the adolescent identity crisis are more suited to a psychodynamic approach. Some conditions, like autism, may be susceptible to both forms of intervention.

We have seen how findings from diverse populations can illuminate specific claims about normal development. But we should also note how the developmental perspective can contribute to the study of these different populations. Erikson's conception of the crisis of trust in infancy contributed to Bettelheim's view of autism. By the same token, behaviorist theory was crucial to Lovaas's efforts to train autistic children. In these cases and in many others, developmental insights have helped other specialists better understand phenomena within their own area. Moreover, unusual conditions pose a difficult but crucial challenge to scholars of human development. Unless they can provide a coherent account of the disorder or condition in question, they cannot claim to have a comprehensive position. For these reasons, the developmental tradition and the study of extreme situations and populations illuminate each other.

PART IV

Middle
Childhood

Middle childhood—the period of primary school—is marked by active mental development. Children become capable of what Piaget calls concrete operations. They can represent physical states mentally and then reverse them. They can appreciate that physical properties, like quantity, remain constant despite differences in appearance. More generally, they become increasingly skillful at adopting the perspective of another individual, understanding how various actions on objects are related to one another, and processing information with speed and precision.

Other cognitive skills prove particularly vital in mastering the lessons of school. The capacities to use language, to classify consistently, and to remember, though present earlier in life, are affected critically by the attainment of operational thought. How and where these capacities are used will vary widely across societies. And formal schooling will profoundly affect the way children use their intellect.

Although middle childhood is a time of relative emotional calm, it is also a period of significant social growth. Children are forming enduring relations with their peers and with a variety of institutions (like schools and clubs) within their society. And they pass through predictable sequences as they relate to peers, interact with authority figures, learn about the principles that regulate society, and develop a more sophisticated notion of the self—its goals, its fears, its motivations. The child is indeed a skill builder, not only in the cognitive realm but also in interactions with, and understandings of, the social world.

CHAPTER TEN

The Intellectual Revolution of Middle Childhood

A child's thinking becomes logical only through the organization of systems of operations.

   –JEAN PIAGET

Ode to a Nonconserver

If one is not enough for you,
Cut it in half
And then you'll have two!
  –EVE MENDELSOHN

To survive in society an individual must understand something about the nature of quantity. Imagine the consequences if we thought that the value of our coins increased when we had spread them out on a table instead of keeping them in a neat pile; or if we thought a pie cut into eight pieces was more food than an identical pie cut into only four pieces. That the amount of money or the amount of pie remains the same in both cases is a fact we know well. But have we always?

What may well be the most famous experiment in developmental psychology speaks directly to this question. It was first described around 1940 by Jean Piaget and his longtime collaborator Bärbel Inhelder. In one variation of the experiment (Piaget, 1965*b*), a child is presented with two identical beakers, both containing the same quantity of a liquid like water. After the child has acknowledged that both containers indeed possess the "same amount," the experimenter pours the contents of one beaker into a third "test" beaker that is taller and thinner than either of the "standard" beakers. The water, of course, rises to a higher level in the test beaker. Then the crucial question is posed: "Does this [test] beaker contain as much water as the untouched [standard] beaker, does it contain more water, or does it contain less?"

Piaget and Inhelder were interested in whether the child would appreciate that the test and standard beakers still contained the same amount of water. To use their terms, would children **conserve continuous** (non-discrete) **quantities** like liquids; would they appreciate that the amount of liquid remains constant? They also wanted to know the child's *reasons* for answering one way or the other. Through scrupulous and careful discussion with the child, Piaget and Inhelder uncovered a pattern of reasoning that has since been confirmed by scores of investigators.

Three- and four-year-olds commonly believe that the total amount of liquid has changed. Attending to only one dimension of the display, they will say, "There's more because it's higher" or "There's more because

the glass is bigger" or "There's less because it was fuller before." The child's assessment seems determined completely by appearance and does not change even when the experimenter points out that no liquid was added or taken away or demonstrates that the amount is the same by pouring the liquid back into its original container.

Children who are five or six have only partially mastered conservation and give ambiguous responses such as, "It looks like there's more but there might not be." They may conserve only when the difference in appearance is minimal or they may correctly predict that "if you pour the water it will still remain the same amount," yet chose the taller beaker when actually observing the seductive visual difference. They may conserve if the water is poured into one test container but lapse to nonconservation if it is further subdivided into a number of smaller containers.

Children at this intermediate stage become

Figure 10.1. A child on the threshold of concrete operations participates in a conservation of liquids task. Notice his careful attention as the contents of the two standard beakers are first equated in amount. The liquid from one standard beaker is then transferred into a taller but thinner test beaker, and he is then asked to indicate whether the water in the test beaker equals that in the remaining standard beaker.

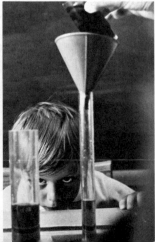

marginally aware that one must attend to two dimensions: width *and* height of a beaker. The child is likely to say of the second beaker, "It's taller but it's also thinner." This insight is crucial: for the first time, the child is exploring the relation between dimensions, rather than attending only to one dimension. A fully developed sense of conservation, however, will only emerge once the child understands that the change in one dimension is compensated for *exactly* by the corresponding change in the other dimension.

This full-fledged conservation ordinarily appears during the third stage, when children are seven or eight years old. Although they are now certain that the amount of liquid has not changed, children offer different reasons. Some stress the **compensation** aspect ("The liquid is higher but it's also thinner: one makes up for the other"). Some emphasize the **identity** across events ("The liquids were equal in the beginning and you didn't add anything or take anything away"). And some focus on **reversibility**—the potential return to the original state ("You could pour it back into the first beaker, and that will show that they were the same all along").

Two further features characterize those children who have mastered conservation. First, when questioned they will offer the whole series of arguments—not just one. In Piaget's phrase, they show understanding of a structured whole, they appreciate all the logical interrelations among the factors of compensation, identify, and reversibility. And second, they will insist on conservation as a logical necessity ("I didn't even have to watch the pouring; as long as I know that you are just pouring, I know that the liquid *cannot* change in amount"). By this time, conservation is resulting from a logical deduction. Empirical observation provides at most a double check that the experimenter has performed no magic.

Piaget's Concrete Operations

Piaget's demonstration is deservedly famous and has inspired hundreds of related studies. The experiment is readily duplicated but at the same time open to numerous explanations; language, mental operations, experience in the real world, and explicit training have all been cited as forces that convert nonconservers into conservers. But perhaps the chief reason for the experiment's long-standing popularity is the central role it occupied in Piaget's own world view. He considered conservation to be crucial and conceded that after thirty years he still did not understand it completely.

To understand Piaget's preoccupation, we must return to his ideas about cognition and his interest in the most basic concepts—time, space, causality, number. As we saw in Chapter 2, infants during the sensorimotor period achieve an initial understanding of these building blocks of human thought, but this understanding extends only to practical knowledge. Children show, through suitable actions and appropriate expectations, that they understand certain physical regularities, but they have no other way to present or represent this knowledge.

After the age of two, during the symbolic or preoperational stage, children learn to represent aspects of their practical knowledge by using symbols. By the time they begin school, children are able to talk about objects, draw them, enact events in symbolic play, tell stories, and assemble three-dimensional constructions. As noted in Chapter 7, they become able to use language to direct their behavior; and they acquire further practical knowledge of the world through observation, imitation, and, above all else, continuous action upon the world of objects.

What five-year-olds lack, according to Piaget, is the intellectual glue with which to join these schemes of knowledge into accurate and unified systems of symbolization and representation. Although they know that one dons boots when it is snowing, they may, nonetheless, claim, "It is snowing because I have my boots on." Individual states of knowledge exist but remain isolated from one another. Children may pour liquids back and forth all the time, but they do not yet mentally represent the logical relations among transformations of this sort. And so, in the conservation task, they cannot readily appreciate the identity between initial and final states, nor the way that decreased width compensates for increased height.

The cognitive challenge facing the five- or six-year-old is to combine these scattered schemes (like identity, reversibility, and compensation) into a structured whole, and to devise mental representations that adequately reflect possible actions and transactions in the physical world. Piaget termed this phase of development **concrete operations. Operations** are those internal mental actions—those schemes carried out in one's head—by which one gains fuller understanding of diverse conceptual realms. These operations are concrete because they are imposed on physical stuff of everyday life like liquids, pies, or pieces of clay, rather than on more abstract matter like words or mathematical symbols (see Figure 10.2). (Operations imposed on more abstract elements are called **formal operations.** We shall consider these highest-level operations in our discussion of adolescent thought in Chapter 13.)

Seven- or eight-year-olds arrive at a correct understanding of conservation because, using a reversing operation, they can mentally pour the contents of the test beaker back into the standard one. They also appreciate that the (potential) action of making the liquid higher is exactly equivalent to the (potential) action of reducing its width. Neither under-

Figure 10.2. Concrete operations are not simply mental abilities useful in solving Piagetian tasks. Only the child who appreciates conservation of number and other principles of measurement can accurately carry out a program of woodworking.

standing can be achieved simply by observing the physical properties of the display. If anything, the perceived array is likely to encourage an incorrect response. Only by looking *through* the displays, by focusing instead on the actions that have actually given rise to present appearances and that can likewise undo them, can the child ferret out the crucial aspects of conservation.

Piaget (1970) believed that during middle childhood the child draws on operations such as compensation, reversibility, and identity to understand the nature of concrete phenomena—not only continuous quantities (like liquids) but also discontinuous quantities (like separate elements in an array) as well as aspects of time, space, and causality. Thus, several conceptual breakthroughs that seem to reflect an underlying set of structures coalesce during middle childhood. Even as the schemes of sensorimotor knowledge were inextricably related during the opening years of life, these unfolding cognitive domains are also intertwined and mutually dependent during the early school years. In exploring conservation, we are charting not an isolated island but the mainland of the child's intellectual life.

An intellectual revolution during middle childhood is an attractive conception that unifies various domains of knowledge. But, as in other realms we have reviewed, research conducted in the wake of Piaget's initial demonstrations has yielded a more complex picture of development, one that is more gradual and less highly integrated than he asserted. In the case of conservation of quantity, and also in such other areas as the child's conception of space and of causality, evidence for understanding of the basic conceptions can be found at an earlier age than Piaget had thought, and the interrelations across domains are less impressive than Piaget claimed (Brainerd, 1978b).

Reactions to Piaget's assertions about concrete operations have accordingly been mixed. Some researchers feel that the basic Piagetian assertions are worth preserving, others feel that the intellectual events of middle childhood are better explained by traditional non-Piagetian accounts, and still other researchers have attempted to suggest a new synthesis, one appropriate to a post-Piagetian era. Some researchers focus on the reasons for naturally occurring changes, while others address the effects of training. In what follows we will review these various perspectives. Finally, having considered the accumulated knowledge about the developmental course of these scientific-logical concepts, we will introduce certain areas that have been relatively neglected by Piaget, including language, memory, and other forms of cognition to be examined more directly in Chapter 11.

CAN CONSERVATION BE TRAINED?

Once conservation had been established as a phenomenon, scientists' curiosity was piqued rather than satisfied. Researchers began to ask why conservation could not be found among preschoolers and whether conservation and other concrete operations could be taught.

Initial attempts to speed up the emergence of concrete operations were mostly unsuccessful (Elkind and Flavell, 1969; S. A. Miller, 1976; Sigel and Hooper, 1968). When they did succeed, the child would either relapse into nonconserving after a few weeks or fail to transfer the ability to a different material or another form of conservation. The first round of experimentation thus suggested that conservation could not be coaxed out; one simply had to await its appearance.

By the mid-sixties, increasing evidence had accumulated that conservation was at least somewhat malleable. In an influential series of experiments, Jerome Bruner varied the classic conservation studies by screening the beakers from view while the pouring took place. While the screen remained in place, the children were asked whether there was still the same amount of water. In general, the children offered conservation-style answers, maintaining that the amount was preserved because nothing had been added or taken away. And their precocious responses persisted even when the test beaker looked quite different from the initial beaker. Children at the threshold of conservation (ages five to seven) were particularly likely to provide conservation responses and to persist even after the screen had been removed. As one child asserted, "Well, it looks like more to drink, but it is only the same, because it's the same water and it was only poured from there to there" (Bruner, Olver, and Greenfield, 1966, p. 107).

Bruner's study was but one of a long series of studies that evoked conservation behavior from diagnosed nonconservers. Researchers have coached children in employing proper verbal reasoning ("When you pour, it remains the same"), in attending to the relevant aspects of the stimulus ("Look at how high and how wide it is"), in handling the materials themselves, in listening to the recommendations of their peers, or in predicting the results of various pourings (Beilin, Kagan, and Rabinowitz, 1966; Brainerd and Allen, 1971; Carey, 1974; Halford, 1970; McGarrigle and Donaldson, 1975; Miller and Brownell, 1975; Murray, 1979). Experimenters have become increasingly successful at producing conservationlike behavior at ages younger than those claimed by Piaget.

Jan Smedslund's Extinction Studies. Although some scholars regard these training successes as refutations of Piaget's account, others draw quite different conclusions. They question the criteria used in labeling a child a conserver; for instance, Bruner counted "same" and "different" answers, not reasons. And they challenge any modification of the basic Piaget demonstration; screening, for instance, prevents the child from witnessing the usually misleading perceptual cues (D. Kuhn, 1974; S. A. Miller, 1976). One harsh critic has been the Norwegian psychologist Jan Smedslund, who himself conducted studies of conservation training in an effort to demonstrate their superficiality.

In one such study, Smedslund (1961) looked at a related understanding called conservation of weight. Children aged five to seven were shown balls of clay and asked to judge whether weight would be conserved after the experimenter had rolled, flattened, or otherwise changed the clay's appearance. Smedslund trained children identified as nonconservers to give conserving responses. In one study, he used a balance to show that a deformed piece of clay continued to weigh the same as a standard piece. After repeated exposures to this demonstration, the nonconservers began to adopt the arguments of conservation of weight ("You just changed the shape. . . . You didn't add anything"), even when the balance was no longer used. Many of Piaget's critics would consider this proof that conservation of weight can be learned in a short time.

But Smedslund then unmasked the precariousness of this learning. Repeating the experiment, he secretly removed a piece of the clay while also changing its shape. When asked which piece of clay would weigh more, the child said they would be the same. Smedslund then placed both on the balance. Naturally, the altered piece now weighed less.

Children's reactions to this and similar situations turned out to reflect quite faithfully their initial conserving abilities. Those who were initially nonconservers invariably accepted the unequal weight without surprise or protest. In traditional learning theory terms, the response that had recently been trained was now readily eliminated or extinguished from the repertoire. But many of the children who had been diagnosed initially as conservers (and who had received no additional training) reacted quite differently. Half of them continued to offer conservation explanations and were even bold enough to challenge the experimenter: "I think you have taken away some of the clay," or "We must have lost some clay on the floor" (see also Robert and Charbonneau, 1978).

Smedslund concluded that children who acquired conservation during training were merely parroting a rather arbitrary law without adequately believing or understanding it. But those who had acquired conservation normally had a firmer and more secure conception and would instead try to account for the unanticipated difference in weight. The actual answers given by conservers and nonconservers were similar. However, the *meaning* embedded in these explanations and the strength of conviction behind it differed markedly, depending on whether the conservation had been acquired as a consequence of training or of natural development.

Focus on Criteria. A few researchers have directed attention to the very criteria used to evaluate conservation. Gerald Gruen, for example, has shown that one secures a much larger percentage of conserving responses if one pays attention only to the responses "same or different" than if one requires an adequate justification of responses (1966). Indeed in one study, Gruen found 37 percent conservers when using Smedslund's criteria, whereas 51 percent were considered conservers according to Bruner's standards.

Building on this idea, Daniel Mossler (1979) has treated the emergence of conservation as a multilevel sequence with each level reflecting one of the criteria that can be invoked. The simplest level is obtained when the child registers surprise at a violation of conservation; here no words are required at all. At a subsequent level the child must simply indicate whether an amount has been conserved. A level-three response requires the child to select an appropriate justification from a set offered by the experimenters, while sophisticated responses at level four include an accurate and spontaneous justification by the child. According to Mossler there is no "sudden thawing" of cognitive structures but rather a gradual linear trend over a number of years. The story one tells about conservation reveals what factors one considers fundamental in cognitive development.

IS CONSERVATION EVER FULLY LEARNED?

Some researchers suspect Piaget's whole account of conservation. They point out many everyday events to which the basic rules of conservation do not apply: water's volume will increase when it is frozen; squashing a ball of clay changes its surface area; astronauts become weightless in space, even though their anatomy is not altered. Perhaps the concept of conservation is less basic (and less unchanging) than the Piagetians have realized. And if conservation is indeed an unreliable phenomenon, perhaps adults will prove as manipulable as Smedslund's children. (For a humorous perspective on this issue, see the box on page 395.)

To explore this view, Vernon Hall and Richard Kingsley (1968) administered conservation tasks to undergraduate and graduate students. Following a set of questions about conservation of weight, an experimenter rolled one of two equal balls of clay into a feather shape and then secretly removed some clay from the feather shape. Weighing revealed that the feather was lighter than the ball. Less than half of the graduate students and only four of seventeen college students gave the correct answer: that clay had been removed or that the scale was somehow faulty. In an effort to fabricate an explanation, nonconserving adults would suggest that a ball had greater density than a feather, that a ball has a different center of gravity, or that there was unequal weight distribution in the two shapes.

From such studies researchers like Hall and Kingsley suggest that conservation is a slippery concept. Apparently the notions of adults—let alone those of children—are quite malleable. Moreover, conservation is not by any means always the rule—for example, the area and the perimeter of a closed figure are not conserved when the figure is elongated. Indeed, part of the complex process of mastering the principles of conservation is determining when matter and amount are conserved and when they are not. Some aspects of conservation require mastery of a logical principle ("If nothing has been added, the amount

Experimenter: Is there the same in these two glasses (*A1 and A2*)?

Edi: Yes.

Experimenter: Your mummy says to you: Instead of giving you your milk in this glass (*A1*), I give it to you in these two (*B1 and B2*), one in the morning and one at night. (*It is poured out.*)

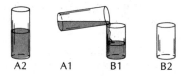

Where will you have most to drink, here (*A2*) or there (*B1 + B2*)?

Edi: It's the same.

Experimenter: That's right. Now, instead of giving it to you in these two (*B1 and B2*), she gives it to you in three (*pouring A2 into C1, C2 and C3*), one in the morning, one at lunch-time and one at night. Is it the same in the two as in the three, or not?

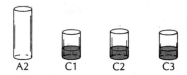

Edi: It's the same in 3 as in 2 . . . No, in 3 there's more.

And if you pour the three (*C1 + C2 + C3*) back onto that one (*A2*) how far up will it come?

(*He pointed to a level higher than in A1.*)

And if we pour these 3 into 4 glasses (*doing so into C1 + C2 + C3 + C4*), with a consequent lowering of the level and then pour it all back into the big one (*A2*), how far up will it come?

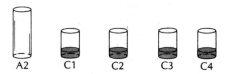

(*He pointed to a still higher level.*)

And with 5?

(*He showed a still higher level.*)

And with 6?

Edi: There wouldn't be enough room in the glass.

Figure 10.3. This dialogue is a clinical interview in the Piagetian tradition. The child is posed a series of puzzles, each related to the one before, but each presenting a somewhat new challenge. In this case, a child reveals his "transitional" status as regards conservation of continuous quantities. At first, he appears to understand the principles of conservation; but when he has to keep three or more vessels in mind, he lapses back to a "nonconservational" mode of responding. (Piaget, 1965)

remains the same") while others require knowledge about what happens in the real world (for instance, the effects of heating versus freezing). Knowledge of trickery, whether by a live experimenter or by photography, is another factor relevant to judgments of conservation (O'Connor, Beilin, and Kose, 1981). In at least one sense, this state of affairs is faithful to the spirit of Piaget. Far from being a static concept that is insensitive to new experiences, conservation emerges as a dynamic principle that can accommodate to new demonstrations (Shultz, Dover, and Amsel, 1979).

The Gestalt of a Cookie: Conservation Challenged

In an article I once wrote for the *New York Times* (Gardner, 1979a), I explained how the appreciation of conservation was one of the major milestones in cognitive development. A week later the editor printed the following letter from a shrewd reader who gave the other side of the argument:

I am struck by Howard Gardner's suggestion ["Getting Acquainted with Jean Piaget," Jan. 3, 1979] that one may teach the conservation of matter to a receptive child by showing that, blindfolded, one cannot tell the difference between a whole and a broken cookie.

There may be a practical difficulty in blindfolding a 4-year-old who is in the act of mourning his cookie: more, though, I am troubled by conceptual problems. *Is* a whole cookie the same as two halves of a broken cookie? Hasn't the broken one, somehow, lost much of its cookieness? To say it tastes the same as a whole one is to say that a banana without a sticker tastes like one with a sticker, that the squared end of a slice of bread tastes like the rounded end, or that orange juice poured by the wrong adult into a cup of the wrong color tastes the same as orange juice offered correctly. How would Mr. Gardner feel, say, about the two halves of a torn "Mona Lisa"?

Besides, if you have the child taste a whole cookie and a broken cookie, the child eats two cookies, which is presumably what you were trying to avoid in the first place. Mr. Gardner says the experiment may have to be repeated a few times.

Cognitively developed or not, most kids ought to be able to see the possibilities *there;* and you could break a cookie in thirds, too, and eat three cookies . . . no, the best thing to do, when the cookie breaks, is to give your child a new one and eat the broken pieces yourself. You even do yourself a favor, for as any adult knows, the two halves don't have nearly as many calories as the whole would.

Alice Mattison

Conservation of Number and Other Concrete Operations

So far we have considered the conservation of continuous physical materials like liquids or clay, whose amounts or weights are described by approximations like "a little" or "lots," "more" or "less." But we also have available a much more precise assessment of quantity, that entailed in using numerical concepts. Confronting two piles of **discontinuous elements** like beads (as opposed to continuous quantities like mounds of clay), the adult can not only declare which pile has more beads; he can also count the beads in each pile, thereby confirming the estimate and providing an exact assessment of quantity. This understanding that the number of elements in an array remains constant irrespective of how the elements are arranged is called conservation of number. Such an understanding proves essential for functioning in any society with a complex economy, and it also constitutes the basis for mathematics and all measurement and scientific thought. Yet it stems from an amazingly simple foundation: the realization that elements in a set can be counted and that the totals of the sets can be compared.

PIAGET'S ORIGINAL STUDY

In the classic Piagetian study of number conservation, children are shown two rows of elements like beads: the rows are identical in both number and appearance (Piaget, 1965*b*). After the child verifies that both rows contain the same number, the experimenter alters one group so that its elements are spread farther apart or pushed closer together than the elements in the other group. The key question: "Do the rows have the same, do you have more, or do I have more?"

As the integrated or structured-whole view of concrete operations must predict, the re-

sults parallel those from the study of conservation of liquids. Three-year-olds make global comparisons: rather than counting the elements, they simply focus on a single property of one group (usually length or density) and make their choice. Five- or six-year-olds, at a point of transition, may try to count or otherwise to match the rows. However, they rarely count properly and are diverted by a misleading perceptual cue like length. At best, they will be aware of contrary impressions ("It looks like more but you didn't add more"), but they will display little confidence in their final judgment, and they are easily swayed by counterarguments.

By seven or eight, children are more certain of their responses, and they are no longer seduced by the appearance of the groups. Because they *know* that nothing has been added or taken away, they cannot possibly conclude that the groups are unequal. Moreover, these children possess an invaluable tool: they have mastered the principle that each element must be counted only once, and they can count the total number in each group to confirm for themselves that they are exactly the same.

Once again Piaget's experiments prompted a barrage of further research (see Brainerd and Allen, 1971; Elkind and Flavell, 1969; Field, 1981; Gelman, 1969; Lovell, 1961; Sigel and Hooper, 1968). Attempts to train number conservation at an earlier age were more successful than those involving liquid conservation, suggesting that this task is somewhat easier for children. Nonetheless, a controversy still remains as to whether preschool children can conserve number. In fact, Peter Bryant (1974) has shown that preschool children can conserve number quite effectively so long as the elements in the two rows are placed directly opposite one another. In that case, the length of the rows does not mislead subjects. Only when perceptual cues contradict each other—when length suggests one answer and counting another—do the children completely lose this apparent sensitivity to number. As was the case with liquids, then, one's criteria determine one's verdict regarding numerical conservation.

WHENCE NUMBER?
ESTIMATORS AND OPERATORS

Rochel Gelman (Gelman, 1972, 1979; Gelman and Gallistel, 1978) has helped clarify the capacities that underlie the mastery of numerical systems. **Estimators** enable people to de-

Figure 10.4. The tendency to array and arrange objects is so pervasive in our world that a child might well hit upon a system of counting even if no one explicitly taught him. This youngster at play with pinecones is clearly taking stock of her inventory—but the accuracy with which she concludes it will depend on whether she has attained the concept of number.

termine quantity: for instance, that a given set contains seven elements rather than six or eight. **Operators** allow them to comprehend the consequences of manipulating elements in various ways, for instance, adding one to a set affects its number whereas rearranging its members does not. In Gelman's view, to understand children's numerical capacities we must first unravel the development of these two capacities.

Gelman traced the development of estimation by pitting the cue of sheer number against other, distracting factors such as length and density. She presented children with a set of three cards, each of which pictured a row of one element (like stars or circles). The cards differed in the number of elements, the length of the row, and the row's density. By asking children which cards were the same or which were different, Gelman could determine the dimension (that is, number, length, or density) on which children based their estimates of amount.

Three-year-olds showed no difficulty in grouping cards by number, provided there were only two or three elements. When there were between five and nine elements, however, they were more likely to focus on length. Thus, for young children number is the dominant dimension when there are few elements, but length takes over when the task is made more complex.

Turning to operators Gelman questioned whether children would notice a change in the number of elements in a set. Once again, she pitted number against other cues. For instance, children were shown two plates, one featuring a row of two mice, the other three. The rows were either the same length, in which case the difference in density signaled the difference in number, or the same density and, thus, different in length.

After showing the child both plates, the experimenter designated one of them as "the winner" and then hid each plate under a can. She mixed them up and then asked the child to guess which can held "the winner," to lift up that can and confirm his choice. Once the child understood the game, the experimenter secretly manipulated the "winner" by changing either the number of elements or the length of the row before placing it under the can. The question was whether the child would recognize the change and would select the altered plate as the "winner." Gelman looked for any signs of surprise and probed the child's reason for concluding that the plate was or was not the "winner."

During the first phase of the experiment, children aged three, four, and five consistently attended to the number of elements hidden under the cans. During the second phase, when the mice were secretly altered, the children's behavior strongly suggested that they understood the relevant operations of addition or deletion. All children confronted with one less mouse noticed it and 80 percent actually searched for it. In contrast, only 66 percent noticed a rearrangement of the mice and none searched for a missing creature. In short, the children behaved as if subtraction or addition, but not displacement, affected number and, hence, being a "winner."

Gelman's findings document that preschool children possess at least primitive estimators and operators. In addition, by the age of two and one-half or three children have also mastered five basic principles of counting: (1) each item in an array must be labeled with one and only one unique word or "tag"; (2) the order of tags remains stable; (3) the last tag in a count represents the total number in the array; (4) any set of items can be counted; (5) the order in which a given object is tagged in a given series is irrelevant, so long as each object is tagged only once per count (Gelman, 1979). To demonstrate such counting, one must gather verbal evidence. But recent sudies raise the remarkable possibility that even infants

may possess rudimentary numerical capacities: when their responses to numerical sets are measured, prelinguistic infants appear able to distinguish between sets of four and five (Collard and Dempsey, 1976; Starkey, Spelke, and Gelman, 1980; Walters and Wagner, 1981). Rather than gaining their sense of number from an ability to count, children may have from the start the ability to appreciate small numbers. They merely learn to apply verbal labels to the quantities they already understand.

The gap between the Piagetian measures of numerical ability and those used by some other researchers has become enormous (Mehler and Bever, 1967). One wonders whether the kinds of abilities now being found in children as young as one or two relate directly to the difficulties exhibited by older nonconserving children or whether fundamentally different processes are at work. Response measures must be taken into account. After all, it is far easier to register surprise at a change in the number of toy figures than to justify a conservation response (Silverman, Rose, and Phillis, 1979). And the task variables are also important to note. Recognizing quantity when numbers are small and there are no competing cues is far easier than recognizing quantity despite deceptive perceptual cues and larger collections of objects (Brainerd, 1977).

Nonetheless, the evidence strongly suggests that children possess a basic sense of discontinuous quantities at a time when the understanding of continuous quantities has not been established. Of what, then, does further numerical development consist? First there is the ability to use numbers, words, and symbols correctly in the course of solving problems posed by others, an ability whose development depends upon the particular oral and numerical systems being used (see the box and Saxe, in press). Equally important, there is the capacity to use numbers on one's own

Counting on Your Fingers . . . and Your Arms and Your Head

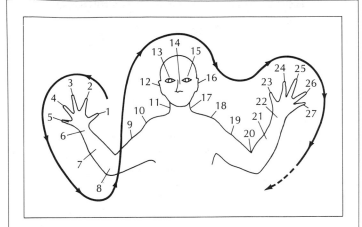

When asked to count a dozen marbles, we will count from one to twelve. An Oksapmin, who lives in the remote villages of Papua New Guinea, is likely to go from "tipana" to "nata"—or from "thumb" to "ear." The Oksapmin people use a counting system that depends on naming body parts. To count, they begin with the right hand thumb and from there enumerate successive parts around the upper half of the body (the other fingers, the wrist, elbow, bicep, and so on) until they reach their other thumb—twenty-seven positions in all.

Geoffrey Saxe was intrigued by this unusual system and he questioned whether Oksapmin and Western children learn a counting system and numerical concepts in a similar way (Saxe, 1977; Russac, 1978). Western children are known to follow a clear progression. First a child is able to count the number of elements in a set; for example, he can count out five marbles. Soon after, he understands that the last number reached refers to the total; now he can say that there are "five" marbles in all. Finally, the child is able to compare quantities; at this point, he not only determines that pile *A* has five marbles and that pile *B* has seven, he can also conclude that pile *B* has more.

Saxe (in press) found that Oksapmin children go through a similar developmental sequence. He asked his subjects to compare the values of different body parts (left elbow versus nose or left shoulder versus right shoulder). All children could use the system for counting, but only older ones could then use their counting to make comparisons. The errors Oksapmin children made, however, differed from those of Western children in ways that reflect the nature of their respective systems. For example, some children continued to identify symmetrical parts (for example, left and right shoulders) as equivalent even after they had learned to label asymmetrical parts (for example, left shoulder and nose) as not equivalent. Physical similarity of body parts had an unwarranted effect on numerical judgments. For Oksapmin children, then, the acquisition of numerical concepts requires understanding that the numerical relation of two body parts is determined by their ordinal position in a counting sequence and not by their physical similarity.

to solve problems that arise spontaneously, for instance, in the course of a game. Finally, unless one has considerable mathematical gifts, one must await more formal instruction before gaining the capacity to carry out more complex arithmetical reasoning.

Representing One's Knowledge of Space

While problems of number are, at least initially, posed to the child by the outside world, the need to find one's way around a spatial environment is the obligation of every animal. Fortunately, a sense of direction and feeling for spatial layouts characterizes every normal child, who can find his way around a familiar environment with little or no difficulty. Yet once environments become more complex and filled with many landmarks, once routes through them become more circuitous, and once the need arises to represent one's spatial knowledge in another medium, the attainment of knowledge about space becomes a challenge. And because spatial environments are themselves quite large, studying the child's emerging conceptions of space has challenged experimental investigators.

Predictably, Piaget was an early contributor to the literature on spatial understanding. We have already seen in Chapter 7 how the preoperational child fails one spatial task: indicating how a complex arrangement of objects such as the three-mountain terrain appears to someone at a different location. We noted in the Introduction the difficulties exhibited by a preoperational child in ordering a set of different-sized sticks so that they progress from the shortest to the longest. Piaget has focused relatively little attention on actual route finding or mapmaking or on the factors that contribute to ease of performance, but his general conceptual framework has contributed to our understanding of these phenomena.

Much of the recent work on spatial understanding has used environments created by an experimenter (Siegel and White, 1975). Nancy Hazen, Jeffrey Lockman, and Herbert Pick (1978) tested children's mastery of an environment consisting of a set of collapsible rooms ($5\frac{1}{2} \times 5\frac{1}{2} \times 6$ feet), each containing four opaque curtain doors. The rooms were uniform except for a distinctive toy animal located at the center of each; these animals served as landmarks to help the children find their way around the artificial layout.

The children were ushered through the space via various routes, and the experimenter called their attention to the different landmarks. Then their knowledge of the spatial environment was tested in a number of ways. They were asked to go through the house in reverse order beginning in the last room and ending up in the first room. As part of this task they had to *predict* which animals they would see in the next room and also to *infer* which animals were located on the other side of doors that led to another room but that they themselves had never entered. Finally, upon exiting the rooms, children were given a set of small boxes and small animals and then asked, "Can you make a house out of these animals and these little rooms so that it looks just like the big house?" (p. 627). Thus the children's capacity to represent their knowledge through the construction of a miniature model could also be assessed.

Children as young as three years performed very well in retracing the route in reverse. This ability seemed to require only motoric (or enactive) knowledge of the direction in which to move. They had more difficulty anticipating which animals would be seen next; this sort of knowledge seemed to involve a greater symbolic or imagistic component, the ability to represent elements not in view. Only children six years of age exhibited some success in inferring which animals were in the rooms that they themselves had never entered. The combination of imaging and deduction proved most challenging.

Data from the model-building task indicated that the spatial representations of the younger children were routelike. That is, the child knew the sequence of the landmarks but could not re-create the shape of the space in which the landmarks were contained. The children showed a strong tendency to *represent* the shape of the house as a single straight line, even though they could indicate by tracing the route with their fingers that the actual route taken was not straight. Older children often knew the overall shape of the house as well as the path on which to travel but even this knowledge did not suffice to make an accurate model. Like nonconservers, these children simply proved unable to integrate and coordinate their various strands of knowledge into a single structured whole.

Results from other laboratories supplement the emerging picture of children's spatial knowledge. In one study Siegel and his colleagues (Siegel et al., 1979) showed that children exposed to a large-scale space proved able to re-create the observed spatial relations in a small-scale model. In contrast, children exposed to a small-scale space and then required to negotiate their way through a large-scale space experienced considerable difficulties in doing so. Other studies reveal that in negotiating their way through a model town, children are aided when their attention is called to the spatial relations within the buildings, when they walk within the center of the town (rather than simply around the periphery), and when they are given practice in constructing the town from memory (Herman, 1980). Younger children (ages five to seven) are helped significantly when a model

environment is bounded by walls, while older children (age ten) apparently do not need such clues in order to master the environment (Herman and Siegel, 1978). In general, landmarks are aids for young children (Cohen and Schuepfer, 1980), though children do not always notice them spontaneously (Anooshian and Owens, 1979) and are not always certain which will prove most helpful (Allen et al., 1979).

We can propose a tentative developmental model of the acquisition of spatial knowledge. Children as young as two years can negotiate their way around simple spaces, avoiding obstacles such as barriers (Heth and Cornell, 1980). Small spaces with landmarks in them can be learned readily by preschoolers, but only school-age children are able to represent the knowledge sufficiently to take indirect routes (Anooshian and Owens, 1979) or to capture their knowledge in maps or models (Presson, 1981). Only older children can (in cartographer fashion) join various routes with one another and integrate them into a more complex map, which allows the inference of routes to landmarks that they have not previously visited (Curtis, Siegel, and Furlong, 1980; Hays and Siegel, 1981).

This model should be seasoned with smidgens of individual differences. First of all, numerous studies suggest that boys have somewhat superior spatial capacities, on the average, than girls (Kail, Carter, and Pellegrino, 1979; Wittig and Peterson, 1979). The reason for this superiority remains undetermined. In addition, youngsters with considerable daily experience in exploring wide spaces perform better on spatial and mapping tasks than those with few such experiences. Appalachian youngsters surpassed middle- and lower-middle-class youngsters in America, suggesting that urban/suburban environments in the United States are not optimal for the development of certain cognitive skills (Norman, 1980; see also Davidson and Klich, 1980).

OTHER OPERATIONS

Tales about conservation of liquids and pellets, perception of spaces, and making of maps can be echoed in several other conceptual domains. In such diverse realms as time, area, length, and causality, Piaget designed basic studies that reveal the gradual emergence, between the ages of six and nine, of the capacity to perform concrete mental operations (see Flavell, 1963; Ginsburg and Opper, 1979; Piaget, 1970). In each case an initial Piagetian demonstration has proved compelling. And in each case further research has revealed origins of the mental operation at a far earlier time in the child's life (Baillargeon, Gelman, and Meck, 1981, Bullock, 1981) and has illuminated the factors that can contribute to the ease or difficulty of the performance (Keil, 1979b; Shultz and Ravinsky, 1977).

One set of tasks called "class inclusion" has proved particularly enigmatic. Asked whether there are more dogs or more animals in the world, the child is likely to say "more dogs." Or, confronted with a set of twelve beads, eight red and four white, and asked whether there are "more red beads or more beads," the child is likely to respond "more red beads." The class-inclusion problem illustrates the role of logical mental operations. In the real world, one can readily compare (by sight) the number of red beads with the number of white beads. However, it is impossible to compare physically a set (all beads) with one of its subsets (red beads); the members of the subset would have to occupy two places simultaneously—in the subset (red beads) and in the total set (all beads). Such a comparison can only take place "in the head." In Piaget's analysis, the child incapable of mental operations cannot mentally construct and compare the two sets—that of all beads and that of all red beads. Instead, drawn by the actual physical contrast, the child reformulates the question as if it were calling for a comparison between red and white beads and answers "red beads."

There may be other reasons for this failure. Through an ingenious set of experiments, James McGarrigle (McGarrigle, Grieve, and Hughes, 1978) demonstrated that the form of the question may pose unnecessary difficulties. He found, for example, that if the child were shown a set of sleeping cows, of which only some were black, and then asked "Are there more black cows or more sleeping cows?" the child would answer correctly. This

Figure 10.5. Presented with this problem, a preoperational child will respond that there are more tulips than flowers. Because he is unable to appreciate at the same time both an overall class (flowers) and one of its subsets (tulips), the child reinterprets this question as "Are there more tulips or more dandelions?"

Flowers

Tulips

Dandelions

Are there more tulips or more flowers?

question is logically equivalent to the question "Are there more black cows or more cows?," one typically failed by children of the same age. McGarrigle suggests that the child can perform correctly so long as his attention is called to the total class (for example, through the addition of the adjective *sleeping*), instead of merely the subclass.

In class-inclusion problems, it appears, the question the children are answering is frequently not the question posed by the experimenter. The experimenter intends one question, and the child perceives another. If this is so, the problem lies not in class inclusion per se but rather in the particular way in which the question has been phrased (Donaldson, 1978). Indeed the class-inclusion question does seem more of a trick than most other Piagetian puzzles (see Siegel et al., 1978; C. L. Smith, 1979) and more readily ameliorated by training, redefinition of the task, or changes in the kinds of classes probed (Horton and Markman, 1979; Kohnstamm, 1963).

An Evaluation of Concrete Operations

Have the variations and reinterpretations of Piaget's studies so fragmented his vision of concrete operations that it is no longer useful? Or is there still a central strand—a small set of mental operations—that underlies the demonstrations and ties them together?

Any consideration of these questions must distinguish between what Piaget claimed and what he did not. To begin with, Piaget noted that all concrete operational capacities do not arise at the same time. They do emerge in a regular order, with conservation of quantity well ahead of conservation of area, space, or volume (see Figure 10.6). Second, Piaget contended that some operations are closely re-

lated; for example, the ability to place an element appropriately in an ordered series is closely tied to the ability to measure. Thus Piaget recognized more than a single family of concrete operations. Finally, Piaget himself placed little importance on the actual age of acquisition. It was the order in which the abilities appeared, the sequence of stages and substages, that was central in his formulation.

Nonetheless, some strong claims remain. In Piaget's view, concrete operations must develop naturally, over time, as a consequence of direct actions on objects. Attempts to train a child in an operation cannot succeed until the child is just about ready to develop that capacity, and by that time training is hardly necessary. In addition, even though the specific operations develop at different rates and at disparate times, Piaget did see them all as interrelated. That is, as we saw in Chapter 7, preoperational children (aged four or five), because of their egocentrism, are unable to overlook deceptive perceptual cues, even as they are incapable of mentally representing elements, sets, or relationships or of thinking of a given element in more than one way. In striking contrast, the concrete operator of eight or nine readily shifts perspectives, is not deceived by misleading cues, can rapidly run through mental operations, and can conceive of elements as belonging simultaneously to several categories.

We cannot resolve here all the debates about concrete operations but we can at least summarize the current state of the controversy. In doing so, we must return once more to the central demonstrations of conservation and to the debate over their significance. Earlier we saw that varying the classic demonstrations can apparently lower the age when concrete operations emerge. However, most of these studies stemmed from the cognitive-structural school, and either changed Piaget's demonstration (as did Bruner) or applied less

CONSERVATION OF SUBSTANCE

The experimenter shows the child two identical clay balls. The child acknowledges that the two have equal amounts of clay.

The experimenter changes the shape of one of the balls and asks the child whether they still contain equal amounts of clay.

CONSERVATION OF LENGTH

Two sticks are aligned in front of the child. The child agrees that they are the same length.

After moving one stick to the left or right, the experimenter asks the child whether they are still equal in length.

CONSERVATION OF AREA

Two identical sheets of cardboard have wooden blocks placed on them in identical positions. The child is asked whether the same amount of space is left on each piece of cardboard.

The experimenter scatters the blocks on one piece of cardboard and again asks the child whether the two pieces have the same amount of unoccupied space.

CONSERVATION OF VOLUME

Two balls are placed in two identical glasses with an equal amount of water. The child sees that they displace equal amounts of water.

The experimenter changes the shape of one of the balls and asks the child whether it will still displace the same amount of water.

Figure 10.6. The capacity to conserve does not develop at a single moment. Indeed, the capacities to conserve area and volume generally emerge only some years after conservation of substance and of length have appeared. Whether it is nonetheless valid to consider all of these capacities as instances of the same level of cognitive development is the central dilemma surrounding Piaget's stage of concrete operations.

stringent criteria for conservation (as did Bryant). But studies in the environmental-learning tradition also probe the same phenomena and cast the controversies over conservation in sharp relief.

IS CONSERVATION SPONTANEOUS OR TRAINED?

Rochel Gelman's Demonstration. In the opinion of many observers, one study speaks with special clarity to the training controversy: Rochel Gelman's (1969) tutoring of five-year-old children in conservation of length and number. Well versed in environmental-learning theory, Gelman was struck by certain parallels to Piaget's approach: both schools focus on children whose ultimate success depends on the capacity to discriminate between features that are crucial and those that are irrelevant.

Gelman took into account studies of discrimination learning such as the investigations of mediation we reviewed in Chapter 7. In one variety, the **oddity-learning problem** (Stevenson, 1974), children learn to pick the "odd" stimulus from a set of three in which only two elements are identical. To answer correctly, children must learn to ignore certain features and focus only on the ones the experimenter has selected. Gelman reasoned that faced with the conservation problem, the child has to overlook cues like length or density and to focus instead on number; or to ignore height and width, focusing instead on the act of pouring. So she sought to wed the technology of oddity learning to the mastery of conservation.

Gelman exposed five-year-old nonconservers to one of three training conditions. In the first, a control, children simply practiced an oddity-learning task and were rewarded for correct responses.

In the second condition, children were again shown three items, two identical and one different. This time, though, half the problems required attention to number (two rows of five chips versus one row of three chips), while the remaining problems required attention to length (two six-inch sticks versus one ten-inch stick). Because Gelman alternated the number and length tasks, the children had to learn to tease out the different features of length and number and to focus on only the relevant feature for any given item. As in the first condition, children were rewarded for correct responses.

The third condition was just like the second except that children received no reinforcement for correct answers and, thus, had no reliable way of learning which dimension required attention. They were merely told at the end of each session that they had played the game very well.

Five-year-olds in the first group performed nearly perfectly in the training (see Figure 10.7). Apparently they had already understood the concepts of "same" and "different" before the start of the training. Children in the second group began to master the required discrimination between number and length immediately; by the twelfth (of thirty-two) trials they were responding correctly 95 percent of the time. In contrast, the children in the third group learned almost nothing about quantity: mere exposure to the relevant dimensions yielded no learning and hence no selections on the basis of number or length.

Considered together, the results suggest that all the children probably had some understanding of length and quantity before training, but that under ordinary circumstances they were often attracted by irrelevant features. The reinforcement for responses in the second condition apparently trained the children to disregard the irrelevant and focus on the relevant cues. The children in the third

Figure 10.7. The dramatic effects achieved by Rochel Gelman in her training of conservation can be seen in these bar graphs. Youngsters in group 1, who received oddity training and reinforcement, demonstrated conservation of length for some weeks following training and even transferred their new understanding to conservation of liquids. Those who received no reinforcement (group 2) or were not trained to focus on number and length (the control group) showed little tendency to become conservers. (Gelman, 1969)

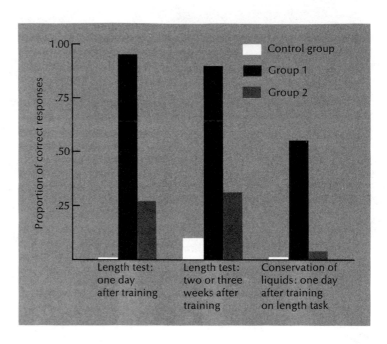

group, who were not suitably reinforced, apparently continued to focus on irrelevant cues.

The following day posttests of conservation yielded dramatic results. Understandably, the children in the first and third groups showed little improvement. The children in the second group performed almost flawlessly on both the length and number tests and also offered adequate explanations for their responses. Furthermore, posttests two to three weeks later testified to the durability of the training. And most children in the second group were able to generalize from their training to conservation of liquid and mass.

Gelman's results suggest that children may solve a variety of conservation tasks with a general rule: locate and use relevant cues of quantity (such as number and length). In fact, Gelman's procedure may have duplicated the crucial steps of attention and discrimination

that children pass through more leisurely on their own "natural" route to conservation (see also Vadhan and Smothergill, 1977). The speed with which the children mastered the oddity problems indicates that they already possessed the requisite concepts of length and number. That idea is strengthened by Gelman's studies, described on pages 397–398, in which children's surprise at secret manipulations of a display conveyed their latent understanding of the relevant operations. Preoperational children may lack only the information (the tricks of the trade) on *how* to use the operations. Or they may succeed only when given a nonverbal way to communicate their understanding.

Evaluating Training Studies. Gelman's demonstration poses a powerful challenge because she invokes environmental-learning theory to explain the rapid mastery of Piagetian problems. Other researchers have also documented instances of precocious performance on and significant "transfer" across conservation tasks (Murray, 1979; Rosenthal and Zimmerman, 1978). Indeed, some thoughtful critics find the training studies so impressive that they question the need for Piagetian theory altogether (Brainerd, 1980*b*). How might a strict cognitive-structuralist meet these challenges?

Deanna Kuhn (1974) stresses that stringent criteria must be met if claims for genuine conservation are to be made. Conservation should be regarded as genuine only when it is accompanied by the child's appropriate explanations, when it persists after training, and when it can be generalized to materials and to problems not specifically involved in training. Children's explanations cannot simply be repeated from training; they must be their own constructions, reflections of a new level of understanding. Similarly, according to the Piagetian theory of the structured whole, certain generalizations should be expected from conservation training, whereas others would be quite unexpected or even deviant. Thus one would expect a link between conservation of number and liquid, but not between conservation of number and the later-appearing conservation of volume. In all, genuine conservation is most likely to be trained when children experience some inconsistency between what they expect (for example, that the liquid will reach a given height) and what actually results (the liquid in fact reaches a much greater height, because the vessel is thinner) (Inhelder, Sinclair, and Bovet, 1974).

Let's examine Gelman's demonstration in terms of Kuhn's strict criteria. The learning lasted for at least a few weeks; there was significant generalization, of the type predicted by the theory; the children's explanations appear to have been appropriate (Gelman does not give much information about this) and, in any case, certainly were not modeled by the nonspeaking experimenter.

Kuhn's analysis helps clarify why Gelman's training succeeded. Gelman suspected that the children had the potential for attending to the appropriate dimensions but did not know which one was relevant. Drawing on her knowledge of training techniques, she devised a game that both made sense to the children and guided their attention to the relevant features. So treated, the children came through with both the relevant discriminations and the appropriate generalizations.

Only one point dilutes the power of Gelman's demonstration. It is quite possible that her five-year-old subjects were on the verge of conservation and would on their own have become conservers within a few months (or even a few weeks). If so, rather than having been elevated a full stage into concrete operations, these children were simply nudged a bit. Perhaps Gelman's demonstrations would have failed with four-year-olds. Lessons from Gelman's study, then, may be consistent with both theoretical viewpoints. As environmental-learning theory would hold, conservation *can* be trained through an attention-directing game. At the same time, as cognitive-structural theory would hold, only children on the verge of an operation can be eased into it through placement in the right environment.

THE RELATIONS AMONG CONCRETE OPERATIONS

As much controversy exists about the adhesiveness of the "glue" holding concrete operations together as about whether they can be taught. Although neither Piaget nor his followers maintain that *all* concrete operations are inextricably related, the entire framework would be weakened if some skills proved to be completely divorced from others or if problem-solving capacities emerged gradually between the ages of three and fifteen, rather than clearly at about seven or eight.

We can question Piaget's claims along a number of lines. First, are these capacities in fact universal, and do children throughout the world acquire them at about the same time? The answer is that they may be universal, but they first emerge anywhere between the age of five and the early years of adolescence (Berry and Dasen, 1974; Bruner, Olver, and Greenfield, 1966; Price-Williams, 1970). In fact, in some societies there is only tenuous evidence that concrete operations are ever attained. This is not to say that equivalent capacities do not exist—only that, as we shall see in the next chapter, children in cultures radically different from ours sometimes give inadequate responses to the Piagetian tasks.

Second, do individual concrete operations appear in the same order across different children, social groups, and cultures? The answer is, very roughly speaking, yes. There seem to be "family resemblances" among certain operators, that tend to emerge at about the same time (Jamison, 1977; Tomlinson-Keasey et al., 1979). But once particular predictions are made about the exact order of emergence among specific concrete operations, Piaget's theory appears to fall down. Empirical studies have generally failed to add much support to, and sometimes they have directly contradicted, Piaget's claims (Dodwell, 1960; Lunzer, 1961). And so, citing numerous findings that contradict Piaget's order of emergence, some critics, notably Charles Brainerd (1978c), have questioned Piaget's whole concept of a structured whole—an interrelated set of operations—at least as it is reflected in the concrete-operational stage.

Piaget's theory of concrete operations may in fact be excessive, a conceptualization no longer in accord with the growing pool of empirical results. Perhaps his particular theory needs revision or even scrapping. Yet all this does not necessarily invalidate the whole enterprise of concrete operations. Rather, in indicating that certain abilities do not always emerge in the order predicted by Piaget, critics like Brainerd have provided valuable empirical information about how this period of development might be better conceptualized.

Even Piaget's harshest critics concur that the issues he confronts in middle childhood are the ones that merit consideration. It is probably unwise to dispense too quickly with the approach that called attention to conservation, the decline in egocentrism, and the growth in the capacity to classify logically. In the view of John Flavell (1971, 1980), one of Piaget's foremost students, many of Piaget's specific claims have not stood up well to empirical investigation, and Piaget may have overlooked the more gradual changes that usher in (and out) the stages of concrete operations. Development is much more heterogeneous than was dreamed of in Piaget's philosophy, and this heterogeneity may be particularly prominent during the school years when so much is being learned.

But, as Flavell suggests, when all is said and done, the concrete-operational child is qualitatively different from the preoperational child—he can for the first time appreciate diverse kinds of equivalencies and assume a variety of perspectives. We are left with two options: either create from scratch a model equivalent in scope to Piaget's or accept Piaget's analysis as a point of departure and then validate, refine, revise, or "operate upon" his claims.

OPERATIONS AND OTHER VIEWS OF COGNITION

For all the disagreement over specifics, most researchers mentioned thus far in this chapter are basically sympathetic with Piaget's goals and many of his central ideas. Some, like Rochel Gelman, are openly critical yet still respectful. But other researchers reflect an entirely different point of view toward cognition and intellect.

The View from Learning Theory. Those from the environmental-learning tradition generally doubt that there is anything special about conservation: like any other behavior, it can be trained (and extinguished) once appropriate stimuli and responses are used. Gelman's research illustrates this general point of view; many other investigations can also be cited in support of it (Berlyne, 1965; Rosenthal and Zimmerman, 1978; J.S.Watson, 1968; Zimmerman and Rosenthal, 1974). Consistent with its conservative scientific orientation, the environmental-learning approach finds little to be gained from positing a special stage like concrete operations or a structured whole underlying disparate tasks.

The so-called skills or cumulative-learning tack, articulated by Robert Gagné (1968), Susan Carey (1974), and Lita Furby (1972), instead tries to break down a complex behavior into its component behaviors or skills. In the case of conservation, one might isolate the child's capacity to note an original equality (or inequality), the nature of the transformation, the relative heights and weights of the liquids, the behaviors of the experimenter, and many other aspects of the phenomenon. One then studies the order in which these components are acquired or combined—an intensive dissection that should yield a finer-grained model of conservation. Such an analysis leads to the conclusion that forms of conservation can be observed during the preschool years; that even adults will fail to conserve under certain circumstances; and that all learning, from the cradle onward, involves a gradual acquisition of increasingly powerful cognitive skills.

The IQ Connection. We have devoted an entire chapter to cognitive capacities without ever mentioning the word **intelligence.** Most of us tend to think of cognitive development as the growth of intelligence; and many think of intelligence as that quality measured by IQ

tests (see the box on page 410). In fact, however, IQ testers and cognitive-structuralists like Piaget are on quite different wavelengths (Block and Dworkin, 1976; Furth, 1981).

Piaget sees the development of cognition, or intelligence, as a universal and spontaneous process beginning with the infant schemes of sucking and looking and continuing with every mental and physical action upon the world. To be sure, individuals differ in how quickly they learn, but Piagetians have little interest in such comparative assessments, in what is usually called "individual differences" or "differential psychology." They are interested instead in the universal characteristics of mental development, in the understandings achieved by all normal humans.

Indeed, the Piagetian and intelligence-testing schools reflect fundamentally different views on the nature of the mind (see Stephens et al., 1972). For Piaget, knowledge derives from the operation: the reversibility of pouring back and forth, the compensation between height and weight, and so on. The essential cognitive act involves taking a state of knowledge (for example, the quantity of water in one beaker), converting it into a second state (the quantity in a second beaker), and deriving knowledge from one's actions about the relation among the states. Piaget's tests highlight the manipulation of physical objects, the alteration of mental schemes, and, eventually, the transformation of symbols that refer to the world. Note that this description of knowledge would be applicable in any society where there are objects and individuals to act upon them.

For Piaget, this form of **operative knowledge** was central in human cognition. He contrasted this operative knowledge, to which he devoted much of his research, with **figurative knowledge**—information about the specific configurations in the world (for example, the color of the liquid, the shape and size of the container). Naturally, as perceivers human beings notice figurative aspects of the world but these do not contribute appreciably to our knowledge; and, in fact, Piaget claimed that emerging operations could actually alter an individual's figurative knowledge. (Recall how the child's reconstruction of a set of sticks changed once he had mastered the operation of seriation). Interestingly, Piaget included all of language within figurative knowledge. As we shall see in Chapter 11, the relegation of language to a domain free of mental operations has not set well with many of his colleagues!

Measuring Smartness: The Mission of IQ Tests

We often describe people (and ourselves) according to how smart, or intelligent, they are. "He is bright." "She is dumb." "I'm a genius." "I'm a moron." What do we mean by such labels? Is intelligence the amount of knowledge a person has, the ability to apply that knowledge appropriately, or the extent of an individual's creativity and resourcefulness? Can we assess intelligence by how "quick" someone is, how he does in school, how much he achieves in life, or how he scores on certain tests? Even without a clear definition of what it is or where it comes from, there seems to be a general consensus that there is some human trait having to do with mental ability. Furthermore, we place great value on mental ability. We recognize, and often emphasize, large individual differences in intelligence, raising ticklish questions about their source, their meaning, and the extent to which they can be altered.

Psychologists have long been interested in these differences and have attempted to understand them in more systematic and scientific ways. They have devised numerous tests that claim to measure or quantify the sometimes elusive quality of mental ability. It is important to remember, however, that a test can only tell us how an individual performs on a given set of question or problems—it is only an assumption that this performance captures the person's underlying mental ability. In short, as E. G. Boring, a psychologist of an earlier era, once quipped, "Intelligence is what the tests test." Nevertheless, these tests are in wide use, they have become an established part of our educational system, and they are considered important indicators of potential and predictors of success.

The need for intelligence tests first arose during the great expansion in public education at the end of the nineteenth century. Faced with growing numbers of students, teachers wanted a means of predicting how well children would do in school. In 1904 two Frenchmen, Alfred Binet and Theophilus Simon, set out to devise a test that would measure a child's expected academic success. Their result, a year later, was the first IQ test—one of the most far-reaching contributions of psy-
(continued)

chology to education and an invention that has led to new awarenessess as well as to new controversies. Today, the Stanford-Binet, an early adaptation, is still in wide use. Other, similar tests have been devised, including three popular Weschler intelligence scales: the Weschler Preschool-Primary Scale of Intelligence (WPPSI) for ages four to six and one-half; the Weschler Intelligence Scale for Children (WISC) for ages seven to sixteen; and the Weschler Adult Intelligence Scale (WAIS) for ages sixteen and over. In order to understand the meaning and significance of these tests, it is helpful to know something about their content and the method and philosophy that led to their creation.

Binet compiled a battery of tests that sampled the wide range of intellectual skills encountered in schools. By administering these tasks to children of various ages, he determined what was "bright," "average," and "below average" for each age. From this he assembled an assortment of tasks that were suitable for different ages; at each level the tests tapped the same range of mental abilities, including reasoning, comprehension, common sense, quickness and abstraction. Nowadays these tests are usually divided into verbal tasks (vocabulary, story comprehension, proverb interpretation, and general information) and nonverbal or performance tasks (maze tracing, puzzle assembly, and picture completion).

In order to assess the capacity to draw abstractions, for example, the tasks require that seven-year-olds describe how two objects (such as wood and coal) are similar; eight-year-olds are asked how they are both similar and different; and eleven-year-olds are asked to compare three objects (such as a cow, a sparrow, and a snake). Memory is tested by asking children to repeat a series of numbers forward and backward, to recall events of a story, and to reproduce geometric figures. Both the complexity of the task and the expected performance vary with age. For instance, older children and adults are asked to define abstract terms such as "obedience" and to elaborate nuances of differences, as between "laziness" and "idleness." (Figure 10.8 shows other examples.)

In order to test a child's intelligence, the tester administers tasks appropriate for the child's age. His performance on these tasks is then compared to that of the average child of the same age. A ten-year-old who performs like most ten-year-olds is said to be "average"; if, however, he performs like most twelve-year-olds, he is said to have a mental age of twelve and to be "above average" or "superior." The intelligence quotient, or IQ, is simply the ratio of mental age to chronological age times 100. Thus a child with an IQ of 100 is average for his age;

(*continued*)

VERBAL REASONING

Each sentence has the first and last word left out. Pick the pair of words that will fill the blanks to make the sentence true and sensible.

1 _____ is to prison as Louvre is to _____

A. warden—paramour
B. warden—museum
C. warden—France
D. Bastille—museum
E. crime—artist

MECHANICAL REASONING

Which chain by itself will not hold up the sign?

A. Chain A
B. Chain B
C. Chain C

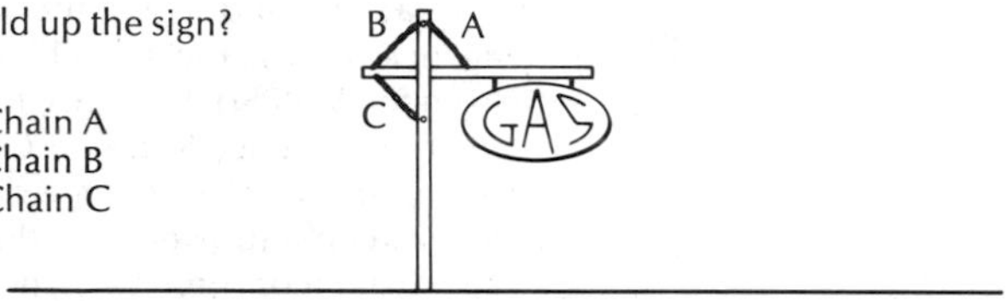

ABSTRACT REASONING

The four figures at left below make a series. Which of the five lettered figures would be the next, that is, the fifth one in the series?

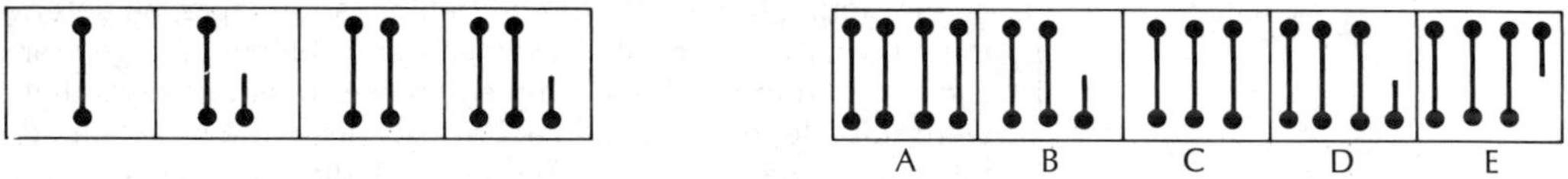

NUMERICAL ABILITY

The tires of Carl's bike should each have 25 pounds of air, but he puts 30 pounds in each. The amount of air he put in was what percent more than he should have put in?

A. 83⅓ %   B. 5%   C. 120%   D. 20%   E. none of these

CULTURALLY UNBIASED TEST ITEM

Fill the blank.

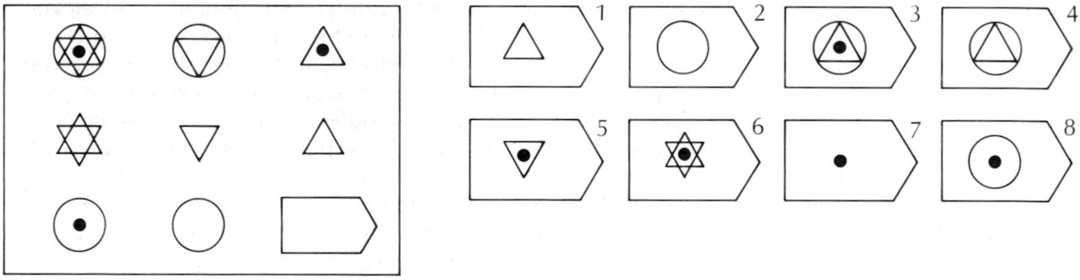

Figure 10.8. As you examine these sample items drawn from intelligence tests, including those items labelled as "culturally unbiased," try to figure out which sorts of general (universal) or specific (culturally dependent) experiences might prove necessary for an accurate solution.

Answers: D, B, C, D, 7

an IQ of 120 shows that the child is at the same level as a child 20 percent older than he is. Our hypothetical "above-average" ten-year-old has an IQ of 120.

Is there a single, unitary ability called intelligence, as the IQ score suggests, or are there different kinds of intellectual skill? A statistical technique known as factor analysis has helped to explain the organization of intelligence. Given a collection of scores from a variety of test items, this procedure reveals a pattern of correlations. The items tend to fall or cluster into several groups. Those items within the same group are considered similar to each other (and demand the same or similar mental abilities) and are relatively independent or different from those in another cluster. There may, for example, be a "visual-spatial ability" cluster, which would include such tasks as block design and maze tracing, whereas the "memory" group would include digit span and story recall. Using factor analysis, Charles Spearman (1904, 1927) found that while there seem to be particular types of intelligence, there is also a common ingredient necessary for all intellectual tasks. His theory, known as the "two-factor theory," suggests that individuals with a high g, or general, factor are "all-around bright" (as in the case of a "Renaissance man"), while those high in a single s, or specific, factor excel in one particular skill (as in the case of a mathematical genius).

Some decades later L. L. Thurstone (1938, 1947) proposed an alternate model: that there are seven primary and independent mental abilities (perceptual speed, numerical ability, word fluency, verbal comprehension, space visualization, associative memory, and reasoning). When he attempted to measure these separate abilities, however, he found that they are to some extent correlated and, therefore, not wholly independent— more proof that there is such a thing as general mental ability, as Spearman had first postulated.

Although we may never know exactly what it means, there does seem to be some trait of general mental ability, and IQ seems to be a plausible way to measure it. A further issue regards the significance and implications of intelligence. What can we expect of smart people? In 1925, Lewis Terman (Terman, 1925; Terman and Oden, 1947, 1959) launched a mammoth longitudinal study of fifteen hundred youngsters whose IQs averaged over 150 and who excelled in nearly all school subjects. He found that as children and adults they were superior in many ways: physically, emotionally, morally, and socially. They retained their intellectual skills and achieved high professional status as compared with their less gifted peers; and, finally, they were generally satisfied with their lives (Sears, 1977; Sears

(*continued*)

and Barbee, 1977). However, none of these individuals made major creative breakthroughs, and life satisfaction was significantly greater among males than females.

"Brains" may not be everything but, evidently, they can't hurt—all else being equal, it is probably better to be bright than stupid. What, then, is the source of intelligence?

Nativists are convinced that intelligence is inborn. Their evidence: Bright parents are more apt to have bright offspring than are less intelligent adults. Furthermore, IQ scores of identical twins are highly correlated with one another (sometimes as high as 0.9) and identical twins reared apart are more alike in IQ than fraternal twins reared together (see Chapter 8).

IQ scores also correlate with race: black children score on the average fifteen points lower than whites. Arthur Jensen (1972, 1979) raised heated controversy when he concluded that IQ is inherited and that blacks are genetically inferior to whites. Most professionals in the area of intelligence testing strongly disagreed; they maintained that the language and content of the IQ tests are biased in favor of white, middle-class children and are inappropriate for blacks (see box on the chitling test, page 331). Additionally, they pointed out that black children who have been raised in white, middle-class homes score an average of fifteen points higher than non-adopted blacks—a further discredit to Jensen's claim and additional support for the environmentalists.

The high correlation between social class and IQ offers additional indication of the role of environmental factors in determining intelligence. Middle-class children on the average score ten to fifteen points higher than those from lower-class families. This may be because middle-class homes are able to offer more "intellectual stimulation": parents talk to their children more and use richer language, they may place greater stress on achievement and encourage intellectual pursuits. Similarly, bright parents may have bright children, not because it is in their genes but because they, too, have intellectually motivating homes.

The debate continues. But the general conclusion is that intelligence is a trait, it is useful for certain predictive purposes in certain social milieus, it does "run in families"—but is not wholly genetically determined or immutable. An individual's experiences and environment will have a strong influence on how this trait emerges and develops. IQ tests have been proven useful for certain predictive purposes, such as expected academic performance. Many scholars hope that tests that tap creativity and that include a focus on the acquisition and utilization of new knowledge will become as influential as the IQ test.

Just as Piaget showed little interest in the specific behaviors that occupied the environmental-learning school (see Chapter 2), he also exhibited little interest in figurative knowledge. In sharp contrast, standard intelligence tests routinely highlight such figurative knowledge, particularly in the verbal portion: definitions, number recall, facts and figures about the world. Rather than probing operations, verbal IQ tests measure the size and fidelity of memory, the acuity of the senses, attention to detail, and the general ability to

focus on figures. Moreover, as we shall see in the next chapter, such figurative skills play an important role in the curricula of our school systems.

To some extent, this line of argument overdraws the differences. Every intelligence test requires some operations—for example, the ability to recognize similarities among words (How are *praise* and *punishment* alike?) or to solve analogies (Dog is to puppy as cat is to _____). By the same token, one could not pass a Piagetian problem without attending to

Creativity

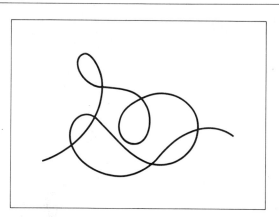

Some people would call this drawing a scribble; others might call it a piece of string; and a few might say it was paint squeezed out of a tube (or three ballerinas completing a dance.) No one answer is right or wrong, but they reflect clearly different degrees of imagination or **creativity**.

For many decades psychologists and educators have sought to measure intelligence (see the box on IQ Tests). More recently, some have sought to study and measure an even more elusive human trait: creativity. On many of the first creativity tests, scores were highly correlated with measures of intelligence; and yet, creativity and intelligence can clearly be distinguished. Indeed, some of the most imaginative artistic minds

(continued)

are surprisingly lacking in logical abilities and even common sense. Similarly, a highly intelligent person, armed with countless facts and a keen memory, may be rigidly conventional and unoriginal. Thus, psychologists have been challenged to devise tests which tease apart creativity and intelligence.

Jacob Getzels and Philip Jackson (1962) launched the mission in the late 1950s when they attempted to identify children who were either highly creative or highly intelligent but not both. Based on limited data, they found some intriguing but inconclusive differences between these populations: creative children tended to have parents who were less conforming and granted their children more independence. In contrast, parents of intelligent but less creative youngsters were more conventional and pressured their children to excel in school.

Hoping to achieve further understanding, Michael Wallach and Nathan Kogan (1965) embarked on new efforts to measure creativity. First they adopted a strict definition of creativity that was distinct from intelligence: when faced with a new task, the creative individual comes up with rich ideas and new associations while assuming a playful and permissive attitude. Wallach and Kogan believed that **associative fluency**—the ability to invent many responses of which a large portion are unusual and original—requires these two characteristics of creativity.

In order to measure creativity, they devised five tests designed to tap associative fluency. Three tests used verbal stimuli and two used nonverbal stimuli. In all cases, children were required to generate as many responses as they could, and a premium was placed on unique answers. (For sample items and responses, see Figure 10.9.) The researchers administered these tasks along with a battery of intelligence tests to 151 ten-year-olds.

The results confirmed that creativity and intelligence are indeed different and separable. The children could be divided into four distinct groups: creative and intelligent; creative but not intelligent; not creative but intelligent; and not creative and not intelligent. Not surprisingly, children in the last group tended to have low self-esteem and were not valued by peers, while those scoring high on both measures were well adjusted, successful, and valued by peers. The profiles of children in the other two groups were more complex.

Intelligent children who scored low in creativity were seen as "addicted" to school. The girls remained withdrawn from peers as they directed their energies to academic achievement. Boys were also conservative and conventional, but they were somewhat defensive and avoided sentimentality.

(continued)

Figure 10.9. In a nonverbal test for associative fluency, children are asked to indicate all the things that the drawing might be. Unique responses are considered significant indices of creativity. (Wallach and Kogan, 1965)

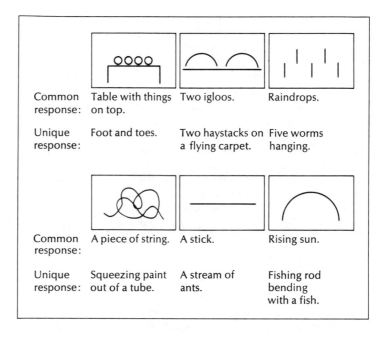

Common response:	Table with things on top.	Two igloos.	Raindrops.
Unique response:	Foot and toes.	Two haystacks on a flying carpet.	Five worms hanging.

Common response:	A piece of string.	A stick.	Rising sun.
Unique response:	Squeezing paint out of a tube.	A stream of ants.	Fishing rod bending with a fish.

Highly creative but less intelligent youngsters tended to be hesitant, insecure, and reluctant to associate with peers. Their anger toward school frequently made them resort to disruptive behavior. These children seemed out of place in the traditional classroom, but in a more open atmosphere which allows expression, they often blossomed.

The findings point to a specific cognitive dimension, associative fluency, that is separate from intelligence and is linked to particular behavior and personality patterns. But this is only part of the picture; there is more to creativity than associative fluency. The ten-year-old who scores well on Wallach and Kogan's tests will not necessarily become a great artist or renowned musician. Just as important is an intimate knowledge of a symbolic medium such as music, clay, or mathematics. For example, the painter must know the properties of his canvas, what effects various brushstrokes achieve, how colors combine, how light is reflected, and how different techniques convey different moods and tones. It is this combination of associative fluency and symbolic sophistication that may well distinguish the average or even intelligent mind from the creative artist.

relevant configurations in the tasks. Indeed, the conservation of quantity tasks contain a compelling example of the interaction of these modes of knowledge. To make progress, and eventually solve such problems, one must ignore some configurations (such as shape or color) and coordinate information from others (for instance, height and width). The ultimate achievement requires operative knowledge (such actions as reversing and compensating). But unless it has been embodied in configurations such operational knowledge remains inaccessible and inapplicable. In the last analysis, the developed individual must have command of both operative and figurative ways of knowing.

Post-Piagetian Approaches

The positions just reviewed—environmental-learning, skills, and intelligence—could each thrive in the absence of Piaget's contributions. Recently, however, a number of scholars influenced by Piaget have proposed approaches to cognition during middle childhood that extend Piaget's insights in new and hitherto unanticipated directions.

One approach, often called **information processing,** attempts to break down the processes that occur during the solution of problems into a series of tiny steps, each step entailing much greater detail than is ordinarily provided in Piagetian accounts. In fact, information-processing psychologists strive to account for solutions as they unfold second by second; and they strive for a degree of accuracy such that they can actually simulate the child's behavior on a computer (Klahr and Wallace, 1976; Seigler, in press, b).

Information-processing scientists pay a great deal of attention to a subject's reaction times, his processes of short-term memory, his scanning patterns, and his capacity to handle several items of information in a short period

of time (Keating, 1979; Schwantes, 1979). The words, pauses, and eye movements in a typical Piagetian protocol are grist for the information-processing mill. Researchers are also occupied with the enormously complex question of what aspects of information processing change with age and which remain relatively constant: the number of bits of information that can be held in mind, the capacity to store bits in memory, the amount of factual knowledge, the individual has, his ability to "assess" different bits of information, the speed with which operations can be carried out, the efficiency with which attention can be allocated and the like (Brown, in press; Chi, 1976; Wilkening, Becker, and Trabasso, 1980). And there is an emphasis on representing the goals as perceived by the subject and on the various steps he takes to lessen the gap between his current understanding and the ultimate achievement of his cognitive goals (Klahr and Wallace, 1976). Clearly, information-processing psychologists have set for themselves an ambitious program, one which is attracting the energies of a growing number of experimental researchers. We will take a closer look at Robert Siegler's version of information processing in Chapter 13.

An approach comparable in scope to the program outlined by Piaget has been put forth by Kurt Fischer (1980). Like Piaget, Fischer describes a framework that covers cognitive development from infancy to adulthood. Fischer also posits a series of hierarchically ordered stages: three at the "sensory-motor" level, three at the "representational" level, and four at the "abstract" level where systems of representations are mapped onto one another. Fischer finds evidence for these ten sequenced stages in the whole gamut of tasks from logical problem solving to social understanding. But in direct opposition to Piaget, Fischer finds no necessary parallel between what occurs at a given moment in one domain and what is occurring elsewhere. Speed and efficiency of development depend chiefly on the amount of experience the child has with materials in a given domain. As Fischer put it, "Unevenness in development is therefore the rule, not the exception" (1980, p. 480). In fact, turning Piaget on his head, Fischer declares that development is characterized by *décalage* (differences in sophistication at a particular stage across domains); when a subject is found at the same level across a number of domains, this is a coincidence rather than proof of a structural principle at work. On Fischer's account, there is no reason to expect conservation of length to co-occur

with any other conservation, but acquisition of all conservations entails parallel stage progressions.

An equally ambitious attempt at synthesis has been attempted by Robbie Case (1978), a researcher strongly influenced by the highly technical theory of Juan Pascual-Leone (1978) and also by the information-processing school. Like Fischer, Case believes that development consists of a series of ordered stages; but, unlike Fischer, Case believes that there is considerably more regularity across domains. For Case, the key concept in explaining development is the amount of "working memory"

Figure 10.10. Four substages of strategies observed in Piagetian tasks as the child becomes capable of concrete operations: Robbie Case's analysis. (Case, 1978)

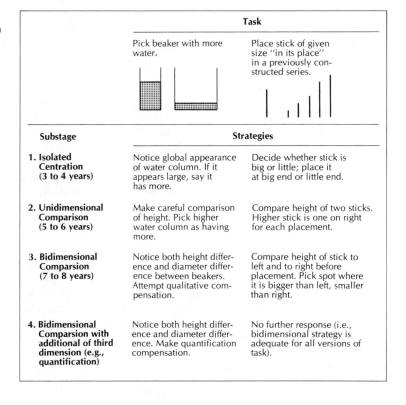

	Task	
	Pick beaker with more water.	Place stick of given size "in its place" in a previously constructed series.
Substage	**Strategies**	
1. Isolated Centration (3 to 4 years)	Notice global appearance of water column. If it appears large, say it has more.	Decide whether stick is big or little; place it at big end or little end.
2. Unidimensional Comparison (5 to 6 years)	Make careful comparison of height. Pick higher water column as having more.	Compare height of two sticks. Higher stick is one on right for each placement.
3. Bidimensional Comparsion (7 to 8 years)	Notice both height difference and diameter difference between beakers. Attempt qualitative compensation.	Compare height of stick to left and to right before placement. Pick spot where it is bigger than left, smaller than right.
4. Bidimensional Comparsion with additional of third dimension (e.g., quantification)	Notice both height difference and diameter difference. Make quantification compensation.	No further response (i.e., bidimensional strategy is adequate for all versions of task).

available to the child. Tasks can be described in terms of the degree of working memory, or "M-Space," that they require, and there is a regular increase with age in the size and availability of this working memory. The M-Space is available for use by one's "executive processes"—the individual's preferred plan, means, or strategy for dealing with a problem. If one knows a subject's M-power, one can predict his performance across a wide range of tasks; and one can enhance the child's performance either by supplementing the memory space available to the child or by reducing the demands made on working memory.

A feeling for the Case approach can be gleaned by considering his analysis of conservation of continuous quantities. Case distinguished four substages through which the child passes, each of which makes increasingly greater demands on working memory.

At the first substage, "isolated centration," the child merely notices the global appearance of a water column. If it appears large, he simply says it has "more."

At a second substage, "unidimensional comparisons" (ages five to six), the child makes a careful comparison of height. He then picks the higher water column as having more liquid. He must now take into account these two heights and retain them for comparison.

A third substage, "bidimensional comparison" (ages seven to eight), entails noticing both height difference and diameter difference between the beakers. Four factors must now be considered. The child is able to appreciate the qualitative compensation that obtains between the two dimensions.

Finally, at the fourth substage, "bidimensional comparison with the addition of a third dimension (or quantification)," the child notices both height and diameter differences but this time is able to make a quantifiable compensation (appreciation that the actual number of units has not changed).

Case isolates a number of factors that contribute to cognitive growth. First the child becomes able to handle a larger number of schemes at one time; thus he can remember and make use of more information in the course of solving problems. This facility comes about because the child becomes able to handle basic operations in a more automatic, less reflective way. As operations become more automatic, they occupy a smaller proportion of the child's total attending capacity. So more of the child's working memory, or computing space, becomes available for attending to other features relevant to the solution of a problem. The overall pace of development is regulated by the gradual increase in the size of working memory; progress during each stage comes about through pratice, highlighting of relevant cues, availability of models, and providing of feedback regarding the attainment of goals.

Case's model is quite complex and, as he himself indicates, it remains to be worked out completely. The model is a blend of classical Piagetian notions, concepts from information theory, approaches from computer modeling (notions such as a set of "executive strategies" and storing of information), and insights gained from various empirical studies conducted by scores of researchers. Case believes that he has preserved the central insight of Piaget: he has shown that if one knows the correct way to analyze tasks, one can successfully predict which tasks will be passed by the child at a particular point in his development. And in recent studies Case has demonstrated structural affinities between tasks in such apparently remote domains as moral judgment and conservation (1981).

Case is not the only researcher to attempt such a synthesis. A number of individuals influenced by Piaget, including Annette Karmiloff-Smith (1979c), feel that the best hope for a model of cognitive development during middle childhood comes from a wedding of Piagetian and computational, or information-processing, approaches.

These approaches, though promising, may suffer from certain weaknesses. For one thing, as many commentators have noted, it is extremely difficult to devise tests which can adjudicate among rival information processing claims: to determine, for example, whether improved performance reflects an increase in working memory, an increase in efficiency, an increase in automaticity, or some combination of these factors (Seigler, in press *b*). Furthermore, as Deanna Kuhn suggests (1980), not all processes of importance can necessarily be represented in terms of short-term information-processing sequences. Also, there is an important difference between the ability to execute a strategy and the realization that a strategy should be invoked; acquiring an understanding of the latter process is the more formidable challenge. Information-processing psychologists have little to say on "how it is that the child knows what to do" and "what" inside the child's head makes the decisions. The existence of strategies may be necessary, but not sufficient, for proper solutions. To account for the child's success or failure to employ the appropriate strategy, one may need recourse to concepts like the "intentions of the child," the child's "level of understanding," his "construction of the tasks," or his ability to "make meaning" (Kuhn, 1980). In their efforts to offer a microscopic explanation for behaviors, researchers must be careful not to dissolve what may be most distinctive—and most important—about children's mental accomplishments.

Signposts

Children at the age of five or six have developed a practical knowledge of the world of persons and objects as well as an initial mastery of such symbol systems as words, gestures, and pictures. Their challenges at the start of schooling and through the years of middle childhood are to organize knowledge about the world on a new, more sophisticated level, to appreciate relationships among units of knowledge, and to capture this form of knowledge in effective symbol systems.

Piaget called this phase of development the mastery of concrete operations, because grasping concepts and relationships involving physical material (rather than abstract symbols) is its hallmark. Experiments designed to test for concrete operations usually probe for the appreciation of a basic property of matter in the physical world. For instance, when a child appreciates that the quantity of a liquid poured from one container to another remains the same, he has mastered the idea of conservation of continuous quantities. He appreciates *identity* despite appearances to the contrary; he realizes, for example, that narrow width acts as compensation for increased height; and, now capable of reversibility, he can mentally return the substance to its original container to show that nothing has changed. By the same token, when the child appreciates that two arrays of six balls each contain the same number of elements, regardless of their perceived crowding, he has attained conservation of number. Piaget believed that these operations permeate a whole cluster of conceptual breakthroughs in understanding space, time, and cause and effect and that they eventually form the basis for all scientific, logical, and mathematical systems. But his position has been increasingly challenged.

Some researchers, although basically sympathetic to Piaget's viewpoint, feel that these abilities may arise earlier than Piaget claims. Jerome Bruner, for example, found that when deceptive differences between containers are eliminated, children appreciate the identity of the contents and can easily acquire conservation. Jan Smedslund, however, contends that children who acquire conservation as a consequence of such training are merely parroting the idea without belief or understanding. This controversy illuminates one of the basic pitfalls of research in this area: experimenters who judge by different criteria are likely to draw different conclusions about a child's cognitive competence and possession of concrete operations.

A similar air of controversy surrounds conservation of number. For instance, several investigators have produced evidence that young children are more aware of number than Piaget suggested. Carefully studying the understanding of number, Rochel Gelman has found among preschool children (and perhaps even among infants) a primitive appreciation of set size and some capacity to perform operations of addition and subtraction. She has also demonstrated an integral link between the ability to pick out the odd element in a group and various forms of conservation. In her view, acquiring conservation need not be spontaneous and untutored; it is simply another form of learning, one that can be taught once the child's attention has been directed toward the relevant dimensions of an array.

Another line of investigation has probed children's understanding of spatial concepts. Children as young as two or three can find their way around simple environments and can even reverse their usual steps through a locale. Older preschoolers use landmarks to find their way around unfamiliar environments. What proves more challenging for children is the ability to make inferences about spaces they have not directly perceived and to represent their knowledge of space in various models, such as maps or three-dimensional constructions—a symbolic rendition of their practical knowledge of the spatial world.

The various critiques of concrete operations have called Piaget's characterization into question. Indeed some critics have questioned the existence of a distinct stage and a characteristic set of structures worthy of the name "concrete operations." By the same token, investigators from the environmental-learning tradition break down concrete operations into component behaviors and contributing skills; they prefer to view the cognitive whole as no more than the sum of its parts.

While some investigators would just as soon dispense with Piaget's formulation, others feel a more promising approach is to build upon Piaget's pioneering insights. Inspired by computer simulation of human thought, several information-processing scientists have developed detailed models of the child's problem-solving processes at various points in development. Kurt Fischer has outlined a broad theory of development that finds a sequence of stages in every domain of knowledge but stresses *décalage,* rather than the integrated-stage aspects of cognitive growth. And, attempting to integrate the information-processing approach with the structural approach, Robbie Case has described the gradual growth of the child's working memory and executive strategies as he negotiates his way through the milestones of cognitive development. Through proper analysis of tasks and a careful attention to the child's information-processing limitations, it may prove possible to predict which tasks can be negotiated at any point in development.

The advent of concrete operations, be it relatively discrete as Piaget believed or much more gradual, uneven, and heterogeneous, as most others now think, is a central milestone of middle childhood. But other events, including some marginally related to operational thought, are also worth noting. For instance, children at this age gain skills in attending to specific details and static properties—the so-called figurative knowledge probed by intelligence tests. These skills prove especially important in the very domains of experience neglected by Piaget: the ability to express oneself clearly; the skills involved in reading and in remembering what one reads; the capacity to relate appropriately to works of art; and a sensitivity to social and emotional cues in interpersonal situations.

In the next chapter, therefore, we will devote particular attention to certain of these figurative capacities—both as they develop naturally and as they are molded by the process of schooling. We will examine how chil-dren, through both formal and informal instruction, acquire the skills valued in their culture. And we will consider some of the ways figurative capacities may interact with the mental operations to which our attention has been directed in this chapter. Taken together, then, the first two chapters of this section on middle childhood will constitute a survey of various approaches to mental development during the school years.

CHAPTER ELEVEN

Skills and Schooling

'Tis education forms the common mind;
Just as the twig is bent, the tree's inclined.

–ALEXANDER POPE

Every theory of education clearly requires a theory of society as a whole
and of how social processes shape education.

–SYLVIA SCRIBNER AND MICHAEL COLE

We take certain activities of daily life for granted. Particularly in Western societies, where individuals have been receiving formal education for generations, we assume that children will begin to attend school at the age of six or seven and will continue on a regular basis for at least a decade. This bias has even permeated the writing of this book, where I refer to the "preschooler," confident that you will understand what I mean and generalize it to all three- or four-year-olds.

In fact, formal schooling has been restricted to only a tiny portion of humanity, and for only a few centuries. Even today, a vast majority of children the world over receive at most a few years of schooling and perhaps one quarter of the children in the world, including some who have attended school, are illiterate. Attendance at high school and university is much rarer; in China, for example, out of nearly one billion individuals, barely one million students were enrolled at a university in 1980.

But education need not take place in institutions deliberately labeled as schools, set off in their own buildings with their own personnel and special curricula. Children have always learned skills, customs, and information from their parents, their peers, and from other knowledgeable individuals. Broaden the definition of schooling to include informal tutelage—through description, through adages, or through demonstrations—and the terms *preschooler* and *school-age child* are more universally applicable.

For in nearly every society, children aged five or six begin to address themselves to the task of mastering those skills and practices needed to cope successfully with life in their culture's context. Studies of other cultures, especially traditional, non-Western cultures, confirm that the period between seven and twelve is a time when children are acquiring skills vital to their society (LeVine, 1970; Seagrim and Lendon, 1980; Super and Harkness, 1980). If their parents are hunters, they will learn how to shoot, lay traps, and prepare meat. If their parents are farmers, they will learn how to plow, harvest, and keep away prey. If their parents fish, they will learn how to handle a boat, navigate, trap, fish, and prepare the catch for eating. The children's instruction is informal, occurring in the course of everyday life. Indeed, youngsters may begin by simply observing, then come naturally to help out, to participate fully, and eventually to supplant their elders altogether.

Some skills, however, do not appear to be acquired in this natural and spontaneous way. Mastery of reading, writing, and arithmetic, understanding of historical and scientific principles, and other skills of the sort being acquired by most youngsters in modern technologically oriented societies seem to depend on a formal education. Moreover, it may be that, in addition to providing these intellectual skills, schooling has certain effects on how individuals solve problems and think about issues. If we are to understand the cognitive changes occuring during middle childhood, we must determine which changes are the natural result of maturation and which depend upon attendance at school. To do so, we should survey a range of abilities used by children everywhere—language, memory, reasoning, classification—in terms of their generic developmental course and in light of the differences that formal schooling might make. Some of these skills—such as the ability to remember a list of words or to recognize objects—depend chiefly on those abilities that Piaget termed figurative (see Chapter 10). Others, such as the capacity to classify objects in terms of multiple dimensions or to reason logically, make considerable use of operative forms of thinking. Schooling surveys a large range of skills and subject matter, covering the gamut of operative and figurative forms of thinking. As a general rule, however, schooling and other kinds of formal training heighten the tendency to use operative modes of thought. Therefore, our account of the effects of schooling centers upon the introduction of more active, operative modes of information processing and upon the training of children to utilize such modes even when they have not been explicitly instructed to do so.

Introducing the Kpelle

Because schooling is almost universal in our society, its effects cannot be assessed by research within our culture. Instead, it is necessary to visit a society in which many children do not attend school. Michael Cole and his associates have studied the Kpelle, a people living in Liberia (Cole et al., 1971). Basically farmers, the Kpelle dwell in thatched huts that are usually no more than a single room with a fire in the center. Some Kpelle live in much the same way as their ancestors did, raising rice, cassava, and other vegetables, letting their children gradually acquire the old-fashioned methods of farming. Other Kpelle have begun to acquire the ways of technologi-

Figure 11.1. In all societies, irrespective of their complexity or degree of industrialization, children spend their middle years acquiring a range of relevant skills. The American youngster at left is carefully screwing a hinge into a piece of wood; the girls from the Kpelle tribe of Liberia are using a mortar and pestle to pound rice.

cally oriented societies. The children go to local schools where they are taught the basic skills of reading and writing.

Over the years, Cole's team has assessed the performance of schooled and unschooled Kpelle youngsters on various tasks. Most of these tasks have been adopted from American experimental psychology. The researchers, however, have striven to make the tests as free from cultural bias as possible by using materials drawn from the region: children are asked to solve tasks about rice and cassava rather than about M&Ms or Coke. In contrast to the tests of conservation, these tasks focus particularly on figurative capacities—on the ability to remember lists of items, to associate

words with one another, and the like. The purpose has been to determine if and when the Kpelle children acquire these capacities.

The Cole team found that both schooled and unschooled Kpelle children performed very poorly on a task where they had to recall a list of words. The result was puzzling. After all, these children display excellent memories in recounting stories and past events. Why did they fail on this task even when the list was repeated several times? Later in this chapter we shall describe how an experimental modification affected performance of the subjects and, in the process, helped to illustrate some of the effects of schooling in a less industrial civilization.

We can better evaluate the significance of Cole's studies among the Kpelle after reviewing the performance of American children on the kinds of linguistic, memory, and classification tasks adopted by the Cole team. Such a review will provide a perspective from which to view the Kpelle findings; it will also complement the examination of classical Piagetian operations that occupied us in the previous chapter; and it will help unravel the mechanisms of certain figurative processes—in particular the use of language and the ability to memorize—that are crucial for the acquisition of knowledge in school. We will also have the opportunity to apply a range of operations within those essentially figurative realms. Such examination can help to explain how schoolchildren memorize facts of geography or names of presidents; how they learn concepts like "gravity," "democracy," "musical harmony"; and how they organize materials in the course of study.

Moving beyond capacities usually considered to be figurative, we will also look at the emergence of the ability to classify objects, which begins with an emphasis on figurative aspects, such as the perceptual properties of the stimuli. With development, operative capacities—such as the consistent application of a set of logical criteria—assume increasing importance in the child's classifications or categorizations. These abilities are particularly important in school, where children are called upon to classify mathematical problems, types of government, or biological species.

Finally, we will address an important set of capacities that develops relatively late: the capacities to reflect upon one's own thought processes, to think about one's own remembering, classifying, and problem solving. This review will again underscore the need for both operative and figurative skills and suggest some of the ways in which they interact productively, in Kpelle children no less than in children being raised in Korea or Kansas.

The Contribution of Language

Of the various tools and symbol systems available, language has been the principal vehicle traditionally used in educational institutions. Students are expected to learn facts and rules announced by the instructor; and once they have learned to read and write, they are expected to draw much of their knowledge from books and to express conclusions in spoken and written language.

In our examination of language during the preschool years (Chapter 4), we saw that children acquire the rudiments of language with tremendous speed and accuracy. This achievement is most impressive and yet, in Piaget's view, it is essentially a figurative form of mastery. That is because an individual can have mastered a great deal of syntax, phonology, and semantics without using language in a logically consistent manner, without being able to use it effectively in argument or to appreciate figures of speech.

In our earlier examination of communication capacities (Chapter 7) we saw how children just beginning school use language to direct their own behavior and to assume the roles of other individuals. Here one encounters initial signs of operations within language, as the child is able to reverse roles or points of view. Yet even after some years of schooling, children still have not mastered all facets of language.

LATER MILESTONES
IN LANGUAGE DEVELOPMENT

While young children use and understand language at a high level, there are still some striking gaps in their competence. For one thing, children in the preschool years display little, if any, awareness that they are actually using language and that this language consists of words that assume various roles in a sentence (Donaldson, 1978; Gleitman, Gleitman, and Shipley, 1972). In one sense, this ignorance is irrelevant, for children are still able to communicate most of their needs adequately. Yet unless they have some awareness of the existence of language and the way that it functions, they will not be able to master reading: reading presupposes the ability to break the stream of sound into individual words and to realize that these words each correspond to a written portion of script (Ferrerio, 1978; Karmiloff-Smith, 1979c; Vygotsky, 1978) (see the box on Reading). Such awareness of words is also necessary in more complex uses of language, such as those entailed in figures of speech or in logical reasoning and argument.

Although the child's grammar advances with astounding speed, islands of ignorance remain. As Carol Chomsky has shown (1969; see also R. J. Harris, 1975; Kessel, 1970) children ranging in age from five to nine have difficulty apprehending the meanings of certain constructions. For example, young schoolchildren will interpret the sentence "The doll is easy to see" as if it meant "The doll can see." They will also assume that "John promised Mary to shovel the driveway," means the same as "John told Mary to shovel the driveway," even as they will fail to appreciate the difference between "Dad asked Johnny what to do" and "Dad told Johnny what to do." They are unable to detect ambiguities, becoming alert to the two meanings of "She hit the man with the glasses" only at about the age of eight or nine and understanding the multiple meanings of "He told her baby stories" somewhere between the ages of nine and twelve (Kessel, 1970). In general, young school-age children show a strong proclivity to rely on their knowledge about the world rather than on any awareness of language per se. In the view of many educators, schooling should commence by recognizing the child's strong interest in the things of

the world and in the actions one can perform on them. But an important goal of most schooling is to facilitate discussion of objects that are absent, to direct attention to language itself, and to promote the use of language for purposes of argument and of artistry.

SENSITIVITY TO METAPHOR AND LOGIC

As an example of what is entailed in children's reflection upon language, consider how one might understand a figure of speech like a metaphor, which equates two elements from different domains of experience. Asked to interpret the sentence "My friend John is a real tiger," most children at the start of school interpret it literally to mean that John is actually a tiger (Winner, Rosenstiel, and Gardner, 1976). Seven- or eight-year-olds will understand that the statement is literally impossible and will attempt to make sense of it in other ways. They may, for example, change the sentence into a story ("John is friendly with a tiger"), or seizing on some property of tigers, they may contend that John has striped shirts or makes a noise like a tiger.

To appreciate this metaphor, however, children must recognize the existence of two separate classes: humans and tigers. Moreover, they must be aware of traits that can cut across these classes, such as ferocity, feline beauty, or impassivity. Only then can they join the two categories while honoring their logical separateness. To accomplish this, the children must be aware of multiple meanings of words and the ways in which classes of words can be related. They must also have a distance from language, an ability to reflect on words and their meaning, which emerges only around the age of ten or eleven.

Related processes can be observed when children are confronted with a verbal tautology, a statement whose truth can be judged solely on logical grounds, without reference to the real world, such as "Either she is tall or

Reading Theory and Practice

Imagine if you could not read: this page would be a meaningless array of hatchmarks; academic study would be impossible and advancement beyond menial occupations very difficult; tax forms, road signs and labels on the supermarket shelf would be confusing if not incomprehensible; merely looking up the schedule of the local movie might be a struggle. In our culture the ability to read is crucial even for routine functioning.

Reading may also affect one's understanding of what has been said. According to the educational psychologist David Olson, preliterate children do not appreciate the difference between literal meaning, or what is *said*, and intent, or what is *meant*. Take, for example, the sentence "You have more than I." If a child understands the intended message, he will likely say that the speaker said, "Give me some." Only once the child reads and can see the sentence before him, will he understand that the speaker *meant*, "Give me some," but actually *said*, "You have more than I." Thus, Olson maintains that the ability to read may unlock a whole new awareness of the language system (Olson and Hildyard, 1980).

Most of us take reading for granted. We may forget that it is a skill which must be acquired and mastered over a number of years. But unlike the ability to walk or eat, reading does not develop naturally; it must be taught. If instruction is inadequate or unavailable, the necessary reading skills will not be attained. Statistics of adult illiteracy suggest that our current educational programs are lacking. Some studies label over one-fifth of the total U.S. adult population as functionally illiterate (*Adult Functional Competency Study,* 1975). In order to design more effective programs of instruction, it is necessary to understand how the brain processes written material and what the act of reading entails. This has been the focus of much recent research and discussion among scholars.

At one time, reading was thought to be a single or holistic process. Although some still hold this view, current theorists generally believe reading to be a complex information processing activity consisting of a number of interrelated subprocesses. There are lower level processes, such as letter and word recognition, word decoding, and syntactic parsing, and there are higher processes, such as drawing inferences and understanding multiple levels of meaning. When these processes (and their representative skills) have been properly mastered and integrated, reading resembles a single or holistic activity. One might compare reading to a game of tennis. A successful forehand shot looks like one sweeping action, but in fact, the player must know how to hold the racket, step into the shot, contact the ball, and follow through with the swing. In addition, he must engage in such strategic activity as anticipating his partner's next shot, accounting for effects of the wind, and compensating for his own weaknesses. How does he do all this?

Our brains can hold and process only a limited amount of information at any one time. Therefore, we must allocate our

(*continued*)

mental energy sparingly and efficiently. If a tennis player must devote all his mental energy to holding his racket properly, he will not be able to focus attention on how to place the ball. The good player has mastered the basic skills to such an extent that they have become automatic; he does not think about how to hold the racket, he just grips it. This allows him to direct his energies to higher skills such as where to place his next shot.

It is much the same with reading. If a person has to direct too much of his limited attention to lower level skills of, say, sounding out words, he will very likely not have much attention left to devote to attaining the full meaning of the text. If, however, his word recognition skills are mastered, he will have resources available for higher level skills of comprehension and inference making. According to Phyllis Weaver, a psychologist of reading at the Harvard Graduate School of Education, a crucial difference between the skilled and the unskilled reader appears to be the degree to which lower level decoding skills and some basic comprehension skills can be performed automatically—that is, rapidly and without attention.

How are the various subskills executed and interrelated during reading? Several schemes have been proposed. According to the "bottom up" or "data driven" scheme, all information is provided in the text. The reader starts with the printed page (the data) and works his way "up," progressing from lower level skills of perceiving visual symbols to converting the symbols to sounds that are then translated into word meanings and combined into phrases and sentences. In the "top down" or "concept driven" model, the reader brings considerable information to the written page, and using his knowledge of the world and of the specific text, he forms predictions about the text's meaning. Lower level skills are only called upon as needed to verify these predictions.

Most likely, reading is neither exclusively data driven nor concept driven; instead, it is an interactive system that simultaneously exploits data and concepts. The facile reader automatically knows how and when to employ higher level processes and lower ones. He may engage in higher processes to develop a mental model of what the text says and then use visual and phonological information to fill out the model. In turn, information gained from recognizing words and phrases informs and refines the mental model, enabling information processing to proceed in an efficient manner.

Theoretical understanding of the reading process has clear and direct implications for instruction. On the assumption that a key to effective reading is automaticity, the aim of reading programs should be to achieve automaticity in as many skills as possible. In teaching almost anything, one begins with the basic skills. One does not teach a player how to place the ball before he knows how to hold the racket. Similarly, with reading it is best to concentrate first on word recognition and then on higher level comprehension skills.   (*continued*)

Two major approaches have been used to teach word recognition skills. Proponents of the phonics method stress that our written language is alphabetic. The key to reading lies in understanding the alphabetic principles and letter-sound relationships which will enable the reader to decode new words. Thus, the phonics approach emphasizes the synthesis of word parts. It typically begins with the smallest unit, first teaching letter names and sounds and then the means of blending them into words. In contrast, the whole word approach focuses on words as the basic unit. It relies heavily on memorization of whole words that are eventually analyzed into parts.

In general, phonics has proved the more successful method. By the third grade, children taught by this approach tend to be better and more independent readers and are more able to use phonic skills to identify untaught words than those instructed by the whole word method. Weaver points out that because it is impossible to memorize every word, the whole word approach presupposes that the child will acquire the requisite phonic knowledge without which he will be unable to decode new words. The able child may do well with the whole word approach probably because he will figure out the letter-sound system or "crack the code" on his own. The less able child will not figure it out and will likely have difficulty advancing beyond an elementary level of reading. Although learning to read by the phonics approach may seem to pose special problems for some children, it is these children who are at risk for reading failure for whom phonics instruction is essential.

Although early instruction should emphasize letter-sound correspondences and decoding skills, it is important to incorporate comprehension skills as well. Children should be able to understand what they decode, and in order to consolidate and automate the essential skills, they should be given ample opportunity to practice reading stimulating, informative materials. Then, once basic skills have been mastered, it is time to shift the focus to higher level comprehension skills and more complex materials. Children should be taught strategies for using their world knowledge effectively. They need to be made aware of how the overall structure of the textual material can provide clues for meaning. Teachers should ask questions that encourage the reader to interpret texts at different levels (for example, literal, inferential, and evaluative).

The timing of reading instruction is crucial. According to Weaver, the major problem with many programs is not so much in *how* skills are taught but *when*. Too often, children are pushed beyond their readiness. Complex texts are introduced before automaticity has been achieved with simpler materials, and higher level skills are taught before the basic ones have been mastered. Effective instruction attends to individual needs and progresses according to the readiness of each child.

(For further reading, see Chall, 1967; Gibson and Levin, 1975; K. Goodman, 1971; Weaver and Shonkoff, 1978.)

she is not tall." Daniel Osherson and Ellen Markman (1975) presented school-age children with a chip and asked them to evaluate various statements by saying "True," "False," or "Don't know." As long as the statement could be empirically verified—as in the case of "This chip is green"—children as young as six or seven performed adequately. But when the experimenter covered the chip and said, "Either this chip is green or it is not green," the same children could not answer correctly. They could not judge such tautologies, statements where empirical considerations (the color of the chip) were irrelevant and the truth was entirely logical, contained within the statement itself. Only youngsters aged eleven or twelve could appreciate the relevant factors and answer correctly of this tautology, "True."

SOME EDUCATIONAL IMPLICATIONS

Implications for schooling follow from these findings. First, it seems clear that children will not understand everything they hear or read, and they may well form misconceptions. This is particularly true when the concrete objects being talked about are not evident, or when statements are primarily abstract or logical. Metaphoric statements are likely to be taken literally; statements that are purely logical in nature are likely to be judged on empirical grounds, or not at all.

Just what enables the child to appreciate these more difficult linguistic forms is not known, but several considerations appear relevant. First, children must understand the precise meanings of terms. A metaphor is effective only when children appreciate that a human being is, under normal circumstances, not equivalent to a nonhuman animal (R. G. Schwartz, 1980). Next, children must be able to think of words (and of language) as other than a literal description of some state of events in the world. For instance, to under-

Figure 11.2. During most of early life, children's learning derives chiefly from their actions in the world of physical objects. One challenge of schooling is to apply accurately those symbol systems devised by the culture (such as mathematical and verbal symbols) to this concrete experience.

stand our metaphor, they must appreciate that John is not really a tiger but that he possesses certain tigerlike traits. To understand a tautology, they must appreciate that a statement can be confirmed without referring to the world, by looking exclusively at the meaning of the expressions in the statement. Though it is certainly possible to understand tautologies without being literate, the capacity to consider statements in terms of their logical implications may be intimately tied to the ability to read (Olson, 1981). Just why this may be so is not understood.

Third, and perhaps most central, these difficult linguistic forms require certain logical capacities (Falmagne, 1975; Scholnick and Wing, 1981; Standenmayer and Bourke, 1977).

Metaphor depends on the appreciation that an element (such as a boy) may be like another element (a tiger) in some but not in other respects. Tautologies require an understanding that an element (a chip) is by definition either green or not green; it cannot be both. Thus children can fully understand poems containing metaphors and scientific works based on logical theories only when they have acquired the necessary operational capacties. Both the figurative capacity to process the linguistic message and the operative capacity to compare classes of objects make essential contributions to such understanding.

Although logical capacities are clearly necessary for appreciating metaphoric and logical sentences, they are probably not sufficient. Children must also be exposed to these kinds of utterances. And, equally crucial, they must acquire some understanding of why such statements are being made. A metaphor presented out of context is much more difficult to evaluate than one that fits into a story (Honeck, Sowry, and Voegtle, 1978; Ortony, 1980); a logical statement uttered in the midst of an argument in which the child has a stake proves easier to evaluate than one presented as an item in an experimenter's test (Pea, 1977; Wason, 1965). Only when children regularly encounter such figurative statements, and are motivated to decode them, will they come to apprehend their intended meanings.

The Capacity to Remember

Like the ability to speak and understand language, the ability to remember is fundamental to all human learning, formal and informal. Indeed, humans could not possibly repeat activities—whether singing, skiing, or spelling—unless they could resurrect what had occurred before.

A well-entrenched view of memory holds that the brain—or the mind—is a receptacle, into which we faithfully pour all our experiences. With suitable stimulation, these memories can be brought back into conscious awareness (Penfield and Roberts, 1959). But as we saw in the introduction to this book, memory is probably a much more active, selective, changing process, in which a person's level of understanding directly determines how information is stored, what is remembered, and under what conditions it can be recalled. To conceptualize this area, psychologists have taken to describing different memory processes. They investigate **verbal memory,** as well as **motor memory** and **visual memory.** They are interested in unusual abilities like eidetic imagery—the capacity to recall a scene or experience with photographic accuracy (see Chapter 9). And they have broken memory down into stages, including **immediate memory** for what has just passed some milliseconds ago; **short-term memory** for the events of the last few minutes; and **long-term memory** for the lasting, unshakable recollections of important events, dates, persons, and feelings (Cermak and Craik, 1979).

Memory has become so rich an area of psychological study that we cannot conceivably review even a tiny bit of the research into memory processes and how they change with age (see A. L. Brown, 1975; Kail, 1979, for recent reviews). Instead, we shall focus on a representative task usually called **free recall.** The underlying ability—to remember a series of items—is used often in the classroom and in daily life. A brief survey can reveal something of the child's capacities for memory—and perhaps also something of our own.

TWELVE WORDS TO RECALL

Following a long tradition, psychologists prefer to test memory with discrete, unfamiliar items, for instance, randomly produced geometric designs, nonsense words, unrelated digits or words. The simplest measure of memory is the number of items recalled. What follows is one such test—a list of a dozen words. Either read them aloud to yourself a few times, or tell them to a friend. Then try to recall the entire list. Keep track of the number of attempts necessary—with correction of errors—until the whole list is correctly related.

Napoleon	car	if
pencil	eighteen	twelve
pair	put	Xerox
beauty	troop	land

You (or your subject) may have taken advantage of what you could recall without special effort—the first and last words (thus documenting "primacy" and "recency" effects), perhaps the numbers, perhaps the most vivid words. But in all likelihood, you will also have attempted some tricks—a sentence, a pictorial image, or some combination—to make the whole message or at least parts of it come together into a more meaningful pattern (see Bartlett, 1932; Rumelhart and Ortony, 1977). Perhaps you have learned to associate a different object with each position in a series (first is always the front door, second is always the doormat, and so on) and have then invented a bizarre but vivid association between Napoleon and the door, pencil and the doormat, and so on. Perhaps you have simply tried to invent a single sentence laced with cues: "In 1812 if troops put a pair of pencils in a beautiful Land Rover car, Napoleon Xeroxed them." Or perhaps your memory is accurate enough that you mastered the list without recourse to any gimmicks.

The less related the words in the list are, the fewer superordinate categories there are and the more difficult the memory task. Experimenters are forever striving to produce lists that thwart even the kind of tricks outlined above—for instance, the nonsense syllables *biv, kor,* and *luv.* But the thinking subject (or the avid game player) will try to make

sense even of these, perhaps transforming them into "bivouac the corporal whom she loves." (Abstract visual patterns motivate similar games between experimenters and subjects.)

AGE CHANGES IN CHILDREN'S MEMORY

The experiment just described and the brief analysis of some common strategies convey some feeling for how adults in our society tackle tasks of free recall. But what of children? Scores of studies have presented children of different ages with such lists of items—words, pictures, objects—and have compared their overall performances and strategies. (For useful reviews see Corsini, 1971; Hagen, 1971*a*; Jablonski, 1974; Kail and Hagen, 1977; Levin, 1980; Pressley, 1977; Rohwer, 1970). The general finding is that, with age, children become better able to devise strategies for remembering new information, to use the strategies appropriately and consistently, and to store information more effectively. Pictures, images, and other forms of elaboration aid children at every age. By the time they reach adolescence or adulthood, individuals have a set of strategies on which they can draw to help them sort or recall whatever information has been presented, and they are generally aware of these strategies.

From Preschoolers to Preadolescents. What of the youngest children? Typical preschoolers, aged three or four, will remember a few items from a list they have heard. On each trial they will remember different words, and their learning will accumulate at a snail's pace. They will process the words as a set of isolated units, not seriously considering their meanings or the possible relations among them. They will not spontaneously rehearse, or they will rehearse only a single word. Eventually they may be able to recall the words in the same order they were presented. In that case, they are learning a figurative pattern—almost like a piece of music, or the garbled version of the pledge to the flag that many of us learned as youngsters. Once it's been mastered, they can echo the pattern back in one seamless unit (Hayes and Schulze, 1977).

It would be misleading to suggest that preschoolers are completely inadequate at recall tasks. Their short-term memory is powerful enough that they can remember groups of pictures or brief lists of words as well as older children can (Brown and Campione, 1972). They may have the basic idea of planning, cuing themselves, or helping themselves to remember in other ways (Wellman, Ritter, and Flavell, 1975), but they do not yet know how best to use or orchestrate these strategies (Kreutzer, Leonard, and Flavell, 1975). They can generally adopt aids, strategies, and cues or rehearse procedures suggested by an experimenter, though they may abandon them with little provocation (Perlmutter et al., 1981). If the words fall readily into familiar categories (for example, two animals, two desserts), they may exploit this fact in their recall (Mansfield, 1977; Perlmutter and Myers, 1979). When cues arise in their everyday settings, they are quick to exploit them (Mitchell et al., 1979), and when children have the opportunity to learn a set of objects in the context of a highly meaningful activity—for example, playing store— their recall improves significantly (Istomina, 1975).

A ready contrast can be seen by considering the behavior of preadolescents, who in most aspects of memory are similar to college students or mature adults. Preadolescents immediately try to make sense of the task and, more specifically, of the list they have heard. They will scan the list to find common properties among the words and will try to sort them by whatever principle suggests it-

self: beginning letter, part of speech, category of experience (Moely et al., 1969). They will adhere to this procedure as much as possible, but if necessary they can add other properties or abandon the original plan altogether (Pellegrino, Posnansky, and Vesonder, 1977).

Having arrived at some strategy, preadolescents will actively rehearse the list so that they can reproduce it successfully when required to do so. When possible, they will cue themselves ("After I say all the names of objects, I'll switch to the little words. Next time I'll start with the four nouns"). They will attempt to convert the information into a sensory pattern or a symbolic medium that lends itself better to memorization: for instance, they may create a picture or song containing a number of the element's names. If allowed, they will simply write down as many words as possible.

Whether the changes in memory capacity between the preschool and preadolescent years are better described as quantitative or qualitative is debatable. From one point of view, preadolescents seem qualitatively different: they exhibit a system and an arsenal of strategies the preschooler does not have and they can invoke them without prompting. Yet traces of these strategies can be identified in preschoolers, or they can be encouraged by the ingenious experimenter. In this sense, the change seems quantitative. But however this shift is described, changes in relatively figurative capacities like memorization do seem less dramatic than the shift in world view associated with a new level of operational thought.

The Contributions of General Understanding. All the same, as children acquire more powerful logical capacities, their ability to remember is affected in instructive ways. The contribution of higher cognitive processes to memory rings out clearly in a study by J. Richard Barclay and Marylou Reid (1975).

Children who thought they were solving a problem were unexpectedly asked to recall sentences like "The artist is taller than the cowboy" and "The fireman is shorter than the cowboy." Seven-year-olds—whose literal understanding of the sentences had been confirmed earlier—recalled only fragmentary "figurative" bits of information, some of which were even inconsistent and contradictory. Ten-year-olds, however, produced a series of ordered relations that even included information not explicitly presented, for instance, "The artist is taller than the fireman." The child's production of a sentence not heard before but factually correct and following from what was heard is evidence that logical reasoning—the capacity to make deductions from available information—has a direct and significant effect on memory (Omanson, Warren, and Trabasso, 1978; Paris and Upton, 1976).

Further support for the contribution of general understanding to memory comes from a study carried out by Scott Paris and Barbara Lindauer (1976). These experimenters asked six- to eleven-year-old children to remember a sentence like "The workman dug a hole in the ground." For half the children, the phrase "with a shovel" was added to the sentence. Memory was tested by requiring the children to recall the sentence when provided with the cue word "shovel," regardless of whether the word had been included in the sentence they had heard. Eleven-year-olds remembered the sentence equally well, whether or not they had heard the word "shovel" in the sentence. They had apparently supplemented the sentence with this information on their own. But six- and seven-year-olds were aided by the cue "shovel" only when they had heard it in the sentence before. Apparently, their memory was not supplemented with this implicit information.

Interestingly, young children's recall improved when, in a variation, they were required to act out the sentences. Having to

demonstrate a workman digging proved as helpful as hearing the word "shovel" itself. Thus, dramatic enactment of a sentence can—like the inclusion of the cue word in the original sentence—close the gap between six- and eleven-year-olds. And when the inference is absolutely central to comprehension of the story, even first graders are likely to make it (Hildyard, 1979). These results suggest to Paris (1978) that young children have the *competence* to make inferences and that they suffer from a "production deficiency"; assuming that a memory task calls for rote recall, not for transforming, they do not spontaneously draw upon the inferential capacities that they have.

EXCEPTIONS TO INCREASING MEMORY

Although memory abilities generally increase with age, some interesting exceptions can be found. In the view of most authorities, recognition memory—the capacity to recognize whether the stimulus in question has been previously encountered—shows relatively little improvement with age (A. L. Brown, 1975; Kagan et al., 1973; K. E. Nelson, 1971; Owings and Baumeister, 1979; Wagner, 1981; but see Dirks and Neisser, 1977). When children are especially expert in a given domain—for example, chess—their memories for displays may actually surpass those of adults (Chi, 1976). And there is at least anecdotal evidence that children's abilities to remember certain kinds of meaningless patterns—for example, the location of matching pairs in the game "Concentration"—is actually better than that of adults. Perhaps older children are actually impaired by their search for a meaningful way of grouping (Somerville and Wellman, 1979).

As we saw in Chapter 9, there is a specific kind of memory—called eidetic imagery—that occurs most frequently among young children and is virtually absent in adulthood, at least in our society. Older persons may be able to describe very well, in general terms, what they have seen, but they are not as proficient at citing exact details. There are at least two plausible explanations: either some neurological changes at puberty actually reduce the child's ability to hold or reproduce stimulation faithfully, or the increasing ability (and tendency) to classify and reclassify items may weaken precise figurative memory (H. Gardner, 1977). Evidence in favor of the latter hypothesis comes from the fact that eidetic imagery is thwarted if a child is required to name items while they are being presented. Rather than enhancing subsequent recall, naming seems to cloud the eidetic imagery (Haber, 1968).

An interesting footnote to this finding comes from the work of John Hagen (1971b). He showed pictures of animals to two groups of children and instructed one group but not the other to name the animals. Such labeling helped children aged seven, eight, and nine in subsequent recall tasks, but it did not help nursery school children. Apparently, these four- and five-year-olds were too young to take advantage of such "encoding" in two sense modalities. At the other end of the age spectrum, the recall of children aged ten was actually harmed by verbal labeling. Perhaps the older children had attained an age where labeling occurs spontaneously and where they had evolved their own strategies for remembering. Even as verbal mediation may undermine an eidetic image, compulsory rehearsal at the direction of the experimenter can interfere with older children's customary memory process.

THE MEMORY THAT IS UNCALLED FOR

In 1954 Harold Stevenson noticed that children who were asked to find a key in a box often remembered other objects in the box. Since there was no reason for them to do so,

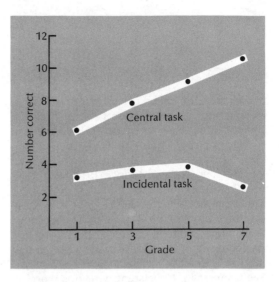

Figure 11.3. Given the overwhelming developmental trend toward improved performance with age, it is of special interest when children's performance *declines* with age. In the task of incidental learning plotted here, children were told to focus on background color but were then asked, unexpectedly, to report which of several pictures had appeared against the background color. Performance on this task of incidental learning declined during the preadolescent years, documenting a lessening ability with age to retain information irrelevant to the task at hand.

this memory was considered to be and later dubbed **incidental learning.**

At first it seemed that incidental learning increased with age. But then Eleanor Maccoby and John Hagen (1965) asked children to attend to the colors of cards that also happened to picture familiar objects. Afterward, the children were asked to pick out the cards portraying certain objects from a larger group of cards. Performance improved slightly between the ages of six and eleven, but decreased significantly between the ages of eleven and thirteen (see Figure 11.3). The experimenters reasoned that children's attention had become more selective or focused. Knowing where to look and having the required mental operations, the older children did so efficiently, thereby neglecting apparently irrelevant figurative information.

In general, incidental learning declines when a person's motivation to perform well on the stated task increases. Perhaps incidental learning represents the persistence of sloppy strategies, a weak orientation toward a specific goal (Hale and Piper, 1973), or the inability to relinquish the "pull" of a dominant stimulus (Hale et al., 1978) or to negotiate one's way among competing tasks (Lane, 1980). More positively, it may also represent the tendency of young children to play freely and to explore their environments more fully (see Chapter 6). Consistent with this more generous view is the finding that incidental learning is more likely to occur when children have time to look around—for example, when the presentation is visual—than when the material is more fleeting, as in verbal presentations (Hale, Miller, and Stevenson, 1968). Whatever its cause, this tendency among young children to pick up incidental details has been found repeatedly, and its emergence and subsequent disappearance may well be basic human milestones during middle childhood.

ALTERNATIVE WAYS TO CONCEPTUALIZE MEMORY

So far, we have emphasized the extent to which memory improves naturally, as a function of age and experience in the world. Primary school children can often remember isolated details of a situation, but the capacities to summarize and integrate information and to arrive at effective strategies for subsequent recall develop only gradually during middle childhood (A. L. Brown, 1975; Elliott, 1980; Mosenthal, 1979). We have also noted that children are particularly limited in recalling information considered by an experimenter to be crucial for a task. Indeed, the child's improving memory can be seen as an increasing sensitivity to the demands of the task, or as a

relinquishing of the task the child would like to perform in favor of that dictated by the experimenter. The declining incidental learner is the budding master of tasks: he becomes ever more sensitive to the requirements of home, school, and the surrounding culture.

A related hypothesis about memory comes from the Soviet school of psychology. This orientation features an interest in how children acquire the signals of the culture—a process we examined in Chapter 7. According to John Meacham (1972), the Soviet psychologists maintain that the culture assumes a crucial role in telling children what they are to remember and how best to remember it. In this view, memory development involves identifying *what* should be remembered as well as providing some *means* for remembering it. Societies have always defined what is important to remember—whether cows, oral verse, the Bible, or navigation routes—and they have equipped young members with procedures for recalling these items (timetables, stories, proverbs, pictures, songs, or diagrams). Our own society, where most children attend school for many years, emphasizes the integration of apparently isolated bits of information about history, geography, economics, politics, and so on. And this is the memory game we eventually master.

Another way to think about memory has grown out of a dispute about the role of mediation. Some experts maintain that preschoolers and kindergartners cannot remember a series of pictures or objects well because they are unable to mediate; that is, as we saw in Chapter 7, they cannot yet generate an internal symbolic response to the stimuli. Even when labels are provided, their performance will not improve because they cannot use such mediators (Reese, 1962). This is the mediation-deficiency view, which holds that children do not have the competence to use labels. In contrast to it, the production-deficiency view maintains that children can use the words and thus have the competence to mediate, but they need prompting if they are to produce the mediators.

John Flavell (Flavell, 1970; Moely et al., 1969) has helped to clarify the production-mediation controversy by characterizing what appears to be the crucial developmental change. Mediation is never totally absent, nor are children completely unable to exploit the mediators provided them. But effective use and production of mediators is aided by general cognitive advances like abilities to plan and discover the relations among apparently disparate elements. Children learn to resort regularly to strategies (such as rehearsal) that will help them complete a task. They learn to devise, implement, and revise plans. The operations of overt labeling, sequencing labels, and even withholding them when necessary are applied more and more effectively to memory. And, of course, as they grow older, children add a variety of serviceable mediators to their repertoires.

METAMEMORY

While the descriptions of memorization we have reviewed are useful in characterizing the child's growing repertoire of strategies (Levin, 1980), they have skirted the child's own perceptions of the activity in which he is involved. Recent interest in **metamemory**—the individual's awareness of and reflection upon his own mnemonic processes—brings to the center of attention the child's own bootstrapping capacities.

The ability to reflect upon one's own activities generally follows the development of those activities themselves. In this sense, metamemory is no exception: it is a relatively late developing capacity (Flavell and Wellman, 1977; Ringel and Springer, 1980). Indeed, at their most proficient levels—for example, when

a subject must continually monitor the efficacy of a particular strategy or when he must decide which portions of a text are least likely to be remembered later—metamemorial skills continue to develop until the adult years (Barclay, 1979; Brown and Smiley, 1978).

Nonetheless, the origins of metamemorial capacities can be found early. By the age of five (and sometimes as young as age three), children already understand that more items make a task harder, that memorization will improve in direct relation to time available for study, and that certain distractions will complicate a task. Interestingly, children at the preschool level do not show metamemorial awareness of the boost that can be provided by cues (for example, drawing a set of pictures so that one can remember them later) (Wellman, 1977). At times the child learns to benefit from unintended cues provided by the experiment: kindergartners are already aware that it is easier to recognize a correct answer from a set of possibilities than to remember it completely on one's own (Speer and Favell, 1979). Quite possibly, this awareness later on encourages children to develop a strategy of converting tasks of recall into tasks of recognition.

The evidence that even young children have incipient metamemorial skills is impressive. Yet there are clear limitations, for example, in estimating the difficulty of a mnemonic task, and so one must be cautious in considering children budding metamnemonists! As Robert Kail (1979) has pointed out, metamemorial sophistication can only be attributed to children whose behaviors change in relation to whether mnemonic capacities are actually being tested. If, for example, a child names a set of pictures spontaneously, one does not know whether he is preparing himself for subsequent recall or just engaging in a naming game. Experimental efforts to tease apart these two behaviors suggest that only during the school years will children consciously adopt different strategies (for example, rehearsing) for conditions where later recall is indicated, as opposed to conditions in which stimuli are being processed for another, nonmnemonic purpose (Appel et al., 1972). Indeed, a great increase in metamemorial knowledge occurs between the ages of six and ten, children become sensitive to the limitations of human memory, the differences among various tasks and the extent to which effort should be expended to recall information that has not been accessed immediately (Kail, 1979; Wellman, 1981).

Though both mnemonic skills and metamemorial knowledge increase with age, they may not be yoked. In fact, good memorizers are not necessarily good metamemorizers. Cavanaugh and Borkowski (1980) independently assessed memory performance, mnemonic strategies, and metamemorial knowledge. They found that within a given grade, there were no significant correlations among these tasks. Subjects' knowledge about strategies did not distinguish those who used from those who did not use the strategies. Two other studies also failed to document a transfer of knowledge about memory to performance on tasks of memory (Kelly et al., 1976; Salatas and Flavell, 1976). Perhaps only among highly self-conscious individuals is task performance actually guided by one's knowledge.

Classification

Children are forever grouping, categorizing, and classifying. Especially in middle childhood, youngsters accumulate numerous collections of cards, stamps, coins, and dolls that they group and regroup into various sets. Baseball cards are sorted by team or league; dolls are sorted by size or country of origin.

In school, children must place information into appropriate categories; the cities of Brazil, the mating habits of various species, the operations of long division. In addition, children develop their own ways of grouping words, objects, and events—whether they are learning number facts, deciding which clothes to wear, or how to arrange their rooms.

We have already noted in Chapters 4 and 7 that children's abilities to classify accurately and logically increase with age. The four-year-old will casually arrange and rearrange forms of various sizes, shapes, and colors, often focusing on patterns that strike his fancy, whereas the eleven-year-old will systematically group the objects by size, shape, or color, shift the basis of grouping on command, and even combine attributes (putting together all the large brown circles). Thus, starting with an attraction to surface, figurative properties, the child gradually adopts logically-consistent modes of classifying that reflect considerable operative intelligence. In the following sections, we will try to determine whether children pass through regular stages of classification, in what ways the earliest forms of classification and those adopted by adolescents are related, and how children's knowledge of language affects classification.

SORTING OBJECTS AND PICTURES

Among cognitive psychologists—including the most illustrious—classification studies abound (Bruner, Olver, and Greenfield, 1966; Inhelder and Piaget, 1964; Kagan, Moss, and Sigel, 1963; Kagan et al., 1964; Vygotsky, 1962; Werner, 1948). In labs the world over, children are shown an array of diverse objects and are asked to put together those that are "most alike" or that "belong together." The task varies in the types of stimuli used and in the number of groupings the children must create; but whatever the case, the general findings are reassuringly similar.

At ages two through four, children often group items haphazardly. Occasionally they group items by their most visible properties, particularly shape, size, or color; or they may group them for highly personal reasons ("I put them together because I like them both").

Children aged five or six often add some other bases for grouping, such as common function ("They both make noise"), common category ("They are both tools"), or some other dimensions transcending what is exclusively perceptible or personal (Currie-

Jedermann, 1981). But they rarely stick with the same rationale throughout a series of grouping. ("Banana and peach are both yellow; peach and potato are both round; potato and meat are served together"). They may select insignificant attributes as their criterion ("Well, a book has got some black printing, a radio and a telephone have printing on them"). They may elaborate on a connection and add new items ("Bell and horn are music things. When you dial a telephone, it's music a little"). Or they weave a story in which all

Figure 11.4. Given the same set of objects, six-year-olds and ten-year-olds will classify them in quite different ways. A typical six-year-old, often proceeding in an unsystematic way, will exhibit a range of thematic and categorical groupings. The ten-year-old is more likely to use a single criterion (like shape) consistently and to account for all objects in an exhaustive manner.

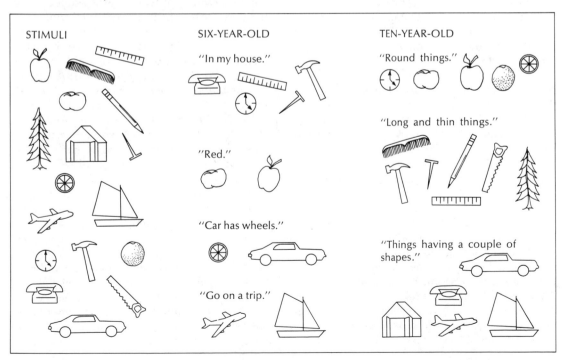

objects figure ("I put together the rabbit and the little girl and the tree because the girl and the rabbit went for a walk and they went to the forest").

Practices of classification change significantly in the next years as children become capable of various concrete operations (see Denney and Moulton, 1976). They may still favor diverse bases of classification, but they will tend to use the same basis throughout a series of trials. They are also capable of, and will come to favor, hierarchical groupings. That is, they can now place one class of objects, like dogs, within a larger class of animals, and then wed animals and plants as members of living things. This ability rests squarely on the operation Piaget calls **class inclusion:** the ability to construe the same object as a member simultaneously of a number of increasingly broad categories (see Chapter 10).

The picture of classification just surveyed may be called the classical view—one put forth by the major theorists of human development and supported by a raft of studies. Recently, a number of noteworthy modifications of this view have been introduced.

First of all, as we have already noted, even preschoolers are capable of some systematic classification. Crucial are the types of objects the subjects are asked to classify. Preschoolers will exhibit difficulties if grouping requires an appreciation of hierarchical or superordinate relations (for example, that terriers are dogs, dogs are animals, animals are living things). Though aware of the broadest distinctions between, say, living and nonliving or thing and nonthing, they cannot appreciate subtler distinctions or the relations that obtain among them (Keil, 1979b; Smith and Kemler, 1977). It is a different story when the objects presented for classification are familiar ones and when possible groupings include the level of basic objects, which is the level at which children customarily name entities. In that case they succeed in putting together all birds, all dogs, or all chairs in the same way as adults, but they will not make a group of all pets or all furniture (Rosch et al., 1976).

Classification also hangs on other factors. Children benefit when categories are closer to their natural experience. It is easier for them to deal with categories whose members are usually found together (the trees of a forest, the members of a family, the troops in an army) than with categories whose members do not necessarily make joint appearances (all collies, all married persons) (Horton and Markman, 1979; Markman, 1979).

Young children frequently zero in on prototypical members of a category (for example, a typical bird) (Rosch, 1974), which provide a point of anchorage. But generally speaking, in determining a prototype young children are restricted to a single feature or a small set of features (Frith and Frith, 1978; Williams, Fryer, and Aiken, 1977). They have difficulty determining which features are prototypical and how to weigh the features that constitute a prototype (Duncan and Kellas, 1978). Possibly for these reasons, they have difficulty appreciating that atypical items can still be members of a category (Thompson and Bjorkjund, 1981). They often confuse features with one another (for example, assuming that all ferocious animals must be male [Feldstein, 1978] or failing to disentangle two cues, such as size and brightness [Smith and Kemler, 1977]).

While age trends are powerful developmental facts, children's groupings still reflect personal style. Some children may focus on specific parts of the stimuli (putting together people who have no shoes), whereas others may focus on relations among individuals (grouping people who are arguing with one another, as a family). Yet children who favor one style can usually adopt another if they are given sufficient examples.

SORTING WORDS

Putting together objects or pictures is an activity familiar to children. But do the same tendencies and principles operate when children face the more artificial task of grouping words? Jeremy Anglin (1970) addressed this question by presenting children with a collection of words, including nouns (such as *horse, boy, idea*), verbs (*eat, listen, sleep*), adjectives (*rich, white, angry*), and adverbs (*sadly, quickly, slowly*), and asking them to group the words that were "most alike." Children aged eight and nine most often classified them according to their common theme, their occurrence in the same situation, or their proximity in ordinary speech. Thus the youngsters linked *white* and *flower* because a flower can be white; *girl* and *grow* because living things grow; *angry* and *laugh* because they are opposites; *listen* and *idea* because one hears ideas. In this, they are reminiscent of young children who, asked to associate freely to a target word, are likely to utter a word that ordinarily follows that target word in normal conversation (K. Nelson, 1977).

In sharp contrast, adolescents and adults overlook these thematic associations and almost always group by part of speech and, within that category, by similar meanings. Given a set of nouns, they are most likely to link *dog* and *cat;* the next most likely pairings are *dog* and *bird,* then *dog* and *tree,* then *dog* and *idea.* Thus, even though children display their grasp of the parts of speech in their everyday speech, and even though they often group pictures of these objects, they do not reflect this knowledge in sorting words until they reach adolescence.

To some extent, different principles appear to govern the sorting of words and objects. Even young schoolchildren will group objects that belong to the same class, but they do not sort words according to the same principle.

Instead, they group words that might occur together in sentences or that make plausible stories. The figurative quality of common utterances dominates the classifying strategies of children until adolescence. Moreover, certain classifying options, such as grouping together words on the basis of phonological similarity, are not relevant for presentation of objects (Gerschitz, 1979).

Nonetheless, common features are apparent in the classification of objects and words. In both cases, younger children's groupings tend to be personal, to stress perceptual or functional relations, and to be inconsistent. In both cases, too, practical and perceptible features lose ground to hierarchical organization as children grow older. Adolescents and adults have evolved a view of the world—an organized dictionary of meaning—within which they can consistently place the whole set of objects (and the nouns that denote them) (Keil, 1979b). In sorting verbs, adjectives, and adverbs they follow similar principles of organization, but of course this process can be tested *only* with words.

LEV VYGOTSKY'S VIEW

A dynamic view of the relationship between objects and words was favored by Lev Vygotsky. To convey his notion, Vygotsky (1962) devised an ingenious task. Children were presented with a series of blocks, each of which was labeled underneath with a single nonsense syllable. All the blocks with the same name shared one set of characteristics, whereas all the blocks with another name shared another set of characteristics. Children were told the nonsense syllable associated with a single block and then allowed to choose other blocks and to guess their names. The child's task was to find all blocks with the same name as the first and then to give the reasons why all blocks so labeled constituted a single class (or concept).

Children exhibited considerable difficulties. Preschoolers linked blocks bearing different labels and gave fanciful reasons for their groupings ("because it's my birthday"). Accordingly, Vygotsky assumed that word meaning at this age was very tenuous. Six- or seven-year-olds would begin to group on a principled basis (for example, placing together all triangles) but would soon expand the concept (to include trapezoids) or limit it (to large triangles). Vygotsky assumed that, for a child at this age, meanings of words remained as flexible as their loose sorting modes (see also Rosner and Poole, 1981).

In middle childhood, groupings came to reflect more rigid classifications but were still subject to the influence of concrete physical likenesses. Thus eight- or nine-year-olds would appear to group all triangles together. But while eliminating a red square from membership, such youngsters might also leave out a red triangle, erroneously inferring that redness had now become a basis for exclusion. Only the adolescent was capable of "true" conceptual groupings, where the elements crucial to a label were identified and then honored faithfully, despite incidental experiences or figurative attractions.

Vygotsky refused to attribute a dominant role either to one's knowledge of the world of objects or to one's knowledge of language and word meanings. Rather he saw the two facets as perpetually interacting: one's knowledge of word meanings reflects one's ability to organize information about the world of objects, even as that knowledge is guided by the categories and groupings embedded in the meanings of words. Thus genuine classification emerges as an achievement that depends on one's level of operational thinking and one's figurative powers. Individuals incapable of operational thinking can only make incom-

plete and haphazard classifications—similarly, their word meanings will prove inadequate and unreliable. And those that cannot reflect upon their knowledge of words may also be incapable of reflecting upon their knowledge of the world.

METACOGNITION

Just as a child's memory processes can be analyzed separately from his capacity (and inclination) to reflect on these processes, so too his cognition can be separated from his metacognition. According to John Flavell (1979), **metacognition** entails the monitoring of one's memory, comprehension, and other cognitive enterprises and products as part of one's knowledge about cognitive phenomena. (One can display metacognition about oneself, one's task, and the strategies at one's disposal.)

Metacognitive skills flower during the school years. A revealing example is offered by Ellen Markman (1977). Subjects in first and third grades participated in a task as an experiment. First the children were asked to inform the experimenter if there was anything at all she failed to state clearly or forgot to tell them. Next, the experimenter in fact left out crucial information about how to execute the task. Older children volunteered, or revealed upon minimal probing, that they were aware of the deficiencies in the instructions. In contrast, first graders had to be induced to repeat an instruction or even to execute it before they realized that anything was wrong. In Markman's view, the younger children were processing the material at a superficial level, not attempting to execute the instructions mentally or to determine the relationship between the instructions and the goals of the task. It is also possible that youngsters were unable to act upon any feelings of uncertainty they might have had (Beal and Flavell, 1981).

The growth of metacognitive skills seems most prominent during the early school years and may in fact be dependent upon schooling and the reflectiveness, questioning, and distancing that it encourages (Ross and Killey, 1977). Yet metacognition, like metamemory, has roots in early life. For example, even preschoolers are aware that it is easier to learn something when one is happy (rather than sad) and alert (rather than tired) (Hayes, Bolin, and Chemelski, 1981); and first graders are able to cue themselves on some simple tasks, taking steps to aid subsequent recall (Gordon and Flavell, 1977). But when it comes to other tasks, such as knowing how to organize a complex review process or to gauge the importance of various forms of information, even much older individuals display difficulties (A. L. Brown, 1975; Brown and Smiley, 1977, 1978; Canney and Winograd, 1980; Elliot, 1980; Mosenthal, 1979).

While certain metacognitive and metamemorial capacities develop naturally, or with only informal tutelage, others are clearly dependent upon inventions of one's culture. Consider, for example, the various notations that have been devised in different cultures over the centuries. Notations for language, music, dance, mathematical understandings, and the like can aid individuals in deciding what is important in a particular display or experience, in organizing this information, and in making it available for later study or revision. The procedures by which individuals learn these cultural notations form a fascinating and as yet little explored area (Bamberger, 1978; Ferrerio, 1978; Goody and Watt, 1962; Karmiloff-Smith, 1979d; Vygotsky, 1978). And the processes by which children sometimes invent their own notations—as it were, their own metacognitive and metamemorial capacities—stand equally in need of elucidation.

The Effects of Schooling

In this chapter we have described a number of significant changes during middle childhood—in the capacities to use language, to remember elements, to classify objects, pictures, and words consistently, and to reflect upon these cognitive capacities. We have examined processes that are inherently figurative and have noted how they are affected and altered by various operative capacities. The changes we have described may occur sooner or later in all individuals; but as we suggested in the opening section of this chapter, it is also possible that they are a direct consequence of lessons taught, either implicitly or explicity, in our schools. Only a comparison embracing children with various amounts of schooling can indicate which is the case.

THE KPELLE REVISITED

You will remember that Kpelle children from Liberia performed very poorly on standard word-recall tasks. In fact, their responses were much like those of far younger American children (see Cole, Frankel, and Sharp, 1971). But were the Kpelle children incapable of these forms of thought, or were the tests simply insensitive measures of the Kpelle's perfectly adequate memories?

To find out, the Cole team modified the original task in several ways. Grouping the original list of words by category boosted performance a little, but recall was still far below that of American children at the same age. But this manipulation revealed an effect of schooling: the Kpelle children who had been to school for two to four years tended to cluster the words according to their semantic category and to remember the first and last items somewhat better than the items in the middle of the list. Researchers discovered two further, unexpected facts: for both schooled and unschooled children, increasing the number of items to be remembered increased the number recalled; and requiring the children to sort the items into cups or to watch while the objects were placed into buckets increased both the number of items recalled *and* the amount of semantic clustering. Such manipulation and observation seemed powerful aids to memory and possibly also served to cue later retrieval of items. (This finding parallels the results of the Paris-Lindauer study described on page 436).

Further systematic variations were conducted in order to determine whether memory could be improved. In one study, children aged ten to fourteen who attended school watched an experimenter hold up each item and then place it on a certain chair. When all the items on a chair belonged to the same category, the children succeeded in using semantic categories in subsequent recall. The Cole group next tried to produce the same effect without the clumsy process of grouping objects on chairs. This time they simply used verbal cuing, listing the categories ("the things will be clothing, tools, food, and utensils") during both the presentation and the recall. The verbal cuing generally had no effect: the children's recall was no better than it had been in earlier conditions.

However, one verbal cuing condition, "constrained recall," significantly enhanced performance. Children were explicitly asked to name and then recall items by category ("Tell me all the tools I named"). Only in this condition did the schooled children remember the items well. More tellingly, the children continued to recall successfully even when the constrained recall was abandoned on the last trials.

As a result of their ingenious and sustained experimentation, Cole and his collaborators identified several factors that enhance the recall abilities of Kpelle children. Experience in touching the objects, in seeing them in specific locations, and in listing the items in a required order improve recall. It seems that schooled Kpelle children resemble younger American counterparts, who need comparable aids. It is not clear whether the difference between American and Kpelle children reflects the emphasis or quality of their educational system, their unfamiliarity with the kinds of tasks devised by Western psychologists, or some other factor. Moreover, since the final and most revealing variations involved only schooled children, the difficulties encountered by unschooled Kpelle are not yet known.

In another study Cole and his colleagues had determined that high school-educated Kpelle aged eighteen to twenty who lived in an urban area were able to recall many items without coaching and tended to cluster the items. Because parallel effects have not been found among unschooled Kpelle of the same age, one may reasonably infer that schooling aids children in organizing what may appear to be disparate items. Cole noted that American children, given to metacognitive speculation, expect that some rule will aid them in sorting and remembering and that the components of a task will be related in a meaningful manner. Thus American children provide their own rules whereas the Kpelle routinely do not.

Invoking a distinction introduced on page 438, Cole firmly believes that the difficulty experienced by the Kpelle is a *production* rather than a *mediation* deficiency. He cites instances in which, within their own meaningful world, Kpelle children's memories are better than American children's. Moreover, in striking analogy to the difficulties experienced by the Kpelle on list recall, a medley of cues fails to help the Americans in tasks drawn from a Kpelle context. Cole concludes that all Kpelle, schooled as well as unschooled, have the potential to mediate but, under the strange conditions of these experiments, seldom resort to such a strategy.

Other studies in other cultures confirm this point: children in each culture, whether schooled or not, are prone to classify in an appropriate manner those materials that are familiar and important to them, while exhibiting difficulties with those materials that bear little significance (Laboratory of Comparative Human Cognition, 1980*a, b;* and references cited therein). Cultures also favor different strategies. For example, aboriginals in Australia, having a long history of geographical exploration, are more likely to use spatial methods in solving problems (Davidson and Klich, 1980). Unschooled Dioula in West Africa solve problems of mental addition successfully by the procedure of regrouping by tens, which is rarely used by Western schoolchildren (Ginsberg, Posner, and Russell, 1979). In some tasks, Westerners perform at inferior levels: Ghanian students have an advantage over New Yorkers at recalling stories (Ross and Millsom, 1970), and rural Eskimo youngsters outperform urban Caucasian children at reproducing complex geometrical designs (Kleinfeld, 1971). And the differences found *within* any culture prove as great as or greater than those found across cultures, thus challenging the notion that one culture reasons or thinks better than another (Cole and Means, 1981).

SCHOOLING AND OPERATIVE TASKS

While Cole's study of recall focuses on a figurative capacity, other cross-cultural investigators have sought to determine the effects of schooling on traditionally operative tasks, particularly those designed by Piaget (Berry and Dasen, 1974).

Patricia Marks Greenfield (1966) examined conservation of liquids among schoolchildren in Senegal and among children of the same age, from the same tribe, who had not been to school. Overall, she found that schooled children aged eight or nine regularly gave conservationlike responses, whereas those who had never been to school offered correct responses only half the time. Moreover, unschooled thirteen-year-olds, the oldest children tested, responded much the same as unschooled eight-to-nine-year-olds, making it unlikely that conservation was simply developing more slowly among the unschooled children.

Examination of the children's reasoning showed that the schooled children rarely cited the appearance of the liquid as a reason for their response. But unschooled children frequently invoked such figurative (and erroneous) reasons, and the tendency to do so in fact increased from 40 percent at age eight to 60 percent among thirteen-year-olds.

According to Greenfield, the unschooled Senegalese children frequently responded as if magic had been at work: "He did it—he made it that way" or "There is more in the glass because you poured it." The spectacle of being involved in the experiment may have been so bizarre to the unschooled Senegalese that it completely overwhelmed any principles they applied to their own lives. Such "magical" responses did not survive schooling. According to Greenfield, "Schooling suppresses such thinking with astonishing absoluteness" (1966, p. 24) (see also Skanes, 1976). And when the unschooled children were allowed to do the pouring themselves, their conservation responses increased dramatically. In Greenfield's view such active participation is needed to counteract the strong magical thinking found among many unschooled children.

From our perspective the contributions of schooling are beneficent, leading to superior performance on both figurative and operative tasks. But we must face the possibility that those living in unschooled societies have equally adaptive cognitive skills and valid

Figure 11.5. The difference between learning in school and learning in the natural context is dramatically illustrated in this scene of hunting in Bechuanaland.

world views. Mangan (1978) suggests two possible approaches to one's experience: the **empiroscientific method** characteristic of Western individuals and the **mythopoetic view** often found in unschooled societies. Many cultures embrace assumptions about life that are quite different from ours: for example, that matter can be changed in various ways and can magically increase, decrease, or change its nature. (Medieval alchemists in the West held these views.) In such societies, views espousing conservation might be regarded negatively and it is not surprising that they would not be found (and would be stamped out when found) among children or even adults in those societies. In an age where atomic theory has challenged so many of our assumptions, can we assert with confidence that ours is the only valid way to describe physical experience?

SCHOOLING AND CULTURE

Several scientists, including Cole, Scribner, Greenfield, and Bruner (Bruner et al., 1966) have sought to identify the features that dif-

ferentiate the experience of the schooled and the unschooled child. In their view, outside of schools children acquire skills through observation and participation in the natural context in which the skills are used. First they watch adults weave or hunt; later they participate as helpers; and eventually they assume the key role themselves. There is little talk, little formal teaching: learning comes from doing. No wonder these youngsters perform best when they become actively involved in a task—be it pouring water in the conservation task or handling objects in a recall task.

For better or worse, the standard classroom is entirely different. There is scarce opportunity for active participation. The teacher talks, often presenting material in abstract, symbolic forms or relying on inanimate sources such as books and diagrams to convey information.

By its very nature, schooled education depends on models. There is no way to see or physically demonstrate abstract concepts and relations among concepts through models in a given symbol system (words, diagrams, and soon). And then they must seek to recapture that aspect of the world in their own imagery. It is not surprising that the schooled Senegalese could use verbal symbols more adroitly than their unschooled peers: they were accustomed to talking in general concepts ("sameness," "addition") and hypothetical events ("If you were to . . .").

Cross-cultural studies like those we have examined illustrate how special an experience schooling can be. Sitting inside a classroom year after year, talking, writing, and reading, seems eventually to produce a special sort of individual. And this schooled person differs qualitatively from one whose learning has come from practical experiences in the physical world and who has used language to achieve immediate wants rather than to describe remote events or entities.

Indeed, for children whose learning occurs entirely outside of school, a word or image

represents a handful of concrete, immediate situations. The word *battle* means a particular battle the child has seen, or perhaps nothing at all. But in school, words and images convey a whole universe of meaning. Battles are discussed and war diagrams are sketched by children who have never been near a battle but who have only read or heard about them.

Schooling, then, favors specific kinds of activities and approaches them in characteristic ways. The schooled individual expects to be presented with problems and tasks—often out of context—that he learns how to tackle just because they have been presented, to look for clues for solutions, to devise strategies and steps, and to look up answers if he does not know them. School provides new tools for tackling tasks—reading, writing, decoding maps. And these new skills can also be put to diverse uses; for instance, once a child can write competently, he can treat almost any topic in written form.

One of the themes to emerge from our review is that operative capacities are enhanced by the experience of schooling. And indeed, in a number of linguistic, classificatory, and mnemonic tasks, attendance at schools increases the likelihood that one can go beyond sheer figurative approaches and adopt appropriate operations. Yet this conclusion should be tempered. First, some operative capacities will develop in all cultures, whether or not they feature formal schooling. Second, operative approaches should not be considered unambiguously superior to figurative ones: there are many areas, ranging from artistic production to scientific observation, where keen figurative capacities are crucial. Some cultures may well cherish these figurative capacities more than we do (Wagner, 1981). It seems preferable to think of figurative and operative skills as complementary, each making contributions to the full mastery of an area of knowledge. (See Table 11.1.)

Figure 11.6. Both education and environment may affect how children perform on short-term recall tasks. Here are plotted the percentage of correct responses from four groups of children on a picture recall task. (D. Wagner, 1978)

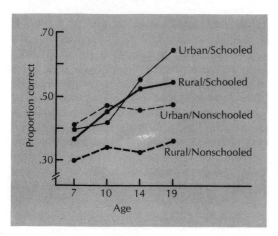

Those who stress the importance of operative thinking have asserted that schooling develops the most general kinds of problem-solving skills, ones that can be brought to bear upon a whole gamut of problems. Indeed, the idea of transfer is intrinsic to education: if one's lessons within the classroom could not be used outside, there would be little point in going to school. As a result of his studies in other, diverse cultures, however, Cole questions this easy assumption. In his view, the existence and desirability of general skills, à la Piaget, has been overemphasized. All intellectual skills are much more fragmented and context-dependent than Piaget would have us believe; they all presuppose a certain kind of environment and will not function in a radically different one. Naturally, we tend to consider our environment the most plausible one and so look askance at those who cannot solve our kinds of problems in our way. But how does a Westerner fare when asked to solve problems of navigation that are second nature to someone raised in the South Seas (Gladwin, 1970)? One culture's "figures" may be another culture's "operations."

For better or worse, schooling places a great value on stating exactly what one means, and investing all "in the words"—whether spoken, written, or read. Whereas in unschooled societies actions can supplement words and a speaker's tone of voice and authority can contribute to the credibility of a message, the emphasis in a schooled environment falls heavily on words. And written words stand up—at least until they have been refuted (or replaced) by a better formulation of the problem or issue at hand. Of course, there may be situations in which words are less effective (or appropriate) than actions—and the overschooled individual may be less likely to recognize them.

The revolutionary effects of literacy have been stressed by many commentators (Goody,

Table 11.1. FIGURATIVE AND OPERATIVE APPROACHES COMPARED

Domain	Task	Figurative approach	Operative approach
Language	Listen to a poem in a foreign language.	Attend chiefly to interesting sound patterns.	Translate the poem into one's native tongue and paraphrase its content.
Classification	Group together various geometric forms.	Attend only to the color of the forms.	Systematically group the forms on the basis of color, shape, and size.
Memory	Remember a list of printed words.	Remember the list eidetically, just as it appeared, in its type face.	Classify the words by category and remember them on that basis.

1977; Olson, 1977). The ability to read and write not only permits access to the events and thoughts of all individuals throughout history but also allows one to supplement or supplant one's memory, organize one's future activities, and communicate with many individuals in novel ways. However, lest the importance of literacy be overstressed, Cole and his associates once again offer an iconoclastic point of view (Laboratory of Human Cognition, 1980*a, b*). These authors examined the effects of four kinds of writing systems that exist among the Vai people of Liberia: two kinds of literacy in Arabic (one used just for prayer, the other used for keeping records); literacy in a Vai syllabary, used primarily for letter writing and record keeping; and "conventional" literacy acquired in Liberian schools. They then administered to individuals competent in each of these systems a set of classification, memory, and logical-reasoning tests. In general, only that "conventional" literacy obtained in schooling had the effects usually associated with schooling; competence in the other forms of literacy did not heighten performance on these diverse tasks. Yet through ingenious probing Scribner and Cole discovered a few fruits of the other literacies: Arabic literacy aided individuals in some forms of rote memory; Vai literacy improved performance on a communication task in which the basic graphic units referred to syllables. Once again, intelligence emerges as a "skill in context," with the context of Western-style conventional schooling most helpful for parrying standard experimental tasks.

Why these effects of schooling? As Scribner and Cole view it (1973), school presents experiences that are unlike those encountered in everyday life and that promote ways of learning and thinking counter to those nurtured in practical activities. The very disengagement of an activity from its customary context encourages its transformation into symbolic form. When education is informal, however, the present context is everything. And because the information to be learned not only is essential for sheer existence but also is transmitted by adults strongly associated with that activity, most teaching is accompanied by potent emotions.

Scribner and Cole do not contend that unschooled children lack important capacities possessed by schooled children. On the contrary, it is their conviction that all cognitive abilities exist in all humans, needing only the proper circumstances or motivation to be elicited.

Other authorities stress somewhat different aspects of this issue. Wagner (1978), for example, indicates that structural features of memory (one's short-term store and one's rate of forgetting) may be universal, while metacognitive processes are probably specific to certain cultures. An individual's cognitive style—for example, the extent to which a child can respond independently of the cues before his eyes—may also reflect schooling. Kagan and Klein (1973) suggest that one's culture determines chiefly the rate at which certain skills will emerge but that "nature will win in the end." In their view, the capacities of perceptual analysis, inference, deduction, symbolism, and memory will eventually appear in sturdy form, for each is an inherent "natural" competence in the human program (see also Kagan et al., 1979). Stevenson and his colleagues (Stevenson et al., 1978) find that schooled children surpass unschooled children in carrying out instructions and in encoding experiences into words, but that unschooled children hold their own in visual discrimination and in handling ordered sequences. Similarly, Sharp, Cole, and Lave (1979), in a study of problem solving among subjects in rural Yucatán, distinguish between two kinds of tasks: those in which education exerts a strong influence (classifying according to taxonomic principles, mastering school-related content such as calculation, handling artificially construed stimuli, or engaging in hypothetical thinking); and those where age seems the primary determinant (classifying according to functional relations, drawing upon real-world knowledge).

Schooling need not create a gap. And yet, inflamed in part by the superior rewards given those who have been to school, a pervasive antagonism often develops between the school's logical, out-of-context knowledge system and that practical participation in daily activities fostered informally by the culture. If this antagonism is to be lessened, schools both here and in less developed regions of the world must be designed and viewed as comfortable and significant environments, rather than as hostile providers of useless knowledge. This means that schools must contain everyday life within their walls, and must make clear the relation between the skills they teach and the problems children find significant.

SCHOOLS UNDER FIRE

Most of the authorities we have cited see the need to make schooling as palatable and nonjarring as possible, but they clearly accept the need for formal education. Yet recent discussions about the very meaning of schooling reflect some much less sympathetic views. Within American society, many critics castigate the "hidden curriculum." Charging that schools are only nominally concerned with the transmission of knowledge, they view schools primarily as socializing agents that inculcate obedience, conformity, and compliance and that seek to stamp out the idiosyncratic values of certain parents and ethnic groups. Such commentators criticize the premium placed upon certain styles of dress and behavior, stereotypical sex roles (such as

those of cheerleader and football quarterback), and competition for popularity. Other critics, who concede that the schools have some educational function, voice a different complaint: they decry the emphasis upon grades and scores on standardized tests. They deplore the fact that one's ultimate status and achievement depends so heavily on these questionable measures. Critics reflecting both perspectives have searched for alternative sets of values and even for alternative forms of education (see the box).

One reaction against the schools of our society has created a nostalgia for a life in which communal values reign supreme and the fragmentary and depersonalized aspects of schools are avoided. Suggesting that figurative knowledge retains a higher value in an unschooled environment, Michael Maccoby and Nancy Modiano (1966) contrast the lives of unschooled peasant children and schooled city children whom they studied in Mexico.

If the peasant child is not dulled by village life, he will experience the uniqueness of events, objects, and people. But as the city child grows older, he may end by exchanging a spontaneous, less alienated relationship to the world for a more sophisticated outlook which concentrates on using, exchanging, or cataloguing. What industrialized urban man gains in an increased ability to formulate, to reason, and to code the ever more numerous bits of complex information he acquires, he may lose in a decreased sensitivity to people and events [p. 269].

Even more extreme is Paolo Freire, another student of Latin American society who sees most schools as elite tools for manipulating oppressed peoples (Freire, 1971). Children's creativity is stunted by the system that treats them as mere receptacles into which teachers pour mostly useless information. And Ivan Illich (1971), who argues in favor of "deschooling society," feels that formal educational institutions should be done away with altogether or, failing that, that they should be used solely to teach the skills people themselves want to acquire. He dismisses schools as arrogant attempts to dictate certain forms of knowledge to an imprisoned audience.

In an indictment of the political and social structures of Western civilization, Freire and Illich see the schools as institutions that fos-

ter neither development of the self nor the acquisition of useful knowledge. They oppose all learning out of context and call for a return to direct means of acquiring knowledge.

Most radical critiques of schooling at least assume that the school accomplishes something, even if that something is evil. Yet the research of Christopher Jencks and his associ-

Home Schooling

At about the age of five, nearly every healthy American child sets out for his first day of school. This long-standing tradition is now facing new challenges: More and more parents are keeping their children at home and initiating their own educational programs.

The home-schooling movement was spurred in part by John Holt, an educational theorist and author of *How Schools Fail* (1964). Since 1977 he has published a bimonthly newsletter about home teaching called "Growing Without Schooling." Holt and his followers condemn the educational establishment for teaching too much, thus making children passive rather than active learners. They object to the "hidden curriculum" that fosters conformity, alienation, and competitiveness at the expense of openness, creativity, and individual growth.

"Home schoolers" argue that parents have the right to decide what kind of education their children should receive and that home teaching can offer both a better education and a healthier outlook on life. Most parents follow a careful curriculum that they sometimes plan with the advice of administrators and educators. These programs may specify when instruction will take place and what subject matter will be taught. In some cases, they include participation in certain school activities such as music classes and sports.

Compulsory education laws require many parents to obtain court approval for their programs. Although thirty-two states now provide nonschool educational alternatives, approval sometimes involves complex legal battles. Yet as dissatisfaction with formal education grows, home schooling is becoming more popular and more recognized. Holt estimates that more than ten thousand families instruct their children at home, and he expects the figure to rise to at least half a million by 1988.

(For further reading see Nagel, 1979; Bumstead, 1979; Arons, 1978; *Time*, 1978).

ates (Jencks, 1972) suggests that schooling cannot even accomplish its purported goal of promoting the attainment of success. Schools have apparently failed in helping the poor but talented youngster and in redressing the society's social and economic inequities. A child's eventual success probably depends more on economic and social status *before* entering school and on the factor of luck. More recent studies confirm that, for the general population, social and economic background of parents is a far better predictor of the ultimate level of success attained in our society than are the actual test scores and school performance of children (DeLone, 1979).

Yet even if schools do not exert a decisive effect on the child's ultimate attainments, it is far from clear that they *cannot* have such an effect. In his influential book *Fifteen Thousand Hours,* a nine-year study of twelve non-selective schools in London, Michael Rutter (1979c) demonstrated that several factors in the schools—the competence of the principal, the resources available, the punctuality of teachers, the rewards issued, the time spent teaching—had clear effects on children's performances on objective tests, the amount of their disruptive behavior, the rate of delinquency, and similar factors (McCall, 1980). Lest it be thought that these findings obtain only in Britain, recent investigators of inner-city schools in New York reach similar conclusions (*New York Times,* 1979). If the principal exerts strong leadership, visits classrooms, and shares commitment with teachers, if the school has a climate that is safe, orderly, and attractive, if objective tests are used to measure progress and make teaching plans, if there are high but attainable expectations for all students and clearly agreed upon and understood teaching objectives, children are likely to perform at a higher level.

Discussions about schooling—pro and con—have a different flavor in cultures where schools have been in existence for a long time and where they are presumably here to stay. Given the trends of modernization, it seems almost inevitable that some form of schooling will be adopted everywhere. Critiques calling for the abolition of schools will, for more than one reason, have a hollow ring in societies that have never built a schoolhouse. If people in these societies are to acquire what those in more technological societies already have, they are most likely to do so in school. But whether they *should* move in the direction of industrialization and what kind of school system is most consistent with the culture's values are questions that scientific research cannot answer.

A DEVELOPMENTAL LOOK AT SCHOOLING

What can developmental psychology bring to these issues of education? According to Lawrence Kohlberg's developmental view (Kohlberg and Mayer, 1972), education—defined broadly to include influences ranging from teachers to television—should undertake two missions. First, the educator must be responsive to the student's developmental level. It is foolhardy to convey the same lesson in the same way to all individuals, irrespective of age and sophistication. Developmental psychology can provide valuable information about what children of different ages know, understand, and believe; what their misconceptions are; and what is likely to guide their thinking in a productive manner.

The second mission of education is to facilitate the achievement of an individual's full intellectual and emotional potential, within that person's chosen setting. Kohlberg is suspicious of attempts to accelerate the acquisition of knowledge; he believes in a natural course of development that will be realized under varied conditions—each child passing at

Figure 11.7. Although schools everywhere attempt to relate their subject matter to goings-on in the rest of the society, schools in the People's Republic of China make a special point of integrating education and work. Here, in a middle school, children design and construct equipment that will be used in the school's tool-making factory.

his own rate through a series of stages. Education in a developmental mode should enable the child to realize each stage fully, allowing each new operation to be expressed in as many different contexts as possible. At the same time, it must set the groundwork for a smooth transition to the next stage.

Such phrasing may make all growth seem narrowly preordained—and, as we shall see in Chapter 13, this criticism of developmental education has some validity. Yet focusing on the *process* of learning rather than on specific desirable (or undesirable) products, Kohlberg

himself regards the child's evolution as open-ended, leading to internal standards of judgment and value that should prove adequate to deal with whatever complexity the child encounters. Similarly, while speaking of development as natural, Kohlberg also acknowledges that its fullest potential can be achieved only under careful guidance. He sums up by saying:

A notion of education for development and education for principles is liberal, democratic, and non-indoctrinative. It relies on open methods of stimulation through a sequence of stages, in a direction of movement which is universal for all children. In this sense it is natural [Kohlberg and Mayer, 1972, p. 494].

Here is a vision of schooling that may hold appeal for both the supporters and the critics of schools.

Signposts

In Chapter 10 we examined some concrete operations that evolve during middle childhood. Now, in this chapter, we have turned our attention to a complementary set of skills including the ability to use language and to remember information. According to Piaget, these skills are considered figurative, rather than operative, for they do not require the same mental operations as the various forms of conservation do. And yet we encountered ample evidence that such figurative abilities are indeed affected by the child's capacity to perform mental operations.

Beginning with a consideration of language use, we found that school-age children are still acquiring the syntax of their native tongue. Furthermore, the individual at this age becomes able for the first time to reflect on language, to appreciate metaphor (realizing that separate classes may be alike in some traits and unlike in others), to detect ambiguity, and to understand how to apply logic without having to refer to the world of objects or to a supporting context. Thus the processes of language that developed so rapidly in early childhood continue to evolve during the school years.

Examining memory, we discovered that as children grow older they become able to devise and use various cues and rehearsal procedures to enhance memory; grouping according to category membership is an especially powerful aid. Although there is in the evolution of this figurative skill no dramatic turning point comparable to achieving a new level of operational thought, some striking trends have been noted. For instance, eidetic (photographic) memory declines, quite possibly supplanted by the child's developing tricks of memorization. Similarly, incidental learning, the recall of objects or details not significant to a task, declines during the latter part of childhood as motivation to succeed focuses the child's attention on relevant details alone. And perhaps most importantly, children become increasingly adept at metamemorial strategies during the school years: awareness of what is entailed in remembering something and the ability to draw on one's own strategies in order to retain information.

Although these and other facts have been widely replicated, contrasting theoretical perspectives have been adopted by researchers in the field of memory. Some scholars focus on the role of mediators—labels and rehearsal strategies that aid the child in recalling lists. Yet these scholars themselves disagree about whether young children are unable to use such labels altogether or whether they can employ labels once the labels have been supplied. Other scholars, including cognitive-structuralists, emphasize the role played by mental operations in affecting the nature and quality of the child's memory. Soviet psychologists stress the effects of the culture in telling the child *what* and *how* to remember.

Turning next to classification, we saw how the child's grouping of elements is at first somewhat haphazard but gradually comes to be based on consistent criteria. In the sorting of physical materials, for example, children first learn to take into account perceptual properties and the functions of a group of objects. There is an emerging ability in the preschool years to sort consistently at the level of basic objects, but little sensitivity to superordinate and subordinate categories. By middle childhood, the child favors hierarchical groups, conceiving of an object as a member of successively broader categories. Only adolescents can classify consistently according to a set of abstract principles.

Although the principles governing the sorting of words are similar to those governing the sorting of objects, there are also some unique features. For instance, eight- and nine-year-olds tend to group words by thematic association, whereas adolescents group them by part of speech and number of shared semantic features. Furthermore, some principle of classification, such as in terms of phonological properties, are possible only in the realm of words.

An important adjunct to improved performance in linguistic, mnemonic, and classification tasks is the advent of metacognitive skills. During the early years of school, children begin to reflect upon their own thought processes and problem-solving skills. Such ability may be signaled by the capacity to indicate when one does not understand something because instructions are incomplete and then to go on, through questioning or some other means, to ferret out the missing information. A principal consequence of schooling may be the fostering of these metacognitive capacities.

One of our goals in this chapter was to assess the effect of attending school on the various cognitive changes taking place in middle childhood. When Michael Cole and his colleagues compared American children with children of the traditional Kpelle culture on tests of recall, they initially found that both schooled and unschooled Kpelle children performed much like American children at the start of school: they showed little tendency to cluster items or to rehearse lists. But the performance of the Kpelle improved markedly when they were allowed to touch the objects to be remembered or to see them in certain

physical settings. This set of results may reflect the fact that Kpelle education is almost always natural and informal, with skilled adults first demonstrating and then participating along with children. Thus Kpelle children find the physical setting and the opportunity to explore to be important aids in the recall of details.

Cross-cultural studies remind us that children's intensive skill acquisition and learning in middle childhood may take place in varied settings. But around the world, skill acquisition is increasingly occurring in schools, where children consider objects out of context, acquire general rules and systems, deal more with models than with materials, and master flexible techniques of problem solving. Language and memory are the key tools; schools provide both the means for exploiting these tools and the often remote materials on which they are to be used. It is there that children learn to apply their developing mental operations in such figurative domains as language and memory.

It may seem that schooling confers a decisive advantage on cognitive performances, at least with respect to abstract, metacognitive, and hypothetical tasks. However, according to Michael Cole and his colleagues, the generalizability of principles mastered in school and the consequences of literacy may have been overrated; all skills have their appropriate contexts, and even different literacies entail different dividends and costs. Moreover, the picture of life endorsed by Western science is not the only valid world view: a mythopoetic perspective on life has proved functional as well.

Those concerned with spiritual and humanistic values sometimes view schooling as inimical. Certainly schools foisted upon traditional cultures often become an alien and distrusted presence in their midst. And some commentators see the school as a manipulative device by which Western nations assault the cultural integrity of other lands and, at home, indoctrinate their own people rather than teach them skills they themselves would like to acquire. However, schooling does introduce a powerful set of cultural artifacts—maps, texts, diagrams, equations, musical scores—that can enhance the range, depth, and generality of an individual's knowledge. Moreover, even though the effects of schools may be less powerful than the effects of socioeconomic background, good principals and comfortable learning environments do matter.

When defined broadly, the goals of education can be seen as consistent with the underlying principles of developmental psychology: the educator must be mindful of the learner's level of understanding and help him to achieve full intellectual and emotional potential within whatever sphere the learner chooses.

The first two chapters of this section have dealt with the child's cognitive skills, at the cost of neglecting the child's social and affective faces. We have reserved for our next chapter consideration of how children's social and affective lives change during middle childhood. In this discussion we will focus on the ways in which children come to know and to relate to the individuals around them: how they form friendships, solve interpersonal problems, and conceive of the society in which they live. Some parallels can be found with knowledge of the physical world but, beyond question, the social milieu is a world of its own.

CHAPTER TWELVE

Relations with Other Selves

A society consists of individuals and groups which communicate with one another.

—CLAUDE LEVI-STRAUSS

Picnic Patterns

At the school my children attend, picnics are held each year for each class. Families gather at a local park to visit with one another, chat with teachers, play informal games, and share food and drink. Over the years I have had the chance to watch my growing children interact with their teachers, their classmates, and with children of different ages.

Differences in play patterns between the ages of five and twelve are striking. When they are five or six, youngsters play alongside one another and interact quite a bit, but these encounters are for the most part momentary physical interactions rather than lasting and meaningful exchanges. One plays with whoever is nearby, often without even knowing the neighbor's name. Parents and teachers are treated as special persons, available whenever help or advice is needed; but other adults, and other children, are treated as virtually interchangeable. When attempts are made to organize games, these tend to fall apart rather quickly, as each child follows his own rules and pays little attention to what others are doing. Clearly, the children have come together because an encounter has been scheduled and, unless injured, they generally have a merry time. When it is "time to go home," they may squawk; but once they are in the car, memories of the picnic quickly fade in favor of the next conversation, television show, or game at home.

Push the clock ahead several years and an observer imbibes an entirely different social atmosphere. Children aged eleven or twelve are "psyched up" for their interactions before even arriving at the party. Someone familiar with their customary friendship networks can already predict who will play with whom, who is attached to whom, and who may be left out. By this age, children have formed strong friendships, typically based on similarities among peers and also on needs that one child may fulfill for another. Popularity is very important. These friendship sets are confirmed at the picnic: children hang around with their good friends and avoid those in the "other " or the "out" group. In their desire to play or just talk with friends, children give their parents short shrift. If there are disputes, they are solved by the disputants themselves, usually through verbal argument, occasionally through physical aggression.

When a game is announced, considerable care is taken in choosing up sides. Much discussion surrounds the use of rules, which must be decided upon ahead of time and carefully adhered to. Good friends maneuver to be on the same side and are devastated if they end up on opposite sides. There is also much talk about schools, friends, hobbies, projects completed this term, plans for the summer, and possible classmates and teachers for the next year. Considerable loyalty has already been built up toward the school, and against the rival school "down the block." There is also considerable secret activity, especially within the clubs and cliques that are constantly springing up.

Success at school has considerable impact on the older children, who already think of themselves in terms of accomplishments, or lack of accomplishments, in the classroom and on the playing fields. One's competence and one's judged personal worth are important, if often unspoken, topics. Close bonds are formed to teachers; but if the teacher is perceived to be incompetent, unfair, or overstrict, children may become quite angry and even cruel toward that teacher. Parents and teachers, like peers, must now earn their children's attention and respect.

By this time, both youngsters and adults are regarded as active agents with their own desires, motivations, and fears, and children invest considerable energy in pondering and negotiating their ways through the network of interpersonal relations. If a friend or enemy does something unexpected, a child will try mightily to puzzle out the reasons for this action. Powerful relations are very important, as children adjust their relations and their perspectives in the light of the authority invested in different figures. Competition and cooperation loom large as well. Indeed, behind every personal relation there is already a history and, in the child's mind, a possible future. This continuity in experience plays an important role in the child's thinking—even as the imminence of a leaving, be it for the evening or for the summer, can sometimes be painful. When you are twelve years old, your mind is no longer so quickly diverted by the next interesting thing that crops up.

Four Facets of Social Cognition

We enter the world of **social cognition**—the child's knowledge of and interaction with significant other persons, particularly those outside his immediate family. At the start of school, the child is already aware of individuals outside his immediate circle, but he has few expectations about them and does not act toward each in a discriminating way. By adolescence, however, the child has had considerable experience in a variety of cooperative and conflicting situations with individuals of different ages, ranging from younger and older peers to authority figures. Understanding of the social world proves as major and perennial a process as knowing the world of physical objects.

In decades past there was a tendency among developmental psychologists to underplay the importance of social cognition and to assume that dealing with human objects was basically the same as dealing with physical objects. That has changed. Nearly all authorities now recognize a number of characteristics of human beings that make them very special kinds of objects, sufficiently different from the liquids and levers studied by Piagetians to warrant separate study.

Consider these features of "knowing other humans." Whereas physical objects are generally immobile and unchanging, humans are constantly moving and often changing in many fundamental ways. Humans have a personality and a set of goals and needs that color all their interactions. One cannot assume that other persons will act and react the same way all the time (as one can assume vis-à-vis a machine) because interactions are dynamic and flexible. One's own words, actions, reactions will influence those of another agent, even as the actions and reactions of the others will in turn influence one's own behaviors. And because individuals communicate with one another, they have the power to undertake actions together or change their line of action as a result of a communication. Human agents also have motivations and intentions. Sometimes these are transparent and readily acknowledged by all participants. But at other times these motives and intentions may not be evident to other individuals and a person has the option (which he may well exercise) of disguising his intentions. The observer is often faced with a difficult task of deduction, one different from the kinds of problems confronting students of physical reality.

In what follows, we will consider facets of the child's knowledge of the social world and his ability to act appropriately within it. We will maintain a comparative perspective in two senses. We will consider the relations between cognition of persons and cognition of objects. And we will contrast behaviors exhibited by young children, when they are still largely innocent of the web of social interaction, with the behaviors exhibited by preadolescents, when they are only too cognizant of the intricate social networks that human beings construct and live in.

As in earlier chapters, we will report experimental studies of various topics. But even more than in the case of physical cognition, the area of social cognition proves difficult to capture in the experimental laboratory. Much has been learned in recent years through sensitive observations of children interacting with one another and through judicious use of the clinical interviewing method developed by Piaget. Accordingly, in much of what follows we will be reviewing stage sequences derived from such socially oriented interviews. (See Figure 12.1 for a comparative summary of principal stage sequences.)

To organize this discussion, we will examine four kinds of interpersonal understanding (cf. Damon, 1977, 1979). First, we will consider relations between individuals who are intimate with one another. We will focus on friendship relations among peers but also touch on authority relations that often obtain between child and valued adult. Next, moving to a more abstract level, we will consider children's construction of rules that govern such interpersonal relations—social conventions like manners, as well as universal principles like justice.

Our third focus falls on the child's growing capacity to conceive of and relate to others in a more generalized way. Instead of focusing on the particular individuals within a child's circle, we will look at the child's ability to attribute motives to others, to appreciate their intentions, to understand "what makes them tick"; and we will consider the factors that

MAJOR MILESTONES IN FOUR SOCIAL DOMAINS

Some common milestones	Understanding of friendships and interpersonal relationships (Selman, Damon, Youniss)	Understanding justice (Damon)	Understanding social institutions (Furth)	Understanding the self and the other (Selman)
LACK OF DIFFER-ENTIATION SIMPLISTIC VIEWS EGOCENTRICITY	All peers treated the same, with unqualified giving and sharing. (I lend money just to do it.)	Justice based on desires. (All children should get as much candy as they want.)	Unaware that social institutions differ; the outside world is conflict-free and rule bound. (When you want money, you go and get it.)	The self is the same as one's physical person. (I am my body, my body is me.) Unaware of others' perspectives.
	Friendships short, depending on time and proximity.	Justice based on external but arbitrary factors. (The bigger child should get more candy.)		Aware of subjective experience but not that one can control feelings. (Whenever I smile, I am happy.)
			Aware that social institutions differ and work differently. (People must work at a job for money.)	Aware of an inner self and of the ability to monitor thoughts. (I can smile without being happy.)
INCREASED DIFFERENTIATION SUBJECTIVE VIEWS AWARENESS OF OTHERS	Peers treated differently from one another; sharing and giving qualified and employed with specific, concrete intent. (I lend someone money to buy a Coke.)	Justice based on equality. (Everyone should get the same amount of candy.)		Aware that others have different perspectives but unable to assume them.
		Justice based on merit and a means of paying someone for work. (The person who worked hardest should get the most candy.)	Recognizes general and limited social functions and obligations. (The purpose of money is to buy things.)	Increased control over the mind. (I won't think about that if I don't want to.) Able to adopt others' perspectives.
		Justice based on several factors; when in conflict, compromise instituted. (He worked harder, but she is younger; they should get the same amount of candy.)		
SELECTIVITY MUTUALITY PSYCHOLOGICAL AWARENESS	Shifts emphasis from physical and material concerns to psychological ones; giving and sharing to offer psychological support. (I lend someone money to make him feel better.) Enduring friendships in which each assumes the other's feelings.	Justice based on evaluation of each factor; some disregarded if irrelevant. (The person who did the best, regardless of age, should get the most candy.)	Understands the general rules of social institutions, which are subject to change and conflict; able to relate the personal to the societal. (Individuals' use of money affects the economic system.)	Aware that people have thoughts, feelings, and unconscious processes. (Whatever I do, there is still more inside of me that remains unconscious and not understood.) Able to understand deeper and more complex perspectives.

Figure 12.1. *Opposite:* As they come to understand various social and interpersonal concepts, children progress through sequenced stages. Instructive commonalities and differences can be discerned across domains. In this chart, principal steps in four domains have been sketched out. Note that the steps across domains do not correspond to one another. Moreover, specific ages cannot be assigned to any of the sequences; children master these concepts at different rates, and some never achieve higher levels.

motivate individuals to act in positive (for example, altruistic) or negative (for example, deceptive) ways toward other individuals. This discussion of relation to "generalized others" will also touch on the child's understanding of certain societywide institutions with which he comes into contact. Finally, we will consider those aspects of personal knowledge that are particularly important in the interpersonal realm: knowledge of one's own competence and of the psychological aspects of the self. Considered as a whole, this survey will illuminate those factors and forces that bring about the dramatic changes seen at a series of school picnics. At the same time, it should suggest some of the ways in which the world of other human beings stands apart from the world of physical objects.

Becoming Friends

If James Youniss (1980) had attended the school picnic, he might have talked to some of the children about friendship. Typically, Youniss asks children to tell a story in which "a child your age does something kind for another child your age" or to tell a story in which "a child your age shows another child your age that they like them" (pp. 63–64). He then searches for recurring patterns in the stories told by children in different age groups. Though the patterns he has discerned in hundreds of interviews are not necessarily tied to specific ages, average ages will be given in the following summaries.

Among the youngest group, children aged six to eight, the theme of unqualified giving or sharing, particularly of valued goods, appears prominently. "Kind" acts include "giving away a lot of candy," "giving some of their snacks," "sharing gum." Playing nicely with another person is also a way in which young children show their positive feelings. When children of this age are asked to make a character "more" or "less" kind, they simply increase the quantity of goods shared or add another "giving" activity; for example, adding "sharing" to "playing together for a while."

Among children aged nine to eleven, actions of sharing and playing are now qualified. Typically, the child notes a material discrepancy between the giver and receivers. For example, a nine-year-old declares, "In class somebody doesn't have a pencil or a book. You lend them one" (p. 67). A thirteen-year-old boy says, "A bunch of kids are out at the Hot Shoppes . . . and you don't have any money. They give you some so you can buy a Coke or something." In the face of an initial inequity, the kind act helps bring the individuals into more of an equivalent position.

Such qualified sharing and playing becomes even more prominent in the stories of youngsters aged twelve to fourteen. But there is another, telling shift. Now youngsters talk less of physical exchanges, more of psychological support for one another. A thirteen-year-old girl indicates, "Someone messes up in diagramming [sentences]. Instead of laughing, she helps out. Help him as an equal and don't look down at him." A twelve-year-old reports, "Jane gets in trouble with her parents. Jill tries to comfort her . . . give her advice" (p. 70).

A number of important shifts are at work here. First of all, there is more attention to the needs and demands of the particular individual who will receive the act of kindness: peers are interchangeable for fives, but this is not the case for preadolescents. Second, there is recognition that two individuals may not initially have the same amount of material or spiritual resources and that one role of friendship and kindness is to bring these resources into better balance. Another factor is the shift from a preoccupation with material goods, like food or toys, to the sharing of psychological riches, like support or advice. Finally, there is an increasing assertion of mutuality: friends must assume one another's troubles, actively caring for one another.

If Robert Selman had attended the class picnic, he might have adopted a less direct approach. Selman (1980) typically poses a dilemma and asks the subject to resolve it. As one such story has it, Kathy and Debby have been best friends since they were five. A new girl, Jeannette, moves into the neighborhood and this causes a crisis in the friendship. It seems that Jeannette invites Kathy to a circus on the one day it is in town. Kathy must then decide whether to go to the circus or to play with her old friend Debby. To make matters worse, Debby, who was not asked, does not like Jeannette because she considers her to be a show-off. Clearly Kathy is in quite a pickle.

Having posed such dilemmas to many children and having asked them a number of questions about how Kathy and Debby should handle this crisis, Selman has arrived at a set of steps through which children's friendships pass during middle childhood. At level 0, "momentary" friendships are based on geographical proximity; there is no understanding of a person's innermost thoughts and feelings. "One-way assistance" friendship, occurring at level 1, is seen as a relationship whose strength is based on reducing conflicts. When a conflict occurs, it is blamed on one participant, who is then expected to reverse his behavior in order to set things right. Thus, in the case of the trio of girls, Kathy is expected to give a present to Debby to make up for her bad feelings about the circus. At this level, then, there is recognition of the psychological effects of a conflict: it is to alleviate these effects that the offending party should make amends. But typifying the one-way perspective of this age, children have difficulty realizing that the problem could have arisen out of the acts or demands of both individuals or that there might be an honest disagreement between participants.

Level 2, "two-way, fair-weather cooperation," typically occurs in preadolescence. Children appreciate that both parties participate psychologically in any interaction or conflict and that both parties must therefore engage actively in its resolution. A satisfactory resolution must require an appeal to each person's responsibilities. Thus, at this age there is much talk about "getting both individuals to agree," finding out "what someone really means," and "working together to talk it out and solve the problem." As for the three girls, one twelve-year-old suggests, "You go up and you ask your old friend if it is O.K. with him. You try to get him to see why you want to go" (p. 110). One presents one's own point of view in an effort to get the other individual to change his own perspective on the situation. Each child is allotted some subjective feelings and each must strive to see the other's point of view. And so, at this age, children focus on the differences in intimacy in the several friendship pairs.

A more advanced approach, found at level 3, entails the understanding that conflicts reside within the relationship itself, in the interaction between the parties, rather than as a consequence of external annoyances. Achieving détente is not enough; each side must feel that both he and the other are truly satisfied and would be satisfied to be in the other's

Figure 12.2. For the preadolescent or young adolescent, friendships increase in importance. While intimate relationships with a single peer or "pal" often develop, there is also a tendency to form clubs or cliques.

place—hence the label for this level, "intimate, mutually shared relationship." There is a recognition that friendship conflicts can be due to differences in personality and that one resolution might be a change in personality. Thus a thirteen-year-old suggests that Debby and Jeannette could only become friends "if one of them changed their personality. Shy people don't usually like show-offs" (p. 111).

At this level, friendship is seen as a deeper, more enduring relationship. Conflicts are inevitable, but they also offer a means of cementing and deepening a relationship. Experiences and superficial solutions are rejected: needs and obligations must be attended to regularly if the friendship is to thrive. Children at this stage realize that a long-term relationship is of a different order than more transitory interactions. In reflecting on the dilemma of the three girls, a twelve-year-old girl contends:

Like you have known your friend so long and love her so much then all of a sudden you are so mad at her you say, I could just kill you, and you still like each other because you have known each other for years and you have always been friends and you know in your mind you are going to be friends in a few seconds anyways [p. 112].

As you may have surmised from this final quotation, there is actually one further level of friendship. At level 4, "autonomous interpersonal friendships," the individual realizes that mutuality can sometimes go too far: if it does, the friendship itself may have to be abandoned in favor of an individual's quest for his own autonomy. Typically, this level of friendship is not encountered in children. It is important to note, however, that it is not age that determines the child's level of friendship understanding but rather the range of his experiences and the degree to which he reflects upon them. Thus, in the passages quoted above we note that some twelve-year-olds can be at one level, while others can be at a more primitive or a more advanced level.

Our two guides to friendship utilize a tool popular in studies of friendship—the open-question, either posed directly (as in the case of Youniss's work) or through a story, (as in the case of Selman's dilemmas) (see Bigelow, 1977). Other psychologists favor a more standardized kind of approach. For instance, Rotenberg (1980) devised stories in which protagonists varied in the amount of help they promised to give and in whether they actually kept their word. After hearing such a story, children of different ages were asked to push a button, indicating how much they trusted the protagonist in each story. As another measure, each child was asked which protagonist merited a favorite toy. The pattern of results turned out consonant with that obtained in clinical interviews. That is, kindergarten subjects focus almost exclusively on the amount of help promised by the protagonist and disregard whether he actually keeps the promise; young children seem to base their test of others on whether others "said nice things." In contrast, the older subjects, aged nine and ten, prove more oriented toward the consistency between the amount of help promised and the extent to which the protagonist follows through with the promise.

While the general pattern of friendships has received much attention, other "friendship" issues have also been explored. A number of investigators have examined sex differences. Ahlgren and Johnson (1979) report that girls tend to place a higher value on cooperation while boys place more stress on competitiveness. During the years of middle childhood, children tend to play primarily with youngsters of their own sex. This trend reaches such intensity in the preadolescent years that some scholars feel there may be a biological predisposition at this age to play primarily with one's own sex (Z. Rubin, 1980). However, such a tendency is not immutable: Serbin, Tonick, and Sternglanz (1977) were able to increase the amount of cooperative play in mixed sex groups, though not at the expense of the amount of play with young-

sters of the same sex. Later, of course, children become more interested in members of the opposite sex, but even at that time there are notable sex differences. Boys seem to want to rebel against authority, while girls have no such avowed wish (Z. Rubin, 1980). On the other hand, girls place a much higher value on having an intimate confidante.

These trends toward privacy and intimacy may not be universal: in more traditional societies, friendships tend to be much more inclusive. And there may also be a social class component, with lower-class children engaging in more spontaneous play with a variety of individuals in the neighborhood. Middle-class children, on the other hand, are more likely to have "handpicked" friends with whom they play in more intimate surroundings. Friendships among middle-class youngsters are more carefully scheduled; like their highly organized parents, they have a full agenda of prescribed activities, which may include playing with special friends.

Certain other themes merit mention. In middle childhood, youngsters are likely to form clubs—groups devoted to specific interests or just to "playing around." Membership is often based on skills or popularity, but also can be based on belonging to certain groups defined arbitrarily on religion, race, or geography. For individuals within the clubs, membership can often be a valuable experience, providing chances to develop skills of taking turns, leading the group, making and revising rules, and sharing with one another. However, the clubs and the cliques that form at about the same time can also have negative effects, particularly for those hapless individuals who are excluded from, or kicked out of, such groups. And even for those fortunate enough to be esteemed club members, the experience involved in rejecting others, treating them cruelly, or engaging in stereotyping may be painful or harmful.

Part of growing up involves losing friends, or moving from one relationship to another. After all, in such shifts children are rehearsing the vicissitudes of more permanent relationships of later life, if they are not already sampling them firsthand. It is a sad experience to lose a friend, particularly when the friend does the rejecting, and it is important for parents, teachers, and other peers to support the child when he has lost a friend, whatever the reason. The blow is no easier to bear when the loss of friendship is due to a friend's move from one town to another. Consider the lament of one twelve-year-old, who threatened to kill herself. "My problem is that I want to go back to my old school and my real home" (Z. Rubin, 1980, p. 81).

Ties to friends occupy the bulk of a youngster's attention, but relations to authority figures, ranging from teachers to parents, remain an important issue at this time. Using dilemmas of the type constructed by Selman, William Damon (1977) has examined the development of authority relations. According to Damon's analysis, issues of authority center on two facets: the legitimacy of the individual who is making a demand on the child and the reasons why the child should obey. Damon has found that the authority relation undergoes a profound revolution from a time when the older authority figure is seen as having a unilateral, total, and unquestioned control over the young individual to a time when the child voluntarily recognizes the elder's legitimate claims to authority. Only the older child comes to appreciate that the role of leadership is a needed but temporary one that persons fill when appropriate, that the leader can merit respect for his personal qualities, and that the leader should take into account the needs and desires of the subordinates. And, among older children, the authority relation itself becomes more flexible, consensual, and equal. For a more detailed account of the steps in the development of authority understanding, see Figure 12.3.

In a way, the two relations we have considered here—peer friendship and relations of authority—complement one another. At the beginning of their lives children are almost always enmeshed in authority relations, where the power of the leader is assumed and the child has little to say. Gradually this relationship becomes more human and more flexible, as the child comes to realize (and accept) when an authority relationship is legitimate and when it is not. In contrast, friendship relations are only transitory at first, but they eventually become as enduring and central as initial authority relations. But if friendships tend to replace parent-child authority ties, certain forms of social understanding continue to affect both kinds of relations. In each case, the older child is better able to appreciate the perspective of others, to attend to their motivations and intentions, and to appreciate the psychological aspects of behaviors (instead of merely focusing on raw issues of amount and power). In this sense, social relations with others are "of a piece."

Regulating Relations Among Persons

There is an unseen hand present in every interpersonal relation, one that comes to assume increasing importance in the lives of children. It is the hand of rule, convention, societal norms—those regulations that operate invisibly in any culture and that are often invoked specifically when a crisis or conflict arises (Durkheim, 1976). These rules are sometimes mere customs or conveniences, as in the case of a greeting or a final handshake; but frequently they involve expectations of how individuals relate to one another, touching on weighty issues like honesty and justice.

Figure 12.3. William Damon outlines six stages through which children pass en route to a mature understanding of the concepts of authority and obedience. (Damon, 1977)

AUTHORITY AND OBEDIENCE RELATIONS: A STAGE DESCRIPTION

Level	Basis of authority	Basis of obedience
0-A	A bond of affection or identity with the authority figure.	A primitive association between commands and subject's desires.
0-B	Physical attributes of the authority figure, such as size or sex.	Pragmatic: Obedience as a means to achieve one's desires.
1-A	Attributes which enable the authority figure to enforce his commands, such as strength or social power.	Respect for the authority figure's power; authority figure is omnipotent.
1-B	Authority figure is a superior person who can do what others cannot.	Reciprocity: If subject obeys authority figure, authority figure will take care of subject.
2-A	Prior training or experience has made authority figure more capable than the subordinates.	Respect for the authority figure and the belief that he cares about subordinates.
2-B	Authority depends on different attributes in different situations; it is not a permanent status but rather is a shared, consensual relation between parties.	A cooperative effort which is situation-specific replaces a general response to a superior person.

William Damon has conceived innovative ways of investigating children's emerging sense of justice. In one study, subjects heard a story about four children who had been asked by some friends of their teacher to make bracelets. As it happens, three of the children were about the same age as the subjects, while George was younger. After about fifteen minutes, the bracelet making stopped and the teacher took stock. Michele made more bracelets than anyone else, and her bracelets were also the prettiest. John, the biggest boy, and Ellen made some nice bracelets as well. George, the youngest, made only half a bracelet and it wasn't very pretty (Damon, 1977).

Thanking the children for making the bracelets, the teacher's friends left them ten candy bars to share. It was up to the children to split up the bars among themselves as they saw fit. And it is the job of the subject in Damon's study to decide how in fact the candy bars ought to be divided. In the resulting inquiry by the experimenter, the child is asked to confront the relative importance of such factors as the child's size and age, his productivity, and the prettiness of the bracelets in contributing to an equitable solution. As a philosopher might put it, each child has to weigh in his own mind, as best he can, the relative claims of *merit* (the child who actually made the prettiest bracelets gets the most candy); *egalitarianism* (all children, as human beings, deserve an equal share of the resources, or at least an equal opportunity to compete); *benevolence* (giving extra weight to an individual who is at some disadvantage, because he is younger, less skilled, or may feel disappointed by his poor performance).

As is customary, Damon outlines three major stages, each in turn consisting of two sublevels. At the most primitive level, called 0-A, the conception of justice is confused with an individual's own desires. Johnny's wants are indistinguishable from what he should get. At level 0-B, choices continue to serve the end of gratifying the self. But now the child considers certain external and observable characteristics. "The biggest should get the most" or "She should have it because she's pretty." Still, at this time, protagonists tend to resolve conflict through preferential treatment for themselves or for individuals associated with them.

At level 1-A, a new principle emerges: everyone should get the same treatment under all circumstances. All persons are considered equivalent and the child does not take into account such factors as the psychological uniqueness, intentions, or motivations of each of the several bracelet makers. This egalitarianism is often motivated less by some abstract principle than by the wish to avoid fussing or fighting in a dog-eat-dog world. The desire for equivalence remains at level 1-B, but now the child regards justice as a means of paying back someone for working hard. And so equity comes to be based on merit—people are treated differently according to their talents, effort, and other criteria of merit. Steven, aged six, indicates that the child who made the most things should get the most, and that if the little child had made some more stuff he'd get more too.

Children aged seven, eight, or nine frequently issue level 2 responses. At 2-A the child acknowledges a number of acceptable claims upon justice, which can lead to a number of morally defensible decisions. The concept of need arising from personal inequality (such as lesser age or skill) is taken into account. But at this stage the child attempts simply to impose compromises on conflicting claims: so if one child made more bracelets, and another child made prettier ones, both children should get more candy bars than the two less productive youngsters. Another way of mediating the claims is quantitative: one awards the most to the child with the strongest claim, granting shares to others in proportion to how productive each is (in his own way). Claims of special need are also taken into account, as this is a good means for establishing ultimate equality (cf. Graziano, Brody, and Bernstein, 1980). When two or more parties conflict, the child is likely to throw up his hands and say "each is right, in a way."

Less Hamlet-like, children at 2-B are willing to bite the bullet and decide which of the competing claims is more justifiable in the present context. Unlike youngsters at earlier stages, the child will exclude certain claims as irrelevant to a particular conflict under consideration. Thus, one seven-year-old excludes all claims except those having to do with the excellence of the bracelet, while an eight-year-old decides that considerations of total equality should have precedence in the present context.

As with the Selman friendship dilemmas, higher stages of reasoning can be found in more sophisticated youngsters. For example, an older subject might assume a more disinterested stance, removing himself altogether from the competing claims of the parties involved. But the progression described here is generally all that one can witness before the years of adolescence (Damon, 1980).

One issue often raised in studies where children indicate what "should be done" or what they "would do" concerns the validity of such assertions. We know all too well that it is easier to mouth a pious course of action than to behave in a moral way. Sensitive to this criticism, Damon followed up his hypothetical stories with a study in a real-life context. Adhering closely to the specifics of the bracelet-making dilemma, Damon actually asked three peers and a younger child (who was not an official subject) to make bracelets for an experimenter. Later the three subjects, in the absence of the younger child, were asked to apportion a reward of ten candy bars among all four children. Damon hypothesized that children at stage 0 would award the child who was biggest and nice; that children at level 1-B and above would pay attention to one or another form of merit. Only children at level 2-B would take into account the claims of the younger child, who, owing to his incompetence, could not possibly make as many bracelets as the others.

Of interest was the relationship between children's responses to the hypothetical situation and their behaviors in the real-life condition. Some subjects received the interview one or two months earlier than the real situation; others received the real situation first. Of course, the specific facts of the stories differed from the particulars of the real-life task.

For 50 percent of the 144 subjects, justice reasoning scores were equal on the real-life and the hypothetical measures. For the remaining 72 subjects, 19 subjects had higher scores in the real-life than in the hypothetical situation, while 52 subjects scored lower. This statistically significant difference—a tendency to respond on a more sophisticated level in the hypothetical dilemma than in the real-life situation—was completely unexpected.

How can we account for the lack of concordance between what a subject *says* ought to be done and how he himself *acts* in a "justice situation"? Damon notes that it is typically in the child's self-interest in the real-life situation to employ a lower level of judgment. The lower modes often tend to be more egocentric and more self-serving, for example, stressing the reason that *happens* to coincide with the child's status. Thus, the child's response features an interaction between his self-interest (which will determine how many candy bars he wants to have) and his social judgment about what kinds of reasons are likely to carry weight in discussion. Interestingly, this finding runs counter to what would be predicted by orthodox Piagetian theory.

According to Piaget, knowledge is first worked through on an action plane; consequently one should expect more sophisticated reasons from the child in the real-life situation than in the hypothetical verbal story. But clearly, self-interest emerges as a more potent variable than developmental stage!

Damon conducted a companion study, in which children's real-life behaviors with respect to authority were compared with their reasoning in a hypothetical dilemma about authority relations. In this case, where children had to decide who should be captain of a team, an extremely close relationship emerged between the children's responses to the dilemmas and their actual behavior in a structurally similar situation. Damon accounts for the discrepancy between the two studies in terms of differences between authority knowledge and justice knowledge. Knowledge about authority has inherent in it one's rational self-interest: at each authority level the child must ask "How does this relation serve my needs?" and answer in such a way that his team will do the best. Thus, in a sense, one's self interest has already been taken into account when one makes a judgment about leadership or authority. On the other hand, as a means of resolving conflicts, justice often necessitates a denial of one's own needs and desires. It is this that is so difficult for young children (and not a few older individuals) to accept (Damon, 1980).

In addressing issues of justice, individuals are dealing with situations having a highly moral flavor—ones that would presumably be similar across different cultures (cf. Enright, Manheim, and Franklin, 1980; but see also Chapter 13, p. 522–526). Other kinds of rules and principles, however, are far more idiosyncratic and arbitrary, as in the case of regulations concerning parking a car or dressing in a certain way. Are children sensitive to differences between universal principles and sociocultural conventions?

To answer this question, Donna Weston and Elliot Turiel (1980) told a series of stories to children ranging in age from five to eleven. The stories outlined various kinds of misdeeds carried out by a young protagonist: hitting another child, undressing on the playground, leaving toys on the floor in the classroom, and refusing to share a snack with another child. Some children at each age regarded each of the actions negatively, but five-year-olds were relatively undisturbed by the actions of undressing and leaving toys around, while eleven-year-olds tended to give these actions a negative evaluation. On the other hand, *virtually every subject* evaluated the act of hitting another child negatively: clearly this action was regarded as qualitatively more reprehensible than the others. From this and other studies (Nucci and Turiel, 1978) Turiel concludes that the difference between moral and social convention is apparent even to preschoolers.

Turiel wanted to see if youngsters' evaluations would alter if the various types of regulations were endorsed by the community. Accordingly, another part of the study focused on the rules adopted by two schools with respect to the behaviors cited in the study. For each story, children were told about one school (the Park School) where youngsters were not allowed to carry out a particular activity (for example, undressing outside) and then about a contrasting school (the Grove School, with different children and different teachers) where children were allowed to perform the activity. In each case, the child was asked whether it was O.K. for the school to have this rule; whether it was O.K. for the child to carry out the questionable behavior; and what the teacher would say to a child following a transgression.

With respect to three of the regulations (undressing, refusing to share, and leaving toys) the majority of subjects at every age approved the policy of the more permissive school. Moreover, children were considered to have acted properly in the schools where the action was permitted. But in contrast, the large majority of subjects at all ages issued a negative evaluation of a school policy that tolerated hitting; most subjects stated that it was not right for a school to permit children to strike one another.

Across ages, subjects' responses to the teacher's behavior conformed to their evaluation of the act. Children ordinarily assumed that the teacher's words and actions would be in accordance with the school policy. However, a greater number of subjects indicated that a teacher would reprimand a child for hitting, even when hitting was officially tolerated by the school. Indeed, the only difference across ages occurred with reference to the progressive school's policy of allowing hitting: younger children were more likely to exonerate the hitting child, while condemning the school; older children tended to reject both the policy and the action (Lockhart, Abrahams, and Osherson, 1977; Nucci and Turiel, 1978).

Despite the early emerging ability to distinguish among different kinds of rules (Nucci, 1981), there are still developmental principles at work. For example, Lockhart, Abrahams, and Osherson (1977) examined the abilities of children to distinguish between regularities based on social convention (for example, the rules of hide-and-seek, the side of the street where cars are driven) and those based on physical causality (for example, whether rocks will float or sink in water). Children were asked whether the regularity had always existed as such, whether it could be changed, and, if so, under what circumstances and how the child would act if the regularity was in fact changed.

Children's abilities to distinguish between various social conventions and the laws of physical reality increased steadily with age. Young children fail to appreciate that social conventions can be changed—"It wouldn't be right . . . God doesn't want it that way" (p. 1528). Third graders feel that conventions can be changed by majority vote. However, they often believe, incorrectly, that physical laws as well as social conventions can be changed. Only fifth graders realize the arbitrariness of conventions and the fact that they can be changed at will; at the same time, unlike younger children, they insist "You can't change nature by a vote." Confirming Turiel's claims, children at every age prove more reluctant to change moral rules than conventions; still they are more likely to suggest that these can be changed than that the laws of nature can be defied.

Such studies provide convincing documentation that relationships among individuals are governed by more than their physical proximity and their immediate activities. Children become quite sensitive to the existence of various relevant principles. Handed down over the centuries, these principles can take diverse forms across cultures but are present in some form in all of them. And so children the world over are occupied in the years of middle childhood in figuring out the nature of these rules and conventions, mastering them, invoking them in their verbal reasoning, at times bending them for their own ends, at times using them in the service of others.

Knowledge of Other Persons

When children come together, they often play, sometimes in the kind of casual way proper to a school picnic, at other times with unbroken attention and commitment for hours at a stretch. They engage in sports like baseball or tennis, card games like war or poker, board games like chess or Monopoly. In one sense, such games are "just" fun; and yet children take them seriously, very seriously. In fact they can be thought of as "rehearsals" for the more critical "games" of adulthood—interpersonal relations with a spouse, a friend, a business colleague—and as rehearsals for the interactions of the marketplace—be it among neighborhood stores or international corporations. Games represent a world in microcosm: the skills needed for successful game playing resemble those necessary for coping in modern commercial society and, possibly, in cultures everywhere.

Consider some of the skills children need to succeed at poker or Monopoly. They must be aware of their own goals, the steps that they should follow to achieve them, the goals of other players, how the other players are striving to achieve them, and the extent to which the goals of the two parties are mutually exclusive. For example, in chess one player's advantage is necessarily the other's disadvantage, but in other board games, like Monopoly, individuals can team up. Children need to assess one another, to figure out when someone is playing straight and communicating directly and when deception is at work. They need to judge when other players are acting from positive or from ill motivation, when acts are intentional or accidental, when an outcome is determined by luck and when it derives from skill. And they must have insights about themselves as players—how good they really are, how likely they are to succeed, where their weaknesses lie.

By adolescence, most individuals have arrived at these adult-like understandings. They have done so not because anyone tells them just what to do but because they have picked up (or themselves hit upon) an informal "folk" or "naive" psychology—a rough-and-ready yardstick of *how* people behave, *why* they behave in the way they do, and *what* makes them tick.

A major task of social psychology has been to define the nature of these adult understandings (Heider, 1958; Kelley, 1967, 1973); developmental psychologists, in turn, have

studied how these understandings evolve (Surber, 1980; Weiner and Peter, 1973; B. Weiner, 1974; Weiner, Kun, and Benesh-Weiner, 1980). Though not usually thought of as a student of social cognition, Piaget (1932) conducted the initial studies that helped to define the basic issues in this area. Much subsequent work has been designed to determine the significance of Piaget's initial demonstrations and to introduce certain crucial distinctions that Piaget failed to make.

In Piaget's original studies, children were told pairs of stories in which protagonists committed acts of destruction. For example, in one story a child broke one cup as he was trying to steal some cookies; in the other story a child broke fifteen cups while he tried to help his mother by drying the dishes. Subjects were asked to evaluate such actions and, in particular, to decide which of the protagonists in the two stories was naughtier and merited more severe punishment.

Piaget outlined a deceptively simple course. In his view, younger children focused only on the amount of damage done: a protagonist who broke fifteen cups was naughtier than a protagonist who broke only one cup. Older children were able to go beyond this *objective orientation* and to take into account the sequence of events that led up to the breakage. Armed with a *subjective orientation*, they might decide that a child who broke only one cup while he was up to mischief was naughtier than a child who broke fifteen cups while trying to help his mother.

In science, progress is often made when two issues that were thought to be a single issue, or two issues that had been confused with one another, can be teased apart. This is what happened when scientists came to distinguish between temperature and heat; it is also what happens when youngsters learn to distinguish between size and weight (C. L. Smith, 1981). And it is what happened with Piaget's studies. Investigators became aware that Piaget had not adequately teased apart two important issues: whether an action is *intentional* and what *motivated* an action (Berndt and Berndt, 1975; Shantz, 1975).

We can get a feeling for the importance of this distinction by returning to the stories about broken cups. A person can break a cup on purpose (intentionally) or he can break it by accident (without meaning to). In either case, we can also consider his motives. For instance, he can intentionally break a cup out of bad motives (say, to hurt his brother) or out of good motive (say, to kill a poisonous spider). Although we seldom consider motives when an act is accidental, the same alternative can be raised. The breakage can occur as a consequence of good motives (an individual was trying to help someone and accidentally knocked over a tray) or out of bad motives (an individual was trying to steal some cookies and happened to knock over a glass).

Perhaps because of this complex set of factors, which they had not fully teased apart, psychologists barked up a number of wrong trees in their initial attempts to illuminate children's understanding of others' behaviors (Karniol, 1978; Keasey, 1978). Reflecting the unwieldy experimental paradigms that were used, initial results concluded that children as old as seven or eight were insensitive to the motivations and intentions of others and paid attention only to the objective amount of damage (or good) that was done.

With a better understanding of the concepts involved, as well as simpler stories and less demanding response measures, a far different picture is emerging. It now appears from adaptations of the Piaget paradigm that even at the age of three, children are sensitive to the motivations of other individuals. They can recognize differences between someone who wants to help or teach another (good motive) and someone who wants to hurt another or make them feel bad (bad motive) (Peterson and Keasey, 1976).

The developmental course of sensitivity to intentions seems slower than that governing motives; still, by the age of six, children are sensitive to the intentions of agents (Armsby, 1971; Berg-Cross, 1975; Farnill, 1974). To elicit such sensitivity it is imperative that experimenters clearly describe the intention: young children will misinterpret actions as stupidity or ineptness unless they are clearly labeled as intentional. A number of other factors can also obscure children's sensitivities. For one thing, young children are very impressed by the consequences of an action. Thus, if an action leads to catastrophic consequences, young children will overlook intention and motive and judge the action negatively. A second relevant factor is that young children prove much more alert to actions that are harmful than to ones that are helpful. (This may be because parents spend more time talking about and reprimanding children for bad acts than rewarding them for good ones.) At any rate, this proclivity to recognize harmful acts as such allows young children to evaluate such acts independently of what happens to a protagonist thereafter; in contrast, they have to see how the authority figure responds to an action before they are prepared to conclude that the action has been positive.

Though a complete account is not yet at hand, it is possible to indicate the general developmental pattern that has emerged in response to the stories initially posed by Piaget. Children as young as three will show some sensitivity to the protagonist's motives, particularly if the motives are very clearly stated. They will not demonstrate sensitivity to intentions until the age of six or so, and then only if the intentions of the protagonist have been stated in unambiguous terms. The ability to judge intentions is much better if the consequences of actions are not described: for when the consequences have large negative effects, they will overwhelm evidence documenting the positive intentions and motives of an agent. Only in middle childhood do children become able to disregard information about consequences and focus exclusively on the intentions and motives of the protagonist (Keasey, 1978).

While the Piagetian paradigm (with its successors) has stimulated the dominant line of research, other investigators have pursued different courses as they attempt to understand how children make social attributions. Shultz (1980) has found evidence that children as young as three may have some awareness of intention. For example, in a card game, where children may sometimes respond by mistake, three-year-olds can readily distinguish between those responses that were issued on purpose and those that were accidental or reflexive. Moreover, they display incipient awareness at age three, and considerable awareness by age five, of whether other individuals' behaviors were accidental or purposeful.

Even if the bare bones of detecting intentionality are present at an early age, a developmental sequence can still be observed (see Karniol, 1978; M. C. Smith, 1978). According to Shultz, three factors are of particular import if the child is to appear sensitive to intention: whether the behavior is real, rather than simply hypothetical; whether the behavior in question was carried out by the child himself; and whether the behavior is spontaneous, rather than staged. An even more complex picture is proposed by Harris (1977). Using a scheme developed by Heider (1958), Harris showed children the film of a destructive action—the breaking of a chair—and presented surrounding contexts suggesting several different levels of responsibility on the part of the actor. At one extreme, the action was completely accidental; at an intermediate level the destroyer had some knowledge of the fragility of a chair; at a higher level the subject was asked to break the chair; and at the highest level the destroyer announced beforehand that she was going to break it.

Only the most mature subjects—eighth graders and college students—fully appreciated these levels of intention and foresight.

Studies have also looked at different aspects of the child's appreciation of motivational factors. Young children tend to make severe judgments about individuals who have been hurt; an injury is considered to be the individual's fault, because he was probably a bad person (Suls and Kalle, 1979). Similarly, younger children are likely to condemn an outright antisocial behavior, for example, one committed by a child who hurts others; older children are more likely to take into account environmental factors and to assume that the antisocial behavior can be changed if environmental forces are altered (Maas, Marecek, and Travers, 1978). Older children also discount an intrinsic explanation when external factors can be identified (Cohen et al., 1979); thus the action of giving something to someone else is not considered to be altruistic in cases where the giver will be rewarded. In contrast, children at kindergarten level are likely to take an additive approach. They credit the giver *both* for making a donation and for receiving a reward. But even at this young age, children have some sense about the reasons awards are given. Children are much less likely to find an activity (like drawing with markers) interesting if they are told that they are going to receive an award for it than if they are simply allowed to participate in it. Even in the nursery school, children have learned to be suspicious of activities to which adults fix awards (Lepper, Greene, and Nisbett, 1973).

What kinds of attributions do children make when an individual behaves in a way incongruous with his usual disposition—for example, when a policeman sees a man stealing a car but does nothing to stop this action? Whiteman, Brook, and Gordon (1977) found an increasing tendency with age for children to provide a motivation that preserved an actor's customary disposition. For example, a sixth grader might claim that the policeman had said to himself, "I'm going to let him do it and then start following." Kindergartners and first graders were more likely to deny the situation altogether, to attribute it to some transient disposition on the part of the actor ("He must have been in a bad mood") or a direct reaction to the event ("His boss told him not to follow the robber"). We see here that younger subjects are less sensitive to the reasons why an individual is likely to behave in a certain way and are more prone to simply invent an *ad hoc* explanation. Nonetheless, if the discrepant behavior is too inconsistent with an individual's customary behavior, even older children will try to account for it with situational, mood, or other kinds of special explanations (Sagotsky and Wondolowski-Svensson, 1981).

The search for consistent accounts of behavior has revealed that older children prove more likely to explain behaviors in terms of long-term dispositions on the part of characters (Wood, 1978). Thus, when a character in a story displayed malicious pleasure, laughing at the misfortune of others, seven-year-olds were likely to explain the behavior in terms of immediately observable facts: "He is laughing because the man is making a funny face." Ten-year-olds were more likely to make a simple interpretation: "He laughed because the man had been told off." In contrast, thirteen-year-olds pointed to a dispositional trait: "He is laughing because he is the sort of man who is glad when someone else gets into trouble." With older subjects, motives become increasingly psychological and dispositional; but even young subjects display some sensitivity to the dispositions of individuals (Berndt and Berndt, 1975) and can infer how they would feel in diverse situations (Green, n.d.).

Reviewing the evidence, we find at a very early age an incipient awareness that individuals behave in specific ways for specific rea-

sons and that their actions may or may not have been carried out intentionally. These understandings are more likely to emerge in situations that are simple, with tasks that require little verbalization. Sensitivity to psychological causes, explanations in terms of individual's general dispositions, attention to the context in which a behavior occurs, awareness of the multiplicity of reasons for a behavior, knowledge that others are cognizant of one's own intentions (Shultz, 1980), and willingness to attribute events to the environment rather than to a person's basic nature—all these increase with age. And, indeed, when one considers the complex motives at work in a poker game or in a negotiation between two partners in a company, it seems safe to say that the development continues throughout the adult years (cf. DiVitto and McArthur, 1978; Kelley, 1967; Sedlak, 1979).

CHILDREN'S ACTIONS TOWARD OTHERS

Children do not, of course, simply judge the behaviors of others; they must constantly make decisions about their own interpersonal behaviors. Raviv, Bar-Tal, and Lewis-Levin (1980) examined children's motivations for helping others (see also Barnett, et al., in press; Grusec and Redler, 1980). Subjects were given an opportunity under four different circumstances to donate prize money to charity. Some children were simply placed in a room with a charity box; some were told that it was nice to make a contribution; other subjects were informed that some of the contributors would win prizes; and some were directed to make a contribution. With age, children were more likely to contribute under the less coercive conditions. Moreover, children contributing voluntarily were more likely to indicate altruistic motives; in contrast (though not surprisingly) the children who contributed under the coercive conditions invoked less altruistic motives, like compliance or desire for a reward.

What of other behaviors that youngsters can direct toward one another? Boys exhibit a greater proclivity toward competitiveness with age, across all situations and tasks. In contrast, girls modulate their behavior in terms of the instructions that they obtain in a given game or task. Moreover, girls become increasingly competitive when pitted against boys while typically exhibiting cooperation in the company of girls (Moely, Skarin, and Weil, 1979; see also Krauss, 1977). Children's abilities to reason about persuasion increase with age, but even young children are able to choose the most effective persuasive argument when offered several alternatives. As the authors comment, "This confusion is quite consistent with information observations; indeed, in real-life settings, parents never cease to be amazed by the conniving persuasive tactics of even their very young offspring" (Howie-Day, 1979, p. 6).

Children are sometimes called on—or feel themselves inspired—to deceive other individuals. Feldman and White (1980) found that, in general, most first graders are pretty good at telling lies when directed to do so and that children gifted at playing different roles also excel in deception. In a similar vein, Krauss and Morency (1980) found that children who are effective communicators are also good deceivers, while interestingly, those most expressive in spontaneous situations prove to be poor deceivers; apparently they have trouble keeping a poker face. DePaulo and colleagues (1980) documented that with age children become increasingly good at detecting when someone is deceiving. And, paradoxically, children are better than adults at detecting deliberate distortions or disguising of one's feelings. Here, finally, is one area of social cognition in which children have it over their

more gullible parents. Perhaps adults are so taken with words that they cannot listen through them to detect the underlying deception—they assume that if an individual talks and acts in a certain way he must *feel* that way. A point for folk wisdom: perhaps it *is* hardest to fool children and animals.

THE PUZZLE OF SOCIAL INSTITUTIONS

Nearly all studies of children's social cognition have focused on how children think about other individuals. One intriguing exception is Hans Furth's investigation of children's conceptions of the social institutions in their community: money, stores, schools, officials, the post office, and government (Furth, Baur, and Smith, 1976). Using Piaget-style clinical interviews, Furth and his colleagues discovered that for most five- and six-year-olds, the outside world appears undifferentiated (there were few distinctions made among roles or among institutions). The social world is seen as free of conflict; all social institutions proceed according to known rules without any accidental contingencies. Actions are executed because people want to carry them out: there is no notion of competing interests, limited supplies of money, vague regulations, or the other nasty ambiguities that pervade a complex industrial society.

The first attempts to go beyond the observed facts are largely imaginative elaborations. Here a child will try to piece together personal observations, plus what he has overheard on television and in adult conversation. For example, asked about the source of money, the child runs through a number of things he has heard, and concludes that it must come from tills in a shop.

A second stage of social understanding involves some limited inferences. Asked where money comes from, a child of six or seven

Figure 12.4. Hans Furth outlined the difficulties exhibited by youngsters in figuring out the purposes of social institutions. Here a group of youngsters receives an inside look at the local police station. Such first-hand exposure may help children better understand this and perhaps other similar social institutions.

no longer simply states that an individual has it or goes and gets it; he is aware that individuals have to work and save up money. Children are aware that an individual is not born to a job but selects it; however, there is still little appreciation that an occupation can be less than permanent.

During a third stage, from around age seven to nine or ten, the child recognizes some general social functions and obligations. He comes to understand that, just as customers pay for goods bought in a store, so too the storekeeper must pay for the goods. Acquisition of an occupational role is seen to involve personal qualities as well as training. Still, because the child lacks overall systematic knowledge, there are many glaring inconsistencies. A child may realize that a school is run by the headmaster and that he uses money to buy goods, but the youngster cannot trace the money beyond the school safe into which the headmaster places his money. There is no appreciation that the money comes from an external source, in this case the state.

At a fourth stage (the final one, at the end of middle childhood) youngsters grasp general rules pertaining to social institutions. For example, asked about job acquisition, an eleven-year-old indicates that people can choose their work situation, but only if there are sufficient jobs (p. 359). The same child appreciates that the head teacher gets money from the local government, which in turn secures money from taxes; like "road taxes, taxes for having a television, the taxes on the house, taxes for having a telephone." The child at this stage hardly possesses a sophisticated understanding of the workings of his government: but he is able to structure his account in terms of definite criteria and he remains consistent in his reasoning. Also emerging at this stage is an ability to relate the personal to the societal: children now understand how an individual's use of money in his own life relates to the passage of money through economic institutions. The child begins to appreciate that the external social world is also governed by rules, that these can be changed, and that there may well be conflicts between various systems within the society.

Unraveling children's views about the numerous social institutions in their world is an enormous task, which researchers have just begun to address. It is also an important one, for practical and theoretical reasons. Social institutions may occupy an intermediate place between the purely physical world, governed by immutable natural laws, and the subjective personal world, where regularities are difficult to ascertain at all.

The Self on the Self

Thoughts about others are important, but thoughts about oneself are equally so, and much more likely to be charged with emotion. How a person thinks about himself influences not only his interactions with others, but also his own accomplishments and his own feelings—in fact, these thoughts about himself in many cases *are* his own feelings.

All is well and good when individuals have basically positive thoughts about themselves. But when these thoughts take a negative turn, the consequences can be quite severe.

Inspired in part by work with animals who had "learned" to become helpless (Seligman and Maier, 1967), Carol Dweck (Dweck and Goetz, 1978; Dweck et al., 1978) became interested in the consequences of an unfavorable view of oneself. In an initial study, two experimenters administered problems to children, one posing solvable problems, the other posing unsolvable ones to the same children. After a time the "failure experimenter" began to administer solvable problems, virtually identical to those administered by the other experimenter. Surprisingly, many children failed to solve these problems. Apparently, children can rather quickly acquire the notion that they are incapable of solving a problem, at least under certain circumstances (Dweck and Reppucci, 1973).

In subsequent research, Dweck and her colleagues have located many children who believe that they are unable to handle certain tasks—they have "learned helplessness." Such children differ in a number of respects from those who have confidence in their own abilities—so-called mastery-oriented children. It turns out that helpless children deride their abilities when they fail but do not credit their competence for their successes: to account for success they are likely to invoke luck or some other external circumstance (cf. Bar-Tal and Darom, 1979). In contrast, mastery-oriented children credit themselves when they succeed on a task and discount their failures as irrelevant to their basic underlying competence. Inasmuch as helpless children don't believe in themselves, it is perhaps not surprising that they are generally unable to cope with unexpected obstacles.

How do mastery-oriented children explain their failures on tasks? According to Dweck, children who persist in the face of failure tend to attribute their poor performance to motivational factors. This attribution is important because it implies that they could do better if they tried harder. It is interesting to note that when the going gets tougher, mastery-oriented children may become even more sophisticated in their strategies, as if the difficulty prods them to greater heights. In contrast, those who do not persist tend to blame their failures on factors they can't control rather than on the degree of effort they have chosen to invest. Note that attributions to unmanageable external factors, as well as an attribution to lack of ability, imply that failure will be difficult to overcome.

There is also a group of children who attain considerable academic success but still evince a low conception of themselves (Phillips, 1981). These children set lower standards for themselves, have lower expectations of success, perceive that their teachers expect less of them, and, in fact, receive lower ratings of expected success from their teachers than do their more self-confident mastery-oriented peers. Such high achieving, low concept children represent an intriguing mixture of the traits of youngsters with learned helplessness and mastery-oriented children. Ignoring the evidence of their own achievements, they act as if they are incapable of attaining success, as if they are their own worst enemies.

In the various paradigms used by Dweck, girls turn out on the average to exhibit more learned helplessness than boys. One promising explanation has been discounted: it can't be the case that girls learn to be helpless because they are told they lack ability. For it turns out that in elementary school, it is *girls* who are more typically told that they are able. In addition, girls usually receive better grades in school, while boys are held in lower esteem and are more criticized by their teachers.

Pursuing the key to learned helplessness, Dweck and her associates examined *all* the feedback provided by teachers toward children (Dweck and Goetz, 1978). And they found striking sex differences that clarify the phenomenon. It turns out that boys receive much more negative feedback than do girls and that the feedback is much more diffuse and ambiguous with respect to the intellectual quality of boys' work. Thus boys apparently learn that they ought to expect criticism, that they have to cope with it, and that it is more likely to concern conduct and other nonintellectual aspects of their work. (In fact, 67 percent of feedback does concern these aspects, compared to 32 percent for intellectual facets of their work.) In contrast, girls receive far less negative feedback, so criticism is much more of a special event. Moreover, a far greater proportion of the negative feedback (88.2 percent) concerns intellectual aspects of their work. Finally, when positive feedback *is* related to the intellectual quality of their work, boys are more likely than girls to be the recipients.

Further research has confirmed this basic point. Regardless of sex, children who receive "failure feedback" about specific problems are far more likely to regard subsequent failure feedback as indicative of their general ability than are children who receive feedback that is irrelevant to the solutions of the problems. The implications are twofold: Boys would also learn to be helpless if they were subjected to the type of negative feedback girls receive; conversely, if girls were socialized like boys, they might well learn mastery rather than helplessness.

Dweck explains why the proclivity toward learned helplessness should have particularly devastating effects in the area of mathematics. According to her analysis, academic subjects differ in the extent to which new problems or assignments call upon a fresh set of skills and are relatively independent of earlier problems. In the language arts, once basic verbal skills have been acquired, a child is rarely confronted with a new unit that puts him at a complete loss. In math, however, a new unit may involve totally new concepts, to which past learning may seem, and may even be, irrelevant (see Parsons, 1981; Reis, 1980). So mathematics provides numerous opportunities for initial failures. This is just the kind of situation that proves devastating for an individual (often a girl) with proclivities toward learned helplessness, while it is stimulating, at least initially, for an individual (often a boy) with a mastery inclination. Of course, nearly all of us eventually learn helplessness in higher mathematics, even as we continue to persevere in verbal domains!

Learned helplessness has proved amenable to laboratory interventions. Children trained to make appropriate attributions following their failures—to attribute their failures to insufficient effort rather than to a fundamental intellectual flaw—prove more successful ultimately than children who are simply given many trials where they are allowed to succeed. Apparently, helpless children are not simply children deprived of success; they are

The Motivation to Achieve

Some people have a drive to excel; they set high goals and strive for continued advancement. Others are content with less success; they prefer a less demanding life. One's actual accomplishments tend to reflect one's motivation—thus, those who *want* to achieve are more apt to be high achievers.

In the 1930s psychologists became interested in learning more about the roots and consequences of high **achievement motivation.** As part of this inquiry, Henry Murray and his colleagues (Murray and Morgan, 1943) developed the Thematic Apperception Test (TAT), a **projective test** that measures a person's motives (such as need for aggression, for dominance, for affiliation, and for achievement). The subject is asked to write stories to accompany simple but somewhat ambiguous pictures. Analysis of the stories then suggests motives that the subject has "projected." For example, when shown a picture of a boy absorbed in thought, a person with a high achievement motivation might say that the child is trying to solve a challenging problem. In contrast, a person with a low achievement motivation might say that the boy is dreaming about a vacation. A reliable indicator of achievement motivation, the TAT is still in wide use.

Researchers have asked *who* achieves in our achievement-oriented society (McClelland, 1961). Parental pressures seem to be a crucial factor in the development of a high achievement motivation. By setting high standards and offering firm but gentle encouragement along with overt expressions of affection, parents foster achievement motivation in their children. In contrast, more domineering parents who exert more control and direction and who display less patience and warmth tend to have low-achievement youngsters (Rosen and D'Andrade, 1959). In the most extreme cases, children become so insecure that they actually develop a motive to fail and even feel a certain degree of happiness (or accomplishment!) when they do fail.

In the past, societal attitudes dictated that high achievement was risky and unattractive for women. This was dramatically illustrated in a study of college students done in the late 1960s (Horner, 1968, 1970, 1972). Women were asked to write a story about a successful female medical student. In 65 percent of the cases, the stories reflected fears of social rejection and loss of femininity. The men, who were asked to write about similar male students did not display such fears; on the contrary, 90 percent showed strong positive feelings.

Recently, the growth of the women's movement has led to changing values and attitudes. As women have advanced into new professions and roles, they have become less fearful of success. At the same time, men appear to have become less achievement-oriented and are under less outside pressure to succeed (L. W. Hoffman, 1972). With these changing patterns, men and women may become more similar in their attitudes toward achievement and, quite possibly, in their actual achievements.

children who cannot properly interpret their successes (and their failures).

Children's conceptions of the realms of effort and mastery have been analyzed by Nicholls (1978). Following the screening of films where individuals solve problems and engage in other kinds of work and leisure activities, Nicholls asked his subjects about the efforts, abilities, and luck of the different protagonists. In general the youngest children did not distinguish effort and outcome as cause and effect. They tended to believe that those who try harder are smarter even if they get a lower score.

At a second level of sophistication, found in seven- and eight-year-olds, effort is considered the prime cause of outcomes; ability does not exist as a separate cause. If people differ in effort and still receive the same score, the child who exerted less effort is assumed to have been working exceptionally hard when he did try.

At the third level, most common around the ages of nine and ten, children do acknowledge that individuals may differ in ability. Yet there is a lingering belief that students are really equally clever if they work as hard as one another. Only at the fourth level, not common until adolescence, is the concept of ability recognized as, in some sense, a limiting factor on performance.

Other age trends have been documented in the area of achievement and mastery. According to Feld, Ruhland, and Gold (1979) fifth graders are much more aware than second graders of social aspects of achievement; they realize that one's performance needs to be considered at least in part in terms of the performances of other individuals. An increasingly large number of situations are seen as arenas where achievement matters. Fourth graders are more likely than kindergartners to appreciate that the outcomes of certain events, such as drawing cards blindly from a

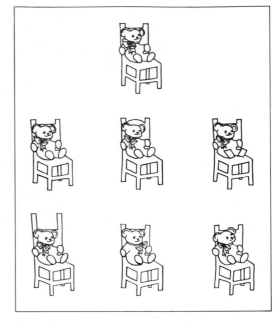

Figure 12.5. Only careful attention to detail permits a youngster to get a high score on the Matching Familiar Figures Test. The impulsive child—noticing a general similarity—is likely to be satisfied by any of the bears; the reflective child is more likely to scan each figure and to make the appropriate match. (Kagan, 1965)

shuffled deck, depend on luck rather than on competence-related factors such as age, practice, intelligence, and effort. Finally, schoolchildren become able by the age of nine to read their teacher's evaluations of a student's performance when he fails a test: they appreciate that if a teacher was angry, he considered the student to have been lazy; whereas, if the teacher showed pity, he believed the student lacked ability (Graham and Stern, 1981).

Conceptual Tempos: Impulsivity Versus Reflectivity

Recall this familiar scene: a classroom during a final exam. Only half the allotted time has elapsed, and yet one impatient student hands in his paper. He has rushed through the entire test scarcely considering his answers. The student beside him plods along, pondering, even obsessing, over every word, and finishes just before the deadline. One student is not necessarily smarter than the other, but the two approach such tasks in clearly different ways, or with different **conceptual tempos.** The first student is **impulsive.** He plunges into situations with little caution or fear of failure; he says and does what comes to mind risking error in the process. In contrast, the **reflective** student is more cautious and critical. He evaluates alternatives and takes more time before answering; he appears more inhibited and more anxious about the outcome in his effort.

Using tests designed to measure conceptual tempos, Kagan and his colleagues (Kagan, 1965, 1966; Kagan et al., 1964; Kagan and Kogan, 1970) have found marked differences even in young children (see Figure 12.5). Kagan postulates that a reflective style may stem from a fear of failure and an inability to disguise this anxiety. Impulsive children may also be anxious, but they mask their insecurities because of a strong drive to appear competent. Those who are spared such anxiety will perform with a moderate conceptual tempo.

Conceptual tempos are not welded into a personality—they can be altered. A child's style of performance can be influenced by extended exposure to adults who are either highly impulsive or strongly reflective. More directly, explicit instructions on how to approach and respond to a given task can change a child's conceptual tempo (Bush and Dweck, 1975; D. Denney, 1972; Meichenbaum, 1971; Ridberg, Parke, and Hetherington, 1971; Yando and Kagan, 1968).

If conceptual tempos can, at least to some extent, be molded, the question arises as to which style, if either, is preferable. After the preschool years, children who are more reflective tend to perform more accurately on certain problem-solving tasks than impulsive children. At least in some situations, then, reflectivity appears to be the superior style. In some social situations, however, (for instance, meeting someone new) a certain amount of impulsiveness (response to first impressions of people) may result in more accurate judgments than labored reflection. At the very least, some flexibility across the impulsive-reflective range seems desirable.

Children's judgments about their own competence are affected by the situation in which they find themselves. Bryant (1977) documents that individual children are more likely to enhance their judgments of themselves when they are placed in a competitive environment, whereas they are more likely to think well of other persons when they have been placed in a cooperative environment. In situations where they ought to attend to the performances of their peers, children younger than second grade fail to use such information in evaluating their own performance. In fact, even when a strong incentive is provided to engage in a comparison of abilities (say a situation where the child can win only if he beats the other children), not until fourth grade can children consistently exploit this "social comparison" information (Ruble et al., 1980). In general, children are able to evaluate their own performances relatively well, though whether it is easier for them to evaluate their own performance or those of other children remains a matter of controversy (Stipek and Hoffman, 1980).

Children's evaluations of themselves at young ages are colored by their desire to place themselves in a favorable light even when that is not appropriate. For example, in a task where second and third graders' donations are actually stimulated by an experimenter's rewards, these children tend to regard themselves as acting out of spontaneous generosity (Smith et al., 1979). Interestingly, however, the expectations of seven- and eight-year-old girls are slightly lower for themselves than for other children, suggesting that learned helplessness may already be setting in (Stipek and Hoffman, 1980).

Children do not just think about themselves as engaged in certain situations; they also think about themselves, and about others, as separate entities. To elicit their thoughts about what the self is like—to probe their intrapsychic awareness—Selman and

Jurkovic (1978) posed dilemmas to children. In one oft-quoted dilemma, Tom is trying to decide what to buy his friend Mike for a birthday party. He learns by chance that Mike's dog has been lost for two weeks. In fact, Mike is so upset that he says he never wants to look at another dog again. Tom then passes a store with a sale on puppies. His dilemma is whether to buy the puppy for Mike, anticipating what Mike's reactions might be.

Once again, we encounter five levels of awareness. At stage 0, roughly spanning the ages three to seven, the child has a purely physical notion of the self. The self inheres in one's own body—particularly, in fact, in one's mouth. Actions are not distinguished from traits; consequently, saying "I'm a good boy" may be the same as saying "I did a good thing." There is no awareness of the perspective of others apart from oneself. Any questions about a character's thoughts or feelings will be answered in terms of the child's own experiences and feelings.

Anytime between age four and age nine the child at stage 1 is aware of his subjective experience, though uncertain as to whether he can hide what he feels. Asked whether Mike meant what he said, a child says, "He meant what he said because he said it"—Mike is not credited with the ability to distort his own observations. Any implication that Mike could say it and not mean it is simply translated into the imputation "He could be lying." If Mike is sad, it is because he looks sad. There is no notion of fooling oneself—this phrase just means that someone will change his beliefs, rather than that he had been unaware of his feelings.

At stage 2 the child is able to view his inner life as clearly distinguishable from his outer experience. This period can begin as early as age six and continue into early adolescence. As posited in traditional theory, the self can now assume the role of a second person and look back upon its inner states.

This revolution in thinking brings about several changes. The child now acknowledges that inner experiences constitute the reality, with outer actions but an appearance of that reality. Mike could put a smile on his face but that wouldn't change his inner feelings.

In addition, at stage 2 the self can now constantly monitor its own thoughts and actions. The child realizes that an individual can fool himself but that it is possible to counter this self-deception through renewed attention to the problem at hand. At this stage the child is aware that one can now consciously put on a façade for others. He realizes it is easier to fool others because they don't share one's own mind. Finally, the child appreciates that awareness of oneself can be used to bolster one's own confidence. Knowing you can do it can help you do it—the power of positive thinking.

Before the preadolescent years, few children go beyond stage 2. For the record, however, the features of the two highest stages should be mentioned. At stage 3, roughly between the ages nine and fifteen, there arises the concept of mind, an entity capable of deciding *which* thoughts are permitted into the domain of awareness and which are kept out. An individual at this stage is aware that you can put something out of your mind because you don't want to know about it: "You still know about it, but you don't think about it or talk about it." The youth believes that self-awareness is always at least potentially available, with the mind or ego playing an active moderating role between inner feelings and outer actions.

Here lies the contrast with the highest stage, which occurs at adolescence. An adolescent sees that individuals have thoughts, feelings, and motivations that resist analysis even by the most introspectively functioning mind. There is awareness of the existence of unconscious processes and the psychological causes of behavior. The youth now realizes that no purposeful act of conscious effort or will can ever yield a total understanding of all the actions of the self.

Selman and Jurkovic provide an elegant portrait of the way in which children gradually come to acquire sophisticated notions about one of the most important, if most elusive, aspects of experience. The stage sequence is a regular one in normal children and one that proves difficult to speed up, as it depends upon experiences that occur in the course of living.

It would be misleading to conclude this review without at least mentioning a few of the factors that complicate this account of the self. First of all, there are tremendous individual differences among youngsters along any number of dimensions, including (but not restricted to) their ability to display creative thinking processes (Wallach and Kogan, 1965), the extent to which they are motivated to achieve (McClelland, 1961), and the speed and accuracy with which they approach and solve problems (Kagan, 1965). (See the boxes on creativity, Chapter 10; achievement motivation; hyperactivity; and conceptual tempos.) While these objective differences are not always apparent at a conscious level, children are often aware of them in a peripheral way. Such differences in style clearly influence the frequency, and the degree of sophistication with which youngsters think about themselves.

Another potent factor in a child's conception of self is the objective fact of his situation. In this chapter we have been dealing primarily with children who are normal and who exhibit adequate relations with peers. Yet as Selman himself has documented, children with cognitive or emotional problems often suffer distorted self-images and have difficulties in thinking coherently about themselves. Training and therapy are often advisable in such situations (Selman, 1980; Selman and Jurkovic, 1978). Similarly, children who have been exposed to unusually stressful situations, such

Hyperactivity

Paul cannot sit still in class. He is intelligent, but he cannot concentrate or learn. His work is poor and erratic; he attacks an assignment aggressively but soon gives it up; he is loud, often disruptive and impulsive and is apt to create chaotic situations about him. At home, Paul is prone to frequent temper tantrums that last anywhere from a few minutes to several days. He tells lies. He is excitable, aggressive, exceptionally clumsy, and has trouble sleeping. In short, he is a problem for both his parents and teachers. On the surface Paul may appear to be a trouble-maker or a bad boy, but in fact, he is a troubled youngster. "He wants to be 'good' and [is] sad that he isn't. It's as if he were divided in half—one part fighting the other" (Feingold, 1975, p. 45).

Like nearly seven hundred thousand other youngsters, predominantly boys, Paul suffers from a behavior disorder known as hyperactivity, or attention deficit disorder (A.D.D.). Until recently, drug therapy was thought to be the prime, if not the only, remedy for A.D.D. Then, in 1973, Dr. Benjamin Feingold sparked both new hope and new controversy by proposing that A.D.D. could be treated by removing additives from a child's diet.

Feingold's claim stemmed from several observations. He noted a high incidence of allergy among hyperactive children compared to normal ones (70 percent to 20 percent) (Rapp, 1978), and he knew of specific cases where diet affected behavior. In addition, the sharp increase in the use of synthetic food additives since World War II coincided with an equally sharp rise in the A.D.D. rate. Feingold concluded that there must be a link between hyperactivity and food additives. Subsequently, he placed A.D.D. children on a diet free of synthetic colorings, flavors, and salicylates and reported marked improvements in 40 to 50 percent of the cases.

Parent diaries and reports document the dramatic success: after eight to nine days on Feingold's diet, the child "seems mellow"; he remains calm even in exciting situations; he is patient and content. He is sometimes irritable, cries easily, and tends to sleep more than usual, but by the fifteenth day he is "more real (no more lying, sneaking, long monologues, and he hasn't done anything outrageous . . .)" (Feingold, 1975, p. 48).

Furthermore, certain foods seem to have direct and immediate effects on behavior. Three hours after drinking punch, for instance, a previously calm child may become hyperactive, bang his head, and display a charged temper. The next day he will be fine again. Foods such as hamburger relish, chocolate, and potato chips, and even flavored medicines have caused similar reactions.

Some researchers, who have been unable to reproduce Feingold's startling results, challenge his theory, and still others adhere to more conventional treatments such as drug therapy and behavior modification. Nevertheless, though Feingold's diet may not be the only answer and it may not help all children, all indications are of a definite association between diet and hyperactivity.

as severe illness, loss of loved ones, or a physical handicap, will also spawn atypical images of self, though their degree of sophistication may sometimes actually be enhanced by these extreme situations. Studies of the sense of self in such atypical populations (Bluebond-Langner, 1978) and also in cultures radically different from our own would be extremely valuable lines of research (Geertz, 1973).

Conclusion: Social Cognition as Cognition

Throughout this chapter we have treated social cognition as if it were a realm unto itself. Yet the child's cognitive powers are growing on many fronts and it would be surprising indeed if no correlations obtained among different domains of knowledge.

According to the classic cognitive-structural position, cognition develops first in relation to physical objects, and only subsequently with reference to the knowledge of the social or the moral realm. There is some evidence to support this claim (Furth, 1978; Kuhn, 1972; Kuhn et al., 1977; Tomlinson-Keasey and Keasey, 1974). However, most of the research on which this conclusion was based did not reflect the more sophisticated views of social cognition developed during the past several years.

Recently, a more complex position has been proposed. According to this account, there is no reason why social cognition should necessarily follow the pattern of other forms of cognition. In fact, as Damon suggests, a child may have some kind of block against mathematical problems yet be a superb classifier when dealing with social objects and relations (1977, p. 322). In Damon's view, tasks in the social realm may call upon the same kinds of operations as do tasks in the physical realm and there is no a priori reason

to assume that one must precede the other. Damon does, as a matter of fact, find close correlations between physical tasks and social tasks, even as he finds considerable intercorrelations among his various social measures; in general, however, he feels that the notion of a unidirectional causality from the physical to the social is unwarranted.

It is possible to adopt an even more radical position on this issue. At times Damon suggests that social interactions with peers may be among the best promoters of intellectual advance, even with respect to purely physical concepts. William Doise, a student of Piaget's, provides particularly vivid instances of the advances in cognitive level that may ensue following discussions among peers at differing levels of sophistication (Doise, Mugny, and Perret-Clermont, 1975, 1976).

And finally, the most radical position of all: the symbolic-interactionist school (Mead, 1934; Cooley, 1902) considers the roots of all knowledge to be social. Left to our own devices, we would never amount to anything at all in the cognitive sphere. Not only are we totally dependent upon the accumulated wisdom of the societies of the past (and the present) but from the very first we rely on other individuals, "significant others," in our world to expose us to objects and events, to show us how to do things, to react to our efforts, prodding, criticizing, guiding, complimenting. Even Piaget's most objective interactions with his infants are at the same time social tutorings revealing not only correct answers (where the ball is hidden) but also modes of interactions with others (how to get attention and reward from one's own father). It is possible to exaggerate this point of view and to neglect the amount of knowledge that the child constructs in relative isolation. Still it is bracing to consider how different the science of developmental psychology would have been if Piaget had been as interested in the social world as in the realm of physical objects.

Signposts

While we tend to think of schools as locales for learning facts and making cognitive strides, they are also the scene of social development, including the child's expanding knowledge of the social world. Our opening vignette contrasted social relations among peers at the start of school with those obtaining at the time of adolescence. Drawing upon the limited experimental evidence available and upon the numerous clinical interviews carried out by investigators of social cognition, we then proceeded to consider the child's progress during middle childhood in four areas of social knowledge.

Turning first to the child's relation with close peers, we considered developmental trends in friendship. Studies by James Youniss and Robert Selman document a series of differences between the friendships of preschool children and those among individuals on the eve of adolescence: from momentary physical encounters to long-term, deeper relationships; from concern with physical possessions and exchanges to an appreciation of psychological needs; from a pursuit of one's own goals to a feeling of mutuality among those involved in a friendship bond.

Other issues also rise in children's friendships. There are considerable sex-role differences, with boys involved in rough-and-tumble play and rebellious activities, girls more interested in cooperativeness and intimate exchanges. There is a strong tendency for children to group together according to sex and to exclude those of the opposite sex. Exclusion also takes other forms: children form clubs, where they may gain positive skills, but also inflict misery on those who are rejected. And loss of friends is difficult for all concerned.

Like other interpersonal relations, friendship relations are mediated by more abstract

concerns. In the second part of this chapter, we turned our attention to certain universal rules that govern interpersonal relations, such as the principle of justice. Reviewing the work of William Damon, we noted that in arriving at a just solution to a social dilemma, children aged five or six exhibit little sense of how to evaluate various factors. In contrast, by the end of middle childhood children are able to approach an issue of justice from a variety of perspectives, to take into account a number of aspects of equity and merit, including the fact that certain individuals may be inherently at a disadvantage in any sharing of goods.

Of course, an individual may speak piously about justice and yet himself behave in an unjust manner. We found that many children were likely to be generous in an abstract situation, while relatively self-serving in a real-life situation. This difference between hypothetical and real-life courses of action proved much more pronounced in the case of justice than in the case of authority relations. Perhaps one's own self-interest is usually taken into account internally in one's judgment about leadership, whether taken hypothetically or "for real," while it is only brought to consciousness in the real-life atmosphere of a decision about justice.

Mounting evidence suggests that young children are quite sensitive to the differences between mere social conventions (such as table manners) and principles of justice. Yet there is developmental progress in the child's ability to distinguish among rules that are impossible to change (such as physical rules), rules that are relatively arbitrary (such as social conventions), and rules that ought not to be changed (such as rules of justice and respect for other persons).

In the third part of this chapter we turned our attention to children's knowledge of the behaviors and actions of other persons. Piaget's studies of how children decide on naughtiness and punishment served as our point of departure. We noted that early studies in the Piagetian tradition were marred by a failure to distinguish between intention and motivation and also by a mistaken belief that young children showed no sensitivity to the reasons for the behaviors of others. Now, in the wake of much work on social attribution, it seems evident that children have an initial sensitivity to motivation (why someone does something) in the preschool years; and that, shortly thereafter, they reveal some understanding of intention (whether the person carried out the action deliberately). However, if the results of an action are overwhelming, children's sensitivities will be masked and they will seem as if they attend only to the ultimate consequences and not to causes.

There are vast strides in the school years. Only the older child can take into account a number of motivations, focus on underlying motivations, and appreciate the particulars of a given social context. Moreover, whereas young children seem to tie behaviors inextricably to the individual who committed them, often blaming the person who happens to be a victim, the older individual is sensitive to factors in an environment that might predispose a person to behave in a prosocial or antisocial way. Finally, the older child looks for consistency in behavior across situations and tries to come up with a plausible motivation for an aberrant act; the younger child is likely to not perceive the incongruity or to invent an *ad hoc* explanation. Only in their ability to detect deception do younger children sometimes outshine their elders.

While most work has been directed to the child's understanding of individuals, Hans Furth has examined children's understanding of more complex social institutions. He finds that young children have little sense of the complexities involved in explaining aspects of the economy or the government; from children's point of view, individuals simply have the jobs they want to have and spend the money they want to spend. By adolescence, youths exhibit some awareness of the general principles that govern economics, the factors that influence choice of occupation, and the relationship between one's personal situation (for example, the amount of money at one's disposal) and the overall economy (for example, how money is secured and spent).

In the fourth and final part of this chapter we examined the individual's appreciation of himself. One intriguing line of evidence came from Carol Dweck's studies of learned helplessness. There is a group of children, more typically girls, who blame their own inadequacies when they fail (even when the fault lies elsewhere) and who are unwilling to credit themselves when they are successful. This personality type comes about, at least in part, because of the different ways in which teachers behave toward girls and boys. If teachers were to subject girls to criticism not so clearly directed at their intellectual performances and to label their successes appropriately, these youngsters might have a better opportunity to achieve mastery.

Children's understanding of mastery has been studied in other quarters as well. The nine- or ten-year-old has come to understand that not only do a person's efforts contribute to success, but his ability and sensitivity to the performances of others are also relevant factors. In judging oneself one must avoid halo effects, but also the tendency to disparage one's own performances.

A final window comes from Robert Selman's studies of the development of the concept of self. A five-stage sequence, three stages of which usually occur during middle childhood, documents progress from a time when the child has no sense of self apart from his physical body to a time when the child appreciates that part of his inner world can reflect upon, monitor, and even control his actions and his thoughts.

Only in the past decade has research on social cognition begun to accumulate, and so the relation of this realm to the other areas of cognition remains in dispute. Most scholars find at least broad relations between the development of physical cognition and that of social cognition, but there is dispute about whether one of these domains must precede or stimulate progress in the other. The most extreme views of social cognition attribute all forms of growth to social interaction and view cognition as social from its origins throughout its entire development.

With this survey of social cognition, we conclude our treatment of the events of mid-

dle childhood. A period of dramatic turbulence in the emotional realm and of equally decisive if less chaotic events in the cognitive realm characterizes adolescence in our society. In the final part of the book we will consider the universal facets of adolescence as well as some features that differ revealingly across cultures. We will revisit many of the issues that have arisen in Part IV, including the connections between knowledge of the physical domain and knowledge of the social sphere and the nature of relations among peers and elders. But before embarking on this final leg of our journey through the life cycle, we will stop to consider in an interlude the major theoretical orientations that have guided us on this journey.

Theories and Facts in Developmental Psychology

Even the most beautiful of theories is never as beautiful as truth or fact.
  —CLAUDE BERNARD

Give us theories, theories, always theories. Let every man who has a theory pronounce his theory.
  —JAMES MARK BALDWIN

Let us suppose that a team of investigators has completed an intriguing study of musical ability. The investigators asked a group of middle-class American youngsters ranging in age from five to ten to listen to two melodies and to indicate whether the two were "the same song." It turned out that five-year-old children cannot appreciate the identity of a melody sung in one key and the same melody transposed to a different key; in contrast, over 80 percent of eight-year-olds do recognize the identity of the two melodies. Moreover, most children become aware of the identity at about the age of seven.

During their studies, the investigators uncovered some additional facts. Over a fifth of the boys like to sing patriotic marches, but only 3 percent care for love songs. The ratio among girls is virtually the reverse: a quarter of the girls like love songs but only 4 percent like the marches. Only two of the youngsters, both boys, are able to arrange four short musical fragments into a melody they have previously known. Over two-thirds of the girls and over half the boys can maintain a tune after the accompaniment ceases. Finally, some youngsters are reluctant to sing any melodies that are unfamiliar or that lack lyrics.

Excited about their findings, particularly the inability of five-year-olds to "conserve melodies," the investigators present a paper at a convention of developmental psychologists. After the presentation, seven scholars representing different approaches to psychology meet informally to discuss the implications of the results. They all agree that the findings have to be considered in the context of the so-called five-to-seven shift (see Chapter 7). But they also interpret the findings in the light of their respective theoretical orientations; and each suggests research techniques that might further illuminate children's musical development. (Representatives of these principal orientations are listed in Table 1 and photographs of leading exponents appear alongside the presentation of their positions.)

In fact, this meeting is fictitious. So are the investigators and their findings. But such an invented occasion allows us to examine how psychologists make sense of what they observe or, to put it more elegantly, how they construct a body of scientific knowledge out of facts they have uncovered and theoretical orientations they have evolved. Accordingly, as we eavesdrop on the participants, we can gain some perspective on the developmental psychologist's daily activity.

Jean Piaget.

A Dialogue Among Seven Developmental Psychologists

A COGNITIVE-STRUCTURALIST INFLUENCED BY PIAGET

I see the changes between the ages of five and seven as reflecting children's ability to perform certain mental actions or operations. Children aged seven or eight can conserve number; they appreciate that nine objects are equivalent to any other nine objects. Now we have secured evidence of their ability to conserve a melody, to appreciate its essential and unchanging properties, even when the key in which it was originally presented has been altered. It makes sense to infer the emergence of an underlying structure, one based on the capacity to recognize identities across two seemingly different patterns.

When we search further, we will probably find that musical ability, like all cognitive realms, develops in a set sequence of stages. The sensorimotor infant who can simply emit and react to sounds slowly matures to become a formal operator who can analyze compositions and freely invent new musical patterns.

I think the researchers have approached this problem well by defining an important end-state—the ability to appreciate musical conservation or constancy—and by posing the same task to subjects of different ages. However, they could have

Table 1. SEVEN ORIENTATIONS TO DEVELOPMENTAL PSYCHOLOGY

Theoretical orientation	Representative	Examples of application
Cognitive-structural	Jean Piaget	Chapter 2 (sensorimotor intellect)
		Chapter 10 (concrete operations)
		Chapter 13 (formal operations)
	Lawrence Kohlberg	Chapter 13 (moral development)
	Deanna Kuhn	Chapter 5 (imitation)
Personality (or dynamic) psychology	Sigmund Freud	Chapter 5 (identification)
	Erik Erikson	Chapter 2 (basic trust)
		Chapter 14 (crisis of identity)
	Bruno Bettelheim	Interlude: Another Perspective on Human Development (autism)
Behaviorist-modeling	B. F. Skinner (operant)	Chapter 2 (operant conditioning)
	Albert Bandura (social learning)	Chapter 5 (imitation)
Environmental-learning; mediationist	Tracy Kendler	Chapter 7 (reversal shifts)
	Alexander Luria	Chapter 7 (language controlling behavior)
Organismic-developmental	Heinz Werner	Interlude: The Model of Development in Psychology (orthogenetic principle)
	Douglass Carmichael	Chapter 13 (irony)
Nativist	Noam Chomsky	Chapter 4 (language development)
	Jerry Fodor	
	Jacques Mehler	Interlude: The Model of Development in Psychology (U-shaped behavior)
	Thomas Bever	
Anthropological	Michael Cole	Chapter 11 (effects of schooling)
	Margaret Mead	Chapter 14 (adolescence in Samoa)
	John Whiting	Chapter 14 (initiation rites)

enriched their data by making greater use of the clinical method. One must pose open-ended questions, observe the child's reaction, probe further when necessary, and offer challenges and counterchallenges. For instance, the investigators should have asked the five-year-olds to name the tunes and challenged them to indicate how two tunes with the same name could still be different.

Children probably acquire musical conservation at about age seven because of an interaction between their developing neuroanatomical structures and the knowledge attained from various musical activities in which they have been participating. But the age and stability of conservation will vary with the nature of such experience; for instance, youngsters will appreciate the identities among familiar patterns earlier than those among less familiar patterns. There may also be a transitional stage when varying the test situation could push children into conserving or not conserving. But establishing these finer points requires careful use of a clinical interview.

A PERSONALITY PSYCHOLOGIST INFLUENCED BY FREUD AND ERIKSON

Although useful, the cognitive developmental view of mental growth neglects children's emotional life as well as pivotal individual differences among youngsters. Between five and seven, children are resolving Oedipal conflicts, forging altered relationships with their parents, and initiating new patterns of interaction with peers. As the latency period begins at about the age of six or seven, children's sexual and aggressive tendencies will become less important and they will turn considerable energies to developing competences. Children's heightened appreciation of music certainly reflects this shift to scholastic and extracurricular activities. At the same time, it reminds us of the importance of art in children's affective life and, possibly, in their unconscious.

A person-centered approach can illuminate some of the individual differences turned up in this study. Children will generally prefer the kind of music favored by others of their sex, particularly parents and other authority figures; thus, boys and girls will naturally exhibit different preferences. Further, the two boys who were able to assemble musical fragments are probably sublimating their libidinal energies through the development of a special skill.

I am fascinated by the few children who would not become involved with unfamiliar works. Perhaps because they feel insecure, these children are afraid to venture into a world that

Sigmund Freud.

honors competence and disparages failure. We would have to undertake intensive case studies of individual children, interviewing them and their parents, observing their play, listening to their stories, monitoring their free associations. The last three techniques are particularly important. Going beyond the clinical questioning of the cognitive-structuralists, such projective measures allow us to probe beneath the surface and examine unconscious motivation and understanding.

A BEHAVIORIST IN THE OPERANT AND SOCIAL-LEARNING TRADITIONS

Talk of cognitive structures, stages, and unconscious motivation is all well and good, but these constructs are so broad, so difficult to operationalize in the laboratory, so elusive to gain evidence *against,* that I sometimes think they basically impede research. We are interested in the major goal of psychology: understanding and predicting behavior. To achieve this, we need to know all the relevant variables and to understand how behaviors are reinforced. We don't need overly broad theories. Different musical preferences are a direct consequence of differences in reinforcement patterns. Girls receive rewards when they behave as girls are expected to behave in our society, that is, when they like romantic music. While girls observe romantic heroines serenaded by romantic ballads, boys see heroes who strut in time to patriotic or martial music. These boys are rewarded when they behave like adult males, including listening to and appreciating exuberant marches. The boy who liked love songs probably experienced unusual or atypical patterns of reinforcement; perhaps he was raised by a single mother, or by parents who wanted a girl.

I am suspicious of the so-called five-to-seven shift. There's nothing special about any particular three-year period—all periods are important. To my mind, the apparent inability of the youngest children to recognize identity from one key to the next only reflects the fact that no one has bothered to teach them that differences in key do not materially alter a piece of music. Before endorsing the five-to-seven shift, I would try to produce the opposite change. What if children were rewarded only when they recognized differences in the keys of two otherwise identical melodies? I'm sure that seven-year-olds would then respond the way five-year-olds do now. And if three- and four-year-olds were rewarded for recognizing the identity among melodies in a different key, I'm equally confident they could master this discrimination. Only by conducting appropriate experiments in modeling and only by carefully vary-

B. F. Skinner.

ing reinforcement contingencies will we be able to determine precisely how these patterns of musical behavior have come about and whether they can be changed or even reversed.

AN ENVIRONMENTAL-LEARNING THEORIST IN THE MEDIATION AND RUSSIAN SCHOOLS

A. R. Luria.

I sympathize with the behaviorist's remarks; yes, global theories tend to interfere with devising careful experiments that incorporate the proper sampling procedures and control groups. But the behaviorist view ignores many changes (including brain reorganization) that occur between the ages of five and seven or eight. Neither schooling nor modeling, nor different reinforcement patterns, can explain them all.

In my view, it is during this time that children cease responding directly to physical stimuli and proceed regularly to mediate their responses, usually through linguistic symbols. Children have apparently learned to describe the properties of musical patterns to themselves in some way. If the descriptions of two melodies happen to coincide, then they will call them "the same." If the mediating labels differ, then the children will declare the melodies "different." At this time, in school, children may learn to attend to new, previously undetected properties of a stimulus—for instance, the relations (or intervals) among the pitches. But it's not clear whether the new discriminations alter their labels or simply exploit the labels they have already evolved on their own.

The earlier speakers neglected the fact that the child is mastering a new medium—music—which is a whole separate symbol system with its own characteristics. It is too simple to say that children transport operations learned in their general activity to the realm of music. They must come to know the unique facets of music—pitches, keys, harmonies, scales—before they can handle musical patterns with some skill. The individual differences uncovered so far reflect not only native endowment in the nervous system, but also, and perhaps principally, the child's prior experience with the medium.

What we really need are some well-designed experiments that probe musical understanding at several ages and with several sets of materials. Especially important is the ability to appreciate relations among pieces of differing familiarity, written in different scales, and using different instruments and lyrics. Because the phrase "the same" is tricky for children, they should simply be trained to pull a lever whenever they think two stimuli are identical and then be reinforced only when they recognize the melody in two different keys.

Once the bases of musical understanding were established by a strict experimental method, I would begin to look for factors, such as modeling or teaching techniques, that enhance or retard attainment of this understanding. I suspect children would progress when their attention was directed to specific properties of music; supplying appropriate labels and pointing out examples of application would probably aid them further.

AN ORGANISMIC-DEVELOPMENTALIST INFLUENCED BY HEINZ WERNER

Although I am in general sympathy with the comments of the Piagetian and the mediationist, I find their explanations inadequate. In my view we are witnessing a fundamental shift in the child's whole relation to the realm of music. Five-year-olds respond to each musical piece as a separate entity; they note only discrete pitches and ignore relations among these tones. In contrast, eight-year-olds attend to the overall musical pattern and appreciate that melodies featuring the same relations among tones share something important. Further—and here I part company with the mediationist—I suspect that this new developmental level could be discerned in every medium dealt with by the child. Once one can focus on relations rather than absolute values, one should be able to do so irrespective of the symbol system involved.

This represents a higher level of psychological maturation, one that depends on neurological as well as environmental factors and allows the achievement of this milestone. The five-to-seven shift can occur because the older child views the whole world in both a more differentiated and a more integrated way. After interacting with the environment for six years, the entire organism is primed for this cognitive advance. Thus, schooling is better viewed as a result, rather than a cause, of the shift.

To establish that these findings represent a genuine developmental step, the test of musical conservation must be administered under diverse conditions and to various populations— including normal adults and individuals who are brain-damaged, retarded, drugged, or traumatized. I think the same developmental stages—one more integrated, the other more primitive—would be found in all these populations.

Heinz Werner.

A NATIVIST IN THE CHOMSKY TRADITION

While I agree with some of the incidental remarks made by the previous speakers, I feel that you all are offering unnecessarily complicated explanations. I prefer to begin with the sim-

Noam Chomsky.

ple observation that all of your subjects are human beings, and that they are programmed by their genetic endowment to develop along certain given lines. It may be part of the plan for early development that a younger child regard notes played in one key as different from those played in another key, but I do not believe that this reflects a fundamentally different attitude toward the music. Rather, at a certain point in development, youngsters are highly attuned to listen for differences and to stress those differences when asked to do so. I am quite certain that if you trained an infant to respond to the melody in one key, you would find that he would respond equivalently to the same melody in another key. The apparent difference in the subject's *competence* is really only a difference in *performance:* as in the case of language or vision, the underlying competence is present at birth and can be demonstrated under the appropriate circumstances.

Why treat the brain differently from other human organs? Why invoke special terminology like "learning" or "interaction" to account for the unfolding of the brain? All of you recognize that the eye is different from the heart and that each evolves according to patterns written down in the genetic code. You would never say that the heart "learns" to beat slower later in life, or that the eyes "learn" to move together as you survey the world. They are just programmed to mature in this way. By the same token, we should think of the brain—and the mind—as programmed to mature in a certain way. In the case of musical perception, this just happens to include a brief period when the differences between two keys are noticed and remarked upon.

The fact that it takes several years until the child answers this question correctly is not evidence of learning or even interaction. After all, the organism does not pass through puberty until the age of twelve or so, but we would never say that the child "learns" to be pubescent. The nervous system is following its own timetable and for many processes (such as senescence) it takes decades for a particular point in the program to be reached.

I do not deny the existence of various individual differences or their possible clinical interest. But from the point of view of a scientific psychology individual differences are really of only marginal importance. If I simply ask the little girls to answer in a different way, and make the reward attractive enough, they will heed my bidding; but that does not reflect anything deep. In every area of cognition, be it language or social understanding, we developmental scientists should direct our attention to the discovery of the programmed sequence of steps from the mental state at birth to the mental state at maturity. We should not be derailed trying to explain idiosyncratic differences that have scant scientific substance.

AN ANTHROPOLOGIST WITH PSYCHOLOGICAL TRAINING

What you all say is interesting, but some remarks, particularly those of the last two speakers, are too narrow. The fact that a certain trend occurs among some middle-class American children hardly indicates that the trend is universal. There are thousands of cultures in the world today, each featuring its own social organization, daily customs, rules of behavior, and set of values. If an individual from another society were to propose a theory that applied to our culture, without actually studying our practices, we would be justifiably suspicious. And so we must be wary of extending any finding beyond the population on which it has been established.

To determine whether this form of musical composition is universal, it is essential to conduct an open-minded investigation using different populations throughout the world. The assertion that everyone develops in the same way because of the genetic code must be examined under the harsh light of cross-cultural evidence. Note, further, that it is completely unjustified to label one answer correct or "more developed" than another. The music of many other cultures is quite different from our own and individuals may relate to music in ways totally unfamiliar to us. They may use different terminology and emphasize other aspects of a composition. All this will dramatically influence anyone's performance on a test, and particularly a test designed by Western psychologists using Western music.

In studying musical understanding in another culture, I would work closely with a member of that culture, who can provide invaluable insights concerning the significance of events and behaviors and can help in translating unfamiliar expressions and rites. I would observe carefully and take notes on how music occurs in natural settings. Then, using that knowledge, I would try to adjust the experimental procedure until it meshed with the practices and expressions of the culture in which I was a guest.

After many such studies in many cultures, some universals of musical conceptions and understanding may emerge, but I doubt it. There may even be evidence in other cultures for the five-to-seven shift, but I doubt that, too. It seems likely that social and cultural variables will account for most of the observed differences among individuals, groups, or sexes.

Margaret Mead.

AFTERTHOUGHTS

Our eavesdropping at this meeting has allowed us to consider how seven psychologists, representing seven different theoretical and investigative traditions, conceptualize a novel set of data. For clarity, we have had them speak as directly as possible, even at the cost of exaggerating features of their own position. Thus it is important to bear a few additional factors in mind.

First, the participants represent only a sample of the theoretical views in child psychology. At least a dozen other perspectives (ranging from ethological psychology to ecological psychology) could have been represented at the meeting. Second, even within each of these schools, many nuances of opinion can be found, and even proponents of the same tradition will often disagree with one another. Third, and perhaps most important, complex parallels and divergencies exist among these schools. For instance, both cognitive-structuralists and personality psychologists favor case studies, though they differ on how these should be pursued and interpreted. Anthropologists and behaviorists both highlight environmental factors, but for entirely different theoretical reasons. Mediationists, cognitive-structuralists, and nativists all focus on cognitive development but tend to interpret phenomena differently. Organismic-developmentalists and personality psychologists embrace elaborate terminologies but often disagree about which phenomena are worth investigating. And so on. Any exhaustive examination of developmental theories would have to examine each theory (as well as the others omitted) on such dimensions.

Joachim Wohlwill's Program for Integrated Research

In contrast to the marked tensions of years past, developmental psychologists of different theoretical orientations have recently been making contact with each other. Perhaps the best evidence of this improved communication is that many younger developmental psychologists, rather than identifying with a single school, have become **eclectic:** they select from diverse schools the assumptions, methods, and concepts that are most appropriate for a particular question.

Although this eclecticism is overall a positive sign, there is a danger. When every psychologist effects his own synthesis, findings may well prove difficult to integrate. In the hope of preventing such chaos, Joachim Wohlwill (1973), an expert in methods of study, has outlined a program of research that can be pursued in diverse areas of psychology, from moral development to understanding music. He describes a sequence of steps that uses five methods of study, each of which should be drawn on at the point when it will prove most useful.

The first step is to define a set of scales or dimensions along which consistent age changes may be observed and mapped. This is the kind of analysis of an end-state at which organismic-developmental researchers and nativists excel. It is necessary to specify both the features that change with age and those that may remain unchanged. In our music experiment, for instance, one might devise measures and tests of specifically musical skills like rhythm perception and melody discrimination. These tests could then be administered to individuals of varying ages and backgrounds in an initial effort to discover the full range of competence in the domain of music.

The second step of this research program entails the descriptive study of age changes, the simple collection of facts. Wohlwill argues that this descriptive phase—at which anthropologists are particularly gifted—is one of the most crucial. Study of both quantitative and qualitative changes, and particularly those along the developmental dimensions established in the first step should form the central task for this phase of research. Our musical researchers seem to have done well in gathering just this sort of indispensable descriptive information.

The third step is the correlational study of age changes, which examines the relations between a given behavior pattern and other simultaneously developing behaviors. Here the question of organized developmental stages arises: do some underlying structures confer coherence on behavior at a given time? Does the child's musical conservation emerge at the same time as other forms of physical and social conservation? Or is musical conservation more integrally related to artistic sensitivity? Answering such questions requires a fine-grained analysis of the interconnections (and distinctions) among a group of responses. Yet focusing on relations among changes should lead one toward identifying structures that may underlie disparate facts; and thus one advances toward an understanding of what factors lead to observed behavioral patterns and correlations. This is an enterprise in which cognitive-structuralists, organismic-developmentalists, and personality psychologists have often made significant strides.

Wohlwill's fourth step is the study of the variables that affect or determine developmental change. This phase would seem to call for the standard experimental approach favored by environmental-learning theorists, in which one chooses a behavior of interest, manipulates variables one at a time, and observes alterations in responses at different age levels. Yet Wohlwill finds this approach limited in usefulness because it is suitable only for studying behaviors that unfold over brief intervals. In Wohlwill's view, it is not possible to manipulate the variables that bring about behaviors as complex as musical conservation. Only with animals can previous experience be totally controlled: only such massive manipulations permit the researcher to uncover the factors governing the emergence (or nonemergence) of such intricate capacities.

Still, it is feasible to secure information on the factors contributing to genuine developmental patterns. One can isolate and study naturally occurring differences in early childhood experience, for example, across social classes, styles of parenting, or different cultural heritages. In the present case, through observing the correlation between type of previous experience and the emergence (or nonemergence) of conservation, one can gain at least some insight about which variables induce developmental changes. And using cross-cultural methods, one can compare groups in which musical conservation emerges at different ages (or in different forms) and at least provisionally identify variables that lead to various patterns. This sort of approach has been used to good advantage by anthropologists.

The fifth and final step in Wohlwill's program is to study individual differences. Individuals may vary markedly on particular developmental measures, as when one child gains conservation ability early and another never does acquire it. Or they may differ on other dimensions, such as how (and how well) they remember melodic fragments. Application of this step would entail inquiry into the contrasting musical performances of girls and boys or studies of the two boys who performed especially well in assembling a tune. Clinicians, anthropologists, and, to some extent, behaviorists all exhibit a special interest in individual differences.

Wohlwill's program is ambitious for two reasons. First, it calls for certain research approaches not presently in favor—for instance, detailed descriptions offered without open allegiance to a single theoretical perspective and qualitative comparisons of subjects from different backgrounds. Second, and more crucial, Wohlwill's program entails a prescribed sequence through the five steps. Only if this sequenced program is followed can maximum advantage be taken of each form of data.

Whether Wohlwill's plan will be adopted throughout developmental psychology as a master plan for future research is difficult to predict. Most researchers are committed to the standard cross-sectional experimental method and might incur difficulty in abandoning it. Moreover, Wohlwill's approach proves time-consuming, costly, and more resistant to analysis than a well-controlled experiment. Yet the need for approaches that orchestrate and integrate diverse forms of data is clear. Therefore, even if researchers do not themselves alter their research style, they may attempt to integrate past findings in the light of the program Wohlwill has recommended.

Facts, Methods, and Theories

In contrasting theories and methods, we have sought to convey how a science of developmental psychology might work. Our discussion has raised severe questions about any naive notion of this process: it is far too simple to maintain that, once accumulated, the facts will speak for themselves. Rather, as we have seen in the example of musical conservation, there are nearly as many interpretations and explanations as there are theorists of development.

A more sophisticated view of the scientific enterprise would hold that facts are what they are, but that the sense one makes of them depends on one's theoretical orientation. But even this view is too simple, for it assumes that all theorists would agree on the facts. Actually the whole notion of fact, let alone a *simple* fact, represents a vexing problem in the philosophy of science.

ARE FACTS AND METHODS NEUTRAL?

The scientist who claims to be simply listing facts is being either naive or deceptive. In truth, he has already made deliberate decisions about what realm to study, what problem to focus on, what measures to use, what data to collect, what scoring method to employ, and what words to use in filing his report. Not that our musical researchers were being dishonest in saying they had gleaned new facts—indeed they had. But different investigators, armed with different problems or theoretical preconceptions, might well report different facts after viewing the same phenomena. Thus a personality psychologist, administering the same tests, might have focused on the kinds of songs children like and completely ignored issues of conservation.

It may even be misleading to say that two sets of investigators would observe the same phenomena. Facts are not given or indisputable. As amply demonstrated in many experiments (and in many family discussions!) two individuals will perceive and interpret the same situation differently and will reap different information from it.

With some training, and with some awareness of one's own biases, it is usually possible to bring about significant agreement in two descriptions of the same display. But experts (and nonexperts) probably will often disagree about which facts are important and which merit separate investigation. And it is just such selection that proves most important in research. The emergence of musical conservation at age seven is a bit of information selected from thousands of other potential candidates. The very item that intrigued the cognitive-structuralist would not have been so striking to someone probing sex differences, emotional disturbances, or cross-cultural values.

In fact, in selecting a method with which to approach a phenomenon, the scientist limits which aspects of the situation he will perceive. For instance, standardized tests will not reveal individual differences in the manner in which a test problem is approached. If everyone receives the same multiple-choice paper-and-pencil test, individuals can be ranked only on how well they did, not on the strategies of reasoning they employed. In contrast, a clinical interview, suited to bring out such differences, proves difficult to use in a standardized way; as a result norms obtained through such an individually tailored method are rightly suspect. Somewhat like strong social or political views, methods are tinted glasses that color one's world. Committed experimentalists are unlikely to ask subjects to write a story about an ambiguous picture, because they would regard such an instrument as subjective and difficult to interpret. Psychoanalysts are unlikely to test memory for nonsense syllables, because they would find this an arbitrary task unrelated to an individual's personality.

DOES PSYCHOLOGY HAVE LEGITIMATE THEORIES?

Even assuming that the facts have been agreed upon and the methods are not at issue, how does one make sense of what has been found? We have already seen that numerous interpretations, each flowing from a separate theory, can be applied to the same facts. Apparently, as our fictitious discussion illustrates, one can assemble an impressive array of facts and still remain at a scientific impasse.

Most (though not all) psychologists feel that theories are good things: a well-worked theory signals a science's sophistication. Moreover, almost everyone agrees that developmental psychology is overrun by facts. What we need are ways of relating these facts, deciding which are worth attending to, organizing them into an explanatory framework, and then devising future research that will resolve remaining gaps. And it is just this guidance that one expects of a coherent scientific theory.

Earlier in this century, psychologists generally assumed that the theoretical orientations developed in the "hard" sciences (physics, chemistry, and the like) represented an appropriate model for a good psychological theory. That meant starting with a few basic elements, stating a series of basic laws, and formulating specific hypotheses that test the validity and relationship of these laws—all of which would culminate in a theory that could predict the specific details of human behavior. (This briefly sketched program was actually undertaken in the 1930s and 1940s by the learning theorist Clark Hull [1943] and his students.)

Although most psychologists once wished such a program well, nearly all now agree that it did not work. Few psychologists would now undertake such an agenda, as they have become suspicious of grand theories.

Given this distaste for overarching theories, one may ask why Piaget and Freud, usually considered theorists, have remained so influential within developmental psychology. But on closer analysis, it becomes apparent that they are not theorists in the strictly scientific sense: they have not stated universal laws, made deductions from them, or made testable predictions. Rather, they have proposed certain abstract principles, a manner of relating these principles to some striking empirical phenomena, a series of related concepts, and a way of anticipating what is likely to happen under different circumstances. Such integrative efforts *are* valued by developmental psychologists, but they are better thought of as "orientations" or "approaches" than as theories. Indeed, all the thinkers (and viewpoints) summarized in this chapter may best be thought of this way.

What is notable is that a host of nontheoretical approaches are currently valued by developmental psychologists. And the features of Piaget's and Freud's work that command the most interest are not the pretensions to an overall grand system but the isolated concepts (like operations or the unconscious) and the compelling phenomena (like conservation or identification). Perhaps the appeal of a theoretical system has simply ceased to be overwhelmingly important to many psychologists. Instead, three fundamental items seem to be at a premium:

1. A series of facts or findings that are provocative and that lead to interesting questions and arguments. Much of the interest in Piaget seems to center in his discoveries of object permanence, egocentrism, and other intriguing phenomena.
2. Some new techniques or methods that allow examination of previously inaccessible phenomena. The appeal of Skinner's methods of shaping behavior through reinforcement seems to lie in the discovery of regularities in behavior and, perhaps even more important, in the potential for eliciting desired behavior changes in retarded or emotionally disturbed children.
3. Some abstract concepts that, although not acounting for all findings, do tie together a group of facts whose interrelations had not been appreciated before. Here we might include the notion of a critical period during infancy when the child's bond to the mother should be formed; or the hypothesized mediating responses that enable a child to categorize stimulus information while on the way to a final response. Many, though probably not most, contemporary development psychologists would cite Piaget as the thinker whose efforts contributed most to this organizational enterprise. Yet, as we have noted in earlier chapters and will see again in Chapter 13, enough difficulties surround Piaget's system to prevent it from taking over the field.

CLOSING THOUGHTS ON POSSIBLE MODELS

At least two possible outcomes may stem from the present state of developmental psychology. Researchers may remain satisfied with an eclectic set of models drawn from different traditions and diverse problems. As these are gradually sorted out, psychologists will come to agree when each is relevant and most appropriate. For instance, a consensus may emerge that Erikson's model is most suited for personality development, Piaget's for cognitive development, learning theory's for the explication of short-term behavior changes, Werner's for describing long-term evolution.

The alternative outcome is that one thinker, or a small group of thinkers, will digest all the empirical research, review all methodological and theoretical approaches, and devise a new theoretical model that satisfactorily integrates the various branches of developmental psychology. It is a subject for speculation whether the new model will arise full-grown or evolve over many years and whether it will resemble a current model (say, Piaget's or Chomsky's) or a current program (say, Wohlwill's).

The historian of science Thomas Kuhn (1962) has studied various sciences and concluded that they typically undergo fundamental changes at certain points in their history. Such a shift occurred in biology with Darwin and in physics with Newton and, later, with Einstein. In each case, inconsistencies and contradictions accumulated steadily until the old theory was clearly inadequate. In its place was constructed a new set of principles and predictions that more adequately took into account the range of data considered relevant by the discipline. In such cases, it is not just that views were refined, or that a single view suddenly received more attention. Rather, the questions asked, the methods employed, and, above all, the whole way of talking about the field changed fundamentally and irrevocably. Such a shift revolutionizes the field, until eventually a new synthesis emerges—one that rewrites the history of the field and renders all previous summaries and textbooks useless.

No such shift has yet occurred in developmental psychology, much less in psychology as a whole. The discipline is young, still amassing facts and concepts. While waiting for a new synthesizing model to emerge, we may be consoled by the following line of thought.

In a way, the whole discipline of developmental psychology consists of an investigation of shifts in explanatory models—namely those accepted by children. Moreover, in more than a superficial way, the evolving mind of the child is reminiscent of model shifts in science. After all, children undergo several fundamental shifts in the way they think about the world. At first, they experience the world completely on the sensorimotor level. Then they encounter it at a symbolic level. And eventually most of them become able to operate and reflect on the symbols themselves. With each change, children see more and know more facts; but they also seem to make sense of the world in a qualitatively different way. What they understood before becomes reformulated and many new insights emerge. And, as in the case of model shifts in the sciences, children at a new level of thought can scarcely reconstruct the ways in which they formerly thought about things. How satisfying it would be if increased understanding of the child's own changing models were to culminate in a convincing model that could reconcile the competing theoretical strands in contemporary developmental psychology.

Adolescence

Adolescence is a time of profound change. Thinking becomes more sophisticated, as young people prove able to reflect on their thought processes, to reason logically, and to deal with abstractions. These qualitative changes characterize the ways adolescents solve scientific problems, reason about moral dilemmas, and even respond to instances of humor. The skill builder, now able to envision the hypothetical, has become a budding scientist and philosopher.

Within our society, adolescence has traditionally been viewed as a period of emotional upheaval that has distinct consequences for work, values, sexuality, and the individual's self-image. Although research has shown that the experiences of adolescents are varied, most adolescents within our culture are confronted with crucial decisions about values, behavior, and relations to others. These concerns cluster about the development of a sense of identity—the feeling that one has made life decisions that are both sensible to oneself and consistent with the values and expectations of the surrounding community. This sense of self will help the individual navigate her way during the adult years.

CHAPTER THIRTEEN

Thought During Adolescence

The thoughts of youth are long long thoughts.
    —HENRY WADSWORTH LONGFELLOW

Adolescence—the period of transition between childhood and adulthood—is marked by several central changes. Most apparent are the physical changes; these, especially when considered with corresponding emotional changes, have suggested that adolescence is a period fraught with turmoil. But there are equally significant alterations in cognition. In this chapter we shall consider the cognitive changes of adolescence. Then, in the next chapter, we shall turn to the broader (and more familiar) picture of the teenager: the rapidly growing, emotionally turbulent seeker of identity.

As we saw in our study of middle childhood, children aged eight through eleven have acquired impressive practical knowledge of the world: they can solve conservation problems; they can master games, crafts, and sports; they exhibit great curiosity about the world. But in the years following middle childhood, youths ordinarily acquire mental powers of a qualitatively different kind.

Let us consider what competent adolescents in our society should be able to accomplish. Adolescents become able to reason not only about elements present to sight or to touch but also about words, groups of words, mathematical equations, and other symbols they cannot physically explore. They can combine and recombine sets of symbols, draw logical inferences from them, go on to construct entire systems of belief in the sciences, in religion, in politics, in the arts. They become actively engaged in the world of ideas rather than just in the world of objects; and they explore this domain as eagerly as they once explored rattles, toys, or seashells. They are performing operations—making, perceiving, and feeling—on strings of symbols (like sentences); they have achieved a perspective on entire symbol systems (like language) that enable them to think about the domain (in the manner of a linguist).

This new level of reasoning is far more complex than the two-year-old's ability to deal directly with objects, the five-year-old's ability to deal directly with symbols—to name the ball, to draw a picture of it—or even the nine-year-old's capacity to unroll a ball of clay in her mind and answer questions about physical conservation of matter. The adolescent can do all these *and* understand the physical laws that govern the behavior of the ball when it has been bounced against the ground or dropped from a high spot. Furthermore, the adolescent can state a group of principles about any set of objects (what forces act on them, how the behavior of such objects is altered by these factors) and explore the relationships among these principles.

The adolescent is a competent experimenter and theoretician. She is a scientist who can reason exclusively in propositions: If "All gases expand when heated" and "Nitrogen is a gas," then "Nitrogen must expand when heated." However, adolescents' mental tools prove serviceable not just in science but in every area of thought that engages their minds. Their span of thought ranges from issues of great seriousness and moment—the themes of philosophy, politics, and religion—to issues of pleasure and entertainment—jokes, anecdotes, lighthearted banter, and wit. Whether dealing with themes that are momentous or only momentary, the adolescent's thought displays a new power and form. To be sure, this sketch of the adolescent is somewhat overdrawn. As we shall see, not every adolescent can carry out all of these functions, and many adolescents only resemble the portrait in an approximate way. Nonetheless, the kinds of capacities listed are the sorts of things adolescents strive to attain and often succeed in attaining.

Figure 13.1. With her serious look and her test tubes and pencil in hand, this adolescent epitomizes the scientific capacities that flower during this stage of life.

You can gain an initial impression of the type of thought characteristic of adolescence by trying to solve three problems, each of which has been posed to adolescents in the course of a psychological experiment. The first problem might be encountered in a science class; the second represents moral or ethical dilemmas about which individuals may have legitimate differences of opinion; the third is a literary passage that has several layers of meanings. While solving these three problems, you can also go beyond the role of subject: you can try out the role of developmental theorist by comparing the abilities needed to solve the problems with those we encountered in our examination of middle childhood.

1. An experimenter presents you with a lever or balance scale, consisting of a fulcrum

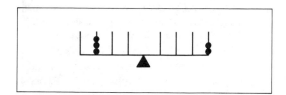

Figure 13.2. A sample balance scale.

and a beam. On the beam are arrayed eight pegs spaced equally apart, four on each side of the fulcrum (see Figure 13.2). Five equal weights are on the balance; three are on the left side of the lever, all on the third peg away from the fulcrum and two are on the right side of the fulcrum, both on the fourth peg from the fulcrum. The question: Which way will the scale tilt?

2. In 1973 it was discovered that Richard Nixon, then president of the United States, had been secretly tape-recording all his meetings in the White House. Investigators thought that these tapes might contain invaluable evidence about whether Nixon had been involved in impeachable crimes. Controversy arose on several issues, but surely one of the most crucial was whether Nixon should destroy the tapes.

   Following are pro and con arguments reflecting three developmental levels of analysis (not necessarily in ascending or descending order). One pair typifies children in middle childhood; a second pair might be voiced by early adolescents (aged twelve to fourteen); a third pair reflects a mature level of thinking found most frequently in late adolescence or early adulthood. Putting aside for the moment your knowledge of events since 1973, and your personal political views, which set of arguments seems most sophisticated and—more important—why?

LEVEL X

Pro: The tapes might contain information that would disrupt the whole society. It's important to keep things going smoothly in our society and not to rock the boat. Therefore, Nixon should destroy the tapes.

Con: It's against the law to destroy government property. Nixon cannot disobey the law—he's a citizen like everyone else and therefore he mustn't destroy the tapes.

LEVEL Y

Pro: Making the tapes public is an empty act. It would undermine the special powers of the president as well as embarrass individuals who thought they were speaking privately. These values are more important than any possible wrongdoing.

Con: Any person can make a mistake, but no person has the right to cover it up. If Nixon has committed impeachable offenses, he should declare his involvement, play the tapes publicly, and offer to resign.

LEVEL Z

Pro: The tapes belong to Nixon, and because they belong to him he has the right to use them in any way he chooses. If he wants to erase them, he should simply do so.

Con: The tapes are very valuable. They cost money to make and they will be worth even more money in the future. To destroy the tapes would be like tearing up money, and Nixon shouldn't be allowed to do that.

3. Read the following passage attributed to the Danish physicist Niels Bohr and explain what it might mean:

   There are two kinds of truth,
   Deep truth and shallow truth
   And the function of Science
   Is to eliminate the deep truth.

   It will be our mission in this chapter to return to each of these problems, to review the ways it is generally approached by adolescents, and, in the process, to arrive at a fuller picture of the thinking adolescent.

Reasoning Like a Scientist

As you may have guessed, the problem of the balance beam is one devised by Jean Piaget and his longtime collaborator Bärbel Inhelder (Inhelder and Piaget, 1958) in an effort to trace the development of scientific thinking in schoolchildren and adolescents. In Piaget's view, the way that adolescents solved this problem, and others also drawn from the world of scientific practice, was different from the way in which younger children approached it. He described this reasoning as formal operations and considered it to be a new stage in the development of cognition.

The general picture of adolescent thought put forth by Inhelder and Piaget is a persuasive one, which we have just sketched and to which we will return. However, the particular portrait of formal operations presented by Piaget has been widely criticized and it would only confuse matters to present it here in detail. Instead, I will describe an approach to such problems that has been taken by the psychologist Robert Siegler (in press, *a*)—an approach that, in my view, preserves much that is worthwhile in Piaget's account of adolescent thought while avoiding some of its weaknesses.

Siegler begins by reminding us that in any problem using a balance beam there are two important perceptual dimensions: the amount of weight on each side of the fulcrum (called the dominant dimension); and the distance of the weights from the fulcrum (called the subordinate dimension). Thus in the problem introduced above, there is more weight on the left side of the scale (three weights versus two), but the weights on the right side of the scale are farther from the fulcrum (four steps versus three). Clearly any individual who

wishes to solve the problem must know how much to attend to the sheer poundage on each side, as compared to the distance of the weights from the fulcrum. And those of us who remember our school science courses or have lots of experience playing with seesaws or levers will know that both dimensions must be taken into account: there is a force of 3 (weights) $\times$ 3 (steps) on the left against 2 (weights) $\times$ 4 (steps) on the right, so the balance beam will tip over on the left.

As young subjects have no way of knowing this, let us trace their route toward this understanding. Siegler has described four rules that children might follow (See Figure 13.3). In invoking the simplest rule, Rule 1, the child bases judgments on a single dominant dimension. If the child simply focuses on the number of weights, she will point to the left side of the balance beam and, in this case, answer correctly. If there is an equal number of weights on both sides of the scale, the child will assert that the beam balances, irrespective of the distances of the respective weights from the fulcrum. In this latter case, of course, the child may or may not answer wrongly.

Rule 2 states that one attends to the values on the dominant dimension when those values are unequal, but that when the values are equal one also considers the subordinate dimension. Thus, so long as there are more weights on one side than on the other, the child will select the side with more weights, irrespective of their distances from the fulcrum. However, if the clue of weight provides no help, the child will, for the first time, attend to distance.

Rule 3 entails a simultaneous consideration of both the dominant and the subordinate dimensions. So long as both dimensions point in one direction, the child readily answers correctly. But when there is a greater value on the dominant dimension on one side (say, more weights on the left) and a greater value

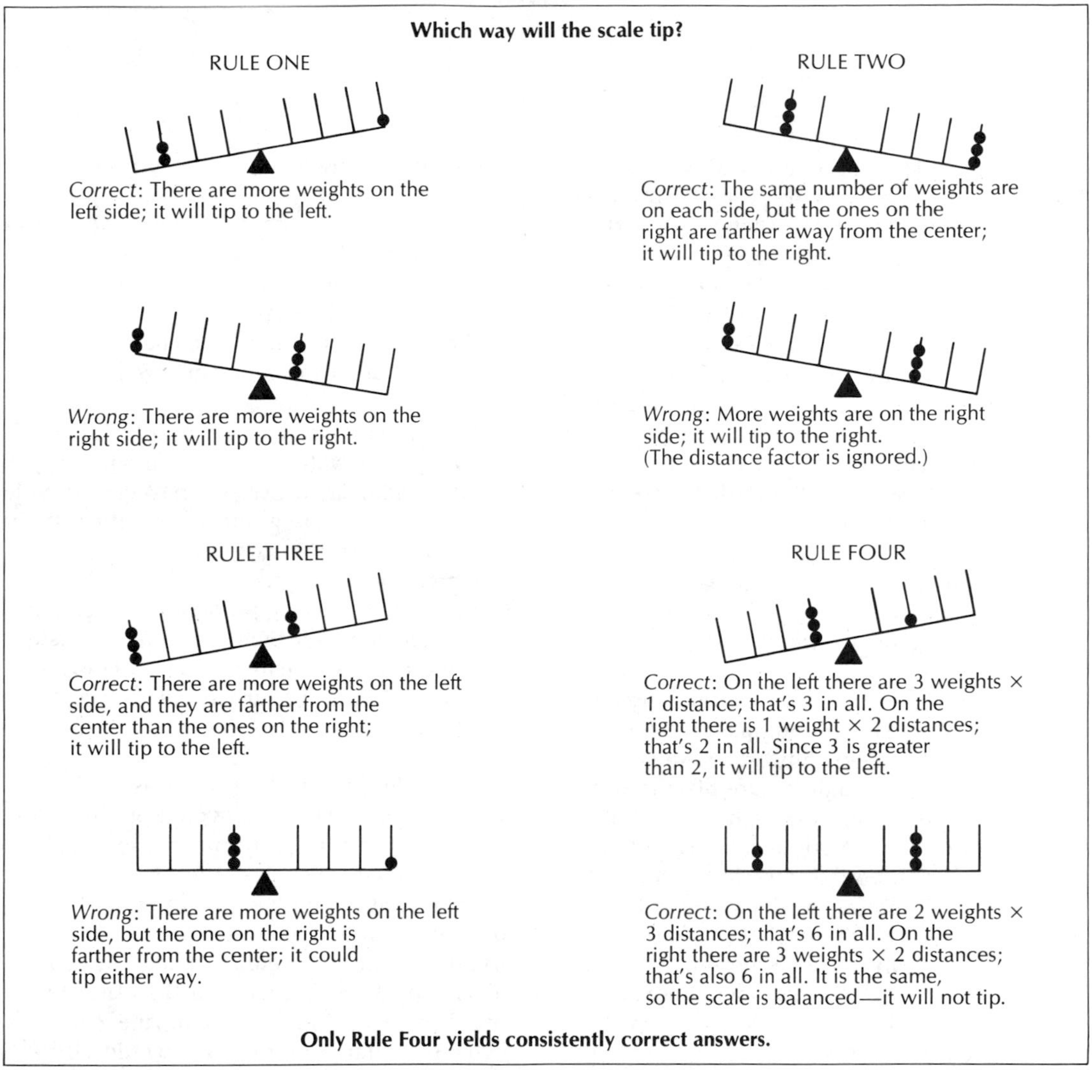

Which way will the scale tip?

RULE ONE

Correct: There are more weights on the left side; it will tip to the left.

Wrong: There are more weights on the right side; it will tip to the right.

RULE TWO

Correct: The same number of weights are on each side, but the ones on the right are farther away from the center; it will tip to the right.

Wrong: More weights are on the right side; it will tip to the right. (The distance factor is ignored.)

RULE THREE

Correct: There are more weights on the left side, and they are farther from the center than the ones on the right; it will tip to the left.

Wrong: There are more weights on the left side, but the one on the right is farther from the center; it could tip either way.

RULE FOUR

Correct: On the left there are 3 weights × 1 distance; that's 3 in all. On the right there is 1 weight × 2 distances; that's 2 in all. Since 3 is greater than 2, it will tip to the left.

Correct: On the left there are 2 weights × 3 distances; that's 6 in all. On the right there are 3 weights × 2 distances; that's also 6 in all. It is the same, so the scale is balanced—it will not tip.

Only Rule Four yields consistently correct answers.

Figure 13.3. The figure outlines rules that children might follow to solve the balance problem. The first three immature rules yield correct answers in some cases, incorrect ones in others. Only Rule Four yields consistently correct answers.

on the subordinate dimension on the other (say, more distance on the right), children lack a consistent rule for resolving the conflict; they simply guess or give up. Clearly, children using this rule would be stymied by our example in Figure 13.2. With weight pointing in one direction (to the left), and dis-

tance pointing to the other dimension (to the right), children will be unable to find a convincing solution.

Rule 4, the final and most sophisticated one, again entails a consideration of both dimensions. But while children using rule 3 do not know how to reconcile inconsistencies, those using rule 4 are aware of the procedure that takes both dimensions properly into account. In the present case, they know that they must multiply the "torques" on both sides of the fulcrum to get the correct answer.

Siegler developed a simple and reliable procedure for determining which of these rules were being used by children in the balance task as well as in other Piagetian measures of scientific thinking. He presented subjects with a number of pictures of sample balance scales such as those shown in Figure 13.2. In each case, the child merely had to indicate whether the beam would fall to the left, fall to the right, or remain balanced. Analogously, in conservation of number problems, children simply had to indicate whether the top row had more buttons, the bottom row had more buttons, or both rows had the same number.

Given such a simple multiple-choice procedure, with only a few choices, one might think that Siegler would secure little information about the subject's thought processes. This method seems more impoverished than the kinds of rich verbal interview techniques Piaget favored, not only with younger subjects but also with the adolescents on whom he tried out balance scale problems.

Enter here Siegler's ingenious innovation. The researcher designed six kinds of problems, which differed from one another in terms of which dimensions were dominant and which of the three possible outcomes would obtain.

1. In equality problems, there were the same values on both dominant and subordinate dimensions for each side of the beam.
2. In dominant problems, there were unequal values on the dominant dimension and equal values on the subordinate dimension.
3. In subordinate problems, there were unequal values on the subordinate

dimension and equal values on the dominant one.
4. In conflict-dominant problems, one side had greater value on the dominant dimension, the other side had greater value on the subordinate dimension, and the side with the superior dominant dimension was correct (as in the problem given in Figure 13.2).
5. In conflict-subordinate problems, one side had greater value on the dominant dimension, the other side had greater value on the subordinate dimension, but this time the side with the superior subordinate dimension was correct.
6. In conflict-equality problems, one side had greater value on the dominant dimension, the other was greater on the subordinate, but the two sides turned out to weigh the same.

According to Siegler's analysis, children who used different rules would produce dramatically different patterns of response on these problems. For example, those who relied on rule 1, attending only to the dominant dimension, would answer correctly on equality, dominant, and conflict-dominant problems, but never correctly on the other three problem types. Children using rule 2 would behave similarly, except they would also solve subordinate problems, because they knew, at least at times when the dominant dimension gave no clear answer, to attend to the subordinate dimension. Those adopting rule 3 would invariably be correct on all three non-conflict problem types but, lacking a way of reconciling conflict, would perform at chance level on the three conflict problems. Those lucky or smart enough to possess rule 4 would perform at or close to 100 percent.

Siegler expected, and obtained, a predictable sequence with age. For example, in one study (1976) half of the children aged four used rule 1; all five-year-olds used rule 1;

older children increasingly used rules 2 and 3; but even among college-age subjects, only a minority used the most sophisticated approach entailed in rule 4. In general, younger children, limited to rules 1 and 2, did not perform as well as older subjects, armed with rules 3 and 4.

Siegler's analysis also uncovered some intriguing paradoxes, which help to clarify the kinds of difficulties children may encounter when they are trying to master a complex new area of study. Consider, for example, the performances on conflict-dominant problems, such as the one illustrated in Figure 13.2. Younger children, using rules 1 or 2, consistently got these problems right, for they simply attended to weight and were done. But the older children, who were using rule 3, did not possess a way of reconciling the conflicting predictions and so answered at chance level. Indeed, performance on the conflict-dominant problems declined from 89 percent for five-year-olds, to 51 percent for seventeen-year-olds. Seventeen-year-olds did less well than five-year-olds on every one of the conflict-dominant items, but not on any other test item. In contrast, performance on subordinate problems improved from 9 percent for five-year-olds to 78 percent for nine-year-olds and 95 percent for seventeen-year-olds; the developmental increments on each subordinate item surpassed those on any other item of the other five problem types. Finally, performance was high for all ages on equality and dominant problems, while improving from below chance to somewhat above chance for the conflict-subordinate and the conflict-equality problems. Thus, while using a simple paradigm Siegler succeeds in ferreting out the reasoning that underlies responses; he thereby displays a sensitivity to the quality of children's thought that is faithful to the spirit of Piaget.

Siegler (1980) characterizes his approach as a **task-analytic** one. He takes a task of the type devised by Piaget and tries to figure out its component parts as precisely as possible. In order to construct a model of children's overall performance, he then seeks to determine how they will carry out each of these parts. Ultimately the task analyst writes out these performances in as precise and unambiguous a language as possible so that they can actually be carried out by a computer, in a simulation of a child's behavior.

Adopting this approach, Siegler examined several of the problems first introduced by the cognitive-structural school and traced the connections among them. He found that rules similar to those used in the balance scale problem are invoked across a wide range of tasks. Based on his analysis, he has also sought to aid his subjects. For example, he determined that young children did not on their own attend to the dimension of distance from the fulcrum; and so he trained them to do so, thereby enhancing their performances.

PIAGET'S CLAIMS ABOUT FORMAL OPERATIONS

In their pioneering original study of thinking in adolescence, Inhelder and Piaget (1958) probed a number of tasks of the balance beam variety. For example, children were given a series of beakers containing colorless liquids and then asked to produce a yellow color by combining the liquids. In another example, children were allowed to play a simple version of billiards; they were then asked to predict the angle at which the ball would rebound after caroming off the edge and to explain *why* the ball behaved as it did. In other problems, children were asked to predict where a shadow would be cast against a screen, and to estimate the probability of choosing a certain color marble from a set of marbles of different colors. Some of the tasks (like the billiards task) seemed to draw primarily on the child's spontaneous learning during childhood;

other tasks (like the balance beam problem) appear more closely tied to schoolroom exercises.

In familiar fashion, Piaget had described a set of three stages through which children pass as they become able to master problems of this sort. In the case of the balance beam, for example, the three stages correspond to rules 1, 2, and 4 of Siegler's analysis. Other investigators have repeated Piaget's demonstrations and have generally found that the phenomena he described were quite robust (Keating, 1980; Martorano, 1977; Neimark, 1975a).

It is with respect to the claims Piaget went on to make that he has been widely criticized (Ennis, 1975; Keating, 1980; Osherson, 1975): in the end, he had to make a retreat. Originally, Piaget claimed that success on one kind of problem was closely related to success on all the other problems in the set. He claimed further that such problems, taken as a group, could be used to diagnose the highest level of cognitive operations, which he called formal operations. Based on a technical analysis of lengthy verbal protocols, Piaget inferred that adolescents could handle a number of different logical forms and deductions, which he went on to express in the language of formal logic. No longer concentrating on the content of the stimulus—its concrete identity, color, odor, height, or weight—the adolescent could reason in a specific logical form, trying out each possibility, isolate and hold all factors constant except one, handle proportions, and make any number of combinations. In short, the adolescent could be a practicing logician. Piaget claimed that this reasoning operated no matter what physical materials or symbols were involved. No longer satisfied with simple practical demonstrations, youngsters would now work deductively: they would envision all possible procedures for a problem—indeed for all problems of this type—and then follow through on them systematically and comprehensively.

FORMAL OPERATIONS DISCONFIRMED

Like other Piagetian claims, his saga of formal operations is attractive. As John Flavell (1980) has commented elsewhere, "One wishes that it were true." Moreover, in the sense sketched at the beginning of this chapter, formal operations do have the ring of truth. The adolescent *is* more like a scientist; she is better able to reason hypothetically, to take into account a wide range of alternatives, to reason "contrary to fact."

Unfortunately, however, attempts to take formal operations more literally, to find strong connections among the various problems studied by Piaget, or to confirm that the logical operations he described are really at work in these classroom-type exercises have run into extremely rough sailing (Brainerd, 1975; Bynum, Thomas, and Weitz, 1972; Ennis, 1975; Falmagne, 1980; Keating, 1980). Some commentators suggest that younger children—say aged eight or nine—understand the scientific laws as well as adolescents but are either ignorant of certain technical language and information or unable to keep track of as many alternatives as the older children. In these instances, the children would have the competence to perform formal mental operations but they would fail because of peripheral conditions.

Another line of criticism surrounds Piaget's claims about the universality of formal thought. Some studies indicate that formal thought is found unpredictably within our own culture, perhaps only among 30 to 40 percent of adolescents and adults (Capon and Kuhn, 1979; Grinder, 1975; Neimark, 1975a). It is rare, as we've seen, even among the college students tested by Siegler. Moreover, this form of thought seems virtually absent in nonliterate cultures (Berry and Dasen, 1974; Neimark, 1975a). As it happens, almost all of Piaget's problems are drawn from the physics or chemistry laboratory and they accordingly favor children who have taken formal science courses and have had experience in scientific procedure and language (though sometimes even the students foul up; see McCloskey, Caramazza, and Green, 1980). By the same token they are biased against children who have not taken science courses, and even more so against those who have not been enrolled in school.

Caught between the claim that formal operational thought would be widespread if it could be tested directly, and the counterclaim that it is available only to a Western scientific elite, Piaget was forced to soften his own statements. In an article written some years before his death, Piaget (1972) conceded that this form of thought might not be found in some societies and that training can strongly influence performance. He also indicated that formal operations may appear only after an individual has had some experience with the medium or domain in which the operations are required. Recognizing that formal thought may not characterize an individual's reasoning in every domain of her life, Piaget recommended that people be tested for such operations in their chosen area of expertise. This advice was in fact taken by DeLisis and Staudt (1980), who demonstrated that students of physics, political science, and English were most likely to think at a formal level in their chosen area of study. Note, however, that these concessions in effect undermine Piaget's original position: an operation cannot be truly formal unless it can be applied willy-nilly to any potential medium. However, except in the case of logicians, whose business it is to reason formally independent of content, considerable evidence suggests that the rest of us reason better about materials that are familiar and that we fall prey to various fallacies when we are required to think in a purely logical vein (Falmagne, 1980; Wason and Johnson-Laird, 1972; Wildman and Fletcher, 1977).

NONFORMAL ACCOUNTS

Given the poor reception accorded formal operations, researchers have set off in a variety of directions in an effort to provide a coherent account of thought past middle childhood. One group of investigators, essentially rejecting the notion of a qualitatively different level of thinking, has focused on the analysis of tasks and the modeling of stages of information processing (Keating, 1980; Siegler, 1980, in press, b; Sternberg, 1977b; see Chapter 10). Such critics speak of greater efficiency in processing, increased working memory, or a superior ability to relate the individual components of a task to one another (Siegler and Vago, 1978). Sometimes the strategies of various age groups are contrasted (Sternberg and Rifkin, 1979). For example, in solving analogies older youths encode the first two terms of the analogy exhaustively and then move swiftly through the remaining steps; in contrast, younger children spend less time in initial encoding, thus reducing their memory load, but much more time in the later steps of comparison or deduction.

SEMIFORMAL ACCOUNTS

Less willing to throw out the baby of formal thought with the excess Piagetian bathwater, other scholars have attempted to salvage parts of the formal operations story. Neimark, for example, examined the order of differences among the various formal operational problems and discerned a regular progression (1975b, 1979; see also Martorano, 1977; Roberge and Flexer, 1979). Neimark also noted certain variables that correlate with formal operational thought, among them the extent to which a subject is reflective or can accept a lack of closure on a task.

Given the relatively low incidence of formal operational thought found in all but the most selected populations, other investigators have focused on how to help individuals. In eliciting formal opertional performance from apparently "concrete" subjects, Danner and Day (1977) have documented the importance of various prompts, such as asking subjects to test variables they have failed to consider or offering various verbal rules to the subjects. Stone and Day (1978) have shown that the opportunity to take formal operational tests increased the likelihood of performance at this level. And Kuhn has suggested a distinction between nonformal subjects in college who immediately benefit from training and can therefore be said to have formal operational thought at a latent level and preadolescent subjects in fifth grade who cannot benefit from such aids and stimulants (Kuhn, Ho, and Adams, 1979).

Another approach to the formal operations conundrum has been to search for other features that might characterize thinking during early adolescence. A number of researchers have pointed out that the adolescent becomes able to attend exclusively to the use of language, for example, noting qualifiers like *usually,* sifting logically relevant from logically irrelevant evidence, recognizing which kinds of information are decisive in a logical context (Bereiter, Hidi, and Dimitroff, 1979), and ignoring certain tentative or situational connotations of words like *space* or *time* in favor of their abstract meaning (Rosenthal, 1979). Eson and Walmsley (1980) stress the flowering of metacognitive abilities during this age, while Moshman (1979) prefers to speak of a metatheoretical orientation, where one comes to know and reflect upon one's own theorizing. Moshman lists a number of features characterizing the thinking of adolescents, such as the urge to isolate variables, the distinction between using and testing hypotheses, the importance of knowing how to disconfirm a hypothesis, and the like. A person is far more likely to solve a formal operations task if she can run through a mental inventory of these notions and then invoke each as needed.

INFORMAL "FORMAL OPERATIONS"

In science, theories do not die just because they have scant support; they fade away because another, better theory has taken their place. While developmental psychologists no longer accept the Piagetian account of formal operations literally, there has not yet been an adequate successor in the theoretical vein. Consequently, many scientists continue to speak of adolescence as the period of formal operations.

Indeed, many developmental psychologists continue to believe that Piaget has identified a set of important phenomena occurring at the time of adolescence. The durability of Piaget's contribution may reflect the recurrent finding that adolescents do seem to reason differently from their preadolescent counterparts. Although many adolescents do not readily make exhaustive deductions from a set of logically impeccable statements, they do approach logical problems systematically, keep track of possibilities, and reason verbally.

According to the informal account of adolescent thought sketched by Inhelder and Piaget (1958) and endorsed by many scholars, changes in scientific reasoning exert a pull on the adolescent's views about other areas of life. For the first time, many adolescents become engrossed in systematic theoretical speculation on such topics as the merits of a new religious sect, the arguments for and against legalized abortion, the quality of an actor's performance. They ponder life's possibilities, revel in bull sessions, speculate, and continuously make inferences, predictions, and idealistic claims. They are now able (and willing) to follow their beliefs to their ultimate conclusion and thus become intensely involved in ideological matters. And, equally important, they seem inclined for the first time to dedicate their lives to ideas to which they are passionately committed. It is the adolescent and the young adult—not the child or the middle-aged person—who has participated centrally in the revolutionary movements of our time. Even if they do not fit strict, formal criteria for scientific thought, the conversations, arguments, and ideas of adolescents can be readily distinguished from those of younger children.

Thinking about Morality: Lawrence Kohlberg's Approach

Although the sciences are a major arena for thought, particularly in our society, they are by no means the only domain in which intellect can be exercised. Piaget himself under scored this fact early in his research career; as we saw in Chapters 5 and 12, he studied children's moral judgments and demonstrated that preadolescents can take account of a person's motivations and intentions when evaluating a course of action. Yet, Piaget never returned to this line of inquiry; he barely crossed the border into the territory of morality.

Now, however, a study of the development of moral thought rivals in scope Piaget's explorations of concrete and formal operations in the sciences. For, taking off from Piaget's pioneering studies, Lawrence Kohlberg has for over twenty years investigated how intellectual capacities are applied to moral thought (Kohlberg, 1958, 1969, 1971). In considering Kohlberg's theory and findings, we have an opportunity both to ponder again the cognitive changes in adolescence and to consider the relation between one's thoughts and feelings and the course of action one pursues.

First, we must understand what Kohlberg means (and does not mean) by moral thought or moral judgment. He has little sympathy for

the once-common practice of examining how individuals behave in a morally charged situation, for example, whether they cheat when given the opportunity to do so. This research approach has repeatedly demonstrated that people cannot be rated simply as "honest" or "cheaters," for nearly everyone cheats at least occasionally, and no one is dishonest all the time (Broughton, 1975b; Hartshorne and May, 1929). Rather, Kohlberg (like Piaget) focuses on the *reasoning* of an individual confronted by a moral or ethical dilemma. Posed with a moral dilemma, subjects must put themselves in the protagonist's place, explaining and justifying a course of action.

In each dilemma, a case can be made for rival courses of action. Analysis focuses on the *reasons* subjects offer rather than the specific actions they might suggest or actually perform in a real situation. At issue in these moral dilemmas are one's recommendations and justifications, not one's morality or immorality. According to Kohlberg, rather than characterizing individuals as moral or immoral, ethical or unethical, the analyst should think of the individual as construing moral dilemmas at a certain level of reasoning.

We gain an initial acquaintance with Kohlberg's enterprise by reconsidering the dilemma of whether Richard Nixon should have destroyed the tapes. Following Kohlberg's analysis, whether the subject did or did not urge destruction of the tapes is of little import. It is the reason behind the recommendation that reflects the subject's morality. For example, two subjects might both have urged destruction but one might have done so because "the tapes belonged to Nixon" (the primitive level of reasoning labeled Z) while the other espoused certain ideals regarding privacy (the sophisticated level of reasoning labeled Y). By the same token, preservation of the tapes might be urged either because "they cost money" (level Z) or because "hiding information is in principle wrong" (level Y).

According to Kohlberg, most individuals who are at or past adolescence should be more attracted by sophisticated pro *and* con arguments than by primitive arguments that happen to be favorable to their own point of view.

Because real and notorious cases like that of the tapes may evoke "canned" arguments, Kohlberg finds it more sensible to study individuals' reasoning about hypothetical moral dilemmas. In numerous studies he and his collaborators have employed ten mundane but intriguing stories. The one we shall examine is by far the most widely quoted; indeed, most of Kohlberg's published reports and data analyses are based on it.

SHOULD HEINZ HAVE STOLEN THE DRUG?

In Europe a woman was near death from cancer. One drug might save her, a form of radium that a druggist in the same town had recently discovered. The druggist was charging $2000, ten times what the drug cost him to make. The sick woman's husband, Heinz, went to everyone he knew to borrow the money, but he could only get together about half of what it cost. He told the druggist that his wife was dying and asked him to sell it cheaper or let him pay later. But the druggist said "No." The husband got desperate and broke into the man's store to steal the drug for his wife. Should the husband have done that? Why? [Kohlberg, 1969, p. 376]

This dilemma has been posed to thousands of people of all ages, socioeconomic groups, intelligence levels, motivations, and apparent degrees of honesty. Nearly all possible reasons and rationalizations have been gathered on it.

According to Kohlberg, whenever such problems are posed, three broad levels of moral development can be discerned. Each of these levels—which were reflected in the three solutions to the Nixon problem—contains in turn two stages. What follows in the box are the six stages and their characteristics, along with illustrations for each stage of pro and con reasoning about Heinz's dilemma.

CLAIMS AND EVIDENCE

In his major writings Kohlberg claims that these stages are universal and fixed, that everywhere youngsters begin by displaying preconventional morality and gradually reason their way up to the level of principled morality. Consistent with cognitive-developmental theory, everyone must pass through the same stages, in the same order, though the ages of stage-attainment vary enormously across subjects. Moreover, each stage is a structured whole: the characteristics of reasoning associated with a stage are related in a sensible manner, giving rise to an integrated world view. Thus, for example, Kohlberg sees the preconventional child's egocentrism, selfishness, and interest in purely physical properties as integrated into a single coherent pattern of thought.

The six-stage sequence has both empirical and logical validity: empirical, in that people can be categorized in terms of it, no matter where they are tested; logical, in that each stage grows naturally out of previous ones, integrating implications that were imperfectly realized earlier. (For instance, the progression from stage 1 to stage 2 involves a logical differentiation. Whereas stage 1 lumps people and property together, stage 2 affords a higher value to human life than to property.)

Kohlberg's assertion that the stages occur in the same order across a variety of populations has secured a good deal of support. Dilemmas like the Heinz problem have been administered to many subjects, and their responses have consistently revealed that children in middle childhood are typically preconventional; that young adolescents (age thirteen to sixteen) are typically at the conventional stage; and that perhaps 50 percent of older adolescents (age sixteen to twenty)

LAWRENCE KOHLBERG'S SIX STAGES OF MORAL REASONING

LEVEL I: PRECONVENTIONAL LEVEL OF MORALITY

Moral value resides in external and physical happenings rather than in persons or in standards. An individual at this stage applies cultural standards of right and wrong without analyzing their meaning.

Stage 1: *Punishment and obedience orientation.* The physical consequences of the action determine its goodness or badness and measures of quantity are paramount. One respects power and acts to avoid trouble and punishment.

PRO: He should steal the drug. It isn't really bad to take it. It isn't like he didn't ask to pay for it first. The drug he takes is only worth $200. He's not really taking a $2000 drug.

CON: He shouldn't steal the drug. It's a big crime. He didn't get permission; he used force and broke and entered. He did a lot of damage, stealing a very expensive drug and breaking up the store too.

Stage 2: *Instrumental relativist orientation.* Right action consists of doing what will satisfy one's own desires and needs, rarely what satisfies others'. Any elements of fairness or reciprocity are interpreted in a wholly pragmatic way: "You scratch my back and I'll scratch yours." But now, purely physical consequences are differentiated from interpersonal aspects of the act.

PRO: It's all right to steal the drug because she needs it and he wants her to live. It isn't that he wants to steal but it's the way he has to use to get the drug to save her.

CON: He shouldn't steal it. The druggist isn't wrong or bad. He just wants to make a profit. That's what you're in business for, to make money.

LEVEL II: CONVENTIONAL LEVEL OF MORALITY

At this level, the individual values group expectations and standards. One conforms to and actively maintains the social order and identifies with the people in it, especially those in positions of power.

Stage 3: *Interpersonal concordance or "good boy–nice girl" orientation.* An action is evaluated in terms of the kind of person likely to perform such an act. If one means well, the action is acceptable; if one has bad motives, it is not. There is considerable conformity to the majority will—to what "people want."

PRO: He should steal the drug. He was only doing something that was natural for a good husband to do. You can't blame him for doing something out of love for his wife; you'd blame him if he didn't love his wife enough to save her.

CON: He shouldn't steal. If his wife dies, he can't be blamed. It isn't because he is heartless or he doesn't love her enough to do everything that he can. The druggist is the selfish or heartless one.

Stage 4: *"Law and order" orientation.* Here there emerges a steadfast adhesion to authority and laws. Motives no longer

(continued)

suffice. A law is a law and must be obeyed, for that is what holds society together.

PRO: You should steal it. If you did nothing you'd be letting your wife die; it's your responsibility if she dies. You have to take it with the idea of paying the druggist.

CON: It is a natural thing for Heinz to want to save his wife, but it's still always wrong to steal. He still knows he's stealing and taking a valuable drug from the man who made it.

LEVEL III: POSTCONVENTIONAL, AUTONOMOUS, OR PRINCIPLED LEVEL

No longer is the group paramount. For the first time, one defines values and principles apart from one's identification with or membership in socially defined groups. The basis of one's actions becomes one's own conscience.

Stage 5: *Social-contract legalistic orientation.* Right action is now defined in terms of general individual rights and standards that have been agreed upon by the whole society. One is aware that values are flexible and that one must aim for reaching a consensus among reasonable people. Thus, the law is seen as a changeable set of principles that may yield to special or unanticipated circumstances. Outside the legal realm, people can arrive at their own agreements and contracts. While circumstances sometimes justify deviant acts, moral standards must be maintained. One's intent in breaking the rules becomes crucial.

PRO: The law wasn't set up for these circumstances. Taking the drug in this situation isn't really right but it's justified to do it.

CON: You can't completely blame someone for stealing, but extreme circumstances don't really justify taking the law in your own hands. You can't have everybody stealing whenever they get desperate. The end may be good but the ends don't justify the means.

Stage 6: *Universal ethical principle orientation.* Abstract, ethical principles now guide one's course of action. The principles result from an appeal to comprehensiveness, universality, and consistency across a wide variety of circumstances. An example would be the Golden Rule—"Do unto others as you would have them do unto you." It may actually be right to deviate from a rule as long as one remains true to one's own moral principles. Moral principles do not allow exceptions; at heart are the universal principles of justice or reciprocity, equality of human rights, and respect for the dignity of human beings as individuals.

PRO: This is a situation which forces him to choose between stealing and letting his wife die. In a situation where the choice must be made, it is morally right to steal. He has to act in terms of the principle of preserving and respecting life.

CON: Heinz is faced with the decision of whether to consider the other people who need the drug just as badly as his wife. Heinz ought to act not just according to his particular feeling toward his wife, but considering the value of all the lives involved.

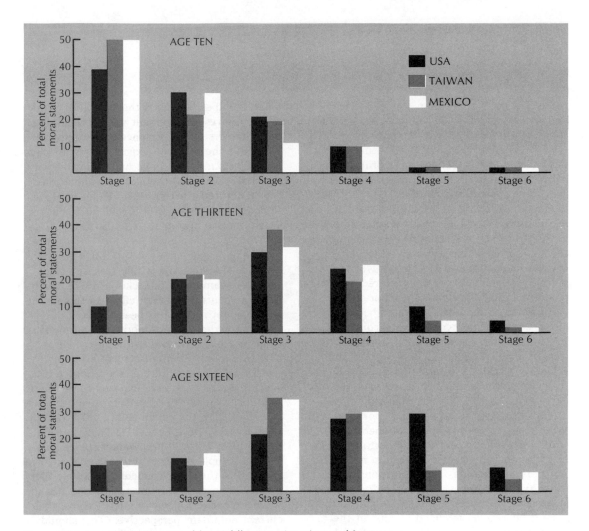

Figure 13.4. The dilemmas posed by Kohlberg to American subjects have been adapted for use in other cultural settings. Results in Taiwan and Mexico lag somewhat behind those in the United States, yet prove remarkably similar to one another. Accounting for these similarities—and differences—is a major challenge confronting students of moral development. (Kohlberg, 1969)

have attained the principled level. The evidence is *cross-sectional*, with more higher stages found among older and wiser subjects (Kohlberg, 1969); *longitudinal*, in that persons seen over a period of years typically advance to a higher stage (Kohlberg and Elfinbein, 1975; Rest, 1975; Rest, Davison, and Robbins, 1978); and **cross-cultural**, in that the same sequence of stages can be found to unfold in certain other cultures (Kohlberg, 1969; Turiel, Kohlberg, and Edwards, 1972), including the United States, Great Britain, Taiwan, Yucatán, and Turkey (see Figure 13.4). That is, when confronted with an appropriate variation on the Heinz dilemma (a man steals food from a store to save a starving wife), Taiwanese respond in the same way as Americans.

Kohlberg and his colleagues seem, then, to have uncovered a sequence of moral development throughout childhood that compares in theoretical power and empirical support with Piaget's description of intellectual development. Indeed, the two efforts are nearly parallel. Not only are Kohlberg's views on processes of development remarkably similar to Piaget's; not only was Kohlberg's work in moral development originally offered as a modification of Piaget's theory; but strong parallels have been demonstrated between moral and logical development (Broughton, 1974; Haier and Keating, 1975; Kohlberg, 1969; Rest et al., 1978; Selman, 1976; Walker and Richards, 1979). In general, these researchers report, children at a given moral stage will also have attained the corresponding cognitive stage. Thus, a conventional moralizer will succeed at all steps of concrete operations and a principled moralizer will perform satisfactorily on conventional Piagetian measures of formal operations. This correspondence is to be expected because the reasoning required at each moral stage is strongly linked to the mental operations assumed to exist at the parallel cognitive stage. The conventional morality of following stated laws and treating all parties equally mimics the set of schemes (identity, reversibility, and compensation) and the strict adherence to rules (as in conservation) seen in concrete operations. And just as principled moralizing depends on the ability to reason about abstract universal principles, formal operations reflect the ability to manipulate abstract strings of symbols or propositions.

The translation between realms is not, however, automatic. Although moral reasoning presupposes certain cognitive skills, individuals at a given cognitive stage will not necessarily be found at the matching moral

stage. Kohlberg explains that moral development requires involvement with diverse social and interpersonal experiences; many people who have the requisite experiences with physical objects may not have had equivalent opportunity for moral thought and operations (see Haier and Keating, 1975; Kuhn et al., 1977; Selman, 1974, 1976; Siegal, 1975; but for an alternative argument, see also Damon, 1975).

Kohlberg has gained many followers and has indeed spawned a whole research tradition (see Damon, 1978; Lickona, 1975). Perhaps the central research effort in this moral-development school has been directed at determining what factors motivate an individual to move from one level to the next higher one. In a manner reminiscent of attempts to teach operational thinking (see Chapter 10), several researchers have exposed subjects to arguments at a level of reasoning either lower or higher than their own (Blatt, 1975; Hickey, 1972; Keasey, 1973; Lee, 1971; Tracy and Cross, 1973; Turiel, 1966; Walker, 1981). In general, people prefer arguments at their own stage or at the stage immediately above their own: They are most likely to advance a stage when exposed to views one level above their current dominant perspective. (This should accord with your own experience in considering the pro and con Nixon and Heinz arguments.) Individuals who are in transition to another stage—that is, who on their own offer a generous mix of reasons from two stages— prove most likely on retesting to espouse arguments of the higher stage. However, they are less prone to respond favorably to arguments two stages above their own; those prove too difficult to grasp. And they tend to view the arguments below their own stage as deficient, lacking comprehensiveness and coherence. Other evidence suggests that individuals fail when asked to explain or paraphrase arguments significantly above their own level, whereas such failures of comprehension are unlikely with arguments from lower levels. It seems from these findings that intense discussions about moral issues, particularly in the company of somewhat sophisticated thinkers, causes feelings of arousal and conflict and enhances one's moral reasoning powers (Blatt, 1975; Crockenberg and Nicolayev, 1979; Gibbs et al., 1981). Presumably, a person in transition will have the opportunity, under this impetus, to bring together into a "structured" whole the facets of the higher cognitive stage.

Those trained in the Kohlberg tradition point to these findings, and others not cited, as evidence that his account or moral development has been validated. However, it must be noted that many of the "training" or "exposure" studies have flaws that make them difficult to interpret (for example, the language spoken by higher-stage models sounds more sophisticated). Moreover, a number of attempts to test the Kohlberg scheme, undertaken by individuals outside the Kohlberg camp, have failed to support it (Rosenthal and Zimmerman, 1978). Surveying this state of affairs, some critics find the empirical support for Kohlberg's theory as flimsy as the support for Piaget's formal operations (Hoffman, 1980).

Although Kohlberg himself originally showed little interest in whether responses to dilemmas affect one's own behavior, considerable research has recently been conducted on the relationship between moral reasoning and moral behavior (Haan, 1978). Some of this research supports the hypothesis that individuals assessed at a high moral stage are more likely to behave in an ethically principled manner. For instance, in one experiment subjects were led to believe that they were administering increasingly severe shocks to another individual (Milgram, 1974). Those subjects who refused to administer the shocks, despite orders to do so from an authoritative scientist, were more likely to be at the principled stage of moral development than were the subjects who administered the shocks. Indeed, 71 percent of individuals at stage 6 refrained from shocking as compared to a mere 13 percent at lower stages (Kohlberg, 1971). Students involved in acts of political civil disobedience at the University of California at Berkeley in the mid-1960's were more likely than their nonactive peers to be at the principled stages of moral development. Eighty percent of stage 6 subjects and 50 percent of stage 5 subjects, but only 10 percent of stage 3 and 4 subjects participated in acts of protest (Haan, Smith, and Block, 1968). And whereas only 20 percent of children at the principled level will cheat in a testing situation, 75 percent of the others will do so (Krebs, 1967).

Although such results certainly show an impressive correlation between moral reasoning and moral action, the behaviors could well have resulted from other unexamined factors such as general intellectual level or even, in the study involving shock, sophistication about psychological experimentation. And, of course, in examples like the Berkeley protests, the question about which course of action is more moral can itself be disputed. In addition, an individual's level of reasoning may be intimately yoked to his own self-interest, to the audience to which his reasoning is directed (Damon, 1978), or to his motivations in a specific situation (Peters, 1971). Clearly, the relation between moral judgment and moral action requires further study.

CRITICISM OF THE KOHLBERG CLAIMS— AND SOME RESPONSES

Although Kohlberg's scheme of moral development has gained considerable research support, and is already being used in many educational programs, it has also generated much controversy. Despite extensive publication of Kohlberg's general approach, so far only he and his associates—and others who have studied with them—have the necessary tools and knowledge to apply the numerous measures and dimensions involved in assessing moral stages. Thus, work that has not received Kohlberg's sanction has unclear status, and those who are not privy to his complicated scoring system are understandably critical of the cult surrounding the Kohlberg group (Hogan, 1973; Kurtines and Greif, 1974; McGeorge, 1973).

A second line of criticism concerns Kohlberg's claims about the universality of stages and their sequence. Elizabeth Simpson (1974) holds that the scheme reflects considerable cultural bias. First, both Western and Taiwanese individuals have been reported to regress to previously held stages. In particular, about one fifth of college-age subjects in American society who have passed through stage 4 revert to a relativistic mode of reasoning, where there is no right or wrong. Their adherence to the response "Do what you can get away with, since there are no absolute standards" should be classified as stage 2. Kohlberg and his colleagues have come up with a number of explanations for this intriguing regression, such as a heightened awareness of differing standards across cultures coupled with growing sensitivity to the inadequacy of the conventions of one's own society (Kohlberg and Kramer, 1969; Turiel, 1974, 1978). Nonetheless, in a strict interpretation of stage theory, subjects should continue to reach higher stages and such regression should not occur.

In addition, principled reasoning has not been found at all among certain groups (Kohlberg, 1971), perhaps because of the criteria used in assessing stages. The stage 5 or 6 person typically refers to abstract principles, universal ideas, and concepts like justice, equality, and reciprocity. Such reasoning (or, at any rate, the words in which it is couched) is not found in many societies and does not even occur often in our own society (Gibbs, 1977). (It is found more frequently among

males than among females, for reasons which are discussed in Chapter 14.) And when principled reasoning does occur, one must be wary of whether the language used is simply a manner of speaking acquired from others. For instance, a college student might acquire abstract language from exposure to fellow students and instructors without actually understanding the principles involved. By the same token, a person assessed at a lower stage of reasoning may understand the principles but not be able to phrase them adequately. Moreover, as Moran and Joniak have shown (1979), findings on moral-judgment tests are closely tied to sophistication of language: indeed, lower-stage responses are actually preferred when they are couched in more sophisticated language. As Simpson exclaims, "Oh pity the poor savages in our ghettos, in villages and tribes abroad, who cannot express themselves so neatly, so profoundly, and so elegantly! By Kohlberg's definition, they may never know principled reasoning" (1974, p. 95).

Kohlberg's supporters argue that they take these language differences into account. Nevertheless, whether responses are scored loosely or conservatively, the risk of misinterpretation remains. Some indication of moral level that is less dependent upon articulateness would be clearly welcome. In one attempt, subjects were asked to rate and rank a series of statements about each dilemma (Rest, 1975; Rest et al., 1974). Although the rich conversation is lost, this procedure allows a person to indicate understanding of relevant issues in a dilemma without the burden of verbalizing them.

Kohlberg's approach may also be insensitive to variations among cultures. For instance, the Western experimenter may be viewed as strange, her methods of testing may simply be inappropriate for certain groups, or the group may have some way of dealing with the dilemma that the outsider would neither recognize nor understand. The moral stances of other cultural groups and societies might have fundamentally different premises, perhaps based on a mythopoetic view (see Chapter 11, pages 447–448). In any case, it is at least debatable whether Kohlberg has devised a culturally unbiased measure. If a measure of moral judgment were devised in, say, Albania or Zaire, how would we fare on it?

Even as some critics find the higher levels of moral reasoning restricted to a tiny and unrepresentative elite, others discern the origins of moral thought at a much earlier time in development; they feel that, shorn of the fancy verbiage, the fundamental insights are available to young schoolchildren. Reflecting the recent rush to locate basic mental operations in very young children, several researchers have demonstrated sensitivity to a protagonist's motivations and intentions as well as to various mitigating circumstances in children as young as four or five (Darley, Klosson, and Zanna, 1978; Gottlieb, Taylor, and Ruderman, 1977; Wellman, Larkey, and Somerville, 1979).

In a very suggestive study, Stein, Trabasso, and Garfin (1979) stripped down the classic Heinz dilemma into a very simple tale: there is a lady who had a sick husband, and who had to steal cat's whiskers in order to make the only medicine that would save his life. According to the researchers' analysis, this tale captures the essentials of the Heinz tale; yet unlike the rather sophisticated Kohlberg version, it poses few linguistic or narrative burdens on the child. Nonetheless, young children still have a great deal of difficulty with the tale. They fail to make obvious inferences (for example, that the medicine will in fact save the husband's life) and they cannot keep this major goal in mind while pursuing the subgoals of securing whiskers or making medicines. Thus, for the young children Kohl-

berg's dilemma does not really exist. In the opinion of this research team, the solution of Kohlbergian dilemmas is so intertwined with the understanding of a complex narrative, including the effects of various courses of action, that it is very difficult to cleave out moral judgments per se.

A final major criticism of Kohlberg's work concerns the relation between moral judgment and moral behavior. While some researchers, cited above, find a relation between an individual's level of reasoning and her moral behavior, recent reviews find only a weak overall relation between what a subject says and how ethically she behaves (Maccoby, 1980; Mischel and Mischel, 1976). More sophisticated subjects often consider more factors and are more thoughtful, but this reflectivity does not necessarily translate into more laudable behavior (Staub, 1970).

Such findings raise sharply the question of how important all this fuss over moral dilemmas really is. William Alston (1971) has pointed out that how a person *reasons* about moral dilemmas may be of only marginal interest; in the last analysis, we want to know how a person will actually *behave*. Thus, in the Milgram experiment (page 527) the crucial factor is simply whether or not a shock was given, not *why*. One who does not give a shock because "It will hurt" (a simple reason) should perhaps be preferred to one who does give a shock because it will "further the pursuit of scientific truth" (a more sophisticated reason). And, indeed, dramatizing the divorce between reasoning and action, when people are asked how they think *others* will behave, they invariably predict far less shocking than actually occurs (Milgram, 1974). Kohlberg may be right in saying that reasoning and action are separate enterprises, but perhaps that in itself is a good reason to disregard reasoning (and rationalization) and to focus instead on actions and consequences.

In fact, because Kohlberg insists that at every stage reasons exist for both opposite (pro and con) actions, some observers view the whole exercise as a bit hollow. One decides what one wants to do, and then simply concocts a reason that justifies one's behavior. In everyday life, or even in the shock experiment, many factors besides reasoning—such as motivation, habit, or emotional state—contribute to our behavior in morally ambiguous situations. By ignoring such pragmatic realities, Kohlberg has presented a fascinating but one-sided view of how one thinks about the proper course of action in situations requiring some self-consciousness about behavior. He may also have significantly underestimated the darker side of human nature—our capacity to reason well and to act poorly. What remains to be done is to disentangle knowledge about morality, the universality of moral principles, the value of higher stages, and the relation of all these to actual behavior.

How, then, should we evaluate the whole Kohlberg enterprise? On the one side, we have seen an impressive body of studies and a persuasive theoretical account documenting basic developmental stages of moral thought that can be tied to other aspects of intellectual growth. On the other side, we have some nagging questions about the way in which scoring decisions are made, the cross-cultural validity of the theory, the interpretation of the responses of the younger subjects, and the relative importance of moral judgments and moral actions.

Of course, it is unfair to maintain that Kohlberg's position is a hard-and-fast stance, unmovable in the face of criticism. In his most recent writings Kohlberg has shown considerable sensitivity to the various criticisms voiced above and has moved quite a way from some of his original pronouncements. For instance, he now concedes that stage 6 is essentially an ideal, a theoretical construct, one rarely encountered in reality even in a sophisticated Western context. Similarly, he takes much more seriously the issues of moral behavior and moral education, declaring that "psychology's abstract concept *moral stage* is not a sufficient basis for moral education" (Kohlberg, 1978, p. 84). And he now believes it is important to deal early with children's antisocial behaviors, by indoctrination if necessary, rather than simply waiting for higher levels of reasoning to evolve.

By the same token, Kohlberg's associates are also involved in a continuing examination of his key ideas. John Gibbs (1979) speaks of the need to transcend a Piaget-based approach in considering the adult phase of moral development. Rejecting Kohlberg's exclusive focus on the *forms* of moral reasoning, Gibbs reminds us of the numerous real-world issues that every adult must face—the choice of vocation, relations with spouse and children, the inevitability of sickness and death. He goes on to argue that in confronting these issues the adult necessarily adopts an *existential* point of view, a kind of metaperspective in which he can reflect on these basic but essentially unsolvable aspects of existence. It is a mistake, in Gibb's view, to assimilate these philosophical dilemmas to a logical stage sequence of moral maturity; they are better viewed as the quest for meaning in which every person will eventually become engaged.

Carol Gilligan and J. Michael Murphy (1979; Murphy and Gilligan, 1980), two other associates of Kohlberg, use the regression in moral judgments described above as a wedge to reconstruct a new version of Kohlberg's theory. In their view, it is progress, not regress, to consider behaviors in a more relativistic way, to take into account personal as well as universal interests, to weight the particulars of a given context (see Perry, 1968).

One acquisition that emerges from years of living is a feeling for the nuances, subtleties, and unpredictable facets of fate that one cannot know as a purely formal-reasoning high school student. The commitment to absolute standards of justice, unchangeable and constant, is replaced by a willingness to take into account particulars of situation and time, to engage in debate, and to consider alternative modes of content.

As an example, Murphy and Gilligan (1980) describe one of their subjects, a Harvard student, who was asked whether Heinz should steal the drug. He responds, "I do think you have certain obligations to your wife or your friends or relatives that are just deeper." Asked whether Heinz should steal for a complete stranger, he takes a cautious approach: "If it were just a question of if the drug would make this guy feel better, maybe it is not so clear there, how deep is the obligation. You can't go around and crusade for everybody. It is just impossible." As to whether he has changed since he went to Harvard, he says that as a result of his experiences in living, he has become "more considerate, taking into account other people's feelings and other people's opinions and other people's lives and how you as a person affect their lives. And seeing whether your effect is a good effect or a bad effect. And before, I didn't really care about [that] too much. My first responsibility was mainly to myself and the other just went along." While not losing the ability to justify judgments according to strictly logical considerations, this subject now tries to consider the actual effects of his actions on other people (Murphy and Gilligan, 1980, p. 99).

One tentative conclusion is that Kohlberg's studies may be particularly revealing about the world of the adolescent. Reasoning about moral situations is decidedly an artificial activity for younger children (Arbuthnot, 1975). Their moral activity seems more appropriately accounted for by the combination of psychoanalytic and social-learning factors portrayed in Chapter 5. But once youths can consider hypothetical worlds and make deductions from principles, their level of reasoning, construction of behavior, and verbal rationalizations become important. Perhaps for the first time, they can consider courses of moral behavior other than their own and make the necessary connection to their own behavior. And so they are able to address a dilemma, like the Heinz drug story, to isolate the relevant variables, and respond appropriately. Yet even as the Kohlbergian dilemmas prove too sophisticated for the young child, they may also miss the important aspects of mature thought: the ability to take into account both logical considerations and the particulars of a given context, to satisfy one's own personal value system while at the same time taking into consideration the feelings and aspirations of others, to ponder one's own place in a social and moral network. For such issues, almost any experimental task may be deficient. One must see how the individual actually leads her life before assessing competence in the moral sphere.

A Look at the Lighter Side

If Piaget's view of the nature of adolescent thought is at all plausible, it should apply to a range of materials. And, as we have just seen, Kohlberg's stages of moral development have an impressive concordance with Piaget's formulations about cognitive development. But what happens in a domain of thought even further removed from logical scientific reasoning—for instance, the arena of humor? Can an approach built on operational thought be discerned even there? Some research undertaken during the past decade suggests that it can.

THE DEVELOPMENT OF
A SENSE OF HUMOR

Accent on Cognition. The notion that humor and thought are integrally related may in itself seem whimsical. After all, isn't humor primarily an emotional event or outlet? A moment's reflection indicates that humor cannot evoke the intended feelings of pleasure unless it is first comprehended. And comprehension is indisputably a cognitive matter.

Reasoning that a person could appreciate and laugh only at what she understood led Edward Zigler and his colleagues to carry out developmental studies of humor (Zigler, Levine, and Gould, 1966, 1967). They expected children's appreciation of cartoons to be enhanced as their capacity to comprehend increased. In a study in which cartoons from children's magazines were shown to youngsters ages seven to eleven, they found that children at a higher cognitive level (such as older children) were more likely to explain the cartoons satisfactorily. But there was first a rise and then a surprising dip in the amount of smiling, laughing, and other "mirth responses." The oldest and youngest subjects reacted similarly while eight- and nine-year-olds displayed more "mirth responses."

The authors interpreted this last result as evidence that one laughs when comprehending a cartoon or joke, except when the item is seen as too simple or even as simpleminded. Just as Kohlberg's subjects reject moral justifications beneath their own level, children scorn humor that they too readily comprehend. The findings require the cognitive hypothesis to be adjusted: cartoons are perceived as funny only when they challenge and thus activate the child's full cognitive repertoire.

Paul McGhee (1971a, b, 1973) suggested a direct link between the subject matter of jokes and the likelihood that children would appreciate them. For instance, the following joke rests on understanding conservation of mass:

Mr. Jones went into a restaurant and ordered a whole pizza for his dinner. When the waiter asked if he wanted it cut into 6 or 8 pieces, Mr. Jones said, "Oh, you'd better make it 6, I could never eat 8 pieces!" [McGhee, 1973]

Children who had not yet attained the relevant conservation neither understood nor appreciated such jokes. Those who had recently acquired the concept laughed most heartily, and college students did not find the jokes funny, presumably because understanding them entailed little cognitive challenge.

While most research on humor has focused on the understanding of various conceptual incongruities, some researchers have focused on jokes in which the meaning inheres in wordplay. For instance, Lila Gleitman and her colleagues (Hirsh-Pasek, Gleitman, and Gleitman, 1978) have examined children's sensitivities to different verbal ambiguities. The easiest jokes turn on transparent semantic properties of the sentences, such as ambiguities in word meaning (for example, How do we know there was fruit on Noah's ark? Because the animals came in *pairs*). Somewhat more challenging are jokes that hinge on ambiguities in the syntactic structure of the sentence (Where would you go to see a *man-eating* fish? A seafood restaurant.) Posing the greatest difficulties are jokes that disrupt the boundaries between words and involve sound distortions (Did you read in the newspaper about the man who ate six dozen pancakes at one sitting? No—*how waffle*.) Clearly, in the latter cases the child needs greater awareness about the principles of language, including the ways in which a stream of sound can be divided. While the relations between such wordplay and the various Piagetian conservations are less evident

(Whitt and Prentice, 1977), strong age trends do emerge in the ability to detect subtle kinds of wordplay in jokes.

We should note, another factor shaping children's behavior in humor contexts. In a series of intriguing investigations, David Brodzinsky and his colleagues have highlighted the contribution of the child's cognitive style (see page 483). In particular, the child's overall tempo—whether she is impulsive or reflective—makes a significant contribution to her mirth response. For impulsive children, the presence of a sound track laced with audience laughter is a significant factor in determining the extent of their response (Brodzinsky, Tew, and Palkovitz, 1979). Moreover, such children (as well as children who are slower but inaccurate) tend to laugh more than others at jokes, regardless of whether they understand them. On the other hand, children who are reflective (as well as those who are speedy but accurate) are less prone to laugh uproariously, and when they do "crack up" they will reveal their level of understanding. One must factor into the humor equation the child's prevalent cognitive style in addition to measures of "pure" comprehension.

Accent on Affect. Clearly, a raft of studies prove that the humor response reflects one's level of conceptual and linguistic understanding (Hirsh-Pasek et al., 1978; McGhee, 1980; McGhee and Chapman, 1980; Schultz, 1972; Schultz and Horibe, 1974; Zigler, Levine, and Gould, 1966, 1967). But it would be misleading to discount the strong affective component of humor. In the view of Martha Wolfenstein (1954) a psychoanalytically oriented researcher, joking transforms "painful and frustrating experiences to exact pleasure from the

Figure 13.5. Children's appreciation of verbal and pictorial humor reflects their level of understanding. Pre-adolescents should enjoy the pun in this cartoon; younger children are more likely to be amused by the incongruous elements, such as the bird peering through the telescope.

same" (p. 12). Examining jokes from pre-schoolers to adolescents, Wolfenstein found that both the form and substance of the joke altered over time.

Preschool children in the Oedipal stage favor jokes that mirror their concerns with size and power relations vis-à-vis their parents and their own genitals and with their relations to the opposite sex (S. Freud, 1938b). Such children will often laugh merely because others are laughing, or merely because the joke violates an expectation. For example, they will laugh uproariously at the story of a family with hundreds of children or the tale of a farmer who buried himself and came up a tomato.

During their early school years, as children become concerned with competence, their wordplay, concentration on riddles, and love of "moron jokes" all reflect a preoccupation with problems of knowing, understanding, and mastery (see Erikson, 1963; R.W. White, 1959).

These youngsters enjoy a simple play on words (You never starve in the desert because of all the sand which is there); formula jokes (Knock, knock. Who's there?); and question-and-answer riddles (Why did the moron take a ladder to school? Because he wanted to attend high school.)

For adolescents, the telling of jokes becomes a performance, a presentation of self as well as the creation of a funny story. Instead of simply mimicking the way they hear a joke, the thirteen- or fourteen-year-olds are concerned with delivery, attempting to associate themselves with the protagonist and imitate the character appropriately (Reid and Stanridge, 1981). Thus, adolescent joking represents a synthesis of the preschooler's playful comic style and her preoccupation with sexual and aggressive themes with the schoolchild's interest in verbal jokes and scrupulous attention to detail. In short, adolescents revisit earlier themes and tones, but on a level of

Figure 13.6. The adolescent who relates a joke is not merely conveying a favorite story; she is also trying out various roles and presenting these contrasting versions of herself to others.

cognition and artistry suited to their capabilities.

Adolescents' capacities to operate upon strings of symbols, to reflect on their own intellectual abilities, and to examine language as an object can all be discerned in their humor. As youths gain distance, they can make jokes about jokes, play on words, laugh at the distortion of a punch line, and tell shaggy-dog stories—those endless jokes whose very appeal lies in the fact that they lack an adequate punch line. The very process of telling becomes the focus of these forms of humor and, at times, the violation of humor conventions itself constitutes the humor.

Wolfenstein's presentation illustrates the strengths of focusing on affect. Although one's approach to humor varies with age, the underlying motive of transforming painful experience can be discerned throughout life. The joke serves as a means of coming to grips with, and rendering manageable, certain themes of overriding importance. Moreover, these themes reoccur in adult humor. Children's mockery of grown-ups reverberates in adult jokes that mock authority (for instance, satires about politicians). Preoccupation with sexual matters persists in the form of sexual allusions and the perennial dirty joke. Such themes endure throughout life. Their garb may change, but their purposes remain similar from childhood to senescence.

THE CAPACITY TO APPRECIATE IRONY

Although the hearing and telling of jokes remain popular throughout life, adolescents become able to appreciate a subtler and more complex form of humor as well. Douglass Carmichael (1966) has investigated the adolescent's emerging skill at appreciating certain intricate verbal passages that require the capacity to reason wholly in terms of linguistic propositions. An example comes from the passage, attributed to the physicist Niels Bohr, which you read at the start of the chapter:

There are two kinds of truth,
Deep truth and shallow truth,
And the function of Science
Is to eliminate the deep truth.

As you may have recognized, this passage exemplifies the literary device of *irony:* the use of words to express something other than their literal meaning, often the opposite of what is apparently being said. While *seemingly* contradictory or contrary to usual beliefs, the statement actually conveys some higher truth or insight. Appreciating irony is one of the most sophisticated of human capacities, one calling for formal operational thought and for a delicate orchestration of the adolescent's abilities to perceive, feel, and make in the realm of symbols.

A Logical Analysis. In Carmichael's view, understanding ironic statements generally involves a series of steps. First, one must be sensitive to the complexity of the passage and realize that it is more than simple criticism or sarcasm. Thus, unless one realizes that Bohr is saying something complex and that he is not merely "putting down" his own discipline, one will never appreciate the intended irony.

One must then proceed to a second level, questioning the writer's intent and probing the content of the statement. Why are these strange, apparently contradictory things being said? One recognizes and tries to relate in an intelligible manner the two perspectives at issue. In Bohr's statement, the two perspectives are (1) the deep (or profound) is ordinarily to be preferred to the shallow (or superficial); and (2) science—which we usually honor—eliminates deepness. How can these rival statements both be true?

The challenge of the third stage is to solve the puzzle with a miniature theory that clarifies the relationship between the two contradictory statements and places them in at least temporary accord. Bohr may mean that science cannot hope to explain everything but can make substantial progress by properly trimming its concerns (not trying to answer every big question). Or he may mean that since "depth" implies ambiguity (obscurity), "deepness" is a perilous label for the scientific domain. So viewed, "deep" and "shallow" become double-edged rather than unambiguously good or bad; and science emerges as having both powers and limitations. Any synthesis at this stage must be viewed as tentative: such statements have a variety of possible meanings and the interpreter must remain aware that she can never fully anticipate the author's conscious (and unconscious) intent.

An Investigation. Following the trails blazed by Piaget and Kohlberg, Carmichael set out to discern the cognitive capacities entailed in appreciating irony. He collected and analyzed various ironic passages. This analysis suggested the existence of the three stages of understanding we have just reviewed:

1. awareness of sarcasm and complexity;
2. explicit interest in the author's intent; identification of two perspectives; and
3. detection of a unified vision that is logically plausible, consistent with experience, and faithful to the author's intent; an awareness of the tentativeness of this synthesis.

Carmichael hypothesized that to understand an ironic statement an individual must pass through these levels in the given order. Older individuals tend to pass through the stages more rapidly, perhaps even at such a pace that the first two appear collapsed into one.

Carmichael tested his claims by presenting ironic passages to intelligent youths ranging from tenth graders (aged fifteen to sixteen) to graduate students. After giving their initial reaction to a statement, they were asked to think aloud while trying to unravel the passage.

Results were very much in line with expectations. Individuals almost invariably responded first at a lower level and then at a higher level. The older (and presumably more cognitively advanced) individuals were more likely to pass through all three levels of analysis and at a faster pace, while younger students were more likely to remain at the first level (seeing the statement as complex but no more), or perhaps to move to the second level (discovering the two perspectives but failing to resolve them).

Formal Operations and Irony. Carmichael did not test his subjects for formal operational thinking, but because they were unusually bright and articulate, it seems likely that nearly all would qualify as formal operators in our informal sense—that is, capable of reasoning on the level of words, treating language itself as an object of analysis. Why, then, did only a minority of the subjects successfully detect and analyze irony?

Our earlier comparison of Piaget's and Kohlberg's problems suggests part of the answer. Piaget's tasks require only general familiarity with the equipment and allow free experimentation to arrive at a systematic approach to the problem. In contrast, handling moral dilemmas at the principled level may well require considerable experience in thinking of the perspectives and principles involved, as well as an understanding of and ability to use abstract terms such as justice and equality.

Mastering ironic passages seems to call for similarly specialized experiences. Because each passage has a different subtopic and because the particular words and content used are crucial, each must be attacked afresh. Furthermore, awareness of the author's intent and familiarity with textual analysis in general as well as the particulars of ironic expression are helpful, if not essential. Thus, the ability to appreciate irony requires a highly developed mind and possibly some specific training in literary studies as well.

The appreciation of irony provides an elegant example of how the individual's three developing systems interact at the formal operational level. To understand irony one needs, first of all, to *perceive* the relationships among sets of propositions. Further, one must *feel* the tensions, contradictions, and intentions behind irony. Even the most logical person will fail to appreciate these unless she has undergone enough experience to relate the passage in question to her own life and, thereby, to make the perspectives come alive (Demorest, Silberstein, and Gardner, 1981). And the person who appreciates one ironic statement may fail to understand another just because the themes of the second are not familiar enough to evoke the required feelings. Finally, one must *make* (or effect) an acceptable union of perceptions and feelings. To succeed, one needs to have undergone many experiences, to know life from several perspectives, to appreciate ambiguities, to detect tensions and resolutions. Formal operations by themselves are not enough.

Conclusion: Beyond Formal Operations

Our consideration of various domains of thought indicates that adolescents, much more than younger children, are able to keep in mind an entire network of ideas. They can consider all possible combinations of liquids, various competing values in an ethical di-

lemma, rival perspectives in an ironic passage. In comparing, transforming, reversing, and unifying, adolescents display their capacities to hold a whole structure in mind at once, notice its parts and their relations, and interchange them.

As we have amply documented, not every adolescent can perform these operations in every domain. Indeed, as many as half of the eighteen-year-olds in our society might fail some of Inhelder's and Piaget's problems, respond below the principled level of morality, and prove unable to detect irony. Nonetheless, if one bears various reservations in mind, it seems justified to characterize adolescent thought as a separate and organized cognitive level: in any domain, the adolescent is better able to deal with abstract concepts and verbal propositions, appreciate hypothetical possibilities, attend to language for its own sake, and note its tensions and ambiguities. Not every adolescent is a formal operator, but every normal adolescent displays some signs of formal operations in science, moral judgment, and literary understanding.

This state of affairs has two new consequences. First, because of the ability to survey a field with some perspective, adolescents become aware of and master distinct bodies of knowledge—like Euclidean geometry or developmental psychology. Second, they can conceive of themselves as wholly separate entities, apart from their families, friends, institutions, and community. This can be frightening: as a separate entity, one may feel isolated and vulnerable. At the same time, however, this new awareness of self holds out enormous possibilities. As never before, the adolescent can now plan her own life, assume responsibility for her own fate, consider all possibilities in career, personal life-style, and systems of beliefs.

Children use the word "I" and understand the concept "myself" long before adolescence, but only when they acquire formal operations can they devise and operate upon a symbol that simultaneously designates the various aspects of themselves. Here lies the reason why one's identity—one's sense of self-worth, strengths, problems, and aspirations—comes forward for the first time during adolescence. We shall examine this process in the next chapter.

But discussing adolescent thought raises inevitable questions: Is there a mental stage beyond formal operations? Is there a stage of moral reasoning after principled morality? Are there levels of humor and irony that transcend those explored by researchers like Carmichael? Did Einstein, Plato, or Shakespeare really reason on a level qualitatively different from that of the adolescent's? Or did they too link propositions, apply principled morality, and unite perspectives just as adolescents do, though perhaps more rapidly or fluently and using more complicated subject matter?

There surely seem to be vast differences between the competent adolescent and the creative scientist. On the one hand, the mature adult is capable of holding a structured yet critical view of a whole domain—a work of art, a scientific theory, a discipline, or one's own life—and is also able to move easily within and beyond that domain, to draw analogies with remote bodies of knowledge, to maintain either a calm objectivity or a critical skepticism (Gilligan and Murphy, 1979; Gruber, 1981; LaBouvie-Vief, 1980; Perry, 1968). On the other hand, the average adolescent has as yet little distance from propositional thought about thought, from the ambiguity of moral judgments, from the full appreciation of irony. She has glimpsed the outlines of the highest forms of reasoning but has not yet fully partaken of them. By the same token, the gifted artist's and scientist's ability to create and follow through on new and powerful images, to find problems and

create fields of knowledge and art seems incomparable with the adolescent's skill at solving given problems or mastering well-delineated fields (Arlin, 1975; Getzels and Csikszentmihalyi, 1976). Each of these observations hints at one or more stages beyond formal operations.

But this is speculation, and it will remain so until researchers can precisely state and empirically differentiate the features of a stage beyond adolescent thought. As we have seen, individuals with formal operations can readily fault the formulations of such seminal thinkers as Piaget or Kohlberg. It is far more difficult to come up with an alternative formulation and with new sources of data, which can themselves be subjected to serious scrutiny.

Signposts

Once more in developmental psychology, Piaget and his colleagues, notably Bärbel Inhelder, have defined and described a new level of thinking—the formal operations of adolescence. According to Piaget, adolescents demonstrate formal operations as they reflect on their own thought, deal with hypotheses and theories, systematically examine propositions, explore relations among propositions, predict outcomes without actually performing trials, and master the internal structure of an entire domain. Formal operational thought—the ability to carry out systematic reasoning independent of particular content—is in fact considered by Piaget the high point of human cognitive development.

Some adolescents in our society accomplish all that Piaget has described. Yet, where Piaget's particular scientific tasks have been widely used, an unsettling picture has emerged. Except in certain highly academic surroundings or when aids are provided, formal operations are not readily elicited, and the logical reasoning characteristic of formal operations may not appear. So, in a strict sense, Piaget's claims do not seem applicable to most adolescents in most cultures. However, his viewpoint does seem to capture the more general reflective, speculative, and analytic nature of adolescent thought.

While some of Piaget's colleagues have attempted to "fix up" and continue to use his conception of formal operations, other scholars have sought alternative ways to conceptualize the adolescent's thinking. Some investigators, adopting the task-analytic approach of Robert Siegler, have sought to describe the rules and strategies followed by adolescent subjects, without addressing the question of whether these necessarily entail a new level of thinking; adopting an information-processing approach, they have focused on the increased efficiency, greater memory space, or superior strategies or combinations of strategies available to older individuals. Still others have underscored the metacognitive and metatheoretical capacities that arise during the years surrounding puberty or have pondered whether there may be levels of thought that go beyond formal operations.

An impressive complementary attempt to indicate the nature of adolescent thought is Lawrence Kohlberg's study of moral reasoning. By posing dilemmas to youths of different ages, Kohlberg has convincingly documented that many individuals in our culture pass through a sequence of levels of moral thought—from preconventional morality, in which moral value lies in externals like physical punishments and rewards; through conventional morality, in which moral value lies in adherence to family, group, or national standards; to the principled judgments characteristic of more experienced adolescents and adults, who have come to view actions by the lights of their own conscience. Examining the factors influencing moral development, Kohl-

berg and his colleagues have found that exposure to individuals operating at the next higher stage and experience in making choices that require moral reasoning seem to be especially important in progressing from one level to the next. Doubts about Kohlberg's scheme center on its claims to universality, the possible contaminating role of linguistic or narrative structures in assessing moral judgments, the complex nature of the dilemmas themselves, and the relation of moral judgment to an individual's actual behavior in morally charged situations. And colleagues of Kohlberg have recently placed greater emphasis on the importance of relativistic judgments that reflect sensitivity to the particular issues and feelings in any given context.

The cognitive changes of adolescence exert their influence even in the affect-tinged domains of humor and irony. An adolescent's level of cognition largely determines her understanding of jokes and ironic passages. Yet cognition is not all. For one thing, there is an individual's cognitive style—what she laughs at and when she laughs. In addition, different themes pervade humor at different ages, and these themes reflect the kinds of problems confronted then. Preschool children, for example, laugh at jokes about size and power, at the unexpected, or at whatever others are laughing at. Children in school, who have become preoccupied with knowing, laugh at jokes about being smart or dumb. Adolescent humor combines aggressive and sexual themes with wordplay in a presentation that conveys self as well as story. And in adolescence, appreciation of irony dawns. The adolescent may sense the complexity of an ironic expression or image, question the creator's intent, and come up with a theory to reconcile apparent contradictions. Appreciating irony requires not only certain logical capacities, but also life experiences varied enough to allow the identification and integration of perspectives relevant to each ironic passage. Indeed, it is in humor—more than in science—that the three developing systems of perceiving, making, and feeling interact in the most comprehensive and developed way with complex symbolic forms.

Out of the emerging ability to deal with comprehensive symbolic structures comes what may be the most impressive and important cognitive attainment of adolescence: the construction of a relatively enduring self or identity. So far we have encountered only the cognitive aspects of identity creation. But adolescence is a time of physical, social, and emotional changes as well, and these also exert their influence. In the next chapter, we will consider how the various components of adolescence actually coalesce into an enduring identity. And to gain a fresh perspective on our notions of the self, we will begin by considering whether our American version of adolescence as a turbulent period is in fact universal.

CHAPTER FOURTEEN

The Experience of Adolescence

. . . that blissful time when childhood is just coming to an end, and out of that vast circle, happy and gay, a path takes shape.

–TOLSTOY, *Anna Karenina*

From the muddy concupiscence of the flesh and the hot imagination of puberty. . . . Both love and lust boiled within me and swept my youthful immaturity over the precipice of evil desires to leave me half drowned in a whirlpool of abominable sins.

–ST. AUGUSTINE

Sometime after the first decade of life, humans become capable of reproducing. That period of life when the reproductive processes mature is usually called **puberty.** Although the most evident and rapid changes during puberty are physical, developments also occur in mental functioning, emotions, social interactions, and conception of the self. This larger series of events—spanning nearly the whole second decade of life—is known as **adolescence.**

Having concentrated thus far exclusively on the cognitive milestones, we shall now turn our attention to other phases of adolescence. We shall begin by examining the physical milestones, including the achievement of

mature sexuality, that occur in every normal child. A change in one's body, and in one's body image, is an important event in the life of a growing individual. But the changes in adolescence are more than skin deep. Indeed, at least in the West, adolescence has traditionally been considered a period of great emotional upheaval. But whether these dramatic emotional changes are universal is a more complex question, one requiring a consideration of adolescence in diverse settings.

Accordingly, in this chapter we will contrast the classical view of adolescence with a picture of adolescence in a very different culture, the island of Samoa in the South Seas. As a further means of gaining perspective on the classical view, we will focus on various aspects of adolescence in contemporary American society. We hope to gain some feeling for what the experience of adolescence is like for those individuals who are experiencing it.

As we undertake our explorations in search of the experience of adolescence, we will touch on a number of topics, including the predominant behaviors and value patterns found among adolescents, the effects of social and ethnic backgrounds, certain cognitive differences between males and females, the sometimes rocky course of family and peer relations, and the changes in world view that often accompany adolescence. To guide us, we will return periodically to three major themes:

A first keystone is the **centrality of sex** in the experience of adolescence. This, of course, begins with changes in the body that evoke strong passions and make possible (and desirable) sexual relations, usually with individuals of the opposite sex. But it entails as well important changes in one's attitudes and values, constant concern with appropriate sex roles, and even possible differences in cognitive profiles and cognitive styles.

A second leitmotiv of adolescence is the **quest for autonomy.** Since early childhood, the youth has been spending an increasing amount of time away from home and has in various ways moved some distance from her parents and siblings. But during adolescence, these trends come to a head as the youth, perhaps for the first time, envisions a permanent separation from the family. The peer group competes with and sometimes replaces the family as the primary reference point. Experimentation with sex, drugs, and alternative life-styles can be another means of declaring autonomy. And, of course, choices about education and career underscore the individual's considerable need for—though sometimes also her fear of—autonomy.

A final compass point in the experience of adolescence is the youth's increasing defini-

tion of her own **identity.** The various changes in sexuality and autonomy came together as the young adult forges for herself (and feels in herself) a new identity—a sense of self that confirms her own goals and, at the same time, her place within a larger community. We will turn to the view of two clinicians, Harry Stack Sullivan and Erik Erikson, as we observe how this search for identity develops and, hopefully, comes to a satisfactory resolution, thereby setting the stage for the rest of life.

Physical Changes in Adolescence

Sometime after children are ten years old, hormonal secretions from the pituitary gland, which lies at the base of the brain, begin to stimulate other endocrine glands: the ovaries (in females), the testes (in males), and the adrenal glands (see Figure 14.1). As hormones from these glands enter the bloodstream, bodily changes that will eventually make the individual capable of reproducing begin to occur.

Reproduction in the male depends on the production of sperm cells, as well as on the capacities to achieve penile erection and to ejaculate the semen in which these cells are contained. These events usually occur between twelve and fifteen years of age. The equivalent reproductive capacity in the female accompanies the first menstrual flow, usually between the ages of eleven and fourteen. The female now produces eggs; when one of these eggs is united with a sperm, the now-fertilized egg develops over a nine-month course into another human being.

Although the youth's initial production of sperm or egg is considered central to the delineation of puberty and thus of adolescence, several associated sexual changes assume importance in the eyes of the community and of the young adolescent. Certain pubescent changes are considered to be **primary sexual changes.** In the young female, in addition to ovulation, the vagina, clitoris, and uterus increase in size. In males the advent of ejaculation is accompanied by the growth of the testes and penis. Along with these primary changes come several **secondary sexual changes.** In both sexes, pubic hair starts to appear. Males develop broader shoulders; an enlargement of the larynx leads to a deepening of the voice (Peterson and Taylor, 1980); and facial hair begins to appear, first on the

upper lip and then on the cheeks and chin. In females the breasts begin to grow larger and the hips widen, while the shoulders remain relatively narrow.

Though dramatic, these sexual changes form but part of a larger pattern of growth in the first part of the second decade of life. Girls experience a growth spurt, usually between ten and one-half and thirteen years of age, somewhat before the start of menstruation (Faust, 1977). During this time, they will gain two to three inches in height and ten to

Figure 14.1. The production of various hormones stimulates the raft of physical changes in both males and females that mark the beginning of adolescence.

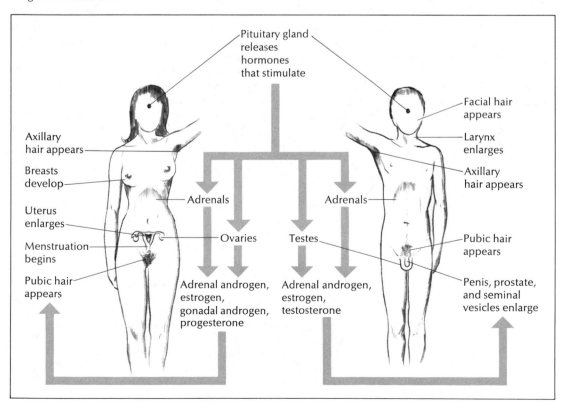

twelve pounds in weight every year. Boys also grow rapidly in a short time. On the average, between twelve and one-half and fifteen years of age, they may grow each year as much as four to five inches, and put on twelve to fourteen pounds. Because the girl's spurt typically occurs before the boys', there is usually a period sometime during early adolescence when girls are actually taller than boys. Yet, by the time they are adults, boys measure 10 percent larger than girls in most dimensions.

Changes in sheer size are accompanied by changes in overall physical shape. Boys acquire wide shoulders and a muscular neck, whereas girls experience an enlargement of the pelvic (hip) region as well as breast development. These different areas of growth can yield curious individual differences, for example, in the contrasting ways in which boys and girls carry books to school (Jenni and Jenni, 1976; see the box). Girls add a layer of fat that softens the curves of the face and the body, whereas boys' faces become more angular and muscular: nose and chin become somewhat more prominent, skin becomes coarser, and the secretion of sweat becomes more pronounced.

In both boys and girls, nearly every region of the body grows. Arms and legs become longer; the chest and abdomen increase in girth; bones grow wider. Thus youths for a time look somewhat long-legged and gawky. Liver, kidneys, and heart all exhibit rapid growth. The lungs' strength and vital capacity (amount of air that can be exhaled after a full inhaling) also increase, particularly among boys. And the strength of muscles greatly increases, again especially among boys. In fact, although no difference is found before puberty in strength of arms or hands, boys become significantly stronger than girls during adolescence. Here lies one reason for the dramatic increase in athletic ability in most boys at this time.

Because the skull bones thicken, adolescents' heads increase somewhat in length and breadth. But their brains, which had attained about 90 percent of adult weight by age five, grow very little. The cognitive changes of adolescents, discussed below, apparently arise from reorganization of brain structures, not from the development of new ones. (For a somewhat different conception, see Epstein, 1973.)

Sex Differences in Carrying Behavior

Stand outside any school or library and watch the people as they come and go. You will notice that men and women carry books differently. "Females usually clasp books against the body with one or both arms wrapped around the books. Males almost always carry books in one hand at the side of the body" (Jenni, 1976, p. 323).

Such were the findings of Mary Jenni (Jenni, 1976; Jenni and Jenni, 1976). In a large group of subjects, ranging in age from eighteen to seventy five and coming from the United States, Canada, and Central America: males consistently used one method of carrying and females another. Furthermore, the size of the load had no significant effect on carrying style.

(continued)

What might account for these differences? Is it body structure? Strength? Custom? Jenni sees social pressure as a major determining factor. Though sex differences were significant at all ages, they were most extreme at adolescence—a time marked by a preoccupation with sexual status and conformity. In contrast, most variation was observed among mixed-aged adults for whom conformity is less of a concern. In addition, men were less likely to use female methods of carrying than vice versa. This fact parallels the general tendency for females to adopt opposite sex-role behaviors more often than men. Perhaps societies are more tolerant of atypical behavior in women.

But social pressure alone cannot explain these different behaviors. One must ask what caused the two styles of carrying to develop. Clearly, men and women have different body structures that may well affect the body positions they assume. The fact that women have wider hips that create a "hip shelf" may make certain carrying positions more comfortable for them than for men. Furthermore, Jenni points out that females in general tend to prefer a more closed position, in which the limbs cover and protect the body, in comparison to males, who leave their bodies more open and accessible (Hewes, 1957). Similar sex differences have also been observed in apes (Wickler, 1969). In light of this evidence, the two methods of carrying may well reflect biological factors as well as social ones. Though how men and women carry books is not of much import in itself, Jenni's dramatic and consistent findings illustrate the powerful influence and interplay of biological and social factors in determining patterns of behavior.

Just what determines or prevents the smooth course of puberty is still not known (Peterson and Taylor, 1980). Evidently, hormonal secretions are important in bringing about the most rapid changes in the second decade of life but the timing of these changes is not rigidly fixed. For example, as a result of emotional stress, the master regulating gland, the pituitary, can be inhibited in which case children will cease growing and remain at a pre-adolescent size (Restak, 1979b). The flexibility of the physical course of puberty is further underscored by two striking facts: over the past century, the age of onset of major pubertal changes has advanced by as much as two years (see Figure 14.2), and the average height of adolescents has increased several inches. Such factors as superior nutrition, better health practices, and cleaner living conditions are often held responsible for these trends, which have occurred chiefly in the developed countries. These trends themselves

result from improvements in our society; they testify to remarkable developmental plasticity, but they can also have certain less desirable consequences. For example, the increased prevalence of unwanted teenage pregnancies can be attributed in part to the lengthened reproductive capacity in the years before the youth normally assumes the status of an adult.

Two Views of Adolescence

THE CLASSICAL VIEW

The dramatic changes accompanying puberty help signal the adulthood that is fast approaching. As boys are becoming men, and girls are becoming women, they begin to regard themselves with new esteem. But this period of rapid change can also become a time of embarrassment, bewilderment, or even despair.

Next to physical changes, the most obvious ones involve emotions. While the feelings of the child during the latency period appear somewhat unfocused and superficial, adolescence sparks deepened sensitivity and passion. More sustained and intense feelings are now directed at one or a few individuals: there is a new capacity for deeper emotional relations and a far stronger desire for sexual union.

The way in which these changes are expressed will inevitably reflect the values and expectations of the adolescent's society. According to one popular nineteenth-century view (see Elder, 1980; Grinder, 1967; Rogers, 1972), adopted by G. Stanley Hall (1904), epochal changes in the child's emotional well-being marked adolescence as a period of great promise as well as exceptional turbulence and stress. Coming to grips with sexual changes and feelings, personality changes, strong conflicts with the older generation, increasing demands and pivotal decisions about work,

Figure 14.2. Median ages at menarche from 1845 to 1969 in selected European countries and the United States. (Roche, 1979)

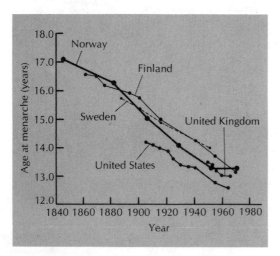

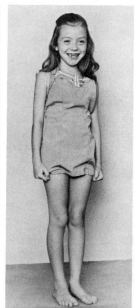

Figure 14.3. Earning the eternal gratitude of students of physical development, photographer Bob Williams photographed his daughter Kristin wearing the same bathing suit at regular intervals for sixteen years. The results speak for themselves.

life-style, friends, and so on—all plagued youths of this age. No normal person could pass through this period unaffected, and many were deeply scarred.

This traditional view was generally accepted by Sigmund Freud (1938b) and his followers. Anna Freud spoke for the psychoanalytic school:

Adolescents are excessively egotistic, regarding themselves as the center of the universe and the sole object of interest, and yet at no time in later life are they capable of so much self-sacrifice and devotion. . . . On the one hand they throw themselves enthusiastically into the life of the community and, on the other, they have an overpowering longing for solitude. They oscillate between blind submission to some self-chosen leader and defiant rebellion against any and every authority. They are selfish and materially-minded and at the same time full of lofty idealism. . . . Their moods veer between light-hearted

optimism and the blackest pessimism. Sometimes they will work with indefatigable enthusiasms and at other times they are sluggish and apathetic [1946, pp. 149–150].

Consistent with the psychoanalytic thesis, the adolescent, like the child during the Oedipal stage, is beset by sexual pressures and strivings. But the sexual urges of adolescents are now directed toward a peer, most typically of the opposite sex, rather than toward the parent of the opposite sex. Though more realistic than those of the toddler, these sexual strivings are punctuated by conflict, strong anxiety, and tensions. Frequently, there are continual and often painful conflicts with one's parents, which may involve repressed sexual feelings on the part of both generations.

Accompanying this traumatic view was the belief that adolescents needed various psychological defense mechanisms, to serve as armor against the full impact of the changes they had to confront. As in earlier periods of life, there would be a need to repress one's strongest and most disturbing feelings; and indeed, it has been claimed by clinicians that adults often have amnesia for the events of puberty, particularly ones that are affectively charged (A. Freud, 1958; Sommer, 1978). Adolescents are characterized by regression, a return to patterns of childhood, as a means of confronting unresolved drives, conflicts, infantile longings, and narcissistic tendencies. But whereas in other life periods regression is deemed a negative process, several students of adolescent psychosexual development consider regression a necessary and helpful part of maturation (Blos, 1968). One can only grow up and become a suitable member of the adult culture if one has satisfactorily come to grips with and worked through the various feelings, desires, and fears of earlier phases of childhood (Adelson and Doehrman, 1980).

THE CLASSICAL VIEW CHALLENGED: MARGARET MEAD IN SAMOA

As a young anthropologist in the 1920s, Margaret Mead set out to challenge the classical view of adolescence. Questioning whether our Western portrait of adolescence was, indeed, universal, Mead embarked upon an investigation of life among preliterate peoples on the island of Samoa in the South Seas (1939).

Focusing on women, Mead found that very young Samoan girls stay near home and cling closely to their mothers or older siblings. By age seven or so, there are strong antagonisms between boys and girls, and children form groups with peers of the same sex. By and large youngsters are left alone, so long as they carry out their chores. Although girls often have to look after younger siblings, they still have time for various activities, which typically include watching childbirth, playing tricks, and "ambushing" pairs of lovers.

With puberty comes entrance into the fabric of society. Both boys and girls are placed into formal groups that are gradually invested with obligations and privileges. Girls, soon to become involved in love relationships, now have specific tasks to perform, and they begin to master the roles that will soon constitute their daily lives.

As Mead described it, the growth of Samoan girls is smooth and natural, in sharp contrast to the adolescent years as traditionally protrayed in our society. As her new role becomes apparent, the young girl assists in adult activities and is charged with responsibilities for child care. She can catch fish, climb, grate fruit, clean house, and participate in dances and rituals.

In Samoa, boys and girls become acquainted at an early age with the biological factors of life, death, and sex. By six or seven, children generally masturbate frequently; by ten they know about the conduct of sexual relations; and by adolescence they are devoting considerable energy to sexual and love relations. There is little hesitation or ambivalence about sexuality, which is approached through both secret and open relationships and through ceremonious courtships. The open, casual manner in which sexuality is treated results in less guilt and shame than in Western culture. The Samoan youth is spared the anxiety and confusion that youth of Western society must typically face and battle.

Growing up in Samoa proves generally easy because life there is apparently uncomplicated. Emotional relations are treated lightly, childrearing is treated casually. There is little competition among relatives, little opportunity—or desire—for changing routines. And, as a consequence, adolescence is uneventful. As Mead concluded:

Adolescence represented no period of crisis or stress but was instead an orderly developing of a set of slowly maturing interests and activities. The girls' minds were perplexed by no conflicts, troubled by no philosophical queries, beset by no remote ambitions. To live as a girl with many lovers as long as possible, and then marry in one's own village, near one's own relatives, and to have many children, these were uniform and satisfying ambitions [Mead, 1939, p. 157].

Mead contrasted the Samoan pattern of growth with the typical picture of American society in the early part of the century. Clearly Samoan children had a much easier, less conflict-ridden life than did their American peers whose lives were filled with opportunities, tensions, desires to achieve, and the neuroses and complexes that result when important goals are thwarted, then as now. Strong feelings occupy a more central role in both adolescent and adult life. Sexuality, autonomy, and identity are simply not major issues for adolescents in Samoa. Moreover, whereas Samoan culture features a closely integrated set of activities, our society is characterized by diversity and fragmentation.

But Mead did not conclude that the Samoan way is problem-free. While our society tolerates diversity, the Samoans leave little opportunity for difference and, indeed, isolate deviants from the group. Whereas we allow and encourage individuality, the Samoans insist on one standard of conduct, thereby reducing the likelihood of clever inventions, novel feelings, or unique interpersonal relations.

Mead discerned a moral in this, one as relevant today as in decades past. Our civilization harbors many stresses that contribute to the pained years of adolescence. But because these stresses may also give rise to growth and strength, we should not strive to erase them. Rather, we should recognize them, seek to understand them, and prepare our youths for the difficult but important personal and societal choices that will confront them. Choice is, after all, the inescapable burden of freedom. From such understanding may well

come increased stability as well as that special capacity for creative change that has been the genius of our civilization.

Varieties of Adolescence and Rites of Initiation

Margaret Mead's study demonstrated that a single view of adolescent experience was untenable: if there could be turbulence (as in America), there could also be stability (as in Samoa). And of course, there are many variations between these extremes. For example, among the Alor of Indonesia, young children are allowed much sexual freedom, but sexual activity is forbidden during the latter years of childhood; in contrast, among the Sirono in South America, no girl is allowed to play sexually before puberty but intercourse becomes customary once she has menstruated (Peterson and Taylor, 1980). Once such cultural differences had been established (see also Benedict, 1949; Goethals and Klos, 1976; Kardiner, 1945; Mead, 1939) social scientists became interested in the *nature* of the differences. They compared the adolescent experiences in various surroundings and attempted to pinpoint the contributing factors. To put it another way, they examined how different cultures modulate the physiological events of puberty.

A popular and intriguing subject for cross-cultural research is the **initiation rite,** a ceremony with which a society marks the passage of a youth from childhood to adulthood. Some cultures perform violent ceremonies in which the sexual organs of men and (less often) women are mutilated or otherwise subjected to stress. Among the Thonga tribe of Africa, for example:

When a boy is somewhere between ten and sixteen years of age, he is sent by his parents to a circumcision school which is held every four or five years. Here, in company with his age mates,

Figure 14.4. As part of an initiation rite in which he will earn full-fledged adult status, this youthful Masai is receiving a ritual haircut at the hands of his mother.

he undergoes severe hazing by the adult males of the society. The initiation begins when each boy runs the gauntlet between two rows of men who beat him with clubs. At the end of this experience, he is stripped of his clothes and his hair is cut. He is next met by a man covered with lion manes and is seated upon a stone facing this "lion man." Someone then strikes him from behind and when he turns his head to see who has struck him, his foreskin is seized and in two movements cut by the lion man. Afterwards he is secluded for three months in the yards of mysteries, where he can be seen only by the initiated. It is especially taboo for a woman to approach these boys during their seclusion; and if a woman should glance at the leaves with which the circumcised covers his wound and which form his only clothing, she must be killed [Whiting, Kluckhohn, and Anthony, 1958, p. 368].

Initiation rites vary widely in length, violence, and elaborateness (Bettelheim, 1962; Grinder, 1975; Rogers, 1972); they may be joyous or traumatic and painful. But whatever their specific features within a given culture, these rites mark the transition to membership in the adult society. Since the actual physical changes are often gradual, initiation rites serve as a dramatic and decisive way for societies to confer adult status on their youths. As such, the rites clearly play a crucial social role, symbolizing the transmitting of love and power to the next generation. But whether the rites serve other functions as well, and why they differ so strikingly from one culture to another, has been the subject of much debate.

RITES AND SEX-ROLE IDENTITY

In an attempt to untangle the mystery of initiation rites, John Whiting and his colleagues (Whiting, Kluckhohn, and Anthony, 1958) hypothesized that initiation rites might occur chiefly in societies in which certain types of family ties prevail. Initially inspired by psychoanalytic theory, the Whiting team suggested that these rites function to sever the powerful Oedipal relation between mother and son and to affirm the boy's membership into male society. They predicted and subsequently confirmed that cultures that foster more intense Oedipal relations (for example, where mother and child share the same bed) would be more likely to practice initiation rites.

Challenging the Oedipal explanation, Frank Young (1962) has proposed that initiation rites are particularly likely in polygamous societies, in which a man must support several women. Such societies emphasize the differences between the sexes by demanding considerable male solidarity. Young believes that stressful initiation rites offer a decisive drama that prepares an adolescent male for life in this society. Like Whiting, Young finds support for his theory in cross-cultural studies.

In response to this rival explanation, Whiting has modified his theory (Burton and Whiting, 1961). Initiation rites are an effort to resolve a conflict in an individual's perceived sexual identity. For example, a boy's strong Oedipal ties to his mother and simultaneous envy of his father's powerful role in patriarchal society will result in deep anxiety during adolescence. Radical action is therefore

thought necessary to counteract this ambivalence. Herein lies a suitable stimulus for initiation rites: they can confirm publicly—perhaps through measures like circumcision—the youth's actual sexual identity.

Despite their different emphases, Whiting, Young, and other observers agree that most cultures are preoccupied with sexual differences at puberty; and each theorist finds in the initiation rites an instrument whereby the adolescent male can explore the meaning and limitations of his sex-role identity. One can also see at work here the kind of "positive regression" described by clinicians such as Peter Blos (1968). In order to assume his proper place within the adult male hierarchy, the youth is subjected to a series of harsh experiences that force him to confront again the strivings and fears of the early years of life.

But what of initiation rites in the young female's life? Why are such ceremonies less frequent and usually less prolonged and less violent? Perhaps it is more vital to mark the male's transition to adulthood because he typically has greater status than the female. Or perhaps the first menstruation serves as a natural and unmistakable indication of adulthood, making further ceremonies unnecessary (Rogers, 1972). It is not surprising that female initiation rites are more likely to occur in societies where the girl continues to live with her parents after marriage. In such cases, the attainment of maturity is less clearly marked, and the need for cultural confirmation accordingly becomes more acute (J. K. Brown, 1963, 1969).

RITES IN OUR CULTURE

An initiation rite achieves one important goal: it removes any doubt in the mind of the youth (or the rest of society) that a decisive step toward adulthood has been taken.

Clearly, a marking of such decisiveness is not essential; neither Samoans nor Americans feature dramatic initiation rites, and yet the transition to adulthood occurs. In the case of Samoa, the absence of a lengthy and intensive attachment between son and mother and the overall smoothness and gradualness of growth seem to make a dramatic initiation rite unnecessary. But in our society, and perhaps in other societies, the absence of an initiation rite may increase the likelihood of a long, somewhat formless, and perhaps difficult adolescence. This may be why a peculiarly difficult adolescence marks the lives of many individuals in Western society.

To be sure, vestiges of initiation rites can be found our culture. Within traditional religions, ceremonies like the Christian First Communion or the Jewish bar mitzvah mark the child's entrance into the adult congregation. Many community organizations celebrate adolescence with special ceremonies or events, such as debutante or "sweet 16" parties. Some organizations even conduct vestiges of initiating activities, such as pledging into fraternities or hazing freshmen. Not infrequently, youths themselves will organize groups that are devoted to marking and smoothing the route to adulthood; consciousness-raising groups of young women are one recent instance. In an informal effort to find signs of their transition to maturity, American youths themselves observe, value, and announce publicly any number of landmarks: the first ejaculation, the start of menstruation, the first date, the first sexual union, the first automobile, graduation from school, marriage. The fact that only some events relate directly to sexual maturity or sex-role identity suggests that growing up in our society may involve more milestones than does coming of age in certain primitive societies.

Each society has definite views of and expectations concerning its youth. In the absence of formal means of announcing these conceptions, youths or parents are likely to improvise suitable formats. The prevalence of informal milestones within our society suggests a felt need among adolescents for some kind of recognition of the transition to adulthood. Formal rites may be more needed, and more likely to occur, where sexual identity has been less well established. And, indeed, studies have indicated that males raised by a single female parent seem more likely to participate in gangs, mysterious rites, and other initiation activities (J. K. Brown, 1969; Glueck and Glueck, 1952). The full significance of this finding is difficult to determine. Life in a single-parent home is also correlated with lower socioeconomic status, and these initiation rites may to some extent reflect social-class membership rather than the absence of the father.

Varieties of Adolescent Experience

Our brief survey indicates the rich variety of cultural patterns during adolescence, including the diverse initiation rites that may mark this special period. Even within our own culture, we encounter staggering diversity. Values are changing rapidly: people come from diverse backgrounds, childrearing practices are varied, emphasis on individual experience is strong. Nonetheless, it is important to discover common patterns within the experiences of American adolescents and, where possible, to make preliminary sense of them. Because of their relatively predictable effects on adolescent experience, we shall begin with a review of physical development and with a discussion of the effects of ethnic background. Then, after a consideration of the special pitfalls surrounding research on adolescent values, behaviors, and thought processes, we shall consider these more elusive yet equally significant facets of the adolescent experience.

Figure 14.5. Many cultures perform ceremonies known as "initiation rites," which mark the youth's entrance to adulthood. Two such examples are the bar mitzvah of the Jewish tradition and initiation in the spirit house in New Guinea.

ONSET OF PUBERTY

The timing of the onset of puberty can create revealing variations in adolescent experience, affecting, for example, the way in which youths think about their bodies and depict themselves in drawings (Koff, Rierdan, and Silverstone, 1978; Koff, Rierdan, and Sheingold, 1980; Rierdan and Koff, 1980a) (see the box). Several studies have shown that American boys who experience the physical changes of puberty early in their second decade have certain advantages over their less precocious peers (Jones and Bayley, 1950; Weatherley, 1964). They are more likely to be rated as attractive and masculine. They are less tense, more in control of themselves, more likely to be treated as leaders, and more likely to have older friends. They are also more likely to have a positive self-image, to succeed in athletics, and to feel comfortable with who they are. Late developers, on the other hand, tend to feel different, vulnerable, and unwanted. And these differences in self-evaluation persist

over many years (Clausen, 1975; Jones, 1957). Apparently, though there may be a certain cost in terms of loss of spontaneity and curiosity (Peskin, 1967), most of the features associated with masculine maturity are valued by the society at large.

A somewhat different picture pertains to adolescent girls. For them, early maturation creates feelings of difference and vulnerability, although occasionally it may bring enhanced social prestige (Faust, 1960; Weatherley, 1964). Their age-mates, still prepubescent, seem more successful with their peers and content with their lot. One possible reason for these consequences is that early maturing girls are often large and may be perceived as masculine. Another is that early maturity prepares girls to participate in sexual relations before they may wish to do so. There may also be an interaction with social class: in one study a positive correlation emerged for middle-class girls between early maturation and self-confidence, while in the case of working-class girls a negative relationship obtained between the

Menarche and Self-Image

For a girl, puberty is marked by menarche, the onset of her first menstrual period, clearly a crucial event in her life. Once a girl, she is now a sexually mature woman able to bear children. But what is the psychological aftereffect of this event? Does it lead the young woman to view herself differently? Is menarche primarily a disruptive and anxiety-producing experience or a positive and integrative one? Is womanhood met with delight, with dread, or with indifference?

By examining drawings of the human figure done by pre- and postmenarcheal women, Elissa Koff and her colleagues have offered some initial answers to these questions (Koff, Rierdan, and Silverstone, 1978; Rierdan and Koff, 1980b). The task was simple: They asked seventh and eighth grade girls first to "draw a person," then to draw a person of the other sex, and finally to give a name to each figure. Using previously designed rating scales, the drawings were first scored for degree of sexual differentiation (how different the male and female figures were from one another) and then for signs of anxiety, as evidenced by aggression and insecurity.

The findings clearly suggest that psychological changes do accompany the biological event of menarche. Postmenarcheal girls produced more sexually differentiated human figures than did premenarcheal girls. (See Figure 14.6.) All postmenarcheal subjects drew a female figure first, while one quarter of the premenarcheal women drew male figures. Only on the anxiety indices were there no reported differences. Menarche, then, seems to signal a greater awareness of one's own sexual identity and a heightened preoccupation with the differences between sexes, a finding consistent with the behavior and attitudes of adolescent females.

Figure 14.6. These two drawings illustrate how a young adolescent girl's self-image changes at the onset of puberty.
The left one was done by a premenarcheal girl at the age of 12 years one month. The right was done by the same girl just six months later but after her first menstrual period.

same two variables (Clausen, 1975). Finally, it is possible that an adolescent's experiences as an early maturer interact with the kind of school she is attending. Early maturers in the elementary school (kindergarten through eighth grade) are out of step with their peers, both male and female; in contrast, if youngsters the same age are attending a junior high school (grades seven through nine), they will be in step with the majority of the population and consequently have a more positive experience (Blyth, Simmons, and Bush, 1978). Whatever the reason, the fact that early maturation exerts different effects on the two sexes and on different social classes, perhaps creating different "deviants," demonstrates the importance of how a phenomenon is perceived by the individual and by others.

ETHNIC BACKGROUND

A second significant contribution to varieties in the experiences of American adolescents is ethnic and cultural differences in the population. One well-known example comes from Francis Hsu's comparison of adolescents from Chinese-American and Anglo-American backgrounds (Hsu, 1953). The latter generally come from households where the ties with parents are strong, where childhood is considered a special time, and where parents are, at best, ambivalent about their offspring's leaving home. Children thus feel an urgent need to break away from their parents. As they strive to affirm their individuality, they often become critical of parents and social values.

In contrast, youths of Chinese extraction are initiated into the adult world early. Less mystique surrounds childhood, parenting is less tense, and parents become less upset when their children eventually withdraw from the household. Because of this early initiation and reduced parental control, Chinese youths are less likely to rebel against parental authority. Paradoxically, Chinese youths are also

more likely to maintain ties with their parents and to honor features of their cultural tradition (Kingston, 1980).

The end result—a highly stressful adolescence for Anglo-Americans and a comparatively benign one for Chinese-Americans. To illustrate this disparity, Hsu points out that Chinese male adolescents commit fewer crimes than Chinese males of any other age, whereas Anglo-American male adolescents commit more crimes than do Anglo-American males of any other age.

Once one ventures beyond the American shores, ethnic differences of course become even more pronounced. Consider, for example, the goals and experiences esteemed by youths from different cultures. Though there are, of course, similarities, Americans stress material well-being, individual achievements, and religious salvation; Australians emphasize peace of mind, an active life, and a cheerful attitude; Israelis strive for individual competence, peace, and national security, while youths in Papua New Guinea value a world at peace and the achieving of salvation. Certainly, the real-world threats and possibilities felt in each culture exert a powerful influence on the goals of youths reared in each (Feather, 1975, 1980; Rokeach, 1973).

VALUES AND BEHAVIORAL PATTERNS

As we have mentioned, adolescence in American society is marked by characteristic difficulties. Though they may appear physically mature, youths of thirteen or even seventeen are not yet equipped to participate as full adults in our society (Keniston, 1971). They still require further education or training, often live at home, and may be reluctant (or unable) to select a mate, vocation, and a lifestyle. As a result, uncertainty, frustration, and tension often prevail.

Despite differences in the timing of puberty, and the facts of one's ethnic heritage, youths raised in America undergo many common experiences. These derive from a number of factors: youths in America witness the same media of communication; they attend schools that present certain subject matters and exhibit a definite set of values; and perhaps most significantly, they are part of a society where one does not generally choose a career, a mate, and a style of living for a number of years after the onset of puberty. As a result of these factors, American youths experience a high degree of uncertainty (and often associated tension) about their sex roles, their attainment of autonomy, and their achievement of identity. Perhaps, indeed, it is in these areas of concern, more than in specific experiences, that one finds the central aspects of American adolescence.

Although the period of adolescence has been much studied, we are still relatively ignorant about adolescents' beliefs and values. In the case of standard experiments, it is hard to secure willing subjects; those who do participate often prove to be self-conscious and suspicious of the experimenters' motives; for a variety of reasons, they may not do their best. Thus, the experimentation that has been conducted often yields questionable results.

Many investigators have used questionnaires to probe adolescents' opinions and attitudes. But these procedures either allow such open responses that it is difficult to find common threads among the data, or they restrict responses to only a few choices and thus may not reflect exactly what is on the subjects' minds. An additional problem surrounding questionnaires is the tendency of individuals to give the answers that they feel they should give, to distort their responses (either consciously or unconsciously) rather than to provide the most candid response. Sometimes systematic observation can yield valuable insights: however, adolescents' desires for secrecy and their sensitivity to outsiders can make such techniques and methods difficult.

These difficulties in studying adolescence have produced mixed and even conflicting results. For instance, some observers stress adolescents' freedom from their parents (Coleman, 1961; Musgrove, 1964); others remark on their continuing dependence (Campbell, 1969; Kandel and Lesser, 1969); and still others feel that the character of the situation determines whether a youth will heed parent or peer (Brittain, 1969). Strong differences have been voiced on the degree of turbulence in American adolescence. The dominant view in both scholarship and the mass media still stresses the many difficulties of the period, but many authorities regard American adolescence as quite free of strains (Offer, 1969). In fact, according to one expert, "Maturation in adolescence most often takes place in steady, silent, and non-tumultuous ways" (Josselson, 1980, p. 189). Because experts disagree so pointedly, generalizations are not always reliable, particularly when millions of adolescents are in question. But some threads of adolescent experience that have been studied merit our attention. These include adolescents' attitudes and beliefs, their values, their thought processes, their relation to family and peers, and their views of the world and of themselves.

MATTERS OF SEX

Much more than was the case in middle childhood, youths in adolescence come to care deeply about societal and personal issues. They become more knowledgeable about political events, religious issues, and social relations and topics. And they are much concerned with ethics and morality: what they should do about interpersonal relations, sexual relationships, personal integrity, or political issues. Much of this concern is expressed in argument and discussion. It also shows in active experimentation, in trying out roles and assessing how they fit.

Although adolescents' political, religious, and social attitudes have been periodically scrutinized (Douvan and Adelson, 1966; Gallatin, 1980; Rogers, 1972), by far the greatest attention has been given to their behaviors and attitudes in the area of sexual relationships. This attention reflects both the adolescents' experiences and the society's concerns.

Decades ago, the traditional view of adolescence was that males and females differed considerably in their sexual beliefs and behaviors. Men were seen as in almost constant need of sexual release. Although some women were thought suitable for sexual adventures, the rest were idealized and sought for marriage. Women were seen as afraid of or at best ambivalent about sex, wanting to preserve their virtue for their husbands, and eventually serving their husbands by tolerating (or submitting to) their sexual demands.

How much validity this extreme view ever possessed is difficult to determine. However, such a caricature holds little relevance for most of American society today. Indeed, some commentators have stressed the extent to which men and women are becoming increasingly similar, approaching an ideal of unisex or **androgyny** (having features of both sex roles) and downplaying the differences among sexes. In some ways, this position may be valid: the double standard is fast disappearing, and sex is considered a private affair that society should not attempt to control (Dreyer, 1975).

Yet, as Joseph Adelson has stressed, reports on the demise of the differences between the two sexes are premature. From early life boys and girls think about themselves and act in divergent ways, and they continue to do so, though in varying ways, throughout life (Feldman, Biringen, and Nash, 1981). In study after study, males emerge as more concerned with action, competition, rationality, and domination, while females stress communal

and interpersonal values such as generosity, sympathy, and artistry (Feather, 1980).

Different attitudes about the pace and course of life are documented in a study by Robert May and Phebe Cramer (cited in Adelson, 1980). When shown an ambiguous picture of male and female acrobats in flight, females characteristically invented stories that move through a time of suffering and doubt, but culminate in an ending that features success and happiness. On the other hand, the typical male story initially features physical and emotional excitement, which eventually gives way to failure and despair. Such differences can be found as early as age six and are well established by the time of adolescence.

SEXUAL ATTITUDES AND BEHAVIORS

No area of study is more private, or more prone to misinterpretation, than that of individual attitudes and behaviors in matters of sex (Kinsey, Pomeroy, and Martin, 1948; Kinsey et al., 1953). This is also an area where attitudes are changing rapidly and generalizations risk being out of date. Indeed, looking just at trends in the past several years, researchers reported a 30 percent increase in the prevalence of premarital intercourse between 1971 and 1976; this comes on top of earlier increases, such as the increase from 21 percent to 34 percent of women engaging in premarital intercourse between 1958 and 1968 (Peterson and Taylor, 1980). Rather than representing a deviant behavior, such sexual experimenting is becoming the behavioral norm.

Few authorities would dispute the increase in sexual involvement during adolescence, particularly among women. Yet the incidence of involvement differs widely across studies. For example, in a study conducted in 1975 in Illinois, about one third of the twelfth grade boys and one half of the girls of the same age indicated that they had engaged in premarital coitus (Jessor and Jessor, 1975); another study reported one in three seventeen-year-olds admitting to coital experiences (Vener and Stewart, 1974). A recent report states that just over 40 percent of all teenagers have had sexual intercourse (Brozan, 1981). But in a survey conducted in New York City, 72 percent of boys and 57 percent of girls between the ages of sixteen and nineteen reported having sexual relations, most on a regular basis (Brozan, 1978).

In the case of the New York study, it proved possible to estimate the accuracy of subjects' responses. Their own ambivalence about sexual behavior comes from the fact that 9 percent of subjects known to have been pregnant reported on the questionnaire that they had never been pregnant. Further, 4 percent of teenage mothers denied that they had ever had sex. Ignorance about sexual matters was striking. In fact, only 28 percent of subjects knew at what point during the month conception is possible (Youth Values Project, 1979).

Certainly, a decisive moment in a youth's life occurs at the time when he or she ceases to be a virgin. In an effort to study the transition from virginity to nonvirginity, Shirley Jessor and Richard Jessor (1975) administered a long questionnaire annually to the same group of several hundred high school and college students. As high school seniors, 27 percent of males and 38 percent of females claimed not to be virgins. By the end of college, 82 percent of males and 85 percent of females were not virgins. (This sample may be somewhat unusual; in most studies the lack of virginity is greater among males than among females.)

Both male and female nonvirgins differed from virgins in several respects. The nonvirgins placed a higher value on independence and were more tolerant of deviation. They were more likely to see their friends as toler-

ant of social and sexual experimentation. At the same time, they were more critical of their society, placed less value on societal goals, and were less involved in traditional activities like churchgoing. Of special interest is the finding that virgins who were shortly to become nonvirgins were more likely to respond like nonvirgins than were those virgins whose status would not soon change. Apparently, the change in attitudes preceded the change in behavior.

In our society the significance of the first sexual bond seems different for males than for females. For females, a love relationship almost always provides the context for the first coital experience. In fact, in one study, 59 percent of the women planned to marry their first partners, and an additional 22 percent were in love though they had no plans to marry (Simon, Berger, and Gagnon, 1972). In contrast, nearly half of the men in the same study were not emotionally involved with their initial partner, and one third of them had coitus with their initial partner but a single time. Men were also more likely to talk to others about their first sexual experience, particularly in cases where there was no strong emotional tie (Miller and Simon, 1980).

In certain areas of sexuality, members of the two sexes necessarily have different interests. For example, while contraception is a concern of both males and females, it is the female who must bear the primary consequence of a failure to practice birth control. Understandably, then, women are more concerned about, and exert more precautions with respect to, contraception. Here, the ability to think ahead and anticipate consequences, usually associated with formal operational thought, may play an important role in preventing unwanted pregnancies (even as it may have another positive effect as a female anticipates the pleasures of carrying a child and becoming a mother) (Feldman and Nash,

1979). Another area of sex variation concerns attitudes toward menstruation. Here, it is the premenarcheal girls who have the most positive attitude of any group, with post-menarcheal girls joining boys of comparable ages in having decidedly negative attitudes about the pains and discomforts connected with menstruation (Clarke and Ruble, 1978).

How individuals regard their own sex and the opposite sex has been much researched of late. At younger ages, children subscribe to the sex-role stereotypes of their culture. Men are expected to have action-filled jobs, to be effective breadwinners, to engage in exercise and sports, to be ambitious, forceful, and daring; women are viewed as emotional, passive, dependent homemakers, or as involved in helping professions like teaching and nursing. These stereotypes are found across many Western cultures (Best et al., 1977). By the teenage years, the amount of sheer **stereotyping** has declined, particularly with regard to members of the adolescent's own sex. In certain areas, stereotyping remains prevalent. For example, in accounting for success in sports, male performance is generally explained in terms of the amount of effort exerted while female performance is generally attributed to luck (Bird and Williams, 1980).

With the coming of college and adult years, adolescents experience a decline in sex-role stereotyping, coupled with an increased willingness to see in themselves (and others) characteristics of the opposite sex (Bem, 1974; Urberg, 1979). Individuals whose reasoning reflects the higher stages of moral development, and who appear to be more socially competent, particularly seem willing to recognize and incorporate in themselves certain features of the opposite sex (Ford and Tisak, 1981; Leahy and Eiter, 1980). Such androgynous individuals seem to be better able to assume the perspectives of other individuals, including those of the opposite sex. The

lessening of sex-role stereotypes may also come about because women become more attracted to certain features of the traditional male role, particularly assertiveness and independence (Hall and Halberstadt, 1980).

Social class modulates these trends (Meyer, 1980). Among working-class children of working mothers, the fact of the mother's employment has relatively little effect on the tenacity with which sex-role stereotypes are upheld; possibly this is because the mother is (correctly) perceived as having little choice about whether she works. On the other hand, the fact of a mother's working exerts a counter-stereotypical effect on the middle-class child's images, quite possibly because the middle-class mother is perceived (again correctly) as working through choice. In both groups, however, older girls' attitudes are more closely related to those held by their own mothers, indicating that general sex-role identification precedes the identification with the particular features of the mother's situation and attitudes.

The emerging sex-role identity can be glimpsed through another window—an individual's behaviors toward infants. As far back as early childhood, members of the two sexes behave differently in the presence of a young infant (Blakemore, 1979), with boys talking less, playing less, and displaying less overall nurturance (Frodi and Lamb, 1978) and girls showing a heightened interest in young babies (Fullard and Reiling, 1976). This difference apparently reaches a height during the high school years, at which time there is a stated disinterest on the part of the male in anything having to do with young children. A modest echoing of this effect is found in girls who have just passed menarche: their interest in babies is suppressed, at least temporarily, in favor of a heightened interest in boys (Frodi et al., 1981). The disparity in attitudes toward babies begins to wane when male youths enter college, but the lack of interest in babies persists among a less well educated group of young males (Feldman and Nash, 1979).

COGNITIVE DIFFERENCES AMONG MALES AND FEMALES?

In addition to their differing attitudes in social and sexual matters, adolescent males and females also exhibit contrasting attitudes toward school subjects. Probably the most dramatic example occurs in the areas of mathematics and science, where girls show a strong disinclination toward enrolling in these subjects and also indicate that they do not like the subjects and feel they are not gifted in them (Fennema and Sherman, 1977; Fox, Brody, and Tobin, 1980; Meece, 1981; Reis, 1980; Sherman, 1978). In contrast, girls tend to prefer and to receive higher scores in the area of language and other humanistic subjects (L. J. Harris, 1978; Vasta, Regan, and Kerley, 1980; Witelson, 1977).

One perspective on this topic holds that these differences are due to patterns of socialization. There has been a long tradition of considering mathematics, science, and spatial reasoning as within the province of men, and so young women are discouraged from entering these fields and are considered to be atypical if they do so (Kolata, 1980). Interesting support for this position comes from the finding that boys whose fathers were absent during childhood (and who were, therefore, raised more like girls) showed college board profiles more similar to those typically shown by girls—higher verbal and lower mathematical scores (Carlsmith, 1964).

Another perspective suggests that the difference may reflect brain organization. Women are said to represent linguistic and spatial abilities in both cerebral hemispheres of their brain, while men are likely to have language unilaterally on the left and spatial abilities unilaterally on the right. Paradoxically, this bilateral representation seems advantageous in the case of linguistic processing, disadvantageous in the area of spatial processing (Witelson, 1977).

Yet another slant on these differences comes from the work of Waber (1976). This investigator examined the test profiles of boys and girls who were either early or late maturers (defined by deviations from the normal emergence of puberty). She found that, regardless of sex, early maturers scored better on verbal materials (thus demonstrating the typical female pattern of performance); late maturers, again regardless of sex, performed better on spatial tasks (thus demonstrating the typical male pattern). This set of results cautions against an easy invoking of genetic or modeling explanations for such well-documented differences in cognitive profiles (see also Newcombe and Bandura, 1981).

A curious result pertinent to this debate concerns the difficulty exhibited by many female subjects on a classic Piagetian test: the capacity to represent accurately the level of water in a glass, when that glass had been tilted. As we noted in the Introduction (page 10), most boys have little trouble ignoring the tilt of the glass and drawing the water parallel to the ground. In contrast, girls tend to draw the water parallel to the tilt of the glass. Sometimes, even when the girl is given a model to copy, or told explicitly to ignore the tilt and to draw the water horizontally, faulty performance continues (Harris, 1978; Liben and Golbeck, 1980).

Struck by this unexpected result, and by the generally poorer performance of women on tests of mathematical and spatial functioning, some authorities have been inclined to invoke a genetic explanation (Benbow and Stanley, 1980; L. J. Harris, 1978; Thomas and Jamison, 1979; see also Burstein, Bank, and Jarvik, 1980, for a review). Others suggest that those women who succeed on these pursuits (as against those who fail) are likely to have a brain organization that is closer to that of the average male (Ray, Georgiou, and Ravizza, 1979).

Explanation in terms of cultural practices can also be offered. Women in our culture have generally been shown to be more **field dependent** (see the box): that is, in responding to a task like drawing the water level, they exhibit a greater tendency to pay attention to the cues from the surrounding field. By contrast, men seem able to disregard these local cues, such as the tilt of the glass, and to take into account the more permanent factor—the physics of the environment; thus they exhibit **field-independent** behavior (Witkin, 1979). Cross-cultural studies reveal that the sex differences in field independence are seldom found in non-Western settings. Moreover, when differences are found, they tend to crop up in cultures that are sedentary and where

there is considerable division of labor, and they are absent in cultures where there is much hunting and migration, with its associated spatial movements (Witkin, 1979). Such a finding casts doubt on the hypothesis that problems in handling spatial relations are an inevitable part of the female condition; if the water/glass task were administered in remote societies, a different pattern of results might well emerge.

Differences in field dependence, then, may be socially rather than genetically determined, perhaps reflecting styles of reasoning rather than overall competence. Other differences in reasoning style have also been put forth. For example, Carol Gilligan (Murphy and Gilligan, 1980) suggests that, confronted with moral dilemmas of the sort devised by Lawrence Kohlberg (see previous chapter), women take into account a different set of considerations

Field Independence in Childhood

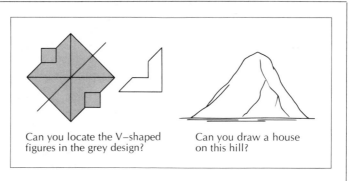

Can you locate the V–shaped figures in the grey design?

Can you draw a house on this hill?

There are two ways in which to approach these problems. A person who is strongly field dependent will draw the house at a slant and will fail to locate the V shapes in the design. A person who is strongly field independent will be able to find the V shapes and will draw the house in its correct, vertical position.

(continued)

Using stimuli similar to these, researchers have established clear individual differences in the way people approach such perceptual and cognitive tasks (Kagan and Kogan, 1970; Liben, 1981; Witkin et al., 1962). People who are field independent will ignore the surrounding perceptual field and zero in directly on the objects in question. Field-dependent people will pay attention to the surroundings, sometimes being helped and sometimes being misled by its cues. Even as early as age five, children often show an inclination toward a particular style, which tends to remain with them throughout childhood (Witkin, Goodenough, and Karp, 1967).

Correlations between field independence and styles of mothering suggest possible causes for these cognitive differences. For example, excessive amounts of parental control contribute to field dependence (Crandall and Sinkeldam, 1964; Witkin et al., 1962). Field-dependent children are more apt to come from overprotective homes in which social conformity is encouraged. These youngsters are often pampered and babied and are given little responsibility. In contrast, field-independent children have less domineering and more supportive mothers who are aware of their children's needs and help them to achieve goals. Thus, children who are granted more independence in their lives also seem to be more cognitively independent of their surroundings.

Different personality profiles accompany the two types of **cognitive styles.** Field-dependent children tend to be more passive and submissive than field-independent children. They are also more sensitive to and influenced by the climate of the situation (for example, they may be unable to perform in a tense or pressured testing session). Finally, while field-independent children tend to engage in intellectualization, rationalization, and isolation, field-dependent children adopt more primitive defense mechanisms including denial, childish behavior, and security seeking.

It is not clear that one cognitive style is preferable to the other. Although field independence seems to correlate with certain analytic and spatial abilities, there is, at best, an ambiguous relationship between cognitive style and overall intelligence or maturity. In general, it is useful to be able to distance oneself from the surroundings rather than to be misled by them. On the other hand, there are times when it is appropriate and necessary to take contextual cues into account. Perhaps the best style is a flexible one, in which one's approach can be carefully fitted to the problem at hand.

and may reach a contrasting set of conclusions. In particular, women are more likely to focus on the need to help others, to take their point of view into account, to be alive to subtle differences across situations and persons, to exhibit concern about an intricate network of social relationships. In contrast, men confront moral issues with an eye focused squarely (and narrowly) on the rights of individuals to noninterference and self-fulfillment; they exhibit considerable concern for abstract rights and obligations and are bent on taking a logically defensible and consistent stance. According to Gilligan, these differences can be located as early as the age of six; in playground games, little boys talk about what "I want" and what "he wants" while little girls talk about *we:* "we agree what we should do; we think it over" (Robb, 1980, p. 71). The question arises once again whether, faced with an opposite set of concerns, men might reason like women, and vice versa; or whether we are dealing here with something sufficiently engrained, sufficiently written into the experience of being male or female, that it is virtually impossible to change.

FAMILY RELATIONS

Even as the attitudes and behaviors of adolescents have changed significantly during this century, so too the relations of boys and girls to their families have undergone alterations. Although families have become smaller—not only with fewer children, but also with fewer relatives—the ties between teenagers and parents at the same time seem to have weakened. This trend reflects less strong ties within the family as well as the heightened influence of the peer group.

Adolescence has been called a time of **dual ambivalence** (Stone and Church, 1973), because parents and children have decidedly mixed feelings about one another. On the one hand, parents want only the best for their children and hope they will succeed in the outside world. On the other hand, parents may doubt whether their children are pursuing the correct course; they may want to continue to control their children's destiny; or they may be envious of their children's greater opportunities and freedom. There may also be unanticipated sexual feelings aroused in parents, fueled by the attractiveness of their children and by resentment concerning the greater sexual freedom now afforded to the younger generation (Adelson and Doehrman, 1980); regressive behaviors on the part of parents sometimes result.

Indeed, to secure a feeling for the dynamics of the parent-child relationship during adolescence, it is useful to contrast their varying perspectives on a number of focal issues. The youth is entering a time of maximum attractiveness, and sexual impulses are new and strong. In contrast, the parents have begun to become less attractive, signs of aging are clear, and there may also be a waning of sexual impulses, with the self-doubt and panic that this sometimes entails. In the area of autonomy, the youth is asserting her need to go forth from the family, while the parents are faced simultaneously with the need to take care of their own elderly parents and retain some control over their still-growing offspring. Finally, in the area of career and lifestyle, the youth is in the process of making pivotal decisions for the future, while the parents have come to the point where they must assess whether they in fact have made the correct choices and whether they can, for the rest of their lives, live with the identity they have long since fashioned.

For their part, despite the desire for autonomy, many youths still feel dependent on their parents. And in fact, there seems to be a desire on the part of youths, even today, to retain strong and positive feelings about their parents (Josselson, 1980). Yet growing children also want to show that they can make it on their own; they resent parental attempts to control them, and they may tend to overestimate the severity of parental reactions to misdeeds. Disputes center on many topics, ranging from using the family car to religious and political attitudes. Among daughters, who often share their parents' values to a greater degree than do sons and who are more susceptible to parental influences as well (Feather, 1980; Kandel, 1981), the conflicts with parents are likely to be about friendship and dating; among boys, responsibility at home and possession of goods (money, car) are paramount (Kinloch, 1970). The contrasting patterns may well reflect different societal expectations, for girls are often viewed as potential spouses (and thus are criticized for their social behavior) and boys are thought of as potential breadwinners (and thus are criticized for their irresponsibility). Occasionally, particularly in a permissive age, some youths will complain that their parents fail to provide sufficient structure or discipline (Bell, 1979).

Parent-child relations are tested anew when the child leaves home, for example to attend college. Sullivan and Sullivan (1980) compared the behaviors of sons who left home to board at college with behaviors of sons who lived at home and commuted to college. Those adolescents who boarded at college exhibited greater affection, ease of communication, satisfaction, and independence in relation to their parents. Mothers expressed increased affection while some fathers became somewhat more dependent on their sons. Apparently the step of separation facilitates the boy's achievement of the developmental goal of gaining independence while retaining emotional ties to his parents. Among the commuters, the relationship between parent and child, still marked by issues of control and depend-

ence, remains more ambivalent and, at least in this case, greater strain resulted.

How the separation of the youth and her family ultimately comes about is of course a complex matter that depends on a variety of factors. Probably the most important factors have to do with the atmosphere of parenting that has been established within the home over many years. To the extent that parents have established a warm relationship with their children, can communicate effectively with them, and have begun a gradual loosening of the ties throughout the preceding years, the final steps toward autonomy will be relatively free of stress. In contrast, in homes where disciplinary tactics have been severe and/or inconstant, where there has been inadequate communication and training, where hostility and lack of trust are found, and where few steps have been taken to lay the groundwork for separation, these times of separation will be fraught with difficulty and conflict (Block, 1971; Conger, 1977).

So far we have been discussing the typical home, where both parents are present and involved in rearing the adolescent. A number of studies portray a single parent's difficulties in raising an adolescent, particularly when that parent is also working, raising other children, or preoccupied with securing another mate. Being raised by a parent of the opposite sex may affect both appropriate cognitive preferences and sex-role identity (see Chapter 5 and also Biller and Bahm 1971). As we have seen, maternal rearing seems to foster verbal skills in males (Carlsmith, 1970). A girl's behavior, in turn, often reflects the reason for her father's absence and the mother's consequent reactions. Daughters of divorcées tend to be sexually promiscuous, whereas daughters of widows prove more inhibited and sexually restrained (Hetherington, 1972).

Family milieu also affects adolescents' conduct. When Sheldon Glueck and Eleanor

Glueck (1952) contrasted delinquent and law-abiding boys, they found that the most important difference lay in the boys' households. Irrespective of social class, the delinquents' homes were less cohesive, featured more hostility between parents and siblings, and were characterized by a confusing combination of extremely severe and extremely permissive discipline. Only when the home was dramatically changed (for instance, by remarriage into a more stable family) or when the child had evolved an unusual set of values (for instance, becoming very religious) did the youths prove able to withstand the conditions that typically give rise to delinquent behavior.

Peer Relations. Relations with peers assume great importance in the lives of most adolescents. It is from their peers that adolescents pick up many of their attitudes, values, and behavioral patterns. It is from their peers that adolescents gain the sustenance and guidance they had previously secured from their immediate family and that they receive signs of belonging, of being a successful (or unsuccessful) person.

Dexter Dunphy (1963) has examined the stages of group development during adolescence. Much like the Samoans studied by Margaret Mead, American preadolescents spend time in groups that are usually composed of only one sex. As adolescence approaches, these groups begin to relate to groups of the opposite sex. A third stage occurs in the early years of adolescence, when the two unisexual cliques engage in specific heterosexual interactions, such as dating (see Figure 14.7). (Usually the individuals with the

Figure 14.7. That period in early adolescence when unisexual groupings are giving way to the first halting attempts at heterosexual coupling is often called the "awkward stage."

highest status in each clique are the first to date.) In the later stages of peer relations, the cliques become exclusively heterosexual. Small clusters of dating couples, who are going steady or are even engaged, come to replace the larger groups of early adolescence.

In Dunphy's view this sequence helps adolescents break away from their parents, spurs healthy competition, and promotes heterosexual attachment. Peer groups demand a high degree of conformity. Membership in such groups can be crucial in forming and defining one's self-image: rejection can be an equally pivotal (but often depressing) influence.

Peer groups have also been studied from an ethological perspective (Weisfeld and Weisfeld, 1981). Richard Savin-Williams (1976) has observed the development of male peer groups in the somewhat controlled setting of a five-week summer camp. He found a rule-governed pattern that resembles the pairings and dominance hierarchies of nonhuman primate groups. Within a few days after the boys arrived at camp, a stable peer hierarchy had emerged. Those boys who were regarded as leaders in the group issued orders and received attention and acclamation. The youngsters in a dominant position had bunks close to the counselors and performed well in sports and on physical fitness measures. (Interestingly, there was *no* relationship between dominance and physical maturity, intelligence, or creativity, at least as these indices were assessed by paper-and-pencil tests.) The dominance hierarchy remained stable through the camping season.

Female campers also adopt dominance hierarchies, which reflect maturation, athletic abilities, and group leadership. However, group structure in the cabins of females is less fixed; dominance is more likely to fluctuate over time, particularly in accordance with situational events (Savin-Williams, 1979). The dominance interactions among the females are more likely to occur in times of special events such as formal banquets, camp-outs, or beach night suppers, while for males they occur in squabbles inside the cabin or at times of contests. In actual interactions, the boys are much more likely to engage in physical encounters and to argue; girls are more likely to compliment, ask favors, imitate, and solicit advice. Over the course of camp, girls decrease the percentage of acts of overt dominance, while boys increase it.

Adolescents pride themselves on their increasing independence and speak in disparaging ways about conformity to adult authority and social convention (Connell et al., 1975; Feather, 1980). Paradoxically, however, in their very opposition to conformity, youngsters often embrace a rigid conformity. In fact, social pressures among peers may be quite severe (Dornbusch et al., 1981; Josselson, 1980). Adolescents continually ask each other, "Do you think I did the right thing?" and find it difficult to tolerate criticism from those on whom they depend for support. Adolescents often feel a desperate need for their friends to approve their choices, views, and preferred patterns of behavior (Chassin, Sherman, and Corty, 1981). They fall easily into cliques and direct a great deal of antipathy and hostility to individuals who have not gained entry into the clique (Coleman, 1961; Schwartz and Merten, 1967).

It is important not to exaggerate the youth's immersion with her peer group, or her alienation from her family. When it comes to espousing religious or political values, or to making major decisions, about education or career, youths still look to their parents. After all, it is their parents who continue to have primary responsibility for them and, in most cases, to support them materially as well as psychologically (Kandel, 1981). Moreover, the break between parents and peers is not as sharp as it might be because, for the most part, peers come from the same social background and espouse the same values and attitudes as the family of the youth herself.

Still, at this age, peers remain supremely important, probably more important than at any other point in the life cycle. This could be because of the roles they assume with respect to the issues that are most central in the experience of American adolescents. Peers initiate one another into the mysteries and pleasures of sexual relationships and serve as the principal sounding boards for discussions of conquests and failures, problems and dreams. Peers prove particularly important factors in whether or not a youth gets involved with illicit drugs, and when parents and peers pull in opposite directions on the drug question, peers frequently prevail (Kandel, 1981). The peer serves as the individual who (like the transitional object) substitutes for parents in the youth's quest for total autonomy; peers also participate in (if they do not instigate) the various social experiments that often serve to declare to others the youth's autonomy. Finally, when it comes to the forging of one's identity, peers serve as models and also as an informal community that reacts, favorably or negatively, to the various roles tried out by the maturing youth.

Changes in World View. Adolescent's attitudes form part of a more pervasive change in world view that is experienced at this time. According to David Elkind (1967), who relates this change to the emergence of formal operations, a new and more comprehensive orientation grows out of adolescents' increased capacities for contemplating possibilities, adopting others' points of view, and reflecting upon the various facets of their own personalities. However, rather than leading adolescents to greater objectivity about themselves and their place in the world, this heightened sensitivity makes their world view more subjective, at least for a while. Adolescents believe that everyone else is focused on them and is busily evaluating them all the time.

Focusing on others' views often stimulates adolescents to fashion a "personal fable," an account of their own life history filled with dramatic, sometimes invented, events. In this fable, they may see themselves as unique, invulnerable, or even immortal. Drawing on this unrealistic image of themselves, youths play to an audience, seeking to win its favor and berating themselves for failure. They may be intensely preoccupied with forbidden acts, on the one hand seeking them out (stealing cars, drinking, having illicit sex), on the other hand obsessing about competing courses of action and feeling intensely guilty (Elkind, 1980). Adolescents may highlight the feeling of specialness by keeping a diary, speaking to God, or writing a novel in which their own life experience forms the sole content (Waterman, Kohutis, and Pulone, 1977).

In this focus on self and on others' views, the adolescent is quite different both from younger children and from adults. Younger children are active and spend little time thinking about themselves as unique and do not believe that they dominate the thoughts of others. On the other side, adults (at least ideally!) have a sense of perspective. They are able to distinguish their own important concerns from trivial ones, and they realize that most of their activities and preoccupations are of little concern to anyone else. Young adolescents, preoccupied with their status in relation to others, veer between feelings of excessive self-importance and deep-seated doubts about their own worth.

Personal Development and the Sense of Self. Because they are increasingly preoccupied with self-development, adolescents are typically concerned with nearly every facet—be it handwriting, clothing, or nicknames—of their own person. These trivial but telling details function as personal statements, determining how adolescents define themselves and how the community defines them. And because adolescents have an unstable image of themselves, they are concerned about how they are regarded by others in their society (Simmons, Rosenberg, and Rosenberg, 1975).

Adolescents are plagued by an array of troubles and worries. They are anxious about their strong sexual desires and secret masturbation, about school performance, peer pressure, and parental tensions. They undergo extremely wide mood swings (Larson, Csikszentmihalyi, and Graef, 1981). They may feel inferior to successful members of their own group and worry that they cannot live up to their own goals.

A number of concerns are heightened during adolescence. There is, for example, a need for solitude; even though youngsters may prefer to be in the company of peers, and feel lonely when by themselves, they find that they return to the company of others, after such solitary respites, feeling more alert, stronger, more involved, and more cheerful (Larson and Csikszentmihalyi, 1978; Sobel, 1980). Perhaps paralleling this need for solitude is an emphasis among many adolescents on asceticism: a renunciation of dating, dancing, drinking, sex, and, indeed, all sources of gratification. Here is one way in which adolescents seek to deal with the pressures they are feeling and to satisfy the demands they make upon themselves. As a temporary phenomenon, asceticism is explicable and perhaps even desirable; such self-renunciation becomes more problematic when it is overemphasized or permanently entrenched (Adelson and Doehrman, 1980).

At times the pressures felt by adolescents, and the demands made upon them, become too severe, and adolescents contemplate, attempt, or even succeed in committing suicide.

Adolescent suicide is in fact on the rise in our society, with one hundred thousand succeeding annually, a threefold increase over the past twenty years. Females attempt suicide three times as often as males, but males succeed three times as frequently as females (I. B. Weiner, 1980). Sometimes the suicide follows upon relatively objective factors, such as the failure to get a job, the dissolution of love relationships, the loss of family members, the breakup of a family, or a financial disaster. As often, however, the pressures are more psychological: a feeling that one is not appreciated by one's family, a feeling that one has no friends, too radical a disjunction between what one thinks one should be like and what one has actually achieved (Kamisher, 1978). The dearth of rituals, of prescribed steps through which to pass in growing up, and the absence of people from whom to seek aid and some means of gaining help are among other possible contributors. Sometimes the suicide attempt is a desperate cry for help that, if answered adequately, can prevent recurrences.

Countering this negative picture is one of adolescence as a rich and pleasurable experience, with many positive emotions. Generous or altruistic impulses guide adolescents to help others. They are capable of great happiness and appreciate humor. They have the opportunity to succeed in school, in sports, or in interpersonal relations and to gain satisfaction from their triumphs (Eisert and Kahle, 1981). And perhaps the most crucial of all, adolescents gain the capacity to care deeply about another person, to love and be loved.

It is difficult to determine just what leads to feelings of satisfaction and well-being among adolescents. Administering a battery of scales to adolescents in high school, Sheryl Pomerantz (1979) found that general satisfaction with one's personal situation correlated with one's achievements and one's self-esteem. Some suggestive sex differences were found. For boys, self-esteem (particularly as reflected in competitive activities) was particularly valued; for girls, physical appearance and those aspects of work and achievement tied to their sense of identity were rated more highly. A study of the ideals held by teenagers in six different Western countries (Block, 1973) found impressive consistency in the values cited by males and females: the males stressed accomplishment and active agency, while the females emphasized communal and interpersonal kinds of experiences.

As we have noted, the achievement of **autonomy**—independence from others—becomes an all-important value during adolescence. Thornburg (1975) describes three forms of autonomy valued by adolescents. The first, **behavioral autonomy,** involves the ability to work, play, spend money, date, and select friends. Each of these pursuits allows the adolescent to make decisions and initiate actions, accepting their consequences. A second and related form is **emotional autonomy,** which requires breaking ties of dependency to one's family. More subtle and more difficult to accomplish than behavioral autonomy, emotional autonomy demands some emotional maturity. It also requires that the new relationship between the youth and the family remain close but that any feelings of dependency become mutual.

The final form, **value autonomy,** has become increasingly important in our complex contemporary society. In years past, attitudes and values usually persisted across generations. This is particularly true for values that were deeply held and established early in life. Increasingly, however, the parents' world is not the children's world, and one generation's values may not coincide exactly with those of the next. For instance, a girl's parents may feel that her goal in life should be to marry and raise a family. But she, growing up in a time when women are beginning to find other acceptable roles, may want to pursue a career. Her new values must arise out of her own experiences, which necessarily include her parents' goals for her. Because values themselves are in flux, it is not surprising that most adolescents have difficulty achieving their own autonomous set of views.

Relation to the Future. Young schoolchildren have quite limited time perspectives: a week in the future seems very distant; a year can scarcely be envisioned. But having lived longer, and having a greater capacity to deal with the hypothetical and the possible, adolescents are able to think and plan in terms of larger time blocks. At the same time, they are also much more aware of the options for the rest of life, including those abilities, skills, and personality traits that are unlikely to change significantly and of the need to make decisions involving long-term goals and commitment of resources.

Deciding one's future course can be unsettling. What work should one do? Where should one live, with whom, and, most subtly, how? How can one draw upon one's skills, values, sex role, aspirations, and knowledge of one's own person, and come up with an occupation and a way of living that is adequate or, better, highly satisfactory? An abundance of life-styles exists; and although nearly everyone has some opportunity for experimenting, decisions with enduring consequences must be made long before alternatives have been sufficiently sampled. Selfish indulgences, personal freedom, worldly success, the demands of parents and community—all these and many more must be considered or not, emphasized or not. Not all these concerns need be conscious; and, indeed, adolescents are often troubled without being sure why. But in our society, where one's destiny seems very largely in one's own hands, decisions about the future constitute a central and weighty burden on the adolescent.

Clinicians' Views
of Adolescence

Most of our observations about American adolescence have come from researchers who deal with normal youths and whose generalizations emerge from a limited contact with many adolescents. Yet psychologists who have worked intensively over a sustained period of time with a comparatively small number of troubled adolescents may well have obtained the keenest insights into the dynamics of this period. Two clinicians, Harry Stack Sullivan and Erik Erikson, stand out among the researchers who have considered adolescence in this way. They offer parallel interpretations of the tensions and possibilities that underlie the experience of adolescence. Whereas Sullivan worked mainly with psychotics and schizophrenics (usually males), Erikson studied less severely impaired youths or ones who had suffered a single severe trauma. Thus, with their contrasting experiences and perspectives, Sullivan and Erikson complement one another; together they furnish some powerful insights into the special characteristics of the adolescent period.

HARRY STACK SULLIVAN'S
STAGES OF CHILDHOOD

Sullivan (1953) views the life course as consisting of a series of stages, each marked by a particular relationship to persons who are significant in the individual's life. These relations, be they early friendships or love unions, each pose particular problems whose resolutions determine the nature and strength of the individual's emerging sense of self.

The Juvenile Era and Others. During the juvenile era—the first years of school—the child ventures into the external world. No longer confined to the home environment, the child is exposed to a variety of new people. In order to form successful and secure friendships, she must learn to accommodate to different persons. The child who behaves precisely the same toward all people is likely to encounter increasingly difficulty in effecting friendships and in accommodating to diverse situations.

Preadolescence and Chums. The juvenile era launches relationships with playmates, while preadolescence is marked by an increasingly strong interest in another person. Now the child chooses a single member of the same sex to be a chum or bosom pal and that person becomes a close and meaningful companion. As we have seen earlier, these preadolescent chums can assume great importance. They allow peers to interact with one another voluntarily, and they involve a kind of mutuality or exchange, which is extremely difficult for children to achieve with adults. A child can collaborate with a special friend of comparable age, sex, skills, interests, and so on, with each child having the opportunity to satisfy her own needs. Moreover, at this age an interchange can be deep and genuinely dynamic, rather than merely reflecting superficially similar attributes or aims (Honess, 1980).

Many preadolescents already suffer from significant personality disorders that Sullivan calls **warps**—extreme egocentrism, childishness, a belief that everyone must like them, or a supercritical attitude toward others. These warps may worsen if the child is unsuccessful in forming a relation with a chum and therefore becomes isolated. Indeed, Sullivan finds that the surest predictor of trouble in adult relations is the absence of such an intimate friendship in preadolescence. Conversely, an effective relationship with a chum can go a long way toward alleviating warps. Children who have hitherto been isolated may be able to reach out to others if they find an extroverted and empathetic chum. The formation of new intimacies provides a kind of affirmation by others: as one looks at oneself through a chum's eyes, one's warps may be alleviated, one's self expanded and bolstered.

Early Adolescence and Lust. Awareness of important sexual body changes marks the beginning of adolescence. And this discovery in turn triggers changes that may have fateful consequences for the individual.

The anxiety brought on by feelings of lust may cause the adolescent to shy away from or even abandon interpersonal relations and resort instead to fantasy or self-stimulation. Conversely, lust may help alleviate anxiety-provoking impulses; rather than seeking isolation, individuals at this time may derive strength from membership in larger groups.

The young adolescent must come to grips with three often conflicting needs: for the satisfaction of lust; for personal security, which may be equated with freedom from anxiety; and for intimate, meaningful, and constant collaboration with at least one other person. To the extent that needs can be met, the adolescent will successfully navigate the stresses of this period. However, should attempts to fulfill one need disrupt or thwart the satisfaction of others, the individual's warps may intensify.

Late Adolescence and the Self. If all goes reasonably well, late adolescence will be marked by establishment of mature interpersonal relations. Adolescents now have a variety of friends toward whom they can behave appropriately and meaningfully. They can now relate to adults on a human level; whereas in early years adults furnished the standards, now youths can see adults as individuals who may also be in need of help and company, who can also make mistakes, and who ought to be treated as friends (Youniss, 1980). Although late adolescence demands an enduring and comfortable sexual relation, equally important is the capacity to blend one's sexual and nonsexual person. And while sexual behaviors remain crucial, Sullivan directs his primary attention to the evolution of self.

The perils of this period include an inadequate sense of self—unrealistic notions of what one is like and equally inappropriate and deficient notions of others. Warps may include feelings of omnipotence or inferiority; attitudes toward others may range from excessive hero worship to unmotivated denigration. Individuals may engage in stereotyping—lumping together a large collection of individuals indiscriminately and, often, rejecting the group in its entirety. Low self-esteem can lead to drug abuse and other forms of hostility toward self and others (Kellam, Ensiminger, and Brown, 1980). The roots of such troubles often extend far back to inadequate relations with a chum or to the first fumbling heterosexual pairings.

Another peril of late adolescence is the emergence of powerful blocks—rejection of wide areas of experience in favor of that exclusive focus upon a narrow realm that permits satisfaction of one's most pressing needs. For instance, there may be a single-minded concentration on academics, self-denial, sexual conquests, or destructive criminal activities. Adolescents may become affixed to routines and rituals so as to avoid unpredictable activities. These blocks ultimately thwart the realization of the diverse potential contained in every individual.

The picture need not be this bleak. Individuals who cope with the challenges of preadolescence and adolescence will emerge as realists, possessing an understanding of others and of themselves. Moreover, and perhaps more important, they will have a sense of self-respect. Having demonstrated a capacity to live among others, and having uncovered activities at which they excel, they do not need to create a sense of self by disparaging others. Instead, they can respect their merit, emulate their strengths, and accept their difficulties and flaws.

Securing empirical data to support this picture of development is not easy. A number of longitudinal studies have investigated the degree of integration and health exhibited during an individual's preadolescence and adolescence, in the light of eventual adult psychological adjustment (Josselson, 1980; Peskin and Livson, 1972). In general, the best predictor of adult adjustment and maturity is a preadolescence marked by independence, self-confidence, and intellectual curiosity. A relatively high degree of adolescent ego strength seems necessary to tolerate the affective turbulence and regression of the process of adolescence. In this context, a period of unrest in early adolescence is also associated with eventual psychosocial maturity—perhaps, in fact, some tumult is necessary, at least in our culture, in order to pave the way for eventual consolidation of ego strength (Josselson, 1980).

ERIK ERIKSON'S CONCEPT OF IDENTITY

Erik Erikson has also evolved a stage theory of personal development. In his scheme, as in Sullivan's, each stage entails warps and insecurities, as well as a more palatable alternative of adjustment, self-respect, and an abiding interest in the world.

Yet important differences characterize the two approaches. Where Sullivan emphasizes sexual and interpersonal relations, Erikson considers a wider variety of personal facets. Where Sullivan describes warps, Erikson discerns a tension or crisis marking each stage of development. And where Sullivan divides adolescence into substages, Erikson considers it to be a single long period that centers on the problem of identity.

We have already encountered Erikson's eight stages of the life cycle in Chapter 1. Each stage of childhood involves a crisis that reflects the themes peculiar to that age: themes of autonomy and shame during the early toddler period; of initiative and guilt during the Oedipal period; of achievement and inferiority during school years. Unsuccessful resolutions typically have repercussions in later development and even adulthood.

The fifth crisis described by Erikson—the identity crisis during adolescence—is considered by many to be the central crisis of all development, at least during the present era of world history. By this time, the youth may already have developed feelings of trust, autonomy, initiative, and achievement—strength will be crucial in specific goals. But who is the person who will attain these goals? How does that person decide which aims to attain and how to evaluate her success in achieving them? Answering such questions requires a unifying concept like the sense of identity.

Introducing this concept, Erikson (1959) recounts an autobiographical essay by the English playwright George Bernard Shaw on his own adolescence. Shaw thought deeply and continuously about who he was. Dissatisfied with his first career in business, he sought deliberately in his late teens and early twenties to carve out a new role for himself, one that would satisfy his own desires and goals as well as the expectations of others. He could evaluate his upbringing and draw upon its influences—snobbism, a dramatic and boisterous household, an atmosphere of religious fervor—in forging the role he wanted to adopt for himself and the world:

I had to become an actor, and create for myself a fantastic personality fit and apt for dealing with men, and adaptable to the various parts I had to play as author, journalist, orator, politician, committeeman, man of the world, and so forth [quoted in Erikson, 1959, p. 109].

Identity Formation. Shaw's growing awareness of decisions with lifelong implications is probably the defining feature of adolescence;

the concern and anxiety that attend these decisions are part and parcel of the identity crisis. Because making choices too quickly can foreclose options, many youths seek a setting where they can "find themselves" by trying out different roles without committing themselves to any one. One toys with possibilities so as to "get a feel" for them, while being careful not to become prematurely ensnared. Potentially fruitful experiments like these, which Erikson calls **moratoriums,** are more likely in some societies than in others. The American and British societies allow a protracted adolescence, whereas most traditional cultures (like that of Samoa) prescribe a particular course shortly after puberty.

Though one's early experiences and influences are important, one's own identity amounts to more than a simple sum of previous identifications. Formation of identity is an active construction, an integration of physical givens, sexual leanings, favored capacities, significant identifications, useful defenses and sublimations, consistent and preferred roles, all stamped with the individual's characteristic style and experiences. In achieving an ultimate sense of identity, individuals who have negotiated the identity crisis achieve a sense of inner continuity with what they were before and what they will become. At the same time, they reconcile their own self-conceptions with the expectations and norms of the surrounding community, and particularly with the desires of significant persons in their lives.

The formation of identity need not be intentional or deliberate as it was for Shaw. Nor does the sense of identity arrive neatly packaged on a given day. Instead, individuals gradually attain a feeling of well-being as elements formerly felt to be independent (and even contradictory) gradually come together. One's choices of occupation, mate, life-style, values, religion, and politics slowly make sense to oneself and to the relevant community.

Challenges to Identity Formation. Establishing a firm, comfortable, and enduring identity is a turbulent and challenging process that can, at times, result in severe stress and even pathology.

The alternative to identity formation is called **role diffusion** (or confusion of identity). Bewildered and distraught by the strong demands made on them—by parents, others, or themselves—youths beset by role diffusion run away, either physically or spiritually, withdrawing from their surroundings into despair. They wander from one pursuit to another; but instead of constructive experimentation, theirs is a kind of mindless "fooling around" with roles—donning the costume of a bum, mimicking the lingo of a criminal, adopting the attitudes of the most diverse (and perverse) groups. Erikson quotes Biff, a young man in Arthur Miller's *Death of a Salesman,* who declares, "I just can't take hold, Mom. I can't take hold of some kind of life."

In the most severe cases of identity confusion, adolescents embrace a negative identity. Convinced that they cannot possibly satisfy others, youths rebel through perverse reaction. They select just those aspects of themselves that they know will trouble the people who care most deeply for them. The daughter of a successful businessman may join a radical political group. The son of a confirmed atheist may enter a seminary. Or the youth may focus *too* exclusively upon herself, displaying a rigid and destructive form of narcissism (Kohut, 1971). Though decidedly negative, these dramatic reactions represent desperate attempts to confirm some kind of autonomy, some manner of self-definition. These youths seem to be saying that, having found themselves in a situation where all the things valued by others prove impossible, this is the only way they can gain some mastery. A young woman says, "At least in the gutter I'm a genius" (Erikson, 1959, p. 132).

This statement captures the adolescent's affirmation that at least *something* has been achieved. An active assertion that one is what one should *not* be makes sense at this moment in one's life history.

A useful approach to measuring the elusive concept of identity is found in the work of James Marcia (1980). This investigator unravels Erikson's unitary concept into a number of principal strands, including the **achievement of identity,** in which the individual is pursuing a self-chosen occupation and ideological goal; **foreclosure,** where career and ideological patterns have been imposed by the parents; **identity diffusion,** marked by no clear occupational or ideological direction; and **moratoriums,** referring to individuals caught in an identity crisis where they are struggling with occupational or ideological issues (Marcia, 1980, p. 16).

Individuals can be classified as belonging to one of these strands. Those involved in moratoriums experience high anxiety, while those having identity achievement or diffusion experience little anxiety. Individuals conforming to the categories of foreclosure and identity diffusion turn out to be more impulsive, while identity achievers and moratorium individuals emerge as more reflective. On a cognitive task administered under stressful conditions, individuals at an identity-achievement level do well, while those with foreclosures do very poorly.

Finally, styles of relating to parents are instructively different. To summarize briefly, foreclosure youths are involved in a "love affair" with their parents whereas identity-diffusion youths are characterized by rejection or detachment from their parents. Moratorium individuals are ambivalent toward their parents; a son tries to free himself from his mother, while a moratorium daughter tries to identify with her father and fulfill his goals. Persons who have achieved identity exhibit fairly balanced views of their parents, having positive though moderately ambivalent relationships with them (Jordan, 1971; Matteson, 1974).

Ideology and Totalitarianism. At no other time are individuals as likely to pass rapidly through a wide sweep of moods, ideals, and aspirations. In the process, an individual may become totally committed to an ideology that, though momentarily appealing, can contain roots of destruction. Many youths are seduced by *isms,* ranging from communism to Zen Buddhism; or by political or religious leaders whose motivation is self-aggrandizement. They may jump at the prospect of quick thrills offered by drugs, sexual experiments, or exotic beliefs. Seeking alternatives and stability, youths may sacrifice their strength or even their lives for a cause doomed to failure.

Of course, this youthful, ideological strain is also admirable—there is no predictable cynicism, no compromise for compromise's sake. As Shaw described his own political involvement, "I was drawn into the Socialist revival of the early eighties, among Englishmen intensely serious and burning with indignation at very real and fundamental evils that affected the world" (quoted in Erikson, 1959, p. 104). In Erikson's view, Shaw's choice of words is not accidental: feelings about injustices and a commitment to set them right are particularly characteristic of this period of life. Thanks in part to youth, dramatic progress in civilization has been made: in our own times it is adolescents in Israeli kibbutzim who have helped build a thriving society in a desert; and it was American youths in the sixties who risked their safety in sit-ins and marches and who inspired many of their elders to change their views. However, one cannot forget the ranks of adolescents who lined up behind Hitler and Mussolini, equally certain that they were right.

As these examples illustrate, the community's role in determining options and in approving roles remains crucial. Moreover, every adequate identity must reflect decisions and roles that make sense to the community in which one resides and the historical epoch in which one lives. All the same, identity formation is essentially a personal, psychological process. So viewed, it is tantamount to the maturation of a sense of self during this period.

CREATING A METAPHOR OF THE SELF

Proceeding from contrasting analytic frameworks and pondering different examples, Sullivan and Erikson have nonetheless arrived at several common conclusions. Both see adolescence as a focal period in an individual's development, one fraught with difficulties yet essential in laying the groundwork for later maturity and health. Although Sullivan is somewhat less optimistic than Erikson, both feel that with support and help even the warped adolescent whose prior crises have not been resolved successfully may establish a tenable identity.

Concern with self or identity may be particularly rampant in Western cultures (Kohut, 1971; Lasch, 1979). In societies where role options are defined and maturity is unequivocally marked by initiation rites, the experimentation entailed in identity formation is less likely, and less necessary (Kernberg, 1976). Yet, at least within the cultures we know, the development of self may well be *the* project for the early stages of life. The young child's task is to acquire a working knowledge of the surrounding physical and social world. The individual in middle childhood increasingly expresses this knowledge in symbols. But only when these abilities flow together in adolescence—only when a youth can handle a symbol system with flexibility

Figure 14.8. Like the toddler peering into the mirror on page 131, this adolescent is involved in constructing a sense of self. But while the toddler is merely discovering and confirming her existence, this adolescent is reflecting on the wealth of possibilities and roles available to her. Soon she will be putting the finishing touches on the metaphor that stands for her physical, emotional, and cognitive self.

and assurance and use this capacity to integrate prior experiences and accumulated knowledge—does it become possible to conceptualize the self, to mold an identity.

The self can be seen as the individual's attempt to integrate interests, capacities, and goals at a time when the major decisions of life must be made. Only in adolescence does the individual become capable of the cognitive operations involved in forming and elaborating a complex concept like the self, one that stands for one's entire being: one's body and mind, past experiences, current needs and fears, aspirations for the future (see Broughton, 1974; Koocher, 1974). From one point of view, the result is nothing more than an intangible figure of speech—the "sense of self"—yet this metaphoric invention comes to constitute the most central aspect of an individual's existence.

Bringing together these notions and impulses during adolescence is a heady challenge. Yet the pressures for solidification, for creating a structure that can represent drives and needs striving for expression and equilibrium, are also considerable. Depending on the social setting, this striving for organization and coherence may be more or less difficult, more or less public, more or less conscious. But success at it may determine prospects and possibilities for the rest of the individual's life.

Signposts

Having described in the previous chapter the principal intellectual changes accompanying the onset of puberty, we have here examined the physical changes and pivotal emotional characteristics of adolescence. Through surveying a large number of topics we paid special attention to three central aspects of the adolescent experience in America: the emergence of sexuality, the need for individual autonomy, and the quest for meaningful identity.

As a means of discovering which aspects of the adolescent experience may be found universally, we first turned our attention to the classical Freudian view. We reviewed the claim that the sexual changes of puberty necessarily result in emotional turmoil and produce characteristic defense mechanisms. Margaret Mead's study of Samoans provides persuasive evidence that adolescents' biological changes do not in themselves cause emotional upheaval. In fact, in a social setting where a smooth transition from childhood to maturity is possible and where the choices at adolescence have been constrained by the culture, adolescence can be a calm and unemotional time. Our complex society engenders adolescent tension and dislocation, but it also allows greater freedom of choice and stimulates growth in intellect and feeling.

Other cross-cultural investigations confirm the wide variety of adolescent experiences. Both abroad and within our own borders, adolescence may be highly turbulent or relatively problem-free, and in each case the surrounding culture and the adolescent's own definition of her situation play crucial roles. We noted that initiation rites, by which the society marks the change from childhood to adulthood, may represent one way a society attempts to confirm the adolescent's sex-role identity. The elaborate and even violent ceremonies in certain cultures can be contrasted instructively with mild rituals of passage—such as Communion or bar mitzvah, sorority or fraternity pledging—in our own society. And even in the absence of any formal rites of passage, cultures or groups of individuals will find ways to ease the transition to adulthood.

Nowhere is the experience of adolescence more diversified than in the United States. Because of variations in the onset of puberty, numerous ethnic and social-class backgrounds, style of cognition, and the rapidly changing fabric of our own society, almost any generalization is rightly suspect. Moreover, a number of problems encountered in studying adolescents further reduce the reliability of characterizations of American youths. Nonetheless, observers and experimenters have attempted to gather and synthesize information about the lives of American adolescents. They have described various changes in attitudes, values, and the perception of self and of others that accompany the cognitive advances of the period.

Certain trends and conflicts typically emerge in sexual attitudes, in relations with parents and with peers, and in the individual's self-concept. Some of these are related to one's sexual identity. For example, females are more likely than males to suffer the consequences (like unwanted pregnancy) of failures to plan. Females may also have different styles of thinking (favoring a sensitivity to context and to the nuances of interpersonal relations), cognitive strengths (linguistic over spatial abilities), and ingredients of satisfaction (focusing on aspects of communal values). During most of childhood, females exhibit greater involvement with infants and child care. And, nowadays, they are more likely to be dissatisfied with traditional sex roles.

Other features cut across the two sexes. Autonomy is dawning: youths want to select their own friends and pastimes, to break emotional ties to the family, and to create their own value system from their own experience. Planning for the future—for work, life-style, and other goals—consumes a great deal of the adolescent's time. The general emerging picture of adolescence in our society confirms the heightened self-awareness of adolescents, their concern about sexuality and autonomy, and their desire to forge an adequate relationship to the wider society while also realizing various personal goals. Yet, ambivalence may be felt with respect to each of these goals, and some anxiety and uncertainty can be expected.

As youths break away from the nuclear family and embark upon a career and lifestyle of their own, peers assume crucial importance. It is to their peers that youths turn for support during periods of trouble, for discussion and guidance about sexual matters, for company at times of social experimentation, for role models, and for reactions to the various identities they are trying out for themselves. Still, the tie to the parents remains important. Adolescents look to their parents for guidance on major life decisions. And if the relation to the parents has been comfortable beforehand, the trials of adolescence can usually be weathered without excessive stress and with positive feelings still in evidence.

The most comprehensive and reliable picture of adolescence may well come from those who have had intensive clinical experience with youths and who view adolescence in a developmental context. Harry Stack Sullivan described the ideal evolution of interpersonal relations throughout childhood—the initial discrimination among new acquaintances at the start of school; the preadolescent friendship with a member of the same sex; the early adolescent reconciliation of sexual desire with participation in a meaningful relationship with another person. Finally, he portrayed the capacity of the young adult to sustain a number of mature interpersonal relationships with peers and elders. At any point, however, tensions and warps may thwart satisfactory development, and much of Sullivan's discussion concerns how these warps may be aggravated or alleviated.

Erik Erikson portrayed the pivotal strains surrounding the definition of identity. By trying out different life-styles and synthesizing various life themes and goals, the adolescent establishes a coherent identity that stands her in good stead for later life. The dangers of the period are role diffusion (withdrawal or superficial playing of nonconstructive roles) and negative identity (deliberate embrace of negative roles as a reaction to possible demands). Every youth undergoes some uncertainty about identity, but the balance between feelings of coherence and diffusion determines the ego strength with which the youth faces subsequent development.

Although a sense of self lies at the core of the individual's affective development, it involves considerable cognitive sophistication as well. Indeed, forming a metaphor that stands for all aspects of the individual appears to entail mental capacities of reasoning and synthesizing that become available only during adolescence. Pivotally located at the intersection of cognitive capacities and affective themes, tying together the aspirations of the individual with the constraints and values of the culture, the developed sense of identity or self serves as a principal signpost for the remainder of one's life.

Adolescence represents both a culmination of the events that occurred during childhood and a preparation for the years of maturity. An adequate survey of development in adulthood would take many pages. Although we cannot undertake such a review, we will in the Epilogue at least touch on some prominent themes that mark later life in the normal individual. Then, in a final glimpse of the panorama of development, we will recapitulate the development of the sense of self throughout life.

The Self
Across the Life Span

Grow old with me
The best is yet to be.

    –ROBERT BROWNING

But of all the thoughts which rushed upon my savage and undeveloped little brain at this crisis, the most curious was that I had found a companion and a confidant in myself. There was a secret in this world and it belonged to me and to a somebody who lived in the same body with me. There were two of us and we could talk to one another. . . . It was a great solace to me to find a sympathizer in my own breast.

    –EDMUND GOSSE

Only in the last few years have developmental psychologists paid much attention to the periods of life following adolescence. Before then, they tended to equate human development with child development, at least in part because the most dominant thinkers in the field, including Jean Piaget and Sigmund Freud, did not consider the adult years. And so they treated the mental and emotional revolutions of adolescence as the last major developments in life. For better or worse, the plan for the rest of life had been launched and was unlikely to alter significantly in the years to come.

But in recent years the rhythm of life in adulthood, particularly in old age, has also intrigued investigators. In this Epilogue, we will consider a few lines of study and conclusions to emerge from research into the adult years. Because this book is primarily about childhood, we can offer only a few broad strokes in our portrait of the later years—certain cognitive and affective facets that will help fill out the patterns described in earlier chapters. Then, following this overview of the later years, we will consider once again the central organizing role of the self in human development. After recapitulating early phases in the development of the self, we will review some efforts to describe a mature end-state of development and consider briefly the final steps taken by the mature human self.

Cognition in Adulthood

Information about adult mental capacities has been obtained chiefly from tests administered to persons of various ages (see Baltes and Schaie, 1973; Chandler, 1976; Denney and Wright, 1976; LaBouvie-Vief, 1980). The measures are sometimes standard intelligence tests (for example, Wechsler, 1955), tests of perceptual and motor capacities (for example, Comalli, Wapner, and Werner, 1959), measures of memory (Cavanaugh and Perlmutter, 1980; Pezdek, 1980; Walsh and Baldwin, 1977), or Piagetian clinical interviews (for example, Papalia, 1972; K. H. Rubin, 1974; Tomlinson-Keasey, 1972). Most of these tests are administered cross-sectionally; that is, adults of different ages receive the same battery and cross-age comparisons are then made. The conventional interpretation of these studies suggests that adult intellect reaches a high point during the twenties and thirties, remains steady or declines gradually until the sixties, and drops off more rapidly during the seventies and eighties. Only in vocabulary and general factual information—sometimes called **crystallized intelligence**—are very old people generally thought to remain at a high level of competence (Horn, 1970; Jarvik, 1973).

But this picture has turned out to be too simple, and it may well be fundamentally misleading. For one thing, as we saw in Chapter 13, the "textbook" level of adult cognition—formal operational thought—is not achieved by a majority of adolescents (Dulit, 1972; Sinnott, 1975). Moreover, both adolescents and adults probably operate cognitively on various levels: sometimes we deal on the abstract or formal level, as when we summarize an evening's reading; but just as often we rely on concrete operations, as in finding our way about a new neighborhood, or even sensorimotor intelligence, as in fiddling with a new machine (Chandler, 1976; Flavell, 1971; Furth, 1973; Piaget, 1972; Riegel, 1973).

A second line of investigation has actually challenged the notion that mental abilities decline in adulthood. K. Warner Schaie and his associates maintain that apparent declines in intellect actually reflect an overall improvement in test performance from one generation to the next (Schaie and LaBouvie-Vief, 1974; Schaie and Parham, 1977). That is, the earlier cross-sectional tests compared the intelligence of a seventy-year-old (born in 1905) and of an eighty-year-old (born in 1895) and concluded that intelligence declined over the decade from seventy to eighty, without taking account of the difference in birth date. Schaie also found that when declines did occur in the same subjects, they were frequently associated with an illness preceding death. This finding alerts testers to take account of the physical condition of subjects: poor health may affect performance on tests of mental ability.

Other researchers have proposed another means of characterizing the abilities of older people. According to their view, apparent declines in old age may reflect how older persons *think* they should perform, in a society where they are scorned (Comfort, 1976). Or their performances reflect less adequate patterns of thinking they have acquired because they have had to retire from active employment (Denney and Wright, 1976). Supporting this notion is the following finding: When institutionalized elderly are placed in more stimulating environments or are encouraged to assume a more active role in their own lives, their performances on standardized tests often go up quite dramatically (Langer et al., 1979).

The picture one obtains of cognitive power in aging individuals depends on a variety of factors, with some research documenting declines (Hooper, Fitzgerald and Paplia, 1971; Pezdek, 1980; Shaps and Nillson, 1980), other investigations suggesting a steady course, particularly in individuals who remain healthy and active (Cavanaugh and Perlmutter, 1980; Labouvie-Vief, 1980; Yussen and Hiebert, 1979). Certainly as researchers have considered the cognitive capacities of older individuals with more care, a more complex picture of their abilities has emerged. Some authorities have in fact tried to identify tasks at which older individuals actually excel. For instance, mature adults may be better able than adolescents to identify new problems in a domain of knowledge (such as science), rather than merely to solve the problems posed by others (Arlin, 1975). The heights of creative invention, and the ability to forge powerful intellectual syntheses, often are not realized until mid-life (Dennis, 1966; Gruber, 1981). And observers have believed for years that the older person can absorb diverse forms of information and call on diverse experiences in reaching a balanced judgment in a way that adolescents and younger adults cannot (Flavell, 1977; Labouvie-Vief, 1980). These claims have not yet been confirmed in experimental investigations: it is no simple matter to stimulate a judicious decision in the experimental laboratory. But the numerous societies (including ours) that confer the greatest responsibilities on individuals of middle and old age seem implicitly to confirm this positive view of their cognitive capacities.

The Quality of Adulthood

Although intellectual trends are readily studied, probably more important for an evaluation of adulthood is the temper or quality of these years: the kinds of experience individuals typically have, the feelings they undergo, the problems they encounter, the lessons they draw, their interactions with other individuals and with major social institutions. The chief sources of information about adult affective development have been intensive interviews and observations by clinicians (Levinson, 1978; Neugarten, 1964, 1966; Scarf, 1976; Sheehy, 1976; Valliant, 1977). Following the customary practices in such investigations, we will view the adult years as a series of periods or episodes: such "phases" correspond roughly to various age bands (as in the twenties), and to various age-related milestones (marriage, death of one's parents, retirement).

During the later teens and early twenties, youths complete the process of breaking away from their own families, often by attending college or serving in the military, and at the same time begin to make the principal decisions governing their own lives. As the decisions fall into place, the period of **young adulthood** may be said to begin. The young adult chooses a mate or does not choose one; becomes a parent or elects not to become one; finds an occupation or fails to find one; and seeks a semblance of social and economic security. Her major challenge is to move from relative noncommitment to comfortable commitment. Often an older person can aid the smoothness and effectiveness of this transition into adulthood. And, frequently, a kind of internal clock registers whether the individual is early or late (compared to peers) in making important decisions and commitments.

Having been launched during the twenties and thirties, the individual arrives at **middle age** in the forties and fifties. This period marks a turning point from the forward-looking perspective of youth. Now the time frame subtly begins to shift, and individuals become aware that at least half of their lives lie behind them. They are aware, not of the vast future before them, but rather of the increasingly limited time that is left (Bortner and Hultsch, 1972; Levinson, 1978; Scarf, 1980; Valliant, 1977). New problems command increasing attention: health, the fate of children and aging parents, the use of leisure, plans for old age (Steuve, 1981).

Whether fifty-year-olds feel frustrated or satisfied with the lives they have led depends on their self-assessment. Physical health, psychological well-being, feelings of sexual competence, family status, role in the community, job competence, security—all these contribute significantly to the way individuals view their finite existence, whether they feel like caring for others or feel that they themselves require care.

An individual's feelings at middle age may also depend on gender. Because female menopause occurs fairly early in the life cycle (usually between the ages of forty-five and fifty), and because it is a decisive event, women may be more sensitive than men to lasting physical changes. For mothers who have been charged with childrearing, middle age is also the time children leave home: some women become markedly depressed as a result of the feelings that their chief mission in life has ended (Scarf, 1980). Yet for others this period provides an opportunity for fresh discoveries and new life experiences.

Men do not undergo the same definite physical changes, but neither do they ordinarily have the sudden opportunity for change in their routines. Thus middle age for them may be a time of boredom, fatigue, and occasional depression, as the chance for major changes in life slips away. Some observers speak of a "mid-life crisis" during the forties: a time when, having achieved the mark of success in one area, but still feeling unfulfilled, men (and an increasing number of women) engineer a decisive shift in their career paths and in their lifestyles. This crisis has some of the trappings of a second adolescence—an identity crisis revisited; yet, though such a characterization suggests that the mid-life crisis is an invention of the contemporary media, the medieval poet Dante reminds us it is not. His *Divine Comedy* begins with these words: "In the middle of the journey of our life, I came to myself within a dark wood, where the straight way was lost. Ah, how hard a thing it is to tell of that wood, savage, and harsh and dense."

One way or another, the individual in mid-life must come to grips with her position in her community and confront the finitude of her own existence. The period of **old age** begins as early as sixty or as late as seventy. At this time most individuals retire or lose their jobs, begin to fail physically (and sometimes mentally), settle firmly in their ways, fear changes, and crave security. In our society, the elderly are typically seen as passive, letting things happen to them but hoping to avoid the unpleasant or unexpected. Men and women are also seen as more alike, with men in particular taking on more of the physical and psychological traits usually associated with women (Hyde and Phillis, 1979). Older individuals turn inward, exhibit increasing interest in the past, and may attach new significance to religion. Old age means losing one's friends and, often, one's spouse through death. It may mean becoming unable to care for one's home or oneself, with the increasing possibility of being placed in a special facility for the elderly.

But is this pattern of aging, so common in American society, natural and inevitable? Based on observations of other societies, particularly preliterate and oriental cultures, some authorities propose that old age could be a much happier and fuller time (see Comfort, 1976; Rosenfeld, 1976). They maintain that mental or physical decline does not have to occur: persons can remain vigorous, active, dignified, and fulfilled until their eighties or even nineties. Further, the older person has vast reservoirs of knowledge, experience, and wisdom, on which the community can (and should) draw.

The Course of the Self

Nearly all scholars concerned with development have emphasized the role of the self (see Brim, 1976; Dickstein, 1977; Geertz, 1973). They allude to the individual's mental representation of her abilities, needs, and goals; her organization of experience; her inner control, which influences decisions and life-style. The factors that contribute to the self—linguistic skills, cognitive capacities, social awareness, ability to take another's perspective, affective sensibilities—date back to the first years of life, but they culminate only toward the end of adolescence in a sense of identity (see Chapter 14). Once formed, the self has a definite and identifiable structure and tone: a person is clearly recognizable to herself. However, the individual's sense of self does not freeze; instead it continues to change and to become more differentiated throughout life, yielding an ever greater number of individual experiences, traits, and goals (Brim and Kagan, 1980). And the sense of self helps determine the individual's thoughts and actions throughout life. Indeed, a developed sense of self seems to be a judicious candidate for the end-state of human development.

Authorities differ on how best to conceive of the self in later life, but they agree that the origins of the self lie in the individual's earliest experience. And so, in an effort to trace the self in later life, we will review the principal phases in its development during childhood and adolescence. At each step, we will be aided by the metaphor proposed earlier in this book as a description of the period.

THE EARLY STAGES

Infancy. Newborns have no sense of self. They are *well-equipped strangers* who lack specific knowledge of the world but have the necessary reflexes and capacities with which to construct this knowledge.

By the end of infancy, children have made great strides toward evolving a sense of self. They can discriminate among other individuals—a necessary step for locating themselves within the world. They are attached to their parents, to other people, and perhaps also to a treasured toy or transitional object. In coming to know others, children see the range of behaviors in which they can engage; and, perhaps aided by a transitional object, they draw a line at least tentatively between "me" and "not-me." They possess an important feeling of trust (or mistrust) that makes a crucial contribution to their eventual feelings about themselves. And each can represent in symbolic form that entity that is herself—a knowledge she demonstrates by using "me" or "I" or by recognizing herself in a mirror.

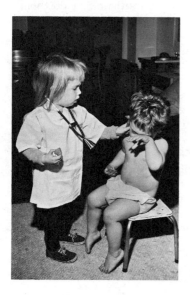

The Preschool Years. Between the ages of two and four children gain an indispensable tool for later life: an initial mastery of the world of symbols. They become able to use and understand words, pictures, gestures, numbers, and other elements that make reference. With these symbols, they can communicate with the world about them, especially with persons close to them, and they can come to know and refer to aspects of themselves. All the sensorimotor knowledge initially acquired is now captured on the level of symbols.

Toddlers are *players,* continually exploring the physical world; trying out symbols; toying with the lines between self and other, between real and fantastic, between order, freedom, and chaos. But their play is by no means frivolous. Rather, it offers a principal means by which the children can order the world and come to understand it. Expecially important here is imaginary play, in which the child tries out the roles of others—firefighter, mother, doctor, teddybear—in an effort to explore options and alight on her own potential role in the society. Children come to correlate the behaviors and states of other persons with their own: by identifying what is good and bad, happy and sad, old and young, they take an important step in defining what they are and what they are not. And, especially important, the child learns to differentiate between male and female, in the process forming a sex-role identification that will govern the child's gender for the rest of life.

The Years from Five to Seven. Self-definition accelerates during the years around the start of school. In the shift from age five to age seven, children no longer simply use but instead become dominated by symbols. Symbols direct their behavior and regulate the kind of sense they make of the world. Children now enter more fully into the social world of others: they can understand what others say, adopt others' perspectives, accept and perform tasks and assignments. They step beyond their immediate families to interact with peers and to assume roles in the larger society. And as they try out new roles, their views of themselves broaden to include influences beyond family.

Yet these children are not yet completely socialized, nor have they wholly embraced the goals and assignments of the

surrounding world. Instead, they can use their growing mastery of symbol systems to explore their own increasingly individual consciousness. They can put words together to tell stories. They can combine lines, shapes, and colors to produce interesting pictures. Often they fashion products of notable power and charm. They begin to exhibit distinctive styles and personalities. Children's special sensitivity to the power of symbols—and their ability to harness symbols in the service of their own ideas and feelings—confers an artistic flair on them at this age.

By school age, children have gained quite an awareness of themselves and their own identities. They have avowed goals and needs (Keller, Ford, and Meacham, n.d.); when they are asked to talk about themselves, they will readily cite their names, their bodies' physical possessions, and favored actions (Mohr, 1978). And yet these children, hardly self-conscious about all this, remain innocently fresh—again partaking of the vision of an *artist*.

Middle Childhood. By the age of eight or nine, children can use symbols fluently. Furthermore, their knowledge of the world extends beyond mere sensorimotor schemes; they can mentally reverse states of knowledge, classify flexibly, and easily take others' points of view. As concrete operators, they talk about and deal with most aspects of the physical world. And, for the first time, children begin to exhibit characteristic cognitive styles: they differ significantly in creativity, confidence, and the motivation to achieve.

These newfound mental powers and styles, coupled with a powerful memory and keen perceptual abilities, equip the child ideally for school. And, indeed, youngsters in middle childhood are enthusiastic and effective learners—*skill builders* who can train like athletes, compete vigorously, drill, rehearse, and improve until they attain a high level of proficiency. Never will children be more capable of collecting information, noticing details, discriminating among elements, and using this knowledge in securing their ends.

Yet this practicality and virtuosity has its limitations (Koocher, 1974; Montemayor and Eisen, 1975; Secord and Peevers, 1974). Often excessively literal-minded, children at this age want words and pictures to mean exactly what they say. They remain impatient with the subtle, the abstract, the aesthetic. Though capable of discussing past and future, they live largely in the present. This cast of mind comes through clearly in schoolchildren's sense of self. Although quite willing to talk about themselves, they continue to do so objectively, primarily in terms of surface impressions, physical traits, and indisputable facts. They equate themselves with the way they look, their possessions, likes and dislikes, and achievements in school and play; and they view others the same way.

Adolescence. Nowhere does the difference between the schoolchild and the adolescent emerge more clearly than in their self-descriptions. In sharp contrast to the schoolchild's emphasis on objective characteristics, the adolescent focuses on psychological traits. Adolescents talk about emotions, ethical and moral qualities, moods, ideas, beliefs, and goals. Their examination of themselves now penetrates surface features, invading the sphere of private beliefs and thoughts, focusing on how one feels about one's past and about one's future prospects . The adolescent's view of herself in time is also lengthened beyond days or weeks to cover the course of a life.

These changes reflect profound alterations in the individual's mental and emotional life that accompany the onset of puberty. Now capable of thinking scientifically and philosophically, adolescents readily engage in hypothetical thought; they can deal with possibilities, with alternatives, with fictional states, with mental experiments. At the same time, they also are subject to deeper and more powerful emotions than they experienced during the latency years of middle childhood. And, in part because they can gain far greater distance from themselves, they can reflect on their own cognitive and affective aspects, even as they can step more completely than ever before into the roles of others. Taken together, these alterations exert a revolutionary effect on the sense of self, which becomes the focus of all energies and attentions. The formation of identity (the ability to create and examine a metaphor that fuses diverse components into a coherent sense of self) is the central mission of adolescence. And the full capacities of the adolescent—*the young scientist-philosopher*—are brought to bear on this assignment.

AT MATURITY

After a sense of identity is formed, at the conclusion of adolescence, the sense of self comes to a point of repose. But this repose is only temporary: developments and alterations in the sense of self continue in later life. But just what form a mature sense of self should take remains difficult and controversial. In this section we will examine briefly the conceptions held by four thinkers in this area.

John Broughton's Studies of Self-Definition. John Broughton (1974, 1975*a*) has examined the ways individuals speak about themselves. As we noted above, preadolescents speak of themselves (as of the natural world) as distinct physical entities. In contrast, adolescents, believing totally in the existence of the self, see it as their essence, the dynamic that makes things happen; for them the body is simply a shadow concealing the true inner substance. Broughton also identifies a period of extreme relativism or skepticism, when some adolescents doubt that a self or a body exists at all and instead view both as mere inventions.

In Broughton's account, the most mature form of identity involves recognizing both a subjective entity called the "self" and an objective entity called the "body." Mental and physical elements are parallel aspects of one domain of knowledge—a set of categories we have devised for interpreting experience. Just as an outside world is seen as necessary for us to have anything to experience, the self is seen as necessary for making sense of our experience. Ultimately, the self emerges as a construction (or metaphor), one neither more nor less real than any other element of experience.

Jane Loevinger's Concept of the Ego. Jane Loevinger (1966, 1976) has attended to the development of the individual's ego—the person's evolving capacity to organize, regulate, and make sense of experiences. Loevinger discerns several primitive ego states that correspond roughly to the sense of self in the early years of life. In the first stage, children are *impulse-ridden*—dependent on others, and yet trying to exploit them. At this time, gaining satisfaction of desires is their major motive in life. Next, during the early school years, children are highly *expedient* and attempt to gain control over others. Most junior high school youngsters and some adults are at the next, *conformist* stage, emphasizing appearances and allegiance to rules, stressing the similarity between themselves and others. A more advanced stage of ego development is the *conscientious* stage, when persons have internalized the society's rules, feel guilty when they disobey, and accept responsibility for their acts. In this stage, reached by many adolescents and adults, individuals become aware of specific feelings in themselves and in others, and they recognize differences among individuals. Although generally obedient, they sometimes choose which societal rules to honor and begin to behave in an autonomous (rather than socially prescribed) manner. However, they may be too driven, too conscientious with respect to what they believe to be right; and they may be too prone to condemn others whose course differs from what they would favor.

Until this point, Loevinger's stages correspond, at least roughly, to the ages of her American subjects. However, unlike the phase sequences reviewed above, Loevinger's theory describes a sequence of structured stages. Whether an individual ever reaches higher steps in the sequence is not a function of age or life milestone, but rather the degree of integration of experiences that an individual may (but may not) be able to achieve. In this sense, Loevinger's theory resembles other stage accounts, such as that put forth by Kohlberg (see Chapter 13), and remains fundamentally different from the age-locked sequence of adult phases we reviewed above (cf. Lasker and Moore, 1979).

Loevinger describes two more advanced—and exceedingly rare—stages of ego development that wait upon considerable growth during the adult years and may be viewed as an endstate, an ideal of ego maturity. At an *autonomous* stage, individuals become more fully aware of the range of choices available and now tolerate rather than condemn those whose choices differ from their own. Their principal goal at this stage is to fulfill their own idealized image of how they should behave. At the same time, in viewing another person they take into account the other's personality, developmental history, and needs. They generally allow others to follow their own course, though they will still assume responsibility when the actions of others become intolerable.

Loevinger refrains from detailing the characteristics of her final, *integrated* stage, because she suspects that analysts would project their own values into a highest stage. But she does indicate that integrated individuals can reconcile their own inner conflicts, remain at peace with what they are, recognize and accept what they cannot attain, and cherish the individuality of others. With the knowledge that one cannot be all things to all individuals, they strive to create an environment in which self-realization becomes a reasonable goal for everyone.

Abraham Maslow's Ideal of Self-Actualization. For a respectable attempt to describe the highest possible levels of ego development, Loevinger recommends the work of Abraham Maslow. Based on case studies and on his own analysis of human development, Maslow (1954, 1962, 1971) has described gifted individuals who have achieved **self-actualization,** the ability to use one's capacities to good purpose, to become fully absorbed in what one deems important, and to do so in a lively yet selfless manner. Self-actualized individuals accept responsibility, are capable of making choices, are honest about their knowledge and limitations. A self-actualizer wishes to grow—to find out "who he is, what he is, what he likes, what he doesn't like, what is good for him and what bad, where he is going and what his mission is" (1971, pp. 48-49). Such individuals recognize their own psychological defenses (whether intellectualizing, denying, or some other distortion of personal experience) and find the courage to give them up. They can take every moment of life seriously and make the most of their own potential without dwelling on their difficulties and inadequacies.

These qualities allow the self-actualizer the elusive but vital capacity to undergo *peak experiences*—moments of ecstasy that occur when one is honest with oneself, willing to strive to realize one's potential, capable of listening to others, and open for discovering what one is. At such times, the individual tends to perceive experience as a whole, valuing the moment for the simple enjoyment of what it is rather than for its usefulness.

During a peak experience, one overcomes tensions, loses anxiety, and lovingly accepts the world with its imperfections. According to Maslow, "the emotional reaction in the peak experience has a special flavor of wonder, of awe, of reverence, of humility and surrender before the experience as before something great" (1962, pp. 87–88). Although he avoids offering a formula for attaining such peaks, Maslow does mention that they grace religious, artistic, mystical, or love experiences.

Erik Erikson's Final Crises. A last window on the mature sense of self is provided by Erik Erikson (Smelser and Erikson, 1980). Three of Erikson's eight stages, or crises, of the life cycle (see Figure 1.14, p. 51) occur during adulthood. After the adolescent crisis of identity versus role diffusion (see Chapter 14), the young adult must make decisions about marriage and family. Erikson characterizes this period as one of *intimacy* (a relatedness with others, especially a loved one) or *isolation* (an inability to form a loving relationship with others). The years of middle age, when a firm life-style has been established, are a period of *generativity* or *stagnation*. One can either enjoy a rich, full, and active life, or one can experience a seemingly stagnant, empty existence.

The final stage is a crisis of summing up—a time for reviewing and evaluating one's past. The alternatives here are stark: a feeling of *integrity*—that one has done one's best and that the events of one's life cohere and make sense; or a feeling of *despair*—that time has run out too soon, that one's contributions do not matter, and that one's life (or life in general) has been painfully futile.

For Erikson, a mature sense of self entails resolving each crisis in the direction of the positive outcome: in adolescence, a sense of identity; in young adulthood, intimacy; in middle age, generativity; and in old age, integrity. But Erikson also characterizes the mature sense of self more broadly. He speaks of the individual's sense of *mutuality*—a feeling that one can both give to others and accept from others (1963). The person capable of mutuality acts to strengthen others as well as herself. While developing her own potential, she facilitates the potentials of others. Clearly, mutuality is based on the Golden Rule: "Do unto others as you would wish them to do unto you." Yet it is also an extension of the Golden Rule, for Erikson stresses that all actions affect not only others but also oneself.

Erikson's original and revealing model for mutuality is the relation between the mother and her child. He sees the mother as enhancing herself and her sense of well-being while she helps her child gain a sense of trust and of self. But, as Erikson points out, it becomes possible (and important for the functioning of society) eventually to extend this general caring relation to any two individuals or groups or societies. Highlighting the integral link between the earliest feelings of trust and the ultimate emergence of integrity and mutuality, Erikson maintains that "the basic fact that will always keep and bring us all closer together is the nakedness and helplessness of the newborn human child" (1974, pp. 81–82).

A Final Signpost

We too must now take final stock. It would be most fitting if, at the end of this journey, we could declare that we have arrived at our destination and now know all about human development. But there are still too many questions not answered, too many paths not followed. We are closer to our goal than when we started, but the road ahead is still long.

What are some paths we might have followed more persistently? Our focus on the psychology of the individual has meant that we sometimes neglected the influences of family, peers, community, and culture. Similarly, our attention to the cognitive and affective events of the individual's development has resulted in an insufficient consideration of the physical, physiological, and genetic underpinnings of the developmental process. Finally, although we took note of dramatic differences among individuals from different settings, our picture of human development now needs to be supplemented by more detailed and extensive portraits of abnormal children or of individuals reared in other, radically different cultures.

What are some possible future directions in developmental psychology? My own guess is that much of the next decade may be spent assessing the possibilities and limitations of Piaget's cognitive-structural view. Such an investigation is likely to dwell on the question of which human capacities are innate, requiring little stimulation from the environment, and which capacities continue to develop in the years following adolescence. The role of central operations like those studied by Piaget may be complemented by more detailed study of how specific media or symbol systems also contribute to mental growth. There will be consideration of the hypothesis that development consists of the growth of several separate cognitive systems, not necessarily linked, and increased concern with the relation among cognitive, social, and personality development. There may also be a more detailed examination of the concept of stages and structures; equally, there may be microscopic probings of the minute-by-minute steps involved in attaining a pivotal mental ability (like conservation) and in effecting a transition from one level of understanding to another.

Although responses to Piaget may occupy much of the developmentalist's attention, there may also be increased involvement with new tools of analysis. The electronic computer will be increasingly used, not merely to aid with complex data analysis, but also to model the processes that children exhibit in the course of problem solving and the stages through which they pass in the course of overall development. Our expanding understanding of the nervous system and the devising of new techniques that make it possible to monitor brain activity in noninvasive ways will inform our understanding of psychological development.

Other trends can be anticipated. Cross-cultural researchers may seek to determine which features of the Western view of development are truly universal and which are distorted by our own parochial measures or observations. Other researchers may try to determine whether there are differences in development stemming from the era in which a person happens to live. The later periods of development, especially middle and old age, may undergo considerably more scrutiny. Finally, the twin disciplines of ethology (the naturalistic observation of children) and ecology (the effect of the individual's natural and cultural environment) may be used more often to yield a fuller portrait of human development. But the advent of new techniques and more technical disciplines can never supplant the role of the alert human researcher: there will always be a central place in developmental psychology for the original thinker who can discover a compelling new phenomenon or synthesize various strands of research into a more comprehensive theory.

The study of human development has been one of the truly exciting areas in social science in the past few decades, and I believe it will remain so. I hope you will also continue to follow events in the field; I would be delighted to learn that some readers of this book have become developmental psychologists. In the meantime, I hope this book has provided some facts and concepts and, more important, some themes with which to organize your own intuitions and conceptions about how individuals develop. As the memories of specific data fade, I hope these themes will remain to help you acquire further knowledge about the world of persons and to enhance your understanding of your own growth.

Glossary

Note: Terms appearing within definitions in **boldface** type are defined elsewhere in the glossary. Page numbers following each definition refer to the place in the text where the term is defined in context.

accommodation: Piaget's term for the process by which a child reworks a **scheme** to fit a new object, idea, or action. (p. 64)

achievement motivation: The need to overcome obstacles and exercise power. (p. 481)

achievement of identity: The point at which an individual is pursuing a self-chosen occupation and ideological goal. (p. 574)

adolescence: The period of life between **puberty** and maturity, during which the individual experiences physical, emotional, and **cognitive** changes (pp. 511, 541)

affective: Pertaining to feelings, emotions, and ties to other persons. (p. 18)

aggression: Overt physical violence toward people or property, the severity of which can be measured either by the amount of destruction or by the intention behind it. The aggression of preschool children is usually instrumental: it arises from frustration and is directed toward objects. Older children's aggression is more often hostile: it follows a threat to the child's self-esteem and is directed toward people. (p. 325)

alert inactivity: *See* states of arousal.

altruism: The selfless regard for others that results in aiding those in distress. (p. 200)

anal stage: According to **psychoanalytic theory,** the second stage of development in the second or third year of life, at the start of toilet training, during which **libidinal energy** is centered on elimination. (*See also* Oedipal stage; oral stage.) (p. 204)

androgyny: Possessing both masculine and feminine characteristics. (p. 557)

anorexia nervosa: A psychological disorder most common among adolescent girls, which is typified by a refusal to eat. (p. 378)

antisocial behavior: Actions performed intentionally to injure or harm another individual (e.g., stealing). (p. 200)

artistic process: A form of activity that includes alertness to traditional art forms and use of the nonpragmatic, expressive properties of **symbols.** (p. 341)

assimilation: Piaget's term for the process by which the child adjusts an object, action, or idea to fit a preexisting **scheme.** (p. 64)

association of ideas: Mental mechanism whereby objects, actions, or ideas become linked so that one elicits the other. A crucial notion in **empiricism.** (p. 81)

associative fluency: The capacity to respond to a task with many unusual and creative associations. (p. 416)

attachment bond: An enduring affectional bond between two organisms—typically a parent and child—arising as a result of intensive interaction over a period of time. (p. 36)

autonomy: Independence from others: an important goal of **adolescence.** (p. 569)

Babinski reflex: An infant's **reflex** consisting of spreading the toes on stimulation of the sole of the foot. (p. 104)

basic object level: An intermediate level of naming or classifying objects between the superordinate and subordinate levels (e.g., using the label "dog" rather than "animal" or "collie"). (p. 185)

behavioral autonomy: The status, sought in **adolescence,** to work, play, spend money, date, select friends, and perform other daily behaviors on one's own. (p. 569)

behaviorism: School of psychological thought based on the study of overt behavior. The major premise is that behavior can be adequately understood by stimulus-response connections without reference to conscious or to mental mechanisms. (p. 83)

bimodal scheme: A mental structure (or **scheme**) involving two sensory modes. (p. 120)

centrality of sex: A keystone of **adolescence** beginning with bodily changes which evoke strong passions and lead to desires for sexual relations. (p. 542)

cerebral cortex: Outer surface of the brain. (p. 280)

chromosome: String of **genes,** within the cell's **nucleus,** bearing genetic information. In humans, twenty-three chromosomes each are donated by the sperm and egg to the zygote. All other cells contain twenty-three pairs, one chromosome in each pair donated by the mother, the other by the father. (p. 100)

circular reaction: Piaget's term for an action

whose completion leads automatically to its repetition, with slight modifications. (*See also* primary, secondary, and tertiary circular reactions.) (p. 68)

classical conditioning: Form of learning in which a neutral **stimulus,** when paired repeatedly with an **unconditioned stimulus,** eventually comes to evoke the original response. (p. 81)

class inclusion: According to Piaget, the **operation** of seeing the same object as a member simultaneously of increasingly broad categories. (p. 442)

clinical approach: A mode of studying human behavior through psychotherapy with disturbed people. (p. 13)

clinical interview: A mode of studying human behavior through loosely structured, lengthy interviews with normal people. (p. 13)

cognitive: Pertaining to mental processes, such as the abilities to reason and to solve problems. (p. 18)

cognitive-structural theory: An orientation in developmental psychology that views the child as an active agent constructing knowledge of the world. Cognitivists focus on rules and patterns governing the physical world and believe development consists of a set of discrete stages. (p. 17)

cognitive style: The way an individual conceptualizes or approaches tasks; a distinctive way of perceiving, feeling, making, and problem-solving that constitutes part of an individual's personality. (p. 562)

compensation: According to Piaget, the **operation** of mentally compensating for changes in appearance, recognizing that they balance each other. (p. 389)

conceptual tempo: A **cognitive style** involving an individual's characteristic rhythm or timing in classification and matching tasks. Conceptual tempo can be either reflective (slow, careful, inhibited, and anxious) or impulsive (rapid, careless, and spontaneous). (p. 483)

concrete operations: According to Piaget, the stage of development during middle childhood when the child begins to use **operations** with reference to physical objects. (p. 390)

conditioned response (CR): In **classical conditioning,** an action or set of actions in response to a **conditioned stimulus.** (p. 82)

conditioned stimulus (CS): In **classical conditioning,** the stimulus that produces a **conditioned response** only if it has been previously paired with an **unconditioned stimulus.** (p. 82)

conditioning: *See* classical conditioning; instrumental conditioning. (p. 81)

conservation: According to Piaget, the knowledge that quantity, number, area, volume, etc., remain the same despite changes in their appearance. (p. 388)

continuous quantity: A quantity of a substance (like liquid or clay) that is not made up of discrete elements. (*See also* discontinuous elements.) (p. 388)

control group: The group of individuals from the **population** in which all variables are held constant. (p. 9)

coordination of secondary schemes: Piaget's term to describe the way an infant combines **secondary circular reactions** and uses them intentionally, with increasing skill, to secure a goal. (p. 69)

creativity: The capacity to discover new ideas and to effect connections among diverse domains. (p. 415)

critical period: A specific interval when certain physical or psychological events must occur if an organism's development is to proceed normally. (*See also* sensitive period.) (p. 34)

cross-cultural: Comparing individuals drawn from different cultures. (p. 525)

cross-modal zones: Regions of the **cerebral cortex** that integrate information relayed by the **primary sensory cortex** and the **secondary processing areas** into an organized experience. (p. 280)

cross-sectional method: Comparing the performances of several subjects of different ages at one time. (*See also* longitudinal.) (p. 12)

crying vocalization: *See* states of arousal.

crystallized intelligence: The part of intellect including vocabulary and general factual information. Old people are thought to retain a high level of this intellectual competence. (p. 580)

decentration: Piaget's term for the child's increasing capacity to transcend **egocentrism** and to view the world as others view it. (p. 63)

defense mechanism: According to **psychoanalytic theory,** a reaction to conflict that protects the person from anxiety by disguising real goals or motives. (p. 203)

denote: Term used when a **symbol** is used to stand for an element in the world, in contrast to when it is used to express feelings or abstract properties. (e.g., the word *dog* denotes the class of canines.) (p. 339)

deoxyribonucleic acid or **DNA:** The substance composing all genes which directs and determines all the activity of living matter—sometimes called the "substance of life." (p. 100)

dependent variable: *See* factors.

developmental: *See* organismic-developmental approach.

developmental psycholinguistics: The study of how children acquire competence in language. (*See also* psycholinguistics.) (p. 160)

differentiation: The development over time of a diffuse whole organism or system into separate parts with specialized functions and structures. (*See also* integration.) (p. 256)

discontinuous elements: Elements like pebbles or beads that are separate from each other but can form a quantity. (*See also* continuous quantity.) (p. 396)

discrepant stimulus: A stimulus that differs materially from an existing **schematic image** but is not totally remote from it. Moderate discrepancies attract more attention than identical stimuli or widely discrepant stimuli. (p. 117)

disequilibrium: In the **organismic-developmental approach,** the state when some of an organism's **mental structures** are competing against others, and tension results. Often fosters advancement to a new stage of development. (*See also* equilibrium.) (p. 262)

dizygotic twins: *See* fraternal twins.

dominant trait: A trait that emerges in the **phenotype** from a dominant gene and hence appears when either parent contributes the gene. (p. 103)

dual ambivalence: A characteristic of both parent and youth during the youth's adolescence, when both struggle to accept the youth's growing **autonomy.** (p. 563)

duos: Word pairs spoken by children toward the end of their second year that express their **sensorimotor** intelligence. (p. 168)

eclectic: An approach to a field of study that draws assumptions, methods, and concepts from various sources. (p. 500)

ectoderm: The outer primary layer of the **embryo**'s skin; it develops into sensory organs, nervous system, outer layer of skin, hair, nails, and part of the teeth. (p. 96)

egocentric speech: Piaget's term for children's speech that is spoken aloud but addressed to no listener in particular, a reflection of children's **egocentrism.** (p. 284)

egocentrism: Piaget's term for the young child's inability to take another person's perspective. (p. 63)

eidetic imagery: A special ability to continue to scan a visual display even after it has been removed from the visual field. Declines after middle childhood. (p. 362)

embryo: The developing human organism during the first eight weeks following conception. (p. 96)

embryonic stage: The eight weeks following the **germinal period** during which the human organism increases in size 2 million percent, begins to take shape, and begins to form various organ systems. (p. 96)

emotional autonomy: A relationship between a youth and the family that involves new closeness; earlier ties of dependence have loosened and any feelings of dependence are now mutual. (p. 569)

empathy: The experience of another person's emotional state. (p. 220)

empiricism: Philosophical stance that knowledge can be derived only from sensation, that is, from experience in the world. (p. 59)

empiroscientific view: The logical approach to one's experience that is characteristic of individuals in the modern West—contrasted with the **mythopoetic view.** (p. 448)

endoderm: The inner primary layer of the **embryo**'s skin; develops into the gastrointestinal tract, vital organs (e.g., liver and lungs), and various glands. (p. 96)

end state: Relatively complete, specific description of the developed form of behavior toward which change is seen to be directed. (p. 260)

environmental-learning theory: An orientation in developmental psychology that views the child as a passive receptacle heavily influenced by the environment. Environmentalists focus on the specific contents of the child's world and regard development as a continuous process. (p. 18)

equilibration: *See* equilibrium.

equilibrium (or equilibration): According to Piaget, the state in which neither **assimilation** nor **accommodation** dominates. In the **organismic-developmental approach,** equilibrium refers to a basic property of organic matter that keeps the biological and psychological organism stable and functioning. (*See also* disequilibrium.) (pp. 65, 260)

errors of growth: Mistakes that result from the overgeneralization of newly learned rules; common in language (e.g., I runned). (p. 173)

estimators: Mental processes by which people determine quantity. (*See also* operators.) (p. 397)

ethology: Observational study of an organism's set of behaviors as they occur in the natural habitat. (p. 33)

experimental group: That group of individuals from the **population** subjected to the independent variable. (p. 9)

exploratory play: *See* play.

extinction: Process by which a **conditioned stimulus,** presented without the **unconditioned stimulus,** gradually ceases to evoke the **conditioned response.** (*See also* classical conditioning.) (p. 82)

factors (or variables): Conditions of the **hypothesis** that are either manipulated by the experimenter (independent variables) or that change as a result of that manipulation (dependent variables). (p. 10)

fetal period: The final stage of prenatal development, which begins in the third month after conception and lasts until birth. (p. 96)

field dependence: A **cognitive style** involving the inability to ignore misleading perceptual cues in certain cognitive tasks and a general tendency to respond to influences in one's immediate environment. (*See also* field independence.) (p. 561)

field independence: A **cognitive style** involving the ability to maintain one's spatial orientation and to ignore misleading perceptual cues. (*See also* field dependence.) (p. 561)

figurative knowledge: According to Piaget, knowledge about specific sensory configurations in the world. (p. 409)

figure: Term used in studies of perception to refer to an entire, organized form—contrasted with isolated features or parts. (p. 116)

five-to-seven shift: Dramatic changes in physical, cognitive, linguistic, motor, emotional, and social development that occur between the ages of five and seven. (p. 278)

foreclosure: Term used by Marcia to describe the type of identity formation in which an individual's career and ideological patterns have been imposed by parents. (p. 574)

formal operations: According to Piaget, the stage of development during **adolescence** when the child begins to use **operations** with reference to abstract elements like verbal propositions. (p. 390)

fraternal twins (or **dizygotic twins):** Twins that result from the union of two separate sperm and eggs and thus do not share identical heredity. (*See also* identical twins.) (p. 308)

free recall: The ability to remember a series of items. (p. 433)

frontal lobes: Area in the front of the brain that controls voluntary motor activities. (p. 280)

gender (psychosexual identity or **sex-role identity):** The sex group (masculine or feminine) with which an individual feels **identification.** (p. 201)

gene: A large, complex molecule that carries the traits of parents and transmits them to offspring. Approximately 20,000 genes make up a chromosome. (p. 100)

generalization: Process by which the response to a specific stimulus becomes the response to a variety of similar stimuli. (*See* classical conditioning.) (p. 82)

genotype: The total genetic makeup contributed by the parent cells. Can give rise to infinite **phenotypes.** (p. 101)

germ cell: A reproductive cell—the sperm or egg cell—containing the **chromosomes,** which carry genetic material. (p. 100)

germinal period: A one- to two-week period following conception during which the **zygote** travels to the uterus, where it is firmly implanted. (p. 96)

grasp reflex: *See* reflex.

habituation: An organism's decreasing responsiveness to a stimulus that has become familiar and predictable by repetition. (*See* classical conditioning.) (p. 83)

hermaphrodity: Possessing both male and female sex charcteristics. (p. 226)

hostile aggression: *See* aggression.

hypothesis: A tentative assumption precise enough to be tested. (p. 7)

identical twins (or **monozygotic twins):** Twins that result from the union of a single sperm and a single egg and thus share identical heredity. (*See also* fraternal twins.) (pp. 100, 308)

identification: A developmental process that results in children's resembling adult figures whom they love or admire. Explanations include those by **psychoanalytic theory, observational-learning theory,** and **cognitive-structural theory.** (*See also* imitation.) (p. 206)

identification with the aggressor: Term used by Freud to describe children who merge their **identities** with, and strive to become like, the individuals whom they most fear. (p. 208)

identity: According to Piaget, the **operation** of mentally equating one quantity with another, knowing they have not been changed in any way. (p. 389). In Erikson's system, an individual's emerging sense of self as it is realized during adolescence. (*See also* identity diffusion.) (p. 542)

identity diffusion: The term used by Erikson to describe the type of **identity** formation in which an individual has no clear occupational or ideological direction. (p. 574)

idiot savants: Individuals of limited or average ability who excel in a single, isolated area such as mathematics or music. (p. 380)

imitation: The tendency of children to duplicate the actions of others. According to **environmental-learning theory,** children are likely to imitate if they are **reinforced** for doing so. (*See also* identification.) (p. 208)

immediate memory: Memory of events happening in the past second. (*See also* long-term memory; short-term memory.) (p. 433)

impelling speech: Language which stimulates a child to perform an action, though not necessarily what was requested. (p. 289)

imprinting: A form of learning that occurs early in life, is resistant to **extinction,** and results in a bond expressed by following and other behaviors that are designed to achieve proximity to a caretaker. (p. 34)

impulsivity: See conceptual tempo.

incidental learning: The tendency to attend to and remember apparently irrelevant aspects of an object or event. (p. 437)

independent variable: See factors.

individual differences: Behaviors or responses that vary consistently among subjects of the same age who come from a homogeneous population. (e.g., individual children differ in whether they are relatively reflective or impulsive.) (p. 12)

infantile autism: A severe childhood disorder characterized by unresponsiveness, constant efforts to maintain sameness in the surroundings, and inability to use language to convey meaning. (p. 371)

information processing: An approach to cognitive psychology in which the process of task execution or problem-solving is broken down into a series of steps. (p. 418)

initiation rite: A ceremony marking a youth's passage from childhood to adulthood, or maturity. (p. 549)

innate releasing mechanism: *See* releaser.

inner speech: According to Lev Vygotsky, the covert use of language as an aid in reasoning; the successor to **egocentric speech.** (pp. 195, 285)

instrumental aggression: *See* aggression.

instrumental conditioning: Form of learning that occurs when an organism's behavior (an **operant)** is **reinforced** by reward. (p. 83)

integration: The process of an organism's separate parts coming together into a new and more highly organized form. (*See also* differentiation.) (p. 257)

intelligence: According to some researchers, the knowledge of vocabulary, general information, and puzzle-solving as measured by IQ tests; currently a controversial area. (p. 409)

interactionism: In the **organismic-developmental approach,** the view that development is the product of an interplay between individual predisposition (genetic factors, current stage, past history) and environmental forces (other people, social factors, cultural traditions). (p. 261)

intersection of social roles: The situation in which the same individual performs more than one **social role** at the same time (e.g., being both a doctor and a father). (p. 247)

internalization: That phase of the process of **identification** in which aspects of one's parents and society become a part of one's **identity.** (p. 206)

intuitive stage: *See* symbolic stage.

irregular sleep: *See* states of arousal.

libidinal energy (or sexual energy): According to **psychoanalytic theory,** a mobile substance that supplies the sexual drive and governs important behaviors and motivations throughout life. (p. 204)

longitudinal method: A study comparing the performances of the same subjects over a period of time. (*See also* cross-sectional.) (p. 12)

long-term memory: Memory spanning hours and longer periods of time. (*See also* immediate memory; short-term memory.) (p. 433)

lower class: *See* social class.

mediating response: A hypothesized internal response that labels a stimulus, recodes it, and guides the outward response to it. (p. 295)

medium: A material or apparatus used to embody **symbols.** (p. 340)

mental structure: A psychological capacity for processing information and analyzing experience; a general way of knowing the world. (*See also* scheme.) (p. 60)

mesoderm: The middle primary layer of the **embryo**'s skin; develops into muscles, skeleton, and excretory and circulatory systems. (p. 96)

metacognition: The individual's awareness of and reflection upon his own **cognitive** processes. (p. 444)

metalinguistic skill: The ability to reflect upon language, rather than simply to use it. (pp. 161, 191)

metamemory: The individual's awareness of and reflection upon his own mnemonic processes. (p. 439)

middle age: The period of an individual's life spanning the time when he is approximately between forty and sixty years old. (p. 582)

middle class: *See* social class.

molar approach: An emphasis on broad issues and concepts, typical of the **cognitive-structural theory.** (*See also* molecular approach.) (p. 293)

molecular approach: An emphasis on specific, narrow elements and step-by-step solution of problems; typical of **environmental-learning theory.** (*See also* molar approach.) (p. 293)

monomatric: A household in which one individual performs the childrearing activities. (*See also* polymatric.) (p. 45)

monozygotic twins: *See* identical twins.

moratorium: According to Erikson, a period during adolescence in which one experiments with various roles but makes no commitment to any single role. (pp. 573, 574)

Moro reflex: An infant's reflex consisting of flinging the arms out, extending fingers, and returning arms to the middle of the body when head position changes suddenly. (p. 103)

morphemes: The smallest units of meaning, including all words and word particles that carry **semantic** weight. (p. 171)

motor memory: The ability to recall learned patterns of movement. (*See also* verbal memory; visual memory.) (p. 433)

mythopoetic view: An approach to one's experience that is found in many unschooled societies and differs from that found in Western societies—contrasted with **empiroscientific view.** (p. 448)

nativism: Philosophical stance based on the belief that all knowledge is already programmed in each newborn and that these inborn capacities will emerge independent of environmental stimulation. (p. 59)

nonreversal shift: A form of **discrimination learning** in which **reinforcement** is changed to reward one pole of a totally new dimension (e.g., black-white instead of small-large). (*See also* reversal shift.) (p. 295)

nucleus: The central portion of every cell. The nucleus of the human **zygote** contains the information-bearing **chromosomes.** (p. 95)

object concept: The term used by Piaget to describe the understanding of the nature and properties of objects, most especially the fact that they continue to exist when no longer in view. (p. 72)

object permanence: Piaget's term for the general **scheme** or **mental structure** of knowing that objects continue to exist even when they disappear from view. (p. 64)

oddity-learning problem: A learning task in which subjects must focus on some stimuli dimensions and ignore others in order to select an "odd" stimulus from a group. (p. 405)

Oedipal stage: According to **psychoanalytic theory,** the third stage of development between the third and sixth years, during which **libidinal energy** centers around the genitals. During this period, the boy desires union with his mother and removal of his father. (*See also* anal stage; oral stage.) (p. 204)

old age: The final period of life, beginning anytime between the ages of sixty and eighty, during which an individual usually retires and often starts to fail both physically and mentally. (p. 583)

operant: In **instrumental conditioning,** a behavior in the repertoire of an organism. (p. 83)

operant conditioning: *See* instrumental conditioning.

operation: Piaget's term for a **scheme** involving internal mental representation; an action performed mentally. (*See* concrete operations; formal operations.) (pp. 63, 390)

operationalization: A step in psychological investigation in which the experimenter defines the procedures used to represent the major concepts in the **hypothesis.** (p. 8)

operative knowledge: According to Piaget, knowledge that derives from **operations** on physical objects or abstract elements. (*See also* figurative knowledge.) (p. 409)

operators: The mental processes by which people comprehend the consequences of manipulating elements. (*See also* estimators.) (p. 397)

oral stage: According to **psychoanalytic theory,** the first stage of development in the first year of life, during which **libidinal energy** is centered around the mouth. Involves needs of gratification. (*See also* anal stage; Oedipal stage.) (p. 204)

organismic: *See* organismic-developmental approach.

organismic-developmental approach: The approach to psychology outlined by Heinz Werner, which is known as "organismic" because it emphasizes the coherence of the whole organism; "developmental," because it assesses the organism in terms of its degree of development. (p. 258)

orthogenetic principle: Principle of the **organismic-developmental approach** holding that development occurs when an organism proceeds from a diffuse whole with little organization to a state of increasing **differentiation,** coordination, and structural **integration.** (p. 259)

penis envy: A Freudian concept which explains what motivates a young girl to seek a strong love attachment to her father: she becomes angry at her mother for not satisfying all her needs and blames her mother for her lack of a penis. (p. 208)

perceptual constancies: *See* shape constancy; size constancy.

periodic sleep: *See* states of arousal.

permissive: A style of childrearing in which parents are reluctant to set firm guidelines, are lax in implementing punishments, and encourage the child to express ideas and fulfill his own wishes, even at the cost of others. (p. 312)

phenotype: An organism's observable characteristics; the environment's determination of the **genotype**'s expression. (p. 101)

phonemes: The basic units of sound that make up language. (p. 158)

phonology: The study of the nature of and relations among sounds of language. (p. 158)

placenta: A fleshy disc rich in blood vessels that attaches the **embryo** to the uterine wall; it transmits essential nutrients to the fetus and returns wastes back to the mother for excretion. (p. 98)

play: Behavior not specifically intended to solve problems, satisfy biological need, overcome an obstacle, or contribute to a ritual; it may be either exploratory (rehearsal of behaviors the child is in the process of mastering) or rule-governed (following a set of cultural rules). (p. 234)

polymatric: A household in which more than one person performs the childrearing activities. (*See also* monomatric.) (p. 45)

population: The group of people to be studied in an experiment. (p. 9)

pragmatics: Term used to refer to the uses to which language can be put. (p. 160)

preoperational stage: *See* symbolic stage.

primary circular reaction: Piaget's term for the infant's early, repetitive actions: the completion of the act triggers the repetition of the act. Sensorimotor substage 2. (p. 68)

primary sensory cortex: Collective term for several areas of the **cerebral cortex** that respond to sensory stimulation. (*See also* secondary processing areas.) (p. 280)

primary sexual changes: Certain pubescent changes considered central to the sexual development of an adolescent. In the female they include the onset of menstruation and an increase in the size of the vagina, clitoris, and uterus. In the male they are the onset of ejaculation along with an increase in the size of the penis and testes. (*See also* secondary sexual changes.) (p. 543)

primary signal system: Pavlovian term referring to an elementary system of signals or stimuli that trigger behavior in animals and humans. (*See also* secondary signal system.) (p. 289)

projective tests: Neutral sets of items to which subjects respond with personal interpretations, thereby revealing aspects of their personalities and motivations. (p. 481)

prosocial behaviors: Actions performed to help another individual or group (e.g., comforting a crying child). (p. 200)

psychoanalysis: A form of treatment for emotional trauma and personality disorders founded by Sigmund Freud. Psychoanalysis involves "talking out" old experiences, analysis of dreams, and free association. (p. 203)

psychoanalytic theory: Sigmund Freud's theory that sexual factors motivate behavior and that treatment for emotional trauma and personality disorders involves exploration of patients' past experiences through techniques like free association and dream analysis. (p. 203)

psycholinguistics: The psychological study of language, the relations between its rules and the mind's operations, and the processes through which people acquire and use **transformations.** (*See also* developmental psycholinguistics.) (p. 160)

psychosexual identity: *See* gender.

puberty: The period between the ages of ten and

fifteen when humans' reproductive systems mature. (p. 541)

quest for autonomy: A central goal of **adolescence** which entails achieving a sense of independence and separation from family ties. (p. 542)

recessive trait: A trait that emerges in the **phenotype** only when both parents contribute the recessive gene. (p. 103)

reflectivity: *See* conceptual tempo.

reflex: A primitive, unlearned, and involuntary action that can be elicited by specific forms of stimulation and has or may once have had survival value. The infant's reflexes include: breathing; blinking; vomiting; coughing; sneezing; rooting (turning head and mouth toward a stimulus applied to the cheek); sucking; swallowing; the **Moro;** grasping (latching firmly to a finger or stick placed in the palm); the **Babinski;** and swimming (paddlelike arm and leg movements when placed in water). (p. 103)

regular sleep: *See* states of arousal.

reinforcement: In **instrumental conditioning,** rewarding an **operant** so it is more likely to occur. (p. 83)

releaser (or innate releasing mechanism—IRM): A key object in the environment that reliably elicits or "releases" a behavior pattern or response in members of a species. (p. 34)

response: An action or set of actions produced when an organism reacts to a **stimulus.** (p. 81)

restrictive: A style of childrearing in which parents set rigid guidelines for behavior, punish infractions, and discourage the expression of impulses or desires for autonomy. (p. 312)

reversal shift: A form of **discrimination learning** in which **reinforcement** is changed to reward the same dimension (e.g., size) but the opposite value of that dimension (small instead of large). (*See also* nonreversal shift.) (p. 295)

reversibility: According to Piaget, the **operation** of mentally returning a quantity to its original state in order to verify its sameness. (p. 389)

role: In play, the part or character assumed by a person, animal, or humanlike prop. (p. 236)

role diffusion: According to Erikson, the alternative to identity formation in which the youth withdraws into **despair** and wanders from one pursuit to another. (p. 573)

rooting reflex: *See* reflex.

rule-governed play: *See* play.

scene: A sequence of play involving **roles** engaged in a series of related activities (e.g., a birthday party). (p. 237)

schedule of reinforcement: In **instrumental conditioning,** a plan describing when and how reinforcement may be applied; **reinforcement** may be scheduled continuously, at a fixed or variable ratio, or at fixed or variable intervals of time. (p. 84)

schema: *See* schematic image.

schematic image: A mental representation, based on experience with an object, that highlights the object's most distinctive elements and serves as reference for subsequent perceptual experiences. (p. 117)

scheme: Piaget's term for the aspect of a capacity that holds constant across all particular realizations of that capacity. A specific way of knowing the world. (*See also* mental structure; operation.) (p. 63)

secondary circular reaction: Piaget's term for an action that indicates the infant's intention: the child repeats actions that have met with success, though the actions are crude and often not well matched to the goal. Sensorimotor substage 3. (p. 69)

secondary processing areas: Regions of the **cerebral cortex** that recognize an object's significance. (*See also* primary sensory cortex.) (p. 280)

secondary sexual changes: Certain pubescent changes considered to be less central than the **primary sexual changes.** They include growth of facial hair, deepening of the voice, and broadening of the shoulders in the male. The female develops larger breasts and wider hips, and in both sexes pubic hair starts to appear. (*See also* primary sexual changes.) (p. 543)

secondary signal system: Pavlovian term referring to the system in humans, based on the **primary signal system,** that draws on verbal and other forms of symbolic knowledge in the culture. (p. 289)

self-actualization: According to Maslow, the ability to make the most of one's potential and to undergo peak experiences, during which one perceives life as a whole. (p. 589)

semantics: The meanings of language; the study of the relationship between words and the concepts they denote. (p. 158)

sense of object permanence: *See* object permanence.

sensitive period: A period during development when the organism is particularly prone to learn or develop in some area. (*See also* critical period.) (p. 34)

sensorimotor stage: According to Piaget, the first stage of **cognitive** development during early childhood. At this time all knowledge derives from motor actions and sensory perceptions; the child gradually becomes able to define goals and to perform actions in an increasingly systematic fashion. (p. 68)

separation anxiety: A common fear among one-year-olds of separation from the mother. (*See also* stranger anxiety.) (p. 36)

sex: An organism's identity as male or female, determined at conception by the combination of X and Y **chromosomes** contributed by the parents (male if XY, female if XX). (*See also* sex-role identity.) (p. 201)

sex role identity: The sex group (masculine or feminine) with which an individual feels **identification.** (*See also* gender.) (p. 227)

sexual energy: *See* libidinal energy.

shape constancy: The perception that an object

is the same object even though its orientation or form in space changes and it looks like a different shape. (p. 115)

shaping: Instrumental conditioning in which behaviors resembling the desired behavior are **reinforced** with increasing selectivity until the precise desired behavior is attained. (p. 83)

short-term memory: Memory of events happening minutes ago. (*See also* immediate memory; long-term memory.) (p. 433)

size constancy: The perception that an object remains the same object, with the same physical size, even when it is nearer and thus looks larger or farther and thus looks smaller. (p. 115)

social class: A group of people whose backgrounds, educations, occupations, and incomes are similar. The class distinctions usually made include upper class (wealthy backgrounds, highly successful executives or professionals); middle class (moderately successful professionals with substantial income but little inherited wealth); working class (blue-collar, lower-level white-color, and semiskilled workers, many of foreign ethnic stock); and lower class (people with near-subsistence incomes, including a disproportionate number of nonwhites). (p. 327)

social cognition: An individual's knowledge of and interaction with significant other persons. (p. 460)

social learning (or observational learning): The learning process of observing the behavior that others model and then carrying out the behavioral sequence witnessed. (p. 203)

social role: A pattern of behavior that reflects an individual's status or place within a group or society. (p. 247)

sociobiology: A school of science which maintains that social behaviors are determined by biological or genetic factors. (p. 201)

somatic cell: A cell that makes up all parts of the body except the **germ cell** (i.e., sperm and egg). (p. 100)

states of arousal: Infant states characterized by definite facial expressions and behaviors, including: regular sleep (slow, even breathing and little facial or bodily movement); irregular sleep (quick, uneven breathing and frequent movements); periodic sleep (rapid, shallow breathing alternating with deep, slow breathing); alert inactivity (regular breathing, relaxed face, visual exploration); waking activity (irregular breathing and diffuse movement); crying vocalization (diffuse movement, eyes tightly closed, crying). (p. 105)

statistical analysis: Mathematical procedures performed on experimental data to determine the validity of the results. (p. 11)

status envy: An explanation of **identification** that states that admiration for a parent leads a child to assume the parent's characteristics. (p. 208)

stereotyping: A person's grouping of many other individuals into a single unrealistic category; often

caused by an inadequate sense of one's own self. (p. 559)

stimulus: A physical event that elicits a **response** or behavior. (p. 81)

stranger anxiety: A common fear among one-year-olds of strangers threatening the **attachment bond** with the mother. (*See also* separation anxiety.) (p. 36)

sucking reflex: *See* reflex.

superego: In **psychoanalytic theory,** the conscience that develops as a result of **identification** with the parent. (p. 206)

surrogate: The term used to refer to a substitute mother. In Harlow's studies, infant monkeys were housed with objects, or surrogates, in place of their biological mothers. (p. 29)

swallow reflex: *See* reflex.

swimming reflex: *See* reflex.

symbol: Any element used to represent, depict, or denote some other element in the world, or to express or exemplify some property or quality of experience. (p. 339)

symbolic stage (or preoperational stage): In Piaget's **cognitive-structural theory,** the period between the ages of two and seven when the child begins to perceive and record experiences on a symbolic level. (p. 342)

symbol system: Combinations of **symbols** that are used together, such as written or spoken language. (p. 340)

synesthesia: The ability or tendency to translate experience perceived in one sense directly and almost automatically into another. (p. 362)

syntax: The rules governing word order in language. (p. 158)

system: A way of viewing the "family" as an organic entity; the focus falls on interactions among family members who have enduring relationships with one another. (p. 315)

systematic observations: The first step in psychological investigation involving the collection of facts about human behavior according to a prepared plan and meeting established standards of objectivity, accuracy, completeness, and reliability. **Observations** can be carried out on one's own behavior or on other people's behavior. (p. 7)

task-analytic: An approach to studying **cognitive** performance in which a task is broken into its component parts to determine how the task is carried out; the performance is then written out by the researcher in a step-by-step model. (p. 517)

temperament: An aspect of personality that reflects an individual's general style of behavior; it consists of such components as attention span, activity level, distractibility, and adaptability. (p. 105)

tertiary circular reaction: Piaget's term for an action that creatively restructures previous **schemes** to meet the demands of a new situation or goals. Sensorimotor substage 5. (p. 70)

transformations: Manipulations of words, word

particles, and word order that allow one to proceed from a basic sentence to related versions. (p. 166)

transitional object: An inanimate physical object that a young child becomes attached to and performs behavioral sequences with in order to satisfy **affective** and **cognitive** needs. (p. 237)

unconditioned response (UR): In **classical conditioning,** the innate, automatic response to an **unconditioned stimulus.** (p. 82)

unconditioned stimulus (US): In **classical conditioning,** a stimulus whose effectiveness does not depend on prior conditioning. (p. 82)

upper class: *See* social class.

value autonomy: A situation in which a child's attitudes and values become increasingly independent of those of the parents and of their generation, and no longer coincide with them. (p. 569)

verbal memory: The ability to recall verbal material, whether spoken or written. (*See also* motor memory; visual memory.) (p. 433)

visual memory: The ability to recall visual im-ages. (*See also* motor memory; verbal memory.) (p. 433)

voice onset time or **VOT:** In speech, the lag time between the parting of the lips and the vibration of the vocal cords which produce the sound. (p. 161)

waking activity: *See* states of arousal.

warp: According to Sullivan, a serious deviation from a healthy course of development. (p. 570)

wh-questions: Questions beginning with *who, what, why, where,* or *when.* (p. 173)

working class: *See* social class.

young adulthood: The period of life following **adolescence;** at this time an individual usually finds an occupation, decides whether or not to find a mate and become a parent, and seeks social and economic security. (p. 582)

zygote: A fertilized egg resulting from the union of a male sperm cell and female ovum. The human zygote contains twenty-three **chromosome** pairs. (p. 95)

References

Abramovitch, R., Corter, C., and Lando, B. Sibling interaction in the home. *Child Development,* 1979, *50,* 997-1003.

Ackerman, B. P. Children's comprehension of presupposed information: Logical and pragmatic inferences to speaker belief. *Journal of Experimental Child Psychology,* 1978, *26,* 92-114.

Acredolo, L. P. Laboratory versus home: The effect of environment on the nine-month-old infant's choice of spatial reference system. *Developmental Psychology,* 1979, *15,* 666-667.

Adams, V. Two verdicts on infant stereotyping. *Psychology Today,* 1980, *14,* 100.

Adelson, J. The dream of androgyny. *The New York Times Book Review.* March 9, 1980, p.3.

Adelson, J., and Doehrman, M. J. The psychodynamic approach to adolescence. In J. Adelson (Ed.), *Handbook of Adolescent Psychology.* New York: Wiley, 1980.

Adult Functional Competency Study. Austin, Texas: University of Texas, 1975.

Ahlgren, A., and Johnson, D. W. Sex differences on cooperative and competitive attitudes from the second through the twelfth grades. *Developmental Psychology,* 1979, *15,* 45-49.

Ährens, R. Beitgrage zur Entwicklung des Physiognomie und Mimikerkennens. *Zeitschrift für Experimentelle und Angewandte Psychologie,* 1954, *2,* 412-94, 599-633.

Ainsworth, M. *Infancy in Uganda.* Baltimore: Johns Hopkins University Press, 1967.

Ainsworth, M. Attachment theory and its utility in cross-cultural research. In P. H. Leiderman, S. R. Tulkin, and A. Rosenfeld (Eds.), *Culture and infancy: Variations in the human experience.* New York: Academic Press, 1977a.

Ainsworth, M. Infant development and mother-infant interaction among Ganda and American families. In P. H. Leiderman, S. R. Tulkin, and A. Rosenfeld (Eds.), *Culture and infancy: Variations in the human experience.* New York: Academic Press, 1977b.

Ainsworth, M. Infant-mother attachment. *American Psychologist,* 1979, *34,* 932-937.

Allen, D. A. The development of propositional speech in young children. Paper presented at the Society for Research in Child Development, New Orleans, March, 1977.

Allen, G. L., Kirasic, K. C., Siegel, A. W., and Herman, J. F. The developmental issues in cognitive mapping: The selection and utilization of environmental landmarks. *Child Development,* 1979, *50,* 1062-1070.

Alschuler, R. and Hattwick, L. *Painting and personality.* Chicago: University of Chicago Press, 1969.

Alston, W. P. Comments on Kohlberg's "From is to ought." In T. Mischel (Ed.), *Cognitive development and genetic epistemology.* New York: Academic Press, 1971.

Ambrose, J. A. The development of the smiling response in early infancy. In B. M. Foss (Ed.), *Determinants of infant behavior* (Vol. 1). New York: Wiley, 1961.

Amsterdam, B. and Greenberg, L. Self-conscious behavior of infants: A video study. *Developmental Psychobiology,* 1977, *10,* 1-60.

Anderson, C. O., and Mason, W. A. Early experience and complexity of social organization in groups of young rhesus monkeys. *Journal of Comparative and Physiological Psychology,* 1974, *87,* 681-90.

Ando, Y., and Hattori, H. Effects of intense noise during foetal life upon postnatal adaptability. *Journal of the Acoustical Society of America,* 1970, *47,* 1128.

Anglin, J. *The growth of word meaning.* Cambridge, Mass.: MIT Press, 1970.

Anglin, J. *Word, object and conceptual development.* New York: Norton, 1977.

Anooshian, L. R., and Owens, C. B. Children's acquisition of spatial location information in an unfamiliar environment. Paper presented at the Society for Research in Child Development, San Francisco, March, 1979.

Anthony, E. J. Psychoneurotic disorders. In A. M. Freedman and H. J. Kaplan (Eds.), *Comprehensive textbook of psychiatry.* Baltimore: Williams and Wilkins, 1967.

Anthony, E. J. The syndrome of the psychologically invulnerable child. In E. J. Anthony and C. Koupernik (Eds.), *The child in his family: Children at psychiatric risk* (Vol. 3). New York: Wiley, 1974.

Antinucci, F., and Parisi, D. Early language acquisition: A model and some data. In C. A. Ferguson and D. I. Slobin (Eds.), *Studies of child language development.* New York: Holt, Rinehart and Winston, 1973.

Apgar, V. A. A proposal for a new method of evaluation of the newborn infant. *Current Research in Anesthesia and Analgesia,* 1953, *32,* 260-267.

Apgar, V. A., and James, L. S. Further observations of the newborn scoring system. *American Journal Diseases of Children*, 1962, *104*, 419-428.

Appel, L. F., Cooper, R. G., McCarrell, N., Sims-Knight, J., Yussen, S. R., and Flavell, J. H. The development of the distinction between perceiving and memorizing. *Child Development*, 1972, *43*, 1365-1381.

Appleton, T., Clifton, R., and Goldberg, S. The development of behavioral competence in infancy. In F. Horowitz (Ed.), *Review of child development research* (Vol. 4). Chicago: University of Chicago Press, 1975.

Arbuthnot, J. Modification of moral judgment through role playing. *Developmental Psychology*, 1975, *11*, 319-24.

Ariès, P. *Centuries of childhood*. London: Jonathan Cape, 1962.

Arlin, P. K. Cognitive development in adulthood: A fifth stage? *Developmental Psychology*, 1975, *11*, 602-606.

Armsby, R. E. A reexamination of the development of moral judgments in children. *Child Development*, 1971, *42*, 1241-1248.

Armstrong, G. *An account of the diseases most incident to children*. London: T. Cadell, 1783.

Arnheim, R. *Art and visual perception*. Berkeley: University of California Press, 1954.

Arnheim, R. The puzzle of Nadia's drawings. *The Art in Psychotherapy*, 1980, *7*, 79-85.

Arnold, A. P. Sexual differences in the brain. *American Scientist*, 1980, *68*, 165-173.

Aronfreed, J. *Conduct and conscience: The socialization of internalized control over behavior*. New York: Academic Press, 1968.

Arons, S. Conformity in the classroom. *Saturday Review*, 1978, *5*, 20.

Aronson, E., and Rosenbloom, S. Space perception in early infancy: Perception within a common auditory-visual space. *Science*, 1971, *172*, 1161-1163.

Bacharach, V. R., and Luszcz, M. A. Communicative competence in young children: The use of implicit linguistic information. *Child Development*, 1979, *50*, 260-263.

Baillargeon, R., Gelman, R., and Meck, B. Are preschoolers truly indifferent to causal mechanisms? Paper presented at the Society for Research in Child Development, Boston, April 1981.

Baldwin, A. L. *Behavior and development in childhood*. New York: The Dryden Press, 1955.

Baldwin, J. M. *Mental development in the child and the race*. New York: Macmillan, 1897.

Ball, S., and Bogatz, G. A. Summative research of *Sesame Street*: Implications for the study of preschool children. In A. Pick (Ed.), *Minnesota Symposium on Child Development* (Vol. 6). Minneapolis: University of Minnesota Press, 1972.

Baltes, P., and Schaie, K. W. (Eds.). *Life-span developmental psychology: Personality and socialization*. New York: Academic Press, 1973.

Bamberger, J. Intuitive and formal musical knowledge: Parables of cognitive dissonance. In S. Madeja (Ed.), *The arts, cognition and basic skills*. St. Louis: CEMREL, 1978.

Bandura, A. Influence of model's reinforcement contingencies on the acquisition of imitative responses. *Journal of Personality and Social Psychology*, 1965, *11*, 587-595.

Bandura, A. Social-learning theory of identificatory processes. In D. A. Goslin (Ed.), *Handbook of socialization theory and research*. Chicago: Rand McNally, 1969.

Bandura, A. (Ed.), *Psychological modelling: Conflicting theories*. New York: Lieber-Athertin, 1974.

Bandura, A. *Social learning theory*. Englewood Cliffs, N.J.: Prentice-Hall, 1977.

Bandura, A. Social learning theory of aggression. *Journal of Communication*, 1978, *28*, 12-29.

Bandura, A., and Huston, A. Identification as a source of incidental learning. *Journal of Abnormal and Social Psychology*, 1961, *63*, 311-318.

Bandura, A., and McDonald, F. J. Influence of social reinforcement and the behavior of models in shaping children's moral judgments. *Journal of Abnormal and Social Psychology*, 1963, *67*, 274-281.

Bandura, A., Ross, D., and Ross, S. Transmission of aggression through imitation of aggressive models. *Journal of Abnormal and Social Psychology*, 1961, *63*, 375-382.

Bandura, A., Ross, D., and Ross, S. Imitation of film mediated aggressive models. *Journal of Abnormal and Social Psychology*, 1963, *66*, 3-11.

Bandura, A., and Walters, R. H. *Social learning and personality development*. New York: Holt, Rinehart and Winston, 1963.

Barash, D. P. Evolution as a paradigm for behavior. In M. Gregory, A. Silvers, and D. Sutch, (Eds.), *Sociobiology and human nature*. San Francisco: Jossey-Bass, 1978.

Barclay, C. R. The executive control of mnemonic activity. *Journal of Experimental Child Psychology*, 1979, *27*, 262-276.

Barclay, J. R., and Reid, M. Logical operations and sentence memory in children. Unpublished paper, University of Colorado, 1975.

Barnett, M. A., Howard, J. A., Melton, E. M., and Dino, G. A. Effect of inducing sadness about self or other on helping behavior in high and low empathic children. *Child Development*, in press.

Barnett, M. A., King, L. M., Howard, J. A., and Dino, G. A. Empathy in young children: Relation to parents' empathy, affection and emphasis on the feelings of others. *Developmental Psychology*, 1980, *16*, 243-244.

Barrera, M. E., and Maurer, D. Recognition of mother's photographed face by three-month-old infants. Paper presented at the International Conference on Infant Studies, Providence, R.I., March, 1978.

Barrera, M. E., and Maurer, D. The perception of facial expressions by the three-month-old. *Child Development*, 1981, *52*, 203-206.

Barrett, D. E. A naturalistic study of sex differences in children's aggression. *Merrill-Palmer Quarterly*, 1979, *25*, 193-203.

Bar-Tal, D., and Darom, E. Pupils' attributions of success and failure. *Child Development*, 1979, *50*, 264-267.

Bartlett, E. J. Sizing things up: The acquisition of the meaning of dimensional adjectives. *Journal of Child Language*, 1976, *3*, 205-219.

Bartlett, F. *Remembering*. Cambridge: Cambridge University Press, 1932.

Bates, E. *Language and context: The acquisition of pragmatics*. New York: Academic Press, 1976.

Bates, E. *Emergence of symbols: Cognition and communication in infancy*. New York: Academic Press, 1979.

Bateson, G. A theory of play and fantasy. *Psychiatric Research Reports*, 1955, *2*, 39-51.

Baumrind, D. Child-care practices anteceding three patterns of preschool behavior. *Genetic Psychology Monographs*, 1967, *75*, 43-88.

Baumrind, D. Current patterns of parental authority. *Developmental Psychology Monographs*, 1971, *1*.

Beagles, J. K., and Greenfield, P. M. The development of structure and strategy in two-dimensional representation. Unpublished paper, University of California, Los Angeles, 1977.

Beagles-Roos, J., and Greenfield, P. M. Development of structure and strategy in two-dimensional pictures. *Developmental Psychology*, 1979, *15*, 483-494.

Beal, C. R. and Flavell, J. H. Knowing a message has problems. Paper presented at the Society for Research in Child Development, Boston, April 1981.

Bearison, D. J., and Isaacs, L. Production deficiency in children's moral judgements. *Developmental Psychology*, 1975, *11*, 732-737.

Bearison, D. J., and Levey, L. M. Children's comprehension of referential communication: Decoding ambiguous messages. *Child Development*, 1977, *48*, 716-720.

Bechtold, A. G., Bushnell, E. W., and Salapatek, P. Infants' visual localization of visual and auditory targets. Paper presented at the Society for Research in Child Development, San Francisco, March 1979.

Becker, W. C. Consequences of different kinds of parental discipline. In M. L. Hoffman and L. W. Hoffman (Eds.), *Review of child development research* (Vol. 1). New York: Russell Sage, 1964.

Beebe, B., and Gerstman, L. J. The "packaging" of maternal stimulation in relation to infant facial-visual engagement: A case study at four months. *Merrill-Palmer Quarterly*, 1980, *26*, 321-339.

Beilin, H., Kagan, J., and Rabinowitz, R. Effects of verbal and perceptual training on water level. *Child Development*, 1966, *37*, 317-330.

Bell, R. Q. Parent, child, and reciprocal influences. *American Psychologist*, 1979, *34*, 821-826.

Bellugi, U. The acquisition of negatives. Ph. D. dissertation, Harvard University, 1967.

Belsky, J. Mother-father-infant interaction: A naturalistic observational study. *Developmental Psychology*, 1979, *15*, 601-607.

Belsky, J. Early human experience: A family perspective: *Developmental Psychology*, 1981, *17*, 3-23.

Belsky, J., and Steinberg, L. D. The effects of day care: A critical review. *Child Development*, 1978, *49*, 929-949.

Bem, S. L. The measurement of psychological androgyny. *Journal of Consulting and Clinical Psychology*, 1974, *42*, 155-162.

Benbow, C. P., and Stanley, J. C. Sex differences in mathematical ability: Fact or artifact? *Science*, 1980, *210*, 1263-1264.

Benedict, R. *Patterns of culture*. New York: Mentor, 1949.

Bennett, E. L. Cerebral effects of differential experience and training. In M. R. Rosenzweig and E. L. Bennett (Eds.), *Neural mechanism of learning and memory*. Cambridge, Mass.: MIT Press, 1976.

Benson, J. B., and Uzgiris, I. C. Self-produced movement in spatial understanding. Paper presented at the Society for Research in Child Development, Boston, April 1981.

Bentler, P. M., Rekers, G. A., and Rosen, A. C. Congruence of childhood sex-role identity and behavior disturbances. *Child Care, Health, and Development*, 1979, *5*, 267-283.

Benton, A. L. *Right-left discrimination and finger localization*. New York: Hoeber, 1959.

Bereiter, C. An academic preschool for disadvantaged children: Conclusions from evaluation studies. In J. C. Stanley (Ed.), *Preschool programs for the disadvantaged*. Baltimore: Johns Hopkins University Press, 1972.

Bereiter, C., Hidi, S., and Dimitroff, G. Qualitative changes in verbal reasoning during middle and late childhood. *Child Development*, 1979, *50*, 142-151.

Berg-Cross, L. G. Intentionality, degree of damage, and moral judgements. *Child Development*, 1975, *46*, 970-974.

Bergman, T., Haith, M. M., and Mann, L. Development of eye contact and facial scanning in infants. Paper presented at the Society for Research in Child Development, Minneapolis, April 1971.

Berlyne, D. E. *Conflict, arousal and curiosity*. New York: McGraw-Hill, 1960.

Berlyne, D. E. *Structure and direction in thinking*. New York: Wiley, 1965.

Berndt, R. J., and Berndt, E. G. Children's use of

motives and intentionality in person perception and moral judgment. *Child Development,* 1975, *46,* 904-912.

Bernstein, B. A sociolinguistic approach to socialization: With some reference to educability. In F. Williams (Ed.), *Language and poverty: Perspectives on a theme.* Chicago: Markham, 1970.

Bernstein, L. Hebb's claim of irreversibility in environmentally restricted rats. *American Psychologist,* 1979, *34,* 802-803.

Berry, J. W., and Dasen, P. (Eds.). *Culture and cognition: Readings in cross-cultural psychology.* London: Methuen, 1974.

Bertenthal, B. I., and Fischer, K. W. The development of self-recognition in the infant. *Developmental Psychology,* 1978, *14,* 44-50.

Best, C. T., and Glanville, B. B. Cerebral asymmetries in speech and timbre discrimination by 2-, 3- and 4-month-old infants. Paper presented at the First International Conference of Infant Studies, Providence, R.I., March 1978.

Best, D. L., Williams, J. E., Cloud, J. M., Davis, S. W., Robertson, L. S., Edwards, J. R., Giles, H., and Fowles, J. Development of sex-trait stereotypes among young children in the United States, England and Ireland. *Child Development,* 1977, *48,* 1375-1384.

Bettelheim, B. *Symbolic wounds.* New York: Collier Books, 1962.

Bettelheim, B. *The empty fortress.* New York: Free Press, 1967.

Bettelheim, B. *The children of the dream.* New York: Free Press, 1969.

Bettelheim, B. *A home for the heart.* New York: Knopf, 1974.

Bettelheim, B. *The uses of enchantment: The meaning and importance of fairy tales.* New York: Knopf, 1976.

Bever, T. G. The cognitive basis of linguistic structures. In J. R. Hayes (Ed.), *Cognition and the development of language.* New York: Wiley, 1970.

Bigelow, B. J. Children's friendship expectations: A cognitive-developmental study. *Child Development,* 1977, *48,* 246-253.

Bijou, S., and Baer, D. *Child development: Universal stage of infancy* (Vol. 2). New York: Appleton-Century-Crofts, 1965.

Biller, H. B., and Bahm, R. M. Father-absence, perceived maternal behavior, and masculinity of self-concept among junior high school boys. *Developmental Psychology,* 1971, *4,* 178-181.

Birch, H. G., and Lefford, A. Intersensory development in children. *Monographs of the Society for Research in Child Development,* 1963, *28,* (Serial No. 89, No. 5).

Bird, A. M., and Williams, J. M. A developmental-attributional analysis of sex role stereotypes for sport performance. *Developmental Psychology,* 1980, *16,* 319-322.

Bixenstine, V. E., DeCorte, M. S., and Bixenstine, B. A. Conformity to peer-sponsored misconduct at four grade levels. *Developmental Psychology,* 1976, *12,* 226-236.

Blakemore, J. E. O. Age and sex differences in interaction with a human infant. Paper presented at the Society for Research in Child Development, San Francisco, March 1979.

Blank, M., Gessner, M., and Esposito, A. Language without communication: A case study. *Journal of Child Language,* 1979, *6,* 329-352.

Blatt, M. Studies on the effects of classroom discussion upon children's moral development. *Journal of Moral Education,* 1975, *42,* 129-161.

Blitsen, D. R. *Human social development.* New Haven: College and University Press, 1971.

Block, J. H. *Lives through time.* Berkeley, Calif.: Bancroft Books, 1971.

Block, J. H. Conceptions of sex-roles: Some cross-cultural and longitudinal perspectives. *American Psychologist,* 1973, *28,* 512-526.

Block, J. H., and Morrison, A. L. The relationship of parental agreement on child rearing orientations to children's personality characteristics. Unpublished paper, University of California, 1978.

Block, N., and Dworkin, G. (Eds.). *The IQ controversy.* New York: Pantheon, 1976.

Bloom, K. Evaluation of infant vocal conditioning. *Journal of Experimental Child Psychology,* 1979, *27,* 60-70.

Bloom, L. *Language development: Form and function in emerging grammars.* Cambridge, Mass.: MIT Press, 1970.

Bloom, L. *One word at a time: The use of single word utterances before syntax.* The Hague: Mouton, 1973.

Bloom, L. An integrative perspective on language development. Unpublished paper, Teachers College, Columbia University, 1980.

Bloom, L., Hood, L., and Lightbown, P. Imitation in language development: If, when, and why. *Cognitive Psychology,* 1974, *6,* 380-428.

Blos, P. Character formation in adolescence. In R. S. Eissler, A. Freud, H. Hartmann, and M. Kris (Eds.), *Psychoanalytic study of the child* (Vol. 23). New York: International Universities Press, 1968, 245-263.

Bluebond-Langner, M. *The private worlds of dying children.* Princeton: Princeton University Press, 1978.

Blurton-Jones, N., and Konner, M. J. Sex differences in behavior of London and Bushman children. In R. P. Michael and J. H. Crook (Eds.), *Comparative ecology and behaviour of primates.* London: Academic Press, 1973.

Blyth, D. A., Simmons, R. G., and Bush, D. The transition into early adolescence: A longitudinal comparison of youth in two educational contexts. *Sociology of Education,* 1978, *51,* 159-162.

Bohannon, J. N., III. Word order discrimination and reading. Paper presented at the Society for Research in Child Development, San Francisco, March 1979.

Booth, C. L. Contingent responsiveness and mutuality in mother-infant interaction: Birth-order and sex difference? Paper presented at the Society for Research in Child Development, Boston, April 1981.

Borke, H. Piaget's mountains revisited: Changes in the egocentric landscape. *Developmental Psychology*, 1975, *11*, 240-243.

Bornstein, M. H. Perceptual development: Stability and change in feature perception. In M. H. Bornstein and W. Kessen (Eds.), *Psychological development from infancy*. Hillsdale, N.J.: Erlbaum, 1978.

Bornstein, M. H. Two kinds of perceptual organization near the beginning of life. Minnesota Symposia on Child Psychology, *18*, October 1979.

Bortner, R., and Hultsch, D. F. Personal time perspective in adulthood. *Developmental Psychology*, 1972, *7*, 98-103.

Botvin, G. J. and Sutton-Smith, B. The development of structural complexity in children's fantasy narratives. *Developmental Psychology*, 1977, *13*, 377-388.

Bower, G. Comprehending and recalling stories. Presidential Address. Presented at the American Psychological Association, Washington, D.C., September 1976.

Bower, T. G. R. Discrimination of depth in premotor infants. *Psychonomic Science*, 1964, *1*, 368.

Bower, T. G. R. Slant perception and shape constancy in infants. *Science*, 1966a, *151*, 832-834.

Bower, T. G. R. The visual world of infants. *Scientific American*, 1966b, *215*, 80-92.

Bower, T. G. R. Perceptual functioning in early infancy. In R. Robinson (Ed.), *Brain and early behavior*. New York: Academic Press, 1969.

Bower, T. G. R. *Development in infancy*. San Francisco: W. H. Freeman, 1974a.

Bower, T. G. R. Repetition in human development. *Merrill-Palmer Quarterly*, 1974b, *20*, 303-318.

Bower, T. G. R. Repetitive processes in child development. *Scientific American*, 1976, *235*, 38-47.

Bower, T. G. R. The infant's discovery of objects and mothers. In S. Trotter and E. B. Thoman (Eds.), *Social responsiveness of infants*. New York: Gardner Press, 1978.

Bower, T. G. R., and Paterson, J. G. Stages in the development of the object concept. *Cognition*, 1972, *1*, 47-55.

Bowerman, M. *Early syntactic development: A cross-linguistic study with special reference to Finnish*. London: Cambridge University Press, 1973.

Bowerman, M. Semantic factors in the acquisition of rules for word use and sentence construction. In. D. M. Morehead and A. E. Morehead (Eds.), *Normal and deficient child language*. Baltimore: University Park Press, 1976.

Bowerman, M. The acquisition of word meaning: An investigation of some current conflicts. In N. Waterson and C. Snow (Eds.), *Proceedings of the third international child language symposium*. New York: Wiley, 1977.

Bowerman, M. Starting to talk worse: Clues to language acquisition from children's late speech errors. In S. Strauss and R. Stavey (Ed.), *U-Shaped behavioral growth*. New York: Academic Press, in press.

Bowlby, J. Psychoanalysis and child care. In J. D. Sutherland (Ed.), *Psychoanalysis and contemporary theory*. London: Hogarth, 1958.

Bowlby, J. *Maternal care and mental health*. New York: Schocken, 1966.

Bowlby, J. *Attachment and loss (Vol. 1, Attachment)*. New York: Basic Books, 1969.

Bowlby, J. *Attachment and loss (Vol. 2, Separation: Anxiety and anger)*. London: Hogarth, 1973.

Bowlby, J. *Attachment and loss (Vol. 3: Loss, sadness, and depression)*. New York: Basic Books, 1980.

Bradley, S. J., Steiner, B., Zucker, J., Doering, R. W., Sullivan, J., Finegan, J. K., and Richardseon, M. Gender identity problems of children and adolescents. *Canadian Psychiatric Association Journal*, 1978, *23*, 175-183.

Braine, L. G. A new slant on orientation perception. *American Psychologist*, 1978, *33*, 10-22.

Braine, L. G., Lerner, C., and Relyea, L. Levels in the identifying of orientation by preschool children. *Journal of Experimental Child Psychology*, 1980, *30*, 171-185.

Braine, M. D. S. Children's first word combinations. *Monographs of the Society for Research in Child Development*, 1976, *41*, (Serial No. 164, No. 1).

Brainerd, C. J. On the validity of propositional logic as a model for adolescent intelligence. Paper presented at the Society for Research in Child Development, Denver, April 1975.

Brainerd, C. J. Effects of spatial cues on children's cardinal number judgments. *Developmental Psychology*, 1977, *13*, 425-430.

Brainerd, C. J. A Markovian analysis of conservation acquisition. Research Bulletin No. 457. Department of Psychology, University of Western Ontario, London, Canada, 1978a.

Brainerd, C. J. *Piaget's theory of intelligence*. Englewood Cliffs, N.J.: Prentice-Hall, 1978b.

Brainerd, C. J. The stage question in cognitive-developmental theory. *The Behavioral and Brain Sciences*, 1978c, *2*, 173-213.

Brainerd, C. J. Effects of group and individualized dramatic play on cognitive development. Paper presented at the American Psychological Association, Montreal, September 1980a.

Brainerd, C. J. Stage II: A review of *Beyond universals in cognitive development*, by D. H. Feldman. 1980b.

Brainerd, C. J., and Allen, T. W. Experimental inductions of the conservation of "first order" quantitative invariants. *Psychological Bulletin*, 1971, *75*, 128-144.

Bray, N. W., and Justice, E. M. Developmental

changes in the effects of instructions on production-deficient children. *Child Development,* 1977, *48,* 1019-1026.

Brazelton, T. B. Early parent-infant reciprocity. In V. C. Vaughn III and T. B. Brazelton (Eds.), *The family—can it be spared?* Chicago: Year Book Medical Publishers, Inc., 1976.

Brazelton, T. B. Introduction in A. J. Sameroff (Ed.), Organization and stability of newborn behavior: A commentary on the Brazelton neonatal behavior assessment scale. *Monograph of the Society for Research in Child Development,* 1978, *43,* (Serial No. 177, Nos. 5-6), 1-13.

Brazelton, T. B., quoted in The wisdom of babies, *Newsweek,* January 12, 1981, p. 71.

Bremner, J. Spatial errors made by infants: Inadequate spatial cues or evidence of egocentrism? *British Journal of Psychology,* 1978, *69,* 77-84.

Bresson, F., Maury, L., Peiraut-Le-Bonniec, G., and de Schonen, S. Organization and lateralization reaching in infants: An instance of asymmetric functions in hands collaboration. *Neuropsychologia,* 1977, *15,* 311-320.

Bretherton, I. Early person knowledge as expressed in gestural and verbal communication: When do infants acquire a "theory of mind"? In M. E. Lamb and L. R. Sherrod (Eds.), *Infant social cognition.* Hillsdale, N.J.: Erlbaum, 1980.

Brewer, W. F., and Stone, J. B. Acquisition of spatial antonym pairs. *Journal of Experimental Child Psychology,* 1975, *19,* 299-307.

Bridger, W. H. Sensory habituation and discrimination in the human neonate. *American Journal of Psychiatry,* 1961, *117,* 991-996.

Bridges, K. A genetic theory of the emotions. *Journal of Genetic Psychology,* 1930, *37,* 514-527.

Brim, O. G. Life-span development of the theory of oneself: Implications for child development. *Advances in Child Development and Behavior,* 1976, *11,* 241-251.

Brim, O. G. Jr., and Kagan, J. (Eds.). *Constancy and change in human development.* Cambridge, Mass.: Harvard University Press, 1980.

Brittain, C. V. A comparison of rural and urban adolescence with respect to peer versus parent compliance. *Adolescence,* 1969, *13,* 59-68.

Brody, J. E. TV Violence cited as bad influence. *The New York Times,* December 17, 1975, p. 20.

Brodzinsky, D. M., Tew, J. D., and Palkovitz, R. Control of humorous affect in relation to children's conceptual tempo. *Developmental Psychology,* 1979, *15,* 275-279.

Bronfenbrenner, U. Freudian theories of identification and their derivatives. *Child Development,* 1960, *31,* 15-40.

Bronfenbrenner, U. *Two worlds of childhood. U.S. and U.S.S.R.* New York: Basic Books, 1970.

Bronfenbrenner, U. Contexts of child rearing: Problems and prospects. *American Psychologist,* 1979, *34,* 844-850.

Bronson, W. The role of enduring orientations to the

environment in personality development. *Genetic Psychology Monographs,* 1972, 86-.

Broughton, J. M. The development of natural epistemology in adolescence and early adulthood. Unpublished doctoral dissertation, Harvard University, 1974.

Broughton, J. M. The cognitive developmental approach to "epistemology" and its relation to logical and moral stages. Paper presented at the Society for Research in Child Development, Denver, April 1975*a.*

Broughton, J. M. The cognitive-developmental approach to morality: A reply to Kurtines and Greif. Unpublished manuscript, Wayne State University, 1975*b.*

Brown, A. L. The development of memory: Knowing, knowing about knowing, and knowing how to know. In H. W. Reese (Ed.), *Advances in child development* (*Vol. 10*). New York: Academic Press, 1975.

Brown, A. L. Knowing when, where, and how to remember: A problem of metacognition. In R. Glaser (Ed.), *Advances in instructional psychology,* Hillsdale, N.J.: Erlbaum, in press.

Brown, A. L., and Campione, J. C. Recognition memory for perceptually similar pictures in preschool children. *Journal of Experimental Psychology,* 1972, *95,* 55-62.

Brown, A. L., and Murphy, M. D. Reconstruction of arbitrary versus logical sequences by preschool children. *Journal of Experimental Child Psychology,* in press.

Brown, A. L., and Smiley, S. S. Rating the importance of structural units of prose passages: A problem of metacognitive development. *Child Development,* 1977, *48,* 1-8.

Brown, A. L., and Smiley, S. S. The development of strategies for studying texts. *Child Development,* 1978, *49,* 1076-1088.

Brown, J. K. A cross-cultural study of female initiation rites. *American Anthropologist,* 1963, *65,* 837-853.

Brown, J. K. Adolescent initiation rites among preliterate peoples. In R. E. Grinder '(Ed.), *Studies in adolescence.* 2nd ed. New York: Macmillan, 1969.

Brown, R. *Words and things.* Glencoe, Ill.: Free Press, 1958.

Brown, R. *A first language: The early stages.* Cambridge, Mass.: Harvard University Press, 1973.

Brown, R., and Bellugi, U. Three processes in the child's acquisition of syntax. *Harvard Educational Review,* 1964, *34,* 133-151.

Brown, R., and Hanlon, C. Derivational complexity and order of acquisition in child speech. In J. R. Hayes (Ed.), *Cognition and the development of language.* New York: Wiley, 1970.

Brozan, N. A new survey of teenage sex—with teenagers asking questions. *The New York Times,* February 25, 1978.

Brozan, N. More teenagers are pregnant despite rise

in contraception. *The New York Times,* March 12, 1981, p. Cl.

Bruch, H. *The gilded cage: The enigma of anorexia nervosa.* Cambridge, Mass.: Harvard University Press, 1978a.

Bruch, H. Obesity and anorexia nervosa. *Psychosomatics,* 1978b, *19,* 208-212.

Bruner, J. S. The course of cognitive growth. *American Psychologist,* 1964, *19,* 1-15.

Bruner, J. S. The growth and structure of skill. Paper presented at the Ciba Conference, London, November 1968.

Bruner, J. S. The nature and uses of immaturity. *American Psychologist,* 1972, *27,* 687-701.

Bruner, J. S. From communication to language—A psychological perspective. *Cognition,* 1975a, *3,* 225-287.

Bruner, J. S. The ontogenesis of speech acts. *Journal of Child Language,* 1975b, *2,* 1-19.

Bruner, J. S. Learning the mother tongue. *Human Nature,* 1978, *1,* 42-49.

Bruner, J. S., Jolly, A., and Sylva, K. *Play: Its role in development and evolution.* London: Penguin, 1976.

Bruner, J. S., Olver, R. R., and Greenfield, P. M. *Studies in cognitive growth.* New York: Wiley, 1966.

Bryan, J. H., and Walbeck, N. Preaching and practicing generosity: Children's actions and reactions. *Child Development,* 1970, *41,* 329-353.

Bryan, J. W., and Luria, Z. Sex-role learning: A test of the selective attention hypothesis. *Child Development,* 1978, *49,* 13-23.

Bryant, B. K. The effects of the interpersonal context of evaluation on self- and other-enhancement behavior. *Child Development,* 1977, *48,* 885-892.

Bryant, B. K., and Crockenberg, S. B. Correlates and dimensions of preschool behavior: A study of female siblings with their mothers. *Child Development,* 1980, *51,* 529-544.

Bryant, P. E. Discrimination of mirror-images by young children. *Journal of Comparative and Physiological Psychology,* 1973, *82,* 415-425.

Bryant, P. E. *Perception and understanding in young children.* New York: Basic Books, 1974.

Buck, R. Nonverbal communication of affect in preschool children relationships with personality and skin conductance. *Journal of Personality and Social Psychology,* 1976, *44,* 225-236.

Bullock, M. Preschoolers' understanding of causal mechanisms. Paper presented at the Society for Research in Child Development, Boston, April 1981.

Bumstead, R. A. Educating your child at home: The *Perchemlides Case. Phi Delta Kappan,* 1979, *61,* 97-100.

Burnham, D. K., and Day, R. H. Detection of color in rotating objects by infants and its generalization over changes in velocity. *Journal of Experimental Child Psychology,* 1979, *28,* 191-204.

Burns, J. M. *Edward Kennedy and the Camelot legacy.* New York: Norton, 1976.

Burns, S. M., and Brainerd, C. J. Effects of constructive and dramatic play on perspective taking in very young children. *Developmental Psychology,* 1979, *15,* 512-521.

Burnstein, E., Bank, L., and Jarvik, L. Sex differences in cognitive functioning: Evidence, determinants, implications. *Human Development,* 1980, *23,* 289-313.

Burton, R. V., and Whiting, J. W. M. The absent father and cross-sex identity. *Merrill-Palmer Quarterly,* 1961, *7,* 85-95.

Bush, E. S., and Dweck, C. S. Reflections on conceptual tempo: Relationship between cognitive style and performance as a function of task characteristics. *Developmental Psychology,* 1975, *11,* 567-574.

Bushnell, E. W. The *decline* of visually-guided reaching in infancy. Paper presented at the Society for Research in Child Development, Boston, April 1981.

Buss, D. M. Predicting parent-child interactions from children's activity level. *Developmental Psychology,* 1981, *17,* 59-65.

Bussey, K. The role of beliefs about self and others in the sex-typing process. In E. E. Maccoby, *Development of children's inferences concerning gender.* Symposium presented at the Society for Research in Child Development, Boston, April 1981.

Butterworth, G. Asymmetrical search errors in infancy. *Child Development,* 1976, *47,* 864-867.

Butterworth, G., and Castillo, M. Coordination of auditory and visual space in newborn human infants. *Perception,* 1976, *5,* 155-160.

Bynum, T. W., Thomas, J. A., and Weitz, L. J. Truth-functional logic in formal operational thinking: Inhelder and Piaget's evidence. *Developmental Psychology,* 1972, *7,* 129-132.

Caldeira, J., Singer, J. L., and Singer, D. G. Imaginary playmates: Some relationships to preschoolers' spontaneous play, language and television viewing. Paper presented at the Eastern Psychological Association, Washington, D. C., March 1978.

Campbell, E. Adolescent socialization. In D. A. Goslin (Ed.), *Handbook of socialization theory and research.* Chicago: Rand McNally, 1969.

Canney, G., and Winograd, P. Schemata for reading and reading comprehension. Paper presented at the American Educational Research Association, Boston, 1980.

Caplan, F., and Caplan T. *The power of play.* New York: Doubleday, 1973.

Caplan, P. J., and Kinsbourne, M. Baby drops the rattle: Asymmetry of duration of grasp by infants. *Child Development,* 1976, *47,* 532-534.

Capon, N., and Kuhn, D. Logical reasoning in the supermarket: Adult females' use of a proportional reasoning strategy in an everyday context. *Developmental Psychology,* 1979, *15,* 450-452.

Carey, S. Cognitive competence. In K. Connolly and J. S. Bruner (Eds.), *The growth of competence.* New York: Academic Press, 1974.

Carey, S. Less is never more. Unpublished lecture, Harvard University, 1976.

Carey, S. The child as word-learner. In M. Halle, J. Bresnan, and G. A. Miller (Eds.), *Linguistic theory and psychological reality.* Cambridge, Mass.: MIT Press, 1977*a*.

Carey, S. "Less" may never mean more. In R. Campbell (Ed.), *Proceedings of Sterling Conference on Psycholinguistics,* 1977*b*.

Carey, S., and Considine, T. Spatial adjectives. Unpublished paper, Massachusetts Institute of Technology, 1976.

Carey, S., and Diamond, R. From piecemeal to configurational representation of faces. *Science,* 1977, *195,* 312-314.

Carey, S., Diamond, R., and Woods, B. Development of face recognition—A maturational component? *Developmental Psychology,* 1980, *16,* 257-269.

Carlsmith, L. Effect of early father absence on scholastic aptitude. *Harvard Educational Review,* 1964, *34,* 3-21.

Carlsmith, L. The effects of early father absence on scholastic aptitude. In L. Hudson (Ed.), *The ecology of human intelligence.* Harmondsworth, Eng.: Penguin, 1970.

Carmichael, D. Irony: A cognitive-developmental study. Ph.D. dissertation, University of California at Berkeley, 1966.

Caron, R. F., and Caron, A. J. Acquisition of face expression concept in infancy. Paper presented at the Society for Research in Child Development, Boston, April 1981.

Carothers, T., and Gardner, H. When children's drawings become art: The emergence of aesthetic production and perception. *Developmental Psychology,* 1979, *15,* 570-580.

Case, R. Gearing the demands of instruction to the developmental capacities of the learner. *Review of Educational Research,* 1975, *45,* 59-87.

Case, R. Intellectual development from birth to adulthood: A neo-Piagetan interpretation. In R. Siegler (Ed.), *Children's thinking: What develops?* Hillsdale, N.J.: Erlbaum, 1978.

Case, R. Intellectual development: A systematic reinterpretation. In F. M. Farley and N. J. Gordon, *New perspectives in educational psychology.* National Society for the Study of Education, Canada, 1980.

Case, R. The search for "horizontal structure" in children's development. In F. S. Kessel, *Cognitive development: Emerging and reemerging themes.* Symposium presented at the Society for Research in Child Development, Boston, April 1981.

Case, R. *Intellectual development: A systematic reinterpretation.* New York: Academic Press, in press.

Caudill, W., and Frost, N. A comparison of maternal care and infant behavior in Japanese-American, American, and Japanese families. In U. Bronfenbrenner and M. A. Mahoney (Eds.), *Influences on human development.* Hinsdale, Ill.: Dryden Press, 1972.

Cavalli-Sforza, L. L. *Elements of human genetics.* 2nd Ed. Menlo Park, Calif.: W. A. Benjamin, 1977.

Cavanaugh, J. C., and Borkowski, J. G. Searching for metamemory-memory connections: A developmental study. *Developmental Psychology,* 1980, *16,* 441-453.

Cavanaugh, J. C., and Perlmutter, M. Age differences in adults' recall of television program content. Presented at the Midwestern Psychological Association. St. Louis, May 1980.

Cermak, L. S., and Craik, F. I. M. *Levels of processing in human memory.* Hillsdale, N.J.: Erlbaum, 1979.

Chaillé, C. The child's conceptions of play, pretending and toys: Sequences and structural parallels. *Human Development,* 1978, *21,* 201-210.

Chall, J. *Learning to read: The great debate.* New York: McGraw-Hill, 1967.

Chamove, A. S. Therapy of isolate rhesus: Different partners and social behavior. *Child Development,* 1978, *49,* 43-50.

Chan, K. S. Contribution of ethnic minority research to ecological approaches to assessment. Paper presented at the Society for Research in Child Development, Boston, April 1981.

Chandler, M. J. Social cognition and life-span approaches to the study of child development. Unpublished paper, University of Rochester, 1976.

Chang, M. W., and Trehub, S. Auditory processing of relational information by young infants. *Journal of Experimental Child Psychology,* 1977, *24,* 324-331.

Chapman, M. Father absence, stepfathers, and the cognitive performance of college students. *Child Development,* 1977, *48,* 1155-1158.

Chase, W. G., and Calfee, R. C. Modality and similarity effects in short-term recognition memory. *Journal of Experimental Psychology,* 1969, *81,* 510-514.

Chassin, L., Sherman, S. J., and Corty, E. Self-images and cigarette smoking in adolescents. Paper presented at the Society for Research in Child Development, Boston, April 1981.

Chen, E. Twins reared apart: A living lab. *The New York Times Magazine,* December 9, 1979, p. 110+.

Chi, M. T. H. Short-term memory limitation in children: Capacity or processing deficits? *Memory and Cognition,* 1976, *4,* 559-572.

Chipman, S. F., and Mendelson, M. Influence of six types of visual structure on complexity judgments in children and adults. *Journal of Experimental Child Psychology: Human Perception and Performance,* 1979, *5,* 365-378.

Chisholm, J. S. Development and adaptation in infancy. In C. M. Super and S. Harkness (Eds.), *New directions for child development: Anthropological perspectives on child development.* No. 8, 1980.

Chomsky, C. *The acquisition of syntax in children from five to ten.* Cambridge, Mass.: MIT Press, 1969.

Chomsky, N. *Syntactic structures.* The Hague: Mouton, 1957.

Chomsky, N. A review of B. F. Skinner's *Verbal Behavior. Language,* 1959, *35,* 26-58.

Chomsky, N. *Aspects of a theory of syntax.* Cambridge, Mass.: MIT Press, 1965.

Chomsky, N. *Reflections on language.* New York: Pantheon, 1976.

Chomsky, N., *Rules and representation.* New York: Columbia University Press, 1980.

Chomsky, N., and Halle, M. *The sound pattern of English.* New York: Harper and Row, 1968.

Chukovsky, K. *From two to five.* Berkeley: University of California Press, 1968.

Cicirelli, V. G. Effects of mother and older sibling on the problem solving behavior of the younger child. *Developmental Psychology,* 1975, *11,* 749-756.

Clark, E. V. What's in a word? On the child's acquisition of semantics in his first language. In T. E. Moore (Ed.), *Cognitive development and the acquisition of language.* New York: Academic Press, 1973.

Clark, E. V. Strategies for communicating. *Child Development,* 1978, *49,* 953-959.

Clark, E. V. The young word-maker: A case study of innovation in the child's lexicon. In L. R. Gleitman and E. Wanner (Eds.), *Language acquisition: The state of the art.* Cambridge: Cambridge University Press, in press.

Clark, E. V., and Anderson, E. A. Spontaneous repairs: Awareness in the process of acquiring language. *Papers and Reports on Child Language Development.* Stanford University, 1979, *16,* 1-12.

Clark, R. What is the use of imitation? *Journal of Child Language,* 1977, *3,* 341-358.

Clarke, A. E., and Ruble, D. N. Young adolescents' beliefs concerning menstruation. *Child Development,* 1978, *49,* 231-234.

Clarke, A. M., and Clarke, A. D. (Eds.). *Early experience: Myth and evidence.* Riverside, N.J.: Free Press, 1977.

Clarke-Stewart, A. Sociability and social sensitivity: Characteristics of the stranger. Paper presented at the Society for Research in Child Development, Denver, April 1975a.

Clarke-Stewart, A. Dealing with the complexity of mother-child interaction. Paper presented at the Society for Research in Child Development, Denver, April 1975b.

Clarke-Stewart, A. And daddy makes three: The father's impact on mother and young child. *Child Development,* 1978, *49,* 466-478.

Clausen, J. A. The social meaning of differential physical and sexual maturation. In S. E. Dragastin and G. H. Elder, Jr. (Eds.), *Adolescence in the life cycle.* New York: Halsted, 1975.

Clifton, R. K. Heart rate conditioning in the newborn infant. *Journal of Experimental Child Psychology,* 1974, *18,* 9-21.

Cochran, M. M., and Brassard, J. A. Child development and personal social networks. *Child Development,* 1979, 50, 601-616.

Cohen, E. A., Gelfand, D. M., Hartmann, D. P., Partlow, M. E., Montemayor, R., and Shigetomi, C. C. Children's causal reasoning. Paper presented at the Society for Research in Child Development, San Francisco, March 1979.

Cohen, L., and Campos, J. J. Father, mother and stranger as elicitors of attachment behavior in infancy. *Developmental Psychology,* 1974, *10,* 146-154.

Cohen, R., and Schuepfer, T. The representation of landmarks and routes. *Child Development,* 1980, *51,* 1065-1071.

Cohn, J. F. Three-month-old infants' reaction to simulated maternal depression. Paper presented at the Society for Research in Child Development, Boston, April 1981.

Cole, M. Epilogue in A. E. Luria (Ed.), *The making of mind.* Cambridge, Mass.: Harvard University Press, 1979.

Cole, M., Frankel, F., and Sharp, D. Development of free recall learning in children. *Developmental Psychology,* 1971, *4,* 109-123.

Cole, M., Gay, J., Glick, J. A., and Sharp, D. *The cultural context of learning and thinking.* New York: Basic Books, 1971.

Cole, M., and Means, B. *Comparative studies of how people think.* Cambridge, Mass.: Harvard University Press, 1981.

Coleman, J. S. *The adolescent society.* New York: Free Press, 1961.

Coles, R. *Children of crisis: A study of crisis and fear.* (Vol. 1). Boston: Atlantic-Little, Brown, 1967.

Coles, R. *Teachers and children of poverty.* Washington, D.C.: Potomac Institute, 1970.

Coles, R. *Children of crisis: Migrants, mountaineers and sharecroppers* (Vol. 2). Boston: Atlantic-Little, Brown, 1972, 1973.

Coles, R. *Children of crisis: The south goes north* (Vol. 3). Boston: Atlantic-Little, Brown, 1972, 1973.

Coles, R. What children know about politics. *New York Review of Books,* February 20, 1975, p. 24.

Coles, R. *Children of crisis: Eskimos, Chicanos, Indians* (Vol. 4). Boston: Atlantic-Little, Brown, 1980a.

Coles, R. *Children of crisis: Privileged ones* (Vol. 5). Boston: Atlantic-Little, Brown, 1980b.

Collard, R., and Dempsey, J. R. Number concept in eight-to twelve-month-old infants. Paper presented at the International Congress of Psychology, Paris, July 1976.

Collins, G. Fathering. *The New York Times Magazine,* June 17, 1979, p. 31 +.

Collins, W. A., Berndt, T. J., and Hess, V. L. Observational learning of motives and consequences for televised aggression: A developmental study. *Child Development,* 1974, *45,* 799-802.

Comalli, P. E., Wapner, S., and Werner, H. Perception of verticality in middle and old age. *Journal of Psychology,* 1959, *47,* 259-266.

Comenius, J. A. *Orbis Pictus.* New York: Bardeen, 1968.

Comfort, A. *A good age.* New York: Crown, 1976.

Conger, J. J. *Adolescence and youth.* New York: Harper and Row, 1977.

Connell, W. F., Stroobant, R. E., Sinclair, K. E., Connell, R. W., and Rogers, K. W. *Twelve to twenty: Studies of city youth.* Sydney, Australia: Hicks Smith, 1975.

Conrad, R. The developmental role of vocalizing in short-term memory. *Journal of Verbal Learning and Verbal Behavior,* 1972, *11,* 521-533.

Cook, M., Field, J., and Griffiths, K. The perception of solid form in early infancy. *Child Development,* 1978, *49,* 866-869.

Cooley, C. H. *Human nature and the social order.* New York: Scribner, 1902.

Cooley, C. H. *Social organization.* New York: Scribner, 1909.

Cooper, C. R. Development of collaborative problem solving among preschool children. *Developmental Psychology,* 1980, *16,* 433-440.

Corballis, M. C., and Zalik, M. C. Why do children confuse mirror-image obliques? *Journal of Educational Child Psychology,* 1977, *24,* 516-523.

Cordua, G. D., McGraw, K. O., and Drabman, R. S. Doctor or nurse: Children's perceptions of sex-typed occupations. *Child Development,* 1979, *50,* 590-593.

Cornell, E. Learning to find things: A reinterpretation of object-permanence studies. In L. S. Siegel (Ed.), *Alternatives to Piaget: Critical essays on the theory.* New York: Academic Press, 1978.

Cornell, E. H. The effects of cue reliability on infants' manual search. *Journal of Experimental Child Psychology,* 1979, *28,* 81-91.

Corsini, D. A. Memory: Interaction of stimulus and organismic factors. *Human Development,* 1971, *14,* 227-235.

Corter, C. M. A comparison of the mother's and a stranger's control over the behavior of infants. *Child Development,* 1973, *44,* 705-712.

Corter, C. M. Infant attachment. In B. M. Foss (Ed.), *New perspectives in child development.* Baltimore: Penguin, 1974.

Corter, C. M., Zucker, K. J., and Galligan, R. F. Patterns in the infant's search for mother during brief separation. *Developmental Psychology,* 1980, *16,* 62-69.

Cowan, P. A., Langer, J., Heavenrich, J., and Nathanson, J. Social learning and Piaget's theory of moral development. *Journal of Personality and Social Psychology,* 1969, *11,* 261-274.

Cox, M. Spatial depth relationships in young children's drawings. *Journal of Experimental Child Psychology,* 1978, *26,* 551-554.

Cramer, P., and Hogan, K. A. Sex differences in verbal and play fantasy. *Developmental Psychology,* 1975, *11,* 145-154.

Crandall, V., and Sinkeldam, C. Children's dependent and achievement behaviors in social situations and their perceptual field dependence. *Journal of Personality,* 1964, *32,* 1-22.

Crassini, B., and Broerse, J. Auditory-visual integration in neonates: A signal detection analysis. *Journal of Experimental Child Psychology,* 1980, *29,* 144-155.

Cravioto, J., and DeLicardie, E. R. Environmental and nutritional deprivation in children with learning disabilities. In W. Cruickshank and D. Hallahan (Eds.), *Perceptual and learning disabilities in children* (Vol. 2). Syracuse: Syracuse University Press, 1975.

Crews, F. American prophet. *New York Review of Books,* October 16, 1975, p. 9.

Crockenberg, S. B., and Nicolayev, J. Stage transition in moral reasoning as related to conflict experienced in naturalistic settings. *Merrill-Palmer Quarterly,* 1979, *25,* 185-192.

Cromer, R. F. The development of language and cognition. In B. M. Foss (Ed.), *New perspectives in child development.* Baltimore: Penguin, 1974.

Cronin, V. Cross-modal and intramodal visual and tactual matching in young children. *Developmental Psychology,* 1973, *8,* 336-340.

Cross, T. G. Mother's speech and its associations with rate of linguistic development in young children. In N. Waterson and C. Snow (Eds.), *The development of communication.* New York: Wiley, 1978.

Crowell, D. H., Blurton, L. B., Kobayashi, L. R., McFarland, J. L., and Yang, R. K. Studies in early infant learning: Classical conditioning of the neonatal heart rate. *Developmental Psychology,* 1976, *12,* 373-397.

Cruikshank, W., and Hallahan, D. (Eds.). *Perceptual and learning disabilities in children.* Syracuse: Syracuse University Press, 1975.

Currie-Jedermann, J. The role of function in conceptual development. Paper presented at the Society for Research in Child Development, Boston, April 1981.

Curtis, L. E., Siegel, A. W., and Furlong, N. E. Developmental differences in cognitive mapping: Configurational knowledge of familiar large-scale environments. Unpublished paper, University of Pittsburgh, 1980.

Curtiss, S. *Genie: A linguistic study of a modern-day wild child.* New York: Academic Press, 1977.

Dale, P. *Language development: Structure and function.* Hinsdale, Ill.: Dryden Press, 1972.

Damon, W. Early conceptions of justice as related to the development of logical operations. Unpublished manuscript, Clark University, 1975.

Damon, W. *The social world of the child.* San Francisco: Jossey-Bass Publishers, 1977.

Damon, W. (Ed.). Moral development. *New Directions for Child Development* (No. 2). San Francisco: Jossey-Bass Publishers, 1978.

Damon, W. The nature of social-cognitive change in the developing child. Paper presented to the Jean Piaget Society, Philadelphia, May 1979.

Damon, W. Patterns of change in children's social reasoning: A two-year longitudinal study. *Child Development,* 1980, *51,* 1010-1017.

Damon, W. Gender and self-understanding in childhood and early adolescence. In E. E. Maccoby, *Development of children's inferences concerning gender.* Symposium presented at the Society for Research in Child Development, Boston, April 1981.

Danner, F. W., and Day, M. C. Eliciting formal operations. *Child Development,* 1977, *48,* 1600-1607.

Dansky, J. L., and Silverman, I. W. Effects of play on associative fluency in preschool-aged children. *Developmental Psychology,* 1973, *9,* 38-43.

Darley, J. M., Klosson, E. C., and Zanna, M. P. Intentions and their contexts in the moral judgement of children and adults. *Child Development,* 1978, *49,* 66-74.

Darwin, C. *On the origin of species.* London: John Murray, 1859.

Darwin, C. A biographical sketch of an infant. *Mind,* 1877, *2,* 286-294.

Davidson, G. R., and Klich, L. Z. Cultural factors in the development of temporal and spatial ordering. *Child Development,* 1980, *51,* 569-571.

Davidson, R., and Fox, N. EEG asymmetry during the perception of positive and negative affect in ten-month-old infants: Frontal versus parietal differences. Paper presented at the Society for Research in Child Development, Boston, April 1981.

Day, M. C. Visual search by children: The effect of background variation and the use of visual cues. *Journal of Experimental Child Psychology,* 1978, *25,* 1-16.

DeLisis, R., and Staudt, J. Individual differences in college students' performance on formal operational tasks. *Journal of Applied Developmental Psychology,* 1980, *1,* 201-208.

DeLoache, J. S., Strauss, M. S., and Maynard, J. Picture perception in infancy. *Infant Behavior and Development,* 1979, *2,* 77-89.

DeLone, R. H. *Small futures: Children inequality and the limits of liberal reform.* New York: Harcourt Brace & Jovanovich, 1979.

Demany, L., McKenzie, B., and Vurpillot, E. Rhythm perception in early infancy. *Nature,* April 21, 1977, *266,* 718-719.

deMause, L. (Ed.). *The new psychohistory.* New York: Psychohistory Press, 1975.

Demorest, A., Silberstein, L., and Gardner, H. From understatement to hyperbole: Recognizing nonliteral language and its intent. Paper presented at the Society for Research in Child Development, Boston, April 1981.

Demos, V. Children's use and understanding of affect terms. Ph.D. dissertation, Harvard University, 1974.

Demos, V. The socialization of affect in early childhood. Unpublished paper, Harvard Medical School, 1975.

Denenberg, V. Animal studies of early experience: Some principles which have implications for human development. In J. P. Hill (Ed.), *Minnesota symposium on child psychology* (Vol. 3). Minneapolis: University of Minnesota Press, 1969.

Denney, D. R. Modelling effects upon conceptual style and cognitive tempo. *Child Development,* 1972, *43,* 105-119.

Denney, D. R., and Moulton, P. A. Conceptual preferences among preschool children. *Developmental Psychology,* 1976, *12,* 509-513.

Denney, N. W., and Wright, J. C. Cognitive changes during the adult years: Implications for developmental theory and research. Unpublished paper, University of Kansas, 1976.

Dennis, M., and Whitaker, H. A hemisphere equipotentiality and language acquisition. In S. Segalowitz and F. Gruber (Eds.), *Language development and neurological theory.* New York: Academic Press, 1977.

Dennis, W. Creative productivity between the ages twenty and eighty years. *Journal of Gerontology,* 1966, *21,* 1-8.

DePaulo, B. M., Irvine, A., Jordan, A., and Laser, P. S. Age changes in the detection of deception. In R. Buck, *Development of nonverbal behavioral skill.* Symposium presented at the American Psychological Association, Montreal, Canada, September 1980.

deVilliers, J. G. The process of rule learning in child speech: A new look. In K. Nelson (Ed.), *Children's language.* (Vol. II). New York: Gardner Press, 1980.

deVilliers, J. G., and deVilliers, P. A. A cross-sectional study: The development of grammatical morphemes in child speech. *Journal of Psycholinguistic Research,* 1973, *2,* 267-278.

deVilliers, J. G., and deVilliers, P. A. *Language acquisition.* Cambridge, Mass.: Harvard University Press, 1978.

deVilliers, P. A., and deVilliers, J. G. Early judgments of semantic and syntactic acceptability by children. *Journal of Psycholinguistic Research,* 1972, *1,* 299-310.

deVilliers, P. A., and deVilliers, J. G. On this, that, and the other: Nonegocentrism in very young children. *Journal of Experimental Child Psychology,* 1974, *18,* 438-447.

deVilliers, P. A., and deVilliers, J. G. Form and function in the development of sentence negation. *Papers and Reports on Child Language Development,* Stanford University, 1979, *17,* 57-64.

deVore, I. (Ed.). *Primate behavior: Field studies of monkeys and apes.* New York: Holt, Rinehart and Winston, 1965.

deVries, R. Constancy of generic identity in the years three to six. *Monographs of the Society for Research in Child Development,* 1969, *34,* No. 3.

Dickens, C. *David Copperfield.* New York: Books, Inc., 1930.

Dickstein, E. Self and self-esteem: Theoretical foundations and their implications for research. *Human Development,* 1977, *20,* 129-140.

DiPietro, J. Rough and tumble play: A function of gender. *Developmental Psychology,* 1981, *17,* 50-58.

Dirks, J., and Gibson, E. Infants' perception of similarity between live people and their photographs. *Child Development,* 1977, *48,* 124-130.

Dirks, J., and Neisser, U. Memory for objects in real scenes: The development of recognition and recall. *Journal of Experimental Child Psychology,* 1977, *23,* 315-328.

DiVitto, B., and McArthur, L. Z. Developmental differences in the use of distinctiveness, consensus and consistency information for making causal attributions. *Developmental Psychology,* 1978, *14,* 474-482.

Dodd, B. J. Effects of social and vocal stimulation on infant babbling. *Developmental Psychology,* 1972, *7,* 80-83.

Dodwell, P. C. Children's understanding of number and related concepts. *Canadian Journal of Psychology,* 1960, *14,* 191-205.

Doise, W., Mugny, G., and Perret-Clermont, A. N. Social understanding and the development of cognitive operations. *European Journal of Social Psychology,* 1975, *5,* 367-383.

Doise, W., Mugny, G., and Perret-Clermont, A. N. Social interaction and cognitive development: Further evidence. *European Journal of Social Psychology,* 1976, *6,* 245-247.

Dollard, J., Doob, L. W., Miller, N. E., Mowrer, O. H., and Sears, R. R. *Frustration and aggression.* New Haven: Yale University Press, 1939.

Dollard, J., and Miller, N. E. *Personality and psychotherapy.* New York: McGraw-Hill, 1950.

Donaldson, M. *Children's minds.* Glasgow: Fontana/ Collins, 1978.

Donaldson, M., and Wales, R. On the acquisition of some relational terms. In J. R. Hayes (Ed.), *Cognition and the development of language.* New York: Wiley, 1970.

Dore, J. The development of speech acts. Ph.D. dissertation, City University of New York, 1973.

Dore, J. Holophrases, speech acts, language universals. *Journal of Child Language,* 1975, *2,* 21-40.

Dore, J. What's so conceptual about the acquisition of linguistic structures? *Journal of Child Language,* 1979, *6,* 129-138.

Dornbusch, S. M., Carlsmith, L., Gross, R. T., Martin, J. A., Jenning, D., Rosenberg, A., and Duke, P. Sexual development, age, and dating: A comparison of biological and social influences upon one set of behaviors. *Child Development,* 1981, *52,* 179-185.

Dorr, D., and Fey, S. Relative power of symbolic adult and peer models in the modification of children's moral choice behavior. *Journal of Personality and Social Psychology,* 1974, *29,* 335-341.

Douvan, E. A., and Adelson, J. *The adolescent experience.* New York: Wiley, 1966.

Dove, A. Taking the chitling test. *Newsweek,* July 15, 1968.

Dowd, I. M., Clifton, R. K., Anderson, D. R., and Eichelman, W. H. Children perceive large-disparity random dot stereograms more readily than adults. *Journal of Experimental Child Psychology,* 1980, *29,* 1-11.

Dreyer, P. H. Changes in the meaning of marriage among youth: The impact of the "revolution" in sex and sex-role behavior. In R. Grinder (Ed.), *Studies in adolescence.* 3rd ed. New York: Macmillan, 1975.

Dulit, E. Adolescent thinking à la Piaget: The formal stage. *Journal of Youth and Adolescence,* 1972, *1,* 281-301.

Duncan, E. M., and Kellas, G. Developmental changes in the internal structure of semantic categories. *Journal of Experimental Child Psychology,* 1978, *26,* 328-340.

Dunphy, D. C. The social structure of urban adolescent peer groups. *Sociometry,* 1963, *26,* 230-246.

Durkheim, E. *The elementary forms of religious life.* 2nd ed. Edison, N. J.: Allen Unwin, 1976.

Dweck, C. S., Davidson, W., Nelson, S., and Enna, B. Sex differences in learned helplessness: II. The contingencies of evaluative feedback in the classroom and III. An experimental analysis. *Developmental Psychology,* 1978, *14,* 268-276.

Dweck, C. S., and Goetz, T. E. Attributions and learned helplessness. In J. Harvey, W. Ickes, and R. Kidd (Eds.), *New directions in attribution research* (Vol. II). Hillsdale, N. J.: Erlbaum, 1978.

Dweck, C. S., and Reppucci, N.D. Learned helplessness and reinforcement responsibility in children. *Journal of Personality and Social Psychology,* 1973, *25,* 109-116.

Eckerman, C. O., and Rheingold, H. L. Infants' exploratory responses to toys and people. *Developmental Psychology,* 1974, *10,* 255-329.

Eckerman, C. O., and Whatley, J. L. Infants' reactions to unfamiliar adults varying in novelty. *Developmental Psychology,* 1975, *11,* 562-567.

Eckerman, C. O., and Whatley, J. L. Toys and social interaction between infant peers. *Child Development,* 1977, *48,* 1645-1656.

Eckerman, C. O., Whatley, J. L., and Kutz, S. L. Growth of social play with peers during the second year of life. *Developmental Psychology,* 1975, *11,* 42-49.

Edwards, C. P., and Whiting, B. B. Differential socialization of girls and boys in the light of cross-cultural research. In C. M. Super and S. Harkness (Eds.), *New directions for child development: Anthropological perspectives on child development.* San Francisco: Jossey-Bass, 1980.

Egeland, B., and Sroufe, L. A. Attachment and early maltreatment. *Child Development,* 1981, *51,* 44-52.

Ehri, L. C. Comprehending and production of adjectives and seriation. *Journal of Child Language,* 1976, *3,* 369-384.

Ehri, L. C. Linguistic insight: Threshold of reading acquisition. In T. G. Waller and G. E. Mackinnon (Eds.), *Reading research: Advances in theory and practice* (Vol.1). New York: Academic Press, 1979.

Eibl-Eibesfeldt, I. *Ethology: The biology of behavior.* New York: Holt, Rinehart and Winston, 1970.

Eimas, P. Speech perception in infancy. Paper presented at the International Congress of Psychology, Paris, July 1976.

Eimas, P., Siqueland, E. R., Jusczyk, P., and Vigorito, J. Speech perception in infants. *Science,* 1971, *171,* 303-306.

Eisenberg-Berg, N., and Lennon, R. Altruism and the assessment of empathy in preschool years. Paper presented at the Society for Research in Child Development, San Francisco, March 1979.

Eisenberg-Berg, N., Murray, E., and Hite, T. Children's reasoning regarding sex-typed toy choices. Paper presented at the Society for Research in Child Development, Boston, April 1981.

Eisert, D. C., and Kahle, L. R. Self-evaluation leads to social comparison during late adolescence: A cross-lagged panel analysis. Paper presented at the Society for Research in Child Development, Boston, April 1981.

Eisner, E. (Ed.). *The arts, human development, and education.* Berkeley: McCutchan, 1976.

Elder, G. H., Jr. Adolescence in historical perspective. In J. Adelson (Ed.), *Handbook of adolescent psychology.* New York: Wiley, 1980.

Elder, J. L., and Pederson, D. R. Preschool children's use of objects in symbolic play. *Child Development,* 1978, *49,* 500-504.

Elkind, D. Cognitive structure and adolescent experience. *Adolescence,* 1967, *2,* 427-434.

Elkind, D. Developmental studies of figurative perception. In L. P. Lipsitt and H. W. Reese (Eds.), *Advances in child development and behavior* 1969, *4,* 2-28.

Elkind, D. Strategic interactions in early adolescence. In J. Adelson (Ed.), *Handbook of adolescent psychology.* New York: Wiley, 1980.

Elkind, D., and Flavell, J. H. *Studies in cognitive development.* New York: Oxford University Press, 1969.

Elliott, S. N. Sixth grade and college students' metacognitive knowledge of prose organization and study strategies. Paper presented at the American Educational Research Association, Boston, April 1980.

Emmerich, W., Goldman, K. S., Kusch, B., and Sharabany, R. Evidence for a transitional phase in the development of gender constancy. *Child Development,* 1977, *48,* 930-936.

Ennis, R. H. Children's ability to handle Piaget's propositional logic: A conceptual critique. *Review of Educational Research,* 1975, *45,* 1-41.

Enright, M. K. The role of context similarity in memory reactivation and generalization in three-month-old infants. Paper presented at the Society for Research in Child Development, Boston, April 1981.

Enright, R. D., Manheim, L. A., and Franklin, C. C. Toward a standardized and objective methodology for studying children's distributive justice reasoning. *The Quarterly Newsletter of the Laboratory of Comparative Human Cognition,* 1980, *2,* 7-10.

Entus, A. K. Hemispheric asymmetry in processing dichotically-presented speech and nonspeech stimuli by infants. Paper presented at the Society for Research in Child Development, Denver, April 1975.

Epstein, H. T. Phrenoblysis: Special brain and mind growth periods. I. Human brain and skull development. *Developmental Psychobiology,* 1973, *7,* 207-224.

Epstein, R., Lanza, P. P., and Skinner, B. F. Symbolic communication between two pigeons (*Columbia livia domestica*). *Science,* 1980, *207,* 543-545.

Erikson, E. H. Identity and the life cycle. *Psychological Issues,* 1959, *1,* 1-171.

Erikson, E. H. *Childhood and society.* New York: Norton, 1963.

Erikson, E. H. Personal communication. March 1964.

Erikson, E. H. *Young man Luther.* New York: Norton, 1968.

Erikson, E. H. *Gandhi's truth.* New York: Norton, 1969.

Erikson, E. H. *Dimensions of a new identity: The 1973 Jefferson lectures in the humanities.* New York: Norton, 1974.

Erikson, E. H. *Toys and reasons.* New York: Norton, 1977.

Ervin-Tripp, S. Imitation and structural change in children's language. In E. H. Lenneberg (Ed.), *New directions in the study of language.* Cambridge, Mass.: MIT Press, 1964.

Escalona, S. K. *The roots of individuality: Normal*

patterns of development in infancy. Chicago: Aldine, 1968.

Escalona, S. K. Basic mode of social interaction: Their emergence and patterning during the first two years of life. *Merrill-Palmer Quarterly,* 1973, *19,* 205-232.

Eson, M. E., and Shapiro, A. S. When 'don't' means 'do': Pragmatic and cognitive development in understanding and indirect imperative. Unpublished paper, State University of New York at Albany, 1980.

Eson, M. E., and Walmsley, S. A. Cognitive and psycholinguistic changes during the transition to adolescence. In the *National Society for the Study of Education Yearbook,* 1980.

Etaugh, C., and Levy, T. Hemispheric specialization for tactile-spatial processing in preschool children. Paper presented at the Society for Research in Child Development, Boston, April 1981.

Evans, P. A visit with John Bowlby. *American Psychological Association Monitor,* May 1977.

Eysenck, H. J. *The IQ argument.* New York: Library Publications, 1971.

Fagan, J. Infants' delayed recognition memory and forgetting. *Journal of Experimental Child Psychology,* 1973, *16,* 424-450.

Fagan, J. Infant memory and the prediction of intelligence. Paper presented at the Society for Research in Child Development, Boston, April 1981.

Fagen, J., Hoffman, M., Rovee-Collier, C. K., and Thompson, S. Reminiscence following reactivation of infant memory. Paper presented at the Society for Research in Child Development, Boston, April 1981.

Fagen, J., Rovee, C. K., and Kaplan, M. G. Psychological scaling of stimulus similarity in three-month-old infants and adults. *Journal of Experimental Child Psychology,* 1976, *22,* 272-281.

Fagot, B. I. The influence of sex of child on parental reactions to toddler children. *Child Development,* 1978, *49,* 459-465.

Falmagne, R. (Ed.), *Reasoning: Representation and process in children and adults.* New York: Halsted Press, 1975.

Falmagne, R. J. The development of logical competence: A psycholinguistic perspective. In R. M. Klueve and H. Spada (Eds.), *Developmental models of thinking.* New York: Academic Press, 1980.

Fantz, R. L. Pattern vision in young infants. *Psychological Review,* 1958, *8,* 43-47.

Fantz, R. L. The origins of form perception. *Scientific American,* 1961, *204,* 66-72.

Fantz, R. L. Visual perception from birth as shown by pattern selectivity. *Annals of the New York Academy of Science,* 1965, *118,* 793-814.

Fantz, R. L. Visual perception and experience in infancy. In *Early experience and visual information processing in perceptual and reading dis-*

orders. Washington, D. C.: National Academy of Sciences, 1970, 351-381.

Fantz, R. L., Fagan, J. F., and Miranda, S. B. Early visual selectivity. In L. B. Cohen and P. H. Salapatek (Eds.), *Infant perception* (Vol. 1). New York: Academic Press, 1975.

Farnhill, D. The effects of social-judgment set on children's use of intent information. *Journal of Personality,* 1974, *42,* 276-289.

Farran, D. C., and Ramey, C. T. Infant day care and attachment behaviors toward mothers and teachers. *Child development,* 1977, *48,* 1112-1116.

Faust, M. S. Developmental maturity as a determination of prestige in adolescent girls. *Child Development,* 1960, *31,* 173-184.

Faust, M. S. Somatic development of adolescent girls. *Monograph of the Society for Research in Child Development,* 1977, *42,* (Serial No. 169, No. 1).

Feather, N. T. *Values in education and society.* New York: Free Press, 1975.

Feather, N. T. Values in adolescence. In J. Adelson (Ed.), *Handbook of adolescent psychology.* New York: Wiley, 1980.

Fein, G. Echoes from the nursery: Piaget, Vygotsky and the relationship between language and play. In E. Winner and H. Gardner (Eds.), *Fact, fiction and fantasy,* New Directions for Child Development, No 6. San Francisco: Josey-Bass, 1979*a.*

Fein, G. Play with actions and objects. In B. Sutton-Smith (Ed.), *Play and learning.* New York: Gardner Press, 1979*b.*

Fein, G., Johnson, D., Kosson, N., Stork, L., and Wasserman, L. Sex stereotypes and preferences in the toy choices of twenty-month-old boys and girls. *Developmental Psychology,* 1975, *11,* 527-528.

Feingold, B. F. *Why your child is hyperactive.* New York: Random House, 1975.

Feiring, C. The social network of three-year-old children. Paper presented at the Society for Research in Child Development, Boston, April 1981.

Feitelson, D., and Ross, G. S. The neglected factorplay. *Human Development,* 1973, *16,* 202-223.

Feld, S., Ruhland, D., and Gold, M. Developmental changes in achievement motivation. *Merrill-Palmer Quarterly,* 1979, *25,* 43-60.

Feldbaum, C. L., Christenson, T. E., and O'Neal, E. C. An observational study of the assimilation of the newcomer to the preschool. *Child Development,* 1980, *51,* 497-507.

Feldman, D. H. *Beyond universals in cognitive development.* Norword, N. J.: Ablex Publishers, 1980.

Feldman, R. S., and White, J. B. Detecting deception in children. *Journal of Communication,* 1980, *30,* 121-128.

Feldman, S. S., Biringen, Z. C., and Nash, S. C. Fluctuations of sex-related self attributions as a function of stage of family life cycle. *Developmental Psychology,* 1981, *17,* 24-35.

Feldman, S. S., and Ingham, M. Attachment behavior: A validation study in two age groups. *Child Development,* 1975, *46,* 319–330.

Feldman, S. S., and Nash, S. C. Changes in responsiveness to babies during adolescence. *Child Development,* 1979, *50,* 942–949.

Feldstein, J. H. Children's classification of animals by sex. Paper presented at the Eastern Psychological Association, Washington, D. C., April 1978.

Fennema, E., and Sherman, J. *Women and mathematics: Research perspectives for change.* Washington, D. C.: National Institute of Education, 1977.

Fenson, L., and Ramsay, D. S. Imitation of meaningful sequences by fifteen- and nineteen-month old children. In L. Nicolich, Mental representation and early language development—Directions for exploring relationships. Conversation hour presented at the Society for Research in Child Development, San Francisco, March 1979.

Fernald, A. Four-month-olds prefer to listen to "motherese." Paper presented at the Society for Research in Child Development, Boston, April 1981.

Fernald, A., and Kuhl, P. Fundamental frequency as an acoustic determinant of infant preference for "motherese." Paper presented at the Society for Research in Child Development, Boston, April 1981.

Ferrerio, E. What is written in a written sentence? A developmental answer. *Journal of Education,* 1978, *160,* 25–40.

Feshbach, S. Aggression. In P. H. Mussen (Ed.), *Carmichael's manual of child psychology* (Vol. 2). New York: Wiley, 1970.

Feshbach, S., and Singer, R. *Television and aggression.* San Francisco: Jossey-Bass, 1971.

Field, D. Can preschool children really learn to conserve? *Child Development,* 1981, *52,* 326–334.

Field, T. Differential behavioral and cardiac responses of three-month-old infants to a mirror and peer. *Infant Behavior and Development,* 1979, *2,* 179–184.

Finley, G. E., and Cheyne, J. A. Birth order and susceptibility to peer modeling influences in young boys. *Journal of Genetic Psychology,* 1976, *129,* 273–277.

Fischer, K. W. A theory of cognitive development: The control of hierarchies of skill. *Psychological Review,* 1980, *87,* 477–531.

Fisher, C. B., and Heincke, S. Remembering the oblique: A matter of degree? Paper presented at the Society for Research in Child Development, Boston, April 1981.

Fiske, E. B. An issue that won't go away. *The New York Times Magazine,* March 27, 1977.

Fitzgerald, H. E., and Brackbill, Y. Classical conditioning in infancy: Development and constraints. *Psychological Bulletin,* 1976, *83,* 353–376.

Fitzhenry-Coor, I. Children's comprehension and inference in stories of intentionality. Paper presented at the Society for Research in Child Development, New Orleans, April 1977.

Flaste, R. Scientists wonder what's on a baby's mind. *The New York Times,* August 27, 1976, p. 18.

Flaste, R. Parents/children: When the youngster says "I hate you." *The New York Times,* July 29, 1977a, p. A16.

Flaste, R. Closeness in the first minutes of life may have lasting effect. *The New York Times,* August 16, 1977b, p. C30.

Flavell, J. *The developmental psychology of Jean Piaget.* Princeton: Van Nostrand, 1963.

Flavell, J. Developmental studies of mediated memory. In H. W. Reese and L. P. Lipsitt (eds.), *Advances in child development and behavior* (Vol. 5). New York: Academic Press, 1970.

Flavell, J. Stage-related properties of cognitive development. *Cognitive Psychology,* 1971, *2,* 421–453.

Flavell, J. *Cognitive development.* Englewood Cliffs, NJ: Prentice-Hall, 1977.

Flavell, J. Metacognition and cognitive monitoring: A new area of cognitive development inquiry. *American Psychologist,* 1979, *34,* 906–911.

Flavell, J. Structures, stages, and sequences in cognitive development. Paper presented at the Minnesota Symposium on Child Psychology, Minneapolis, October 1980.

Flavell, J., Botkin, P. T. and Fry, C. L. *The development of roletaking and communication skills in young children.* New York: Wiley, 1968.

Flavell, J., and Wellman, H. Metamemory. In R. Kail, Jr., and J. Hagen (Eds.), *Perspectives on the development of memory and cognition.* Hillsdale, N. J.: Erlbaum, 1977.

Fodor, J. A. *The language of thought.* New York: Crowell, 1975.

Fogel, A. Peer versus mother-directed behavior in one- to three-month-old infants. *Infant Behavior and Development,* 1979, *2,* 215–226.

Fogel, A. Face-to-face interactions with two-month-olds: Mother versus stranger. Paper presented at the Society for Research in Child Development, Boston, April 1981.

Fogelson, R. *Violence as protest.* New York: Doubleday, 1970.

Ford, M. E. and Tisak, M. S. Adolescent androgyny and its relationship to social competence, identity status, and academic achievement. Paper presented at the Society for Research in Child Development, Boston, April 1981.

Forrest, D. L., and Waller, T. G. Language, metalanguage and reading. Paper presented to the International Reading Association Research Seminar on Linguistic Awareness and Learning to Read, Victoria, British Columbia, 1979.

Fowler, W. Cognitive learning in infancy and early childhood. *Psychological Bulletin,* 1962, *59,* 116–153.

Fox, L. H., Brody, L., and Tobin, D. (Eds.). *Women*

and the mathematical mystique. Baltimore: Johns Hopkins University Press, 1980.

Fraiberg, S. H. *The magic years*. New York: Scribner, 1959.

Fraiberg, S. H. *Every child's birthright*. New York: Basic Books, 1977.

Freedman, D. G. Infancy biology and culture. In L. P. Lipsitt (Ed.), *Developmental Psychobiology: The significance of infancy*. New York: Wiley, 1976.

Freedman, D. G. Ethnic differences in babies. *Human Nature*, 1979, *2*, 36-43.

Freeman, N. H. *Strategies of representation in young children*. London: Academic Press, 1980.

Freeman, N. H., and Janikoun, R. Intellectual realism in children's drawings of a familiar object with distinctive features. *Child Development*, 1972, *43*, 1116-1121.

Freire, P. *Pedagogy of the oppressed*. New York: Seabury, 1971.

Freud, A. *The ego and the mechanisms of defense*. New York: International Universities Press, 1946.

Freud, A. Certain types and stages of social maladjustment. In K. R. Eissler (Ed.), *Searchlights on delinquency*. New York: International Universities Press, 1949.

Freud, A. Adolescence. In R. S. Eissler, A. Freud, H. Hartmann, and M. Kris (Eds.), *Psychoanalytic study of the child* (Vol. 13). New York: International Universities Press, 1958.

Freud, A. *Normality and pathology in childhood*. New York: International Universities Press, 1965.

Freud, S. *Beyond the pleasure principle*. New York: Boni and Liveright, 1927.

Freud, S. *The interpretation of dreams*. New York: Boni and Liveright, 1938*a*.

Freud, S. Three contributions to the theory of sex. In A. A. Brill (Ed.), *The basic writings of Sigmund Freud*. New York: Random House, 1938*b*.

Freud, S. In J. Rickman (Ed.), *A general selection from the writings of Sigmund Freud*. Garden City, N. Y.: Doubleday Anchor, 1957.

Freud, S. The relation of the poet to day-dreaming. In B. Nelson (Ed.), *On creativity and the unconscious*. New York: Harper, 1958.

Freud, S. Civilization and its discontents. In *The standard edition of the complete psychological works of Sigmund Freud* (Vol. XXI). London: Hogarth, 1961.

Freud, S. Dissection of the personality. In *New introductory lectures on psychoanalysis*. New York: Norton, 1965*a*.

Freud, S. Femininity. In *New introductory lectures on psychoanalysis*. New York: Norton, 1965*b*.

Freud, S. *New introductory lectures on psychoanalysis*. New York: Norton, 1965*c*.

Friedrich, L. K., and Stein, A. H. Aggressive and prosocial television programs and the natural behavior of preschool children. *Monographs of the Society for Research in Child Development*, 1973, *38*, (Serial No. 151, No. 4).

Frith, C. D., and Frith, U. Feature selection and classification: A developmental study. *Journal of Experimental Child Psychology*, 1978, *25*, 413-428.

Frodi, A. M., and Lamb, M. E. Sex differences in responsiveness to infants: A developmental study of psychophysiological and behavioral responses. *Child Development*, 1978, *49*, 1182-1188.

Frodi, A. M., Murray, A. D., Lamb, M. E., and Steinberg, J. Behavioral responsiveness to infants in pre- and postmenarcheal girls. Paper presented at the Society for Research in Child Development, Boston, April 1981.

Fromkin, V. A. Krashen, S., Curtiss, S., Rigler, D., and Rigler, M. The development of language in Genie: A case of language acquisition beyond the "critical period." *Brain and Language*, 1974, *1*, 81-107.

Fullard, W., and Reiling, A. M. An investigation of Lorenz's "Babyness." *Child Development*, 1976, *47*, 1191-1194.

Furby, L. Cumulative learning and cognitive development. *Human Development*, 1972, *15*, 265-286.

Furman, W., and Bierman, K. L. A features model theory of children's conceptions of friendship. Paper presented at the Society for Research in Child Development, Boston, April 1981.

Furrow, D., Nelson, K., and Benedict, H. Mothers' speech to children and syntactic development: Some simple relationships. *Journal of Child Language*, 1979, *6*, 423-442.

Furth, H. G. *Thinking without language: Psychological implications of deafness*. Englewood Cliffs, N. J.: Prentice-Hall, 1966.

Furth, H. G. Piaget, I. Q., and the nature-nuture controversy. *Human Development*, 1973, *16*, 61-73.

Furth, H. G. Children's societal understanding and the process of equilibration. *New Directions for Child Development*, 1978, *1*, 101-123.

Furth, H. G. *Piaget and knowledge*. 2nd ed. Chicago: University of Chicago Press, 1981.

Furth, H. G., Baur, M., Smith, J. E. Children's conception of social institutions: A Piagetian framework. *Human Development*, 1976, *19*, 351-374.

Gagné, R. M. Contributions of learning to human development. *Psychological Review*, 1968, *75*, 177-191.

Gaines, R. Matrices and pattern detection by young children. *Developmental Psychology*, 1973, *9*, 143-150.

Galin, D., Johnstone, J., Nakell, L., and Herron, J. Development of the capacity for tactile information transfer between hemispheres in normal children. *Science*, 1979, *204*, 1330-1333.

Gallatin, J. Politcal thinking in adolescence. In J. Adelson (Ed.), *Handbook of adolescent psychology*. New York: Wiley, 1980.

Gallup, G. G. Self-recognition in primates: A comparative approach to the bidirectional properties of consciousness. *American Psychologist,* 1977, *32,* 329–338.

Garber, H., and Heber, F. R. The Milwaukee Project: Indications of the effectiveness of early intervention in preventing mental retardation. In P. Mittler (Ed.), *Research to practice in mental retardation* (Vol.1). Baltimore: University Park Press, 1977.

Gardner, B. T., and Gardner, R. A. Two way communication with an infant chimpanzee. In A. M. Schrier and F. Stollnitz (Eds.), *Behavior of non-human primates* (Vol.4). New York: Academic Press, 1971.

Gardner, H. Problem-solving in the arts. *Journal of Aesthetic Education,* 1971, *5,* 93–114.

Gardner, H. Style sensitivity in children. *Human Development,* 1972, *15,* 325–338.

Gardner, H. *The arts and human development.* New York: Wiley, 1973.

Gardner, H. Metaphors and modalities: How children project polar adjectives onto diverse domains. *Child Development,* 1974, *45,* 84–91.

Gardner, H. *The shattered mind.* New York: Knopf, 1975.

Gardner, H. Senses, symbols and operations: An organization of artistry. In D. Perkins and B. Leondar (Eds.), *The arts and cognition.* Baltimore: Johns Hopkins University Press, 1977.

Gardner, H. Getting acquainted with Jean Piaget. *The New York Times,* January 3, 1979*a,* p. 61.

Gardner, H. U-shaped behavior changes basic concepts of development. *The New York Times,* September 25, 1979*b,* p. C3.

Gardner, H. *Artful scribbles: The significance of children's drawings.* New York: Basic Books, 1980*a.*

Gardner, H. The strange career of Alexander Luria. *Psychology Today,* 1980*b, 14,* 84–96.

Gardner, H. *The quest for mind: Piaget, Lévi-Strauss, and the structuralist movement.* 2nd ed. Chicago: University of Chicago Press, 1981.

Gardner, H. Children's perceptions of works of art: A developmental portrait. In D. O'Hare (Ed.), *The psychology of art.* London: Harvester, in press.

Gardner, H., and Winner, E. First intimations of artistry. In S. Strauss (Ed.), *U-shaped behavioral growth.* New York: Academic Press, 1981.

Gardner, H., Winner, E., Bechofer, R., and Wolf, D. The development of figurative language. In K. Nelson (Ed.), *Children's language.* New York: Gardner Press, 1978.

Gardner, J., and Gardner, H. A note on selective imitation by a six-week-old infant. *Child Development,* 1970, *41,* 1209–1213.

Garmezy, N. Vulnerable and invulnerable children: Theory, research and intervention. Master lecture on developmental psychology presented at the American Psychological Association, Washington D. C., September 1976.

Garner, A. M., and Wenar, C. *The mother-child interaction in psychosomatic disorders.* Urbana: University of Illinois Press, 1959.

Garvey, C. *Play.* J. Bruner, M. Cole, and B. Lloyd (Eds.), *The developing child.* Cambridge, Mass.: Harvard University Press, 1977.

Garvey, C. Communication controls in social play. In B. Sutton-Smith (Ed.), *Play and learning.* New York: Gardner Press, 1979.

Garvey, C., and Berndt, R. The organization of pretend play. In *Structure in play and fantasy.* Symposium presented at the American Psychological Association, Chicago, September 1975.

Gazzaniga, M. *The bisected brain.* New York: Appleton-Century-Crofts, 1970.

Geertz, C. *The interpretation of culture.* New York: Basic Books, 1973.

Geffen, G., and Wale, J. Development of selective listening and hemispheric asymmetry. *Developmental Psychology,* 1979, *15,* 138–146.

Gelfand, D. M., and Hartmann, D. P. The prevention of childhood behavior disorders. In B. Lahey and A. Kazdin (Eds.), *Advances in child clinical psychology.* New York: Plenum, 1977.

Gelman, R. Conservation acquisition: A problem of learning to attend to relevant attributes. *Journal of Experimental Child Psychology,* 1969, *7,* 176–187.

Gelman, R. The nature and development of early number concepts. In H. W. Reese (Ed.), *Advances in child development and behavior* (Vol. 7). New York: Academic Press, 1972.

Gelman, R. Cognitive development. *Annual Review of Psychology,* 1978, *29,* 297–332.

Gelman, R. Preschool thought. *American Psychologist,* 1979, *34,* 900–905.

Gelman, R., and Gallistel, C. R. *The child's understanding of number.* Cambridge, Mass.: Harvard University Press, 1978.

Gentner, D. What looks like a jiggy but acts like a zimbo? A study of early word meaning using artificial objects. Paper presented at the Stanford Child Language Research Forum, Stanford, April 1978.

Gerschitz, E. M. Modes of representation, the epistemic subject, and developmental word association phenomena. Paper presented at the Eastern Psychological Association, Philadelphia, April 1979.

Geschwind, N. The development of the brain and the evolution of language. *Monograph Series on Languages and Linguistics,* 1964, *17,* 155–169.

Gerschwind, N. Neurological foundations of language. In H. R. Myklebust (ED.), *Progress in learning disabilities.* New York: Grune and Stratton, 1967.

Getzels, J. W., and Csikszentmihalyi, M. *The creative vision: A longitudinal study of problem finding in art.* New York: Wiley, 1976.

Getzels, J. W., and Jackson, P. W. *Creativity and intelligence.* New York: Wiley, 1962.

Gewirtz, J. L. A learning analysis of the effects of normal stimulation, privation, and deprivation on the acquisition of social motivation and attachment. In B. M. Foss (Ed.), *Determinants of infant behavior* (Vol. 1). New York: Wiley, 1961.

Gewirtz, J. L. Mechanisms of social learning: Some roles of stimulation and behavior in early human development. In D. A. Goslin (Ed.), *Handbook of socialization theory and research.* New York: Rand McNally, 1969.

Ghiselin, B. *The creative process.* New York: Mentor, 1952.

Gholson, B. *The cognitive-developmental basis for human learning: Studies in hypothesis testing.* New York: Academic Press, 1980.

Gibbs, J. C. Kohlberg's stages of moral judgment: A constructive critique. *Harvard Education Review, 1977, 47,* 43–61.

Gibbs, J. C. Kohlberg's moral stage theory: A Piagetian revision. *Human Development, 1979, 22,* 89–112.

Gibbs, J. C., Widaman, K. F., Colby, A., and Fenton, E. Construct validation of the socio-moral reflection measure. Unpublished paper, Ohio State University, 1981.

Gibson, E. J. *Principles of perceptual learning and development.* New York: Appleton-Century-Crofts, 1969.

Gibson, E. J., and Levin, H. *The psychology of reading.* Cambridge, Mass.: MIT Press, 1975.

Gibson, E. J., Owsley, C. J., and Johnston, J. Perception of invariants by five-month-old infants: Differentiation of two types of motion. *Developmental Psychology, 1978, 14,* 407–415.

Gibson, J. J. *The senses considered as perceptual systems.* Boston: Houghton Mifflin, 1966.

Gilligan, C., and Murphy, J. M. Development from adolescence to adulthood: The philosopher and the dilemma of the fact. In D. Kuhn (Ed.), Intellectual development beyond childhood, *New Directions for Child Development* (No. 5). San Francisco: Jossey-Bass, 1979.

Ginsberg, H. P., Posner, H. K., and Russell, R. L. The development of mental addition: A cross-cultural study. Paper presented at the American Psychological Association, New York, September 1979.

Ginsburg, H., and Opper, S. *Piaget's theory of intellectual development.* 2nd ed. Englewood Cliffs, N. J.: Prentice-Hall, 1979.

Gladwin, T. *East is a big bird.* Cambridge, Mass.: Harvard University Press, 1970.

Gleason, H. A. *An introduction to descriptive linguistics.* New York: Holt, Rinehart and Winston, 1965.

Gleitman, L., Gleitman, H., and Shipley, E. The emergence of the child as grammarian. *Cognition, 1972, 1,* 137–164.

Gleitman, L., and Rozin, P. The structure and acquisition of Reading I: Relations between orthographics and the structure of language. In A. S. Reber and D. L. Scarborough (Eds.), *Toward a psychology of reading.* Hillsdale, N.J.: Erlbaum, 1977.

Glenn, C. G. Memory for multi-episode stories: A developmental study. Paper presented at the Psychonomics Meeting, November 1977.

Glueck, S., and Glueck, E. *Delinquents in the making.* New York: Harper, 1952.

Gobbel, G., and Rider, B. Meaningfulness, semantic category knowledge, and recall of young children. Paper presented at the Society for Research in Child Development, Boston, April 1981.

Goethals, G. W., and Klos, D. (Eds.). *Experiencing youth: First-person accounts.* Boston: Little, Brown, 1976.

Golding, W. *Lord of the flies.* New York: Crowell, 1962.

Goldman, P. Development and plasticity of frontal association cortex in the infrahuman primate. In C. Ludlow and M. E. Doran-Quine (Eds.), *The neurological bases of language disorders in children: Methods and directions for research.* Publication No. 79-440. Bethesda, Md.: National Institute of Health, 1979.

Goldman-Rakic, P. S. Inner and outer limits of CNS plasticity. In A. H. Parmelee, Jr., *Brain plasticity—What is it?* Symposium presented at the Society for Research in Child Development, Boston, April 1981.

Goldsmith, H. H., and East, P. L. Parental perception of infant temperament: Validity and genetics. Paper presented at the Society for Research in Child Development, Boston, April 1981.

Golinkoff, R. Semantic development in infants: The concepts of agent and recipient. *Merrill-Palmer Quarterly, 1975, 21,* 181–193.

Golinkoff, R. A comparison of reading comprehension processes in good and poor comprehenders. *Reading Research Quarterly, 1976, 11,* 623–659.

Golinkoff, R. M., and Kerr, J. L. Infants' perception of semantically defined action role changes in filmed events. *Merrill-Palmer Quarterly, 1978, 24,* 53–61.

Golomb, C. Children's representation of the human figure: The effects of models, media, and instruction. *Genetic Psychology Monographs, 1973, 87,* 197–251.

Golomb, C. *Young children's sculpture and drawing: A study in representational development.* Cambridge, Mass.: Harvard University Press, 1974.

Golomb, C. Representation and reality: Their origin and determinants of young children's drawings. Paper presented at the National Symposium for Research in Art. Urbana, Ill., October 1980.

Golomb, C., and Cornelius, C. Symbolic play and its cognitive significance. *Developmental Psychology, 1977, 13,* 246–252.

Gombrich, E. H. *Art and illusion.* New York: The Bollingen Foundation, 1960.

Goodglass, H., and Geschwind, N. Language disorders (aphasia). In E. Carterette and M. Freidman (Eds.), *Handbook of perception* (Vol. 7). New York: Academic Press, 1976.

Goodman, K. Decoding—From code to what? *Journal of Reading*, 1971, *14*, 455-462.

Goodman, N. *Languages of art*. Indianapolis: Bobbs-Merrill, 1968.

Goodman, S. H. A sequential functional analysis of preschool children's private speech. Paper presented at the Society for Research in Child Development, New Orleans, March 1977.

Goodman, S. H. The integration of verbal and motor behavior in preschool children. *Child Development*, 1981, *52*, 280-289.

Goodnow, J. Auditory-visual matching: Modality problem or translation problem? *Child Development*, 1971a, *42*, 1187-1201.

Goodnow, J. The role of modalities in perceptual and cognitive development. In J. Hill (Ed.), *Minnesota symposium on child development* (Vol. 5). Minneapolis: University of Minnesota Press, 1971b.

Goodnow, J. *Children drawing*. Cambridge, Mass.: Harvard University Press, 1977.

Goody, J. *The domestication of the human mind*. Cambridge: Cambridge University Press, 1977.

Goody, J., and Watt, I. The consequences of literacy. *Comparative Studies in Society and History*, 1962, *5*, 304-345.

Gordon, F. R., and Flavell, J. H. The development of intuitions about cognitive cueing. *Child Development*, 1977, *48*, 1027-1033.

Goren, C. Form perception, innate form preferences, and visually mediated head-turning in human newborns. Paper presented at the Society for Research in Child Development, Denver, April 1975.

Gorney, C. Twins with a language of their own. *The Boston Globe*, July 23, 1979, p. 21.

Gottfried, A. W., Rose, S. A., and Bridger, W. H. Cross-modal transfer in human infants. *Child Development*, 1977, *48*, 118-123.

Gottlieb, D. E., Taylor, S. E., and Ruderman, A. Cognitive bases of children's moral judgments. *Developmental Psychology*, 1977, *13*, 547-556.

Gottman, J. M., and Parkhurst, J. T. Developing may not always be improving: A developmental study of children's best friendships. Paper presented at the Society for Research in Child Development, New Orleans, March 1977.

Gouin-Décarie, T. *Intelligence and affectivity in early childhood*. New York: International Universities Press, 1965.

Gould, R. *Child studies through fantasy: Cognitive-affective patterns in development*. New York: Quadrangle Books, 1972.

Gould, S. J. Biological potential versus biological determinism. *Natural History*, 1976, *85*, 12-22.

Gove, F. L., and Keating, D. P. Empathic role-taking precursors. *Developmental Psychology*, 1979, *15*, 594-600.

Grace, J., and Suci, G. Attentional priority of the agent and the acquisition of word reference. Paper presented at the Society for Research in Child Development, Boston, April 1981.

Graham, S., and Stern, P. Children's attributional reasoning about affective reactions of others. Paper presented at the Society for Research in Child Development, Boston, April 1981.

Gratch, G. On levels of awareness of objects in infants and students thereof. *Merrill-Palmer Quarterly of Behavior and Development*, 1976, *22*, 157-176.

Graziano, W. G. Standards of fair play in same-age and mixed-age groups of children. *Developmental Psychology*, 1978, *14*, 524-530.

Graziano, W. G., Brody, G. H., and Bernstein, S. Effects of information about future interaction and peer's motivation on peer reward allocations. *Developmental Psychology*, 1980, *16*, 475-482.

Green, R. Children's quest for sexual identity. *Psychology Today*, 1974, *8*, 45-51.

Green, S. K. Causal attribution of emotion as a role-taking skill in children. Unpublished paper, George Washington University, n.d.

Greenfield, P. M. On culture and conservation. In J. S. Bruner, R. R. Olver, and P. M. Greenfield (Eds.), *Studies in cognitive growth*. New York: Wiley, 1966.

Greenfield, P. M. Structural parellels between language and action in development. In A. Lock (Ed.), *Action, symbol and gesture: The emergence of language*. London: Academic Press, 1978.

Greenfield, P. M., Geber, B., Beagles-Roos, J., Farrar, D., and Gat, I. Television and radio experimentally compared: Effects of the medium on imagination and transmission of content. In P. M. Greenfield, *Cognitive impact of media on children*. Symposium presented at the Society for Research in Child Development, Boston, April 1981.

Greenfield, P. M., and Schneider, L. Building a tree structure: The development of hierarchical complexity and interrupted strategies in children's construction activity. *Developmental Psychology*, 1977, *13*, 299-213.

Greenfield, P. M., and Smith, J. *The structure of communication in early language*. New York, Academic Press, 1976.

Greenough, W. T. Enriched environments and brain anatomy: The results and the assumptions. In A. H. Parmelee, Jr., *Brain-plasticity—What is it?* Symposium presented at the Society for Research in Child Development, Boston, April 1981.

Gregory, M. S., Silvers, A., and Sutch, D. *Sociobiology and human nature*. San Francisco: Jossey-Bass, 1978.

Greven, P. *The Protestant temperament: Patterns of child rearing, religious experience, and the self in early America*. New York: New American Library, 1979.

Griffin, G. A., and Harlow, H. F. Effects of three months of total social deprivation on social adjustment and learning in the rhesus monkey. *Child Development,* 1966, *37,* 533-547.

Grinder, R. E. *A history of genetic psychology.* New York: Wiley, 1967.

Grinder, R. E. (Ed.). *Studies in adolescence.* 3rd ed. New York: Macmillan, 1975.

Gruber, H. E. Darwin's theory of nature and other images of wide scope. In J. Wechsler (Ed.), *On aesthetics in science.* Cambridge, Mass.: MIT Press, 1978.

Gruber, H. E. *Darwin on man.* Chicago: University of Chicago Press, 1981.

Gruen, G. Note on conservation: Methodological and definitional considerations. *Child Development,* 1966, *37,* 977-983.

Gruendel, J. M. Referential extension in early language development. *Child Development,* 1977, *48,* 1567-1576.

Grusec, J. E., and Kuczynski, L. Direction of effect in socialization: A comparison of the parent's versus the child's behavior as determinants of disciplinary techniques. *Developmental Psychology,* 1980, *16,* 1-9.

Grusec, J. E., and Redler, E. Attribution, reinforcement, and altruism: A developmental analysis. *Developmental Psychology,* 1980, *16,* 525-534.

Gunnar-vongnechten, M. R. Changing a frightening toy into a pleasant one by allowing the infant to control it. Paper presented at the Society for Research in Child Development, New Orleans, March 1977.

Gunnar-vongnechten, M. R. Changing a frightening toy into a pleasant toy by allowing the infant to control its actions. *Developmental Psychology,* 1978, *14,* 157-162.

Guthrie, K., and Hudson, L. M. Training conservation through symbolic play: A second look. *Child Development,* 1979, *50,* 1269-1274.

Gutmann, D. Parenthood: A key to the comparative study of the life cycle. In N. Datan and L. H. Ginsberg (Eds.), *Life-span developmental psychology.* New York: Academic Press, 1975.

Haan, N. Two moralities in action contexts: Relationships to thought, ego regulation, and development. *Journal of Personality and Social Psychology,* 1978, *36,* 286-305.

Haan, N., Smith, M. B., and Block, J. Moral reasoning of young adults: Political social behavior, family background, and personality correlates. *Journal of Personality and Social Psychology,* 1968, *10,* 185-201.

Haber, R. N. Personal communication, October 1968.

Haber, R. N. Commentary on motor-sensory feedback and geometry of visual space: An attempted replication by J. Gyr, R. Wiley, and A. Henry. *The Behavioral and Brain Sciences,* 1979, *2,* 59-94.

Haber, R. N., and Haber, R. B. Eidetic imagery. I.

Frequency. *Perceptual and Motor Skills,* 1964, *19,* 131-138.

Hadamard, J. *The psychology of invention in the mathematical field.* Princeton: Princeton University Press, 1945.

Hagen, J. W. Some thoughts about how children learn to remember. *Human Development,* 1971*a,* *14,* 262-71.

Hagen, J. W. Is incidental recall perceptually or cognitively determined? Paper presented at the Society for Research in Child Development, Minneapolis, April 1971*b.*

Haier, E., and Keating, D. Moral reasoning, formal operations, and intellectual precocity. Unpublished research, University of Minnesota, 1975.

Hainline, L. Developmental changes in visual scanning of face and nonface patterns by infants. *Journal of Experimental Child Psychology,* 1978, *25,* 90-115.

Hainline, L., and Feig, E. The correlates of childhood father absence in college-aged women. *Child Development,* 1978, *49,* 37-42.

Haith, M. M. Organization of visual behavior at birth. Paper presented at the International Congress of Psychology, Paris, July 1976.

Hale, G. A., Miller, L. K., and Stevenson, H. W. Incidental learning of film content: A developmental study. *Child Development,* 1968, *39,* 69-77.

Hale, G. A., and Piper, R. A. Developmental trends in children's incidental learning: Some critical stimulus differences. *Developmental Psychology,* 1973, *8,* 327-335.

Hale, G. A., Taweel, S. S., Green, R. Z., and Flaugher, J. Effects of instructions on children's attention to stimulus components. *Developmental Psychology,* 1978, *14,* 499-506.

Halford, G. S. A theory of the acquisition of conservation. *Psychological Review,* 1970, *77,* 302-316.

Hall, G. S. *Adolescence.* New York: Appleton, 1904.

Hall, G. S. *Aspects of child life and education.* New York: Appleton, 1907.

Hall, G. S. *Life and confessions of a psychologist.* New York: Appleton, 1923.

Hall, J. A., and Halberstadt, A. G. Masculinity and feminity in children: Development of the children's personal attributes questionnaire. *Developmental Psychology,* 1980, *16,* 270-280.

Hall, V. C., and Kingsley, R. C. Conservation and equilibration theory. *Journal of Genetic Psychology,* 1968, *113,* 195-213.

Halliday, M. A. K. *Learning how to mean—Explorations in the development of language.* London: Edward Arnold, 1975.

Halmi, K. A. Anorexia nervosa: Recent investigations. *American Review of Medicine,* 1978, *29,* 137-148.

Halverson, H. M. An experimental study of prehension in infants by means of systematic cinema records. *Genetic Psychology Monographs,* 1931, *10,* 107-286.

Hampson, J. M. Determinants of psychosexual orientation. In F. A. Beach (Ed.), *Sex and behavior.* New York: Wiley, 1965.

Harlow, H. The formation of learning sets. *Psychological Review,* 1949, *56,* 51-65.

Harlow, H. The nature of love. *American Psychologist,* 1958, *13,* 637-85.

Harlow, H. *Learning to love.* New York: Ballantine Books, 1971.

Harlow, H. "Harry, you are going to go down in history as the father of the cloth mother." A conversation with Carol Tavris. *Psychology Today,* 1973, *8,* 65-77.

Harlow, H., and Harlow, M. K. Social deprivation in monkeys. *Scientific American,* 1962, *207,* 136-144.

Harlow, H., and Harlow, M. K. Effects of various mother-infant relationships on rhesus monkey behaviors. In B. M. Foss (Ed.), *Determinants of infant behavior* (Vol. 4). New York: Barnes and Noble, 1969.

Harlow, H., and Zimmerman, R. R. Affectual responses in the infant monkey. *Science,* 1959, *130,* 421-432.

Harnick, F. The relationship between ability level and task difficulty in producing imitation in infants. *Child Development,* 1978, *49,* 209-212.

Harper, L., and Sanders, K. M. Preschool children's use of space: Sex differences in outdoor play. *Developmental Psychology,* 1975, *11,* 119.

Harrington, D. M., Block, J. H., and Block, J. Intolerance of ambiguity in preschool children: Psychometric considerations, behavioral manifestations, and parental correlates. *Developmental Psychology,* 1978, *14,* 242-256.

Harrington, M. *The other American.* New York: Macmillan, 1964.

Harris, B. Developmental differences in attribution of responsibility. *Developmental Psychology,* 1977, *13,* 257-265.

Harris, L. J. Sex differences in spatial ability. In M. Kinsbourne (Ed.), *Asymmetrical functions of the brain.* Cambridge: Cambridge University Press, 1978.

Harris, L. J., Hanley, C., and Best, C. Conservation of horizontality: Sex differences in sixth-graders and college students. Paper presented at the Society for Research in Child Development, Denver, March 1975.

Harris, P. Development of search and object permanence during infancy. *Psychological Bulletin,* 1975a, *82,* 332-344.

Harris, P. Object permanence and object perception. Paper presented at the Society for Research in Child Development, Denver, April 1975b.

Harris, R. J. Children's comprehension of complex sentences. *Journal of Experimental Child Psychology,* 1975, *19,* 420-433.

Harris, S. L. Teaching language to nonverbal children—with emphasis on problems of generalization. *Psychological Bulletin,* 1975, *82,* 565-580.

Hartshorne, H., and May, M. *Studies in character.* New York: Macmillan, 1929.

Hartup, W. W. Friendship states and the effectiveness of peers as reinforcing agents. *Journal of Experimental Child Psychology,* 1964, *1,* 154-162.

Hartup, W. W. Peer interaction and social organization. In P. H. Mussen (Ed.), *Carmichael's manual of child psychology* (Vol. 2). New York: Wiley, 1970.

Hartup, W. W. Aggression in childhood: Developmental perspectives. *American Psychologist,* 1974, *29,* 336-341.

Hartup, W. W. Toward a social psychology of childhood: From *Patterns of child-rearing to 1984.* Paper presented at the American Psychological Association, Washington, D.C., September 1976a.

Hartup, W. W. Peer interaction and behavioral development of the individual child. In E. Schopler and R. J. Reichler (Ed.), *Child development, deviations, and treatment.* New York: Plenum, 1976b, Reading 37.

Hartup, W. W. Issues in child development. Peers, play, and pathology: A new look at the social behavior of children. In J. D. Osofsky (Ed.), *Newsletter of the Society for Research in Child Development,* Fall 1977.

Harvey-Darton, F. J. *Children's books in England.* Cambridge: Cambridge University Press, 1960.

Hatano, G., Miyake, K., and Tajima, N. Mother behavior in an unstructured situation and child's acquisition of number conservation. *Child Development,* 1980, *51,* 379-385.

Hay, A. Children's comprehension of the author's point of view in stories. Paper presented at the Society for Research in Child Development, Boston, April 1981.

Hay, D. F. Cooperative interactions and sharing between very young children and their parents. *Developmental Psychology,* 1979, *15,* 647-653.

Hay, D. F., Ross, H. S., and Goldman, B. D. Social games in infancy. In B. Sutton-Smith (Ed.), *Play and learning.* New York: Gardner Press, 1979.

Hayes, D. S. Cognitive bases for liking and disliking among preschool children. *Child Development,* 1978, *49,* 906-909.

Hayes, D. S., Bolin, L. J., and Chemselski, B. E. Preschoolers' understanding of physical and emotional states as memory-relevant variables. Paper presented at the Society for Research in Child Development, Boston, April 1981.

Hayes, D. S., and Schulze, S. A. Visual encoding in preschoolers' serial retention. *Child Development,* 1977, *48,* 1066-1070.

Haynes, H., White, B., and Held, R. Visual accommodation in human infants. *Science,* 1965, *148,* 528-530.

Hays, J. D., and Siegel, A. Way finding and spatial representation: A test of a developmental model of cognitive mapping of large-scale environments. Paper presented at the Society for Research in Child Development, Boston, April 1981.

Hazen, N. L., Lockman, J. J., and Pick, J. L., Jr. The

development of children's representations of large-scale environments. *Child Development,* 1978, *49,* 623-636.

Hebb, D. O. *The organization of behavior.* New York: Wiley, 1949.

Heider, F. *The psychology of interpersonal relations.* New York: Wiley, 1958.

Henig, R. M. The child savers. *The New York Times Magazine,* March 22, 1981, pp. 34-44.

Herman, J. F. Children's perspective taking and mental rotation abilities in large- and small-scale spaces. Paper presented at the Psychonomic Society, Phoenix, November 1979.

Herman, J. F. Children's cognitive maps of large-scale spaces: Effects of exploration, direction, and repeated experience. *Journal of Experimental Child Psychology,* 1980, *29,* 126-143.

Herman, J. F., and Siegel, A. W. The development of cognitive mapping of the large-scale environment. *Journal of Experimental Child Psychology,* 1978, *26,* 389-406.

Herrnstein, R. J. *IQ in the meritocracy.* Boston: Little, Brown, 1973.

Hershenson, M. Visual discrimination in the human newborn. *Journal of Comparative and Physiological Psychology,* 1964, *58,* 270-276.

Hess, R. D. Social class and ethnic influences on socialization. In P. H. Mussen (Ed.), *Carmichael's manual of child psychology* (Vol. 2). New York: Wiley, 1970.

Hess, R. D., and Shipman, V. C. Early experience and the socialization of cognitive modes in children. *Child Development,* 1965, *36,* 869-886.

Heth, C. D., and Cornell, E. H. Three experiences affecting spatial discrimination learning in ambulatory children. *Journal of Experimental Child Psychology,* 1980, *30,* 246-264.

Hetherington, E. M. Effects of father absence on personality development in adolescent daughters. *Developmental Psychology,* 1972, *7,* 313-326.

Hetherington, E. M. Divorce: A child's perspective. *American Psychologist,* 1979, *34,* 851-858.

Hewes, G. The anthropology of posture. *Scientific American,* 1957, *196,* 123-132.

Hiatt, S., and Campos, J. Fear, surprise and happiness: The patterning of facial expression in infants. Paper presented at the Society for Research in Child Development, New Orleans, March 1977.

Hickey, J. The effects of guided moral discussion upon youthful offenders' level of moral judgement. Ph. D. dissertation, Boston University, 1972.

Higgins, E. T. Communication development as related to channel, incentive, and social class. *Genetic psychology monographs,* 1977, *96,* 75-141.

Hildyard, A. Children's production of inferences from oral texts. *Discourse Processes,* 1979, *2,* 33-56.

Hinde, R. A. *Biological basis of human social behavior.* New York: McGraw-Hill, 1974.

Hirsch, H. The perfectible brain: The role of ex-sensory stimulation during development. In A. H. Parmelee, Jr., *Brain plasticity—What is it?* Symposium presented at the Society for Research in Child Development, Boston, April 1981.

Hirsch, J. Behavior-genetic analysis and its biosocial consequences. *Seminars in Psychiatry,* 1970, *2,* 89-105.

Hirsh-Pasek, K., Gleitman, L. R., and Gleitman, H. What did the brain say to the mind? A study of the detection and report of ambiguity by young children. In A. Sinclair, R. J. Janella, and W. J. M. Levelt (Eds.), *The child's conception of language.* New York: Springer-Verlag, 1978.

Hiscock, M., and Kinsbourne, M. Asymmetries of selective listening and attention switching in children. *Developmental Psychology,* 1980, *16,* 70-82.

Hochberg, J., and Brooks, V. Pictorial recognition as an unlearned ability: A study of one child's performance. *American Journal of Psychology,* 1962, *75,* 624-628.

Hoffman, L. W. The father's role and the child's peer-group adjustment. *Merrill-Palmer Quarterly,* 1961, *7,* 97-105.

Hoffman, L. W. The professional woman as mother. Paper presented at the Conference of Successful Women in the Sciences, New York Academy of Sciences, New York, May 1972.

Hoffman, L. W. Maternal employment: 1979. *American Psychologist,* 1979, *34,* 859-865.

Hoffman, M. L. Moral development. In P. H. Mussen (Ed.), *Carmichael's manual of child psychology* (Vol. 2). New York: Wiley, 1970.

Hoffman, M. L. Moral development in adolescence. In J. Adelson (Ed.), *Handbook of adolescent psychology.* New York: Wiley, 1980.

Hogan, R. Moral conduct and moral character: A psychological perspective. *Psychological Bulletin,* 1973, *79,* 217-232.

Holden, C. Twins reunited. *Science 80,* 1980, *1,* 55-59.

Hollinshead, A. B. *Two factor index of social position.* New Haven: Privately printed, 1957.

Holt, J. *How schools fail.* New York: Dell, 1964.

Honeck, R. P., Sowry, B. M., and Voegtle, K. Proverbial understanding in a pictorial context. *Child Development,* 1978, *49,* 327-331.

Honess, T. Self-reference in children's descriptions of peers: Egocentricity or collaboration? *Child Development,* 1980, *51,* 476-480.

Hong, K. M., and Townes, B. D. Infants' attachment to inanimate objects: A cross-sectional study. *Journal of the American Academy of Child Psychiatry,* 1976, *15,* 49-61.

Hooker, D. The development of behavior in the human fetus. In W. Dennis (Ed.), *Readings in child psychology.* 2nd ed. Englewood Cliffs, N. J.: Prentice-Hall, 1963.

Hooper, R., Fitzgerald, J., and Paplia, D. Piagetian theory and the aging process: Extensions and speculations. *Aging and Human Development,* 1971, *2,* 3-20.

Horn, J. L. Organization of data on life-span development of human abilities. In L. R. Goulet and P. B. Baltes (Eds.), *Life-span developmental psychology.* New York: Academic Press, 1970.

Horner, M. S. Sex differences in achievement motivation and performance in competitive and noncompetitive situations. Ph. D. dissertation, University of Michigan, 1968.

Horner, M. S. Femininity and successful achievement: A basic inconsistencey. In J. M. Bardwick, E. Douvan, M. S. Horner, and D. Gutman (Eds.), *Feminine personality and conflict.* Belmont, Calif.: Brooks-Cole, 1970.

Horner, M. S. Towards an understanding of achievement related conflicts in women. *Journal of Social Issues,* 1972, *78,* 157-176.

Horton, M. S., and Markman, E. M. Children's acquisition of basic and superordinate-level categories from intensional and extensional information. Paper presented at the Society for Research in Child Development, San Francisco, March 1979.

Howe, C. J., The meanings of two-word utterances in the speech of young children. *Journal of Child Language,* 1976, *3,* 29-47.

Howes, E. R. Twin speech: A language of their own. *The New York Times,* September 11, 1977, p. 54.

Howie-Day, A. M. Metapersuasion: The development of reasoning about persuasive strategies. Paper presented at the Society for Research in Child Development, San Francisco, March 1979.

Hsu, F. L. K. *Americans and Chinese: Two ways of life.* New York: Abelard-Schurman, 1953.

Hubel, D. H. Brain: with biographical sketch. *Scientific American,* 1979, *14,* 44-53.

Hudson, W. The study of the problem of pictorial perception among unacculturated groups. *International Journal of Psychology,* 1967, *2,* 89-107.

Hughes, R., Tingle, B. A., and Sawin, D. B. Development of empathetic understanding in children. *Child Development,* 1981, *52,* 122-128.

Huizinga, J. *Homo ludens: A study of the play element in culture.* Boston: Beacon Press, 1955.

Hull, C. L. *Principles of behavior.* New York: Appleton-Century-Crofts, 1943.

Hulsebus, R. C. Operant conditioning of infant behavior: A review. In H. W. Reese (Ed.), *Advances in child development and behavior* (Vol. 8). New York: Academic Press, 1973.

Hurlock, E. *Developmental psychology.* 4th ed. New York: McGraw-Hill, 1975.

Hutt, C. Exploration and play in children. *Symposia of the Zoological Society of London,* 1966, *18,* 61-81.

Hutt, C. Exploration and play (#2). In B. Sutton-Smith (Ed.), *Play and learning.* Gardner Press, 1979.

Hutt, C., and Bhavani, R. Predictions from play. *Nature,* 1972, 237.

Hutt, S. J., Hutt, C., Leonard, H. C., Benuth, H. V., and Muntjewerff, W. J. Auditory responsivity in the human newborn. *Nature,* 1968, *218,* 888-890.

Huttenlocher, J. The origins of language comprehension. In R. L. Solso (Ed.), *Theories in cognitive psychology.* Potomac, Md.: Erlbaum, 1974.

Huttenlocher, J., and Presson, C. Mental rotation and the perspective problem. *Cognitive Psychology,* 1973, *4,* 277-299.

Huttenlocher, P. K., and Huttenlocher, J. A study in children with "hyperlexia." Unpublished manuscript, Yale University School of Medicine, 1975.

Hyde, J. S., and Phillis, D. E. Androgyny across the life span. *Developmental Psychology,* 1979, *15,* 334-336.

Iannotti, R. J. The many faces of empathy: An analysis of the definition and evaluation of empathy in children. Paper presented at the Society for Research in Child Development, Denver, April 1975.

Illich, I. *Deschooling society.* New York: Harper and Row, 1971.

Inglis, R. *Sins of the fathers: A study of the physical and emotional abuse of children.* New York: St. Martin's Press, 1978.

Inhelder, B., and Piaget, J. *The growth of logical thinking from childhood to adolescence.* New York: Basic Books, 1958.

Inhelder, B., and Piaget, J. *The early growth of logical thinking.* New York: Norton, 1964.

Inhelder, B., Sinclair, H., and Bovet, M. *Learning and the development of cognition.* Cambridge, Mass.: Harvard University Press, 1974.

Istomini, Z. M. The development of voluntary memory in preschool age children. *Soviet Psychology,* 1975, *13,* 5-64.

Ives, W., and Houseworth, M. The role of standard orientations in children's drawing of interpersonal relationships: Aspects of graphic feature marking. *Child Development* 1980, *51,* 591-593.

Izard, C. E. *The face of emotion.* New York: Appleton-Century-Crofts, 1971.

Izard, C. E. Huebner, R. R., Risser, D., McGinnes, G. C., and Dougherty, L. M. The young infant's ability to produce discrete emotion expressions. *Developmental Psychology,* 1980, *16,* 132-140.

Jablonski, E. M. Free recall in children. *Psychological Bulletin,* 1974, *81,* 522-539.

Jacklin, C. N., and Maccoby, E. F. Social behavior at thirty-three months in same-sex and mixed-sex dyads. *Child Development,* 1978, *49,* 557-569.

Jackowitz, E. R., and Watson, M. W. The development of object transformations in early pretend play. *Developmental Psychology,* 1980, *16,* 543-549.

Jacobson, S. W., and Kagan, J. Interpreting "imitative" responses in early infancy. *Science,* 1979, *205,* 215-217.

Jakobson, R., and Halle, M. *Fundamentals of language.* The Hague: Mouton, 1956.

James, W. *Principles in psychology.* New York: Dover, 1950.

Jamison, W. Developmental interrelationships among concrete operational tasks: An investigation of Piaget's stage concept. *Journal of Experimental Child Psychology,* 1977, *24,* 235-253.

Jarman, R. F. Matching of auditory-visual and temporal-spatial information by seven-and nine-year-old children. *Child Development,* 1979, *50,* 575-577.

Jarvik, L. F. Discussion: Patterns of intellectual functioning in later years. In L. F. Jarvik, C. Eisdorfer, and J. C. Blum (Eds.), *Intellectual functioning in adults.* New York: Springer, 1973.

Jeffrey, W. E., and Cohen, L. B. Habituation in the young infant. In H. W. Reese (Ed.), *Advances in child development and behavior* (Vol. 6). New York: Academic Press, 1971.

Jencks, C. *Inequality.* New York: Basic Books, 1972.

Jenni, D. A., and Jenni, M. A. Carrying behavior in humans: Analysis of sex differences. *Science,* 1976, *199,* 859-860.

Jenni, M. A. Sex differences in carrying behavior. *Perceptual and Motor Skills,* 1976, *43,* 323-330.

Jennings, K. D. People versus object orientation, social behavior, and intellectual abilities in preschool children. *Developmental Psychology,* 1975, *11,* 511-519.

Jennings, K. D., Harmon, R. J., Morgan, G. A., Gaiter, J. L., and Yarrow, L. J. Exploratory play as an index of mastery motivation: Relationships to persistence, cognitive functioning, and environmental measures. *Developmental Psychology,* 1979, *15,* 386-394.

Jensen, A. How much can we boost IQ and scholastic achievement? *Harvard Educational Review,* 1969, *39,* 1-123.

Jensen, A. The IQ controversy: A reply to Layzer. *Cognition,* 1972, *1,* 33-105.

Jensen A. *Bias in mental testing.* Riverside, N. J.: Free Press, 1979.

Jessor, S., and Jessor, R. Transition from virginity to nonvirginity among youth: A social-psychological study over time. *Developmental Psychology,* 1975, *11,* 473-484.

Jones, M. C. The later careers of boys who were early or late maturing. *Child Development,* 1975, *28,* 113-128.

Jones, M. C., and Bayley, N. Physical maturing among boys as related to behavior. *Journal of Educational Psychology,* 1950, *41,* 129-148.

Jones-Molfese, V. J. Responses of neonates to colored stimuli. *Child Development,* 1977, *48,* 1092-1095.

Jordan, D. Parental antecedents and personality characteristics of ego identity statuses. Ph.D. dissertation, State University of New York at Binghamton, 1971.

Josselson, R. Ego development in adolescence. In J.

Adelson (Ed.), *Handbook of Adolescent Psychology.* New York: Wiley, 1980.

Kagan, J. The concept of identification. *Psychological Review,* 1958, *65,* 296-305.

Kagan, J. Impulsive and reflective children: Significance of conceptual tempo. In J. Krumboltz (Ed.), *Learning and the educational process.* Chicago: Rand McNally, 1965.

Kagan, J. Reflection-impulsivity: The generality and dynamics of conceptual tempo. *Journal of Abnormal Psychology,* 1966, *71,* 17-24.

Kagan, J. Attention and psychological change in the young child. *Science,* 1970, *170,* 826-832.

Kagan, J. *Change and continuity infancy.* New York: Wiley, 1971.

Kagan, J. Discrepancy, temperament, and infant distress. In M. Lewis and L. Rosenblum (Eds.), *The origins of fear.* New York: Wiley, 1975.

Kagan, J. Family experience and the child's development. *American Psychologist,* 1979, *34,* 886-981.

Kagan, J., Kearsley, R. B., and Zelazo, P. R. The effects of infant day-care on psychological development. In *The Effect of Early Experience on Child Development.* Symposium presented at the American Association for the Advancement of Science, Boston, February 1976.

Kagan, J., Kearsley, R. B., and Zelazo, P. R. *Infancy: Its place in human development.* Cambridge Mass.: Harvard University Press, 1978.

Kagan, J., and Klein, R. E. Cross-cultural perspectives on early development. *American Psychologist,* 1973, *28,* 947-961.

Kagan, J., Klein, R. E., Finley, G. E., Rogoff, B., and Nolan, E. A cross-cultural study of cognitive development. *Monographs of the Society for Research in Child Development,* 1979, *44,* No. 5.

Kagan, J., Klein, R. E., Haith, M. M., and Morrison, F. J. Memory and meaning in two cultures. *Child Development,* 1973, *44,* 221-223.

Kagan, J., and Kogan, N. Individual variation in cognitive process. In P. H. Mussen (Ed.), *Carmichael's manual of child psychology* (Vol. 1). New York: Wiley, 1970.

Kagan, J., and Moss, H. *Birth to maturity: A study in psychological development.* New York: Wiley, 1962.

Kagan, J., Moss, H., and Sigel, I. Psychological significance of styles of conceptualization. *Monographs of the Society for Research in Child Development,* 1963, *28,* 73-112.

Kagan, J., Rosman, B., Day, D., Albert, J., and Phillips, W. Information processing in the child: Significance of analytic and reflective attitudes. *Psychological Monographs,* 1964, *79,* 1-36.

Kail, R. *The development of memory in children.* San Francisco: W. H. Freeman, 1979.

Kail, R., Carter, P., and Pellegrino, J. The locus of sex differences in spatial ability. *Perception and Psychophysics,* 1979, *26,* 182-186.

Kail, R. V., Jr., and Hagen, J. W. *Perspectives on the*

development of memory and cognition. Hillsdale, N. J.: Erlbaum, 1977.

Kalnins, I., and Bruner, J. S. The coordination of visual observation and instrumental behavior in early infancy. *Perception,* 1973, *2,* 307-314.

Kamin, L. J. Psychology as social science: The Jensen affair ten years after. Unpublished paper, Princeton University, 1979.

Kamin, L. J. Jensen's last stand. *Psychology Today,* 1980, *14,* 117+.

Kamisher, M. Why suicide? *Boston Sunday Globe/ New England Magazine.* April 2, 1978, 28+.

Kandel, D. B. Peer influences in adolescence. In T. J. Brendt, *The influence of friendships on social behavior and development.* Symposium presented at the Society for Research in Child Development, Boston, April 1981.

Kandel, D. B., and Lesser, G. S. Parental and peer influences on educational plans of adolescents. *American Sociological Review,* 1969, *34,* 213-223.

Kanner, L. Autistic disturbances of affective contact. *Nervous Child,* 1943, *2,* 217-250.

Kanner, L. Early infantile autism. *Journal of Pediatrics,* 1944, *25,* 211-217.

Kaplan, B. Mediations on genesis. *Human Development,* 1967, *10,* 65-87.

Kaplan, B. Strife of systems: The tension between organismic and developmental points of view. Unpublished paper, Clark University, 1970.

Kaplan, B. Genetic psychology, genetic epistemology, and theory of knowledge. In T. Mischel (Ed.), *Cognitive development and epistemology.* New York: Academic Press, 1971.

Kardiner, A. *The psychological frontiers of society.* New York: Columbia University Press, 1945.

Karmiloff-Smith, A. A functional approach to child language: A study of determiners and reference. *Cambridge Studies in Linguistics,* No. 24. Cambridge: Cambridge University Press, 1979*a*.

Karmiloff-Smith, A. Language as a formal problem-space for children. Paper prepared for the Conference on "Beyond description in child language." Nijmegen, Holland, June 1979*b*.

Karmiloff-Smith, A. Micro- and macrodevelopmental changes in language acquisition and other representational systems. *Cognitive Science,* 1979*c*, *3,* 91-117.

Karmiloff-Smith, A. Modifications in children's representational systems and levels of accessing knowledge. Paper presented at the Conference on "Knowledge and Representation" at the Netherlands Institute for Advanced Study in Humanities and Social Sciences, Wassenan, Holland, 1979*d*.

Karniol, R. Children's use of intention cues in evaluating behavior. *Psychological Bulletin,* 1978, *85,* 76-85.

Katz, J. J. *Semantic theory.* New York: Harper and Row, 1972.

Katz, P. A. The development of female identity. *Sex Roles,* 1979, *5,* 155-175.

Kavanaugh, R. D. On synonymy of *more* and *less:* Comments on methodology. *Child Development,* 1976, *47,* 885-887.

Kaye, H. Conditioning during infancy: New milk, old bottles. In A. J. DeCasper, *Infant conditioning and development: New perspectives for the 1980s.* Symposium presented at the meeting of the Society for Research in Child Development, Boston, April 1981.

Kaye, K. The maternal role in developing communication and language. In M. Bullowa (Ed.), *Before speech: The beginnings of human communication.* Cambridge: Cambridge University Press, 1979.

Keane, T. G., and Swartz, K. B. Visual habituation to sad and happy expressions in three- and six-month-old infants. Paper presented at the Society for Research in Child Development, Boston, April 1981.

Keasey, C. B. Social participation as a factor in the moral development of preadolescents. *Developmental Psychology,* 1971, *5,* 216-220.

Keasey, C. B. Experimentally induced changes in moral opinions and reasoning. *Journal of Personality and Social Psychology,* 1973, *26,* 30-38.

Keasey, C. B. Children's developing awareness and usage of intentionality and motives. In H. E. Howe, Jr. and C. B. Keasey (Eds.), *Nebraska Symposium on Motivation* (Vol. 15). Lincoln, Nebr.: University of Nebraska Press, 1978.

Keating, D. P. Toward a multivariate life-span theory of intelligence. In D. Kuhn (Ed.), Intellectual development beyond childhood. *New Directions for Child Development,* No. 5, 1979, 69-84.

Keating, D. P. Thinking processing in adolescence. In J. Adelson, *Handbook of Adolescent Psychology.* New York: Wiley, 1980.

Keil, F. The development of the young child's ability to anticipate outcomes of simple causal events. *Child Development,* 1979*a*, *50,* 455-463.

Keil, F. *Semantic and conceptual development: An ontological perspective.* Cambridge, Mass.: Harvard University Press, 1979*b*.

Kellam, S. G., Ensiminger, M. E., and Brown, C. H. Epidemiological research into the antecedents in early childhood of psychiatric symptoms and drug use in adolescence. *Society for Research in Child Development News,* 1980, 6-7.

Keller, A., Ford, L. H., and Meacham, J. A. Dimensions of self-concept in preschool children. Unpublished paper, State University of New York, Buffalo, n.d.

Kellogg, R. *Analyzing children's art.* Palo Alto, Calif.: National Press Books, 1969.

Kelley, H. H. Attribution theory in social psychology. In D. Levine (Ed.), *Nebraska Symposium on Motivation.* (Vol. 4). Lincoln, Nebr.: University of Nebraska Press, 1967.

Kelley, H. H. The process of causal attribution. *American Psychologist,* 1973, *28,* 107-128.

Kelly, H., and Gardner, H. Viewing children through

television. *New Directions for Child Development,* 1981, *13.*

Kelly, H., and Meringoff, L. A comparison of story comprehension in two media: Books and television. Paper presented at the American Psychological Association, New York, September, 1979.

Kelly, M., Scholnick, E. K., Travers, S. H., and Johnson, J. W. Relations among memory, memory appraisal, and memory strategies. *Child Development,* 1976, *47,* 648-659.

Kempe, R. S., and Kempe, C. C. *Child abuse.* Cambridge, Mass.: Harvard University Press 1978.

Kendler, H. H., and Kendler, T. S. Vertical and horizontal processes in problem-solving. *Psychological Review,* 1962, *69,* 1-16.

Kendler, H. H., and Kendler, T. S. Developmental processes in discrimination learning. *Human Development,* 1970, *13,* 65-89.

Kendler, T. S. Verbalization and optimal reversal shifts among kindergarten children. *Journal of Verbal Learning and Verbal Behavior,* 1964, *31,* 428-36.

Kendler, T. S. An ontogeny of mediational deficiency. *Child Development,* 1972, *43,* 1-17.

Keniston, K. *Youth and dissent: The rise of a new opposition.* New York: Harcourt, Brace and Jovanovich, 1971.

Kennedy, J. M. *A psychology of picture perception.* San Francisco: Jossey-Bass, 1974.

Kennedy, R. *Times to remember.* New York: Doubleday, 1974.

Kernberg, O. *Object-relations theory and clinical psychoanalysis.* New York: Jason Aronson, 1976.

Kessel, F. S. The role of syntax in children's comprehension from ages six to twelve. *Monographs of the Society for Research in Child Development,* 1970, *35,* (Serial No. 139, No. 6).

Kessen, W. *The child.* New York: Wiley, 1965.

Kessen, W. Questions for a theory of cognitive development. *Monographs of the Society for Research in Child Development,* 1966, *31,* 55-70.

Kessen, W. Sucking and looking: Two organized congenital patterns of behavior in the human newborn. In H. Stevenson (Ed.), *Early behavior: Comparative and developmental approaches.* New York: Wiley, 1967.

Kessen, W. (Ed.). *Childhood in China.* New Haven: Yale University Press, 1975.

Kessen, W. The American child and other cultural inventions. *American Psychologist,* 1979, *34,* 815-821.

Kessen, W., Haith, M. M., and Salapatek, P. H. Infancy. In P. H. Mussen (Ed.), *Carmichael's manual of child psychology* (Vol. 1). New York: Wiley, 1970.

Kessen, W., Levine, J., and Wendrich, K. A. The imitation of pitch in infants. *Infant Behavior and Development,* 1978, *2,* 93-99.

Kiefer, M. *American children through their books.* Philadelphia: University of Pennsylvania Press, 1948.

Kilbride, H. W., Johnson, D. L., and Streissguth, A. P. Social class, birth order, and newborn experience. *Child Development,* 1977, *48,* 1686-1688.

Kingston, M. H. *China men.* New York: Knopf, 1980.

Kinloch, G. C. Parent-youth conflict at home: An investigation among university freshmen. *American Journal of Orthopsychiatry,* 1970, *40,* 658-664.

Kinsey, A. C., Pomeroy, W. B., and Martin, C. E. *Sexual behavior in the human male.* Philadelphia: Saunders, 1948.

Kinsey, A. C., Pomeroy, W. B., Martin, C. E., and Gebhard, P. H. *Sexual behavior in the human female.* Philadelphia: Saunders, 1953.

Kirschenblatt-Gimblett, B. Speech play and verbal art. In B. Sutton-Smith (Ed.), *Play and learning.* New York: Gardner Press, 1979.

Kitchener, R. F. Epigenesis: The role of biological models in developmental psychology. *Human Development,* 1978, *21,* 141-160.

Klahr, D. Problem-solving and planning by preschool children. Paper presented at the Society for Research in Child Development, San Francisco, March 1979.

Klahr, D. Nonmonotone assessment of monotone development: An information processing analysis. In S. Strauss and R. Stavey (Eds.), *U-shaped behavioral growth.* New York, Academic Press, in press.

Klahr, D., and Wallace, J. F. *Cognitive development: An information processing view.* Hillsdale, N.J.: Erlbaum, 1976.

Klaus, M. H., and Kennell, J. Mothers separated from newborn infants. *Pediatric Clinics of North America,* 1970, *17,* 1015-1037.

Kleiman, D. Preschool program is called beneficial. *The New York Times,* December 14, 1980, p. 35.

Klein, M., Hermann, P., Isaacs, S., and Riviere, J. *Developments in psychoanalysis.* London: Hogarth, 1952.

Kleinfeld, J. Visual memory in village Eskimo and urban Caucasian children. *Arctic,* 1971, *24,* 132-137.

Koestler, A. *The act of creation.* New York: Macmillan, 1964.

Koff, E., Rierdan, J., and Sheingold, K. Memories of menarche: Age and preparedness as determinants of subjective experience. Paper presented at the Eastern Psychological Association, Hartford, April 1980.

Koff, E., Rierdan, J., and Silverstone, E. Changes in representation of body image as a function of menarcheal status. *Developmental Psychology,* 1978, *14,* 635-642.

Kohlberg, L. The development of modes of moral thinking and choice in the years ten to sixteen. Ph.D. dissertation, University of Chicago, 1958.

Kohlberg, L. A cognitive-developmental analysis of children's sex-role concepts and attitudes. In E. Maccoby (Ed.), *The development of sex differences.* Stanford, Calif.: Stanford University Press, 1966.

Kohlberg, L. Stage and sequence: The cognitive-developmental approach to socialization. In D. A. Goslin (Ed.), *Handbook of socialization theory and research.* New York: Rand McNally, 1969.

Kohlberg, L. From is to ought: How to commit the naturalistic fallacy and get away with it in the study of moral development. In T. Mischel (Ed.), *Cognitive development and genetic epistemology.* New York: Academic Press, 1971.

Kohlberg, L. Revisions in the theory and practice of moral development. In W. Damon (Ed.), *Moral development. New Directions for Child Development* (No. 2). San Francisco: Jossey-Bass, 1978, *10,* 83–88.

Kohlberg, L., and Elfinbein, D. The development of moral judgments concerning capital punishment. *American Journal of Orthopsychiatry,* 1975, *45,* 614–640.

Kohlberg, L., and Kramer, R. Continuities and discontinuities in childhood and adult moral development. *Human Development,* 1969, *12,* 93–120.

Kohlberg, L., and Mayer, R. Development as the aim of education. *Harvard Educational Review,* 1972, *14,* 449–496.

Kohnstamm, G. A. An evaluation of part of Piaget's theory. *Acta Psychologica,* 1963, *2,* 303–315.

Kohut, H. *The analysis of the self.* New York: International Universities Press, 1971.

Kolata, G. B. Math and sex: Are girls born with less ability? *Science,* 1980, *210,* 1234–1235.

Konner, M. Newborn walking: Additional data. *Science,* 1973, *178,* 307.

Konner, M. Infancy among the Kalahari Desert San. In P. H. Leiderman, S. R. Tulkin, and A. Rosenfeld (Eds.), *Culture and infancy: Variations in the human experience.* New York: Academic Press, 1977.

Koocher, G. P. Emerging self-hood and cognitive development. *Journal of Genetic Psychology,* 1974, *125,* 79–88.

Korzenik, D. Children's drawings: Changes in representation between the ages of five and seven. Ph.D. dissertation, Harvard University, 1972.

Kosslyn, S. *Image and mind.* Cambridge, Mass.: Harvard University Press, 1980.

Kotelchuck, M. The nature of the child's tie to his father. Ph.D. dissertation, Harvard University, 1972.

Kotelchuck, M. The nature of the infant's tie to his father. Paper presented at the Society for Research in Child Development, Philadelphia, March 1973.

Kotelchuck, M. The infants relationship to the father: Experimental evidence. In M. Lamb, *The role of the father in child development.* New York: Wiley, 1976.

Krauss, I. K. Some situational determinants of competitive performance on sex-stereotyped tasks. *Developmental Psychology,* 1977, *13,* 473–480.

Krauss, R. M., and Glucksberg, S. The development of communication: Competence as a function of age. *Child Development,* 1969, *40,* 255–266.

Krauss, R. M., and Morency, N. L. The nonverbal encoding and decoding of affect in first and fifth graders. In R. W. Buck, *Developmental aspects of nonverbal behavior.* Symposium presented at the American Psychological Association, Montreal, 1980.

Krebs, R. L. Some relationships between moral judgment, attention, and resistance to temptation. Ph.D. dissertation, University of Chicago, 1967.

Kreutzer, M. A., Leonard, C., and Flavell, J. H. An interview study of children's knowledge about memory. *Monographs of the Society for Research in Child Development,* 1975, *40,* (Serial No. 159, No. 1).

Kuczaj, S. Evidence for a language learning strategy: On the relative ease of acquisition of prefixes and suffixes. *Child Development,* 1979, *50,* 1–13.

Kuenne, M. R. Experimental investigtion of the relation of language to transposition behavior in young children. *Journal of Experimental Psychology,* 1946, *36,* 471–490.

Kuhl, P. K., and Miller, J. D. Speech perception by the chinchilla: Voiced-voiceless distinction in alveolar plosive consonants. *Science,* 1975, *190,* 69–72.

Kuhn, D. Mechanisms of change in the development of cognitive structures. *Child Development,* 1972, *43,* 833–844.

Kuhn, D. Imitation theory and research from a cognitive perspective. *Human Development,* 1973, *16,* 157–180.

Kuhn, D. Inducing development experimentally: Comments on a research paradigm. *Developmental Psychology,* 1974, *10,* 590–600.

Kuhn, D. The development of developmental psychology. Unpublished paper, Harvard University, 1980.

Kuhn, D., Ho, V., and Adams, C. Formal reasoning among pre- and late adolescents. *Child Development,* 1979, *50,* 1128–1135.

Kuhn, D., Langer, J., Kohlberg, L., and Haan, N. S. The development of formal operations in logical and moral reasoning. *Genetic Psychology Monographs,* 1977, *95,* 97–188.

Kuhn, D., Nash, S. C., and Brucken, L. Sex role concepts of two- and three-year-olds. *Child Development,* 1978, *49,* 445–451.

Kuhn, T. S. *The structure of scientific revolutions.* Chicago: University of Chicago Press, 1962.

Kuo, Z. Y. *Dynamics of behavior development.* New York: Random House, 1967.

Kurdek, L. A. An integrative perspective on children's divorce adjustment. *American Psychologist,* in press.

Kurdek, L. A., Blish, D., and Siesky, A. E., Jr. Chilren's long-term divorce adjustment. Paper presented at the Society for Research in Child Development, Boston, April 1981.

Kurtines, W., and Greif, E. B. The development of moral thought: Review and evaluation of Kohlberg's approach. *Psychological Bulletin,* 1974, *81,* 453-470.

Laboratory of Comparative Human Cognition. *Culture and intelligence.* 1980*a*.

Laboratory of Comparative Human Cognition. *Intelligence as a cultural practice.* 1980*b*.

LaBouvie-Vief, G. Beyond formal operations: Uses and limits of pure logic in life-span development. *Human Development,* 1980, *23,* 141-161.

Labov, W. *The study of non-standard English.* Washington, D.C.: ERIC Clearinghouse for Linguistics, 1969.

LaFreniere, P. A nine-month longitudinal study of dominancy, attention, and affiliation in a preschool group. Paper presented at the Society for Research in Child Development, Boston, April 1981.

Lamb, M. Twelve-month-olds and their parents: Interaction in a laboratory playroom. *Developmental Psychology,* 1976, *12,* 237-246.

Lamb, M. Father-infant and mother-infant interaction in the first year of life. *Child Development,* 1977*a*, *48,* 167-181.

Lamb, M. The development of the mother-infant and father-infant attachments in the second year of life. *Developmental Psychology,* 1977*b*, *13,* 637-648.

Lamb, M. Parental influences and the father's role: A personal perspective. *American Psychologist,* 1979, *34,* 938-944.

Landauer, T. K., and Whiting, J. W. M. Infantile stimulation and adult stature of human males. *American Anthropologist,* 1963, *66,* 1007-1028.

Landreth, C. *Early childhood behavior and learning.* New York: Knopf, 1967.

Lane, D. M. Incidental learning and the development of selective attention. *Psychological Review,* 1980, *87,* 316-319.

Lane, S. G. *Down the rabbit hole.* New York: Atheneum, 1971.

Langer, J. *Theories of development.* New York: Holt, Rinehart and Winston, 1969.

Langer, J. Werner's comparative-organismic theory. In P. H. Mussen (Ed.), *Carmichael's manual of child psychology* (Vol. 1). New York: Wiley, 1970.

Langer, J. Interactional aspects of cognitive organization. *Cognition,* 1975, *3,* 9-28.

Langer, J. *The origin of logic: From six to twelve months.* New York: Academic Press, 1979.

Langer, J. The structural development of concept and symbol formation. Paper presented at the First Biennial Conference of the Heinz Werner Institute of Developmental Psychology, Worcester, Mass., June 1981.

Langer, J., Rodin, J., Beck, P., Weinman, C., and Spitzer, L. Environmental determinants of memory improvement in late adulthood. *Journal of Personality and Social Psychology,* 1979, *38,* 2003-2013.

Langer, S. *Philosophy in a new key.* Cambridge, Mass.: Harvard University Press, 1942.

Langford, P. E. The development of the concept of development. *Human Development,* 1975, *18,* 321-332.

Langlois, J. H., and Downs, A. C. Mothers, fathers, and peers as socialization agents of sex-typed play behaviors in young children. *Child Development,* 1980, *51,* 1237-1247.

Larson, R., and Csikszentmihalyi, M. Experimental correlates of time alone in adolescence. *Journal of Personality,* 1978, *46,* 677-693.

Larson, R., Csikszenmihalyi, M., and Graef, R. Mood variability and the psycho-social adjustment of adolescents. *Journal of Youth and Adolescence,* 1981, in press.

Lasch, C. *Culture of narcissism: American life in an age of diminishing expectations.* New York: Norton, 1979.

Lasker, H. M., and Moore, J. F. Current studies of adult development: Implications for education. Unpublished paper, Harvard University, 1979.

Lasky, R. E. The ability of six-year-olds, eight-year-olds, and adults to abstract visual patterns. *Child Development,* 1974, *45,* 626-632.

Lawson, K. R. Spatial and temporal congruity and auditory-visual integration in infants. *Developmental Psychology,* 1980, *16,* 185-192.

Leahy, R. L., and Eiter, M. Moral judgment and the development of real and ideal androgynous self-image during adolescence and young adulthood. *Developmental Psychology,* 1980, *16,* 362-370.

Leask, J., Haber, R. N., and Haber, R. B. Eidetic imagery in children. *Psychonomic Monograph Supplements,* 1969, *3,* 25-48.

Lee, L. C. The concomitant development of cognitive and moral modes of thought: A test of selected deductions from Piaget's theory. *Genetic Psychology Monographs,* 1971, *85,* 93-146.

Leiderman, P. H., and Leiderman, G. F. Affective and cognitive consequences of polymatric infant care in the East African highlands. In A. Pick (Ed.), *Minnesota symposium on child development* (Vol. 8). Minneapolis: University of Minnesota Press, 1974.

Leiderman, P. H., and Seashore, M. J. Mother-infant neonatal separation: Some delayed consequences. In R. Porter and M. O'Connor (Eds.), *Parent-infant interaction.* CIBA Foundation Symposium 33 (new series). Amsterdam: Associated Scientific Publishers, 1975.

Lempers, J. D., Flavell, E. R., and Flavell, J. H. The development in very young children of tacit knowledge concerning visual perception. Unpublished paper, University of Minnesota, 1975.

Lenneberg, E. H. *Biological foundations of language.* New York: Wiley, 1967.

Lenneberg, E. H., Rebelsky, F. G., and Nichols, I. A. The vocalizations of infants born to deaf and hearing parents. *Human Development,* 1965, *8,* 23–37.

Leopold, W. F. Patterning in children's language learning. *Language Learning,* 1953, *5,* 1–14.

Lepper, M. R., Greene, D., and Nisbett, R. E. Undermining children's intrinsic interest with extrinsic reward. *Journal of Personality and Social Psychology,* 1973, *28,* 129–137.

Lester, B. M. Spectrum analysis of the cry sounds of well-nourished and malnourished infants. *Child Development,* 1976, *47,* 237–241.

Lester, B. M., Kotelchuck, M., Spelke, E., Sellers, M. J., and Klein, R. E. Separation protest in Guatemalan infants: Cross-cultural and cognitive findings. *Developmental Psychology,* 1974, *10,* 79–85.

Levin, J. R. The mnemonic 80s: Keywords in the classroom. Madison: Wisconsin Research and Development Center for Individualized Schooling, 1980.

Levine, L. E., and Hoffman, M. L. Empathy and cooperation in four-year-olds. *Developmental Psychology,* 1975, *11,* 533–534.

LeVine, R. A. Cross-cultural study in child psychology. In P. H. Mussen (Ed.), *Carmichael's manual of child psychology* (Vol. 1). New York: Wiley, 1970.

Levine, S. Infantile stimulation: A perspective. In J. A. Ambrose (Ed.), *Stimulation in early infancy.* New York: Academic Press, 1969.

Levinson, D. *The seasons of man's life.* New York: Knopf, 1978.

Lewis, M. The meaning of fear. Paper presented at the Society for Research in Child Development, Denver, April 1975.

Lewis, M. The social determinants of play. In B. Sutton-Smith (Ed.), *Play and learning.* New York: Gardner Press, 1979.

Lewis, M., and Brooks, J. Infants' reaction to people. In M. Lewis and L. Rosenblum (Eds.), *The origins of fear.* New York: Wiley, 1975.

Lewis, M., and Kreitzberg, V. S. Effects of birth order and spacing on mother-infant interactions. *Developmental Psychology,* 1979, *15,* 617–625.

Lewis, M., and Rosenblum, L. (Eds.). *The origins of fear.* New York: Wiley, 1975.

Lewis, O. *La vida.* New York: Random House, 1966.

Lewkowicz, D. J., and Turkewitz, G. Cross-modal equivalence in early auditory-visual intensity matching. *Developmental Psychology,* 1980, *16,* 597–607.

Lewkowicz, D. J., and Turkewitz, G. Hemispheric specialization in processing auditory information during infancy. Paper presented at the Society for Research in Child Development, Boston, April 1981.

Lewontin, R. Race and intelligence. *Bulletin of the Atomic Scientists,* 1970, *26,* 2–8.

Lewontin, R. *The genetic basis of evolutionary change.* New York: Columbia University Press, 1974.

Liben, L. S. Operative understanding of horizontality and its relation to long-term memory. *Child Development,* 1974, *45,* 416–424.

Liben, L. S. Long-term memory for pictures related to seriation, horizontality, and verticality concepts. *Developmental Psychology,* 1975a, *11,* 795–806.

Liben, L. S. Evidence for developmental differences in spontaneous seriation and its implications for past research on long-term memory improvement. *Developmental Psychology,* 1975b, *11,* 121–125.

Liben, L. S. The facilitation of long-term memory improvement and operative development. Paper presented at the Jean Piaget Society, Philadelphia, June 1976.

Liben, L. S. An investigation of long-term memory regressions in Piagetian research. Paper presented at the Society for Research in Child Development, New Orleans, March 1977.

Liben, L. S. Perspective-taking skills in young children: Seeing the world through rose-colored glasses. *Developmental Psychology,* 1978, *14,* 87–92.

Liben, L. S. Copying and reproducing pictures in relation to subjects' operative levels. *Developmental Psychology,* 1981, *17,* 357–365.

Liben, L. S., and Golbeck, S. L. Sex differences in performance on Piagetian spatial tasks: Differences in competence or performance? *Child Development,* 1980, *51,* 594–597.

Liben, L. S., and Signorella, M. L. Gender-related schemata and constructive memory in children. *Child Development,* 1980, *51,* 11–18.

Liberman, A. M. The grammars and speech and language. *Cognitive Psychology,* 1970, *1,* 301–323.

Lickona, T. (Ed.). *Morality: Theory, research, and social issues.* New York: Holt, Rinehart and Winston, 1975.

Liebert, R. M., Neale, J. M., and Davidson, E. S. *The early window: Effects of television on children and youth.* New York: Pergamon, 1973.

Liebow, E. *Tally's corner.* Boston: Little, Brown, 1967.

Light, P. H., and MacIntosh, E. Depth relationships in young children's drawings. *Journal of Experimental Child Psychology,* 1980, *30,* 79–87.

Liles, B. Z., Shulman, M. D., and Bartlett, S. Judgments of grammaticality by normal and language-disordered children. *Journal of Speech and Hearing Disorders,* 1977, *42,* 199–209.

Lingle, K. M., Gonska, K., and McGillicuddy-DeLisis, A. V. Cognitive distancing demand differences in cross-gender parent-child interaction. Paper presented at the Society for Research in Child Development, Boston, April 1981.

Lipsitt, L. Developmental psychobiology comes of age: A discussion. In L. P. Lipsitt (Ed.), *Developmental psychobiology: The significance of the infant.* Hillsdale, N.J.: Erlbaum, 1976.

Lipsitt, L. Critical conditions in infancy. *American Psychologist,* 1977, *34,* 973-980.

Lipsitt, L. Infants at risk: Perinatal and neonatal factors. *International Journal of Behavior Development,* 1979, *2,* 23-42.

Ljung, B. O., Bergsten-Brucefors, A., and Lindgren, G. The secular trend in physical growth in Sweden. *Annals of Human Biology,* 1974, *1,* 245-256.

Lloyd, B. Young children's understanding of gender. In E. E. Maccoby, *Development of children's inferences concerning gender.* Symposium presented at the Society for Research in Child Development, Boston, April 1981.

Locke, J. *An essay concerning human understanding.* London: Dent, 1961. (Originally published, 1690).

Lockhart, K. L., Abrahams, B., and Osherson, D. N. Children's understanding of uniformity in the environment. *Child Development,* 1977, *48,* 1521-1531.

Lodge, A. Determination and prevention of infancy brain dysfunction: Sensory and nonsensory aspects. In R. N. Walsky and W. T. Greenough (Eds.), *Environments as therapy for brain dysfunction.* New York: Plenum Press, 1976.

Loevinger, J. The meaning and measurement of ego development. *American Psychologist,* 1966, *21,* 195-206.

Loevinger, J. *Ego development: Conceptions and theories.* San Francisco: Jossey-Bass, 1976.

Lord, A. B. *The singer of tales.* Cambridge, Mass.: Harvard University Press, 1960.

Lorenz, K. Companionship in bird life. In C. Scholler (Ed.), *Instinctive Behavior.* New York: International Universities Press, 1957.

Lorenz, K. *On aggression.* New York: Harcourt, Brace and World, 1966.

Lorenz, K. *Studies in animal and human behavior* (Vol. 1). Cambridge, Mass.: Harvard University Press, 1971.

Lovaas, O. I. Considerations in the development of a behavioral treatment program for psychotic children. In D. W. Churchill, G. D. Alpern, and M. K. DeMyer (Eds.), *Infantile autism.* Springfield, Ill.: Thomas, 1971.

Lovaas, O. I. Conversation with Paul Chance. *Psychology Today,* 1974, *8,* 76-84.

Lovaas, O. I. *The autistic child: Language development through behavior modification.* New York: Halstead Press, 1977.

Lovaas, O. I., Berberich, B., Perloff, P. F., and Schaefer, B. Acquisition of imitative speech by schizophrenic children. *Science,* 1966, *151,* 705-707.

Lovell, K. *The growth of basic mathematical and scientific concepts in children.* New York: Philosophical Library, 1961.

Lowenfeld, V. *Creative and mental growth.* New York: Macmillan, 1957.

Lunzer, E. A. Some points of Piagetian theory in the light of experimental criticism. *Journal of Child Psychology and Psychiatry,* 1961, *1,* 191-202.

Luquet, G. *Le dessin enfantin.* Paris: Alcan, 1927.

Luria, A. R. *The role of speech in the regulation of normal and abnormal behavior.* New York: Boni and Liveright, 1961.

Luria, A. R. *Higher cortical functions in man.* New York: Basic Books, 1966.

Luria, A. R. *The mind of the mnemonist.* New York: Basic Books, 1968.

Luria, A. R. *The making of mind.* Cambridge, Mass.: Harvard University Press, 1979.

Lyle, J., and Hoffman, H. R. Children's use of television and other media. In E. A. Rubenstein (Ed.), *Television and social behavior* (Vol. 4). Washington, D. C.: U. S. Government Printing Office, 1972.

Lyons, R. D. Study finds first borns having higher I. Q.'s. *The New York Times,* February 6, 1979, C-1.

Lyons-Ruth, K. Bimodal perception in infancy: Response to auditory-visual incongruity. *Child Development,* 1977, *48,* 820-827.

Lytton, H. Do parents create, or respond to, differences in twins? *Developmental Psychology,* 1977, *13,* 456-459.

Maas, E., Marecek, J., and Travers, J. R. Children's conceptions of disordered behavior. *Child Development,* 1978, *49,* 146-154.

McCall, R. Michael Rutter: Challenging the status quo. *American Psychological Association Monitor,* 1980, *11,* 8-9.

McCall, R. B., Parke, R. D., and Kavanaugh, R. D. Imitation of live and televised models by children one to three years of age. *Monographs of the Society for Research in Child Development,* 1977, *42,* No. 5.

McClearn, G. E., and DeFries, J. C. *Introduction to Behavioral Genetics.* San Francisco: W. H. Freeman, 1973.

McClelland, D. C. *The achieving society.* New York: VanNostrand, 1961.

McClelland, D. C., Atkinson, J., Clark, R., and Lowell, E. *The achievement motive.* New York: Appleton-Century-Crofts, 1953.

McClosky, M., Caramazza, A., and Green, B. Curvilinear motion in the absence of external forces: Naive beliefs about the motion of objects. *Science,* 1980, *210,* 1139-1141.

Maccoby, E. (Ed.). *The development of sex differences.* Stanford, Calif.: Stanford University Press, 1966.

Maccoby, E. *Social development.* New York: Harcourt, Brace and Jovanovich, 1980.

Maccoby, E., and Hagen, J. W. Effect of distortion upon central versus incidental recall: Developmental trends. *Journal of Experimental Child Psychology,* 1965, *2,* 280-289.

Maccoby, E., and Jacklin, C. N. *The psychology of sex differences.* Stanford, Calif.: Stanford University Press, 1974.

Maccoby, M., and Modiano, N. On culture and equivalence. In J. S. Bruner, R. R. Olver, and

P. M. Greenfield (Eds.), *Studies in cognitive growth*. New York: Wiley, 1966.

McConaughy, S. H. A developmental model for story comprehension in reading and listening. Paper presented at the Boston University Conference on Language Development, Boston, October 1978.

Macfarlane, A. Olfaction in the development of social preferences in the human neonate: Parent-infant interaction. *Ciba Foundation Symposium*, Elsevier Excerta Medica, 1975.

McGarrigle, J., and Donaldson, M. Conservation accidents. *Cognition*, 1975, *3*, 341-350.

McGarrigle, J., Grieve, R., and Hughes, M. Interpreting inclusion: A contribution to the study of the child's cognitive and linguistic development. *Journal of Experimental Child Psychology*, 1978, *26*, 528-550.

McGeorge, C. Situational variation on level of moral judgement. Unpublished paper, University of Canterbury, New Zealand, 1973.

McGhee, P. E. Cognitive development and children's comprehension of humor. *Child Development*, 1971*a*, *42*, 123-138.

McGhee, P. E. The role of operational thinking in children's comprehension and appreciation of humor. *Child Development*, 1971*b*, *42*, 733-741.

McGhee, P. E. Children's appreciation of humor: A test of the cognitive-congruency principle. Paper presented at the Society for Research in Child Development, Philadelphia, March 1973.

McGhee, P. E. Development of the sense of humour in childhood: A longitudinal study. In P. E. McGhee and A. J. Chapman (Eds.), *Children's humour*. New York: Wiley, 1980.

McGhee, P., and Chapman, T. (Eds.). *Children's humour*. London: Wiley, 1980.

McGillicuddy-DeLisis, A. V. The role of parent belief systems in the development of children's representational thinking. In J. E. Johnson, *The role of parent belief systems as influences on parent-child interactions and children's cognitive competence*. Symposium presented at the Society for Research in Child Development, Boston, April 1981.

McGurk, H., Turnure, C., and Creighton, S. J. Auditory-visual coordination in neonates. *Child Development*, 1977, *48*, 138-143.

Mackworth, N. H., and Bruner, J. S. How adults and children search and recognize pictures. *Human Development*, 1970, *13*, 149-177.

Macnamara, J. Cognitive basis of language learning in infants. *Psychological Review*, 1972, *79*, 1-14.

McNeill, D. Developmental psycholinguistics. In F. Smith and G. Miller (Eds.), *The genesis of language*. Cambridge, Mass.: MIT Press, 1966.

McNeill, D. *The acquisition of language*. New York: Wiley, 1970*a*.

McNeill, D. The development of language. In P. H. Mussen (Ed.), *Carmichael's manual of child psychology* (Vol. 1). New York: Wiley, 1970*b*.

Mahler, M. On early infantile psychosis. *Journal of the American Academy of Child Psychiatry*, 1965, *4*, 554-568.

Mahler, M., Pine, F., and Bergman, A. *The psychological birth of the human infant*. New York: Basic Books, 1975.

Malinowski, B. *The sexual life in savages in north-western Melanasia*. New York: Eugenics, 1929.

Malone, P., and Beller, E. K. The effects of different learning environments on creativity in children. Paper presented at the Society for Research in Child Development, Philadelphia, April 1973.

Mandler, J. M., and Johnson, N. S. The remembrance of things parsed: Story structure and recall. *Cognitive Psychology*, 1977, *9*, 111-151.

Mandler, J. M., and Robinson, C. A. Developmental changes in picture recognition. *Journal of Experimental Child Psychology*, 1978, *26*, 122-136.

Mangan, J. Piaget's theory and cultural differences: The case for value-based modes of cognition. *Human Development*, 1978, *21*, 170-189.

Mansfield, A. F. Is the preschool child's memory perceptually organized? Paper presented at the Society for Research in Child Development, New Orleans, 1977.

Maratsos, M. P. The bases of formal syntax. Paper presented at the meeting of the Society for Research in Child Development, Boston, April 1981.

Maratsos, M. P., and Chalkley, M. A. The internal language of children's syntax: The ontogenesis and representation of syntactic categories. In K. Nelson (Ed.), *Children's language* (Vol. 2). New York: Gardner Press, 1980.

Maratsos, M. P., Kuczaj, S. A., and Fox, D. E. C. Some empirical studies in the acquisition of transformational relations. In W. A. Collins (Ed.), *The Minnesota symposium on child development* (Vol. 12). Hillsdale, N. J.: Erlbaum, 1978.

Maratsos, M. P., Kuczaj, S. A., Fox, D. E. C., and Chalkley, M. A. Some empirical studies in the acquisition of transformational relations: Passives, negatives, and the past tense. In W. A. Collins (Ed.), *Children's language and communication. The Minnesota Symposium on Child Psychology.* (Vol. 12). Hillsdale, N. J.: Erlbaum, 1979.

Marcia, J. Identity in adolescence. In J. Adelson (Ed.), *Handbook of Adolescent Psychology*. New York: Wiley, 1980.

Marcus, D. E., and Overton, W. F. The development of cognitive gender constancy and sex role preferences. *Child Development*, 1978, *49*, 434-444.

Markman, E. Realizing that you don't understand: A preliminary investigation. *Child Development*, 1977, *48*, 986-992.

Markman, E. M. Classes and collections: Conceptual organization and numerical abilities. *Cognitive Psychology*, 1979, *11*, 395-411.

Marks, L. On colored-hearing synesthesia. Cross-modal translations of sensory dimensions. *Psychological Bulletin*, 1975, *82*, 303-331.

Marquis, D. P. Can conditioned responses be established in the newborn infant? *Journal of Genetic Psychology,* 1931, *39,* 479-492.

Martino, M. *Emergence: A transsexual autobiography.* New York: Crown, 1977.

Martorano, S. C. A developmental analysis of performance on Piaget's formal operations tasks. *Developmental Psychology,* 1977, *13,* 666-672.

Maslow, A. *Motivation and personality.* New York: Harper, 1954.

Maslow, A. *Toward a psychology of being.* Princeton: Van Nostrand, 1962.

Maslow, A. *Farther reaches of human nature.* New York: Viking Press, 1971.

Masters, J. C., Barden, R. C., and Ford, M. E. Affective states, expressive behavior, and learning in children. *Journal of Personality and Social Psychology,* 1979, *37,* 380-390.

Masters, J. C., Ford, M. E., Arend, R., Grotevant, H. D., and Clark, L. V. Modeling and labeling as integrated determinants of children's sex-typed imitative behavior. *Child Development,* 1979, *50,* 364-371.

Masterson, J. F. *The psychiatric dilemma of adolescence.* Boston: Little, Brown, 1967.

Matas, L., Arend, R., and Sroufe, L. A. Continuity of adaptation in the second year: The relationship between quality of attachment and later competence. *Child Development,* 1978, *49,* 547-556.

Matteson, D. R. Alienation versus exploration and committment: Personality and family corrolaries of adolescent identity statuses. Report from the Project for Youth Research. Copenhagen: Royal Danish School of Educational Studies, 1974.

Matthews, W. S. Modes of transformation in the initiation of fantasy play. *Developmental Psychology,* 1977, *13,* 212-216.

Mattison, A. The gestalt of a cookie. *The New York Times,* January 3, 1979.

Maudry, M. and Nekula, M. Social relations between children of the same age during the first two years of life. *Journal of Genetic Psychology,* 1939, *54,* 193-215.

Maurer, D., and Barrera, M. Normal and distorted faces: When do infants see the difference? Paper presented at the International Conference on Infant Studies, Providence, R. I., March 1978.

Maurer, D., and Barrera, M. Infants' perception of natural and distorted arrangements of schematic faces. *Child Development,* 1981, *52,* 196-202.

Maurer, D., Siegel, L. S., Lewis, T. A., Kristofferson, M. W., Barnes, R. A., and Levy, B. Long term memory improvement? *Child Development,* 1979, *50,* 106-118.

May, R. *Sex and fantasy.* New York: Norton, 1980.

Meacham, J. A. The development of memory abilities in the individual and in society. *Human Development,* 1972, *15,* 205-228.

Meacham, J. A. Verbal guidance through remembering the goals of actions. *Child Development,* 1978, *49,* 188-194.

Mead, G. H. *Mind, self, and society.* Chicago: University of Chicago Press, 1934.

Mead, M. *Sex and temperament in three primitive societies.* New York: Morrow, 1935.

Mead, M. *From the South Seas: Studies of adolescence and sex in primitive societies.* New York: Morrow, 1939.

Meece, J. L. Sex differences in achievement-related affect. In A. Huston, *Sex differences in achievement motivations: Where are we now?* Symposium presented at the Society for Research in Child Development, Boston, April 1981.

Mehler, J., and Bever, T. G. Cognitive capacity of very young children. *Science,* 1967, *158,* 141-142.

Mehler, J., and Bever, T. G. The study of competence in cognitive psychology *International Journal of Psychology,* 1968, *3,* 273-280.

Meichenbaum, D. The nature and modification of impulsive children: Training impulsive children to talk to themselves. Paper presented at the Society for Research in Child Development, Minneapolis, April 1971.

Meltzoff, A. N., and Borton, R. W. Intermodal matching by human neonates. *Nature,* 1979, *282,* 403-404.

Meltzoff, A. N., and Moore, M. K. Imitation of facial and manual gestures by human neonates. *Science,* 1977, *198,* 75-78.

Mendelson, M. J. Acoustic-optical correspondences and auditory-visual coordination in infancy. *Canadian Journal of Psychology,* 1979, *33,* 334-346.

Mendelson, M. J., and Haith, M. M. The relation between audition and vision in the human newborn. *Monographs of the Society for Research in Child Development,* 1976, *41,* (No. 4.).

Menig-Peterson, C. L. The modification of communicative behavior in preschool-aged children as a function of the listener's perspective. *Child Development,* 1975, *46,* 1015-1018.

Menten, J. M., and Cohen, L. B. Infant perception of auditory-visual synchrony. Paper presented at the meeting of the American Psychological Association, New York, September 1979.

Menyuk, P. *The acquisition and development of language.* New York: Prentice-Hall, 1971.

Meringoff, L. K. Influence of the medium on children's story apprehension. *Journal of Educational Psychology,* 1980, *72,* 240-249.

Meringoff, L. K., Vibbert, M., Kelly, H., and Char, C. How shall you take your story, with or without pictures? In P. Greenfield, *Cognitive impact of media on children.* Symposium presented at the Society for Research in Child Development, Boston, April 1981.

Meyer, B. The development of girls' sex-role attitudes. *Child Development,* 1980, *51,* 508-514.

Michel, G. Right handed: A consequence of infant supine head orientation preference? *Science,* 1981, *212,* 685-687.

Milgram, S. *Obedience to authority.* New York: Harper and Row, 1974.

Milgram, S., and Shotland, R. L. *Television and anti-social behavior*. New York: Academic Press, 1973.

Millar, S. *The psychology of play*. London: Penguin, 1968.

Millar, W. S. Conditioning and learning in early infancy. In B. M. Foss (Ed.), *New perspectives in child development*. Baltimore: Penguin, 1974.

Miller, L. The idea of conflict: A study of the development of story understanding. In E. Winner and H. Gardner (Eds.), *Fact, fiction and fantasy in childhood*. New Directions for Child Development, No. 6, San Francisco: Jossey-Bass, 1979.

Miller, L. B., and Dyer, J. L. Four preschool programs: Three dimensions and effects. *Monograph for the Society for Research in Child Development*, 1975, 162.

Miller, N. E., and Dollard, J. *Learning and imitation*. New Haven: Yale University Press, 1941.

Miller, P. Y., and Simon, W. The development of sexuality in adolescence. In J. Adelson, *Handbook of Adolescent Psychology*. New York: Wiley, 1980.

Miller, S. A. Nonverbal assessment of Piagetian concepts. *Psychological Bulletin*, 1976, *83*, 405–430.

Miller, S. A., and Brownell, C. A. Peers, persuasion, and Piaget: Dyadic interactions between conservers and nonconservers. *Child Development*, 1975, *46*, 992–997.

Miller, S. A., Shelton, J., and Flavell, J. H. A. A test of Luria's hypothesis concerning the development of verbal self-regulation. *Child Development*, 1970, *41*, 651–665.

Milner, E. *Human neural and behavioral development: A relational inquiry with implications for personality*. Springfield, Ill.: Thomas, 1967.

Mischel, W. *Personality and assessment*. New York: Wiley, 1968.

Mischel, W. Sex-typing and socialization. In P. H. Mussen (Ed.), *Carmichael's manual of child development* (Vol. 1). New York: Wiley, 1970.

Mischel, W., and Mischel, H. A cognitive social-learning approach to morality and self-regulation. In T. Lickona (Ed.), *Moral development and behavior*. New York: Holt, Rinehart and Winston, 1976.

Mitchell, D. B., Hazen, N., Cavanaugh, J. C., and Perlmutter, M. Exhaustive search and picture cues enhance two-year-olds' memory. Paper presented at the American Psychological Association, New York, September 1979.

Mitchell, G., Redican, W., and Gomber, J. Males can raise babies. *Psychology Today*, 1974, *8*, 62–68.

Mitchell, G., and Schroers, L. Birth order and prenatal experience in monkey and man. In H. W. Reese (Ed.), *Advances in child development and behavior* (Vol. 8). New York: Academic Press, 1973.

Moely, B. E., Olson, F. A., Halwes, T. G., and Flavell, J. H. Production deficiency in young children's clustered recall. *Developmental Psychology*, 1969, *1*, 26–34.

Moely, B. E., Skarin, K., and Weil, S. Sex differences in competition-cooperation behavior of children at two age levels. *Sex Roles*, 1979, *5*, 329–342.

Moerk, E. L. The mother of Eve—as a first language teacher. Paper presented at the Society for Research in Child Development, San Francisco, March 1979.

Moessinger, P. Piaget on equilibrium. *Human Development*, 1978, *21*, 255–267.

Mohr, D. M. Development of attributes of personal identity. *Developmental Psychology*, 1978, *14*, 427–428.

Molfese, D. L., and Molfese, V. J. Hemisphere and stimulus differences as reflected in the cortical responses of newborn infants to speech stimuli. *Developmental Psychology*, 1972, *15*, 505–511.

Moltz, H. Imprinting: Empirical basis and theoretical significance. *Psychological Bulletin*, 1960, *57*, 297–314.

Mondell, S., and Tyler, F. B. Parental competence and styles of problem-solving play behavior with children. *Developmental Psychology*, 1981, *17*, 73–78.

Money, J. Biological and behavioral aspects of sexual differentiation. In N. Kretchmer and D. N. Walcher (Eds.), *Environmental influences on genetic expression*. Washington, D. C.: U. S. Government Printing Office, 1971.

Money, J. An interview with John Money. *American Psychological Association Monitor*, 1976, *7*, 10–11.

Money, J., and Ehrhardt, A. *Man and woman/boy and girl*. Baltimore: Johns Hopkins University Press, 1972.

Montemayor, R., and Eisen, M. The development of self-perception in children and adolescents. Paper presented at the Society for Research in Child Development, Denver, April 1975.

Moore, M. K. The genesis of object permanence. Paper presented at the Society for Research in Child Development, Philadelphia, March 1973.

Moran, J. J., and Joniak, A. J. Effect of language on perference for response to a moral dilemma. *Developmental Psychology*, 1979, *15*, 337–338.

Morison, P., and Gardner, H. Dragons and dinosaurs: On distinguishing the realms of reality and fantasy. *Child Development*, 1978, *49*, 642–648.

Morris, J. *Conundrum*. New York: Harcourt, Brace, and Jovanovich, 1974.

Moscovitch, M., Strauss, E., and Olds, J. Children's production of facial expressions. Paper presented at the American Psychological Association, Montreal, September 1980.

Mosenthal, P. Children's strategy preferences for resolving contradictory story information under two social conditions. *Journal of Experimental Child Psychology*, 1979, *28*, 223–343.

Moshman, D. To really get ahead, get a metatheory. In D. Kuhn (Ed.), *Intellectual development beyond childhood*. New Directions for Child Development, No. 5, San Francisco: Jossey-Bass, 1979.

Moskowitz, B. A. The acquisition of language. *Scientific American,* 1978, *239,* 92-108.

Moss, H. A. Sex, age, and state as determinants of mother-infant interaction. *Merrill-Palmer Quarterly,* 1967, *13,* 19-53.

Mossler, D. G. The emergence of concrete operations. Paper presented at the Society for Research in Child Development, San Francisco, March 1979.

Mossler, D. G., Marvin, R. S., and Greenberg, M. T. Conceptual perspective taking in 2- to 6-year-old children. *Developmental Psychology,* 1976, *12,* 85-86.

Mossler, D., Van Devender, T., Miscione, J., and Marvin, R. How and when children use verbal and nonverbal cues in an ongoing social interaction. Paper presented at the Northeastern Conference on Human Development, Atlanta, 1978.

Mount, R., Kagan, J., Hiatt, S., Reznick, J. S., and Szpak, M. Right visual preference correlates with early language development. Paper presented at the Society for Research in Child Development, Boston, April 1981.

Mowrer, O. H. *Learning theory and the symbolic processes.* New York: Wiley, 1960.

Mueller, E., Bleier, M., Hegedus, K., and Cournoyer, P. The development of peer-verbal interaction among two-year-old boys. *Child Development,* 1977, *48,* 284-287.

Mueller, E., and Brenner, J. The origins of social skills and interaction among playgroup toddlers. *Child Development,* 1977, *48,* 854-861.

Mueller, E., and Lucas, T. A developmental analysis of peer interaction among toddlers. In M. Lewis and L. A. Rosenblum (Eds.), *Friendship and peer relations.* New York: Wiley, 1975.

Muir, D., and Field, J. Newborn infants orient to sounds. *Child Development,* 1979, *50,* 431-436.

Mulford, R. Prototypicality and the development of categorization. *Papers and Reports on Child Language Development,* Stanford University, 1979, *16,* 13-25.

Murphy, J. M., and Gilligan, C. Moral development in late adolescence and adulthood: A critique and reconstruction of Kohlberg's theory. *Human Development,* 1980, *23,* 77-104.

Murray, F. B. The conservation paradigm: The conservation of conservation research. Technical Report No. 2, University of Delaware Studies in Education, Newark, Delaware, December 1979.

Murray, H. A. *Explorations in personality.* New York: Oxford University Press, 1938.

Murray, H. A., and Morgan, C. *Thematic apperception test.* Cambridge, Mass.: Harvard University Press, 1943.

Musgrove, F. *Youth and the social order.* Bloomington, Ind.: Indiana University Press, 1964.

Mussen, P. H. Early sex-role development. In D. A. Goslin (Ed.), *Handbook of socialization theory and research.* Chicago: Rand McNally, 1969.

Mussen, P. H., and Eisenberg-Berg, N. *Roots of caring, sharing and helping: The development of prosocial behavior in children.* San Francisco: Freeman, 1977.

Nagel, E. Home schooling: The epitome of parental involvement. *The Interstate Compact for Education,* 1979, *13,* Backcover and p. 31.

Nauta, W. The problem of the frontal lobe: A reinterpretation. *Journal of Psychiatric Research,* 1971, *8,* 167-187.

Neimark, E. D. Intellectual development during adolescence. In F. D. Horowitz (Ed.), *Review of child development research* (Vol. 1). Chicago: University of Chicago Press, 1975a.

Neimark, E. D. Longitudinal development of formal operations thought. *Genetic Psychology Monographs,* 1975b, *91,* 171-225.

Neimark, E. D. Current status of formal operations research. *Human Development,* 1979, *22,* 60-67.

Neisser, U. *Cognitive psychology.* Englewood Cliffs, N. J.: Prentice-Hall, 1967.

Nelson, K. Structure and strategy in learning to talk. *Monographs of the Society for Research in Child Development,* 1973, *38,* (Serial No. 149, No. 2).

Nelson, K. The syntagmatic-paradigmatic shift revisited: A review of research and theory. *Psychological Bulletin,* 1977, *84,* 93-116.

Nelson, K. Explorations in the development of a functional semantic system. In W. A. Collins (Ed.), *Children's language and communication. The Minnesota Symposia on Child Psychology,* (Vol. 12). Hillsdale, N. J.: Erlbaum, 1979.

Nelson, K. Individual differences in language development: Implications for development and language. *Developmental Psychology,* 1981a, *17,* 170-187.

Nelson, K. The development of event representation. In M. T. H. Chi, *What is memory development in the development of? A look after a decade.* Symposium presented at the Society for Research in Child Development, Boston, April 1981b.

Nelson, K., Rescorla, L., Gruendel, J., and Benedict, H. Early lexicons: What do they mean? *Child Development,* 1978, *49,* 960-968.

Nelson, K. E. Memory development in children: Evidence from nonverbal tasks. *Psychonomic Science,* 1971, *25,* 346-348.

Nelson, K. E. Studies in child language and multilingualism. *Annals of the New York Academy of Sciences,* 1980, *345,* 46-67.

Nelson, K. E. Experimental gambits in the service of language acquisition theory: From the Fiffin Project to operation input swap. In S. Kuczaj (Ed.), *Language development: Syntax and semantics.* Hillsdale, N. J.: Erlbaum, 1981.

Nelson, K. E., Denninger, M., and Messe, M. Memory parameters in language acquisition. Paper presented at the Society for Research in Child Development, Boston, April 1981.

Neugarten, B. *Personality in middle and later life.* New York: Atherton Press, 1964.

Neugarten, B. Adult personality: A developmental view. *Human Development,* 1966, *9,* 61–73.

Newcombe, N., and Bandura, M. M. The effect of age at puberty on spatial ability in girls: A question of mechanism. Presented at the Society for Research in Child Development, Boston, April 1981.

Newell, A., and Simon, H. A. *Human problem-solving.* Englewood Cliffs, N. J.: Prentice-Hall, 1972.

Newman, H. H., Freeman, R. N., and Holzinger, K. J. *Twins: A study of heredity and environment.* Chicago: University of Chicago Press, 1937.

Newport, E. L. Motherese: The speech of mothers to young children. In N. Castellan, D. P. Pisoni, and G. Potts (Eds.), *Cognitive theory* (Vol. 2). Hillsdale, N. J.: Erlbaum, 1977.

Newport, E. L., Gleitman, L., and Gleitman, H. Mother, I'd rather do it myself: Some effects and noneffects of maternal style. In C. Snow and C. Ferguson (Eds.), *Talking to children: Language input and acquisition.* Cambridge: Cambridge University Press, 1977.

Newton, N., and Modahl, C. Pregnancy: The closest human relationship. *Human Nature,* 1978, *1,* 40–56.

The New York Times. Boy with immune deficiency upsets theories in three years in plastic bubble. October 10, 1974, p. 41.

The New York Times. Nearly all autistic twins are identical twins. April 24, 1977, IV, p. 6.

The New York Times. Studies dispute view of limits on inner city schools. December 26, 1979.

The New York Times. Mistaken identity leads to a surprising discovery. September 19, 1980.

Nicholls, J. G. The development of the concepts of effort and ability, perception of academic attainment, and the understanding that difficult tasks require more ability. *Child Development,* 1978, *49,* 800–814.

Nicolich, L. M. Beyond sensorimotor intelligence: Assessment of symbolic maturity through analysis of pretend play. *Merrill-Palmer Quarterly,* 1977, *23,* 89–99.

Nicolich, L. M. Symbolic play: Sequences of development and methods of assessment. Unpublished paper, Rutgers University, New Brunswick, 1978.

Ninio, A., and Bruner, J. The achievement of antecedents of labeling. *Journal of Child Language,* 1978, *5,* 1–15.

Nolan, E., and Kagan, J. Psychological factors in the face-hand test. *Archives of Neurology,* 1978, *35,* 41–42.

Norman, D. K. A comparison of children's spatial reasoning: Rural Appalachia, suburban, and urban New England. *Child Development,* 1980, *51,* 288–291.

Novak, M. A. Social recovery of monkeys isolated for the first year of life. *Developmental Psychology,* 1979, *15,* 50–61.

Novak, M. A., and Harlow, H. F. Social recovery of monkeys isolated for the first years of life. I. Rehabilitation and therapy. *Developmental Psychology,* 1975, *11,* 453–465.

Novey, M. Personal communication, April 1975.

Nowlis, G. H., and Kessen, W. Human newborns differentiate differing concentrations of sucrose and glucose. *Science,* 1976, *191,* 865–866.

Nucci, L. Conceptions of personal issues: A domain distinct from moral or societal concepts. *Child Development,* 1981, *52,* 114–121.

Nucci, L. P., and Turiel, E. Social interactions and the development of social concepts in preschool children. *Child Development,* 1978, *49,* 400–407.

Nussbaum, M., Shenker, I. R., Marc, J., and Klein, M. Cerebral atrophy in anorexia nervosa. *Journal of Pediatrics,* 1980, *96,* 867–869.

Oates, J. *Early cognitive development.* New York: Halsted Press, 1978.

O'Connor, J. M., Beilin, H., and Kose, G. The effects of media on logical operations. Paper presented at the Society for Research in Child Development, Boston, April 1981.

Offer, D. *The psychological world of the teenager.* New York: Basic Books, 1969.

Olson, D. *Cognitive development.* New York: Academic Press, 1970.

Olson, D. (Ed.). *Media and symbol.* Chicago: University of Chicago Press, 1974.

Olson, D. The language of instruction: On the literate bias of schooling. Paper presented at the Conference on Schooling and the Acquisition of Knowledge, San Diego, November 1975.

Olson, D. On the nature and achievement of human competence. Unpublished paper, Ontario, Institute for Studies in Education, 1976.

Olson, D. From utterance to text: The bias of language in speech and writing. *Harvard Educational Review,* 1977, *47,* 257–282.

Olson, D. Cognitive development: Implicit and explicit knowledge. In F. S. Kessel, *Cognitive development: Emerging and reemerging themes.* Symposium presented at the Society for Research in Child Development, Boston, April 1981.

Olson, D. and Hildyard, A. Literacy and the comprehension of literal meaning. Paper presented at the Conference "The development and use of writing systems." Bielfeld, Germany, June 1980.

Olson, G. M. Infant recognition memory for briefly presented visual stimuli. *Infant Behavior and Development,* 1979, *2,* 123–134.

Omanson, R., Warren, W., and Trabasso, T. Goals, inferential comprehension, and recall of stories by children. *Discourse Processes,* 1978, *1,* 337–354.

Omark, D. R., and Edelman, M. Peer group social interactions from an evolutionary perspective. Paper presented at the Society for Research in Child Development, Philadelphia, March 1973.

Oppenheimer, L., and Strauss, S. Filiation of operational structures and imagery. *Journal of Genetic Psychology*, 1975, *127*, 179-190.

Ornitz, E. M. Neurophysiologic studies. In M. Rutter and E. Schopler (Eds.), *Autism: A reappraisal of concepts and treatment.* New York: Plenum Press, 1978.

Ortony, A. Some psycholinguistic aspects of metaphor. In R. P. Honeck and R. R. Hoffman (Eds.), *Cognitive and figurative language.* Hillsdale, N. J.: Erlbaum, 1980, 69-86.

Osgood, C. A behavioristic analysis of perception and language as cognitive phenomena. In H. E. Gruber, K. R. Hammond, and R. Jessor (Eds.), *Contemporary approaches to cognition.* Cambridge, Mass.: Harvard University Press, 1957.

Osherson, D. N. *Logical abilities in children.* Reasoning in adolescence: Deductive inference, Vol. 3. Hillsdale, N. J.: Erlbaum, 1975.

Osherson, D. N. and Markman, E. Language and the ability to evaluate contradictions and tautologies. *Cognition*, 1975, *2*, 213-226.

Ostwald, P. The sounds of infancy. *Developmental Medicine and Child Neurology*, 1972, *14*, 350-361.

Owings, R. A., and Baumeister, A. A. Levels of processing, encoding strategies, and memory development. *Journal of Experimental Child Psychology*, 1979, *28*, 100-178.

Oyama, S. The concept of the sensitive period in developmental studies. *Merrill-Palmer Quarterly*, 1979, *25*, 83-103.

Palermo, D. S. More about less: A study in language comprehension. *Journal of Verbal Learning and Verbal Behavior*, 1973, *12*, 211-221.

Palermo, D. S. Still more about the comprehension of "less." *Developmental Psychology*, 1974, *10*, 827-829.

Papalia, D. E. The status of several conservation abilities across the life span. *Human Development*, 1972, *15*, 229-243.

Papousek, H. Experimental studies of appetitional behavior in human newborns and infants. In H. W. Stevenson, E. H. Hess, and H. L. Rheingold (Eds.), *Early behavior.* New York: Wiley, 1967.

Papousek, H., and Bernstein, P. The functioning of conditioning stimulation in human neonates and infants. In J. A. Ambrose (Ed.), *Stimulation in early infancy.* New York: Academic Press, 1969.

Paris, S. G. The development of inference and transformation as memory operations. In P. Ornstein (Ed.), *Memory development in children.* Hillsdale, N. J.: Erlbaum, 1978.

Paris, S. G., and Lindauer, B. K. The role of inference in children's comprehension and memory for sentences. *Cognitive Psychology*, 1976, *8*, 217-227.

Paris, S. G., and Upton, O. Children's memory for inferential relationships in prose. *Child Development*, 1976, *47*, 600-668.

Pariser, D. Children's drawings of wrecked cars: A study in the development of form. Ph.D. dissertation, Harvard University Graduate School of Education, 1976.

Park, C. Review of *Nadia: A case of extraordinary drawing ability in an autistic child* by Lorna Selfe. *Journal of Autism and Childhood Schizophrenia*, 1978, *8*, 457-472.

Parke, E. M., 1972, as cited in G. Collins, Fathering. *The New York Times Magazine*, June 17, 1979, p. 31.

Parsons, J. E. Attributions, learned helplessness, and sex differences in achievement. In S. Yussen (Ed.), *The development of reflection.* New York: Academic Press, 1981.

Parsons, T. Family structure and the socialization of the child. In T. Parsons and R. F. Bates (Eds.), *Family socialization and interaction process.* Glencoe, Ill.: Free Press, 1955.

Pascual-Leone, J. Compounds, confounds, and models in developmental information processing: A reply to Trabasso and Foellinger. *Journal of Experimental Child Psychology*, 1978, *26*, 18-40.

Passman, R. H. Arousing reducing properties of attachment objects: Testing the functional limits of the security blanket relative to the mother. *Developmental Psychology*, 1976, *12*, 468-469.

Passman, R. H. Providing attachment objects to facilitate learning and reduce distress: Effects of mothers and security blankets. *Developmental Psychology*, 1977, *13*, 25-28.

Passman, R. H., and Erck, T. W. Permitting maternal contact through vision alone: Films of mothers for promoting play and locomotion. *Developmental Psychology*, 1978, *14*, 512-516.

Passman, R. H., and Weisberg, P. Mothers and blankets as agents of permitting play and exploration by young children in a novel environment: The effects of social and nonsocial attachment blankets. *Developmental Psychology*, 1975, *11*, 170-177.

Patterson, C. J., and Kister, M. C. The development of listener skills for referential communication. In. W. P. Dickson (Ed.), *Children's oral communication skills.* New York: Academic Press, in press.

Patterson, C. J., and Massad, C. M. Facilitating referential communication among children: The listener as teacher. *Journal of Experimental Child Psychology*, 1980, *29*, 357-370.

Patterson, F. G. The gesture of a gorilla: Language acquisition in another pongid. *Brain and Language*, 1978, *5*, 72-97.

Pavlov, I. *Conditioned reflexes.* New York: Dover, 1927.

Pea, R. D. The development of truth-functional language: one and one-half to three years. Paper presented at the Society for Research in Child Development, New Orleans, March 1977.

Peery, J. C. Neonate-adult head movement: No and yes revisited. *Developmental Psychology, 1980, 16,* 245-250.

Peiper, A. *Cerebral functions in infancy and childhood.* New York: Consultants Bureau, 1963.

Pellegrino, J. W., Posnansky, C., and Vesonder, G. T. Developmental changes in free recall: The interaction of task structure and age. *Journal of Experimental Child Psychology, 1977, 24,* 86-96.

Penfield, W. Some mechanisms of consciousness discovered during electrical stimulation of the brain. *Proceedings of the National Academy of Sciences, 1958, 44,* 51-66.

Penfield, W., and Roberts, L. *Speech and brain mechanism.* Princeton: Princeton University Press, 1959.

Pepler, D. J. The effects of play on convergent and divergent problem-solving. Paper presented at the American Psychological Association, Montreal, September 1980.

Pepler, D. J. Naturalistic observations of teaching and modeling between siblings. Paper presented at the Society for Research in Child Development, Boston, April 1981.

Perlmutter, M., Hazen, N., Mitchell, D. B., Grady, J. G., Cavanaugh, J. C., and Flook, J. P. Picture cues and exhaustive search facilitate very young children's memory for location. *Developmental Psychology, 1981, 17,* 104-110.

Perlmutter, M., and Myers, N. A. Development of recall in 1- to 4-year-old children. *Developmental Psychology, 1979, 15,* 73-83.

Perry, D. G., and Bussey, K. The social learning theory of sex differences. *Journal of Personality and Social Psychology, 1979, 37,* 1699-1713.

Perry, W. B. *Forms of intellectual and ethical development in the college years: A scheme.* New York: Holt, Rinehart and Winston, 1968.

Peskin, H. Pubertal onset and ego functioning. *Journal of Abnormal Psychology, 1967, 72,* 1-15.

Peskin, H., and Livson, N. Pre- and postpubertal personality and adult psychologic functioning. *Seminars in Psychiatry, 1972, 4,* 343-354.

Peters, R. S. Moral development: A plea for pluralism. In T. Mischel (Ed.), *Cognitive development and epistemology.* New York: Academic Press, 1971.

Peterson, A. C., and Taylor, B. The biological approach to adolescence. In J. Adelson (Ed.), *Handbook of adolescent psychology.* New York: Wiley, 1980.

Peterson, C. L., Danner, F. W., and Flavell, J. H. Developmental changes in children's response to three indications of communicative failure. *Child Development, 1972, 43,* 1463-1468.

Peterson, W. C., and Keasey, C. B. Preschoolers' conceptions of intentionality and motives. Unpublished manuscript, University of Nebraska, Lincoln, 1976.

Petretic, P. A., and Tweney, R. D. Does comprehension precede production? The development of children's responses to sentences of varying grammatical adequacy. *Journal of Child Language, 1977, 4,* 201-209.

Pezdek, K. Life span differences in semantic integration of pictures and sentences in memory. *Child Development, 1980, 51,* 720-729.

Phillips, D. A. High-achieving students with low academic self-concept: Attitudinal and behavioral correlates. Paper presented at the Society for Research in Child Development, Boston, April 1981.

Phillips, J. Syntax and vocabulary of mothers' speech to young children: Age and sex comparisons. *Child Development, 1973, 44,* 182-187.

Phillips, S., King, S., and DuBois, L. Spontaneous activities of female versus male newborns. *Child Development, 1978, 49,* 590-597.

Piaget, J. *The child's conception of the world.* New York: Harcourt, Brace, 1929.

Piaget, J. *The moral judgment of the child.* New York: Harcourt, Brace, 1932.

Piaget, J. *The construction of reality in the child.* New York: Basic Books, 1954.

Piaget, J. *The language and thought of the child.* New York: Meridian Books, 1955.

Piaget, J. *Play, dreams, and imitation.* New York: Norton, 1962a.

Piaget, J. Comments on Vygotsky's critical remarks. In L. Vygotsky (Ed.), *Thought and language.* Cambridge, Mass.: MIT Press, 1962b.

Piaget, J. *The origins of intelligence in children.* New York: Norton, 1963.

Piaget, J. *The child's conception of the world.* Totowa, N. J.: Littlefield, Adams, 1965a.

Piaget, J. *The child's conception of number.* New York: Norton, 1965b.

Piaget, J. *Biologie et connaissance.* Paris: Gallimard, 1967.

Piaget, J. *On the development of memory and identity.* Worcester, Mass.: Clark University Press, 1968.

Piaget, J. *On the development of memory and identity.* Worcester, MA: Clark University Press, 1968b.

Piaget, J. Piaget's theory. In P. H. Mussen (Ed.), *Carmichael's manual of child psychology* (Vol.1). New York: Wiley, 1970.

Piaget, J. *Insights and illusions of philosophy.* New York: World, 1971.

Piaget, J. Intellectual evolution from adolescence to adulthood. *Human Development, 1972, 15,* 1-21.

Piaget, J. *The grasp of consciousness.* Cambridge, Mass.: Harvard University Press, 1976.

Piaget, J. Language within cognition. In M. Piatelli-Palmarini (Ed.), *Language and learning: The debate between Jean Piaget and Noam Chomsky.* Cambridge, Mass.: Harvard University Press, 1980.

Piaget, J., and Inhelder, B. *The child's conception of space.* London: Routledge and Kegan Paul, 1956.

Piaget, J., and Inhelder, B. *The psychology of the child.* New York: Basic Books, 1968.

Piaget, J., and Inhelder, B. *Memory and intelligence.* New York: Basic Books, 1973.

Piatelli-Palmarini, M. (Ed.). *Language and learning: The debate between Jean Piaget and Noam Chomsky.* Cambridge, Mass.: Harvard University Press, 1980.

Pick, H. L., and Pick, A. Sensory and perceptual development. In P. H. Mussen (Ed.), *Carmichael's manual of child psychology* (Vol. 1). New York: Wiley, 1970.

Piers, M. (Ed.). *Play and development.* New York: Norton, 1973.

Pines, M. Super kids. *Psychology Today,* 1978, *12,* 53–63.

Pinker, S. Formal models of language learning. *Cognition,* 1979, *7,* 217–283.

Pipp, S. L, and Van Giffen, K. Parameters of scanning in the first three months of life. Paper presented at the Society for Research in Child Development, Boston, April 1981.

Plomin, R., and Rowe, D. C. Genetic and environment etiology of social behavior in infancy. *Developmental Psychology,* 1979, *15,* 62–72.

Polak, P. R., Emde, R. N., and Spitz, R. A. The smiling response and the human face. *Journal of Nervous and Mental Disorders,* 1964, *139,* 103–109, 407–415.

Pomerantz, S. C. Sex differences in the relative importance of self-esteem, physical self-satisfaction, and identity in predicting adolescent satisfaction. *Journal of Youth and Adolescence,* 1979, *8,* 51–61.

Prather, P. Centration: An issue of perceptual or postperceptual processing? Paper presented at the Society for Research in Child Development, Boston, April 1981.

Premack, D. *Intelligence in ape and man.* Hillsdale, N. J.: Erlbaum, 1976.

Pressley, M. Imagery and children's learning: Putting the picture in developmental perspective. *Review of Educational Research,* 1977, *47,* 585–622.

Presson, C. C. The development of map-reading skills. Paper presented at the Society for Research in Child Development, Boston, April 1981.

Price-Williams, D. R. (Ed.). *Cross-cultural studies.* Baltimore: Penguin, 1970.

Prior, M. R., and Bradshaw, J. L. Hemisphere functioning in autistic children. *Cortex,* 1979, *15,* 73–82.

Prizant, B. M. The functions of immediate echolalia in autistic children. Unpublished paper, Southern Illinois University at Carbondale, 1978.

Provence, S., and Lipton, R. C. *Infants in institutions.* New York: International Universities Press, 1963.

Purpura, D. Quoted in L. K. Altman, Fetal brain said to live at twenty-eight weeks. *The New York Times,* May 9, 1975, p. 30.

Rabin, A. I. *Growing up in the kibbutz.* New York: Springer, 1965.

Radin, N. Wives of child-rearing men. Paper presented at the Society for Research in Child Development, Boston, April 1981.

Ragozin, A. S. Attachment behavior of day-care children: Naturalistic and laboratory observations. *Child Development,* 1980, *51,* 409–416.

Rajecki, D. W., Lamb, M., and Obmascher, P. Toward a general theory of infantile attachment: A comparative view of aspects of the social bond. *The Behavioral and Brain Sciences,* 1978, *3,* 417–464.

Rapp, D. J. Does diet affect hyperactivity? *Journal of Learning Disabilities,* 1978, *11,* 383–389.

Raviv, A., Bar-Tal, D., and Lewis-Levin, T. Motivations for donation behavior by boys of three different ages. *Child Development,* 1980, *51,* 610–613.

Ray, W. J., Georgiou, S., and Ravizza, R. Spatial abilities, sex differences, and lateral eye movements. *Developmental Psychology,* 1979, *15,* 455–457.

Read, P. B., and Jenness, D. Some neglected aspects of social development in childhood. *Social Science Research Council Annual Reports,* 1974–1975, pp. 17–35.

Rebelsky, F. Personal communication, June 1976.

Reese, H. W. Verbal mediation as a function of age level. *Psychological Bulletin,* 1962, *59,* 502–509.

Reese, H. W., and Overton, W. F. Models of development and themes of development. In L. R. Goulet and P. B. Baltes (Eds.), *Life-span developmental psychology.* New York: Academic Press, 1970.

Reid, P. T., and Stanridge, L. R. Children's production of humor related self-concept and the use of ambiguity. Unpublished paper, University of Tennessee, Chattanooga, 1981.

Reis, H. T. A longitudinal study of quantitative-verbal interests. Unpublished paper, University of Rochester, 1980.

Reisman, J. M., and Shorr, S. T. Friendship claims and expectations among children and adults. *Child Development,* 1979, *49,* 913–916.

Rescorla, L. A. Overextension in early language development. *Journal of Child Language,* 1980, *7,* 321–336.

Rest, J. R. Longitudinal study of the Defining Issues Test of moral judgment: A strategy for analyzing developmental change. *Developmental Psychology,* 1975, *11,* 738–748.

Rest, J. R., Cooper, D., Coder, R., Masanz, J., and Anderson, D. Judging the important issues in moral dilemmas: An objective measure of development. *Developmental Psychology,* 1974, *10,* 491–501.

Rest, J. R., Davison, M. L., and Robbins, S. Age trends in judging moral issues: A review of cross-sectional, longitudinal, and sequential studies of the Defining Issues Test. *Child Development,* 1978, *49,* 263–279.

Rest, J. R., Turiel, E., and Kohlberg, L. Level of

moral development as a determinant of preference and comprehension of moral judgments made by others. *Journal of Personality,* 1969, *37,* 225-252.

Restak, R. Male, female brains: Are they different? *Boston Globe,* September 9, 1979*a,* p. A1.

Restak, R. Psychosocial dwarfism: The evidence grows, the kids don't. *The New York Times,* November 18, 1979*b,* p. E20.

Revész, G. Über audition colorée. *Zeitschrift für Angewandte Psychologie,* 1923, *21,* 308-332.

Rheingold, H. The effect of a strange environment on the behavior of infants. In B. M. Foss (Ed.), *Determinants of infant behavior* (Vol. 4). New York: Barnes and Noble, 1969.

Rheingold, H. Helping by two-year-old children. Paper presented at the Society for Research in Child Development, San Francisco, March 1979.

Rheingold, H., and Cook, K. The contents of boys' and girls' rooms as an index of parents' behavior. *Child Development,* 1975, *46,* 459-483.

Rheingold, H., and Eckerman, C. O. Fear of the stranger: A critical examination. In H. Reese (Ed.), *Advances in child development and behavior* (Vol. 7). New York: Academic Press, 1973.

Rheingold, H., Gewirtz, J. L., and Ross, H. W., Social conditioning of vocalization in the infant. *Journal of Comparative and Psychological Psychology,* 1959, *52,* 68-73.

Ribble, M. A. Infantile experience in relation to personality development. In J. M. Hunt (Ed.), *Personality and behavior disorders* (Vol. 2). New York: Ronald Press, 1944.

Rice, R. D. Premature infants respond to sensory stimulation. *American Psychological Association Monitor,* November 1975, pp. 8-9.

Richards, M. M. Sorting out what's in a word from what's not: Evaluating Clark's semantic features acquisition theory. *Journal of Experimental Child Psychology,* 1979, *27,* 1-47.

Ridberg, E., Parke, R., and Hetherington, E. M. Modification of impulsive and reflective cognitive styles through observations of film-mediated models. *Developmental Psychology,* 1971, *5,* 369-377.

Riegel, K. F. Dialectic operations: The final period of cognitive development. *Human Development,* 1973, *16,* 346-370.

Rierdan, J., and Koff, E. Body image of early and late adolescent girls. Paper presented at the Eastern Psychological Association, Hartford, April 1980*a.*

Rierdan, J., and Koff, E. The psychological impact of menarche: Integrative versus disruptive changes. *Journal of Youth and Adolescence,* 1980*b,* *9,* 49-57.

Rieser, J., Yonas, A., and Wikner, K. Rodent localization of odors by human newborns. *Child Development,* 1976, *47,* 856-859.

Riesman, D., Glazer, N., and Denney, R. *The lonely crowd.* New Haven: Yale University Press, 1950.

Rimland, B. *Infantile autism.* New York: Appleton-Century-Crofts, 1964.

Rimland, B. Recent research on infantile autism. *Journal of Operational Psychiatry,* 1972, *3,* 35-39.

Rimland, B. Where does research lead? Paper presented at the meeting of the National Society for Autistic Children, San Diego, 1975.

Ringel, B. A., and Springer, C. J. On knowing how well one is remembering: The persistence of strategy use during transfer. *Journal of Educational Child Psychology,* 1980, *29,* 322-333.

Rinkoff, R. F., and Corter, C. M. Effects of setting and maternal accessibility on the infant's response to brief separations. *Child Development,* 1980, *51,* 603-606.

Robb, C. Vive la difference. *The Boston Globe Magazine,* October 5, 1980, pp. 11+.

Roberge, J. J., and Flexer, B. K. Further examination of formal operational reasoning abilities. *Child Development,* 1979, *50,* 478-484.

Robert, M., and Charbonneau, C. Extinction of liquid conservation by modeling: Three indicators of its artificiality. *Child Development,* 1978, *49,* 194-200.

Robinson, E. J. The child's understanding of inadequate messages in communication failure: A problem of ignorance or egocentrism? Paper given at the Wisconsin Conference on Children's Oral Communication Skills, Madison, Wisconsin, October 1978.

Robinson, E. J., and Robinson, W. P. Development in the understanding of causes of success and failure in verbal communication. *Cognition,* 1977, *5,* 363-378.

Robinson, P. (Ed.). *Brain and early behavior.* New York: Academic Press, 1969.

Roche, A. F. Secular trends in human growth, maturation and development. *Monograph of the Society for Research in Child Development,* 1979, *44,* (Serial No. 179, Nos. 3-4).

Rogers, D. *The psychology of adolescence.* Englewood Cliffs, N. J.: Prentice-Hall, 1972.

Rohwer, W. D. Images and pictures in children's learning: Research results and educational implications. *Psychological Bulletin,* 1970, *73,* 393-403.

Rokeach, M. *The nature of human values.* New York: Free Press, 1973.

Rondal, J. A. Investigation of the regulatory power of the impulsive and meaningful aspects of speech. *Genetic Psychology Monographs,* 1976, *94,* 3-33.

Rorty, R. *Philosophy and the mirror of the nature.* Princeton: Princeton University Press, 1980.

Rosch, E. On the internal structure of perceptual and semantic categories. In T. E. Moore (Ed.), *Cognitive development and the acquisition of language.* New York: Academic Press, 1973.

Rosch, E. Basic level concepts in natural categories. Paper presented at the Psychonomic Society, Boston, November 1974.

Rosch, E. Cognitive representations of semantic categories. *Journal of Experimental Psychology,* 1975, *104,* 192-233.

Rosch, E., Mervis, C. B., Gray, W. D., Johnson, D. M., and Boyes-Braem, P. Basic objects in natural categories. *Cognitive Psychology, 1976, 8,* 382-439.

Rose, S. *The conscious brain.* New York: Knopf, 1973.

Rose, S. A. Infants' transfer of response between two-dimensional and three-dimensional stimuli. *Child Development,* 1977, *48,* 1086-1091.

Rose, W. R., Gottfried, A. W., and Bridger, W. J. Cross-model transfer in six-month-old infants. Paper presented at the Society for Research in Child Development, Boston, April 1981.

Rosen, B. C., and D'Andrade, R. The psychological origins of achievement motivation. *Sociometry,* 1959, *22,* 185-218.

Rosen, M. G. The secret brain: Learning before birth. *Harpers,* 1978, *256,* 46-47.

Rosenblatt, D. Learning how to mean: The development of representation in play and language. Conference on the Biology of Play. Farnham, Eng., June 1975.

Rosenblatt, P. C., and Skoogberg, E. L. Birth order in cross-cultural perspective. *Developmental Psychology,* 1974, *10,* 48-54.

Rosenfeld, A. *Prolengevity.* New York: Knopf, 1976.

Rosenthal, D. A. Language skills and formal operations. *Merrill-Palmer Quarterly,* 1979, *25,* 133-143.

Rosenthal, T. L., and Zimmerman, B. J. *Social learning and cognition.* New York: Academic Press, 1978.

Rosenzweig, M. Environmental complexity, cerebral change, and behavior. *American Psychologist,* 1966, *21,* 321-332.

Rosner, S., and Poole, D. Category attributes and item inclusion. Presented at the Society for Research in Child Development, Boston, April 1981.

Ross, D. G. *Stanley Hall: The psychologist as prophet.* Chicago: University of Chicago Press, 1972.

Ross, H. The effects of increasing familiarity on infant reactions to adult strangers. *Journal of Experimental Child Psychology,* 1975, *20,* 226-239.

Ross, H. S., and Killey, J. C. The effect of questioning on retention. *Child Development,* 1977, *48,* 312-314.

Ross, N. M., anad Millsom, C. Repeated memory of oral prose in Ghana and New York. *International Journal of Psychology,* 1970, *5,* 173-181.

Rotenberg, K. J. "A promise kept, a promise broken": Developmental bases of trust. *Child Development,* 1980, *51,* 614-617.

Rothman, S. R. The influence of moral reasoning on behavioral choices. *Child Development,* 1976, *47,* 397-406.

Rousseau, J. J. *The Emile of Jean Jacques Rousseau* (W. Boyd, Ed.). New York: Columbia Teacher's College, 1962. (Original publication, 1762).

Rowland, G. L. The effects of total isolation upon the learning and social behavior of rhesus monkeys. Ph.D. dissertation, University of Wisconsin, 1964.

Rubin, K. H. The relationship between spatial and communicative egocentrism in children and young and old adults. *Journal of Genetic Psychology,* 1974, *125,* 295-301.

Rubin, K. H., Fein, G. C., and Vandenberg, B. Play. In. P. H. Mussen (Ed.), *Carmichael's manual of child psychology.* 2nd ed. New York: Wiley, in press.

Rubin, K. H., and Maioni, T. L. Play preference and its relationship to egocentrism, popularity, and classification skills in preschoolers. *Merrill-Palmer Quarterly,* 1975, *21,* 171-179.

Rubin, S., and Gardner, H. Once upon a time: The development of sensitivity to story structure. Unpublished paper. Harvard University, 1979.

Rubin, S., and Wolf, D. The development of maybe: The evolution of social roles into narrative roles. *New Directions for Child Development,* 1979, *6,* 15-28.

Rubin, Z. *Children's friendships.* Cambridge, Mass.: Harvard University Press, 1980.

Rubinstein, E. A. Television and the young viewer. *American Scientist,* 1978, *66,* 685-693.

Ruble, D. N, Boggiano, A. K., Feldman, N. S., and Loebl, J. H. Developmental analysis of the role of social comparison in self-evaluation. *Developmental Psychology,* 1980, *16,* 105-115.

Ruble, D. N., Feldman, N. S., and Boggiano, A. K. Social comparison between young children in achievement situations. *Developmental Psychology,* 1976, *12,* 192-197.

Rumbaugh, D., Glasersfeld, E., Werner, H., Pisani, P., and Gill, T. Lana (chimpanzee) learning language: A progress report. *Brain and Language,* 1974, *1,* 205-212.

Rumelhart, D. E. Notes on a schema for stories. In D. G. Bobrow and A. Collins (Eds.), *Representation and understanding.* New York: Academic Press, 1975.

Rumelhart, D. E., and Ortony, A. The presentation of knowledge in memory. In R. C. Anderson, R. J. Spiro, and W. E. Montague (Eds.), *Schooling and the acquisition of knowledge.* Hillsdale, N. J.: Erlbaum, 1977.

Ruppenthal, G. C., Arling, G. L., Harlow, H. G., Sackett, G. P., and Suomi, S. J. A one-year perspective of motherless-mother monkey-behavior, *Journal of Abnormal Psychology,* 1976, *85,* 341-349.

Rushton, J. P. Effects of prosocial television and film materials on the behavior of viewers. In L. Berkowitz (Ed.), *Advances in experimental social psychology* (Vol. 12). New York: Academic Press, 1979.

Russac, R. J. The relation between two strategies of cardinal numbers: Correspondence and counting. *Child Development,* 1978, *49,* 728-735.

Rutter, M. The development of infantile autism. *Psychological Medicine*, 1974, *4*, 147-163.

Rutter, M. Maternal deprivation, 1972-1978: New findings, new concepts, new approaches. *Child Development*, 1979a, *50*, 283-305.

Rutter, M. Protective factors in children's responses to stress and disadvantage. In M. W. Kent and J. Rolf (Eds.), *Primary prevention of psychopathology: Social competence in children* (Vol. 3), Hanover, N. H.: University Press of New England, 1979b.

Rutter, M. *Fifteen thousand hours*. Cambridge, Mass.: Harvard University Press, 1979c.

Rutter, M., and Schopler, E. (Eds.). *Autism: A reappraisal of concepts and treatment*. New York: Plenum Press, 1978.

Ryan, E. B. Identifying and remediating failure in reading comprehension: Toward an instructional approach for poor comprehenders. In T. G. Waller and G. E. MacKinnon (Eds.), *Reading research: Advances in theory and practice* (Vol. 2). New York: Academic Press, in press.

Ryan, E. B., and Ledger, G. W. Children's awareness of sentence grammaticality. Paper presented at the Psychonomic Society, Phoenix, November 1979.

Rybash, J. M., Roodin, P. A., and Hallion, K. The role of affect in children's attribution of intentionality and dispensation of punishment. *Child Development*, 1979, *50*, 1227-1230.

Saarni, C. Children's understanding of display rules for expressive behavior, *Developmental Psychology*, 1979, *15*, 424-429.

Sachs, J. The role of adult-child play in language development. In K. H. Rubin (Ed.), *Children's play*. New Directions for Child Development, No. 9. San Francisco: Jossey-Bass, 1980.

Sachs, J., and Truswell, L. Comprehension of two-word instructions by children in the one-word stage. *Journal of Child Language*, 1978, *5*, 17-24.

Sack, W. H. Children of imprisoned fathers. *Psychiatry*, 1977, *40*, 163-174.

Sackett, G. P., Ruppenthal, G. C., Fahrenbruch, C. E., Holm, R. A., and Greenough, W. T. Social isolation rearing effects in monkeys vary with genotype. *Developmental Psychology*, 1981, *17*, 313-318.

Sagi, A., and Hoffman, Y. L. Empathic distress in the newborn. *Developmental Psychology*, 1976, *12*, 175-176.

Sagotsky, G., and Wondolowski-Svensson, S. Explaining discrepant and nondiscrepant social situations. Presented at the Society for Research in Child Development, Boston, April 1981.

Salapatek, P. Visual investigation of geometric patterns in the human newborn. Paper presented at the Society for Research in Child Development, Philadelphia, March 1973.

Salatas, H., and Flavell, J. H. Behavioral and meta-mnemonic indicators of strategic behaviors under remember instructions in first grade. *Child Development*, 1976, *47*, 81-89.

Saltz, E. Pretend play: A complex of variables influencing development. Paper presented at the American Psychological Association, Montreal, September 1980.

Saltz, E., Dixon, D., and Johnson, J. Training disadvantaged preschoolers on various fantasy activities: Effects on cognitive functioning and impulse control. *Child Development*, 1977, *48*, 367-380.

Sameroff, A. J. The components of sucking in the human newborn. *Journal of Experimental Child Psychology*, 1968, *6*, 607-623.

Sameroff, A. J. Can conditioned responses be established in the newborn infant? *Developmental Psychology*, 1971, *5*, 1-12.

Sameroff, A. J. Learning and adaptation in infancy. In H. W. Reese (Ed.), *Advances in child development and behavior* (Vol. 7). New York: Academic Press, 1972.

Sameroff, A. J. (Ed.). Organization and stability of newborn behavior: A commentary on the Brazelton neonatal behavior assessment scale. *Monograph of the Society for Research in Child Development*, 1978, *43*, (Serial No. 177, Nos. 5-6).

Sameroff, A. J., and Kelly, P. Socio-economic status, racial and mental health factors in infant temperament. Unpublished manuscript. As cited in A. Thomas and S. Chess, *Temperament and development*. New York: Brunner/Mazel, 1977.

Sanders, K. M., and Harper, L. V. Free-play fantasy behavior in preschool children: Relations among gender, age, season, and location. *Child Development*, 1976, *47*, 1182-1185.

Savin-Williams, R. C. An ethological study of dominance formation and maintenance in a group of human adolescents. *Child Development*, 1976, *47*, 972-979.

Savin-Williams, R. C. Dominance hierarchies in groups of early adolescents. *Child Development*, 1979, *50*, 923-935.

Saxe, G. B. A developmental analysis of notational counting. *Child Development*, 1977, *48*, 1512-1520.

Saxe, G. B. Body parts as numerals: A developmental analysis of numeration among Oksapmin in Papua New Guinea. *Child Development*, 1981, *52*, 306-316.

Saxe, G. B. Culture and the development of numerical cognition: Studies among the Oksapmin of New Papua New Guinea. In C. J. Brainerd (Ed.), *Children's logical and mathematical cognition*. New York: Springer-Verlag, in press.

Saxe, G. B. Children's counting: The early development of numeration. Unpublished paper, City University of New York, n.d.

Scarf, M. *Body, mind, and behavior*. Washington, D.C.: New Republic, 1976.

Scarf, M. *Unfinished business: Pressure points in the lives of women*. New York: Doubleday, 1980.

Scarlett, W. G. Social isolation from age-mates among nursery school children. *Journal of Child Psychology and Psychiatry.* 1980, *21,* 231-240.

Scarlett, W. G., Fucigna, C., Ware, E., and Nelson, M. The development of expressivity in early childhood. Paper presented at the American Educational Research Association, Boston, April 1980.

Scarlett, W. G., and Wolf, D. When it's only make-believe: The construction of a boundary between fantasy and reality in storytelling. *New Directions for Child Development,* 1979, *6,* 29-40.

Scarr-Salapatek, S. Race, social class, and IQ. *Science,* 1971, *174,* 1285-1295.

Scarr-Salapatek, S. IQ: Methodological and other issues. *Science,* 1972, *178,* 229-240.

Scarr-Salapatek, S. Genetics and the development of intelligence. In F. Horowitz (Ed.), *Review of child development research* (Vol. 4). Chicago: University of Chicago Press, 1975.

Scarr-Salapatek, S., and Weinberg, R. A. Narrowing the uncertainty about racial differences in IQ. Paper presented at the International Congress of Psychology, Paris, July 1976.

Schachter, D., and Gollin, E. S. Spatial perspective taking in young children. *Journal of Experimental Child Psychology,* 1979, *27,* 467-478.

Schachter, S. *The psychology of affiliation.* Stanford: Stanford University Press, 1959.

Schaefer, E. S. A circumflex model for maternal behavior. *Journal of Abnormal and Social Psychology,* 1959, *59,* 226-235.

Schaefer, E. S. A configurational analysis of children's reports of parent behavior. *Journal of Consulting Psychology,* 1965, *29,* 554-557.

Schaefer-Simmern, H. *The unfolding of artistic activity.* Berkeley: University of California Press, 1948.

Schaffer, H. R., and Emerson, P. The development of social attachments in infancy. *Monographs of the Society for Research in Child Development,* 1964, *29,* (Serial No. 94, No. 3).

Schaie, K. W., and LaBouvie-Vief, G. Generational versus ontogenetic components of change in adult cognitive behavior: A fourteen year cross-sequential study. *Developmental Psychology,* 1974, *10,* 305-320.

Schaie, K. W., and Parham, I. A. Cohort-sequential analyses of adult intellectual development. *Developmental Psychology,* 1977, *13,* 649-653.

Schieffelin, B. Getting it together: An ethnographic approach to the study of the development of communicative competence. In E. Ochs and B. B. Schefflin (Eds.), *Developmental Pragmatics.* New York: Academic Press, 1979.

Schlesinger, I. M. Production of utterances and language acquisition. In D. Slobin (Ed.), *The ontogenesis of grammar.* New York: Academic Press, 1971.

Schlesinger, I. M. The role of cognitive development and linguistic input in language acquisition. *Journal of Child Language,* 1977, *4,* 153-169.

Schliefer, M., and Douglas, V. I. Effects of training on the moral judgment of young children. *Journal of Personality and Social Psychology,* 1973, *28,* 62-67.

Schmeck, H. M., Jr. Brains may differ in women and men. *The New York Times,* March 25, 1980, p. Cl.

Schneiderman, M. H. "If that's what you mean, why didn't you say so?" Differential uses of maternal action-directive sub-types. Paper presented at the Society for Research in Child Development, Boston, April 1981.

Scholnick, E. K., and Wing, C. S. Evaluating presuppositions and propositions. Paper presented at the Society for Research in Child Development, Boston, April 1981.

Schramm, W., Lyle, J., and Parker, E. B. *Television in the lives of our children.* Stanford: Stanford University Press, 1961.

Schuberth, R. E., Werner, J. S., and Lipsitt, L. P. The stage IV error in Piaget's theory of object concept development: A reconsideration of the spatial localization hypothesis. *Child Development,* 1978, *49,* 744-748.

Schwantes, F. M. Cognitive scanning processes in children. *Child Development,* 1979, *50,* 1136-1143.

Schwartz, G., and Merten, D. The language of adolescence: An anthropological approach to youth culture. *American Journal of Sociology,* 1967, *72,* 453-468.

Schwartz, J. C. Childhood origins of psychopathology. *American Psychologist,* 1979, *34,* 879-885.

Schwartz, M., and Day, R. H. Visual shape perception in early infancy. *Monograph of the Society for Research in Child Development,* 1979, *44,* (Serial No. 182, No. 7).

Schwartz, R. G. Presuppositions and children's metalinguistic judgments: Concepts of life and the awareness of animacy restrictions. *Child Development,* 1980, *51,* 364-371.

Scott, J. P. *Aggression.* Chicago: University of Chicago Press, 1958.

Scott, J. P., Stewart, J. M., and De Ghett, V. J. Critical periods in the organization of systems. *Developmental Psychobiology,* 1974, *7,* 489-513.

Scribner, S., and Cole, M. Cognitive consequences of formal and informal education. *Science,* 1973, *182,* 553-559.

Seagrim, G., and Lendon, R. *Furnishing the mind: A comparative study of cognitive development in central Australian aboriginies.* New York: Academic Press, 1980.

Searle, J. *Speech acts.* Cambridge: Cambridge University Press, 1970.

Sears, R. R. Sources of life satisfactions of Terman gifted men. *American Psychologist,* 1977, *32,* 119-128.

Sears, R. R., and Barbee, A. H. Career and life satisfactions among Terman's gifted women. In J. C. Stanley, W. C. George, and C. H. Solano (Eds.), *The gifted and the creative: A fifty-year perspec-*

tive. Baltimore: Johns Hopkins University Press, 1977.

Sears, R. R., Maccoby, E. E., and Levin, H. *Patterns of child rearing.* Evanston, Ill.: Row, Peterson, 1957.

Sears, R. R., Rau, L., and Alpert, P. *Identification and child rearing.* Stanford: Stanford University Press, 1965.

Sebeok, T. A. *The sign and its masters.* Austin: University of Texas Press, 1979.

Secord, P., and Peevers, B. H. The development and attribution of person concepts. In T. Mischel (Ed.), *Understanding other persons.* Totowa, N. J.: Rowman and Littlefield, 1974.

Sedlak, A. J. Developmental differences in understanding plans and evaluating actors. *Child Development,* 1979, *50,* 536-560.

Seeley, J. *Creative heights.* New York: Basic Books, 1956.

Segal, J., and Yahraes, H. *A child's journey: Forces that shape the lives of our young.* New York: McGraw-Hill, 1979.

Segalowitz, S. J., and Chapman, J. S. Cerebral asymmetry for speech in neonates: A behavioral measure. *Brain and Language,* 1980, *9,* 281-288.

Selfe, L. *Nadia: A case of extraordinary drawing ability in an autistic child.* London: Academic Press, 1977.

Seligman, M. E. P. On the generality of the laws of learning. *Psychological Review,* 1970, *77,* 406-418.

Seligman, M. E. P., and Maier, S. F. Failure to escape traumatic shock. *Journal of Experimental Psychology,* 1967, *74,* 1-9.

Selman, R. L. *The development of conceptions of interpersonal relations.* Boston: Harvard Judge Baker Social Reasoning Project, 1974.

Selman, R. L. Toward a structural analysis of developing interpersonal relations concepts. In A. Pick (Ed.), *Minnesota Symposium on Child Psychology* (Vol. 10). Minneapolis: University of Minnesota Press, 1976.

Selman, R. L. *The growth of interpersonal understanding: Developmental and clinical analyses.* New York: Academic Press, 1980.

Selman, R. L., and Jurkovic, G. J. The child as a budding psychotherapist: What children understand of introspective processes. Presented at the Wheelock/Bank Street Conference on the Developmental-Interaction Point of View, Boston, June 1978.

Serbin, L. A., Tonick, I. J., and Sternglanz, S. H. Shaping cooperative cross-sex play. *Child Development,* 1977, *48,* 924-929.

Shantz, C. U. The development of social cognition. In E. M. Hetherington (Ed.), *Review of child development research* (Vol. 5). Chicago: University of Chicago Press, 1975.

Shapira, A., and Madsen, M. C. Cooperative and competitive behavior of kibbutz and urban children in Israel. *Child Development,* 1969, *40,* 609-617.

Shaps, L. P., and Nillson, L. G. Encoding and retrieval operations in relation to age. *Developmental Psychology,* 1980, *16,* 636-643.

Sharp, D., Cole, M., and Lave, C. Education and cognitive development: The evidence from experimental research. *Monograph of the Society for Research in Child Development,* 1979, *44,* (Serial No. 178, Nos. 1-2).

Shatz, M. On the development of communicative understanding: An early strategy for interpreting and responding to messages. *Cognitive Psychology,* 1978, *10,* 271-301.

Shatz, M., and Gelman, R. The development of communication skills: Modifications in the speech of young children as a function of listener. *Monographs of the Society for Research in Child Development,* 1973, *152,* (Serial No. 152, No. 2), 1-38.

Sheehy, G. *Passages,* New York: Dutton, 1976.

Sherman, J. *Sex related cognitive differences.* Springfield, Ill.: Charles C. Thomas, 1978.

Sherman, T. Categorization skills in infants. Paper presented at the Society for Research in Child Development, Boston, April 1981.

Shigetomi, C. C., Hartmann, D. P., Gelfand, D. M., Cohen, E. A., and Montemayor, R. Children's altruism: Sex differences in behavior and reputation. Paper presented at the Society for Research in Child Development, San Francisco, March 1979.

Shinn, M. Father absence and children's cognitive development. *Psychological Bulletin,* 1978, *85,* 295-324.

Shotwell, J., Wolf, D., and Gardner, H. Styles of achievement in early symbolization. In M. Foster and S. Brandes (Eds.), *Symbol as sense: New approaches to the analysis of meaning.* New York: Academic Press, 1980.

Shultz, T. R. The role of incongruity and resolution in children's appreciation of cartoon humor. *Journal of Experimental Child Psychology,* 1972, *13,* 456-477.

Shultz, T. R. Development of the concept of intention. In W. A. Collins (Ed.), *Development of cognition, affect, and social relations. Minnesota Symposia on Child Psychology* (Vol. 13). Hillsdale, N. J.: Erlbaum, 1980.

Shultz, T. R., Dover, A., and Amsel, E. The logical and empirical bases of conservation judgments. *Cognition,* 1979, *7,* 99-123.

Shultz, T. R., and Horibe, F. The development of the appreciation of verbal jokes. *Developmental Psychology,* 1974, *10,* 13-20.

Shultz, T. R., and Ravinsky, F. B. Similarity as a principle of causal inference. *Child Development,* 1977, *48,* 1552-1558.

Siegal, M. Spontaneous development of moral concepts. *Human Development,* 1975, *18,* 370-383.

Siegel, A. W., Herman, J. F., Allen, G. L., and Kirasic, K. C. The development of cognitive maps of large- and small-scale spaces. *Child Development,* 1979, *50,* 582-585.

Siegel, A. W., and White, S. H. The development of spatial representations of large-scale environments. In H. W. Reese (Ed.), *Advances in child development and behavior* (Vol. 10). New York: Academic Press, 1975.

Siegel, L. S., McCabe, A. C., Brand, J., and Matthews, J. Evidence for understanding of class inclusion in preschool children: Linguistic factors and training effects. *Child Development,* 1978, *49,* 688-693.

Siegler, R. S. Three aspects of cognitive development. *Cognitive Psychology,* 1976, *4,* 481-520.

Siegler, R. S. Recent trends in the study of cognitive development: Variations on a task-analytic theme. *Human Development,* 1980, *23,* 278-285.

Siegler, R. S. Development sequences within and between concepts. *Monographs of the Society for Research in Child Development,* in press *a.*

Siegler, R. S. Information processing approaches to development. In P. Mussen (Ed.), *Manual of child psychology* (Vol. 1). New York: Wiley, in press *b.*

Siegler, R. S., and Vago, S. The development of a proportionality concept: Judging relative fullness. *Journal of Experimental Child Psychology,* 1978, *25,* 371-395.

Sigel, I., and Hooper, F. *Logical thinking in children.* New York: Holt, Rinehart and Winston, 1968.

Silberstein, L. Thinking about imagination: The child's perspective. Paper presented at the Society for Research in Child Development, Boston, April 1981.

Silverman, I. W., Rose, A. P., and Phillis, D. E. The "magic" paradigm revisited. *Journal of Experimental Child Psychology,* 1979, *28,* 30-42.

Silverman, J., Winner, E., and Gardner, H. On going beyond the literal: The development of sensitivity to artistic symbols. *Semiotica,* 1976, *18,* 291-312.

Simmons, A. G., Rosenberg, F., and Rosenberg, M. Disturbance in the self-image at adolescence. *American Sociological Review,* 1975, *38,* 553-568.

Simmons, W. A cultural practice theory in domestic subcultural research. Paper presented at the National Institute of Education Conference on Cognitive Skills, Pittsburgh, October 1980.

Simner, M. L. Newborn's response to the cry of another infant. *Developmental Psychology,* 1971, *5,* 136-150.

Simon, W., Berger, A. S., and Gagnon, J. S. Beyond anxiety and fantasy: The coital experiences of college youth. *Journal of Youth and Adolescence,* 1972, *1,* 203-222.

Simpson, E. E. L. Moral development research: A case study of scientific cultural bias. *Human Development,* 1974, *17,* 81-106.

Sims, V. M. *SCI occupational rating scale.* New York: Harcourt, Brace, and World, 1952.

Sinclair, H. Sensorimotor action patterns as a condition for the acquisition of syntax. In R. Huxley and E. Ingram (Eds.), *Language acquisition: Models and methods.* London: Academic Press, 1971.

Sinclair-de-Zwart, H. *Acquisition de langage et dévelopment de la pensée.* Paris: Dunod, 1967.

Singer, J. *The child's world of make-believe.* New York: Academic Press, 1973.

Singer, J. L., and Singer, D. G. Television viewing, family style, and aggressive behavior in preschool children. Paper presented at the American Association for the Advancement of Science, Houston, January 1979*a.*

Singer, J. L., and Singer, D. G. The values of imagination. In B. Sutton-Smith (Ed.), *Play and learning.* New York: Gardner Press, 1979*b.*

Singer, J. L., and Singer, D. G. Imaginative play in the preschooler: Some research and theoretical implications. Paper presented at the American Psychological Association, Montreal, September 1980.

Sinha, C. The development of word meaning. Unpublished paper, University of Bristol, Bristol, Eng., 1978.

Sinnott, J. D. Everyday thinking and Piagetian operativity in adults. *Human Development,* 1975, *18,* 430-443.

Siqueland, E. R. Reinforcement patterns and extinction in human newborns. *Journal of Experimental Child Psychology,* 1968, *6,* 431-442.

Siqueland, E. R. Biological and experimental determinants of exploration in infancy. In L. J. Stone, H. T. Smith, and L. B. Murphy (Eds.), *The competent infant.* New York: Basic Books, 1973.

Siqueland, E. R., and Lipsitt, L. P. Conditioned head-turning in human newborns. *Journal of Experimental Child Psychology,* 1966, *3,* 356-376.

Skanes, G. R. Conservation and environment. *Canadian Journal of Behavioral Science,* 1976, *8,* 243-250.

Skinner, B. F. *The behavior of organisms: An experimental analysis.* New York: Appleton-Century-Crofts, 1938.

Skinner, B. F. *Science and human behavior.* New York: Macmillan, 1953.

Skinner, B. F. *Verbal behavior.* New York: Appleton-Century-Crofts, 1957.

Skinner, B. F. *Beyond freedom and dignity.* New York: Knopf, 1972.

Skinner, B. F. About behaviorism. New York: Knopf, 1974.

Slaby, R. G., and Frey, K. S. Development of gender constancy and selective attention to same-sex models. *Child Development,* 1975, *46,* 849-856.

Slade, P. D., and Russell, G. F. M. Awareness of body dimension in *anorexia nervosa:* Cross-sectional and longitudinal studies. *Psychological Medicine,* 1973, *3,* 188-199.

Slobin, D. Cognitive prerequisites for the development of grammar. In C. A. Ferguson and D. Slobin (Eds.), *Studies of child language development.* New York: Holt, Rinehart and Winston, 1973.

Sluckin, A. M., and Smith, P. K. Two approaches to the concept of dominance in preschool children. *Child Development*, 1977, *48*, 917–923.

Smedslund, J. The acquisition of conservation of substance and weight in children. *Scandinavian Journal of Psychology*, 1961, *2*, 11–20.

Smelser, N. J., and Erikson, E. H. (Eds.). *Themes of work and love in adulthood.* Cambridge, Mass.: Harvard University Press, 1980.

Smilansky, S. *The effects of socio-dramatic play on disadvantaged preschool children.* New York: Wiley, 1968.

Smith, C., and Lloyd, B. Maternal behavior and perceived sex of infant: Revisited. *Child Development*, 1978, *49*, 1263–1265.

Smith, C. L. Children's understanding of natural language hierarchies. *Journal of Experimental Child Psychology*, 1979, *27*, 437–458.

Smith, C. L. A study of the differentiation of the concepts of size and weight. Paper presented at the Society for Research in Child Development, Boston, April 1981.

Smith, C. L., Gelfand, D. M., Hartmann, D. P., and Partlow, M. E. Children's causal attributions regarding help-giving. *Child Development*, 1979, *50*, 203–210.

Smith, C. L., and Tager-Flusberg, H. The relationship between language comprehension and the metalinguistic awareness in preschoolers. Paper presented at the Boston University Conference on Language Development, Boston, October 1980.

Smith, L. B., and Kemler, D. G. Developmental trends in free classification: Evidence for a new conceptualization of perceptual development. *Journal of Experimental Child Psychology*, 1977, *24*, 279–298.

Smith, M. C. Cognizing the behavior stream: The recognition of intentional action. *Child Development*, 1978, *49*, 736–743.

Smith, P. K. Social and fantasy play in young children. In B. Tizard and D. Marvey (Eds.), *Biology of play.* Clinics in Developmental Medicine (No. 62). London: William Heinemann Medical Books, 1977.

Smith, P. K. A longitudinal study of social participation in preschool children: Solitary and parallel play reexamined. *Developmental Psychology*, 1978, *14*, 517–523.

Smith, P. K., and Dutton, S. Play and training in direct and innovative problem solving. *Child Development*, 1979, *50*, 830–836.

Snow, C. E. Mothers' speech to children learning language. *Child Development*, 1972, *43*, 549–565.

Snow, C. E. Mothers' speech research: From input to interaction. In C. E. Snow and C. A. Ferguson (Eds.), *Talking to children: Language input and acquisition.* Cambridge: Cambridge University Press, 1979.

Snow, C. E., Arlman-Rupp, A., Hassing, Y., Jolse, J., Joosten, J., and Vorster, J. Mothers' speech in three social classes. *Journal of Psycholinguistic Research*, 1976, *5*, 1–20.

Snow, M. E. Birth and differences in young children's intentions with mother, father, and peer. Paper presented at the Society for Research in Child Development, Boston, April 1981.

Snyder, S. S., and Feldman, D. H. Internal and external influences on cognitive developmental change. *Child Development*, 1977, *48*, 937–943.

Sobel, D. Solitude emerges as blessing in research on adolescents. *The New York Times,* August 19, 1980, p. C1.

Somerville, S. C., and Wellman, H. M. The development of understanding as an indirect memory strategy. *Journal of Experimental Child Psychology*, 1979, *27*, 71–86.

Sommer, B. *Puberty and adolescence.* New York: Oxford University Press, 1978.

Sonnenschein, S., and Whitehurst, G. J. The development of communication: When a bad model makes a good teacher. *Cognition*, 1980, *3*, 371–390.

Sowell, T. New light on Black IQ. *The New York Times Magazine,* March 27, 1977.

Spearman, C. "General intelligence" objectively determined and measured. *American Journal of Psychology*, 1904, *15*, 201–293.

Spearman, C. *The abilities of man: Their nature and measurement.* New York: MacMillan, 1927.

Speer, J. R., and Flavell, J. H. Young children's knowledge of the relative: Difficulty of recognition and recall memory tasks. *Developmental Psychology*, 1979, *15*, 214–217.

Spelke, E. S. Perceiving bimodally specified events in infancy. *Developmental Psychology*, 1979, *15*, 626–636.

Spelke, E. S., and Owsley, C. J. Intermodal exploration and knowledge in infancy. *Infant Behavior and Development*, 1979, *2*, 13–27.

Spiker, C. C. Research methods in children's learning. In P. H. Mussen (Ed.), *Handbook of research methods in child development.* New York: Wiley, 1960.

Spiro, M. E. *Children of the kibbutz.* New York: Schocken, 1965.

Spitz, R. A., and Wolf, K. M. Anaclitic depression. *Psychoanalytic Study of the Child*, 1946, *2*, 313–342.

Sroufe, L. A. The coherence of individual development: Early care, attachment, and subsequent development issues. *American Psychologist*, 1979, *34*, 834–841.

Sroufe, L. A., and Waters, E. The ontogenesis of smiling and laughter: A perspective on the organization of development in infancy. *Psychological Review*, 1976, *83*, 173–189.

Sroufe, L. A., Waters, E., and Matas, L. Contextual determinants of infant affective response. In M. Lewis and L. Rosenblum (Eds.), *The origins of fear.* New York: Wiley, 1974.

Stamps, L. E. Temporal conditioning of heart-rate response in newborn infants. *Developmental Psychology*, 1977, *13*, 624-629.

Stamps, L. E., and Porges, S. W. Heart-rate conditioning in newborn infants: Relationships among conditionability, heart-rate variability, and sex. *Developmental Psychology*, 1975, *11*, 424-431.

Standenmayer, H., and Bourne, L. E., Jr. Learning to interpret conditional sentences: A developmental study. *Developmental Psychology*, 1977, *13*, 616-623.

Starkey, P., Spelke, E., and Gelman, R. Number competence in infants: Sensitivity to numeric invariance and numeric change. Paper presented to the International Conference on Infant Studies, New Haven, Conn., April 1980.

Starr, R. Child abuse. *American Psychologist*, 1979, *34*, 872-878.

Starr, S. The relationship of single-word to two-word sentences. *Child Development*, 1975, *46*, 701-708.

Starr, S., and Eshlemen, S. Contexts of language listener and topic. Paper presented at the Society for Research in Child Development, Denver, April 1975.

Staub, E. A. A child in distress: The effects of age and number of witnesses on children's attempts to help. *Journal of Personality and Social Psychology*, 1970, *14*, 130-140.

Staub, E. A. Uses of role playing and induction in training for prosocial behavior. *Child Development*, 1971, *42*, 805-816.

Steeg, J. (Ed.). *Introduction to Émile*. New York: D. C. Heath, 1886.

Stein, A. H., and Friedrich, L. K. Television content and young children's behavior. In J. P. Murray, E. A. Rubenstein, and G. A. Comstock (Eds.), *Television and social behavior* (Vol. 2). Washington, D. C.: U. S. Government Printing Office, 1972.

Stein, N. The concept of a story: A developmental psycholinguistic analysis. Paper presented at the American Educational Research Association, San Francisco, April 1979.

Stein, N. L., Trabasso, T., and Garfin, D. Comprehending and remembering moral dilemmas. In S. Goldman, *Understanding discourse: interactions between knowledge and process*. Symposium presented at the American Psychological Association, New York, September 1979.

Stephens, B., McLaughlin, J. A. Miller, C. K., and Glass, G. V. Factorial structure of selected psycho-educational measures and Piagetian reading assessments. *Developmental Psychology*, 1972, *6*, 343-348.

Stern, C. *Principles of Human Genetics*. 3rd ed. San Francisco: W. H. Freeman, 1973.

Stern, D. The first relationship: Infant and mother. In J. Bruner, M. Cole, and B. Lloyd (Eds.), *Developing Child Series*. Cambridge, Mass.: Harvard University Press, 1977.

Sternberg, R.J. Component processes analogical reasoning. *Psychological Review*, 1977a, *84*, 353-378.

Sternberg, R. J. *Intelligence, information processing, and analogical reasoning: The componential analysis of human abilities*. Hillsdale, N. J.: Erlbaum, 1977b.

Sternberg, R. J., and Rifkin, B. The development of analogical reasoning processes. *Journal of Experimental Child Psychology*, 1979, *27*, 195-232.

Steuve, A. The elderly mother-daughter bond: Two streams of thought. Paper presented at the Society for Research in Child Development, Boston, April 1981.

Stevens, S. S. *Handbook of experimental psychology*. New York: Wiley, 1951.

Stevenson, H. Latent learning in children. *Journal of Experimental Child Psychology*, 1954, *47*, 17-21.

Stevenson, H. Learning in children. In P. H. Mussen (Ed.), *Carmichael's manual of child psychology* (Vol. 1). New York: Wiley, 1970.

Stevenson, H. *Children's learning*. New York: Appleton-Century-Crofts, 1974.

Stevenson, H. W., Parker, T., Wilkinson, A., Bonnevaux, B., and Gonzalez, M. Schooling, environment, and cognitive development: A cross-cultural study. *Monograph of the Society for Research in Child Development*, 1978, *43*, (Serial No. 175, No. 3).

Stewart, R. B. Sibling attachment relationships: An observation of child-infant interaction in the stranger-situation. Paper presented at the Society for Research in Child Development, Boston, April 1981.

Stipek, D. J., and Hoffman, J. M. Development of children's performance-related judgments. *Child Development*, 1980, *51*, 912-914.

Stoller, R. I. *The transsexual experiment*. London: Hogarth, 1975.

Stone, C. A., and Day, M. C. Levels of availability of a formal operational strategy. *Child Development*, 1978, *49*, 1054-1066.

Stone, L. The massacre of the innocents. *New York Review of Books*, November 14, 1974.

Stone, L., and Church, J. *Childhood and adolescence*. 3rd ed. New York: Random House, 1973.

Strauss, M. S. The abstraction of prototypical information by adults and ten-month-old infants. *Journal of Experimental Psychology: Human Learning and Memory*, 1979, *5*, 618-635.

Strauss, M. S. Infant memory of prototypical information. Presented at the Society for Research in Child Development, Boston, April 1981.

Strauss, M. S., and Cohen, L. B. Infant immediate and delayed memory for perceptual dimensions. Unpublished manuscript, University of Illinois, 1978.

Strauss, M. S., Deloache, J. S., and Maynard, J. Infants' recognition of pictorial representations of real objects. Paper presented at the Society for

Research in Child Development, New Orleans, March 1977.

Strauss, S. U-shaped behavioral growth: Implications for theories of development. In W. Hartup (Ed.), *Review of Child Development Research* (Vol. 6). Chicago: University of Chicago Press, 1980.

Strauss, S., and Rimalt, I. Effects of organizational disequilibrium training on structural elaboration. *Developmental Psychology,* 1974, *10,* 526-533.

Strauss, S., and Stavy, R. U-shaped behavioral growth: Implications for theories of development. In W. W. Hartup (Ed.), *Review of child development research* (Vol. 6). Chicago: University of Chicago Press, 1979.

Strutt, G. F., Anderson, D. R., and Weil, A. D. A developmental study of the effects of irrelevant information on speeded classification. *Journal of Experimental Child Psychology,* 1975, *20,* 127-135.

Sullivan, H. S. *The interpersonal theory of psychiatry.* New York: Norton, 1953.

Sullivan, K., and Sullivan, A. Adolescent-parent separation. *Developmental Psychology,* 1980, *16,* 93-96.

Sulloway, F. R. The role of cognitive flexibility in science. Unpublished paper, Cambridge, Mass., Harvard University, 1972.

Suls, J., and Kalle, R. J. Children's moral judgements as a function of intention, damage, and an actor's physical harm. *Developmental Psychology,* 1979, *15,* 93-94.

Suomi, S. Adult male-infant interactions among monkeys living in nuclear families. *Child Development,* 1977, *48,* 1255-1270.

Suomi, S. J., and Harlow, H. F. Social rehabilitation of isolate-reared monkeys. *Developmental Psychology,* 1972, *6,* 487-496.

Suomi, S. J., and Harlow, H. F. Monkeys without play. In J. S. Bruner, A. Jolly, and K. Sylva (Eds.), *Play: Its role in development and evolution.* London: Penguin, 1976.

Super, C. M. and Harkness, S. (Eds.). Anthropological perspectives on child development. *New Directions for Child Development,* No. 8, 1980.

Super, C. M., and White, S. H. Studies of the simultaneity of behavior change in the five to seven range. Unpublished research, Harvard University, 1970.

Surber, C. F. The development of reversible operations in judgments of ability, effort, and performance. *Child Development,* 1980, *51,* 1018-1029.

Surgeon General's scientific advisory committee on television and social behavior. *Television and growing up: The impact of televised violence.* Washington, D. C.: U.S. Government Printing Office, 1972.

Sutton-Smith, B. The importance of the storyteller: An investigation of the imaginative life. *The Urban Review,* 1975, *8,* 82-95.

Sutton-Smith, B. Introduction. In B. Sutton-Smith (Ed.), *Play and learning.* New York: Gardner Press, 1979a.

Sutton-Smith, B. (Ed.). *Play and learning.* New York: Gardner Press, 1979b.

Sutton-Smith, B., Botvin, G., and Mahoney, D. Developmental structures in fantasy narratives. *Human Development,* 1976, *19,* 1-3.

Sutton-Smith, B., and Rosenberg, B. *The sibling.* New York: Holt, Rinehart and Winston, 1970.

Suzuki, S. *Nurtured by love: A new approach to education.* Hicksville, N. Y.: Exposition Press, 1969.

Swann, W. B., Jr., and Pittman, T. S. Initiating play activity of children: The moderating influence of verbal cues on intrinsic motivation. *Child Development,* 1977, *48,* 1128-1132.

Sylva, K., Bruner, J. S., and Genova, P. The role of play in the problem-solving of children three to seven years old. In J. S. Bruner, A. Jolly, and K. Sylva (Eds.), *Play: Its role in development and evolution.* London: Penguin, 1976.

Taniuchi, L. K. The creation of prodigies through special early education: Three case studies. Unpublished paper, Laboratory of Human Development: Harvard Project on Human Potential, Harvard Graduate School of Education, 1980.

Tanner, J. M. Physical growth. In P. Mussen (Ed.), *Carmichael's manual of child psychology* (Vol. 2). New York: Wiley, 1970.

Tanner, J. M. Trend toward earlier menarche in London, Oslo, Copenhagen, the Netherlands and Hungary. *Nature,* 1973, *243,* 95-96.

Tauber, M. A. Parental socialization techniques and sex differences in children's play. *Child Development,* 1979, *50,* 225-234.

Taylor, H. O. *The medieval mind.* Cambridge, Mass.: Harvard University Press, 1949.

Taylor, M., and Bacharach, V. R. The development of drawing rules: Metaknowledge about drawing influences performance on nondrawing tasks. *Child Development,* 1981, *52,* 373-375.

Terman, L. M. *Genetic studies of genius: Mental and physical traits of a thousand gifted children* (Vol. 1). Stanford, Calif.: Stanford University Press, 1925.

Terman, L. M., and Oden, M. H. *Genetic studies of genius: The gifted child grows up: Twenty-five years' follow-up of a superior group* (Vol. 4). Stanford, Calif.: Stanford University Press, 1947.

Terman, L. M., and Oden, M. H. *Genetic studies of genius: The gifted child grows up: Thirty-five year follow-up* (Vol. 5). Stanford, Calif.: Stanford University Press, 1959.

Terrace, H. S., Petitto, C. A., Sanders, R. J., and Bever, T. G. Can an ape create a sentence? *Science,* 1979, *206,* 891-902.

Thomas, A., and Chess, S. *Temperament and development.* New York: Brunner/Mazel Publishers, 1977.

Thomas, A., Chess, S., and Birch, H. G. The origin of personality. *Scientific American,* 1970, *223,* 102–109.

Thomas, A., Chess, S., Birch, M. G., Hertzig, M. E., and Korn, S. *Behavior individuality in early childhood.* New York: New York University Press, 1963.

Thomas, H., and Jamison, W. On acquisition of understanding that still water is horizontal. *Merrill-Palmer Quarterly,* 1975, *21,* 31–44.

Thomas, H., and Jamison, W. Ability to know that the surface of still water is invariantly horizontal appears to be sex-linked. Unpublished paper, Pennsylvania State University, 1979.

Thomas, H., Jamison, W., and Hummel, D. Observation is insufficient for discovering that the surface of still water is invariantly horizontal. *Science,* 1973, *181,* 173–174.

Thompson, B. E., and Bjorkjund, D. F. Children's judgments and processing of typical and atypical category exemplars. Presented at the Society for Research in Child Development, Boston, April 1981.

Thompson, R. A., and Hoffman, M. L. Empathy and the development of guilt in children. *Developmental Psychology,* 1980, *16,* 155–156.

Thompson, J., and Chapman, R. S. Who is "Daddy"? The status of two-year-olds' overextended words in use and comprehension. *Papers and Reports on Child Language Development,* Stanford University, 1975, *10,* 59–68.

Thornburg, H. *Development in adolescence.* Wadsworth, Calif.: Brooks-Cole, 1975.

Thorndike, E. L. *Educational psychology.* New York: Columbia University Press, 1913.

Thurstone, L. L. Primary mental abilities. *Psychometric Monographs,* 1938, No. 1.

Thurstone, L. L. *Multiple-factor analysis: A developmental and expansion of "The vectors of mind."* Chicago: University of Chicago Press, 1947.

Tieger, T. On the biological basis of sex differences in aggression. *Child Development,* 1980, *51,* 943–963.

Tighe, T. J., and Tighe, L. Stimulus control in children's learning. In A. Pick (Ed.), *Minnesota Symposium on Child Development* (Vol. 6). Minneapolis: University of Minnesota Press, 1972.

Time. Teaching children at home. 1978, *112,* 78–81.

Tinbergen, N. *The study of instinct.* London: Oxford University Press, 1951.

Tizard, B., and Hodges, J. The effect of early institutional learning on the development of eight-year-old children. *Journal of Child Psychology and Psychiatry,* 1978, *19,* 99–118.

Tomikawa, S. A., and Dodd, D. H. Early word meaning: Perceptually or functionally based? *Child Development,* 1980, *51,* 1103–1109.

Tomlinson-Keasey, C. Formal operations in females from eleven to fifty-six years of age. *Developmental Psychology,* 1972, *6,* 364.

Tomlinson-Keasey, C., Eisert, D. C., Kahle, L. R.,

Hardy-Brown, K., and Keasey, B. The structure of concrete operational thought. *Child Development,* 1979, *50,* 1153–1163.

Tomlinson-Keasey, C., and Keasey, C. B. The mediating role of cognitive development in moral development. *Child Development,* 1974, *45,* 291–298.

Torgersen, A. M. Temperamental differences in infants: Illustrated through a study of twins. Paper presented at a conference on Temperament and Personality, Warsaw, Poland, 1974.

Townsend, D. J. Do children interpret "marked" comparative adjectives as their opposites? *Journal of Child Language,* 1976, *3,* 385–396.

Townsend, D. J., and Erb, M. Children's strategies for interpreting complex comparative questions. *Journal of Child Language,* 1975, *2,* 1–17.

Tracy, J. J., and Cross, H. J. Antecedents of shift in moral judgment. *Journal of Personality and Social Psychology,* 1973, *26,* 238–244.

Trehub, S. E. Reflections on the development of speech perception. *Canadian Journal of Psychology,* 1979, *33,* 368–381.

Trehub, S. E., and Abramovitch, R. Less is not more: Further observations on nonlinguistic strategies. *Journal of Experimental Child Psychology,* 1978, *25,* 160–167.

Trehub, S. E., Bull, D., and Schneider, B. A. Infant speech and nonspeech perception: A review and reevaluation. Unpublished paper, Center for Research in Human Development, Erindale College, University of Toronto, Mississauga, Ontario, 1979.

Trevarthen, C. Descriptive analyses of infant communicative behavior. In H. R. Schaffer (Ed.), *Studies in mother-infant interaction.* New York: Academic Press, 1977.

Tronick, E., Als, H., Brazelton, T. B. Monadic phases: A structural descriptive analysis of infant-mother face-to-face interaction. *Merrill-Palmer Quarterly,* 1980, *26,* 1–24.

Trotter, S. Zajonc defuses IQ debate: Birth order wins prize. *American Psychological Association Monitor,* May 1976, *7,* 1.

Turiel, E. An experimental test of the sequentiality of developmental stages in the child's moral development. *Journal of Personality and Social Psychology,* 1966, *3,* 611–618.

Turiel, E. Developmental processes in the child's moral thinking. In P. Mussen, J. Langer, and M. Covington (Eds.), *New directions in developmental psychology.* New York: Holt, Rinehart and Winston, 1969.

Turiel, E. Conflict and transition in adolescent moral development. *Child Development,* 1974, *45,* 14–79.

Turiel, E. Social regulations and the domains of social concept. In W. Damon (Ed.), *Social cognition. New Directions for Child Development,* 1978, *1,* 45–74.

Turiel, E., Kohlberg, L., and Edwards, C. Cross-cultural study of development of moral judgement. In L. Kohlberg and E. Turiel (Eds.), *Recent research in moral development*. New York: Holt, Rinehart and Winston, 1972.

Turnbull, C. M. *The mountain people*. New York: Simon and Schuster, 1974.

Unger, R. K. Toward a redefinition of sex and gender. *American Psychologist*, 1979, *34*, 1085-1094.

Ungerer, J. A., Brody, L. R., and Zelazo, P. R. Long-term memory for speech in two- to four-week-old infants. *Infant Behavior and Development*, 1978, *1*, 177-186.

Urberg, K. Sex role conceptualizations in adolescents and adults. *Developmental Psychology*, 1979, *15*, 90-92.

Urberg, K., and Docherty, E. The development of role-taking skills in young children. *Developmental Psychology*, 1976, *12*, 198-203.

Vadhan, V. P., and Smothergill, D. W. Attention and cognition. *Cognition*, 1977, *5*, 251-263.

Valliant, G. E. *Adaptation to life*. Boston: Little, Brown, 1977.

Vandell, D. L. Effects of a play-group experience on mother-son and father-son interaction. *Developmental Psychology*, 1979, *15*, 379-385.

Vandell, D. L. Encounters between infants and their preschool-aged siblings during the first year. Unpublished paper, University of Texas, 1981.

Vandenberg, B. Play, problem-solving, and creativity. In K. H. Rubin (Ed.), *Children's play. New Directions for Child Development*, No. 9, San Francisco: Jossey-Bass, 1980.

van den Daele, L. Qualitative models in developmental analysis. *Developmental Psychology*, 1969, *1*, 303-310.

van den Daele, L. Infrastructure and transition in developmental analysis. *Human Development*, 1974, *17*, 1-23.

Vargha-Khadem, F., and Corballis, M. C. Cerebral asymmetry in infants. *Brain and Language*, 1979, *8*, 1-9.

Vasta, R., Regan, K. G., and Kerley, J. Sex differences in pattern copying: Spatial cues or motor skills? *Child Development*, 1980, *51*, 932-934.

Vaughn, B., Gove, F. L., and Egeland, B. The relationship between out-of-home care and the quality of infant-mother attachment in an economically disadvantaged population. *Child Development*, 1980, *51*, 1203-1214.

Vener, A. M., and Stewart, C. S. Adolescent sexual behavior in middle America revisited: 1970-1973. *Journal of Marriage and Family*, 1974, *36*, 728-735.

Von Hofsten, C., and Lindhagen, K. Observations on the development of reaching for moving objects. *Journal of Experimental Child Psychology*, 1979, *28*, 158-173.

Vygotsky, L. *Thought and language*. Cambridge, Mass.: MIT Press, 1962.

Vygotsky, L. Play and the role of mental development in the child. *Soviet Psychology*, 1967, *5*, 6-18.

Vygotsky, L. *Mind in society*. Cambridge, Mass.: Harvard University Press, 1978.

Waber, D. P. Sex differences in cognition. *Science*, 1976, *192*, 572-574.

Wagner, D. A. The effects of formal schooling on cognitive style. Paper presented at the Society for Cross-Cultural Research, New Haven, February 1978.

Wagner, D. A. Culture and memory development. In H. Triandos and A. Heron (Eds.), *Handbook of cross-cultural psychology* (Vol. 4). Boston: Allyn and Bacon, 1981.

Wagner, S., Winner, E., Ciccetti, D., and Gardner, H. "Metaphorical" mapping in human infants. *Child Development*, 1981, *52*, 728-731.

Walker, L. J. The sequentiality of Kohlberg's stages of moral development. Paper presented at the Society for Research in Child Development, Boston, April 1981.

Walker, L. J., and Richards, B. S. Stimulating transitions in moral reasoning as a function of stage of cognitive development. *Developmental Psychology*, 1979, *15*, 95-103.

Wallach, M., and Kogan, N. *Modes of thinking in young children*. New York: Holt, Rinehart and Winston, 1965.

Wallerstein, J. S., and Kelly, J. B. The effects of parental divorce: The adolescent experience. In A. Koupernik (Ed.), *The child in his family: Children at a psychiatric risk* (Vol. 3). New York: Wiley, 1974.

Wallerstein, J. S., and Kelly, J. B. The effects of parental divorce: Experiences of the preschool child. *Journal of the American Academy of Child Psychiatry*, 1975, *14*, 600-616.

Walsh, D. A., and Baldwin, M. Age differences in integral semantic memory. *Developmental Psychology*, 1977, *13*, 509-514.

Walters, J., and Wagner, S. The earliest numbers. Paper presented at the Society for Research in Child Development, Boston, April 1981.

Warner, W. L., Meeher, M., and Eells, K. *Social class in America*. Chicago: Science Research Associates, 1949.

Wason, P. C. The contexts of plausible denial. *Journal of Verbal Learning and Verbal Behavior*, 1965, *4*, 7-11.

Wason, P. C., and Johnson-Laird, P. M. *The psychology of reasoning: Structure and content*. Cambridge, Mass.: Harvard University Press, 1972.

Waterman, A. S., Kohutis, E., and Pulone, J. The role of expressive writing in ego identity formation. *Developmental Psychology*, 1977, *13*, 286-287.

Watson, J. B. *Psychology from the standpoint of a behaviorist*. Philadelphia: Lippincott, 1919.

Watson, J. S. Conservation: An S-R analysis. In I. Sigel and F. Hooper (Eds.), *Logical thinking in children*. New York: Holt, Rinehart and Winston, 1968.

Watson, J. S. Reactions to responsive contingent stimulation in early infancy. *Merrill-Palmer Quarterly*, 1972, *18*, 219-227.

Watson, M. W., and Fischer, K. W. Development of social roles in elicited and spontaneous behavior during the preschool years. *Developmental Psychology*, 1980, *16*, 483-494.

Watson, P. Uncanny twins. *London Sunday Times Weekly Review*, May, 25, 1980, pp. 1-6.

Weatherley, D. Self-perceived rate of physical maturation and personality in late adolescence. *Child Development*, 1964, *35*, 1197-1210.

Weaver, P. A., and Shonkoff, F. *Research within reach: A research-guided response to concerns of reading educators*. Newark, Del.: International Reading Association, 1978.

Wechsler, D. *The Wechsler Adult Intelligence Scale*. New York: Psychological Corporation, 1955.

Wedemeyer, D. Poor little rich children? Study shows they often are. *The New York Times*, August 3, 1976, p. 34.

Wehren, A., and DeLisis, R. Self and other gender constancy: A dimensional analysis. Paper presented at the Society for Research in Child Development, Boston, April 1981.

Weiner, B. (Ed.). *Achievement motivation and attribution theory*. Morristown, N. J.: General Learning Press, 1974.

Weiner, B., Kun, A., and Benesh-Weiner, M. The development of mastery, emotions, and morality from an attributional perspective. In W. A. Collins (Ed.), *Development of cognition, affect, and social relations. The Minnesota Symposia on Child Psychology* (Vol. 13). Hillsdale, N. J.: Erlbaum, 1980.

Weiner, B., and Peter, N. A cognitive-developmental analysis of achievement and moral judgments. *Developmental Psychology*, 1973, *9*, 290-309.

Weiner, I. B. Psychopathology in adolescence. In J. Adelson (Ed.), *Handbook of adolescent psychology*. New York: Wiley, 1980.

Weiner, S. On the development of *more* and *less*. *Journal of Experimental Child Psychology*, 1974, *17*, 271-287.

Weinraub, M., and Frankel, J. Sex differences in parent-infant interaction during free play, departure, and separation. *Child Development*, 1977, *48*, 1240-1249.

Weinraub, M., and Lewis, M. The determinants of children's responses to separation. *Monographs of the Society for Research in Child Development*, 1977, *42*, (Serial No. 172, No. 4).

Weisfeld, G. E., and Weisfeld, C. C. Dominancy among adolescent boys: Who evaluates whom? Presented at the Society for Research in Child Development, Boston, April 1981.

Weisler, A., and McCall, R. B. Exploration and play. *American Psychologist*, 1976, *31*, 492-508.

Weisz, J. R. Developmental change in perceived control: Recognizing noncontingency in the laboratory and perceiving it in the world. *Developmental Psychology*, 1980, *16*, 385-390.

Wellman, H. M. Preschoolers' understanding of memory-relevant variables. *Child Development*, 1977, *48*, 1720-1723.

Wellman, H. M. Metamemory revisited. In M. T. H. Chi, *What is memory development the development of? A look after a decade*. Symposium presented at the Society for Research in Child Development, Boston, April 1981.

Wellman, H. M., Larkey, C., and Somerville, S. C. The early development of moral criteria. *Child Development*, 1979, *50*, 869-873.

Wellman, H. M., and Lempers, J. D. The naturalistic communicative abilities of two-year-olds. *Child Development*, 1977, *48*, 1052-1057.

Wellman, H. M., Ritter, K., and Flavell, J. H. Deliberate memory behavior in the delayed reactions of very young children. *Developmental Psychology*, 1975, *11*, 780-787.

Wellman, H. M., and Somerville, S. C. The everyday memory performance of toddlers. In M. Perlmutter, *A naturalistic view of young children's memory*. Symposium presented at the American Psychological Association, New York, September 1979.

Werner, H. *Comparative psychology of mental development*. New York: Harper and Row, 1948.

Werner, H. The concept of development from a comparative and organismic point of view. In D. Harris (Ed.), *The concept of development*. Minneapolis: University of Minnesota Press, 1957.

Werner, H., and Kaplan, B. *Symbol formation*. New York: Wiley, 1963.

Werner, J. S., and Wooten, B. R. Human infant color vision and color perception. *Infant Behavior and Development*, 1979, *2*, 241-274.

Wertham, F. C. *Seduction of the innocent*. New York: Holt, Rinehart and Winston, 1954.

Wertheimer, M. Psychomotor coordination of auditory and visual space at birth. *Science*, 1961, *134*, 1962.

Wertlieb, D., and Rose, D. Maturation of maze behavior in preschool children. Developmental Psychology, 1979, *15*, 478-479.

Wertsch, J. V. Inner speech revisited. Paper presented at the Society for Research in Child Development, New Orleans, March 1977.

Wertsch, J. V. From social interaction to higher psychological processes: A clarification and application of Vygotsky's theory. *Human Development*, in press.

Weston, D. R., and Turiel, E. Act-rule relations: Children's concepts of social rules. *Developmental Psychology*, 1980, *16*, 417-424.

Wetstone, H., and Friedlander, H. The effect of word order on young children's responses to simple gestures and commands. *Child Development*, 1973, *44*, 734-740.

Wexler, K., and Culicover, P. *Formal principles of*

language acquisition. Cambridge, Mass.: MIT Press, 1980.

Whalen, P. *The founding father.* New York: New American Library, 1965.

White, B. An experimental approach to the effects of experience on early human behavior. In J. P. Hill (Ed.), *Minnesota Symposium on Child Psychology* (Vol. 1). Minneapolis: University of Minnesota Press, 1967.

White, B. *Human infants: Experience and psychological development.* Englewood Cliffs, N. J.: Prentice-Hall, 1971.

White, B. *The first three years of life.* Englewood Cliffs, N. J.: Prentice-Hall, 1975.

White, B., Castle, P., and Held, R. Observations on the development of visually directed reaching. *Child Development,* 1964, *35,* 349-364.

White, N., and Kinsbourne, M. Does speech output control lateralize over time? Evidence from verbal-manual time-sharing tasks. *Brain and Language,* 1980, *10,* 215-223.

White, R. W. Motivation reconsidered: The concept of competence. *Psychological Review,* 1959, *66,* 297-333.

White, S. Evidence for a hierarchical arrangement of learning processes. In L. P. Lipsitt and C. C. Spiker (Eds.), *Advances in child development and behavior* (Vol. 2). New York: Academic Press, 1965.

White, S. Some general outlines of the matrix of developmental changes between five and seven years. *Bulletin of the Orton Society, 1970a, 20,* 41-57.

White, S. The learning theory approach. In P. H. Mussen (Ed.), *Carmichael's manual of child psychology* (Vol. 1). New York: Wiley, 1970*b.*

White, S. Personal communication, 1975.

White, S. Children in perspective: Introduction. *American Psychologist,* 1979, *34,* 812-814.

White, S., and Olds, A. R. Unpublished analysis of cross-cultural files. Harvard University, 1964.

Whitehurst, G. J. Comprehension, selective imitation, and the CIP hypothesis. *Journal of Experimental Child Psychology,* 1977, *23,* 23-28.

Whiteman, M., Brook, J. S., and Gordon, A. S. Perceived intention and behavioral incongruity. *Child Development,* 1977, *48,* 1133-1136.

Whiten, A. Assessing the effects of perinatal events on the success of the mother-infant relationship. In H. R. Schaffer (Ed.), *Studies in mother-infant interaction.* London: Academic Press, 1977.

Whiteside, M. F., Busch, F., and Horner, T. From egocentric to cooperative play in young children: A normative study. *Journal of the American Academy of Child Psychiatry,* 1976, *15,* 294-313.

Whiting, B. (Ed.). *Six culture series.* New York: Wiley, 1966.

Whiting, J. W. M. Resource mediation and learning by identification. In I. Iscoe and H. W. Stevenson (Eds.), *Personality development in children.* Austin: University of Texas Press, 1960.

Whiting, J. W. M., Kluckhohn, C., and Anthony, A. The function of male initiation ceremonies at puberty. In E. E. Maccoby, T. M. Newcomb, and E. L. Hartley (Ed.), *Readings in social psychology.* 3rd ed. New York: Holt, Rinehart and Winston, 1958.

Whitt, J. K., and Prentice, N. M. Cognitive processes in the development of children's enjoyment and comprehension of joking riddles. *Developmental Psychology,* 1977, *13,* 129-136.

Whyte, W. H. *The organization man.* New York: Doubleday, 1956.

Wickes, F. G. *The inner world of childhood.* Rev. ed. New York: Mentor, 1968.

Wickler, W. Socio-sexual signals and their intraspecific imitation among primates. In D. Morris (Ed.), *Primate Ethology.* New York: Doubleday, 1969.

Wildman, T. M., and Fletcher, H. J. Developmental increases and decreases in solutions of conditional syllogism problems. *Developmental Psychology,* 1977, *13,* 630-636.

Wilkening, F., Becker, J., and Trabasso, T. *Information integration by children.* Hillsdale, N. J.: Erlbaum, 1980.

Willerman, L. Effects of family on intellectual development. *American Psychologist,* 1979, *34,* 923-929.

Williams, T. M., Fryer, M. L., and Aiken, L. S. Development of visual pattern classification in preschool children: Prototypes and distinctive features. *Developmental Psychology,* 1977, *13,* 577-584.

Wilson, B., and Wilson, M. An iconoclastic view of the imagery sources in the drawings of young people. *Art Education,* 1977, *30,* 5-11.

Wilson, E. O. *Sociobiology: The new synthesis.* Cambridge, Mass.: Harvard University Press, 1975.

Wilson, E. O. *On human nature.* Cambridge, Mass.: Harvard University Press, 1978.

Wilson, R. S. Twin mental development in the preschool years. *Developmental Psychology,* 1974, *10,* 580-588.

Wilson, R. S. Twins and siblings: Concordance for school age mental development. *Child Development,* 1977, *48,* 211-216.

Wilson, R. S. Synchronies in mental development: An epigenetic perspective. *Science,* 1978, *202,* 939-948.

Winitz, H., and Irwin, O. C. Syllabic and phonetic structure of infants' early words. *Journal of Speech and Hearing Research,* 1958, *1,* 250-256.

Winner, E. New names for old things: The emergence of metaphoric language. *Journal of Child Language,* 1979, *6,* 469-492.

Winner, E., and Gardner, H. (Eds.), *Fact, fiction, and fantasy.* New Directions for Child Development, No. 6. San Francisco: Jossey-Bass, 1979.

Winner, E., and Gardner, H. The art in children's drawings. *Review of Research in Visual Arts Education,* in press.

Winner, E., McCarthy, M., and Gardner, H. The on-togenesis of metaphor. In R. P. Honeck and R. R. Hoffman (Eds.), *Cognitive and figurative language*. Hillsdale, N. J.: Erlbaum, 1980.

Winner, E., Rosenstiel, A. K., and Gardner, H. The development of metaphoric understanding. *Developmental Psychology*, 1976, *12*, 289-297.

Winnicott, D. *The child, the family, and the outside world*. London: Penguin, 1964.

Winnicott, D. *Playing and reality*. New York: Basic Books, 1971.

Winnicott, D. W. *The piggle*. New York: International Universities Press, 1977.

Witelson, S. F. Sex differences in the neurology of cognition: Psychological, social, educational, and clinical implications. In E. Sullerot and C. Escoffier (Eds.), *Le Fait Feminin*. Paris: Fayard, 1977.

Witkin, H. A. Socialization, culture, and ecology in the development of group and sex differences in cognitive style. *Human Development*, 1979, *22*, 358-372.

Witkin, H. A., Dyk, R. B., Faterson, H. D., Goodenough, D. R., and Karp, S. A. *Psychological differentiation*. New York: Wiley, 1962.

Witkin, H. A., Goodenough, D. R., and Karp, S. A. Stability of cognitive style from childhood to young adulthood. *Journal of Personality and Social Psychology*, 1967, *7*, 291-300.

Wittig, M. A., and Peterson, A. C. (Eds.). *Sex-related differences in cognitive functioning: Developmental issues*. New York: Academic Press, 1979.

Wohlwill, J. *The study of behavioral development*. New York: Academic Press, 1973.

Wolf, D. P. Understanding others: The concept of independent agency. In G. Forman (Ed.), *Action and thought: From sensorimotor schemes to symbolic operations*. New York: Academic Press, in press.

Wolf, D. P., and Gardner, H. Style and sequence in early symbolic play. In N. R. Smith and M. B. Franklin (Eds.), *Symbols functioning in children*. Hillsdale, N. J.: Erlbaum, 1979.

Wolf, D. P., and Gardner, H. On the structure of early symbolization. In R. Schiefelbush and D. Bricker (Eds.), *Early language intervention*. Baltimore: University Park Press, 1981.

Wolfenstein, M. *Children's humor*. Glencoe, Ill.: Free Press, 1954.

Wolff, P. H. Observations on the early development of smiling. In B. M. Foss (Ed.), *Determinants of infant behavior* (Vol. 2). London: Methuen, 1963.

Wolff, P. H. The causes, controls, and organization of behavior in the neonate. *Psychological Issues*, 1966, *5*, 17.

Wolff, P. H. Sucking patterns of infant mammals. *Brain, behavior, and evolution*, 1968, *1*, 354-367.

Wood, M. E. Children's developing understanding of other peoples' motives for behavior. *Developmental Psychology*, 1978, *14*, 561-562.

Woodworth, R. S. *Heredity and environment: A cul-tural study of recently published materials on twins and foster children*. New York: Social Science Research Council Bulletin, 1941.

Wozniak, R. H. Verbal regulation of motor behavior: Soviet research and non-Soviet replications. *Human Development*, 1972, *15*, 13-57.

Wynn, R. L., and Lawrence, W. W. Dominance status and its relationship to friendship choice. Paper presented to the Society for Research in Child Development, Boston, April 1981.

Yando, R. M., and Kagan, J. The effects of teacher tempo on the child. *Child Development*, 1968, *39*, 27-34.

Yarrow, L. J. Emotional development. *American Psychologist*, 1979, *34*, 951-957.

Yarrow, M. R., Scott, P., and Waxler, C. Z. Learning concern for others. *Developmental Psychology*, 1973, *8*, 240-260.

Yates, B. T., and Mischel, W. Young children's preferred attentional strategies for delaying gratification. *Journal of Personality and Social Psychology*, 1979, *37*, 286-300.

Yawkey, T. D. Sociodramatic play and cognitive abilities in young children. Paper presented at the Society for Research in Child Development, Boston, April 1981.

Young, F. W. The function of male initiation ceremonies: A cross-cultural test of an alternative hypothesis. *American Journal of Sociology*, 1962, *67*, 379-391.

Young, G., and Décarie, T. G. An ethology-based catalogue of facial/vocal behavior in infancy. *Animal Behavior*, 1977, *25*, 95-107.

Young, G., and Lewis, M. Effects of familiarity and maternal attention on infant peer relations. *Merrill-Palmer Quarterly*, 1979, *25*, 105-119.

Young, W. C., Goy, R. W., and Phoenix, C. H. Hormones and sexual behavior. *Science*, 1964, *143*, 212.

Youniss, J. *Parents and peers in social development*. Chicago: University of Chicago Press, 1980.

Youth Values Project, 1979. Available from S. Ross, Director, RFD 3, Putney, Vt.

Yussen, S. R., and Hiebert, E. H. Moral reasoning in adult years. Presented at the American Psychological Association, New York, September 1979.

Zachry, W. Ordinality and interdependence of representation and language development in infancy. *Child Development*, 1978, *49*, 681-688.

Zahn-Waxler, C., Radke-Yarrow, M., and King, R. A. Child rearing and children's prosocial initiations towards victims of distress. *Child Development*, 1979, *50*, 319-330.

Zajonc, R. B., and Markus, G. B. Birth order and intellectual development. *Psychological Review*, 1975, *82*, 74-88.

Zazzo, R. Le problème de l'imitation chez le nouveau-né. *Enfance*, 1957, *10*, 135-142.

Zeaman, D., and House, B. An attention theory of retardate discrimination learning. In N. R. Ellei (Ed.), *Handbook of mental deficiency*. New York: McGraw-Hill, 1963.

Zelazo, P. R. From reflexive to instrumental behavior. In L. Lipsitt (Ed.), *Developmental psychology: The significance of infancy*. Hillsdale, N. J.: Erlbaum, 1976.

Ziegler, M. E. The father and his child's academic and cognitive performance. Unpublished paper, University of Michigan, Ann Arbor, 1981.

Zigler, E., Levine, J., and Gould, L. Cognitive processes in the development of children's appreciation of humor. *Child Development*, 1966, *37*, 507-518.

Zigler, E., Levine, J., and Gould, L. Cognitive challenge as a factor in children's humor appreciation. *Journal of Personality and Social Psychology*, 1967, *6*, 332-336.

Zigler, E., and Muenchow, S. Mainstreaming: The proof is in the implementation. *American Psychologist*, 1979, *34*, 993-996.

Zilbach, J. I. Family development. In J. Marmor (Ed.), *Modern psychoanalysis*. New York: Basic Books, 1968.

Zimmermann, B. J., and Rosenthal, T. L. Conserving and retaining equalities and inequalities through observation and correction. *Developmental Psychology*, 1974, *10*, 260-268.

Zivin, G. On becoming subtle: Age and social rank changes in the use of facial gestures. *Child Development*, 1977, *48*, 1314-1321.

Zucker, K. J., Doering, R. W., Bradley, S. J., and Finegan, J. K. Sex-typed play in gender-disturbed children and their siblings. Paper presented at the meeting of the American Psychological Association, New York, September 1979.

Zussman, J. S. U. Situational determinants of parental behavior. Ph.D. dissertation, Stanford University, 1977.

Acknowledgments (*continued*)

ure 3.4: From the article, "Plasticity of Sensory Motor Development" by B. L. White and R. Held. *Figure 3.5:* Michal Heron. *Figure 3.6:* From Louise Hainline, "Developmental Changes in Visual Scanning of Face and Nonface Patterns by Infants," *Journal of Experimental Child Psychology*, 1978, *25*, 90-115. *Figure 3.7:* From A. N. Meltzoff and R. W. Borton, "Intermodal Matching by Human Neonates." Reprinted by permission from *Nature*, 1979, *282*, 403. Copyright © 1979 Macmillan Journals Limited. *Figure 3.8:* David Linton. *Figure 3.9:* Suzanne Szasz. *Figure 3.10:* Bill Ives. *Figure 3.11:* Shelton/Monkmeyer. *Figure 3.12:* Anna Kaufman Moon.

Page 136: Frank Siteman. *Page 137:* Historical Pictures Service, Chicago. *Page 141:* Scala/Alinari. *Page 143:* Kunsthistorisches Museum. *Page 144:* The Bettmann Archive. *Page 149:* Clark Communications, Clark University. *Page 153:* Henry Moore. *Family Group* (1948-49). Bronze (cast 1950), $59\frac{1}{4}$ x $46\frac{1}{2}''$, at base, 45 x $29\frac{7}{8}''$. Collection, The Museum of Modern Art, New York. A Conger Goodyear Fund.

Page 154: Top, Bonnie Freer/Photo Researchers; bottom, Julie O'Neil/The Picture Cube. *Page 155:* Top left, Erika Stone/Peter Arnold; bottom left and top right, Jean Smith; bottom right, Burk Uzzle/Magnum.

Page 157: Peter Vandermark/Stock, Boston. *Figure 4.1:* Jean Smith. *Figure 4.2:* Jean Smith. *Figure 4.4:* William MacDonald, *Developmental Psychology Today*, 2nd Ed. © 1975, CRM Books, a Division of Random House, Inc. *Figure 4.5:* Roger S. Fouts. *Page 180:* Robert Burroughs, *The New York Times. Figure 4.6:* Marjorie Pickens.

Page 199: Daniel S. Brody. *Figure 5.1:* Top, Derek Bayes; bottom, Henry Grossman. *Figure 5.3:* Burk Uzzle/Magnum. *Figure 5.4:* Erika Stone/Peter Arnold. *Figure 5.6:* Jean Smith *Figure 5.7:* Ellis Herwig/Stock, Boston. *Figure 5.8:* Ellis Herwig/Stock, Boston. *Figure 5.9:* Adapted from *The Psychology of Sex Differences* by Eleanor Emmons Maccoby and Carol Nagy Jacklin with the permission of the publishers, Stanford University Press. © 1974 by the Board of Trustees of the Leland Stanford Junior University.

Page 231: Anestis Diakopoulos/Stock, Boston. *Figure 6.1:* Left, George Zimbel/Monkmeyer; right, Judith Sedwick. *Figure 6.2:* Marjorie Pickens. *Figure 6.3:* Suzanne Szasz. *Figure 6.4:* Ray Shaw/Photo Trends. *Figure 6.5:* Bonnie Freer/Photo Researchers.

Page 256: Bruce Coleman, Inc. *Page 257:* Dr. Landrum B. Shettles. *Page 271:* Top left: Picasso, Pablo. *Mother with Dead Child on Ladder*. May 9, 1937. Guernica study. Pencil on white paper, $17\frac{7}{8}$ x $9\frac{1}{2}''$. On extended loan to The Museum of Modern Art, New York, from the artist's estate. Top center: Picaso, Pablo. *Mother with Dead Child on Ladder*. May 10, 1937. Guernica study. Color crayon and pencil on white paper, $17\frac{7}{8}$ x $9\frac{1}{2}''$. On extended loan to The Museum of Modern Art, New York, from the artist's estate. Top right: Picasso, Pablo. *Guernica*. (1937, May-early June.) Oil on canvas, $11'5\frac{1}{2}''$ x $25'5\frac{3}{4}''$. On extended loan to The Museum of Modern Art, New York, from the artist's estate. Detail Bottom: Picasso, Pablo. *Guernica*. (1937, May-early June.) Oil on canvas, $11'5\frac{1}{2}''$ x $25'5\frac{3}{4}''$. On extended loan to The Museum of Modern Art, New York, from the artist's estate.

Page 274: Top, Peter Southwick/Stock, Boston; bottom, B. Griffith/The Picture Cube. *Page 275:* Top, Stephanie Dinkins/Photo Researchers; middle, Richard Balzer/Stock, Boston; bottom, Dan Budnick/Woodfin Camp.

Page 277: Marjorie Pickens. *Figure 7.4:* From Diana Korzenik, "Children's Drawings: Changes in Representation between the Ages of Five and Seven." Unpublished doctoral dissertation, Harvard University, 1972. *Figure 7.5:* From A. R. Luria, *The Role of Speech in the Regulation of Normal and Abnormal Behavior* (New York: Liveright, 1961), p. 69. © 1961 Pergamon Press. *Figure 7.7:* From H. H. Kendler and T. S. Kendler, "Vertical and Horizontal Processes in Problem Solving," *Psychological Review*, 1962, *69*, 1-16. Copyright 1962 by the American Psychological Association. Reprinted by permission of the publisher and author. *Figure 7.8:* Judith Sedwick.

Page 305: David S. Strickler/The Picture Cube. *Page 306:* Chas. Addams © *The New Yorker.* May 4, 1981, p. 43. *Figure 8.1:* From L. Longstreth, *Psychological Development of the Child,* Second Edition, pp. 433, 434, 436; based on D. Baumrind, "Current Patterns of Parental Authority" from *Developmental Psychological Monographs,* 1971. Copyright 1971 by the American Psychological Association. Reprinted by permission. *Figure 8.3:* Elizabeth Hamlin/Stock, Boston. *Figure 8.4:* From E. Hilgard, R. Atkinson, and R. Atkinson, *Introduction to Psychology,* p. 91. © 1975 Harcourt, Brace Jovanovich, Inc., New York. Adapted from R. E. Nisbett, "Birth Order and Participation in Dangerous Sports," *Journal of Personality and Social Psychology,* 1968, *8,* 351-353. Copyright 1968 by the American Psychological Association. Adapted by permission of the publisher and author. *Figure 8.5:* Peter Southwick/Stock, Boston. *Figure 8.6:* From William Kessen, ed., *Childhood in China* (New Haven: Yale University Press, 1975). *Figure 8.7:* Dr. Albert Bandura.

Page 338: Mimi Forsyth/Monkmeyer. *Figure 9.1:* Dan Budnick/Woodfin Camp. *Figure 9.2:* Taken from L. Selfe, *Nadia: A Case of Extraordinary Drawing Ability in an Autistic Child.* London: Academic Press, 1977, No. 24. *Figure 9.3:* From N. H. Mackworth and J. S. Bruner, "How Adults and Children Search and Recognize Pictures," *Human Development,* 1970, *13,* pp. 149-177 (Karger, Basel). *Figure 9.4:* Adapted from L. G. Braine, "A New Slant on Orientation Perception." *American Psychologist,* 1978, *33,* p. 16. Copyright 1978 by the American Psychological Association. Adapted by permission of the publisher and author. *Figure 9.5:* Tom Davey and Robert Coles. *Figure 9.6:* From Claire Golomb, *Young Children's Sculpture and Drawing* (Cambridge: Harvard University Press, 1974), pp. 38, 46, 135, 167. Copyright © 1974 by the President and Fellows of Harvard College. By permission. *Figure 9.7:* Stephanie Dinkins/Photo Researchers.

Page 374: From Bruno Bettelheim, *The Empty Fortress.* Copyright 1967 The Free Press, New York. Reproduced with permission of the author. *Page 381:* Gabriel Polonsky. *Page 382:* Top left and bottom, from Rhoda Kellogg, *Analyzing Children's Art* (Palo Alto: National Press Books), pp. 214, 99. Copyright © 1970 by Rhoda Kellogg. Right, reprinted with permission of Macmillan Publishing Co., Inc. from *Truants From Life: The Rehabilitation of Emotionally Disturbed Children* by Bruno Bettelheim. Copyright © 1955 by The Free Press, a Division of Macmillan Publishing Co., Inc.

Page 384: Top, David S. Strickler/The Picture Cube; bottom, Suzanne Szasz. *Page 385:* Top left, David S. Strickler/Monkmeyer Press Photo Service; top right, Horst Shafer/Photo Trends; bottom right, Ken Heyman. *Page 387:* Bohdan Hrynewych. *Figure 1:* NYT Pictures. *Figure 10.2:* Ken Heyman. *Figure 10.3:* From *The Child's Conception of Number* by Jean Piaget. First published in Switzerland in 1941. Published in English translation in 1952. Reprinted by permission of Humanities Press, Inc. and Routledge and Kegan Paul Ltd. *Page 395:* © 1981 by The New York Times Company. Reprinted by permission. *Figure 10.4:* Suzanne Szasz. *Page 399:* From G. B. Saxe, "Body Parts as Numerals: A Developmental Analysis of Numeration Among Oksapmin in Papua New Guinea." *Child Development,* 1981, *52,* pp. 306-316, Fig. 1. © The Society for Research in Child Development, Inc. *Figure 10.5:* Adapted from *Developmental Psychology Today,* 2nd Ed., p. 211, © 1975 CRM Books, a Division of Random House, Inc. *Figure 10.7:* From R. Gelman, "Conservation acquisition: A prob-

lem in learning to attend to relevant attributes," *Journal of Experimental Child Psychology,* 1969, *7,* 167-187. *Figure 10.8:* Top to bottom: Sample question taken from the Differential Aptitude Test, Form T, Copyright 1947, 1948; © 1972. Reproduced by permission of The Psychological Corporation. New York, NY. All rights reserved. Sample question from the Cureton Multi-Aptitude Test, Form B, © 1955. Reproduced by permission of The Psychological Corporation, New York, NY. All rights reserved. Sample question from the Differential Aptitude Test, Form S © 1972. Reproduced by permission of The Psychological Corporation. New York, NY. All rights reserved. Sample question from the Lorge-Thorndike Intelligence Test, Verbal Battery, Level 4, Form B, © 1954. Reproduced by permission of the Riverside Publishing Company. Bias-free question taken from Raven's Advanced Progressive Test. Set II, © 1962. Reprinted by permission of J. C. Raven Limited. *Figure 10.9:* From Michael A. Wallach and Nathan Kogan, *Modes of Thinking in Young Children.* Copyright © 1965 by Holt, Rinehart, and Winston. Adapted by permission of Holt, Rinehart and Winston. *Figure 10.10:* From R. Case. Intellectual development from birth to adulthood: A neo-Piagetian interpretation. In R. Siegler (ed.), *Children's thinking: What Develops?* Lawrence Erlbaum, 1978, 46-47. Reprinted by permission of the author and publisher.

Page 424: Donald Dietz/Stock, Boston. *Figure 11.1:* Left, Suzanne Szasz; right, Harrison Owen. *Figure 11.2:* Jean-Claude Lejeune/Stock, Boston. *Figure 11.3:* From E. E. Maccoby and J. W. Hagen, "Effects of Distraction upon Central versus Incidental Recall: Developmental Trends," *Journal of Experimental Child Psychology,* 1965, *2,* 285. *Figure 11.5:* Nat Farbman/Life. *Figure 11.6:* From D. Wagner, "Memories of Morocco: The Influence of Age, Schooling and Environment on Memory." *Cognitive Psychology,* 1978, *10,* 10. *Figure 11.7:* From *Childhood in China,* William Kessen, ed. (New Haven: Yale University Press, 1975).

Page 459: Ellis Herwig/Stock, Boston. *Figure 12.2:* Ellis Herwig/Stock, Boston. *Figure 12.3:* Adapted from W. Damon, *The Social World of the Child.* San Francisco: Jossey-Bass, 1977, 178-179, Table 3. *Figure 12.4:* Hays/Monkmeyer. *Figure 12.5:* From Jerome Kagan, "Impulsive and Reflective Children: Significance of Conceptual Tempo," Figure 1, in J. D. Krumboltz (ed.), *Learning and the Educational Process,* p. 135. Copyright © 1965 by Rand McNally College Publishing Company, Chicago. Reprinted by permission.

Page 492: Yves de Braine/Black Star. *Page 494:* Sigmund Freud Copyrights Ltd. *Page 495:* Ken Heyman. *Page 496:* Ellen T. Rosenthal. Courtesy Basic Books, Inc., New York. *Page 497:* Courtesy of Professor Seymour Wapner, Heinz Werner Institute of Developmental Psychology, Clark University. *Page 498:* Courtesy of Professor Noam Chomsky, MIT. *Page 499:* Ken Heyman.

Page 508: Top, James H. Karales/Peter Arnold, Inc.; bottom, Mimi Forsyth/Monkmeyer Press Photo Service. *Page 509:* Top, Daniel S. Brody/Stock, Boston; bottom, Peter Southwick/Stock, Boston

Page 511: Lou Jones. *Pages 523-524 and Figure 13.4:* From L. Kohlberg, "Stage and Sequence: The Cognitive-Developmental Approach to Socialization," from D. Goslin (ed.) *Handbook of Socialization Theory and Research.* Copyright © 1969 by Rand McNally & Company. Reprinted by permission of Houghton Mifflin Co. The Taiwan data are adapted. *Figure 13.5:* From Roy Doty, *Q's Are Weird O's.* Copyright © 1975 by Roy Doty. Reprinted by permission of Doubleday & Co., Inc. *Figure 13.6:* J. Berndt/Stock, Boston.

Page 541: T. C. Fitzgerald/The Picture Cube. *Page 545:* From D. A. Jenni and M. A. Jenni, "Carrying Behavior in Humans: Analysis of Sex Differences," *Science,* November 19, 1976, *194,* pp. 859–860, Figure 1. Copyright 1976 by the American Association for the Advancement of Science. *Figure 14.2:* From A. F. Roche, "Secular Trends in Stature, Weight, and Maturation," in A. F. Roche (Ed.), Secular Trends in Human Growth, Maturation, and Development. *Monographs of the Society for Research in Child Development,* 1979, *44,* No. 3-4, p. 20. © The Society for Research in Child Development, Inc. *Figure 14.3:* Bob Williams. *Fig-ure 14.4:* From Mirella Ricciardi, *Vanishing Africa* published by William Collins. *Figure 14.5a:* Betsy Cole/The Picture Cube. *Figure 14.5b:* Malcolm Kirk/Peter Arnold. *Figure 14.6a and b:* From E. Koff, J. Rierdan, and E. Silverstone. *Figure 14.7:* Mimi Forsyth/Monkmeyer. *Figure 14.8:* Frank Siteman/The Picture Cube.

Page 582: Mary Ellen Mark/Magnum. *Page 584:* Anna Kaufman Moon. *Page 585:* Ray Shaw/Photo Trends. *Page 586:* Marjorie Pickens. *Page 587:* Frank Siteman/The Picture Cube. *Page 590:* Elliott Erwitt/Magnum.

Index of Authors

Index of Subjects